History of Astronomy

Garland Encyclopedias in the History of Science (Vol. 1)
Garland Reference Library of Social Science (Vol. 771)

History of Astronomy
An Encyclopedia

Edited by
John Lankford

GARLAND PUBLISHING, INC.
New York & London
1997

Library of Congress Cataloging-in-Publication Data

History of astronomy : an encyclopedia / edited by John Lankford.
p. cm. — (Garland encyclopedias in the history of science ; vol. 1)
(Garland reference library of social science ; v. 771)
Includes bibliographical references and index.
ISBN 0-8153-0322-X (alk. paper)
1. Astronomy—History—Encyclopedias. I. Lankford, John, 1934–
II. Series. III. Series: Garland reference library of social science ; v. 771.
QB15.H624 1997
520'.3—dc20 96-28558
CIP

Cover art: Constellation of Orion from *Uranometria* by Johann Bayer (Augsburg: 1603).
Reprinted by permission of Adler Planetarium and Astronomy Museum.

Cover design: Lawrence Wolfson Design, New York.

Printed on acid-free, 250-year-life paper.
Manufactured in the United States of America.

To the Memory of My Friend and Colleague

LeRoy E. Doggett

We have loved the stars too fondly
to be fearful of the night.

Contents

General Introduction

Since World War II, the historical study of science has grown enormously. Once the domain of a few scientists interested in their intellectual genealogy and a scattering of intellectual historians, philosophers of science, and sociologists of knowledge, it is now a mature and independent discipline. However, historians of science have not had a way until now to make the essentials of their subject accessible to high school and college students, scholars in other disciplines, and the general public. The encyclopedias in this series will furnish concise historical information and summarize the latest research in a form accessible to those without scientific or mathematical training.

Each volume in the series will be independent from the others. The focus of a particular volume may be a scientific discipline (for example, astronomy), a topic that transcends disciplines (for example, laboratories and instruments, science in the United States), or a relationship between the science and another aspect of culture (for example, science and religion). The same entry title may appear in a number of volumes, perhaps with a different author, as individual volume editors/co-editors approach the subject from a different context.

What is common to each of the volumes is a concern for the historiography of the history of science. By historiography, I mean the recognition that there is never an undisputed explanation of past events. Instead, historians struggle to come to a consensus about the facts and significant issues, and argue over the most valid historical explanation(s). The authors of the entries in this and the other volumes in the series have been asked to provide entries that are accurate and balanced, but also cognizant of how historical interpretations have changed over time. Where historiographic debate has occurred, authors have been asked to address that debate. They have also been given the freedom to express their own positions on these issues.

The extent to which historiographic issues are prominent in the entries varies from entry to entry, and from volume to volume, according to the richness of the historical literature and the depth of the debate. Even for a subject with a rich historiographic literature, such as science in the United States, there are topics for which there is little scholarship. The one or two scholars working on a particular topic are still laboring to uncover the facts and get the chronology correct. For other fields, there have been too few active scholars for the development of a complex debate on almost any topic.

Each entry also provides a concise, selected bibliography on the topic. Further bibliographic information can be obtained from the volumes in the Garland series Bibliographies on the History of Science and Technology, edited by Robert Multhauf and Ellen Wells.

Marc Rothenberg
Smithsonian Institution

Acknowledgments

This project could never have been completed without the advice and help of a number of colleagues. Brenda Corbin, librarian of the U.S. Naval Observatory, provided bibliographic information and checked obscure references. Joseph N. Tatarewicz ferreted out a number of NASA photographs for use in the volume. Charles J. Peterson used his computer skills to provide diagrams that illustrate numerous entries. Leif Robinson of *Sky & Telescope* provided several key illustrations. Ronald S. Brashear and Edwin C. Krupp furnished photographs from the files of the Huntington Library and Griffith Observatory. Deborah J. Warner and her staff at the Smithsonian Institution were very helpful in locating photographs. Owen Gingerich suggested a number of contacts, many of whom agreed to write for the project. Charles J. Peterson, Joseph N. Tatarewicz, and George E. Webb stepped in to provide entries at critical points. Without their willingness to volunteer for some tough assignments, this volume would have been very much impoverished. Dr. David Wisner translated several entries from the French. Many colleagues cheerfully answered questions, suggested possible authors, and agreed to participate in the project themselves. To each, my most hearty thanks.

Series editor Marc Rothenberg watched over the development of the volume, made timely suggestions, and was patient when I relocated twice in the course of bringing the project to fruition. During my years at West Virginia University, Gregory Good, himself an editor in this series, and I shared the trials and tribulations of the job, and I thank him for helping me to smile even when problems piled up higher than the ridges that surround Morgantown. Morgan McCollough served as an able assistant in preparing the manuscript, patiently solving many problems (both textual and with the computer).

Preface

How this Encyclopedia is Organized and How to Use It Effectively

This volume is designed to be simple to use. It will help, however, if users understand its organization. Entries are arranged in alphabetical order, but we have not loaded everything under *A* for *astronomy* or *astronomical*. For example, to find out about astronomical instruments, look up *Instruments, Astronomical*. Within articles, words in bold type cross-reference other articles. The index will also help readers to locate information quickly.

Each entry provides references for further reading. References range from classic books and papers to the most recent monographs. For current references, readers are referred to the *Isis Annual Bibliography* of the history of science. That volume is published each year by the History of Science Society as part of its quarterly journal, *Isis*. College and university libraries will have it in their collections, as will larger public libraries.

The focus of this encyclopedia is the period from the beginning of the Scientific Revolution to the present. Synoptic entries deal with astronomy in the ancient and medieval periods and introduce readers to its development in Islamic and Oriental cultures as well.

In an ideal world, this encyclopedia would have been much longer. Limitations of space and the availability of contributors were serious constraints. For some subjects, such as astronomy in many national contexts, or the history of major astronomical institutions, there simply were no knowledgeable scholars available to submit articles. Perhaps these lacunae will stimulate fresh research initiatives.

Entries fall into five broad categories. Those in the first category provide a historical overview of astronomy. They range from twelve hundred to five thousand words and make up the core of the encyclopedia. Take the most basic entry, *Astronomy*. Here readers gain an understanding of its historical and cultural development. Another example is *Time and Time Keeping Instruments,* which examines the ways people have devised for measuring time. *Calendars* looks at time in a different way, tracing its subject from antiquity. Astronomy is a science driven by innovations in instrumentation. Hence telescopes receive special treatment. A series of entries trace the telescope from its invention through the late twentieth century, while other entries deal with specialized telescopes and auxiliary equipment such as photometers, cameras, and spectroscopes.

Entries on astronomy in various national contexts make up a second major category. From England, France, and Latin America to China and Japan, distinguished historians have explored the development of astronomy in many different nations. Readers of these entries will soon see that political, social, religious, and economic developments, as well as patronage and instrumentation, have played an important role in shaping the organization and goals of astronomy—and sometimes its content as well.

The history of observatories forms a third category. Entries are included on national observatories such as the Royal Greenwich Observatory and the Paris Observatory as well as on leading private research institutions and on astronomy at major universities. There, especially, we might have wished for much fuller coverage. There are many important observatories—public, private, and academic—for which histories have yet to be written. Academic observatories are not listed by the name of the observatory, but rather by the name of the institution. For example, the history of the Steward Observatory at the University of Arizona is found under *University of Arizona, Astronomy at*.

Entries on the social history of astronomy form another category. These deal with topics such as *Women in Astronomy*, *Literature and Astronomy*, the *Catholic Church, Astronomy and* or the *Reward System in Modern Astronomy*. This group of entries puts readers in touch with cutting edge research in the history of science and are an important aspect of the encyclopedia.

The last category is biographies. Here the editor had a difficult time. He did not wish to duplicate existing biographical encyclopedias, such as the *Dictionary of Scientific Biography*, the *Dictionary of National Biography*, or the *Dictionary of American Biography*. Biographies have been kept short and have been selected because of their relationship to larger entries, such as *Amateurs in Astronomy* or *Scientific Revolution, Astronomy in*.

There are many possible tours. Let your imagination and the index be your guides. First-time users may wish to take an introductory tour of the subject. They might try starting with the entry on *Astronomy* in order to gain an overview. Then proceed to the three major entries that examine the primary divisions of astronomy since the Scientific Revolution: *Astrometry*, *Astrophysics*, and *Celestial Mechanics*. From there move on to *Observatories*. To deepen your understanding, proceed to *Photometry, Astronomical; Solar Physics;* and *Spectroscopy, Astronomical. Radio Astronomy*, *Double Star Astronomy*, *Galaxies*, and *Variable Star Astronomy* should also be on this list.

A second tour might be motivated by questions concerning astronomy before the Scientific Revolution. If that is the case, start with *Archaeoastronomy* to gain an understanding of the role astronomy played in preliterate cultures and then move on to such entries as *Ancient World, Astronomy in; Medieval Astronomy; Arabic/Islamic Astronomy; Chinese Astronomy;* and *Babylonian Astronomy*. *Star Names* and *Constellations* will also provide important information.

Should you wish to gain an understanding of the history of astronomical instrumentation, begin your inquiry with *Instruments, Astronomical* and then move on to the three entries that trace the telescope from its invention to our own day. A number of entries deal with specialized instruments. Examples include *Radio Telescopes*, *Meridian Instruments*, *Sextant*, *Micrometer*, and *Multiple Mirror Telescopes*. Pretelescopic instruments of the medieval and early modern period are also discussed in entries such as *Astrolabe*.

Astronomy in the age of space-based observatories is well covered. If you are curious, start with *Optical Astronomy from Space* and then move on to more specialized entries dealing with *Gamma-Ray Astronomy*, *Infrared Astronomy*, *Ultraviolet Astronomy*, and *X-Ray Astronomy*. Of course, the *Hubble Space Telescope* is discussed. Since World War II, observations from beyond the earth have redefined our understanding of the solar system. Begin with *Solar System Astronomy* and move on to entries on each of the planets plus *Asteroids*, *Planetary Satellites*, and *Moon (Earth's)*. *Cometary Astronomy* and *Meteoric Astronomy* are also important here, as are entries on the *National Aeronautics and Space Administration* (NASA) and the *Jet Propulsion Laboratory, Astronomy at* (JPL).

Advanced users will find entries on specialized topics, from *Extraterrestrial Intelligence* and the *SETI* project (whose funding was discontinued by Congress in 1994) to *Physics and Astronomy; Catalogues, Astronomical; Planetariums;* or the *Moscow Observatory*. Some topics, such as cosmology, require a series of entries to trace the subject from ancient times to the present. There are entries on both *Russian Astronomy* and *Soviet Astronomy*.

Many entries include a discussion of the scholarly literature and interpretative debates. Advanced students will find these historiographical discussions valuable. To be sure, many topics have yet to be treated in enough depth for a historiographical tradition to develop. Those are candidates for further research, and readers looking for topics will find interesting possibilities in the pages that follow. The historiography of American astronomy is discussed by Rothenberg in the first volume of the new series of *Osiris* (1985), which is devoted to American science. The history of astronomy as a research field has grown rapidly in the past fifteen years and now includes investigations organized chronologically and thematically, as well as those that focus on various national cultures.

A variety of units of measurement are used in the entries that follow. The Preface concludes with a table that identifies and explains selected units of measurement.

Units of Measurement

Unit	*Explanation*
Astronomical Unit (AU)	A measure of distance most often used in the solar system. It is the length of the semimajor axis of earth's orbit. One AU is equal to approximately 149,597,870 kilometers or 499.005 light seconds.
Angstrom Unit (Å)	Unit of measurement for wavelengths of light and X-rays developed in the nineteenth century. One angstrom is 10^{-8} centimeter or one ten-millionth of a millimeter, or 0.3937×10^{-8} inch. The unit was named for the Swedish physicist A.J. Ångström, who made the first accurate measurements of wavelengths of light.
Arcminute (') Arcsecond ('')	Minutes and seconds of arc as units of angular measurement. An arcsecond is equal to $^1/_{3600}$ of a degree. An arcminute is equal to $^1/_{60}$ of a degree.
B.C.E. Before the Common Era	Used in place of B.C. (before the Christ).
Centimeter (cm)	Metric unit equal to 0.01 meter, or approximately 0.39 inch.
C.E. The Common Era	Used in place of A.D., which comes from the latin *Anno Domini*, meaning Year of the Lord, indicating that the event took place in the Christian era.
Degree of Arc (°)	A unit of angular measurement that is 60 arcminutes. The full moon subtends an angle of about one-half a degree (30 arcminutes) in the sky.
F/Ratio (i.e., f/10)	The ratio of the focal length to the diameter of a telescope lens or mirror. The smaller the F ratio the faster the telescope as a photographic instrument.
Kilometer (km)	Metric unit equal to 1,000 meters, or about 0.62 mile.
Light year (ly)	A unit of distance equal to the distance light travels through space in one tropical year (365.242,19 days). The speed of light in a vacuum is 299,792 km/s, and thus a light year equals 9.4605×10^{12} km.
Meter (m)	Basic unit in the metric system equal to approximately 39.32 inches. The meter is defined by international convention as the length of the path traveled by light in a vacuum during an interval of $^1/_{299,792}$ second.
Parsec (pc)	Unit of length generally used outside the solar system. One parsec equals 30.857×10^{12} km, 206,265 AU, or 3.2616 ly.

Units of measurement in modern astronomy are defined in the *Facts on File Dictionary of Astronomy.* 2nd ed. Edited by V. Illingworth. New York: Facts on File Publications, 1985. See also *The Facts on File Dictionary of Physics*. Edited by J. Daintith. New York: Facts on File Publications, 1981, and later editions.

Contributors

Agar, Jon
History of Science Unit
University of Kent at Canterbury

Andrewes, Will
Collection of Historical Scientific Instruments
Harvard University

Ashworth, William B. Jr.
Department of History
University of Missouri at Kansas City
and Linda Hall Library

Bausch, Judy L.
Yerkes Observatory
The University of Chicago

Becker, Barbara J.
Southwest Regional Laboratory

Bedini, Silvio A.
Smithsonian Institution

Bennett, James A.
University of Oxford

Brashear, Ronald S.
Henry E. Huntington Library

Bronshten, Vitaly A.
Institute of Astronomy
Russian Academy of Sciences

Chapman, Allan
Wadham College
University of Oxford

Crowe, Michael J.
Program of Liberal Studies
University of Notre Dame

Débarbat, Suzanne
Observatoire de Paris

DeVorkin, David H.
National Air and Space Museum
Smithsonian Institution

Dick, Steven J.
U. S. Naval Observatory

Doel, Ronald E.
University of Alaska

Doggett, LeRoy E.
Late of the U. S. Naval Observatory

Drummeter, Louis F. Jr.
Independent Scholar

Eisberg, Joann
Independent Scholar

Evans, David S.
Department of Astronomy
University of Texas at Austin

Gascoigne, S. C. B.
Department of Astronomy
Australia National University

Genuth, Sara Schechner
Department of History
University of Maryland at College Park

Gingerich, Owen
Harvard-Smithsonian Center
for Astrophysics
Harvard University

Gossin, Pamela
School of Arts and Humanities
University of Texas–Dallas

Greenstein, Jesse L.
Robinson Laboratory of Astrophysics
California Institute of Technology

Gurshtein, Alexander
Institute of Astronomy
Russian Academy of Sciences

Harwit, Martin
National Air and Space Museum
Smithsonian Institution

Hashimoto, Takehiko
Department of the History and
Philosophy of Science
Tokyo University

Hearnshaw, J. B.
Department of Physics and Astronomy
University of Canterbury, Christchurch,
New Zealand

Hirsh, Richard F.
Department of History
Virginia Polytechnic and State University

Hoffleit, Dorrit
Department of Astronomy
Yale University

Huang, Yi-Long
Institute of History
National Tsinghua University, Taiwan

Hufbauer, Karl
Department of History
University of California, Irvine

Jaki, Stanley L.
Seaton Hall University

Jarrell, Richard A.
Department of Natural Science,
Atkinson College
York University

Kidwell, Peggy A.
Division of Mathematics
National Museum of American History
Smithsonian Institution

Krisciunas, Kevin
Joint Astronomy Center,
Hilo, Hawaii

Krupp, Edwin C.
Griffith Observatory

Kunitzsch, Paul
Institute of Semitic Studies
University of Munich

Lankford, John
Office of the Provost
Kansas State University

Lattis, James M.
Space Astronomy Laboratory
University of Wisconsin-Madison

Mattei, Janet A.
American Association of
Variable Star Observers

McCluskey, Stephen C.
Department of History
West Virginia University

McCutcheon, Robert A.
Computer Sciences Corporation

Osterbrock, Donald E.
Lick Observatory
University of California, Santa Cruz

Palmeri, Joann
Independent Scholar

Pang, Alex S.-K.
Independent Scholar

Paul, E. Robert
Late of Department of
Mathematical Sciences
Dickinson College

Peterson, Charles J.
Independent Scholar

Plotkin, Howard N.
Department of Philosophy
The University of Western Ontario

Ragep, F. Jamil
Department of the History of Science
University of Oklahoma

Rochberg, F.
Department of History
University of California, Riverside

Rothenberg, Marc
Joseph Henry Papers
Smithsonian Institution

Saridakis, Voula
Department of History
Virginia Polytechnic
and State University

Sheehan, William
Independent Scholar

Slotten, Hugh R.
Institution of Electrical and Electronics Engineers-Rutgers Center for the History of Electrical Engineering
Rutgers University

Smith, Julian A.
Institute for the History and Philosophy of Science and Technology, University of Toronto and Ryerson Polytechnic University

Smith, Robert W.
National Air and Space Museum
Smithsonian Institution
and the Johns Hopkins University

Strauss, David
History Department
Kalamazoo College

Sullivan, Woodruff T., III
Department of Astronomy
University of Washington at Seattle

Sweetnam, George
Department of History
Princeton University

Tatarewicz, Joseph N.
Independent Scholar

Taub, Liba C.
Whipple Science Museum
University of Cambridge

Van Helden, Albert
Department of History
Rice University

Waff, Craig B.
Independent Scholar

Wali, K. C.
Department of Physics
Syracuse University

Warner, Deborah Jean
Division of Physical Sciences
National Museum of American History
Smithsonian Institution

Webb, George E.
Department of History
Tennessee Technological University

Whyte, Nicholas
Department of Social Anthropology
Queens University at Belfast

Wilkins, George
Her Majesty's Nautical Almanac Office
Royal Greenwich Observatory

Will, Clifford M.
Department of Physics
Washington University,
St. Louis

Williams, Thomas R.
Department of History
Rice University

Wilson, Curtis
St. John's College
Annapolis

Wooley, Frank E.
Science and Technology Division
Corning Incorporated

Worley, Charles E.
U. S. Naval Observatory

Yeomans, Donald K.
Jet Propulsion Laboratory

History of Astronomy

Adams, Walter Sydney (1876–1956)

American astrophysicist and science administrator. Adams graduated from Dartmouth (1898) and studied at Chicago (1898–1904). He worked under **George Ellery Hale** at **Yerkes Observatory** (1898–1904) and Mount Wilson Observatory (1904–1923). Adams became director of Mount Wilson in 1923 and retired in 1946. With Arnold Kohlschütter, Adams discovered spectroscopic parallax and established a program of determining the absolute magnitudes of six thousand stars. Additionally, Adams and his colleagues measured the radial velocities of over seven thousand stars. Adams also found time for short-term projects in **stellar spectroscopy** and planetary atmospheres. Undoubtedly, Adams's greatest contribution to astronomy was his position as director of Mount Wilson during a period of tremendous growth in American astronomy.

Ronald S. Brashear

Bibliography

Joy, A.H. "Walter Sydney Adams." *Biographical Memoirs of the National Academy of Sciences* 31 (1958): 1–31.

Airy, George Biddell (1801–1892)

English Astronomer Royal. George Biddell Airy, who began his career as director of Cambridge University's observatory in 1828, was appointed Astronomer Royal following John Pond's resignation in 1834. Although four individuals directed the **Royal Greenwich Observatory** during the nineteenth century, Airy has come to epitomize English professional astronomy of that period. He transformed Greenwich during his lengthy tenure (1835–1881). His passion for efficiency, precision, and uniformity led him to adapt commercial and industrial methods to the observatory's work. He introduced a factory-style division of labor to speed collection, reduction, and dissemination of observational data by breaking down complex tasks into repetitive, specialized steps requiring little training to complete successfully. He developed self-registering instruments to reduce disparities resulting from individual sensory differences, and hired a retinue of assistants to perform routine data reduction.

Although Airy has figured prominently in histories of Greenwich and accounts of Neptune's discovery, no in-depth biography has yet been written. Recently, science historians have drawn attention to the analytical richness of examining Airy within the context of the political and social dynamics of his time. One of the few professional scientists employed by the government, Airy worked hard to maintain Greenwich's hegemony in British science through a period of great change in astronomy's goals and methods. His efforts to balance his own need for programmatic rigidity against pressures to modify the observatory's scope and style of work present opportunities to probe professional and political tensions arising from government support for scientific research in the nineteenth century.

Barbara J. Becker

Bibliography

Airy, G.B. *Autobiography of Sir George Biddell Airy*, edited by Wilfrid Airy. Cambridge: Cambridge University Press, 1896.

Chapman, A. "Sir George Airy (1801–1892) and the Concept of International Standards in Science, Timekeeping and Navigation." *Vistas in Astronomy* 28 (1985): 321–328.

——— "Public Research and Private Duty: George Biddell Airy and the Search for Neptune." *Journal for the History of Astronomy* 19 (1988): 121–139.

Meadows, A.J. *Greenwich Observatory, Volume 2: Recent History (1836–1975)*. London: Taylor & Francis, 1975.

Schaffer, S. "Astronomers Mark Time: Discipline and the Personal Equation." *Science in Context* 2 (1988): 115–145.

Smith, R.W. "The Cambridge Network in Action: The Discovery of Neptune." *Isis* 80 (1989): 395–422.

———. "A National Observatory Transformed: Greenwich in the Nineteenth Century." *Journal for the History of Astronomy* 22 (1991): 5–20.

Aitken, Robert Grant (1864–1951)

American double star astronomer and observatory director. A graduate of Williams College in 1887, Aitken served four years as professor of mathematics at the University of the Pacific before continuing on to the **Lick Observatory**, where his entire astronomical career was spent, culminating as its director (1930–1935). In 1899 he and William J. Hussey resolved to survey all the *Bonner Durchmusterung* stars down to ninth magnitude for new double stars in a systematic search upon which statistical investigations could be based. After Hussey left Lick, Aitken finished the work in 1915; his new discoveries then exceeded 3,103 pairs, nearly all discovered with the 36-inch refractor. The interpretation of this work was published in his book *The Binary Stars,* which became the authoritative reference for every aspect of double stars.

In addition to measurement of binary stars, Aitken also took over the double star card file begun by **Sherburne W. Burnham** (1838–1921) and continued by Eric Doolittle (1869–1920). Published in 1932, this famous double star catalogue earned him the Gold Medal of the Royal Astronomical Society.

Other honors bestowed on Aitken included first presidency of the double star commission of the **International Astronomical Union** (1922–1925) and the presidency of the American Astronomical Society (1937–1940).

Charles E. Worley
Charles J. Peterson

Bibliography

Aitken, Robert G. *A New General Catalogue of Double Stars Within 120° of the North Pole*. Washington, D.C.: Carnegie Institution of Washington Publication 417, 1932.

———. *The Binary Stars*. New York: D.C. McMurrie, 1918; New York: McGraw-Hill, 1935 (2nd ed.).

Van den Bos, W.H. "Robert Grant Aitken." *National Academy of Sciences Biographical Memoirs* 32 (1958): 1–30.

Alfonsine Tables

The most widely used astronomical tables of the Middle Ages, circulated under the name of Alfonso X, *el sabio,* King of Castille and Leon (1252–1284). Their exact relationship to an earlier set of astronomical tables in Castillian, now lost, which were based upon original observations commissioned by the king, is uncertain. The Latin Alfonsine Tables first appeared in Paris around 1320, accompanied by a number of different canons, or instructions, for their use written by such astronomers as John of Saxony.

The appearance of the tables signaled the assimilation of geometrical astronomy into the university curriculum. The astronomy of the tables is fundamentally Ptolemaic, although they introduced a complicated motion of the equinoxes, combining a steady motion around the zodiac in forty-nine thousand years with an oscillation of ±9 degrees every seven thousand years, which confounded astronomers until the time of Copernicus.

Stephen C. McCluskey

Bibliography

Comes, M., et al., ed. *De Astronomia Alphonsi Regis.* Proceedings of the Symposium on Alfonsine Astronomy held at Berkeley (August 1985). Barcelona: Instituto "Millás Vallicrosa" de Historia de la Ciencia Arabe, 1987.

Poulle, E., ed. *Les Tables Alphonsines avec les canons de Jean de Saxe.* Paris: Éditions du Centre National de la Recherche Scientifique, 1984.

Thoren, V., and E. Grant., trans. "Extracts from the Alfonsine Tables and Rules for Their Use." In *A Source Book in Medieval Science,* edited by Edward Grant, 465–487. Cambridge: Harvard University Press, 1974.

Almanacs, Astronomical

Astronomical almanacs are annual publications comprised of astronomical data on the positions of celestial bodies for regular intervals or specific dates for a given year and locale (the calendar) and various items of literary information (the filler).

The makers of the earliest almanacs generally obtained the astronomical data in their publications from ephemerides, which were compendia, usually covering periods of about a decade, of astronomical data calculated for the geographic coordinates of a single location. The almanac makers could often directly copy data on solar and planetary motions from an ephemeris calculated for any nearby location. Because the daily motions of the sun and planets are relatively slow, the differences of their times of appearence do not vary much for locations relatively close together, such as the cities and towns in Europe or those in the British colonies in New England. On the other hand, the motion of the moon is sufficiently rapid to produce significant differences in its position resulting from the differences in longitude between the locations of the almanac and the ephemeris. The almanac-makers thus had to add a correction factor to the lunar positions provided in an ephemeris.

The makers of ephemerides in turn computed the data in their publications from tables of the motions of the various celestial bodies. An ephemeris was more difficult to produce than an almanac, because the computation of data for an ephemeris required familiarity with logarithms, proportions, and the principles of computational astronomy, and the ability to use a variety of tables of astronomical data.

Up to the end of the seventeenth century, the makers of tables of the motions of the sun, the moon, and the planets based them on assorted geometrical models developed from many years of observation. No physical theory, however, was available to explain the patterns of motion represented by the models. After Isaac Newton proposed the theory of gravitation (1687), table-makers gradually adopted it as the foundation for their tables. Gravitational theory implies that the motions of the sun, the moon, and the planets are subject to perturbative effects. Because the determination of the motions of three or more mutually attracting bodies has no exact solution, mathematicians have resorted to approximations. As mathematicians developed gravitational theory to higher orders of approximation, theories of the motions of the various solar-system bodies became increasingly complex. Consequently, the construction of tables and ephemerides over the years has required an increasing amount of computation.

Publishers began printing almanacs shortly after the invention of movable type in the mid-fifteenth century. The calendar portions of the earliest printed almanacs listed times of solar and lunar eclipses and the solar and lunar conjunctions and oppositions during the year. In the seventeenth century, almanacs also included the daily celestial longitudes of the sun, moon, and planets, and the positions of the planets relative to each other.

Almanacs also included the times of the sun's rising and setting each day, the phases of the moon, and the positions of specific stars. Because such data had practical applications, especially in agriculture and timekeeping (particularly in earlier centuries, when clocks and watches were relatively scarce), almanacs became a very popular publication. For example, Italian presses published at least forty-four almanacs in the last quarter of the fifteenth century, and more than one hundred in the following forty years. German presses produced more than 750 prior to 1600. In the sixteenth century, at least 151 almanacs were published for the Belgian city of Antwerp, and more than six hundred for various English locations. Almanacs were also printed in France, Denmark, and Sweden. Publication of almanacs in North America began in 1639, after Harvard College set up the first printing press in the British colonies. Eighty-one other American almanacs were published prior to 1701.

Almanacs became even more popular with the addition to their filler section, in the late sixteenth and early seventeenth centuries, of astrological and weather predictions, as well as essays and poetry. More than two thousand different almanacs were published in England in the seventeenth century. The press runs of individual almanacs were sometimes quite large. In 1664, for example, booksellers sold forty thousand copies of Vincent Wing's Almanack and more than 360,000 copies of other almanacs.

Continental publishers printed most of the early ephemerides and tables of the motions of the sun, the moon, and the planets. Independent ephemerides and tables began appearing in England in the 1650s with the work of Vincent Wing, Jeremy Shakerley, and Thomas Streete. The early ephemerides were generally the work of a single individual.

Gravitational theory, however, increased the amount of computation required to produce them far beyond what a single person could handle in a reasonable amount of time. For that reason, and because navigators increasingly made use of ephemerides, various national governments began officially sponsoring the production of ephemerides computed by teams of calculators.

The first such national ephemeris was the *Connaissance des Temps* for the year 1679; this publication appeared initially under the auspices of the French Academy of Sciences and, after the French Revolution, the *Bureau des Longitudes*. Accurate determination of longitude at sea (to within one degree by the method of lunar distances), however, became possible only after the middle of the eighteenth century, with improvements in the design of astronomical and nautical instruments and increased accuracy in tables of the motion of the moon. Using lunar tables by the German astronomer Tobias Mayer, the British Astronomer Royal Nevil Maskelyne gained the approval of the British Board of Longitude to compute and publish *The Nautical Almanac and Astronomical Ephemeris,* first issued for the year 1767. Other national ephemerides include the *Berliner Astronomisches Jahrbuch* (1776), the Spanish *Ephemerides Astronomicas* (1791), *The American Ephemeris and Nautical Almanac* (1855), the *Astronomical Yearbook of the USSR* (1923), the *Japanese Ephemeris* (1943), and the *Indian Ephemeris and Nautical Almanac* (1958).

For many years, the makers of these national ephemerides often used different theories of the motions of the solar-system bodies, different astronomical constants, different geographical coordinate systems, and different time scales. International cooperation in recent years, however, has led to uniformity in these areas, avoidance of duplication in the computational work, and, in the case of the British and U.S. ephemerides, a common publication since 1981, *The Astronomical Almanac.*

John T. Kelly examined the mathematical basis of the early almanacs as part of a study examining the development of computational astronomy from about 1500 to 1800 in the British colonies in North America, England, and, to a lesser extent, Continental Europe. J. Weeks has compiled an extensive listing of the theories used in the British and American national ephemerides from their respective beginnings to the present. Kelly's book includes an extensive bibliography.

Craig B. Waff

Bibliography

Forbes, E.G. "The Foundation and Early Development of the Nautical Almanac." *Journal of the Institute of Navigation* 18 (1965): 391–401.

Kelly, J.T. *Practical Astronomy during the Seventeenth Century: Almanac-Makers in America and England.* New York: Garland, 1991.

Marguet, F. "La 'Connaissance des Temps' et son histoire." *Revue génerale des sciences pures et appliques* 23 (1912): 133–140.

Seidelmann, P.K., et al. "The Almanacs—Yesterday, Today and Tomorrow." *Navigation: Journal of the Institute of Navigation* 24 (1976–1977): 303–312.

Waff, C.B. "Charles Henry Davis, the Foundation of the American Nautical Almanac, and the Establishment of an American Prime Meridian." *Vistas in Astronomy* 28 (1985): 61–66.

Weeks, J., comp. "Historical Information." In *Explanatory Supplement to the Astronomical Almanac: A Revision to the Explanatory Supplement to the Astronomical Ephemeris and the American Ephemeris and Nautical Almanac. Prepared by the Nautical Almanac Office, U.S. Naval Observatory with Contributions from H.M. Nautical Almanac Office, Royal Greenwich Observatory, Jet Propulsion Laboratory, Bureau des Longitudes, and the Time Service and Astrometry Departments, U.S. Naval Observatory*, edited by P. Kenneth Seidelmann, 609–665. Mill Valley, Calif.: University Science Books, 1992.

Amateurs In Astronomy

Amateur astronomers made substantial contributions to the progress of astronomy in the past two centuries. Often, while working in areas that professional astronomers considered less important, amateurs were rewarded with discoveries of fundamental importance. At minimum, amateurs provide continuity of observational records that prove useful to researchers.

Late in the eighteenth century, nearly all astronomy was practiced by individuals with private observatories. These astronomers, for example **John Goodricke** and **William Herschel**, established patterns of research that later emerged as important areas of amateur contribution.

As paid positions for astronomers gradually became more common in the early nineteenth century, the profession of astronomy began to emerge, and with it, the need to distinguish those who were amateur astronomers. An amateur astronomer is one who practices astronomy as a science but without pay, a meaningless distinction before about 1800.

Observation from private observatories continued after 1800 but many individuals were observing only for recreational purposes. The gathering and reporting of scientifically valuable data distinguishes the astronomer, both amateur and professional, from these recreational sky observers.

Prior to the 1970s the historiography of astronomy is clouded by inappropriate references to the deeds of nonastronomers as amateurs, and less than candid acknowledgment of the actual contributions of amateur astronomers.

The Emergence of Amateurs in Astronomy—1800 to 1860

Visual observation and positional astronomy dominated the work of astronomers in the early nineteenth century. An English amateur, Stephen Groombridge, developed a catalogue of the positions of 4,243 circumpolar stars. It is a model for accuracy and thoroughness, that remained an important tool for many years. A successful merchant, Groombridge equipped an excellent observatory in his home.

A few early amateurs were attracted to the sun. In 1843, Samuel Heinrich Schwabe, an apothecary in Dessau, Germany, discovered the sunspot cycle of approximately eleven years. The English brewer, Richard Christopher Carrington, used his measurements of sunspots to quantify the rotational period of the sun and accurately locate the sun's pole.

Double stars were important to nineteenth-century studies of stellar evolution. The prodigious output of double star discoveries and measurements by the Reverend William Rutter Dawes (1799–1868) in England, demonstrated the value of a dedicated, keen-eyed observer with a moderate sized telescope.

John Herschel conducted the first extensive telescopic survey of the southern skies. Observing at the Cape of Good Hope, South Africa, from 1834 to 1838, Herschel discovered and catalogued thousands of double stars and nebulae.

An English paper manufacturer, Warren De La Rue, clearly established the value of photography as an astronomical technique. In 1857 De La Rue captured exceptional detail in lunar photographs using the new wet collodion process. At the 1860 solar eclipse in Spain, he used photographs taken from stations located 400 km apart to prove that prominences were associated with the sun and not the moon.

From 1800 to 1860, a typical amateur observatory was equipped with a 3- to 6-inch refracting telescope. However, following the example of William Herschel, a few amateurs experimented with large **reflecting telescopes**. **William Parsons, Third Earl of Rosse**, observed detailed structure in the nebulae with 36- and 72-inch telescopes. Parsons's telescopes were limited to observations close to the meridian.

An English brewer, William Lassell, first mounted large reflecting telescopes equatorially. Using 24- and 48-inch equatorial reflectors, Lassell discovered four satellites of Uranus and Neptune, and hundreds of **nebulae**.

Parsons and Lassell demonstrated the advantage of the increased light grasp and resolution available with larger apertures. However, the excessive weight of the speculum metal mirrors they were forced to use limited further progress in this direction until the development of lighter, silvered glass mirrors.

There were not many theoreticians among amateur astronomers. A noteworthy exception was the German physician Heinrich Wilhelm Mathias Olbers. Olbers was highly respected for his simplified method of computing comet orbits.

The Golden Age of Amateur Astronomy—1860 to 1920

By 1860, it was clear that a profession of astronomy was emerging. Amateurs were more conscious of their status. Disputes with professional astronomers arose over technical issues as they attempted, unsuccessfully in most cases, to compete with professional astronomers. In spite of tensions, amateurs continued to make substantial contributions to astronomy.

Some amateurs were recognized for their contributions and became professionals. In the United States, **Sherburne Wesley Burnham** and **Edward Emerson Barnard** epitomize amateurs whose accomplishments (in double star and comet discoveries respectively) led to their eventual employment as professionals.

English amateurs during this period were particularly effective in their contributions, focusing mainly in areas of astronomy that were neglected by professional astronomers. **Arthur Stanley Williams**, a barrister, discovered the variations in rotation of Jupiter's atmosphere as a function of latitude.

A 6-inch refracting telescope constructed by the Cleveland firm of Warner and Swasey between 1890 and 1910. It is mounted on a permanent pier. Its owner would have had a permanent observatory building of some sort. Many amateurs would have used a wooden tripod and carried the telescope outside when they wanted to observe. The equatorial mounting and clock drive (seen through the glass door at the top of the pier) indicate this was a quality instrument. With refracting telescopes like this, amateurs observed variable stars, searched for double stars, and observed features on the moon and planets. (Courtesy of the National Museum of American History)

Williams also discovered a number of **variable stars**. An accountant, William Frederick Denning, is best remembered for his extensive observations of meteors and discovery of permanent radiants for meteor showers. Denning's radiants were instrumental in associating meteors with debris in the orbits of comets.

Family and occupational requirements conflicted with an amateur's astronomical interests. For example, a South African teacher, Alexander William Roberts, worked routinely with only two or three hours of sleep. Using his astonishingly precise observations, Roberts was able to show that stars in eclipsing binaries are prolate spheroids that are in contact in some cases. Roberts was the first astronomer to calculate the densities of individual stars.

The development of **astrophysics** as a separate field within astronomy owed much to the experimentation of amateur astronomers, particularly in spectroscopy and photography. When the analytical power of **spectroscopy** became apparent in the 1860s, amateurs were quick to exploit its value in astronomy.

An English silk merchant, **William Huggins**, with his wife, Margaret Lindsey Huggins, made fundamental discoveries using visual and photographic recording of spectral observations. Huggins discovered that some of the nebulae were tenuous clouds of gas, while others (now known to be **galaxies**) had the spectral characteristics of stars.

In the United States, attorney Lewis Morris Rutherfurd and physician **Henry Draper** pioneered in photography and combined it with a spectroscope to achieve permanent records of spectra.

Two English amateurs, Isaac Roberts and Frank McClean, were particularly active in applying photography to astronomy. Roberts's photographic portraits of nebulae demonstrated that important morphological differences existed among these objects. McClean prepared the first wide-field spectrographic atlas of the night sky and discovered oxygen in the spectrum of Beta Crucis and other helium stars.

Many amateur astronomers observed with telescopes that had been manufactured by others, usually with smaller, more affordable apertures. Those astronomers who constructed their own telescopes progressed rapidly to larger apertures for greater light grasp and resolution. They were frequently rewarded with discoveries, and eventually led professional astronomers into similar advances

Several amateur telescope-makers published their techniques. Henry Draper's paper, in a Smithsonian Institution annual report, described improved techniques for making lightweight, parabolic, silvered-glass mirrors. The Reverend William Frederick Archdall Ellison in England gave more complete instructions on mountings as well as optics. As these publications became available, more individuals accepted the challenge of making their own telescopes.

While amateur astronomers were observing, constructing, and experimenting, some were also theorizing. William Henry Stanley Monck, a bankruptcy judge, economist, and ethicist, pointed out a relationship between the spectral characteristics of stars and their radial velocities. Monck speculated that this might indicate the presence of streams of stars, anticipating by at least ten years the more broadly publicized and accepted star-streaming theories of **Jacobus Kapteyn**.

Amateur astronomers popularized astronomy, helping professional astronomers gain public support for new observatories. For example, the Reverend Alden Walker Quimby, a dedicated sunspot observer, lectured widely and wrote articles for Philadelphia newspapers. Torvald Köhl lectured to over 300,000 individuals in Denmark, and found time for planetary, variable star, and meteor observations. Connecticut lawyer William Tyler Olcott was instrumental in the organization of American variable star observers, and he wrote a number of popular books on astronomy. His *Field Book of the Stars* was updated and remained in print for several decades after his death.

The Transition to Cooperation—1920 to the Present

As the twentieth century progressed, the role of the amateur in astronomy began to change. By 1920, the profession of astronomy was well established. Without academic credentials, one's transition from amateur to professional became unlikely. The mathematics involved at the frontiers of astronomy exceeded the grasp of most amateurs and, for the first time, professional astronomers used telescopes with apertures far exceeding those of the largest amateur telescopes. New strategies by which amateurs could contribute to astronomy without competing with professionals were clearly needed.

Late in the nineteenth century, organizations devoted to the amateur astronomer appeared. Some of these organizations were broad in scope, for example the British Astronomical Association (BAA). Others were organized around one branch of astronomy, such as meteors or variable stars. These organizations provided a framework within which amateur contributions were encouraged, collected, and reported with credibility. The pattern of amateur work shifted from competition with professional astronomers to active cooperation based on the amateur's equipment and available time.

The usual form of cooperation was routine observation of known astronomical objects, although searching for new objects continued as a competitive field. BAA observers, under the leadership of Theodore Evelyn Reece Phillips and Bertrand Meigh Peek, provided the only continuous and reliable record of Jupiter for many decades.

Similarly, amateurs contributed by monitoring variations in the brightness of thousands of variable stars that would otherwise not have been observed. Dedicated amateurs like Reginald Purdon DeKock of South Africa and Cyrus F. Fernald and Leslie C. Peltier of the United States made discoveries of comets and of novae while making routine observations for the American Association of Variable Star Observers (AAVSO). AAVSO observers now provide guidance on variable star activity to professional astronomers controlling earth-orbiting astronomical observatories.

Discovery of new objects by amateurs has gained in importance. Early discovery of an extragalactic supernova allowed astronomers to study these transient objects, important both for their use as distance indicators and for understanding of the final stages of stellar evolution. The Reverend Robert Evans of Australia demonstrated the value of the skilled amateur in scanning a large number of galaxy fields to detect the presence of new stars. Evans is credited with discovery of more than twenty-five extragalactic supernovae.

Another form of contribution through cooperative work took advantage of the relative portability of an amateur's telescope. Instrument portability is essential for observing a total solar eclipse, or a grazing lunar or asteroid occultation. Members of the International Occultation Timing Association improved knowledge of the moon's position and polar diameter, the diameter of the sun, and the size and shape of several asteroids.

A wave of interest in amateur telescope-making in the United States spread quickly to other parts of the world. In a series of *Scientific American* articles beginning in 1926, editor Albert Graham Ingalls and Russell Williams Porter, an amateur telescope maker, inspired thousands to make telescopes and observe the night skies. Interest in telescope-making continued after World War II, but commercial instruments replaced homemade telescopes for many amateurs. Photoelectric photometers and charge-coupled detectors connected to personal computers became useful observational tools for amateurs, encouraging more sophisticated cooperative observing projects.

Over the past two centuries, amateur astronomers have made substantive contributions to the progress of astronomy. These contributions varied from introduction of new observational methods and interpretations to popularizing astronomy, and have included substantial routine observational data gathering as well as discoveries of new objects. With the advent of electronic image processing techniques, amateurs will continue these contributions and expand their efforts in new areas.

Thomas R. Williams

Bibliography

DeVorkin, D.H. "Community and Spectral Classification in Astrophysics: The Acceptance of E.C. Pickering's System in 1910." *Isis* 72 (1981): 29–49.

Lankford, J. "Amateur versus Professional: The Transatlantic Debate over the Measurement of Jovian Longitude." *Journal for the British Astronomical Association* 86 (1979): 574–582.

———. "Amateurs versus Professionals: The Controversy over Telescope Size in Late Victorian Science." *Isis* 72 (1981): 11–28.

———. "Amateurs and Astrophysics: A Neglected Aspect in the Development of a Scientific Specialty." *Social Studies of Science* 11 (1981): 275–303.

———. "Astronomy's Enduring Resource." *Sky and Telescope* 76 (1988): 482–483.

Rothenberg, M. "Organization and Control: Professionals and Amateurs in American Astronomy, 1899–1918." *Social Studies of Science* 11 (1981): 305–325.

Stebbins, R.A. "Avocational Science: The Amateur Routine in Archeology and Astronomy." *International Journal of Comparative Sociology* 21 (1980): 34–48.

———. "Looking Downwards: Sociological Images of the Vocation and Avocation of Astronomy." *Journal of the Royal Astronomical Society of Canada* 75 (1981): 2–14.

Williams, T.R. "Criteria for Identifying an Astronomer as an Amateur." In *Stargazers—The Contributions of Amateurs to Astronomy,* edited by S. Dunlop and M. Gerbaldi. Berlin: Springer-Verlag, 1988.

———. "A Galaxy of Amateur Astronomers." *Sky & Telescope* 76 (1988): 484–486.

Ambartsumian, Viktor Amazaspovich (b. 1908)

Soviet astrophysicist. Ambartsumian studied at Leningrad State University (LSU) and **Pulkovo Observatory**. In 1934 he organized a department of astrophysics at LSU, and in 1946 he founded the Biurakan Observatory. Elected a member of the USSR Academy of Sciences in 1939, Ambartsumian has also been president of the Armenian Academy of Sciences since 1947. He has served as vice president (1948–1955) and later as president (1961–1964) of the **International Astronomical Union**.

Ambartsumian carried out one of the first studies of stellar radiation transfer in gaseous nebulae. He developed methods to compute star cluster decay times and the time required to establish statistical equilibrium in double star systems. In 1947 Ambartsumian discovered the existence of unstable stellar associations, which pointed to the conclusion that star formation is still taking place in the galaxy.

Robert A. McCutcheon

Bibliography

Kolchinskii, I.G., A.A. Korsun', and M.G. Rodriges. "Ambartsumian, Viktor Amazaspovich." In *Astronomy, biograficheskii spravochnik* [Astronomers, a Biographical Handbook], 2nd ed., 15–17. Kiev: Naukova dumka, 1986.

Turkevich, J. "Ambartsumian, Viktor Amazaspovich." In *Soviet Men of Science.* Academicians and Corresponding Members of the Academy of Sciences of the USSR, 13–18. Princeton: Van Nostrand, 1963.

Ancient World, Astronomy in

Many ancient civilizations have left evidence of interest in astronomical events. Such interests were motivated by the numerous concerns of daily life, including timekeeping and calendar-making, agriculture, navigation, religion, politics, and the desire to comprehend the world. A distinction between literate societies (such as the Babylonian, Egyptian, Greek, Chinese, and Mayan) and nonliterate societies (including, geographically, Polynesia, Micronesia, Britain, Peru, and northern Europe) is suggested by the types of evidence of astronomical activity that survive—namely literary texts or archaeological remains. However, the dichotomy is not absolute. Literate societies also erected various sorts of astronomical monuments, which are typically associated with nonliterate societies (as apparently occurred, for example, in ancient Egypt).

Nevertheless, the distinction between literate and nonliterate societies, and the different skills required to study the evidence of written texts versus physical remains, is indicative of a division of labor that has occurred among scholars seeking to understand astronomy in the ancient world. While ancient societies produced many written accounts about the heavens, historians of astronomy have tended to focus their efforts on works of technical mathematical astronomy. Additionally, historians have profited from the examination of more general mathematical works that discuss methods that may be applied to astronomy. However, the textual and archaeological approaches are not mutually exclusive. In some cases, archaeological evidence has been examined using the technical mathematical approaches of historians and astronomers who more frequently work with written evidence. There have also been various attempts to correlate literary evidence with archaeological remains, which may provide a context for understanding; studies of early instruments have benefited from this approach.

Because of the paucity of surviving evidence of any type, both the approaches of the technical historians and of those studying physical remains are somewhat limited; both groups could benefit by the examination of other types of evidence. In some cases, texts that are not obviously astronomical in content must be relied upon to provide information regarding the contexts of ancient astronomy. This becomes evident once the question is raised regarding the motivations for interest in astronomy in antiquity. Many standard accounts point to practical considerations: weather-forecasting, farming, the establishment of civil calendars (important for politics and diplomacy), religious observance, and **astrology**. Some scholars attribute to the ancient Greeks especially a strong intellectual interest in the heavens.

There are, however, limitations on what can be learned regarding the social, cultural, and intellectual contexts of ancient astronomy, much less about individuals engaged in astronomical practice. In the case of nonliterate societies, no knowledge of the individuals involved is available; even in the case of literate cultures (notably ancient Greece), often very little biographical information, sometimes only a name, survives. As Neugebauer pointed out, it is sometimes impossible to find evidence to support many of the favorite clichés of the history of astronomy, including the emphasis on Alexandria as a center of scientific activity (Neugebauer, *History*, vol. 2, 571–572). Significantly, in some cases information about a particular person or idea is available only through what may seem to be unlikely sources, such as poetry. These examples highlight the necessity of examining a wide variety of ancient texts for information that may be relevant to the history of ancient astronomy.

Perhaps the lack of information about the individuals engaged in astronomical activities has helped determine that the study of ancient astronomy be largely concerned with the problems, ideas, and methods as they have been recorded in written documents. The choice of texts for study has been in many cases determined by the definition of astronomy adopted by scholars. Astronomical bodies and events were described in many ancient texts that would be regarded as belonging to different genres, including the mythological, poetic, practical, speculative, philosophical, and mathematical. Each class of texts yields a different approach to and view of **astronomy**. For the study of ancient Greek astronomy, it is certainly significant that some of the Greek authors considered astronomy to be a branch of mathematics; nevertheless, the historian must consider whether mathematical texts are the only ones appropriate for study, or whether other forms of literary evidence, including poetic and philosophical writings, should also be examined. Such decisions rest on the understanding of the term *astronomy* and such questions as whether the study of ancient astronomy should consider, for example, cosmological writings and folk astronomy. Certainly, one approach need not preclude others.

Within the study of the written evidence concerning ancient astronomy, there have been several important questions around which much scholarly work has been focused, particularly with regard to the transmission of astronomical information (including observations and methods) between ancient cultures; the relationship between cosmology (natural philosophy) and astronomy (a branch of mathematics) within the Greek tradition; the status of observations in astronomical practice; and the place of astral piety and astrology.

Among those ancient civilizations that left written records of their astronomical work, the Babylonians and the Greeks are particularly noteworthy. By the standard account, Babylonian astronomy used arithmetical methods to predict astronomical events, while the Greeks sought to explain the apparent motions of the heavenly bodies using geometrical models. Recently, the important role of numerical methods in Hellenistic astronomy has been recognized (Jones, 441).

Many ancient Greek authors, including **Plato** (427–348/347 B.C.E.) and **Aristotle**

(384–322 B.C.E.), traced the origin of their astronomy to the East; modern scholarship, to some extent, echoes this account. The extensive debt of Greek astronomy to the Babylonians continues to be investigated and understood, with regard to the transmission of both observational data and astronomical methods. While knowledge remains sketchy, certainly the large-scale transmission that apparently occurred could not have been accomplished through any one route. Several scholars have argued convincingly that the second-century B.C.E. Greek astronomer **Hipparchus** seems to have played an enormous role in the transmission of Babylonian astronomy (Jones, 448–449).

In the Hellenistic period, the Greeks made use of Babylonian data and astronomical methods, yet certain approaches to the study of the heavens are recognized as distinctively Greek. Examples include the application of geometrical methods to the problem of accounting for the apparent motions of the heavenly bodies and the intertwining of natural philosophy and astronomy. The latter approach is shown in the reliance of geometrical models on cosmological postulates and an interest in physical questions, demonstrated, in part, by attempts to determine cosmic distances.

Astronomy was traditionally considered to be a branch of mathematics by the Greeks. The formulation of the classical problem of Western astronomy, which was to last until the early modern period, has been variously attributed to the Pythagoreans and Plato. Simplicius (sixth century C.E.), in his commentary on Aristotle's treatise *On the Heavens*, reported that Plato posed the following problem to his students: to account for (save) the seemingly irregular planetary phenomena (appearances) using only uniform, circular motions. The relationship between the phenomena and geometrical accounts of the heavenly motions has been the topic of an extended debate, in which questions have been raised concerning the correspondence of the mathematical account to sensory experience and to the physical world itself.

Consideration of the nature of the cosmos was a standard topic in many of the writings of the ancient Greek philosophers. The relationship of these physical accounts (from the Greek word for nature, *physis*) to mathematical astronomical works is complicated and difficult to assess in general terms. That ancient Greek astronomy relied on certain natural philosophical postulates as a foundation is clear (for example, the cosmological principle of the sphericity of the heavens). Further significant connections between astronomy and philosophy seem to have been at work as well. In a seminal article on early Greek astronomy, Bowen and Goldstein suggested that for the Pythagoreans and Plato, "The circular motions of the heavenly bodies manifested a *moral* order that was ultimately analyzable by means of the same whole-number ratios as melodious sound" (Bowen and Goldstein, 332–333). The assumption of an important connection between ethics and the organization of the natural world was not uncommon in the writings of the ancient Greek authors, and such assumptions suggest that the accounts were meant to describe the universe in terms which, on some level, must be regarded as real.

The intended correspondence between the mathematical astronomical models and the sensory world undoubtedly varied from author to author in antiquity. Further, the role of observations with regard to astronomical theory has been the subject of long and heated discussion, by philosophers as well as by historians. In the twentieth century, the debate has been fueled by the work of Pierre Duhem, who suggested that the astronomical models can be regarded either as convenient fictions devised by mathematicians to aid in making calculations of the celestial motions or as descriptions of the motions of physically real bodies. In the first case, Duhem claimed, the mathematical account need only account for, or save, the appearances. In the second case, the account given by the astronomer must agree with natural philosophical (physical) claims about the nature of the universe (Duhem, 28). In Duhem's view, the major Greek astronomers (with the exception of Aristotle) were interested simply in providing explanations that did not contradict the phenomena. He saw this methodological approach continuing throughout the history of science in the West, up to his own day. His thesis has been adopted by many scholars and criticized by others; Lloyd has provided a careful critique of Duhem's original statement, concluding that it is impossible to determine with any certainty the views of most of the important figures in Greek astronomy regarding the relationship between astronomy and physics. What evidence does survive often contradicts Duhem's position. The testimony of astronomical writers and practitioners, including Ptolemy (second century C.E.), indicates that astronomers routinely started from philosophical assumptions regarding the physical makeup of the universe, including the generally accepted ideas regarding the regularity, uniformity, and circularity of the motions of the heavenly bodies, as well as assumptions about which bodies were in motion and which were at rest (Lloyd, 274).

While the concerns of the mathematicians and those of natural philosophers were, to some extent, distinguished by their different approaches, Greek astronomers did not advocate a mathematical approach completely separated from physics. Mathematicians may have simplified their problems for the sake of computational convenience, but Duhem's position was too extreme. While aesthetic considerations, such as simplicity, might help decide between competing astronomical models, so too did physical considerations play a role in the adoption and rejection of theories, as indicated by the lack of support for the suggestion by Aristarchus of Samos (third century B.C.E.) that the earth is in motion around the sun. Tensions regarding the relationship between astronomy and natural philosophy, as well as questions regarding the status of the phenomena, continued in astronomy well beyond the ancient period.

The development and description of observational instruments in antiquity suggest that making observations was an important part of the work of some astronomers. Other instruments, which utilized astronomical events but which were not intended for observing purposes, such as **sundials**, were also developed. The gnomon (a vertical stick used to cast a shadow of the sun in order to tell time) was one of the earliest astronomical instruments, possibly dating from prehistory. Herodotus (fifth century B.C.E.) claimed that the Greeks learned about it from the Babylonians; Anaximander (sixth century B.C.E.) was credited as the inventor by Diogenes Laertius (third century C.E.); **Ptolemy** discussed the gnomon in the *Almagest*.

Detailed descriptions of several observing instruments were given by Ptolemy and by the fourth-century commentators on his work, Pappus and Theon of Alexandria, as well as by Proclus in the fifth century C.E. Each instrument was designed to make a particular observation—for example, the star-taking instrument (called an astrolabe by Ptolemy, but which is an equatorial **armillary sphere** in modern terminology) used to determine the dates of the equinoxes. He described two such instruments in use at a public site in Alexandria, suggesting the reliance on observations for calendrical needs.

The practical uses of astronomy, as well as the intellectual challenges, address only some of the motivations for pursuing astronomy in antiquity. Ancient spirituality incorporated many forms of astral piety, the veneration of the heavenly bodies as divine or eternal. Literary works and architectural monuments provide evidence for many forms of astral piety, which also found expression in the writings of many ancient authors. The Greek philosophical tradition, in particular, elaborated on the theme of the veneration of the astral deities, often to the disgust of Jewish and Christian theologians.

The earliest extant Greek texts, the Homeric and Hesiodic poems of the eighth century B.C.E., suggest important relationships between celestial phenomena and divinity. In the Homeric poems, the actions and activities of the gods serve to explain many of the phenomena of the sky; the Homeric understanding of celestial phenomena is intimately connected to the behavior of the gods.

In some cases, Greek astral piety did not simply entail the veneration of celestial divinities; notably, a particular form of astral piety was linked to an ethical teaching that emphasized the benefits to be derived from the study of the heavens. Examples may be found in the writings of Plato, Aristotle, and their followers, including Ptolemy. According to this view, the intellectual work of the astronomer is a striving for a noble and disciplined character, which enables the astronomer to become more similar to the celestial divinities.

The celestial bodies were also regarded as divinities within several Near Eastern religious traditions. While there is evidence that these religions influenced Greek ideas regarding celestial divinity, the nature and extent of this influence is not well known, neither in general terms nor with regard to the possible influence of local religious practice on particular communities or individuals. Within the Hellenistic astral religions generally, there was an emphasis on ritualized practices, salvation, and the afterlife.

But the importance of the celestial divinities was not seen as restricted to influence in the hereafter; rather, the view that the celestial bodies affect events on earth was an important one, which took many forms. Within the Greek philosophical tradition, many authors discussed the relationship between the heavens and earth, suggesting that the entire universe is intimately connected physically. In a separate tradition, celestial phenomena were used to predict the weather.

Astrological practice was based on the notion that celestial events influence what occurs on earth and that such influences could be predicted using astronomical knowledge and techniques.

Astrology seems to have first emerged in Mesopotamia, during the second millennium B.C.E., as part of the literature of omens, in which celestial phenomena were correlated with events of state. Very little is known about the early history of astrology, even though a large number of omen texts survive. Belief in astrology has been cited as one of the important factors motivating the transmission of astronomical knowledge between cultures (Neugebauer, *Exact Sciences*, 168). During the Hellenistic period, there was an increased interest in astrology, which relied on the production of numerical astronomical tables. The importance of astrology in Hellenistic Alexandria is indicated by the fact that the most important astronomers of the period are associated so closely with the practice. Hipparchus is mentioned often in the literature; Ptolemy devoted an entire treatise to astrology, which he explained is a second type of astronomical prediction, secondary to and less effective than the type described in the *Almagest*. Nevertheless, he considered the study of astrology to be worthwhile, since it is concerned with the configurations of the sun, moon, and stars, and the changes that result from those configurations. According to the principles of Hellenistic astrology, events on earth could be predicted by the physical influence of the motions of the celestial bodies. The theoretical basis that underlay Hellenistic astrology found a wide and sympathetic audience within the philosophical community, particularly among Stoic philosophers, who regarded astrology as a natural correlate of the principle of cosmic sympathy, in which all things in the universe are intimately connected. Regarding the significance of ancient astrology, Neugebauer reminded us that study of ancient astronomy quite properly includes a consideration of astrology (Neugebauer, *Exact Sciences*, 171).

As the discussion of astrology indicates, the modern understanding of what constitutes the subject matter of astronomy is quite different from that of the ancients. Any consideration of astronomy in the ancient world must include those ideas and practices that were important to the ancients themselves. The modern concept of astronomy as a scientific discipline cannot be anachronistically applied to antiquity; the modern understanding of how the ancients regarded the celestial phenomena should be informed by the examination of texts and sources that may not be considered scientific but that indicate widely held views or areas of controversial opinion regarding the heavens.

The paucity of complete astronomical texts requires the study of many sorts of texts, including those that are generally regarded as literary or philosophical. However, these texts should not simply be studied for the astronomical bits that can be gleaned from them; rather, an understanding of astronomy in the ancient world will be enhanced by a consideration of why some literary authors included detailed information about the heavens and the practice of astronomy. Certainly, astronomically based imagery is a commonplace among poets, but the ancient authors stand at the beginning of that tradition. At the least, the examination of such works provides some knowledge of the probable state of astronomical knowledge among educated people in antiquity. Further, the study of such texts will yield information regarding folk astronomy and popular conceptions of the heavens, information that broadens our understanding of ancient civilizations. The consideration of the intellectual contexts of ancient astronomy must also involve an examination of the philosophical background, interpreted in the broadest sense, to include natural philosophy, cosmology, metaphysics, ethics, and aesthetics.

By increasing understanding of the intellectual, social, and cultural background of ancient astronomy, insights will be gained regarding the place of astronomy in the ancient world. Some of this work must rely on specialists in ancient civilizations; there remain many aspects of ancient life that are little studied by scholars, not always for a lack of materials, but rather for a lack of interest. For example, detailed studies of the agrarian economy have been few and far between (though there does seem to be a slight increase in interest recently, perhaps tied to more general interest in environmental issues). As agricultural needs are cited as a motivation for acquiring astronomical and calendrical knowledge, that would seem to be a profitable avenue for future research.

Because there is little possibility of learning about the individuals engaged in astronomical activity in antiquity, it becomes imperative to try to gain an understanding of the contexts of the ancient world, in order to understand the place of astronomical knowledge within that world. In order to understand the contexts of ancient astronomy, the cooperation of scholars across different disciplines will be required, including archaeologists and specialists in ancient civilizations, as well as historians of astronomy.

Liba C. Taub

Bibliography

Bowen, A., and B. Goldstein. "A New View of Early Greek Astronomy." *Isis* 74 (1983): 330–340.

Brecher, K., and M. Feirtag. *Astronomy of the Ancients*. Cambridge: MIT Press, 1979.

Cumont, F. *Astrology and Religion among the Greeks and Romans*. New York: Dover, 1960.

Duhem, P. *To Save the Phenomena: An Essay on the Idea of Physical Theory from Plato to Galileo*. Translated by Edmund Doland and Chaninah Maschler. Chicago: University of Chicago Press, 1969.

Heath, T. *Aristarchus of Samos: The Ancient Copernicus*. Oxford: Clarendon Press, 1913.

Hodson, F.R., ed. *The Place of Astronomy in the Ancient World*. London: Oxford University Press, 1974.

Jones, A. "The Adaptation of Babylonian Methods in Greek Numerical Astronomy." *Isis* 82 (1991): 441–453.

Krupp, E.C. *In Search of Ancient Astronomies*. London: Chatto and Windus, 1979.

Lloyd, G.E.R. "Saving the Appearances." In *Methods and Problems in Greek Science*. Cambridge: Cambridge University Press, 1991.

Neugebauer, O. *The Exact Sciences in Antiquity*. 2nd edition. New York: Dover, 1969.

———. *A History of Ancient Mathematical Astronomy*. 3 vols. Berlin: Springer-Verlag, 1975.

North, J. *The Fontana History of Astronomy and Cosmology*. London: Fontana Press, 1994.

Pannekoek, A. *A History of Astronomy*. New York: Dover, 1961.

Price, D.J. "Precision Instruments: to 1500." In *A History of Technology*, edited by Charles Singer, E.J. Holmyard, A.R. Hall, and Trevor I. Williams, vol. 3: 582–619. Oxford: Clarendon Press, 1957.

Ruggles, C.L.N., ed. *Archaeoastronomy in the 1990s: Papers derived from the third 'Oxford' International Symposium on Archaeoastronomy, St. Andrews, U.K., September 1990*. Loughborough, U.K.: Group D, 1993.

Anglo-Australian Observatory

The Anglo-Australian Observatory (AAO) was established in 1973 as the instrumentality that operates the Anglo-Australian Telescope (AAT). It is responsible to the Anglo-Australian Telescope Board, an intergovernmental authority with three members appointed from each country. In 1988 the AAO took over the UK Schmidt Telescope, a southern counterpart of the Palomar Schmidt. The total staff, at present (1993), is fifty-eight, of whom some thirty-five work at a headquarters in Epping, Sydney, the remainder at the telescopes. Those are located at Siding Spring Observatory in northern New South Wales.

The AAT was first proposed in 1960 as a large optical telescope to be built jointly by Australia and Great Britain. It was to be in the 150-inch range and to be located in Australia. Costs and observing time were to be shared equally. Authority to proceed was given in 1967.

The question of how to run it was first raised at a board meeting in March of 1970 by Olin Eggen, director of the Mount Stromlo and Siding Spring Observatory (MSSSO). He proposed that the Australian National University (ANU) operate the telescope on behalf of the board. The case was that ANU had the expertise, that by incorporating the AAT into their existing structure they could run it more economically, and that they owned the mountain. Underlying it was MSSSO's determination to defend at all costs its near monopoly of Australian optical astronomy.

It was a strong case which with better handling might have won. But the British astronomers were lukewarm. They wanted direct access to the telescope—access by right, not via the ANU—which they maintained could be achieved only by operating it through a separate body directly responsible to the board. They thought too that the ANU had badly underestimated the costs and the technical difficulties. So began a bitter dispute that embroiled many people. Exacerbated by personal and institutional rivalries, it became notorious throughout the astronomical world, created deep rifts in Australian astronomy, and at times threatened the future of the whole project. The dispute was not resolved until June of 1973, when the board was at last given a mandate to appoint its own staff and to manage and develop the AAT. In retrospect, it is generally agreed that ANU played their cards badly, and that MSSSO was well out of it: Running that complex and sophisticated instrument would have imposed a much greater burden on the observatory than they ever anticipated, and changed its character profoundly.

Regularly scheduled observing began in mid-1975. The success of the telescope was immediate, nowhere more so than in the computer control system. It had been planned from the outset for full computer control (hence the superbly designed and executed polar axis), and its unprecedented setting accuracy, the ease with which it could be moved from star to star, and the flexibility that allowed operations like beam switching and automatic focusing all came as a revelation.

A comparable impression was created by the new fast spectrograph and electronic detector. It was built by Joe Wampler, the telescope's first director, and was a copy of one he and his collaborator Lloyd Robinson had made for the **Lick Observatory**. It too was fully computer controlled, and that, together with its ability to subtract sky backgrounds accurately and to display current signals on a video screen, were new and revolutionary concepts for Australian astronomers.

These new systems made the telescope so easy to operate that suddenly it was open to a much wider circle of users. Not surprisingly, it transformed optical astronomy in both Britain and Australia, especially in Britain, where observational astrophysics had languished for many years. Its success was a direct stimulus to the building of the British 4.2-meter William Herschel Telescope and the Australian 2.3-meter, which set new standards in mechanical precision and pointing accuracy. The power of the 2.3's control system established beyond doubt the practicability of the altazimuth mounting, now universally used for large telescopes.

The AAO has also pioneered major instrumental advances. These include a suite of versatile, sensitive infrared instruments, the state-of-the-art photometric system and a coudé echelle spectrograph with extremely high resolution. It pioneered the application of optical fibers for multiobject spectroscopy; a recent and ambitious project uses a 2-degree high-definition field at prime focus, created by a newly designed optical corrector, to obtain spectra of up to four hundred objects in one exposure. The facility is unique, and likely to remain so for a considerable time.

This continuously evolving instrumental program has played an essential part in the success of the AAO, and here and elsewhere the observatory has had the support of a strong and farsighted board. It has been an encouraging example of binational cooperation. The division of the staff into an on-site unit and the "laboratory" (as it is known) at Epping has also worked well. The laboratory provides offices, laboratories, computing facilities, and a library. There scientific work, instrument and software development, and administration are carried on, and visiting astronomers are accommodated. With a total strength of about ten, the computing staff is especially strong.

In 1971 the British decided to build a 1.2-meter Schmidt telescope on Siding Spring Mountain. It was to serve as a complement and a search instrument for the AAT in the same way that the Palomar Schmidt has done for the 200-inch Hale Telescope. The telescope was installed in 1973. It was similar in design to the Palomar Schmidt, but improved optics, particularly an achromatic corrector plate, enabled it to cover a much wider wavelength range and also to obtain objective prism spectra. Its main initial task, shared with the somewhat smaller Schmidt at the **European Southern Observatory** in Chile, was to map the southern sky from −17° to the South Pole with a mosaic of 606 photographic plates. The UK Schmidt took the blue plates, the ESO Schmidt the red. Subsequently it has carried out other surveys, done much observing for special projects, and recently was equipped with a fiber system for multiobject slit spectroscopy that can accommodate up to ninety-two objects. The combination of the Schmidt, the AAO, and the large Australian radio telescopes has proved particularly effective for studying quasars, and it has contributed a large part of our current knowledge of quasar astronomy.

In 1988 it was decided to transfer the telescope from the UK Science and Engineering Research Council to the AAO, where, like the AAT, it operates under the AAO director and is funded jointly by the two governments. The final destination of all Schmidt plates remains, as from the beginning, the Plate Library at the Royal Observatory, Edinburgh. Other U.K. facilities, such as high-speed measuring machines, maintain their close links with Schmidt operations in Australia.

S.C.B. Gascoigne

Bibliography

Annual Reports of the Anglo-Australian Telescope Board. Epping, Australia: Anglo-Australian Observatory.

Gascoigne, S.C.B., K.M. Proust, and M.O. Robins. *The Creation of the Anglo-Australian Observatory*. Cambridge: Cambridge University Press, 1990.

Hoyle, F. *The Anglo-Australian Telescope*. University College–Cardiff: Cardiff Press, 1982.

Arabic/Islamic Astronomy

Arabic/Islamic astronomy refers to a complex group of related traditions that dealt in a variety of ways with celestial phenomena; they were cultivated for approximately a millennium—from the eighth to the eighteenth centuries—in the lands dominated by Islamic civilization that stretched from Spain to Central Asia. Both the terms *Arabic* and *Islamic* are here in need of explanation and qualification. Arabic is not meant as an ethnic but rather a linguistic term, in recognition of the large numbers of non-Arabs who wrote their works in Arabic. It should be noted, though, that many astronomical works were produced, particularly in the later centuries, in other Islamic languages (especially Persian and Turkish). As for the term *Islamic*, it should be taken in the sense of the civilization rather than the religion, because much of the astronomy was secular, and also in acknowledgment of the many non-Muslims who worked within these traditions.

As in other civilizations, celestial phenomena were dealt with in a variety of ways in Islam, and distinct genres can be identified, among which we can include: (a) folk astronomy, much of which predated Islam and was associated with the star lore of the pre-Islamic Arabs; (b) religious cosmologies that were inspired by the Qur^cān and sacred traditions; (c) astrology, which in the main was rooted in the Hellenistic period; (d) the philosophical literature (derived, for the most part, from Plato's *Timaeus*, Aristotle's *De Caelo*, and their later commentators), which delved into the essential nature of the universe; (e) practical astronomy that used mathematical means to solve the problems of planetary positions, timekeeping, religious ritual, and so on; and (f) theoretical astronomy, which sought a coherent physical cosmography based on mathematical models without analyzing the underlying philosophical basis. Especially after the eleventh century, most medieval sources identified a distinct subject called *ᶜilm al-hay'a* as one of the mathematical, secular disciplines that included (e) and (f), and that can be roughly identified with the tradition of Hellenistic astronomy. In what follows, it is mostly that tradition that will be discussed.

Sources of Islamic Astronomy

As a result of the Islamic conquests of the seventh and eighth centuries, intellectual life in the Mediterranean basin and the Middle East was revitalized. In these conquered regions, there were, no doubt, indigenous scholars among the Persian-, Syriac-, and Greek-speaking peoples who had maintained a modest scientific tradition. But the major impetus to this Islamic renaissance of science came from the patronage of certain elite segments of the new ᶜAbbāsid caliphate that came to power in 750 C.E. and soon established itself in the newly founded capital of Baghdad. These patrons, which included several caliphs as well as Arab notables, not only employed a number of these indigenous people as court astrologers and astronomers but, more important, also effected numerous translations of Indian, Greek, Syriac, and possibly Persian works into Arabic using their multilingual talents. The importance of these translations cannot be overemphasized; with ancient scientific texts available in Arabic, a rather significant number of the Islamic literate public, which was not insubstantial, as a result of widespread schooling among all classes and the availability of cheap paper, were both aware and influenced by these secular traditions.

The Persian and Syriac astronomical traditions played relatively minor roles; from what is known of them, both traditions seem to be derivative (the former from Greek and especially Indian astronomy, the latter mainly from Greek material). On the other hand, Indian astronomy was quite influential in the early stages of Islamic astronomy. There apparently were several translations of Sanskrit works; the most important of these came to be known as the *Sindhind*. This became the basis for an important tradition in Arabic that included the *Zīj* (astronomical handbook) of Muḥammad ibn Mūsā al-Khwārizmī (fl. 813–833), who was also one of the key figures in the history of algebra. This tradition, though originally centered in Baghdad, had its greatest long-term influence in Muslim Spain and western Europe through the incorporation of some of its material in the Toledan Tables and later in the **Alfonsine Tables**.

But in Eastern Islam, Indian astronomy was supplanted toward the end of the ninth century by the astronomy of the Greeks and in particular that of **Claudius Ptolemy**, the great Alexandrian scientist of the second century C.E. Four of his books were crucial for the development of astronomy in Islam: the *Almagest*, the *Handy Tables*, the *Planetary Hypotheses*, and the *Tetrabiblos*. With only minor distortion, it is possible to see these as serving as the basis for four distinct traditions of the Islamic astronomical corpus: (a) general works on mathematical astronomy; (b) the *zīj* literature; (c) works falling under the rubric of *hay'a* (cosmography—see below); and (d) astrology. In addition, a group of minor Greek texts called the *Little Astronomy* (more commonly known in Arabic as the *Middle Astronomy*, as they were supposed to be studied between Euclid's *Elements* and the *Almagest*) were also translated into Arabic.

It is important to note that this triumph of Ptolemaic astronomy, prominently marked by the appearance in the early tenth century of the *Zīj* of Abū ᶜAbdallāh Muḥammad al-Battānī, was not inevitable. Indian astronomical techniques were preferred by some Islamic astronomers even after Ptolemy's works were widely available, and one also has the report from sixth-century (that is, pre-Islamic) Persia of the astronomers of the ruler Khusrau Anūshirwān basing their new *zīj* on an Indian astronomical text rather than Ptolemy's *Almagest*. From a modern perspective this may seem surprising, but in fact Indian astronomy, tending as it did to eschew broader metaphysical, physical, philosophical, and cosmological considerations, was more suited to astronomers who desired practical, straightforward methods of determining celestial positions that could be used for astrological prognostications. On the other hand, Greek astronomy, and that included Ptolemaic astronomy, came with considerable baggage inasmuch as it insisted upon retaining its connections with cosmology, which took the form of geometrical modeling using spherical orbs and circles, rules from natural philosophy that insisted upon uniform circular motion in the heavens, and metaphysical (that is, theological) considerations that made a Prime Mover the ultimate source of motion. One must therefore see the success of Ptolemaic astronomy in Islam as part of a larger Hellenization of intellectual life that occurred in the ninth century, a trend that far from being marginal engaged important segments of the elite including the Caliph al-Ma'mūn himself (ruled 813–833) and the Arab notable al-Kindī. In this scheme, astronomy was one of the philosophical sciences and provided both a means for salvation of the soul through intellectual activity and the mathematical underpinning to the cosmology of spheres and intelligences that was the backbone of not only the Neoplatonic worldview but also astrology and the emerging astral magic of the Sabians. It may in fact not be at all a coincidence that Thābit ibn Qurra and al-Battānī, who were key figures in ensuring the success of Ptolemaic astronomy, were members of this group of protected Hellenized pagans of northern Mesopotamia.

Observational/Practical Astronomy

Islamic astronomers developed, refined, and added to the computational techniques that had previously been invented to bring under control the complexities of astronomical phenomena. Among their most important contributions was to trigonometry, which became, for the first time in Islam, an independent mathematical discipline; by the tenth century, the six trigonometric functions, some of which had been inherited from India, were clearly defined and tabulated, and many important theorems and identities were enunciated that considerably simplified the tedious computations necessitated by the Greek chord function, which was generally discarded. A number of other elegant methods were developed to facilitate the setting up and use of astronomical tables. Another interesting development was universal solutions (that is, for all locations) of a number of problems in spherical astronomy.

Already in the ninth century, astronomical observations, several under the patronage of the Caliph al-Ma'mūn, were made that either led to the confirmation or modification of earlier parameters. Among these were improved values for the obliquity of the ecliptic, the precession of the equinoxes, the motion of the solar apogee, the solar eccentricity, and the size of the earth (which was the yardstick for measuring the size of the universe). The latter is particularly instructive as regards the methods and precision reached in Islamic astronomy as compared with Greek astronomy. Ptolemy, as well as other Greek astronomers and geographers, used rough, ready, and transparently approximate numbers for the circumference of the earth; on the other hand, Ma'mūn's astronomers conducted the first known scientific expedition to determine its size and came up with a figure within a few hundred kilometers of the modern value.

Star mapping generally followed the Ptolemaic tradition, but there was also a folk tradition of Arabic star names preserved as the lunar mansions. A beautiful and well-known text is al-Ṣūfī's *Book of Fixed Stars* (tenth century). Most *zīj*es include lists of stellar coordinates; a notable one is that of the fifteenth-century prince/astronomer **Ulugh Beg** of Samarqand, who oversaw a revised star catalogue based on new observations.

Various observational instruments were inherited from the Greeks, such as the celestial and armillary spheres, the parallactic ruler, and the mural quadrant. Muslim astronomers added to and improved them in various ways; for example, large-scale sextants were built, the largest, having a radius of 40 meters, being located at Ulugh Beg's Samarqand observatory. It should be noted that in addition to this one, there were a number of other large-scale observatories, in particular one built under the patronage of the Mongols at Marāgha in northwest Iran in the thirteenth century and another in Istanbul in the sixteenth. Indeed, the **observatory** as an institution was an Islamic innovation that seems to have influenced later efforts in Europe. Non-observational instruments, which included analogue computers such as the **astrolabe**, various **quadrants**, **sundials**, and equatoria, were used for solving problems of spherical astronomy, mathematics, timekeeping, and planetary positions. Two of these, the astrolabe and sundial, were of Greek provenance but were considerably developed and improved. Of especial interest are the universal astrolabes and quadrants, which could be used at any location.

Theoretical Astronomy and Modeling

Theoretical treatments tended to emphasize, especially after the eleventh century, that the subject matter of astronomy was the simple physical bodies, both celestial and sublunar. Its purpose was to understand the external makeup—or configuration (*hay'a*)—of the universe. This was contrasted with both the natural philosophical tradition of Aristotle's *De Caelo* and the astrological corpus, both of which dealt with the essential (or internal) aspects of the bodies. Note that this new categorization meant that astronomy should also deal with the configuration of the four sublunar elements; thus most general treatments of astronomy after the eleventh century came to have a section on the configuration of the earth that included general discussions of geography. The prevalent view was that the universe was a plenum composed of nine contiguous, solid, spherical bodies called orbs, all concentric with an immobile, spherical earth. The lowest of these, that of the moon, enclosed the four sublunar levels of the four elements, namely fire, air, water, and earth. Each of the concentrics had embedded within it additional orbs called eccentrics and epicycles. There was one concentric each for the seven planets in the following order: Moon, Mercury, Venus, Sun, Mars, Jupiter, Saturn—another for the fixed stars, and a starless ninth that was the source of the daily motion. Opinions varied as to how motion occurred, but generally it was held to result from a combination of the proper motion effected by the orb's own soul and the accidental motion that was a consequence of being contained inside other orbs. All the celestial orbs were composed of a special fifth element called aether; unlike the four sublunar elements, it could rotate only with uniform motion.

Although this general picture derived for the most part from Ptolemy's *Planetary Hypotheses*, Islamic theoreticians found much to complain about and proposed numerous alternatives that were meant to reform or supersede Ptolemy's models. Driven by the conflicts between the values for precession and the obliquity of the ecliptic found by Ma'mūn's observers and those of Ptolemy, several "trepidation" models were proposed from the ninth through twelfth centuries to account for these variations. Later Islamic astronomers usually rejected them, correctly attributing the problem to Ptolemy's poor observations. On the other hand, they continued to have currency in Europe up to and even after Copernicus.

Another type of difficulty with Ptolemy concerned certain devices that he had introduced in the *Almagest*, such as the equant, that violated the principle of uniform circular motion. Ibn al-Haytham (d. ca. 1040), known principally for his great work *Optics*, also wrote the *Configuration of the World*, in which he attempted to show how one could make the mathematical models of the *Almagest* into physical models; in a later work, *Doubts about Ptolemy*, he set out to prove that this was not possible given such devices as the equant. In the thirteenth century, a number of writers, beginning with the Persian polymath Na'īr al-Dīn al-Ṭūsī, who was the first director of the Marāgha observatory, proposed alternative models that were meant to reform the Ptolemaic system. These efforts continued for at least three more centuries and included the work of his colleague Mu'ayyad al-Dīn al-ᶜUr4ī, his student Quṭb al-Dīn al-Shīrāzī, Ibn al-Shāṭir, the timekeeper of the Umayyad Mosque in Damascus who proposed an astronomy without eccentrics, and a number of people associated with the Samarqand observatory in the fifteenth century.

In Islamic Spain, the astronomical tradition was rather different than in the East. The continuation of the *Sindhind* tradition has already been noted. In addition to Abū Isḥāq al-Zarqāllu (eleventh century), who is known for his universal astrolabe, trepidation theory, and accurate value for the motion of the solar apogee, and Jābir ibn Aflaḥ (twelfth century), who wrote a rather critical commentary on the *Almagest*, Spain was the scene of an interesting twelfth-century episode in which a number of Aristotelians, including the famous philosopher Averroes, sought a radical reform of Ptolemaic astronomy that would rid it of epicycles and eccentrics altogether. The motivation was to return to a purer astronomy in which there was only a single center of celestial motion. The end product of this movement was the work of al-Biṭrūjī. His system, reminiscent of that of Eudoxus, was not very successful from a mathematical point of view, but it was quite influential in the Latin West.

The Historiography of Islamic Astronomy

Islamic astronomy had a profound effect upon Byzantine and medieval European astronomy, and a somewhat smaller impact on Indian astronomy. In Spain in the twelfth century, not only original works but even Greek works such as the *Almagest* were translated into Latin from Arabic. This influence is attested to by the almost two hundred modern star names with Arabic origins, technical terms such as zenith, nadir and azimuth, the introduction into Europe of trigonometry, and the widespread medieval and Renaissance interest in the problems of mathematizing cosmology. Even into the seventeenth century, Europeans were studying Islamic astronomy for its contemporary significance. By the nineteenth century, a historical interest had replaced a scientific one. These studies tended to be dominated by strongly positivistic and judgmental attitudes that berated Islamic scientists for not doing more for the progress of science. Though some orientalist scholars came to the defense of their subjects, the dominant attitudes, often colored by anti-Semitism, were firmly fixed by the beginning part of this century. Typical of this period is the remark that "Islamic science is in large part the plundered spoils of decadent Greek science" (Duhem, vol. 2, 179); more charitable commentators noted the role of preservation and transmission played by Islam.

After World War II, a large number of studies appeared that took their inspiration from Otto Neugebauer; these emphasized the advances in computational techniques and the notable achievements of the eleventh-century universal scholar al-Bīrūnī, who exhibited a decidedly practical bent in his astronomy. Meanwhile it was discovered that the models of Ibn al-Shāṭir and of Copernicus were virtually identical, and it was rediscovered that Copernicus's device for generating straightline from uniform circular motion had originally been invented by al-Ṭūsī. These discoveries and others, coupled with an increased awareness of the importance of cosmological considerations for both Ptolemy and Copernicus, have tended to place the Islamic contribution to theoretical astronomy in a new light. Other recent historiographical trends have emphasized the specific Islamic context. Some have claimed that this context is at base a religious quest for unity in the cosmos that informs all Islamic science. Others, basing themselves on newly discovered manuscript sources, have argued that scientific advances may have been inspired by religious problems such as determining prayer times, finding the sacred direction of Mecca, and predicting the beginning of the lunar month, but that the methodology and results were decidedly secular. The Islamic context has also been shown to have played an important role in leading to an astronomy that separated itself from astrology as well as philosophy.

The problem of context is intimately tied with other historiographical problems. That Islamic science is simultaneously Western and non-Western points to the inadequacy of this dichotomy, but no clear alternative has emerged that would allow its particular aspects to be integrated into a general account of astronomy. Transmission is another problematic area. The notion that Islamic astronomy is only important insofar as it contributed to European science is now generally discredited, but an overly contextualized approach runs the risk of marginalizing its contributions. This is particularly the case for the possible links between late Islamic astronomy and Copernicus mentioned above. Some historians have emphasized the Copernican connection to the exclusion of the Islamic context, while others have insisted that these models are part of Islamic history with only a coincidental connection with Copernicus. This post twelfth-century tradition has raised another issue, that of decline. The standard view has been that Islamic science ceased when its role as transmitter was completed in the twelfth century; religious fanaticism was usually taken to be the culprit. But then how does one explain the continuation and vigor of Islamic science and astronomy into at least the sixteenth century?

This last question, to which no one has yet offered an adequate answer, is meant to emphasize how little of the mass of manuscript material existing in libraries throughout the world has been looked at, much less edited, translated, or studied, and how few serious researchers there are. The past twenty-five years have witnessed numerous discoveries and new insights, but much more needs to be done before an adequate history of Islamic astronomy can be written.

F. Jamil Ragep

Bibliography

al-Biṭrūjī, Nūr al-Dīn abū Isḥāq. *On the Principles of Astronomy*. Edited, translated, and with a commentary by Bernard Goldstein. 2 vols. New Haven: Yale University Press, 1971.

Duhem, P. *Le Système du monde*. 10 vols. Paris: Hermann, 1913–1959.

Hartner, W. *Oriens-Occidens: Ausgewählte Schriften zur Wissenschafts- und Kulturgeschichte*. 2 vols. Hildesheim: George Olms, 1968, 1984.

Kennedy, E.S., et al. *Studies in the Islamic Exact Sciences*. Edited by David A. King and Mary Helen Kennedy. Beirut: American University of Beirut, 1983.

King, D.A. *Islamic Mathematical Astronomy*. London: Variorum Reprints, 1986; 2nd. rev. ed., Aldershot (U.K.): Variorum Reprints, 1993.

———. *Islamic Astronomical Instruments*. London: Variorum Reprints, 1987.

———. *Astronomy in the Service of Islam*. Aldershot (U.K.): Variorum Reprints, 1993.

Kunitzsch, P. *The Arabs and the Stars: Texts and Traditions on the Fixed Stars, and Their Influence in Medieval Europe*. Northampton (U.K.): Variorum Reprints, 1989.

Langermann, Y.T. *Ibn al-Haytham's "On the Configuration of the World."* New York: Garland (Harvard Dissertations in the History of Science), 1990.

Nallino, C. "Sun, Moon and Stars (Muhammadan)." In *Encyclopaedia of Religion and Ethics*, edited by J. Hastings, vol. 12, 94–101. Edinburgh: T.&T. Clark, 1921.

Neugebauer, O. *A History of Ancient Mathematical Astronomy*. 3 vols. Berlin: Springer-Verlag, 1975.

Pingree, D. "The Greek Influence on Early Islamic Mathematical Astronomy." *Journal of the American Oriental Society* 93 (1973): 32–43.

Ragep, F.J. "Duhem, the Arabs, and the History of Cosmology." *Synthese* 83 (1990): 201–214.

———. *Naṣīr al-Dīn al-Ṭūsī's Memoir on Astronomy (al-tadhkira fī ᶜilm al-hay'a)*. Sources in the History of Mathematics and Physical Sciences. 2 vols. New York: Springer-Verlag, 1993.

Sabra, A.I. "An Eleventh-Century Refutation of Ptolemy's Planetary Theory." In *Studia Copernicana* 16, 117–131. Warsaw: Ossolineum, 1978.

———. "The Andalusian Revolt Against Ptolemaic Astronomy: Averroes and al-Biṭrūjī." In *Transformation and Tradition in the Sciences*, edited by E. Mendelsohn, pp. 133–153. Cambridge: Cambridge University Press, 1984.

———. "The Appropriation and Subsequent Naturalization of Greek Science in Medieval Islam: A Preliminary Statement." *History of Science* 25 (1987): 223–243.

Saliba, G. *A History of Arabic Astronomy: Planetary Theories during the Golden Age of Islam*. New York: New York University Press, 1994.

Samsó, J. *Islamic Astronomy and Medieval Spain*. Aldershot (U.K.): Variorum Reprints, 1994.

Sayili, A. *The Observatory in Islam*. Ankara: Turkish Historical Society, 1960.

Sezgin, F. *Geschichte des arabischen Schrifttums*. Vol. 6: *Astronomie*. Leiden: E.J. Brill, 1978.

Archaeoastronomy

Archaeoastronomy is the interdisciplinary study of prehistoric, ancient, and traditional astronomies worldwide within their cultural context. It includes both written and archaeological records. It embraces calendrics; practical observation; sky lore and celestial myth; symbolic representation of celestial objects, concepts, and events; astronomical orientation of tombs, temples, shrines, and urban centers; symbolic displays involving celestial phenomena in the natural environment; traditional cosmology; and ceremonial application of astronomical tradition. Although archaeoastronomy is most often associated with astronomical alignments in monumental architecture—for example **Stonehenge**, North American medicine wheels, prehistoric Pueblo buildings in the American Southwest, Mesoamerican temple platforms, and Egyptian pyramids and temples—its true scope establishes it as an "anthropology of astronomy" (Aveni 1989, 7).

If astronomy is "the means by which societies seek to make their observations of the heavens intelligible" (McCluskey, 214), archaeoastronomy is a systematic, cross-cultural attempt to understand how prehistoric, ancient, and traditional societies do that. The exploration of this "interaction between the brain and sky" (Krupp 1981, 59) emphasizes the cultural component of astronomy, which is expressed in temples, tombs, iconography, costume, seasonally timed or astronomically inspired ritual and ceremony, myth, calendars, clocks, urban planning, agriculture, hunting and gathering practices and prohibitions, divination, systems of kinship, royal protocol, vision quest shrines, transcendental journeys of the soul, world view, and even astronomical observatories.

Ethnoastronomy is the study of traditional astronomies through ethnographic and ethnohistoric resources. The history of astronomy is generally taken to be the study of the historic development of literate, mathematical, "scientific" astronomy (Neugebauer, 35). Both are usually judged to embrace realms of knowledge different from archaeoastronomy, but both actually overlap the concerns, methods, and data of archaeoastronomy.

Intentional astronomical alignment of some prehistoric monuments of Europe is generally accepted, but the purpose, complexity, and precision of these elements of megalithic architecture are controversial, unresolved issues. These alignments are judged to be directed to the horizon and to rising or setting points of important celestial objects, especially the sun. The seasonal excursion of the position of sunrise and sunset establishes annual northern and southern limits for this event. The summer (Northern Hemisphere) solstice sun rises and sets in the north, and the winter (Northern Hemisphere) solstice sun rises and sets in the south. At any given latitude, sunrise and sunset never occur outside these solstitial limits. Equinox sunrise and sunset, in spring and autumn, take place midway between the solstice limits.

Stonehenge, in southern England, probably incorporated an axis symbolically oriented toward the summer solstice sunrise. Sites like Kintraw and Ballochroy in western Scotland include upright stones, or menhirs, that have been interpreted as components of precise solar observatories, but skeptics argue that the evidence for high precision is subjective. The alignment near Minard, Scotland, on Brainport Bay, includes quartz scatters and other signs of prehistoric ritual, along with a pair of upright, socketed stones that establish a line to a horizon feature that marks summer solstice sunrise.

Lunar alignments have also been identified in prehistoric monuments. Through each month the moonrise and moonset shifts between northern and southern limits that are analogous to the annual turning points, or solstice limits, of the sun. Gravitational effects, however, induce a cyclical swiveling of the moon's orbit. In 18.61 years, the moon's monthly limits vary from a maximum spread (major standstill) to a minimum spread (minor standstill) and back to maximum. Lunar standstill alignments at Stonehenge have been advocated. The southern major standstill moon skirts the horizon at Callanish, on the Isle of Lewis, in Scotland's Outer Hebrides, and stones in the central circle frame the southernmost full moon dramatically. Most of the stone circles in northeast Scotland, in the general vicinity of Aberdeen, have one stone that lies on its side and is flanked by two uprights. The main axis of these circles is indicated by the recumbent stone, and the majority of these recumbent stones are located toward the south, between the major standstill southern moonrise and moonset. In these circles, at the major standstill, the summer full moon would appear to rise from, hover over, or set upon the recumbent stone. If any of these lunar alignments—from Stonehenge, Callanish, or northeast Scotland—are real, their accuracy and precision suggest a symbolic, rather than observational, purpose.

A number of standing stones and stone alignments have been explained as genuine prehistoric lunar observatories, precise enough to discern the semiannual solar perturbation of the moon's orbit. In Scotland, these include the Kilmartin stones near the Temple Wood stone circle, the Ballinaby stone on Islay, and several more. Massive upright stones and the vast stone rows at Carnac, in Brittany, France, have also been interpreted as lunar observatories. The varying effects of atmospheric refraction, however, appear to be large enough to have prevented such precise observations of the moon from being made in the Stone and

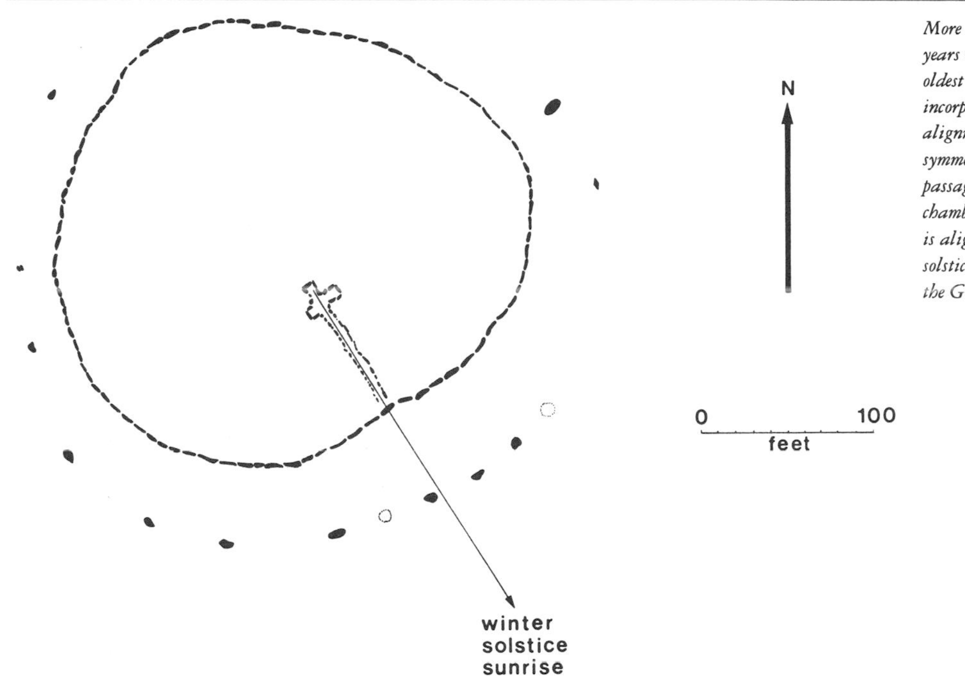

More than five thousand years old, Newgrange is the oldest monument thought to incorporate an astronomical alignment. The axis of symmetry and the main passage of this prehistoric chambered tomb in Ireland is aligned with winter solstice sunrise. (Courtesy of the Griffith Observatory)

Bronze ages with megalithic observatories. Critics also judge that such precise observations of the moon have no obvious function in the culture of the megalith builders.

Prehistoric chambered passage graves are found throughout Europe, and many of them are older than most of the stone rings and standing stones. Newgrange, in Ireland, was constructed around 3300 B.C.E. Its main axis, which is defined by its axis of symmetry, by the passage that leads to its central chamber, and by two elaborately decorated stones lodged in its exterior curbing, is aligned with the winter solstice sunrise. Although the first light of the winter sun cannot enter the chamber through the passage entrance, a window that was constructed just above the entrance does permit the winter solstice sunlight to bathe the inner sanctum. This seasonally significant symbolic alignment is a plausible and convincing example of prehistoric astronomy. If it was intended, Newgrange is the oldest known astronomically aligned monument. Other passage graves and chambered tombs, including Knowth in Ireland, Bryn Celli Ddu in Wales, Maes Howe and the Clava Cairns in Scotland, and La Roche-aux-Fées and Gavr'inis in Brittany, are oriented on important seasonal stations of the sun.

Folk calendars of Europe recognize not only the solstices and equinoxes but also the dates that fall more or less midway between those dates. For that reason, the sun's position in early February, early May, early August, and early November may have been noted in Antiquity. Some prehistoric monuments, including the neolithic (2900 B.C.E.) temple at Godmanchester, near Cambridge, England, have alignments for the sun that correspond to these intermediate calendar dates.

Just how long human beings have systematically observed the sun, moon, and stars is not known, but circumstantial evidence

Newgrange is fronted with an elaborately carved entrance stone. Above the door behind it, a modest window, known as the roof box, allows light from the winter solstice rising sun to beam through the tomb and to reach the back chamber. (Courtesy of E.C. Krupp)

from the Upper Paleolithic suggests the tradition is tens of thousands of years old. Seasonal symbolism and lunar tallies have been recognized in the art and notations of Ice Age Europe.

Written evidence for systematic astronomy and an accurate calendar in China dates to the Bronze Age Shang dynasty and about 1300 B.C.E. Seasonal ritual linked with the solstices was in place at least by the Zhou dynasty and the third century B.C.E. The cardinal directions originate from the daily rotation of the sky around the north celestial pole, and by the era of Qin Shihuang di (third century B.C.E.), China's first emperor, imperial tombs were designed with cardinal orientation. In the Han dynasty, which followed Qin, much of China's traditional astronomical imagery emerged in a conventionalized form. Through the rest of China's history, until the declaration of the Chinese Republic in 1912, astronomy was institutionalized in an official capacity at the service of the emperor.

Archaeoastronomical studies of the Hindu tradition in India have been limited, but the cardinal orientation, seasonal festivals, and astronomical symbolism of the Sun Temple at Konarak have been studied. Solstitial and cardinal alignments of hills and temples at Vijayanagara, the fourteenth century medieval Hindu capital, have been identified and understood in terms of spiritual cosmology and sacred authorization of kingship. A rich tradition of Hindu star names, celestial myths, and sky lore also survives.

Cuneiform records from Mesopotamia demonstrate the presence of systematic observation and mathematical astronomy by the seventh century B.C.E. and imply a quantitative knowledge of the cyclical behavior of Venus as early as the eighteenth century B.C.E. Omen texts also demonstrate the early use of astronomical observation for astrological interpretation of events on earth. Much of this material is often classified as part of the history of astronomy, but it is accompanied by an old tradition of celestial symbolism. This iconography is found in Mesopotamian religion and political organization from at least the beginning of the second millennium B.C.E., and the continuing use of star names of Sumerian origin suggests that much of the Mesopotamian astronomical lore and symbolism originated even earlier. Astronomical alignment of Mesopotamian architecture remains unstudied. In the sixth century B.C.E., Persepolis, the capital of the Persian empire, incorporated lion and bull constellation symbolism that related to the New Year vernal equinox festival and that probably was based upon a Middle Eastern tradition rooted in the Neolithic Era of the fourth millennium B.C.E.

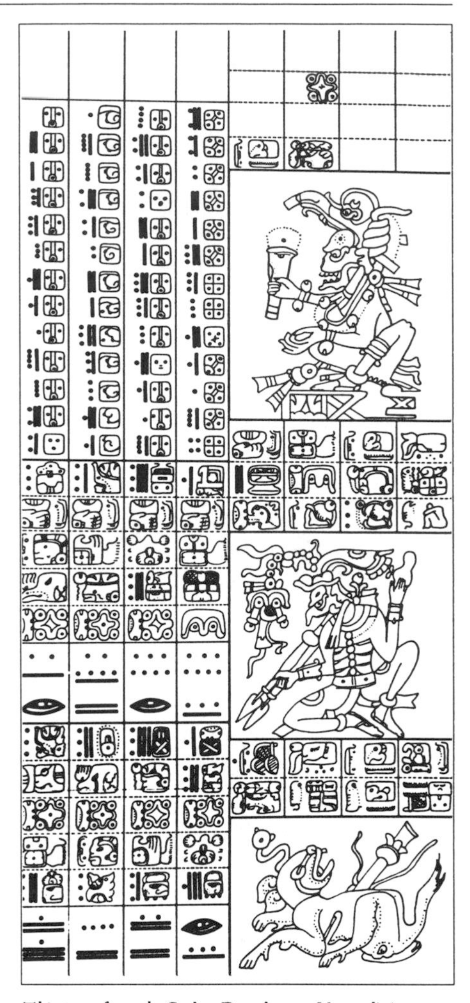

This page from the Codex Dresden, *a Maya divinatory almanac from northern Yucatán, includes a table that permits calculation of the date in the 260-day calendar of significant junctions in the 584-day cycle of the motion of Venus as seen from the earth. Venus is personified as a god in the two pictorial panels. The speared creature in the bottom panel is a victim of the dangerous influence of Venus in Maya astrological belief. (Courtesy of the Griffith Observatory)*

Ancient Egypt is known to have been the source of the solar calendar that evolved into the Gregorian calendar in use today, and Egyptian astronomical conventions were responsible as well for the concept of a 24-hour day. Texts relating to astronomy or incorporating astronomical symbolism are known from as early as the Old Kingdom period in the third millennium B.C.E. Most of these sources were found in a funereal context. Old

Kingdom pyramids are cardinally aligned, and unusual shafts built into the Great Pyramid at Giza appear to have been pointed toward stars of great importance in the Egyptian calendar and timekeeping systems and in Egyptian concepts of the destiny of the soul. By the New Kingdom, in the middle of the second millennium B.C.E., some Egyptian temples were aligned toward the winter solstice sunrise and possibly other celestial targets.

A tradition of literate astronomy in the New World prevailed among the Maya of southern Mexico and central America. A 365-day calendar based on the tropical year, a 260-day sacred calendar, and a system for keeping track of the phases and movement of the moon were used by the Maya, although their predecessors, the Olmec, are credited with having devised the counting system and the calendars. Divinatory almanacs that include tables that relate to the movement of the planet Venus and to the recurrence of eclipses survive from the Postclassic period. Astronomical alignments on extreme horizon positions of Venus have been measured from the House of the Governor at Uxmal in Yucatán. The upper tower of the **Caracol, at Chichén**

The last couple of hours of equinox sunset at Chichén Itzá, a late Maya ceremonial center in northern Yucatán, transform the western balustrade of the north stairway of the Castillo pyramid into a descending serpent with triangles of light. This building was known to the Maya as the Temple of Kukulcán, the Maya equivalent of the god the Aztecs called Quetzalcóatl. Quetzalcóatl sometimes took the form of a feathered rattlesnake, and the Yucateco rattlesnake has distinctive diamondback markings that from the side look like the serpent of sunlight on the Castillo stairs. (Courtesy of E.C. Krupp)

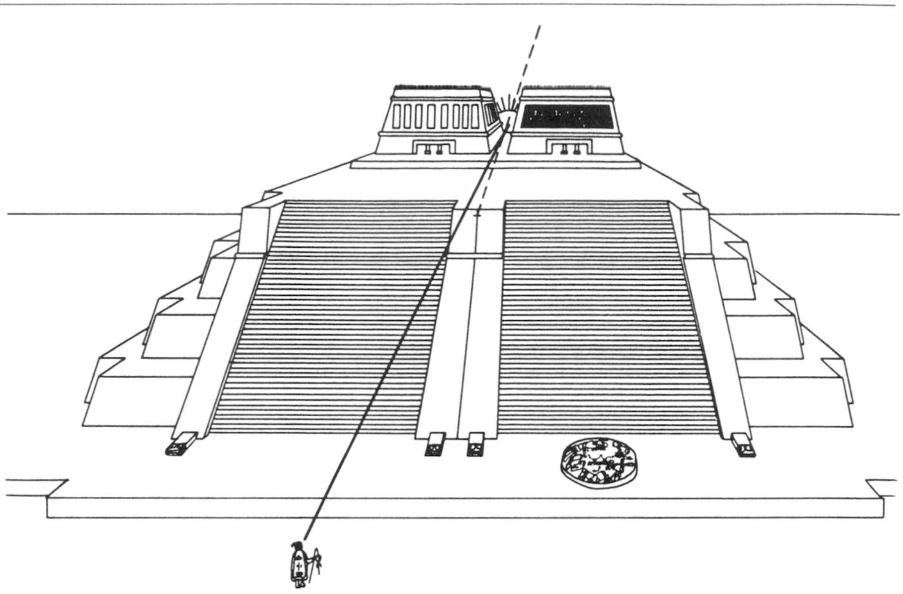

Tenochtitlán equinox sunrise over Templo Mayor. Templo Mayor was the primary stage for ritual in Tenochtitlán, the Aztec capital. This pyramid in part symbolized the hill of creation where the tribal god of the Aztecs was born with the full strength of the sun. He defeated his sister, Coyolxauhqui, who is shown dismembered and dead in the large sculpted disk at the foot of the stairs on the right. The entire building was oriented to allow the equinox sun to rise and appear above the temples on its summit. (Courtesy of the Griffith Observatory)

Itzá, may have functioned as a Venus observatory. Astronomical alignments and symbolism have been proposed for many other Maya structures. A "diamondback serpent" of light and shadow descends the west balustrade of the north stairway of the Castillo, or main pyramid, at Chichén Itzá in the late afternoon, at the time of the equinoxes. This event is consistent with other seasonal and astronomical symbolism of Mesoamerica. It may have been part of public ritual related to renewal and the return of the rains after the vernal equinox. Translation of Maya texts has revealed part of the role of astronomy in Maya life. Important dynastic events were linked, through astronomical and calendrical cycles, to mythic events in the distant past. Through these relationships, the prerogatives of the Maya elite were legitimized. Warfare and sacrifices timed by appearances of the planet Venus were conducted.

The Aztecs and other peoples of ancient Mexico used basically the same calendrical system as was kept by the Maya, although evidence for the same level of astronomical calculations and long-range calendrics is absent. A number of native pictorial manuscripts from central Mexico, pre-Conquest and post-Conquest, include images and day names that appear to link the documents to cycles of the sun and Venus and to celestial mythology. Astronomically aligned architecture may have been part of Tenochtitlán, the Aztec capital. The city plan seems to have been based upon cosmological concepts. Its main temple symbolized the mountain where Huitzilopochtli, the tribal patron god of the Aztecs, was born and fought the battle that established his supremacy—and therefore Aztec sovereignty. Huitzilopochtli was not the sun, but solar power was part of his identity. On the mountain of his birth, he killed his sister, Coyolxauhqui, who embodied some aspects of the moon. A massive stone relief depicting the slain and dismembered Coyolxauhqui was excavated from the lower foundations of the main temple, Templo Mayor. This temple is also aligned to allow the equinox sun to appear to rise from it as seen from the plaza to the west.

Although there was no known literate astronomy north of Mexico, symbolic depiction of astronomical events by North American Indians is abundant. The crescent moon accompanied by a star is found in rock art of the American Southwest, the Great Basin, and California. At first thought to represent eyewitness observations of the Crab supernova of 1054 C.E, these petroglyphs and pictographs are judged by other researchers to symbolize moon/Venus conjunctions. Astronomically aligned architecture is found in the Southwest. **Chaco Canyon**, in northwest New Mexico, appears to confirm prehistoric interest in cardinal directions, solstice sunrises and sunsets, and possibly the lunar standstills. Solar alignments produced light-and-shadow effects through ports in the walls of prehistoric Pueblo structures at Hovenweep, in the Four Corners region. A line of upright stones at Yellow Jacket, in the same area, points to the place on the mountain horizon where the sun rises on summer solstice. Another distinct horizon feature, near the summer solstice sunrise, allows a sunwatcher to anticipate the coming solstice by observing the sun's arrival there several days before the solstice. This technique is known to have been employed by the Hopi Sun Chief at the village of Walpi in order to alert the community to the need to begin preparations for the coming winter solstice ceremonies.

The main axis of the Bighorn Medicine Wheel, a boulder construction above the treeline on Medicine Mountain, Wyoming, is oriented toward the summer solstice sunrise. Several other mountaintop or hilltop medicine wheels also have features that indicate astronomical sightlines.

Cahokia (700–1500 C.E.), across the Mississippi River from St. Louis, was the major settlement of the Mississippian Era in North America. The Sun Circle, a timber post circle constructed to the west of Monks Mound (the largest indigenous monument north of Mexico), includes solstice and equinox sunrise alignments.

Ethnographic studies verify the existence of sun, moon, and star observation, celestial mythology, seasonal ritual, and other aspects of traditional astronomy among American Indian groups. Detailed research on the ethnoastronomy of the Chumash of California, the Skidi Pawnee of Kansas and Nebraska, and the Mescalero Apache of New Mexico has been published. The native astronomy of many other American Indians has been partially examined. Light-and-shadow effects, primarily associated with the solstices, have been discovered at a number of California rock art sites.

In South America, ethnohistoric information and archaeological data have been combined to reconstruct the astronomical system and calendrical traditions of the Inca. Cuzco's Coricancha, or Temple of the Sun, occupied the center of a radial set of lines of shrines, and some of these lines had astronomical significance. Towers were constructed on the horizon to mark the position of the rising or setting sun at the solstices, at key dates in the agricultural cycle, and at other important stations in the calendar. At Machu Picchu, the famous Inca settlement, windows of the Torreon appear to be associated with June solstice sunrise and important stars. A nearby cave known as Intimachay has a rock-cut window that admits the light of the December solstice sun. The *intihuatana*, or "hitching post of the sun," is an elaborately

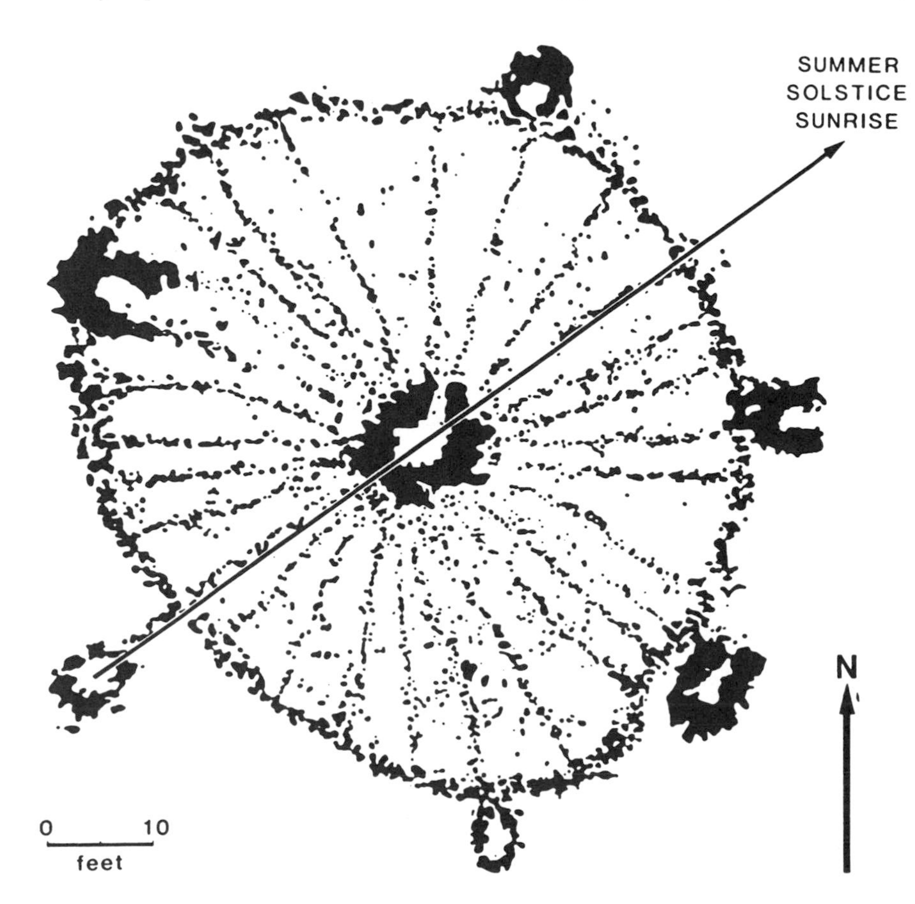

Summer solstice sunrise aligns with axis of symmetry of the Bighorn Medicine Wheel, a design laid out in stones and cairns on Medicine Mountain, in Wyoming. The southwest cairn occupies the end of an extended spoke that also coincides with the figure's main axis. (Courtesy of the Griffith Observatory)

carved outcrop associated with Inca sunwatching, but no astronomical function for it has been deduced.

The overall design of Cuzco was based upon the intercardinal directions, which were associated with the solstice limits and with the Milky Way's intersections with the horizon. Many of these concepts are preserved along with traditional Andean star lore by Quechua speakers today, and the ethnoastronomy of the Quechua-speaking people of the village of Mismanay has been studied comprehensively and published.

Although the astronomical knowledge and cosmological concepts of other South American peoples have not received the same attention, some information on the native astronomical knowledge and cosmology of the Bororo, the Guajiro, the Shipibo, the Desana, the Kogi, and the Warao has been synthesized. There is a great deal of native astronomy still embedded in the mythology of many other South American Indians.

Modern archaeoastronomical studies began in 1894, when the British astronomer Sir **Norman Lockyer** published *The Dawn of Astronomy.* In it, Lockyer reported the results of field work in Egypt, where he measured temple orientations and analyzed their possible alignment with the stars and the sun. Actually, Lockyer first outlined some of his key results in papers that he presented in 1891 and 1892, and H. Nissen, a German scholar, had suggested the possibility of astronomical temple alignment as early as 1885. Lockyer's study of Egyptian astronomy was accompanied by a short commentary on the possibility of astronomical significance in Greek temples. In 1906, Lockyer's first edition of *Stonehenge and Other British Stone Monuments Astronomically Considered* extended the concept of celestial alignment in monumental architecture to prehistoric structures in Europe. Although both books emphasized astronomical orientation, Lockyer supported and developed his ideas about ancient and prehistoric astronomy with other kinds of evidence. Egyptian history, religion, and myth were incorporated into *The Dawn of Astronomy*. British folklore and the peasant astronomy of Europe found their way into Lockyer's Stonehenge book. In both instances, Lockyer's work was too undisciplined for the specialists. Because his discussion of the cultural expressions of astronomy were flawed, his ideas about alignments were ignored, and except for the work of Alexander Thom, archaeoastronomy remained dormant until the 1960s.

Alexander Thom, a Scottish professor of engineering science, had been studying prehistoric sites in Britain and had carefully surveyed hundreds of them since the 1930s. His analysis led him to three principal conclusions. He believed that the rings and related monuments had been designed and constructed with a universal prehistoric unit, the megalithic yard. He recognized geometric design, possibly based upon Pythagorean triangles, in noncircular rings. He found a variety of astronomical alignments in the monuments and eventually argued in favor of highly precise solar and lunar observatories that could establish a reliable calendar and permit the direct prediction of lunar eclipses.

Widespread interest in prehistoric astronomy was stimulated in 1963 by Gerald S. Hawkins, a British astronomer and later a naturalized U.S. citizen. Hawkins reexamined the astronomical potential of Stonehenge and concluded that it contained solstitial alignments and lunar standstill alignments. He also explained the ring of fifty-six Aubrey holes, located just inside the monument's circular earthen bank, as a lunar eclipse computer.

Hawkins's work at Stonehenge inspired controversy and hostility from archaeologists. In time, Hawkins followed up his research with other field studies of New Kingdom temples in Egypt and of the Nazca lines on the southern coastal deserts of Peru.

Research on Mesoamerican astronomy had primarily involved the decipherment of Maya texts. The first real breakthrough in that area had occurred in 1880, when Ernst Förstemann, the head librarian of the Royal Public Library of Dresden, recognized that several pages in a Maya manuscript in the library's collection had something to do with the 584-day cycle of the planet **Venus**. Astronomical symbolism was recognized in art and ritual throughout Mesoamerica, and various researchers continued to try to crack the hieroglyphic record preserved in the few surviving Maya codices. The astronomical potential of the Caracol was considered by Oliver Ricketson in 1928. In 1970, Colgate University astronomer Anthony F. Aveni organized his first field expedition to Mexico, and he began publishing papers on astronomical alignments in Mesoamerican monuments in 1972.

By the early 1970s, a small group of independent investigators had emerged. Astronomer John A. Eddy surveyed and analyzed the Bighorn Medicine Wheel in 1972. At about the same time, Alexander Marshack published his first study of European Upper Paleolithic notations. Archaeologist Jonathan Reyman included commentary on possible astronomical elements of prehistoric Pueblo architecture in his 1971 Ph.D. thesis, and he prepared an unpublished report on astronomical alignments in Chaco Canyon's Pueblo Bonito in 1975. Astronomer Ray Williamson and his collaborators began measuring alignments in Chaco Canyon in 1972. Earlier, in the 1960s, Warren Wittry had made his preliminary findings at Cahokia's Sun Circle.

The Royal Society and the British Academy sponsored the first meeting specifically organized to discuss ancient and prehistoric astronomy. Held in December 1972, "The Place of Astronomy in the Ancient World" included papers dealing with both the written and the unwritten record. Mesopotamia, Egypt, the Maya region, China, prehistoric Europe, Peru, and the Pacific were discussed.

"Archaeoastronomy in Pre-Columbian America," a symposium organized by Aveni and Horst Hartung, who was a professor of city planning and pre-Columbian architecture at the University of Guadalajara, was held in Mexico City in June 1973. Despite the name of the meeting, papers on the American Southwest, the Great Basin, Midwestern mounds, and Egypt and Peru were included.

In 1977, two American astronomers, John Carlson and Ray Williamson, inaugurated the *Archaeoastronomy Bulletin,* a modest quarterly newsletter intended to keep those interested in the subject in touch with each other and informed about ongoing developments and events. In August 1978, the *Archaeoastronomy Bulletin* announced the formation of the Center for Archaeoastronomy. It was based at the University of Maryland, directed by Carlson, and responsible for publishing the newsletter, which was evolving into a journal.

Through the 1970s, additional meetings on archaeoastronomy were held. Each time the number of participants grew, and the scope of the studies widened. In 1979, "Archaeoastronomy in the Americas" drew an attendance of 150 people to Santa Fe, New Mexico, where forty papers were presented. Time at this meeting was consciously dedicated to a discussion of the identity, character, standards, and future of archaeoastronomy.

The *Journal for the History of Astronomy* began publishing archaeoastronomical papers by Alexander Thom and his son A.S. Thom as early as October 1971, but by 1979 the volume of archaeoastronomical research justified the establishment of a companion journal, *Archaeoastronomy*. The first issue was dominated by papers on North American rock art and on megalithic alignments in Britain.

The first truly international symposium on archaeoastronomy was held at the Queen's College in Oxford, England, in September 1981. Selected papers were published in two volumes, one dedicated to Old World sites and the other restricted to New World material. The Old World collection dealt exclusively with the astronomical alignment of archaeological monuments. The New World papers differed by their inclusion of ethnographic, ethnohistoric, iconographical, and textual data.

Although a variety of other conferences and symposia have been held since the Oxford conference, most have emphasized regional concerns. The most significant exceptions include the First International Conference on Ethnoastronomy, held in Washington, D.C., in September 1983, and the ongoing Oxford series (Mérida, Yucatán, Mexico—January 1986; St. Andrews, Scotland—September 1990; Stara Zagora, Bulgaria—August 1993). The interdisciplinary and international character of the field has been affirmed by sessions and symposia organized under the auspices of the Historical Astronomy Division of the American Astronomical Society, the American Association for the Advancement of Science, the International Congress of Americanists, the New York Academy of Sciences, and universities and other institutions in the United States, Canada, Mexico, Guatemala, Hungary, Poland, France, Italy, and India.

Edwin C. Krupp

Bibliography

Aveni, A.F., ed. *Archaeoastronomy in Pre-Columbian America.* Austin: University of Texas Press, 1975.

———. *Native American Astronomy.* Austin: University of Texas Press, 1977.

———. *Archaeoastronomy in the New World.* Cambridge: Cambridge University Press, 1982.

———. *New Directions in American Archaeoastronomy.* Oxford: B.A.R., 1988.

———. *World Archaeoastronomy.* Cambridge: Cambridge University Press, 1989.

Hadingham, E. *Early Man and the Cosmos.* New York: Walker, 1984.

Heggie, D.C., ed. *Archaeoastronomy in the Old World.* Cambridge: Cambridge University Press, 1982.

Hodson, F.R., ed. "The Place of Astronomy in the Ancient World." *Philosophical Transactions of the Royal Society of London* 276, 1257 (1974): 1–276.

Krupp, E.C. "A Glance into the Smoking Mirror." In *Archaeoastronomy in the Americas,* edited by Ray A. Williamson, 55–59. Los Altos, Calif., and College Park, Md.: Ballena Press and Center for Archaeoastronomy, 1981.

———. *Echoes of the Ancient Skies.* New York: Harper & Row, 1983.

———. *Beyond the Blue Horizon—Myths and Legends of the Sun, Moon, Stars, and Planets.* New York: HarperCollins, 1991.

———., ed. *In Search of Ancient Astronomies.* Garden City, N.Y.: Doubleday, 1978.

———. *Archaeoastronomy and the Roots of Science.* Boulder, Colo./Washington, D.C.: Westview Press/American Association for the Advancement of Science, 1984.

Lockyer, Sir J.N. *The Dawn of Astronomy.* London: Cassell and Company, 1894.

———. *Stonehenge and Other British Stone Monuments Astronomically Considered.* 2nd ed. London: Macmillan, 1909.

McCluskey, S.C. "Science, Society, Objectivity, and the Astronomies of the Southwest." In *Astronomy and Ceremony in the Prehistoric Southwest,* edited by John B. Carlson and W. James Judge, 205–217. Albuquerque, N.M.: Maxwell Museum of Anthropology, 1987.

Neugebauer, O. "The History of Ancient Astronomy: Problems and Methods." *Journal of Near Eastern Studies* 4 (1945): 1–38.

Argelander, Friedrich Wilhelm August (1799–1875)

Stellar astronomer of Prussian-Finnish descent, Argelander was educated in Konigsberg, where he was encouraged by Friedrich Wilhelm Bessel to study astronomy. Between 1823 and 1836 he was the director of Turku and then Helsinki observatories in Finland, before taking up a professorship in Bonn. His main contributions were an analysis of solar motion from stellar **proper motion**, the study of the light curves of variable stars, and, above all, the cataloguing of stellar positions and magnitudes.

Argelander's reputation rests more on his systematic thoroughness as an observer using simple instruments than on any single notable discovery. In Finland he determined proper motions for several hundred stars and later used that data to greatly improve the value for the solar motion among the stars.

In Bonn his first notable program was the *Uranometria Nova* catalogue of 1843, giving the positions and magnitudes of 3,256 naked-eye stars north of −35 degrees declination. Magnitudes were estimated to about one-third of a magnitude, using notation such as 2, 2.3, 3.2, 3 for successively fainter stars. He also developed Herschel's method of sequences, or step estimation method, and applied it to the study of variable stars, encouraging amateur astronomers to use this technique to obtain light curves.

Argelander's greatest work was the *Bonner Durchmusterung,* a huge survey of the northern sky, complete to magnitude 9.5 and undertaken with no more than a 76-mm refractor. The observations were undertaken over seven years starting in 1852 with his assistants in Bonn, with magnitudes estimated to about ±0.24 in the best cases at the zenith.

The significance of the *Bonner Durchmusterung* is that thousands of stars were catalogued for the first time, thus providing a statistical base for later astronomers to use to analyze their numbers and distribution to different magnitude limits.

J. B. Hearnshaw

Bibliography

Sticker, B. "Argelander, Friedrich Wilhelm August." In *Dictionary of Scientific Biography*, edited by C.C. Gillispie, vol. 1, 240–243. New York: Scribner, 1970.

Argentine National Observatory

The Argentine National Observatory at Cordoba was founded in 1870 and opened the following year by President Domingo Faustino Sarmiento, under the direction of the American astronomer Benjamin Apthorp Gould. For the first sixty-five years, it was run by expatriate Americans studying astrometry. Their efforts culminated in the influential star catalogue *Cordoba Durchmusterung* in 1930. From 1936 onward the observatory was led by Argentines, who directed it toward astrophysics and galactic astronomy. But it was soon overtaken by larger observatories and ultimately absorbed by the University of Cordoba in 1955.

President Sarmiento provided the first support for the observatory. A strong advocate of public education, industrialization, and development, he offered Gould the directorship in hopes that Americans would increase the level of scientific and technical knowledge in Argentina. Gould, founder of the *Astronomical Journal*, had served as executive officer (1855–1858) and director (1858–1859) of the Dudley Observatory. During the 1860s he charted stars near the north celestial pole, and by about 1865 decided to extend his observations to the largely neglected southern skies. Sarmiento's invitation was ideal for his plans.

Gould began astronomical research in Argentina long before the observatory was constructed. Cordoba, over 600 km northwest of Buenos Aires in the remote Argentine interior, was chosen because it was free from both coastal hurricanes and Andean earthquakes. After charting the skies with naked eye and binoculars, Gould realized the site had excellent seeing conditions and transparency as well. Over the next few years, Gould and four North American assistants compiled the *Uranometria Argentina*, which catalogued the positions and magnitudes of stars brighter than the seventh magnitude within 100 degrees of the South Pole.

Meanwhile, Gould ordered telescopes for the new observatory from France, but the 1870 Franco-Prussian War delayed their arrival. It was not until October 1871 that the Argentine National Observatory was finally dedicated. It was equipped with a 12-inch refractor, a 5-inch photographic refractor (with a Clark object lens), and a small meridian circle.

During its early years, the observatory concentrated on the **astrometry** of the southern skies. Despite frequent political upheavals, irregular financing (in 1880, Gould paid his staff from his own funds), and unpredictable weather (assistant Charles William Stevins was struck by lightning and killed at his desk!), Gould and his staff carried out a remarkably thorough program of observation. The *Uranometria Argentina* was finally released in 1879, establishing Gould's Belt, a broad band of bright stars inclined approximately 20 degrees to the galactic equator. Between 1872 and 1877, observatory staff made their first zone observations of southern stars, published as the 1884 *Catalogo de las zonas estelares* (73,160 stars) and the 1886 *Catalogo general* (32,448 stars).

The observatory's most significant achievement, however, was its general catalogue of all Southern Hemisphere stars brighter than the tenth magnitude. The enormous *Cordoba Durchmusterung* (CD), with positions of 613,953 stars, became the southern equivalent of the influential northern *Bonner Durchmusterung*. Observations for CD began in the 1870s and continued for many years; it was not completed until 1930.

Gould returned to the United States in 1885. He was succeeded by John Macon Thome, who had previously been one of the observatory's most productive assistants. Thome continued astrometric research throughout the 1890s but was hampered by increasing Argentine economic uncertainty and the constant threat of war with Chile. Meanwhile, the rival Argentine observatory at La Plata (founded 1882) failed to keep its commitment to the international *Carte du Ciel* project. Consequently, its region of sky (between –24 and –31 degrees) was reassigned to Cordoba. Because all stations were to have identical instruments for the project, Cordoba received a 13-inch photographic refractor from the Paris instrument makers Paul Gauthier and the Henry Brothers in 1902. The observatory's results were published between 1925 and 1932.

After Thome's death in 1908, the facility was headed by former Lick Observatory astronomer Charles Perrine. The last American to direct the observatory, Perrine rehabilitated the facility and moved it into the twentieth century, finishing the old positional astronomy programs and initiating galactic research and astrophysical investigations. However, his tenure was cut short by a rising wave of Argentine nationalism. Resentment of the American control of the national observatory led to an assassination attempt in 1931, his demotion in 1933, and his retirement three years later.

Perrine spent over two decades attempting to construct a 60-inch reflecting telescope for the observatory. This ill-fated project consumed far too much time, effort, and money, and left the staff short of resources for many years. It was not until 1942 that a 60-inch reflector was finally installed at nearby Bosque Alegre.

In 1936, control of the observatory passed into Argentine hands with the appointment of Felix Aguilar as director. Aguilar, the founder of La Plata's first astronomy school, promoted spectroscopic work during his tenure. In 1940 the physicist Ernesto Gaviola became director, moving the observatory toward astrophysical research and instrument development; the first all-reflection optics spectrograph was constructed there by R. Platzeck in 1943, and in 1944 the observatory saw the foundation of the Argentine Physics Association.

After World War II, the observatory continued to play an active role in the development of South American science. Native Argentines like Livio Gratton, Jorge Sahade, Carlo Cesco, and J.L. Sersic studied galactic astronomy at Cordoba, Bosque Alegre, and elsewhere. But the observatory's days as an independent research center were numbered.

In 1955 the Argentine National Observatory was absorbed by the University of Cordoba, becoming part of its research and teaching facilities. The Cordoba site was largely relegated to astrometry, occultations, and computing cometary and asteroid orbits. During the 1960s and beyond, most of the ongoing research work in stellar spectroscopy and faint objects was carried out by the larger Bosque Alegre telescope instead. The Argentine National Observatory passed into history.

Julian A. Smith

Bibliography

Berendzen, R., and D. Seeley. "Perrine, Charles Dillon." In *Dictionary of Scientific Biography*, edited by C.C. Gillispie, vol. 10, 526–527. New York: Scribner, 1974.

Evans, D.S. "Astronomical Institutions in the Southern Hemisphere, 1850–1950." In *The General History of Astronomy: Volume 4: Astrophysics and Twentieth-Century Astronomy to 1950: Part A*, edited by O. Gingerich. Cambridge: Cambridge University Press, 1984.

———. *Under Capricorn: A History of Southern Hemisphere Astronomy*. Bristol and Philadelphia: Adam Hilger, 1988.

Hodge, J.E. "Charles Dillon Perrine and the Transformation of the Argentine National Observatory." *Journal for the History of Astronomy* 8 (1977): 12–25.

Marsden, B.G. "Gould, Benjamin Apthorp." In *Dictionary of Scientific Biography*, edited by C.C. Gillispie, vol. 5, 477–478. New York: Scribner, 1972.

Page, T. *Observatories of the World*. Cambridge, Mass: Smithsonian Institution, 1967.

Rigaux, F. *Les Observatoires Astronomiques et Les Astronomes*. Bruxelles: L'Union Astronomique Internationale, 1959.

Sersic, J.L. "Observatorio Astronomico, Cordoba." *Information Bulletin for the Southern Hemisphere*, no. 12, 12.

———. "The First Century of the Observatorio Astronomico de Cordoba." *Information Bulletin for the Southern Hemisphere*, no. 42, 347.

Aristarchus of Samos (ca. 310–230 B.C.E.)

Aristarchus of Samos succeeded Theophrastus (ca. 371–ca. 287 B.C.E.) as head of the Peripatetic school. A man of great learning and varied interests, his work in astronomy is especially noteworthy. He was credited in Antiquity (by the first-century-B.C.E. architect Vitruvius) with the invention of a concave hemispherical sundial known as a *skaphe*.

His only extant treatise, *On the Sizes and Distances of the Sun and Moon,* was part of the collection of astronomical treatises used in teaching referred to by Pappus (fourth century C.E.) as the "Little Astronomy" (in contrast to "The Great Astronomy," the second-century-C.E. *Mathematical Syntaxis* of **Ptolemy**). Here, following explicitly stated assumptions, Aristarchus used geometrical methods to calculate ratios of the relative sizes and distances of the sun and moon to the earth. His assumptions included the following: that when the moon appears to be halved, the eye of an observer is on the great circle that divides the dark and light areas of the moon and, that when the moon appears to be halved, the distance of the moon from the sun is less than a quarter of a circle (90 degrees) by 1/30 (in other words, the angular distance of the moon to the sun is 87 degrees). Starting from these and other stated assumptions, Aristarchus then proceeded to prove three propositions, including one concerning the ratios of the distances of the sun and moon from the earth, stating that the distance of the sun from the earth is greater than eighteen times, but less than twenty times, the distance of the moon from the earth. While acknowledging that Aristarchus' results were far from the actual figures, historians have pointed to the importance of his approach (the combined use of observation with both geometrical and arithmetical methods), while recognizing the difficulties inherent in judging the precise moment of dichotomy (cutting in half) of the moon and also in estimating the difference between small angles.

Aristarchus is also renowned for his suggestion that the earth travels around the sun, reported in *The Sand-Reckoner*, written by Archimedes (287–212 B.C.E.), a younger contemporary. Aristarchus reasoned that the size of the universe is very large, starting from assumptions that included the idea that the fixed stars and the sun are stationary, while the earth moves around the sun in a circular orbit, with the sun in the center of the earth's orbit. Aristarchus assumed the size of the sphere of the fixed stars to be so great that the circle of the earth's orbit has "such a proportion to the distance of the fixed stars as the centre of the sphere bears to its surface" (translated by Heath, 302). While the precise meaning of this last phrase is somewhat problematic, as Archimedes pointed out, the idea of the large size of the universe is clear. Aristarchus' heliocentric hypothesis was not widely adopted in Antiquity; for the most part it was rejected because it seemed to fit with neither the phenomena nor natural philosophical accounts. Plutarch reported that the Stoic philosopher Cleanthes (331–232 B.C.E.) accused Aristarchus of impiety, because of his suggestion that the earth is in motion. It is interesting to note that Copernicus (1473–1543) was aware of Aristarchus' heliocentric hypothesis.

Liba C. Taub

Bibliography

Heath, T. *Aristarchus of Samos: The Ancient Copernicus. A History of Greek Astronomy to Aristarchus together with Aristarchus's Treatise on the Sizes and Distances of the Sun and Moon.* Oxford: Clarendon Press, 1930; reprint, New York: Dover, 1981.

Helden, A. van. *Measuring the Universe: Cosmic Dimensions from Aristarchus to Halley*. Chicago: University of Chicago Press, 1984.

Knorr, W.R. "Aristarchus of Samos." In *Encyclopedia of Cosmology: Historical, Philosophical and Scientific Foundations of Modern Cosmology*, edited by N.S. Hetherington, 17–19. New York: Garland, 1993.

Neugebauer, O. *A History of Ancient Mathematical Astronomy*. 3 vols. Berlin: Springer-Verlag, 1975.

Stahl, W.H. "Aristarchus of Samos." In *Dictionary of Scientific Biography*, edited by C.C. Gillispie, vol. 1, 246–250. New York: Scribner, 1970.

Aristotle, the Astronomy of

Aristotle's contemporaries would not have considered him an astronomer. Yet we can recognize in his discussion of the heavens something like, and profoundly unlike, modern astronomy. He did not share the ancient astronomer's concern with developing mathematical models of the heavens, but sought to treat the phenomena that astronomers observed and the models they used in their predictions as subjects for his physical and metaphysical inquiries. Like his master, Plato, Aristotle recognized the importance of geometry in the study of the heavens. But he added to Plato's concern for the formal cause his own characteristic emphasis on the physical causes of the heavens' distinctive motions, especially the material and final causes.

Aristotle inferred the material nature of the heavens from their observed characteristics. The stars, he claimed, were unchanging: "Throughout all past time . . . we find no trace of change either in the whole of the outermost heaven or in any one of its proper parts" (*de Caelo,* 270b 13ff). From this, he concluded that the heavens must be made of a substance different from the ordinary material that makes up the ephemeral things of our everyday experience. The heavens were seen to turn continuously with circular motion, while heavy things naturally fall straight to earth and light things like fire naturally rise straight to the sky. From these two observed differences he concluded that the heavens must be made of a different material substance, which he called aether, that by its nature moves in circles and is not subject to growth and decay.

If aether provided the heavens' material substance, Aristotle deferred to the findings of the mathematical astronomers Eudoxus and Callippus for the heavens' geometrical form. These astronomers had developed simple geometric models that accounted qualitatively for the motions of the sun, moon, and planets by systems of concentric spheres that Aristotle transformed into a single physical model of concentric, nesting, aetherial spheres.

For the sun, Eudoxus had used two spheres, one for the daily motion and another, inclined some 24 degrees to the first, that carried the sun around the zodiac each year. For the moon he used three spheres: an outer one for the daily motion, a second, inclined some 24 degrees to the first, corresponding to the zodiac; and a third, inclined some 5 degrees to the second, along which the moon moves each month. For the planets he used four spheres, the outer two similar to those of the sun, plus two more that produced an oscillatory motion intended to account for the planets' retrograde motion and variations in latitude.

Callippus added two further spheres each for the sun and moon, possibly to account for the variations in their motion along the zodiac that would later be explained by Ptolemy's eccentric spheres, and one additional sphere each for Mercury, Venus, and Mars, although their function is not known.

To transform these separate geometric models into a single physical cosmos, Aristotle added additional counteracting spheres so that the inferior planets would not be influenced by the motion of the planets above them, making a total of fifty-five concentric spheres. Having determined their material substance and the form that orders their motion, Aristotle still needed to discuss the physical cause of the continuous, unchanging motion of the celestial spheres.

Continuous, unchanging motions required continuously acting, unchangeable causes. Aristotle asserted that the only such unchanging action was thought, which implied that the ultimate causes of the fifty-five motions of the heavens were fifty-five unchanging thinking beings—that is, gods—who acted as the final causes of the motions of the fifty-five aetherial spheres that carried around the sun, moon, and planets. In time, monotheistic Aristotelians would demote all but one of these movers to the status of created spiritual beings, leaving only one as the first or prime mover.

Stephen C. McCluskey

Bibliography

Aristotle. *De Caelo*; *Metaphysica*; *Physica*. Various editions.

Dicks, D.R. *Early Greek Astronomy to Aristotle*. Ithaca, N.Y.: Cornell University Press, 1970.

Lloyd, G.E.R. *Aristotle: The Growth and Structure of His Thought*. Cambridge: Cambridge University Press, 1968.

Armillary Sphere

The armillary sphere was produced both as an instrument of observation and a tool for demonstrating astronomical principles. Both forms were composed of rings (or *armillae*) representing the great circles of the celestial sphere. In the observational armillary, these rings were kept to a minimum, and one or two carried sights. In the demonstrational armillary, the polar circles, tropics, equator, and ecliptic were delineated. Although observational armillaries were as much as 3 meters in diameter, didactic armillaries were typically much smaller and occasionally made of wood and pasteboard instead of brass. They were sometimes mounted on handles, but often were set like globes into cradles so that the sphere could be adjusted to represent the heavens as seen from any latitude. To illustrate the geocentric system, a small terrestrial globe was fixed to an ecliptic-polar axis in the center of the sphere, while rings carried images of the moon, sun, and planets around it.

Ptolemaic armillary sphere. Italian, late sixteenth to seventeenth century (M-11). (Courtesy of the Adler Planetarium, Chicago, Illinois)

Early armillaries were derived from Ptolemy's *astrolabon*, which enabled astronomers to find the ecliptic coordinates of stars without having to convert from altazimuth measurements. Later forms gave positions directly in equatorial coordinates. Both types were used in medieval Islamic observatories. During the fifteenth and sixteenth centuries, Bernard Walther, **Nicolas Copernicus**, and **Tycho Brahe** employed zodiacal armillaries, but Tycho was happier with the equatorial form and built three. The observational armillary developed independently in China, where it was also a key piece of observatory equipment.

Although planetary rings may have been added to the armillary as early as the fourth century, no record of the demonstrational instrument has been found in the Islamic world.

The didactic Ptolemaic instrument appeared in the Latin West during the thirteenth century and was used for teaching up through the nineteenth century. Beginning in the late seventeenth century, Copernican armillary spheres were paired with Ptolemaic ones as teaching tools, and their uses were described (along with that of globes) in numerous manuals.

Sara Schechner Genuth

Bibliography

King, H.C., and J.R. Millburn. *Geared to the Stars: The Evolution of Planetariums, Orreries, and Astronomical Clocks.* Toronto: University of Toronto Press, 1978.

Needham, J., with W. Ling. *Science and Civilization in China.* Vol. 3, *Mathematics and the Sciences of the Heavens and the Earth.* Cambridge: Cambridge University Press, 1959.

Nolte, F. *Die Armillarsphäre.* Abhandlungen zur Geschichte der Naturwissenschaften und der Medizin, 2. Erlangen: M. Mencke, 1922.

Poulle, E. *Les sources astronomiques (textes, tables, instruments).* Typologie des sources du Moyen Âge Occidental, 39. Turnhout, Belgium: Brepols, 1981.

Price, D.J. "A Collection of Armillary Spheres and Other Antique Scientific Instruments." *Annals of Science* 10 (1954): 172–187.

Turner, A. *Early Scientific Instruments: Europe 1400–1800.* London: Sotheby's, 1987.

Asada, Goryu (1734–1799)

Born the fourth son of a feudal family, Asada had no officially assigned job and studied astronomy and medicine by himself. As an amateur astronomer, he devised his own calendar, which predicted the solar eclipse in 1763 better than the official calendar. In 1767, Asada was ordered to become an official doctor of the clan. But he was by then a dedicated astronomer and decided to leave the clan to become an independent scholar. After he moved to Osaka, Asada concentrated on astronomical research, constructing instruments, making observations, and devising a new calendrical system. He attracted many excellent disciples, the most notable being the theoretician Yoshitoki Takahashi and the instrument maker Shigetomi Hazama. A wealthy merchant, Hazama also helped Asada financially. Learning of the reputation of the Asada school, the Tokugawa government requested Asada develop a new official calendar. Instead of doing so himself, Asada told Takahashi to carry out the assignment. Along the way, they consulted a Chinese astronomical treatise edited by a Jesuit astronomer, that explained Kepler's three laws of planetary motion. Deeply impressed by the precise agreement between theory and observation, Asada and his students committed themselves to the research of Western astronomy and used it for their development of the new *Kansei* calendar.

Takehiko Hashimoto

Bibliography

Watanabe, T. *The History of Modern Japanese Science and Goryu Asada* (in Japanese). Tokyo, 1983.

Association of Universities for Research in Astronomy (AURA)

The Association of Universities for Research in Astronomy, Inc. (AURA) was created in 1957 as a consortium of seven universities to develop and manage a new national optical observatory under contract to the National Science Foundation (NSF). The **Kitt Peak National Observatory** (KPNO) near Tucson, Arizona, was developed by AURA (1958–1960), followed by the **Cerro Tololo Inter-American Observatory** in Chile (1960–1967). AURA assumed management of the Sacramento Peak (solar) Observatory in New Mexico from the U.S. Air Force in 1976, and developed the Space Telescope Science Institute at the Johns Hopkins University in Baltimore (1981) for NASA. The consortium expanded to twenty-two member universities by 1992, and continues to operate these multipurpose astronomical facilities for use by all qualified researchers.

Historical accounts (chiefly Edmondson, Goldberg) cite **Yerkes Observatory** director **Otto Struve**'s 1940 appeal, "Cooperation in Astronomy" (*Scientific Monthly* 50, 142–147), as the antecedent for the concept that became AURA. Concerned over the decline in astronomical facilities and research, especially east of the Rockies, Struve proposed that several universities collaboratively secure private foundation money to develop new instruments at McDonald observatory in Texas, where Yerkes already had a cooperative venture. Struve's idea was not followed up until after the disruption of World War II, when federal government patronage became a new force in astronomy, and it is unclear whether Struve's idea was simply forgotten or became influential in the new climate. Indiana University astronomer John B. Irwin attempted in 1952 to interest Eastern U.S. astronomers and the newly established National Science Foundation (NSF) in building a cooperative facility for photoelectric research in Arizona.

Irwin's idea led to a conference the following year in Flagstaff, Arizona, where it was enlarged under prodding from Leo Goldberg to encompass a general purpose telescope available to all researchers. The NSF then appointed an advisory panel for a national astronomical observatory in 1954 under Michigan's Robert R. McMath. While the McMath Panel investigated the various scientific, financial, and administrative issues, Aden B. Meinel (Yerkes Observatory) and Helmut Abt (McDonald Observatory) searched the entire Southwestern United States, developing a list of 150 potential sites, out of which five were selected for extensive testing. In 1955 the concept of a simple "observing station" expanded under NSF pressure to become a full "new observational scientific center" (Edmondson 1991, 74). Apparently, NSF was interested in going beyond individual research and training grants to support of major facilities and saw astronomy as a suitable test case. Working in a similar manner with Associated Universities, Inc., NSF was developing a National Radio Astronomy Observatory as well (Needell 1987, 1991).

While NSF was interested in developing new scientific facilities, it did not have legal authority to operate them. Hence a proper organization to receive the NSF funding was needed. During 1955–1956, NSF and the McMath panel worked out the chief issues, agreeing that while NSF would retain title to the observatory, a new organization would be created to receive NSF funding and to develop and manage the observatory. Underlying this was the new notion that NSF would provide long-term support for facilities, not just small grants for research, training, or equipment. With a letter of intent from NSF, Leo Goldberg began late in 1956 to organize the legal and administrative apparatus. In March 1957 representatives of the original seven universities met to work out the articles of incorporation, and by May all had agreed to sign on. In September, the National Science Board authorized NSF to negotiate with AURA, which incorporated the following month. In December 1957 the AURA board of directors approved the NSF contract and in March 1958 selected Kitt Peak, near Tucson, as the site for the observatory. Throughout, many of the leaders of U.S. astronomy were actively involved as members or consultants of the several organizing groups and NSF committees.

At Kitt Peak the initial 0.9-meter telescope went into operation in 1960, followed by a 2.1-meter (1964), and a 4-meter (1973). In addition, a variety of other optical telescopes, associated auxiliary instrumentation, shops, support facilities, and other resources were provided on the mountain or in Tucson. Solar astronomy as well was part of the plan. McMath was a pioneer in solar astronomy, and at his urging an immense solar tower telescope was included. A 203-cm heliostat mirror on a tower nearly 305 meters high fed the sunlight along a 244-meter temperature-controlled path partly above and partly below ground, where other optics formed a solar image 90 cm in diameter. Construction of the McMath Solar Telescope began at the dedication of the observatory and was completed in late 1962.

While Kitt Peak was being developed, **Gerard P. Kuiper** at the University of Chicago had secured U.S. Air Force funding for a large telescope in Chile. When Kuiper left Chicago for Arizona in 1960, AURA and NSF agreed to take over the project. **Cerro Tololo Interamerican Observatory** was developed and inaugurated in 1967. Whereas AURA had managed the development of Kitt Peak, it had to become in effect the general contractor for developing the Chile observatory. In addition to the initial 0.9-meter and 1.5-meter instruments, a 4-meter instrument was added in 1976, with the assistance of the Ford Foundation. Several other telescopes followed.

Between 1952 and 1976 the U.S. Air Force built and operated the Sacramento Peak Observatory (SPO) near Sunspot, New Mexico, dedicated to geophysical research into solar activity and terrestrial interactions. As the military agencies, under congressional and budget pressure, divested themselves of many basic research activities in the early 1970s, NSF agreed in 1976 to take over the observatory and provide most of its operating budget. AURA became its temporary and then permanent manager.

In 1978, shortly after the NASA Space Telescope program began in earnest, AURA undertook a lengthy series of studies to develop a bid for the scientific institution that would mediate the astronomical community's use of the instrument. In 1981 NASA selected the AURA proposal, which included choosing the Johns Hopkins University in Baltimore as the site of the proposed institute. The

Space Telescope Science Institute (STScI) was deliberately patterned after the other national observatories operated by AURA, the exception being that actual control of the telescope would take place from the nearby NASA Goddard Space Flight Center. As at the other AURA-operated observatories, the STScI maintains a scientific staff who both support and use the instrument for research; manage solicitation, review, and selection of proposals; schedule observations; and assist the users in acquiring and interpreting data.

Most recently, AURA has become manager of the Gemini 8-meter Telescopes Project, an international venture (United States, United Kingdom, Canada, Chile, Brazil, and Argentina) to develop twin 8-meter telescopes on Mauna Kea, Hawaii, and on Cerro Pachon, Chile. The telescopes are expected to become operational in 1998 and 2000, respectively. This marks AURA's move from managing national facilities with some international participation to developing and managing truly and substanially international enterprises in astronomy.

Frank K. Edmondson (1994) provides the most comprehensive and detailed treatment of AURA's history. Early installments may be found in Edmondson (1982, 1983, 1991). Leo Goldberg recounts his involvement in "The Founding of Kitt Peak" and in oral history interviews at the Center for History of Physics (College Park, Maryland) and the National Air and Space Museum. J. Merton England (1983) documents the NSF activities. Allan Needell (1987, 1991) recounts the important influence of Associated Universities, Inc., and its management of the Brookhaven National Laboratories as precedents for the creation of AURA. Kloeppel (1983) provides a basic but somewhat problematic account of the development of KPNO; see Edmondson (1984) for an authoritative corrective. AURA's early but curtailed ambitious plans in the 1950s for space astronomy and its successful bid around 1980 to develop and operate the Space Telescope Science Institute are discussed in Smith (1993).

The most comprehensive body of historical manuscript materials is in the collection of Frank K. Edmondson at Indiana University. A key actor in the creation and development, Edmondson augmented his own large collection of personal papers with numerous manuscripts, copies, and oral history interviews used in writing his history of AURA (Edmondson 1994). Some corporate records are in storage at the KPNO offices in Tucson, and others at the corporate headquarters, which moved to Washington, D.C. in 1983. Manuscript materials are in the collections of the individuals involved, especially at the university archives of Michigan (McMath, Mohler, Goldberg), Wisconsin (Whitford), Harvard (Goldberg), and Arizona (Kuiper). Papers of the AURA board members may be found at their home institutions, and one should not overlook the university administrative officials who served alongside astronomers as board members. Collections at the various funding agencies (NSF, Ford Foundation, NASA, and so on) also contain materials of interest.

Joseph N. Tatarewicz

Bibliography

Association of Universities for Research in Astronomy, Inc. *AURA: The First Twenty-five Years 1957–1982*. Tucson, Ariz: Association of Universities for Research in Astronomy, 1983.

Edmondson, F.K. "Association of Universities for Research in Astronomy, Inc. (AURA)." In *Research Institutions and Learned Societies*, edited by J.C. Kiger, 154–158. The Greenwood Encyclopedia of American Institutions. Westport, Conn.: Greenwood Press, 1982.

———. "Observatory at Kitt Peak." Book review of Kloeppel, J.E. *Realm of the Long Eyes: A Brief History of Kitt Peak National Observatory* (San Diego: Univelt, 1983). *Journal for the History of Astronomy* 15 (1984): 139–141.

———. "AURA and KPNO: The Evolution of an Idea, 1952–58." *Journal for the History of Astronomy* 22 (February 1991): 69–86.

———. "AURA, Kitt Peak and Cerro Tololo—The Early Years (A Personal Review)." 1994.

———. *Personal Papers*. Manuscript Collection. Bloomington: Indiana University Archives.

England, J.M. *A Patron for Pure Science.* Vol. 1. *The National Science Foundation's Formative Years, 1945–1957*. Washington, D.C.: National Science Foundation, 1983.

Goldberg, L. "The Founding of Kitt Peak." *Sky & Telescope* 65 (March 1983): 228–230.

Kloeppel, J.E. *Realm of the Long Eyes: A Brief History of Kitt Peak National Observatory*. San Diego: Univelt, 1983.

Needell, A.A. "Lloyd Berkner, Merle Tuve, and the Federal Role in Radio Astronomy." *Osiris* 3 (1987): 261–288.

———. "The Carnegie Institution of Washington and Radio Astronomy: Prelude to an American National Observatory." *Journal for the History of Astronomy* 22 (February 1991): 55–67.

Smith, R.W., with contributions by P.A. Hanle, R. Kargon, and J.N. Tatarewicz. *The Space Telescope: A Study of NASA, Science, Technology, and Politics*. New York: Cambridge University Press, 1993.

Asteroids

Asteroids, the swarm of small, rocky bodies orbiting the sun between Mars and Jupiter, have garnered astronomical and geophysical attention far out of proportion to their diminutive size and scant total bulk. The first four asteroids were discovered at the beginning of the nineteenth century, and many hundreds more were discovered, catalogued, and tracked after the introduction of photography in the second half of the century. For more than a century they were studied almost solely with **celestial mechanics** techniques, **photometry**, and some optical diameter measurements. Beginning early in the present century, radiometry, colorimetry, and **spectroscopy** were applied in hopes of determining their mineralogical composition and possible relationships to **comets** and meteorites. Studies of their orbital characteristics were largely done to facilitate tracking and recovery, to apply to questions in cosmogony, and much later to associate cratering episodes on the inner planets with particular populations. Studies to determine their mineralogical composition were important for identifying populations that might have come from hypothetical common parent bodies and the degree of evolution of those bodies before fragmentation, and to associate various asteroid populations with groups of meteorites.

In 1772 J.E. Bode drew attention to a simple numerical relationship among the sizes of the orbits of the six known planets. First proposed by J.D. Titius, the formula fit nicely, except for a conspicuous gap between the orbits of Mars and Jupiter. The discovery of Uranus at an appropriate solar distance in 1781 increased faith in the law. While Baron von Zach organized several astronomers to search systematically for the missing planet, **Giuseppe Piazzi** at Palermo noticed an unusual starlike object lacking cometary nebulosity on January 1, 1801. After noting its motion over six weeks, he christened the new planet Ceres, after the patron deity of Sicily. Piazzi was unable to compute an orbit from the small number of observations made before it was lost in the solar glare, but Carl Friedrich Gauss developed an entirely new method of orbit computation. This method could be applied to only three observations and did not require hypothesizing the shape of the orbit beforehand. Gauss's calculations enabled Wilhelm Olbers to recover Ceres at the end of the year.

Before astronomers could take too much consolation in the gap being filled with a single planet, Olbers in April 1802 discovered another similar object, later named Pallas. In 1804 K.L. Harding discovered yet another, Juno, and in 1807 Olbers added Vesta. Because of the similarity of their orbital elements, and the erroneous supposition that the orbits intersected, Olbers hypothesized that these asteroids, as **William Herschel** called them, were the remains of a single disrupted planet.

No new asteroids were discovered until the 1840s, when the Berlin Academy resurrected von Zach's so-called Celestial Police, subdividing the zodiac among participating astronomers for accurate star surveys down to the ninth magnitude. The number of asteroids increased rapidly to more than a hundred by the 1870s, when photography was introduced. By 1900 more than 450 had been found, by 1950 more than fifteen hundred, and by 1980 in excess of three thousand. While Gauss's method was sufficient for recovering an observed asteroid, keeping track of this multitude of ever smaller bodies was a serious burden on astronomical resources. The Berlin Computing Office, Copernicus Institute, took care of the work until severe disruption during World War II. After that, the center for computation moved to the University of Cincinnati, where the celestial mechanician and friend of minor planets **Paul Herget** nursed the enterprise. In 1978 the Minor Planet Center moved to the Harvard-Smithsonian center in Cambridge, Massachusetts.

While somewhat of a burden, the increasing numbers of asteroids stimulated new research initiatives. Daniel Kirkwood proposed as an alternative to Olbers's hypothesis that the asteroids represented a ring of material that had failed to coalesce into a planet, using this to bolster the Laplacian nebular hypothesis. In the 1850s, as Kirkwood became the chief American defender of the nebular hypothesis, he drew attention to the uneven distribution of the asteroids' periods of revolution, particularly at one-half and one-third the period of Jupiter. He elaborated this theory in the late 1860s, identifying several Kirkwood Gaps, and hypothesizing that the gravitation of Jupiter acting on the bodies always at the same points of these orbits would tend to eject particles, perhaps even supplying thereby material for the coalescence of asteroids in adjacent areas. Analysis of such orbital resonances, and modeling of asteroidal orbit evolution to determine possible predecessor planet bodies, have continued to be important areas of research to this day.

The asteroids also supplied other puzzles for celestial mechanics. In 1873 Aethra, the first known Mars-crossing asteroid, was discovered but subsequently lost. In 1898 another, Eros, was discovered. The first namesake of the earth-approaching Amor group, it was predicted to come within 0.27 astronomical unit of earth in 1900–1901 and a scant 0.17 AU in 1930–1931. Data from the latter approach, which was observed by some forty observatories in a coordinated international effort, took ten years to reduce and provided the highest-precision value for the solar parallax until the introduction of radar and space probe techniques in the late 1950s. Beginning in the 1930s, other asteroids were found that approached the earth at even smaller distances, but their size and consequent brightness was so small they could be observed only near close-approach, and computation of reliable orbits was problematic. In 1932, Apollo, the first of a group of asteroids that lay entirely within the earth's orbit, was discovered, followed by Icarus, Geographos, and others.

Beginning in 1906 asteroids were discovered with periods equal to that of Jupiter, but at the so-called Lagrangian points of equilibrium some sixty degrees in longitude leading and following the planet. They were named after heroes of the Trojan War—Achilles, Hector, and so on—and constitute the Trojan Group.

Within the Mars-Jupiter main asteroid belt various groupings were discerned. **K. Hirayama** proposed a number of families in 1918, based on similarities in selected orbital elements. The many perturbations and the difficulty of modeling so many mutually interacting bodies has kept research on such groupings from reaching consensus. Beginning in the early 1970s, a classification roughly by inferred mineralogical or observed spectral characteristics was introduced by Clark Chapman and colleagues, and later modified by Edward Bowell and colleagues. The vast majority are C (carbonaceous, after their similarity to carbonaceous chondrite meteorites) or S (after their similarity to stony meteorites) types. Others include M (metallic), R (red), E (enstatite achondrite), and U (unclassifiable).

Asteroid research was stimulated to a new level of activity after 1970 by developments in the space program. Plans for the first interplanetary spacecraft to travel beyond Mars drew attention to the asteroid belt as a potential hazard as well as a zone of opportunity. In 1983 the Infrared Astronomical Satellite (IRAS) surveyed two thousand asteroids and added a host of discoveries. It also found complex bands of zodiacal dust thought to be associated with them. In 1989, the first ground-based radar images of an asteroid, 4769 Castalia, were obtained, and, at the end of 1992, high-resolution radar imaging revealed 4179 Toutatis to be a close-contact binary. While numerous proposals for asteroid flyby or rendezvous missions were unsuccessful, late in 1991 the *Galileo* spacecraft, en route to Jupiter, obtained the first images of an asteroid—951 Gaspra. In mid 1993 the spacecraft obtained images of 243 Ida.

Cratering records studied on the moon and inner planets during the 1970s called forth studies of asteroid groups and families, and especially searches for additional earth-approaching asteroids. In 1980 abnormally high levels of iridium were found to be associated with a catastrophic mass extinction of many species of life (including the dinosaurs) on earth 65 million years ago. Luis Alvarez hypothesized that the iridium arrived via a large asteroid impact, setting off a controversy that continues to this day, but which further stimulated asteroid study.

Only selected episodes and topics in asteroid astronomy have garnered the attention of professional historians. Jaki and Nieto treat the Titius-Bode law. Forbes has treated the role of Gauss in determining the orbit of Ceres and facilitating its recovery, as has Buhler. Numbers discusses extensively the work of Daniel Kirkwood and resonance theory in relation to the nebular hypothesis. Glen analyzes the debates after 1980 concerning the role of asteroids in catastrophic events in earth history. Professional astronomical reviews found in Binzel et al., Gehrels et al., and Chapman et al. provide authoritative summaries and references, even to older published literature.

Cunningham provides a good historical overview and useful capsule biographies of contemporary leaders in asteroid research.

Joseph N. Tatarewicz

Bibliography

Binzel, R.P., T. Gehrels, and M.S. Matthews, eds. *Asteroids II*. Space Science Series. Tucson: University of Arizona Press, 1989.

Buhler, W.K. *Gauss: A Biographical Study*. New York: Springer-Verlag, 1981.

Chapman, C.R., J.G. Williams, and W.K. Hartmann. "The Asteroids." *Annual Review of Astronomy and Astrophysics* 16 (1978): 33–75.

Cunningham, C.J. *Introduction to Asteroids: The Next Frontier*. Richmond, Va.: Willmann-Bell, 1988.

Doel, R.E. *Unpacking a Myth: Interdisciplinary Research and the Growth of Solar System Astronomy, 1920–1958*. Ph.D. diss. Princeton: Princeton University, 1990.

Forbes, E.G. "The Correspondence between Carl Friedrich Gauss and the Rev. Nevil Maskelyne (1802–05)." *Annals of Science* 27 (1971): 213–237.

———. "Gauss and the Discovery of Ceres" *Journal for the History of Astronomy* 2 (1971): 195–199.

Gehrels, T., and M.S. Matthews, eds. *Asteroids*. Space Science Series. Tucson, Ariz.: University of Arizona Press, 1979.

Glen, W. *The Mass Extinction Debates: How Science Works in a Crisis*. Stanford, Calif.: Stanford University Press, 1994.

Jaki, S.L. "The Original Formulation of the Titius-Bode Law." *Journal for the History of Astronomy* 3 (1972): 136–138.

Nieto, M.M. *The Titius-Bode Law of Planetary Distances: Its History and Theory*. New York: Pergamon, 1972.

Numbers, R.L. "The American Kepler: Daniel Kirkwood and His Analogy." *Journal for the History of Astronomy* 4 (1973): 13–21.

Watson, F.G. *Between the Planets*. Rev. ed. Natural History Library. Cambridge: Harvard University Press, 1962, 1941.

Astrograph

In the nineteenth century, *astrograph* became the name for refracting telescopes designed to take photographs. **David Gill** began in 1882 to take astronomical photographs with commercial portrait lenses, and vigorously promoted the use of photography for astrometry. At the **Paris Observatory**, Prosper and Paul Henry, encouraged by Admiral E.B. Mouchez, who realized the value of Gill's work, began using photography for astrometry, and designed a refractor for the purpose. The instrument, a 34-cm f/10 objective. This design was chosen for use by participants in the *Carte du Ciel* project agreed on in 1887 at the Astrographic Congress.

It was not accidental that the initial astrographic telescopes, as well as later ones, had objective designs that were closely related to those for camera lenses, which provided fields wide (5 to 20 degrees) and flat, and well corrected for aberration, with f-numbers between 5 and 10. Astrographs remained refractors, rather than reflectors, because the two-, three- or four-element objectives were well suited for the correction of spherical aberration (chromatic aberration was a different problem). They were also, mechanically, more stable than reflectors—a major factor when system stability was required over a period of years. Key designers included Frank E. Ross, Paul and Prosper Henry, H. Dennis Taylor, and C.S. Hastings. Harvard's 24-inch f/5.5 Bruce doublet, and the 20-inch, f/7, four-element Ross objective at Lick are good examples. A number of firms produced standardized astrographs, including Grubb in Britain and Zeiss in Germany. The astrograph's importance for astrometry began to fade when the Schmidt telescope appeared in the thirties.

Louis F. Drummeter Jr.

Bibliography

Gill, D. "The Applications of Photography in Astronomy." In *Astronomy*, edited by Sir Bernard Lovell, vol. 1, 314–328. Barking, Essex: Elsevier, 1970. *The Royal Institution Library of Science (being the Friday Evening Discourses in Physical Sciences held at the Royal Institution: 1851–1939).*

König, A. "Astrometry with Astrographs." In *Astronomical Techniques*, edited by W.A. Hiltner, 461–462. Chicago and London: University of Chicago Press, 1962.

Lankford, J. "The Impact of Photography on Astronomy." In *Astrophysics and Twentieth-Century Astronomy to 1950: Part A*, edited by O. Gingerich, *The General History of Astronomy*, vol. 4, edited by M. Hoskin, 27–29. Cambridge: Cambridge University Press, 1984.

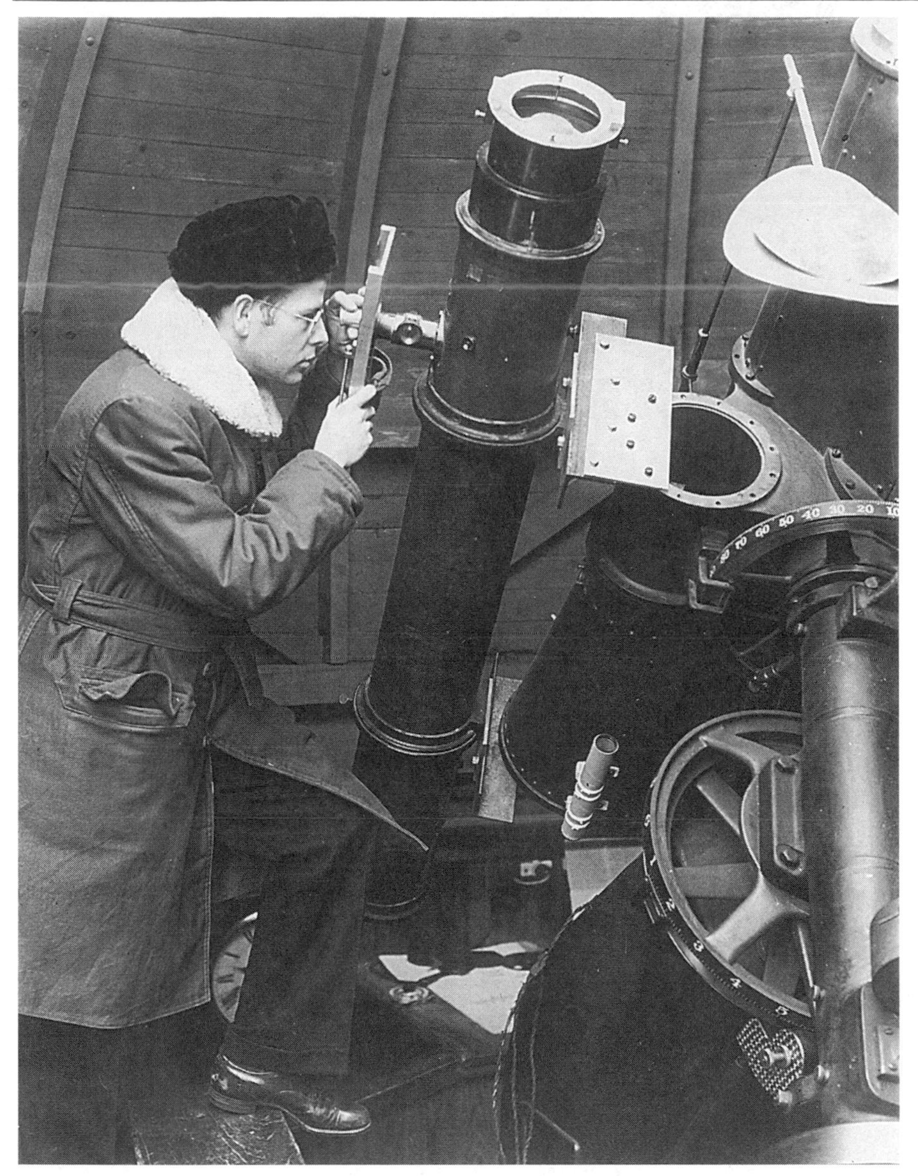

Astronomer William W. Morgan using the Bruce Astrograph of the Yerkes Observatory. Here the instrument has been modified for wide-field spectroscopy. (Courtesy of the Yerkes Observatory of the University of Chicago)

Miczaika, G.R., and W.M. Sinton. *Tools of the Astronomer*. Cambridge: Harvard University Press, 1961.

Turner, H.H. *Astronomical Discovery*. Berkeley and Los Angeles: University of California Press, 1963.

Weimer, T. *Brève Histoire de la Carte du Ciel en France*. Paris: Observatoire de Paris, 1987.

Astrolabe

The planispheric astrolabe—typically made of brass—is an analogue computer and portable model of the heavens. Its construction employs stereographic projections of both the heavens and the altazimuth coordinates for a particular latitude. In operation, the astrolabe simulates the apparent rotation of the stars around the celestial north pole. It was used for locating stars in the sky and finding the times of their risings and settings; for determining the hour, day or night; for making astrological calculations; for finding latitude or longitude; for surveying; and, in Islamic regions, for determining the hours of prayer and the direction of Mecca.

Reaching its standard form by the late fourth century, the astrolabe likely developed in the first or second century at or near Alexandria. It was widely used in the Islamic world, and transmitted to the Latin West through Spain in the tenth century. By the mid-thirteenth century, the astrolabe was familiar to European scholars as a teaching, cal-

Astrolabe by Gualterus Arsenius, Louvain, 1558 (M-23). (Courtesy of the Adler Planetarium, Chicago, Illinois)

culating, and observing instrument. Production peaked during the fifteenth and sixteenth centuries, and numerous texts introduced readers to its manifold functions. Prominent makers included Jean Fusoris of Paris, Gualterus Arsenius of Louvain, and Georg Hartmann of Nuremberg. By the seventeenth century, however, the astrolabe had come to be replaced by more specialized instruments for star-finding, time-finding, surveying, and teaching. Hence, the production of instruments and companion textbooks slackened in Europe but remained high in the Islamic world, where the instrument continued to be a tool of religion.

Hundreds of astrolabes have been preserved worldwide. Superb research collections are to be found at the Museum of the History of Science in Oxford, the Adler Planetarium in Chicago, and the National Maritime Museum in Greenwich, England. Much has been written about the astrolabe. Based in Paris, the Société Internationale de l'Astrolabe publishes a journal, *Astrolabica*, and organizes conferences. In recent years, scholars have debated whether the instrument was ever truly a tool of investigation, or simply a sophisticated calculating device and pedagogical model.

Sara Schechner Genuth

Bibliography

Gibbs, S., J. Henderson, and D. Price. *A Computerized Checklist of Astrolabes*. New Haven: Department of History of

Science and Medicine, Yale University, 1973.

Gibbs, S., with G. Saliba. *Planispheric Astrolabes from the National Museum of American History*. Washington, D.C.: Smithsonian Institution Press, 1984.

Gunther, R.T. *The Astrolabes of the World*. 2 vols. Oxford: Oxford University Press, 1932.

Hartner, W. "The Principle and Use of the Astrolabe." In *A Survey of Persian Art*, edited by A.U. Pope, vol. 3, 2530–2554. London: Oxford University Press, 1939; reprinted in Willy Hartner, *Oriens-Occidens*, 2 vols. (Hildesheim: G. Olms, 1968–1984), vol. 1, 287–311.

Michel, M. *Traité de l'Astrolabe*. Paris: Gauthier-Villars, 1947.

Pedersen, O. "Astronomy." In *Science in the Middle Ages*, edited by D.C. Lindberg, 303–337. Chicago: University of Chicago Press, 1978.

Poulle, E. *Walcher de Malvern et son astrolabe (1092)*. Centro de Estudos de Cartografia Antiga, Secção de Coimbra, 132. Coimbra: Junta de Investigações Científicas do Ultramar, 1980.

Turner, A.J. *Astrolabes, Astrolabe Related Instruments*. Time Museum: Catalogue of the Collection, edited by Bruce Chandler. Vol. 1. *Time Measuring Instruments*, part 1. Rockford, Ill.: Time Museum, 1985.

Astrology

A method of divination based on the apparent movements and positions of the planets and stars; in particular the pseudoscientific methods of Babylonian origins (via Hellenic and Islamic intermediaries) that are used by Western astrologers to relate the appearance of the sky to matters of personal or national fate.

Astrological Methods

The signs of the zodiac and the dates on which the sun passes through them each year can be found in any newspaper. The twelve with which we are familiar appear to have been amalgamated from an earlier Babylonian tradition of eighteen signs about the fifth century B.C.E. The effects of precession have long since separated the stars composing the zodiacal constellations from the parts of the ecliptic they are supposed to rule, and although some medieval astrologers agonized over this problem, most modern astrologers have simply ignored it. The signs are only one of a number of divisions of the zodiac used by astrologers. Some traditions subdivide the twelve signs themselves into thirds, ninths, tenths, or twelfths. A different division of the 360 degrees of the ecliptic is the lunar mansions, twenty-seven or twenty-eight asterisms corresponding to the location of the moon on each day of the lunar month. These have not been prominent in the Western tradition, but appear in Islamic astrology and so have been transmitted to the Indian subcontinent.

The twelve astrological houses are quite distinct from the twelve signs of the zodiac. The houses appear to have been developed in the first centuries C.E. from an Egyptian tradition of attaching significance to the four cardinal points. They are usually based on dividing in three the four arcs of the ecliptic demarcated by the ascendant and the mid-heaven (the degrees of the ecliptic respectively rising—that is, east, and culminating south, at the time of interest) and the points opposite to them. There has never been widespread agreement among astrologers as to how the houses themselves should be determined, and most systems encounter problems at high (terrestrial) latitudes because of their dependence on the ascendant.

It will be apparent that a competent astrologer needed a considerable amount of mathematical training to produce a satisfying interpretation of the positions of the planets in this framework of signs and houses. Since the ascendant and mid-heaven change by a degree every four minutes and are very dependent on the geographical location for which the horoscope is being cast, every chart will have a unique interpretation, very sensitive to small changes in detail. Besides their own carefully mathematical data, however, astrologers were expected to interpret other celestial omens such as comets, novae, the aurora borealis, and unusual appearances of the sun or moon.

Genethliac astrology, based on the appearance of the sky at the birth (or, more rarely, the conception) of an individual, is still used to make predictions about the health, character, and future prospects of that person. Mundane astrology predicts or interprets world events from planetary configurations: In 1186 and 1524, storms and floods (with consequent political turmoil) were predicted respectively from conjuctions of all five known planets, the sun and the moon in Libra (ruled by the element of air) and Pisces (ruled by water). Horary astrology is used to answer a client's specific query, based on a chart cast for the moment the question is asked. A development of this, elective astrology, is used to choose a suitable time for the start of some enterprise such as a journey or marriage, and relates the future appearance of the sky to the birth-chart of the client.

Together these practices are referred to as judicial astrology. The methods used to answer such queries remain surprisingly constant over the millennia, and so has the uneasy tension within astrology between its scientific, mathematical apologists and those practitioners who take a more magical, divinatory approach. Both were condemned as fraudulent, superstitious, or even demonically inspired by writers such as Cicero, Augustine, and Calvin—all of whom were prepared to admit that the stars might have some relevance to weather-forecasting or medical treatment—and in more recent times by scientists less prepared to make such concessions.

History of Astrology

The roots of astrology are in the lists of astral omens and their consequences for rulers, harvests, wars, and so on, compiled in Mesopotamia up to the fifth century B.C.E.; the earliest surviving horoscope using the twelve-sign zodiacal system was calculated for April 29, 410. The Babylonians also developed considerable skill in predicting eclipses and made extensive observations of planetary movements. Astrology soon thrived in the neighboring Hellenic civilization, though it always retained an Oriental mystique. Astrological treatises are known to have been among the lost works of Hipparchus (fl. 127 B.C.E.); the earliest surviving astrological works date from the first century of our era. **Claudius Ptolemy**, though not a practicing astrologer himself, compiled an encyclopedic selection of astrological methods and lore in the *Tetrabiblos*, written about 180 as a sequel to the *Almagest*. Also in Egypt at about the same time the Hermetic magical writings were being compiled from a mixture of Aristotelianism and folk religion.

The place of astrology in the classical world was similar to that of the examination of the entrails of sacrifices and the interpretation of dreams and thunderstorms; it was the most developed system of divination, both in potential breadth of application and in complexity for the student. Cramer describes the unpleasant political consequences for those casting the horoscopes of their rulers to try to discover when they would die. However, the practice of astrology in what became the Christian world declined after Augustine's vigorous denunciation of it in his *City of God*, written soon after the fall of Rome to the Goths in 410.

To the East, astrology flourished under the last century of Sasanid rule in Iran (until 630) but was somewhat subdued after the Muslim conquest. Its revival came with the ascendancy of the Abbasid dynasty after 749; the new capital of Baghdad was founded on a date determined by astrologers in 762. The caliph al-Ma'mun founded a research institute (the House of Wisdom) including an observatory in 828. Baghdad's pluralist and enlightened atmosphere encouraged scholars of many religious backgrounds; the synthesis of Sasanid, Hellenic, Hermetic, and Indian astrological teachings by Abu Ma'shar (787–886) was probably the most durable contribution to astrology. Astrology in Islam became considerably more mathematically refined than it had been in the Hellenic world. The need for better calculations of planetary positions created a market for the mathematical skill of al-Khwarizmi (780–850), whose name became garbled by Europeans into the word algorithm.

Western Europe discovered Islamic astrology only around 1200 C.E., although it is argued that an independent tradition of astral magic had survived the Christian onslaught. Translations of the works of Abu Ma'shar by Adelard of Bath and others in the first half of the twelfth century augmented a general renewal of interest in Aristotle. Doctors began to examine their patients' horoscopes as well as their urine—medical astrology was not just permitted by the Church but widely regarded as common sense. European monarchs were attracted to astrology for the same reasons as their predecessors in Baghdad, Ctesiphon, and Rome; when Michael Scot became Frederick II's court astrologer in Sicily in the early thirteenth century, he became part of a long tradition at that Norman court on the edge of the Arab world.

The Church hierarchy cautiously welcomed the Islamic astronomical data as new evidence in the ongoing controversy about the date of Easter; Robert Grosseteste, Albertus Magnus, and Roger Bacon all advocated calendar reform but differed on the efficacy of astrology. Most theologians disliked the implications of astrology for free will but were prepared to make exceptions for medicine and meteorology. Even the critics of astrology, such as Thomas Aquinas and, a century later,

Nicole Oresme, admitted that the stars and planets had some causative effects on the state of human affairs; what they denied was the ability of astrologers to predict these effects accurately. The English writer Geoffrey Chaucer wove sophisticated astrological themes into many of his works, though it is not known how many of his audience would have been conscious of them.

The philosophical attack on astrology in the Renaissance was opened by the Platonists Marsilio Ficino and Pico della Mirandola, who pointed to the numerous internal contradictions of astrological procedure and its poor record of useful predictions as reasons to distrust it. Although their polemics informed centuries of intellectual debate, they made little difference to the widespread general acceptance of astrology. More theological attacks by John Calvin and Martin Luther were provoked by the widespread panic caused in Germany and Italy in anticipation of the conjunction of 1524. Both the notorious French occultist Nostradamus and the English mathematician and magician John Dee were still able to gain considerable influence at their respective courts in the sixteenth century through their astrological skills. Dee was also a mathematical innovator who advocated the Copernican system and advised Elizabeth I on calendar reform.

The Renaissance debate did inspire some practitioners to try to purify astrology by eliminating sources of errors. Francis Bacon advocated stripping it of its superstitious baggage, leaving only a rational core of established beliefs; the Franciscan Tommaso Campanella actually published such a purified astrological system. But it was their contemporary **Johannes Kepler** whose attempts to rid astrology of its mathematical errors laid the groundwork for the physical discoveries that led to its terminal decline.

In England, astrology thrived on the unstable political situation between 1640 and 1690; William Lilly's Christian Astrology was published in 1647 and its author continued practicing as a professional astrologer through both Cromwell's regime and the Restoration. It was at this period that the publication of astrological almanacs peaked; at one point they outsold the Bible. However, this was the last generation in which a professional astrologer could claim the right to participate in debates about astronomy. Under pressure from the Newtonian view of the universe, which actually dared to quantify the forces between the planets, astrologers sought refuge in the magical traditions from which their discipline had sprung. For almost two hundred years after 1700, astrology was once again relegated to the status of superstition.

The revival of astrology as a popular phenomenon in the last hundred years is linked with a general increase of interest in the paranormal, spurred by the appearance of newspaper horoscopes in the 1930s and the much more recent New Age movement. Some scientists have reacted by seeing astrology as a threat to rationalism that must be countered on all occasions; in 1975, the astronomer Bart Bok orchestrated the publication of an anti-astrology statement signed by 186 eminent scientists, including nineteen Nobel laureates. A number of impressive attacks on astrology's historical and scientific pretensions have been produced by psychologists, astronomers, and philosophers. That has had no discernable effect on the astrologers themselves, many of whom argue that their systematic interpretation of computer-generated horoscopes is a perfectly scientific practice.

The only novel contribution in modern times to the astrological debate has come from Michel Gauquelin, a French researcher who claims to have found nonrandom variations in the positions of planets at the time of birth of a sample of people who became athletes. He claims to have found similar results for other professions as well. His results have not been generally accepted, and even if true would still be a very long way from traditional astrology.

Historiography

Unfortunately, Tester's recent attempt to write a comprehensive history of astrology was prematurely abridged by the author's death, and it includes very little social context; no historical survey exists. Two interesting and relatively accessible primary sources are the textbooks by Al-Biruni (973–1050) and William Lilly (1602–1681). Many more remain in manuscript or early editions; there is no modern edition of Abu Ma'shar, for instance. Recent work by North has shown that useful information can be gained by analyzing the techniques used for calculating the houses in historical horoscopes.

Bouché-Leclercq's account seems likely to remain the standard discussion of Greek astrology. The political and legal role of astrology in the Roman empire is entertainingly though somewhat speculatively described by Cramer. For Sasanian and Arabic astrology, one must fall back on the standard works of Sarton and Thorndike, supplemented by

Carmody's critical bibliography of the Arabic manuscripts in Latin translation.

The wealth of the manuscript heritage has left Western medieval astrology less shrouded in mystery; there have been recent studies of its connections with the English court and with the writings of Chaucer, and of its intellectual context. As the surviving material tends to be linked with the ruling classes, little is known about the practice of astrology at other levels of society. The invention of printing facilitated both the distribution of astrological ideas and their subsequent survival for discussion by scholars; although the bones of the Renaissance debate have been picked clean by Allen and Garin, work continues on the role of astrology in the Reformation and its social meaning in Renaissance Europe.

The vernacular tradition of the early modern period has shown even greater resilience; this is clear from Sir Keith Thomas's masterly survey of astrology as it was practiced in England in the sixteenth and seventeenth centuries, and from the numbers of other recent books on astrology in England, Germany, and Italy about that time. The published and unpublished writings of astrologers steering round the changing political winds in England between 1640 and 1690 have proved fertile ground for several scholars; there has been little research on the American almanacs of the same period.

There has been very little investigation of the nature of astrology since 1700 apart from anthropological research into its role in non-Western cultures; most that has been written is fiercely partisan. The 1975 anti-astrology statement of Bok and Jerome was accompanied by articles by both that did not differ very much from what Pico della Mirandola or Cicero might have written. Among other critics, it should be noted that the psychologists Eysenck and Nias attack astrology as a whole but, unusually, support Gauquelin's findings. Finally, the sociologist Theodor Adorno has attacked astrology as a means of social control; he points out that horoscopes never instruct their readers to challenge the world, but rather tend to encourage a passive acceptance of one's fate.

Nicholas Whyte

Bibliography

Adorno, T.W. "Stars down to Earth." *Telos* 19 (1974): 13–90.

Allen, D.C. *The Star-Crossed Renaissance: The Quarrel about Astrology and its Influence in England.* Durham, N.C.: Duke University Press, 1941.

Bok, B.J., and L.E. Jerome. *Objections to Astrology.* Buffalo: Prometheus, 1975. Mostly reprinted from their articles in *The American Humanist*, September/October 1975.

Bouché-Leclercq, A. *L'Astrologie Grecque.* Paris: Leroux, 1899. reprint, Aalen: Scientia, 1979.

Capp, B. *Astrology and the Popular Press: English Almanacs 1500–1800.* London and Boston: Faber and Faber, 1979.

Carey, H. *Courting Disaster: Astrology at the English Court and University in the Later Middle Ages.* London: Macmillan, 1992.

Carmody, F.J. *Arabic Astronomical and Astrological Manuscripts in Latin Translation: A Critical Bibliography.* Berkeley: University of California Press, 1956.

Castagnola, R., ed. *I Guicciardini e le scienze occulte.* Florence, Studi e testi (Istituto nazionale di studi sul Rinascimento) vol. 19: Olschki, 1990.

Cramer, F.H. *Astrology in Roman Law and Politics*, vol. 37. Philadelphia: Memoirs of the American Philosophical Society, 1954.

Culver, R.B., and P.A. Ianna. *The Gemini Syndrome: A Scientific Evaluation of Astrology.* Buffalo: Prometheus, 1979.

Curry, P. *Prophecy and Power: Astrology in Early Modern England.* Cambridge, UK: Polity, 1989.

———, ed. *Astrology, Science and Society.* Woodbridge, U.K.: Boydell, 1987.

Eade, J.C. *The Forgotten Sky: A Guide to Astrology in English Literature.* Oxford: Clarendon, 1984.

Eysenck, H.J., and D.K.B. Nias. *Astrology: Science or Superstition?* London: Temple Smith, 1982.

Flint, V.I.J. *The Rise of Magic in Early Medieval Europe.* Oxford: Clarendon, 1991.

Garin, E. *Lo Zodiaco della Vita.* Bari: Laterza, 1976. Translated by C. Jackson and J. Allen as *Astrology in the Renaissance: The Zodiac of Life.* London: Routledge and Kegan Paul, 1983.

Gauquelin, M. *The Cosmic Clocks.* London: Owen, 1969.

Haskins, C.H. *Studies in the History of Medieval Science.* Cambridge: Harvard University Press, 1927.

Hunter, M., and A. Gregory. *An Astrological Diary of the Seventeenth Century: Samuel Jeake of Rye 1652–1699.* Oxford: Clarendon, 1989.

Lemay, R.J. *Abu Ma'shar and Latin Aristotelianism in the Twelfth Century.* Beirut: American University, 1962.

Lilly, W. *Christian Astrology*. London: Regulus, 1985.

North, J.D. *Horoscopes and History*. London: Warburg Institute, 1986.

———. *Chaucer's Universe*. Oxford: Clarendon, 1988.

Sarton, G. *Introduction to the History of Science.* 3 vols. in 5. Baltimore, Carnegie Institution: Williams and Wilkins, 1927–1948.

Talkenberger, H. *Sintflut: Prophetie und Zeitgeschehen in Texten und Holzschnitten astrologischer Flugschriften, 1488–1528.* Tubingen: Niemeyer, 1990.

Tester, S.J. *A History of Western Astrology*. New York: Ballantine, 1987.

Thomas, K. *Religion and the Decline of Magic: Studies in Popular Beliefs in Sixteenth and Seventeenth-century England.* London: Weidenfeld and Nicolson, 1971.

Thorndike, L. *A History of Magic and Experimental Science.* New York: Columbia University Press, 1922.

Wright, R.R., ed. and tr. *The Book of Instruction in the Elements of the Art of Astrology by . . . Al-Biruni*. London: Luzac, 1934.

———, ed. *Astrologi Hallucinati: Stars and the End of the World in Luther's Time.* Berlin and New York: de Gruyter, 1986.

Zambelli, P. *The Spectrum Astronomiae and its Enigma: Astrology, Theology, and Science in Albertus Magnus and His Contemporaries*. Dordrecht and Boston: Kluwer, 1992.

Astrometry

Astrometry is the precise measurement of the positions, motions, and apparent sizes of celestial bodies, and may also be taken to encompass the many research programs and conclusions derivable from this data. The term *astrometry* itself dates only from the nineteenth century, but the practice of positional astronomy is the oldest part of astronomical science. In the broadest sense, **Stonehenge** and other stone circles and alignments are believed to have been constructed to mark the motions of the sun and moon. The Babylonians tracked the motions of Venus and other celestial bodies, and the Greeks are reputed to have produced the first star catalogue in the second century B.C.E. These were pioneering and valiant efforts, but only since the sixteenth century have a variety of new techniques infused astrometric science with steadily increasing accuracy. This enterprise continues to the present day, even in the midst of the new astronomy of **astrophysics**. Indeed, modern astrometry is sometimes driven by astrophysical problems and aided by studies at nonoptical wavelengths, developments undreamt of by its earlier practitioners. Despite the multifaceted nature of modern astronomy, it is indisputably true that of the forty centuries of astronomy since Stonehenge, and the twenty-five since classical Greece, only in the last century has astrophysics dethroned astrometry as the predominant theme of celestial science. The importance of astrometry to the history of astronomy cannot therefore be overemphasized, nor should its relevance to modern astronomy be underrated.

Astrometry is an observational science par excellence, but it is closely related to the theoretical science of **celestial mechanics**. From Babylonian algebraic models and Greek epicyclic models of planetary motions, to the Newtonian and relativistic dynamics characteristic of modern celestial mechanics, astrometric observations have always provided the raw material for models and theories of celestial motions. The interplay between theory and observation is thus an important hallmark of astrometry. More broadly, while astrometric positions may be an end in themselves in providing products such as a stellar reference frame, the usefulness of the field extends far beyond the determination of positions. Carefully measured over time, these positions have revealed the scale of the solar system through **solar parallax**, the distances of the stars from **stellar parallax**, stellar masses through measures of double star motions, the motion of the sun and galactic rotation through stellar **proper motions**, and unseen stellar and perhaps even planetary companions through perturbations in proper motions. Moreover, the stellar reference frame itself has for centuries been essential for determining civil time and for navigational and geodetic purposes; more recently, the extragalactic reference frame allows unprecedented accuracy in measuring the whole range of motions of our own earth, as well as motions on the earth caused by plate tectonics.

To analyze all of the developments of astrometry in a brief compass is an impossible task, so we shall concentrate on certain patterns of achievement, method, and research programs that emerge from its long and checkered history. In order to provide an overview, we first distinguish three eras of astrometry, each characterized by unique methods and precisions achieved. Narrowing our focus to the more modern second and third eras, we then discuss instruments and techniques, and conclude with a discussion of institutions and their research programs as a means of exploring the driving forces, uses and patronage of astrometry through history.

From Hipparchus to HIPPARCOS: Three Eras of Astrometry

From the Greek astronomer Hipparchus of Rhodes (fl. 140 B.C.E.) to the *Hipparcos* satellite dedicated to gathering astrometric data in the 1990s, three eras of astrometry may be distinguished. In terms of method, they may be designated as the naked eye, telescopic, and interferometric/space eras; in terms of precision achieved, they correspond to the minute of arc, second of arc, and milliarcsecond regimes, a factor of about a million increase in precision over the last two millennia. The table on the opposite page demonstrates this increased precision, and also shows some of the means by which this was achieved, as well as the resulting discoveries of each era. It is important to note that the table represents precisions actually achieved at each period, rather than those theoretically achievable; especially as the second of arc regime was approached, theoretically achievable precisions due to technological breakthroughs were not always realized because of other errors of observation. Thus, while half-arcsecond precision might have been achievable because of improvements in divided circle technology by 1800, precisions actually achieved were still at the arcsecond level, an important consideration in explaining why stellar parallax was not detected until 1838. Moreover, precisions even with one particular instrument will be affected by the skill of the observer, the number of observations of a single object, the care with which the observations were analyzed, atmospheric seeing and transparency, and even stellar magnitude. Increasingly after 1800, the theory of errors, closer attention to the peculiarities of each instrument, and the combination of observations contributed to precision improvements as much as technological advance.

Even so, the history of astrometry is characterized by several sudden technological breakthroughs, followed by long periods of routine work with more minor modifications. Thus, through innovative instrumentation **Tycho Brahe** in the sixteenth century improved over the Greeks by more than a factor of ten. At the beginning of the nineteenth century techniques of precision dividing and reading of full circles (as opposed to sextants or quadrants) produced another order of magnitude jump. After that, a combination of painstaking modifications in technique and analysis (such as the moving wire micrometer and screens to dim the brightest stars) brought the errors still lower, until in the 1980s and 1990s the techniques of interferometry and spacecraft produced yet another order of magnitude jump.

The Naked Eye Era

Stonehenge and its successors aside, the era of naked-eye positional observations spanned eighteen hundred years, from the time of Hipparchus to the mid-seventeenth century. Already in this era we see one astronomical discovery closely linked to improvements in precision. Hipparchus' observations produced the first great surprise of positional astronomy—the apparent motion of the sphere of fixed stars around earth's pole at the rate of about 50 arcseconds per year, the phenomenon we now know as the precession of the equinoxes, which is due to the motion of the earth's axis. Hipparchus could make this discovery only by comparison of the bright star Spica with a position from about 160 years earlier, and only because of the cumulative nature of precession; his instruments were certainly unable to discern 50 arcseconds, but he could take the 2-degree (7,200–arcsecond) difference in positions and divide by 160 years to come up with about 1 degree/century. Hipparchus is often credited as the author of the first star catalogue, later elaborated by Ptolemy (150 C.E.) in his *Almagest*. Modern scholarship differs widely on this point, however, with one author (G.J. Toomer) claiming Hipparchus had no star catalogue at all similar to the form of Ptolemy's, and another (R.R. Newton) claiming that Ptolemy used Hipparchus wholesale and fabricated his own data. Nevertheless, Ptolemy's star catalogue is the first passed down to us from ancient times.

Although the Islamic culture produced the star catalogues of Al-Sufi (960) and **Ulugh Beg** (1430), and although in the West Bernard Walther and perhaps others made considerable instrumental progress, the great breakthrough in precision observations is generally accorded to Tycho Brahe. Supported by Frederic II of Denmark, Tycho constructed a variety of instruments at Uraniborg on the island of Hven, using improved sights and diagonal scales on quadrant- and sextant-type

Improvement in Precision of Astrometric Measurements

Method	Representative Observer/ Institution	Date	Precision[1] (Arcsec)	Instrument	Refinements	Representative Discoveries
Naked Eye	Hipparchus	150 B.C.E.	1200"	armillary		*precession*
	Ptolemy[2]	150 C.E.		sphere		(50"/yr)
	Ulugh Beg[3]	1437	1200"	same		
	Walther[4]	1503	600"	same		
	Tycho Brahe[5]	1600	15"	quadrant/ sextant	improved sights & diagonal scales	
	Hevelius[6]	1670s	15–20"	same		
Telescopic visual						*proper motion* (Halley, 1718)
	Flamsteed[7]	1700	15"	quadrant	telescopic sight	*aberration, 20"*
		1725	8"		& micrometer	(Bradley, 1728)
	Greenwich[8]	1800	1"	transit circle	divided circle	
						parallax, .3"
	Bessel[9]	1838	.02"	heliometer	small field	(Bessel, 1838)
	Pulkovo[10]	1855	.7"	transit circle	6 circle microscopes	*unseen stellar companions*
						polar motion, .5"/yr
	USNO[11]	1910	.3"	transit circle		(Chandler, 1885)
	USNO[12]	1980s	.07"	transit circle	movable wire micrometer	
photographic						
	Gill	1886–	2"–	astrograph	photographic	*star streams*
	Kapteyn[13]	1900	4"		plate	(Kapteyn, 1904)
	22 obsys[14]	1891–	.17"	astrograph	same	*galactic rotation*
	Carte du Ciel	1950	.40"			(Oort, Lindblad, 1920s)
	Schlesinger[15]	1910	.02"	long-focus	small	*planetary*
	USNO[16]	1980s	.004"	telescopes	field	*companions?* 1960s
	USNO[17]	1980s	.15"	astrograph	fine emulsions	
electronic					measuring machines	
	USNO[18]	1990s	sub-.001"	61-inch reflector	digital imaging charge-coupled device	
Interferometric						
radio	NASA, USNO, NRL, NGS[19]	1980s	.001"	VLBI	combined data from several instruments	
optical	USNO/NRL[20]	1994	.005"			
Space						
	HIPPARCOS[21]	1989–93	.002"	satellite	no atmosphere	

[1]In this table the internal accuracy, or "precision," of a given instrument with its random errors must be distinguished from the true accuracy, which takes into account systematic errors. The distinction between the terms *precision* and *accuracy* is of recent origin, and although not always used consistently, the concept is important. As Boss (1937) explained, "Simultaneous observations of the same star by two different telescopes might each yield a probable error of plus or minus 0.15" [arcsecond] for each series of observations, yet the two mean positions might disagree by 0.4". This may be due to outstanding instrumental errors, to differential refraction, to differences in the methods of reduction, and to other factors" (Boss, p. 49). To cite a more recent example, the first Hubble Space Telescope mirror is an example of precision without accuracy:

a mirror precisely shaped to the wrong figure. Through most of the seventeenth century internal accuracy depended on the graduated scales of the instrument. With the introduction of the micrometer, the precision attainable by an instrument no longer bore a direct relation to the interval between its graduated divisions. Precision is almost always an underestimate of the true accuracy, which includes systematic errors detectable only by using several instruments. As a general rule, at least since the nineteenth century, the systematic error is often about the same order of magnitude as the random error. Since errors add vectorially, the total error, and thus the accuracy, may be the square root of two times the precision. The distinction between "probable error" used into the early twentieth century and the "mean error" or "standard error" used today has little effect on our table; the former is 74 percent the size of the latter. In this table we use precision in the modern sense of internal accuracy, also known as "random error" and "accidental error." The precisions given are state-of-the art for the best instrument and selected stars; they are not necessarily routinely achievable, especially for the earlier periods.

[2]There is wide variation among accuracy estimates of ancient observations, in part because some authors do not specify internal or external accuracy. Pannekoek (1961, 157), points out that while the instruments of Hipparchus and Ptolemy were probably divided to fourths or sixths of a degree, the mean errors of observations were greater than these divisions, corresponding to 35 minutes of arc in longitude (2100") and 22 minutes of arc in latitude (1320"). Podobed (1964, 8), gives plus or minus 15' [arcminutes] (900") as the accuracy of the first star catalogues observed by armillary spheres. It is well known that the systematic error in the longitudes of Ptolemy's star catalog is about 1 degree, or 3600" (see, for example, Toomer, 1984, 328, note 51). Shevchenko (1990) gives –78' as the mean systematic error in longitude for Ptolemy; he finds 21' (1260") for random errors in longitude and 17 minutes for latitude—both for zodiacal stars. See also Evans (1987, esp. 162–65). Note the value quoted for precession is the approximate modern value; Ptolemy may have used 36"/year.

[3]Shevchenko (1990) gives random errors for Ulugh Beg's catalogue as plus or minus 20' (1200") in longitude and plus or minus 17' in latitude—both for zodiacal stars—essentially the same as Ptolemy's results. He finds systematic errors in longitude of +13', but demonstrates how this varies by constellation. Krisciunas (1993) confirms this result. He gives systematic errors of about 11' in longitude and about 8' in latitude, a significant improvement over Ptolemy's one degree.

[4]Kremer (1980). Kremer (180) comments that these random errors of 10' "result from inherent structural limitations of the armillary, determined by the readability of the calibrations, the size of the holes or slits in the alidade, and the flexure of the rings due to their weight or to temperature variations." Since on the armillary sphere different rings are used to measure longitudes and latitudes, Kremer separated Walther's data into two independent populations. Comparing Walther's positions with a modern computation, he finds that the latitudes were relatively free of systematic error, while the total error in longitude (including the systematic error, thus giving the true accuracy) may have been as large as 13', including the error in the position of the reference object. The accuracy in longitude relative to the reference star was about 5' (300"), and the accuracy in latitude was .7' (42"). Thoren (1990, 155), states that 10 minutes of arc is "generally regarded as the best accuracy achieved before Tycho's time." Kremer's data shows that 10' was also the best precision achieved before Tycho.

[5]Wesley (1978), especially Table 1. The value quoted is for the mural quadrant. By comparison Tycho's precision for the Jacob's staff had been 35', causing him to discard it. According to Kremer (176), the precision for Tycho's equatorial armillary was 3'. Thoren (1990, 190), finds that Tycho had 1 minute of arc accuracy with his new instruments by 1585, compared to 4 minutes of arc he achieved before 1581. Wesley (Table 4) shows that Tycho's accuracy was around 35". See also Thoren (1973).

[6]Chapman (1990, 32).

[7]Chapman (1983, 135), and Chapman (1990, 120).

[8]Chapman (1983, 135), and Chapman (1990, 120). Chapman in the latter reference states that "In the 1790s the 'ceiling of accuracy' had passed beyond the 1" of arc barrier, and by 1820, Pond's observing books [at Greenwich] displayed consistent reading to places of 1/10 of an arcsecond." This may have been true of the accuracy of graduated scales on the full circle, but does not take into account the random errors of observation (the observational precision), nor the systematic errors (yielding the observational accuracy).

[9]Fricke (1970, 101). This mean error applies to the precision of Bessel's measurement of the stellar parallax of 61 Cygni. Pannekoek (1961, 343), notes the importance of systematic errors is emphasized by the fact that while Bessel after many years found the parallax value for 61 Cygni to be 0.35", Struve independently found it to be 0.51" for the same star. Note the heliometer can make only small field measurements. Monet (1988, 415), notes that small-angle techniques may give ten times the accuracy of large field measurements.

[10]Eichhorn (1974, 147).

[11]Eichelberger and Morgan (1920, lxxix; cxxxix), and Eichhorn (1974, 157). Note again this is only mean error; systematic error is probably another .4". Eichhorn (278) also states that the typical mean error of a meridian position around 1890 was .5" in either coordinate.

[12]U.S. Naval Observatory, average mean error with six observations of a star with the six-inch transit circle telescope. Van Altena (1983, 157), notes that refraction of the Earth's atmosphere places a limiting accuracy of 0.13" on accuracy obtainable from one transit circle observation.

[13]Gill (1913, lvii). This is the precision of positions in the Cape Photographic Durchmusterung, containing some 454,000 stars. For the context see Pannekoek (1961, 469).

[14]Eichhorn (1974, 280). By comparison the mean

errors of the Cape Photographic Catalogue for 1950 range from .15 to .22", but the positions may be subject to an additional .3" systematic error. Eichhorn (1974, 274).

[15]Schlesinger (1911, 26). Note again that this is small field astrometry.

[16]Harrington, et al. (1985). Average internal error for parallax plates taken with the U.S. Naval Observatory 61-inch astrometric reflector. External error is stated as also about the same.

[17]Douglass and Harrington (1990). Internal error of star positions based on photographic plates with U.S. Naval Observatory 8-inch double astrograph.

[18]Dahn, Monet, et al. (1990). Internal error for parallax obtained with U.S. Naval Observatory 61-inch astrometric reflector with CCD detector.

[19]Ma (1990). Abbreviations: VLBI: Very Long Baseline Interferometry. NASA: National Aeronautics and Space Administration. USNO: U.S. Naval Observatory. NRL: Naval Research Laboratory. NGS: National Geodetic Survey.

[20]Predicted precision of USNO/NRL instrument in progress.

[21]Perryman (1990).

instruments that he constructed anew. Tycho's principal achievement was almost entirely observational, due to his skill in constructing and using improved instrumentation. But his painstaking observational work had an almost immediate impact on broader aspects of astronomy. World views hinged on these minute measurements; Tycho's inability to measure stellar parallax led to doubts about the Copernican theory, and resulted in his own Tychonic system of the world. And it was the 8 minutes of arc discrepancy between theory and observation of the motion of Mars that motivated **Johannes Kepler** to abandon Greek epicycles for the ellipse, one of the foundation stones of modern astronomy. The German astronomer **Johannes Hevelius** in his private observatory at Danzig (now Gdansk) took Tycho's techniques to their limit. As Chapman (1990) points out, Hevelius was the last representative of the Tychonic instrument school—that is, he was the last major user of large sextants and quadrants without telescopic sights. With Tycho and Hevelius, naked-eye astrometry reached its highest form and its physical limit; as the English natural philosopher Robert Hooke found experimentally at the time, the Tychonic school had reached the resolution of the human eye of about 1 arcminute.

The Telescopic Era

The link between improved accuracy and astronomical discovery accelerated remarkably with the second era. Supported by royal patronage, the first great national observatories were founded at Paris (1667), Greenwich (1675), Berlin (1701), and St. Petersburg (1725). At the Royal Observatory, Greenwich **John Flamsteed** produced the first great star catalogue observed using telescopic sights; the value of the *Historiae Coelestis* (1725) may be appreciated from Newton's strenuous efforts to obtain it for his use. The accuracies represented in Flamsteed's work were beginning to bear fruit in unexpected ways. Taking precession into account, the man who within two years would become Flamsteed's successor at Greenwich, **Edmond Halley**, showed (1718) that the bright stars Aldebaran, Sirius, and Arcturus were displaced from their positions in Antiquity by large fractions of a degree, the phenomenon that became known as stellar proper motion. No longer were the fixed stars of the Greeks so fixed, opening a whole new area of research into stellar motions and their implications. Halley's successor, James Bradley, discovered a stellar aberration of 40 arcseconds (1728), interpreted as due to the earth's orbital motion, and two decades later became the first to detect the nodding wobble of the earth known as nutation, an effect amounting to about 18 arcseconds (1748). When in 1783 **William Herschel** detected, from an analysis of stellar **proper motions**, the motion of the sun toward the constellation Hercules, astrometry added yet another triumph to its growing list of discoveries.

Further improvements in accuracy aided by refined telescopic practice allowed much smaller effects to be discovered in the nineteenth century. Attempts to measure **stellar parallax** had been sporadically undertaken since the seventeenth century, and there were several celebrated claims that it had been measured in the early nineteenth century, culminating in a controversy between John Brinkley at Dublin and John Pond at Greenwich (1814–1822). But only with the independent work of **Friedrich Wilhelm Bessel**, **Wilhelm Struve**, and Thomas Henderson, announced during the years 1838–1840, were measurements made that stood the test of time. The measurements of only a few tenths of an arcsecond solved one of the great mysteries of astronomy, proving definitively that a star shifted position as the observer changed position in the earth's orbit. This demonstrated at last the truth of the Copernican theory, and opened yet another research program for astrometry, for the determination of

Prospect of the Royal Greenwich Observatory from Greenwich Park, ca. 1676. From Flamsteed's Historia Coelestis *(1725). National observatories such as Greenwich were the chief patrons of positional astronomy. (Courtesy of the U.S. Naval Observatory)*

the minute shifts was a method for directly measuring accurate stellar distances. Meanwhile the measurements of proper motions yielded another surprise: Bessel first announced in 1844 that unseen stellar companions were producing variations in proper motion of a few seconds to few tenths of a second amplitude in the stars Procyon and Sirius; the companions were confirmed by direct telescopic observation later in the century. Later in the nineteenth century, Chandler detected through stellar measurements the motion of the earth's pole amounting to only 0.5 arcsecond/yr (1885). By the mid-twentieth century, the discovery of unseen planetary companions, producing perturbations in proper motions or double star orbits of a few hundredths of a second of arc amplitude, was claimed. Like parallaxes before 1838, the claim of planetary companions has been controversial and is still very much in doubt. These advances went hand in hand with a plethora of advances in instrumentation and technique; the most important of these are discussed further in the section on instruments and methods, as well as in the entry on meridian instruments.

The Era of Space and Interferometry

Just as precisions for the naked-eye era eventually ran up against the inherent resolution of the human eye at about one arcminute, the traditional techniques of the telescopic era by the 1980s were producing diminishing returns despite heroic efforts, as atmospheric effects at optical wavelengths made it difficult to go beyond precisions of several hundredths of an arcsecond. Although lack of perspective often makes it difficult to declare the dawn of a new era during one's own time, modern astrometry is certainly entering such an era. The use of the transit circle, the prime instrument of large-angle astrometry for two centuries, has been on the decline for several decades, and is now in danger of extinction, as space satellites and the technique of interferometry (interference of light waves) are ushering in a new regime of accuracy that can circumvent or surmount the effects of the earth's atmosphere. The European Space Agency's *Hipparcos* (High Precision Parallax Collecting Satellite) is measuring positions, proper motions and parallaxes for more than 100,000 stars to magnitude 13, with a mean error of about 0.002 arcsecond. The United States has plans for an Astrometric Imaging Telescope, and the Russians have announced a dedicated astrometric instrument known as *Lomonosov*. While funding is still uncertain for these spacecraft, the pioneering *Hipparcos* shows that astrometry above the earth's atmosphere is one of the waves of the future. Meanwhile, ground-based optical and radio interferometry are also beginning to show results at the milliarcsecond level.

Interferometry in space promises even better accuracies in the future—one American proposal known as *Points* (Precision Optical Interferometer in Space) calls for 5 microarcsecond accuracy. With these techniques, the modern era holds the promise of producing the holy grail of astrometry—an inertial reference system—that is, one that does not change perceptibly over time—against which all other stellar, planetary, and earth motions may be measured. What new phenomena may emerge out of this new regime of accuracy and stability cannot be predicted.

Transitions between Eras

Inflection points in history always produce controversy, and the transitions between astrometric eras are no exception. The major controversy between the naked-eye and the telescopic era involved Hevelius and Flamsteed. Hevelius, the aging German astronomer of the Tychonic instrument school, used the quadrant with normal sights, but Flamsteed, the English Astronomer Royal still in his twenties, used a telescope with micrometer eyepiece on his quadrant and sextants. During the 1670s Hooke became the champion of telescopic sights, and in 1678 the Royal Society of London sent Halley to Hevelius's observatory at Danzig to adjudicate the issue of telescopic sights. If Hevelius did better than the one arcminute that Hooke argued was the resolution of the human eye, it was not much better, and more a testament to the remarkable eyesight of one man than a path to the future. It soon became clear that the future lay elsewhere.

A similar argument was gathering steam three hundred years later during the transition from the telescopic to the interferometric and Space Age. In this case, however, there was little doubt that the new methods were more accurate, but two hundred years' worth of refined technique do not die easily. The controversy revolved around how much overlap should exist between the old and new techniques, as well as the relative merit of proven versus nonproven techniques, and the economics and reliability of ground-based versus space-based techniques. Once again, however, it is likely that these were merely the arguments of a transition phase, and that the instruments that can prove themselves to produce reliable milliarcsecond accuracies will win out until the transition to the interferometric/space era of astrometry is as complete as the transition from the naked-eye to the telescopic era of astrometry. This is already the case for the photographic zenith tube (PZT), which has been completely superseded by radio Very Long Base Interferometry (VLBI) for determining earth orientation parameters.

Instruments and Techniques: The Methods of Astrometry

The achievements of astrometry are intimately linked to improved instrumentation, and eventually to a theory of errors and procedures for combining observations to the best advantage. We now address in more detail—for the period beginning with telescopic sights—the development of the instruments and techniques to which astrometric achievement is so clearly tied.

Visual Methods. Visual methods—the combination of eye and telescope—dominated astrometry through the eighteenth and nineteenth centuries, and have been important through most of the twentieth century. Founded on the increasing mechanical and optical skills, particularly of British instrument-makers John Bird, John Dollond, Edward Troughton, and Jesse Ramsden, visual astrometric instrumentation took many forms in the constant drive for increasing precision. The large quadrants gradually gave way early in the nineteenth century to full divided circles, which could be read by microscopes at several points and analyzed for errors. A Troughton mural circle (so called because it was mounted on a wall) was installed at Greenwich in 1812. Zenith instruments (more accurate because they were fixed) date back to the seventeenth century, were developed in their telescopic forms throughout the eighteenth century, and achieved notable form in Airy's reflex zenith tube (1851), which culminated in the photographic zenith tube used for the determination of variation of latitude and time. The equatorial refractor itself was an important astrometric instrument, especially when accompanied by refinements like the filar micrometer, or in specialized forms such as the heliometer, which originated with Dollond and utilized a split lens for astrometric measurement. By the end of the nineteenth century, the merits of long-focus refractors for astrometry were becoming clear, not for the large-angle task of determining a coordinate system, but for differential work in small fields, including the determination of double star orbits.

But for large-angle work no instrument was more important to astrometry than the transit instrument and its later development, the transit circle. It was first used by Ole Roemer in Copenhagen in 1689, and Halley mounted England's first transit instrument at Greenwich in 1721. A transit instrument could provide only right ascension, but when provided with a circle, it could also provide declination, and to such accuracy in both coordinates that it would eventually supersede the mural circle. The first successful transit circle was made by Troughton in 1806 for Groombridge. This form of instrument proved so successful that by the mid-nineteenth century no respectable observatory was without one. For 150 years they were the prime instrument of large-angle astrometry. During its century of operation beginning in 1851, the Airy transit circle at Greenwich made some 675,000 individual observations. Today, there are fewer than a dozen transit circles in operation in the world, and most of these are no longer visual instruments.

The prominence of the English instrument makers was gradually overshadowed by events on the Continent. Faced with purchasing new instrumentation, both **Pulkovo Observatory** (1834) and the **U.S. Naval Observatory** (1842) turned primarily to the instrument-makers of Germany. Both purchased achromatic refractors and smaller comet seekers from Merz and Mahler in Munich. Both purchased prime vertical transits, Pulkovo from Repsold and the Naval Observatory from Pistor and Martins in Berlin. And both purchased transit instruments from Ertel, successor to Reichenbach in Munich. In addition, Pulkovo purchased a large vertical circle from Ertel and a heliometer from Merz and Mahler. Only for the mural circle did the Naval Observatory turn to the English instrument maker Troughton and Simms; Pulkovo placed its faith in Repsold for its large meridian circle.

The English school differed from the German school in more than instrumentation. **Bessel** was the first to insist on the importance not merely of good instrumentation, but also of systematically understand-

The 8.5-inch transit circle of the U.S. Naval Observatory, mounted in 1866. The transit circle, standard equipment at most observatories during the nineteenth century, was used for the precise measurement of the positions of celestial objects in both coordinates. The instrument is now being superseded, even at the great national observatories. (Courtesy of the U.S. Naval Observatory)

The 26-inch Alvan Clark refractor of the U.S. Naval Observatory was the largest telescope in the world when it became opera-tional in 1873. In this photograph, taken in that year, Simon Newcomb is at the eyepiece. Observatory Superintendent Benjamin F. Sands is also pictured. Long focus refractors like the 26-inch were used for small-field astrometry, especially visual and photographic measurements of planetary satellites, double stars, and stellar parallax. (Courtesy of the U.S. Naval Observatory)

ing the peculiarities of each instrument, so that its errors could be taken into account to ensure maximum accuracy. This philosophy extended even to analyzing the observer; Bessel is credited with introducing the term *personal equation* to characterize the differences among observers in registering times of transit, a phenomenon found also in other measurements. It was not without reason that Bessel was among the first to detect stellar parallax and unseen companions; the combination of instrumentation and analytical methods that he championed brought astrometry to its heights by the end of the nineteenth century.

PHOTOGRAPHIC METHODS. Photographic methods have been applied to astrometry for about a century. Seen by some as a method for abolishing personal equation, this goal was not entirely met because of the need to measure the star images on the plates—at least not until the 1960s, when automatic measuring engines came into use. Nevertheless, photography did provide immediately a permanent record and a faster technique whereby thousands of star images might be captured simultaneously. Photographic astrometry began with David Gill, who undertook at the end of the nineteenth century his own photographic survey of the southern sky at the Cape Observatory, the results of which were measured and analyzed by **J.C. Kapteyn**. But as with visual astrometry, photographic astrometry could also be beneficially used for small fields or individual objects; in the first decades of the twentieth century, **Frank Schlesinger** at **Yerkes**, Allegheny, and **Yale observatories** pioneered the application of photography to the determination of parallaxes using long-focus refractors.

Gill was also a key player in organizing the International Astrophotographic Congress held in Paris in 1887, a conference that coordinated the first international photographic survey of the sky. The resultant *Carte du Ciel* and its accompanying Astrographic Catalogue were landmarks in astrometric photographic technique. Twenty-two observatories around the world participated, and although the work stretched over many decades, the result is still valuable today.

The photographic technique has been steadily improved by better emulsions sensitive to various wavelengths, improved measuring machines, and new developments with telescope design, including the wide-angle reflecting telescope first developed by Berhnard Schmidt in 1932. Today the photographic method, both for surveys such as the National Geographic-Palomar Sky Survey and for long-focus work, is an essential aspect of astrometry. Though many images may be obtained on a photographic plate, compared with the single observations made with the transit circle, the latter (or its successors) is still necessary to provide reference stars for measuring the images on the photographic plate.

PHOTOELECTRIC METHODS AND CCDS. Photoelectric methods are relatively new to the field of astrometry, becoming widespread only in the 1980s. Although several forms of photoelectric detectors exist, most are being superseded for astrometry by the charge-coupled device (CCD), a high-quantum, efficiency solid-state detector. Applied to transit circles or more traditional telescopes, the CCD will capture images much fainter than is possible with traditional photographic methods and increase accuracies five to ten times. Although CCDs are not yet available for wide-field work, CCD arrays will put the photographic method in danger of extinction.

Interferometry and the Space Age

Interferometry—which uses the interference of light waves for its measurements—was a method developed by **Albert A. Michelson** in the late nineteenth century. The first stellar **interferometer** was not built until 1920, and only in the 1970s did it begin to be used for astrometry other than double star measurements. In the radio region of the spectrum, Connected Element Interferometry (CEI) uses nearby telescopes to collect data simultaneously, while Very Long Baseline Interferometry (VLBI) combines data from distantly located telescopes. As techniques of radio interferometry were refined in the 1980s, optical interferometry also began to be developed for astrometric uses. For small-field work such as double star measurements, the technique of speckle interferometry combines very fast freeze-frame images to surmount some of the problems of atmospheric turbulence.

Spacecraft may potentially make use of photoelectric, CCD, or interferometric methods of astrometry. Though few are yet funded for actual construction, over the long term astrometric spacecraft will undoubtedly play an important part. Considering the expense of spacecraft design, construction, and operations, ground-based astrometry, especially interferometry, will also continue to play an essential role.

It is important to recognize that not all astrometric methods are useful for all purposes, and therefore the precisions quoted in Table I are not achievable for all applications. Visual transit circles can measure stars only to about tenth magnitude, but they can determine so-called fundamental catalogues in that they can also determine the origins of their coordinate systems. Photographic methods can measure many more stars and much fainter (the Astrographic Catalogue includes stars to the twelfth magnitude, and the First Palomar Sky Survey to the twenty-first), but reference stars are still needed. CCD methods can go even fainter, but only for very small fields. Similarly, long-focus astrometry is applicable only to small fields because such telescopes have only small fields. While very useful for double star, parallax, and unseen companion work, it is therefore not possible in practice to achieve milliarcsecond accuracy using a long-focus refractor except for such specialized purposes. Moreover, it is not possible for the *Hipparcos* satellite, for example, to produce by itself a fundamental reference frame (one whose origin is independently determined), unless it is linked by other means to a terrestrial or extragalactic reference frame. The latter is the subject of much work today.

Computer Methods for Analysis

An important characteristic of astrometric work is the care needed to analyze the observations; it is a maxim of the discipline that for every hour spent at the telescope, ten hours must be spent in analysis of the observations. For most of its history this has meant tedious hand calculations, sometimes aided by mathematical tables or a mechanical calculating device. No overview of methods in astrometry would be complete without mention of this aspect, or the complete revolution that electronic computers brought to the field. Beginning at about the dawn of the Space Age in 1957, large computers began to become widely available in astronomical institutions. The routine work of calculating star positions by rigorous methods was an excellent match for the computer's ability to process many steps quickly and accurately.

The last thirty-five years, therefore, have seen a radical change in the analysis of the observations of positional astronomy, as well as in the day-to-day routine of astronomers. The astrometrist has had to become adept at programming and has had to keep abreast of the constant improvements in computer methods. In addition to this routine reduction of observations, the ability of the computer to acquire and handle large sets of data, and to apply more sophisticated mathematical models and techniques, has allowed analyses to be undertaken that would have been prohibitively time consuming before.

Institutions and Their Research Programs: The Uses of Astrometry

The achievements of positional astronomy did not occur in a vacuum, but within institutions subject to a variety of political, social, and economic effects, all of which affected the extent to which technical advances could be implemented, and the means of implementation. Although we cannot here study the multitude of external effects that have impinged on astrometric science, in this section we clarify the context in which astrometric research programs are undertaken and the goals that drive the field.

PATRONAGE. By contrast to the naked-eye era of positional astronomy, the telescopic era was motivated by navigational needs and so from an early date gained the patronage of national governments. National observatories were founded for just this reason. The royal warrant for the Greenwich Observatory specifically stated that its purpose was to provide data essential for navigation. At that time this meant the method of lunar distances, which required a detailed knowledge of the motion of the moon and the positions of the background stars. The **Berlin Observatory** was founded in the early eighteenth century to make observations necessary for calendar reform. And aside from navigation, the Paris, St. Petersburg, and Pulkovo observatories were deeply involved in triangulation methods of surveying their national lands by way of astronomical observation. It is no surprise, then, that national governments have traditionally been one of the primary supporters of astrometric work. The same still holds true today, although the celestial connections to navigation, for example, are no longer so direct, and astrometric work at observatories such as Greenwich has suffered as a consequence. In some countries, new government-supported research programs have arisen; in the United States, **NASA**, the U.S. Naval Observatory, the **Jet Propulsion Laboratory**, and the Naval Research Laboratory are still the prime supporters of new astrometric instrumentation and data analysis necessary for spacecraft navigation, geodesy, and astrophysics. In Europe the consortium of the governments that comprise the European Space Agency supports Hipparcos.

At the same time, other institutions have supported astrometric research, but their support has declined in proportion to the rise of astrophysics. While most university astronomy departments and observatories are unable to undertake the long-term programs characteristic of positional astronomy, a few (Yale, Yerkes, Lick) are still heavily involved, for example, in parallax and proper motion work, or in analyzing the results based on the larger programs. And while government agencies often take the lead financially, they are supported by university expertise, which may in turn be supported by government grants or contracts. The *Hipparcos* investigative teams are drawn from both government and universities all over Europe. But, in general, modern astrometry has become too much of a big science, and the output of its research programs too long term, to be heavily supported by universities.

RESEARCH PROGRAMS. The primary goal of astrometry has always been to provide more accurate positions for more stars at increasingly fainter magnitudes, and, after the discovery of galaxies and quasars, to provide an inertial reference system based on objects that appeared to be fixed. With such a reference system everything else could fall into place: parallaxes and proper motions could be determined, a reference system would exist for the motions of comets, asteroids, and planets, and the myriad motions of the earth could be measured. The shelves of any observatory library are lined with the results of this work of positional determination, from Ptolemy's catalogue of 1,022 stars to Flamsteed and the Hubble Space Telescope. The Smithsonian Astrophysical Observatory Catalogue (1966) contains positions and proper motions of 258,997 stars, and the Space Telescope Guide Star Catalogue contains millions of stars. These are the long-term programs today largely undertaken by government institutions. The development and types of these catalogues are discussed further in the entry on astronomical catalogues.

From stellar proper motions, the motion of the sun through space and the rotation of the galaxy may be determined. The former was determined in the eighteenth century, and the latter was successful in the twentieth century, but these results are always subject to further refinement. These are not large research programs, and it is an interesting characteristic of the field that these analyses are often not undertaken by the data gatherers themselves, but by other workers at universities or observatories who are the data users. This is undoubtedly a reflection of manpower requirements, specialization, and constraints on mission-related work of government institutions.

Since the first valid determinations of stellar parallax in 1838, some fifteen thousand parallaxes have been measured. The goal behind these routine parallax programs is clear: Astrophysically interesting conclusions can be drawn only when stellar distances are known, and the entire cosmic distance scale rests on trigonometric parallaxes. Parallaxes were relatively slow in coming during the nineteenth century, but with the application of photography to the long-focus refractor by Schlesinger as early as 1910, the great parallax programs began. Some six thousand parallaxes were known by 1938, more than half of them determined at Allegheny, McCormick, and Yale (Johannesburg) observatories. Adriaan van Maanen was the first to use the reflecting telescope for parallaxes, making use of both the 60-inch and 100-inch Mt. Wilson telescopes for more than four hundred determinations. For much of the twentieth century, refractors continued in use for this purpose, but the 61-inch astrometric reflector of the U.S. Naval Observatory now is considered the standard ground-based instrument for stellar parallaxes. On the space-based side, *Hipparcos* will make an enormous contribution to the field. Like parallaxes, double star programs are very relevant to astrophysics because they provide the chief means of determining stellar masses; nevertheless, this demanding and long-term undertaking is now being carried out by only a few individuals.

Even though during the nineteenth century some observatories sold time as a means of financial support, the determination of time and the motions of the earth have become almost exclusively the province of government agencies because of their relevance to navigation and geodesy. Pure research goals are also met by these programs; NASA's Crustal Dynamics Program is a prime example.

Aside from these major programs, astrometry embodies a variety of special studies. In the nineteenth century, for example, many countries sent expeditions to determine the solar parallax, particularly by the method of the transit of Venus, a very rare phenomenon that occurs in pairs only once a century. A study of the internal motions of clusters of stars may lead to a determination of their ages. Early in the twentieth century, Adriaan van Maanen claimed that internal motions in spiral nebulae proved they were internal to our own galaxy. But in a cautionary note on the difficulties of astrometric work, van Maanen was proven wrong—the spiral nebulae were later proven to be independent galaxies. One of the more exciting claims of astrometry is the possible existence of planetary systems that might contain earthlike planets. Once again, these are extremely difficult measurements, and the existence of such systems is as yet unproven.

Finally, we should not lose sight of the human aspect of astrometry. The achievements of the discipline are the result of centuries of painstaking individual and team efforts at data gathering, not always the most glamorous of scientific endeavors, but surely among the most necessary. Hundreds of astronomers, opticians, and technicians, collectively working some millions of hours, have been seriously involved in astrometry over the course of history, not a large number in the course of human events, but certainly a good fraction of the astronomical community's efforts. Gradually extracting nature's secrets through some of the most difficult measurements known to science, they have produced multitudes of star catalogues and almanacs, measured the universe from the solar system to the quasars, determined the structure of the galaxy, and perhaps detected the effects of remote planets on which life might dwell. Finally, the field now stands on the verge of producing astrometry's Holy Grail—an inertial reference system better than ever before, though never perfect. These achievements are no small tribute to the past, and no small legacy for the future.

Because astrometry has comprised so much of the field of astronomy since its beginnings, the general histories of astronomy cover broad aspects of the development of astrometry. More specific aspects are covered in biographies of key figures (concisely in the *Dictionary of Scientific Biography* or in more detail in volumes such as Thoren's biography of Tycho Brahe), in institutional histories of the national observatories, in annotated translations of seminal works (such as Toomer's on Ptolemy's *Almagest*), and in modern astrometric conferences with historical components (see Débarbat et al. and Lieske and Abalakin cited below). Very little research, on the other hand, has been undertaken with broad analytic questions in mind. The problems of patronage, research programs, institutional cooperation, interaction of astrometry and astrophysics, and many others remain ripe for historical inquiry.

Because astrometry was so important to national governments, key archival collections will be found in the archives of the national observatories, such as the U.S. Naval Observatory (U.S. National Archives), Royal Greenwich Observatory (Cambridge University Library), and the Paris Observatory. Much more of interest will be found in collections of individual practitioners or their institutions scattered around the world.

Steven J. Dick

Bibliography

Boss, B. *General Catalogue of 33,342 Stars.* Washington: Carnegie Institution, 1937.

Chapman, A. "The Accuracy of Angular Measuring Instruments Used in Astronomy between 1500 and 1850." *Journal for the History of Astronomy* 14 (1983): 133–137.

———. *Dividing the Circle: The Development of Critical Angular Measurement in Astronomy, 1500–1850.* New York: Harwood, 1990.

Dahn, C.C., D.G. Monet, et al. "Results from the First List of USNO CCD Parallaxes." *Bulletin of the American Astronomical Society* 22 (1990): 820.

Débarbat, S., J.A. Eddy, H.K. Eichhorn, and A.R. Upgren, eds. *Mapping the Sky: Past Heritage and Future Directions.* International Astronomical Union Symposium 133. Dordrecht: Kluwer, 1988.

Douglass, G.G., and R.S. Harrington. "The U.S. Naval Observatory Zodiacal Zone Catalog." *Astronomical Journal* 100 (1990): 1712–1715.

Eichelberger, W.S., and H.R. Morgan. *Results of Observations with the Nine-Inch Transit Circle, 1903–1911, Publications of the United States Naval Observatory.* Vol. 9, part I. Washington: Government Printing Office, 1920.

Eichhorn, H. *Astronomy of Star Positions.* New York: Frederick Ungar, 1974.

Evans, J. "The Origin of the Ptolemaic Star Catalogue, Part 1." *Journal for the History of Astronomy* 18 (1987): 155–172.

Forbes, E.G. (vol. 1), A.J. Meadows (vol. 2), and D. Howse (vol. 3). *Greenwich Observatory: The Royal Observatory at Greenwich and Herstmonceux, 1675–1975.* London: Taylor and Francis, 1975.

Fricke, W. "Bessel." In *Dictionary of Scientific Biography*, edited by C.C. Gillispie, vol. 2, 97–102. New York: Scribner, 1970.

Gill, D. *A History and Description of the Royal Observatory, Cape of Good Hope.* London: His Majesty's Stationery Office, 1913.

Harrington, R.S., C.C. Dahn, et al. "U.S. Naval Observatory Parallaxes of Faint Stars. List VII." *Astronomical Journal* 90 (1985): 123–129.

Kremer, R.L. "Bernard Walther's Astronomical Observations." *Journal for the History of Astronomy* 11 (1980): 174–189.

Krisciunas, K. "A More Complete Analysis of the Errors in Ulugh Beg's Star Catalogue." *Journal for the History of Astronomy* 24 (1993): 269–280.

Lieske, J.H., and V.K. Abalakin. *Inertial Coordinate Systems on the Sky.* International Astronomical Union Symposium 141. Dordrecht: Kluwer, 1990.

Ma, C. "Realization of an Inertial Reference Frame from Mark III VLBI." In *Inertial Coordinate Systems on the Sky,* International Astronomical Union Symposium 141, edited by J.H. Lieske and V.K. Abalakin, 271–280. Dordrecht: Kluwer, 1990.

Monet, D.G. "Recent Advances in Optical Astrometry." In *Annual Review of Astronomy and Astrophysics*, edited by G. Burbidge, D. Layzer, and J.G. Phillips, vol. 26, 413–440. Palo Alto: Annual Reviews, 1988.

Newton, R.R. *The Crime of Claudius Ptolemy.* Baltimore: Johns Hopkins University Press, 1977.

Pannekoek, A. *A History of Astronomy.* London: George Allen and Unwin, 1961.

Perryman, M.A.C. "In-Orbit Status of the Hipparcos Astrometry Mission." In *Lieske and Abalakin* (1990): 297–305.

Podobed, V.V. *Fundamental Astrometry.* Chicago: University of Chicago Press, 1964.

Schlesinger, F. "Photographic Determinations of Stellar Parallax Made with the Yerkes Refractor." *Astrophysical Journal* 33 (1911): 8–27.

Shevchenko, M. "An Analysis of Errors in the Star Catalogues of Ptolemy and Ulugh Beg." *Journal for the History of Astronomy* 21 (1990): 187–201.

Thoren, V. "New Light on Tycho's Instruments." *Journal for the History of Astronomy* 4 (1973): 25–45.

———. *The Lord of Uraniborg: A Biography of Tycho Brahe.* New York: Cambridge University Press, 1990.

Toomer, G.J., trans. and ann. *Ptolemy's Almagest.* New York: Springer-Verlag, 1984.

Van Altena, W.F. "Astrometry." In *Annual Review of Astronomy and Astrophysics*, edited by G. Burbidge, D. Layzer, and J.G. Phillips, vol. 21, 131–164. Palo Alto: Annual Reviews, 1983.

Wesley, W.G. "The Accuracy of Tycho Brahe's Instruments." *Journal for the History of Astronomy* 9 (1978): 42–53.

Astronomers Royal

As England vied with other European nations for hegemony in the seventeenth century, the accurate determination of longitude at sea became a national priority. Just as pressing was the need to establish an observatory in England, especially after reports that a Frenchman had solved the longitude problem by astronomical means. **John Flamsteed** argued that current ephemerides and star catalogues were not sufficiently accurate to support the French claim. Charles II named Flamsteed his Astronomical Observer and agreed to build an observatory at Greenwich. Thus England's first government-supported scientific post was dedicated to applied research.

Defining the boundaries of appropriate research at Greenwich always has been a matter of negotiation, with each Astronomer Royal molding the observatory's program to suit his own personality, interests, and abilities. Although bound by royal warrant to the task of providing astronomical data for the good of the nation, the role of England's Astronomer Royal has evolved in response to changing conceptions of the nature of astronomical science. An examination of the changing role of the Astronomer Royal in British science provides historians of science with a way to examine several important questions.

Colin Ronan's narrative history of the Astronomers Royal from Flamsteed through Richard van der Riet Woolley recounts episodes that shaped the position's social and scientific agenda. Ronan's objective was to justify government support of astronomical research at a time when British astronomers appeared to be producing little of practical value. A more analytical examination can be found in the tercentenary history by Forbes, Graham-Smith, McCrea, and Meadows. The restructuring of British astronomy after World War II invites historical reflection on the Astronomers Royal, not as a succession of eccentric personalities, but rather as critical points in a debate over the position of science in British society across three centuries.

When Flamsteed became Astronomer Royal in 1676, the crown was unaccustomed to purchasing scientific expertise. Consequently, no one knew how much scientific information should cost, what the product might look like, or how long it might take to produce. Although the king funded the construction of the observatory building and granted Flamsteed an annual salary of £100, he provided no money for the purchase of instruments or for the hiring of assistants, an arrangement that caused considerable confusion over the ownership of observational records.

Flamsteed obtained some instruments through gifts and constructed others himself.

His self-sufficiency, coupled with the lack of contractual guidelines, reinforced Flamsteed's belief that the data were his own, a belief that placed him at odds with other astronomers. To gain administrative control over the work of the observatory, Queen Anne established the Board of Visitors in 1710. The board, consisting of members of the Royal Society, was charged with ensuring that instruments were in working order, replacing them as necessary, and reviewing the annual report of the Astronomer Royal.

The Board of Visitors, however, did not resolve the problem of ownership. Both **Edmond Halley** and his successor, James Bradley, treated observational data as personal property, actions seen by other astronomers as obstructing the continuity of work at Greenwich and limiting their access to important resources. Bradley's records required such extraordinary efforts to recover that the Council of the Royal Society drafted a set of regulations codifying the Astronomer Royal's rights and responsibilities in 1764. By that time, there was a growing recognition in the British scientific community of the permanence of the institution in contrast to the transience of the individual occupant.

The 1764 regulations were welcomed by Nevil Maskelyne, the fifth Astronomer Royal, whose long tenure smoothed the institution's transition to a more mature and routine phase of its work. Maskelyne operated within the new regulations to build a positive relationship between the observatory and the Board of Visitors as well as its fiscal agent, the Board of Ordnance. But there were two developments during Maskelyne's tenure that permanently altered the institution's scientific purpose and research agenda: the claim by John Harrison to have constructed a marine chronometer of sufficient accuracy to solve the longitude problem and the discovery of a new planet by **William Herschel**.

The suggestion that the longitude problem had been solved by mechanical means raised serious questions about the future direction of research at Greenwich. After all, astronomers had long assumed that the problem would be solved only through observational and theoretical work in **astrometry** and **celestial mechanics**. Maskelyne's personal and professional bias in favor of astronomical methods for finding longitude at sea was unshaken by the performance of Harrison's chronometer in exacting trials and embroiled Maskelyne in many disputes. Indeed, his fervor led him to intensify efforts to provide mariners with lunar tables so accurate that they would rival the new chronometers. Maskelyne determined the precise coordinates of standard reference stars and instituted an annual ephemeris for navigators, the *Nautical Almanac*, a task that became so labor intensive that it eventually required the employment of additional staff. As navigators' reliance on chronometers increased, the Admiralty, which assumed administrative control over Greenwich in 1818, assigned the Astronomer Royal responsibility for rating those instruments bound for naval service.

The second development, William Herschel's discovery of the planet **Uranus** in 1781, won the patronage of King George III and the title of Royal Astronomer. Like the Astronomer Royal, Herschel was provided with an observatory and a salary, but unlike his counterpart, Herschel served the crown as a natural historian of the heavens. Herschel's telescope was less an instrument of measurement than a novel cabinet of curiosities through which he made marvelous objects in the night sky accessible to the royal family. Herschel's catalogues of nebulae seemed to justify his claims concerning the light-gathering power of large reflecting telescopes.

Though Herschel's discoveries increased popular interest in descriptive astronomy and fueled cosmological speculation, they exemplified for Maskelyne all that astronomical research at Greenwich was not. His commitment to serve as Britain's chief timekeeper and master of astrometry insulated the Astronomer Royal from other currents in astronomy. Questions regarding cosmology, stellar evolution, or the physical composition of celestial bodies, which interested a growing number of astronomers in Britain, were deemed too theoretical to be worthy of government support or the Astronomer Royal's time. Maskelyne's literal interpretation of the Royal Warrant of 1675 informed his decision to restrict observations at Greenwich to those that would improve navigation, an adaptive, albeit limiting, choice, leading to a highly specialized research niche for the Royal Observatory.

A similar brand of conservatism governed the acquisition of instruments and the application of new research methodologies by the nineteenth century Astronomers Royal. Maskelyne and his successors, John Pond and **George Biddell Airy**, developed methods that enhanced precision, while leaving programs that involved riskier, discovery-oriented projects to astronomers in the private sector. Telescopes with apertures comparable in size to William Herschel's, for example, had no place at the Greenwich Observatory until the twentieth century. Likewise, astronomical photography and spectroscopy were resisted at Greenwich until the last quarter of the century.

John Pond, who became Astronomer Royal in 1811, continued the course set by his predecessor, but encountered challenges calling for greater administrative flexibility than he could muster. It was during Pond's tenure that Greenwich ceased to be the principal seat of British astronomical research. Growing numbers of astronomers, many of them amateurs with wide-ranging research interests, resources, and expertise, vainly sought leadership and intellectual support from the Astronomer Royal. The year 1820 saw the founding of two institutions: the Royal Astronomical Society (RAS), which supported positional and descriptive astronomy, and the Royal Observatory at the Cape of Good Hope, charged with mapping the southern skies.

Although a talented observer, Pond was hampered in his success in fulfilling his obligations as Astronomer Royal by the slovenliness of the chief assistant, poor health, and inadequate administrative skills. Pond became the first Astronomer Royal to retire from office and the only one to have done so involuntarily. His successor, George Biddell Airy, director of the Cambridge University Observatory, was selected for the post because of his reputation as an efficient administrator.

Airy's management style became legendary, his lengthy tenure marked by anecdotes illustrating ways of doing science efficiently in an age of progress and increasing specialization. Historians are beginning to analyze Airy's incremental, often situation-bound, management style in a broader social, political, and economic context. Airy's obsession with positional astronomy can be profitably understood in terms of institutional survival and the art of designing a productive research niche.

Wedded by duty and personal preference to a program of precise, efficient, and uniform measurement, Airy streamlined the collection, reduction, and publication of observational data by breaking down complex tasks into repetitive, specialized steps that required little training. To assist in managing the observatory's activities (and to forestall the discipline problems Pond had encountered), Airy created the post of chief assistant. He developed self-registering instruments to mechanize observations and reduce disparities resulting from perceptual differences between observers. These systemic changes in the practice of astronomy at Greenwich made it possible for Airy to delegate what he viewed as the tedium of mere observation and computation to lower-level staff.

Like his predecessors, Airy was one of the government's only paid scientists when he began his forty-six-year reign in 1835. But unlike them, he had no other source of income. This practical matter combined with the government's growing thirst for expert scientific information and Airy's indefatigable sense of duty, transformed the Astronomer Royal into a general science advisor. Although other scientists would join the civil service, Airy steadfastly asserted the Astronomer Royal's position as chief scientific consultant to the crown, giving advice on scientific and technical issues, ranging from the structural integrity of bridges in high winds to science education.

By mid-century, Airy's passion for organization was no longer sufficient to keep Greenwich competitive. Although astrometry was the backbone of research at the great observatories of Paris, Berlin, and St. Petersburg, it did not constrain their activities in the way that Airy's routine, limited operations at Greenwich did. Continental astronomers applied positional methods and instruments to projects in which Airy saw little purpose. In the end, his programmatic rigidity became an institutional liability.

Indeed, important astronomical discoveries were made by astronomers working outside the boundaries Airy deemed appropriate for research in a national observatory. For example, in 1838, **Friedrich Wilhelm Bessel** announced the first determination of a stellar parallax, a project Airy would not have encouraged at Greenwich.

Perhaps the most memorable and disquieting astronomical discovery made during Airy's tenure was that of the planet Neptune. Coordinates for this object were determined independently by two celestial mechanicians—**Urbain Jean Joseph Le Verrier** in France and John Couch Adams in England—and the planet was located by Johann Gottfried Galle of the Berlin Observatory, using Le Verrier's data. Adams had asked Airy to search for the planet, but the Astronomer Royal was not interested and passed the information on to the director of the Observatory at Cambridge University, who bungled the search. When sole credit for the discovery was awarded to Le Verrier, the Astronomer Royal was exposed to public criticism. The discovery of Neptune aside, Airy's administration provides opportunities for historians to explore his sense of stewardship for British astronomy.

In the last decade of Airy's tenure, a group of vocal observers, attracted by **astrophysics**, questioned the adequacy of Greenwich to contribute to the new astronomy. The Astronomer Royal's authority had been diluted by the success of British astronomers working on projects in **astronomical spectroscopy**, celestial photography, and **solar physics**. Many believed that the decentralization of British astronomy jeopardized the programmatic continuity essential to the development of astrophysical theory. In their view, ephemeral phenomena like sunspots, solar prominences, **novae**, and **variable stars** demanded routine, coordinated observations at a network of national astrophysical observatories located throughout the empire. Many RAS members argued the necessity of government support for astrophysics to preserve Britain's leadership in astronomy. Airy understood that government financial support for research at other facilities would divert resources from Greenwich, and he actively opposed government patronage for astrophysical observatories.

Airy was not opposed to the methods and research interests of the new astronomy. In the first decade of his tenure, growing international acceptance of meteorology, solar physics, and especially terrestrial magnetism as legitimate astronomical concerns had fanned his interest in the collection and analysis of such data. Although never a practitioner, he was an early advocate of **astronomical photography**, and encouraged research in stellar spectroscopy. Nevertheless, Airy felt keenly his responsibility to the British public. In his opinion, individuals with private means were free to pursue projects of their own design. Indeed, the rapid development of astrophysics exemplified the benefits of keeping discovery-oriented scientific activity in the private sector. Still, Airy could no longer ignore the call to diversify the research program at Greenwich, particularly after the astrometric value of celestial photography and spectroscopy was demonstrated. More important, he recognized the need for the Astronomer Royal to project a new style of leadership if the post were to retain its stature in an increasingly competitive scientific market. Firm assurances from Airy that Greenwich had already begun astrophysical observations, combined with the support of key figures in the RAS and the Royal Society, delayed the establishment of an independent government astrophysical observatory until shortly before Airy's retirement in 1881.

When John Couch Adams declined the invitation to become the eighth Astronomer Royal, the post was offered to Airy's chief assistant, William Henry Mahoney Christie, the first Greenwich staff member to be promoted to the post. Sharing neither Airy's disdain for observation nor his skepticism of the new astronomy, Christie had directed research on **stellar radial velocities**. And, though he benefited from his predecessor's example and good counsel during the first decade of his term—a luxury no other Astronomer Royal had enjoyed—Christie interpreted the position in his own way and pursued research suited to his own interests. While not neglecting astrometry, Christie moved the observatory in new directions.

Christie's diversification of the Greenwich research agenda complicated, but did not interrupt, activities associated with the institution's traditional duties such as chronometer rating and maintenance of the national time service. Research on problems relevant to the new astronomy expanded under Christie's successor, Frank Watson Dyson. Born after the first pioneering discoveries of astronomical spectroscopy, Dyson enthusiastically incorporated astrophysics into the Greenwich research program, an action viewed by some as too speculative, or holding insufficient promise for practical benefit to the nation. Defining the limits of the observatory's research program is one important element in a complex array of concerns that informed astronomers and politicians as they debated the future of government-sponsored astronomical research in twentieth-century Britain.

By the end of the nineteenth century, Greenwich was no longer a satisfactory observing site. A burgeoning network of electric railway lines interfered with the observatory's magnetic studies, corrosive industrial aerosols damaged instrumentation, while gas, and, later, electric light obscured the night sky. In 1939, Dyson's successor, Harold Spencer Jones, recommended relocating to a more favorable site.

The success of new observatories in the United States caused some in Britain's astronomical community to consider abandoning observational astronomy at the Royal Observatory in favor of building a research niche based upon expertise in theoretical astronomy. Physical damage to observatory buildings and instruments during World War II, as well as the overwhelming burdens of Britain's war effort, forced a lengthy hiatus in astronomical research at Greenwich. And, like spectroscopy in the nineteenth century, the development of **radio astronomy** by individuals working outside the purview of the Astronomer Royal provided new ways of studying the heavens. The growth of radio astronomy signaled the beginning of a lively competition with Greenwich for resources and scientific talent.

In light of the damage sustained at Greenwich and Spencer Jones's own commitment to optical astronomy, interest in finding a new site was rekindled after the war. While some advocated removing the Royal Observatory to a less overcast climate, the faction wanting to remain in England, on or near the prime meridian, prevailed. In the 1940s, overseas travel and communications made the support of a research facility outside of England impractical and expensive. In 1945, Herstmonceux Castle in Sussex was selected because of its improved observing conditions and proximity to the University of Sussex. The move was not completed until 1958, under the direction of Spencer Jones's successor, Richard van der Riet Woolley, and the Royal Observatory at Greenwich became officially known as the Royal Greenwich Observatory at Herstmonceux (RGO).

While astronomers contemplated the selection of a new observing site, Henry Plaskett, in his 1945 presidential address to the RAS, suggested that a large reflecting telescope be built in England comparable in size to those in the United States and Australia. Spencer Jones convinced both his colleagues and the treasury of the need for a telescope at least 100 inches in diameter. By the end of 1946, serious discussion was under way over the design of the telescope, but a decade passed before agreement could be reached that would best satisfy the broadest range of political and professional needs. Financial constraints contributed to further delays, and the instrument, the Isaac Newton Telescope (INT), a 98-inch reflector, was not completed until 1967.

In the meantime, English radio astronomers began planning a large-aperture telescope. In 1955, this expensive project, undertaken by scientists at the University of Manchester, received (from both government and private sources) over five times the funds allocated to the INT project. The 250-foot radio telescope at Jodrell Bank was completed in just two years, a decade before the INT. Acclaim over discoveries made with this instrument accelerated a shift in power in the British astronomical community from the RGO and the Astronomer Royal toward the RAS and the universities.

A 1963 government inquiry into the organization of civil service in the U.K. led to the establishment of the Science Research Council (SRC; later the Science and Engineering Research Council, or SERC). The SRC placed the RGO under its authority, and, although Woolley directed the observatory until 1971, the position of director was separated from that of Astronomer Royal. Under this new administrative arrangement, the director was responsible for ground-based observational facilities for U.K. astronomers, as well as astronomy-based services to the general public. The Astronomer Royal became a figurehead, a change that took place partially by design and partially in consequence of the relative inactivity of Woolley's successor, Martin Ryle, whose activities were limited by ill health.

Although Woolley reduced the manpower and resources devoted to meridian astronomy and the time service, his personal interest in the motion of nearby stars kept research at the RGO optically based, a focus that continues to the present day, in spite of the rapid expansion of astronomical research to other areas of the electromagnetic spectrum and the appointment of radio astronomers Ryle and Francis Graham-Smith to the post of Astronomer Royal. Indeed, it was during the tenures of Ryle and Graham-Smith that efforts were undertaken to establish an overseas optical observatory that would provide Northern Hemisphere observers with observing capabilities similar to those available to astronomers working in the Southern Hemisphere.

The suggestion to build such a facility came not from England's Astronomer Royal, but from the Astronomer Royal of Scotland, Hermann Brück. While Woolley endorsed the plan, it was slow in getting off the drawing boards. Teams from the Royal Observatory at Edinburgh and the RGO conducted a worldwide search for a site. Finally, eleven years after the original proposal, a treaty was signed with Spain to allow Britain, Sweden, the Netherlands, and Denmark to build an observatory complex on *San Miguel de la Palma* in the Canary Islands, in exchange for a share of the observing time. Directed by Spain's *Instituto de Astrofisica de Canarias* and known as the *Observatoria del Roque de los Muchachos*, the facility opened in 1985. The RGO transferred the INT from Herstmonceux to La Palma to conduct spectroscopic research, and a 4.2-meter telescope, appropriately named in honor of William Herschel, was designed to study faint objects.

By the time La Palma became operational, the RGO was emerging from a decade of administrative flux. The effect of this interruption in administrative continuity on public, political, and professional attitudes toward government support for astronomy presents interesting challenges to historians who seek to understand the interplay of personality, chance, programmatic vision, and competition for resources in the process of institutional change.

When the INT became operational in its new location, most tasks at the RGO centered on the construction and maintenance of British telescopes and equipment at La Palma. Traditional activities now occupy only about 10 percent of staff time. Herstmonceux was sold by the SERC in 1988, and the RGO was moved to Cambridge University in 1990 along with all its archival records.

Today, the Astronomer Royal's post involves no set function, although its occupant is expected to respond to public inquiries and represent British astronomy both at home and abroad. Arnold Whittaker Wolfendale, a high-energy-particle physicist, was Astronomer Royal from 1991 to 1995. Wolfendale's appointment came on the heels of the RGO's move to Cambridge. The RGO director, Alec Boksenberg, is also a physicist by training. Appointed to the post in 1981, Boksenberg was lured into astronomical research by the dearth of employment in physics and the opportunity to administer the operation of the new observatory facilities at La Palma. In 1995 Martin Rees became Astronomer Royal.

In recent years, astronomy has borne the brunt of the SERC's cost-cutting measures, particularly as funds for big projects—the proposed collaboration with the United States and Canada to build two new 8-meter optical telescopes, for example, or the gravity wave observatory being planned with German astronomers—have come under scrutiny in order to make money available for smaller grants. Britain's withdrawal from active collaboration in the *Hipparcos* project has deepened fears that belt-tightening measures will adversely affect the international reputation of British astronomy. While the Astronomer Royal possesses no political power, members of Britain's astronomical community view it as his responsibility to serve as their spokesman, to publicize the results of ongoing astronomical research, and to justify financial support for future projects. As longtime chairman of the SERC's Astronomy and Planetary Sciences Board, Wolfendale was not shy about exerting his influence, but only time will tell if his efforts were successful.

Barbara J. Becker

Astronomers Royal

Name	*Dates*	*Dates Served*
John Flamsteed	1646–1719	1675–1719
Edmond Halley	1656–1742	1720–1742
James Bradley	1693–1762	1742–1762
Nathaniel Bliss	1700–1764	1762–1764
Nevil Maskelyne	1732–1811	1765–1811
John Pond	1767–1836	1811–1835
George Biddell Airy	1801–1892	1835–1881
William Henry Mahoney Christie	1845–1922	1881–1910
Frank Watson Dyson	1868–1939	1910–1933
Harold Spencer Jones	1890–1960	1933–1955
Richard van der Riet Woolley	1906–1986	1956–1971
Martin Ryle	1918–1984	1972–1982
Alan Hunter (RGO Acting Director)	1912–1995	Jan–July 1972
E. Margaret Burbidge (RGO Director)	1919–	July 1972–Nov 1973
Alan Hunter (Director)	1912–1995	1973–1975
Francis Graham-Smith (RGO Director)	1923–	1976–1981
Francis Graham-Smith	1923–	1982–1990
Alec Boksenberg (RGO Director)	1936–	1981–
Arnold Whittaker Wolfendale	1927–	1991–1995
Martin Rees	1942–	1995–

Bibliography

Chapman, A. "Public Research and Private Duty: George Biddell Airy and the Search for Neptune." *Journal for the History of Astronomy* 19 (1988): 121–139.

Forbes, E. *Greenwich Observatory: Origins and Early History 1675–1835*. London: Taylor and Francis, 1975.

Graham-Smith, F., et al. "Three Hundred Years of Greenwich." *Nature* 255 (1975): 581–606.

Howse, D. *Nevil Maskelyne: The Seaman's Astronomer*. Cambridge: Cambridge University Press, 1989.

McCrea, W.H. "The Royal Greenwich Observatory 1675–1975." *Quarterly Journal of the Royal Astronomical Society* 17 (1976): 4–24.

Meadows, A.J. *Greenwich Observatory: Recent History, 1836–1975*. London: Taylor and Francis, 1975.

Ronan, C.A. *Their Majesties' Astronomers: A Survey of Astronomy in Britain between the Two Elizabeths*. London: Bodley Head, 1967.

Smith, R.W. "The Cambridge Network in Action: The Discovery of Neptune." *Isis* 80 (1989): 395–422.

———. "A National Observatory Transformed: Greenwich in the Nineteenth Century." *Journal for the History of Astronomy* 22 (1991): 5–20.

Urania, the ancient Muse of astronomy, flanks an allegorical personification of astronomy with Ptolemy, the Alexandrian astronomer who was regarded, until the Copernican Revolution, as the primary authority on astronomy in Antiquity. This scene, glorified by the sun, moon, stars, and firmament, was designed by Johann Santritter for a 1490 Venetian edition of De Sphaerae mundi *by Sacrobosco. Sacrobusco's work served as the introductory text in astronomy for generations of students between the thirteenth and sixteenth centuries. (Courtesy of the Griffith Observatory)*

Astronomy

Astronomy is the only science the Romans personified with a Greek Muse. The rest of the Muses presided over endeavors that today would be classified as performing arts, and the ancients attributed to the Nine Muses the power to inspire the creative impulse in those engaged in metrical pursuits. To the ancients, the cyclic movements of the stars and planets qualified astronomy as a metrical pursuit. Monitoring the rhythms of heaven and the music of the spheres, astronomy kept company with the theater, music, poetry, and the dance.

Harmonious celestial movement allied astronomy with music and with the gods. Traveling far above the earth, celestial objects surveyed the scene below with the perspective of gods. The sun, moon, planets, and stars were remote. Independent travelers, they blazed their own trails through heaven. Although visible to all, they answered to none. Pattern and regularity made them eternal. They obeyed laws, but the laws were their laws. The Greek roots of the word astronomy refer to star law and tell us what mattered most about the sky. Its behavior was orderly and predictable.

Astronomy's Muse was Urania. Her name means heavenly, and she was usually depicted with a celestial globe and a measuring compass. These symbols of her jurisdiction link her with observation and measurement. Although systematic observation and mathematical astronomy were developed in Mesopotamia, scientific astronomy seems to be a Greek invention. The Greeks tried to explain and predict the movements of objects in the sky with geometric models. They tested their explanations with data obtained through precise measurement, and they abandoned their explanations when the match failed. The heavens were, in fact, the one realm where measurement and prediction were reasonably successful in providing an accurate portrait of nature. Astronomy's result-oriented reputation and practical applications helped preserve the methods and goals developed in Antiquity. Historian of science Otto Neugebauer emphasizes this: "Astronomy is the only branch of the ancient sciences which survived almost intact after the collapse of the Roman Empire" (Neugebauer, 20).

Although our understanding of the character and components of Urania's domain has evolved considerably since Antiquity, the prerogative of astronomy is very much the same. Aristotle, for example, underscored the mathematical character of astronomy and said that astronomy's territory began at the moon. Everything beyond it, he added, was celestial, unchanging, eternal, and divine.

A modern definition of astronomy is as close as any standard dictionary. *The Random House Dictionary of the English Language*, for example, omits those references to unchanging, eternal, and divine but informs us that astronomy is "the science that deals with the material universe beyond the earth's atmosphere." It is a definition that would have satisfied Aristotle, for he regarded the zone below the moon and above the earth as atmospheric. College textbooks on elementary astronomy also offer a definition, usually in the glossary. Despite the specialized character of academic texts, George Abell's fourth edition of *Exploration of the Universe*, one of the most successful modern texts, adds only a little more detail than the dictionary: Astronomy is "the branch of science that treats of the physics and morphology of that part of the universe that lies beyond the earth's atmosphere" (Abell, 664). The mandate is somewhat greater than that given by Aristotle, but the principle is the same.

Long before the Greeks decided the heavens were eternal and divine, however, divinity was already attributed to the objects in the sky. The sky was regarded as the realm of the gods, and astronomy exposed its practitioners to the divine. Through contact with divinity, astronomy inspired the soul. This transcendental vision of astronomy finds no authorized function in the domain of a modern materialist science that describes the universe according to physical principles, but scientific astronomy retains its power to inspire awe and to propel the imagination far beyond the concerns of everyday life. This occurs, in part, because astronomy directs our attention to things on the grandest scale we can measure or imagine. Through astronomy, we are eyewitnesses to the largest things in the universe, the farthest things in the universe, and the most exotic things in the universe. That is the source of astronomy's emotional dimension in our own era. Accordingly, the stage is still set for grand opera in many nontechnical and popularly oriented accounts of astronomical discovery.

Today's nontechnical astronomy books for the general reader rarely tell us what astronomy is, but almost always emphasize its importance. Carl Sagan's *Cosmos* (1980), a publishing and television landmark, embraces the history, content, and significance of astronomy but never defines it. *The Amazing Universe*, published by the National Geographic Society in 1975, informs us that astronomy "is a great human endeavor" (Friedman, 19). A. Pannekoek, the Dutch historian of astronomy, declared the science to be "a work of culture, an adventure of the mind" (Pannekoek, 15). Patrick Moore, a linchpin of popular astronomy for half a century, called astronomy "the oldest science in the world" (Moore, 11). According to Donald Goldsmith, astronomy is also "the second-oldest profession" (Goldsmith, 49). Goldsmith further defined astronomy in terms of public perception. It is, he wrote, "just three things—the man in the moon, the rings of **Saturn**, and Halley's comet" (Goldsmith, 50). These are the fundamentals—the exotic charged with the grandeur of distance and time.

These relatively recent commentaries continue a well-established romantic tradition. At the turn of the century, Herbert Howe's *Study of the Sky* (1896) opened with a familiar fanfare: "Astronomy is at once the most ancient and the noblest of the physical sciences." In the same era, **Camille Flammarion** (1), the celebrated French astronomer and popularizer, emphasized astronomy's lofty attractions. "Astronomy is the science which concerns us most, the one most necessary for our general instruction, and at the same time the one which offers for our study the greatest charms and keeps in reserve the highest enjoyments." The English poet and essayist Edwin Arnold predicted astronomy would be "the chief educator and emancipator of the human race" (Olcott and Putnam, 7). In *Field Book of the Skies*, a best-selling practical guide to astronomy in the first half of this century, William Tyler Olcott and Edmund W. Putnam enthusiastically wrote that astronomy is "the most ancient, the most uncommercial, and the most unselfish" of all sciences (8). In a further lapse of restraint, they added that astronomy involves "the supreme and superlative manifestations of natural law" (8) and is no less than "the mother of all thought" (7). Jermain G. Porter, director of the Cincinnati Observatory, underscored the aesthetic, historical, and philosophical value of astronomy. More than any other science, he judged, it enlarges the mind and gives "a true conception of the relation of man to his physical environment" (ix).

Although many authors have found it difficult to maintain a disciplined distance from astronomy's emotional appeal, we might depend upon historians to deal less breathlessly with astronomy. In this respect, Otto Neugebauer does not fail us. He narrows his definition of astronomy to "only those parts of human interest in celestial phenomena which are amenable to mathematical treat-

Babylonian astronomers study the heavens from the summit of a ziggurat in this romantic portrayal of astronomical observation included in Astronomical Myths *by John F. Blake, who based the book on Camille Flammarion's* History of the Heavens. *Systematic skywatching and mathematical astronomy were both legacies of Mesopotamia, where celestial objects also were regarded as divine. (Courtesy of the Griffith Observatory)*

ment" (2). Stephen C. McCluskey broadens the definition to cover all the ways societies "make their observations of the heavens intelligible" (214) and spotlights the importance of systematic, integrative thought. Neither indulges "the romance of astronomy," but other historians, including Pannekoek, have been attracted to that flame that seems to ignite astronomy with greater meaning. **J.L.E. Dreyer** recognized the link between the maturity of astronomical knowledge, the evolution of Western thought, and the history of Western civilization: "Among the branches of physical sciences there is no other which in its historical development so closely reflects the general progress of civilisation as the doctrine of the position of the earth in space and its relation to the planetary system" (vii).

Colin Ronan's popular history *Science* begins by quoting the poetry of Alfred Noyes, who, near the end of World War I, likened the discoveries of astronomy to battles in a war against ignorance. As a writer of science history, Ronan saw the development of astronomy as a "thread guiding us through the labyrinth of cultural differences in various civilizations" (17). Like McCluskey, he spotlighted the cross-cultural character of astronomy. Everyone watched the sky and made use of it.

The French historian Charles-Albert Reichen continued the courtship with the transcendental component of astronomy in *A History of Astronomy*. "Astronomy," he reminded readers,"by its very nature, touches on the most sacred mysteries of creation" (6). According to Pannekoek, the study of the stars was "the unfolding" of a higher world and "the noblest object that human thinking and spiritual effort could find" (13).

Certainly we can trace these ideas back to the Greeks. In the second century C.E., **Ptolemy** stressed the value of mathematics in *The Almagest*, the most important compilation of Greek astronomy. Only mathematics provides "sure and unassailable knowledge" (van der Waerden, 2), and in Ptolemy's view, astronomy was the branch of mathematics that "deals with knowledge of the divine celestial bodies" (van der Waerden, 2). Ptolemy was actually echoing ideas advanced by Plato about five centuries earlier. In the *Republic*, Plato classified astronomy as one of the four branches of mathematics (Dicks, 92), and later, in the *Laws*, he argued that everyone should command some knowledge of it (Dicks, 93). The historian George Sarton summarized Plato's view on astronomy. It is "the basic knowledge for wisdom, health, and happiness" (Sarton, 421). Plato recognized the rationality of the universe in the regularity of celestial motions. Rational regularity in heaven provided the foundation for the calendar—the orderly, numbered progression of time. This regulates society and inspires proper reverence for the divine.

The ancients, we see, continued to tell the same story. Astronomy developed from a primordial recognition of the cyclic behavior of the sky into a quantitative study of the motions of celestial objects. These motions conferred order upon the landscape of time and space and were judged to reveal the nature of celestial gods. As handiwork of the divine, the pattern of celestial events directed the sacred to earth and stitched it to the affairs of the world.

This notion is the core of all traditional astronomy. For example, indigenous Chinese astronomy operated as an imperial institution, but it, too, defined the sacred character of the cosmos. The Chinese emperor acted ritually as an intermediary with the divine to preserve the dynamic balance between heaven and earth. His tools included the calendar, seasonal ceremony, and precise astronomical measurement. In Imperial China, precision was the handmaiden of imperial authority.

Similar expressions of sacred order may be extracted from cultural applications of astronomy all over the world. From the soothsayers of Babylon to the shamans of Siberia, from the calendar-keeping priests of Egypt to the bloodletting kings of the Maya, people have extracted from celestial events messages that organized and stabilized their lives.

The complexity of what we mean by astronomy is, in part, a product of its historical development. Modern scientific astronomy is not the same thing as the astronomy of the ancients or even the astronomy romanticized by its many interpreters. For that reason, historians have tried to distinguish different approaches to the sky by considering the goals, techniques, and results of each enterprise. Without denying the cultural significance of cosmogony, celestial mythology, sky lore, cosmovision, and astrological inquiry, Neugebauer (19) identifies mathematical analysis as the real difference between skywatching and genuine astronomy. B.L. van der Waerden is more interested in the cultural motivations for early astronomy and examines the links between astronomical knowledge, calendrics, and cosmic religion. In the early era, according to van der Waerden, the mathematical predictability of celestial events and the sublimity of the celestial realm stimulated the growth of cosmic religion. This religion invested the sky with divinity and attributed to astrologers the ability to discern celestial will.

W.M. O'Neil, an Australian authority on the history and philosophy of science, identified three types of early astronomical activity—prescientific astronomy, proto-scientific astronomy, and scientific astronomy. Prescientific astronomy involves simple recognition and classification of celestial events. The discovery of cyclical regularity in the behavior of celestial objects and a rough quantitative appreciation of them are credited to proto-scientific astronomy. Scientific astronomy exploits mathematical analysis in the pursuit of accurate prediction. As long as scientific astronomy was associated with the symbolic applications of astronomy, which primarily serve traditional religion, it differed from modern scientific astronomy, which is founded on astrophysics.

The astronomy of the ancients is, at its heart, a reflection of their recognition of the sacred in celestial order and of the divine in the remote territory of the sky. Astronomy in this sense is the night sky, an alert eye, and long memory. With these tools, the objects in heaven could be observed. Some of their conduct became predictable, but their physical nature remained out of reach.

The ancients saw a link between the macrocosm of the universe and the microcosm of their own lives. This analogy anchored the world view of European civilization until the **Copernican Revolution** triggered a complete revision in the way we think about our place in the universe. That conceptual transformation in turn altered what people once meant by astronomy.

Aristotle formulated the cosmology and the approach to nature that governed Western thought until the Renaissance. In the sixteenth century, the view of Aristotle still prevailed, but then the telescopic discoveries of **Galileo** and acceptance of the Copernican system propelled Europe toward a new astronomy. When Galileo saw craters on the moon, changing phases of Venus, spots on the sun, and a miniature solar system of satellites in orbit around Jupiter, he realized that the authoritative work of Ptolemy and Aristotle was contradicted. Supported by Galileo's telescopic observations, the heliocentric system of **Copernicus** re-established the need for detailed observation of the movements of the planets. **Tycho Brahe**, already persuaded that Aristotle's notion of an eternal, unchanging celestial kingdom was compromised by the appearance of a new star—a supernova—in 1572, undertook a vigorous observational campaign. His engraved metal instruments provided more accurate information and greater observational precision, and **Johannes Kepler** extracted three laws of planetary motion from Tycho's data. Kepler realized that the motions of the planets could be understood in dynamical terms, as products of a central attractive force, presumably centered in the sun. Isaac Newton completed the cosmological metamorphosis by formulating a mathematical law of

Quantitative manipulation of celestial cycles also evolved among the Maya, an indigenous Mesoamerican people. This detail from one of four surviving hieroglyphic screenfold Maya texts appears to depict an ancient Maya skywatcher. He is surrounded by a sphere of stars, and his eye reaches out like a crescent wrench to get a grip on the cosmos. (Courtesy of the Griffith Observatory, redrawn from the Codex Madrid*)*

Frequently mistaken as a sixteenth-century representation of the transcendental mechanisms that order the heavens through cyclical motion, this illustration was actually contrived by the French astronomer Camille Flammarion and first appeared in the nineteenth century. (Courtesy of the Griffith Observatory)

universal gravitation that described and predicted the trajectories of planets in heaven and apples on earth. Astronomy was still mathematical, but physics was replacing geometry. To Newton, the ultimate regulator of this system was transcendent and divine, but the planets were worlds, not gods. In time, telescopes and space probes would expose more and more of their true nature.

Through mathematical science, Isaac Newton demonstrated that the behavior of celestial objects can be understood in terms of general physical law. His achievement was extraordinary, and it continues to be appreciated. This British postage stamp was issued in 1987 to commemorate the three hundredth anniversary of the publication of Newton's Principia. *(Courtesy of E.C. Krupp)*

Newton convinced us that the observable universe could be understood in terms of general physical laws. In time, a deeper understanding of the nature of matter and radiation transformed astronomy again. No longer preoccupied solely with measurement of position and the monitoring of motion, astronomers analyzed starlight. Again applying known physical laws, this time to measurements of brightness, color, and the character of the spectrum, astronomers became astrophysicists and deduced the true nature of stars.

With particle physics and quantum mechanics, the cosmos departed further from common sense and everyday experience, but conformed to experiment and physical law. Now, specialized instruments extend our sight beyond the reach of the eye to the invisible realms of infrared, ultraviolet, radio light, and X-rays. Background microwave energy completely curtains us with light let loose not long after an explosive birth of space-time, begun perhaps 15 billion years ago. Titanic telescopes reveal the extraordinary scale of a cosmos filled with galaxies and clusters of galaxies and clusters of clusters of galaxies. Their systematic universal recession tells us the entire universe is expanding.

By looking out into the darkness, we look back into time, and every star, every galaxy, and every quasar is a separate message from a different moment in a universe we never see at one time. It is a cosmos where gravity is arm-wrestling with momentum, and no one knows yet who has won the match.

It's a very different astronomy from what it used to be, but it still has an emotional dimension. It still makes people stop and think about things far removed from daily life. And for some, it still has a transcendental appeal. That is not the intention of modern scientific astronomy, but it is probably an inevitable consequence of asking questions about first and last things. The origin, evolution, and fate of celestial objects, and of the entire universe, are fair game in astronomy. We employ astronomy to ask how our world—and life on it—began, for the answers must, in part, be found in the origin of the solar system. Astronomy also lets us inquire of the stars—their births in nurseries of interstellar gas and dust, their lives sustained by the energy of thermonuclear furnaces in their cores, and their tranquil or violent deaths. Astronomy probes the galaxies and allows us to ask how long the universe we see has been behaving this way and how long it will all keep going.

George Cornewall Lewis, who in 1862 tried to synthesize the astronomical traditions of Antiquity in *Historical Survey of the Astronomy of the Ancients*, believed the modern astronomy of his day was deeply rooted in the past. This bond with the ancients, according to Lewis, makes something special out of astronomy. It has, he says, "this peculiarity that it is conversant with subjects which from the earliest ages attracted the daily attention of mankind and gave birth to observation and speculation before they were treated by strictly scientific methods" (1). Even though modern astronomy has departed from this ancestral path, it remains a product of inquiries that were framed by the sky's symbolic meaning and the spiritual purpose of understanding that meaning.

Astronomy, if nothing else, has increased in an extraordinary way our understanding of the scale—in physical extent and in time—of the universe we inhabit. When this information is digested philosophically or emotionally, it confronts us, as the sky once confronted the ancients, with great mysteries and great beauty. Despite the dramatic changes that have occurred in the astronomical enterprise since Antiquity, astronomy's history nourishes a sense of continuity in the thought and emotion astronomy inspires. That sense of continuity of human experience prompts us still to listen to the music of its Muse.

Edwin C. Krupp

Bibliography

Abell, G.O. *Exploration of the Universe.* Philadelphia: Saunders College Publishing, 1982.

Dicks, D.R. *Early Greek Astronomy to Aristotle.* London: Thames and Hudson, 1970.

Dreyer, J.L.E. *A History of Astronomy from Thales to Kepler.* New York: Dover, 1906.

Flammarion, C. *Popular Astronomy*, translated by J.E. Gore. New York: D. Appleton, n.d.

Friedman, H. *The Amazing Universe.* Washington, D.C.: National Geographic Society, 1975.

Goldsmith, D. *The Astronomers.* New York: St. Martin's Press, 1991.

Heath, T.L. *Greek Astronomy.* London: J.M. Dent and Sons, 1932.

Hodson, F.R., ed. "The Place of Astronomy in the Ancient World." *Philosophical Transactions of the Royal Society of London* 276: 1–276.

Howe, H. *A Study of the Sky.* New York: Flood and Vincent, 1896.

Krupp, E.C. *Echoes of the Ancient Skies.* New York: Harper and Row, 1983.

———. *Beyond the Blue Horizon—Myths and Legends of the Sun, Moon, Stars, and Planets.* New York: HarperCollins, 1991.

———, ed. *In Search of Ancient Astronomies.* Garden City, New York: Doubleday, 1978.

———. *Archaeoastronomy and the Roots of Science.* Boulder, Colo./Washington, D.C.: Westview Press/American Association for the Advancement of Science, 1984.

Lewis, G.C. *An Historical Survey of the Astronomy of the Ancients.* London: Parker, Son, and Bourn, West Strand, 1862.

McCluskey, S.C. "Science, Society, Objectivity, and the Astronomies of the Southwest." In *Astronomy and Ceremony in the Prehistoric Southwest*, edited by J.B. Carlson and W.J. Judge, 205–217. Albuquerque: Maxwell Museum of Anthropology, 1987.

Moore, P. *The Picture History of Astronomy.* New York: Grosset and Dunlap, 1961.

Neugebauer, O. "The History of Ancient Astronomy: Problems and Methods." *Journal of Near Eastern Studies* 4 (1945): 1–38.

Olcott, W.T., and E.W. Putnam. *Field Book of the Skies*. New York: G.P. Putnam's Sons, 1936.
O'Neil, W.M. *Early Astronomy from Babylonia to Copernicus*. Sydney: Sydney University Press, 1986.
Pannekoek, A. *A History of Astronomy*. New York: Interscience, 1961.
Porter, J.G. *The Stars in Song and Legend*. Boston: Ginn, 1902.
Reichen, C-A. *A History of Astronomy*. New York: Hawthorn Books, 1963.
Ronan, C.A. *Science*. New York: Facts on File Publications, 1982.
Sagan, C. *Cosmos*. New York: Random House, 1980.
Sarton, G. *A History of Science*. Vols. 1 and 2. New York: Norton, 1952.
van der Waerden, B.L. *Science Awakening II*. Leyden: Noordhoff, 1974.

Astrophysics

The first use of the term astrophysics has been attributed to Johann Carl Friedrich Zöllner of Leipzig in 1865. He defined it as a coalescence of physics and chemistry with astronomy (Herrmann, 1984, 70; Hufbauer, 1991, 64). Greenwich astronomer Edwin Dunkin in 1869 introduced the astrophysicist as an astronomer who performed spectroscopic observations of the sun and stars, comparing these celestial spectra to laboratory spectra of metals and gases. Toward the end of the century, Zöllner's definition was broadened by practitioners such as the Princeton astronomer C.A. Young, who stated in 1888 that astronomical physics, or astro-physics, was the study of the physical characteristics of heavenly bodies, which could include measures of brightness as well as spectrum to deduce temperatures and other physical characteristics of stellar atmospheres and planetary surfaces, and all phenomena that indicate or depend on their physical condition (3).

By Young's definition, the roots of astrophysics date back at least to Newton, John Mitchell, Henry Cavendish, and especially **William Herschel** and his exploration of matter theory, its cosmical ramifications, and his speculations on the solar constitution. Most definitely one can find elements of astrophysical investigation in Newton's speculation on the gravitational history of the stellar system; Kant and Laplace's **nebular hypothesis**; William Herschel's observations of the nebulae and his speculation on the evolution of stellar systems; Joseph Fraunhofer's observations of the spectra of the sun and stars; Pouillet's, **John Herschel**'s, or Forbes's measurement of the solar constant; Edward Sabine's suggestion that geomagnetism was influenced by variations in solar activity; or R. Joule's, J.R. Mayer's, H. von Helmholtz's, and William Thomson's applications of kinetic theory and thermodynamics to the problem of the maintenance of the sun's heat. Most commonly, astrophysics is regarded as developing from 1860, when **Kirchhoff** and Bunsen demonstrated that spectral line position indicates chemical identity, making it possible to identify the compositions of celestial objects. It is at this point that the term astrophysics appears, reflecting the acquisition of a new set of observational and theoretical tools.

Creating Astrophysics

In only a few years, spectrum analysis applied to astronomy (variously called astrophysics, solar physics, astronomical spectroscopy, the new astronomy, or cosmical physics) revealed new knowledge of the sun's constitution and the composition of its photosphere, the existence of truly gaseous nebulae, the solid nature of comet nuclei, and provided the ability to classify stars by their spectra. The application of **photometry** and **spectroscopy** to astronomy, and the resulting stimulus to theoretical speculation on the solar constitution, also created a new cohort of specialists attracted from physics, chemistry, and astronomy. The group included both professionals and amateurs. Transition figures who became specialists in the new realm include **William Huggins, Norman Lockyer, Angelo Secchi,** and Zöllner as observationalists, and Hervé Faye, Herbert Spencer, Helmholtz, and William Thomson as theorists. Although the observationalists, who explored solar as well as stellar phenomena, soon identified themselves with the new specialty, few if any of the theorists did.

Astrophysics became one of the most active applications of spectroscopic technique in the second half of the nineteenth century (McGucken, 133). Prominent physicists, such as Kirchhoff, Ångstrom, Thalén, Cornu, and Rowland, produced ever more detailed maps of the solar spectrum. They contributed mainly to solar physics, but their work resulted in improved techniques in laboratory spectroscopy and led to systems of wavelength determination that had great impact on stellar astrophysics, and in the hands of Johnstone Stoney, Balmer, and Rydberg, contributed to atomic theory. Indeed, the lessons and techniques of **solar physics** informed astrophysics in its earliest years (Meadows 1984, 59; Hufbauer 1991, 59). The close connection between the fields of physics, spectroscopy, solar physics, and astrophysics was best represented by the impassioned plea of **Charles Piazzi Smyth**, Astronomer Royal for Scotland, who argued that they shared a common need of standardization, element identification, and systematic mapping. Smyth also called for standardized practice.

Smyth's plea demonstrates that although astrophysics was a growing field, it lacked coherence as a specialty. The specialty had not coalesced by 1890, even though there were a half-dozen observatories established explicitly for astrophysical research (Hufbauer 1991, 66). What made the difference was the emergence of a central journal and international organization. Both were the product of **George Ellery Hale**, who established the *Astrophysical Journal* in the 1890s and used it as a platform to campaign for a systematic way to generate and publish spectroscopic data. The campaign lasted for more than a decade, until the major observatories agreed to cooperate under the auspices of Hale's new International Union for Cooperation in Solar Research.

The growth of institutions devoted to astrophysics, capped by Hale's marshaling of forces in both physics and astronomy to establish the *Astrophysical Journal*, the Astronomical and Astrophysical Society of America, the International Union for Cooperation in Solar Research, and the Mount Wilson Solar Observatory, all by 1905, marks the emergence of astrophysics as a specialty within astronomy at the very least; or as a separate discipline, as its most ardent supporters argued. The first ten volumes of the premiere bibliographical review, the *Astronomische Jahresbericht*, for instance, placed astronomy and astrophysics in wholly separate sections, but at the same hierarchical level. This produced an unwieldy bibliographical structure, however, requiring duplicate entries for many subjects, and so after 1910, under new editorship, astrophysics was absorbed into the astronomical categories.

Up to World War I, astrophysics was almost completely driven by observation; a vast amount of data on the spectra, brightness, colors, and radial velocities of the stars was being amassed. Most of these observations were collected and published in volumes issued by observatories. The majority of papers published in the first fifteen years of the *Astrophysical Journal* were devoted to observational or laboratory technique or the reduction and empirical analysis of observations. Since 1865, 50 percent of the papers in the *Astronomische Nachrichten* used spectroscopic techniques, and 13 percent examined colors or performed colorimetry or photometry of some sort (Herrmann and Hamel).

Looking closely at these studies, however, one finds that much of the work was rooted in traditional astronomical practice, augmented by an additional set of tools. In addition to classifying stars by magnitude and color, stars could now be classified by spectrum. The measurement of radial velocities was a new form of traditional positional astronomy. Radial velocity programs, pioneered in Europe but raised to mass production status at American observatories like Lick and Yerkes, were the real heart of astrophysics at the turn of the century. These programs held out the possibility of making rapid inferences about the kinematic characteristics of the sidereal universe, something that would take generations using traditional astrometric methods.

Correlation in Astrophysics

Following Kirchhoff's operational dictum of "one element, one spectrum," astrophysical knowledge depended upon correlations between celestial spectra and laboratory analysis. There were detractors, like Norman Lockyer, who argued from laboratory studies that increased temperature broke elements down into more fundamental constituents and thus changed their spectral signatures. But Lockyer's arguments found few adherents, especially after a number of his claims for line coincidences were either refuted or hotly contested by rivals like William Huggins, or by more sober workers like C.A. Young (Meadows 1972, 66, 154–155).

Even though most stars could be classified by their spectra, there were still many problems that concerned astronomers. Secchi and H.C. Vogel needed two separate classes to describe all types of red stars, while the solar type and white type required only a single category each. There were also many absorption and emission lines in celestial spectra that could not be found in the laboratory. Lockyer's helium in the sun, the enigmatically strong coronium lines high in the solar atmosphere, and nebulium in the brightest nebulae, defied identification, though there was much effort to do so. Astrophysicists also puzzled over the fact that calcium lines appeared higher in the solar atmosphere than lines of hydrogen, when the former was an element of greater atomic weight (Clerke, 115).

By World War I, observational astrophysicists were concerned that many of the correlations found in the data lacked rational explanation. No one could say with confidence why some spectral lines required high temperature to be visible when excited by laboratory arcs and sparks, or why others could be observed at low temperature in laboratory flames. On the astronomical side, Hale and his Yerkes staff demonstrated that sunspot spectra were characteristic of stars of spectral types later, or cooler, than the sun, and **Karl Schwarzschild** and his colleagues at Potsdam developed precision colorimetry, informed by Planck's radiation theory, that supported the empirical relation. Although these combined observatory and laboratory studies had shown that the sequence of stellar spectra organized at Harvard was a temperature sequence, no one could say why on physical grounds (DeVorkin and Kenat, 102–132).

There were also striking correlations between the magnitudes of the stars and their spectral class, found independently by **Ejnar Hertzsprung** and by **Henry Norris Russell** between 1905 and 1913. Both claimed that giant stars existed, Russell incorporating them into a theory of stellar evolution that was a revival of a scheme suggested by Lockyer. Russell envisioned stars collapsing through gravitational contraction and heating until they achieved densities too great to allow them to behave as perfect gases. Thereafter stars would continue to contract, and cool. Russell's theory did not agree with the concept of a linear temperature descent from nebulae through contraction and cooling, which had recently gained support from **J.C. Kapteyn**'s studies of the kinematics of the different stellar classes (Meadows, 1972; DeVorkin, 1984, 90–108; Paul).

But Kapteyn's deductions were also correlations without theoretical foundation. While the meaning of his star streams was being debated, Russell's giant suns and his vision of their place in the order of stellar development found favor in **Arthur Stanley Eddington**'s early studies of giants as perfect gas-spheres in radiative equilibrium, and in another discovery made by **Walter Sydney Adams** and Arnold Kohlschütter at Mount Wilson. Using high-dispersion spectra of scores of stars made with Mount Wilson's new 60-inch Cassegrain reflector, they found that stars of the same spectral class, but with high and low luminosity, could be distinguished by differences in line intensities in their spectra, something that Harvard's Antonia Maury first detected. Their spectroscopic parallax technique became not only a valuable new tool for estimating stellar distances, distances far greater than trigonometric parallaxes or proper motions could match, but the luminosity effect also confirmed the existence of Russell's and Hertzsprung's extremely luminous giant stars. Adams, however, was far from comfortable with what he had discovered. Like all empirical correlations this one had no known reason to exist. There was laboratory evidence showing that reduced pressure could produce the characteristics seen in giant stars. But this was another empirical correlation without a physical basis.

Faced with these problems at the outset of World War I, astronomers like Russell and Eddington knew that stronger ties with physics were needed. How well did stars approximate black-body radiation? What really governed the changes seen in the spectral classes of the stars? During the war, Russell called for increased attention to theory and by 1919 was sufficiently convinced to tell his former student Harlow Shapley that "Eddington and Jeans have shown us that the time is ripe for fundamental work in theoretical astrophysics" (DeVorkin and Kenat, I, 110).

The Rise of Theoretical Astrophysics

Theoretical astrophysics today is typically the study of physical processes in stellar interiors, atmospheres, the interstellar medium, and in stellar and galactic systems. At the turn of the century, however, it was defined by the *Astronomische Jahresbericht* as the theoretical foundations of photometry and spectroscopy, including Doppler's principle and anomalous dispersion. Theorists had attempted to describe the structure, evolution, and source of energy of the sun and stars in the nineteenth century either through dynamical studies of rotating figures in gravitational equilibrium or idealized models in convective equilibrium. Few if any astronomers paid attention, nor were they equipped to do so (Hufbauer 1981, 277–303). When Robert Emden's milestone *Gaskugeln* appeared in 1907, which gave full expression to the work of Homer Lane, August Ritter, and William Thomson, it was received with caution even by mathematical theorists like **James H. Jeans**.

Contemporary with Emden, Arthur Schuster and Karl Schwarzschild attempted to describe the solar atmosphere using radiative transfer theory. Schwarzschild returned to the problem in 1914 armed with Bohr theory and the conviction that stellar atmospheres could be studied best by determining the actual amount of energy absorbed or reemitted, which required measuring spectrophotometric line profiles, and deriving from Bohr theory mechanisms of both line and continuum absorption and reemission.

Physical theory thus became useful in astrophysics mainly through its ability to interpret astrophysical observations. Hale looked for the Zeeman effect in sunspots to verify the existence of magnetic fields. Hertzsprung used Planck's radiation law in 1905 to predict the angular diameter of Antares. And when Bohr explained the so-called second spectrum of hydrogen in stars of the Zeta Puppis type as due to ionized helium, Alfred Fowler, though initially skeptical, realized by 1914 that it made sense only if the Rydberg constant was adjusted. Fowler's success soon converted him to the Bohr model and to a new framework of thinking within which to interpret spectra (Robotti, 123–145; McGucken).

The old quantum theory could not do more than predict the presence of spectral lines. Thus when, in 1916, Eddington embarked on a program to explore radiative equilibrium in the interiors of giant stars, which were assumed to be in the perfect gas state, his physics was limited to the standard gas laws and the concept of local thermodynamic equilibrium developed by Kirchhoff. These elements dominated Eddington's theoretical methodology, culminating a decade later in his *Internal Constitution of the Stars*, which gave full expression to the idea that stars could be described as spheres of gas existing in a state of convective equilibrium, based on his discovery that all stars, not just giants, behave as perfect gases and follow a mass-luminosity law detected observationally but given theoretical meaning by him in 1924.

In spite of the success of his radiative models, Eddington was constantly frustrated by his lack of knowledge of the mechanism of absorption, embodied in the opacity of the gaseous stellar interior. Simply put, absorption coefficients derived from Eddington's models based on astrophysical data differed widely from theoretical values derived by H.A. Kramers. The opacity disparity blocked Eddington, and kept him from wholly embracing quantum theory in astrophysics. Even when quantum theory could better handle the interaction of radiation and matter after the appearance of Bohr's correspondence principle, the vector model of the atom, and Einstein's development of a quantum theory of absorption, most astrophysicists did not respond quickly to these opportunities. Eddington resisted the use of Kramers' theory of absorption until the early 1930s.

The reticence in applying quantum theory to astrophysics diminished in the 1920s, after a series of spectacular events convinced astronomers and physicists alike of the interpretive powers of physical theory. Beyond the confirmation of the gravitational deflection of starlight by the sun, and direct observational evidence that stars indeed approximate black-body radiators, was the realization by physical chemist John Eggert in Berlin and Indian physicist **Meghnad Saha** that physical conditions in stellar interiors and atmospheres could be described by an ionization equilibrium process. Saha's theory of thermal ionization equilibrium finally provided a theoretical foundation for the Harvard system of spectral classification embodied in the famous **Draper Catalogue of Stellar Spectra**, and drew the attention of observational astrophysicists to the interpretive value of Bohr theory. Saha found that for a gas consisting of only one element, at a given temperature and pressure, a specific degree of ionization was maintained due to a set rate of absorption and emission of photons. By the mid-1920s, the refinement and application of ionization theory to the stars by Russell, E.A. Milne, R.H. Fowler, and Cecilia Payne not only confirmed the Harvard classification as a temperature sequence, but also revealed the extremely low pressures in stellar atmospheres and provided the first hints that they were composed primarily of hydrogen (DeVorkin and Kenat, I, 102–132; II, 180–222). These successes set an example for young physicists, such as Svein Rosseland, Herman Zanstra, Ira S. Bowen, and Albrecht Unsöld: Astronomy was a field ripe for modern physics.

The ripeness of astrophysics in the 1920s is demonstrated by the fact that the field was rapidly growing, acquiring new theoretical tools, and finally developing a literature. Prior to that time, few textbooks and training programs existed. The **Potsdam Astrophysical Observatory** had developed one of the first training programs in the 1890s where Julius Scheiner prepared his *Die Spectralanalyse der Gestirne* (1890), soon translated into English by E.B. Frost, followed closely by Gustav Müller's *Die Photometrie der Gestirne* (1897). But these texts eschewed theory. James Jeans's second edition of *The Dynamical Theory of Gases* (1916) was extensively rewritten in light of the quantum theory, although it was less appreciated by astronomers than his 1919 *Problems of Cosmogony and Stellar Dynamics*, which utilized little modern physics. The first elementary textbook in English to integrate some modern physics into astrophysics was volume 2 of Russell, Dugan, and Stewart's *Astronomy*, which appeared in 1927, two years after F.J.M. Stratton's higher-level monograph *Astronomical Physics* and Herbert Dingle's popular *Modern Astrophysics*. Eddington's 1926 *Internal Constitution of the Stars*, however, set the pace for physicists, who needed summaries at the level of Sommerfeld's classic text *Atombau und Spektralinien*. By the early 1930s, the first volumes of the monumental *Handbuch der Astrophysik* were appearing, and the *Zeitschrift für Astrophysik* had started publication, followed later in the decade by the advanced textbooks of Svein Rosseland, Albrecht Unsöld, and **Viktor Ambartsumian**, and by the inauguration of the quarterly *Annales d'Astrophysique*.

The ripeness of astrophysics can also be measured in its institutions. In the Soviet Union, astrophysics was equated with the new regime, but few new observational facilities were constructed until midcentury. The purges of the 1930s and the effects of World War II wiped out both observatories and approximately 20 percent of the Soviet astronomical community (Graham, 220–224). During these years, the strength of Soviet astrophysics lay in theoretical astrophysics.

In America, by the 1920s, Hale's Mount Wilson Observatory was closely associated with the California Institute of Technology, making it one of the strongest institutions for research at the interface of astrophysical observation and physical theory. With patronage from the National Academy and the International Education Board, Pasadena became a mecca for physicists looking for new fields to conquer. Zanstra, for example, discovered a fluorescence mechanism that describes the transfer of radiation from stars to nebulae. Then came Svein Rosseland, a student of Bohr, who was interested in applying physics to a wide range of astrophysical phenomena. He was followed by Albrecht Unsöld, a student of Arnold Sommerfeld, who visited Mount Wilson in 1928 to use the hydrogen line profile data to determine absolute elemental abundances in stellar atmospheres. Stimulated by some of Rosseland's speculations, California Institute of Technology physicist Ira S. Bowen migrated to astrophysics and demonstrated how a metastability mechanism could explain why certain forbidden spectral lines were the strongest features in gaseous nebulae, thus making possible line identifications that had defied solution for more than half a century.

Unsöld established the methodology for the modern study of stellar atmospheres. He calculated the number of atoms active in producing a line; how the intensity of a spectral line changes with abundance, which came to be called the curve of growth technique. In the 1930s the problem was to identify the many ways lines could be broadened to refine the curve of growth technique. Thermal effects and turbulence as well as abundances could be involved. In the late 1930s, after Rupert Wildt demonstrated that the chief source of continuum opacity came from the negative hydrogen ion, workers like Unsöld and Bengt Strömgren felt that a final general solution was at hand. But there were still many puzzles to solve. Unraveling these problems with improved theory and automated means of numerical analysis constitutes the bulk of modern theoretical studies of stellar atmospheres. Theory and numerical technique, however, were not the only factors to combine to explain stellar atmospheres. Quantitative methods of spectral classification also proved useful.

Physics as the Basis for Astrophysics

Zanstra, Bowen, Rosseland, and Unsöld were all trained in physics, and set an example for the type of training and skills that were going to be required to make significant contributions to astrophysics. Their success demonstrated that astrophysics was highly fertile ground for an ambitious physicist. A good example is Bengt Edlén, who made a conscious decision to enter astrophysics to solve the enigma of the coronium lines—the strongest features in the solar corona—ultimately associating them with highly ionized lines of common elements in much the same way Bowen had identified the nebulium lines a decade earlier (Hufbauer 1993, 203–205).

Small-scale migrations from physics to astrophysics also occurred in many European countries, often the result of one or two individuals influenced by visits to major astrophysical centers. For example, the Italian Giorgio Abetti moved into solar physics after working at Potsdam, Mount Wilson, and **Yerkes**.

As physicists entered astrophysics, they campaigned for new institutions for research and training, such as Rosseland's Institute for Theoretical Astrophysics, established in the early 1930s in Oslo. Although most astrophysical work remained observational, theory was strong at Cambridge University, and by the end of the decade was strengthening at places like Harvard, where Donald Menzel was actively building a group of theorists, and at Yerkes, where **Otto Struve** campaigned for a campus-based theoretical institute that would include **Subrahmanyan Chandrasekhar**.

To make effective use of theory, an astrophysicist must be a competent mathematical physicist (McCrea, 343). Otto Struve certainly knew this when in the late 1920s he spent a postdoctoral year with Eddington studying radiative transfer processes. From that point, Struve focused on mechanisms of line broadening in stellar spectra. Becoming director of the Yerkes Observatory in the early 1930s, Struve also set about creating a strong theoretical group and using the Yerkes directorship as a platform, frequently spoke about the needs of astronomical spectroscopy. Struve's essays served as guides for physicists looking for fertile ground.

As new branches of physics grew, they found application in astrophysics. Thus nuclear physicists were drawn to the study of the constitution and energy source of the sun and stars. There was not much physicists could say in 1900, when astronomers realized that the maximum lifetime of the sun, assuming it consumed gravitational energy only, was woefully inadequate to account for geological or biological time scales. During the ensuing three decades, astrophysical theorists realized that even without knowing the specific mechanism, realistic stellar models had to account for a power source acting in the stellar interior, and that such a source required convective transport to remain stable. The trend in the 1930s—led by Rosseland and Ludwig Biermann—was to concentrate the power source at the stellar center, removing energy by convection. This stimulated the use of composite polytropic models, developed in the late 1920s and early 1930s by Thomas Cowling, **Milne**, **Strömgren**, and **Russell**, which allowed stars to be described by a series of concentric polytropic distributions. This new versatility eventually paved the way for Cowling to construct a stable point-source model, which, by the mid-1930s, envisioned a small convective core surrounded by a radiative envelope. This was the intellectual framework within which astrophysicist Carl F. von Weizsäcker, a student of Heisenberg, and nuclear physicists such as Hans Bethe, George Gamow, and Edward Teller examined nuclear processes in stars, based upon the transformation of hydrogen into heavier elements.

The landmark contributions of Bethe and von Weizsäcker had immediate consequences. Matter annihilation was no longer needed, so the main sequence no longer could be thought of as an evolutionary track. Astronomers could opt for an intermediate time scale on the order of 10^{10} years, which agreed reasonably with cosmological and geological time scales. Another benefit was that their successes attracted nuclear physicists like Edwin Salpeter, a Cornell graduate, to astrophysics in the early 1950s. Salpeter showed that the fusion of three helium nuclei could form carbon, and helium fusion was capable of acting as a new source of energy after hydrogen exhaustion. Salpeter's work highlighted the importance of improving communication between nuclear physicists and astrophysicists. The best example of the collaborative approach was the work of California Institute of Technology nuclear physicist William A. Fowler, Margaret Burbidge, an observational astrophysicist, Geoffrey Burbidge, a theoretical physicist, and Fred Hoyle, a theoretical astrophysicist. They developed a theory explaining the creation of heavy elements in stars and inaugurated the study of stellar nucleosynthesis.

Astrophysics as a Branch of Physics

Although Hale used the metaphor as early as the 1890s, astrophysicists in the 1920s frequently characterized their objects of study as cosmic crucibles that might reveal the fundamental properties of matter. The ultimate aim of the astrophysicist, both Eddington and Jeans argued, was as much the reductionist search for the ultimate state of matter as it was the ultimate nature of the universe. Astrophysics was extrapolated physics, but it was also the realm where new physics might be found (Ginzberg, 265–266).

By the early 1940s, influential observatory directors like Otto Struve believed that astronomy was on the threshold of profound change. Astrophysics and physics were merging. As more and more physicists crossed over, they brought new standards of practice to astrophysics. Physicists told Struve it was incomprehensible that astronomy could afford to continue expensive data-gathering projects that were not driven by theory. Struve feared that the traditional controls exercised by observatory directors would decline, leading to less survey work. The challenge was to change the nature of survey work by letting individuals informed by physical theory design and direct these projects. Large-scale data collecting had to continue, especially as new regions of the spectrum were opening up, but these programs required new forms of organization, new approaches to research, and new sources of patronage. Some form of government support was needed; but Struve feared it would further diminish traditional patterns of autonomy and control (Struve, 474).

The changes Struve envisioned helped to make astrophysics more like physics. After World War II, military patrons were interested in physical applications, and when the National Science Foundation (NSF) began operation in the 1950s, its activities changed the traditional power structure of the American astronomical community. National funding strategies required national planning, especially as facilities became larger and more expensive. In a cooperative effort by NSF and individuals representing special interests within each of the scientific disciplines it served, national facilities were planned that would, in theory, provide access to state-of-the-art equipment. In astronomy, this meant observatories for both radio and optical research that were almost completely dedicated to astrophysics.

National planning, although still involving observatory directors, meant a loss of traditional control and an increased emphasis upon finite projects. Proposals for funding, or for telescope time at national facilities, were now competitively evaluated by peer review panels. These panels looked for proposals leading to publishable results and proposals that examined questions of astrophysical significance. These constraints were wholly different from those that had existed before the war, when the funding programs were mainly concerned with proposals that fit into the agenda of an observatory director, rather than independent investigators.

These changes promoted new behavioral patterns. Although there is as yet little historical work in this area, it appears that proposal competitiveness depended more and more on the likelihood of a publishable product. As Struve predicted, astronomers had to be able to design projects that provided solutions of acknowledged problems.

The Soviet *Sputnik* also accelerated the process of making astrophysics a branch of physics. As only a very few astronomers had expressed an interest in using balloons, rockets, and satellites to conduct astronomical research prior to *Sputnik*, the skills and techniques to build optical and electronic devices for research from orbit were found among physicists. The pioneers in ultraviolet solar spectroscopy were all physicists who knew how to build vacuum spectrographs. The X-ray realm was opened up by physicists who migrated into astrophysical research bringing special skills. And as cosmic-ray physics lost place to accelerator-based high-energy physics, many of its practitioners migrated into astrophysics via space research (DeVorkin, 1992).

Access to space has increased astronomy's dependence upon the newest forms of technology, and so opened up new avenues for specialists from physics. As a result, approximately half of those entering astronomy in the 1960s were physics Ph.D.s. Many of them, like V.L. Ginzburg, Edlén, Bruno Rossi, Bethe, or Richard Tousey, retained their identity as physicists. Others, like Chandrasekhar, Salpeter, Martin Ryle, and Riccardo Giacconi, chose to align themselves with astrophysics (Goldberg, 21–22; Berendzen and Moslen, 50–51).

Astronomy was a part of big science in the postwar era. National optical and radio observatories began to compete for funding with huge new facilities created by consortia of universities and nations, as well as with space-based observatories such as the **Hubble Space Telescope**. These developments suggest the political and institutional complexity of modern astronomy as it approached the scale of high-energy physics. The role of the individual scientist has also changed. Astronomy as a big science offers historians and sociologists of modern science an interesting venue in which to study the impact of new forms of patronage, instrumentation, and cognitive interests.

In sum, in the past 150 years the history of astrophysics has paralleled the growth of physics itself, both in intellectual scope and organizational behavior. Just as astrophysics incorporated spectroscopy in the nineteenth century, it later added atomic physics, quantum mechanics, and nuclear physics. In the process, more and more areas within astronomy became dependent upon physics.

In their continuing search for new fields to conquer, physicists have increasingly looked to astrophysics. "Opportunities for physicists cluster at the frontiers of astronomy" one writer claimed in 1981. Acknowledging that resistance still existed among traditional astronomers, he concluded that "any physicist with a powerful new instrumental or theoretical technique can quickly find himself making contributions at the forefront of astrophysics" (Harwit, 187).

The recent history of **cosmology** certainly mirrors this view. In its early-modern phases in the 1920s and 1930s, its most important questions were informed by radial velocity studies. Then, in the 1940s, theoretical nuclear physicists began to look at conditions in the early universe, which also provided links to abundance and time scale problems. Many theorists now rejoice that particle physicists are looking closely at the first moments of the Big Bang, some claiming that the field lacked legitimacy prior to their entry. A center for such studies has, appropriately, emerged at the Fermi National Accelerator Laboratory in Illinois, and a new international journal of *Astroparticle Physics* has appeared. Accordingly, the American Physical Society formed a cosmic physics division in 1970, changing its name to astrophysics in 1983.

Historical studies of the impact astrophysics has had on astronomy have yet to appear. But it is clear, as **W.W. Campbell, Lick Observatory** director, pointed out as early as 1908, that much of the parent discipline of astronomy has been consumed in the growth process. In many universities, astrophysics is pursued as actively in physics departments as it is in traditional astronomy departments.

David H. DeVorkin

Bibliography

Berendzen, R., and M.T. Moslen. "Manpower and Employment in American Astronomy." In *History of and Education in Modern Astronomy*, edited by R. Berendzen. Annals of the N.Y. Academy of Sciences, 198 (1972): 50–51.

Clerke, A.M. *Problems in Astrophysics*. London: Adam and Charles Black, 1903.

DeVorkin, D.H. "Stellar Evolution and the Origins of the Hertzsprung-Russell Diagram in Early Astrophysics." In *Astrophysics and Twentieth-Century Astronomy to 1950*, edited by O. Gingerich, 90–108. Cambridge University Press, 1984.

———. *Science with a Vengeance: How the Military Created the US Space Sciences after World War II*. New York: Springer-Verlag, 1992.

DeVorkin, D.H., and R. Kenat. "Quantum Physics and the Stars (I); (II)." *Journal for the History of Astronomy* 15 (1983): 102–132; 180–222.

Ginzberg, V.L. "Does Astronomy Need 'New Physics'?" *Quarterly Journal of the Royal Astronomical Society* 16 (1975): 265–281.

Goldberg, L. "Quantum Mechanics at the Harvard Observatory in the 1930s." In *Problems in Theoretical Physics and Astrophysics: A Collection of Essays dedicated to V.L. Ginzberg on his 70th Birthday.* Moscow, 1989.

Graham, Loren R. *Science in Russia and the Soviet Union*. New York: Cambridge University Press, 1993.

Harwit, M. "Physicists and Astronomy—Will You Join the Dance?" *Physics Today* 34 (1981): 172–187.

Herrmann, D.B. *The History of Astronomy from Herschel to Hertzsprung*. Translated and revised by K. Krisciunas. Cambridge: Cambridge University Press, 1984.

Herrmann, D.B., and J. Hamel. "Zur Frühentwicklung der Astrophysik das Internationale Forscherkollektiv 1865–1899." *NTM-Schriftenreihe für Geschichte der Naturwissenschaften, Technik und Medizin* 12 (1975): 25–30.

Hufbauer, K. "Astronomers Take Up the Stellar-Energy Problem, 1917–1920." *Historical Studies in the Physical Sciences* 11 (1981): 277–303.

———. *Exploring the Sun: Solar Science since Galileo*. Baltimore: Johns Hopkins, 1991.

———. "Breakthrough on the Periphery: Bengt Edlén and the Identification of the Coronal Lines, 1939–1945." In *Center on the Periphery: Historical Aspects of 20th-Century Swedish Physics*, edited by S. Lindqvist, 199–237. Cambridge, Mass.: Science History Publications, 1993.

———. "Artificial Eclipses: Bernard Lyot and the Coronagraph, 1929–1939." *Historical Studies in the Physical and Biological Sciences* 14 (1994): 337–394.

Kidwell, P.A. "Prelude to Solar Energy: Pouillet, Herschel, Forbes and the Solar Constant." *Annals of Science* 38 (1981): 457–476.

McCrea, W.H. Review of S. Rosseland. "Theoretical Astrophysics." *Mathematical Gazette* 20 (1936): 343.

McGucken, W. *Nineteenth Century Spectroscopy*. Baltimore: Johns Hopkins, 1969.

Meadows, A.J. *Science and Controversy: A Biography of Sir Norman Lockyer*. Cambridge, Mass.: MIT Press, 1972.

———. "The New Astronomy." In *Astrophysics and Twentieth-Century Astronomy to 1950,* edited by O. Gingerich, 59–72. The General History of Astronomy, edited by M. Hoskin. Cambridge: Cambridge University Press, 1984.

Paul, E.R. *The Milky Way Galaxy and Statistical Cosmology 1890–1924.* New York: Cambridge University Press, 1993.

Robotti, N. "The Spectrum of [Zeta] Puppis and the Historical Evolution of Empirical Data." *Historical Studies in the Physical Sciences* 14 (1983): 123–145.

Struve, O. "Fifty Years of Progress in Astronomy." *Popular Astronomy* 51 (1943): 469–481.

Young, C.A. *General Astronomy.* Boston: Ginn, 1888.

Atlases, Astronomical

As collections of star maps and pictures, usually bound together in book form, astronomical atlases first appeared during the Renaissance. They served as finding aids by conveying star-catalogue information in graphic form. Stars identified with respect to the constellation figures could be readily located by astronomers, even if they lacked the expensive apparatus to spot a star directly from its celestial coordinates. Conversely, the coordinates for a new celestial object could be found by measuring the angular distance between it and known stars, and plotting these measurements on charts.

Pictures of individual constellations have illustrated astronomical and mythological works since Antiquity. In some pictures—such as those to be found in the tenth-century manuscript of Abu'l-Husayn al-Sufi's *Book of the Fixed Stars* (preserved in the Bodleian Library at Oxford University)—stars were positioned correctly within the constellation figures, but no coordinates were provided and the cartographic projections were not obvious. The earliest atlases were part of this tradition, being collections of pictures rather than maps of the constellations. Alessandro Piccolomini published the first atlas, *De le stelle fisse*, in Venice in 1540. While its pages lacked usable coordinate scales with which to locate stars according to either the ecliptic or equatorial systems, the stars were well graduated according to their magnitudes. Piccolomini also pioneered the use of letters to identify prominent stars in each constellation, and this practice was later adopted by Johann Bayer in 1603, and, through him, by all later astronomers.

The first atlas from which star coordinates could be read was the *Theatrum mundi, et temporis* of Giovanni Paolo Gallucci (Venice, 1588). Gallucci, however, charted his stars as they would appear on a celestial globe—that is, he used an external rather than a geocentric projection—and this made his atlas difficult to use as a finding aid. After Gallucci, the most notable atlases were those by Bayer, Johannes Hevelius, **John Flamsteed**, and Johann Elert Bode.

To a certain extent, atlases were only as good as the star catalogues on which they were based. Sixteenth-century cartographers drew mainly on the Ptolemaic catalogue of 1,025 stars (as revised by Nicolas Copernicus and others), whereas seventeenth-century mapmakers, like Bayer, took advantage of **Tycho Brahe**'s catalogue of northern stars and Pieter Dircksz Keyser's catalogue of southern stars. Bayer plotted over two thousand stars in his *Uranometria* (Augsburg, 1603). In another atlas, *Firmamentum Sobiescianum* (Danzig, 1687), **Hevelius** made use of his own remarkable, naked-eye observations, along with the telescopic observations of **Edmond Halley**, who improved on the work of Keyser and Frederik de Houtman in the Southern Hemisphere. The first telescopic catalogue of the northern sky was produced at Greenwich by Flamsteed, and its three thousand stars formed the basis of the maps in his *Atlas coelestis* (London, 1729). Flamsteed took care to place stars within the constellations as Ptolemy had described them, and criticized Bayer for reversing human figures in many cases so that Ptolemaic stars that had formerly been in a right hand or leg now fell in the left. Bode continued in Flamsteed's tradition with his impressive *Uranographia* (Berlin, 1801). To Flamsteed's stars, he added those observed by **Nicolas-Louis de Lacaille** in the Southern Hemisphere and **Joseph-Jérôme Lefrançais de Lalande** in the Northern. His atlas was the first to depict almost all stars visible to the naked eye (down to the sixth magnitude), plus many other stars as faint as the eighth magnitude. About 17,240 stars were charted in over one hundred star groups.

In these atlases, images of the stars were graduated according to stellar magnitudes. Bayer assigned Greek and Latin letters to the stars in order of their brightness within each northern constellation. Lacaille extended Bayer's system to the southern constellations in 1763, and Francis Baily assigned letters to new northern stars in 1845. The so-called Flamsteed numbering system for identifying stars was introduced by Lalande in 1783 in a French edition of Flamsteed's catalogue. Today, astronomers use Flamsteed numbers to identify stars for which there is no Bayer letter.

Each of these cartographers favored different projections. Gallucci borrowed a tech-

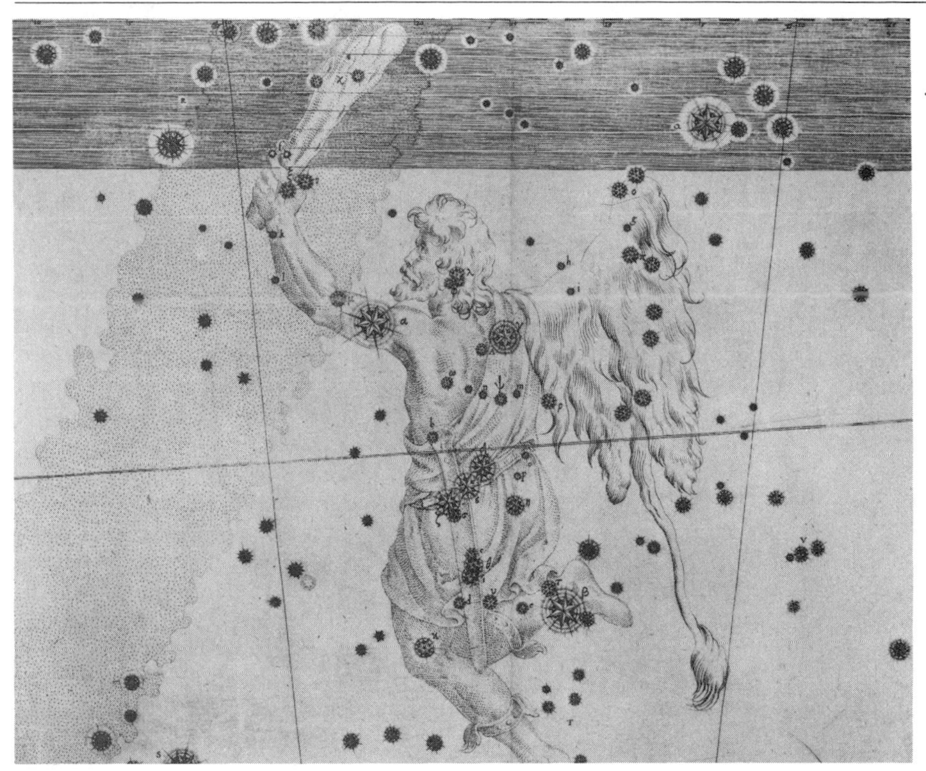

Constellation of Orion from the astronomical atlas of Johann Bayer, Uranometria *(Augsburg, 1603). (Courtesy of the Adler Planetarium, Chicago, Illinois)*

nique used by terrestrial mapmakers when he employed trapezoidal projections on his maps. Parallels of latitude were drawn as equidistant straight lines, whereas circles of longitude appeared as sloping vertical lines. Bayer and Hevelius used this projection as well. The gnomic projection—in which great circles were projected as straight lines—was adopted by Christoph Grienberger (Rome, 1612), and Ignace-Gaston Pardies (Paris, 1674). Flamsteed preferred the Sanson-Flamsteed sinusoidal projection. In this conical projection, parallels of declination were drawn as equidistant straight lines, and hour circles were drawn as sine curves to either side of a vertical straight line in the center of the map. In his great atlas, Bode followed a suggestion of Lalande and drew parallels of declination as curved lines, and circles of right ascension as sloping vertical lines (similar to those in a trapezoidal projection). Atlases sometimes contained planispheres, too. These circular maps were centered on either the equatorial or ecliptic poles. Most covered one hemisphere, but some extended well below the equator to 40 degrees south declination. The stars were charted according to a polar stereographic or polar equidistant projection.

A beautiful feature of early modern atlases is the remarkable variety of constellation figures and the ways they are embellished. While the earliest cartographers—such as Piccolomini and Gallucci—worked only with the forty-eight Ptolemaic constellations, later cartographers took pleasure in forming fresh constellations from newly catalogued, non-Ptolemaic stars. The new constellations depicted mundane or mythical animals, illustrated Biblical stories, flattered political patrons, and glorified scientific research.

Adorned with ninety-nine constellations, Bode's atlas marked the end of an era. By 1800, celestial objects had become too numerous to be grouped effectively into constellations. After Bode, atlases have placed less emphasis on constellation figures, and more on precision measurement of position, brightness, and other physical properties of stars.

Little has been written about astronomical atlases, and the most meticulous and comprehensive work to date is Warner's catalogue of celestial cartographers. This work provides an excellent foundation for further research and outlines some of the historical questions that closer scrutiny of the atlases could answer: namely, about the state of information about celestial objects at a given time; how it was communicated; which cartographic projections were favored and why; the connections between star catalogues and star maps; who invented and adopted new constellations; the aesthetic traditions and iconographic conventions used in embellishing the figures of constellations; the degree to which astronomers drew or supervised the preparation of the maps; the roles printers and publishers played; whether there were specific centers for the production of astronomical atlases; to what extent the activities of celestial cartographers differed from those of terrestrial cartographers; and how the maps reflected social, political, and religious values.

As the foregoing list makes clear, astronomical atlases are a rich resource, but historians of science and art have yet to utilize them fully.

Sara Schechner Genuth

Bibliography

Brown, B. *Astronomical-Atlases, Maps & Charts*. London: Dawsons of Pall Mall, 1968.

Snyder, G.S. *Maps of the Heavens*. New York: Abbeville Press, 1984.

Warner, D.J. *The Sky Explored: Celestial Cartography, 1500–1800*. New York: Alan R. Liss, 1979; Amsterdam: Theatrum Orbis Terrarum, 1979.

Australia and New Zealand, Astronomy in

Astronomy has been associated with Australia since Captain Cook discovered its eastern seaboard in 1770, on a voyage made ostensibly to observe the 1769 transit of Venus from Tahiti. Settlement followed. The first Australian observatory arrived with First Fleet in 1788. It was sent by the British Board of Longitude to observe the predicted return of a comet, but the comet failed to materialize and no other observations survive. The first permanent observatory, the first such in the Southern Hemisphere, was established as a private venture by Governor Brisbane in 1822 in Parramatta, west of Sydney. It had its successes, but after he returned to England it closed in 1847.

State observatories were set up in Melbourne in 1853, Sydney in 1856, Adelaide in 1874, and Perth in 1896. Established to provide accurate time for ships' chronometers, their responsibilities soon grew to include geodetic surveying, meteorology, the surveillance of tides and the earth's magnetism, and the custody of weights and measures. They were the principal scientific agencies of their governments, and their directors were men of standing. Melbourne was noted for its catalogues of star positions, praised by the Astronomer Royal. In 1888 H.C. Russell, director of Sydney, used a commercial portrait lens to make a series of long-exposure photographs of the Milky Way and the Magellanic Clouds that were widely acclaimed. He also carried out seminal work in meteorology. He is the only Australian named in Pannekoek's *History of Astronomy*.

In 1869 Melbourne acquired a 48-inch reflector, for forty years the biggest working telescope in the world. It ran into trouble, partly because of problems with its metal mirror, and partly because it could not be used for photography. By 1890 it was obsolete and did no effective work until the 1950s, when, overhauled and modernized at Mount Stromlo, it was at last put to good use.

At the turn of the century, the observatories went into a long decline. They had been hard hit by an economic downturn in the 1890s. Then in 1908 they were obliged, under a provision in the newly adopted federal constitution, to transfer their meteorological functions to a new Commonwealth Bureau. This cost them not only much of their income, but also the channel through which they were best known to the public. Finally, in 1890 they had agreed to take part in the *Carte du Ciel* project for the photographic mapping of the whole sky. With a population of barely two million, Australia was made responsible for three of the eighteen zones, more than any other country except France. It was an immense burden that precluded the observatories from taking part in any other branch of astronomy. Ultimately all closed except Perth-Adelaide in 1940, Melbourne in 1945, and Sydney in 1982.

The Commonwealth government established the Commonwealth Solar Observatory (CSO) in 1924 and Radio Research Board (RRB) in 1926, both as purely research institutes. The CSO made an early mark with C.W. Allen's photometric atlas of the solar spectrum. In 1939 Richard Woolley became its director, with the explicit intention of leading it out of solar and terrestrial physics into stellar astronomy. These plans were delayed by the outbreak of World War II, with which both institutions became heavily involved.

The RRB was a most successful organization, and when in 1940 steps were taken to set up a laboratory to work on the new and secret system of radar, the RRB was a natural starting-point. Thus the Radiophysics Laboratory (RPL), which was to bring such luster to Australian science. At the end of the war the decision was made to keep it in being, to study peacetime applications of radio science.

Wartime radar observers had noted peculiar radio noise emanating from the sun, and J.L. Pawsey and his group decided to follow this up.

They soon discovered that sunspots emitted much more radio power than could be explained by the physicists. The key observations were made with the famous sea interferometer, the first interferometer used in radio astronomy. So encouraged, the group embarked on a full-scale investigation of solar radio emission. It led them to W.N. Christiansen's high-resolution linear arrays of spaced, steerable paraboloids, his invention of earth rotation synthesis, J.P. Wild's dynamic spectrograph, and finally to his solar radioheliograph, an early synthesis radio telescope. Their results completely altered perceptions of the solar corona.

Using the same sea interferometer, J.G. Bolton and his group discovered a number of pointlike radio sources, three of which they identified with optical objects, two of them extra-galactic. These were the first radio galaxies, which were to revolutionize extragalactic astronomy. This too led to major instrumental developments, such as the Mills Cross, a transit instrument with the then-unprecedented beamwidth of 48 arcminutes. With it, B.Y. Mills produced the first reliable survey of radio sources.

The discovery of the 21-cm spectral line of neutral hydrogen in 1951 was immediately taken up by RPL. One program, conducted in collaboration with the Dutch, produced the first overall picture of the spiral structure of our own galaxy. Another gave a new view of the Magellanic Clouds, confirmed that the Large Cloud was a flat rotating system not unlike our own, and yielded the first estimate of its mass.

In the mid-1950s, and largely at the instigation of E.G. Bowen, director of RPL, it was decided that the next major instrument would be a large steerable paraboloid. It was a critical decision with important ramifications—the beginning of Big Science in Australia, and the end of a traditional style of operating in small groups with single-purpose, inexpensive equipment. Both Pawsey and Bowen had a case, though in Mills's opinion, "The real troubles . . . were political rather than scientific . . . and related to the progressive undermining of Pawsey as leader of the radio astronomy group, which was much resented by his supporters" (Robertson, 205). As it was, Christiansen, Mills, and others left for the University of Sydney, Pawsey for the U.S.A. Pawsey was to have been the first director of National Radio Observation at Greenbank, West Virginia, but a fatal illness intervened and he died in 1962. The dispute changed the structure of Australian astronomy. With three of its leading figures gone, RPL's stock diminished to some extent, while Sydney University's rose, its significant position in the field dating from that time.

The Parkes Radio Telescope was commissioned in 1961, with Bolton as its first director; for five years he had been director of the Owens Valley Radio Observatory in California. He later described the telescope as one of the most successful research instruments ever built. Much of the credit must go to Bowen, who played a key role in its funding, design, and construction. The Parkes Telescope was the prototype for the three space communications telescopes built for NASA's Deep Space Network. It is notable, among much else, for a catalogue of some eight thousand southern sources. The telescope played a key role in the discovery of quasars, and again in the Apollo lunar and other missions.

The return to peace found the Mount Stromlo Observatory with a much-expanded staff and some first-class technical facilities. But unlike the radio astronomers with their brand-new subject, the Mount Stromlo staff had to find their way into optical astronomy, one of the oldest and best established of the sciences. That took time. Nevertheless, by 1955, when Woolley returned to England, several lines of work had been established. They included studies of emission nebulae, especially the discovery by C.S. Gum of the great Vela Nebula, since named after him; S.C.B. Gascoigne and G.E. Kron made the first photoelectric observations of cepheids and clusters in the Magellanic Clouds; and G. de Vaucouleurs studied aspects of extragalactic astronomy previously untouched in the south.

Woolley had the observatory transferred to the new Australian National University (ANU), a much more congenial home, and had obtained a 74-inch reflector, which, with its sister instrument at Pretoria, was for twenty years the biggest telescope in the south. He also founded the country's first graduate school in astronomy. The 74-inch was especially important because it brought the staff face-to-face with important contemporary problems, and the experience gained with it had much to do with the success of the Anglo-Australian Telescope (AAT).

Woolley was succeeded by Bart Bok, who largely completed what Woolley had begun—

that is, made Mount Stromlo Observatory a significant force in world astronomy. Bok early recognized the need to move from Canberra's growing light pollution, and within a few years had created a field station that quickly became the Siding Spring Observatory. He had T.E. Dunham build a coudé spectrograph for the 74-inch, a fine instrument that introduced the observatory to the study of stellar atmospheres. Bok thought his most important success was creating a first-class graduate school with emphasis on optical and radio astronomy. It changed the ambience of the observatory, becoming the pivot about which much of its research effort turned, and it may well have supplied the edge that enabled Mount Stromlo Observatory to catch up with the Radiophysics Laboratory.

At the University of Sydney, Mills built a new radio telescope with much improved sensitivity and resolution. Located at Molonglo near Canberra and funded largely by the U.S. National Science Foundation, it came on line just as the first pulsars were discovered in England, and proved an ideal instrument for finding more; it soon discovered the greater part of those known. Later it was converted to a synthesis telescope. Christiansen's group converted his radio telescope array into another synthesis instrument that for many years provided the highest resolution in the south, 23 arcseconds.

Another unique instrument at Sydney was the stellar intensity interferometer. Built by R. Hanbury Brown's group, it used a new optical principle to determine the diameters of the brighter blue stars. Having measured all within reach, it was succeeded by an updated and greatly extended version of the classical Michelson interferometer. With a maximum baseline of 640 meters, it has realized a century-old dream, and is the first instrument of its kind to have gone into regular operation.

The advent of the Anglo-Australian Telescope (AAT) in 1975 had a profound effect on Australian astronomy, not only because it was so powerful, so well instrumented, and so easy to use, but also because it was declared a national facility and hence made available to all comers. The other major observatories soon followed suit with their telescopes. Smaller institutions could now compete on much more favorable terms than before, and observers, including graduate students, could move freely from installation to installation and could frame their programs accordingly.

Two other large instruments followed the AAT. In 1986 a 2.3-meter optical telescope was completed by Mount Stromlo Observatory. Its alt-azimuth mounting, fast primary, full computer control, and rotating building make it very much state of the art. It was designed at Mount Stromlo Observatory, funded by Australian National Observatory, and, except for specialist components, made in Australia. In 1988 observing began with the Australia Telescope, the first large synthesis radio telescope built in the south. The basic compact array consists of six 22-meter dishes spaced along a 6 kilometer baseline. It can be extended to longer baselines by utilizing the 64-meter Parkes radio telescope (320 kilometers south) and the 70-meter NASA telescope (275 kilometers south of Parkes). Emphasis has been given to wide frequency cover (0.3 GHz to 115 GHz, or 90 cm to 2.6 mm) and good spectral and polarization performance.

Astronomy in New Zealand is conducted on a smaller scale than in Australia. There are two main observatories, one on Mount John in the middle of the South Island, the other, the Carter Observatory, in Wellington. Mount John Observatory possesses a well-appointed 40-inch telescope, the biggest in the country, and is owned and operated by the University of Canterbury. It was established in 1965, initially in cooperation with the universities of Pennsylvania and Florida. The Carter Observatory is a government establishment that goes back to 1941. It has an observing station at Black Birch, at the northern end of the South Island, which is also the site of a substantial astrometric observatory established by the U.S. Naval Observatory in 1983 (it is due to close in 1995). Amateurs have always been strong in New Zealand, with two at least, F.M. Bateson and A.F.A.L. Jones, well known for their observations of double stars. There are about a dozen expatriate New Zealanders, well established in their fields, working at various observatories around the world.

Amateurs have also been prominent in Australia, from the days of Governor Brisbane onward, and the roll includes at least two world figures. John Tebbutt discovered the great comets of 1861 and 1881, besides much else; Robert Owen has, to date, found more than thirty supernovae in external galaxies.

Historically, Australian astronomy falls into three periods. Before 1900 the state observatories reached their zenith: They were essential to their governments and in good standing with the public. Between 1900 and the outbreak of World War II, they lost their strong position and almost vanished from the public scene. After World War II astronomy rose miraculously from nothing to become one of the strongest sciences in the country. Here it is possible to comment only on a few major points.

First, for the most part British influence has been minimal; thus, only three Australian directors have been appointed on British advice, the last in 1864. The state observatories were shaped rather by their access to the southern third of the sky, the interests and perceptions of various governors, the vicissitudes of politics and the economy, the needs of mariners, surveyors, and meteorologists, the changing personalities and research currents within astronomy itself, and, last but not least, the fortunes of World War II.

One of the most interesting aspects of the Melbourne telescope is how a town as new and remote as Melbourne came to have the world's largest telescope, a 48-inch reflector. The reasons include the affluence and euphoria generated by the new goldfields; the great comets of 1859 and 1862 and the enthusiasm they aroused with the public; the presence on the observatory board of powerful figures like the state governor and the state treasurer, the latter an old associate of Ellery's; and some strenuous lobbying by Professor Wilson, newly appointed to Melbourne University from Ireland (where the telescope was built).

Finally, why did Australian astronomy explode so dramatically in the immediate postwar years? Its resurgence was led by radio astronomers who had the ability to capitalize on the unique opportunities created by wartime radar. But they could not have done so without the high-level decisions that created the Radiophysics Laboratory in the first place, kept it in being after the war, and supported the redirection of Mount Stromlo into stellar as opposed to solar astronomy. Again, the war produced a new breed of scientists, of which Bowen and Woolley were good examples. They were accustomed to authority, knew about money, moved easily in the upper echelons of government, and had established good contacts there; their institutions reaped the benefit.

In the longer run, success bred success. It meant continued government support, led to more powerful instruments, and attracted the best students. Perhaps Pawsey expressed it best: "Research in this field has been very generously supported by the Australian authorities, but financial support, though essential, must be supplemented by something else. The reasons must involve personalities, methods of organisation, historic background, and such complex factors, and all of these appear to have been particularly favorable in Australia" (Pawsey, 18)

With a population of seventeen million, Australia supports about a dozen active astronomical institutions. The Astronomical Society of Australia, founded in 1966, has some 250 members, almost all professional astronomers, with a sprinkling of serious amateurs. If there is one feature that characterizes Australian astronomy it is the diversity and degree of innovation that has gone into its major telescopes. Some are unique, and many have introduced designs or practices widely adopted elsewhere.

The *Australian Dictionary of Biography* (Melbourne, Melbourne University Press, 1966–) and the *Proceedings of the Astronomical Society of Australia* (1967–) contain biographical, historical, and autobiographical information on the history of astronomy in Australia.

S.C.B. Gascoigne

Bibliography

Bhatal, R., and G. White. *Under the Southern Cross: A History of Astronomy in Australia*. Sydney: Kangaroo Press, 1991.

Gascoigne, S.C.B. "Australian Astronomy Since the Second World War." In *Australian Science in the Making*, edited by R.W. Home, 308–344. Cambridge: Cambridge University Press, in association with the Australian Academy of Science, 1988.

Gascoigne, S.C.B., K.M. Proust, and M.O. Robins. *The Creation of the Anglo-Australian Observatory*. Cambridge: Cambridge University Press, 1990.

Pawsey, J.L. "Australian Radio Astronomy." In *The Australian Scientist* 181–186, Sydney, 1961.

Robertson, P. *Beyond Southern Skies: Radio Astronomy and the Parkes Telescope.* Cambridge: Cambridge University Press, 1992.

Sullivan, W.T. III, ed. *The Early Years of Radio Astronomy,* New York: Cambridge University Press, 1984.

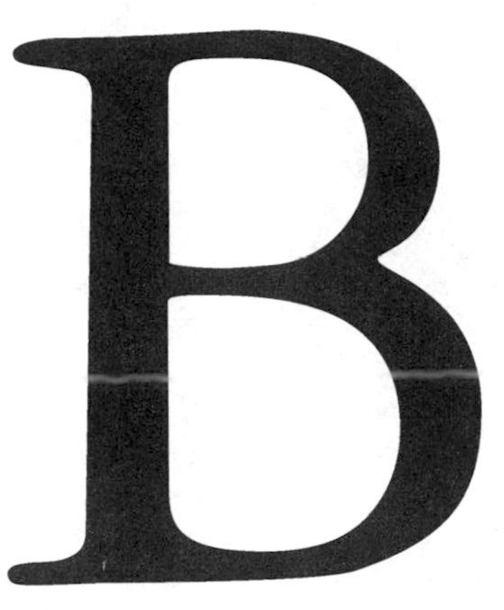

Baade, Wilhelm Heinrich Walter (1893–1960)

German astronomer. Baade studied at Göttingen (1913–1919) and worked at the Hamburg Observatory (1919–1931). Baade's duties at Hamburg mainly involved solar system astronomy, but he studied variable stars whenever he could. Baade went to the Mount Wilson Observatory in 1931 to pursue studies in stellar and extragalactic astronomy, subjects more to his liking. When World War II began, Baade, an enemy alien, had to obtain special permission to use the telescopes on Mount Wilson. With red-sensitive plates and the wartime blackout of Los Angeles, Baade was able to resolve the central portions of M31 and its satellites into stars. He discovered that spiral galaxies contained two distinct types of stars: younger, blue stars in dusty galactic regions (Population I) and older, redder stars in dust-free regions (Population II). When the 200-inch Hale Telescope entered service, Baade's inability to resolve RR Lyrae stars in M31 forced him to increase the distance to the galaxy by a factor of two. Baade's other research projects included the optical identification of radio sources (with Rudolph Minkowski) and the development of the Schmidt-type telescope for wide-field photography. Baade died with most of his research still unpublished. This work was eventually completed by colleagues at Mount Wilson and the Leiden Observatory.

Baade's work is central to the development of stellar and galactic astronomy from the 1940s onward. Unfortunately, his career and work have not received adequate historical treatment. Some of Baade's papers are at the Huntington Library, but most of his letters are to be found only in the archives of his correspondents.

Ronald S. Brashear

Bibiliography

Dieke, S.H. "Baade, Wilhelm Heinrich Walter." In *Dictionary of Scientific Biography*, edited by C.C. Gillispie, vol. 1, 352–354. New York: Scribner, 1970.

Jackson, J. "The President's Address on the Award of the Gold Medal to Dr. Walter Baade." *Monthly Notices of the Royal Astronomical Society* 114 (1954): 370–383.

Babylonian Astronomy

In the first decades of the twentieth century, the decipherment of Babylonian astronomical texts led to the realization of their relation to Greek astronomy and, by extension, Arabic, Indian, and European astronomy. Babylonian astronomy then had to be fitted not only into the history of astronomy, but also the history of science in general. And because of the striking line of continuity between the Babylonian and Greek astronomical traditions, the question of the origins of Western science, hitherto considered to be definable in terms exclusively of ancient classical tradition, had to be reopened.

Under the rubric Babylonian astronomy is included all the attempts, for which written evidence is extant, to systematize, describe, predict, or compute celestial (lunar, solar, planetary, even meteorological) phenomena. In the astronomical tradition, two basic methods characterize the Babylonian approach to celestial phenomena: observation and mathematical schematization. Some texts are primarily observational or computational, but both methods are found from the earliest period for which there is written evidence of celestial inquiry, and they are often integrated within the same text. Many computational texts are based on schematic mathematical descriptions of lunar or planetary behavior, which, in their general applicability, have a kind of theoretical status. Of course, much observational data provided the foundation for the mathematical treatment of lunar and planetary phenomena. Nevertheless, the character of the Babylonian astronomical sources, as of their chronological distribution, does not support a linear progressive model that has observation preceding and being superseded by mathematical theoretization.

In this overview, the focus will be on the textual sources, in order to present a complete picture of the materials available. The scholarly traditions of ancient Mesopotamian celestial inquiry have necessarily been classified in modern terms as astronomical or astrological, since some sources focus on the phenomena alone while others are explicitly aimed at the prognostication of the future of the state (or king as its representative) or an individual's life. Because the cuneiform record gives us access to contemporary astronomical texts from a period spanning the late second to the end of the first millennium B.C.E., the development and constant interrelationship between the two closely related disciplines of astronomy and **astrology** (celestial divination) is clear. To eradicate altogether the distinction between astrology and astronomy would be to ignore the Babylonian scribes' own classification of texts. Further, to differentiate texts in any modern (or post-seventeenth century) way (as, for example, between science and pseudo-science) would equally distort the ancient evidence.

The sources are presented in two basic groups, defined chronologically. Among the astronomical sources, the separation between early and late is determined by a methodological distinction. Among the astrological sources, the difference is also methodologically definable, but stems from a turn toward personal astrology and a more comprehensive use of astronomy than is evident in the omens. For both, the chronological divide occurs around 500 B.C.E., roughly coincident with the end of the native Babylonian or Neo-Babylonian empire and the beginning of Persian rule in Mesopotamia. The astronomy of both early and late periods bears relation to celestial divination (astrology): in the early period to the astral omens, and in the late to omens as well as horoscopes.

The Early Period

The interests of early Babylonian astronomy are chiefly planetary and stellar risings and settings, daylight length, and lunar visibility. Many of these phenomena appear in the protases of the celestial omens of the period (see below under *Enūma Anu Enlil*). A number of the phenomena also received schematic mathematical treatment already in the early period. The sources are the Astrolabes, a compendium of descriptive astronomy entitled MUL.APIN ("The Plough Star"), the omen series *Enūma Anu Enlil*, and various observational texts, among which are the Reports and the earliest Diaries. Texts containing true (that is, contemporary and datable) observations do not appear until relatively late in the early period (see below under Reports and Diaries).

Astrolabes

The Babylonian name for this text is the "Three Stars Each," because it presents a fixed star calendar in which months of heliacal risings are given for three fixed stars per month in a twelve-month schematic year. The stars are assigned to three paths in the sky, named for the three gods Anu, Enlil, and Ea. The paths are defined with respect to the eastern horizon, where one could see the stars rising in their monthly sequence. The attempt to place the stars in their appropriate places in the sky and to describe their cyclical return to their places accounts for the modern title "**Astrolabe.**" Part of the Astrolabe text is a religious calendar. It assigns to the months various activities dedicated to gods associated with the particular month, as in the following excerpt from month II: *Ajaru* (is the month) of the Pleiades, the seven great gods. (The month of) the opening of the earth, (month in which) the oxen go in procession, the water sluices are opened, the plows are flooded. The month of Ningirsu, the hero, the great *issakku*-priest of Enlil.

The month sections of the Astrolabe texts also contain numerical values (probably in time degrees [1 degree = 4 minutes]) for the variation in length of day through the year in accordance with a scheme that assigns the longest day, 4, to month III (=summer solstice), the shortest day, 2, to month IX (=winter solstice), and the mean values of 3 correspond to the equinoctial months VI and XII. The ratio of longest to shortest day is obviously 2:1.

MUL.APIN

The astronomical compendium MUL.APIN focuses directly on cataloguing and systematizing a wide variety of celestial phenomena. Subjects found in MUL.APIN include names and relative positions in the sky of fixed stars, dates of their heliacal risings, simultaneous risings and settings of certain stars and constellations, stars that cross the meridian, stars in the path of the moon, astronomical seasons, luni-solar intercalation rules with fixed stars, stellar calendar, appearances and disappearances of the five planets, periods of planetary appearance, length of day scheme, lunar visibility scheme. Despite its primary interest in the phenomena themselves, hence our classification of the text as astronomical, the final section of MUL.APIN is devoted to celestial omens, and thus represents a part of celestial divination or astrology.

The Celestial Omens of Enūma Anu Enlil

Celestial divination emerged in the context of Old Babylonian scribal scholarship (ca. 1800 B.C.E.) with a series of omens from the eclipses of the moon. These took the general form "if an eclipse occurs on the fourteenth day and (the moon) was red, downfall of the army in battle." The omen series was subsequently expanded into a compendium entitled *Enūma Anu Enlil*, standardized as a reference handbook for all celestial omens, and preserved as such until the end of the Seleucid period. In the form preserved in the version from Assurbanipal's library at Nineveh of the seventh century B.C.E., *Enūma Anu Enlil* numbered seventy tablets organized into four sections according to the phenomena of interest: the first section (EAE 1–22) pertains to phenomena of the moon god, Sin, such as lunar visibility, halos, eclipses, and conjunctions with planets and fixed stars; the second section (EAE 23–36) refers to the phenomena of the sun god, Samas, such as coronas, parhelia, and eclipses, third (EAE 37–49/50) contains meteorological phenomena of the storm god, Adad, such as lightning, thunder, rainbows, cloud formations, and winds; and the fourth section (EAE 50/51–70) contains planetary *omina* such as first and last visibilities, stations, acronychal risings, as well as *omina* for fixed star phases.

Tablet Fourteen on Lunar Visibility

The Fourteenth Tablet of *Enūma Anu Enlil* concerns the daily change in duration of lunar visibility throughout a schematic (thirty-day) month, which is a function both of the monthly change in lunar elongation from the sun as well as the variation in the length of the night throughout the year. The values for the daily change in visibility tabulated in this text are calculated on the basis of a mathematical scheme built on the assumption that the moon is invisible at conjunction (day 30), visible the entire night at opposition (day 15), and in between steadily increases or decreases its duration of visibility after sunset at the rate of 1/15th night. The values given in the text may be represented graphically by a zigzag function. The value 1/15th night will itself vary throughout the year because of the change in the length of night. The Babylonian scheme for the change in length of night presumes a ratio 2:1 for longest to shortest night.

Reports

From the scholars of the seventh century Assyrian court comes an archive consisting of observations of the appearances of the moon and planets reported with the corresponding *omina* from *Enūma Anu Enlil*. The ostensible purpose of these short Reports was to inform the king of approaching events forecasted from the stars, appropriate measures to take in the event of bad omens, and propitious times for certain activities (cultic, military, and so on). These sources reveal a knowledge of the underlying periodicities of many lunar and planetary synodic phenomena. On this basis, occasionally an appearance will be predicted and the corresponding omen checked ahead of time.

Observations

The largest corpus of Babylonian astronomical observations are termed Astronomical Diaries. Although extant only from the seventh century, these texts were probably already being compiled, in Babylon primarily, in the eighth century, and were contemporaneous with the activity of observation and celestial divination by scholar-scribes of the Neo-Assyrian period. The diary-writing tradition persisted well beyond the seventh century to the first century B.C.E. and so practically to the end of the cuneiform tradition itself.

A standard diary collected lunar, planetary, meteorological, economic, and occasionally political events night by night for one half of a Babylonian year. For each night and with respect to time designations such as "beginning of night," or "in the last part of night," the position of the moon is given, as well as any planets that may be visible. Dates are given for the cardinal points of the year, solstices and equinoxes, eclipses, and much weather data is included such as cloud formations, rain, or mist. The water level of the Euphrates as well as the prices of grain, wool, and other commodities are included at the end of each month section. For further discussion of the Diaries in the late period, see below.

The Late Period

The interests of astronomy in the late period are more comprehensive than can be documented in texts prior to 500 B.C.E. Predicting the dates and positions (giving ecliptical longitudes by degrees within zodiacal signs) of the synodic phenomena of all five planets (**Jupiter**, **Venus**, **Saturn**, **Mercury**, and **Mars**) as well as conjunctions and oppositions (for the purpose of predicting lunar eclipses) of sun and moon are of greatest interest. Both observations and predictions (computed) of these phenomena are the subjects of a number of text types. These divide first into tabular (ephemerides) and nontabular (diaries, almanacs, and other) classes. A classificatory separation may also be defined methodologically, in which case the ephemerides and procedure texts belong to the mathematical astronomy, while the diaries and other nontabular texts belong to nonmathematical astronomy. The tabular form of the ephemerides is a consequence of its underlying mathematical structure, which is not found in the diaries or in any of the other nonmathematical genres. At the same time, it should also be clear that nonmathematical is not synonymous with observational. The distinction between mathematical and nonmathematical is also not simply a way of distinguishing computation and prediction from observation. Virtually all the nonmathematical text genres contain predictions of phenomena—predictions, however, which were not obtained by the methods of the mathematical tables. The only nonmathematical genre that is noted for its recording of astronomical observations is the one termed diaries, and even those regularly include predicted data.

Nonmathematical Astronomy

The bulk of the sources for this type of astronomy are the Astronomical Diaries. The Diaries archive has been introduced above. This archive was maintained throughout the Achaemenid, Seleucid, and Arsacid periods, and represents, therefore, an eight-hundred-year archive of consistent astronomical observations. Of primary importance was the progress of the moon each month through the sidereal ecliptic. This daily progress was charted by means of distances between the moon and the normal stars. In addition, dates of certain lunar visibility intervals were also observed at key times during the month, specifically around conjunction and opposition of moon and sun. The interest here was presumably in calendar dates of first and last visibilities, and syzygies, which occur at intervals of not less than twenty-nine and not more than thirty days apart. When one of these lunar phenomena could not be observed because of adverse weather, and a prediction was made, the following is typical: "interval from sunrise to moonset was 17 degrees; I did not keep watch; the sun was surrounded by a halo." Predictive control of these dates belongs to the most sophisticated level of Babylonian lunar theory, since visibility considerations are of the highest complexity. This kind of control is attested only in the lunar ephemerides of the mathematical astronomy.

Goal-year texts present a variety of astronomical phenomena whose dates and positions were culled from Diaries a particular number of years before the goal year. The number of years was determined by the period appropriate to the given planet (or moon) as follows: Jupiter, seventy-one (synodic period) and eighty-three years (the sidereal period); Venus, eight years; Mercury, forty-six years; Saturn, fifty-nine years; Mars, forty-seven and seventy-nine years (the sidereal period), and finally, for the moon, the data is collected for eighteen years before the goal year (the Saros cycle).

Other compilations of consecutive lunar eclipses covering a period from the eighth century up to the Seleucid period, as well as less extensive collections, usually arranged in eighteen-year groups, are also known. Such compilations are preserved only in Seleucid copy. Individual reports of observed eclipses were also made. The eclipse phenomena of the reports are similar to those in the eclipse *omina* of *Enūma Anu Enlil*—that is, date (year, month, day) of occurrence, time of beginning of eclipse, direction of the shadow, magnitude (in fingers). The position of the moon relative to some fixed star (usually a "*ziqpu*" or culminating star) at the time of the eclipse is sometimes also given, as is the presence or absence of planets.

The Diaries and Goal-year texts fit together well as source and derivative, while two other types of nonmathematical astronomical texts present data in quite a different manner. These are the Almanacs and Normal-star almanacs. An Almanac presents in twelve (or thirteen) month-sections the location of each planet in the zodiac through the year. The tablet is organized by the month, and the first line of each month section contains the zodiacal sign in which each planet is found on the first day of the month. Degrees within signs are never given. These positions are registered in the standard order of the planets found also in Goal-year texts and horoscopes—that is, Jupiter, Venus, Mercury, Saturn, and Mars. Thereafter, the dates of predicted entries of the planets into the next sign are given. The prediction of these dates would be of importance since it is precisely the boundaries between signs that are impossible to observe, and the crossing from one zodiacal sign to another is very likely an astrologically important event.

In addition to predicting the positions in the zodiac of the planets month by month for one Babylonian year, dates of synodic phenomena are included in the appropriate order, as are the lunar visibility intervals on day 1, the day of opposition (usually day 14 or 15), and the day of last lunar visibility (usually day 28 or 29), and the dates of equinoxes or solstices. Occasionally also the heliacal appearances of Sirius are predicted, and so too are eclipses. The chronological range for the almanacs, taken from the datable texts, is from 261 B.C.E. to 75 C.E.

Mathematical Astronomy

The Babylonian mathematical astronomy of the last three centuries B.C.E. is, from the modern point of view, the most significant achievement of Babylonian science. Within this group of sources may be found astronomical concepts (longitude, latitude, anomaly, regression of lunar nodes), parameters (lunar and planetary periods and period relations), and units (degrees of arc) that are continuous with those of the Western tradition represented by Ptolemy and Copernicus. As a result of the work of decipherment of the mathematical astronomical texts by J. Epping, J.N Strassmaier, and F.X. Kugler around the turn of the century, followed by the further analysis and publication of the entire corpus by O. Neugebauer, as well as the contributions of historians such as A. Aaboe and B.L. van der Waerden, modern history of science was forced to redefine the origins of Western astronomy, no longer in terms exclusively of the ancient classical tradition, but in terms of the Babylonian tradition and its influence upon the Greeks.

The bulk of the texts are lunar or planetary ephemerides, which are supplemented by a smaller group of procedure texts outlining the steps necessary to generate ephemeris tables. The ephemeris tables contain parallel columns of numbers in specific sequences that represent occurrences of characteristic lunar and planetary phenomena. In a given ephemeris, pertaining to some individual planet, or the moon, each column represents a different periodic phenomenon—for example, in a lunar ephemeris separate columns generate positions or dates for new moons, eclipses, and so on; for a planetary ephemeris, columns may refer to particular synodic appearances, such as first visibilities or stationary points. The mathematical astronomical texts use a fixed continuous luni-solar calendar based on the nineteen-year cycle of intercalation, where years are of the Seleucid Era, and months are lunar (that is, the first day is determined by the first visibility of the lunar crescent on the western horizon just after sunset). Where positions (longitudes) are given, the zodiac is the frame of reference.

While no general physical theory of celestial motion, especially in spherical geometric terms, was articulated as such, the computational methods built upon a foundation of the period relations governing the occurrences of the phenomena of interest to the Babylonian astronomers—that is, the synodic phenomena of the moon and planets were applicable to all the phenomena of all the celestial bodies. Within Babylonian lunar and planetary theory coexisted two different systems, designated A and B, which are defined according to their particular arithmetical methods of computing longitudes; System A by means of a piecewise constant step function, System B by a zigzag function. The goal of Babylonian astronomy was to predict when the moon or planets would be visible. It can be no coincidence that the visible appearances of the heavenly bodies that formed the basis for celestial omens were the central focus of Babylonian astronomy. In preserved colophons of the mathematical ephemerides, the scribes who mastered this astronomy held the professional title "Scribe of Enūma Anu Enlil."

Late Astrological Texts

The *Enūma Anu Enlil* series continued to be transmitted well into the Seleucid Era, but the introduction of personal predictions from celestial phenomena at the time of birth, both in the old form of omens and in the new form of horoscopes, can be identified after about 500 B.C.E. But in the Babylonian horoscopes, as in the later Greek, the actual personal predictions are rarely given. Because astronomical data is provided for the birthdate and time of birth of the subject, it can be assumed that these celestial phenomena are the important signs for the future of the child. Our assumption that the purpose of producing a record of celestial phenomena at the time of birth was to obtain a prediction about an individual's future is based on the fact that this was already an established practice, evidenced by the corpus of nativity omens that begin to appear around the same time as the earliest horoscopes. These have the form "if a child is born and Jupiter comes forth" or "if a child is born in the middle of Aries" and the like.

A corpus of horoscopes is extant that numbers a mere thirty-two texts, and, with the exception of two documents from the fifth century B.C.E., belongs for the most part to the last three centuries B.C.E. The chronological range is from the oldest at 410 B.C.E. to the youngest at 69 B.C.E. With five documents from the first century B.C.E., these are among the youngest cuneiform texts known. Horoscopes appear only after the significant turning point in the development of Babylonian positional astronomy marked by the invention of the zodiac in roughly 500 B.C.E. It is clear that the astronomical data—planetary positions as well as other phenomena regularly recorded in the horoscopes, such as equinox and solstice dates, lunar longitudes, and eclipses—derive from a variety of astronomical texts in which such data are collected (e.g., Diaries, Almanacs, Goal-year texts). Contemporary Babylonian astronomical practices, observational as well as computational, are therefore reflected in the horoscope texts, much as the descriptive astronomy of MUL.APIN is reflected in *Enūma Anu Enlil.*

F. Rochberg

Bibliography

Aaboe, A. "On Babylonian Planetary Theories." *Centaurus* 5 (1958): 209–277.

———. "On Period Relations in Babylonian Astronomy." *Centaurus* 10 (1964): 213–231.

———. "Observation and Theory in Babylonian Astronomy." *Centaurus* 24 (1980): 14–35.

Hunger, H. *Astrological Reports to Assyrian Kings.* State Archives of Assyria Volume VIII. Helsinki, 1992.

Hunger, H., and D. Pingree. *MUL.APIN: An Astronomical Compendium in Cuneiform.* Archiv für Orientforschung Beiheft 24. Vienna, 1989.

Neugebauer, O. *Astronomical Cuneiform Texts.* Vols. I–III. London: Lund Humphries, 1955.

———. *A History of Ancient Mathematical Astronomy.* Vols. I–III. New York: Springer-Verlag, 1975.

Pinches, T.G., J.N. Strassmaier, and A. Sachs. *Late Babylonian Astronomical and Related Texts.* Providence: Brown University Press, 1955.

Reiner, E., and D. Pingree. *The Venus Tablet of Ammisaduqa.* Babylonian Planetary Omens 1. Malibu: Undena Publications, 1975.

———. *Enūma Anu Enlil Tablets 50–51.* Babylonian Planetary Omens 2. Malibu: Undena Publications, 1981.

Rochberg-Halton, F. *Aspects of Babylonian Celestial Divination: The Lunar Eclipse Tablets of Enūma Anu Enlil.* Archiv für Orientforschung Beiheft 22. Vienna 1988.

———. "Babylonian Horoscopes and Their Sources." *Orientalia* 58 (1989): 102–123.

Sachs, A. "Babylonian Horoscopes." *Journal of Cuneiform Studies* 6 (1952): 49–75.

Sachs, A. J., and H. Hunger. *Astronomical Diaries and Related Texts.* Vols. I and II. Vienna: Österreichische Akademie der Wissenschaften, 1988–89.

van der Waerden, B.L. *Science Awakening II: The Birth of Astronomy.* Leiden: Noordhoff International Publishing, and New York: Oxford University Press, 1974.

van Soldt, W.H. *Solar Omens of Enūma Anu Enlil: Tablets 23 (24)–29 (30).* Nederlands Historisch-Archaeologisch Instituut te Istanbul, 1995.

Banneker, Benjamin (1731–1806)

Benjamin Banneker, tobacco farmer, amateur astronomer, and the first African-American man of science, was the son of Robert Banneky, a freed African slave, and Mary Banneky, daughter of a freed slave named Bannka and a white English woman named Molly Welsh. Born in Baltimore County, Maryland, on November 9, 1731, he was taught to read and write from a Bible by his white grandmother, and his only formal school was attendance for several weeks in a Quaker one-room schoolhouse. From his youth he demonstrated considerable skill in mathematics. Becoming interested in astronomy in his later life, he taught himself, without assistance, from borrowed texts, including Leadbetter's *A Complete System of Astronomy,* Mayer's *Tabulae Motuum Solis et Lunis,* and Ferguson's *Easy Introduction to Astronomy*. He proceeded to calculate an ephemeris successfully for an **almanac** for the year 1790.

Selected in 1791 by the surveyor Andrew Ellicott as his assistant on the survey of the Federal Territory, a ten-acre site in Virginia and Maryland for the new national capital, Banneker worked in the field observatory tent for the first three months of the survey. He was responsible for making nightly observations of the transit of stars with the zenith sector, correcting and maintaining the field observatory clock, and recording his observations for Ellicott's use for the following day's survey. In his leisure hours he completed calculations for an ephemeris for an almanac for 1792, which he sold to a Baltimore printer. Promoted by the Pennsylvania and Maryland abolitionist societies, it sold widely in the United States and England. Banneker continued to calculate ephemerides for almanacs that were published through 1797. A recent computerized comparison with ephemerides made by others in the same period revealed that Banneker's calculations were consistently accurate and competent. Banneker died in his sleep on the morning of October 9, 1806, one month before his seventy-fifth birthday.

Silvio A. Bedini

Bibliography

Bedini, S.A. *The Life of Benjamin Banneker.* New York: Scribner, 1972; reprint, Rancho Cordova, Calif.: Landmark Enterprises, 1985.

Tyson, M.E. *A Sketch of the Life of Benjamin Banneker. From Notes Taken in 1836. Read by J. Saurin Norris, before the Maryland Historical Society, October 1854*. Baltimore: John D. Toy, n.d.

———. *Banneker, the Afric-American Astronomer. From the Posthumous Papers of Martha E. Tyson. Edited by Her Daughter*. Philadelphia: Friends' Book Association, 1884.

Barnard, Edward Emerson (1857–1923)

American astronomer. Born in Nashville, Tennessee, Barnard acquired a reputation for comet discoveries with a small telescope, which in 1883 led to a fellowship at Vanderbilt University and in 1888 to appointment to the **Lick Observatory** staff. At Lick he discovered (1892) the fifth satellite of Jupiter, which made his international reputation. Barnard also devoted time to planetary observations. He pioneered the wide-angle photography of comets and the Milky Way. After 1895 he was on the staff of **Yerkes Observatory**. A versatile and tireless observer, he is renowned for his keenness of sight and dedication to astronomy.

William Sheehan

Bibliography

Sheehan, W. *The Immortal Fire Within: The Life and Work of Edward Emerson Barnard*. Cambridge: Cambridge University Press, 1995.

Barringer Meteor Crater

Located 40 miles southeast of Flagstaff, Barringer Meteor Crater contributed significantly to the acceptance of impact theory as the leading explanation for lunar and terrestrial cratering phenomena. Scientists began to investigate the crater in the 1890s but interpreted the structure as a volcanic phenomenon. This theory represented the scientific consensus of the period, with both lunar and terrestrial craters defined as volcanic events.

An important alternative to this interpretation came from mining entrepreneur Daniel Moreau Barringer. The existence of a large collection of meteoritic material in the area (the famous "Canyon Diablo" meteorites) led Barringer to suggest an extraterrestrial origin of the crater in 1906. He further believed that the primary mass of the meteor lay buried beneath the crater and represented a potential profit of some $250 million from nickel and other metals. Despite his devotion to proving the meteoritic origin of the crater, Barringer remained unable to capitalize on his theory and failed to recover the wealth he anticipated.

In his attempt to prove the meteoritic origin of the crater, however, Barringer approached many leading scientists of the early twentieth century. Although astronomers and geologists rejected the idea of a profitable meteoritic mass, by the time of Barringer's death the meteoritic origin of the crater was generally accepted. Over the next quarter century, several more impact craters were identified and, after 1940, lunar craters were increasingly explained in terms of impact theory as well.

George E. Webb

Bibliography

Barringer, D.M. "Coon Mountain and Its Crater." *Proceedings of the Academy of Natural Sciences of Philadelphia* 57 (1906): 861–886.

Hoyt, W.G. *Coon Mountain Controversies: Meteor Crater and the Development of*

Impact Theory. Tucson: University of Arizona Press, 1987.
Shoemaker, E.M. "Asteroidal and Comet Bombardment of the Earth." *Annual Review of Earth and Planetary Science* 11 (1983): 461–494.

Berlin Observatory

The Berlin Observatory has a remarkable history of continuous development spanning nearly three centuries in various incarnations. In 1706 the *Societät der Wissenschaften* (which later became the *Königlich Preussischen Akademie der Wissenschaften*) in Berlin had Martin Grünberg design and build an observatory. It was completed in 1711. This structure, which was also to serve as a meeting place for the society, took the form of a tower rising above the royal stables in *Dorotheenstrasse.* The tower configuration was common for late-seventeenth- and eighteenth-century European observatories. The Paris and Bologna observatories were, for example, tower structures. The first of the building's three floors served as the society's meeting hall, and the two higher floors were the observatory proper. In addition, the roof of the tower was used as an observing platform. Later modifications increased the height of the tower to keep the observers above newer buildings nearby.

Ironically, the academy's first astronomer, Gottfried Kirch, died before the observatory was ready, so his collaborator and successor, J.H. Hoffmann, was its first observer. A string of observers, including Gottfried's son Christfried Kirch, followed Hoffmann in rapid succession until Johann Elert Bode, who began as an assistant, became director in 1787. Bode's work in reviving the Academy's *Astronomisches Jahrbuch* (begun by Johann Lambert) and his compilation of two major star atlases first brought fame to the work of the Berlin Observatory. Bode had the original observatory extensively refurbished in 1800.

Johann Franz Encke became director of the observatory in 1825 and brought about its first major transition. Steady growth in the size and importance of telescopes, as well as the growth of the city of Berlin, prompted the abandonment of the old tower observatory. Its successor, located near the modern *Enckeplatz*, was designed in 1828 by Karl Friedrich von Schinkel and began operations in 1835. Schinkel flanked a large telescope-housing dome between two adjoining structures north and south. On the west he put a room for a meridian circle and in the east wing were offices, workrooms, and the astronomer's dwelling. This basic plan became the archetype of many nineteenth-century observatories in Europe and North

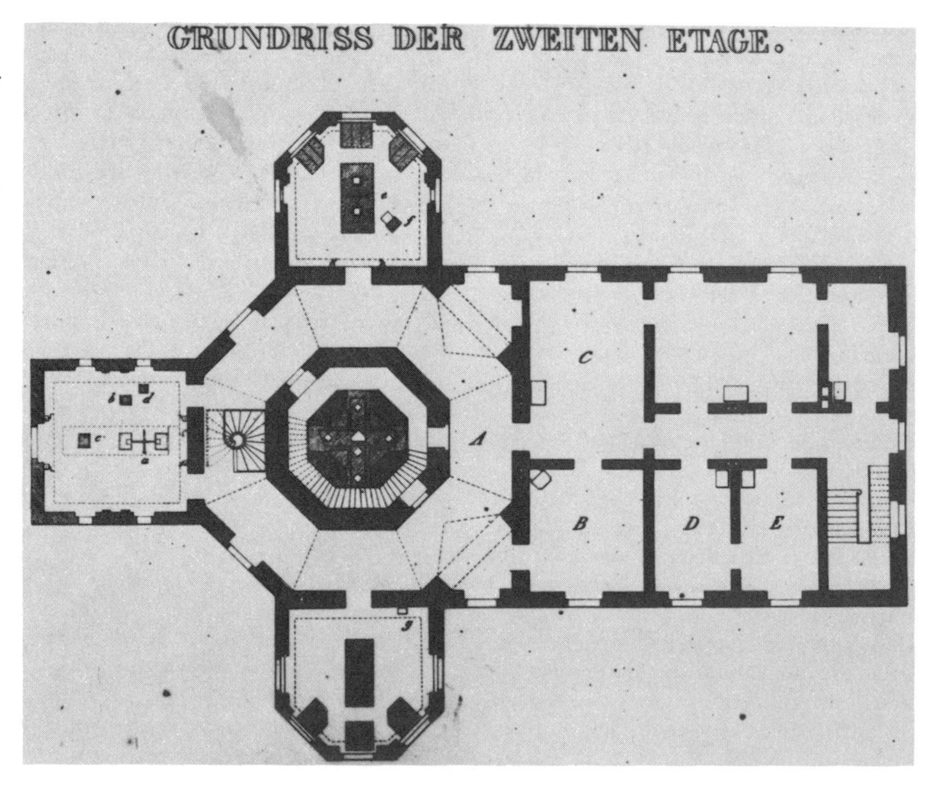

Floor plan of the Berlin Observatory. This became the model on which a number of continental and U.S. observatories were constructed. Taken from J.F. Encke, ed., Astronomische Beobachtungen auf der Koeniglichen Sternwarte zu Berlin. *Volume One, Berlin, 1840. (Courtesy of J.M. Lattis)*

America. The observatory's principal instruments were a heliometer and a 9-inch Fraunhofer refractor. The 27-inch Zeiss refractor, which came in 1879, required some modifications and rebuilding of the central dome. The building was demolished in 1915 after the establishment of the Berlin-Babelsberg Observatory. Encke's important work on comets and asteroids, his vigorous agenda of astrometry, and star chart production all enhanced the reputation of the Berlin Observatory. Encke also edited the academy's yearbook and used it to publish his research results in addition to its traditional, popular contents. Encke's program of star charting was intended largely to advance the search for asteroids, which became a specialty of the Berlin astronomers. The charts also aided in the discovery of the planet Neptune by Encke's observers Johann Gottfried Galle and Heinrich Louis d'Arrest after Urbain Leverrier in Paris had sent Galle predictions of the planet's position.

Encke's successor was Wilhelm Foerster, who strongly promoted the funding and growth of astronomy and astrophysics in Germany. His successor, **Karl Hermann Struve**, who took over in 1904, oversaw another major relocation—this time to the modern Babelsberg site, situated near Potsdam and thus well outside of the ever-expanding city of Berlin. The new observatory was constructed between 1911 and 1913. Its primary instrument was a 27-inch Zeiss refractor later augmented by a 50-inch Zeiss reflector in an additional dome. Located in the German Democratic Republic (East Germany) for many years after World War II, the Babelsberg Observatory served as the seat of the *Zentralinstituts für Astrophysik*.

Most of the historical work on the Berlin Observatory is to be found in treatments of its directors and other major figures, such as Bode, Encke, and Galle. However, some important works on the observatory as an institution have appeared, most notably in the collections of articles cited in the bibliography. Particularly important is J. Hamel and Klaus-Harro Tiemann, "Die Vertretung der Astronomie an der Berliner Universität in den Jahren 1810 bis 1914" (in Jürgen, *Beiträge*), which contains an important summary of astronomy teachers, courses, and academic publications of the Berlin University. Also important is I. Baumgart, "Dokumente zur Geschichte der Sternwarte Berlin-Babelsberg aus den Jahren 1700–1945 in Zentralen Archiv der Akademie der Wissenschaften der DDR" (in Jackisch, *Sternzeiten* 2), which provides a historical summary of the observatory and an overview of the documentation for its early history.

James M. Lattis

Bibliography

Hamel, J., et al. *Beiträge zur Geschichte der Astronomie in Berlin.* Archenhold-Sternwarte Berlin-Treptow Vorträge und Schriften 69. Berlin-Treptow, 1988.

Jackisch, G., ed. *Sternzeiten: Zur 275jährigen Geschichte der Berliner Sternwarte, der heutigen Sternwarte Babelsberg.* Band 1. Akademie der Wissenschaften der DDR, Veröffentlichungen des Forschungsbereichs Geo- und Kosmoswissenschaften. Heft 6. Berlin: Akademie-Verlag, 1977.

———. *Sternzeiten: Zur 275 jährigen Geschichte der Berliner Sternwarte, der heutigen Sternwarte Babelsberg.* Band 2. Akademie der Wissenschaften der DDR, Veröffentlichungen des Forschungsbereichs Geo- und Kosmoswissenschaften. Heft 7. Berlin: Akademie-Verlag, 1977.

Müller, P. *Sternwarten in Bildern: Architektur und Geschichte der Sternwarten von den Anfängen bis ca. 1950.* Berlin: Springer-Verlag, 1992.

Bessel, Friedrich Wilhelm (1784–1846)

Known as the founder of the German school of practical astronomy, Bessel demonstrated the success of his methodology by making one of the first valid measurements of **stellar parallax**. Stimulated by an interest in navigation, Bessel studied astronomy and mathematics on his own, and impressed the astronomer W. Olbers by his calculation of the orbit of Halley's comet in 1804. On Olbers's recommendation, in 1806 Bessel became an assistant at J.H. Schröter's private observatory near Bremen; there he learned observational astronomy, studied celestial mechanics, and began the analysis of the observations of James Bradley. His widely recognized abilities led to his appointment in 1809 as director of the observatory in Königsberg being built by Friedrich Wilhelm III of Prussia. There he remained for the rest of his life.

In addition to the necessity of precision instruments in positional astronomy, Bessel and his followers in the German school emphasized the importance of rigorous analysis and the determination of all observational errors. This led to improved values for the **astronomical constants** of precession, nutation, and aberration; it further enabled Bessel to detect variations in the proper motions of certain stars, which he correctly deduced were caused by unseen companion stars, and yielded his early measurement of stellar parallax in 1838. Using the **heliometer** for differential measurements between two stars, Bessel found a parallax for 61 Cygni of 0.314 arcsecond, with a mean error of only 0.02 arcsecond, a value very close to the modern parallax. With this achievement Bessel opened the way for distance determinations for the nearest stars. Bessel undertook many other specialized investigations in astronomy, mathematics, and geodesy. His rigorous methods set the standard for those who followed.

Steven J. Dick

Bibliography

Fricke, W. "Bessel, Friedrich Wilhelm." In *Dictionary of Scientific Biography*, edited by C.C. Gillispie, vol. 2, 97–102. New York: Scribner, 1970.

Bethe, Hans Albrechte (1906–)

German-born American theoretical physicist. Bethe, who earned his Ph.D. at Munich University (1928), emigrated from Germany after the Nazis came to power. In 1934, he went to Cornell University, which became a premier graduate center for theoretical physics under his leadership. Bethe took up the **stellar-energy** problem in 1938 at the urging of George Gamow and Edward Teller. His identification of two thermonuclear reaction chains as the power sources of main-sequence stars was a decisive turning point in research on stellar structure and evolution. This breakthrough served as the justification for Bethe's 1968 Nobel Prize in physics.

Karl Hufbauer

Bibliography

Bernstein, J. *Hans Bethe: Prophet of Energy*. New York: Basic Books, 1980.

Black Holes

Term coined by John A. Wheeler for an object so compact that nothing, not even light, can escape its gravitational attraction. Although discussions of the capture of light by massive objects can be dated to John Michell and **Pierre Simon Laplace** in the eighteenth century, a proper understanding lies in the realm of general relativity theory. **Karl Schwarzschild** calculated the boundary radius, or event horizon, of such a theoretical (nonrotating) body to be about 3 km for a

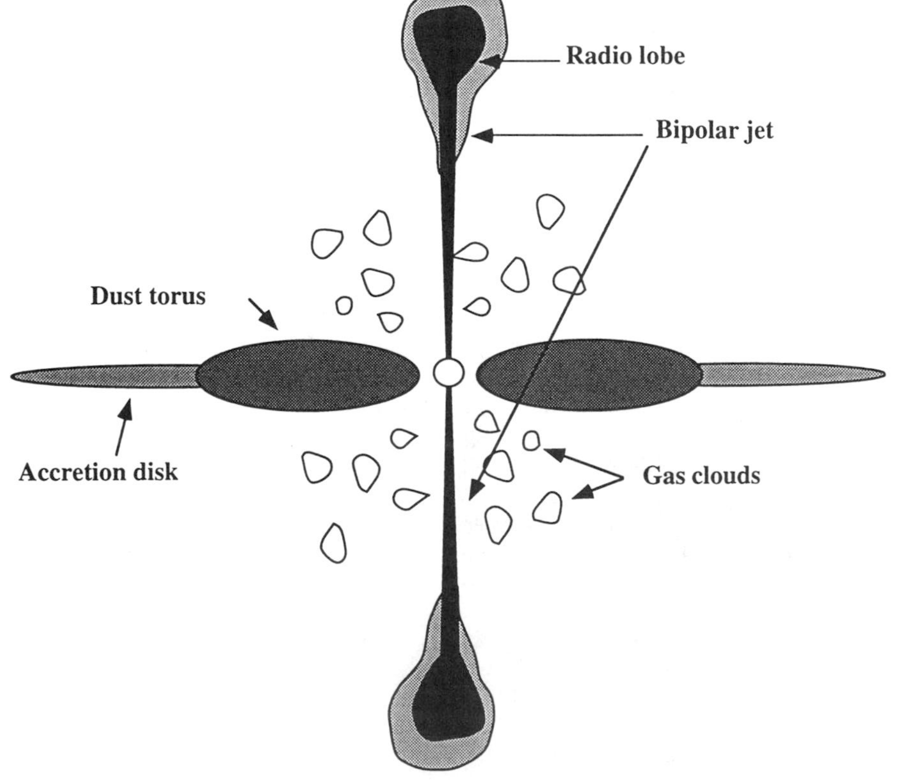

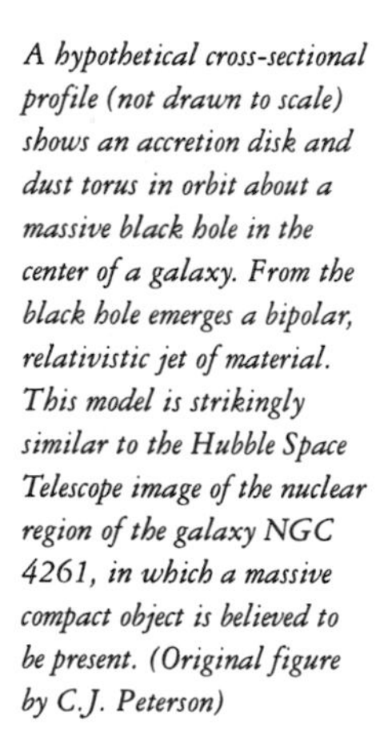
A hypothetical cross-sectional profile (not drawn to scale) shows an accretion disk and dust torus in orbit about a massive black hole in the center of a galaxy. From the black hole emerges a bipolar, relativistic jet of material. This model is strikingly similar to the Hubble Space Telescope image of the nuclear region of the galaxy NGC 4261, in which a massive compact object is believed to be present. (Original figure by C.J. Peterson)

body of one solar mass. Interior to the event horizon, relativity theory suggests that any matter collapses into an infinitesimally small volume or singularity. In 1963, a solution for a rotating object was provided by Robert P. Kerr. Stephen W. Hawking in the 1970s applied quantum mechanical concepts to the theory of black holes to show that they may not exist forever, but can radiate energy.

To address the physical origin for black holes, J. Robert Oppenheimer and Hartmann Snyder in 1939 first considered the collapse of a star. Modern astronomical inquiry identifies two observational classes of black hole candidates, stellar black holes in X-ray binary systems and massive black holes in the nuclei of galaxies. A dozen or more black hole candidates are known, including Cygnus X-1 and Scorpius X-1. The second category, a few million to a few billion solar masses, is postulated as the central engine responsible for a wide range of energetic phenomena (radio, X-ray, and gamma-ray emission, jets, and others) associated with the nuclei of some galaxies. Such active galactic nuclei objects include Seyfert galaxies, radio lobe galaxies, and quasars. Massive black holes also may be present in the centers of some nonactive galaxies.

Charles J. Peterson

Bibliography

Cowley, A.P. "Evidence for Black Holes in Stellar Binary Systems." *Annual Review of Astronomy and Astrophysics* 30 (1992): 287–310.

Misner, C.W., et al. *Gravitation*. San Francisco: Freeman, 1973.

Oppenheimer, J.R., and H. Snyder. "On Continued Gravitational Contraction." *Physical Review* 56 (1939): 455–459.

Rees, M.J. "Black Hole Models for Active Galactic Nuclei." *Annual Review of Astronomy and Astrophysics* 22 (1984): 471–506.

Bowen, Ira Sprague (1898–1973)

American physicist, astrophysicist, and science administrator. Bowen served as Robert Andrews Millikan's graduate assistant at Chicago and the **California Institute of Technology**. After receiving his Ph.D. in 1926, Bowen stayed at Caltech as a professor in the physics department. Bowen's work in spectroscopy included his discovery in 1927 of the true nature of the "nebulium" lines in gaseous nebulae. He continued to study gaseous nebulae, developing the image slicer in the process. Bowen became involved in the 200-inch Telescope Project because of his expertise in optics and spectroscopy. In 1946, Bowen was named director of the Mount Wilson Observatory and personally managed the completion of the 200-inch telescope.

Ronald S. Brashear

Bibliography

Babcock, H.W. "Ira Sprague Bowen." *Biographical Memoirs of the National Academy of Sciences* 53 (1982): 83–119.

Brahe, Tycho (1546–1601)

Danish aristocrat and astronomer, born in Skaane, Denmark (now Sweden) December 14, 1546, into a family of long-established Danish nobility. He attended the University of Copenhagen and subsequently studied at universities in Leipzig, Wittenberg, Rostock (where in 1567 he lost his nose in a duel), Basel, and Augsburg before returning to Denmark in 1570. Achieving great fame with his observations of the nova of 1572, Tycho was granted the island of Hven in the Sound off Copenhagen in 1576 by King Frederick II. There Tycho established an observatory named Uraniborg, which he turned into a superbly equipped research facility. From 1580 to 1597 Uraniborg was the premier observatory in Europe. Following a disagreement with the new king, Christian IV, Tycho left Uraniborg and, after spending time at Rostock and Wandesbeck, arrived in 1599 in Prague at the invitation of the Emperor Rudolph II, who granted him the title of Imperial Mathematician. In 1600 the young Johannes Kepler met Tycho and soon joined him as an assistant. Their collaboration was cut short by Tycho's death, on October 24, 1601.

Tycho was first and foremost an observational astronomer, perhaps the greatest before the telescope changed the nature of observational astronomy. His goal was to effect a complete restoration of astronomy based on the best possible observations. To that end he designed and had crafted at Uraniborg over twenty superb instruments, any one of which would have been the envy of contemporaries. Nearly all of his instruments were accurate to within a minute of arc, and some approached a limit of 30 seconds of arc. The best instruments were the mural quadrant, completed in 1582, and a steel revolving quadrant, finished in 1588. To get the maximum from these precision instruments, Tycho invented new sights, new methods of inscribing scales, and new mounts. He also understood, as did few of his contemporaries, that the accuracy of these large instruments could be even further improved by taking long series of observations over extended periods of time, so that human and random errors could be reduced.

Tycho entered the cosmological arena with the appearance of the nova of 1572. By repeated measurements he determined that the star exhibited no parallax whatsoever and must be in the eighth sphere of the fixed stars, which suggested that Aristotle's doctrine of the immutability of the heavens was empirically suspect. The comet of 1577 did exhibit a parallax, but it was less than that of the moon, indicating that it too was a celestial object, not a denizen of the elemental world as Aristotle had argued. The fact that the comet seemed to move across several planetary orbits subsequently led Tycho (1587) to take the remarkable step of denying the reality of celestial spheres and, in effect, casting the planets loose.

Tycho greatly admired **Copernicus** and the way the Copernican system explained the many links between planetary models and the position of the sun. But he could not accept Copernican cosmology because of the lack of stellar parallax, incompatibility with Scrip-

Tycho Brahe's largest instrument, the mural quadrant, from Tycho Brahe, Astronomiae instauratae mechanica *(Prague, 1602). (Courtesy of the History of Science Collection, Linda Hall Library, Kansas City, Missouri)*

DE COMETA ANNI 1577. 183

Nova Mundani Systematis Hypotyposis ab Authore nuper adinuenta, qua tum vetus illa Ptolemaica redundantia & inconcinnitas, tum etiam recens Coperniana in motu Terræ Physica absurditas, excluduntur, omniaq; Apparentiis Cœlestibus aptißime correspondent.

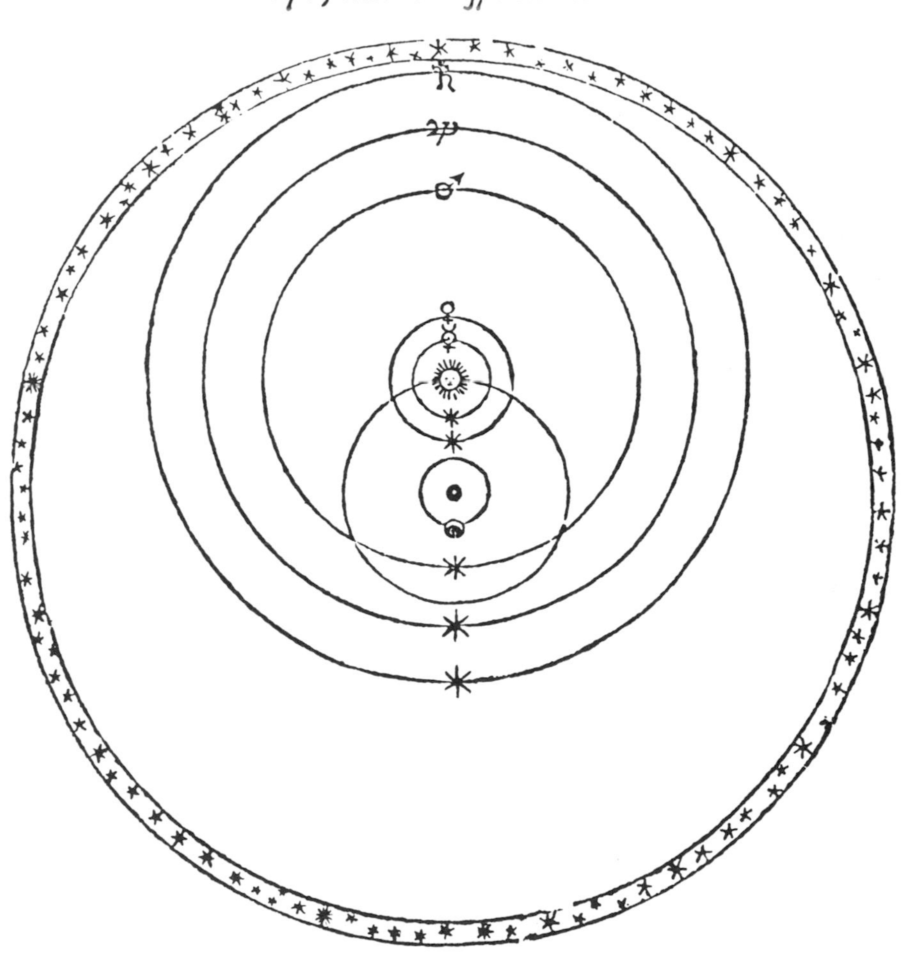

The Tychonic system from Tycho Brahe, De Mundi *(Prague, 1603). (Courtesy of the History of Science Collection, Linda Hall Library, Kansas City, Missouri)*

ture, and the physical repugnance of a moving earth. So in 1588 Tycho proposed a compromise system, with the five planets orbiting the sun, and the sun, moon, and stars circling a stationary, central earth. This Tychonic, or geoheliocentric, cosmology was considered by Tycho to be his greatest legacy.

Tycho has always been admired as an instrument maker and an observer, but frequently depicted as an astronomer who lacked the ability to do theoretical research in the Copernicus/Kepler mode. Recent research, principally by Thoren, has demonstrated that Tycho was, in fact, one of the great theorists of the period; his lunar theory, in particular, was brilliant and without precedent. What Tycho lacked was time, not genius.

William B. Ashworth Jr.

Bibliography

Blair, A. "Tycho Brahe's Critique of Copernicus and the Copernican System." *Journal of the History of Ideas* 51 (1990): 355–377.

Dreyer, J.L.E. *Tycho Brahe: A Picture of Scientific Life and Work in the Sixteenth Century.* New York: Dover, 1963.

Gingerich, O., and R.S. Westman. *The*

Wittich Connection. Transactions of the American Philosophical Society. Vol. 78, Pt. 7. Philadelphia: American Philosophical Society, 1988.
Hannaway, O. "Laboratory Design and the Aim of Science: Andreas Libavius versus Tycho Brahe." *Isis* 77 (1986): 585–610.
Hellman, C.D. *The Comet of 1577: Its Place in the History of Astronomy.* New York: Columbia University Press, 1944.
———. "Brahe, Tycho." In *Dictionary of Scientific Biography*, edited by C.C. Gillispie, vol. 2, 401–416. New York: Scribner, 1970.
Shackelford, J. "Tycho Brahe, Laboratory Design, and the Aim of Science: Reading Plans in Context." *Isis* 84 (1993): 211–230.
Thoren, V.E. "Tycho Brahe." In *Planetary Astronomy from the Renaissance to the Rise of Astrophysics, Part A: Tycho Brahe to Newton,* edited by R. Taton and C. Wilson, vol. 2A: 3–21. *The General History of Astronomy*. Cambridge: Cambridge University Press, 1989.
———, with contributions by J.R. Christianson. *The Lord of Uraniborg: A Biography of Tycho Brahe.* Cambridge: Cambridge University Press, 1990.
Wesley, W.G. "The Accuracy of Tycho Brahe's Instruments." *Journal for the History of Astronomy* 9 (1978): 42–53.

Brashear, John Alfred (1840–1920)

American optician and educator. He left school to work in Pittsburgh steel mills, and began to make and sell small telescopes as a hobby. In 1881 he opened an optical shop as a full-time business sponsored by philanthropist William Thaw, and with John McDowell and Charles Hastings he built it into a world-renowned optical company. He acquired wealthy and powerful friends, and later became influential and active in Pittsburgh professional and educational affairs. He was a trustee of the University of Pittsburgh, served for two years as chancellor, and chaired the observatory committee. He headed the Frick educational committee, and served as president of several engineering and arts and science organizations.

Astronomer **Frank Schlesinger** noted that Brashear's company made much of the astronomical equipment in use in the United States. For example, Brashear made a 30-inch refractor for Allegheny Observatory; a 72-inch reflector for Victoria Observatory; spectroheliographs for **George Ellery Hale**; and the Mills spectroscope at **Lick Observatory**. They provided precision equipment, such as bolometers and rock-salt prisms for Samuel Langley, astronomical doublets (photographic objectives) for Maximilian Wolf and **Edward Barnard**, astronomical cameras for Frank L.O.Wadsworth, interferometric components for **A.A. Michelson**, and precision grating blanks for **Henry Rowland**. Brashear personally developed a famous chemical silvering process used for coating reflectors. For many years, Brashear's company provided optical components for Warner and Swasey telescopes.

Louis F. Drummeter Jr.

Bibliography

Brashear, J.A. *John A. Brashear, The Autobiography of a Man who Loved the Stars*. Edited by W. L. Scaife. New York: American Society of Mechanical Engineers, 1924.
Gaul, H.A., and R. Eiseman. *John Alfred Brashear: Scientist and Humanitarian 1840–1920*. Philadelphia: University of Pennsylvania Press, 1940.
Schlesinger, F. "John Alfred Brashear, 1840–1920." *Popular Astronomy* 28 (1920): 372–379.

Brouwer, Dirk (1902–1966)

Dutch/American dynamical astronomer. After receiving a Ph.D. at Leiden in 1922, Brouwer spent a year at the University of California, Berkeley, before settling at Yale. From 1941 to his death he served as chairman of Yale's Department of Astronomy and director of the observatory. He was editor of the *Astronomical Journal* from 1941 to 1958 and co-editor with **G.M. Clemence** to 1965. Brouwer made the Yale department a leading center of dynamical astronomy by attracting outstanding faculty and graduate students at a time when the field was challenged by new requirements from the space program and new opportunities of electronic computation. Brouwer made research contributions to planetary theory, differential correction of orbits, the rotation of the earth, artificial satellite theory, resonance theory, and **astrometry**. *Methods of Celestial Mechanics* by Brouwer and G.M. Clemence remains a standard textbook.

LeRoy E. Doggett

Bibliography

Clemence, G.M. "Dirk Brouwer." *Biographical Memoirs of the National Academy of Sciences* 61 (1970): 69–87.

Brown, Ernest William (1866–1938)

British/American celestial mechanician. Brown joined the mathematics faculty at Haverford College in 1891 after receiving B.A. and M.A. degrees from Cambridge University. He received a D.Sc. from Cambridge in 1897. Brown moved to the mathematics department at Yale in 1907, where he served until retirement in 1932 and subsequently as professor emeritus. He was president of the American Astronomical Society, 1928–1931. Brown's study of the lunar theory, following Hill's methods, incorporated perturbations due to planetary attractions and the departure of the earth and moon from sphericity. His lunar tables became the standard for national ephemerides in 1923. In computerized form, with adjusted parameters, they served until 1984. Brown also studied minor planet orbits and the orbits of Uranus, Neptune, and Pluto.

LeRoy E. Doggett

Bibliography

Schlesinger, F., and D. Brouwer. "Ernest William Brown." *Biographical Memoirs of the National Academy of Sciences* 21 (1939): 243–273.

Burnham, Sherburne Wesley (1838–1921)

American double star astronomer. Burnham, a self-trained amateur, spent only four years of his career (1888–1892) as a professional, on the staff at **Lick Observatory**. The remaining time he supported himself first as a court stenographer and later as clerk of the Federal Circuit Court in Chicago. From 1897 to 1914, however, he was professor of practical astronomy at the **Yerkes Observatory**, making a weekly commute to use its large refractor.

Early in his adult life, Burnham became interested in astronomy, particularly double stars. He devoted his free time to double stars and his discoveries, due to keen eyesight, diligence, and possession of a fine Clark refractor, soon ensured astronomical fame. His efforts showed that the potential for visual double-star discovery had not been exhausted by earlier workers. In time he used nearly all of the great refractors in the United States. By the end of his career, he was credited with discovering more than twelve hundred close pairs, as well as many more wide, faint ones.

Burnham, about 1880, also began a card catalogue listing all discoveries and measures, many of which were his own. This resulted in his elegant *General Catalogue of Double Stars,* which became the standard reference work. For his work, Burnham received many honors, including the Gold Medal of the Royal Astronomical Society (1894) and the Lalande Prize of the French Academy of Sciences (1904).

Charles E. Worley
Charles J. Peterson

Bibliography

Burnham, S.W. "A General Catalogue of 1290 Double Stars Discovered from 1871 to 1899 by S.W. Burnham, Arranged in Order of Right Ascension with All the Micrometrical Measures of Each Pair." *Publications of Yerkes Observatory* 1 (1900).

———. *A General Catalogue of Double Stars Within 121° of the North Pole.* Washington, D.C.: Carnegie Institution of Washington, 1906.

Frost, E.B. "Sherburne Wesley Burnham, 1838–1921." *Astrophysical Journal* 54 (1921): 1–8.

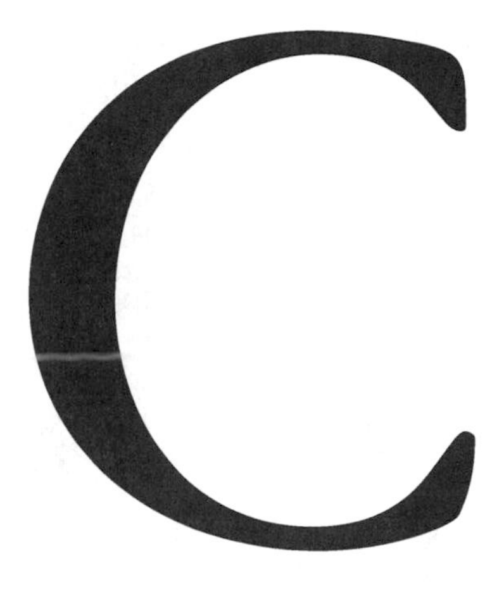

Calendars

A calendar is a system for grouping days to reckon time over extended periods. Division of the day into smaller units is classified as timekeeping. Calendars have provided the basis for agricultural, hunting, and migration activities, for divination and prognostication, and for maintaining cycles of religious and civil events. In addition, calendars satisfy a deep psychological desire to organize and control time.

Although the function of a calendar is social rather than scientific, many calendars replicate astronomical phenomena to a degree that seems to go beyond any practical value. Only a purely observational calendar maintains synchrony with astronomical phenomena. However, an observational calendar exhibits short term uncertainty because the natural phenomena are complex and the observations are subject to error. Furthermore, an observational calendar does not provide secure extrapolation for regulating future activities, and it requires careful record-keeping to maintain an unambiguous chronology.

The principal astronomical cycles are the year, based on the revolution of the earth around the sun, and the month, based on the revolution of the moon around the earth. These cycles are not composed of an integral number of days, and they are neither constant nor perfectly commensurable with each other. As a result calendars that attempt to reconcile these cycles must be correspondingly complex.

The tropical year, defined as the mean interval between vernal equinoxes, corresponds to the cycle of the seasons. Over several millennia, the length of the tropical year is given by

$$365^{d}.24218\ 96698 - 0.00000\ 61535\ 9\ T - 7.29 \times 10^{-10}\ T^{2} + 2.64 \times 10^{-10} T^{3}.$$

where T is measured in centuries from 2000. However, the interval from a particular vernal equinox to the next may vary from this mean by several minutes.

The synodic month, the mean interval between conjunctions of the moon and sun, corresponds to the cycle of lunar phases. It is given by

$$29^{d}.53058\ 88531 + 0.00000\ 02162\ 1\ T - 3.64 \times 10^{-10}\ T^{2}.$$

where again T is measured in centuries from 2000. Any particular phase cycle may vary from the mean by up to seven hours. Twelve synodic months (sometimes called a lunar year) equal approximately 354.4 days; 235 synodic months equal, to within a few hours, nineteen tropical years. The latter relation, known as the Metonic cycle, is used in calendrics and eclipse prediction.

A solar calendar, of which the Gregorian calendar in its civil usage is an example, is designed to maintain synchrony with the tropical year. To do so, a day is periodically intercalated, producing a leap year.

A purely lunar calendar, such as the Islamic calendar, follows the lunar phase cycle without regard for the tropical year. Thus the months of the Islamic calendar systematically shift with respect to the months of the Gregorian calendar.

A third type of calendar, the lunisolar calendar, has a sequence of months based on the lunar phase cycle. Every few years a whole month is intercalated to bring the calendar back in phase with the tropical year. The Hebrew and Chinese calendars are lunisolar calendars, as is the Christian system for dating Easter.

Nonastronomical elements, such as numerical cycles, local environmental observations, or decisions by political authorities also appear in calendars. Although the seven-day week is now a nonastronomical unit, it may originally have had astronomical associations. Seven is the number of wandering stars known to the ancients and is the closest integer to quartering the moon's phase cycle.

The development of the Gregorian calendar illustrates the calendrical interplay of scientific and societal concerns. To understand it we must briefly examine the Hebrew and Julian calendars. Although it now serves as the worldwide standard for communications, the Gregorian calendar was created to satisfy the ceremonial requirements of the Roman Catholic Church. A crucial aspect of the requirements was defined when early Christians decided that their celebration of Easter should be independent of the Hebrew calendar.

In the Gospels, the Resurrection of Christ was stated to occur on the Sabbath following the Passover feast. Passover began at sundown on the fourteenth day of the springtime month of Nisan, which began with the first sighting of the lunar crescent. Christians living by the Julian calendar (a purely solar calendar) of the Roman empire had to determine a lunisolar date on a solar calendar.

The Julian calendar, introduced by Julius Caesar in 46 B.C.E., had normal years of 365 days, with a leap year of 366 days occurring every fourth year. While the resulting average calendar year of 365.25 was understood to be longer than the tropical year, the system had the virtue of simplicity.

The Hebrew calendar of that time began each month with the first sighting of the crescent moon. Since there are approximately 354 days in twelve lunar months, a thirteenth month was occasionally added to ensure that holidays occurred during the appropriate seasons. Decisions concerning when to introduce a thirteenth month were made by a calendar committee. Rules governing intercalation, formerly secret, were generally disseminated in the fourth century C.E., so that Jews, however widely scattered, could maintain a common set of holidays. Rules for intercalation have evolved since then. Today, a year of the formalized Hebrew calendar consists of twelve or thirteen months of twenty-nine or thirty days, with seven intercalary months occurring in nineteen years, to fit the Metonic cycle. Ordinary years have 354, 353, or 355 days, while leap years have 384, 383, or 385 days. The resulting average month is 29.530594 days, and the average calendar year is 365.246822 days.

As Christianity spread, the problem of dating Easter became acute, with a variety of methods being used to calculate the lunar months. In 325 C.E., the Council of Nicea adopted a specific set of rules that served as a standard for the following centuries. March 21 was adopted as the date of the vernal equinox, and the Metonic cycle was used to calculate moon phases. But because the Julian calendar year was too long, Easter gradually drifted from its springtime position and lost its relation with the Jewish Passover.

Realization of this produced a debate, both theological and scientific, over when to celebrate Easter. Although the length of the synodic month was well established, there was uncertainty over the length of the tropical year. The calendar reform commission of Pope Gregory XIII eventually recommended a leap year system consisting of a four-hundred-year cycle with ninety-seven leap years. Leap years would occur every fourth year, except in century years that were not evenly divisible by four-hundred. Thus 1700, 1800, and 1900 are not leap years; 1600 and 2000 are. The resulting average calendar year is 365.2425, a value that is consistent with the ***Alphonsine Tables*** of more than two centuries earlier. In addition, adjustments were made to the tables of moon phases for determining the date of Easter.

The recommendations of the commission were instituted in 1582. Ten days were deleted from the calendar so that October 4, 1582, was followed by October 15, 1582, thereby causing the vernal equinox of 1583 and subsequent years to occur about March 21. Despite the deletion of ten days from the month, the cycle of weekdays was not interrupted.

The new calendar was promulgated through the Roman Catholic world. Protestant states initially rejected, but gradually accepted the Gregorian calendar. The Eastern Orthodox churches rejected the new calendar and continued to use the Julian calendar with traditional lunar tables for calculating Easter. Because the purpose of the Gregorian calendar was to regulate the cycle of Christian holidays, its acceptance in the non-Christian world was initially not at issue. But as international communications developed, the civil rules of the Gregorian calendar were gradually adopted around the world. The process of adoption, however, continued into the early twentieth century.

The desire for calendar reform continues today. Proposals usually address one or more of the following concerns: redistribution of the number of days in months to equalize divisions of the year, synchronization of week days with the days of the months, specification of an initial epoch that does not glorify a particular individual or historical event, more accurate replication of astronomical cycles. Despite many ingenious proposals, the difficulties of successfully instituting a worldwide reform seem daunting.

LeRoy E. Doggett

Bibliography

Bickerman, E.J. *Chronology of the Ancient World.* Ithaca: Cornell University Press, 1968.

"Calendars." In *Explanatory Supplement to the Astronomical Ephemeris and the American Ephemeris and Nautical Almanac*, 3–10, 175–202. London: H.M. Stationery Office, 1961.

Coyne, G.V., M.A. Hoskin, and O. Pedersen. *Gregorian Reform of the Calendar.* Vatican City: Specola Vaticana, 1983.

Doggett, L.E. "Calendars." In *Explanatory Supplement to the Astronomical Almanac*, edited by P.K. Seidelmann, 575–606. Mill Valley, Calif.: University Science Books, 1992.

Spier, A. *The Comprehensive Hebrew Calendar.* New York: Behrman House, 1952.

California Institute of Technology, Astronomy at

Negotiations culminating in 1933 resulted in the International Education Board of the Rockefeller Foundation giving $5.5 million to the California Institute of Technology (Caltech) to construct a 200-inch/5-meter reflecting telescope on Mount Palomar in Southern California. This action made Caltech a leading astronomical center. Twice the diameter of its Mount Wilson predecessor, the 200-inch has been surpassed by twin ten-meter (400-inch) telescopes on Mauna Kea, located on the island of Hawaii and given to Caltech by the William R. Keck Foundation. The first 10-meter telescope went into operation in 1992, the second in 1996. They will be operated by Caltech and the University of California under a joint agreement. Private patronage has kept optical astronomy in Southern California at the forefront of Big Science during the twentieth century.

The Mount Palomar telescope was saved from obsolescence (the fate of many Big Science projects, such as high-energy particle physics accelerators) by its great light gathering power and superb engineering. It has always been cost effective to upgrade the Palomar instrument with new auxiliary equipment. Successive generations of photometers, spectrographs, and cameras have benefited from Cold War research into new photon detectors, especially charge-coupled diodes (CCDs) and infrared arrays. The CCD has largely supplanted photographic plates. These auxiliary instruments depend on computers to handle digitized data. The accessible wavelength range has expanded, providing new windows for ground-based astronomy. The 200-inch is fully scheduled and used by hundreds of astronomers. It remains one of the most important telescopes in the world. Palomar Mountain also has a 1.5-meter Ritchey-Chrétien reflector, and two Schmidt telescopes of 0.7 and 1.9 meters. The big Schmidt is currently photographing the northern sky in three colors; these survey plates will be scanned and digitized, and then made available for worldwide distribution.

In 1904, **George Ellery Hale**, father of the 200-inch, organized the Mount Wilson Observatory of the Carnegie Institution of Washington. Mount Wilson soon had a wide range of important instrumentation: solar tower telescopes as well as a 60-inch/1.5-meter (1908) and 100-inch/2.5 meter (1919) reflector. The Mount Wilson staff helped plan the 200-inch; however, its construction and operation were the responsibility of Caltech. Difficulties in manufacturing and figuring the 200-inch glass disk, as well as World War II, delayed its completion until 1948.

Caltech assumed full responsibility for a research and instructional program in astronomy. But, in the beginning, only **Fritz Zwicky**, professor of physics, was interested in astronomy, while Mount Wilson had a large staff. A joint operating plan provided for reciprocity between Palomar and Mount Wilson staff members and graduate students. This plan ensured that all parties would have access to the telescopes on Mount Wilson and Mount Palomar. This plan remained in effect from 1947 to 1980. The first director of the Palomar Observatory was the Caltech physicist **Ira S. Bowen**.

Caltech hired Jesse L. Greenstein from the Yerkes Observatory of the University of Chicago in 1948. He was charged with organizing graduate instruction in astronomy. Greenstein assembled the professorial and research staffs for the Robinson Astrophysical Laboratory at Caltech. Like Hale, Greenstein was part of a movement of astronomers from the Midwest to California.

Since no endowment accompanied the Rockefeller gift, astronomy at Caltech remains a general-budget item, requiring continuous institutional support. Greenstein's plan for Caltech was outlined in a letter to Dean Ernest C. Watson in 1947. Greenstein perceived the future of graduate education in astronomy as involving atomic, nuclear, and mathematical physics, as well as thermodynamics and theoretical astrophysics. Student research was to be with large telescopes and faculty research would emphasize applications of modern physics. Undergraduate preparation was largely in physics, with introductory courses in astrophysics, astronomical instrumentation, and, later, radio astronomy.

The astronomy program and observatory grew rapidly after World War II with the first appointments coming from the Yerkes staff or Chicago Ph.D.s trained at Yerkes. Among those best suited for faculty positions and to carry out research with the 200-inch were young theorists, just discovering the joys of observational astronomy. Perhaps a discovery made with the 200-inch was more satisfying than a mathematical theory! From its initial professorial staff of two, the Robinson Laboratory became the nucleus of a campus-wide effort. Greenstein served as informal head (a position now filled by the executive officer) from 1948 to 1972, followed by Maarten Schmidt. Schmidt served as division chairman, then director of the Hale Observatories (the combined Mount Palomar and Mount Wilson operations), until the joint operating agreement terminated in 1980. In 1992, the Robinson Laboratory bulletin board pictured twenty-seven graduate students, seventeen faculty, plus twenty-four senior research fellows, professional staff, and visiting scientists. Names of astronomy faculty and research personnel in the 1992 Caltech catalog total forty-eight, but numbers are vague because Caltech's divisional structure blurs affiliations.

The teaching department was rated by the American Council on Education as best in the United States in 1967 and 1971, for quality of its faculty and effectiveness of its graduate education program. One Caltech Ph.D., Robert Wilson, won a Nobel Prize in physics (with his colleague Arno Penzias of the Bell Telephone Laboratories) for discovery of the 3-degree Kelvin background radiation left over from the Big Bang. Mount Wilson spectroscopist Olin C. Wilson received a physics Ph.D. (1937), the first in astronomy before a curriculum existed. Well-known Ph.D.s include Helmut Abt (1952), editor of the *Astrophysical Journal*; Halton C. Arp (1953), a skeptic who doubts the red shift/distance relation; and Allan R. Sandage, who accepts this relationship and calibrates it. Sandage, a leader in observational cosmology, received the Crafoord Prize (1991). The percentage of women in the graduate program remains low; the first female Ph.D.s were Susan E. Kayser (1966) and Virginia L. Trimble (1968). Senior faculty women include Professor Judith G. Cohen (1971) and Senior Research Associate Anneilla I. Sargent (1977). Meaningful statistics on the distribution of Ph.D. thesis topics are difficult to assemble. Individual stars and galaxies were the most frequent targets; optical spectroscopy was the most frequently used technique. But the growth of infrared, centimeter, and submillimeter radio techniques will soon rival work in the optical region. The graduate student population has stabilized at about twenty-five. Over 130 theses are in the Robinson library, and more are in related departmental libraries.

Under a division chairman (Gerry Neugebauer), an executive officer (Anthony Readhead) supervises astronomy (1992). Director Neugebauer and a large resident support and technical staff manage the observatory. Astronomical and astrophysical research is carried out at Mount Palomar by Caltech students and faculty from the astronomy division as well as from the divisions of physics and planetary sciences. Recent contractual arrangements permit astronomers from the Observatories of the Carnegie Institution of Washington and Cornell University to use Palomar telescopes.

Keck Observatory headquarters are at Kamuela, Hawaii, and the director reports to the joint Caltech/University of California board. Over a period of twenty-five years, the University of California's operating support will match Caltech's initial capital contribution, while Caltech increases the number of faculty and research fellows.

Caltech astronomy includes more than telescopes on Palomar Mountain. In addition to the Keck Observatory, there are a number of other facilities. The Owens Valley Radio

Observatory (1958) was a natural follow-on to Palomar, arising from interest in the identification of distant radio sources. It was the first Caltech astronomy facility to be funded by the federal government (at first by the Office of Naval Research, currently by the National Science Foundation). Its first director was John Bolton, an English radar expert on loan from Australia. The Owens Valley operation emphasized variable-spacing, high-resolution interferometry. Starting at decameter and centimeter wavelengths for accurate positions and continuum spectroscopy, it has progressed to submillimeter interferometry, using five variable-spacing 10-meter dishes. Much time has been devoted to the investigation of molecular lines and low-temperature sources such as protostars. A high-precision 10-meter dish operates on Mauna Kea in Hawaii to take advantage of low residual water vapor. Caltech staff are developing ultra-high-frequency detectors and receivers for the Hawaii radio telescope for research dealing with radial velocities and identifications of molecular lines that will link radio and infrared research techniques. The Owens Valley group was a pioneer in Very Long Baseline Interferometry (VLBI), participating in many successful international VLBI experiments under Marshall H. Cohen. The Owens Valley interferometer revealed the giant extended lobes of radio galaxies and quasars. VLBI experiments working at milliarcsecond resolution monitor the apparently faster-than-light motions near the heart of quasars and active galactic nuclei. The Big Bear Solar Observatory was founded by Harold Zirin in 1969, with both foundation and federal support. On a lake, the solar observatory benefits from the excellent daytime seeing. Its staff regularly monitor flares, magnetic fields, and the solar interior, the latter by helioseismology.

But even this review does not encompass all of the astronomical research carried out at Caltech. Theoretical astrophysics and relativity were not emphasized in early planning, but today they receive considerable attention. Under Roger Blandford and Kip Thorne, research in these areas has produced important findings and has been supplemented by the Laser Interferometric Gravitational Observatory (LIGO) headed by Rochus Vogt. Pioneering work in the infrared was undertaken by Caltech physicist Robert B. Leighton, whose Two Micron Infrared Survey was based on Mount Wilson observations. He designed and built the 10-meter dishes used at Owens Valley and on Mauna Kea. Infrared research was continued by Caltech physicists under Neugebauer and became a major area of investigation using the 200-inch, and it became an important factor in the design of the Keck 10-meter telescope. Neugebauer headed the successful Infrared Astronomical Satellite (IRAS) survey (1983). The National Aeronautics and Space Administration established a nearby independent facility where visiting scientists use elaborate computer programs to study IRAS data. Nuclear Astrophysics in the Kellogg Laboratory, under William A. Fowler (Nobel Laureate, 1983), investigates the systematics and cross-sections for reactions between light nuclei. The original goals were energy-producing reaction rates, and predictions of elemental and isotope abundances in stellar environments. Much of current nucleosynthesis theory resulted from work in the Kellogg Laboratory, including abundances predicted after the Big Bang. The Abundance Project (1950–1970) under Greenstein provided stellar spectroscopic data based on observations with the 100-inch and 200-inch telescopes. In the Division of Planetary Sciences, geochemical studies are carried out dealing with the age of the solar system, dating of minerals and meteorites, and anomalous abundance and isotope ratios that are useful for nucleosynthesis theory. This work is directed by Gerald J. Wasserburg, a Crafoord Laureate in 1986. James A. Westphal has been a leader in developing the Wide Field and Planetary Camera for the Hubble Space Telescope and provided important concepts and hardware for auxiliary instrumentation at Palomar.

Caltech's astronomy and astrophysics are truly interdisciplinary, carried out at four remote observing locations, in six campus buildings and by many independent research teams. Caltech scientists have made a large and important contribution to astronomical knowledge.

The Caltech Archives in the Beckmann Institute hold important collections of letters and manuscripts of over one hundred faculty members and are available to scholars with the approval of the Archivist. The papers of George E. Hale are in the Huntington Library. There is also a microfilm edition of the Hale Papers. A Caltech Oral History Project includes many interviews with astronomers and physicists.

Jesse L. Greenstein

Bibliography

Goodstein, J.R. *Millikan's School: A History of the California Institute of Technology.* New York: Norton, 1991.

Greenstein, J.L. "An Astronomical Life." *Annual Reviews of Astronomy and Astrophysics* 22 (1984): 1–35.
Preston, R. *First Light*. New York: Atlantic Monthly Press, 1987.
Sullivan, W.T. III, ed. *The Early Years of Radio Astronomy*. New York: Cambridge Univ. Press,1984.
Woodbury, D.O. *The Glass Giant of Palomar*. New York: Dodd, Mead, 1939.
Wright, H. *Explorer of the Universe: A Biography of George Ellery Hale*. New York: Dutton, 1966.
———. *The Great Palomar Telescope*. London: Faber and Faber, 1953.

Cambridge University, Astronomy at

Astronomy, as a systematically cultivated discipline, came quite late to Cambridge, for not until after 1700, by which time the university was almost five hundred years old, did a distinct tradition in the science emerge. While Nicholas of Lynn, William Holbrook, and others in the fourteenth and fifteenth centuries had calculated tables, the medieval university never developed a mathematical and astronomical community like that which flourished at Oxford.

Renaissance Cambridge did produce mathematicians of distinction, such as the occult geometer John Dee, William Oughtred, and John Bainbridge, though the established scientific contributions of these men took place away from their *alma mater*, and Bainbridge became the first holder of the Savilian Professorship of Astronomy at Oxford in 1619. Cambridge's most intellectually far-reaching astronomer of the pre-Newtonian period was **Jeremiah Horrocks** of Emmanuel College. Leaving Cambridge in 1635 and living in his native Lancashire, Horrocks demonstrated the elliptical shape of the lunar orbit and became the first person to observe a transit of Venus, in 1639. Cambridge University in the seventeenth century, somehow, never developed those bonds of affinity between scientific men that produced bodies like the Royal Society in 1660, and one of the notable characteristics of the university's most celebrated scientist, Isaac Newton, of Trinity College, was his isolation within the immediate academic community, in spite of being Lucasian Professor of Mathematics. Quite apart from Newton's natural secretiveness, even toward his mathematical mentor, Isaac Barrow, there was no body of scientists to which he could relate within the university. Indeed, his work in optics and dynamics was virtually incidental to his presence within the university, while the manuscript of *Principia Mathematica* (1687) first received the imprimatur of the Royal Society of London in 1686, before it had any serious impact upon Cambridge. But Newton's achievement transformed astronomy and related studies in Cambridge, for the acclaim that came in the wake of *Principia* and *Opticks* (1704) led to the establishment of a university tradition in astronomy and mathematics that would extend down to the present day.

Though astronomy was never a curricular subject in its own right within the basic arts degree of Cambridge University (any more than it was at Oxford), the subject did secure an associated status in undergraduate teaching. By 1800, those students who were trained to compete in the Mathematical Tripos Examination encountered problems in dynamics and planetary theory, though no practical or observational acquaintance with astronomy was required.

In 1704, the Plumian Professorship of Astronomy and Experimental Philosophy was endowed in Cambridge. That professorship, which was important in the academic community of astronomy, was to be held by some of the most distinguished figures in the astronomical world over nearly three centuries. Cambridge's other astronomically related chairs include the Lucasian Professorship of Mathematics (founded 1663, and Newton's chair) and the Lowndean Professorship of Astronomy and Geometry.

Eighteenth-century Cambridge saw the creation of several semiprivate astronomical observatories that were owned by colleges, yet which were not corporate university property. An observatory associated with the Plumian professorship was established in Trinity College at the beginning of the eighteenth century, while another was built next door to Trinity, at St. John's College, in 1765. William Ludlam of St. John's College was an assiduous private collector of scientific instruments and precision tools, and his surviving manuscripts provide an invaluable guide to the cost and accuracy-tolerances of eighteenth-century precision devices.

Cambridge did not build a university observatory (as opposed to the semiprivate college observatories) until 1822. Its first effective director (who was also Plumian professor) was **George Biddell Airy**. Between 1828 and 1835, Airy established observing procedures at Cambridge that transformed English practical astronomy and that he extended to the **Royal Observatory, Green-**

wich, after becoming Astronomer Royal in 1835. Airy was also the motivating force behind the building of the 11-inch-aperture Northumberland refracting telescope at Cambridge in 1838, which was used by Airy's successor, James Challis, to search for John Couch Adams's Planet "X" in 1846. Indeed, Adams's calculation of the place of what was to become the planet Neptune, from the perturbations of Uranus, was one of the great triumphs of nineteenth-century Cambridge mathematics, and provided a clear proof of the predictive power of Newtonian gravitation theory. It is unfortunate that Challis's overstretched resources at the Cambridge Observatory led to the visual discovery of Neptune being made in Berlin on the quite separate calculations of **Urbain Jean Joseph Le Verrier** in September 1846. In 1858, however, Adams succeeded to the Lowndean professorship and in 1861, the directorship of the observatory.

Though only residing in the university between 1811 and 1816, and conducting his famous researches into binary stars, nebulae, and the structure of the Milky Way at his private observatories at Slough and the Cape of Good Hope, **John Frederick William Herschel** is always seen as part of the Cambridge astronomical establishment, and of St. John's College in particular.

In the twentieth century, Cambridge became one of the world's foremost centers of astronomical research. Continuing the celestial mechanics work of Newton and Adams, the faculty of mathematics, including later the Department of Applied Mathematics and Theoretical Physics, has produced a succession of internationally distinguished figures, such as George Howard Darwin, Harold Jeffreys, and Stephen William Hawking.

Visual observational astronomy in Cambridge developed with particular emphasis on stellar and solar physics. Fred Hoyle is renowned not only for his original researches into cosmology (and advocacy of the Steady State Theory in 1948) but also as a gifted popularizer: a trait he shared with his Cambridge predecessor Robert Stawell Ball. The university observatory was substantially reequipped after World War II with a 36-inch reflecting telescope, and a 17/24-inch aperture Schmidt camera. In 1967, the Institute of Theoretical Astronomy, with funds from the Wolfson Foundation, was built on the grounds of the university observatories with Fred Hoyle as its director. The separate institutions were combined in 1972 to form the present Institute of Astronomy of the university. Since 1990, the Royal Greenwich Observatory has operated from Cambridge.

Cambridge University's Cavendish Laboratory had begun investigations into radio physics under John Ashworth Ratcliffe in the 1930s, and that work was resumed in 1945. It was with Martin Ryle, Francis Graham-Smith, and others, however, that **radio astronomy** took off in Cambridge, especially after Mullard Ltd. provided their support to create the Mullard Radio Astronomical Observatory in 1956.

Originally using an array of fixed receivers, which were supplemented in the 1960s by the One-Mile and Half-Mile arrays of dishes that operated on railway tracks, the Mullard Radio Observatory began to map the radio universe. The aperture synthesis technique developed by Martin Ryle made it possible not only to detect feeble radio sources, but also to establish their angular positions with great accuracy, so that in some cases it was possible for visual astronomers to identify radio sources photographically. The discovery of pulsars by Susan Jocelyn Bell Burnell and Antony Hewish in 1967 remains one of the outstanding achievements of Cambridge radio astronomy.

Considering Cambridge University's contributions to astronomy, the amount of historiographical discussion has been surprisingly sparse. Richard S. Westfall's biography of Newton, and Gunther Buttmann's of John Herschel, are important biographical studies of two Cambridge astronomers, but Robert Theodore Gunther's *Early Science in Cambridge* still provides the most complete overall history. Frederick John Marrian Stratton's *History of the Cambridge Observatories* provides a major institutional source, while the Institute of Astronomy's *Annual Reports* contain the very recent history. David W. Dewhirst of the Institute of Astronomy is actively engaged in research into Cambridge astronomy in the nineteenth and twentieth centuries. The principal archival holdings are to be found in the Institute of Astronomy Library, and in the Cambridge University Library, which now also houses the records of the Royal Greenwich Observatory.

Allan Chapman

Bibliography

Airy, G.B. *Autobiography.* Edited by W. Airy. Cambridge: Cambridge University Press, 1896.

Buttmann, G. *The Shadow of the Telescope: A Biography of John Herschel.* Translated by

B.E.J. Pagel. New York: Scribner, 1970.

Chapman, A. "Private Research and Public Duty: George Biddell Airy and the Search for Neptune." *Journal for the History of Astronomy* 19 (1988): 121–139.

———. "Jeremiah Horrocks and the Transit of Venus, 1639." In *1991 Yearbook of Astronomy*, edited by Patrick Moore. London: Sidgwick and Jackson, 1990.

———. "An Occupation for an Independent Gentleman: Astronomy in the Life of John Herschel." *Vistas in Astronomy* 36 (1993): 71–116.

Dewhirst, D.W. "The Greenwich-Cambridge Axis." *Vistas in Astronomy* 20 (1976): 109–111.

———. "Mullard Radio Astronomy Observatory." In *Encyclopaedia of Astronomy*, edited by P. Moore. London: Mitchell Beazley, 1988.

Feingold, M. *The Mathematicians' Apprenticeship: Science, Universities and Society in England, 1560–1640*. Cambridge: Cambridge University Press, 1984.

Gunther, R.T. *Early Science in Cambridge*. Oxford: Oxford University Press, 1937.

McLean, A. *Humanism and the Rise of Science in Tudor England*. London: Heinemann, 1972.

Stratton, F.J.M. *The History of the Cambridge Observatories*. Cambridge: Cambridge University Press, 1949.

Westfall, R.S. *Never at Rest. A Biography of Isaac Newton*. New York: Cambridge University Press, 1980.

Campbell, William Wallace (1862–1938)

American stellar and nebular spectroscopist. Born on a farm near Fostoria, Ohio, Campbell graduated from Michigan (1886) and taught at Colorado (1886–1888) and Michigan (1888–1891) before joining the **Lick Observatory** staff in 1891. He became its acting director in 1900, and then its director (1901–1930), during which time he also became president of the University of California (1923–1930). He studied the spectra of hot stars, gaseous nebulae, and especially pioneered in the measurement of stellar radial velocities. He led seven solar eclipse expeditions, culminating in the accurate measurement (with Robert J. Trumpler) of the general relativistic deflection of light in Australia in 1922. Campbell was an outstanding observational astronomer who set the course of the Lick Observatory for years past his own death.

Donald E. Osterbrock

Bibliography

Wright, W.H. "Biographical Memoir of William Wallace Campbell 1862–1938." *Biographical Memoirs of the National Academy of Sciences* 25 (1949): 35–70.

Canadian Astronomy

European astronomy played a part in Canada's exploration from the early seventeenth century. Once permanent settlement by the French began in 1605, astronomy was necessary for navigation and surveying. Jesuit missionaries made observations and recorded native astronomical lore. The need for pilots on the St. Lawrence River required the teaching of astronomy at the Collège de Québec as early as 1666, leading to a professorship of hydrography. The last incumbent, Joseph de Bonnécamps, armed with instruments from France, made observations throughout the colony and planned to erect an observatory in Québec. His plan was forestalled and the college closed after the British conquest of Canada in 1759–1760.

British explorers of the Arctic and Hudson's Bay Company trading areas also relied on astronomy. William Wales and Joseph Dymond traveled to Hudson's Bay to observe the transit of Venus in 1769, simultaneously observed by Capt. James Cook in Newfoundland. Other prominent practitioners during the early British period included Surveyor-General Samuel Holland of Québec and hydrographers Henry W. Bayfield and the Owen brothers, Edward and William.

Apart from astronomical work in relation to boundary surveys, no official interest appeared until the late 1840s. The Toronto Observatory was established in 1840 only to measure terrestrial magnetism. Québec required accurate time for shipping; cooperation between the Royal Greenwich Observatory and the Canadian legislature led to the creation of the Quebec Observatory in 1850, under the superintendency of Edward Ashe, R.N. By 1854, a time ball was installed. Over the next few years, a small network of observatories appeared. In 1855, local subscribers built a small observatory in Kingston; in 1863, an amateur meteorologist in Montreal, Dr. Charles Smallwood, moved his instruments to the campus of McGill University. These observatories were supported by small annual grants from the Canadian parliament.

Time and meteorological observations were their primary interest. When the British North American colonies confederated in 1867, the observatories passed into federal hands. During the 1870s, one more small observatory with a time ball was added in Saint John, New Brunswick, but soon all were drawn together as part of the Canadian Meteorological Service and their astronomical functions receded or disappeared.

Boundary surveys, especially the 49th parallel survey, were under British control but included Canadian participants. By the 1870s, the Dominion of Canada, as part of its survey of its vast, newly incorporated western lands, began to utilize astronomical observations in the field in connection with the telegraph to determine longitudes. In 1890, the Department of the Interior created an Astronomical Branch. Its chief, William F. King, and his assistant, Otto J. Klotz, both veterans of the western survey, pressed for a national observatory. Thanks to an economic boom and surging nationalism, this goal was attained: In 1905, the Dominion Observatory opened in Ottawa.

The observatory provided a time service, undertook geophysical research into seismology, gravity, and geomagnetism, and made meridian telescope observations. With a 15-inch refractor and horizontal solar telescope, **John Stanley Plaskett** and staff inaugurated astrophysical research, primarily spectroscopic binaries and solar rotation. By 1910, with newly designed spectrographs, they reached the limits of the telescope and lobbied for a new instrument. In 1913, the government approved construction of a 72-inch reflector, with optics by Brashear and mechanical parts by Warner and Swasey. The **Dominion Astrophysical Observatory** (DAO), in Victoria, British Columbia, opened in 1918 with Plaskett as director. The telescope was briefly the world's largest.

During the interwar years, the DAO concentrated upon spectroscopic binaries, radial velocities, and spectroscopic parallaxes of early-type stars, galactic dynamics, and the interstellar medium. Plaskett and Joseph A. Pearce were the first to corroborate Jan Hendrick Oort's model of the Milky Way. Carlyle S. Beals investigated **Wolf-Rayet stars**. Robert M. Petrie and others extended these lines after World War II, while Andrew McKellar developed laboratory astrophysics.

In the 1920s and 1930s, the Dominion Observatory continued limited work on solar rotation and variable stars but turned increasingly to geophysics. After Beals became Dominion Astronomer in 1946, staff branched into new areas (meteor impact structures, solar photography) while continuing to improve the time service. Positional astronomy was served by Photographic Zenith Tubes and experiments with a mirror transit instrument. By the late 1950s, Peter M. Millman organized meteor photography with super-Schmidt cameras; between 1966 and 1971, a dozen small automated meteor cameras were installed on the Prairies to locate meteorite falls.

In the university sector, the establishment of the **David Dunlap Observatory** of the University of Toronto in 1935 created a second center of astrophysical work. The 74-inch telescope, with the earliest large pyrex mirror, was similar in design to the DAO instrument and was employed for spectroscopic studies under Reynold K. Young, Frank S. Hogg, and others, and Helen S. Hogg's work on variables in globular clusters.

Postwar astrophysical research at the two major observatories broadened in scope with the advent of new auxiliary equipment and larger staffs. At the same time, large-scale observing programs gave way to individual research projects. By the 1960s, under the leadership of Petrie, astronomers began planning for the 150-inch Queen Elizabeth II telescope, to be located on Mt. Kobau in British Columbia. The planners soon envisaged a Canadian national observatory similar to Kitt Peak. Escalating cost estimates and objections from university-based astronomers who wanted a better site led the government to cancel the project in 1968.

Canadians made pioneering efforts in **radio astronomy**, with the first experiments by Arthur Covington at the National Research Council of Canada (NRC) in Ottawa in 1946. Covington's group concentrated upon detecting and recording solar flux at 10.7 cm. In 1947, he established a daily solar patrol, which has continued to date and provides one of the primary daily measurements of solar activity. His group also devised a series of innovative interferometers for high-resolution studies of the solar disk. Also in 1947, Donald W.R. McKinley and Millman launched optical and radar studies of meteor trails. During the 1950s, and especially during the International Geophysical Year (1957–1958), several groups at the NRC, Defence Research Board, and the University of Saskatchewan investigated upper atmospheric phenomena by radar and radio methods. George Harrower at Queen's University observed scintillation of radio stars, while Donald McRae and collaborators at Toronto's electrical engineering department erected a number of experimental antenna systems at the David Dunlap Observatory in the late 1950s and early 1960s.

In 1956, both the Dominion Observatory and the NRC sought quiet sites for radio observatories. The former opened the Dominion Radio Astrophysical Observatory (DRAO) in Penticton, British Columbia, in 1960 at the same time the latter established the Algonquin Radio Observatory (ARO) in Ontario. The DRAO staff focused on surveys at 21 cm with a 26-meter paraboloid and at low frequency with a fixed array. In the 1970s, work began on an aperture synthesis array that eventually comprised seven antennas. The ARO developed a number of systems for solar and galactic work. A 46-meter antenna for microwave work, similar to that at Parkes, Australia, began operation in 1966 and was employed during the 1970s and 1980s to discover many complex interstellar molecules. In 1967, radio astronomers from the NRC, DRAO, Defence Research Board, and Toronto and Queen's Universities were the first to demonstrate continent-wide Very Long Baseline Interferometry (VLBI) by measuring the size of quasars with the Penticton and Algonquin antennas.

As part of a major overhaul of science machinery in 1970, government astronomy was consolidated. Previously, the Observatories Branch of the Department of Energy, Mines and Resources had operated the two Dominion observatories and the DRAO. With reorganization, the Ottawa observatory was closed, its geophysics staff remaining with the department; all other facilities were amalgamated with the NRC. The national time service was assumed by the NRC physics division. By 1975, all federal astronomy was directed by the NRC's Herzberg Institute of Astrophysics, including the DAO, DRAO, ARO, Shirley Bay solar telescope, meteor stations, and laboratories for spectroscopy and laboratory astrophysics. With the concentration of federal research, major installations evolved from departmental centers to national facilities, open to university researchers.

During this transition, the dream of new optical facilities, dashed in 1968, was achieved by Canada's agreement with France to build and operate a 3.6-meter telescope in Hawaii; the Canada-France-Hawaii Telescope (CHFT) opened in 1979. Located at a superb site, with superior optical and mechanical design, the CFHT quickly emerged as one of the world's finest instruments. The DAO instrumentation group continues to develop improved equipment for it.

Funding cuts accelerated in the 1980s. One result was a shift to cooperative international ventures rather than the construction of new, large facilities in Canada. A plan for a cross-Canada chain of **radio telescopes** for VLBI was one victim of contraction; another was the closure of the Algonquin Radio Observatory, replaced by joint ownership of the James Clerk Maxwell Telescope (JCMT) in Hawaii. More recently, two other cooperative ventures have emerged, one optical, the Gemini new technology telescopes, and one radio, the RADIOASTRON project with Russia.

During the nineteenth century, astronomy was a cultural subject in Canadian universities. Several universities, such as King's, New Brunswick, McGill, Laval, Queen's, Victoria, and Woodstock, maintained small observatories, most of which disappeared in the early twentieth century. No Bachelor's-level degree program in astronomy emerged before Clarence Augustus Chant introduced an astronomy specialty within physics at the University of Toronto in 1904. By 1907, his program included **astrophysics**. Until the years following World War II, most universities offered astronomy courses as options within physics but no degree programs, although Queen's, McGill, and British Columbia graduated a number of physics students who entered astronomy. Toronto was effectively the training center for two generations of graduates. Until 1950, approximately 70 percent of all astronomers who trained and worked in Canada were graduated by Toronto.

Toronto enrolled a handful of Master's students before World War II, but did not introduce a full-scale Ph.D. program until 1947. The Ph.D. was not a common requirement for most astronomical work before 1950, and of those who obtained it (or a physics Ph.D.), 70 percent did so in the United States, at Harvard, Chicago, Princeton, Michigan, or California. Toronto emerged in the 1950s as the primary center for graduate study. During the higher education boom of the 1960s and 1970s, new universities and new astronomy programs appeared at many schools, with Ph.D. programs at Montréal, Laval, Victoria, British Columbia, Alberta, Calgary, Waterloo, Western Ontario, Queen's, and York. Despite the number of institutions providing advanced training, the total enrollment remained modest: By 1980, the total graduate population was approximately 150. The expansion of universities initially absorbed many of the graduates, but opportunities decreased in the 1980s. Most university-based staff were observational astronomers. By the 1970s, interest in theoretical work led to informal summer institutes and, in 1982, a permanent Canadian Institute for Theoretical Astrophysics in Toronto.

With the availability of federal science funds, several universities developed modest research facilities or expanded existing observatories. Given funding limitations and available sites, the largest of these were a 1.2-meter reflector at Western Ontario and a 1.5-meter reflector at the jointly administered Mont-Mégantic Observatory in Québec. Optical astronomers, like their radio counterparts, began observing at high-quality sites overseas. Two Canadian-supported facilities, the University of Toronto's 0.6-meter reflector installed in the 1960s at Las Campanas Observatory in Chile—where Supernova 1987A was discovered—and the Canada-France-Hawaii telescope, have been facilities of choice. The Dominion Astrophysical Observatory, reorganized as a national facility, attracts visiting researchers from across Canada and from elsewhere. Radio astronomers resort to the two federally supported facilities, the DRAO and the JCMT in Hawaii, but are as likely to visit foreign observatories, particularly the Very Large Array in New Mexico.

Astronomical organization took a unique turn in Canada. Amateurs first organized themselves in Toronto in 1867. After a precarious existence, the club reorganized as the Astronomical and Physical Society of Toronto in 1890; by 1907 it was chartered as the Royal Astronomical Society of Canada (RASC). Its leading light for a half-century was Chant, who edited its *Journal* as well as creating its popular *Observer's Handbook* in the same year (1907). Although the RASC began as a Toronto-based, English-language, and mostly amateur organization, it rapidly took on a more national character by adding centers in other cities, beginning with Ottawa. It currently has branches in twenty-two cities, two operating in French. An unusual feature of the RASC has been the union of amateurs with professionals; its journal has published both technical and popular articles from the beginning. In more recent years, the nature of the journal has been widely debated.

Also starting in the 1960s, several Canadian cities and governments built major planetaria and several science centers, such as the Ontario Science Center, the Edmonton Space Sciences Centre, and the National Museum of Science and Technology in Ottawa, with important astronomy exhibits or installations.

Professional organization was more difficult to achieve due to the profession's structure, dispersal, and small size. At the turn of the century, the Royal Society of Canada publications provided a limited outlet for professional papers. Canadians were active in the American Astronomical Society throughout the century and the RASC provided a common meeting place for some. Canada formed its first national committee for the International Astronomical Union (IAU) in 1920. Until the government reorganization in 1970, a federal ministry was the IAU adhering body. This task passed to the NRC, which immediately created for astronomy an associate committee, a structure linking its own scientists with academic or industrial scientists. The National Committee acted as the Associate Committee; at its 1970 meeting, the rapidly growing community recognized the need for a separate professional organization. In 1971, the Canadian Astronomical Society/Société canadienne d'astronomie (CASCA) formed. During the 1960s, the National Committee meetings were, in fact, annual professional conferences in all but name. CASCA took up this activity, as well as acting as a national planning and lobbying organization for astronomy.

Funding of Canadian astronomy has always been the responsibility of the state. Because there is almost no tradition of private philanthropy for science in Canada, few facilities—with the notable exception of the David Dunlap Observatory—owe themselves to nonpublic funding. Parliamentary grants supported the small nineteenth-century observatories. The two dominion observatories were established and operated as divisions of federal departments. Few colleges and universities could provide equipment out of their meager resources. By the twentieth century, private or church-supported higher education essentially disappeared, and research overheads were (and are) supplied by provincial government education grants to institutions.

From the 1920s, the NRC has provided small research grants to individuals in universities. In the postwar era, the NRC became the primary conduit for federal research funds to universities, and those funds expanded considerably. Military-supported research was never a feature of Canadian astronomy. Military research undertaken by the NRC during and immediately after World War II ceased with the establishment of the Defence Research Board in 1947. This organization supported only some small-scale, in-house work in radio astronomy. The embryonic Canadian space agency, with an orientation toward nonmilitary space research, emerged from within the NRC.

With further reorganization in the 1980s, funding responsibilities were severed from the NRC and entrusted to the Natural Science and Engineering Research Council (NSERC). Planning and prioritizing of funding for astronomy became a complex proposition, involving the NRC (operating federal facilities), NSERC (providing funds for university-based researchers and graduate and postdoctoral fellowships), CASCA (where government and university astronomers discussed issues), and government (essentially the Treasury Board). CASCA has emerged as the venue for discussion and as the primary lobbying body.

Richard A. Jarrell

Bibliography

Jarrell, R.A. *The Cold Light of Dawn: A History of Canadian Astronomy*. Toronto: University of Toronto Press, 1988.

Hodgson, J.H. *The Heavens Above and the Earth Beneath: A History of the Dominion Observatories. Part I to 1946.* Ottawa: Geological Survey of Canada, 1989; *Part II to 1970* (1993).

Canals of Mars

From the seventeenth century to the present, astronomers have been able to discern increasingly fine details on the surface of Mars. As early as 1830, Father **Angelo Secchi** found markings in the form of straight lines that he identified as *canali,* or channels. In 1877, a much larger network of these straight lines was discovered by the Italian astronomer **Giovanni Schiaparelli**, who adopted Secchi's terminology. Two years later, Schiaparelli reported on the doubling of the canals. While he refused to speculate publicly about the origin of the *canali*, historians have recently determined that Schiaparelli believed they were the work of intelligent beings.

The systematic exploration of the canals was taken up by an inexperienced amateur, Percival Lowell, who, in collaboration with the Harvard astronomer W.H. Pickering, built the **Lowell Observatory** in Flagstaff, Arizona, in 1894 to take advantage of the good seeing in an elevated desert location. Lowell systematically pursued the observation of the canals over the next twenty-two years, identifying not only those seen by his predecessors but many more. Altogether, he claimed to have documented the existence of over five hundred canals. The discovery of the canal network, in turn, became the basis for an elaborate theory about the existence of intelligent life on a dying planet—a theory that Lowell defended until his death in 1916.

From the beginning, Lowell's claims were challenged by professional astronomers who concerned themselves with two related issues: whether Mars had an atmosphere that would support life and whether the lines Lowell saw through his telescope actually existed on the surface of Mars. By 1909, the preponderance of professional opinion in the astronomical community weighed in against Lowell. Spectroscopic studies revealed that Mars was too dry to support life, while astronomers using large telescopes discovered that the fine lines supposed to represent canals actually dissolved into nonlinear features under greater magnification. Following these revelations, the issue receded from scientific journals and the headlines, only to return during the *Mariner* and *Viking* expeditions in recent years. Their findings have laid to rest the issue of intelligent life on Mars and, along with it, the matter of the canals. Astronomers still hold out some hope that microorganismic life might be found, but even the appearance on Mars of enormous channels that once carried water has not vindicated Lowell's claims about the canals. As it happens, the location of the channels coincides only occasionally with the lines drawn by Lowell on his maps of the planet.

The issue of canals on Mars was linked in complicated ways with the development of modern astronomy. This development involved tensions between old and new techniques as well as between amateur and professional astronomers. Indeed, extraterrestrial life, which the canals were alleged to prove, had been a matter of speculation among scientists and philosophers for centuries. The wildest speculations ended in the mid-nineteenth century. The discovery of the canals of Mars may be regarded as a new chapter in that story.

Lowell wished to put the study of extraterrestrial life on a more scientific basis by using the new techniques available from astrophysics. Through spectroscopy and photography, he believed, it would be possible to accurately determine the composition and features of the Martian surface. Lowell also hoped to ally astronomy with other scientific disciplines including geology and zoology in order to investigate the evolution of planets as worlds. He called this new discipline planetology. Furthermore, by locating the observatory in a remote area where mountains and air

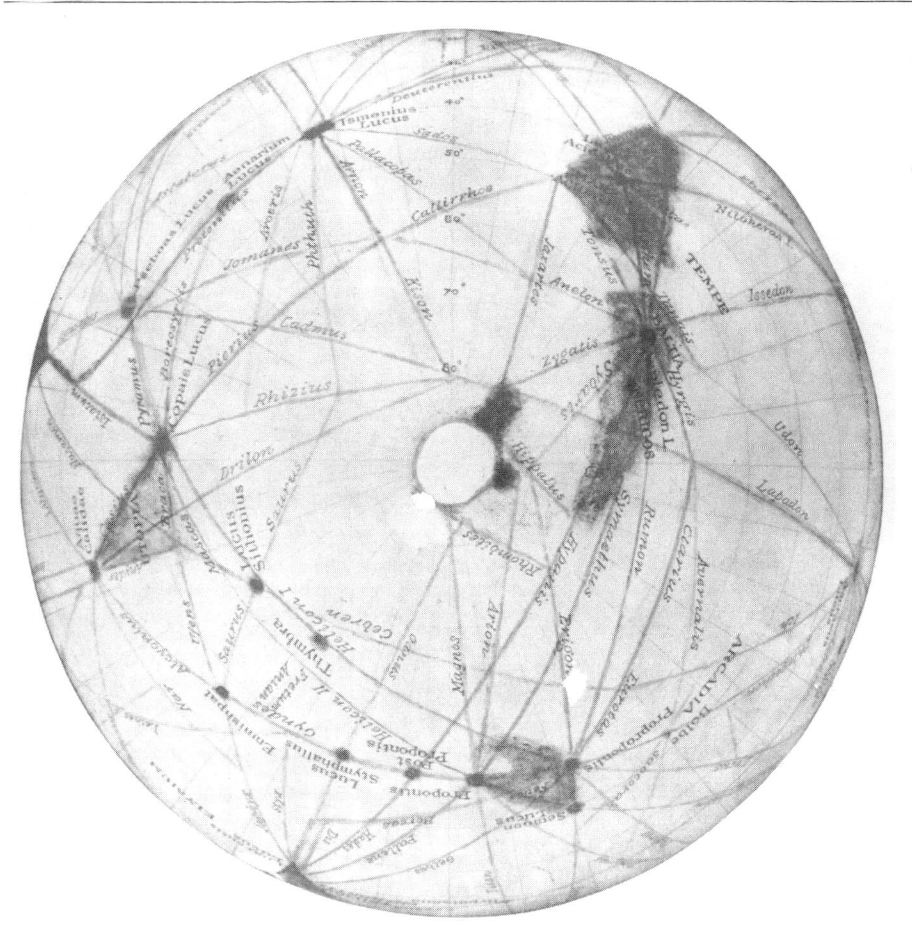

A 1901 drawing of the canals of Mars by Percival Lowell. The north polar cap is in the center of the drawing. Lowell and his followers believed that the canals were the work of intelligent beings. (*Courtesy of* Sky & Telescope)

would collaborate to permit better seeing, Lowell hoped to make the earth's atmosphere a contributing factor in his work. And, even though his observatory was smaller than some university counterparts, the focus on planetary rather than stellar astronomy promised systematic attention to a relatively neglected area.

Despite his receptivity to some modern approaches, Lowell pursued the evidence of canals on Mars in ways that violated the norms of professional astronomers. Even though the 24-inch Clark refractor with which he equipped the observatory was one of the largest and finest of its era, Lowell frequently reduced the aperture of his telescope, claiming, along with British amateurs of the 1880s, that this practice improved the viewing. He systematically resisted evidence that in using larger telescopes, the linear features of the canals dissolved into myriad confusing detail. Lowell also involved several inexperienced amateurs in the campaign to achieve acceptance of his views on Mars.

While the necessity of refuting Lowell's findings diverted a number of astronomers from other research to the canal issue, it could be argued that, in the end, Lowell's work produced several advances. Among them was the testing of the idea that seeing could be improved by locating observatories in areas where atmospheric conditions were favorable. Lowell was also responsible for focusing more attention on planetary astronomy, which, in turn, led to the collection of more data on the surface features and atmospheric conditions of Mars as well as other planets.

Since 1976, historians of science, responding no doubt to the *Viking* and *Mariner* probes, have given considerable attention to Lowell's work. That they have generated less controversy among themselves than Lowell's work did among astronomers of his era has much to do with the conclusive results of the probes, which seem to have settled the issue of the canals and intelligent life once and for all. William Graves Hoyt has offered a sympathetic portrait of Lowell's activities, on the one hand praising him for his energetic pursuit of the canals while on the other acknowledging that Lowell's predisposition toward the canals' existence affected his objectivity. Michael J. Crowe has been a harsher critic, pointing to the way in which Lowell took up a sensational topic and reaped not only criticism but also much attention from the public. William Sheehan has pursued the question of perception in great detail, showing how Lowell arrived at certain conclusions based largely on the small size of his telescope. These three book-length works, which, taken together, provide a comprehensive consideration of the canals, put into perspective an early interdisciplinary approach to the question of extraterrestrial life. Further attention should be given to the research of astronomers who, following Lowell's death in 1916, continued to support his claims regarding life on Mars.

The best source of information on the canals is the Lowell Observatory Archives, which houses the papers of Percival Lowell as well as those of his collaborators, including A.E. Douglass, V.M. Slipher, and C.O. Lampland. Virtually all of these papers are available on microfilm.

David Strauss

Bibliography

Annals of the Lowell Observatory, Vols. I–III. Boston: Houghton, Mifflin, 1898.

Baker, V.R. *The Channels of Mars*. Austin: University of Texas Press, 1982.

Crowe, M.J. *The Extraterrestrial Life Debate, 1750–1900: The Idea of a Plurality of Worlds from Kant to Lowell*. Cambridge: Cambridge University Press, 1986.

Hoyt, W.G. *Lowell and Mars*. Tucson: University of Arizona Press, 1976.

———, ed. *Early Correspondence of the Lowell Observatory, 1894–1916*. Microfilm Edition.

Lowell, P. *Mars*. Boston: Houghton, Mifflin, 1895.

———. *Mars and Its Canals*. Boston: Macmillan, 1906.

Schiaparelli, G.V. *Osservazioni astronomiche e fisiche sull' asse di rotazione e sulla topografia del pianeta Marte*. Roma: Reale Academia dei Lincei, 1878; memoria seconda, Roma, 1881; memoria terza, Roma, 1886.

Sheehan, W. *Planets and Perceptions: Telescopic Views and Interpretations, 1750–1900*. Tucson: University of Arizona Press, 1988.

Cannon, Annie Jump (1863–1941)

American astronomer. Cannon attended Wellesley College in Massachusetts, spent several years at home, and then returned to Massachusetts to work first at Wellesley and then under **Edward C. Pickering** of the **Harvard College Observatory**. At Harvard, Cannon spent her days classifying the spectra shown on photographic plates and her evenings searching for variable stars. She received her M.A. from Wellesley in 1907.

Working with Pickering and **Wilhelmina Fleming,** Cannon devised a system of classifying stellar spectra that is still used, in modified form. She first applied this scheme to stars of the Southern Hemisphere. The Harvard system of spectral classification was adopted as a standard by the International Solar Union in 1913. Between 1918 and 1924, Cannon and her associates published a nine-volume catalogue listing the spectral classification of a quarter of a million stars. Cannon continued her work in stellar classification, as well as her study of variable stars, until shortly before her death.

Cannon received numerous honorary degrees, including the first doctorate of science awarded to a woman by Oxford University. Nonetheless, she received an official appointment from the Harvard Corporation only in 1938 and was never made a member of the Harvard faculty.

Peggy A. Kidwell

Bibliography

Gingerich, O. "Cannon, Annie Jump." In *Dictionary of Scientific Biography*, edited by C.C. Gillispie, vol. 3, 49–50. New York: Scribner, 1971.

Mayall, M.W. "The Candelabrum." *Sky* (1941): 3–5, 14.

Caracol at Chichén Itzá

The Caracol is a two-story circular tower supported by a monumental two-terrace platform at Chichén Itzá, a Maya ceremonial center in northern Yucatán, Mexico. It was first associated with Maya astronomy in 1875 by the pioneer explorer Augustus Le Plongeon, but his motivation for calling the Caracol an observatory remains obscure. By the time Le Plongeon encountered the Caracol, it had fallen into ruin. The upper section of the cylindrical tower looked more like a dome, and it is possible Le Plongeon was inspired by its similarity to the great domes of nineteenth-century observatories.

The Caracol (snail) derives its name from the staircase that winds through the upper tower and mimics the spiral character of a snail shell. The building probably originated as a rectangular platform in the Classic era, be-

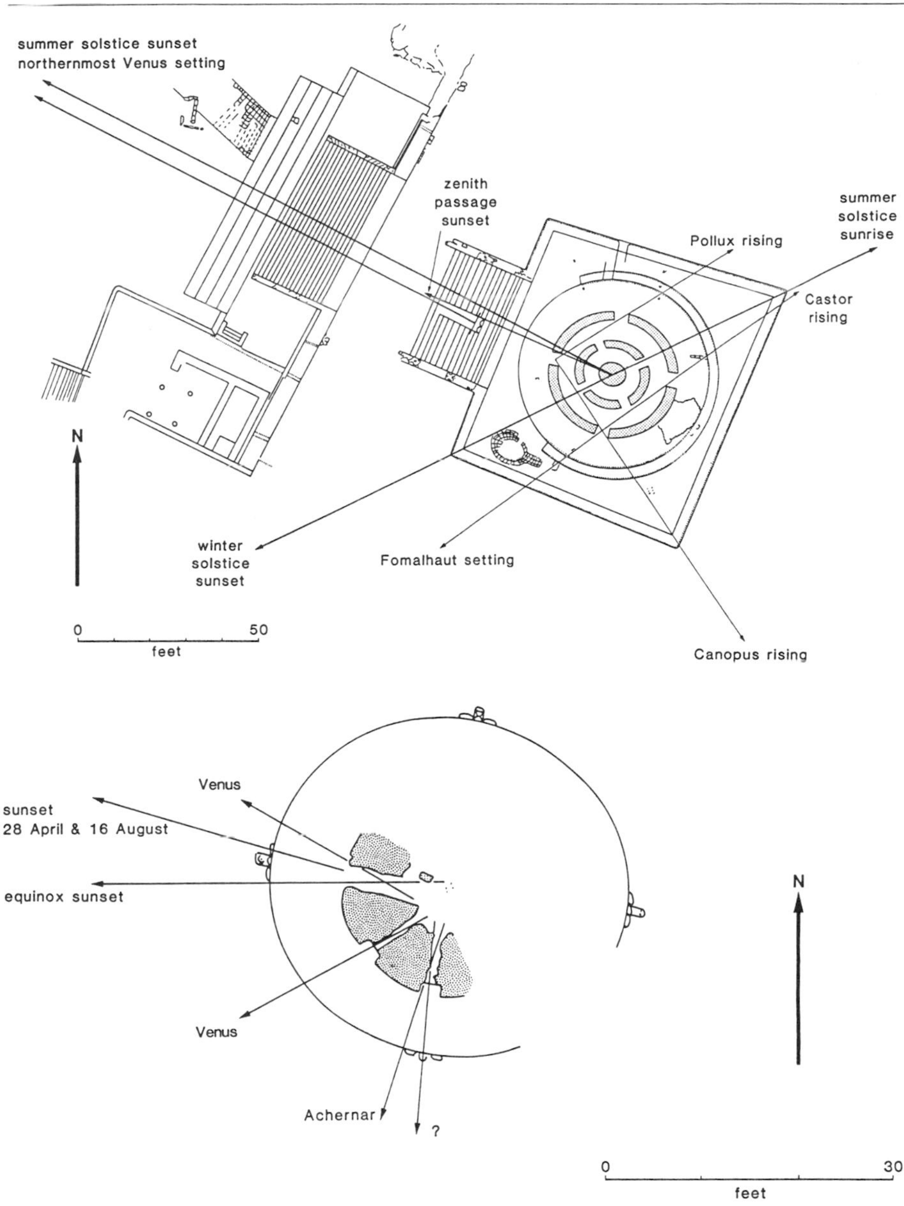

This plan of the platforms and lower tower of the Caracol demonstrates numerous possibilities of astronomical use. The zenith passage sunset line, the northernmost Venus setting, and the solstice diagonal are perhaps the most plausible. (Courtesy of the Griffith Observatory)

Three windows survive with half of the Caracol's upper tower. Several astronomical alignments have been attributed to these apertures. The most persuasive are the lines for the extreme settings of Venus and August 16 sunset. That date in August falls within a few days of the foundation date for the Long Count, the parade of days the Maya judged to have passed since the beginning of the present era of time. (Courtesy of the Griffith Observatory)

tween the seventh and tenth centuries C.E. This platform faces the position of summer solstice sunset, and a platform diagonal falls within 1.5 degrees of summer solstice sunrise. In the Postclassic period, Chichén Itzá fell under the control of Mexicanized Putún Maya, who originated from the Gulf Coast. A sequence of two circular platforms, followed by the construction of the upper platform and the tower, is attributed to the later phase of construction. There are four outer doorways and four inner doorways, offset from the outer entrances, in the lower section of the tower. Three windows, two of them quite small, are preserved on the surviving western half of the upper tower. The eastern portion is destroyed, but it was still present when Alfred P. Maudslay studied the site. He reported the presence of three more tower windows.

In 1925, Oliver Ricketson judged that the function of the upper tower was astronomical. He thought a diagonal sightline across jambs of the larger, western window was targeted on the equinox sunset. He interpreted the other diagonal across the jambs of the western window as an alignment for the northernmost moonset in the moon's 18.61-year cyclical regression of nodes. The southernmost moonset was indicated in his analysis by a diagonal through the southwest window, and the south window's diagonal pointed south.

Karl Ruppert's careful survey of the Caracol in 1930 demonstrated that Ricketson's moon alignments and south-pointing diagonal missed their targets by a degree in the first case and three degrees in the second. Although this work clouded the Caracol's performance as an observatory, prestigious Mayanists like Sylvanus Morley and J. Eric S. Thompson mentioned it in discussions of Maya astronomy.

No serious study of Caracol astronomical alignments was undertaken again until 1975, when Anthony F. Aveni, Sharon Gibbs, and Horst Hartung published a comprehensive review of the structure supported by new field measurements. They showed that some platform and stairway features faced the northernmost setting point of Venus in the era of the building's use and the position of sunset on the days the sun passes through the zenith at the latitude of Chichén Itzá. The southwest-northeast diagonal of the upper platform indicates first gleam of summer solstice sunrise. Alignments with Castor, Pollux, and Fomalhaut are created by some of the door-to-door sightlines through the lower tower, but these appear to have little practical value. The cross-jamb equinox sunset line of the upper tower's western window was confirmed, but the inner corner that forms this line appears to have slipped from its original position. Ricketson's lunar lines were shown to have been impossible, but they agree instead with the northernmost and southernmost settings of Venus. The centerline of the large, western window indicates the position of sunset on April 28 and August 16. The August 16 date suggests that the window might have been intended to frame the setting sun on August 13. That day, or one close to it, was the starting date in the Maya Long Count calendrical system and was associated with the mythical creation of the world in 3113 B.C.E.

Aveni and his collaborators have identified Venus alignments at other Maya sites and emphasized the planet's importance in Mesoamerican ritual, myth, warfare, and sacrifice. The presence of Venus tables in the *Dresden Codex*, a Postclassic divinatory almanac apparently prepared in northern Yucatán, supports the notion that the Maya observed Venus systematically. It may not be possible to prove that astronomical observations were performed at the Caracol, but the Maya had to watch Venus from somewhere. The Caracol's elevated platforms and tower would have lifted a Maya skywatcher above tree-level for a clear view of the flat Yucatán horizon. Whether the building was functional or symbolic, plausible astronomical alignments that would have been meaning-

Superficially, the tower of the Caracol resembles an observatory because it seems to have a dome. In fact, the structure has fallen into ruin. Both upper and lower towers were originally cylindrical. (Courtesy of E.C. Krupp)

ful to the Maya are found within its architecture.

Edwin C. Krupp

Bibliography

Aveni, A.F. *Skywatchers of Ancient Mexico.* Austin: University of Texas Press, 1980.

Aveni, A.F., S.L. Gibbs, and H. Hartung. "The Caracol Tower at Chichén Itzá: An Ancient Astronomical Observatory?" *Science* 188 (1975): 977–985.

Krupp, E.C. *Echoes of the Ancient Skies.* New York: Harper and Row, 1983.

———, ed. *In Search of Ancient Astronomies.* Garden City, N.Y.: Doubleday, 1978.

Carnegie Institution of Washington, Observatories of

American astronomical institution created, funded, and administered by the Carnegie Institution of Washington. It was founded in 1904 as the Mount Wilson Solar Observatory, located on Mount Wilson, California, 5,714 feet /1,742 meters above sea level and eight miles northeast of the city of Pasadena, where the observatories' offices are located.

Upon the formation of the Carnegie Institution of Washington (CIW) in 1902, its trustees began the process of deciding what fields of basic science it should fund with Andrew Carnegie's large endowment and in what manner the money should be disbursed. Eventually deciding to support research through the establishment of a number of special departments in certain scientific fields, the Carnegie trustees agreed to establish an observatory as one of its scientific departments. The observatory they chose to create was the one proposed to them by its Advisory Committee on Astronomy, the Mount Wilson Solar Observatory. The Carnegie trustees officially established the observatory on December 20, 1904, and selected as its director **George Ellery Hale**, the observatory's main proponent.

Hale, director of the **Yerkes Observatory**, had occupied Mount Wilson since 1903 in the hopes that the Carnegie Institution would fund the proposed solar observatory. Hale felt that the Southern California location was an excellent site, with much better skies for astronomical observing than those at Yerkes. Over the next two years, Hale erected first a temporary telescope and then the permanent Snow solar telescope. Hale staffed his observatory with hand-picked associates from Yerkes Observatory, including **Walter Sydney Adams** and George Willis Ritchey. When the Carnegie Institution provided the funding, Hale resigned as the Yerkes Observatory's director and used the foundation he had laid in 1903 as the basis for the new Mount Wilson Solar Observatory.

Hale had a distinct research agenda for the Mount Wilson Solar Observatory. Originally a solar physicist, Hale had become interested in the general problem of stellar evolution. He felt that Mount Wilson could contribute to the solution of this problem by making diverse studies that would contribute to the knowledge of the physical constitution and evolution of stars. As a result, Hale's plan for Mount Wilson was that, instead of being a dedicated solar observatory, it should be an observatory where astronomers could observe the sun, stars, and star systems with the hope of solving the problem of stellar evolution.

The first permanent telescope on Mount Wilson was the horizontal Snow solar telescope that suffered from convection currents caused by ground heating. Because of this, Hale constructed a tower telescope in 1907 that placed the coelostat mirrors 60 feet/18 meters above the ground. For stellar and nebular research, Hale completed a 60-inch /1.5-meter reflecting telescope the following year using a mirror that his father had purchased for him in 1894. Other support structures were also constructed on the mountain: a physical laboratory, power house, battery house, and staff lodging (the Monastery). Since Hale did not want his astronomers and their families living permanently on the mountain, he constructed an office building and instrument shop in the city of Pasadena.

Initial research at Mount Wilson covered a broad range of subjects: direct photography of the sun, spectra of sunspots, stellar spectroscopy, photography of nebulae and clusters, and relations between solar and magnetic phenomena. Hale's discovery of the Zeeman effect in sunspot spectra in 1908 provided the impetus to search for the sun's general magnetic field, and to that end he constructed a 150-foot/45-meter tower telescope. This telescope, completed in 1912, provided greater spectral dispersion than the 60-foot tower telescope, and by 1913 Hale believed, incorrectly, that he had detected the sun's general magnetic field.

With the completion of the 60-inch reflecting telescope, Mount Wilson became the premiere site for stellar spectroscopy. Hale placed his second-in-command, Adams, in charge of this research. Under Adams, research projects included bright star spectra, stellar **radial velocity** measurements, spectroscopic binaries, and variable star spectra. The 60-inch telescope demonstrated the advantage of the reflecting over the refracting telescope as well as the great possibilities for even larger reflectors. A larger telescope was a distinct possibility, for even before the 60-inch telescope had been completed, John D. Hooker gave the observatory enough money to purchase a mirror 100 inches (2.5 meters) in diameter. Hale, however, still needed additional funding to build the telescope mounting and dome. When Andrew Carnegie increased the endowment of the CIW in 1911, Hale was finally given the money, and construction began in earnest. Although delayed by problems in casting the mirror and the diversion of resources due to World War I, the Hooker telescope finally saw first light in November 1917 and began regular observation runs in September 1919. With the presence of the Hooker and 60-inch telescopes on Mount Wilson, the word *Solar* was dropped from the observatory's name.

In addition to constructing new telescopes, Hale took great care in making sure that the observatory was adequately staffed. He made a point of hiring astronomers and physicists who could pursue independent research and could easily meld into the community that made up the observatory staff. The observatory also counted among its staff a cadre of over a dozen computers, almost always women, whose job it was to reduce the observational data provided by the research staff. The Mount Wilson Observatory staff was also supplemented by Research Associates of the Carnegie Institution. These Research Associates were visiting scientists funded separately by the institution and their work was often carried out in connection with one of the institution's departments. The observatory was also regularly visited by astronomers and physicists who would spend a few months collaborating with the observatory staff. With its imposing array of large telescopes and its growing network of scientific collaboration, by 1920 the Mount Wilson Observatory had become one of the leading centers of observational astronomy. The staff shied away from theoretical astronomy, leaving it to their collaborators either from the newly created California Institute of Technology (Caltech) or visiting from other institutions.

In 1923, following many bouts with ill health, Hale resigned as director and was succeeded by Adams. The latter was the logical choice, having taken charge of the observatory during Hale's repeated absences. During Adams's tenure, the observatory staff greatly expanded their research programs in solar, stellar, and nebular astronomy. Perhaps the most significant scientific breakthrough achieved at Mount Wilson was the birth of observational cosmology. In 1923, **Edwin Powell Hubble** discovered Cepheid variable stars in M31, enabling him to determine their distance and show that the spiral nebula was external to the Milky Way. Following up on this research, Hubble, with the assistance of Milton Lasell Humason, was able to show that all distant spiral nebulae were receding from us with a velocity proportional to their distance from the Milky Way (Hubble's law).

Most of the observatory staff were involved in military research during World War II, causing a relative period of scientific dormancy with the exception of work done by Walter Baade, an enemy alien, and a few others. War research at Mount Wilson centered on optical topics, mainly for aerial photography and gun sights.

With the end of World War II, the Mount Wilson Observatory underwent a number of significant changes. In 1946, Adams retired as director and many people assumed that Hubble would succeed him. Instead of Hubble, however, the Carnegie Institution selected a physicist, **Ira Sprague Bowen** of the California Institute of Technology, as director. Bowen, a spectroscopist and protégé of Robert Andrews Millikan, had worked on astronomical problems and had the optical expertise to bring the 200-inch/5-meter Telescope Project to completion. Although the 200-inch telescope was to be owned by Caltech, the actual administration of the instrument, as well as the other telescopes on Palomar Mountain, would devolve upon the staff of the Mount Wilson Observatory. In 1948, therefore, with the dedication of the 200-inch telescope as the Hale Telescope, the observatory changed its name to the Mount Wilson and Palomar Observatories. The observatories also instituted a policy of accepting guest investigators using a selection committee, rather than the informal invitations issued in the past. The observatories' research programs concentrated more and more on stellar and extragalactic research during the 1950s, and the solar observing program waned. In 1959, the observatories curtailed their solar research except for solar magnetic studies.

The 1960s was a decade of expansion for the observatories. Upon Horace Welcome

Babcock's installation as director in 1964, plans got underway for an observatory in the Southern Hemisphere. After site testing, the decision was made in 1968 to construct an observatory on Las Campanas, a mountain in Chile, 8,100 feet/2,469 meters above sea level. The land was obtained the following year and construction began on the 40-inch/1-meter Swope Telescope at the Las Campanas Observatory. In the meantime, with the assistance of funding from the National Science Foundation and the Oscar G. Mayer family, a 60-inch telescope was built on Palomar Mountain and began operation in 1972. Caltech's Big Bear Solar Observatory in Big Bear, California, was dedicated in 1970 and was affiliated with the observatories. And in honor of its first director, the name was changed to the Hale Observatories in 1969.

The construction of a large telescope on Las Campanas began in 1970 after the Hale Observatories received additional funding from Carnegie trustee Crawford Greenewalt and his wife. The 100-inch Irénée DuPont telescope saw first light in 1976 and went into general use the next year. In 1978, a new director, Maarten Schmidt, was named, and shortly thereafter the observatories underwent a dramatic change. The joint operation of the Carnegie and Caltech Observatories, which had been in effect since 1948, was terminated in 1980, mainly due to the complex differences in operating styles between the two institutions. The Palomar and Big Bear Observatories were to be administered completely by Caltech. The Carnegie-owned part of the observatories was renamed the Mount Wilson and Las Campanas Observatories, with George W. Preston as director.

The observatories, continuing the emphasis on stellar and extragalactic astronomy, decided in 1985 to decommission the Hooker telescope and phase out support of the solar telescopes on Mount Wilson. The resources of the observatories were redirected into instrument development for the telescopes at the darker skies of Las Campanas. When Ray J. Weymann became director in 1986, plans were announced for the construction of the 8-meter Magellan Telescope on Las Campanas, to be funded by a consortium originally consisting of the Carnegie Institution, the University of Arizona, and the Johns Hopkins University (the latter withdrew from the project in 1991 and the telescope was scaled down to a 6.5-meter mirror). In 1989, the observatories, under a new director, Leonard Searle, handed over operation of the Mount Wilson Observatory to the private Mount Wilson Institute. With their resources now focused on Las Campanas, the observatories changed their name in 1989 to the Observatories of the Carnegie Institution of Washington.

The Observatories of the Carnegie Institution of Washington were created during a period when wealthy Americans, for various reasons, were willing to patronize basic science research. This period also illustrated the rising prestige of American astronomy. With the advent of the Carnegie Observatories, European astronomers found it more and more necessary to turn to the United States for research and instruction. The Carnegie Observatories remained as the leading center of observational astronomy until the second half of the twentieth century, when governmental funding surpassed that of private research centers. Even with the significance of the Carnegie Observatories, however, no institutional history has ever been written. While the observatories have been well covered in other works, it has always been in the context of specific research activities or scientific biographies. An institutional history of the Carnegie Observatories is necessary, especially to place it in context with the other large observatories of its time.

The archives of the Carnegie Observatories have been placed on permanent deposit at the Huntington Library in Pasadena, California. The Carnegie Observatories Collection consists of the papers of the directors: Hale (except for his personal papers, which are in the Caltech Archives and Yerkes Observatory Archives in Wisconsin), Adams, and Bowen. The papers of some of the astronomers are also in the collection, as well as other miscellaneous items pertaining to the observatories. The Huntington Library also has the Edwin Powell Hubble Collection, which has a great deal of material pertaining to the observatories.

Ronald S. Brashear

Bibliography

Adams, W.S. "Early Days at Mount Wilson [in 2 parts]." *Publications of the Astronomical Society of the Pacific* 59 (1947): 213–231, 285–304.

———. "The Founding of the Mount Wilson Observatory." *Publications of the Astronomical Society of the Pacific* 66 (1954): 267–303.

———. "Early Solar Research at Mount Wilson." *Vistas in Astronomy* 1 (1955): 619–623.

Carnegie Institution of Washington Year Book, Nos. 1–82. Washington, D.C.: Carnegie Institution of Washington, 1903–1983.

Hale, G.E. *Ten Years' Work of a Mountain Observatory*. Washington, D.C.: Carnegie Institution of Washington, 1915.

Osterbrock, D.E. "The Appointment of a Physicist as Director of the Astronomical Center of the World." *Journal for the History of Astronomy* 23 (1992): 155–165.

Smith, R.W. *The Expanding Universe: Astronomy's 'Great Debate,' 1900–1931*. Cambridge: Cambridge University Press, 1982.

Van Helden, A. "Building Large Telescopes." In *Astrophysics and Twentieth-Century Astronomy to 1950: Part 4A*, edited by O. Gingerich, 134–152. Cambridge: Cambridge University Press, 1984.

Wright, H. *Explorer of the Universe: A Biography of George Ellery Hale*. New York: E.P. Dutton, 1966.

Wright, H., J.N. Warnow, and C. Weiner, eds. *The Legacy of George Ellery Hale*. Cambridge: MIT Press, 1972.

Cassini de Thury, César-François (1714–1784)

French geodist and astronomer sometimes referred to as Cassini III. Cassini de Thury was born in France and educated at the family home at the Paris Observatory under the tutelage of his granduncle Giacomo Filippo Maraldi. He became a member of the French Academy of Sciences in 1735 and eventually succeeded his father, Jacques Cassini, as director of the Paris Observatory.

Cassini de Thury at first supported his family's long-held belief in the Cartesian conception of the figure of the earth as a spheroid elongated at the poles. In this regard he assisted (1733–1734) his father in determining the arc of the great circle perpendicular to the meridian of Paris, determined (1735–1736) the two demiperpendiculars to the meridian of Paris, and verified (with Nicolas-Louis de Lacaille in 1739–1740) the meridian of Paris. This work, however, eventually led him to support the Newtonian conception of an earth flattened at the poles.

Cassini de Thury's most important work was in cartography. Using the various geodetic work conducted by academy teams in France between 1733 and 1740 as a foundation, he published (ca. 1746) a new map of France in eighteen sheets on the scale 1:870,000. Subsequently, Cassini de Thury and his collaborators produced a more detailed map in 182 sheets on the scale 1:86,400.

Craig B. Waff

Bibliography

Berthaut, H.M.A. *La carte de France (1750–1898)*, vol. 1, 16–65. Paris, 1898.

Dainville, F. de. "La carte de Cassini et son intérêt geographique." *Bulletin de l'association des géographiques français* 521 (1955): 138–147.

Drapeyron, L. "La vie et les travaux géographiques de Cassini de Thury." *Revue de géographie* 20 (1896): 241–254.

———. "Projet de jonction géodésique entre la France et l'Italie." *Bulletin de l'Union géographique du Nord de la France* 19 (1898): 289–295.

Gallois, L. "L'Académie des sciences et les origines de la carte des Cassini." *Annales de géographie* 18 (1909): 193–204, 289–310.

Sueur-Merlin, A. "Mémoire sur les travaux géographiques de la famille Cassini." *Journal des voyages, découvertes et navigations modernes* 15 (1812): 174–191.

Taton, R. "Cassini de Thury, César-François (Cassini III)." In *Dictionary of Scientific Biography*, edited by C.C. Gillispie, vol. 3, 107–109. New York: Scribner, 1971.

Cassini, Gian Domenico (Jean-Dominique) (1625–1712)

French astronomer and geodist sometimes referred to as Cassini I. Born in Italy, Cassini studied at Vallebone, the Jesuit college in Genoa, and the abbey of San Fructuoso. After receiving an invitation to work in the observatory of the Marquis Cornelio Malvasia, a rich amateur astronomer and senator from Bologna, Cassini studied under the astronomer Giovan Battista Riccioli and physicist Francesco Maria Grimaldi. The senate of Bologna appointed Cassini professor of astronomy at the university in 1650, and after carrying out several technical missions for Bolognese authorities, he was appointed superintendent of fortifications (1663) and inspector for Perugia (1665). His early astronomical work earned Cassini invitations from the French finance minister, Jean Baptiste Colbert, to become (1667) a corresponding member of the French Academy of Sciences and to visit Paris to set up the academy's observatory. Cassini arrived in 1669 and ultimately decided to stay. He became the director of the observatory, a post that he held until his death and that passed on to three generations of his descendants.

One of his first instruments was a large **sundial** of his own design constructed atop the church of San Petronio of Bologna. With it he made numerous observations of the sun concerning the speed of its apparent motion, the obliquity of the ecliptic, and the exact positions of the solstices and the equinoxes; these formed the basis of new tables of the motion of the sun, which he published in 1662. Other observations led to his formulation of the first major theory of atmospheric refraction.

New telescopes of long focal length and good definition, which Cassini began obtaining in 1664 from the Roman lens-makers Giuseppe Campani and Eustachio Divini, enabled him to make detailed observations of the surfaces of the planets **Jupiter**, **Mars**, and **Venus** that led to his determination of their rotation periods (in the first two cases, very close to presently accepted values). He also observed Jupiter's flattening and bands and spots in its atmosphere. Navigators and astronomers used Cassini's tables of the motions of the satellites of Jupiter (1668 and 1693) for many decades; the Dane Olaus Römer used them in 1675 to demonstrate the finite speed of light.

In Paris, using telescopes with focal lengths ranging from seventeen to 136 feet, Cassini continued to concentrate on solar system objects. He discovered the Saturnian satellites Lapetus (1671), Rhea (1672), Tethys (1684), and Dione (1684), and explained the variation of brightness of Lapetus as the result of its always turning the same face toward **Saturn**. He observed a narrow band (Cassini's division) separating the planet's ring into two parts; spectroscopy and the *Voyager* space probes subsequently verified his thesis that the two parts are composed of a large number of particles revolving around the planet. Cassini observed a band in the atmosphere of Saturn and many features on the moon's surface and in 1679 drew a large map of the moon. Observations of the zodiacal light led him to propose the phenomenon was cosmic rather than meteorological, but later observers disproved his theory that it was part of the solar structure.

Simultaneous observations of Mars during the 1672 opposition by Cassini (in Paris) and Jean Richer (in Cayenne) enabled them to determine the planet's parallax and in turn the **solar parallax** with sufficient accuracy to permit for the first time a fairly accurate estimation of the astronomical unit and, in turn, the dimensions of the other planetary orbits.

A major concern of Cassini's was the figure of the earth. When Richer observed that the length of a pendulum with a frequency of once a second was less at Cayenne than at Paris, he (followed by Christiaan Huygens and Isaac Newton) theorized that this difference was due to the flattening of the earth at the poles. Cassini, on the other hand, believing in the sphericity of the earth, suggested temperature differences as the cause. As a means of resolving this dispute, Cassini persuaded (1683) Colbert and King Louis XIV to fund the measurement of an arc of the meridian approximately 8 degrees 30 minutes between the northern and southern borders of France. The results of this project (completed in 1700 after delays caused by the death of Colbert and an inadequate state support) led Cassini to propose a terrestrial spheroid elongated at the poles, a view favored by the Cartesians and defended with great vigor by his son Jacques and initially by his grandson César-François Cassini de Thury.

Although a skillful observer, Cassini was an extremely conservative theorist. He initially believed in a Tychonic planetary system, and apparently later accepted a Copernican system in only a limited way. He also vigorously opposed Newton's theory of universal gravitation.

Craig B. Waff

Bibliography

Cohen, I.B. "G.D. Cassini and the Number of the Planets: An Example of 17th-Century Astro-Numerological Patronage." In *Nature, Experiment, and the Sciences: Essays on Galileo and the History of Science in Honour of Stillman Drake*, edited by T.H. Levere and W.R. Shea, 199–205. Dordrecht: Kluwer Academic, 1990.

Débarbat, S., and C. Wilson. "The Galilean Satellites of Jupiter from Galileo to Cassini, Römer, and Bradley." In *Planetary Astronomy from the Renaissance to the Rise of Astrophysics. Part A. Tycho Brahe to Newton. The General History of Astronomy,* vol. 2A, 144–157. Cambridge: Cambridge University Press, 1989.

Delambre, J.B.J. *Histoire de l'astronomie moderne,* vol. 2, 686–804. Paris, 1821.

Grillot, S. "L'emploi des objectifs italiens à l'Observatoire de Paris à la fin du 17eme siecle." *Nuncius* 2 (1982): 145–155.

Taton, R. "Cassini, Gian Domenico (Jean-Dominique) (Cassini I)." In *Dictionary of Scientific Biography*, edited by C.C. Gillispie, vol. 3, 100–104. New York: Scribner, 1971.

———. "L'Observatoire de Paris à l'époque de Roemer." In *Roemer et la vitesse de la lumière*. Paris: Vron, 1978.

Cassini, Jacques (1677–1756)

French astronomer and geodist sometimes referred to as Cassini II. Born in Paris, Cassini was educated at the Collège Mazarin, where, at the age of fourteen, he defended a thesis on optics under Varignon. The son of Gian Domenico (Jean-Dominique) Cassini, the director of the Paris Observatory, he traveled widely in his youth. The publication of the astronomical observations and geodetic operations that he performed during these trips led to his election to the French Academy of Sciences in 1699. During the next decade, as his father's health declined, he gradually took over the management of the Paris Observatory. He in turn relinquished this post to his son César-François Cassini de Thury a few years before his death.

Like his father and the remaining Cartesians of the early eighteenth century, Cassini firmly believed that the terrestrial spheroid was elongated along the line of the poles, as opposed to the Newtonian view that the earth was flattened at the poles. Measurements of the meridian of Paris to the southern border of France in 1700–1701 (with his father) and to the northern coastal city Dunkerque in 1718 confirmed Cassini's views on this matter, which he described in his book *De la grandeur et de la figure de la terre* (1722).

Newtonians such as John Theóphilus Desaguliers (1725), Pierre-Louis Moreau de Maupertuis (1732), and Giovanni Poleni (1733), however, criticized the Cassini/Cartesian viewpoint. Poleni in particular argued that possible errors of measurement could be as large as the differences established by the Cassinis between the lengths of the different arcs of the meridian, and he suggested that measurements of an arc of latitude between two well established points of longitude be made. Cassini and his son César-François undertook such measurements along the great circle perpendicular to the meridian of Paris, determining the western portion between Saint-Malo and Paris in 1733 and the eastern portion between Paris and Strasbourg in 1734. Once again, Cassini found support for his views in these measurements. The Newtonians, however, disputed this conclusion and persuaded the Academy of Sciences to send out expeditions to Peru (1735–1744) and Lapland (1736–1737) to measure arcs of the meridian at more widely separated points on the globe. After the Lapland expedition (headed by Maupertuis) returned and announced measurements that supported the Newtonian position, Cassini, although still unconvinced, left the defense of his position to his son.

Cassini's astronomical interests were, like his father's, primarily in the solar system. He studied the inclinations of the orbits of the satellites of Jupiter and Saturn, the structure of Saturn's rings, comets, and terrestrial tides. In 1740 he published his *Tables astronomiques du soleil, de la lune, des planètes, des étoiles fixes et des satellites de Jupiter et de Saturne,* as well as an astronomy textbook, *Elements d'astronomie.* During his last few years he assisted his son in the geodetic operations that served as a foundation for a new map of France.

Craig B. Waff

Bibliography

Delambre, J.B.J. *Histoire de l'astronomie au XVIIIe siècle*, 250–275. Paris, 1827.

Taton, R. "Cassini, Jacques (Cassini II)." In *Dictionary of Scientific Biography*, edited by C.C. Gillispie, vol. 3, 104–106. New York: Scribner, 1971.

Cassini, Jean-Dominique (1748–1845)

French geodist and astronomer sometimes referred to as Cassini IV. Born in Paris, Cassini attended the Collège du Plessis in Paris and the Oratorian Collège at Juilly. He subsequently studied under the physicist Nollet, the mathematician Antoine Mauduit, and the astronomers Giovanni Maraldi and Jean-Baptiste Chappe d'Auteroche (whose posthumous *Voyage in Californie pour l'observation du passage de Vénus sur la disque du soliel, le 3 juin 1769* he edited in 1772). Cassini was elected to the French Academy of Sciences in 1770 and formally succeeded his father, César-François Cassini de Thury, as director of the Paris Observatory in 1784.

Cassini headed the testing of the marine chronometer of Pierre Le Roy during an Atlantic cruise in 1768, completed the map of France begun by his father, and participated (with Adrien-Marie Legendre and Pierre-François-André Méchain in 1787) in the geodetic operations joining the Paris and Greenwich meridians.

King Louis XVI agreed in 1784 to Cassini's request that the Paris Observatory be restored and reorganized, but this work was only partially completed at the beginning of the Revolution. Cassini's growing hostility toward the Revolution and to reforms at the observatory led to his resignation as director on September 6, 1793. Although elected to the experimental physics and astronomy sections of the new Academy of Science in 1798 and 1799, Cassini devoted most of the rest of his life to local politics in the area around the family chateau of Thury in the Oise.

Craig B. Waff

Bibliography

Chapin, S.L. "The Vicissitudes of a Scientific Institution: A Decade of Change at the Paris Observatory." *Journal for the History of Astronomy* 21 (1990): 235–274.

Delacour, C. "Le dernier des Cassini." *Mémoires de la Société académique . . . de l'Oise* 2 (1853): 67–92.

Devic, J.F.S. *Histoire de la vie et des travaux scientifiques et littéraires de J.D. Cassini IV*. Clermont, 1851.

Taton, R. "Cassini, Jean-Dominique (Cassini IV)." In *Dictionary of Scientific Biography*, edited by C.C. Gillispie, vol. 3, 106–107. New York: Scribner, 1971.

Widmalm, S. "Accuracy, Rhetoric, and Technology: The Paris-Greenwich Triangulation, 1784–88." In *The Quantifying Spirit in the 18th Century*, edited by T. Frängsmyr et al., 179–206. Berkeley: University of California Press, 1990.

Catalogues, Astronomical

Astronomical catalogues are compilations of observational data relating to positions, brightnesses, motions, spectra, and other characteristics of celestial bodies. One or several types of data may be published in a single catalogue. An essential tool of the astronomer, these catalogues reflect the evolution of astronomical techniques and the progress of astronomy itself, and may themselves be the result of major research programs. Until the seventeenth century, all catalogues were based on naked-eye observations. Subsequently, catalogues were based on refinements of apparatus attached to telescopes. The development of photography, spectroscopy, and photometry in the nineteenth century brought new techniques and new types of catalogue data, as did interferometry, space exploration, and the new astronomies of the twentieth century, yielding information about objects across the entire electromagnetic spectrum. Catalogues should be distinguished from almanacs, which contain predicted positions of celestial bodies, and from celestial charts or atlases, which contain information in graphic form. Sometimes celestial data may be published in both catalogue and atlas form. In this article we concentrate primarily on positional catalogues, which have been the primary type of catalogue for most of the history of astronomy.

Positional Catalogues and Their Derivatives

The earliest extant star catalogues, found in the works of **Ptolemy**, **Tycho Brahe**, and **Johann Hevelius** (as well as several Islamic authors), gave naked-eye positions made with the **armillary sphere**, **quadrant**, or **sextant**, techniques that could give accuracies only to about the minute of arc range at best. Flamsteed was the first to publish a star catalogue using telescopic sights; his *Historia Coelestis* (1725) included three thousand stars and brought positional astronomy firmly into the arcsecond regime. Hundreds of positional catalogues were published in subsequent centuries, with instrumental refinements that brought optical positions to a few hundredths of an arcsecond. Finally, modern techniques of radio interferometry have generated catalogues of selected radio objects with positional accuracies in the milliarcsecond region. At optical wavelengths the *Hipparcos* spacecraft is dedicated to producing milliarcsecond positions of more than 100,000 stars, and ground-based optical interferometry holds the promise of the same accuracy. With the discovery of quasars, a catalogue of objects forming an inertial (nonrotating) reference frame is nearing fruition; the need to tie the optical frame into the radio frame is at present an important problem of star cataloguing.

Three notable developments in the nineteenth century had important implications for all modern star catalogues of position. At mid-century the German astronomer **F.W.A. Argelander** undertook a massive survey, or *Durchmusterung*, of all stars visible to about magnitude 9.5 between declinations +90 and –2 degrees. The resulting *Bonner Durchmusterung* (1859–1862) contains 324,189 stars and is still in use today. Its southern extension, the *Cordoba Durchmusterung*, was not completed to the South Pole until 1930. The second development began with Argelander's proposal to the German Astronomische Gesellschaft for an international program of more precise star positions determined by transit circles; this was subsequently undertaken by some twenty observatories and published as the AGK1 (*Astronomische Gesellschaft Katalog* 1). Largely completed about 1910, it contains some 144,000 stars. A more select *Fundamental Catalog* (FC) of 539 stars was published by Arthur Auwers in 1879; its purpose was to give the best primary reference system possible. The third development was the application of photography to astrometry at the end of the nineteenth century. The largest project to result from this innovation was the Astrographic Catalogue, which contained about 1.5 million objects down to 11th magnitude, measured at an accuracy of about 0.2–0.4 arcsecond, though their equatorial coordinates did not become generally available until the advent of the computer.

Modern star catalogues, rooted in nineteenth century work, are three-tiered in terms of accuracies and numbers of stars catalogued. The primary tier, consisting of compilations to produce a homogeneous system of most accurate star positions available, is represented by the so-called FK5 catalogue (1988), including its faint extension to 9.5 magnitude, containing altogether positions of some five thousand stars, some to a few hundredths of an arcsecond at the time of observation. This catalogue is heir to the series of *Fundamental Catalogues* produced by the Germans since Arthur Auwers's first *Fundamental Catalogue* (FC) in 1879. The secondary tier, known as the International Reference Stars (IRS), is comprised of observations of some forty thousand stars (almost all 7th to 9th magnitude) from the Northern and Southern Hemispheres with positions accurate to about one-tenth of an arcsecond at the epoch of observation. The resulting catalogues, known as the AGK3R and the *Southern Reference Stars* (SRS), are heir to the AGK1 suggested by Argelander, coordinated by the German Astronomische Gesellschaft, and completed for the northern sky only in 1912. The tertiary tier are the photographic catalogs, such as the AGK2 and AGK3 for the Northern Hemisphere, and the *Cape Photographic Catalogue* for the Southern Hemisphere, and the *Yale Catalogue*. The most general compilations of star catalogues include Benjamin Boss's *General Catalogue of 33,342 Stars* (1937), *The Smithsonian Astrophysical Observatory Star Catalog of 258,997 Stars* (1966), the *Astrographic Catalog Reference Stars* (ACRS, containing 325,416 stars), and the German *PPM-Positions and Proper Motions of 181,731 Stars North of -2.5 Degrees Declination* (1989). *The Space Telescope Guide Star Catalogue*, containing some twenty million objects in the 9th to 16th magnitude range, was constructed for the use of the Space Telescope but has much broader applications and lower accuracy. Modern catalogues also exist in the radio, infrared, X-ray, and gamma ray regions of the spectrum.

Catalogues of star positions are important not only in themselves, but also for what can be derived from them—namely, the proper motions of the stars. These are generally also published in the same positional catalogues. Parallaxes are another datum that can be derived from position, but in this case the observations must be specially planned and made roughly six months apart. Following up on the compilation of **Frank Schlesinger** in the 1930s, Louise Jenkins published the *General Catalogue of Trigonometric Stellar Parallaxes* (1952), with 5,822 parallaxes, and its *Supplement* (1963), adding six hundred more. These will soon be superseded by a new catalogue of parallaxes compiled by Yale astronomer William van Altena. Meanwhile the U.S. Naval Observatory has published since 1970 many lists of parallaxes obtained with its 61-inch astrometric reflector, considered the standard in the field.

Catalogues of Specialized Data

The rise of astrophysics in the late nineteenth century brought a new kind of catalogue, one whose primary purpose was not to specify position, but spectral type, related to temperature and composition. **E.C. Pickering** and **A.J. Cannon** at Harvard produced the first great compilation of spectral types, published as the ***Draper Catalogue of Stellar Spectra*** (1918–1924) and the *Henry Draper Extension* (1925–1936 and 1949), together containing more than 350,000 spectra of individual stars. Spectroscopy also gave rise to catalogues of stellar and galactic radial velocities. The rise of photometric methods also generated catalogues of stellar magnitudes of ever-increasing accuracy. Catalogues of special types of stars began to proliferate, most notably double star catalogues including Burnham's *General Catalogue of Double Stars* (1906) and Aitken's *New General Catalogue* (1932). These double star catalogues have been superseded by the World Double Star database, maintained at the U.S. Naval Observatory.

The first well-known catalogue of celestial objects other than stars was **Charles Messier**'s catalogue of diffuse objects (1774, and further supplements), containing about one hundred objects. These objects are now known to range from nebulae within the galaxy to globular clusters surrounding it and other galaxies near and far. The rapid pace of nonstellar observational astronomy is evident in John Herschel's *General Catalogue of Nebulae* (GC, 1864), which contained 5,079 objects. By 1888 J.L.E. Dreyer had compiled his *New General Catalogue of Nebulae and Clusters of Stars,* (NGC) supplemented by the *Index Catalogues* (IC) of 1895 and 1908. Altogether, these catalogued more than thirteen thousand nonstellar objects, providing the NGC and IC designations still prevalent today. Since then numerous other catalogues of galaxies, nebulae, and virtually every astronomical object have appeared, and in many wavelength regimes, as astronomical discovery has accelerated. So great has the amount of astronomical data become that it must take advantage of all the modern advances in computer data-handling and is now coordinated and disseminated from World Data Centers. This includes data from many regions of the electromagnetic spectrum, too numerous to mention here.

Although catalogue work is often routine, it is a first and necessary step toward discovery, and has consumed a significant fraction of astronomical effort. Issues of data gatherers and data users, of comparative techniques of data gathering, and of cataloguing as impetus for international cooperation in astronomy remain issues open to historical research.

Steven J. Dick

Bibliography

Debarbat, S., J.A. Eddy, H.K. Eichhorn, and A.R. Upgren. *Mapping the Sky: Past Heritage and Future Directions.* Dordrecht: Kluwer, 1988.

Lieske, J.H., and V.K. Abalakin, eds. *Inertial Coordinate System on the Sky.* Dordrecht: Kluwer, 1990.

Catholic Church, Astronomy and

In the eyes of anyone acquainted, however vaguely, with astronomy and the Roman Catholic Church, their first major interaction coincides with the rise of modern astronomy in terms of Copernicus's heliocentric theory. Yet the involvement of the Catholic Church in astronomy had long antedated Copernicus. Also, the patronizing by the Church of astronomy during the more than four centuries that had gone by since Copernicus was not at all conditioned by that historic clash between heliocentric theory and the Church.

In its first phase the clash was a most harmonious encounter. Nothing could seem less revolutionary than the gathering in the Vatican gardens that, with Cardinal Schönberg in the lead, listened in the summer of 1534 to **Nicholas Copernicus**, a canon of the faraway cathedral of Frauenburg, about the beauty and advantages of looking at the system of planets as centered on the sun and not on the earth. Nor did Copernicus mean to offer anything revolutionary in the sense of wreaking havoc, a principal meaning of revolutions in modern times.

Copernicus first made a name for himself by his efforts to prevent a financial havoc, a runaway depreciation of the coinage. To establish a lasting harmony between real seasons and the calendar was also a chief aim of his plea in behalf of his heliocentric theory. The latter, both in its geometrical formalism and in its meager recourse to physical considerations (chiefly to the medieval impetus theory), included so many traditional notions as to prompt historian Herbert Butterfield to speak of the conservatism of Copernicus. Originally submitted as the *Narratio prima,* the theory was published in full form under the title *De revolutionibus orbium coelestium.* It stood for that stability that the revolutions of celestial orbs, and especially the sphere of the fixed stars, had symbolized since time immemorial.

Most important, the introductory chapter in Copernicus's book exuded an age-old conviction of Catholic faith in that stability of existence that is on hand as long as existence is fully attributed to a most benevolent and intelligent Creator. Such an attribution is the basis of Catholic creed and had been thematically voiced by Augustine and Thomas Aquinas. Existential stability implied that whatever could be safely known by natural reason about things natural was to serve as a standard of explanation whenever the text of the Bible seemed to imply something to the contrary.

In view of this it is rather academic to settle the question as to what extent Copernicus was a realist. He did not take issue with the idea of astronomical explanation as a mere formalism—namely, that its devices were but so many abstract means to save the phenomena. This nutshell summary of astronomical method, first enunciated by Plato, had been the expression of the mainstream of astronomical research in classical Antiquity. The study of astronomy continued in that spirit during medieval centuries in the Latin West, where the Catholic Church was the sole framework of higher studies through its establishment of a uniform educational system, first through the cathedral and monastery schools and later through the universities. This medieval study of Ptolemaic astronomy received an unsurpassed analysis in Pierre Duhem's two masterpieces. In *To Save the Phenomena*, he set forth the importance that the formalistic approach played during medieval times. In the ten volumes of his *Système du monde,* he set forth, largely from until-then unexplored manuscript sources, the eager study of Ptolemaic astronomy during the four centuries prior to Copernicus.

Nothing was said about Copernicus and heliocentric theory when the Catholic Church made its most tangible contribution to astronomy by implementing the calendar reform. Decreed by the Council of Trent, the reform was worked out by the Jesuit Christopher Clavius and implemented through the energetic action of Pope Gregory XIII in 1582. For the truth was that the heliocentric theory as given by Copernicus did not provide greater accuracy in predicting heavenly motions than the geocentric system of Ptolemy. During the sixteenth century, only one astronomer, Thomas Digges, endorsed the Copernican system, though without giving any hint about the solution of the physical problems it created. The relatively few who referred to Copernicus found it so wanting in demonstrative strength as to decry it as absurd and ridiculous. Among these were such progressive thinkers as Jean Bodin, hardly a devotee of Christian and Catholic orthodoxy.

As to Giordano Bruno, he advocated Copernicus's theory only insofar as it discredited geocentric stability, but opposed it insofar as it replaced geocentric stability with heliocentric ordering. Bruno, in fact, harangued against that meager measure of stability that is the distinction between planets and stars. Bruno was a forerunner of those who called in science, or religion, or politics, for revolutions as a means of promoting change for change's sake. The endless changes championed in Karl Popper's and especially in Alfred North Whitehead's cosmologies had been fully anticipated in the cosmology of Bruno, an unabashed pantheist.

This is still to be pondered by those who decry Bruno's fate in the hands of the papacy. They should also realize that without papal authority there would have been no chance at that time, and for many years afterwards, for that most needed calendar reform. Until as late as the mid-1750s, Protestant countries resisted the new calendar, a marvel in accuracy and reliability. They did so for the simple reason that it was a popish innovation. Such Protestant luminaries of the new Copernican astronomy as **Kepler**, Huygens, **Horrocks**, Newton, **Halley**, Gregory, and **Flamsteed** did not go out on a limb to oppose that bigoted attitude.

With the exception of a few individuals, such as Maestlin and Kepler, Protestantism was still to come forth with its championing of Copernicanism when the Catholic Church came into a notorious conflict with it. What started as a harmony turned into a conflict, owing to a mistaken strategy into which Protestantism lured the Catholic Church. Since the Reformers replaced the teaching authority of the hierarchy with the authority of the Bible, it seemed to many counterreformers, especially to leading Jesuit theologians, that nothing could be more effective in vanquishing the Reformers than to meet them on their own chosen battlefield, a tactic never recommended by experts in military art.

In practice, the tactic could amount to removing from focus the priority of Church authority over the Bible insofar as the latter did not claim to decide the question of which books were inspired or not. At the minimum the tactic imposed the duty not to give any further pretext to Protestants that the Catholic Church readily departed from the Bible. Such a duty seemed to be threatened when **Galileo** began his crusade, shortly after his telescopic discoveries, in behalf of the Copernican system. His crusade had all the ingredients of crusades, invariably a baffling mixture. He failed to realize that he had contradicted the first three books of his great *Dialogues on the Two Chief World Systems* when in its fourth book he proposed the tides as an experimental proof of the earth's twofold motions. Worse, it became immediately clear that the proof was wrong. In formulating the proof, Galileo confused two coordinate systems: one with the earth, the other with the sun in its center.

The other parties were no less free from involvement in contradictions. One of those parties, the Protestant, had already too many voices, though, with respect to the Galileo case, it spoke in fairly one tone and took one approach. The tone, insofar as it touched upon the Catholic Church's handling of Galileo, is best left aside. The approach was a classic in dissimulation. Protestants hardly ever recall that it became Luther's privilege to call, for the first time, Copernicus a fool as one who had brazenly departed from truths imparted by biblical revelation. They are equally taciturn about Melanchthon, the first to denounce in print Copernicus as foolhardy. Melanchthon did so in his *Elementa doctrinae physicae,* which for many years served as the primary textbook of science instruction in Lutheran schools. The approach of Milton was both notable and typical. He took Galileo's side inasmuch as this promoted his virulent anti-Catholicism, but did not champion Galileo to the extent of parting with the biblically revealed truth of the stability of the earth. About the same time, the famed Protestant biblical scholar John Lightfoot endorsed that truth with all the parade of a literalist exegesis.

Catholics still have to learn, by and large, that the only comfort they can take from the Galileo case is that papal infallibility escaped, as if by a hair's breadth, from being involved in the stance taken against heliocentrism and Galileo in 1616. Not the pope but the Holy Office made the following two doctrinal declarations: (1) to take the sun for the immovable center of the world was "absurd, philosophically false, and formally heretical, because it is expressly contrary to the Holy Scripture"; (2) to remove the earth from the center of the world by attributing to it local as well as diurnal motion was "absurd, philosophically false, and, theologically considered, at least erroneous in faith." Galileo himself was enjoined not to teach the heliocentric theory. For teaching that theory in his *Dialogue on the Two Chief World Systems,* published in 1632, Galileo was sentenced to house arrest and had to abjure the theory.

Tellingly, none of the prominent Ptolemaists of the 1630s and 1640s, with Riccioli in the van, referred to Galileo's condemnations as being the official, irrevocable Catholic teaching. At worst, it was a teaching enforceable in the Papal States and other strictly Catholic countries. Freedom in Protestant countries to voice the Copernican truth did not make one immune, at least for another generation, from theological denunciations. Between the two condemnations of Galileo, an Anglican convocation in Oxford in 1622 denounced Copernicus's doctrine in a tone compared to which the strictures of the Holy Office should seem conciliatory. It took an enlightened Protestant, Leibniz, to muster courage and warn his correligionists that Galileo's condemnation did not imply an official (and therefore irrevocable) teaching on the part of the Catholic Church.

The doctrinal declarations of the Holy Office were suspended by Benedict XIV in 1754 and repealed, in full consistory, by Pius VII in 1818. Six years later Galileo's *Dialogues* as well as Copernicus's great work were removed from the Index of prohibited works. For the sentences against Galileo the papacy offered a noble apology when John Paul II addressed, on October 31, 1992, the Pontifical Academy of Sciences and set forth the conclusions of a high-ranking committee, set up in 1980 to reexamine the Galileo case. Catholics would, of course, wrongly expect that the Protestant world, let alone the secularistically scientific world, would now cease casting science and the Catholic Church at loggerheads by further insisting on the Galileo case. While, as Cardinal John Henry Newman said, it is a "one-stock argument," many will eagerly keep it in stock.

Catholics (and Christians for that matter) cannot ponder long and hard enough the truth of a dictum born in the decade preceding the start of Galileo's heliocentric crusade. Galileo himself quoted that dictum in defense of his crusade, which had its first high water mark when, following his first condemnation in 1616, he wrote, and let it circulate in manuscript, his *Letter to Grand Duchess Cristina.* It contains the phrase, formulated by Cardinal Baronius, possibly under the influence of his reading of Augustine's commentaries on Genesis, that the Bible teaches man not about how the heavens go but how to go to Heaven.

The phrase may help cast in proper light the relation between the Catholic Church and astronomy (or science, for that matter). Ever since its growing robust in the seventeenth century, science has been gaining an increasingly prominent place in cultural esteem. The place is now not only prominent but overweening. It has indeed become a fashion to appreciate other cultural factors only inasmuch as they serve and promote science. To do this in respect to the Catholic Church would be to cast it in a light in which it never was its official intention to appear.

The readiness of Catholics to gain respect in an increasingly scientific culture by references to scientific achievements of Catholics should be seen in this light. There are, of course, a great many Catholics who can be invoked as prominent in science or in the science of astronomy in particular. **Giuseppe Piazzi**, the discoverer of the first asteroid,

Angelo Secchi, the famed investigator of the sun, George Lemaître, the first to submit the idea of an expanding universe and of a Big Bang, were not only Catholics, but priests as well. Among practicing lay Catholics who were prominent in astronomy (Laplace and many others who were, at least during much of their lives though not in their last hours, nominal Catholics, may be left aside) were **Joseph Fraunhofer**, the pioneer of stellar spectroscopy, and **Urbain Jean Joseph Le Verrier**, the discoverer of Neptune. Among the living are Hermann Brück, retired Astronomer Royal of Scotland, and the cosmologist Charles Misner of the University of Maryland.

If the distinction between practicing and nominal is kept in mind, the list with which Protestants and Jews might come up would not include Newton and Einstein, to mention only two. Long would be the list composed of prominent astronomers who belong to the church of agnostics and of pantheists. Even the church of atheists could claim some prominent astronomers. An incautious reference to prominent Catholic astronomers may indeed turn into an unintended tool of demonstrating the truth of any non-Catholic and non-Christian ideology.

Caution serves one well even when the subject is not the relation of individual Catholics but of the official Catholic Church to astronomy. The word *official* is particularly appropriate, because, unlike other Christian churches, to say nothing of other major religions, the Catholic Church alone has an official, clearly identifiable voice. This voice is very distinct, at times very different, from the voice of this or that prominent Catholic writer or thinker, or this or that opinion popular among Catholics. Thus while many Catholics, even some eminent ones, thought that the antipodes were impossible, the Church never endorsed that impossibility. Much less did the Church endorse the flatness of the earth, various aspects of Aristotelian cosmology, such as the incorruptibility of superlunary material, or the existence of the sphere of the fixed stars.

The official teaching of the Catholic Church has always been faithful to the dictum that its duty was to teach how to go to Heaven and not to enlighten mankind about how the heavens go or about other matters astronomical and scientific. The official teaching of the Church has, however, an important, though indirect rapport (and contribution) to astronomy in particular and science in general. The very foundation of that official teaching is the doctrine that all visible and invisible entities owe their existence to a strictly creative and free act (performed in time) of a personal God whose creation has to be fully coherent. Such a view, wholly alien to pagan Greek philosophy, provided, in the long run, Western Christendom with crucial insights for the fortunes of physical science, astronomy included.

One such insight was the medieval impetus theory of motion, formulated by John Buridan at the Sorbonne around 1330. From there it quickly spread to all European universities. Copernicus learned about it while a student at the University of Cracow and later used it as the chief answer to the physical problems of the earth's twofold motions. Buridan's insight also made ultimately possible the formulation of the first of Newton's three laws, long antedating Newton. Another insight was the recognition that all bodies were of the same nature, which found its crowning in the connection made by Newton between the fall of the moon and of an apple.

It is the same doctrine of the creation of all and in time (which means that the past history of the universe is strictly finite) that stands in the way of most unscientific efforts very much in vogue nowadays. One is to prove scientifically the eternity of the universe, as if such a proof would not require an experiment going on for eternity. The other is to trace the existence of the universe to a so-called quantum-creation, to say nothing of the self-contradictory idea of multiple universes. Such universes are either in interaction (and in this case they form one universe) or not. In the latter case they are mutually unknowable to one another and therefore cannot be the subject of scientific considerations.

A further consequence of that official teaching is the doctrine that the investigation of the natural realm is a religious, nay sacred duty, although always subordinate to one's obligation to seek eternal salvation. Thus the Church implemented that duty, in modern times, by tackling the very difficult task of founding Catholic universities with various science departments. About astronomy proper, the Catholic Church notably promoted it by the activities of the Vatican Observatory.

Established in 1888 in the Vatican, the observatory served as a successor to the astronomical instruments of the Collegio Romano (the Jesuit University in Rome), duly expropriated by Garibaldi's troops in 1870. In its relocation in the Vatican's Leonine Tower, the observatory had for its chief task to contribute to the international *Carte du Ciel* project.

Deterioration of atmospheric conditions in a metropolis like Rome made imperative the move in the 1930s to the Papal Summer Residence in Castelgandolfo, right above Lake Albano. There research included the spectroscopic investigation of the chemical constitution of stars and astrometry, through the installment of a Schmidt telescope that began its operation in 1962. At that time the instruments of the Astrophysical Laboratory included a Jarrell-Ash spectrograph, a G-80 spectrograph, and a large grating spectrograph. A most interesting work of the earlier years was the investigation of the green flash, visible in clear atmospheric conditions around the sun's crescent at sunset and sunrise. The work, largely done by the papal astronomer Father Daniel O'Connell between 1954 and 1957, was published in a splendidly illustrated volume, *The Green Flash and Other Low Sun Phenomena,* in 1958.

The deterioration of atmospheric conditions during the postwar expansion of greater Rome soon hindered astronomical observations at Castelgandolfo. Several alternatives had to be considered. One plan was the transportation of the Schmidt telescope either to Sardinia or to the Canary Islands. Another was to reestablish the observatory in the Andes in Chile. Both plans would have been prohibitively costly. The fact that the Rev. George W. Coyne, S.J., papal astronomer since 1978, directed in the late 1960s the Catalina Observatory of the University of Arizona, Tucson, was instrumental in moving part of the staff of the observatory to Tucson. The Vatican Observatory thus became part of the great astronomical research establishments at the University of Arizona in Tucson and in the high mountains surrounding. The Vatican Advanced Technology Telescope will be inaugurated in the near future on the top of Mount Graham northeast of Tucson.

The Catholic Church also promotes astronomy by study weeks, held under the auspices of the Pontifical Academy of Sciences. Papers and discussions are frequently published. Among the recipients of the Pius XI Gold Medal for astronomical research are Allan Sandage and Martin Rees.

Stanley L. Jaki

Bibliography

Butterfield, H. *The Origins of Modern Science 1300–1800.* London: G Bell and Sons, 1957.

Coyne, G.V., M.A. Hoskin, and O. Peterson, eds. *Gregorian Reform of the Calendar: Proceedings of the Vatican Conference to Commemorate Its 400th Anniversary, 1582–1982.* Città del Vaticano: Pontificia Academia Scientiarum, Specola Vaticana, 1983.

Drake, S., ed. and trans. *Discoveries and Opinions of Galileo.* New York: Doubleday, 1957.

Duhem, P. *Le système du monde histoire des doctrines consologiques de Platon a Copernic.* 10 vols. Paris: A. Hermann, 1913–1959.

———. *To Save the Phenomena.* Chicago: University of Chicago Press, 1969.

Jaki, S. *Genesis 1 through the Ages.* London: St. Thomas More Press, 1992.

———. *Is There a Universe?* New York: Wethersfield Institute, 1993.

Maffeo, S. *In the Service of Nine Popes: A Hundred Years of the Vatican Observatory.* Translated by G.V. Coyne. Vatican City: Pontifical Academy of Sciences and Specola Vaticana, 1991.

Shea, W.R. *Galileo's Intellectual Revolution: The Middle Period, 1610–1632.* New York: Science History Publications, 1972.

Celestial Mechanics

Celestial mechanics, a term introduced by **Pierre-Simon Laplace** at the end of the eighteenth century, is the science that analyzes the behavior of celestial bodies interacting under the force of gravitation. The history of celestial mechanics begins with the theory of gravitation and laws of motion that Isaac Newton presented in the *Philosophiae Naturalis Principia Mathematica* (1687). Until the rise of astrophysics, celestial mechanics was the theoretical side of astronomy, engaging the principal astronomers of the eighteenth and nineteenth centuries. Although it suffered a period of decline coinciding with the rise of astrophysics, celestial mechanics has enjoyed a remarkable renascence since the 1950s, providing basic data needed for space research and new insights into the behavior of planetary and stellar systems.

Celestial mechanics has also played an important role in the history of mathematics, requiring and inspiring the development of increasingly powerful mathematical tools. From Leonhard Euler to George D. Birkhoff, mathematicians regarded celestial mechanics as an especially interesting area for research. Through the early twentieth century, astronomy and mathematics were closely linked in university curricula, with celestial mechanics serving as the common denominator.

In the *Principia*, Newton demonstrated that the laws that determine motion near the earth are the same as those that govern the motions of the planets. He showed that Johannes Kepler's laws of planetary motion were consistent with a very large point mass (the sun) and a very small point mass (a planet) acting under universal gravitation. Newton demonstrated that uniform spherical masses can be treated as point masses. He determined the mass of Jupiter by applying Kepler's laws (modified to include the masses of the bodies as parameters) to the Galilean satellites. He recognized that planets (particularly **Jupiter** and **Saturn**) must perturb each other's motions, though he could not determine the long-term effects on their orbits. He explained the cause of precession, though his analysis was flawed. He explained the known anomalies in the moon's motion as being caused by solar perturbations, though his analysis was not completely successful. He stated that comets must travel in conic sections (probably ellipses of high eccentricity) and developed a graphical method for deriving a parabolic orbit from a set of three observations.

Yet, despite these amazing accomplishments, celestial mechanics could not develop without major innovations in both mathematical theory and astronomical observation. On the theoretical side, the mathematical methods of the *Principia* stifled progress for half a century. Newton presented and explored his laws through geometrical methods because he could not write them in the form of differential equations and, had he done so, lacked the mathematical tools to solve them.

On the observational side, the planetary perturbations that Newton posited were not observable because the determination of planetary positions was not sufficiently precise to reveal such small quantities. Then James Bradley made major observational breakthroughs with the discoveries of aberration (1729) and nutation (1737). When these effects were removed from observations, planetary positions could be determined with enough accuracy to reveal the effects of planetary perturbations.

Theoretical breakthroughs came from the Continent, where mathematicians were not tied to Newton's mathematical tools and system of notation. In England, Newtonian analysis was laboriously carried out by applying limiting ratios of infinitesimals in a geometrical analysis. The notation of Gottfried Leibniz, with an explicit symbol for the independent variable, was more promising. Even so, progress in analyzing perturbations was slow.

Laying the Foundation

Celestial mechanics began to develop rapidly in the middle of the eighteenth century. By 1739, **Leonhard Euler** had developed the concept of trigonometric functions and shown how they could be used in calculus. Eight years later, Euler, **Alexis-Claude Clairaut**, and Jean d'Alembert independently wrote Newton's laws of motion in the form of differential equations. These methods were applied to resolving two observational anomalies that challenged Newton's laws: an acceleration in the moon's longitude, discovered by **Edmond Halley** in 1693; and gradual changes in the mean motions of Jupiter and Saturn, which Kepler noticed in comparing ancient and modern observations. Prizes for the solution of these problems were offered by the academies of Paris, Berlin, and St. Petersburg.

The differential equations of motion for two bodies acting under Newton's laws can be integrated to produce formulas that give the positions of the bodies for all time. This is not true for three or more bodies. However, since the planets follow paths that approximate two-body motion, Euler successfully replaced factors in the equations by infinite series of sine/cosine terms. A finite number of these terms were then integrated term by term to provide an approximate solution of the differential equations. The resulting formulas, called a planetary (or satellite) theory, can be evaluated for specific times to calculate an ephemeris of the body.

Because of the moon's importance for finding geographic longitude, there were immediate attempts to develop a lunar theory. Newton's work on the moon, a combination of geometric derivation of perturbations and empirical adjustment of **Jeremiah Horrocks**'s elliptical parameters, failed, particularly in representing the motion of apogee. Clairaut's solution of the apogee problem in 1748 was an early victory of Newtonian theory and Eulerian analysis. By 1753, Tobias Mayer developed tables for the moon's motion that were accurate to one minute of arc.

A distinction should be noted between a planetary (or satellite) theory and tables. A theory is a set of trigonometric series that give the position as a function of time. Because of the difficulty in evaluating the trigonometric functions, much effort was spent recasting the theory into a form that merely required standard arithmetic operations. A successful

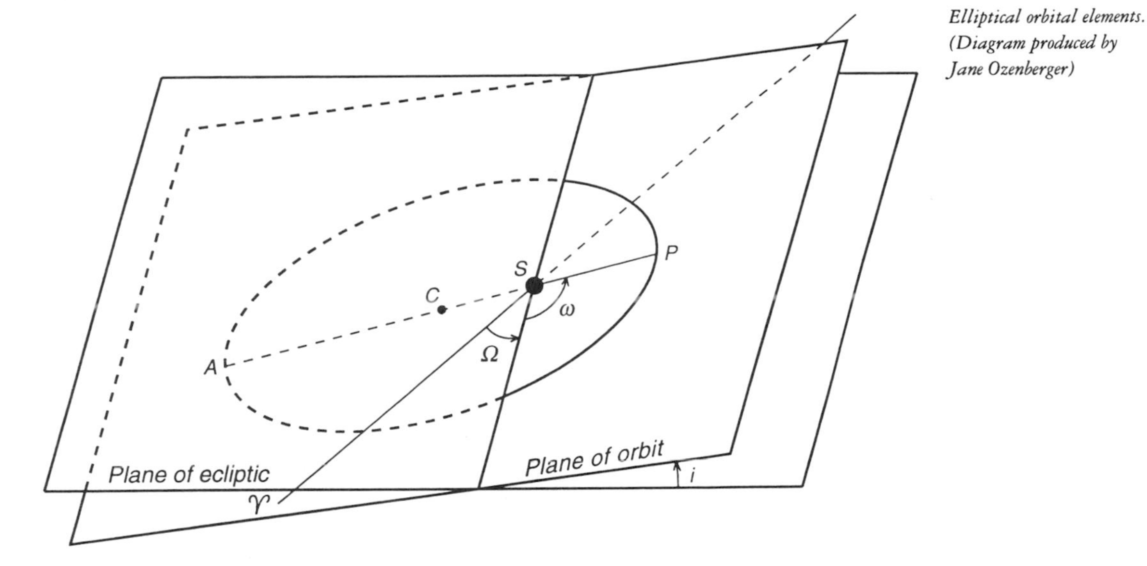

Elliptical orbital elements. (Diagram produced by Jane Ozenberger)

S: The Sun
C: Center of the Orbit
P: Perihelion Point
♈: Vernal Equinox
i: Inclination of the Orbit

Ω: Longitude of the Node
$\Omega + \omega$: Longitude of Perihelion
CP = AC: Semimajor Axis
CS/CP: Eccentricity

set of tables greatly reduced the work of the computer, while maintaining the integrity of the original theory. Today, with electronic computers performing the computations, tables are no longer needed.

Mayer's success derived partly from using equations of condition, derived by Euler, to determine values of a set of parameters of a theory. The equations of condition relate observational residuals (the differences between observed positions and positions calculated from a theory) and errors in the orbital elements. Although a firm basis for using equations of condition would have to wait for the theory of least squares, astronomers quickly began applying them, with intuitive averaging concepts, to adjust orbital elements. Soon it became possible to incorporate an increasing number of new observations (particularly from the Royal Observatory at Greenwich) in solving for orbital elements.

From the late 1740s through the mid-1780s, the Jupiter/Saturn problem was studied by Euler, **J.L. Lagrange**, and Laplace. Halley's posthumously published tables (1749) incorporated a secular acceleration for Jupiter and deceleration for Saturn. Doubting that mutual attraction could totally explain their motions, Laplace investigated the possibilities of perturbations by comets, retardation of motion by a resisting aether, and propagation of gravity at finite speed. All these explanations failed. When J.H. Lambert announced in 1773 that Jupiter's acceleration and Saturn's deceleration were both decreasing in magnitude, the matter was further muddled.

Much effort went into transforming the equations of motion to find the most tractable form for integration. For example, polar coordinates might be used instead of rectangular coordinates; or time might be replaced as the independent variable by a related quantity, such as the position angle of the body in its orbit. By 1766, Euler and Lagrange had, in stages, developed differential equations for the six elements of the Keplerian orbital ellipse: longitude of the node, longitude of aphelion, inclination, eccentricity, semimajor axis, and time of perihelion passage. Under perturbations, the static Keplerian ellipse could be visualized as evolving in orientation, shape, and size as the six orbital elements changed. This powerful approach became known as the variation of orbital parameters.

Two types of terms were noted in the series representing the perturbed elements. Periodic terms, with purely oscillatory sine or cosine functions, depended directly on the positions of the planets. Secular terms, which are independent of the positions of the planets, either increased (or decreased) proportionally with time or were of very long period.

The meaning of secular terms was a great puzzle. Of particular concern was the semimajor axis, for if it were to increase without bound, the planet would escape from the solar system. In the 1770s, Lagrange and Laplace demonstrated that, at least to the first order of approximation in the perturbing forces, the semimajor axis did not have secular terms. In other words, the solar system was stable—at least to the first order of perturbations.

Because one body normally dominates the perturbations, work on lunar and planetary theories was facilitated by considering a system of three bodies, free of perturbations from other sources. The moon could be treated as a body orbiting the earth, with perturbations from the sun. Similarly, Jupiter and Saturn were considered to perturb each other as they orbited the sun. The three-body problem, as it is known, is of fundamental importance in celestial mechanics.

Unlike the two-body problem, the three-body problem does not have a set of formulas that completely describe the motion for all time. However, as discussed below, there are five equilibrium solutions in which the geometric configuration hold for all time. In addition, a certain number of algebraic expressions can be derived that describe fundamental features of the motion. A set of six equations specify that the center of mass of the system is stationary or moves with constant velocity, not affecting behavior within the system; three more specify that the total angular momentum of the system is constant; an equation specifies that the total energy of the system is constant. These integrals of motion were known to Euler in the 1760s. Euler discovered three equilibrium solutions in which the three bodies revolve around their common center of mass in straight-line configurations. Lagrange, in a seminal paper in 1772, derived two equilibrium configurations in which the bodies revolve as an equilateral triangle. One of these has the third body leading; in the other, the third body trails. Collectively, the equilibrium points are known as the Lagrangian points.

Efforts to improve the theories and tables of the planets progressed slowly, because masses of the planets, required for calculating perturbations, were still poorly known. Newton had derived the masses of Jupiter, Saturn, and the earth from the periods of their satellites. Although his values for Jupiter and Saturn were reasonably close, that for the earth was in error by almost a factor of two. For the other planets, there was only speculation. Thus it is not surprising that, as late as 1771, J.-J.L. Lalande based his tables for Mercury, Venus, and Mars on Keplerian ellipses, while only his tables of Jupiter and Saturn contained periodic terms due to their mutual perturbations. Even in the 1780s, Lagrange derived masses from the ad hoc assumption that the density of a planet was inversely proportional to its distance from the sun.

William Herschel's discovery of Uranus in 1781 posed a new challenge. After the initial failure of attempts to fit the observations with a parabolic orbit, Anders J. Lexell found that the orbit was nearly circular, at twice the distance of Saturn. Nearly two years after the planet's discovery, Laplace determined elliptical elements. Using prediscovery observations, Jean-Baptiste Delambre was able to construct a theory in 1790.

Finally, in 1785, Laplace announced the resolution of the Jupiter/Saturn problem. Following Lagrange's suggestion, he searched for high-order, periodic terms depending on near commensurability of the motions of the planets. In the case of Jupiter and Saturn, two orbital revolutions of Saturn are nearly equal to five revolutions of Jupiter. A feature of planetary theories is that coefficients of the trigonometric terms include a factor $1/(jn + kn')$, where j and k are integer numbers and n and n' are the mean motions of two planets. If n is the mean motion of Jupiter and n' is the mean motion of Saturn, $5n'$ is approximately equal to $2n$. Then for the term with $j=2$ and $k=-5$, the denominator is nearly zero, and the term (that is, the perturbation) is very large. For Jupiter and Saturn it corresponds to a long-term perturbation of approximately nine hundred years. For half that time Jupiter accelerates while Saturn decelerates, then they switch roles. This inequality produces a perturbation of 48.5 minutes of arc in the longitude of Saturn and 19.9 minutes in the longitude of Jupiter. The planets are said have a small divisor, resulting from a 5:2 resonance.

Another case of resonance was found in the orbits of Jupiter's satellites, which had challenged astronomers since their discovery by Galileo. Ole Römer explained some of the observed anomalies by the hypothesis that light travels at a finite speed. However, it was also necessary to consider perturbations by the sun, by the oblateness of Jupiter, and by the mutual attraction of the satellites. After Lagrange made a preliminary study, Laplace published a full theory, establishing the importance of the orbital resonances. In this case, Io, Europa, and Ganymede have mean motions that satisfy the relation $n - 3n' + 2n'' = 0$ to nine significant digits. As in the case of Jupiter and Saturn, this means that the theories have small divisors.

In 1787, Laplace announced the solution to the lunar acceleration problem. It was caused, he said, by the secular decrease in the eccentricity of earth's orbit. Thus the two major problems at the middle of the century were solved—or so it seemed. Newtonian astronomy, developed according to the analytical methods of Euler, Lagrange, and Laplace, had triumphed. Laplace fittingly concluded the century by compiling the first four volumes of *Mécanique Céleste*. During the next century, the methods developed by Laplace would be carefully explored and developed. Celestial mechanics would experience a golden age in which it became the very symbol of the power of science.

The Golden Age

On the night of January 1, 1801, **Giuseppe Piazzi** discovered a planetary object that soon passed behind the sun. To aid recovery, Carl Friedrich Gauss derived a method for determining orbital elements from a small number of observations over a short arc of the orbit. Gauss determined that the object, the minor planet Ceres, occupied an orbit between Mars and Jupiter.

Gauss and Adrien Legendre vied for priority in deriving a means of rigorously using a number of observations to correct orbital elements. Making use of Euler's equations of condition, they adjusted the elements to minimize the sum of the squares of residuals. This method of least squares eliminated the practice of determining orbital elements from small sets of observations, artfully or arbitrarily selected from a large collection.

Asteroids provided special challenges to celestial mechanicians. First of all, as new ones were discovered—more than 450 by the end of the century—the computational workload increased. While preliminary elliptical elements could be determined from a few observations, they had to be updated to account for new observations and perturbations by Jupiter. Failure to do so would result in losing and then spuriously rediscovering the asteroid. Furthermore, because the eccentricities and inclinations of their orbits were often sizable, series developed in powers of these parameters would converge very slowly, requiring the calculation of many terms. Fortunately, Johann Encke did much to improve the rigor and efficiency of computational methods.

The drudgery of calculating minor planet orbits paid off when Daniel Kirkwood examined orbital periods of the minor planets. Instead of a uniform distribution, he found gaps at periods that were nearly simple fractions ($1/2$, $1/3$, $2/5$) of that of Jupiter. Kirkwood incorrectly argued that since conjunctions with Jupiter would recur in the same part of the orbit, the orbital eccentricity would increase, with the result that the planet would eventually fall into the sun.

A standard tool in dealing with intractable equations is to simplify them by creating new variables from factors in the original equations. In the 1840s, William R. Hamilton and Karl Gustav Jacobi developed a canonical form for the equations of motion and a systematic procedure for transforming to a new set of variables. A sequence of transformations produces increasingly simplified sets of canonical equations, until a solvable set is obtained. The theory consists of the solution of the simplified equations plus the sequence of transformations. This method was successfully used by Charles Delaunay to construct a lunar theory, though the labor was daunting. After twenty years of work, the theory was published between 1860 and 1867. Despite the difficulties of applying transformation methods, they became a powerful tool for studying dynamical systems.

Celestial mechanics achieved its greatest triumph when Neptune was discovered on the basis of predictions made by **Urbain J.J. Le Verrier**. Sharing in the honors was J.C. Adams of Cambridge University. Le Verrier and Adams had to solve the inverse of the accustomed problem of planetary orbits. Normally, perturbations were calculated from known positions of known bodies, but in this case, the effects of the perturbations were analyzed to derive their cause. Certain initial assumptions had to be made concerning the mass and the orbit of the perturbing planet. While the assumptions of Le Verrier and Adams were not really accurate, it is now generally agreed that their predictions were based on valid analyses.

Le Verrier devoted his life to analyzing the orbits of all the planets, for by mid-century they were in need of more accurate theories. He found that the observed motion of the perihelion of Mercury was 565 seconds of arc per century, instead of 527 seconds of arc, as predicted from Newtonian perturbations by other planets. This result, announced in 1859, elicited a number of possible explanations: an undiscovered planet inside the orbit of

Mercury, a ring of matter around the sun, a small correction to the inverse-square law. Despite a host of reported sightings, the intra-Mercurial planet, Vulcan, was never found, and none of the other explanations was fully satisfactory.

Another problem was reported when J.C. Adams found that Laplace's explanation of the moon's secular acceleration was inadequate. Laplace had argued that the acceleration, roughly 12 seconds of arc per century, resulted from the secular decrease in the eccentricity of the earth's orbit. Adams showed that theory could explain only 5.7 seconds. After considerable debate, William Ferrel and Delaunay independently found that the discrepancy was caused by tidal interaction between the earth and moon. The mutual attraction between the moon and the high tide on earth serves to impede the earth's rotation, while pulling the moon forward. As a result, the rotation of the earth is slightly slowing, as the moon becomes more distant. Since time was measured by the rotation of the earth, the moon appeared to accelerate.

When **Simon Newcomb** became director of the American Nautical Almanac Office in 1877, he saw a need to create a unified system of theories and astronomical constants. The planetary theories of Le Verrier and his predecessors had incorporated a hodgepodge of inconsistent observations and reduction methods. Newcomb collected observations from the principal observatories, determined improved values of astronomical constants, and began a program of developing new planetary theories on a consistent system. With the aid of assistants who did the computing, he undertook theories for the inner planets, Mercury through Mars, and the outer planets, Uranus and Neptune. Jupiter and Saturn were assigned to G.W. Hill, who preferred to work without assistance. The resulting theories of the inner planets were used in American almanacs until 1984; those of the outer planets were used until 1960.

Newcomb and Hill worked independently on different aspects of the lunar theory. From an analysis of observations, Newcomb found and corrected defects in the lunar theory of **Peter Hansen**, which was used in the British and American almanacs. Having collected observations going back to Antiquity, Newcomb explored apparent irregularities in the moon's longitude. For a time, he suspected but could not prove that he was really seeing variations in the earth's rotation. His suspicion was confirmed in the 1930s, when the same irregularities were found in the observed motions of the inner planets and the satellites of Jupiter.

Hill began development of an entirely new lunar theory, which came to fruition in the hands of **E.W. Brown** in 1919. As his starting solution, Hill considered the earth and sun to move at a constant rate in circles around their center of mass, with a hypothetical, massless moon following an orbit that returned to its original starting position with respect to the earth and sun. That is, Hill's first approximation was a periodic solution of the restricted three-body problem.

As the name implies, the restricted three-body problem is a special case of the three-body problem. In the general case, three bodies of finite mass move under their own mutual attraction. In the restricted problem, two restrictions are imposed: (a) one of the bodies is of infinitesimally small mass, and (b) the two bodies of finite mass revolve in circular motion around their center of mass with the same mean motion. Hill determined the first periodic orbit of this system since Lagrange, and he explored the regions of possible motion that depend on the initial energy of the infinitesimal body.

Questions about the stability of the solar system, originally raised by Lagrange and Laplace, engaged mathematicians throughout the century. In 1809, Simeon Poisson proved that semimajor axes of the planets had no secular terms through the second order in the perturbations, thereby adding assurance that the solar system was stable. In the 1880s, studies by C. Haretu, D. Eginitis, and François Tisserand verified Poisson's conclusion but found secular terms in the third order. By then, however, Newcomb demonstrated that planetary theories could be developed purely in periodic terms, without the secular terms that had raised questions about the stability of the solar system. Unfortunately, **Jules Henri Poincaré** proved that small divisors caused the trigonometric series in Newcomb's theories to diverge. Hence they could not describe the motions of the planets for all time. However, as demonstrated in practice by astronomers, planetary theories were useful, as long as the perturbations remained small.

Extending Hill's work, Poincaré determined theoretically that there are an infinite number of periodic orbits in the restricted three-body problem. By considering the behavior of orbits that begin very close to a periodic orbit, he established a new way of thinking about stability. He considered an orbit to be stable if the body would pass infinitely often through positions as near as one chose to its initial position.

Despite the artificiality of the restricted problem, it has proved to be a good first approximation to many examples of orbital motions. One of Poincaré's findings was that stable periodic orbits should exist in the vicinity of the Lagrangian equilibrium points. This was confirmed in 1906, when a minor planet was discovered near a Lagrangian point of the sun/Jupiter system. It was the first of the Trojan asteroids.

As the nineteenth century closed, Newcomb pointed out several unsolved orbital problems. The most vexing was the excess perihelion motion of Mercury. Like Le Verrier, Newcomb tested a variety of hypotheses to explain the phenomenon. One of the most tempting was an almost inverse-square law in which the power of the distance was -2.0000001574 rather than -2, exactly. However, Newcomb, along with many other astronomers, eventually accepted a proposal by **Hugo von Seeliger** that orbits were being perturbed by the interplanetary matter that produced the zodiacal light. By adjusting the parameters describing the cloud, it was possible to reduce most of the troublesome anomalies.

Meanwhile, physicists were proposing a variety of gravitational theories, mostly inspired by advances in electrodynamic theory. For them, Mercury's perihelion was not a major issue. Although Einstein was aware of the problem, he did not emphasize it until 1915, when he found that the general theory of relativity explained the total excess of 42 arcseconds per century. Of course, Mercury's perihelion was not the only element affected. The largest effect was about 2 arcseconds per century in the perigee and node of the moon, which was within the accepted limits of observational accuracy. Therefore relativistic corrections were applied as necessary to Newtonian planetary theories.

Despite the discovery of Neptune, the motion of Uranus was still not satisfactorily accounted for by theory. Percival Lowell, William Pickering, and others analyzed residuals between observations and theory in search of a ninth planet. The residuals, however, were much smaller than those discussed by Le Verrier and Adams. Numerous solutions resulted in a wide variety of predicted positions. When Pluto was finally discovered in 1930, there was good reason to praise the thoroughness of the search rather than the rigor of the prediction. When the true mass of Pluto was finally determined, after discovery of its satellite in 1978, it was found to be much smaller than any prediction and far too small to have caused the alleged perturbations.

Decline and Renascence

Following Poincaré, the study of the three-body problem, based on Newton's laws, took on a life of its own. G.H. Darwin, **F.R. Moulton**, Svante Elis Strömgren, and their students undertook tedious calculations of periodic orbits, while George D. Birkhoff worked on the topological theory of orbits.

Although Poincaré was interested in practical aspects of celestial mechanics, his work introduced a new level of mathematical abstraction into the field. However, astrophysicists came to regard celestial mechanics as a tedious search for an *n*th digit of precision or for arcane theorems of purely mathematical relevance. At the same time, mathematicians were coming to view celestial mechanics as merely a special case of dynamical systems theory.

At the beginning of the twentieth century, celestial mechanics was established in both astronomy and mathematics curricula. By mid-century it had largely disappeared from both, and perhaps twenty people in the world engaged in research in the field. This would change with the development of electronic computers and the beginning of the space age.

In the late 1920s, L.J. Comrie, at the British Nautical Almanac Office, successfully used tabulating machines to evaluate Brown's lunar tables for use in the *Nautical Almanac*. Inspired by this example, Wallace Eckert and **Paul Herget** automated a variety of orbital calculations. In the 1940s astronomers at Yale, Columbia, Cincinnati, and the U.S. Naval Observatory cooperated in numerical integrations and construction of planetary theories. This led to the numerical integration of the orbits of the five outer planets over a period of four hundred years, which set an example for future work.

Numerical integration was crucial for calculating the motion of Pluto. Because its orbit passes inside that of Neptune, a traditional planetary theory, with factors involving the ratio of the heliocentric distances of Neptune and Pluto, would not converge. Close approaches of the two planets are prevented by a 3:2 resonance that constrains conjunctions to times when Pluto is near aphelion, well outside the orbit of Neptune.

With electronic computers to handle the drudge work, a few young scientists were again attracted to the field and more entered after the first artificial satellites were launched. **Dirk Brouwer**, Yoshihide Kozai, and John Vinti led the way in developing the theory of a satellite orbiting an oblate earth. This was soon extended to include drag caused by earth's atmosphere. There was an immediate need to study orbits in a new three-body problem: earth, moon, and space probe. Electronic computers were applied to calculating orbits of the three- and *n*-body problems, and transformation methods for solving perturbation problems were adapted for computerized calculations. André Deprit, Victor Szebehely, and their students were pioneers in these efforts.

At the same time, breakthroughs in observing technology challenged theorists. Modern transit circle observations determined the position of Mars to about 100 km, but radar ranging determined distances to a few hundred meters. Analysis of transponder signals from the *Viking* spacecraft on Mars yielded distances to less than 10 meters. Today laser ranging to the moon is done to a few centimeters.

Since traditional planetary theories failed to meet these levels of precision, the Jet Propulsion Laboratory (JPL), charged with producing ephemerides for space missions, performed numerical integrations of relativistic equations for all the planets and the moon. Prior to this work, planetary theories were developed from Newtonian models, with relativistic corrections applied as necessary. The JPL integration designated DE200/LE200 continues to serve as a worldwide standard, although it has been superseded for some purposes by more recent integrations.

Computers have also been employed in constructing analytical planetary theories. In the 1940s **G.M. Clemence** generated an analytical theory for Mars, since Newcomb's theory had never been entirely satisfactory. At the *Bureau des Longitudes*, theories for the moon and all planets except Pluto were generated, with parameters adjusted for consistency with JPL's DE200/LE200. Currently a number of workers are exploring techniques that may avoid the occurrence of small divisors and that will produce more accurate theories with fewer terms.

Missions to the planets also required improved orbits for natural satellites. Theories developed by Tisserand, Newcomb, Adams, Hermann and Georg O.H. Struve, Ralph Sampson, and Frank Ross were now out of date. In the 1970s, new observational programs and theoretical developments brought about a general upgrading of satellite theories. These were used for the *Voyager* space mission, which resulted in the discovery of new satellites and of unexpected dynamical features of the rings of Saturn.

The stability of orbits in the solar system remains an unresolved issue, though there has been progress on both theoretical and computational fronts. Following work by Carl Ludwig Siegel on the problem of small divisors, A.N. Kolmogorov in 1954 and then V.I. Arnol'd and Jürgen Moser in the 1960s showed that motion in a hypothetical solar system with sufficiently small planetary masses, orbital eccentricities, and inclinations would be in large measure quasiperiodic. Unfortunately the conditions of what has come to be known as the KAM theorem are too strict to apply to a realistic solar system.

Since the 1970s, work on stability has been done by computer simulations that model the motions of planets over millions of years. It is found that two orbits that begin arbitrarily close together can diverge exponentially with time. Such behavior is called chaotic. In the simulations, an orbit that seems well behaved for hundreds of thousands of years can suddenly undergo unexpected changes in its orbital eccentricity. Although this chaotic behavior does not occur randomly, in defiance of the laws of motion, it cannot be fully predicted, because it depends so critically on initial coordinates and velocity. An orbit calculated to fifteen significant digits might behave quite differently than the same orbit calculated to sixteen digits.

Conditions that result in chaotic behavior are associated with resonances, such as those found in the asteroid belt. A large change in an asteroid's eccentricity could send it close to a major planet, from which it might pick up enough energy to cause its ejection from the solar system. This may, at last, offer an explanation for the Kirkwood gaps.

The nature of chaos is one of the most active areas of contemporary research. However, there is always concern about the degree to which mathematical models represent the dynamics of an actual physical system. Celestial mechanics, which for more than two centuries has predicted the motions of planets and satellites with ever-increasing accuracy, has now revealed that the behavior of a gravitational system, while deterministic, is ultimately unpredictable.

Historiography

The history of celestial mechanics has passed from generation to generation as footnotes in great survey works and textbooks: Laplace's *Mécanique Céleste* (especially in Nathaniel Bowditch's English translation with extensive commentary, 1829–1839), Tisserand's *Traité de Mécanique Céleste* (1889–1896), **Yusuke Hagihara**'s *Celestial Mechanics* (1970–1976), Moulton's *Introduction to Celestial Mechanics* (1902), Brouwer's and Clemence's *Methods of Celestial Mechanics* (1961). However, these can scarcely be considered historical studies. While historians of science have examined Kepler and Newton in detail, there has been very little research on their successors. The exception is Curtis Wilson, who has explored aspects of celestial mechanics from Kepler to the nineteenth century. Wilson's scholarship is mathematically technical and not accessible to a general audience. Treating a highly mathematical subject without recourse to mathematics, as attempted in this essay, may result in misrepresentations. Even so, the attempt must be made.

Several historical problems are ripe for study. One is the attempt to test the validity of gravitational theories, beginning with Newton's, and extending to relativistic theories. Another concerns the institutional context in which celestial mechanics is practiced. Do different institutional contexts lead to different approaches or results? Patronage is also an interesting avenue for investigation. Initial discoveries in celestial mechanics were inspired by prizes sponsored by European scientific academies. Since then, patronage has come from universities, national almanac offices, aerospace companies, the military, and national space agencies.

Finally, there are questions of the broader cultural significance of celestial mechanics. Through the early twentieth century, prominent celestial mechanicians brought scientific values to discussions of cosmology, philosophy, and even economics and politics. The sense of order implied by successful explanations of celestial phenomena was invoked as evidence of divine authorship, or was used to argue that a universe based on laws of nature did not require a deity.

At the end of the twentieth century, celestial mechanics symbolizes the ambivalent status of science in the public mind. The science that guides spacecraft to distant planets can also guide intercontinental ballistic missiles. From the certitude that Newton's laws initially seemed to imply, celestial mechanics has progressed to exploring the limits of predictability.

LeRoy E. Doggett

Bibliography

Bowditch, N. *Laplace's Mécanique Céleste.* 5 vols. (Translation with commentary.) Boston: Gray, Little and Wilkins, 1829–1839.

Brouwer, D. "Review of Celestial Mechanics." *Annual Review of Astronomy and Astrophysics* 1 (1963): 219–234.

Brown, E.W., G.D. Birkhoff, A.O. Leuschner, and H.N. Russell. "Report of the Committee on Celestial Mechanics of the National Research Council." *Bulletin of the National Research Council* 4 (1922): 1–22.

Fontenrose, R. "In Search of Vulcan." *Journal for the History of Astronomy* 4 (1973): 145–158.

Gautier, A. *Essai historique sur la problème des trois corps*. Paris, 1817.

Grant, R. *History of Physical Astronomy*. 2nd ed. London: Henry G. Bohn, 1852.

Morando, B. "The Golden Age of Celestial Mechanics from Laplace to Poincaré." In *Planetary Astronomy from the Renaissance to the Rise of Astrophysics, Part B,* edited by R. Taton and C. Wilson. *The General History of Astronomy,* vol. 2B, edited by M. Hoskin. Cambridge: Cambridge University Press, in press.

———. "Laplace and the Mécanique Céleste." In *Planetary Astronomy from the Renaissance to the Rise of Astrophysics, Part B,* edited by R. Taton and C. Wilson. *The General History of Astronomy,* vol. 2B, edited by M. Hoskin. Cambridge: Cambridge University Press, in press.

Moyer, A.E. *A Scientist's Voice in American Culture: Simon Newcomb and the Rhetoric of Scientific Method.* Berkeley: University of California Press, 1992.

Roseveare, N.T. *Mercury's Perihelion from Le Verrier to Einstein*. Oxford: Clarendon Press, 1982.

Wilson, C. "Perturbations and Solar Tables from Lacaille to Delambre: The Rapprochement of Observation and Theory." *Archive for History of Exact Sciences* 22 (1980): 53–188; 189–304.

———. "The Great Inequality of Jupiter and Saturn: From Kepler to Laplace." *Archive for History of Exact Sciences* 33 (1985): 15–290.

———. "Clairaut's Calculation of the Eighteenth-Century Return of Halley's Comet." *Journal for the History of Astronomy* 24 (1993): 1–15.

———. "The Problem of Perturbation Analytically Treated: Euler, Clairaut, d'Alembert." *Planetary Astronomy from the Renaissance to the Rise of Astrophysics, Part B,* edited by R. Taton and C. Wilson. *The General History of Astronomy,* vol. 2B, edited by M. Hoskin. Cambridge: Cambridge University Press, in press.

Wisdom, J. "Urey Prize Lecture: Chaotic Dynamics in the Solar System." *Icarus* 72 (1987): 241–275.

Cerro Tololo Interamerican Observatory

The Cerro Tololo Interamerican Observatory (CTIO) is the southern equivalent of the Kitt Peak National Observatory. Along with the Sacramento Peak National Solar Observatory, the Space Telescope Science Institute, and the Advanced Telescope Program (the National New Technology Telescope), CTIO is part of the National Optical Astronomy Observatories (NOAO). The NOAO in turn is operated by the Association of Universities for Research in Astronomy and funded by the National Science Foundation.

CTIO is located near the coastal city of La Serena in the north central region of Chile, and its observing facilities are divided three ways among Chilean, staff, and visiting astronomers. It was originally inspired by the University of Chile, which needed a new observatory for astronomical research, and American astronomer **Gerald P. Kuiper**, who wanted to set up a large telescope at the best site on earth to carry out lunar and planetary observing programs. Kuiper's criteria included clear and dark skies, low humidity, excellent seeing, and accessibility to major urban centers. After a three-year site survey (1960–1963), German astronomer Jurgen Stock recommended Cerro Tololo, a 2,200-meter mountain 485 km north of Santiago and 80 km east of La Serena. During this early period a 1-meter reflector was installed at Cerro Tololo in a joint program with the University of Chile's Cerro Calan National Observatory; Chilean astronomers H. Moreno and C. Torres employed it to take photometric observations of the Scorpio-Centaurus region. The University of Chile continued its close cooperation with Cerro Tololo throughout the early years of CTIO.

Construction of the observatory began in 1963. CTIO was officially founded in 1965, though the facility was not dedicated until November 6, 1967. By that time the site's telescopes were already studying stellar spectra and colors. CTIO was originally equipped with two 41-cm f/18 and one 91-cm f/13 Cassegrain reflectors, a 61/91-cm f/3.5 Curtis Schmidt telescope, and a 152-cm Ritchey-Chretien reflecting telescope with f/7.5 and f/13.5 secondary mirrors. Also included were a dormitory and lounge for about a dozen astronomers, a dining hall, warehouses, offices, a machine shop, an electronics office, a power generator, and an independent water supply. The administrative headquarters of CTIO were located in La Serena.

During its first decade of operation, the observatory did much more than Kuiper's projected planetary and lunar astronomy. Among its early observing programs were planetary nebulae and the **Magellanic Clouds**. The Curtis Schmidt telescope was used by Warner and Swasey Observatory astronomers to compile a catalogue of 5,132 highly luminous O and B type stars along a band 20 degrees wide in the southern Milky Way. Portions of the influential ***Henry Draper Catalogue*** were also revised at Cerro Tololo. In cooperation with Soviet astronomers, CTIO undertook simultaneous spectroscopic and photometric studies of southern red dwarf flare stars, and short period Cepheid variables.

The facility quickly became popular with the international astronomical community, and pressure increased for the installation of more telescopes. CTIO Director Victor M. Blanco and the seven staff astronomers worked alongside a steadily increasing number of visitors; by 1973 almost one hundred researchers came to CTIO from forty-four institutions. They were served by a staff of about 150, of whom approximately 125 were Chilean.

To meet the rising demands, CTIO added an infrared liquid helium cooled photometer. A 1-meter reflecting Ritchey-Chretien telescope was contributed by Yale University in 1973. But the most spectacular advance was the installation of a 4-meter reflecting telescope the following year. This was the twin of a 4-meter telescope installed at Kitt Peak, both of which took thirteen years to build. It arrived at Coquimbo harbor in Chile in June 1973 in eighty-six boxes weighing almost 500 tons. The mirror was ground in the optical shop at Kitt Peak; instead of the traditional quartz, the makers used Cervit, a ceramic material with a much lower thermal coefficient. Hence it was almost completely unaffected by temperature changes. It arrived from Kitt Peak on September 2, 1974, and was taken to Cerro Tololo the next day and aluminized. The first prime focus photograph was made by Australian CTIO staff astronomer John Graham on September 18.

The installation of this telescope made CTIO the largest observatory in the Southern Hemisphere, surpassing its two neighbors, the **European Southern Observatory (ESO)** at Cerro La Silla (with a 3.6-meter telescope, completed in 1976), and Las Campanas Observatory (with a 2.5-meter Irénee du Pont telescope, installed in 1977). Its success led to a flood of new research at CTIO. Astronomers like P.S. Osmer and Barry M. Lasker (using the 4-meter telescope), along with James Hesser and Nolan Walborn (working with the 1.52-meter Ritchey-Chretien) investigated various types of stars, galaxies, globular clusters, nebulae, HII regions, and other gaseous objects. CTIO became famous for its work on the Magellanic Clouds, the central regions of the Milky Way galaxy, and high-energy cosmic radio and X-ray sources in the 1970s and 1980s.

By the late 1980s and early 1990s, the CTIO site supported six telescopes. The larger telescopes had been fitted with charge-coupled devices (CCDs) for optical imaging, various optical spectrographs, and photometers. Infrared imaging, spectroscopy, and photometry were well supported. A first-aid center, library, and computer systems (for both data reduction and telescope control) were also added. The facility remains highly popular among visiting astronomers, and despite an allocation of 60 percent of CTIO's observing time (staff researchers get 30 percent and Chilean astronomers 10 percent), there is still not enough telescope time to satisfy the many observing proposals received each year.

Julian A. Smith

Bibliography

Blanco, V.M. "The Inter-American Observatory in Chile." *Sky & Telescope* 35 (1968): 72–76.

Classen, J., and N. Sperling. "Telescopes for the Record." *Sky & Telescope* 61 (1981): 303–307.

Colbeck, L.A. *Facilities Manual of the Cerro Tololo Inter-American Observatory*. National Optical Astronomy Observatories, 1990.

Donnelly, M.C. *A Short History of Observatories*. Eugene: University of Oregon Books, 1973.

Evans, D.S. *Under Capricorn: A History of Southern Hemisphere Astronomy*. Bristol and Philadelphia: Adam Hilger, 1988.

Irwin, J.B. "Chile's Mountain Observatories Revealed." *Sky & Telescope* 47 (1974): 11–16.

Krisciunas, K. *Astronomical Centers of the World*. Cambridge: Cambridge University Press, 1988.

Marx, S., and W. Pfau. *Observatories of the World*. New York: Blandford Books, 1982.

Walker, M.F. "Image-Tube Observations at Cerro Tololo." *Sky & Telescope* 40 (1970): 132–138.

Chaco Canyon

Between the tenth and thirteenth centuries C.E., the Anasazi, prehistoric Pueblo Indians of the American Southwest, built numerous multistory communal houses and ceremonial structures in Chaco Canyon, in the northwest corner of New Mexico. The canyon became the ceremonial and trade hub for 20,000 square miles of the San Juan Basin and the Colorado Plateau. Chaco culture was connected with the canyon by a 250-mile system of roads. Although the apartment towns of Chaco Canyon were once thought to have been fully occupied by a permanent resident population, archaeological opinion has shifted. The canyon is thought to have served as the site of periodic assembly and economic exchange, activated by ritual, for a widely dispersed population. Permanent residents may have been limited to a small number of caretakers and esoteric specialists.

Anasazi astronomical traditions seem to have been incorporated into the public architecture of Chaco Canyon and into more modest sites associated with prehistoric rock art. Practical astronomy and astronomical symbolism are known components of the culture of the descendants of the Anasazi, the historic Pueblo. The astronomical connotations of prehistoric Pueblo sites in Chaco Canyon are important because they help to reveal how the Chaco system operated and how it was ritually sustained.

Pictographs of a crescent, star, and hand on an overhang near the Penasco Blanco ruin have been interpreted as an eyewitness record of the Crab supernova of 1054 C.E. On the morning of July 5, 1054, the brilliant new star rose in the dawn in the company of the waning crescent moon. The supernova interpretation of the rock art has been evaluated critically by archaeologist Jonathan Reyman. He

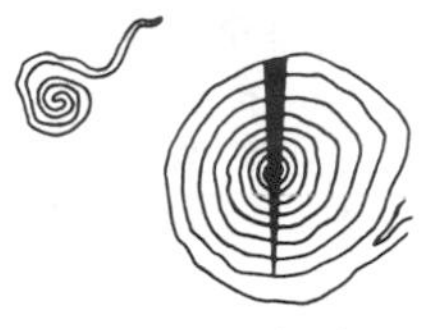

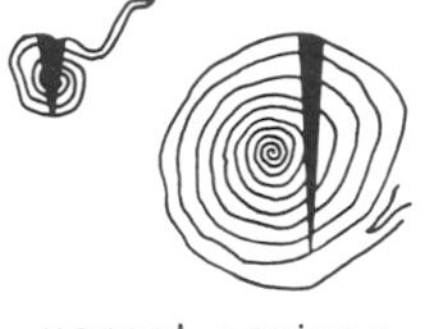

Fajada Butte, Chaco Canyon, New Mexico. Three slabs of rock that lean against the face of the cliff near the top of Fajada Butte allow the light that passes between them at near midday to form daggers of light that appear to interact seasonally with petroglyphs carved upon the back wall. (Courtesy of the Griffith Observatory)

Pueblo Bonito, a multistory complex of apartments, plazas, and subterranean ceremonial chambers, is accurately aligned with the cardinal directions. The wall that splits the large central plaza in two establishes the north-south line. (Courtesy of E.C. Krupp)

concluded that the site was more likely a shrine where the Anasazi sunwatcher placed offerings after calendric observations of the sun were performed at a site intended for that purpose. Among the historic Pueblo Indians, the crescent stands for the waning moon, and the star stands for the Morning Star.

A canyon ledge near Wijiji pueblo operates as a backsite for winter solstice sunrise, which is aligned with a natural rock chimney across the rincon from the ledge. Prehistoric Anasazi petroglyphs and more recent Navajo rock art are present. The ledge is long enough to permit calendric observations of the sunrise before the winter solstice. The Hopi Sun Chief is known to have anticipated the winter solstice by making horizon observations of the sun from a chosen spot in the village of Walpi. Jonathan Reyman has underscored the importance of astronomical and calendrical observations in establishing and maintaining priestly authority and power in Pueblo society. Astronomer Michael Zeilik identifies the Sun Chief's ability to anticipate key dates in the socioceremonial cycle as the most essential element of the Sun Chief's knowledge.

The most publicized astronomical interpretation of Chaco Canyon involves a spiral petroglyph on Fajada Butte, a conspicuous natural landform. In 1979, Anna Sofaer, Volker Zinser, and Rolf Sinclair reported a seasonal pattern of light and shadow created by three stone slabs leaning vertically against the petroglyph panel near the summit of the butte. The most eyecatching event occurs at summer solstice, near local noon, when a dagger of sunlight slices through the spiral. Although the team interpreted the site as a precise solar observatory, the effect, if intentionally exploited by prehistoric Indians, appears to serve as a less-precise symbolic display. Erosion of the earth footing around the slabs has since allowed them to slip out of place, and the effect no longer performs as first reported.

The main axis of Pueblo Bonito, a large D-shaped apartment town, is aligned within 45 arcminutes of cardinal north-south. A section of its straight south wall is only 8 arcminutes south of east. Accurate cardinal alignment is found in other Chaco structures, and the accuracy of these alignments indicates the symbolic value of the cardinal directions. Pueblo Bonito also effectively exploits the principles of passive solar heating and the seasonal variation of the sun's path to provide rooms and plazas that are comfortable year round. Jonathan Reyman identified two rooms with corner apertures that could have been used to make observations of winter solstice sunrise.

Casa Rinconada, a Great Kiva or community subterranean ceremonial chamber, is also cardinally oriented. Its architectural elements echo organizing principles of the Pueblo cosmos, as described by the Acoma Indians of New Mexico. Solstitial light and shadow effects have been observed at Casa Rinconada, but these appear to be accidental products of site reconstruction.

Cosmological and mythological symbolism, related to underworld and emergence themes, has been attributed to the Great North Road, which terminates abruptly in the badlands of Kutz Canyon, 35 miles due north of Chaco Canyon.

Lunar standstill alignments have also been attributed to some Chaco Canyon buildings and Chaco outliers, notably Chimney Rock in Colorado, but the meaning of these remains in dispute.

Edwin C. Krupp

Bibliography

Gabriel, K. *Roads to Center Place—A Cultural Atlas of Chaco Canyon and the Anasazi.* Boulder, Colo.: Johnson Books, 1991.

Krupp, E.C. *Echoes of the Ancient Skies.* New York: Harper and Row, 1983.

———, ed. *In Search of Ancient Astronomies.* Garden City, N.Y.: Doubleday, 1978.

Malville, J.M. "Prehistoric Astronomy in the American Southwest." *Astronomy Quarterly* 8 (1991): 1–34.

Malville, J.M., and C. Putnam. *Prehistoric Astronomy in the Southwest.* Boulder, Colo.: Johnson Books, 1989.

Sofaer, A., V. Zinser, and R.M. Sinclair. "A Unique Solar Marking Construct." *Science* 206, no. 4416 (1979): 283–291.

Williamson, R.A. *Living the Sky—The Cosmos of the American Indian.* Boston: Houghton Mifflin, 1984.

Zeilik, M. "The Sunwatchers of Chaco Canyon." *Griffith Observer* 47 (1983): 1–12.

Chamberlin-Moulton Hypothesis

Descriptive theory of the origin of the solar system, also known as the Planetesimal Hypothesis, proposed 1901–1905 to replace the Laplacian nebular hypothesis. As early as 1897, University of Chicago geologist Thomas Chrowder Chamberlin developed misgivings about the nebular hypothesis based on geological considerations. To address the astronomical aspects, Chamberlin turned to Chicago astronomer **Forest Ray Moulton,** the two proposing that the solar system originated in a manner involving a stage in which it would have appeared very like the spiral nebulae photographed by James E. Keeler at **Lick Observatory**.

In their planetesimal theory, the material of the planets came from the sun during a close gravitational encounter with a passing star. At closest approach, huge tidal bulges were produced which, with internal solar forces such as produce solar prominences, resulted in repeated ejections of material. Due to the influence of the passing star, this material would have formed two spirallike arms extending outward from the sun. Part of the ejected material may have escaped, and another fraction fell back into the sun, ensuring its rotation in the same sense as the revolution of the planets but with a relatively small angular momentum, a major factor that had led Chamberlin, Moulton, and others to reject the Laplacian model. The material remaining in orbit about the sun underwent rapid cooling, some remaining as uncondensed gas and the rest forming numerous small solid bodies (planetesimals) and a few larger ones (protoplanets), each group of objects being the result of a different prominence eruption. The subsequent accretion of smaller bodies by the larger formed the planets and their lunar systems. Circular planetary orbits were produced from the eccentric orbits of the original material through interaction with the smaller debris. Ultimately the gas and dust

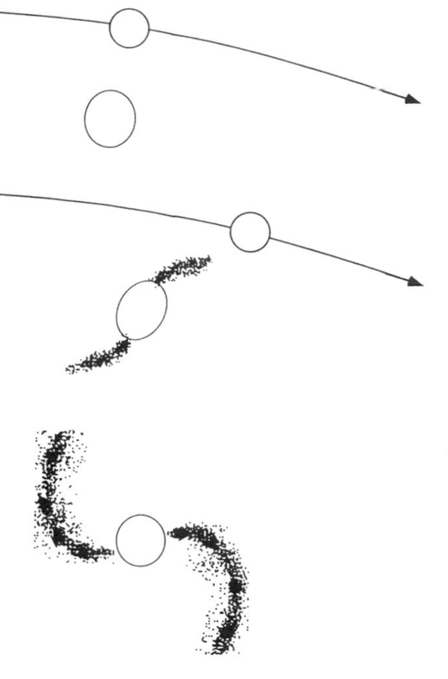

A passing star (at top) was envisioned as raising a tidal bulge upon the sun. Internal disturbances ejected a series of pulses of material from the solar bulges (middle), which quickly cooled into planetesimal bodies (bottom) and subsequently amalgamated into the planetary bodies. (Figure by Charles J. Peterson)

was dispersed from the solar system or was swept up by the planets; comets and asteroids are the debris that remain.

Chamberlin and Moulton succeeded in refuting the Laplacian hypothesis, but reception of their own theory was mixed, with favorable support received over several decades primarily in the United States. Critics, however, raised questions about the ability of planetesimal-protoplanet interaction to produce circular orbits, the observed angular momentum distribution of the solar system, and cometary objects. In 1917 the need for solar eruptions to actually eject material during the tidal encounter was disputed by **James H. Jeans**. Harold Jeffreys also argued that planetesimal collisions would induce vaporization and hence lead to a Laplacian nebula; two decades later, in 1939, Lyman Spitzer showed that a filament drawn from the sun would dissipate rather than condense. Tidal-based theories such as the original Chamberlin-Moulton hypothesis and the Jeans-Jeffreys revision nevertheless held a prominent place for nearly a third of a century in the debate, but passed out of favor by the late 1930s when it became clear that no contemporary theory of the origin of the solar system was satisfactory. Within another decade, theories that considered planetary formation as a corollary of formation of the sun gained general acceptance; the concept of planetesimals introduced by Chamberlin and Moulton is incorporated into modern theory.

Charles J. Peterson

Bibliography

Brush, S.G. "A Geologist among Astronomers: The Rise and Fall of the Chamberlin-Moulton Cosmogony." *Journal for the History of Astronomy* 9 (1978): 1–41, 77–104.

———. *Fruitful Encounters: The Origin of the Solar System and the Moon from Chamberlin to Apollo.* vol. 3 of *A History of Modern Planetary Physics.* New York: Cambridge University Press, 1996.

Chamberlin, T.C. "Fundamental Problems of Geology." *Carnegie Institution Yearbook for 1904* (1905): 195–258.

Jaki, S.L. *Planets and Planetarians: A History of Theories of the Origin of Planetary Systems.* New York: Wiley, 1977.

Moulton, F.R. "On the Evolution of the Solar System." *Astrophysical Journal* 21 (1905): 165–181.

Russell, H.N. *The Solar System and Its Origin.* New York: Macmillan, 1935.

Chandrasekhar, Subrahmanyan (1910–1995)

One of the most eminent astrophysicists of the twentieth century. Known as *Chandra* throughout the scientific world, his early education was under the tutelage of his parents and private teachers. He got a B.Sc. from Presidency College, Madras (1930) and a Ph.D. from Cambridge University, England (1933). Chandra was elected a Fellow of the Trinity College, Cambridge (1933–1936). In 1937 he joined the staff of the **Yerkes Observatory** of the University of Chicago. Elected Fellow of the Royal Society of London (1944) and named as Morton D. Hull Distinguished Service Professor (1946), Chandra has spent his career at Chicago. Chandra served as editor of the *Astrophysical Journal* from 1952 to 1971. Among the honors bestowed on him are the Nobel Prize in Physics (1983) and the Copley Medal of the Royal Society of London (1984).

Chandra's first important discovery (1930) was the limit on the mass of a star that can become, in its terminal stage, a white dwarf. The limit, known as the *Chandrasekhar limit* (1.44 solar mass), has been hailed as one of the important discoveries in astrophysics. It paved the way to the discovery of the other two terminal stages of a stellar evolution: neutron stars and black holes. Subsequently, Chandra's distinctive pattern of research encompassed several areas, to which he has devoted five to ten years, resulting in a sequence of papers and ending with a monograph. Chandra's monographs have had lasting effect on astronomy and astrophysics, providing not only numerical results for comparison with observations but also mathematical models and techniques.

In brief, Chandra's major contributions to astrophysics include studies of stellar structure and stability as they relate to the evolution of stars; stellar dynamics dealing with matter and motion in galaxies and star clusters; the principles of radiation transfer and radiation equilibrium in stellar atmospheres; the theory of the illumination and polarization of the sunlit sky; and the theory of the negative ion of hydrogen, which resolved a long-standing controversy pertaining to the solar spectrum and the abundance of hydrogen in the sun.

Since 1960, Chandra's main interests have been in Einstein's general theory of relativity in relation to astronomy. He developed the post-Newtonian scheme to systematically take into account general relativistic effects and established, theoretically, the existence of black holes. Chandra's contributions to the mathematical theory of black holes and his continuing studies of the exact solutions of Einstein's equations have provided new and important physical and mathematical insights into the richness and beauty of Einstein's theory.

Chandra is often thought of as a scientist in the tradition of Lord Rayleigh or Jules Henri Poincaré. Most of his research papers are collected together in six volumes. A book entitled *Truth and Beauty* by Chandra is a collection of seven lectures that express his thoughts on aesthetics and motivations in science.

K.C. Wali

Bibliography

Chandrasekhar, S. *Truth and Beauty: Aesthetics and Motivations in Science.* Chicago: University of Chicago Press, 1987.

Chandrasekhar, S. *Selected Papers.* 6 vols. Chicago: University of Chicago Press, 1989–1991.

Wali, K.C. *Chandra: A Biography of S. Chandrasekhar.* Chicago: University of Chicago Press, 1991.

Chinese Astronomy

The history of Chinese astronomy is as old as written Chinese history itself. Records of eclipses and novae are found among the Shang (ca. 1562–ca. 1066 B.C.E.) oracle bones. The Imperial Astronomical Bureau also played an important function in almost every ruling house ever since at least the Han dynasty (206 B.C.E.–220 C.E.).

Ancient monuments and artifacts connected with astronomy are quite rich in China. Artifacts discovered in one of the well-known Han tombs at Mawangdui in Changsha include a picture of eighteen different comets drawn in the fourth century B.C.E. and an astronomical work recording the movements of the planets from 246 to 179 B.C.E. Numerous star maps, gnomons, clepsydras, **armillary spheres, celestial globes,** and calendar books are also available. Some of them show strong evidence of the cultural exchange between China and other countries. For instance, *Qiyao Li* (Seven Luminaries Calendar) of the Tang dynasty (618–907) was imported from India. A star map on the ceiling of a tomb of 1116 C.E. displays the twelve Greek zodiac signs. Several astronomical instruments preserved at the old Beijing Observatory were made by Jesuit missionaries.

Because the ancient Chinese believed that sky phenomena were closely related to the sovereign power of the emperor, the Son of Heaven, common people were usually forbidden to learn astronomy privately. The nomenclature of stars and constellations, which were a projection of the ruling class, the government organizations, and provinces of the Chinese empire, clearly reflects the astrological characteristics of ancient Chinese astronomy.

Supported and administered by the government, Chinese astronomers maintained an assiduous watch of the sky and became the most persistent and accurate observers of celestial phenomena anywhere in the world in ancient times. In fact, Chinese records are almost the only ones available at least from about the fifth century B.C.E. to the tenth century C.E. According to recent statistics, there are more than ten thousand special astronomical events recorded in the literature, including roughly 270 on sunspots, 300 on auroral displays, 300 on meteorites, 1,600 on solar eclipses, 1,100 on lunar eclipses, 200 on lunar occultations, 100 on novae and supernovae, 1,000 on comets, 400 on meteor showers, and 4,900 on meteors. In addition, thousands of records on the movements of the planets and the moon are extant. Since most astronomers in ancient China were government employees, the large amount of records was therefore a result of activities of the bureaucratic state rather than of priests or independent scholars in the Western world.

The discovery of the Crab pulsar in 1967, which was associated with the guest star (nova) of 1054 in Chinese literature, stirred renewed interest in Chinese records. In addition to providing valuable information on galactic novae and supernovae, the abundance of the records allows modern astronomers to make significant progress in studying the nongravitational accelerations of the earth and moon from solar eclipses and solar variability using records of sunspots and auroras.

Aside from making observations and interpreting celestial portents, the Astronomical Bureau also was responsible for government timekeeping devices and for the selection of auspicious times and sites for various imperial functions. Another main responsibility of imperial astronomers was the promulgation of a yearly calendar. Being indispensable reference tools for daily life, millions of civil calendars were printed and sold every year in ancient China. Apart from setting the beginning date as well as length of each month and year, traditional Chinese civil calendars were aimed at providing people with advice about what to do and what not to do.

The system that permitted only astronomers in the bureaucracy ensured the continuity of astronomical activities but discouraged causal speculations. The ties between astronomy and the occult sciences limited the development of astronomical science.

The decline of astronomy happened especially in Ming (1368–1644) China. Imperial astronomers failed to accurately predict several solar and lunar eclipses using the official Datong calendar or the Muslim calendar, both of which were run side by side for reference purposes since 1450. Although there were instances where members of the bureau were punished because of incorrect calculations, the two systems were allowed to persist because there was a shortage of competent calendar-makers in the bureau. The worsening situation forced the Ministry of Rites to ask the emperor for permission to make a countrywide search for calendar experts in 1559. However, the effort was in vain.

The greatest impact on the Ming Astronomical Bureau came with the arrival of the Jesuit Matteo Ricci in China at the end of the sixteenth century. Knowing that astronomy was highly respected in China, the Jesuits decided to use it as a way of teaching Christianity. The prediction of the solar eclipse of June 21, 1629, allowed the traditional Chinese method, the Muslim method, and the Western method to be compared. Xu Guangqi, a Chinese Christian convert and a high-ranking scholar and official, succeeded in demonstrating the superiority of the Western method. In November of the same year, a calendar bureau was instituted. As the director of this new bureau, Xu organized more than fifty Chinese scholars and astronomers, most of whom were or later became Christians, to carry out the most far-reaching astronomical reform since the time of Guo Shoujing in the Yuan dynasty (1206–1368).

The Jesuits brought with them ideas that were new to the Chinese, such as that of a spherical earth. European theories of planetary and lunar motions, together with their algebraic and geometrical techniques, also provided improved predictions of planetary positions and eclipses. Xu persuaded the Jesuits who were officially appointed as consultants of the Calendar Bureau to undertake the introduction of scientific works from the West through translation during the reform. *The Chongzhen Lishu* (Astronomical Encyclopedia of the Chongzhen Reign Period) was the achievement of this effort, which marked the first large-scale introduction of Western sciences into China in modern times.

Christian astronomers in China made numerous observations in the late Ming period to test the astronomical system thus incorporated, and tried to demonstrate the superiority of the new method over the traditional Chinese and Muslim systems. Although the new method had been proved more accurate than traditional ones, the new system was promulgated just before the fall of the Ming dynasty and had not yet been used in the making of calendar books.

When the Manchus assumed the reins of government in China, the German Jesuit Adam Schall von Bell was appointed as the director of the Imperial Astronomical Bureau. He proposed to adopt Western almanacs in China; however, this idea was not favored by the government. Nonetheless, certain innovations were included in civil calendars.

In part because these reforms were contradictory to the traditional experience, and in part because they did not conform to the rationale of occult sciences, Schall's new calendars incurred great hostility. In time Schall became more tolerant toward Chinese astrology and the divinatory expressions in traditional civil calendars. Practical as the attitude might be, the Church condemned Chinese occult science as superstition.

Schall was accused by Yang Guangxian of making incorrect civil calendars and of selecting an inauspicious time to bury a deceased heir to the throne. Consequently, Schall and most Christian Chinese astronomers were removed from office in 1664; some of them were later beheaded.

Yang Guangxian presided over the Astronomical Bureau from 1665 to 1669. The traditional Chinese method and the Muslim method were resumed during the period. However, Schall's case was redressed in 1669, and the top posts in the bureau were given to the Jesuit Ferdinand Verbiest and his associates. To comply with the Church's attitude toward Chinese occult sciences, Western astrology was stealthily introduced into China by the Jesuit astronomers who were struggling between divination and the pope's command. After Verbiest, Jesuit astronomers controlled official astronomical practice in the bureau until 1826.

Except for the period of 1665–1669, the Tychonic world system was regarded as the tacitly recognized cosmology in China in the seventeenth and eighteenth centuries. Because of the character of Jesuit science, they opposed Copernicanism. The domination of the Tychonic system was seriously challenged only in the nineteenth century. However, because Chinese faith in astrology remained undiminished until the end of the Qing (1644–1911) period, Chinese astronomy was static at a time of major scientific advances in the West.

Only under the influence of the Self-Strengthening Movement (1861–1895) and the May Fourth Movement (1919) did astronomical science revive in China. In 1922, the Chinese Astronomical Society was founded in Beijing. Gao Lu of the Central Observatory was elected president at the inaugural meeting. When the society was set up, the Central Observatory, operated by the Chinese government, was limited to compiling almanacs. It lacked both funds and equipment for scientific research. In contrast, the Xujiahui, Sheshan, and Qingdao observatories as well as the Astronomy and Mathematics Department at Qilu University, set up by foreign countries, were concentrated on time service, photographic astrometry, and astronomy teaching.

In 1924, the Chinese government took over the Qingdao Observatory from Germany. In 1926, the Mathematics Department of Sun Yatsen University in Guangzhou was expanded and turned into the Mathematics and Astronomy Department and an affiliated observatory was set up in 1929. The Institute of Astronomy was founded in Nanjing in 1928 and the Purple Mountain Astronomical Observatory in 1934. After the outbreak of the Sino-Japanese War in 1937, the equipment and research workers of the Purple Mountain Observatory were moved to Kunming, and the Phoenix Hill Astronomical Observatory was established in Kunming by the Institute of Astronomy. During the war, the equipment in these institutions suffered destruction and loss, and work came to a standstill. Those engaged in astronomical research and teaching did not exceed thirty in number for the whole country at the end of World War II.

In 1949, China was divided into two parts because of the civil war: Taiwan, ruled by the Nationalist government, and Mainland China, ruled by the Communist government. Few astronomers moved to Taiwan in 1949, and astronomical activity in Taiwan before the seventies was very limited.

Only in 1977 did Central University in Chungli found the Institute of Physics and Astronomy, which provided the first graduate program of astronomy in Taiwan. A reflector of 60-cm aperture was set up at the Central University and used mainly for students. The astronomy program became an independent graduate institute in 1992. In addition, there is an active solar physics research group in Tsinghua University in Hsinchu.

Due to the involvement of Chinese-American astronomers led by Frank H. Shu, the development of astronomy has made great progress in recent years. A planning committee was set up in 1992, charged with creating an Institute of Astronomy and Astrophysics in the Academia Sinica, Taipei. This proposed institute will become the prime mover for the advancement of astronomy in Taiwan.

The development of astronomy on the mainland has been more rapid than that in Taiwan during the last forty years. Especially after the Communist Party promoted the opening and reform policy in 1980, astronomy has seen the unprecedented development of facilities for research and teaching. Since the early 1980s, a network of astronomical institutions has been structured. This system consists of five observatories (Purple Mountain Observatory, Shanghai Observatory, Beijing Astronomical Observatory, Yunnan Observatory, and Shaanxi Observatory), one factory (Nanjing Astronomical Instrument Factory), three departments (Department of Astronomy in Nanjing University, Department of Astronomy in Beijing Normal University, and Astronomy Section of the Department of Geophysics in Beijing University), three research divisions (the Astrophysical

Division of China Science and Technology University, the High Energy Astrophysics Division in the High Energy Physics Institute, and the Division of Historical Astronomy in the Institute for History of Sciences), and four stations (a Time Service Station in Wuhan Institute for Geodesy and Geophysics, the Astronomical Station in Urumqi, and Satellite Observation Stations in Guangzhou and Changchun).

New equipment and facilities have been allocated to these institutions. From 1984 to 1989, a synthesis aperture radio telescope consisting of twenty-eight dishes, a solar magnetic field telescope, a 1.26-meter infrared telescope, and a 2.16-meter telescope were installed in Beijing Astronomical Observatory. In 1987, a 25-meter radio dish and a 1.56-meter astrometric telescope were built in Shanghai Observatory. A 13.7-meter millimeter-wave radio telescope was mounted in Delingha Station of Purple Mountain Observatory in Qinghai Province. Among them, the performance of the solar magnetic field telescope is regarded as one of the best in the world, and the 2.16-meter telescope is the largest telescope in East Asia. Most instruments mentioned above were made in domestic factories and observatories, which marked a great leap forward in the manufacturing capability of China.

There are two professional journals of astronomy available in China: one is *Acta Astronomica Sinica,* first published in 1953; the other is *Acta Astrophysica Sinica,* first published in 1981. There is also a journal, *Chinese Astronomy and Astrophysics,* edited in Britain, which translates important Chinese papers into English.

More observational facilities were built in this decade than were constructed in the preceding eighty years, and the membership of the Chinese Astronomical Society is approaching two thousand; but the excellence of research in many fields of astronomy in China has not yet reached an internationally competitive level. However, increasing exchanges and collaboration between Taiwan and Mainland China astronomers as well as between Chinese and foreign astronomers may improve the situation in the near future.

Yi-Long Huang

Bibliography

Chen, Z. *Zhongguo Tianwenxue Shi* (History of Chinese Astronomy). 4 vols. Shanghai: Shanghai Renmin Chubanshe, 1980–1989.

Clark, D.H., and F.R. Stephenson. *The Historical Supernovae*. Oxford: Pergamon Press, 1977.

Hashimoto, K. *Hsü Kuang-Ch'i and Astronomical Reform*. Osaka: Kansai University Press, 1988.

Ho, P.Y. "Ancient and Mediaeval Observations of Comets and Novae in Chinese Sources." *Vistas in Astronomy* 5 (1962): 127–225.

———. *The Astronomical Chapters of the Chin Shu*. Paris: Mouton, 1966.

Huang, Y.-L. "Court Divination and Christianity in the K'ang-Hsi Era." *Chinese Science* 10 (1991): 1–20.

———. "An Examination on the Correctness of Chinese Chronological Tables—A Case Study of the Period using the Linde Calendar." *Hanxue Yanjiu* (Chinese Studies) 10, no. 2 (1992): 279–306.

Jiang, X. *Tianxue Zhenyuan* (The True Meaning of Astronomy). Shenyang: Liaoning Jiaoyu Chubanshe, 1991.

Needham, J., and W. Ling. *Science and Civilisation in China*, vol. 3. Cambridge: Cambridge University Press, 1959.

Pan, N. *Zhongguo Hengxing Guance Shi* (An Observational History of Stars in China). Shanghai: Xuelin Chubanshe, 1989.

Schafer, E.H. *Pacing the Void, T'ang Approaches to the Stars*. Berkeley: University of California Press, 1977.

Sivin, N. "Copernicus in China." In *Colloquia Copernicana, II,* edited by Union Internationale d'Histoire des Sciences, 63–122. Warsaw, 1973.

Xi, Z., and S. Po. "Ancient Oriental Records of Novae and Supernovae." *Science* 154 (1966): 597–603.

Yabuuchi, K. *Chugoku No Tenmon Rekiho* (Chinese Astronomy and Calendrical Science). Tokyo, 1969.

Yamada, K. *Jujireki No Michi* (The Road to the Shoushih Calendar System). Tokyo: Misuzu Shobo, 1980.

Zhongguo Tianwenxue Zai Qianjin (Chinese Astronomy on the March, in Commemoration of the Sixtieth Anniversary of the Foundation of the Chinese Astronomical Society, 1922–1982). Nanjing: Chinese Astronomical Society, 1982.

Zhongguo Tianwenxue Zai Qianjin (Chinese Astronomy on the March, in Commemoration of the Seventieth Anniversary of the Foundation of the

Chinese Astronomical Society, 1922–1992). Hefei: Press of the University of Science and Technology of China, 1992.

Zhuang, W., and L. Wang, eds. *Zhongguo Gudai Tianxiang Jilu Zongji* (A Compilation of the Astronomical Records in Ancient China). Nanjing: Jiangsu Kexue Jishu Chubanshe, 1987.

Chronograph

A device for recording the moment at which an observation is made. Its basic feature is a cylinder driven by a spring-powered or electrical mechanism to rotate uniformly once per minute. A pen, moved along the cylinder by a rotating screw, traces a continuous line on a piece of paper wrapped about the cylinder. Time marks or notches along the line are produced by tying the pen to the armature of an electromagnet in an electrical circuit which, on the one hand, is interrupted momentarily once every second by a mechanical circuit breaker in a clock, and on the other hand by a signal key held by an observer, say to record precisely the time of transit of a star as it passes the wire in the eyepiece of a transit telescope.

The need for the chronograph stemmed from the introduction as early as 1844 of electrical signals for comparing time between distant sites for longitude determination in the United States. In 1848, William Cranch Bond of **Harvard College Observatory** conceived the idea of an automatic circuit interrupter so that a clock would produce a signal at second intervals (there ensued a bitter debate between Bond and John Locke of Cincinnati over priority of this invention). In 1850, Bond added a governor to his chronograph to eliminate spacing irregularities between second marks on the paper record. Replacing the older practice of timing observations by interpolation between second counts by listening to a clock with automatic timing of observations for longitude determination—quickly termed the American method—made that task easier and more accurate, with random errors reduced to below 0.1 second of time. Automatic timing was quickly extended to astronomical observations for other purposes.

Use of chronographs has been replaced by more accurate electronic clocks and computer technologies.

Charles J. Peterson

Bibliography

Bond, W.C. "History and Description of the Astronomical Observatory of Harvard College." *Annals of the Harvard College Observatory* 1 (1856): xxiii–xxx, xlix–lv.

Holden, E.S. *Memorials of William Cranch Bond and of His Son George Phillips Bond.* San Francisco: C.A. Murdock, 1897.

Clairaut, Alexis-Claude (1717–1765)

French mathematician and celestial mechanician. As a child prodigy, Clairaut was educated by his father, a mathematics teacher in Paris. He played a large part in the first translation of Newton's *Principia* into French, incorporating some of his own research in the discussion. With Euler and d'Alembert he developed the

Chronograph formerly used by astronomers at the Georgetown College Observatory (Georgetown University) in Washington, D.C. Special paper was attached to the drum and a pen placed in the holder. The astronomer noted the time when the chronograph was started. The governor on the right ensured uniform motion. The astronomer pressed a button that sent a signal to the instrument that moved the pen upward. Later the astronomer could read the exact time of an observation from the sheet on the chronograph. (Courtesy of the National Museum of American History)

analytical methods that became the basis for celestial mechanics, in which he made important contributions to lunar theory and planetary theory. In anticipation of the return of Halley's Comet in 1759, he numerically integrated the perturbations due to Jupiter and Saturn to determine the date of perihelion passage. It was the first large-scale numerical integration of orbital motion.

LeRoy E. Doggett

Bibliography

Brunet, P. *La vie et l'oeuvre de Clairaut*. Paris: Presses Universitaires de France, 1952.

Itard, J. "Alexis-Claude Clairaut." In *Dictionary of Scientific Biography*, edited by C.C. Gillispie, vol. 3, 281–286. New York: Scribners, 1971.

Clark, Alvan (1804–1887)

Premier American telescope maker. Born in Ashfield, Massachusetts, Clark attended a local grammar school, worked briefly for a wagon maker, and spent many years engraving cylinders used to print textiles, before opening a portrait studio in Boston in 1836. Alvan Clark & Sons was established in Cambridgeport, Massachusetts, around 1850. It was incorporated in 1901, taken over by the Sprague-Hathaway Mfg. Co. in 1933, and dissolved in 1958.

In 1844, young **George Bassett Clark**'s attempt to make a small reflecting telescope interested his father in telescope construction. A few years later, his ability to locate the slight errors in the objective of the Harvard 15-inch refractor gave Clark the courage he needed to begin making telescopes. At that time, there was only one other commercial telescope maker (**Henry Fitz**). Popular interest in astronomy was growing rapidly and with it a market for telescopes.

Before the development of the Hartmann test, astronomers often tested their objectives by observing double stars. In the course of testing their objectives, Alvan and **Alvan Graham Clark** discovered several new doubles. In 1851 Alvan Clark detected an eighth-magnitude double in Canis Minor that was not listed in Admiral Smyth's catalogue, but which, he later found, had been discovered by **F.G.W. Struve**. William R. Dawes, a well-known English double star observer who would become Clark's first important customer, published measures of Clark's doubles, descriptions of his instruments, and commented on Clark's visual acuity.

The first recorded sale of a Clark telescope, a 5-inch achromatic refractor, came in 1848. By 1855 the Clarks had produced a dozen objectives ranging from 4 to 7 inches. By 1860 they had made a 12-inch objective that showed Mimas, the innermost satellite of Saturn. In 1860 the Clarks received an order from the University of Mississippi for an 18-inch lens, 3 inches larger than the Harvard and Pulkovo instruments. This was the first of five times that the Clarks would surpass the world's record and construct the largest telescope in existence. In 1873 they finished a 26-inch lens for the **United States Naval Observatory**; twelve years later a similar telescope was erected at the University of Virginia. In 1883 they provided the 30-inch lens for the Russian Observatory at Pulkovo. The 36-inch lens for the **Lick Observatory** was sent to California in 1887. And the 40-inch objective, mounted at the **Yerkes Observatory** in 1897, is still the largest objective ever mounted.

Alvan Clark joined the American Association for the Advancement of Science in 1850. At the 1856 meeting he read a paper describing a powerful double eyepiece micrometer that could measure celestial distances too great to be brought within the field of view of a single eyepiece powerful enough to see the objects.

Alvan Clark received many honors. In 1867 he was awarded the Rumford Medal of the American Academy of Arts and Sciences for his ability to figure nearly perfect lenses and for his method of local correction. Because even the best glass was irregular, the Clarks used local correction to obtain the sharpest possible focus rather than mathematically true curves. They apparently had been using this method for several years before the French physicist J.-B.-L. Foucault announced that he had developed the method in 1859.

To locate the figure errors the Clarks developed a test similar, but prior, to Foucault's knife-edge test for mirrors. Their test was made either on an actual star or, more conveniently, on an artificial star in the cellar of their workshop. Photographic lenses were tested photographically. After the irregularities were marked with red powder, the lens was laid flat and an optician would retouch the offending areas. Alvan Clark's sense of touch was said to be so acute that when a lens appeared perfect to the eye his fingers could still detect slight irregularities. Unable to find a cloth sufficiently soft for the final rub, Alvan Clark used his bare thumbs.

Most of the Clark objectives were figured like simple Fraunhofer lenses. The outer, crown glass lens was equiconvex; the flint lens was biconcave, with the side toward the eyepiece nearly flat. The inner surfaces had equal but opposite curves, and were separated by a distance that might be as much as several inches. The Clarks did not join the search for mathematically perfect lens configurations, and were little concerned with the new forms described by theoreticians. They made only one large lens, the 9-inch lens for Princeton, according to Gaussian curves. They found that the meniscus components were difficult to make, and they disagreed that they gave better color correction and sharper definition.

In the 1880s the Clarks developed two forms of photographic refractors. The Lick 36-inch is an ordinary visual achromat, with a third element that adapts the instrument for photography. For the Boyden telescope at Harvard, the Clarks produced a new combination of two lenses that could be arranged one way for photography and another way for visual observations.

Alvan Clark, who was also a renowned marksman, obtained a patent for a false loading muzzle in 1840. In 1851 he obtained a patent for a "simple and substantial eye-piece wherein ready access may be easily had to the glasses or lenses in order either to cleanse or repair them, as the case may require."

As business grew, the Clarks hired a half-dozen or so assistants, most of them European immigrants. The most important was Carl Axel Robert Lundin, a Swedish optician and mechanician who joined the Clarks in 1874 and remained until his death forty-one years later. In recognition of his work with telescopes Lundin received a medal at the 1876 Philadelphia Centennial Exhibition and a diploma from the 1893 Columbian Exposition.

Deborah Jean Warner

Bibliography

Warner, D.J. *Alvan Clark & Sons: Artists in Optics.* Washington, D.C.: Government Printing Office, 1968; reprint, Richmond, Va.: Willmann-Bell, 1996.

Clark, Alvan Graham (1832–1897)

American telescope maker. The younger son of **Alvan Clark**, he went to work in a machine shop at age sixteen. A few years later he joined his father and brother and spent the rest of his career with Alvan Clark & Sons, the renowned telescope makers of Cambridgeport, Massachusetts. Alvan Graham's forte was optics and, working with his father, he figured or tested most of the large objective lenses produced in the Clark factory. After Alvan Clark's death in 1887, Alvan Graham took responsibility for such important objectives as the 20-inch for the Denver Observatory, the 24-inch for the **Lowell Observatory**, the 24-inch Bruce photographic lens for the **Harvard College Observatory**, the 36-inch visual achromatic objective lens and its photographic corrector installed at the **Lick Observatory** in 1887, and the 40-inch installed at the **Yerkes Observatory** in 1897. Actual work on these instruments, however, was probably done by C.A.R. Lundin, who had been with the Clarks since 1874 and who would take over the operation of the firm after Alvan Graham Clark's death.

In January 1862, while testing the 18½-inch telescope, Clark discovered the companion of Sirius, a star whose existence the German astronomer Bessel had predicted in 1844. In honor of this discovery the Paris Academy of Sciences awarded Clark the Lalande Prize in 1862. In subsequent years Clark found more than a dozen other double stars, but he left the determination of their separations and position angles to others.

Clark went on three solar eclipse expeditions, and in 1870, using a single-prism spectroscope, Clark charted the spectrum of the aurora borealis.

In 1893, at the meeting of the Congress of Astronomy and Astrophysics, Clark speculated on telescopes of the future. He was then working on the 40-inch telescope for the Yerkes Observatory, and was confident that refractors would continue to prove superior to reflectors. Moreover, he doubted there was any practical limit to their size.

Deborah Jean Warner

Bibliography

Burnham, S.W. "Double-Stars Discovered by Mr. Alvan G. Clark." *American Journal of Science* 17 (1879): 283–289.

Clark, A.G. "Great Telescopes of the Future." *Astronomy and Astro-Physics* 12 (1893): 673–678.

———. "Possibilities of the Telescope." *North-American Review* 156 (1893): 48–53.

Wendell, O.C. "Alvan Graham Clark." *Proceedings, American Academy of Arts and Sciences* 33 (1897): 520–524.

Clark, George Bassett (1827–1891)

American telescope maker. The eldest child of **Alvan Clark**, George attended school in Cambridge, Massachusetts, and spent some time at Phillips Academy in Andover, preparing for Harvard, but he was always more interested in technical than classical pursuits.

Clark's mechanical bent was already apparent in childhood, when he used a lathe to make toys for his friends. While at Phillips Academy, he melted a piece of bell metal and made a 5-inch telescope mirror that revealed the satellites of Jupiter. After graduation he worked briefly as a civil engineer. In 1848 he joined the gold rush to California, but returned East after a few months, "richer in experience than in worldly goods." He then opened a shop in East Cambridge where he made and repaired scientific instruments. His father and brother soon joined the business, and they began trading as Alvan Clark & Sons in the mid-1850s.

George Bassett Clark was the mechanician of the firm and, although he never attracted the sort of public attention his father and brother enjoyed as optical craftsmen, he was appreciated by the astronomers for whom he made such complex and sophisticated apparatus as telescope mounts, spectroscopes, photometers, and photographic instruments. Astronomers at the **Harvard College Observatory** considered Clark a valuable resource. Clark's contributions to the Harvard instrumentation began with the spring-governor-controlled clock drive for the 15-inch refractor that made possible the first stellar photographs in 1857. When E.C. Pickering became director of the observatory, he called on Clark to make several photometers and the large instruments for the Henry Draper study of stellar spectra.

The **U.S. Naval Observatory** had the Clarks rework and repair much of their European apparatus in the 1860s and then produce important new equipment in the 1870s. While George Clark's work was often obscured by the large telescopes built by the firm, astronomers at the Naval Observatory viewed the micrometer he made for the 26-inch refractor as one of the finest ever made. George Clark also shouldered most of the responsibility for the various instruments ordered by the U.S. commission for the 1874 transit of Venus, pushing himself so hard to meet the deadlines that he ruined his health. Clark also produced the apparatus with which **Simon Newcomb** measured the velocity of light.

Deborah Jean Warner

Bibliography

Brashear, J.A. "George Bassett Clark." *Astronomy and Astro-Physics* 11 (1892): 367–371.

"George Bassett Clark." *Proceedings, American Academy of Arts and Sciences* 27 (1891–1892): 360–363.

Clemence, Gerald M. (1908–1974)

American dynamical astronomer. After receiving a Bachelor's degree in mathematics from Brown University in 1930, Clemence joined the staff of the **U.S. Naval Observatory**. He was appointed director of the Nautical Almanac Office in 1945 and then scientific director of the Naval Observatory in 1958. After retirement, he joined Yale University as a senior research associate and became a professor of astronomy in 1966. He served as president of the American Astronomical Society, 1958–1960.

Combining on-the-job experience with self-training, Clemence mastered the methods of planetary and lunar theory. Using early punched-card machines, he developed a new theory of Mars to replace the flawed theory of Simon Newcomb. Later, Clemence worked with **Dirk Brouwer** and **Wallace Eckert** to numerically integrate the orbits of the five outer planets, covering the period of telescopic observations and projecting a century into the future.

Brouwer and Clemence produced *Methods of Celestial Mechanics*, which remains a standard advanced textbook. Beginning in 1949, Clemence assisted Brouwer in editing the *Astronomical Journal*. Upon the death of Brouwer, he served as editor from 1966 to 1973.

LeRoy E. Doggett

Bibliography

Duncombe, R.L. "Gerald M. Clemence." *Physics Today* 28 (1975): 59–60.

Herget, P. "The Keeper of Mars." *Sky & Telescope* 49 (1975): 215–216.

Coast and Geodetic Survey

A legislative act of 1807 established what became known, in 1878, as the United States Coast and Geodetic Survey. Before 1878, when a decision was first made to connect the surveys on the Atlantic and Pacific coasts by a triangulation extending across the country, the institution was officially known as the U.S. Coast Survey. In 1982, the Coast and Geodetic Survey lost its separate existence when it became part of the National Ocean Survey.

This entry will focus on the history of the survey during the period when the connection with astronomy was especially important, the years from 1843 to 1867 when Alexander Dallas Bache served as superintendent. A discussion of the role of the Coast Survey in the development of astronomy during this period helps illuminate a number of major themes in the social and institutional history of modern science.

Under Bache's command, the Coast Survey became the most important scientific institution in the United States. Bache used the survey to provide financial and material support for the nascent scientific community. He also took advantage of his position to influence or gain control of other key scientific institutions, including the American Association for the Advancement of Science, the American Philosophical Society, and the National Academy of Sciences. Bache thus became the leader of the scientific community in the United States.

The astronomer Charles A. Young recalled that under Bache's command the Coast Survey encouraged astronomy more than any other branch of the federal government. The Coast Survey needed precise astronomical observations—including occultations, moon culminations, and eclipses—from both American and European observatories, in order to measure the shape of the earth and to determine the latitude and longitude of its survey stations. The Coast Survey experimented with a number of different instrumental and computational techniques to improve the accuracy of astronomical practice. In order to determine longitudes, the survey transported chronometers between England and the United States, and used a telegraphic connection to compare the timing of astronomical events at two different locations. The latter technique became known as the American method of longitude determination.

Bache sought to link Coast Survey activities with research in geodesy in Europe. European savants responded by praising the work of the survey. Astronomical research on the survey was pursued in connection with hydrography, geodesy, terrestrial magnetism, the study of the tides, meteorology, and natural history. Susan F. Cannon has coined the term "Humboldtian science" to characterize this interrelated complex of interests in which astronomy was linked to geophysical knowledge.

Bache used the Coast Survey to support American astronomy in a number of ways. Bache helped create and sustain a network of observers and observatories across the country. Although the Coast Survey operated hundreds of temporary observing stations, Congress forbade the survey to build permanent observatories. Bache reacted by connecting the survey to existing observatories, providing them with patronage in exchange for data. Coast Survey patronage supplemented the private patronage that had been especially important in building observatories but that often failed to support day-to-day astronomical research.

The best university observatories in the country participated in the astronomical work of the survey. Harvard, Brown, Amherst, and Dartmouth colleges cooperated in New England. In New York, Columbia College and the U.S. Military Academy also contributed data. The College of New Jersey and Georgetown supplied observations from the Middle Atlantic region. In the Middle West, Bache received data from Western Reserve College in Cleveland and the University of Michigan at Ann Arbor. There was no decent observatory in the southern United States for Bache to use, so he helped establish one of the first high-quality observatories in the South—at the College of Charleston, South Carolina.

Important observations used by the survey came from private observatories including the Dudley Observatory in Albany and the Cincinnati Observatory. Bache provided the Cincinnati Observatory with a transit instrument costing approximately $3,000. The director of the Central High School Observatory in Philadelphia, E. Otis Kendall, was paid $300 annually for data sets during the early 1850s.

The survey helped coordinate astronomical research in the United States not only by loaning instruments to individuals making observations for the survey but also by borrowing the best instruments from other astronomers. A prominent lawyer in New York City, Lewis M. Rutherfurd, provided the survey with instruments and a building that assistants used as a temporary observatory. While working in Nantucket in 1845, a Coast Survey observer used instruments owned by the survey, the Military Academy at West Point, the U.S. Navy, and a local amateur astronomer.

The Coast Survey supported all levels of astronomical research, including the important work of data reduction, which frequently was performed by college and university faculty members. The Harvard mathematician Benjamin Peirce analyzed important data and supervised the work of other calculators, especially after 1852 when he became the director of longitude determinations for the survey. A number of other mathematicians and scientists made calculations for the survey, including Sears Walker, John Downes, and Eugene Nulty, all from Philadelphia, and Stephen Alexander of the College of New Jersey. Outside calculators generally received $50 to $80 a month for work on a single project, such as occultations of stars computed for a particular station.

Because of the presence of Benjamin Peirce and other experts who served as consultants for the Coast Survey, Cambridge, Massachusetts, became a second center for the astronomical work of the survey (the Coast Survey office was located in Washington, D.C.). Bache supported the work of George and William Bond at the **Harvard College Observatory** and funded the consulting work of Benjamin A. Gould, the first American to receive a German Ph.D. in astronomy. The two permanent consultants at Cambridge, Benjamin Peirce and Benjamin Gould, annually received approximately $1,500 from the Coast Survey during the 1850s. The close connection between Cambridge and the Coast Survey led, in 1849, to the establishment at Cambridge of the Nautical Almanac Office. One of Peirce's students, the naval officer Charles Henry Davis, became the director of this institution after seven years as an assistant on the survey.

The early history of the survey underscores the importance of government patronage for astronomy. Historians have correctly emphasized the role of private philanthropy during the nineteenth century, but government patronage also needs to be considered. A history of the survey also provides a better understanding of crucial developments in the organization of astronomical research during the nineteenth century. The Coast Survey helped transform astronomy from an individualistic activity into a hierarchically organized large-scale enterprise involving a division of labor and managerial control. Actions of the Coast Survey also reveal how astronomy served the career interests of Alexander Dallas Bache and other scientist-entrepreneurs.

The manuscript records of the U.S. Coast and Geodetic Survey are held by the National Archives (Record Group 23).

Hugh R. Slotten

Bibliography

Bruce, R.V. *The Launching of Modern American Science, 1846–1876*. New York: Knopf, 1987.

Cannon, S.F. *Science in Culture: The Early Victorian Period*. New York: Dawson and Science History Publications, 1978.

Dupree, A.H. *Science in the Federal Government: A History of Policies and Activities to 1940*. Baltimore: Johns Hopkins University Press, 1986.

Manning, T.G. *U.S. Coast Survey vs. Naval Hydrographic Office: A 19th Century Rivalry in Science and Politics*. Tuscaloosa: University of Alabama Press, 1988.

Reingold, N. "Research Possibilities in the U.S. Coast and Geodetic Survey Records." *Archives Internationales d'Histoire des Sciences* 11 (1958): 337–346.

———. *Science in Nineteenth-Century America: A Documentary History*. Chicago: University of Chicago Press, 1964.

Slotten, H.R. "The Dilemmas of Science in the United States: Alexander Dallas Bache and the U.S. Coast Survey." *Isis* 84 (1993): 26–49.

———. *Patronage, Practice, and the Culture of American Science: Alexander Dallas Bache and the U.S. Coast Survey*. New York: Cambridge University Press, 1994.

Cometary Astronomy

Several times a century, a bright comet provides an impressive, naked-eye, display in a night sky. The solid nucleus of a comet, composed of dust particles embedded in frozen ices, is only a few miles across and far too small to be seen with the naked eye. However when a comet approaches the sun, the ices vaporize into gases and these gases expand away to form an enormous cometary atmosphere. Dust particles entrained in the expanding gas are pushed back in the antisolar direction by solar radiation pressure to form dust tails; the ion, or gas, tails result when the comet's gases are first ionized by the sun's radiation and then blown back in the antisolar direction by high-speed charged solar wind particles. Even a comparatively small cometary nucleus can generate an atmosphere as large as the sun and gas and dust tails that stretch over distances comparable to the separation between the sun and earth. Although their gas and dust densities are extremely low, the atmosphere and tails of an impressive comet can dwarf the dimensions of other solar system objects.

With the single exception of periodic comet Halley, all impressive naked-eye com-

Comet Ikeya-Seki, November 1, 1965. The exposure was 3 minutes on Kodak Royal X Pan Recording Film and a K-37 areal camera. (Courtesy of the National Aeronautics and Space Administration)

ets have orbital periods about the sun that are measured in thousands or millions of years. These objects arrive in the earth's neighborhood on no particular schedule, their motions are not confined to the ecliptic plane of the planets, and they appear to fade from view as mysteriously as they arrived.

Because of their unusual, infrequent, and unpredictable appearances, it was not until the era of **Edmond Halley** and Isaac Newton that comets were treated in the same manner as the other planetary bodies. This period marks a rough transition in cometary thought from a belief that comets were not celestial objects to a realization that indeed they are members of our solar system. This period also marked a change in the perception of comets as heavenly signs (usually malefic) to a realization that the elliptic nature of cometary paths about the sun would allow collisions with the earth itself. Before the work of Halley and Newton, comets were often considered as warning signs to a sinful earth from a vengeful God. Subsequent to this work, comets were most often feared because they might be celestial missiles capable of striking the earth.

Among the ancient Greeks, Aristotle was the dominant scientific authority, and his influence on subsequent cometary ideas would be difficult to overestimate. Aristotle did not regard comets as celestial phenomena and so did not include them in his work on heavenly bodies (*De Caelo*), but rather in his treatise on terrestrial phenomena (*Meteorologica*). He believed comets would form when the sun, or planets, warmed the earth causing the evaporation of dry, warm exhalations from the earth itself. These exhalations rose up through the airy sphere and upon reaching the border of the fourth fiery sphere, the friction of their motion ignited them and the resultant comet, along with neighboring dry exhalations, was carried about the earth by the circular motion of the heavens in the fifth sphere. The form and duration of the comet depended upon the amount and form of the exhalation. Expressed in the fourth century B.C.E., the Aristotelian view of comets went nearly unchallenged for two millennia.

Astrological interpretations of comets were promoted by the second century Roman scholar **Ptolemy**, who wrote in his *Tetrabiblos* that comets should be regarded as mysterious signs or portents that provoke discord among men and give rise to wars and other evil consequences. During the Middle Ages, the bulk of cometary literature was astrological in nature. Writers were unwilling to deviate from Aristotle's views on the origin of comets or Ptolemy's reported relationship between comets and adversity. During this period, scholars did not discuss the physical nature of comets but rather their meaning.

Because of the astrological importance of comets as portents, Chinese court astrologers frequently scanned the skies for new signs that might guide their astrological interpretations. For centuries, they made and recorded observations of cometary apparitions including detailed notes on cometary positions with respect to the neighboring stars.

It was not until the great comet of 1577 that the techniques and instrumentation were accurate enough to decide whether comets were terrestrial phenomena or celestial objects beyond the moon. **Tycho Brahe**, Michael Mästlin, and Cornelius Gemma all made distance, or parallax, measurements of this comet and each inferred the comet's position as beyond the moon. Tycho gathered many of the parallax measurements together and published the results in a 1588 Latin treatise whose short title is *De Mundi*. Tycho placed the comet of 1577 in a circular orbit about the sun just outside the heliocentric orbits of Mercury and Venus, but, in an attempt to maintain the geocentric view of Aristotle, the sun itself was put in motion about the stationary earth.

Though Tycho's work departed somewhat from Aristotelian dogma, subsequent works by **Galileo Galilei** and **Johannes Kepler** were based largely upon the traditional Aristotelian views. Prompted by a 1619 treatise on comets by the Jesuit scholar Horatio Grassi, Galileo argued that there was no evidence that comets travel in closed orbits, and that the observations of the recent comets of 1618 could be explained by assuming rectilinear motion. In his 1619 work *De Cometis Libelli Tres*, Kepler also argued that comets are ephemeral bodies and travel in straight lines. At the time, there were no accurate techniques for computing the orbital paths of comets, and Galileo and Kepler could, in fact, approximately represent the observed phenomena by assuming rectilinear motion for comets.

In the decades prior to the 1687 publication of Isaac Newton's *Principia*, there were diverse opinions on the nature and motion of comets. However, a few common opinions were evident. The celestial nature of comets was no longer seriously questioned since an increasing number of parallax determinations had demonstrated that comets were not below the moon. However, Aristotelian cometary ideas were still pervasive and most contemporary savants considered the origin of comets to be due to agglomerations or exhalations from the heavenly bodies. In many contemporary theories, the all-pervasive aether took an active role in either the appearance or dynamics of comets. Robert Hooke suggested the aether as a mechanism for dissolving a comet's head and providing the tail curvature, while **Johannes Hevelius** offered the aether as a resisting medium capable of explaining the observed nonuniformity of cometary motions.

More important than the Aristotelian concepts of exhalations and the all-pervasive aether was the notion that transitory objects have rectilinear orbits and that permanent bodies travel upon circular paths. This principle was not questioned and often provided a starting point for a particular theory. In the pre-Newtonian era, most scholars first decided whether comets were permanent or transitory and then tried to fit the observations to the appropriate path. Hence, two schools of cometary thought were evident. The first believed, a priori, that comets were permanent celestial objects and hence had circular (or at least closed) orbits. To this school belonged **Jean-Dominique Cassini**, Adrien Auzout, Pierre Petit, Giovanni Alfonso Borelli, and others. The second school, which included Hevelius and Christiaan Huygens, considered comets as transitory objects whose motions were uniform and rectilinear.

For those comets observed through most of the seventeenth century (for example, 1607, 1618, 1652, 1664, 1665), only a segment of their paths was observed and their motions on the sky could be crudely fit with either a closed orbit or one that was nearly rectilinear. However, the comet seen in November and December 1680 was observed both before and after perihelion and its apparent motion was completely inconsistent with a rectilinear path.

In one of his final efforts prior to the publication of his *Principia* in 1687, Isaac Newton developed a technique for computing parabolic orbits of comets from three position observations. Although Newton himself applied the technique only to John Flamsteed's observations of the comet of 1680, Edmond Halley used Newton's technique for two dozen comets that had been well observed between 1337 and 1698 and noted that the comets seen in 1531, 1607, and 1682 had remarkably similar orbital characteristics. In his *Synopsis of the Astronomy of Comets* (1705), Halley boldly predicted that this was a single comet making periodic returns and that the comet, which would one day bear his name, should return in 1758. **Alexis-Claude Clairaut** refined Halley's prediction by taking into account the perturbative effects of Jupiter and Saturn. His prediction for the comet's time of perihelion passage in early 1759 was in error by only thirty-three days. Cometary research in the eighteenth century focused upon the dynamics of these objects.

For much of his professional career, Johann Franz Encke studied the motion of the periodic comet that now bears his name. In 1819, Encke showed that comets seen in 1786, 1795, 1805, and 1819 were one and the same object. The subsequent prediction for this comet's return in 1822 was the first success to follow Halley's 1705 prediction. When Encke's comet did return in 1822, Encke noted that the observed perihelion passage was a few hours earlier than his prediction and he postulated that a resisting medium, which his computations had not taken into account, might be responsible for the slight shrinkage of the comet's orbit.

In the eighteenth and early nineteenth centuries, the success with which Newtonian mechanics had been applied to the motions of comets increased the veneration of Newton's ideas concerning the physical nature of comets. According to Newton, comets were solid, permanent, celestial bodies. Newton acknowledged Kepler's notion of tail particles being carried along into the tail region by the action of solar rays. However Newton's own ideas on cometary tails began with an analogy with smoke rising from a chimney. Cometary tail particles were heated by the sun's rays and these particles then heated the surrounding aether. The subsequent rarefaction of the aether caused it to ascend away from the sun, carrying along the tail particles. In one final speculation on cometary tails, Newton suggested that the tail vapors, continually rarefied and dispersed, would spread throughout the heavens, be gradually accreted by the planets, resupplying them with vital fluids spent upon "vegetation and putrefaction." Thus, cometary vapors became essential for life on earth.

The development of polarization and spectroscopic techniques in the late nineteenth century provided the diagnostic tools necessary for investigating the physical nature of comets. Dominique F.J. Arago observed the tail region of comet 1819 II Tralles with a doubly refracting prism attached to a small telescope. The two tail images, representing two states of polarization, were of slightly different intensities, indicating that at least some of the light coming from the tail was polarized and hence reflected sunlight. Early spectroscopic investigations by Giovanni Battista Donati and **William Huggins** established that comets do emit their own radiation as well as reflect the sun's rays, and some success was achieved in attributing broad spectral emission features to the carbon molecule. However, an understanding of the complex structure and the identification of various molecular bands did not progress very far until the development of quantum mechanics in the late 1920s. Hence the early interpretations of cometary spectroscopic observations were often confused. Nevertheless, the mere presence of molecular bands in a cometary spectrum implied that gases were present in an excited state. The additional presence of continuum radiation in a comet's spectrum implied that its atmosphere contained solid reflecting surfaces.

By the late nineteenth century, the connection between comets and meteor streams was well established. In 1866, **Giovanni Virginio Schiaparelli** noted the orbital similarities between comet Swift-Tuttle (1862 III) and the meteor stream giving rise to the annual Perseid meteor showers. The following year a similar relationship was noted between comet Tempel-Tuttle and the Leonid meteor stream. Largely as a result of these identifications, Newton's model of a solid cometary body was supplanted by a model of a comet as a cloud of individual particles.

The year 1950 marked distinct turning points in the cometary paradigm for the cometary physical model and the origin of comets. In a 1950 paper, Fred L. Whipple put forward his icy conglomerate model for the cometary nucleus. One of the principal motivations for this model was to explain the so-called nongravitational effects that had been first noted in the motion of periodic comet Encke. Whipple suggested that the cometary nucleus was indeed a solid body made up of several frozen ices, including water, with embedded dust particles. When these dirty ice balls approach the sun, the vaporization of their ices introduce a small, rocketlike thrust upon the nucleus itself, and this effect had caused comet Encke to consistently arrive at perihelion prior to the predicted times that were based upon purely Newtonian mechanics. Also in 1950, **Jan H. Oort** analyzed the orbital characteristics of very long period comets and concluded that they must arrive in the inner solar system from a reservoir, or cloud, of 190 billion comets surrounding the sun out to distances of 50,000 to 150,000 astronomical units. Oort noted that the observed numbers and orbits of long-period comets could be explained if occasional stars passed through the cloud and perturbed comets into the inner solar system.

In March 1986 a total of five spacecraft flew past the nucleus of comet Halley, and the images returned from the European spacecraft revealed a black, irregularly shaped object that emitted dust and gas from vents covering only about 10 percent of its surface area. Water ice was identified as making up 80 percent of the volatile ices with a roughly equal amount by

Great Comets since 1550 C.E.

First Date Reported	*Observational Interval*	*Perihelion*		*Perigee*		*Maximum Brightness*		*Notes*
		Date	*Dist.*	*Date*	*Dist.*	*Date*	*Mag.*	
1556 Feb. 27	73	4/22	0.49	3/13	0.08	3/14	–2	
1577 Nov. 1	79	10/27	0.18	11/10	0.63	11/08	–3	
1607 Sept. 21	35	10/27	0.58	9/29	0.24	9/29	1–2	Halley
1618 Nov. 16	67	11/08	0.40	12/06	0.36	11/29	0–1	
1664 Nov. 17	75	12/05	1.03	12/29	0.17	12/29	–1	
1665 Mar. 27	24	4/24	0.11	4/04	0.57	4/20	–1	1
1668 Mar. 3	27	2/28	0.07	3/05	0.80	3/08	1–2	
1680 Nov. 23	80	12/28	0.01	11/30	0.42	12/29	1–2	2
1682 Aug. 15	40	9/15	0.58	8/31	0.42	8/31	0–1	Halley
1686 Aug. 12	30	9/16	0.34	8/16	0.32	8/27	1–2	
1743 Nov. 29	45	3/01	0.22	2/27	0.83	2/20	–3	3
1769 Aug. 15	100	10/08	0.12	9/10	0.32	9/22	0	4
1807 Sept. 9	90	9/19	0.65	9/27	1.15	9/20	1–2	
1811 Apr. 11	260	9/12	1.04	10/16	1.22	10/20	0	
1843 Feb. 5	48	2/27	0.006	3/06	0.84	3/07	1	5
1858 Aug. 20	80	9/30	0.58	10/11	0.54	10/07	0–1	
1861 May 13	90	6/12	0.82	6/30	0.13	6/27	0	4
1865 Jan. 17	36	1/14	0.03	1/16	0.94	1/24	1	6
1874 June 10	50	7/09	0.68	7/23	0.29	7/13	0–1	
1882 Sept. 1	135	9/17	0.008	9/16	0.99	9/08	–2	7
1901 Apr. 12	38	4/24	0.24	4/30	0.83	5/05	1	
1910 Jan. 13	17	1/17	0.13	1/18	0.86	1/30	1–2	8
1910 Apr. 10	80	4/20	0.59	5/20	0.15	5/20	0–1	Halley
1927 Nov. 27	32	12/18	0.18	12/12	0.75	12/08	1	9
1965 Oct. 3	30	10/21	0.008	10/17	0.91	10/14	2	10
1970 Feb. 10	80	3/20	0.54	3/26	0.69	3/20	0–1	11
1976 Feb. 5	55	2/25	0.20	2/29	0.79	3/01	0	12

Notes

1. Last observed on April 20 as it approached solar conjunction.

2. Discovered with the aid of a telescope on November 14. On December 18, it was observable 2° from the sun at noon.

3. Visible in daylight only 12° from the sun on February 27.

4. Tail reported as longer than 90° at closest approach to earth.

5. On the date of perihelion this sungrazing comet was observed in daylight nearly 1° from the sun.

6. Comet observed in Southern Hemisphere.

7. The Great September comet was a brilliant object that was observed very close to the sun, and split into at least four separate pieces near perihelion. This comet and comet Ikeya-Seki in 1965 are believed to be members of the same family of sungrazing comets.

8. This comet was easily observed on January 17 only 4.5° from the sun. It is often confused with the later apparition of comet Halley in mid-1910.

9. On December 18, this comet was seen in daylight only 5° from the sun. At the end of December, the tail was reported to be nearly 40° in length.

10. Sungrazing comet Ikeya-Seki split into two or possibly three pieces near perihelion. Toward the end of October, the impressive tail reached lengths in excess of 45°.

11. The tail of comet Bennett reached 10° in mid-March.

12. Comet West's impressive broad tail reached a length of 30° on March 8. Near perihelion, the comet split into four pieces.

weight of dark silicate dust particles. These spacecraft images dramatically validated the ideas that Whipple had put forward almost forty years earlier and put to rest the model of a comet as a cloud of discrete particles.

In a 1980 paper by Luis Alvarez and colleagues, the suggestion was made that an asteroidal impact was responsible for a major biological extinction event sixty-five million years ago. Natural satellite images returned from the *Voyager* spacecraft revealed heavily cratered landscapes in the outer solar system, and there followed a growing perception of comets and asteroids as major evolutionary forces within the solar system. In 1961, John Oró suggested that cometary impacts with the earth were responsible for depositing the water-and-carbon bearing molecules that allowed life to form. By the end of the twentieth century, comets were perceived as possibly playing a major role in the evolution of life itself—a notion first hinted at by Isaac Newton three centuries earlier.

Great Comets: A Checklist

A relative few comets are so visually impressive as to be termed "great comets." Just the right set of circumstances must occur. Far from the sun, the solid portions of comets, which consist mostly of water ice and embedded dust particles, are inactive. They are not large enough to be seen with the naked eye. However, when near the sun, the icy cometary surfaces vaporize and throw off large quantities of gas and dust thus forming the enormous atmosphere and tails that make comets so visually striking. It is the fluorescing of these gases, and particularly the reflection of sunlight from the minute dust particles in the comet's atmosphere and tail, that can make these objects so impressive. However, this activity by itself does not ensure that a comet will become a great comet. An active comet can become great only by making a particularly close approach to the sun so that it produces enormous quantities of gas and dust or by making a close approach to the earth so that its tail can be easily viewed. In either case, great comets must be seen in a dark sky.

While applying the appellation "great comet" to a particular cometary return is a subjective process, the table on page 158 is an attempt to list the great naked-eye comets that have been reported since 1550 C.E.. With the single exception of periodic comet Halley, all the tabulated comets have passed through the inner solar system either for the first time, or the intervals between their returns are measured in thousands or millions of years. The first tabular entry gives the approximate date the comet was first reported as a naked-eye object. The following column gives the approximate observational interval (in days) during which the comet remained a naked-eye object. The next two columns give the date and distance in astronomical units when the comet reached its closest point to the sun (perihelion). One astronomical unit is the mean distance between the sun and earth. The following columns give the date and distance when the comet reached its closest point to the earth (perigee), and the date and apparent magnitude when the comet reached its brightest in a dark sky. A diffuse cometary image becomes visible to the naked eye when it reaches a magnitude of approximately 4 in a dark sky. Compared with a comet whose magnitude is 4, a 3rd magnitude comet would appear 2.5 times brighter, and a magnitude 2 comet would appear 2.5 × 2.5 = 6.3 times brighter still, and so on. The brightest star in the sky (Sirius) has an apparent magnitude of –1.5. At its brightest, the planet Jupiter appears at magnitude –2.7. For the two sixteenth-century comets the Julian calendar is used, while the dates for the remaining comets are referred to the Gregorian calendar.

Donald K. Yeomans

Bibliography

Alvarez, L.W., W. Alvarez, F. Asaro, and H.V. Michel. "Extraterrestrial Cause for the Cretaceous—Tertiary Extinction." *Science* 208 (1980): 1095–1108.

Hellman, C.D. *The Comet of 1577: Its Place in the History of Astronomy*. New York: AMS Press, 1971.

Jervis, J.L. *Cometary Theory in Fifteenth-Century Europe*. Dordrecht: D. Reidel, 1985.

Oró, J. "Comets and the Formation of Biochemical Compounds on the Primitive Earth." *Nature* 190 (1961): 389–390.

Ruffner, J.A. *The Background and Early Development of Newton's Theory of Comets*. Bloomington: Indiana University Press, 1966.

———. "The Curved and the Straight: Cometary Theory from Kepler to Hevelius." *Journal for the History of Astronomy* 2 (1971): 178–194.

Yeomans, D.K. *Comets, a Chronological History of Observation, Science, Myth, and Folklore*. New York: John Wiley and Sons, 1991.

Constants, Astronomical

Astronomical constants are certain defined, observed, and derived fundamental quantities adopted by international agreement. They are used for a variety of purposes, including production of astronomical tables of the sun, moon, and planets. They include the masses of the planets, the astronomical unit (earth-sun distance), precession, nutation, aberration, and the velocity of light, among others. The idea of a system of constants to be used internationally seems to have originated with **Simon Newcomb** by the time he became superintendent of the U.S. Nautical Almanac Office in 1877. Despite their name, values for the astronomical constants have evolved over time with improved data; those adopted at the Paris international congress of 1896, based on Newcomb's work, were used in the British and American ephemerides beginning in 1901. In 1938 Willem de Sitter and **Dirk Brouwer** for the first time analyzed the entire system of constants as a unified whole, pointing out their relationships and inconsistencies. Except for the replacement of Universal Time by Ephemeris Time in the principal almanacs in 1960, most of Newcomb's system remained intact until 1968, when new constants (IAU, 1964 system) were introduced with the approval of the **International Astronomical Union** (IAU). Rapid progress in theory and observation necessitated the IAU (1976) system of constants, which were officially introduced in 1984.

Astronomical constants are important because the ephemerides generated from the theories in which they are used are the basis for navigational almanacs and predictions of phenomena such as eclipses, occultations, and moon rise and set. More generally, accurate constants permit valid comparison of ephemerides with observation, highlighting discrepancies such as the advance in the perihelion of Mercury that may need to be explained by new theories. For these reasons, the determination of more accurate astronomical constants has been a major theme in the history of astronomy, evident, for example, by the immense effort of the eighteenth- and nineteenth-century transit of Venus expeditions to determine the solar parallax, and thereby the distance from the earth to the sun and the scale of the entire solar system.

Steven J. Dick

Bibliography

Clemence, G.M. "The System of Astronomical Constants." In *Annual Review of Astronomy and Astrophysics*, edited by L. Goldberg, A. Deutsch, and D. Layzer, vol. 3, 93–112. Palo Alto: Annual Reviews, 1965.

Seidelmann, P.K., ed. *Explanatory Supplement to the Astronomical Almanac*. Mill Valley, Calif.: University Science Books, 1992.

Constellations

Constellations are arbitrary groupings of stars that are perceived as figures or patterns and named after characters from classical mythology, common animals, and objects.

Precisely when and where the practice of dividing the sky into constellations first occurred is not known, but it was very long ago. Astronomical ceilings in Egyptian tombs, which date back to 1470 B.C.E., depict constellations such as the Hippopotamus, Crocodile, and Bull. In the eighth century, Homer and Hesiod mentioned a few familiar star groups, including Orion, Ursa Major, the Hyades, and the Pleiades (today an asterism in Taurus). And the Babylonian star list, known as the ^{mul}APIN series (ca. 700 B.C.E.), recorded the twelve zodiacal constellations among eighteen star groups in the path of the moon. Current research suggests that the constellations known to the Babylonians originated much earlier—perhaps with the Sumerians before 2000 B.C.E.—and that transmission to the Babylonians, and from them to the Greeks, involved more than one culture and a process of innovation as well as adaptation.

The earliest-known systematic description of the Greek constellations, which are still used today, was by Eudoxus of Cnidus. Eudoxus wrote two books to accompany a celestial globe (all now lost). Nonetheless, our understanding of the Eudoxan constellations is aided by the work of Aratus of Soli and the Farnese Atlas (a late second-century statue). Aratus versified the *Phaenomena* of Eudoxus, and his poem was immensely popular. It prompted at least twenty-seven commentaries; was translated into Latin and later Arabic; helped to make the figures of the constellations conventional; and along with the works of Pseudo-Eratosthenes, Hyginus, and Marcus Manilius, contributed to constellation lore and mythology well into the early modern era. Unearthed in the sixteenth century and preserved today in the Museo Archeologico Nazionale in Naples, the Farnese Atlas is a Roman copy of a Greek statue. The celestial globe borne on the shoulders of the Atlas appears to be a direct descendant of the Eudoxan globe. Analysis of these works has led some historians to argue that the Eudoxan/Aratean constellations were arranged as they would have appeared to people living near the latitude of 36 degrees north in about 2000 B.C.E. The human figures were drawn from a geocentric point of view—that is, they turned their faces and bodies in toward the earth.

Since Antiquity, the constellations have served as finding aids. **Ptolemy**, for instance, catalogued stars according to their positions within the figures of forty-eight constellations. Any stars left over were grouped with nearby constellations. While not the first to use constellations in this way, Ptolemy's catalogue became the starting point for all later divisions of the sky. Because the constellations served as reference systems, they kept their basic shapes from one map to another, even though depictions of them reflected the artistic conventions and dress of different times and places in the Eastern and Western worlds. In Persia, Abu'l-Husayn al-Ṣūfī clothed each Ptolemaic figure in Arabic dress and illustrated it as it appeared in the sky, and in reverse, as it would appear on a star globe. Many Persian and Arabic copies of his *Book of the Fixed Stars* have been preserved. His orientalized designs influenced later cartographers, for whom classical, scientific depictions of the constellations were generally unavailable. In the Renaissance, European cartographers continued to follow the lead of Islamic artists, but often replaced oriental attire with classical garb and fixed mythological inaccuracies (for example, by substituting the head of Medusa for the bearded ghoul held by Perseus in Islamic astronomical works). They also borrowed imagery from illustrated texts of Aratus and Hyginus, even though this mythography differed from that in the Ptolemaic corpus.

For over fourteen hundred years, European and Islamic astronomers focused their attention on Ptolemy's stars and a few faint stars noted by Bedouins. Beginning in the sixteenth and seventeenth centuries, however, many non-Ptolemaic stars—both inside and outside the borders of the Ptolemaic constellations—were catalogued by **Tycho Brahe** and astronomers in Europe; by navigators and astronomers such as Pieter Dircksz Keyser and Frederik de Houtman, who traveled to the East Indies between 1595 and 1602; and by **Galileo Galilei** and others using the newly invented telescope. These stars were formed into new constellations.

In 1536, Kaspar Vopel may have been the first to add to the list of constellations handed down by Ptolemy, when he charted Coma Berenices and Antinous on a celestial globe (currently in the Kölnisches Stadtmusuem). Some of the new constellations represented real or fabulous animals, but many more glorified voyages of exploration, reinforced religious and political values, served the patronage system, or celebrated scientific achievements.

In order to commemorate recent discoveries, for example, the Dutch geographer Petrus Plancius, grouped the southern stars observed by Keyser into Indus (an Indian), Tucana (a toucan), Piscis Volans (a flying fish), and other exotic creatures of the New World. The same sentiment was expressed two hundred years later, when William Croswell of Boston charted the Bust of Columbus.

As an act of religious devotion, Renaissance navigators had introduced the Southern Cross. Plancius, who was a Calvinist theologian as well as a geographer, grouped other field stars into seven constellations with biblical connotations; these included Columba (Noah's dove) and the rivers Jordanus and Tigris. Argo Navis, the ship, he renamed for Noah's Ark. During the Reformation and Counterreformation, others tried to rid the heavens of pagan associations. Wilhelm Schickard of Tübingen printed a biblical gloss of traditional constellations on his maps, whereas Julius Schiller, a Catholic lawyer of Augsburg, replaced the twelve signs of the zodiac with the Apostles, the northern constellations with New Testament figures, and the southern constellations with Old Testament figures.

Some astronomers took a more political course. In a tradition established by Galileo, who had named the Jovian satellites the Medicean stars, celestial cartographers used their maps to lionize monarchs, archbishops, and patrons. Edward Sherburne, a Catholic royalist in Britain, charted Cor Caroli for the heart of Charles I. **Edmond Halley** created Robur Carolinum to represent the oak at Boscobel in which Charles II hid from Republican soldiers. **Johannes Hevelius** charted Scutum Sobiescianum, the shield of John Sobiesci III, King of Poland. Ignace-Gaston Pardies and Augustin Royer of Paris charted Lilium and Sceptrum, respectively, in honor of Louis XIV. This pattern continued to the end of the eighteenth century, when Johann Elert Bode of Berlin created Friedrichs Ehre in honor of Frederick the Great.

Scientific research, achievements, and craftsmanship were also recognized by the cartographers. In a tribute to their instruments, Hevelius charted Sextans (sextant); Joseph-Jérôme Lefrançais de Lalande created Quadrans Muralis (mural quadrant); and Nicolas-Louis de Lacaille charted Horologium (pendulum clock), Reticulum (his micrometer), Telescopium, and Mensa (Table Mountain, where he worked at the Cape of Good Hope, 1751–1752). On either side of the place where Uranus was first sighted, Maximilian Hell defined Tubus Herschelii Minor and Tubus Herschelii Major (for William Herschel's small and large telescopes).

Northern and southern constellations as depicted on planispheres by Johannes Honter of Kronstadt in 1532. (Courtesy of the Adler Planetarium, Chicago, Illinois)

Constellations in Bode's 1801 atlas commemorated the Montgolfiers' balloon flights and the invention of movable type. He joined Lacaille in depicting philosophical apparatus, artists' tools, and mathematical instruments.

By the turn of the nineteenth century, when Bode published his atlas, *Uranographia*, there were at least ninety-nine constellations, and astronomers realized that the proliferation of new star groups had become unmanageable. During the course of the nineteenth century, the newer constellations began to be dropped from atlases. Another problem persisted, however. There was no consensus on the boundary lines between constellation figures. Cartographers snaked dotted lines between star groups, but these lines differed from map to map. The **International Astronomical Union** took action at its first general assembly in 1922. It officially adopted a list of eighty-eight constellations, which are still in use today. Eugène Delporte, a Belgian astronomer, was commissioned to draw up a definitive list of boundaries, and his work, *Délimitation scientifique des constellations* (1930), was tantamount to an international scientific treaty. Constellations have since been regarded as precisely defined areas of the sky; their boundaries follow arcs of right ascension and declination.

From the nineteenth century until very recent times, most research on the history and mythology of celestial constellations has been carried out by art historians, mythologists, and philologists, rather than historians. In general, their more erudite publications have been targeted at classicists. The less scholarly books have been aimed at coffeetables. In the last thirty years, however, a small number of astronomers and historians of science have begun to examine the history of constellations, making use of archaeological, philological, scientific, historic, literary, and art-historical sources. Their work can be divided into two main groups: (a) studies of the origin of constellations; and (b) surveys of celestial cartography.

IMAGINES CONSTELLATIONVM
AVSTRALIVM.

In the first group, scholars have considered when, where, why, and how ancient people divided the sky into constellations. In examining different cultures, many archaeologists and anthropologists have speculated that the origin of constellations was connected to the importance of stars in the routine lives of indigenous or early peoples, particularly in determining the times for agricultural tasks, or in finding their way in undifferentiated terrains (such as water, desert, or snow). What counts as evidence for the existence of a system of constellations has itself been the subject of controversy; archaeoastronomers, for instance, have debated whether prehistoric cup marks on stones in Europe could be representations of constellations.

For many years, the starting point for studies of the origin of the current system of constellations has been the work of Aratus and the puzzling fact that the Eudoxan globe he described was more than fifteen hundred years out of date (as a result of precession) and designed for a latitude south of Greece and north of Egypt (where Eudoxus did not live). How Eudoxus came to possess this historical artifact or why he failed to notice its incongruity with the heavens of his day has been the subject of some interesting speculation. Whereas many historians have avoided drawing conclusions from Aratus about the development of the constellations long before Eudoxus, others have more boldly suggested that all the classical constellations were designed at one definite time and place according to a preconceived plan. Recent studies of cuneiform texts do not support that position, however, for they reveal that the Babylonians used some star groups not mentioned by Eudoxus, even though his globe predated them. Consequently, most historians of science have come to recognize that the constellations were invented, developed, transmitted, and adapted within and across various cultures.

To learn more about the processes by which constellations have been invented, developed, and transmitted in more recent times, scholars can turn to books in the second historiographic category—namely, historical surveys of celestial cartography. The main drawbacks are that most works in this category are catalogues of maps, atlases, and globes, and many treat terrestrial and celestial cartography together. As essential reference works, these are useful starting points for research, but the scholar has to ferret out the information of interest. They excel, however, in providing historical images of the constellations.

Although many devoted amateurs have tried to fill the gap, a thorough study of the history and mythology of the constellations has yet to be written.

Sara Schechner Genuth

Bibliography

Allen, R.H. *Star Names: Their Lore and Meaning*. New York: Dover, 1963.

Dekker, E. "Early Explorations of the Southern Celestial Sky." *Annals of Science* 44 (1987): 439–470.

Delporte, E. *Délimitation scientifique des constellations (tables et cartes)*. Cambridge: Cambridge University Press, 1930.

Harley, J.B., and D. Woodward, eds. *The History of Cartography*. Chicago: University of Chicago Press, 1987–.

Kunitzsch, P. *The Arabs and the Stars*. Northampton, U.K.: Variorum Reprints, 1989.

Ridpath, I. *Star Tales*. New York: Universe Books, 1988.

Roy, A.E. "The Origin of the Constellations." *Vistas in Astronomy* 27 (1984): 171–197.

Savage-Smith, E. *Islamicate Celestial Globes: Their History, Construction, and Use*. Washington, D.C.: Smithsonian Institution Press, 1985.

Snyder, G.S. *Maps of the Heavens*. New York: Abbeville Press, 1984.

Thiele, G. *Antike Himmelsbilder. Mit Forschungen zu Hipparchos, Aratos und seinen Fortsetzern und Beiträgen zur Kunstgeschichte des Sternhimmels*. Berlin: Weidmann, 1898.

Waerden, B.L. van der. *Science Awakening*. Vol. 2, *The Birth of Astronomy*. Leiden: Noordhoff International, 1974; New York: Oxford University Press, 1974.

Warner, D.J. *The Sky Explored: Celestial Cartography, 1500–1800*. New York: Alan R. Liss, 1979; Amsterdam: Theatrum Orbis Terrarum, 1979.

Copernican Revolution

The name applied, not always consistently, to the period and events encompassing the introduction and ultimate acceptance of a heliocentric astronomy and cosmology. This entry begins with a brief explanation of the state of astronomy on the eve of the Copernican revolution.

Renaissance astronomy before **Copernicus** was a classical mathematical science, practiced according to the precepts of the *Almagest* of **Ptolemy**. This meant that astronomers attempted to predict planetary positions using models that were geocentric and that utilized epicycles, deferents, eccentrics, and other devices that preserved uniform circular motion, as well as the Ptolemaic equant, a device that produced uniform motion about an off-center point. The seventy-five years prior to Copernicus saw a concerted attempt to recover the pure Greek text of the *Almagest* (medieval astronomers had used an Arabic version). The year 1496 witnessed the publication of the first usable summary of Ptolemaic astronomy, the *Epitome*, begun by Georg Peurbach and finished by Johannes Regiomontanus. The *Almagest* itself was published in 1515 in a medieval Latin translation, again in 1528 in a new Renaissance translation, and finally in 1538 in the original Greek. The principal novelty of pre-Copernican astronomy was the attempt to give physical reality to epicycles and deferents in the form of spheres within shells within spheres; this innovation, although actually Arabic in origin, was credited to Peurbach and his *New Theories of the Planets* (first published by Regiomontanus in 1571 and many later editions). Throughout this period Ptolemaic astronomy worked very well, and it was never, contrary to what is sometimes claimed, in a state of crisis.

The revolution began with the publication of Copernicus's *On the Revolutions of the Heavenly Orbs* in 1543. In this work, intended as a replacement for the *Almagest*, Copernicus offered planetary models that replaced a static earth with a static sun. The earth itself became a planet and was given a simple circular orbit around an off-center sun. Copernicus further proposed that the diurnal motion of the heavens could be better explained by a rotating earth, and that even precession could be accounted for by a conical wobble of the earth's axis.

These are the familiar features of his astronomical system. But there are other elements that are as, if not more, important in the ensuing debate: (a) Copernicus continued to use the traditional Ptolemaic elements of epicycles, deferents, and eccentrics. By placing the earth in motion Copernicus was able to eliminate the five large planetary epicycles that accounted for each planet's changing relationship with the earth, but otherwise the Copernican models were in general constructed along the same lines as the Ptolemaic ones. (b) Copernicus strongly rejected the equant, on the grounds that it violated the canon of uniform circular motion. To achieve the same effects, Copernicus had to utilize secondary epicycles. Thus the simplification seemingly achieved by eliminating the large planetary epicycles was in reality negated by the addition of smaller ones. There is no real sense in which the Copernican models are simpler than their Ptolemaic predecessors. (c) Some of the Copernican models are equivalents of the Ptolemaic ones, achieved by a simple change of coordinates. But the lunar model and the model that accounted for precession were notable improvements over traditional versions. (d) Copernicus utilized trigonometry in calculating planetary positions, instead of the chord system of the ancients, making his models easier to use. (e) The Copernican models are not really heliocentric, but rather heliostatic. The center for each planetary orbit was the center of the earth's orbit, called the mean sun, rather than the true sun. In addition, the planes of the planetary orbits all passed through the mean sun, not the true sun.

The last feature to be noted deserves special consideration: (f) Copernicus believed that his heliocentric astronomy was physically true, and thus the basis for a heliocentric cosmology. The entire Book I of *Revolutions* is devoted to defending a real moving and rotating earth, and arguing that his system, unlike Ptolemaic astronomy, is a true system, with each planet's place in the scheme fully and uniquely determined. The fact that this system could, for the first time, explain the order and the sizes of the planetary orbits was, for Copernicus, convincing evidence of its truth. This introduction of physical realism into astronomy was partially offset by an unsigned preface to *Revolutions* that claimed the models proposed were hypothetical, devised merely to aid in computation and not meant to be physically true. We now know that this prefatory note was written by Andreas Osiander without the permission of Copernicus, but contemporary readers might well assume otherwise.

Within a decade after its publication, *Revolutions* began to acquire a small following, located almost exclusively at the University of Wittenberg in Germany. Interestingly, what these astronomers liked about Copernicus was his abolition of the equant, since it seemed to purify astronomy by reestablishing uniform circular motion as its basic axiom. They also admired certain Copernican models, such as his lunar model, and account of precession. Copernicus's heliocentrism, and especially his argument that it was a true system, were passed over in silence. Erasmus Reinhold did produce a set of tables (the *Prutenic Tables*, 1551) that used exclusively Copernican models, and, while it was widely employed, it produced no better predictions than the old ***Alphonsine Tables*** based on Ptolemy. Of this first generation of Copernicans, only Joachim Rheticus, who in 1539 had galvanized Copernicus into publishing his great work, seemed to realize, admire, and accept the full revolutionary impact of Copernicus.

By the 1580s, however, Copernicus was beginning to be perceived as a cosmological innovator, rather than just a skillful mathematician who restored the purity of uniform circular motion to astronomy, and his heliocentrism began to receive serious attention. A few accepted it cautiously, such as Michael Maestlin (Kepler's teacher) and Christoph Rothmann at the court of Hesse-Cassel. Thomas Digges was the English Rheticus who enthusiastically embraced all aspects of Copernicanism, including its status as a true depiction of the universe. Digges's engraving of a heliocentric cosmos (1576), with the addition of an infinite stellar region, has been often reproduced by modern scholars, but it is not clear who, if anyone, became a Copernican because of Digges. Be that as it may, we have now almost exhausted the list of sixteenth-century Copernican astronomers. Most others followed the lead of **Tycho Brahe**, who read Copernicus, admired him greatly, and flatly rejected his cosmology. Tycho found the idea of a moving earth physically absurd, the lack of observed stellar parallax impossible to explain, and the unconformity with Scripture disturbing. Tycho went further and proposed his own cosmology (1588), which had five planets orbiting the sun, and the sun in turn, and the moon, orbiting a central and unmoving earth. This cosmology offered all the explanatory power of the Copernican hypothesis while preserving a stationary earth. The Tychonic system attracted many followers during the next fifty years.

A diagram of the Copernican model for Jupiter, from Nicholas Copernicus, De Revolutionibus *(Nuremberg, 1543). It illustrates the most powerful argument for the Copernican system, namely that the ratio between the size of Jupiter's orbit and the size of the earth's orbit (BS/SE) is absolutely determined by the model. It is also of interest that the center of the diagram, E, is the center of the earth's orbit; the position of the sun is not even indicated. (Courtesy of the History of Science Collection, Linda Hall Library, Kansas City, Missouri)*

NICOLAI COPERNICI

A D B, & connectantur rectæ lineæ B D, B E, F E. Quoni
in triangulo B D E duo latera data ſunt D E part. 687. q
eſt 10000. compræhendentia datum angulum B D E p
ſcrup. L I X. Demõſtrabitur ex eis B E, baſis partiũ ear
10543. & angulus q ſub D B E par
XXI. quibus B E D diſtat ab A D I
ergo E B F angulus partium erit
pul. XXII. Igitur in triangulo E
eſt ipſe angulus E B F, cum duo
bus ipſum compræhendentibu
tium 10543, quarum B F, 229
parte ipſius D E diſtantia, quar
eſt B D 10000. Sequitur reliquun
eis F E partium 10373. & angulus
pul. L. Secantibus autem ſe line
in X ſigno, erit D X E angulus
differentia inter F E D, & B D
uerisq motus, quem componu
& B E F partium III. ſcrupul. X
lata partibus XXXIX. ſcrup. I. r
F E D, angulum partium XXXV. ſcrupul. L. à ſum
eccentri ad ſtellam. Sed ſummæ abſidis, locus era
CLX. faciunt coniunctim partium CXCIIII. ſcrupul
rat uerus locus Iouis reſpectu E centri, ſed uiſus e
tibus CCV. ſcrupul. IX. differentiæ igitur partium
XIX. ſunt commutationis. Explicetur iam orbis t
E centrum R S T, cuius dimetiens R E T, ad D B co
ut ſit R apogæum commutationis. Aſſumatur quoq
cumferentia ſecundum menſuram mediæ anomaliæ
tionis partium CXI. ſcrup. XV. & extendatur F E V

One reason for the slow progress of Copernicanism was that, as a set of astronomical models, its accuracy of prediction was not really an improvement over older schemes. Its principal advantage—that it locked the planets into a unified system, with a definite order and spacing—was not seen as a virtue by astronomers whose traditional job was the prediction of planetary positions, one planet at a time. And the physical absurdity of a moving earth was hard to overcome.

In the early seventeenth century, Copernicanism also began to elicit religious objections. Tycho had been the first to raise such objections in print, but he was a Lutheran. The Catholic Church seems to have been unaware of any problems—after all, astronomy traditionally dealt with hypotheses, not reality—until Giordano Bruno appeared. Bruno was by no means an astronomer, but he was a Copernican and a heretic. When he was burned at the stake in 1600, the possibility that Copernicanism might be dangerous was raised for the first time.

Enter the Italian physicist and mathematician **Galileo Galilei**. Galileo claimed to have been a Copernican since at least 1597, but he kept his convictions to himself until 1610, when the newly invented telescope began, in Galileo's hands, to call certain cosmological doctrines into question. The moon was revealed as a mountainous, cratered body, not at all like the perfect ethereal globe called for by traditional cosmology. The sun was blemished with spots. Jupiter was the center of its own system of four moons. None of these discoveries was evidence of heliocentrism, but they did call for a cosmological reevaluation, and, for Galileo, this meant a commitment to Copernicanism. When he discovered that Venus has phases, a fact incompatible with any geocentric scheme (although fully compatible with the Tychonic system), Galileo became a Copernican, really its first highly visible advocate. Moreover, he took it upon himself to show that Copernicanism and Scripture were not in conflict. In widely circulated letters after 1613, Galileo argued that the language of the Bible was designed to accommodate the understanding of ordinary persons, and passages that imply a stationary earth should consequently not be taken literally. Galileo's assumption of the mantle of biblical exegete immediately aroused the interest of Church authorities, and Cardinal Roberto Bellarmine was appointed to look into the matter. He concluded in 1616 that there was no proof of the earth's motion, and therefore no reason to read those relevant passages other than literally. In addition, a commission pronounced that key elements of heliocentrism were heretical or dangerous to the faith, and *Revolutions* was placed on the Index of Forbidden Books.

Galileo, believing that he could still discuss Copernicanism hypothetically, published in 1632 the *Dialogue Concerning the Two Chief World Systems,* in which he presented the arguments on both sides of the cosmological issue. His partiality to Copernicanism was obvious, and, as a result of his ensuing trial for defying Church orders, Galileo was forced to recant his heliocentric views and *The Dialogue* joined the *Revolutions* on the Index. The Church was now publicly in opposition to Copernicanism.

It is not clear exactly how the Galileo affair, as this whole contretemps has been called, affected the Copernican revolution. Certainly the progress of Copernicanism was slowed in Italy, where scientists turned their attention to less contentious subjects, such as mechanics and pneumatics. However, Galileo's book attracted wide attention in other countries, especially France and the Netherlands, and was partially responsible for the growth of Copernicanism.

Galileo's most important contribution to Copernicanism was in providing a physics compatible with a moving earth. By introducing the principle of inertia, Galileo was able to show that objects on a rotating earth will behave exactly the same way as on a stationary earth and that one can no longer call the earth's motion physically absurd. This argument is introduced in the *Dialogue* and worked out more systematically in the *Discourse on Two New Sciences* (1638).

Galileo has been considered the most visible Copernican, but there is little doubt that the decisive role in the reception of Copernicanism was played by **Johannes Kepler**. An enthusiastic Copernican, Kepler changed the nature of the debate by providing heliocentrism with advantages it never had under Copernicus. Replacing each planet's system of epicycles and eccentrics with one simple ellipse, Kepler was able to improve planetary predictions dramatically. In his system, the sun became central for the first time; all planetary planes passed through the true sun, and the foci of each planetary ellipse lay in the same true sun. Planetary latitude and longitude could be accounted for by the same model. Kepler's improved orbit for the earth and his period law allowed the recalculation of most planetary parameters with much greater precision. And with his suggestion that the planets were moved in their orbits by a force emanating from the sun, Kepler radically transformed astronomy by inventing a new subdiscipline, celestial physics.

If one has to define any single moment when Copernicanism turned the corner, it might well have been in 1631 when Pierre Gassendi observed a transit of Mercury across the sun. Kepler had predicted the event, and his prediction was more accurate by several orders of magnitude than those based on the Ptolemaic or Copernican models. The superiority of Kepler's astronomy, and its explicit heliocentrism, was now evident to all.

The Copernican revolution was essentially complete by 1650. To be sure, at about that time the Jesuit Giovanni Battista Riccioli published his monumental *New Almagest*, defending a modified geocentrism, but Riccioli was the swan song for traditional cosmology. Elsewhere in Europe, astronomers such as Hevelius, Lansberge, and Boulliau or cosmologists such as Descartes had long been fully committed to Copernicanism. The burning question was no longer, Is heliocentrism true? It was rather, How much of Kepler's elliptical orbits, celestial physics, and architectonic cosmology had to be accepted in order to retain his improved predictions? Heliocentrism would receive its fullest exposition when Newton allied it with universal gravitation in the *Principia* (1687). By that time, heliocentrism had already achieved general acceptance.

William B. Ashworth Jr.

Bibliography

Gingerich, Owen. "Johannes Kepler." In *Planetary Astronomy from the Renaissance to the Rise of Astrophysics, Part A: Tycho Brahe to Newton*, edited by R. Taton and C. Wilson. *The General History of Astronomy,* vol. 2A, 54–78. Cambridge: Cambridge University Press, 1989.

———. *The Eye of Heaven: Ptolemy, Copernicus, Kepler.* New York: American Institute of Physics, 1993.

———. ed. *The Nature of Scientific Discovery. A Symposium Commemorating the 500th Anniversary of the Birth of Nicolaus Copernicus.* Washington, D.C.: Smithsonian Institution Press, 1975.

Jardine, N. "The Significance of the Copernican Orbs." *Journal for the History of Astronomy* 13 (1982): 168–194.

Krafft, F. "The New Celestial Physics of Johannes Kepler." In *Physics, Cosmology, and Astronomy, 1300–1700: Tension and Accommodation*, edited by S. Unguru, 185–227. Dordrecht: Kluwer, 1991.

Kuhn, T.S. *The Copernican Revolution: Planetary Astronomy in the Development of Western Thought.* New York: Vintage, 1959.

Westman, R.S., ed. *The Copernican Achievement.* (*Contributions of the UCLA Center for Medieval and Renaissance Studies, Vol.* 7). Berkeley: University of California Press, 1975.

Copernicus, Nicholas (1473–1543)

Polish astronomer and mathematician. Born in Torun, Poland, on February 19, 1473, Copernicus entered the University of Cracow in 1491, where he received a humanist education. Appointed a canon of the cathedral of Frombork in 1495, he received permission to pursue studies in Italy, first in canon law at Bologna, then in medicine at Padua, finally receiving a doctorate from Ferrara in 1503. His first astronomical observations were made in Italy. Some time thereafter he returned to Poland, finally taking up residence in Frombork in 1513, where he would spend the next forty years as an ecclesiastical administrator.

A short treatise, the *Commentariolus*, written before 1514, contains the basic elements of a new heliocentric astronomy and cosmology. Copernicus argues there that the sun and not the earth is the center of planetary motion, and that the earth rotates on its axis, producing the appearance of the daily rotation of the planets and stars. The treatise was circulated but not published, and Copernicus turned his attention to church matters, no easy task with the onset of the Protestant revolution.

In 1539 Copernicus was visited by a young Lutheran astronomer, Georg Joachim Rheticus, who wished to learn the details of heliocentric astronomy. This new disciple immediately arranged the publication of a *First Narration* (1540), an announcement and advertisement for the new system. Perhaps invigorated by his disciple, Copernicus began the preparation of his own detailed treatise on heliocentric astronomy, intended as a replacement for the *Almagest* of Ptolemy. *On the Revolutions of the Heavenly Orbs* was published early in 1543; Copernicus suffered a stroke and died on May 24 of that same year. Tradition has it that he received the first copy on his deathbed; there is no evidence for this, but it is not improbable.

Copernican reforms called for new planetary models based on sun-centered orbits. The earth, now a planet, also required a model. The daily rotation of the earth not only removed the necessity of the daily motion of the heavens, but, with an additional wobble, could now be used to account for the precession of the equinoxes. Copernicus also refused to use the equant point, the Ptolemaic device that allowed an epicycle to circle about one center while maintaining uniform speed about another. All his models utilize pure uniform circular motion. Some of them, however, are quite different from the Ptolemaic prototypes.

The other novelty of *Revolutions* lies in Book 1. There Copernicus maintained that his was a physically true system, and he tried to

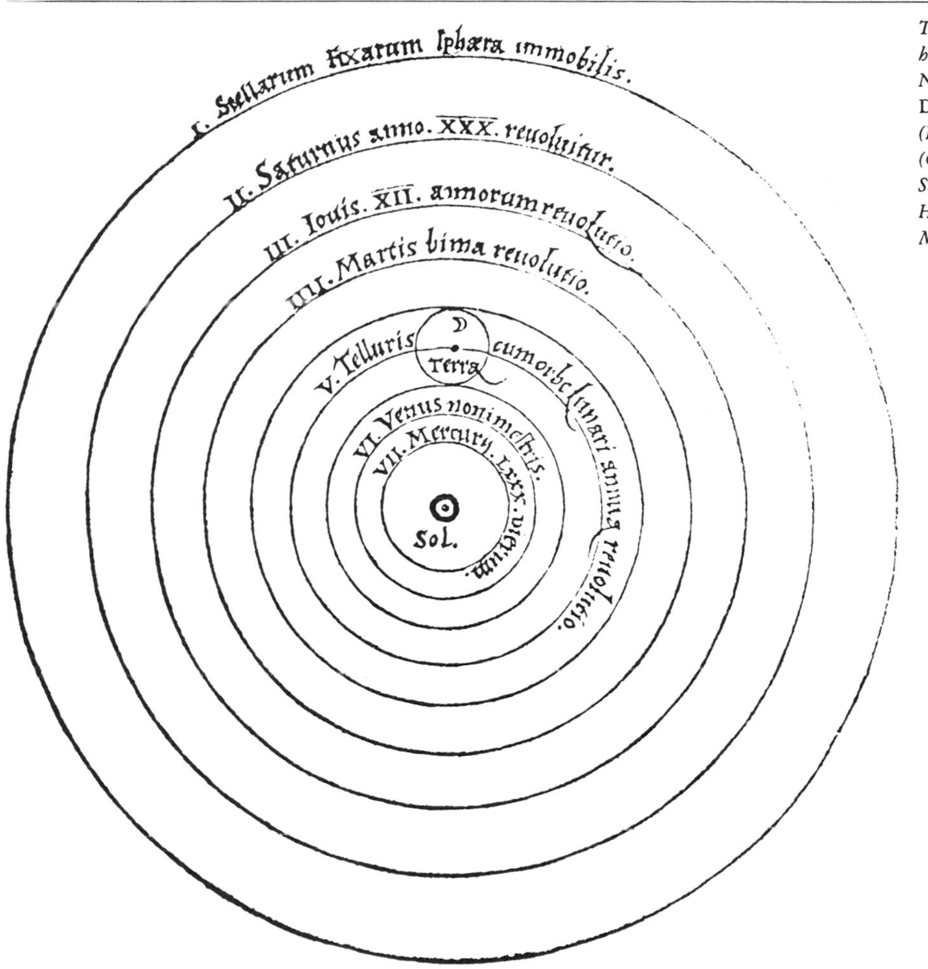

The simplified heliocentric system from Nicholas Copernicus, De Revolutionibus *(Nuremberg, 1543). (Courtesy of the History of Science Collection, Linda Hall Library, Kansas City, Missouri)*

demonstrate that the earth could actually rotate, even though common sense cries out against it. This novelty was somewhat obscured by an anonymous preface, written by Osiander, which claims that Copernicus is merely trying to provide a new set of hypotheses that will simplify computations.

In Book 1 Copernicus also gives reasons for preferring a heliocentric system; these include the fact that the order and distances of the planets are, for the first time, uniquely determined; that retrograde motion, where a planet appears to stop and move backwards against the stars, is easily explained as the result of viewing a planet from a moving earth; and the close correlation of Mercury and Venus with the sun can be understood as a result of these two planets orbiting the sun.

The genesis of the Copernican heliocentric system is obscure. One plausible suggestion is that Copernicus began by trying to construct models that could be physically real; this required the abolition of the equant, since a real sphere cannot rotate uniformly about an off center point. In turn, this may have led to the heliocentric conjecture as the best way of avoiding intersecting spheres.

Revolutions marks a milestone in Western thought, but it should be understood that it was a highly technical treatise, comprehensible only to someone already skilled in mathematics and Ptolemaic astronomy and hardly a work that by itself could inaugurate a general reformation of cosmology. It is also notable that Copernicus retained most of the elements of traditional astronomy, including epicycles, spheres, uniform circular motion, and a finite stellar sphere, and that many of his models are physically implausible. Much more work had to be done before the Copernican innovation could become a revolution.

William B. Ashworth Jr.

Bibliography

Beer, A., and K.A. Strand, eds. *Copernicus, Yesterday and Today. Proceedings of the Commemorative Conference held in Washington in Honour of Nicolaus*

Copernicus. Vistas in Astronomy 17 (1975).

Copernicus, N. *On the Revolutions*. In *Complete Works of Copernicus, vol. 2,* edited by J. Dobrzycki, translated and with a commentary by E. Rosen. London: Macmillan, 1978.

Gingerich, O. *The Eye of Heaven: Ptolemy, Copernicus, Kepler.* New York: American Institute of Physics, 1993.

———. ed. *The Nature of Scientific Discovery. A Symposium Commemorating the 500th Anniversary of the Birth of Nicolaus Copernicus*. Washington, D.C.: Smithsonian Institution Press, 1975.

Jardine, N. "The Significance of the Copernican Orbs." *Journal for the History of Astronomy* 13 (1982): 168–194.

Kuhn, T.S. *The Copernican Revolution: Planetary Astronomy in the Development of Western Thought*. New York: Vintage, 1959.

Rosen, E. "Copernicus, Nicholas." In *Dictionary of Scientific Biography,* edited by C.C. Gillispie, vol. 3, 401–411. New York: Scribner, 1970.

———. *Three Copernican Treatises*. 3rd ed. New York: Octagon, 1971.

Swerdlow, N.M. "The Derivation and First Draft of Copernicus's Planetary Theory: A Translation of the 'Commentariolus' with Commentary." *Proceedings of the American Philosophical Society*, 117 (1973): 423–512.

Swerdlow, N.M., and O. Neugebauer. *Mathematical Astronomy in Copernicus's "De Revolutionibus."* 2 vols. (*Studies in the History of Mathematics and Physical Sciences, vol. 10*). New York: Springer Verlag, 1984.

Westman, R.S., ed. *The Copernican Achievement. (Contributions of the UCLA Center for Medieval and Renaissance Studies, vol.* 7). Berkeley: University of California Press, 1975.

Cosmology, Ancient Greek

The study of the cosmos is the subject of cosmology. The word *cosmos* comes from the Greek verb *kosmeo*, which means "to arrange." Cosmology, therefore, is concerned with the arrangement of the heavens, and studies the nature of the heavens in physical terms—for example, the material constitution of the heavenly bodies and the order and distances of the planets. While many Greek writers had something to say about the cosmos, some of those thinkers who are usually referred to by modern writers as philosophers were particularly interested in the cosmos. Indeed, for at least two of the major schools of Hellenistic philosophy, the Epicureans and the Stoics, the treatment of cosmology was crucially connected to other aspects of their philosophical systems.

Astronomy was considered by many important ancient Greek authors, including Plato, to be a branch of mathematics. This distinction between astronomy and cosmology may account for the fact that modern historians of astronomy have tended to focus on the mathematical achievements of the ancient Greek astronomers, leaving the study of ancient Greek cosmology to specialists in ancient philosophy. But while astronomy and cosmology in some cases were distinct approaches to studying the heavens in antiquity, they were not divorced from one another. Rather, ancient Greek astronomers developed their mathematical models within certain cosmological guidelines; for this reason particular attention must be paid to the relationship between philosophical discussions of the cosmos and astronomy.

The earliest extant texts of the Greeks, the eighth-century B.C.E. poems of Homer and Hesiod, make repeated reference to the celestial phenomena, which were regarded as divinities. For Homer, the phenomena of the sky were epiphanies of the gods; Hesiod was concerned with describing the origin of the universe and the role of the divinities. Those thinkers known collectively as the pre-Socratic philosophers talked and wrote about the natural world; unfortunately only fragments of their texts survive, referred to or quoted in works by later writers. For the most part, only scattered references to the celestial phenomena are known. (Even for later writers, in many cases no writings survive and it is necessary to rely on the reports of even later authors.)

The celestial bodies visible to the naked eye are the sun, **moon**, the fixed stars, which keep their positions relative to one another as they appear to move across the sky, and the five stars that seem to wander or move somewhat erratically and are known as planets (from the Greek *planeo*, "to wander"); these latter are **Venus**, **Mercury**, **Mars**, **Jupiter**, and **Saturn**. The apparent motions (phenomena) of the celestial bodies include the following: all celestial bodies rise in the east and set in the west daily; the sun, moon, and planets move slowly eastward in relation to the fixed stars, seeming, as it were, to drift. Further, the planets, in their drifting from west to east, seem to slow down, reverse their direction (that is, travel westward), then slow down again, reverse direction and continue to travel eastward; this is known as retrograde motion or retrogression.

The earliest texts concerned with describing the cosmos in any detail appear to have been written by Pythagoreans. The fragments of the fifth-century Pythagorean Philolaus suggest a conception of the universe as a sphere, in which a fire occupies the center, around which the earth, an invisible counter-earth, the moon, the sun, the five wandering planets, and the fixed stars circle. The Pythagorean conception of the universe is probably also reflected in the *Timaeus*, a dialogue written by Plato (427–348/347 B.C.E.) and one of the earliest extended cosmological accounts to survive. Here, Timaeus, the primary speaker, relates his views of the origin and organization of the cosmos. The universe was created and designed according to mathematical principles. Further, the celestial bodies function as a heavenly clock providing the measure of time, thereby benefiting human beings. Order and purpose characterize the cosmos of the *Timaeus*; this teleological (Greek *telos*, "end," or "purpose") approach to cosmology became common in Greek accounts of the universe.

From at least the fourth century B.C.E., those thinkers concerned with celestial phenomena generally regarded cosmology as providing the postulates from which mathematical models could be constructed. In antiquity, Plato was credited with posing what would become the classical problem of astronomy: how to account for the seemingly irregular motions of astronomical bodies using only uniform, circular motions. The solutions proposed by several of his students have been preserved. Eudoxus of Cnidus (ca. 400-ca. 347 B.C.E., who probably heard Plato lecture) and Aristotle (384–322 B.C.E.) both adopted the following cosmological postulates: The earth was regarded as stationary and in the center of the universe. Further, the circular motions used to account for the phenomena must be uniform with regard to speed and direction and share the same geometrical center. In other words, the universe was described as geostatic and geocentric, while the geometrical account was based on a principle of uniformity and homocentricity.

Aristotle provided a detailed account of the nature and organization of the cosmos, which he divided into two separate regions, each composed of distinct types of matter and experiencing different types of motion. The terrestrial region (also known as the sublunar realm, for it lies below the orbit of the moon) is made of four elements—namely, fire, air, water, and earth; natural motion in this region is rectilinear—that is, toward or away from the center of the universe. The celestial region (or superlunar realm, above the orbit of the moon, reaching to the sphere of the fixed stars) is composed of a distinct element known as the *aither* (in Latin, aether), which is the only element present there. The celestial bodies are composed of *aither*, which also fills the spaces between them. The natural motion of the celestial region is circular and continuous; Aristotle explained that the word *aither* means always running.

While some cosmological principles were widely accepted, a certain flexibility and willingness to consider new ideas was characteristic of the intellectual tradition of the Greeks and found expression in cosmology as well. Alternative cosmologies were presented by philosophers, probably in response to a variety of problems. In some cases, the traditional cosmological postulates did not always fit the mathematical needs of astronomers and various adjustments were made. As is too often the case with ancient sources, only sketchy details survive.

Celebrated deviations from the traditional earth-centered cosmology are associated with two ancient writers. Heraclides of Pontus (fourth century B.C.E.), a possible student of Plato and a contemporary of Aristotle, has been regarded by some as having suggested that the earth is in the center of the universe and rotates daily. He has also been credited with the idea that Mercury and Venus circle the sun, which in turn travels around the earth. Such ideas would represent a clear break with the principles of geostaticity, geocentricity, and homocentricity. **Aristarchus of Samos** (ca. 310–230 B.C.E.) was reported by Archimedes (287–212 B.C.E.) to have adopted the view that the sun is at the center of the universe, with the earth circling around it. The Stoic philosopher Cleanthes (331–232 B.C.E.) regarded the traditional geocentric cosmology so highly that he stated that Aristarchus should be accused of impiety for suggesting that the earth is in motion.

Yet, the traditional cosmological postulates were regarded by others as problematic for descriptions of the intricate motions of the celestial bodies. In the fourth century B.C.E., Aristotle and Eudoxus utilized only circular motions that were uniform and concentric; their astronomical solutions could not account for the varying brightness of the planets. Believing this effect to be the result of changing distance from the earth, subsequent astronomers gradually developed new geometrical models that permitted greater flexibility but that abandoned the principle of homocentricity. However, these new mathematical models allowed astronomers to more adequately describe the phenomena. Apollonius of Perga (fl. ca. 200 B.C.E.) is usually associated with the development of the eccentric circle (in which the center of the circle is not the center of the earth) and the deferent-epicycle model (in which a planet is described as moving on a point on a circle, known as an epicycle, whose center is moving on yet another circle, known as a deferent). These models were further developed by **Hipparchus** (second century B.C.E.) and **Ptolemy** (second century C.E.), who also introduced the use of a point from which motion appears to be uniform, while allowing the center of the epicycle to move along the deferent at varying speeds; this point was later referred to as the equant. Nevertheless, astronomers did not completely abandon the traditional cosmology, which provided a framework and underlying principles for their work, as Ptolemy showed at the beginning of the *Almagest*.

Philosophical interest in cosmology continued throughout the Hellenistic period, even among those philosophers who were not particularly concerned with natural philosophy, much less the mathematical approach to astronomy. In particular, Epicurean and Stoic philosophers formulated cosmologies that were distinctly different from those of Plato and Aristotle. While the importance of these cosmologies for particular astronomical writers must be individually assessed and will not be considered here, two points will be mentioned because of their general relevance to astronomical theory. The Stoics rejected the Aristotelian division of the cosmos into two distinct regions, claiming that a cosmic sympathy unites the entire universe, in which every event affects other events occurring throughout the universe. For some writers, cosmic sympathy provided a physical explanation to account for the influence of celestial bodies on terrestrial events, described and predicted by astrology, a practice that had both supporters and detractors in Antiquity. That there was no universally held cosmology is significant, yet there were some ideas that were widely accepted. The attitude of Epicurus (341–270 B.C.E.) regarding the validity of explanations of celestial phenomena is noteworthy here; he claimed that multiple explanations must always be considered, since there is no direct access to the phenomena themselves. His views, which were repeated by Lucretius (probably 94–55 B.C.E.) in his widely read poem *On the Nature of Things*, may have encouraged or justified the development of alternative explanations and further cosmological speculation.

In the second century C.E., the astronomer Ptolemy presented a cosmology that showed the influence of his predecessors, particularly Plato, but which was strikingly eclectic and original. Ptolemy clearly enunciated his commitment to the ideal of "exhibiting the uniform circular motions" (*Almagest* 9.2; 3.1) at the same time that he adopted the geometrical models of Apollonius and Hipparchus. At the beginning of his great astronomical work known as the *Almagest*, Ptolemy took pains not only to present his cosmological postulates, but also to justify their adoption. He explained at the outset that the following points should be assumed in advance: that heaven is spherical in shape and moves spherically; that the earth is spherical, with regard to the senses, when taken as a whole; that the earth is in the middle of the universe, having the ratio of a point with regard to size and distance to the sphere of the fixed stars; that the earth experiences no motion involving change of place; and that there exist two primary motions in the heavens (the daily motion from east to west and the motion of the planets from west to east). While his cosmological postulates are generally in agreement with those of many of his predecessors, including Aristotle, he often approached physical questions from a mathematical perspective; in this way his treatment of physical considerations differs from that of the philosophers. His justifications for adopting certain physical postulates vary, but he made it clear that these assumptions must be in agreement with the phenomena. Given the importance of the *Almagest* in the history of astronomy, it is significant that Ptolemy chose to begin his work with a discussion of the basis for adopting the cosmological assumptions that underlie the mathematical work of the astronomer; these first sections of the book would have found a wider audience than the more technical sections of the work. Here, in the treatise that represents the culmination of ancient Greek astronomy, Ptolemy emphasized the important and complicated relationship between cosmology and astronomy, philosophy and mathematics.

Liba C. Taub

Bibliography

Cornford, F.M. *Plato's Cosmology: The "Timaeus" of Plato Translated with a Running Commentary*. London: Routledge and Kegan Paul, 1937.

Dicks, D.R. *Early Greek Astronomy to Aristotle*. Ithaca: Cornell University Press, 1970.

Heath, T. *Aristarchus of Samos: The Ancient Copernicus. A History of Greek Astronomy to Aristarchus together with Aristarchus's Treatise on the Sizes and Distances of the Sun and Moon.* Oxford: Clarendon Press, 1930; reprint, New York: Dover, 1981.

Kirk, G.S., J.E. Raven, and M. Schofield. *The Presocratic Philosophers*. 2nd ed. Cambridge: Cambridge University Press, 1983.

Lloyd, G.E.R. *Greek Science: Thales to Aristotle*. London: Chatto and Windus, 1970.

———. *Greek Science after Aristotle*. London: Chatto and Windus, 1973.

———. "Greek Cosmologies." In *Methods and Problems in Greek Science: Selected Papers*, 141–163. Cambridge: Cambridge University Press, 1991.

Long, A.A., and D.N. Sedley. *The Hellenistic Philosophers*. 2 vols. Cambridge: Cambridge University Press, 1987.

Munitz, M.K. *Theories of the Universe from Babylonian Myth to Modern Science*. New York: Free Press, 1957.

Pannekoek, A. *A History of Astronomy*. New York: Dover, 1989.

Sambursky, S. *The Physical World of the Greeks*. London: Routledge and Kegan Paul, 1956.

———. *The Physical World of Late Antiquity*. Princeton: Princeton University Press, 1987.

Taub, L.C. *Ptolemy's Universe: The Natural Philosophical and Ethical Foundations of Ptolemy's Astronomy*. Chicago: Open Court, 1993.

Cosmology, Contemporary

Defined as the scientific study of the origin, evolution, and large-scale properties of the physical universe, cosmology since the 1940s has developed on foundations built in the prewar period. What astronomers mean by the universe and the questions they ask about its nature are constrained by the fundamental premises on which twentieth-century cosmology is constructed. Since the 1930s, general relativity and the recession (red shift of spectral lines) of distant galaxies provide a mutually reinforcing theoretical and observational framework for cosmological inquiry, a framework within which belief in a static cosmos has been transformed into a vision of a dynamic, evolving universe.

In the postwar period, the goal of cosmology has been to reconstruct the temporal history of the universe. Since this involves both elucidation of the geometric properties of the expanding fabric of space-time and a characterization of the physical constituents of the universe at various epochs, cosmology has been influenced by physics, astronomy, and astrophysics. Indeed, these influences were an impetus to George Gamow who, in collaboration with Ralph A. Alpher and Robert Herman in the 1940s and 1950s, established the theoretical foundations for what came to be called the Big Bang theory of the origin and evolution of the universe. While the current standard model has its origins in this work, the history of cosmological inquiry since the 1940s is a more richly nuanced and complex subject than generally presented.

For Gamow, the early history of the universe held the key to the origin of the chemical elements. Approaching cosmology from this perspective, the result was a persuasive physical theory of the evolution of the universe from its beginnings in an initial explosion. Gamow's idea of a decoupling time (the transition from a radiation- to a matter-dominated universe) provided a cornerstone on which scientists have built temporal histories. To be sure, the original theory has been considerably modified.

In 1948, the same year that a key paper introducing the Big Bang theory appeared, an alternative, Steady State cosmology, was proposed by Hermann Bondi, Thomas Gold, and Fred Hoyle. They were dissatisfied with cosmologies that postulated a beginning for the universe. While Steady State proponents accepted the red shift in the spectrum of distant galaxies as evidence for expansion, they rejected the view that this expansion implied an earlier, more condensed primordial state. Instead, Bondi and his colleagues proposed the perfect cosmological principle: a universe whose properties remained uniform over time. They postulated the continual creation of matter to reconcile uniformity with the dispersion of matter that resulted from expansion. While epistemological and philosophical concerns motivated the development of Steady State theory and remained a feature in subsequent debates, problems such as the origin of the elements and the age of the universe emerged as critical issues for which the theory could not provide acceptable answers.

While some scientists maintained that element formation, or nucleosynthesis, occurred as a result of cooking processes in the primordial universe, others advocated astrophysical scenarios. When Hoyle and Margaret Burbidge, Geoffrey Burbidge, and William Fowler proposed a model for the creation of elements in supernovae, their ideas were viewed not as an either/or proposition, but as compatible with both Steady State and Big Bang cosmologies. An early problem with the Big Bang theory was an inconsistency between the predicted age of the universe and that of the earth based on geological studies. Clearly, the earth could not be older than the universe. This discrepancy for the earth was eliminated by Walter Baade, whose research led to an increase in the cosmic distance scale and, thus, the age of the universe.

Throughout the 1960s key observational discoveries, many linked to the development of radio astronomy, were influential in shaping the outcome of the debate between the two cosmologies. Quasars (extremely distant objects that emit more energy than anything else in the universe), discovered in 1963, provided observational evidence that indicated the early universe looked very different than the universe today, a result incompatible with Steady State cosmology. Later, the discovery of the cosmic microwave background radiation (interpreted as a remnant of the Big Bang itself) was seen as confirmation of Big Bang cosmology. The discovery of cosmic background microwave radiation by Arno Penzias and Robert Wilson is often characterized as the crucial turning point in the debate between the rival cosmologies, legitimating the Big Bang as the canonical view of the scientific community. While the shift is more complex than typically portrayed, it is true that most subsequent research has focused on refining Big Bang theory. From the 1970s, this process has been influenced by major theoretical and observational developments in physics and astronomy.

The influence of theoretical physics on the field can be seen in the emergence of research specialties in quantum and particle cosmology as well as applications of general relativity. Given impetus by the work of Steven Weinberg and others, the very early universe emerged in the 1980s as a prime research site for elementary particle physicists. The condition of the very early universe, once primarily the testing ground for theories of the formation and distribution of the elements, has become the arena in which theories of particle creation and the distribution of photons and baryons are evaluated. Further, the early universe has proved fruitful for scientists working on grand unified theories that aim to unify the four basic forces of nature.

While the realm of the very small has provided impetus to cosmological research, so too has the realm of the very large. Observational and theoretical studies of the large-scale structure of the universe have become significant for cosmology. Theories of galaxy formation and the evolution of large-scale structures raised questions about the assumptions underlying Big Bang cosmology, especially homogeneity and isotropy as requirements for the cosmological principle. The characterization of cosmology as "a search for two numbers" illustrates the overlap between theoretical and observational cosmology (Harrison, 339). The Hubble constant (the present rate at which the expansion velocity of the universe changes as a function of distance) and the deceleration parameter (the rate at which the expansion of the universe slows as a result of gravitation) are key elements in cosmological models, and their determination has been closely linked to fundamental techniques and premises of theoretical and observational astronomy. For instance, the determination of the type of universe we inhabit (open, flat, or closed) is dependent on the ratio of the values for average and critical mass density of the universe. In turn, these values are dependent on theories concerning the nature and distribution of energy and matter in the universe (including controversial issues such as dark matter and missing mass).

The mutual relevance of physics, astronomy, and cosmology has become increasingly evident as scientists reconstruct earlier and earlier epochs of cosmic history and attempt to account for present features of the universe on the basis of previous conditions. In the context of Big Bang cosmology, this means dealing with questions about the beginning of the universe. As many historians have pointed out, the lack of a beginning was the most appealing feature of Steady State cosmology.

The problem of initial conditions underlies one of the most interesting developments in recent cosmology, the rise of the anthropic principle. While there is a lack of precision and consistency of usage, its defining feature is the belief in a fundamental connection between the presence of human beings and the basic parameters and physical properties of the universe. The fascination of the anthropic principle is reflected in a flood of papers and books on the topic since Brandon Carter's 1974 paper. While Carter coined the term "anthropic principle" and articulated its weak and strong versions, the exploration of cosmic coincidences is not entirely new. From the mid-1970s, discussion of such coincidences (including the seemingly remarkable features of the universe that have permitted the emergence of life) was motivated by concerns with problematical aspects of Big Bang theory.

For instance, in 1973 C.B. Collins and Stephen Hawking considered the relevance of initial conditions to the present isotropy of the universe and concluded that an exceedingly low probability existed for the occurrence of such a universe. Consequently, the very existence of such a universe deserved explanation. That such a universe was uniquely suited to human life added the anthropic component to the problem. Many-universe theory came to function as an explanatory device. The fact that the universe is uniquely suited for the emergence of human life is explained satisfactorily (for some scientists) by postulating that our universe is only one of an infinite variety of possible universes.

Scientific literature on the anthropic principle consists of technical elaborations of the problem, evaluations of its explanatory value for cosmology, and critiques of its status as scientific explanation. Philosophers have joined in the debate, providing some of the most intriguing accounts of the historical significance of this episode. Ernan McMullin characterizes the anthropic principle as a shift away from long-held Cartesian ideas of acausality between initial and present cosmic conditions. However, he sees the development of the most significant modification to Big Bang theory—the inflationary universe—as a reaffirmation of the Cartesian approach to cosmic origins.

Proposed in 1981 by Alan Guth and subsequently modified by Andrei Linde, Andreas Albrecht, and Paul Steinhardt, the concept of the inflationary universe significantly altered scientists' views of the very early universe. As the name implies, this model calls for a period of rapid and extraordinary change in the early development of the universe. The inflationary model was influenced by particle physics and grand unified theory. In this theory, the accelerated pace of the cosmic expansion is attributed to a gravitational repulsion caused by a false vacuum state—a state whose existence rests on phase transition as defined by elementary particle theory. The existence of an inflationary epoch in the early universe has provided the means by which certain problems could be resolved. And, as Alan Lightman notes, the theory "provides a physical mechanism by which the initial conditions of the universe may have been irrelevant—a notion that pleases and relieves many physicists" (Lightman and Brawer, 44).

Cosmological inquiry since the 1940s has attracted scholarly attention, but a synthetic historical treatment has yet to emerge. Particular episodes in the development of contemporary cosmology have raised intriguing questions for scholars engaged in the historical, philosophical, and sociological study of science, and case studies of important episodes constitute much of the literature. For the most part scholarly efforts have concentrated on the immediate postwar decades. Historians have focused on the development and status of competing cosmologies, especially rivalry between Steady State and Big Bang theories. In addition, they have analyzed major theoretical and observational developments such as the development of the anthropic principle and the discovery of cosmic background radiation.

A common concern underlying many of these accounts is how science grows and changes. Often, specific theories of scientific change have been employed to evaluate episodes of controversy with the analysis centered on factors involved in the acceptance or rejection of theories. Cosmic background radiation has provided a key focus for many studies. Helge Kragh places this event in historical context by showing how labeling the findings of Penzias and Wilson as a discovery "depended crucially on the theoretical interpretation by the Princeton physicists [Robert Dicke and James Peebles] and the entire theoretical context in which the measurements were incorporated" (Kragh, "Cosmic Microwave Background Radiation," 103). While some effort has been made to place the Steady State versus Big Bang debates in wider scientific and historical contexts, much more can be done with this episode as well as with other developments in theoretical and observational cosmology. In a field that is rooted in fundamental but often tenuous assumptions, fruitful areas for research might include the examination of alternative interpretations of the red shift, as well as the history and continuing influence of alternative cosmologies. In addition, the role of instrumentation, experiment, and techniques of computer modeling and data reduction in shaping cosmological inquiry remains largely unexplored. While the influence of radio astronomy has been recognized, the impact of space and satellite technology on cosmology has yet been thoroughly examined.

A second theme in historical studies of cosmology has been the role of nonscientific factors. Epistemological, ideological, philosophical, professional, and religious factors, as well as personalities, have influenced the development and acceptance or rejection of theories. The validity or interpretation of fundamental premises have led to acrimonious debates among participants and in the wider scientific and intellectual communities. This has been shown in the Steady State versus Big Bang debate and more recently in discussions of the meaning of beginning and creation in cosmology, and of the tenability of the anthropic principle. The significance of such factors in shaping cosmology is acknowledged by most historians, but varying emphasis has been placed on their influence in scientific debates.

While it is convenient to categorize factors as nonscientific or scientific, it is also valuable to recognize as historically contingent the twentieth-century belief in compartmentalization of domains of knowledge. As **McMullin** argues in his discussion of cosmology, metaphysics, and theology, the boundaries between such domains tend in practice to be quite permeable (McMullin, 387). Indeed, the issue of legitimacy has itself been an important underlying theme in the development of contemporary cosmology.

Many accounts of twentieth-century cosmology emphasize the emergence of the field as a genuine science. The beginnings of scientific cosmology are alternatively placed with the achievements of **Edwin Hubble**, with the recognition of the significance of the background radiation, or with the integration of particle physics into cosmological inquiry. Yet, by failing to acknowledge that the criteria for scientific explanation have themselves changed over time, far too many accounts leave readers with the impression that pre-twentieth century cosmology was not part of the scientific enterprise, a view that is inconsistent with rich traditions of scholarship in the history of science. When approached with historical sensitivity, the task of analyzing the circumstances under which cosmology gained recognition as a legitimate science reveals much about the technical development of cosmology as well as the place of this discipline among the sciences and in a wider cultural context.

Beginning in the 1970s, important changes in cosmology occurred on the institutional and professional levels (Kragh, "Big Bang Cosmology," 40). A valuable area for study would involve exploring ways in which scientific communities concerned with cosmological inquiry have interacted, shaping the field into a more cohesive activity. This would entail examination of the problems recognized by these groups, and the ways in which consensus has been achieved, both in defining problems and methods for their solution. Such investigations should also include an examination of the role of women and other traditionally excluded groups in the cosmological enterprise. Traweek's study of high energy physics provides a good model.

With respect to the wider cultural context, cosmology offers a unique window for viewing late-twentieth century conceptions of the meaning and place of science in society. A science that raises (and offers answers to) questions about the origin and ultimate fate of the universe says as much about that society as it does about nature. Reflections on the meaning and value of cosmological inquiry and its relationship to religion continue to be incorporated into scientific as well as more general literature. An understanding of the cultural significance of cosmological thought remains an important goal for historical scholarship.

An extensive literature has been generated by participants, while the experiences of contemporary astronomers, astrophysicists, and cosmologists have been documented through systematic oral history programs, most notably that of the Center for the History of Physics at the American Institute of Physics in College Park, Maryland and at the National Air and Space Museum in Washington, D.C. In addition, Alan Lightman and Roberta Brawer have provided a valuable source for historians in their book based on interviews with modern cosmologists.

Joann Palmeri

Bibliography

Brush, S.G. "Astronomy in the Twentieth Century." In *The History of Modern Science: A Guide to the Second Scientific Revolution, 1800–1950*, 487–529. Ames: Iowa State University Press, 1988.

———. "Prediction and Theory Evaluation: Cosmic Microwaves and the Revival of the Big Bang." *Perspectives on Science* 1 (Winter 1993): 565–602.

Copp, C.M. "Professional Specialization, Perceived Anomalies, and Rival Cosmologies." *Knowledge: Creation, Diffusion, Utilization* 7 (1985): 63–95.

Harrison, E. "A Century of Changing Perspectives in Cosmology." *Quarterly Journal of the Royal Astronomical Society* 33 (1992): 335–349.

Hetherington, N.S. *Encyclopedia of Cosmology: Historical, Philosophical, and Scientific Foundations of Modern Cosmology*. New York: Garland, 1993.

Kragh, H. "Big Bang Cosmology." In *Encyclopedia of Cosmology: Historical, Philosophical, and Scientific Foundations of Modern Cosmology*, edited by N.S. Hetherington, 31–42. New York: Garland, 1993.

———. "Cosmic Microwave Background Radiation." In *Encyclopedia of Cosmology: Historical, Philosophical, and Scientific Foundations of Modern Cosmology*, edited by N.S. Hetherington, 100–105. New York: Garland, 1993.

Lightman, A., and R. Brawer. *Origins: The Lives and Worlds of Modern Cosmologists.* Cambridge: Harvard University Press, 1990.

McMullin, E. "Indifference Principle and Anthropic Principle in Cosmology." *Studies in the History and Philosophy of Science* 24 (1993): 359–389.

North, J.D. *The Measure of the Universe: A History of Modern Cosmology*. Oxford: Oxford University Press, 1965.

Toulmin, S. *The Return to Cosmology.* Berkeley: University of California Press, 1982.

Traweek, S. *Beamtimes and Lifetimes: The World of High Energy Physicists.* Cambridge, Mass.: Harvard University Press, 1988.

Weart, S.R., and D.H. Devorkin. "Interviews as Sources for History of Modern Astrophysics." *Isis* 72 (1981): 471–477.

Cosmology, Medieval

Within a variety of medieval cosmologies, there was general agreement on a shared view that saw the cosmos as something like an onion. A spherical earth lay at its center, surrounded by a series of spherical shells that carried around the **sun**, **moon**, and other planets embedded within them. Above these planetary spheres was the sphere of the stars (and for some, one or more invisible spheres to account for the motion of the starry sphere) and below them were the turbulent elementary spheres of fire, air, water, and earth.

The modern historical myth that a scripturally based belief in a flat earth had any significant influence in medieval cosmology finds no support in the historical record. Only two Greek theologians, Cosmas Indicopluestes and Lactantius, maintained clearly that the earth was flat, and their works were not translated into Latin until the Renaissance. Throughout the Middle Ages there are frequent allusions to the sphericity of the earth.

If there was general agreement on the broad frame of the cosmos, fine details offered many opportunities for disagreement. Before the recovery of **Aristotle** in the twelfth century, most cosmologists accepted a secondhand Aristotelian view that the spheres were made of aether. But **Plato** had maintained in his *Timaeus* (40a), one of the few ancient philosophical works known in the early middle ages, that the celestial bodies were made of a subtle fire. Thus Martianus Capella in the fifth century and Bernard Silvestris in the twelfth followed Plato's view on this point. Others, such as William of Conches in the twelfth century, sought to blur the disagreement by identifying the celestial fire with aether.

Related to this philosophical question of the material substance of the spheres were biblically based questions concerning the creation of the firmament and the waters above the firmament described in Genesis. Here scriptural commentators asked whether the highest heaven was made of water or aether.

The authorities differed as much on the order and size of the celestial spheres as they did on their substance. Ptolemy and his followers had arranged the planets at increasing distance from the earth in the order moon, **Mercury**, **Venus**, Sun, **Mars**, **Jupiter**, and **Saturn**. Plato, however, had placed the moon and sun nearer to the earth, followed by the other planets. Martianus Capella added further complications to the matter by placing the center of the circles of Mercury and Venus in the sun, rather than the earth. From the ninth century on, medieval commentators struggled with these inconsistencies.

There was general agreement that the earth was so small it could be considered as an insignificant point in the center of the universe, but the exact dimensions of the remaining spheres was another matter of disagreement, depending on the approach taken to the problem. Plato in *Timaeus* (35b–36a) had proposed an obscure relationship connecting the celestial spheres to the numbers two and three and their squares and cubes. Macrobius, seeking to reinforce the ethical lesson of the unimportance of earthly things, interpreted Plato in a way that placed Saturn at a great distance from the earth:

Planet		*Distance from Earth*
Moon		1
Sun	1×2 =	2
Venus	2×3 =	6
Mercury	6×2^2 =	24
Mars	24×3^2 =	216
Jupiter	216×2^3 =	1,728
Saturn	$1{,}728 \times 3^3$ =	46,656

Chalcidius, rather than discussing distances, considered the relative sizes of the earth, sun, and moon, based on Hipparchus's analysis of how the shadows of the earth and moon caused eclipses. He gave the volume of the moon as 1/27th the volume of the earth and the volume of the earth as 1/1880th the volume of the sun.

Figures of this sort provided the basic dimensions of the cosmos until the arrival of Ptolemaic astronomy in the twelfth century. In his *Planetary Hypotheses,* Ptolemy had derived a set of distances for the planets, beginning with an observation to determine the distance of the moon, followed by an assumption that each of the planets was embedded in a solid sphere, the thickness of which was determined by the planet's eccentricity and the size of its epicycle. A number of slightly different versions of these Ptolemaic dimensions by al-Farghānī, al-Battānī, and Ptolemy himself reached medieval Europe, but we may take the dimensions that Campanus of Novara gave (in miles) as typical.

Ptolemaic Dimensions by Campanus of Novara

Planet	*Distance from Earth to Planet's Sphere (in miles)*	*Planet's Diameter (in miles)*
Moon	107,936 20/33	1,896 26/33
Mercury	209,198 13/33	230 26/33
Venus	579,320 28/33	2,884 28/33
Sun	3,892,866 55/66	35,700
Mars	4,268,629 11/66	7,572 24/33
Jupiter	32,352,075 42/66	29,641 27/33
Saturn	52,544,702 28/66	29,209 3/33
fixed stars	73,387,747 10/66	

Despite this tradition, extending from Macrobius to Campanus, of treating the celestial spheres as real objects with measurable dimensions, there was some question regarding the sense in which these spheres should be considered as solid. Michael Scot, in his commentary on Sacrobosco's *Sphere*, posed three alternatives: They could be hard like earth, they could be continuous (thus all the elements, including fire, air, and water, are solid), or they could merely be three-dimensional (geometrical solids as opposed to plane figures). Medieval philosophers never fully resolved the sense in which the celestial spheres were to be considered as solid. Furthermore, some Aristotelian natural philosophers, especially those who followed the great Spanish Arab commentator Averroes, cast doubts upon the spheres' physical reality.

Al-Biṭrūjī, influenced by Averroes and others of the rigorous Spanish Aristotelian tradition, tried to create a cosmology that would replace the Ptolemaic epicycles and eccentrics. His system employed several principles. The first was that the heavens had a single motion from east to west, rather than two opposed motions (an east to west daily motion and an eastward motion through the zodiac) as had been affirmed by Plato, Ptolemy, and even Aristotle himself. In al-Biṭrūjī's model, as the planets got farther from the first mover, they increasingly lagged behind this single westward motion rather than opposing it with a contrary eastward motion.

Secondly, he implemented this lagging motion with a complex system of concentric spheres, which could not account in detail for all the astronomical phenomena. Despite its serious astronomical flaws, al-Biṭrūjī's system was cited by Latin Aristotelians who shared his philosophical misgivings with Ptolemaic cosmology. It was generally rejected by practicing astronomers, but in the dispute some philosophers couched the argument in terms of the superiority of philosophy to astronomy. They maintained that astronomy cannot yield the truth about the configuration of the heavens, but merely posits a combination of uniform circular motions that saves the phenomena.

Besides the issue of epicycles and eccentrics against concentric spheres, al-Biṭrūjī's model also raised the issue of the physical cause of the motions of the heavens. Aristotle himself had been somewhat inconsistent on the point, arguing in the *Physics* for a single mover, and in the *Metaphysics* for fifty-five. As noted above, al-Biṭrūjī and his followers favored a single mover, whose influence became weaker at greater distances.

More popular among both philosophers and poets was the view that transformed the multiple divine movers of the *Metaphysics* into immaterial thinking creatures called intelligences, who moved the nine celestial spheres. These were identified by figures as diverse as Thomas Aquinas and Dante Alighieri with the nine choirs of angels described by the sixth-century Greek theologian pseudo-Dionysius.

In his commentary on the *Physics*, John Buridan proposed another alternative, suggesting that intelligences might not be necessary to move the spheres. Since the celestial spheres, by their nature, offered no resistance to movement, the impetuses that God impressed upon them at the creation would continue undiminished without the need for any further cause. Buridan's discussion makes it clear that the medieval cosmological models of spheres and movers, despite those elements that overlap significantly with theology, also had elements that he and his contemporaries saw as falling clearly within a physics of the heavens.

The study of medieval cosmology has made significant steps in the past decades, yet that progress has largely been restricted to the bounds of scholastic Aristotelian natural philosophy. The transition from the Platonic cosmologies of the twelfth century to the Aristotelian cosmologies has been somewhat neglected. Even more important, however, would be an examination of the relations between the cosmology expressed in commentaries on Aristotelian texts and the tacit cosmologies found in texts of the *corpus astronomicum*.

Stephen C. McCluskey

Bibliography

Aristotle. *Physica, Metaphysica*. (various editions)

Benjamin, F.S., and G.J. Toomer. *Campanus of Novara and Medieval Planetary Theory: Theorica planetarum*. Madison: University of Wisconsin Press, 1971.

Duhem, P. *Le Système du Monde: Histoire des doctrines cosmologiques de Platon à Copernic*. Vols. 2–4. Paris: Hermann, 1954.

Goldstein, B. *Al-Biṭrūjī: On the Principles of Astronomy*. 2 Vols. New Haven and London: Yale University Press, 1971.

Grant, E. *Planets, Stars, and Orbs: The Medieval Cosmos, 1200–1687*. London and New York: Cambridge University Press, 1993.

Hetherington, N., ed. *Encyclopedia of Cosmology*. New York: Garland, 1993.

Macrobius. *Commentarii in Somnium Scipionis*. Edited by J. Willis. Leipzig: B.G. Teubner Verlag, 1970.

Pedersen, O. *Early Physics and Astronomy: A Historical Introduction*. Rev. ed. Cambridge: Cambridge University Press, 1993.

Plato. *Timaeus*. (various editions)

Russell, J.B. *Inventing the Flat Earth: Columbus and Modern Historians*. New York: Praeger, 1991.

Thorndike, L. *The Sphere of Sacrobosco and Its Commentators*. Chicago: University of Chicago Press, 1949.

Cosmology, Modern

The subject matter of cosmology includes the origin, evolution, and large-scale properties of the physical universe. This definition did not achieve widespread usage until the 1930s, following what might be described as the remaking of cosmology. The cosmological enterprise has been such that the basic concepts of the universe, as well as the goals of cosmologists, have been dependent on many factors. Jacques Merleau-Ponty has suggested that these factors include "the means of astronomical observation, the prevailing mathematical techniques, the general trend of ideas about nature, the relationship between science and philosophy or religion, and so on." (Merleau-Ponty, 1977, 283). To this list, historians of science might add social context, forms of patronage, and the interests of particular groups.

The history of modern cosmology includes a number of historiographically sophisticated works, but the dominant approach has been the history of scientific ideas. A great deal of attention has been paid to the philosophical issues associated with cosmological topics, but historians have yet to place the history of cosmology in a broader intellectual and social context or to examine the local production of cosmological knowledge. A useful historical introduction is the *Encyclopedia of Cosmology* (Hetherington 1993).

In the middle of the eighteenth century, many natural philosophers, astronomers, and mathematicians judged the cosmic order to lie beyond scientific examination. For instance, in the famous *Encyclopédie*, J.R. d'Alembert argued that cosmology consists of the laws of nature and the sequence of mechanical events in the universe. However, D'Alembert noted that the main interest of cosmology was to show that the world is put in order by God. The "sincerity of that statement is very doubtful" (Merleau-Ponty, 1965, 286); it was probably included only for the sake of the censors. Sincere statement or not, it accurately portrays how recent historians have viewed many of the speculations about the cosmos during the eighteenth century, speculations produced by, among others, Thomas Wright, Immanuel Kant, and J.H. Lambert. There were, however, significant differences between these cosmologies. It would, for example, be a mistake to assume that all of them reckoned the universe to be static. Kant and Wright broke with this idea and advocated permanent cosmological development.

Between 1785 and 1830, what has been termed romantic cosmology was also important. Members of this school sought to replace what seemed to them an overly mechanical universe, devoid of God, with one that revealed nature's continual transformation from an absolute divine unity. Thus, the Dane H.C. Oersted emphasized the key role that his belief in the unity of all physical forces played in the discovery of electromagnetism. For the romantics, "The general order of the world is the result of the conflict of forces that find their ultimate source in God" (Wilson, 601). The British experimental physicist Michael Faraday also was committed to a view of the universe in which the forces of nature have one common origin and are mutually dependent. Faraday speculated about and experimented on the existence of a relation between electricity and gravity, and in so doing, Wilson argued, was making the first attempt to construct a field-theoretical scientific cosmology. In adopting such a viewpoint, "The field-theoretical cosmology of Einstein's general theory of relativity can be seen as the latest scientific expression of a philosophical view of the world whose history does not begin with special relativity or with Maxwell's mathematical presentation of field theory, but rather reaches back to Faraday and through him to Oersted and the metaphysical and theological concerns of the German romantics" (Wilson, 604).

Eighteenth-century cosmology contained many strands. The great French mathematical astronomer P.-S. Laplace was a cosmologist of a different sort from Wright, Lambert, or the romantics. He eschewed theological issues, and in thinking of the entire universe, Laplace "probably imagined it as the indefinite repetition, in endless space, of gravitating systems more or less analogous to the solar system, either in the process of condensation, or having already reached an ultimate and steady-state" (Merleau-Ponty, 1977, 290). However, for Laplace, natural science was not concerned with the order and structure of the universe, but, as for d'Alembert, with laws and the connections of events.

This is a decidedly more restricted view of cosmology than that offered by **William Herschel**, at the core of whose thought were questions about the construction of the heavens and whose scientific practice was as a self-styled natural historian of the heavens. In his speculations on nebulae and their life histories, Herschel presented an audacious and novel vision, one that many natural philosophers and astronomers found overly ambitious. While the nature of the nebulae became a significant issue in the middle of the nineteenth century, particularly following observations made with a new generation of large reflecting telescopes, cosmology, in the sense of the structure and evolution of the universe, was relatively little studied. Merleau-Ponty has characterized the general position at the end of the nineteenth century: "As for knowing how the universe as a whole is constituted, or what its overall configuration is, these are questions which are probably insoluble and which had best not be raised. The only thing that astronomy shows us unquestionably, beyond the frontiers of the solar system, is a very large number of stars grouped in a mass with a distinctive shape—the galaxy" (Merleau-Ponty and Morando, 92).

In the first decade of the twentieth century, astronomers and physicists rarely used the term cosmology. Even the concept of the universe acquired a new meaning during the early years of the century. To astronomers in 1900, the universe often implied what would now be termed the Milky Way system. This usage rested on the view that our galaxy was the only such aggregation of stars visible to even the largest telescopes. Occasionally astronomers speculated on whether or not other galaxies lay beyond our stellar system, but in 1900 few astronomers thought there was convincing evidence that external galaxies had actually been observed. In the early years of the twentieth century it was, according to historian Stanley L. Jaki, "customary to picture the universe as consisting of two parts: one visible and confined to the Milky Way, and another, truly infinite, which was believed to be forever beyond the reach of visible observations" (Jaki, 270). Around the turn of the century, astronomers such as **J.C. Kapteyn** and **Hugo von Seeliger** developed statistical methods for analyzing data on the distribution of stars in space in order to map the structure of our stellar system. E.R. Paul has lately examined the history of statistical cosmology and rescued the topic from obscurity.

There are two main elements in the historiography of early-twentieth-century cosmology: the debate on the nature of the spiral nebulae and the value of general relativity as a means of interpreting the large-scale properties of the physical universe. Historians generally agree that the debate over the spiral nebulae (Are the spirals remote galaxies of stars grown milky through their great distance, or are they small, relatively nearby clusters of stars, or perhaps genuinely nebulous objects?) was brought to an end by **Edwin P. Hubble**. In the 1920s, Hubble concluded that the spirals are indeed galaxies.

Historians agree that Hubble was the leading observational cosmologist in this era. He was also influential in setting the terms within which most historians and astronomers have sought to understand this debate, a legacy that has worked to marginalize efforts of others who contributed to the field. Hubble has also been accorded pride of place in establishing the red shift–distance relationship, and, by extension, the discovery of the expanding universe. In 1927, when Hubble took up the problem of the red shifts of galaxies, the observational evidence for an expanding universe was ambiguous. For a decade there had been speculation about a red shift–distance relation for external galaxies. A few scientists had even tried to determine observationally the form (if any) of the relationship. But the evidence presented was not convincing; plots of red shifts (generally interpreted as indicators of radial velocity) versus distance had the appearance of scatter diagrams.

Using red shifts secured at the Mount Wilson Observatory by Milton Humason, as well as data obtained earlier by **V.M. Slipher** at the **Lowell Observatory**, together with his own estimates of the distances of the galaxies, Edwin Hubble persuaded his colleagues that there was indeed a red shift–distance relation and that, at least in the first approximation, it was linear. Soon Hubble's observational research on the red shift–distance relation was meshed with the calculations of various theorists who had predicted a velocity–distance relation as a consequence of applying Einstein's theory of general relativity to the entire universe. Although some astronomers were skeptical about interpreting the red shift as a Doppler effect, the red shift–distance relation was rapidly transformed into a velocity–distance relation. Harrison has argued that the failure of cosmologists and historians "to distinguish between the linear-red shift distance law (an empirical approximation of limited validity) and the velocity-distance law (a theoretical derivation of unlimited validity) leads to confusion and obscuration of the fundamental concepts of modern cosmology" (Harrison, 28). The relationship between red shift and distance became known as Hubble's law and the constant linking the two as the Hubble constant. Determining the value of the Hubble constant has been one of the major concerns of cosmology.

In a seemingly endless stream of textbooks and popular works, Hubble has been portrayed as the discoverer of the expanding universe. This view distorts the historical record. However, the temptation to transform a complex historical process into a myth recounting the heroic work of a lone individual, whose story can be exploited to comfort the old, educate and inspire the young, and affirm community values, has generally proved irresistible. Not only does such a myth ignore observational researches that defined the context for Hubble's own investigations, it also omits the means by which Hubble and others sought to interpret their findings.

The theory within which the red shift–distance law was usually interpreted was general relativity. In 1917 Albert Einstein solved the field equations of general relativity for a static model of the entire universe. The model was finite but unbounded. Astronomers had assumed for centuries that the universe was infinite and its geometry Euclidean, hence Einstein was proposing a major conceptual shift. Mathematicians and astronomers had earlier considered non-Euclidean geometries, but the physical underpinnings of Einstein's non-Euclidean geometries were very different. Further, the static model came at the price of introducing a new constant into the field equations, the so-called cosmological constant. Although later repudiated by Einstein, the cosmological constant remains today an unresolved problem.

The Dutch astronomer Willem de Sitter soon found other solutions to the field equations. One was Einstein's, another corresponded to a solution for the flat space-time of special relativity, but the third became known by de Sitter's name. Although it would later turn out that de Sitter had found one of the simplest models of an expanding universe, at the time he believed the solution to be static. He was quickly joined by **A.S. Eddington**, Hermann Weyl, and others in exploring the properties of what became known as the de Sitter model. In the early 1920s, the Soviet theorist **Aleksandr Friedmann** discovered further solutions, solutions that were nonstatic. But initially these investigations drew little interest.

The 1920s saw other important theoretical researches. In 1927, for example, Georges Lemaître published a seminal paper on the expanding universe. But such was the novelty of the idea, as well as the obscurity of its author and place of publication, that, like Friedmann's earlier papers, it initially caused little comment. Historian Helge Kragh has argued persuasively in a reappraisal of Lemaître's cosmology that the Belgian scientist was the first to connect theory and observation in a way that would come to be seen as physically meaningful and that lay within the general framework of the expanding universe. The physicist H.P. Robertson also helped to set the stage for the concept of the expanding universe. In 1928, he argued that adding to Einstein's theory the restrictions that space-time was homogeneous and isotropic led to an expanding universe of sorts. Hence, before Hubble's 1929 paper and the mythic discovery of the expanding universe, such a concept had been explored by a number of scientists.

Historians of science have examined these critical events and attempted to develop wider perspectives on the history of early-twentieth-century cosmology. John North's monumental *Measure of the Universe* and Merleau-Ponty's *Cosmologie du XXe Siècle* signaled that by the mid-1960s historians were writing on modern cosmology with new depth and sophistication. Kerszberg also provides an important discussion on the beginnings of relativistic cosmology. Smith has examined the so-called great debate and evaluated the role of Hubble in these events.

Hubble was always careful to avoid in print definitely interpreting red shifts as velocity shifts. But on the basis of the writings of Eddington and others, the calculations of Lemaître and various theorists, and Hubble's observational researches, the red shift–distance relation was soon established, and the notion of the expanding universe was swiftly accepted. However, the concept of the expanding universe entailed the puzzling and fundamental question: What started the expansion? One of those to explore this problem was A.S. Eddington, probably the most influential astrophysicist of his generation. For Eddington, the "most attractive" case was one in which the mass of the universe is equal to the mass of the Einstein universe—that is, the mass of the universe in the static solution Einstein had discovered over a decade earlier. The idea was that the world had evolved from an Einstein universe and so had developed "infinitely slowly from a primitive uniform distribution in unstable equilibrium" (Eddington, 1930, 672). So there was a beginning to the expansion, but Eddington shied away from a creation for the universe when he considered the possibility of a universe with a mass larger than Einstein's model. This Eddington explicitly rejected because "it seems to require a sudden and peculiar beginning of things." He went on, "As a scientist I simply do not believe that the present order of things started off with a bang; unscientifically I feel equally unwilling to accept the implied discontinuity in the divine nature" (Eddington, 1932, 85).

During the early 1930s, several scientists, including California Institute of Technology mathematical physicist R.C. Tolman, examined possible physical mechanisms to explain the expansion. An alternative explanation suggested that expansion really did start with the beginning of the universe. Lemaître introduced this concept. In 1931, he suggested the first detailed account of what later became known as Big Bang cosmology. But unlike modern Big Bang theories, Lemaître's universe did not evolve from a true singularity, but from a material pre-universe that Lemaître referred to as the primeval atom. For Lemaître, a cosmic singularity was a non-physical concept in which neither time nor space existed; Lemaître insisted that cosmology could and should be understood in physical terms. For Lemaître, "The last two thousand million years are slow evolution: they are ashes and smoke of bright but very rapid fireworks" (Lemaître, 705). These arguments mark the introduction of the beginning of the universe as a legitimate subject for scientific discourse.

During the 1930s, as John North has argued, theoretical cosmology divided into two steams. One stream started from the question of "the stability of the Einstein universe, a question which might, it was thought, throw light on the beginning of the universe—and even, perhaps, on its 'cause.' These questions turned to matters of purely astrophysical interest—condensations in interstellar gas, cosmic radiation, and the synthesis of the chemical elements—and to speculation on the so-called primeval atom introduced by Lemaître. Those who followed the other stream of thought (such as **E.A. Milne**) argued from geometrical and kinematic premises. They tended (for example, in the appeals to symmetry) to a rigid idealization of the situation. Often this was not accompanied by any but the slightest reference to astronomical practice" (North, 126).

One aspect of the latter stream was a renewal of interest in Newtonian cosmology—that is, the use of Euclidean space, Newtonian gravitation, and many of the principles of Newtonian mechanics to explain the large-scale properties of the universe. By the end of the nineteenth century, Newtonian ideas, it was widely agreed, led to inconsistencies when applied to an infinite universe. But in 1934, the leading proponent of Newtonian cosmology, E.A. Milne, aided by W.H. McCrea, derived correspondences between the Newtonian equations of an expanding universe and certain fundamental equations of relativistic cosmology. However, critics emphasized that although Newtonian and relativistic cosmology might produce apparently similar formulae, their physical interpretation was so different that any correspondence was physically meaningless. Milne also developed kinematic relativity. This was perhaps the most significant of the rivals to relativistic cosmology, although other cosmologies were advanced.

The key point, however, is that by the early 1930s, the discussion of the expanding universe had produced an exchange between theorists and observers that was undreamed of only a few years before. Although pitifully meager by present-day standards, the discussion encouraged some astronomers and mathematicians to believe that they could ultimately explain the entire history of the universe. In the first three decades of the century, the content of cosmology had been reshaped and extended; indeed, the practice and very nature of the enterprise had been redefined. However, many of the conceptual problems of cosmology were far from new.

In addition to the debate over what triggered the expansion of the universe, there was also renewed interest in its fate. The idea of the heat death of the universe had been introduced in 1854 by Hermann Helmholtz, based on ideas of William Thomson (Lord Kelvin) concerning the dissipation of energy. Very simply, the heat death theory suggested that as the universe aged, energy was lost. The second law of thermodynamics defines this process as irreversible. Time's arrow moves only in one direction, and as the universe grows old its heat is forever lost.

In the late 1920s, the heat death of the universe reached a broad audience through popular writings and the press. This idea was widely discussed when it became enmeshed in a debate on one of the hottest scientific topics of the late 1920s—the nature of cosmic rays. This debate was conducted chiefly between two scientific nabobs, the British mathematical physicist Sir **James Jeans** and the Nobel Prize–winning American experimental physicist Robert Millikan. For Millikan, cosmic rays were telltale signs of the conversion of radiation into matter. This view led Millikan to develop a grand cosmological theory characterized by a continual cycle of the birth and death of the elements in a kind of steady-state universe. Jeans challenged both Millikan's particular theory, as well as the implied rejection of the unidirectionality of the evolution of the universe, which in turn rested on the second law of thermodynamics. Later cosmologists incorporated the second law into cosmological models based on general relativity. This was one of the goals of R.C. Tolman's influential *Relativity, Thermodynamics, and Cosmology* (1934).

We have already noted that during the 1930s a number of scientists were concerned with how the expansion of the universe might have started. A related issue was the time-scale problem. According to theories of stellar evolution and dynamical theories of the evolution of double stars and star clusters, the ages of the stars seemed to be much greater than the age of the universe as estimated from the value of the Hubble constant. On this basis, even the age of the earth derived from radioactive dating seemed to be greater than the age of the universe. The value of the constant in Hubble's 1929 paper was 500 kms per second per megaparsec, which, if one simply extrapolated the present expansion back in time and took no account of a possible acceleration in the expansion, implied there was a time about 2×10^9 years ago when all the material in the universe had been packed much closer together than now. The choice of a suitable time scale became "the nightmare of the cosmologists." As de Sitter pointed out, the "temptation is strong to identify the epoch of the beginning of the expansion with the 'beginning of the world,' whatever that might mean." If so, the "stars and the stellar systems must be some thousands of times older than the universe!" He concluded reluctantly that the "expansion has only been going on during an interval of time which is as nothing compared with the duration of the evolution" (De Sitter, 705).

During the 1930s—and indeed for some years after—cosmology was not academically respectable. This aspect of the history of cosmology has been little studied, but will prove important for understanding its development. The low standing of cosmology probably turned many scientists away from the field. Also, relativistic cosmology was somewhat marginal because general relativity itself was not widely accepted. Further, as Kragh has suggested, the marginality of cosmology was due to important issues that competing cosmologies raised, but failed to resolve. Among these was the time-scale problem.

The time-scale problem was one of the concerns of those who developed Steady State cosmology in the late 1940s, although the driving force behind its invention was what its authors regarded as objectionable features in the standard relativistic cosmology. The central idea of Steady State cosmology was that, except for local irregularities, the universe is in a steady state. As galaxies are born, age, and disperse, matter is continually created so that the steady state is not disturbed. The formulation of H. Bondi and T. Gold was based on the perfect cosmological principle, that is, that the universe presents the same aspect to every fundamental observer, wherever the observer is, at all times. From this principle they deduced that the universe must always expand. Fred Hoyle's approach was different. He too accepted the perfect cosmological principle, but sought to explain the distribution of matter in the universe by modifying the field equations of general relativity. The Steady State theory, implying the universe's infinite age, avoided the time-scale problem. By the late 1950s, due to revisions in the cosmic distance scale, the age of the universe had been increased and a strong reason for adopting the theory had disappeared.

Through the efforts of George Gamow, Ralph Alpher, and Robert Herman in the late 1940s and 1950s, Big Bang theory advanced far beyond Lemaître's ideas. In particular, their account offered a convincing explanation of how helium and other elements could be manufactured from hydrogen under extreme conditions of temperature and pressure during the very early stages of a Big Bang universe. But in 1957, Hoyle, together with Margaret and Geoffrey Burbidge and William Fowler, provided a convincing demonstration of how heavy elements could be synthesized by nuclear reactions inside stars, particularly during supernovae explosions, thereby undercutting the need for a Big Bang origin of the elements. But what most scientists saw as decisive evidence against the Steady State theory was discovered in 1965 in the form of the cosmic background radiation. This radiation was generally interpreted as the relic of a Big Bang origin to the universe. Excellent overviews of the history of both Steady State cosmology and Big Bang cosmology have been written by Kragh.

By the end of the 1950s, cosmology was a well-defined field of study and there was an active group of scientists who can be identified as cosmologists, something that was not the case in 1900. The questions pursued by cosmologists were of far greater scope than had seemed possible earlier in the century, and these questions were being addressed with much more powerful observational and theoretical tools. Whether one adopted the Big Bang or Steady State cosmology, the views of the universe held by astronomers and cosmologists after World War II were radically different from those of 1900. While historians of science have examined some of these changes, much important research remains to be done. We are only just beginning to understand the complex development of modern cosmology.

Robert W. Smith

Bibliography

Alpher, R.A., and R. Herman. "Early Work on 'Big Bang' Cosmology and the Cosmic Background Radiation." In *Modern Cosmology in Retrospect*, edited by B. Bertotti et al., 129–157. Cambridge: Cambridge University Press, 1990.

Berendzen, R., R. Hart, and D. Seeley. *Man Discovers the Galaxies*. New York: Science History Publications, 1976.

Bondi, H. "The Cosmological Science, 1945–1952." In *Modern Cosmology in Retrospect*, edited by B. Bertotti et al., 189–196. Cambridge: Cambridge University Press, 1990.

De Maria, M., and R. Russo. "Cosmic Rays and Cosmological Speculations in the 1920s: The Debate between Jeans and Millikan." In *Modern Cosmology in Retrospect*, edited by B. Bertotti et al., 401–410. Cambridge: Cambridge University Press, 1990.

De Sitter, W., "The Evolution of the Universe." *Nature* 128 (1931): 700–721.

Eddington, A.S. "On the Instability of Einstein's Spherical World." *Monthly Notices of the Royal Astronomical Society* 90 (1930): 668–678.

———. *The Nature of the Physical World.* Cambridge: Cambridge University Press, 1932.

Harrison, E. "The Redshift-Distance and Velocity-Distance Laws." *Astrophysical Journal* 403 (1993): 28–31.

Hetherington, N. "The Delayed Response to Suggestions of an Expanding Universe." *Journal of the British Astronomical Association* 84 (1973): 22–28.

Hetherington, N.S., ed. *Encyclopedia of Cosmology: Historical, Philosophical, and Scientific Foundations of Modern Cosmology.* New York: Garland, 1993.

Hoskin, M. *William Herschel and the Construction of the Heavens*. New York: Norton, 1964.

Hoyle, F. "An Assessment of the Evidence against the Steady-State Theory." In *Modern Cosmology in Retrospect*, edited by B. Bertotti et al., 221–232. Cambridge: Cambridge University Press, 1990.

Hubble, E. *The Realm of the Nebulae*. New Haven: Yale University Press, 1936.

Jaki, S.L. *The Milky Way: An Elusive Road for Science*. Newton Abbot: David and Charles, 1973.

Kerszberg, P. *The Invented Universe: The Einstein–De Sitter Controversy (1916–17) and the Rise of Relativistic Cosmology.* Oxford: Clarendon Press, 1989.

Kragh, H. "The Beginning of the World: Georges Lemaître and the Expanding Universe." *Centaurus* 32 (1987): 114–139.

———. "Big Bang Cosmology." In *Encyclopedia of Cosmology,* edited by N.S. Hetherington, 31–42. New York: Garland, 1993.

———. "Steady State Theory." In *Encyclopedia of Cosmology,* edited by N.S. Hetherington, 629–636. New York: Garland, 1993.

Lemaître, G. "The Evolution of the Universe." *Nature* 128 (1931): 700–721.

Merleau-Ponty, J. *Cosmologie du XXe Siècle; Etude Epistemologique et Historique des Theories de la Cosmologie Contemporaire.* Paris: Gallimard, 1965.

———. *La Science de l'Univers a l'Age du Positivisme: Etude sur les Origines de la Cosmologie Contemporaire*. Paris: Vrin, 1983.

———. "Laplace as Cosmologist." In *Cosmology, History and Theology. Based on the Third International Colloquium held at Denver*, edited by W. Yougrau and A.D. Breck. New York: Plenum, 1977.

Merleau-Ponty, J., and B. Morando. *The Rebirth of Cosmology*. Translated by H.Weaver. New York: Knopf, 1976.

North, J. *The Measure of the Universe: The History of Modern Cosmology*. Oxford: Clarendon Press, 1965.

Paul, E.R. *The Milky Way Galaxy and Statistical Cosmology, 1890–1924.* New York: Cambridge University Press, 1993.

Schaffer, S. "The Phoenix of Nature: Fire and Evolutionary Cosmology in Wright and Kant." *Journal for the History of Astronomy* 9 (1978): 180–200.

———. "The Great Laboratories of the Universe: William Herschel on Matter Theory and Planetary Life." *Journal for the History of Astronomy* 11 (1980): 81–111.

———. "Herschel in Bedlam: Natural History and Stellar Astronomy." *British Journal for the History of Science* 13 (1980): 211–239.

Smith, R.W. "The Origins of the Velocity-Distance Relation." *Journal for the History of Astronomy* 10 (1979): 133–165.

———. *The Expanding Universe: Astronomy's 'Great Debate' 1900–1931.* Cambridge: Cambridge University Press, 1982.

———. "Edwin P. Hubble and the Transformation of Cosmology." *Physics Today* 43 (1990): 52–58.

Tolman, R.C. *Relativity, Thermodynamics and Cosmology.* Oxford: Clarendon Press, 1934.

Tropp, E.A., V.Y. Frenkel, A.D. Chernin. *Alexander Friedmann: The Man who Made the Universe Expand.* Cambridge: Cambridge University Press, 1993.

Wilson, A.D. "Romantic Cosmology." In *Encyclopedia of Cosmology,* edited by N.S. Hetherington, 596–604. New York: Garland, 1993.

Crabtree, William (1610–1644?)

English mathematician and celestial mechanician. William Crabtree, a successful clothier, was the key figure in a trio of early seventeenth-century provincial English astronomical observers that included **Jeremiah Horrocks** and William Gascoigne. Crabtree believed that rigorous observation of the heavens with improved instruments was essential to generating reliable ephemerides and a description of the true nature and structure of the physical universe. A collector and reader of books on scientific subjects, Crabtree served as a conduit into England for the ideas and theories of contemporary Continental natural philosophers. He became aware of Johannes Kepler's *Rudolphine Tables* shortly after they were published. His own observations convinced him of their superiority over others in use at the time. Crabtree was one of the first in England to adopt Kepler's laws of planetary motion and embrace the physical theory on which they were based. He was also among the first English observers of sunspots.

By 1636, Crabtree had made the acquaintance of young Horrocks. The two began an extensive correspondence sharing observations and ideas on improving instruments. They occasionally collaborated on observational projects, the most notable being the transit of Venus in 1639, which Horrocks had predicted. Around that same time, Crabtree learned of Gascoigne's invention of the telescopic sight and eyepiece micrometer. He immediately recognized the potential of these instruments for improving the precision with which both positions and angular separations of celestial bodies could be measured. Crabtree and Gascoigne corresponded on observational problems and instrument improvements, which information Crabtree shared with Horrocks.

Barbara J. Becker

Bibliography

Chapman, A. *Three North Country Astronomers*. Manchester: Neil Swinton, 1982.

———. "Jeremiah Horrocks, the Transit of Venus, and the 'New Astronomy' in Early Seventeenth-Century England." *Quarterly Journal of the Royal Astronomical Society* 31 (1990): 333–357.

Horrocks, J. *The Transit of Venus across the Sun 1639*. Translated by A.B. Whatton. London: Macintosh, 1859.

———. *Opera Posthuma*. Edited by J. Wallis. London: R. Scott, 1672–1673; M. Pitt, 1678.

Crimean Astrophysical Observatory

Modern astronomical equipment and a location with good astronomical seeing make the Crimean Astrophysical Observatory one of the most important in the former USSR. It is a research institution with no teaching responsibilities. Its leading staff members were educated at Moscow and Leningrad (now Saint Petersburg) universities.

Before the fall of the Soviet Union, the observatory was administered by the USSR Academy of Sciences. Now it is outside the borders of Russia and controlled by Ukraine. The principal instruments include a 2.6-meter reflector, several smaller reflectors, a double 40-cm Zeiss astrograph, a large solar tower telescope, and radio telescopes. Main areas of research interest include astrophysics, solar-terrestrial relations, observations of asteroids, space experiments, radio astronomy, and the design of new instrumentation.

At the beginning of the twentieth century, the **Pulkovo Observatory** was given a well-equipped amateur observatory. After the 1917 revolution the observatory was enlarged, and, due to efforts of Pulkovo astronomer **Grigorii A. Shain**, a 40-inch reflector by Grubb-Parsons was installed in 1926. Unfortunately, the observatory was destroyed by fascists during World War II.

Academician Grigorii A. Shain led the restoration of the observatory. He visited the United States to gather information on site selection and new forms of instrumentation. The location for the new observatory was in the Crimean Mountains near the famous Tartar city of Bakhchisarai. The Crimean Astrophysical Observatory came into existence in 1945, under the supervision of the USSR Academy of Sciences. G.A. Shain was the first director. He was responsible for the construction of a 2.6-meter reflector; in 1961 the instrument was named the Shain Telescope. The second director was academician Andrey B. Severny, an expert in solar physics and vice president of the International Astronomical Union (1964–1970).

Associate director Alexander A. Boyarchuck, a specialist in astrophysics, became chairman of the Astronomical Council of the USSR Academy of Sciences. Under his leadership the Astronomical Council became the Institute of Astronomy of Academy of Sciences of the USSR (now Russian Academy of Sciences). In 1991 academician Boyarchuck became president of the International Astronomical Union.

Many distinguished Russian astronomers have been associated with the Crimean Astrophysical Observatory, including astrophysicist Solomon B. Pickel'ner and the first director of the Special Astrophysical Observatory, Ivan M. Kopylov.

Alexander Gurshtein

Bibliography

Pickel'ner, S.B. "G.A. Shain." In *Researches on History of Astronomy*, edited by P. Kulikovsky, vol. 3, 551–610. Moscow: Nauka, 1957.

Ponomarev, D.N. *Astronomical Observatories of the USSR*. Moscow: Nauka, n.d.
Struve, O., and V. Zebergs. *Astronomy of the 20th Century*. New York: Macmillan, 1962.

Cross-Staff

Invented by Levi ben Gerson in the early fourteenth century, the cross-staff consisted of a wooden or brass staff, roughly 3- to 14-feet long. In the early stages of its development, one or more perforated cross-pieces slid along the staff; in the later stages, a single, fixed cross-piece was employed. In the mid-sixteenth century, it became known as the *radius astronomicus*, the astronomer's staff, to distinguish it from the specialized cross-staves being employed by surveyors and navigators. All staves measured angles. To use the most common form, one end of the staff was positioned on the cheekbone just below the eye, and a cross-piece was slid along the staff until its ends touched the two objects whose angular distance was to be measured. Sides of the staff were calibrated for angles subtended by each cross-piece at the eye.

The cross-staff was first used by Levi ben Gerson to measure the altitudes of stars and planets, their separations, and the diameters of the sun and moon. During the sixteenth and seventeenth centuries, at the height of its popularity, it was also used to fix the positions of novae and comets, to measure the diameters of comets and the lengths of their tails, to determine lunar distances, and to note the degree of lunar eclipses.

Johann Werner, Regiomontanus, Peter Apian, Gemma Frisius, and above all, Thomas Digges were among those who helped to make the astronomer's cross-staff more accessible, accurate, and free from errors caused by the eccentricity of the eye (that is, the fact that rays of light from a distant object converge in the eye, and not at the start of the scale, which is positioned below the eye).

Cross-Staff by Johannes van Keulen en Zoonen, Amsterdam, 1765 (A-172). (Courtesy of the Adler Planetarium, Chicago, Illinois)

Whereas the cross-staves of mariners are to be found in museum collections, few astronomers' staves have been preserved.

Sara Schechner Genuth

Bibliography

Cotter, C.H. *A History of the Navigator's Sextant*. Glasgow: Brown, Son and Ferguson, Nautical Publishers, 1983.
Roche, J.J. "The Radius Astronomicus in England." *Annals of Science* 38 (1981): 1–32.
———. "The Cross-Staff as a Surveying Instrument in England, 1500–1640." In *English Map-Making, 1500–1650*, edited by S. Tyacke, 107–111. London: British Library, 1983.
Stimson, A.N., and C. St. John Hume Daniel. *The Cross Staff: Historical Development and Modern Use*. London: Harriet Wynter, 1977.

David Dunlap Observatory

The David Dunlap Observatory has been the focal point of university-based Canadian astronomy during the twentieth century. As the research center for the Department of Astronomy of the University of Toronto, since its opening in 1935 it has been the training ground for the majority of Canadian astronomers.

Toronto was the first Canadian university with a formal curriculum in astronomy. The subject was taught as a mathematics course from the mid-nineteenth century. In 1890, Toronto graduated Clarence Augustus Chant in physics, appointing him lecturer the following year. In 1904, he introduced an honors option in astronomy, thus inaugurating modern astronomy teaching in Canadian universities. After obtaining a Harvard Ph.D. in physics, he began investigating current lines of astrophysical research, asking **William W. Campbell** for permission to spend the summer of 1907 at **Lick Observatory** to learn techniques. That autumn he organized courses in astrophysics. Over the next few years, he trained a number of future astronomers who worked at the Dominion Observatory and the Dominion Astrophysical Observatory. Astrophysics was a separate subdepartment within physics by 1913, and soon there was an independent department of astronomy.

As early as 1905, Chant began enquiring into the possibility of an observatory for Toronto. The Toronto Magnetic and Meteorological Observatory, then located on campus, had a small refractor, purchased to observe the transit of Venus in 1882, but this was insufficient for serious research. By 1911, Chant was negotiating with the Royal Astronomical Society of Canada, of which he was at various times president and editor of its *Journal* and *Observer's Handbook*, and the city to create a joint public-university observatory in a city park. The site, well within the city, would have been practically useless for research purposes. Funds were impossible to raise.

In the 1920s, he was able to elicit the interest of financier David Dunlap. When Dunlap died, Chant approached his widow, Jessie Donalda Dunlap, for support. She was enthusiastic, and a site in Richmond Hill, several miles north of Toronto, was chosen. When she gave final financial approval in 1930, a 74-inch reflector, modeled on **J.S. Plaskett**'s telescope at the **Dominion Astrophysical Observatory**, was ordered from Grubb-Parsons. Corning cast its pyrex disk as a test run for Hale's 200-inch telescope; this was completed in 1933. The telescope, operating as an f/18 Cassegrain and also with an f/4.9 Newtonian focus, was designed primarily to continue the research lines of Victoria: binary stars and spectroscopy. When it opened in 1935, it was the world's second largest reflector and a model for other Grubb-Parsons telescopes.

During the 1920s, Chant had only one associate, R.K. Young, his former student, who had worked with Plaskett at Ottawa and Victoria. With the approaching completion of the observatory, Chant was able to augment the staff with former students Frank S. Hogg, Peter M. Millman, and J.F. Heard. Helen S. Hogg came with her husband from Victoria as a research associate. Chant retired in 1935; Young became department head and first director. Young's research program followed Victoria's lead: radial velocities and spectroscopic binary orbits were the mainstay, though Millman experimented with meteor spectroscopy, Frank Hogg worked in spectrophotometry and Helen Sawyer Hogg observed Cepheids in globular clusters.

Before World War II, the department typically enrolled more than one hundred students in its courses. On the graduate level, only the M.A. was offered—there was no Ph.D. in astronomy anywhere in Canada until the department introduced it in 1947—but rarely was more than one graduate student in residence.

During the war, with Heard and Millman away, the women on staff, Helen Hogg and Ruth J. Northcott, took a greater share in the routine work. At war's end, Hogg succeeded as director and head. Millman was lost to the Dominion Observatory.

During the 1950s, the department's horizons expanded. Ralph Williamson arrived in 1947, introducing the new field of radio astronomy. A former Toronto graduate, Donald McRae, put the new field into practice in the late 1950s with a number of experiments at the observatory in collaboration with the Electrical Engineering department. The radio astronomy group relocated its equipment to the Algonquin Radio Observatory after 1960; it was prominent in the Canadian Very Long Baseline Interferometry experiment in 1967. Although Toronto no longer maintains its own instruments, the radio group remains very active.

Original plans called for three small domes on the administration building (the 74-inch telescope was housed in its own dome). Young had constructed a 0.5-meter reflector with equatorial mount during the late 1920s in anticipation of an observatory. This telescope, the original Toronto Observatory refractor, and a 0.6-meter reflector donated to the university during the 1960s became the occupants of the domes. Only the last, employed in photometric work, was a useful research tool.

As the DDO was exposed to increasing light pollution with the expansion of suburbs, the staff turned to other observing sites, including their 0.6-meter telescope (recently named the Helen Sawyer Hogg Telescope) erected at Las Campanas in Chile in 1971 and the Canada-France-Hawaii Telescope. With widening interests and enlarged staff, Toronto pursued theoretical studies and became permanent host to the Canadian Institute for Theoretical Astrophysics in the 1982.

Now, with one of the largest astronomy departments in the world, Toronto provides a full range of research and teaching topics, including spectroscopy, photoelectric photometry, radio astronomy, theoretical astrophysics and extragalactic studies. The DDO's main telescope, the second largest in the world when it was completed, is now a middle-range instrument at a limited site but continuing improvements have ensured its productivity.

Richard A. Jarrell

Bibliography

Jarrell, R.A. *The Cold Light of Dawn: A History of Canadian Astronomy*. Toronto: University of Toronto Press, 1988.

Delambre, Jean-Baptiste Joseph (1749–1822)

French astronomer, geodist, and historian of astronomy. Born in Amiens, Delambre studied literature and history at the Collège du Plessis in Paris. In 1780, he began attending the astronomy lectures of Joseph-Jérôme Lefrançais de Lalande at the Collège Royale. On the recommendation of Lalande, Geoffroy d'Assy (*receveur générale des finances,* whose son Delambre was tutoring) built a private observatory for Delambre, whose first observation was the 1786 transit of Mercury. Delambre was elected a member of the French Academy of Sciences in 1792, after winning the academy's prize in 1790 (on the theory of the motion of the recently discovered planet Uranus). He later became a member of the newly organized academy and an inital member (1795) of the Bureau des Longitudes. Delambre succeeded Lalande as professor of astronomy at the Collège de France in 1807 and published two books (1813 and 1814), derived from his lectures. He established several lycées and in 1814 became a member of the Conseil Royal d'Instruction Publique. Delambre retired a year later.

In addition to his 1790 prize work, Delambre demonstrated expertise in positional astronomy through the publication of various tables of the motions of the sun, Jupiter, Saturn, and the satellites of Jupiter. He continued to make observations from his private observatory until 1808, primarily to check stellar positions in major catalogues.

In 1792, the academy appointed Delambre and Pierre-François-André Méchain to carry out the geodetic work that would serve as the foundation for the fundamental unit of length in the new decimal-based metric system. An academy commission decided that that unit would be one-quarter of a terrestrial meridian and thus requested that an arc of the meridian from Dunkerque to Barcelona be accurately measured. Despite the revolutionary times, Delambre persevered in his portion of the measurement (from Rodez to Dunkerque) and completed the work in 1799. After subsequent laborious calculations, Delambre wrote the final three-volume report.

With the publication (1806) of the historical first volume of this report, Delambre embarked on a new career as a historian. He published a *Rapport historique sur le progrès des sciences mathématiques depuis 1789* (1810) and a historical manuscript on the *Grandeur et figure de la terre* (published posthumously in 1912). His major historical work was a six-volume history of astronomy published between 1817 and 1827. Two volumes were devoted to ancient astronomy, and subsequent volumes dealt with astronomy in the Middle Ages, the Renaissance, the seventeenth century, and the eighteenth century, respectively. Because of Delambre's detailed analysis of one treatise after another, these volumes are considered by I. Bernard Cohen (Cohen 1971, 17) to be "the greatest full-scale technical history of any branch of science ever written by a single individual." Nevertheless, as Cohen observes, Delambre's lack of synthesis and generalization make it difficult to trace a particular topic over a long period.

Craig B. Waff

Bibliography

Caulle, J. "Delambre—sa participation à la détermination du mètre." *Recueil des Publications de la Société Havraise d'Études Diverses.* 103e année (1936): 143–157.

Cohen, I.B. Introduction to facsimile reprint of Delambre's *Histoire de l'astronomie moderne*. New York: Johnson Reprint, 1969.

———. "Delambre, Jean-Baptiste Joseph." In *Dictionary of Scientific Biography*, edited by C.C. Gillispie, vol. 4, 14–18. New York: Scribner, 1971.

Jacquinet, P. "Commémoration du deuxcentième anniversaire de la naissance de J.B. Delambre—son oeuvre astronomique et góodésique." *Bulletin de la Société Astronomique de France.* 63e année (1949): 193–207.

Delisle, Joseph-Nicolas (1688–1768)

French astronomer, known for his vast correspondence coordinating observations of the transit of Venus in 1761, the first observed for determining the sun's distance through measurement of solar parallax. Influenced by Jacques Cassini at an early age, he set up an observatory at the Palais de Luxembourg (1710–1715) and taught mathematics and astronomy at the Collège de France beginning in 1718. At the invitation of Peter the Great, Delisle founded the observatory at St. Petersburg in 1725. He remained there for twenty-two years, successfully applying the practical problems of navigation and mapping to the vast Russian empire, and teaching others to do so. On his return to Paris in 1747, he once again taught at the Collège de France until succeeded by his student Jèrôme de Lalande in 1761.

Steven J. Dick

Bibliography

Chapin, S.L. "Delisle, Joseph-Nicolas." In *Dictionary of Scientific Biography*, edited by C.C. Gillispie, vol. 4, 22–25. New York: Scribner, 1972.

Woolf, H. *The Transits of Venus: A Study of Eighteenth-Century Science*. Princeton: Princeton University Press, 1959.

Dembowski, Ercole (1812–1881)

Double star observer. The son of a Polish nobleman, the Baron Ercole Dembowski was born in Milan. After retiring from the Austrian Navy in 1843, he moved to Naples, where his interest in astronomy was stimulated by the astronomer Antonio Nobile. Dembowski acquired a 5-inch telescope with which he began to observe double stars in 1852 at his own observatory at San Giorgio a Cremano near Naples. Later he moved to the Milan area, where he observed with a 7-inch Merz refractor at his second observatory at Monte di Albuzzate.

Dembowski was an assiduous observer, even though he was afflicted both by inferior equipment and by gout. He systematically reobserved the double stars discovered by **Friedrich George Wilhelm Struve**, producing an uninterrupted twenty-five-year period of highly accurate observations. His total of nearly twenty-one thousand measures was collected posthumously into two large volumes. Unmatched in either quality or quantity in this period of time, these data are of special importance for double star studies. The Royal Astronomical Society honored him in 1874 with their Gold Medal.

Charles E. Worley
Charles J. Peterson

Bibliography

Dembowski, Ercole. *Misure Micrometriche di Stelle Doppie e Multiple, Fatte negli Anni 1852–1878*, edited by G.V. Schiaparelli and O. Struve. Roma: Coi tipi del Salviucci, 1883–1884.

Dominion Astrophysical Observatory

By the 1910 meeting of the International Solar Union in Pasadena, **John Stanley Plaskett** had impressed both **George Ellery Hale** and **William W. Campbell** with his efforts in astrophysics at the Dominion Observatory, Ottawa. Particularly involved in radial velocity work, Plaskett recognized that the 15-inch Ottawa refractor, even with his own fast and efficient spectrograph, had reached its limit. He and his chief, William F. King, lobbied the government, which, in 1911, agreed to fund a new instrument, but the project was not secured until the spring of 1913. Plaskett approached the Brashear and Warner and Swasey firms, who had supplied the optical and mechanical parts for the Ottawa 15-inch telescope, providing a design for a 72-inch reflector. The telescope had novel features, including electric drives, self-aligning ball bearings, and a quickly changed front end to change from Cassegrain to Newtonian for prime focus work.

A site was selected just north of Victoria, British Columbia, in 1914, with construction beginning the following year. The plate glass blank, cast at the St. Gobain works in France, was shipped just before the outbreak of war. The telescope saw first light in May 1918 and was, for a short time, the world's largest.

The Dominion Astrophysical Observatory (DAO) was considered a division of the Ottawa observatory, but Plaskett was effectively independent. His initial staff was small, just William E. Harper and Reynold K. Young, who both transferred from Ottawa. The research programs, strictly spectroscopic at first, centered upon obtaining orbits of spectroscopic binary stars and measuring radial velocities and spectroscopic parallaxes of hot (mostly O-type) stars. Plaskett's son, Harry H. Plaskett, brought the staff complement to four in the early 1920s, participating in the general programs. Despite the staff size, their output was extraordinary, much of it appearing in the *Publications*, inaugurated in 1922 as a series separate from that of Ottawa.

When Young moved to Toronto in 1925, Joseph A. Pearce joined Plaskett in a new radial velocity survey of B-stars. This work was substantially finished when Jan Oort announced his galactic rotation model in 1927. Plaskett and Pearce were the first to corroborate the model observationally. They also tackled the question of interstellar sodium and calcium clouds, investigated by both Plaskett and Young in the 1920s. Other contributors to the stellar spectroscopy programs in the 1930s were Roderick O. Redman, Frank S. Hogg, and Carlyle S. Beals, the last of whom concentrated upon the nature and classification of Wolf-Rayet and P Cygni stars, as well as exploring the interstellar gas problem. Throughout the period, the DAO attracted visitors from Canada and abroad, most of whom undertook spectrographic work. One exception was Helen Sawyer Hogg, whose research on variable stars in globular clusters was the only photographic work performed at the telescope's Newtonian focus.

After Plaskett's retirement, Harper, then Pearce succeeded him, but the primary programs continued. A new B-star program, initiated by Pearce, continued under Robert M. Petrie (director, 1951–1966). From the 1940s, the observatory broadened its scope. Andrew McKellar, hired, like Petrie, in the mid-1930s, introduced laboratory astrophysics, applying it to problems in stellar atmospheres. He studied carbon bands in the spectra of R and N stars in an attempt to find the C^{12}/C^{13} ratio, planetary atmospheres, and comets. He discovered evidence of CH, CN, and NaH in space, and (unwittingly) was the first to measure the cosmic background radiation. Stellar atmosphere studies by Kenneth O. Wright and Anne B. Underhill supplemented the traditional fare during the 1940s and 1950s. Binary star work waned during the postwar period, although Alan Batten continued the tradition, publishing in 1967 the *Catalogue of the Orbital Elements of Spectroscopic Binary Systems*, originally edited by Lick Observatory.

The DAO staff always excelled in designing instrumentation. The original universal spectrograph, designed by Plaskett, could use one or more prisms or a grating. During the 1940s, the spectrograph was fitted with a grating in Littrow form. In 1952, an optical plate was installed in the spectrograph, allowing for testing and interchanging of optical components. This has allowed for continuous upgrading. During Petrie's administration, a 48-inch Grubb-Parsons reflector featuring a large horizontal coudé spectrograph was installed. By the early 1970s successive refinements of this instrument, particularly by Harvey Richardson, had made it as effective an instrument as the

Hale 200-inch telescope for spectrographic work. A new optical shop with a testing tower was erected in 1973. The observatory's optical team replaced the original 72-inch plate glass mirror with Cer-Vit (1974) and later ground and polished the mirror for the Canada-France-Hawaii Telescope (1979). With state-of-the-art optical and electronic equipment, the DAO was able to remain fully competitive, and, by the 1970s, distinctly different research lines emerged, although spectroscopy lay at the heart of most research.

Until 1970, the DAO was part of the Observatories Branch of the federal Department of Energy, Mines, and Resources. In that year, federal government astronomy was reorganized and concentrated in the National Research Council of Canada. With the simultaneous closing of the Dominion Observatory in Ottawa, the DAO became the only government-supported optical astrophysical observatory. Wright was the last director (1966–1977) to rise from the ranks. His successor, Sydney van den Bergh, was lured from Toronto, while the current director (since 1986), James Hesser, is a relatively recent appointment from outside. During the last decade, the span of research interests expanded to include extragalactic studies, solar system work, and a rich variety of galactic and stellar inquiries.

Richard A. Jarrell

Bibliography

Jarrell, R.A. *The Cold Light of Dawn. A History of Canadian Astronomy.* Toronto: University of Toronto Press, 1988.

Double Star Astronomy

The majority of stars in the solar neighborhood, and perhaps in our own and other galaxies, appear to be members of double and multiple star systems. While we see a few objects that appear double owing purely to perspective, these optical pairs are not numerous compared with the true binary stars, where the pair is gravitationally bound and revolves around a common center of mass. That most doubles must be physical pairs was established by statistical arguments as early as 1767 by John Michell. Historically, binary stars also have been subdivided into classes of objects defined by the observational techniques used to discover and study them. Thus, we have the visual binaries, where the components can be seen as distinct points of light in a telescope; spectroscopic binaries, where duplicity is revealed by the periodic shifts of the spectrum lines; photometric binaries, detected by periodic light variations as one component comes in front of the other; and astrometric binaries, found from small but periodic variations in their proper motions. However, these separate categories are beginning to merge as new observational methods are applied. In particular, the advent of speckle and long baseline optical interferometry, as well as the development of much more accurate radial velocity spectrometers, is resulting in the resolution of many spectroscopic pairs, which now may be regarded as visual objects. This trend is expected to accelerate as more large optical interferometers come on line.

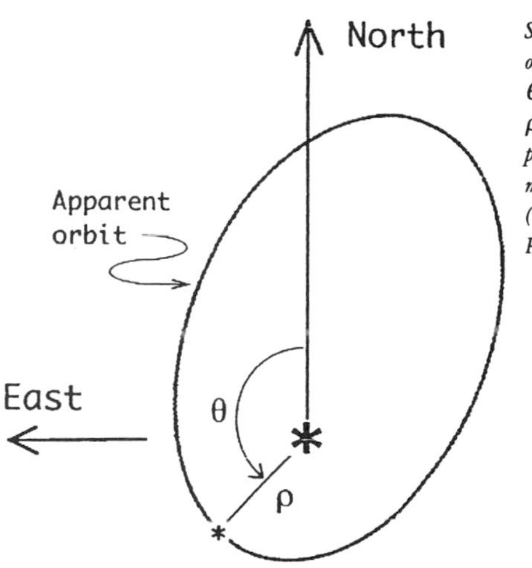

Schematic diagram of the orbit of a visual double star. θ is the position angle and ρ the distance between the primary and secondary measured in seconds of arc. (Figure by Charles J. Peterson)

Visual binary stars are very important to astrophysics for two basic reasons. First, they yield much more information on stellar parameters than do single stars. Only binary stars can yield direct determinations of stellar masses, one of the two initial parameters upon which evolution of a star depends (the other is chemical composition). In turn, combined with other empirically determined quantities, the luminosities, radii, and effective temperatures can be obtained. Second, surveys of the stellar population reveal that a large proportion of the stars are bound in binary or multiple systems. For example, the nearest star, α Centauri, is a triple system, while among the stars nearer than five parsecs, at least fifty-eight reside in double or triple systems, compared with only thirty-four single objects (of which several are suspected to have astrometric companions). Thus binary stars provide important information concerning star formation and evolution.

Visual binaries traditionally have been measured in polar coordinates, θ (position angle) and ρ (the separation in seconds of arc),

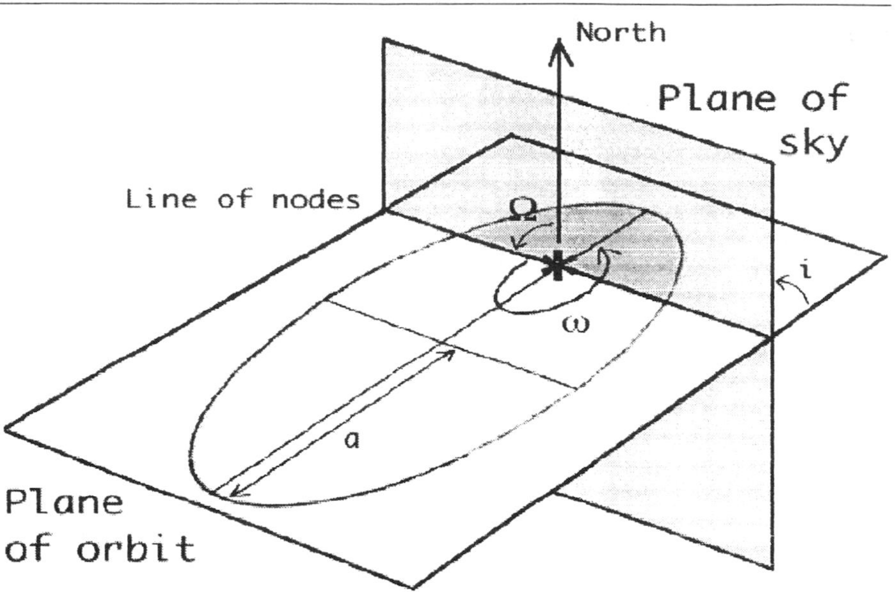

The elements of this ellipse define its shape and orientation in space. Included in this schematic are the semi-axis major axis expressed in arcseconds (a), the inclination of the orbit to the line-of-sight (i), the position angle where the orbit cuts the plane of the sky (Ω), called the node, and the angle in the plane of the true orbit between the line of nodes and major axis (ω). Astronomers have calculated orbits for about nine hundred visual binary star systems. (Figure by Charles J. Peterson)

centered on the primary or brighter component, as illustrated. If there is orbital motion, the successive measures will be found to define an ellipse. While we ordinarily see a projection of the true ellipse on the plane of the sky, called the apparent orbit, it is not difficult to determine the true orbit. The elements of this ellipse define its shape and orientation in space. The classical elements are the period in years (P), the time of periastron passage (T), the eccentricity of the ellipse (e), the semi-axis major expressed in arcseconds (a), the inclination of the orbit to the line-of-sight (i), the position angle where the orbit cuts the plane of the sky (Ω), called the node, and the angle in the plane of the true orbit between the line of nodes and major axis (ω). This latter quantity is measured in the direction of the companion's motion, and is usually called the longitude of periastron. Orbits of varying degrees of accuracy now exist for about nine hundred visual systems.

Having determined the period and major semi-axis of a binary, we can derive the total mass of the system in terms of the sun's mass, by Kepler's harmonic relation: $P^2/a^3 = (m_1 + m_2)$. However, we must first be able to convert a, measured in seconds of arc, into astronomical units. This can be done only if we can reliably measure the parallax of the binary. Finally, if we wish to divide the total mass between the components, we must measure the mass-ratio of the system. Both parallax and mass-ratio can be measured, given sufficient lapsed time, by referring the positions of the binary components to a background reference frame of stars. The number of visual binaries for which good orbits, parallaxes, and mass-ratios have been determined is still small, perhaps fifty systems.

There is a general relation observed between the quantity of matter contained in a star (its mass) and its luminosity. This mass-luminosity relation is of fundamental importance in studying the structure and evolution of stars. Some stars, such as white dwarfs, deviate from the relation, and such deviations provide additional insights into stellar evolution.

Although the first telescopic discovery of a double star is attributed to Giambattista Riccioli about 1650, it was not until late in the eighteenth century that serious attention was paid to this kind of object, with the near-simultaneous publication of double star catalogues by Christian Mayer and **William Herschel**. Herschel continued his observations for some decades and was able to show by 1801 that some double stars exhibited orbital motion and were therefore true binaries.

The study of binary stars was limited, however, by the quality of telescopes and auxiliary instrumentation. This changed in 1824 when **Friedrich George Wilhelm Struve** at the Dorpat Observatory received the famous Fraunhofer refractor, equatorially mounted and equipped with a good driving mechanism and micrometer. Struve shortly embarked on what was the first systematic survey for discovery of double stars and their measurement, which ultimately yielded 3,134 pairs. In 1837 he published his monumental *Mensurae Micrometricae* double star catalogue.

Following Struve's work, astronomers were content to simply observe the known pairs, although casual new discoveries were made. About 1870 American astronomer

Sherburne Wesley Burnham turned his attention to the discovery of new pairs and showed that earlier surveys were far from complete. Using large refractors, Burnham discovered more than 1,300 pairs, of which many were close and in rapid motion. He also began the systematic collection of double star data, which eventually was published as a catalogue in 1906. This collection has been continued by successive generations of astronomers and forms a valuable data base.

Burnham's example led to the great visual surveys of the twentieth century. **Robert Grant Aitken** and William J. Hussey used the 36-inch refractor at **Lick Observatory** to survey the sky north of declination –30 degrees, while the southern sky received attention from South Africa by Willem H. van den Bos and William S. Finsen at the Union Observatory, and Richard A. Rossiter and colleagues at the Lamont-Hussey Observatory. When the latter group finished their work about 1945, visual doubles catalogued over the whole sky exceeded fifty-thousand. In 1927 Robert T.A. Innes issued a catalogue of southern pairs, and Aitken did the same for the northern doubles in 1932, although he omitted many of the wide pairs.

Following World War II, technology advanced rapidly, and the Lick and Union Observatory astronomers agreed to combine their resources, first to create a machine-readable catalogue embodying all data accumulated since the Aitken and Innes catalogues, and second to produce a new, up-to-date catalogue. This was accomplished in 1963 with the publication of the "Index Catalogue of Visual Double Stars," (known by its acronym IDS) listing all known pairs, which then totaled 64,237 objects.

Visual resurveys continue to result in further discoveries. The Northern Hemisphere has been almost completely redone by Paul Couteau, Wulff D. Heintz, and Paul Muller in recent years, and thousands of new pairs found. In addition, Heintz has surveyed a small portion of the Southern Hemisphere overlooked in the initial surveys. There have also been a number of special surveys. In the 1930s, **Gerard P. Kuiper** looked at both the bright and nearby stars, and discovered a number of important pairs. Later, Charles Worley looked at a sample of M-dwarfs and discovered several interesting objects.

Photographic surveys began before the turn of the century when the sky was photographed for the *Carte du Ciel*. Because of the small scale of this survey, the pairs discovered are generally wide and faint. Later, observational programs aimed at discovery of common proper motion pairs were undertaken, notably by Willem J. Luyten and Henry L. Giclas. These programs have added many thousands of pairs.

Introduction of new observational techniques has always produced new discoveries. The application of photography to stellar spectroscopy allowed the detection of spectroscopic binaries, with **Edward C. Pickering** finding in 1889 the duplicity of Mizar and **Hermann C. Vogel** establishing the orbital motion of Algol in the same year. Radial velocity programs, extending over many years, particularly at **Lick Observatory** and the **Dominion Astrophysical Observatory**, have paid particular attention to spectroscopic binary stars.

Development of new techniques is also contributing new visual pairs. High-speed photometry of lunar occultations has revealed a number of binaries. However, such observations provide only a one-dimensional representation of the position angle and separation of the pair, and therefore are not suitable for orbit calculations. Nevertheless, they do prove duplicity, as well as giving valuable information on the magnitude difference in the system. Harold A. McAlister and colleagues have surveyed many bright stars by speckle interferometry, and have found more than two hundred new binaries. Many of these are very close and in rapid orbital motion, and a number of new orbits have already been calculated. A group has also used the experimental long baseline optical interferometer at the Mount Wilson Observatory to resolve a number of double-lined spectroscopic binaries. Combining the astrometric and spectroscopic results leads to the parallax and masses of the component stars. Charge-couple devices are being used both in the discovery and routine measurement of double stars by several groups.

The European astrometric satellite *Hipparcos* has completed a very successful survey that has produced thousands of new binary stars. Following final reductions and publication of the results, these pairs will swell the total of known visual binaries considerably.

As discoveries and measurements of visual binaries continued to accumulate, astronomers increasingly felt the need for a central archive to both preserve and distribute this data. Such an archive had, in fact, been informally established by Burnham, who compiled a manuscript catalogue containing all data known to him. This passed to Eric

Doolittle of Flower Observatory, who transferred the manuscript to file cards. Subsequently, Aitken became the conservator and, upon his death, Hamilton M. Jeffers of Lick Observatory became responsible. Southern pairs were cared for by Innes, and later van den Bos. As mentioned before, the two data sets were combined later to form the first all-sky double star catalogue. In 1965 the entire data base was transferred to the United States Naval Observatory. The data is now kept in computer files, which have been continually expanded and updated, so that today a very nearly complete data base exists. It now contains more than 440,000 observations of more than 77,000 visual double and multiple stars.

To an observer, visual binaries present a varied scenario. Pairs with a small difference of brightness abound, because they are the easiest to discover, but many of large brightness and color difference also are seen. α Centauri appears as two bright, solarlike stars, revolving in a very elliptical orbit with a period of eighty years. More than two degrees away is the faint M-dwarf companion Proxima, visible only through a telescope. An apparently analogous system in the north is the bright pair Castor, with a period of a few hundred years. It too, is accompanied at a distance by a red dwarf companion. But appearances are deceiving! In this case, each of the bright components is known to be a spectroscopic binary, while the red dwarf is the eclipsing binary YY Geminorum. Thus the system is sextuple. Several surprises in recent years have been provided by speckle interferometry. For example, the bright component of Albireo (β Cygni) has an 0.4 arcsecond companion exhibiting orbital motion, and the famous double-double ε Lyrae has a fifth component. Both Sirius and Procyon have white dwarf companions, first discovered as astrometric pairs, but later resolved. A third naked-eye star, o^2 Eridani, is itself single, but is accompanied at a distance by a red-white dwarf binary.

These systems are examples of the normal kind of multiple system, called hierarchical because the separations between the close and wide companions are greatly different. But there exists another class, called trapezia, named after the famous Trapezium in the Orion nebula. In trapezia, the separations of the components are more or less the same, not hierarchical. Such systems are dynamically unstable and will disintegrate in a relatively short time.

The mechanism of star formation is still not well understood, because the early stages take place in heavily obscured regions that were inaccessible to observation until recently. For binaries, several mechanisms have been suggested: fission, capture, and fragmentation. There are serious theoretical difficulties with fission. Recent work shows that in some conditions it would be possible to form binaries from circumstellar disks, so capture may still play a role. At the present time, the fragmentation mechanism seems the most promising. It involves a break-up of a dense molecular cloud core during the dynamical collapse phase, which leads to the formation of protostellar objects. Depending on the shape of the cloud, it is possible to produce not only binary, but multiple star systems as well.

Nearly a century ago, the distinguished historian of astronomy Agnes M. Clerke wrote, "The members of binary systems may fairly be regarded as contemporaneous. Their origin was in common; their destinies are indissoluble; they are identically circumstanced; they must be similarly composed. They should then be exceptionally trustworthy guides to the unravelment of evolutionary time-relations" (Clerke, 275–276). This is still relevant today, as we endeavor to fully understand not only the formation, but also the evolution of the binary and multiple stars.

Charles E. Worley
Charles J. Peterson

Bibliography

Abt, H.A. "Normal and Abnormal Binary Frequencies." *Annual Review of Astronomy and Astrophysics* 21 (1983): 343–372.

Aitken, R.G. *The Binary Stars.* New York: D.C. McMurrie, 1918; 2nd ed. New York: McGraw-Hill, 1935.

———. *A New General Catalogue of Double Stars Within 120° of the North Pole.* Washington, D.C.: Carnegie Institution of Washington, 1932.

Batten, A.H., J.M. Fletcher, and D.G. MacCarthy. "Eighth Catalogue of the Orbital Elements of Spectroscopic Binary Systems." *Publications of the Dominion Astrophysical Observatory* 17 (1989): 1–317.

Burnham, S.W. *A General Catalogue of Double Stars within 121° of the North Pole.* Washington, D.C.: Carnegie Institution of Washington, 1906.

Clerke, A.M. *Problems in Astrophysics.* London: Adam and Charles Black, 1903.

Innes, R.T.A., B.H. Dawson, and W.H. van den Bos. *Southern Double Star Catalogue,*

–19° to –90°. Johannesburg: Union Observatory, 1927.

Jeffers, H.M., W.H. van den Bos, and F.M. Greeby. "Index Catalogue of Visual Double Stars, 1961.0." *Publications of the Lick Observatory* 21 (1963): Parts 1 and 2.

McAlister, H.A. "High Angular Resolution Measurements of Stellar Properties." *Annual Review of Astronomy and Astrophysics* 23 (1985): 59–87.

Struve, F.G.W. *Stellarum Duplicium et Multiplicium Mensurae Micrometricae per magnum Fraunhoferi Tubum annis a 1824 ad 1837 in Specula Dorpatensi Institutae: Adjecta est Synopsis Observationum de Stellis Compositis Dorpatis annis 1814 ad 1824 par Minora Instrumenta Perfectarum*. Petropoli: Typographia Academica, 1837.

Worley, C.E., and W.D. Heintz. "Fourth Catalog of Orbits of Visual Binary Stars." *Publications of the U.S. Naval Observatory* 24, Part 7 (1983).

Draper Catalogue of Stellar Spectra

A monumental spectrographic catalogue that includes the spectral type of virtually all stars brighter than magnitude 9.0. It was the brainchild of **Edward C. Pickering**, the director of the Harvard Observatory, and was financed by Mrs. Anna Palmer Draper, who wished to memorialize her husband, Henry, a pioneer astrophysicist.

The first classification scheme was developed by **Williamina Paton Fleming** under Pickering's supervision. Studying the stars visible from Cambridge, she arranged their spectra into classes A through Q on the basis of increasing complexity. When **Annie Jump Cannon** later studied the bright southern stars, she followed this system.

But when Antonia C. Maury, a niece of **Henry Draper**, examined the brighter northern stars, she developed her own scheme. Maury placed the stars into twenty-two groups identified by Roman numerals, and appended additional information on the appearance and total strength of their lines. This system was the first attempt at a two-dimensional classification, and provided evidence that led to the discovery of giants and dwarfs.

The Fleming/Cannon one-dimensional scheme was so simple and versatile, however, that Cannon decided to use it when she classified a quarter-million stars for the ***Draper Catalogue of Stellar Spectra***. The Draper classification system was adopted for worldwide use by the International Union for Cooperation in Solar Research in 1913. The *Draper Catalogue of Stellar Spectra* produced spectacular results; it not only brilliantly memorialized Henry Draper's name, but also propelled Harvard to a position of world leadership in astrophysics.

Howard N. Plotkin

Bibliography

DeVorkin, D.H. "A Sense of Community in Astrophysics: Adopting a System of Spectral Classification." *Isis* 72 (1981): 29–49.

Hoffleit, D. "The Evolution of the Henry Draper Memorial." *Vistas in Astronomy* 34 (1991): 107–162.

Plotkin, H.N. "Edward C. Pickering, the Henry Draper Memorial, and the Beginnings of Astrophysics in America." *Annals of Science* 35 (1978): 365–377.

———. "Henry Draper, Edward C. Pickering, and the Birth of American Astrophysics." *Symposium on the Orion Nebula to Honor Henry Draper*. In *Annals of the New York Academy of Sciences* 395 (1982): 321–330.

Draper, Henry (1837–1882)

American astronomer. Born in Prince Edward County, Virginia, he lived in New York City from age two until his death. He graduated from the medical department of the University of the City of New York in 1858, and then became a faculty member.

Draper's interest in astronomy was sparked by a visit to the Earl of Rosse's six-foot telescope in Ireland. Acting on the advice of **John Herschel**, he began experimenting with silvered glass mirrors. By 1862 he had succeeded in constructing a 15½-inch glass mirror, and by 1872 had successfully installed a 28-inch mirror in his Hastings-on-Hudson observatory.

His greatest success was in the area of astronomical photography. In 1872, he used his 28-inch telescope to take the first photograph of a star (Vega) that exhibited Fraunhofer lines, beating out his closest rival, **William Huggins**, by four years. A decade later, he used an 11-inch **Alvan Clark** photographic refractor to take a superb 137-minute exposure of the Orion Nebula.

His greatest blunder occurred in 1877, when he announced the discovery of oxygen in the sun and a new theory of the solar spectrum. Unfortunately, he had been too quick to interpret data at the very limits of his instrument's capabilities and had apparently misunderstood Kirchhoff's law of radiation.

Although Draper was an amateur, his pioneering astrophysical research placed him on the cutting edge of that fledgling discipline. The New York Public Library houses five boxes of Draper's correspondence. To date, there is no full-length published biography.

Howard N. Plotkin

Bibliography

Gingerich, O. "Henry Draper's Scientific Legacy." *Symposium on the Orion Nebula to Honor Henry Draper*. In *Annals of the New York Academy of Sciences* 395 (1982): 308–320.

Plotkin, H.N. *Henry Draper: A Scientific Biography*. Unpublished Ph.D. dissertation, Johns Hopkins University, 1972.

———. "Henry Draper, Edward C. Pickering, and the Birth of American Astrophysics." *Symposium on the Orion Nebula to Honor Henry Draper*. In *Annals of the New York Academy of Sciences* 395 (1982): 321–330.

Whitney, C.A. "Henry Draper." In *Dictionary of Scientific Biography*, edited by C.C. Gillispie, vol. 4, 178–181. New York: Scribner, 1971.

Dreyer, Johann Louis Emil (1852–1926)

Danish-born Johann Louis Emil Dreyer studied mathematics and astronomy at Copenhagen University. In 1874 he began work in Ireland as an assistant to Lawrence Parsons, Fourth Earl of Rosse, where he gained experience observing nebulae with Rosse's famed 72-inch reflector. Dreyer served as an assistant at the Dunsink Observatory in Dublin (1878–1882) and then as director of the Armagh Observatory until his retirement in 1916.

Dreyer contributed to an understanding of nebulae through two extensive projects. After completing a supplement to John Herschel's nebular catalogue in 1878, Dreyer undertook the demanding task of renumbering the nebulae discovered up to 1888 at the request of the Royal Astronomical Society. His *New General Catalogue of Nebulae and Clusters of Stars* (1888) provided new positions adjusted for precession since Herschel's day, new descriptions to reflect current thinking on nebular form and physical structure, as well as new objects. Dreyer prepared two additional indexes in 1895 and 1908, bringing the total number of nebulae catalogued to thirteen thousand.

Dreyer made substantial contributions to the history of astronomy. He wrote a biography of **Tycho Brahe** (1890), and collected and edited all of the Dane's work and correspondence (1913–1929). In 1906, Dreyer prepared a comprehensive history of astronomy from ancient times to the advent of modern astronomy, and, in 1912, he edited the scientific papers of Sir **William Herschel,** prefacing the volumes with a detailed biography. He collaborated with Herbert Hall Turner to edit a centenary history of the Royal Astronomical Society (1923).

Barbara J. Becker

Bibliography

Dreyer, J.L.E. *Tycho Brahe. A Picture of Scientific Life and Work in the Sixteenth Century*. Edinburgh: A. and C. Black, 1890; reprint, New York: Dover, 1963.

———. *A History of the Planetary Systems from Thales to Kepler*. Cambridge: Cambridge University Press, 1906; republished as *A History of Astronomy from Thales to Kepler*. New York: Dover, 1953.

———. *The Scientific Papers of Sir William Herschel.* 2 vols. London: Royal Society and Royal Astronomical Society, 1912.

———. *Omnia opera Tychonis Brahe Dani.* 15 vols. Copenhagen: Nielson and Lydich, 1913–1929.

Dreyer, J.L.E., H.H. Turner, et al. *History of the Royal Astronomical Society 1820–1920*. London: Wheldon and Wesley, 1923; reprint, Oxford: Blackwell Scientific Publications, 1987.

E

Eclipses of the Sun

Total solar eclipses are among the most spectacular of astronomical phenomena. They are also among the most difficult to observe. Solar eclipses occur approximately once a year and are often visible only in areas far from established observatories. Totality lasts only a few minutes, and the objects revealed—the solar corona and prominences—are delicate, subtle, and difficult to observe under the best of circumstances.

Solar eclipses have been observed by Europeans for centuries, but only since 1860 have they been pursued aggressively by astronomers and solar physicists. Previously they were observed when they were visible in Europe (1836, 1842, and 1851), but astronomers did not travel overseas to observe eclipses. Eclipses became valuable with the rise of **solar physics** after 1859. Eclipses were a source of unique knowledge about the physical constitution of the sun, knowledge that could not be produced before the invention of the spectroscope. The sun is the nearest star and can provide important information about stellar developments, but only during a total eclipse can the solar atmosphere and corona be directly viewed and analyzed. Other astronomers refined their models of solar and lunar motion with data on the timing of the phases of an eclipse, or searched the area around the sun for intramercurial planets (Fontenrose). Efforts to use eclipses to pinpoint the times and locations of biblical and other events of ancient history added further interest to contemporary eclipses.

Nineteenth- and early twentieth-century eclipse research went through several phases. These phases are by no means distinct; instruments and interests from one era often survived to the next. Before 1836 observers concentrated on timing the contacts of the sun and moon. With Francis Baily's description in 1836 of the phenomena later called Baily's Beads, astronomers began to cast a wider observational net. During eclipses visible over Europe in 1842 and 1851, Baily, **George Biddell Airy**, and other astronomers and naturalists engaged in a natural history of eclipses, writing about meteorological phenomena, optical effects, changes in the landscape and atmosphere during totality, and the prominences and corona. In 1860 and 1868, photography and then spectroscopy were applied to eclipse observation, marking the ascendance of physical research in observing programs. The most important discoveries about the corona were made in the first years of physical observations. In 1870 Charles Young observed the reversing layer for the first time. Eight years later the corona's size and spectrum were discovered to vary with the sunspot cycle. In the same period observers began to experiment with instruments specially designed for eclipse observation. At first these were relatively modest. For example, Thomas Alva Edison invented an instrument to observe the eclipse of 1878, and Amherst astronomer David Todd developed automatic cameras to photograph the corona (Eddy 1979). In 1893 a new generation of eclipse instruments, larger and more expensive and involving more labor but producing larger amounts of data, was unveiled by American and British astronomers (Eddy 1971). Before the 1890s, professional and amateur astronomers had worked as equals in the field, but as instruments became more specialized, amateurs were pushed to the margins.

The history of eclipse observation demonstrates the complex ways theories and instruments interact in shaping observational practice and records produced by eclipse observers. Perhaps the most theory-laden records were the photographs and drawings alleged to represent the appearance of the corona. After decades of careful observation of solar system objects and nebulae, reinforced by the dominance of John Ruskin's ideas about the value of realism in art, astronomers came to place high value on detailed, realistic pictures of the corona. The scope of observing programs changed as technologies and theories changed. Prominences attracted as much attention as the corona until 1868, when **Pierre Janssen** and **J. Norman Lockyer** discovered a means of observing prominences out of eclipse. After that, observers concentrated exclusively on the corona and search for intramercurial planets. In 1919, efforts to test Einstein's theory of general relativity forced observers to shift focus from the corona to the star fields around the sun in a search for stellar deflections. Theoretical interests even shaped instruments: Norman Lockyer's prismatic camera generated data suited to his scheme of spectral analysis and theories about solar structure.

Solar eclipse expeditions are also notable for the ways they used and reflected colonial culture and expectations. Expeditions relied so heavily on railroads and steamships to get them and their delicate instruments safely into the field that they chose their observing sites on the basis of their proximity to stations and docks. They also relied on commercial transportation and national navies to provide reduced shipping rates and special accommodations for instruments. They made field camps using material borrowed from colonial armies and colonial civil services. Finally, a comparison of European and non-Western reactions to eclipses reflected scientists' ideas about the superiority of Europeans over their colonial subjects. In a period in which scientific and technological achievements were increasingly used as measures of men, European ability to successfully predict eclipses—treated (according to Europeans) by non-Westerners as fantastic, uncontrollable phenomena—represented an especially potent triumph of Western culture over non-Western superstition. Further, in these accounts European scientists reacted to totality with a mixture of awe and self-discipline, respecting the majesty of nature but still making their observations, while non-Westerners were described as surrendering to superstition, terror, and primitivism.

Solar eclipses and solar eclipse expeditions have received little attention from historians of science. Scholars have examined particular instruments (Eddy 1971, 1979) or the history of expeditions sponsored by particular institutions (Osterbrock et al.). Others have paid close attention to the eclipses that verified Einstein's theory of general relativity (Crelinstein; Earman and Glymour). More recent work has taken an explicitly sociological and political approach, examining the role of the new imperialism, the rise of tourism, and changes in instrumentation and recording practices to expeditionary experiences and observations.

Alex S.-K. Pang

Bibliography

Crelinstein, J. "William Wallace Campbell and the 'Einstein Problem': An Observational Astronomer Confronts the Theory of Relativity." *Historical Studies in the Physical Sciences* 14 (1983): 1–91.

Earman, J., and C. Glymour. "Relativity and Eclipses: The British Eclipse Expeditions of 1919 and Their Predecessors." *Historical Studies in the Physical Sciences* 11 (1980): 49–85.

Eddy, J. "The Schaeberle 40-Foot Eclipse Camera of Lick Observatory." *Journal for the History of Astronomy* 2 (1971): 1–22.

———. "Edison the Scientist." *Applied Optics* 15 (November 1979): 3737–3749.

Fontenrose, R. "In Search of Vulcan." *Journal for the History of Astronomy* 4 (1973): 145–158.

Hufbauer, K. *Exploring the Sun: Solar Science since Galileo*. Baltimore: Johns Hopkins University Press, 1991.

Osterbrock, D., J.R. Gustfason, and W.J.S. Unruh. *Eye on the Sky: Lick Observatory's First Century*. Berkeley: University of California Press, 1988.

Pang, A.S.-K. "Spheres of Interest: Imperialism, Culture, and Practice in British Solar Eclipse Expeditions, 1860–1914." Ph.D. thesis, University of Pennsylvania, 1991 (UMI #9200379).

Eddington, Arthur Stanley (1882–1944)

English astronomer and physicist. Educated at Trinity College, Cambridge, Eddington became chief assistant at the Royal Greenwich Observatory in 1906. From 1913, he was Plumian Professor of Astronomy at Cambridge and from 1914, director of the Cambridge Observatory. Eddington became a fellow of the Royal Astronomical Society in 1906, and president from 1921 to 1923. From 1913 he was an owner and editor of *The Observatory*. Eddington was knighted in 1930.

Eddington organized expeditions to Brazil and Principe to photograph the eclipse of 1919. Using the eclipse photographs to measure the deflection of the starlight passing near the sun, Eddington provided empirical confirmation of general relativity. From 1916, Eddington engaged **James Jeans** in debates concerning the physical conditions in the interior of a star in radiative equilibrium. In 1924, he derived a stellar mass-luminosity relationship. In 1926, he published *The Internal Constitution of the Stars*, containing his influential standard model of the structure of idealized polytropic stars and identifying nuclear processes as a probable source of stellar energy. Eddington became famous for popular lectures and books. During the 1930s, however, the scientific community rejected his final project, *Fundamental Theory*, an attempt to construct a measurement-free account of the physical world, unifying quantum mechanics and relativity.

Historians have written on Eddington's relationship to other figures and events; however, biographical discussions centering on him are mainly obituaries and memorial lectures by colleagues. Most of Eddington's personal papers were burned at his death, though the Trinity College preserves a one-volume journal combining partial professional records with a lifelong log of bicycle trips.

Joann Eisberg

Bibliography

Chandrasekhar, S. *Eddington: The Most Distinguished Astrophysicist of His Time.* Cambridge: Cambridge University Press, 1983.

DeVorkin, D.H., and R. Kenat. "Quantum Physics and the Stars (II)." *Journal for the History of Astronomy* 14 (1983): 180–222.

Douglas, A.V. *The Life of Arthur Stanley Eddington*. London: Thomas Nelson, 1956.

Hufbauer, K. "Astronomers Take up the Stellar-Energy Problem, 1917–1920." *Historical Studies in the Physical Sciences* 11 (1981): 277–303.

Stachel, J. "Eddington and Einstein." *The Prism of Science*, edited by E. Ullmann-Margalit, 225–250. Dordrecht: D. Reidel, 1986.

Education of Astronomers

The education of astronomers is a subject about which there is too much unfounded speculation and too little reliable knowledge. For example, it is incorrect to assume that entry into the astronomical community (or many other scientific communities for that matter) has always depended on completion of graduate studies leading to the Ph.D. (in England the D.Sc.). Neither does possession of a graduate degree distinguish amateur from professional. Until relatively recently, graduate work was not a prerequisite for professional standing in astronomy. Indeed, even in the first half of the twentieth century, many leading astronomers had no more than a baccalaureate degree and, in some cases, only a high school education. As a group, astronomers who were honored with stars in successive editions of the *American Men of Science* series between 1906 and 1944 included a larger number of individuals whose highest level of educational attainment was a high school certificate than almost any other scientific community. The following discussion focuses primarily on astronomers in the United States.

Lack of graduate credentials did not hamper the careers of many elite American astronomers. Until recently, the Ph.D. was not a prerequisite for assuming the directorship of a major research observatory. **Harlow Shapley**, who became director of the **Harvard College Observatory** in 1921, was the first Ph.D. (Princeton 1913) to hold that office. Only when **Walter S. Adams** retired from the directorship at the Mount Wilson Observatory in 1946 did a Ph.D. scientist assume the directorship. Nor was the lack of graduate credentials an impediment to membership in the National Academy of Sciences.

From the 1870s, graduate education in the United States was linked to the dramatic expansion of higher education. By 1920 the astronomy department at the University of California at Berkeley was the major producer of graduate degrees in astronomy, followed by the University of Chicago. At Berkeley and Chicago, students had the advantage of working at a major research observatory under the supervision of leading astronomers. Very few Americans went abroad for graduate training in astronomy. Indeed, more non-American-born students earned astronomy Ph.D.s in the United States than did Americans studying abroad.

Lankford has found that in nineteenth-century American astronomy, the educational credentials of the founders of astrophysics were often limited to a high school diploma, while workers in astrometry and celestial mechanics tended to have baccalaureate degrees. After 1900, however, there was a tendency for astrophysicists to acquire the doctorate in greater numbers than those who devoted themselves to more traditional fields.

Several of the post–Civil War women's colleges developed strong astronomy departments. The most important of these programs include Vassar (Maria Mitchell), Mount Holyoke (Elizabeth Bardwell), Smith (Mary Bryd), and Wellesley (Sara Whiting). These departments were feeders, their graduates often going on for advanced work in public or private universities.

In the early nineteenth century, higher education in Germany was reorganized and the modern state-supported German university soon became the idealized model for many other nations. Astronomy in German universities was located in research institutes or observatories. Indeed, German universities were not organized into academic departments as was the case with higher education in the United States. The Ph.D. became normative for admission to the German astronomical community at a relatively early date.

In England, graduate work and the expansion of higher education came relatively late. Until after World War II, the D.Sc. was not required for admission to the astronomical community or positions on university faculties or at state-operated observatories. In France, the situation was unique. The modern French system of higher education dates only from the 1890s. Historians of science have given little attention to academic credentialing in the French astronomical community.

Undergraduate and graduate education in astronomy are aspects of the history of American science that deserve scholarly attention. Students in astronomy were exposed to a sequence of courses beginning at the introductory level and going on to explore both observational and theoretical aspects of the science. Until well into the twentieth century, undergraduate training most often focused on the traditional fields of astrometry and celestial mechanics.

As Rothenberg suggests (245), by the 1870s professors of astronomy were no longer presenting their subject as a part of general education, designed to produce well-rounded graduates. Rather, they were engaged in recruiting and training the next generation of professional astronomers. In the last quarter of the nineteenth century, new American graduate programs in astronomy consisted of courses in celestial mechanics and astrometry as well as mathematics and physics, plus practical training with the transit circle and refracting telescope. At both the University of Chicago and the University of California at Berkeley, there was a curious division of labor between the campus astronomy department and the off-campus observatory. Astrometry and celestial mechanics were the primary concerns of the campus department, while students gained a knowledge of astrophysics at the observatory, primarily through participation in faculty research projects, seminars, and directed reading programs. In comparison to the situation after World War II, early graduate education in astronomy, at least in America, was comparatively informal. Hands-on observatory experience formed a major component and was often considered more important than accumulating credits based on formal course work.

In the early twentieth century, more courses in physics (especially optics, theory of light, and spectroscopy) were added and practical experience expanded to include the application of photography in various research fields from astrometry to spectroscopy and photometry and the use of the reflecting telescope. In the 1930s, astronomers at Harvard, the Yerkes Observatory of the University of Chicago, and the University of Michigan established summer schools at which European scientists shared their knowledge of quantum mechanics and relativity. Only after World War II did the education of American astronomers routinely include advanced work in theoretical physics.

The education of scientists is a field in which there are many research opportunities. The subject provides important materials for scholars seeking to understand science in its social and institutional context. A good example of this approach is Rothenberg's Bryn Mawr doctoral dissertation on the education of American astronomers. We need studies that range from detailed examinations of departments of astronomy in various types of institutions to cross-cultural comparative investigations. Especially valuable would be an inquiry into European graduate education in astronomy grounded in archival research. Biographical memoirs published by various national academies provide valuable information; so do obituaries, biographical dictionaries, and encyclopedias.

John Lankford

Bibliography

DeVorkin, D.H. "The Harvard Summer School in Astronomy." *Physics Today* 37 (1984): 48–55.

Geiger, R.L. *To Advance Knowledge: The Growth of American Research Universities, 1900–1940*. New York: Oxford University Press, 1986.

———. *Research and Relevant Knowledge: American Research Universities since 1940*. New York: Oxford University Press, 1992.

Guralnick, S.M. "The American Scientist in Higher Education, 1820–1910." In *The Sciences in the American Context: New Perspectives*, edited by N. Reingold, 99–142. Washington, D.C.: Smithsonian Institution Press, 1979.

Kohler, R.E. "The PhD Machine: Building on the Collegiate Base." *Isis* 81 (1990): 638–662.

Lankford, J. *American Astronomy: Community, Careers and Power, 1859–1940*. Chicago: University of Chicago Press, forthcoming.

Lankford, J., and R.L. Slavings. "Gender and Science: The Experience of Women in American Astronomy, 1859–1940." *Physics Today* 43 (1990): 58–65.

Lundgreen, P. "Differentiation in German Higher Education." In *The Transformation of Higher Learning, 1860–1930*, edited by K.H. Jarausch, 149–179. Chicago: University of Chicago Press, 1983.

Ringer, F.K. *Education and Society in Modern Europe*. Bloomington: Indiana University Press, 1979.

Rothenberg, M. *The Education and Intellectual Background of American Astronomers*. Ph.D. dissertation, Bryn Mawr College, 1974.

Eratosthenes (ca. 276 B.C.E.–ca. 195 B.C.E.)

The head of the library at Alexandria, and a scholar who wrote on a variety of subjects, including geography and mathematics, Eratosthenes used a geometrical argument to determine the circumference of the earth. According to Cleomedes (dates disputed, ranging from first century B.C.E. to second century C.E.), Eratosthenes' argument relied on several key ideas. At midday on the summer solstice a gnomon (a shadow caster, such as a vertical stick) casts no shadow in Syene, while in Alexandria at the same time a shadow will be cast creating an arc that is 1/50 of a complete sphere. He assumed that the two towns were on the same meridian and estimated the distance between them to be five thousand stades; taking this to be 1/50 of the circumference of the earth, the total circumference would be 250,000 stades (according to Cleomedes). Other ancient authors (including Pliny the Elder, d. 79 C.E.) reported that Eratosthenes' figure for the circumference of the earth was 252,000 stades.

Hipparchus (second century B.C.E.) wrote a work, "Against the Geography of Eratosthenes," arguing that while, in theory, this method would work, it relies on the accuracy of the data. The exact length of the unit of measurement (stade) used by Eratosthenes is not known, so that no real comparison to other estimates of the size of the earth can be made. Looking at the ancient reports of Eratosthenes' work, Neugebauer and Goldstein have each argued that differences in the number of stades given for the distance between Syene and Alexandria, as well as for the circumference of the earth, indicate that Eratosthenes' numbers should be taken only as estimates that do not reflect actual measurement. (Neugebauer, 652–654; Goldstein, 411–416.) No account by Eratosthenes of his method survives; however, Cleomedes provides a detailed description in *De motu circulari* (Thomas, vol. 2, 267–273).

Liba C. Taub

Bibliography

Dicks, D.R. "Eratosthenes." In *Dictionary of Scientific Biography*, edited by C.C. Gillispie, vol. 4, 388–393. New York: Scribner, 1971.

Goldstein, B. "Eratosthenes on the 'Measurement' of the Earth." *Historia Mathematica* 11 (1984): 411–416.

Helden, A. van. *Measuring the Universe: Cosmic Dimensions from Aristarchus to Halley*. Chicago: University of Chicago Press, 1984.

Neugebauer, O. *A History of Ancient Mathematical Astronomy*. 3 vols. Berlin: Springer-Verlag, 1975.

Thomas, I., trans. *Selections Illustrating the History of Greek Mathematics*. 2 vols. London: William Heinemann, 1951.

Euler, Leonhard (1707–1783)

Swiss/German/Russian mathematician. Euler was educated at the University of Basel, receiving a Master's degree in philosophy in 1723. His career was spent as a member of the St. Petersburg Academy of Science (1727–

1741, 1766–1783) and Berlin Academy of Science (1741–1766). Although he made significant contributions to nearly every area of mathematics, his work in celestial mechanics was particularly important. In the late 1730s he developed the calculus of trigonometric functions. A decade later, when Euler, Clairaut, and d'Alembert independently wrote Newton's laws of motion in the form of differential equations, Euler's mathematical methods provided the means for solving the equations. Euler worked extensively on the lunar theory and the mutual perturbations of Jupiter and Saturn. His methods served as the basis for succeeding generations of celestial mechanicians.

LeRoy E. Doggett

Bibliography

Youschkevitch, A.P. "Leonhard Euler." In *Dictionary of Scientific Biography*, edited by C.C. Gillispie, vol. 5, 467–484. New York: Scribner, 1971.

European Southern Observatory (ESO)

In spring 1953 the Dutch astronomer **Jan Oort**, with **Walter Baade** of the Mount Wilson and Mount Palomar observatories, informally proposed to key European astronomers a joint program to establish a southern observatory. Many objects of astronomical interest, such as the **Magellanic Clouds** and the galactic center, lay in the southern sky. Furthermore, the political context of the reconstruction of postwar Europe, along with the construction of European institutions such as CERN (Centre Européean de Recherche Nucléaire), favored joint projects. A statement signed in Leiden in 1954 by leading astronomers from six countries (German Federal Republic, Belgium, France, Great Britain, the Netherlands, and Sweden) called for a joint observatory in South Africa with a telescope of 3-meter primary mirror, and a Schmidt telescope of 1.2-meters, a combination imitative of Mount Palomar. Astronomers extensively tested sites in South Africa for atmospheric and optical quality, and negotiated a draft convention, heavily influenced in form by that of CERN.

However, the project stalled: It was expensive, Britain withdrew, favoring a Commonwealth observatory, and political instability meant the short-lived French governments were unlikely to commit themselves. The catalyst to the eventual signing of the convention in 1962 was the promised injection of nongovernmental money: The Ford Foundation offered one-fifth of the estimated cost of the project. Also in 1962 the site was switched to Chile: Tests revealed excellent seeing conditions, and the ESO Committee was concerned about future South African unrest. Committee member Otto Heckmann reached a quick agreement with the Chilean government facilitated by the strong German sympathies of Chilean scientists. Land and mining rights were bought around a 2,400-meter ridge called Cerro Chincado, or colloquially *La Silla* ("the saddle"). Heckmann was appointed first director general of ESO when the more obvious candidate, French astronomer Charles Fehrenbach, declared that he had too many commitments to French observatories. The ESO headquarters were located at Santiago, 240 km from La Silla.

Instrumentation tended to be distributed along national lines: The photometric telescope became a concern of Dutch astronomers at the Kapteyn Laboratory at Groningen, and the spectrographic telescope was delegated to the French. This trend was officially recognized in a series of national telescopes that were owned by universities and institutes rather than ESO. The two key ESO telescopes, a 3.6-meter modified Ritchey-Chrétien reflector and a 1.62-meter Schmidt, were started in 1962. Slow progress on these projects led to reorganization of ESO in 1969, with the construction of the telescopes being managed from a Telescope Project (TP) Division based at CERN, and with Adriaan Blaauw's succeeding Heckmann as director general.

In 1974–1975, ESO was again extensively restructured. The headquarters went, with expanded responsibilities, to Garching near Munich, partly to satisfy the demand of the German government for a major European scientific center, but also because of the serious economic problems of Chile. This disruption meant that during the mid-1970s ESO staff concentrated on existing projects. However, money from new members Italy and Switzerland in 1982 meant that a new project could be undertaken: the 3.58-meter New Technology Telescope (NTT). The NTT possessed a very thin active mirror, with optical distortion removed by image analysis. The NTT was a test project for the ESO Very Large Telescope (VLT), which incorporated both active optics and adaptive optics: the use of computers to remove distortion caused by the earth's atmosphere. The plan involved four 8-meter telescopes, connected into an interferometer with equivalent diameter of 16 meters.

ESO's astronomical program has centered on the use of the 3.6-meter telescope, guided by the wide field surveys of the **Schmidt telescope**. Surveys included a collaboration with Siding Spring in Australia to produce the Southern Sky Survey, explicitly designed to complement the Palomar Sky Survey, and the Faint Galaxy Survey, a extension of the northern Uppsala General Catalogue of Galaxies. Unusual Dwarf Irregular Galaxies (DIG) were discovered in Sculptor and Sagittarius. In 1976 fuzziness on an ESO plate around a red star provided strong evidence that at least some quasars were galactic nuclei. Research has also been done on solar system astronomy: The Schmidt plates revealed numerous minor planets, and in 1975 the naked-eye Comet West was discovered. ESO astronomers participated in the long-term photographic project to track Halley's Comet, and Garching provided the Space Telescope European Coordination Facilities.

There are few accounts of ESO's history, and there has been no full, contextual study by a historian of astronomy. The early years of ESO figure in the autobiographies of Heckmann and Fehrenbach, against the background of, respectively, German and French astronomical communities. The years 1953–1975 have been described well by Blaauw in a series of articles for the ESO journal, *The Messenger*. Blaauw's account is closely referenced with documentary sources, and he brings extensive inside knowledge from his early involvement in the ESO project and from his appointment as director general of ESO from January 1970 to January 1975. However, it must be borne in mind that the two crucial disjunctures in ESO's history, that of the setting up of the TP Division at CERN in 1969 and the establishment of a large headquarters at Garching at the persuasive invitation of the West German government in 1975, were both associated with the appointments of new ESO director generals.

The history of the later years is scant. Some uncritical history, as well as photographs of the instrumentation and sites, are included in Laustsen et al., a pictorial collection of research at ESO largely displaying to advantage color photography with the 3.6-meter telescope and the Schmidt. The audience intended for such accounts necessarily circumscribes historical discussion. Important aspects are unstudied: the extent that ESO mimicked existing organizations and programs such as that at CERN and Mount Palomar, and the tension between ESO as an expression of postwar European scientific collaboration typified by ESO's hosting of the pan-European journal *Astronomy and Astrophysics* and the national interests of astronomical cultures as expressed in the national telescope programs.

Jon Agar

Bibliography

Blaauw, A. "ESO's Early History, 1953–1975." *The Messenger* 54–64 (1988–1990).

Fehrenbach, C. *Des Hommes, des Télescopes, des Étoiles*. Paris: Presses du CNRS, 1990.

Heckmann, O. *Sterne, Kosmos, Weltmodelle.* Munich: Verlag Piper, 1976.

Laustsen, S., C. Madsen, and R.M. West. *Exploring the Southern Sky: A Pictorial Atlas from the European Southern Observatory (ESO)*. Berlin: Spinger-Verlag, 1987.

Expeditions, Astronomical

Astronomical expeditions have been conducted by scientists since the seventeenth century. Expeditions provide a window on the growing technical complexity of scientific observation, the history of scientific institutions, and the politics of modern Western science. Expeditions can be divided into three kinds. The first and earliest were geodetic surveys organized to study the earth itself. The second pursued rare phenomena visible only in restricted areas, like transits of **Mercury** or **Venus** or total solar eclipses. The third took astronomers to high-altitude sites to escape the interference of earth's atmosphere.

Expeditions were children of the revolutions in science, the rise of capitalism, and European politics. The first important astronomical expeditions were to measure arcs of the meridian or carry out trigonometric surveys sponsored by the French Academy of Sciences from 1672. These expeditions were of great scientific interest, but the absolutist monarchy of Louis XIV supported them as part of its program to expand the power of the crown. National trigonometric surveys were undertaken by European countries in the eighteenth century. Magnetic surveys were also conducted to determine the effect of local magnetic variations on navigation.

The expansion of global trade and European overseas empires in the eighteenth and nineteenth century created service roles and opportunities for astronomical fieldwork around the world. Measurements of meridian arcs spread to Africa, Peru, and India. Trigonometric surveys revised older maps and applied geometric precision to mapping Europe, America, and overseas colonial holdings. In the same era, a new kind of astronomical expedition emerged with the transit of Venus expeditions of 1761 and 1769. Transits of Venus were extremely rare, and offered eighteenth century astronomers a chance to "complete the Newtonian system by determining . . . one of the basic natural constants of physical astronomy, the solar parallax" (Woolf, vii). They opened a new chapter in the history of astronomy. National governments provided funding and instruments, chose observers, and set travel and observing agendas, thus linking expeditions to international politics. In the nineteenth century, solar eclipses joined transits of Venus as rare subjects of great interest. Solar eclipses had been casually observed in the eighteenth and early nineteenth centuries, but the development of solar physics made them valuable for the physical information they could yield. After 1860, European astronomers and governments organized expeditions to observe eclipses all over the world.

The rise of astrophysics and the application of photography to astronomical research drove some astronomers to mountaintops in search of better seeing conditions. The potential value of mountains as observing sites had been discussed since Newton's day, but only with instrumental innovations in the mid-nineteenth century did good seeing conditions become important enough to observers to justify arduous journeys. **Charles Piazzi Smyth**'s 1865 expedition to Tenerife was one of the first to investigate mountaintop observing conditions. A number of astronomers spent time in the Alps, Rockies, Andes, or Himalayas in subsequent decades. Most conducted observations that would have been difficult in lower altitudes or investigated the effect of the atmosphere itself on the solar spectrum. These expeditions established the value of high-altitude observing sites and thus opened the way to the building of permanent mountaintop observatories.

Astronomical expeditions demonstrate the ways technologies, theories, institutions, and politics shape research agendas and scientific practice. Expeditions to measure arcs of the meridian became popular after the invention of new instruments—the filiar micrometer, pendulum clock, and telescopic sight—ushered in a revolution in positional astronomy. Theoretical concerns also determine the value of astronomical events: Interest in transits of Venus declined after their value came into dispute in the nineteenth century, but astrophysics brought solar eclipses from the margins to the center of the discipline. Expeditions were also shaped by the demands of commerce and geopolitics. Captain James Cook's 1761 expedition to the South Pacific carried orders to observe the transit of Venus, search for the legendary Southern Continent, and evaluate commercial opportunities in the region. European and colonial governments supported geodetic research and trigonometric surveys for the commercial and military benefits they could provide. Even astrophysical fieldwork followed the expansion of European spheres of political influence and technological systems. Railroads, time and telegraph services, and industrial workshops provided support services for field parties, and opened areas of the world that would not previously have been accessible to astronomers.

Historians of astronomy have devoted less attention to expeditions than to the intellectual history of astronomy. This mirrors the history of science's preference for studies of laboratory science and theory over the field sciences. However, it also reflects inherent difficulties in the subject. Much astronomical research has been conducted on expeditions with nonscientific aims, and other expeditions have turned into field stations. Further, the very definitions of both astronomical research and expeditions has changed over time. What was astronomy in 1700 may be geography in 1900, and a trip from France to Southern Africa was an expedition in 1680 but not 1880. Nonetheless, important work has been done in the area. Most notable is Harry Woolf's *Transits of Venus* and studies of solar eclipse expeditions that tested Einstein's theory of general relativity (Earman and Glymour; Crelinstein). The history of geodesy and national surveys has been explored by historians of cartography and geography. Expeditions were also important in the early history of astronomy in the Southern Hemisphere (Evans).

Alex S.-K. Pang

Bibliography

Brown, L. *The Story of Maps*. Boston: Little, Brown, 1949.

Crelinstein, J. "William Wallace Campbell and the 'Einstein Problem': An Observational Astronomer Confronts the Theory of Relativity." *Historical Studies in the Physical Sciences* 14 (1983): 1–91.

Earman, J., and C. Glymour. "Relativity and Eclipses: The British Eclipse Expeditions of 1919 and Their Predecessors." *Historical Studies in the Physical Sciences* 11 (1980): 49–85.

Evans, D.S. *Under Capricorn: A History of Southern Hemisphere Astronomy*. Philadelphia: Adam Hilger, 1988.

Gill, I. *Six Months in Ascension: An Unscientific Account of a Scientific Expedition*. London: John Murray, 1878.

Olmstead, J.W. "The Scientific Expedition of Jean Richer to Cayenne (1672–1673)." *Isis* 34 (1942): 117–128.

Sandes, E. *The Military Engineer in India*. Chatham: Institution of Royal Engineers, 1935.

Smyth, C.P. *Report on the Teneriffe Astronomical Expedition of 1865*. London, 1858.

Woolf, H. *The Transits of Venus: A Study of Eighteenth-Century Science*. Princeton: Princeton University Press, 1959.

Extraterrestrial Intelligence

Interest in whether extraterrestrial intelligent beings exist, or, as it was long known, the question of the plurality of worlds, has been present in nearly all periods of history. The intensity and range of this interest are suggested by statements made by scholars as different as Albertus Magnus (in the twelfth century) and Sir David Brewster (in the nineteenth century). The medieval scholastic wrote that "since one of the most wondrous and noble questions in Nature is whether there is one world or many, . . . it seems desirable for us to inquire about it" (Crowe, 6). Six centuries later, the Scottish scientist proclaimed: "There is no subject within the whole range of knowledge so universally interesting as that of a Plurality of Worlds" (305).

The debate over extraterrestrial life dates back to classical Antiquity, when such advocates of atomist philosophy as the Greek philosophers Leucippus, Democritus, and Epicurus, as well as the Roman poet Lucretius, wrote on the existence of other inhabited worlds. Plato and Aristotle opposed the claim. Saint Augustine of Hippo was among the first Christian authors to discuss the idea, which he opposed, as did most medieval Christian authors, including Albertus Magnus and Thomas Aquinas. After the Condemnation of 1277, in which one of the propositions denounced was that "the First Cause [God] cannot make many worlds," Nicole Oresme, eventually the bishop of Paris, expressed openness to the idea. Moreover, Cardinal Nicholas of Cusa advocated extraterrestrials, including solarians, in his classic work *Of Learned Interest.*

If it be asked who opened the door to the extraterrestrials of the modern world, the curious answer is that it was a Polish canon with a passion for mathematics who introduced the heliocentric system. That system created by **Nicholas Copernicus** changed our earth into a planet and gradually transformed stars into other suns, which many authors assumed are surrounded by inhabited planets. Although no evidence indicates that Copernicus recognized the ramifications that his hypothesis would have for belief in extraterrestrial intelligences, others soon saw such implications. As early as 1550, the Lutheran reformer Philip Melanchthon warned against the Copernican cosmology and the idea that Christ's incarnation and redemption could have occurred on another planet. Moreover, by century's end, Giordano Bruno championed the Copernican system and embellished it with an abundance of extraterrestrials. **Galileo Galilei** and René Descartes, although recognizing the issue, were far more cautious, as was **Johannes Kepler**, who nonetheless published his *Somnium,* a treatise filled with speculations about life on the moon. Because of this and a comparable volume published in 1638 by the English scientist-cleric John Wilkins, the moon became a battleground regarding lunar life for over two centuries.

Near the end of the seventeenth century, two books, both written within the Cartesian tradition in physics, dramatically placed the issue of extraterrestrial life before the public. In 1686, Bernard le Bovier de Fontenelle created a sensation by championing extraterrestrials in his *Entretiens sur la pluralité des mondes.* The Vatican deemed this volume dangerous, placing it on the Index of Forbidden Books in 1687, but the public proclaimed it a delight. By 1800, the popularity of this presentation had carried the work through dozens of editions as well as translation into at least nine languages. However gifted Fontenelle was in literary matters, he lacked the credibility accorded to scientists. Thus it was particularly striking when in 1698 there appeared a volume advocating extraterrestrials written by one of the leading scientists of the century, Christiaan Huygens. Huygens's posthumous *Cosmotheoros,* or, in its English title, *Celestial Worlds Discover'd: or, Conjectures concerning the Inhabitants, Plants and Productions of the Worlds in the Planets*, would within two decades be available in five languages in addition to the original Latin version. The success of these books, despite the slimness of the scientific evidence on which they were based, guaranteed the debate would go on for a long time.

Moreover, even though Cartesian physics gradually lost out to the system developed by Isaac Newton, the change had little effect on belief in life elsewhere in the universe. The era of the extraterrestrials had begun.

Historical research has shown that a majority of eighteenth-century intellectuals entered the extraterrestrial life debate, most taking the positive side. Poets as diverse as Alexander Pope, Edward Young, Friedrich Klopstock, and Thomas Gray incorporated extraterrestrials into their poetry, Pope, for example, suggesting in his *Essay on Man* that though "the proper study of mankind is man," the proper way to study man must include consideration of extraterrestrials. Religious writers were scarcely less enthusiastic, frequently seeing extraterrestrials as evidence of God's generosity or, at times, seeing God's generosity as evidence that extraterrestrials must exist. Such discussions became standard in the large number of treatises on physicotheology, aimed at illustrating God's attributes from the consideration of nature. The views of Emanuel Swedenborg, however, were far from standard; this Swedish scientist turned prophet, reporting conversations with inhabitants of various planets. These and other remarkable aspects of his life and thought led his followers to found a major new religion, the Church of the New Jerusalem. Quite a different position was taken by Thomas Paine, who in his *Age of Reason* (1794) charged that the existence of extraterrestrials necessitates the rejection of the central Christian notions of the divine incarnation and redemption.

Philosophers, whether empiricists such as John Locke or Voltaire or idealists such as Gottfried Wilhelm Leibniz and George Berkeley, managed to incorporate the plurality of worlds doctrine into their systems. Immanuel Kant discussed the doctrine in at least eight of his publications, most notably in *Allgemeine Naturgeschichte und Theorie des Himmels* (1755).

Many astronomers of the eighteenth century, apparently untroubled by the absence of direct empirical evidence for extraterrestrials, included them in their publications. This was true of Thomas Wright, one of the pioneers of stellar astronomy, as well as of Johann Lambert, who discussed them in his *Cosmological Letters* (1761), now recognized as a major source for the disk theory of the Milky Way. **William Herschel**, famous for his discovery of the planet Uranus, was heavily involved with ideas of life elsewhere. The intensity of Herschel's interest in such beings is suggested by the fact that in the 1770s, he believed that he had detected a forest on the moon. He restrained himself from publishing these observations but in 1795 went into print in support of inhabitants of the sun and stars. Moreover, the contributions made by Kant, Wright, Lambert, and Herschel to stellar astronomy in general and especially to the idea that other galaxies exist provided additional locales for extraterrestrial civilizations.

Some eighteenth-century dissenters from the new orthodoxy appeared, for example, religious leader John Wesley, philosopher David Hume, and mathematician Leonhard Euler, but their cautions were heeded by few. Yet it is now clear that the widespread eighteenth-century belief in extraterrestrials rested on a frail astronomical foundation. Broad analogy more than detailed astronomy, physicotheology more than physics, teleology more than the telescope, and metaphysics more than measurement led so many to accept the pluralist doctrine.

During the early decades of the nineteenth century, belief in the widespread existence of extraterrestrial life reached a peak. One reason for this was that a Scottish minister, Thomas Chalmers, published in 1817 an eloquent and successful response to Paine's claim that belief in extraterrestrial life is irreconcilable with Christianity. Thus Chalmers's *Astronomical Discourses on the Christian Revelation in Connection with Modern Astronomy* served to put at ease many Christians' suspicious of the idea of extraterrestrial intelligences. Moreover, by the 1830s, such prominent scientists as John Herschel, Johann Bode, François Arago, and Pierre-Simon Laplace had endorsed the doctrine. Indeed, Laplace provided a theory of the origin of the solar system (the nebular hypothesis) according to which most stars should be surrounded by planetary systems. The adaptability of the idea of extraterrestrial intelligences to various religious systems is suggested by the fact that two major new religions founded during the middle third of the nineteenth century, the Church of Jesus Christ of Latter-day Saints (or Mormonism) and the Seventh-day Adventist Church, gave the doctrine a central place in their beliefs. So widely accepted had the plurality-of-worlds doctrine become that when Richard Locke, a New York journalist, published in 1835 a satirical report that life had been discovered on the moon, nearly everyone missed the satire and took the report seriously.

The situation began to change somewhat when William Whewell published in 1853 his *Of the Plurality of Worlds: An Essay*, in which he challenged the overconfident pluralism of that period. Whewell showed that a careful examination of the conditions prevailing on the other planets of our solar system indicates that these bodies almost certainly lack life forms comparable to humans. On a more abstract level, he countered the claim of those who maintained that all planets must be inhabited because, were that not the case, God's efforts in creating them would have been wasted. Whewell noted that throughout most of its history the earth itself was without intelligent life, and that apparent waste appears to be part of God's plan. Numerous authors, both scientists and religious writers, challenged Whewell's claims; yet it is now clear not only that Whewell's solar system is far closer to that revealed by twentieth-century astronomy, but also that the densely inhabited solar systems of his opponents had been constructed with almost no attention to scientific evidence.

During the last third of the nineteenth century, the two most widely read authors on astronomical topics were France's **Camille Flammarion** and Britain's **Richard Proctor**. Each had established himself by publishing a book advocating extraterrestrials, and each continued to treat this topic. Yet differences arose. Flammarion uncritically championed belief in extraterrestrials and devoted two massive books to recording supposed changes on Mars as evidence of Martian life; Proctor gradually moved in what he called a "Whewellite" direction, as he came to see the correctness of Whewell's claim that other planets in the solar system have conditions hostile for intelligent beings.

Near century's end, Mars emerged as the last best hope for providing evidence of life elsewhere in the solar system. Such hopes gained strength when the prominent Italian astronomer **Giovanni Schiaparelli** reported that, during the opposition of 1877, he detected *canali* on the Martian surface. Schiaparelli's claim, at first viewed skeptically, gradually won increased support as others confirmed his sightings. No one did more to encourage belief in the Martian canals than Percival Lowell, who founded an observatory dedicated to proving their existence. Nonetheless, by 1913, Edward Walter Maunder, Eugène Antoniadi, and **W.W. Campbell** had convinced nearly the entire astronomical community that Mars lacks not only canals but also an atmosphere suitable for living beings.

By 1916, when Lowell died, the extraterrestrial life debate had gone on for centuries. Over 140 books and thousands of articles had been devoted to the topic. After Lowell's death, proponents of extraterrestrial life could no longer point to Mars as an abode of life. The rejection of the **nebular hypothesis** of planetary formation in favor of encounter theories also weakened the case for extraterrestrial beings. According to the encounter theory, planetary systems form very rarely. During the 1940s, however, the nebular hypothesis was revived and improved, which gave new impetus to those favoring extraterrestrial life. An even more important development came after World War II with radio astronomy, which made it possible to conduct electronic searches for extraterrestrial intelligences.

Michael J. Crowe

Bibliography

Crowe, M.J. *The Extraterrestrial Life Debate 1750–1900: The Idea of a Plurality of Worlds from Kant to Lowell.* Cambridge: Cambridge University Press, 1986.

Dick, S.J. *Plurality of Worlds: The Origins of the Extraterrestrial Life Debate from Democritus to Kant.* Cambridge: Cambridge University Press, 1982.

———."Plurality of Worlds." In *Encyclopedia of Cosmology*, edited by N.S. Hetherington, 502–512. New York: Garland, 1993.

———. *The Biological Universe: The Twentieth Century Extraterrestrial Life Debate and the Limits of Science.* New York: Cambridge University Press, 1996.

Guthke, K.S. *The Last Frontier: Imagining Other Worlds from the Copernican Revolution to Modern Science Fiction.* Ithaca: Cornell University Press, 1990.

Hoyt, W.G. *Lowell and Mars.* Tucson: University of Arizona Press, 1976.

Jaki, S. *Planets and Planetarians: A History of Theories of the Origin of Planetary Systems.* Edinburgh: Scottish Academic Press, 1978.

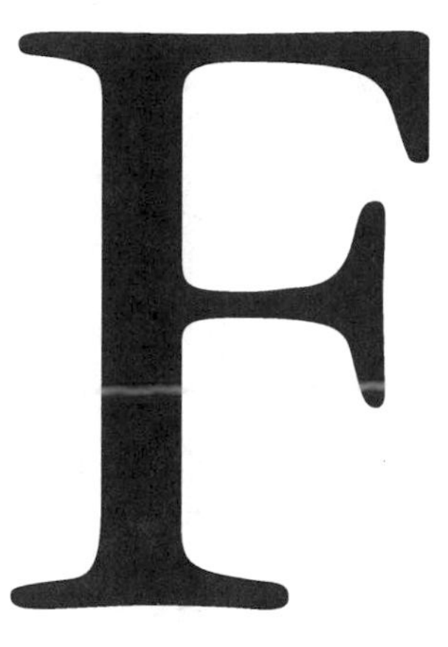

Fesenkov, Vasilii Grigor'evich (1889–1972)

Soviet astrophysicist. Fesenkov received his degree in astronomy from Khar'kov University in 1911. He directed the State Astrophysical Institute (1922–1931) and the Shternberg Astronomical Institute (1936– 1939). He organized and directed (1942–1964) the Institute of Astronomy and Physics of the Kazakh Academy of Sciences, and he also organized and directed (1945–1972) the Committee on Meteorites of the USSR Academy of Sciences. Fesenkov founded and edited (1924–1972) the *Astronomicheskii zhurnal*, the most important astronomy journal during the Soviet period of Russian history.

Fesenkov is widely regarded as one of the founders of Soviet astrophysics. His scientific activity included works in photometry; physics of the sun, stars, and nebulae; atmospheric optics; the zodiacal light; meteoritics; and cosmogony. Solar system formation was one of his first interests. Later (1935) he discovered the dependence between position angle and degree of light polarization in the solar corona. In his later career, Fesenkov determined the speed and direction of solar motion based on a study of radial velocities.

Robert A. McCutcheon

Bibliography

Kolchinskii, I.G., A.A. Korsun', and M.G. Rodriges. "Fesenkov, Vasilii Grigor'evich." In *Astronomy, biograficheskii spravochnik {Astronomers, a Biographical Handbook}*. Kiev: Naukova dumka, 1986.

Fitz, Henry (1808–1863)

American telescope maker. A successful locksmith, he began making telescopes in 1835, turned professional in 1845, and became the best-known maker of telescopes and achromatic objectives in the United States before the Civil War. The poor quality of available glass caused him to minimize lens thickness in order to reduce light scattering, and to invent zone-polishing to overcome local index inhomogeneities. Professionals judged Fitz's telescopes equal to ones from the best European makers. He made many 6- to 9-inch objectives. His largest objective was 16 inches, but at the time of his sudden death he was planning a 24-inch objective.

Louis F. Drummeter Jr.

Bibliography

Bates, R.S. "Henry Fitz—Early American Telescope Maker." *Sky & Telescope* 1 (1941): 18.

Howell, J.F. "Henry Fitz." Contributions from the Museum of History and Technology, Paper 26. *Bulletin of the United States National Museum* 228 (1963): 164–170.

Lankford, J. "In Search of Henry Fitz." *Sky & Telescope* 68 (1984): 214–218.

Flammarion, Camille (1842–1925)

French amateur astronomer and popularizer of astronomy. Flammarion was trained as an engraver in Paris. Always fascinated by astronomy, Flammarion joined the *Bureau des Calculs* at the **Paris Observatory** in 1858, but was dismissed by Le Verrier four years later. He then worked as a computer at the *Bureau* *des Longitudes* until 1863, when he left for a highly successful career in journalism, specializing in science and literature. In 1880 Flammarion published his most prestigious popular work, *Astronomie populaire*, the title of which he borrowed from the four-volume work by the astronomer D.F. Arago, whom Flammarion admired. In 1882 he launched *Astronomie*, a review dedicated to popular astronomy, which became the official journal of the *Société de Astronomique de France,* founded by Flammarion in 1887. A wealthy patron helped Flammarion build a private observatory at Juvisy in 1883, equipped with a 42-cm refracting telescope. The observatory welcomed the famed specialist in planetary astronomy E.M. Antoniadi at a time when Flammarion was fascinated by the study of the canals of Mars. His collected publications gave him enduring fame. In 1975 a facsimile edition of *Astronomie populaire* sold in astounding numbers.

Suzanne Débarbat

Bibliography

Duplay, A. "La vie de Camille Flammarion," *L'Astronomie* 89 (1975): 405–419.

Flammarion, C. *Mémoires biographiques et philosophiques d'un astronome*. Paris: Editeur Ernest Flammarion, 1911.

Pecker, J.-C., and J. Pernet, "L'Observatoire de Juvisy." *L'Astronomie* 101 (1987): 331–342.

Flamsteed, John (1646–1719)

First British Astronomer Royal, Flamsteed pioneered in the systematic application of telescopic sights to positional astronomy, and achieved a wide reputation for the accuracy of his star positions. Lacking university education, Flamsteed studied astronomy on his own and became known through his correspondence. When in 1625 King Charles founded the Royal Observatory at Greenwich, Flamsteed received the appointment at the age of twenty-eight. He held the position until his death, almost forty-five years later.

With the mandate to improve methods of navigation, two related activities dominated Flamsteed's scientific life: observing the motion of the moon and the positions of the stars. Unlike Hevelius and the Tychonic school, the young Flamsteed accomplished this with a variety of instruments with telescopic sights, including a sextant accurate to about 10 arcseconds, with which he made twenty-thousand observations from 1676 to 1689, and after 1689 with a 140-degree mural arc. Because the accuracies of his observations were unsurpassed, Flamsteed became embroiled in a bitter controversy with Isaac Newton and **Edmond Halley**, who wanted quick access to these observations. His full observations were published only posthumously in the *Historia coeleste Brittanica* (1725), containing three thousand stars, and in the *Atlas coelestis* (1729).

Plagued by ill health and financial problems, Flamsteed earned himself an important place from the point of view of institutions, instruments, and the general history of astronomy. An edition of his letters is in progress at the **Royal Greenwich Observatory**, Cambridge.

Steven J. Dick

Bibliography

Forbes, E.G., and D. Howse. *Greenwich Observatory: The Royal Observatory at Greenwich and Herstmonceux, 1675–1975*. London: Taylor and Francis, 1975.

Thoren, V. "Flamsteed, John." In *Dictionary of Scientific Biography,* edited by C.C. Gillispie 5: 22–26. New York: Scribner, 1972.

Fleming, Williamina Paton (1857–1911)

American astronomer. Born and raised in Dundee, Scotland, Fleming immigrated to the United States with her husband in 1878, but they soon separated. Fleming went to work for **Edward C. Pickering**, first in his household and then, in 1881, as an assistant at the **Harvard College Observatory**. She began doing simple copying and computing, but went on to develop an empirical system for the classification of the stellar spectra photographed with Harvard telescopes. In 1890, she published her empirical classification of the spectra of over ten thousand stars. In addition to finding general patterns of spectral classification, Fleming drew attention to peculiar stars, novae, and variable stars. From 1899 until her death, she was curator of astronomical photographs at Harvard. She had one son, an engineer, Edward P. Fleming.

Peggy A. Kidwell

Bibliography

Cannon, A.J. "Williamina Paton Fleming." *Astrophysical Journal* 34 (1911): 314–317.

Mack, P.E. "Women in Astronomy in the United States 1875–1920." B.A. thesis. Harvard University, 1977.

France, Astronomy in

Empirical knowledge of the sidereal universe began in 1610, with the *Sidereus nuncius* published by **Galileo**, whose observations were made with a small telescope. Emulators of Galileo sprang up throughout Europe, including Pierre Gassend (Gassendi) in France, who made the first observation of a transit of Mercury in 1631. A friend of Gassendi, Nicolas Claude Fabri de Peiresc, observed the four Galilean moons of Jupiter in 1610 and recognized their importance for the determination of longitude. For this purpose, however, the motions of the moons needed to be determined, and, in 1668, a Bolognese professor, **Jean-Dominique Cassini**, published the first complete tables of the moons of Jupiter.

In 1666 the French Academy of Science and in 1667 Louis XIV's Royal Observatory were created, with the goal of stimulating and supporting scientific research. Paris counted more than twenty private observatories (often run by religious orders), but all were poorly equipped. The reputation of Cassini was such that he was called to the **Paris Observatory** in 1669; soon he would reside there as its de facto director.

Thanks to the excellent objective lenses obtained from Italian opticians, Cassini brought fame to the Observatory through numerous discoveries, including four moons of Saturn and the division of its rings (the Cassini Division), and by his great map of the moon (1679). He continued to observe Jupiter's moons and improved his tables. Differences between the observed and predicted times for eclipses of the Jovian moon Io led to the discovery of the finite velocity of light. This discovery, published in the *Journal des savants* on December 7, 1676, was made by the young Danish astronomer Ole Römer, working at the Paris Observatory.

Newton's *Principia* (1687) opened up new ways of understanding the universe. The *Entretiens sur la pluralité des mondes*, published in 1686 by Bernard Le Bovier de Fontenelle, popularized new ideas about astronomy in an original way.

Geodesy and Positional

Colbert, Louis XIV's minister, requested the Academy of Science to construct a map of France, a project that demanded new instrumentation. The collaboration of Adrien Auzout and Jean Picard led to the construction of the filar micrometer and precision instruments (sectors, quadrants, levels), which were used for over a century. The vernier was conceived by Pierre Vernier in 1630 and provided an exact way of reading divided circles. The new instruments, used to observe eclipses of Jupiter's moons, made possible precise determination of longitude in France and elsewhere.

Several geodetic expeditions led to important results. The measurement of the arc of the meridian (led by Picard, 1667–1670) provided a new value for the radius of the earth that agreed with Newton's law. An expedition to Cayenne furnished the first modern determination of the **solar parallax**. Further, the length of the pendulum counting seconds was shorter in Cayenne, providing an argument for the flattening of the earth. Mapping the French coast (led by J.-D. Cassini and others, 1679–1680) led to an important modification of the dimensions of France.

Later expeditions, supported by the Academy of Science, measured arcs of the meridian toward the equator and the north pole to determine the flattening of the earth. The results, reported and analyzed by P.L. de Maupertuis and **A.-C. Clairaut**, along with collaborators from France and Spain, corroborated Newton's views of the shape of the earth.

As positional astronomy developed, French astronomers begin compiling star catalogues. In 1763, observing at the Cape of Good Hope, Nicolas-Louis de Lacaille produced the first catalogue of southern stars (nearly two thousand objects) and defined a number of constellations. The *Histoire céleste française*, a catalogue of fifty thousand stars observed principally from Paris by Michel le Français de Lalande and calculated by his wife, Marie Harlay, was directed by Michel's uncle, Joseph Lalande. The latter produced the great *Traité d'astronomie* of 1764, and the *Bibliographie astronomique* (1801), which remains useful and is the ancestor of modern bibliographies.

Celestial Mechanics

After the publication of Newton's *Principia*, the scientific world, which on the Continent remained committed to Cartesian views, needed to decide between the two systems. The opposition to Newton lost its leader with the death of Leibniz in 1716, and while Voltaire—who attended Newton's funeral in 1727—returned a warm supporter of Newtonian theory, it was up to the French Academy of Science to take action. In 1734 the academy awarded a prize for the first analytic application of the law of gravitation to Daniel Bernoulli. In 1735 the academy sponsored expeditions that confirmed the flattening of the earth. The power of Newtonian mechanics was dramatically demonstrated by the return of Halley's Comet within a month of the date predicted by A.-C. Clairaut.

Meanwhile, research in celestial mechanics grew more important. **Jean-Baptiste Delambre** studied the precession of the equinox and the nutation of the earth's axis. J.L. Lagrange spent twenty years (1764–1786) developing a theory of the moon and the planets. Similarly, **Pierre-Simon Laplace** published (1799–1825) the *Traité de mécanique céleste* as well as his famous *Exposé du système du monde*. **Charles Messier** published a catalogue of 103 nebulae and star clusters (objects now labeled with the letter *M*, bringing him lasting fame). Tables and theories of solar system objects appeared in rapid succession. Delambre and Alexis Bouvard tackled Jupiter, its moons, Saturn, and Uranus.

A stunning confirmation of Newton's theory was made in 1846. While working on problems posed by the planet Uranus, **Urbain Le Verrier** calculated the position of an unknown planet disturbing the orbit of Uranus, thus corroborating the law of universal gravitation and leading to the discovery of Neptune. Le Verrier then developed his general theory of the solar system (1877), and Charles-Eugène Delaunay produced important work on the theory of the moon (1860–1867). **François-Félix Tisserand**'s *Traité de mécanique céleste* appeared between 1889 and 1896. Celestial mechanics in France culminated with *Les méthodes nouvelles de la mécanique céleste* (1899) by **Henri Poincaré**, which is still used today.

The Metric System

The *Système International d'unités*, which was adopted in 1960 and enables researchers and engineers throughout the world to communicate, is based on the metric system developed as a result of the royal decree of May 8, 1790, designed to do away with various incoherent units of measurement then in use in Europe. What role did astronomers play in developing the metric system?

The essential problem was to base the unit of length on a natural, indestructible element. The length of the pendulum counting seconds, susceptible to variation even at a fixed latitude, was eliminated in favor of a fraction of the terrestrial meridian, presumably constant. Since the work of J. Picard and J.-D. Cassini, geodesy remained an important field in France, especially thanks to several generations of the Cassini family, who directed the **Paris Observatory**. While **Jacques Cassini** was both an astronomical observer and a geodesist, **César-François Cassini de Thury** and his son, Jean-Dominique Cassini, devoted nearly their entire careers to the first general map of France (1756–1790), presented to the Constituent Assembly. The Cassinis also worked on determining longitude, and on measuring the distance between the meridians of Paris and Greenwich. These map-making operations became the basis of European cartography and led to greater agreement between maps of various countries.

Two astronomers, J.-B.J. Delambre and P. Méchain, were responsible for the geodetic measurements between Dunkirk and Barcelona, which led to the definition of the meter in 1799. As for the calibration of the unit of weight, the kilogram, laboratory measurements relating this unit to the unit of length were conducted in part in the building housing the Paris Observatory by A. Lavoisier.

Physics and Photography

Physical astronomy (for example, the study of planetary surfaces, the observation of sun spots, or the discovery of the Orion Nebula in 1610 by N.C.F. de Peiresc), to which J.-D. Cassini and others devoted an important part of their careers, declined in the eighteenth century. Work in this domain was begun anew in the nineteenth century with Dominique F.J. Arago and his studies of the photometry and of polarimetry of the sun, stars, and the earth's atmosphere. An eminent leader in French astronomy, Arago became director of observations of the Paris Observatory in 1834. He played a particularly important role in teaching younger researchers, encouraging them to undertake research that would prove of great significance. Arago guided Augustin Fresnel toward the study of light, important for the physical understanding of astronomical instruments. Fresnel demonstrated the wave theory of light. He supported French instrument makers, aiding Gambey and Bréguet, whose transit circles, refracting telescopes, and pendulum clocks were purchased by the Paris Observatory. Arago understood the importance of photography, reporting to the academy in January 1839 on the invention of the daguerréotype and predicting its value to astronomy.

In 1845 the first daguerréotype of the sun was obtained by Armand H.L. Fizeau and Jean B.L. Foucault. Arago also encouraged Fizeau to develop new ways for measuring the speed of light. Experiments were carried out by Fizeau in 1849 and in 1862 by Foucault. Working as a volunteer at the Paris Observatory, Foucault developed what became known as the Foucault pendulum, which demonstrated the earth's rotation. One of these devices was installed in the vault of the Panthéon in 1851, allowing Parisians to watch the earth turn. Foucault also invented the gyroscope, as well as a method of testing the figure of astronomical mirrors while they were being ground and polished. French contributions to photography and instrumentation lifted astronomy to a new plane.

In the mid-nineteenth century, it was decided to develop observatories in several French towns. In Marseille the Jesuit observatory was transformed into a branch of the Paris Observatory by Le Verrier in 1862; this particular establishment became independent in 1873. Similarly, observatories were created in Toulouse (1873), Lyons (1878), Bordeaux (1879), and Besançon (1882). These were often founded on sites of earlier establishments, and later attached to universities in these cities. These new establishments received modern equipment for research in astrometry and photographic astronomy. Important international congresses in these fields were often held in Paris. In 1887, for example, an international conference decided to map the entire sky using photography. The *Carte du Ciel* was directed by an international committee and the Paris Observatory served as its informal headquarters. Later congresses, such as that of 1896, adopted the system of astronomical constants proposed by **Simon Newcomb**, director of the United States Nautical Almanac Office. By 1900 an international system defined astrometry and celestial mechanics. As for the *Carte du Ciel*, its chief merit was a vast collection of plates, which, remeasured using modern techniques, provide an important source of information on stellar **proper motion**.

The Sun

Solar research provided the motivation for the creation of the Meudon Observatory by **Jules Janssen**. In 1876 Janssen first photographed solar granulations. In 1919 systematic observation of solar activity was organized. This project resulted in a rich collection of spectroheliograms that now cover nearly seven solar cycles and permit long-term studies of the sun's dynamic structure. The study of the chromosphere at various wavelengths was carried out with instruments invented by Henri Deslandres (**spectroheliograph**, 1894) and Bernard Lyot (polarizing filter, 1931). The corona, previously observed only during total eclipses, now could be studied on a regular basis thanks to the coronograph, invented at Meudon by Lyot in 1933. A solar eclipse lasts for a few minutes at any given location on earth. However, the eclipse of 1973 was observed for some eighty minutes from a Concorde jet specially equipped for the event.

Solar activity (including sunspots, faculae, coronal condensation, flares and filaments, spicules, and eruptions) is the object of continuous observation and theoretical research. Observations are made using various instruments at the **Meudon Observatory**, including classic siderostats and the coelostat on the solar tower situated in a wooded enclosure ensuring particularly steady images. Observations are also made at the Pic-du-Midi Observatory, created in 1878 by two pioneers of high-elevation observing, Charles-Marie-Etienne Champion de Nansouty and Célestin-Xavier-Vaussenat, located in the Pyrénées Mountains at an altitude of nearly 3,000 meters. Radio observations of solar activity at various wavelengths are also monitored at the **Nançay Radio Astronomy Station**. The Meudon Observatory collects observations of solar activity from fifty centers around the world and is responsible for the prediction of solar activity. Satellites also contribute observations of the sun, especially in the ultraviolet and X-ray range.

Time

Time is a subject of enduring interest to astronomers. In 1891, legal time in France became the mean time for Paris, as determined by astronomers at the Paris Observatory. Starting in May 1910, the Eiffel Tower was used to broadcast signals from the time service of the Paris Observatory. The importance of these signals, especially for navigation, was recognized at the International Conference on Time held in Paris in 1912, which proposed the creation of a *Bureau International de l'Heure* to be located at the Paris Observatory. Delayed by World War I, the *Bureau* was not established until 1919, under the aegis of the International Astronomical Union. The Paris Observatory helped finance the *Bureau* and furnished its personnel and equipment. French astronomers have played an important role in the determination and dissemination of time.

A Brief View of the Present

French astronomy has a long tradition of research in celestial mechanics. Work in this field continues, principally in Nice and at the *Bureau des Longitudes*. Astrophysics was introduced late in France, where the emphasis was traditionally on fundamental astronomy. It began with Janssen's work in solar physics. Deslandres transferred experimental spectroscopy from Paris to Meudon at the turn of the century and created a laboratory that became the base of the experimental and theoretical activities of the Meudon Observatory. A team of researchers from the Paris Observatory established the *Institut d'Astrophysique de Paris* (1936–1937), administered by the *Centre National de Recherches Scientifiques*. Notable work was done there by Daniel Chalonge, Daniel Barbier, and Henri Mineur. Mineur demonstrated in 1944 that previous research had underestimated galactic distances.

Galactic studies benefited from research on radial velocities, first introduced at the Meudon Observatory by Deslandres. Radial velocity research is a specialty of the Marseille Observatory, which is also known for the discovery of comets. The observation of double stars, the basis of the determination of mass in the universe, was formerly carried out at Paris and more recently at the Nice Observatory, where numerous planetary discoveries also have been made.

Astronomical photography, pursued in Bordeaux, Paris, and Toulouse as part of the *Carte du Ciel*, also led to the lunar atlas (1896–1910) of Maurice Loewy and Pierre Puiseux, using the great coudé equatorial of the Paris Observatory. Today photography is the specialty at three French observatories ideally located and equipped with large instruments (apertures between 100 and 200 cm). These are the Haute-Provence Observatory, created in 1936, the Pic-du-Midi Observatory, and the *Centre d'Etudes et de Recherches Géodynamiques et Astronomiques,* established in 1974 near Grasse. The Grasse Center is equipped with state-of-the-art instruments, including the French moon laser, the solar astrolabe, and an optical interferometric station.

The field of electronphotography developed in France from the work of Gilbert Rougier and André Lallemand. Lallemand, while pursuing research at the Paris Observatory, constructed electron photomultipliers and the electronic camera—equipment permitted the observation of ever fainter objects. An infrared camera was developed at the Lyon Observatory.

Aside from the Nançay Radio Astronomy Station, French radio astronomers have at their disposal the *Institut de Radioastronomie Millimétrique*, a Franco-Hispanic-German collaboration created in 1979 and located both in the Alps on the *Plateau de Bure* and in Spain at Pico Velata.

Several international undertakings have been launched, such as the creation of the *Centre de Données Stellaires* (1972) at the Strasbourg Observatory and the laboratory for the *Machine Automatique à Mesurer pour l'Astronomie* located at the Paris Observatory (1983). The European Space Agency's astrometric satellite was designed by Pierre Lacroute at the Strasbourg Observatory. This satellite has been used by several French research teams. *Hipparchos* will produce definitive astrometric data.

Almost all fields related to astrophysics are covered by equipment carried on space vehicles, often launched by the French rocket *Ariane,* operated by the *Centre National d'Etudes Spatiales*, created in 1961. French participation frequently involves cooperation with Europe, America, and Russia. In the Space Age, ground-based astronomy has not lost its importance. France participated in the formation of the **European Southern Observatory** (1962) and also entered into a joint project with Canada and the University of Hawaii to erect an observatory on Mauna Kea, which since 1974 has permitted French astrophysicists to make observations from an altitude of over 4,000 meters.

Suzanne Débarbat

Bibliography

Bigourdan, G. *Histoire de l'astronomie d'observation et des observations en France.* Paris: Gauthier-Villars, 1930.

Bluche, F, ed. *Dictionnaire du Grand Siècle.* Paris: Fayard, 1990.

Montucla, J.-E. *Histoire des mathématiques.* Paris: Henri Agasse, reprint, Paris: Librairie scientifique et technique Albert-Blanchard, 1968.

Taton, R., ed. *Histoire générale des sciences.* Paris: Presses Universitaires de France, 1957–1964.

Funding Astronomy

The science of astronomy is funded in a variety of ways. Sources of patronage are not mutually exclusive. Often astronomers depend on several different patrons to support their activities.

The oldest and probably most enduring source of support for astronomy is government patronage. The Paris Observatory (1667) represents the first government establishment for modern astronomical research. It was soon followed by the Royal Greenwich Observatory (1675). The process of creating government-funded observatories continued well into the nineteenth century and includes the **U.S. Naval Observatory** (1830) and the Imperial Observatory at **Pulkovo** (1839).

From the mid-seventeenth to the mid-nineteenth centuries national governments established observatories with specific missions. These institutions were dedicated to the solution of practical problems associated with navigation and timekeeping. In Europe, they were also frequently involved with research in geodesy, geophysics, and map making. To be sure, important theoretical investigations were carried out at government observatories, but the justification for state support lay in providing information useful for overseas trade and commerce and colonial expansion. In time, celestial mechanics and astrometry as practiced in national observatories reached levels of perfection and complexity that were far in access of the needs of the state.

With the emergence of astrophysics in the nineteenth century, national governments in Europe responded by creating new research institutions. Among the best known were the astrophysical observatories at **Meudon** (1876), **Potsdam** (1876), and South Kensington (1879). Until the mid-twentieth century, however, government observatories dedicated to astrometry and celestial mechanics remained the primary beneficiaries of state patronage. In the United States, for example, only after World War II were federal dollars made available to support astrophysics.

The second phase of government patronage for astronomy begins after 1945. The American experience illustrates many of these new trends. The Cold War led to major innovations in funding American science. Both the military (such as, the Office of Naval Research and the Air Force) and new federal agencies such as the National Science Foundation (1950) and the **National Aeronautics and Space Administration** (1958) became major patrons of astronomical research. National optical and radio observatories were established. Solar system astronomy and astronomy from space became active research fields. American astronomy expanded rapidly as a result of the postwar infusion of federal funds.

Private patronage provides a second source of funding for astronomy. In the eighteenth and nineteenth centuries, wealthy individuals built observatories. Some patrons undertook observational work themselves. The career of British telescope-maker and planetary observer William Lassell illustrates this pattern. In other cases, patrons, even if active observers, staffed their observatories with astronomers. The private observatory of Johann Schröter at Lilienthal is a case in point. An enthusiastic lunar and planetary observer, Schröter also employed young scientists such as Karl Ludwig Harding and **Friedrich Wilhelm Bessel**, both of whom became leaders of German astronomy in the nineteenth century. One of the last examples of the individually funded research institution was the McMath-Hulbert Solar Observatory, which became a part of the University of Michigan in the 1930s. By the late nineteenth century, as astronomy became more technology-intensive, relying on larger and larger telescopes and expensive auxiliary equipment, as well as a large scientific staff to collect and analyze data, few individuals could command resources to support private astronomical research institutions.

Individuals also supported astronomy through gifts and bequests. The financial history of the **Harvard College Observatory** through World War I has been reconstructed by Jones and Boyd. The bequest of Uriah Boyden (1879), for example, made possible the Harvard station at Arequipa, Peru, and the generosity of Henry Draper's widow resulted in the great spectroscopic surveys that bear his name. Catherine Wolfe Bruce aided a number of Harvard projects and eventually her generosity extended to astronomers around the world. While individual benefactions still play a role in funding astronomy, the magnitude of the research enterprise is such that their role is relatively minor.

Philanthropic foundations are an American invention of the early twentieth century. Captains of industry diverted some of their wealth to create foundations that were often dedicated to education and scientific research. The Carnegie Institution of Washington (CIW) was one of the first to support astronomy. The CIW became the parent of the Mount Wilson Observatory and supported astrometric research at the Dudley Observatory. The Rockefeller General Education Board paid for the planning and construction of the 200-inch telescope and, in the 1990s, the great 10-meter reflectors in Hawaii are the result of the generosity of the Keck Foundation. However, as was the case with individual philanthropy, the scale and expense of astronomy has grown to the point where not even the richest foundation can provide adequate resources.

University and college budgets also financed astronomy. Departments of astronomy and associated observatories, professors, and astronomers, assistants and graduate students all have some claim on institutional resources. In Germany, with a state-supported system of higher education, public money payed the bills. In the United States, with a mixed system, private resources and state treasuries supported astronomy. As a result of the Cold War, federal dollars were channeled into universities in order to strengthen the sciences. Astronomy benefited from this practice.

The research grant developed after World War II. However, we can find nineteenth-century precursors. Many learned societies managed endowment funds dedicated to the support of scientific research. This was true for the American Academy of Arts and Sciences, the American Philosophical Society, and the National Academy of Sciences in the United States. The National Academy, for example, held endowments to support work in celestial mechanics and astrometry (the Gould Fund), the Smith Fund for research in meteoric astronomy, and the Henry Draper fund for astrophysical research. Grants from these sources were small, but often critical to the success of individual research projects. The French Academy of Sciences and the Royal Society of London also held or administered funds on which scientists could draw to support research. The French Academy of Sciences encouraged astronomical research by sponsoring competitions to solve set problems (in the nineteenth century, most often in celestial mechanics), the winner of which received a cash award.

Of the physical sciences, astronomy probably received the most support. Astronomers drew on all four sources of patronage. Their projects either appealed to patrons or were viewed as essential to the state. Geology, geophysics, and the biological sciences depended on government and private patronage. Chemical research was generally supported by industry. Physics, until the early twentieth century, depended almost exclusively on private patrons or colleges and universities.

Patronage provides a useful vehicle for many important historical investigations. A deeper understanding of patronage since the beginning of the nineteenth century would enrich our knowledge of the growth of science and its relationship to the social, economic, and political context. For example, there are only a few time series detailing support for the physical sciences. Reingold and Brodansky and Kevles have attempted the task for the sciences in America, but their results are not easily compared. Time series showing support for astronomy in several countries based on a clearly defined constant dollar benchmark would be of great value. So would data that compared support for astronomy with that for other sciences during the period. With the exception of the history of the Harvard College Observatory by Jones and Boyd, we have no detailed information of the funding of an observatory. Nor are there studies of the finances of major astronomy departments. It would be interesting to develop data on foundation support for astronomy in twentieth-century America. Which foundations led the way? What kinds of research did they support? Clearly, the place to begin is with CIW support for the Mount Wilson and Dudley observatories. Another useful investigation would focus on support from learned societies and academies. Much of the data are available in printed reports, but must be supplemented by archival research.

Long-range planning for federal support of astronomy in the United States developed in the 1960s. Astronomy advisory panels sponsored by the National Academy of Science and the National Science Foundation formulated ten year plans, ranking projects according to priority. These plans rested on a community-wide consensus. This process of consensus-building is worthy of detailed investigation, since it is virtually unique to astronomy among the sciences in America. Attempts at long-range planning in other scientific communities have not been successful. Both archival and oral history sources (such as Greenstein's oral history memoir) would be useful for research in this area.

John Lankford

Bibliography

Bilstein, R.E. *Orders of Magnitude: A History of the NACA and NASA 1915–1990.* Washington, D.C.: NASA SP-4406, 1989.

Débarbat, S., S. Grillot, and J. Lévy. *Observatoire de Paris—Son histoire (1667–1963).* Paris: Observatoire de Paris, 1984, 1990.

DeVorkin, D.H. *Science with a Vengeance: How the Military Created the U.S. Space Sciences after World War II.* New York: Springer-Verlag, 1992.

Dick, S.J. "How the United States Naval Observatory Began, 1830–1865." In

Sesquicentennial Symposia of the United States Naval Observatory, edited by S.J. Dick and L.E. Doggett, 167–181. Washington, D.C.: USNO, 1983.

Doel, R.E. *Solar System Astronomy in America: Communities, Patronage, and Interdisciplinary Research, 1920–1960.* New York: Cambridge University Press, 1996.

Forbes, E.G., A.J. Meadows, and D. Howse, eds. *Greenwich Observatory: The Royal Observatory at Greenwich and Herstmonceaux, 1675–1975.* 3 vols. London: Taylor and Francis, 1975.

Greenstein, J.L. *Astronomy and Astrophysics for the 1970s.* Astronomy Survey Committee of the Committee on Science and Public Policy, National Academy of Sciences. Washington, D.C.: NAS, 1972.

———. *Oral History Interview.* New York, American Institute of Physics, Center for the History of Physics, 1977–1978.

Jones, B.Z., and L.G. Boyd. *The Harvard College Observatory: The First Four Directorships, 1839–1919.* Cambridge: Harvard University Press, 1971.

Kevles, D.J. "The Physics, Mathematics, and Chemistry Communities: A Comparative Analysis." In *The Organization of Knowledge in Modern America, 1860–1920,* edited by A. Oleson and J. Voss, 139–172. Baltimore: Johns Hopkins University Press, 1978.

Lankford, J. "Private Patronage and the Growth of Knowledge: The J. Lawrence Smith Fund of the National Academy of Sciences, 1884–1940." *Minerva* 25 (1987): 269–281.

———. "Financing American Astronomy: An Overview." *Griffith Observer* 55 (1991): 16–18.

Miller, H.S. *Dollars for Research: Science and Its Patrons in Nineteenth Century America.* Seattle: University of Washington Press, 1970.

Reingold, N., and J.N. Brodansky. "The Sciences, 1850–1900: A North Atlantic Perspective." *Biological Bulletin* 168 (1985): 44–61.

Tatarewicz, J.N. *Space Technology and Planetary Astronomy.* Bloomington: Indiana University Press, 1990.

Wolf, C. *Histoire de l'Observatoire de Paris de sa création à 1793.* Paris: Gauthier-Villars, 1902.

Galaxies

Until the mid-1960s, the history of galaxies and extragalactic astronomy was largely the uncritical product of whiggish historians of science or the accounts of astronomers intent on constructing histories to buttress priority claims. A good example of the latter is **Edwin P. Hubble**'s *The Realm of the Nebulae*. By the mid-1960s, younger historians, interested in more than linking contemporary astronomy to earlier efforts, thus demonstrating that science is an inevitable road to truth, started to examine the history of galactic astronomy. The work of Cambridge historian Michael Hoskin provides a good example of the new approach. Although whiggish histories continue to be written (an egregious but still valuable example is Jaki's *Milky Way*), these began to be balanced by more critical and nuanced accounts. To be sure, by current standards, these accounts often were limited to intellectual developments and paid relatively little attention to instrumentation or institutional context.

By the early 1980s, the history of galaxies through the early 1930s had been reasonably well described. Subsequent scholarship filled in details, but has not offered radically new perspectives. While the history of contemporary cosmology has drawn some scholarly attention, as yet only the sketchiest understanding of the history of extragalactic astronomy from the 1930s has emerged.

As historians of astronomy currently understand matters, the history of galaxies stretches back to the seventeenth century. Perhaps Christopher Wren was referring to nebulae as distant star systems when he spoke of future astronomers who might find "every nebulous star appearing as if it were the firmament of some other world" in his 1657 inaugural lecture as professor of astronomy at Gresham College (Jones, 33). In his posthumously published lecture notes, *Syntagma philosophicum* (1658), Pierre Gassendi suggested that nebulae might be other Milky Ways, but dismissed the notion as dreamy speculation. It was not until the eighteenth century that the question of whether or not there are collections of stars comparable in size to but lying outside the Milky Way—island universes as they were sometimes called in the nineteenth and early twentieth centuries, or galaxies in modern terminology—was extensively discussed. The question attracted the attention of thinkers such as Thomas Wright and Immanuel Kant, who sought to reconcile their conceptions of God with their views on the physical universe. But for the great majority of astronomers and natural philosophers, the issue of the arrangement of the stars was of little concern. For them, the stars were of interest only as a backdrop against which to measure the motions of solar system bodies.

For **William Herschel**, however, this was far from the case. His approach to the study of the heavens was very different from those adopted by Kant and Wright. In many respects Herschel was a natural historian of the heavens for whom speculation and observation with powerful telescopes were separate aspects of the same quest. The most sophisticated account of Herschel as a natural historian is Schaffer (1980). Although he had made repeated examinations of the Orion Nebula from 1774 on, Herschel in 1783 began to pay systematic attention to nebulae as objects worthy of study in their own right. In 1784 he added 466 of these objects to the roughly one hundred previously catalogued, and he would later catalogue many more.

Through painstaking counts of stars in various regions of the sky, Herschel concluded that the Milky Way is a huge, but limited, stratum of stars. He decided that unresolved nebulae are systems beyond the Milky Way, many of which are in all probability as big as the Milky Way. By the mid-1780s, Herschel had largely set, and brought to the attention of a wide audience, the terms of a debate on the nature of the nebulae that would continue through the 1920s. First, were these dim patches of light remote star systems whose light merges to give a milky effect, or were they made of a luminous fluid? And second, if they were groups of stars, were these star systems part of or associated with the Milky Way Galaxy, or were they vast, independent galaxies?

Even during the period (1784–1790) when he equated all nebulae with star clusters, Herschel was puzzled by what he termed planetary nebulae. Were they, as he proposed, really star clusters reaching the final stages of their development? However, in 1790, Herschel came upon what was to him a very curious object: a star surrounded by a roughly circular patch of nebulosity that resisted his attempts to resolve it into stars. The star and nebulosity seemed physically linked, not the product of a chance alignment. Herschel interpreted this juxtaposition as proof of the existence of a luminous fluid. If so, nebulae that withstood Herschel's attempts to resolve them might, after all, be genuinely nebulous, not star systems beyond the Milky Way grown misty at great distances. Since the nineteenth century, astronomers and historians have debated the extent to which Herschel retreated from his earlier advocacy of island universes. It seems likely, however, that he never abandoned the idea that some nebulae were distant galaxies.

John Herschel pursued the same astronomical interests as his father and, in the 1820s, began to search systematically for nebulae and star clusters. By 1833, he had compiled a catalogue of some 2,306 objects. But these included only clusters and nebulae visible from England's northerly position. Herschel embarked for South Africa in 1833 with a rebuilt version of his father's 20-foot reflector, to sweep the southern skies.

Before his researches in the Southern Hemisphere, John Herschel had argued that the great majority of clusters and nebulae were star systems, although he was prepared to admit that some nebulae—the Orion and the Andromeda nebulae for example—were truly nebulous. John's observations in South Africa, however, transformed his thinking. Especially important were observations of the Magellanic Clouds, in which he detected nebulosity in every stage of resolution. Herschel regarded all of the Large Cloud's stars and nebulae as at essentially the same distance from earth. The enormous variation he saw between objects in the Large Magellanic Cloud were, he reasoned, probably due to genuine differences in size and brightness. In fact, Herschel was persuaded that there was no limit to the variety of celestial objects. While his father had ruthlessly exploited simplifying assumptions in his cosmological investigations, John shied away from doing so. John nevertheless decided that our galaxy is a member of a system of nebulae, and that the center of the system lies in the direction of a great concentration of nebulae in the constellation Virgo.

For some, the debate over the resolution of the nebulae, because it related to the larger issue of the existence of nebulous fluid in the universe, was, as Schaffer (1989, 131–164) emphasized, a highly charged political issue. Laplace's **nebular hypothesis**, with its assumption of nebulous fluid, had been seized on by reformers, such as the British political economist and astronomer John Pringle Nichol. For Nichol, the nebular hypothesis—with its developmental view of the solar system—provided a general model of universal progress, a model that could be pressed into service to help justify political reform in England. Reformers used astronomy to support progressive changes in human society.

Some astronomers, for example the politically conservative Irishman Thomas Romney Robinson, strongly objected to Laplace's nebular hypothesis. Even before Lord Rosse's giant telescope became operational, Robinson contended that the great reflector would undermine the nebular hypothesis by resolving all nebulae into systems of stars. Once the telescope came on line in 1845, Robinson quickly decided that given an instrument of sufficient light grasp, all nebulae were potentially resolvable (Bennett, 104–108).

The data gathered with big speculum metal reflectors were nevertheless ambiguous and did not settle the debate over the existence of nebulous fluid in space. Even the reported resolution of the Orion Nebula did not disconcert such a staunch advocate of nebular fluid and cosmic evolution as Nichol. He pointed to the discovery of a new kind of nebula—the spiral nebulae—as compelling evidence for nebular fluid.

In 1864, the debate over the nature of the nebulae took an unexpected turn when the British astrophysicist **William Huggins** directed his spectroscope toward a planetary nebula in the constellation Draco. Huggins found the spectrum was composed of a single bright line. Such lines, Huggins argued, are characteristic of a luminous gas, not clusters of stars. Huggins found similar results for other nebulae. Here was very strong evidence that at least some nebulae are indeed genuinely nebulous. However, not all nebulae, nor even a majority of the nebulae Huggins examined, possessed bright emission lines in their spectra (Becker, 126–145). His spectroscopic results ensured that observational resources deployed in the debate over the nature of the nebulae would henceforth involve more than raw light-gathering power.

Huggins's findings, when taken in conjunction with other evidence, led to a general decline in the island universe theory. By the end of the century, it was widely accepted that nebulae were not equally distributed, but seemed to avoid the plane of the Milky Way. If the nebulae were truly independent galaxies, it would be curious indeed for them to avoid just that region of the sky that the Milky Way marked out. **James E. Keeler** of the **Lick Observatory** photographed nebulae and clusters of nebulae with the 36-inch Crossley telescope. Keeler estimated the total number of nebulae observable with the Crossley at around 120,000, an entire order of magnitude higher than the previously accepted figure. Keeler also held that most possessed a spiral structure. As historian Agnes Clerke put it in 1905, "[The] relationship between the various orders of nebulae is manifest. The tendency of all to assume spiral forms demonstrates their close affinity; so that to admit some to membership of the sidereal system while excluding others would be a palpable absurdity. And since those of a gaseous constitution must be so admitted, the rest follow inevitably" (Clerke, 350). In addition, in 1885 a nova had flared in the Andromeda Nebula. Since the Andromeda nebula was so large, astronomers assumed it was nearer the earth than faint nebulae. Whatever the cause of the nova, it seemed inconceivable that the nebula could be composed of millions of stars, for at its brightest the nova had reached about one-tenth of the brightness of the entire nebula. How, astronomers asked, could a single star rival the luminosity of an immense stellar assembly? When the evidence was reviewed, "The island universe theory of nebulae, partially abandoned by Herschel after 1791 . . . but brought into credit again by Lord Rosse's discoveries . . . scarcely survived the spectroscopic proof of the gaseous character of certain nebulae" (Berry, 405).

If astronomers generally rejected the existence of visible galaxies, that does not mean that they necessarily rejected the existence of galaxies. By the end of the nineteenth century it had become customary to divide the universe into a visible region confined to the Milky Way and its members, and an infinite region presumed to lie beyond the reach of observations (Jaki, 270). In this latter realm there might well be galaxies.

In the first decade of the twentieth century, there was renewed interest in visible galaxies prompted by new observational evidence. In 1898, **Julius Scheiner** at Potsdam obtained a spectrogram of the Andromeda Nebula that he interpreted as the product of a large body of stars. E.A. Fath, first at Lick and then the Mount Wilson Observatory, secured spectrograms that suggested that the spirals are star systems lying far beyond the boundaries of the Milky Way (Smith 1982, 9–11). There was no consensus on where these boundaries lay, but with the sun believed to be close to the center of the galactic system, the system itself was often reckoned to be shaped like a thin lens, perhaps 10,000 light years in diameter. A few astronomers, such as Max Wolf at Heidelberg and **Sir David Gill** at the Cape of Good Hope, proposed that our galaxy was arranged in a spiral pattern. If so, it seemed plausible that the spiral nebulae were themselves galaxies.

As a consequence of these findings and speculations, galaxies once again became an important topic in astronomy. By about 1910, two main versions of the island universe theory had developed. The first merely stated that there are independent stellar systems beyond the confines of our own galaxy. The second might be better termed the comparable galaxy theory, since it carried the implication that the island universes are comparable in size with our galactic system (Smith 1982, 15, 86–89).

In 1912, a new approach that would eventually lead to a novel and immensely important method of calculating distances to spiral nebulae was developed by **Vesto M. Slipher** of the **Lowell Observatory**. Slipher became the first to measure the radial velocity of a spiral nebula. The Lowell astronomer hoped that the spiral nebulae would provide clues to the origin of the solar system, but the radial velocities he detected persuaded some of his colleagues that the speeds of the spirals were altogether too great for them to be gravitationally bound to our stellar system (Hoyt, 147–150; Smith 1982, 17–22). Slipher's results also indicated that, by the second decade of the twentieth century, path-breaking observations of spiral nebulae frequently were being made at observatories in the western United States (Smith 1979, 53–54).

Another important body of evidence emerged at Mount Wilson in 1916, when Adriaan van Maanen began comparing photographs of spirals to determine internal motions (Berendzen et al., 118–131). Van Maanen detected motions, and, although at first the results did not contradict the theory of the spirals as galaxies, they clearly clashed with the idea of the spirals as comparable galaxies. This issue was thrown into sharp relief when, in 1917, **Harlow Shapley** presented his radical theory of the galactic system (Smith 1982, 55–77), in which the sun was tens of thousands of light years from the center. If our galaxy were anything like as big as Shapley claimed (about 300,000 light years in diameter), and if van Maanen's measures were accurate, the larger spiral nebulae were very much smaller than, and inside of, the Milky Way. By 1920, Shapley was also speculating that the peculiar distribution of the spirals, and their systematic recession from our galaxy, could be explained by supposing them to be masses of nebulous material repelled in some manner from the galactic system, which he presumed to be moving through a vast field of such nebulae.

Shapley's criticisms of the island universe theory led him to participate in 1920 in the so-called great debate on the scale of the universe, which Shapley chose to interpret as the scale of the Milky Way Galaxy, but which his opponent, Heber Curtis of the Lick Observatory, took to mean the existence of other galaxies as well. At stake was not simply the status of particular astronomical objects, but even more important, what constituted sound astrophysical practice, with Shapley representing new ways of doing business, and Curtis the conservative traditions of the Lick Observatory. At the time of the great debate, it is likely that most astronomers supposed the spiral nebulae to be independent galaxies outside of our galaxy. But the combination of Shapley's galactic theory and van Maanen's measures was a fairly potent mix. It persuaded some people to rethink their views (Smith 1982, 97–103).

With the benefit of hindsight, we can see that what was required to settle the issue was a means of determining distances that was widely accepted as accurate by the practitioners of nebular astronomy. Until such a method could be found, the existence of island universes would remain problematic. Mount Wilson astronomer Edwin P. Hubble provided the method in the early 1920s.

In 1923, Hubble found a Cepheid variable in the Andromeda Nebula. Using the 100-inch reflector, Hubble quickly found Cepheids in other nebulae as well. Within a year or so, Hubble had accumulated enough evidence using Cepheids and the other distance indicators, to convince almost all astronomers that the outer regions of the Andromeda Nebula consisted of clouds of stars and that the nebula was indeed an external galaxy. Following these and similar discoveries, the debate over the existence of visible galaxies was all but over (Smith 1982, 97–136).

A few years later Hubble presented convincing evidence that the galaxies (extragalactic nebulae, in his terminology) exhibited a red shift–distance relation, and that, at least in the first approximation, it was linear. His initial paper on the red shift–distance relation appeared in 1929 and was followed by a much more extensive discussion in 1931. Hubble was always careful in print to avoid definitely interpreting the red shifts as Doppler shifts. But the writings of **Arthur Stanley Eddington** and others soon meshed the calculations of Georges Lemaître and other theorists with Hubble's research on the red shift–distance relation. The notion of the expanding universe was swiftly accepted by many, and the linear relationship between red shift and distance was later widely accepted as Hubble's law, despite the fact that others had predicted such a relationship before Hubble. To many astronomers, it was Hubble who had provided the proof of the relationship's existence.

Among the key questions that arose were: Do galaxies form in clusters and, if so, how big are the clusters? How did the galaxies form and how do they evolve? Answers to these and other questions shaped extragalactic astronomy from the 1930s. In what ways these questions are linked to social, institutional, and instrumental issues has not yet been explored. One set of developments that will surely need to be integrated into any well-rounded account is the post–World War II development of instruments to observe the universe at wavelengths other than those of visible light. For example, the rapid growth of radio astronomy—itself a product of the greatly increased willingness of many national governments to support science—did much to reshape astronomers' conceptions of galaxies and to see them as possible sites of incredibly violent events. A balanced account of the recent history of extragalactic astronomy will need to reach far beyond the history of science and technology narrowly defined.

Robert W. Smith

Bibliography

Becker, B. *Eclecticism, Opportunism, and the Evolution of a New Research Agenda: William and Margaret Huggins and the Origins of Astrophysics.* Unpublished Ph.D. dissertation, Johns Hopkins University, 1993.

Bennett, J.A. "Church, State, and Astronomy in Ireland. 200 Years of Armagh Observatory." Armagh: Armagh Observatory, 1990.

Berendzen, R., R. Hart, and D. Seeley, *Man Discovers the Galaxies.* New York: Science History Publications, 1976.

Berry, A. *A Short History of Astronomy.* London: John Murray, 1898.

Clerke, A. *The System of the Stars.* 2nd ed. London: Black, 1905.

Dreyer, J.L.E., ed. *The Scientific Papers of Sir William Herschel.* 2 vols. London: Royal Society and Royal Astronomical Society, 1912.

Herrmann, D.B. *Geschichte der Astronomie von Herschel bis Hertzsprung.* Berlin: Deutscher Verlag der Wissenschaften, V.E.B, 1975.

Hetherington, N. *The Edwin Hubble Papers: Previously Unpublished Manuscripts on the Extragalactic Nature of Spiral Nebulae. Edited, Annotated, and with a Historical Introduction.* Tucson: Pachart, 1990.

Hoskin, M. *William Herschel and the Construction of the Heavens.* London: Oldbourne, 1963.

———. *Stellar Astronomy: Historical Studies.* Chalfont St. Giles: Science History Publications, 1982.

———. "John Herschel's Cosmology." *Journal for the History of Astronomy* 18 (1987): 1–34.

Hoyt, W.G. *Lowell and Mars.* Tucson: University of Arizona Press, 1976.

Hubble, E.P. *The Realm of the Nebulae.* New Haven: Yale University Press, 1936.

Jaki, S.L. *The Milky Way: An Elusive Road for Science.* Newton Abbott, U.K.: David and Charles, 1973.

Jones, K. "The Observational Basis for Kant's Cosmogony: A Critical Analysis." *Journal for the History of Astronomy.* 2 (1971): 29–34.

Osterbrock, D.E. *James E. Keeler, Pioneer American Astrophysicist, and the Early Development of American Astrophysics.* Cambridge and New York: Cambridge University Press, 1984.

Osterbrock, D.E., J.R. Gustafson, and W.J.S. Unruh. *Eye on the Sky: Lick Observatory's First Century.* Berkeley: University of California Press, 1988.

Schaffer, S. "Herschel in Bedlam: Natural History and Stellar Astronomy." *British Journal for the History of Science* 13 (1980): 211–239.

———. "The Nebular Hypothesis and the Science of Progress." In *History, Humanity, and Evolution*, edited by J. Moore, 131–164. Cambridge: Cambridge University Press, 1989.

Smith, R.W. "The Origins of the Velocity-Distance Relationship." *Journal for the History of Astronomy* 10 (1979): 133–164.

———. *The Expanding Universe: Astronomy's 'Great Debate' 1900–1931.* Cambridge: Cambridge University Press, 1982.

———. "Edwin P. Hubble and the Transformation of Cosmology." *Physics Today* 18 (1990): 52–58.

Galilei, Galileo (1564–1642)

Italian astronomer, mathematician, and physicist. Galileo enrolled in 1581 at the University of Pisa to study medicine. His attention diverted by mathematics, Galileo left school, studied privately in Florence and did some tutoring, and acquired enough of a reputation to secure the chair of mathematics at Pisa in 1589. He moved to Padua in 1592, and taught there until 1610. Most of his work during these years concerned the physics of moving bodies and bodies in equilibrium. He appears to have had little interest in astronomy, although he told Kepler in 1597 that he was sympathetic to Copernicanism. He also gave public lectures during the appearance of the supernova of 1604, attacking the idea of the immutability of the heavens.

Galileo become an astronomer in 1609, when, at the age of forty-five, he heard about the newly invented telescope, constructed his own crude nine-power instrument, and turned it on the heavens. He discovered that the

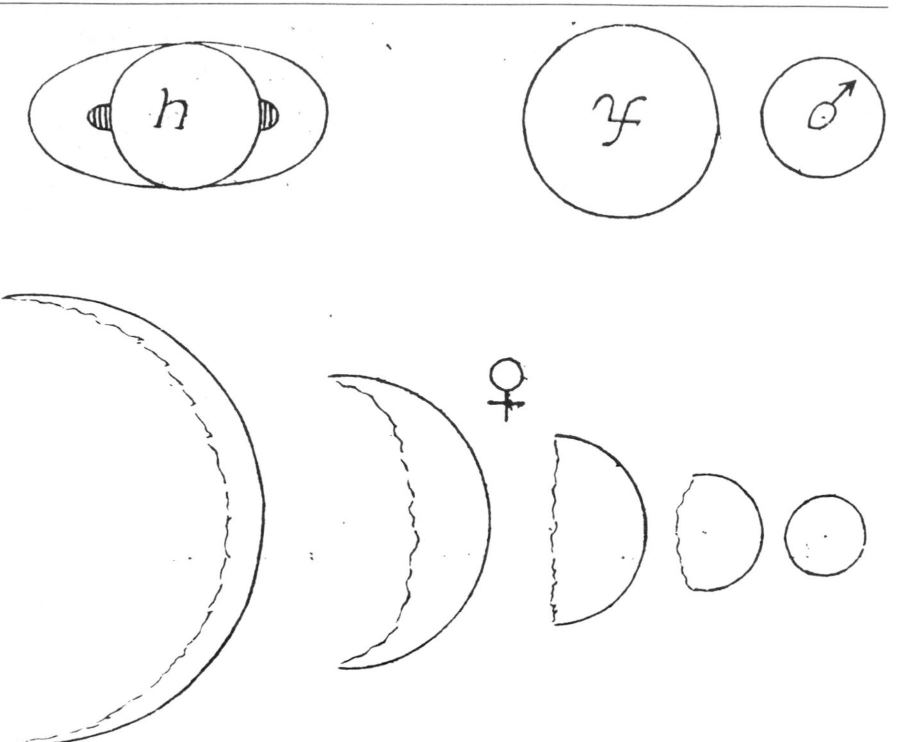

A diagram showing the appearances of the planets as viewed through Galileo's telescope, from Galileo Galilei, Il Saggiatore *(Rome, 1623). Galileo's discovery that Venus exhibits phases, illustrated in the lower half of the diagram, convinced him of the truth of the Copernican system, since they can not be explained by a Ptolemaic geocentric model. Top row shows (from left to right) views of Saturn, Jupiter, and Mars. (Courtesy of the History of Science Collection, Linda Hall Library, Kansas City, Missouri)*

moon was cratered and mountainous, not at all the perfect quintessential sphere of Aristotelian cosmology. Turning to Jupiter, he found four small stars that soon proved to be Jovian satellites. Realizing the sensational nature of these discoveries, Galileo quickly published a pamphlet announcing his findings, the *Sidereus Nuncius* (*Starry Messenger*) of 1610. For the occasion, he christened the Jovian satellites the Medicean stars, in honor of the Medici family of Florence. This overt bid for patronage did not go unrewarded. Later that year Galileo moved to Florence as philosopher and mathematician to the Medici court.

In 1610 Galileo also discovered sunspots, the rotation of the sun, and the phases of Venus. The latter phenomenon, which can be explained only if Venus orbits the sun, turned Galileo into a public Copernican, and he first defended heliocentrism in his *Letters on Sunspots* (1613).

In 1613 Galileo began arguing in widely circulated letters that Scripture and Copernicanism are compatible, provided one realizes that the Bible was written to accommodate the understanding of the common person and need not be taken literally. Galileo's venture into Scriptural exegesis came to the attention of Church authorities. Cardinal Roberto Bellarmine was asked to look into Galileo's specific claims and the entire question of Copernicanism as well. In 1616, a commission declared that the doctrines of a moving earth and a central, fixed sun were heretical and erroneous in faith; Copernicus's *Revolutions* was placed on the Index of Forbidden Books; and Galileo was given a warning by Bellarmine, the exact nature of which would later be in dispute.

In 1624, following the election of Pope Urban VIII, whom Galileo found sympathetic to the new ideas, the scientist began composition of a treatise that would eventually become the *Dialogue Concerning the Two Chief World Systems* (1632). In this brilliantly written work, Galileo allowed three interlocutors, Salviati, Sagredo, and Simplicio, to discuss the merits and problems of heliocentric and geocentric cosmologies. To answer the common sense argument against a moving earth, Galileo here introduced the tenets of an inertial physics and the relativity of motion that would emerge more fully in the *Discourse on Two New Sciences* (1638).

Galileo secured all the proper permissions and imprimaturs, but the *Dialogue* apparently infuriated Urban VIII, and the matter was turned over to the Inquisition. In 1633, after a stormy investigation, Galileo agreed to recant his views, submit to a lifelong house-arrest, and see his book banned.

The events from 1613 to 1633 are commonly called the Galileo affair, and for three and a half centuries scholars and theologians have disagreed over just what Bellarmine said to Galileo, whether he violated a Church order, whether the *Dialogue* was indeed an impartial examination of cosmologies, and whether the Church acted properly in bringing Galileo to trial. Some have suggested that Galileo's real crime was not heliocentrism, but an atomic philosophy that undermined the sacrament of the Eucharist. Others maintain that Galileo was simply guilty of over-ambition and that his personal strivings ran afoul of the papal court. All agree that the outcome was unfortunate, especially for the Church, which took a public stand against heliocentrism, a principle embraced by most scientists by the end of the century.

Galileo spent his last years composing the *Two New Sciences*, which laid the foundation of modern physics, and presiding over a school of talented disciples.

William B. Ashworth Jr.

Bibliography

Biagioli, M. *Galileo Courtier: The Practice of Science in the Culture of Absolutism.* Chicago: University of Chicago Press, 1993.

Blackwell, R.J. *Galileo, Bellarmine, and the Bible.* Notre Dame: University of Notre Dame Press, 1991.

De Santillana, G. *The Crime of Galileo.* Chicago: University of Chicago Press, 1955.

Drake, S. "Galilei, Galileo." In *Dictionary of Scientific Biography*, edited by C.C. Gillispie, vol. 5, 237–250. New York: Scribner, 1973.

———. *Galileo at Work: His Scientific Biography.* Chicago: University of Chicago Press, 1978.

Finocchiaro, M.A., ed. *The Galileo Affair: A Documentary History.* Berkeley: University of California Press, 1989.

Galilei, Galileo. *Dialogue concerning the Two Chief World Systems.* 2nd ed. Translated by Stillman Drake. Berkeley: University of California Press, 1967.

———. *Sidereus Nuncius, or The Sidereal Messenger.* Translated and with an introduction, conclusion, and notes by A.V. Helden. Chicago: University of Chicago Press, 1989.

Langford, J.L. *Galileo, Science, and the Church.* Rev. ed. Ann Arbor: University of Michigan Press, 1971.

Redondi, P. *Galileo Heretic.* Translated by Raymond Rosenthal. Princeton: Princeton University Press, 1987.

Van Helden, A. "Galileo, Telescopic Astronomy, and the Copernican System." In *Planetary Astronomy from the Renaissance to the Rise of Astrophysics, Part A: Tycho Brahe to Newton*, edited by R. Taton and C. Wilson, vol. 2A, 81–105. *The General History of Astronomy.* Cambridge: Cambridge University Press, 1989.

Westfall, R.S. *Essays on the Trial of Galileo.* Vatican Observatory Publications, Studi Galileiani, 1(5). Vatican City: Specola Vaticana, 1989.

Gamma-Ray Astronomy

Gamma-rays were first identified and named late in the nineteenth century as one of the penetrating radiations emitted by radioactive substances and X-ray machines. Astronomically, it came to be a generic category for radiation beyond the X-ray region, with energies of about 1,000,000 electron volts (1MeV) and beyond—the most energetic photons in nature. Gamma-rays reveal themselves by interacting with various media—the atmosphere of the earth, crystals, liquids, or gases in various detectors—and producing charged particles or visible flashes or tracks. Simple electrometers revealing ionization of the surrounding air were first carried to various heights to determine whether the sources of gamma-rays were radioactive substances in the earth, the atmosphere itself, or perhaps of cosmic origin. Mountaintops, towers, balloons, and aircraft were used in the first half of the century, joined later by rockets and satellites, to raise detectors to greater altitudes. The cosmic origin of some gamma-radiation was accepted by the 1930s, although theorists were initially at a loss to understand what physical mechanisms might produce such energetic radiation.

The growing awareness of violent astronomical processes and exotic objects (**supernovae**, quasars, neutron stars, **black holes**, and so on) joined with detector developments and spaceflight technology after the mid-1950s to make gamma-ray astronomy an active and vigorous specialty. During the 1960s balloons and rockets were joined by satellites as carriers of gamma-ray astronomical instruments. By the 1970s the first all-sky maps in gamma-rays had been produced from satellite observations, followed by individual investigations of a variety of objects.

During a series of 1911–1912 high-altitude balloon ascents, Victor Hess of Vienna obtained electrometer measurements that convinced him that gamma-rays were of cosmic origin as well as emitted from radioactive substances on and in the earth. Robert Millikan in the United States carried out a series of measurements from automated balloons, aircraft, and on various locations on the earth that led him initially to challenge Hess's conclusion. There followed an intense debate and a variety of other measurements by Auguste Picard of Brussels and Erich Regener of Stuttgart, among others. By 1932 the various complications and sources of error had been unraveled, and consensus on the cosmic origin emerged.

Means of detecting cosmic gamma-radiation—either indirectly or directly—diversified. Gamma-ray detectors must discriminate their quarry from the much more populous background of cosmic rays. A variety of spark chambers were developed in which a liquid or crystal substance reacting to all of the radiation (gamma and cosmic) was surrounded by another detector insensitive to gamma-rays. The resulting flashes, or scintillations, were recorded and counted visually, photographically, or electronically, and those not due to gamma-rays subtracted.

Gamma-rays interacting with the atoms of the upper atmosphere produce a cascading shower of secondary gamma-rays and charged particles, which can then be detected with Geiger or scintillation counters at high-altitude sites or carried by balloons or rockets. Gamma-rays also produce a feeble Cherenkov radiation, visible in the optical region, for which ground-based telescopes have been built.

Beginning in the 1960s, more sophisticated spark chambers, scintillation counters, and other specialized solid-state detectors were flown using high-altitude balloons, small rockets, and various satellites. These included Defense Department satellites designed to detect bursts of gamma-rays from nuclear explosions on earth or in orbit as well as civilian satellites devoted to other kinds of astronomy. Groups with expertise in this extremely specialized area grew at universities, the **National Aeronautics and Space Administration**, industry, and at Defense Department military and civilian scientific laboratories. X-ray and gamma-ray astronomy interacted with astrophysics and cosmology as much as with high-energy physics, nuclear science, and defense engineering.

The United States Small Astronomy Satellite (SAS-2, 1972) and the European COS-B in 1975 were the first satellites devoted entirely to gamma-ray astronomy; they allowed researchers to produce crude all-sky maps. These showed a diffuse background, heightened intensity in the galactic plane, and about thirty individual sources. Because the resolution of these maps was not much more than a degree of arc, only a few of the sources could be identified with conspicuous optical objects (such as the Crab Nebula, an optical pulsar in the constellation Vela, and the X-ray source Cygnus X-3).

Following the general pattern of space astronomy, a much more sophisticated observatory was designed to study this spectral region in greater detail—with better angular and spectral resolution. The paths of charged cosmic rays (protons, neutrons, and heavy nuclei) are altered in their passage through the universe, but not so the highly energetic gamma-rays, and hence they were important in pointing unambiguously to the sources of cosmic radiation.

The High Energy Astronomical Observatories (HEAO) flown primarily for X-ray astronomy during the 1970s carried instruments sensitive to the lower-energy gamma-rays, and a gamma-ray spectrometer. The international Compton Gamma Ray Observatory (GRO) was deployed from the Space Shuttle in 1991. It mapped more precisely the gamma-ray emission from the galactic plane, obtained measurements of emission from quasars, observed gamma radiation from solar flares, and identified a few more of the enigmatic objects known as gamma-ray bursters.

Only cosmic ray studies enjoy a developed historiography, and the allied field of X-ray astronomy has been the subject of some professional historical scrutiny. Ziegler (1989) analyzes the discovery of cosmic radiation and the interaction of instrumental and balloon technology, finding it to be a complex and protracted interplay rather than a simple event in 1912. De Maria, et al. analyze the international controversy over interpretation of various results during this period. DeVorkin extensively and thoroughly discusses these and later observations made from balloons over half a century. Hirsh provides some discussion of gamma-ray astronomy but concentrates primarily on the early history of X-ray astronomy. Russo discusses the history of the European gamma-ray satellite COS-B.

For gamma-ray astronomy from ground-based instruments and spacecraft, one is generally limited to a few memoirs, journalistic accounts, and scientific review articles. Tucker and Tucker (1986) devote three chapters to gamma-ray astronomy in their readable and informative but sparsely documented volume, providing highlights of ground-, balloon-, rocket-, and satellite-based developments and personalities. Tucker (1984), Tucker and Giacconi (1985), and Rossi discuss gamma-ray astronomy peripherally, while dealing mainly with the allied field of X-ray astronomy, in which they were themselves participants. Weeks, Field and Chaisson, and various articles in *Annual Review of Astronomy and Astrophysics* provide scientific reviews ranging from popular to professional.

Joseph N. Tatarewicz

Bibliography

Annual Review of Astronomy and Astrophysics. Palo Alto, Calif.: Annual Reviews, 1963–.

De Maria, M., M.G. Ianniello, and A. Russo. "The Discovery of Cosmic Rays: Rivalries and Controversies between Europe and the United States." *Historical Studies in the Physical and Biological Sciences* 22 (1991): 165–192.

DeVorkin, D.H. *Race to the Stratosphere: Manned Scientific Ballooning in America.* New York: Springer-Verlag, 1989.

Field, G.B., and E. Chaisson. *The Invisible Universe: Probing the Frontiers of Astrophysics.* Boston: Birkhauser, 1985.

Henbest, N., ed. *Observing the Universe.* London: Basil Blackwell, 1984.

Hirsh, R.F. *Glimpsing an Invisible Universe: The Emergence of X-ray Astronomy.* New York: Cambridge University Press, 1983.

Rossi, B.B. *Moments in the Life of a Scientist.* New York: Cambridge University Press, 1990.

Russo, A. "Choosing Big Projects in Space Research: The Case of ESRO's Scientific Satellite COS-B." *History and Technology* 9 (1992). Also published in *Choosing Big Technologies*, edited by J. Krige. Berkshire, U.K.: Harwood Academic Publishers.

Tucker, W.H. *The Star Splitters: The High Energy Astronomy Observatories.* NASA SP-466. Washington, D.C.: GPO, 1984.

Tucker, W.H. and R. Giacconi. *The X-Ray Universe: The Quest for Cosmic Fire—From Black Holes to Intergalactic Space.* Cambridge: Harvard University Press, 1985.

Tucker, W.H. and K. Tucker. *The Cosmic Inquirers: Modern Telescopes and Their Makers.* Cambridge: Harvard University Press, 1986.

Weeks, T.C. "The Gamma-Ray Universe: Taking a Long, Hard Look." In *Infinite Vistas: New Tools for Astronomy*, edited by J. Cornell and J. Carr, 231–253. New York: Scribner, 1985.

Ziegler, C. "Technology and the Process of Scientific Discovery: The Case of Cosmic Rays." *Technology and Culture* 30 (1989): 939–963.

Gerasimovich, Boris Petrovich (1889–1937)

Soviet astrophysicist. Gerasimovich studied at Khar'kov University, where he served as a professor and senior astronomer in the 1920s. At the invitation of **Harlow Shapley**, Gerasimovich spent three years (1926–1929) at the **Harvard College Observatory**. In 1933 he was named director of **Pulkovo Observatory**, which he directed until his arrest and execution in 1937 at the time of the Great Purges.

Together with V.G. Fesenkov, Gerasimovich is regarded as one of the founders of Soviet astrophysics. His scientific research included variable stars, emission nebulae (in particular planetary nebulae), interstellar absorption, galactic structure, and theoretical astrophysics. Gerasimovich served in a number of Soviet and international astronomical organizations, coordinated the writing of the first Soviet textbook on astrophysics and stellar astronomy, and coordinated the international effort to observe the 1936 total solar eclipse in the Soviet Union.

Robert A. McCutcheon

Bibliography

Eremeeva, A.I. "Zhizn' i tvorchestvo Borisa Petrovicha Gerasimovicha (k 100–letiiu so dnia rozhdeniia)." *Istoriko-astronomicheskie issledovaniia* 21 (1989): 253–301.

Kulikovsky, P.G. "Gerasimovich, Boris Petrovich." In *Dictionary of Scientific Biography*, edited by C.C. Gillispie, vol. 5, 363–364. New York: Scribner, 1981.

Germany, Astronomy since 1600

German culture has produced famous astronomers since the Middle Ages. Some historians judge the early eighteenth century to have been a time of crucial transition in German astronomy, in which the social status of the astronomer (whose roles included calendar-making and astrological prognostication) became less associated with crafts, trades, and guilds. Astronomy was seen as an endeavor for those with academic training. Furthermore, this transition seems to have initiated the exclusion of women, who were important figures in German astronomy of the late seventeenth century. Schiebinger has argued that the career of Maria Winkelmann Kirch, wife and mother of Berlin Academy astronomers Gottfried and Christfried Kirch, illustrates how fading guild traditions left women unable to maintain the status they had held in the astronomy of earlier generations: "As astronomy moved more and more out of the private observatories and into the public world, women lost their toehold in modern science" (Schiebinger, 190–191).

The German astronomical community developed in new directions during the eighteenth century. For example, the Berlin Academy (founded in 1700) early employed a professional astronomer. Johann Tobias Mayer, discoverer of lunar librations, established the Göttingen Observatory (1751), where he confirmed and measured the secular acceleration of the moon, and published solar and lunar tables. Johann Heinrich Lambert founded the *Berliner astronomisches Jahrbuch* (1776) as a means of promoting communications between astronomers. He also published his *Cosmologische Briefe über die Einrichtung des Weltbaues* (1761), a theoretical discussion of star systems and the sun's place among the stars, and *Photometria* (1760), which established the foundations of photometry. Johann Bode, director of the **Berlin Observatory**, continued Lambert's *Jahrbuch* and published two important star atlases. In the early 1780s, **Johann Schröter** built a major observatory at Lilienthal, and in 1788 Duke Ernest II founded an observatory near Gotha. In 1796 Gotha was the site of an astronomical congress, and in 1800 Franz Xaver von Zach founded *Monatliche Korrespondenz*, the first German astronomical journal. The international *Astronomischen Nachrichten*, founded in 1823 by Heinrich Schumacher, became the most important German astronomical journal after the *Korrespondenz* ceased in 1826.

An excellent thematic study of German Enlightenment astronomy is available in Baasner, *Lob der Sternkunst*. The work and career of Mayer have received serious study in a major biographical work by Forbes, which establishes his great influence in Germany's scientific development and illuminates the interconnections between astronomy, academic mathematics, cartography, and instrument construction. Schröter and the Lilienthal observatory are unifying themes of a collection of essays edited by Drews and Schwier, exploring a variety of topics and presenting important source material on German astronomy. Schröter and astronomy at Lilienthal have also been studied at some length by Gerdes.

During the nineteenth century, as Germany became a nation-state, its astronomy reached world class status. This is reflected in the founding of major research institutions and observatories, the establishment of professional societies, and the growth of the German optical industry. German astronomers excelled in the exacting observational and mathematical work that helped place positional astronomy and **celestial mechanics** on a firm quantitative footing. Modern astrophysics, especially the development of spectroscopy and photometry, has some of its most important roots in the work of German scientists and technicians. Good surveys of this period are available in English by Herrmann and Chapman.

The remarkable growth of astronomy in Germany, and especially its great flowering in the nineteenth century, has not gone unnoticed by historians of science. Attempts to place the topic in a larger perspective take two approaches. One is an essentially Marxist historical view interpreting the development of astronomy as a natural consequence of the social and economic evolution of modern Europe. A more sociological approach places emphasis on the internal development of German academic institutions and the institutionalization of academic research as major factors in the rapid rise of German science.

Dieter Herrmann, a historian of modern astronomy, sees a causal relationship between the socioeconomic evolution of early modern Europe and the development of modern science. He views the rise of modern astronomy as a result of the growth of European capitalist economies. The rise of the middle class created a need for the fruits of science, while European industrialization provided, in turn, tools for the advancement of science such as improved production methods, materials, machine tooling, and the like. Early capitalism, he argues, needed astronomical data for practical tasks—most crucially for navigation, but also for geographical surveys and timekeeping. But middle-class enthusiasm for science was not constant. In Herrmann's view, the bourgeoisie favored science only as long as it could provide antiecclesiastical ammunition needed in the struggle to destroy feudalism. Once ecclesiastical power declined, "the attitude of the bourgeoisie became necessarily disunited concerning the sciences" (Herrmann 1984, 6).

Herrmann insists that, in the nineteenth century, as Europe was transformed by the forces of industrialization, society still had a need, rooted in socioeconomic development, for the services of astronomers. He notes that half of all German astronomers in the period 1800–1850 were occupied with geographical and geodetic research (Herrmann 1969–1970, 326–327). Yet, correlations are not causes, and other reasons, such as disciplinary associations or institutional traditions, could produce similar results. Herrmann does recognize other forces operating in the development of eighteenth- and nineteenth-century German astronomy. There was, for instance, an urgent need for refined astrometric data. This demanded, in turn, an understanding of such factors as stellar aberration, precession, nutation, and atmospheric refraction. It also required an understanding of observational errors, both of the instrument and observer. Herrmann also points out that work on **comets, asteroids**, and **astrometry** suggested the benefits of cooperative research—that is, groups of observers dividing the labor and sharing the data.

The German astronomical community responded to this organizational problem by creating scientific journals and by cooperative projects in astrometry, asteroid orbit determinations, and the like (Herrmann 1969–1970, 327). This leaves us with a view of German astronomy's developing largely in response to the socioeconomic evolution of Europe, but conditioned by other factors including technological capacities and, not surprisingly, the nature of the discipline's subject matter.

Sociologist Joseph Ben-David has studied German academic institutions, and the development of the German astronomical community in the nineteenth century follows closely the pattern he identified: "The transformation of science into a status approaching that of a professional career and into a bureaucratic, organized activity took place in Germany between 1825 and 1900" (Ben-David, 108). Ben-David emphasizes the influence of the German *Naturphilosophie* movement that viewed natural science as only one segment of the spectrum of human knowledge. In this view, no field of knowledge, including astronomy, was required to be directly useful for political or economic ends. Rather, learning was valuable for its own sake. Scientific research that had no social or economic value could be an important activity for astronomers because it was essential to comprehending nature as a whole.

Reforms in the German university system in the early nineteenth century enhanced the place of mathematical sciences, including astronomy. By the 1830s, structural changes in the university system established a place and professional independence for researchers pursuing experimental and mathematical science. Ultimately that led to a demand for professional researchers, thus making it a realistic career choice. Ben-David concludes that the emergence of university research in Germany between 1825 and 1870 was a development internal to academic society and virtually independent of external socioeconomic factors.

Though both offer fruitful insights, neither of these perspectives provides a completely satisfactory explanation. Political and cultural movements, for example, were very influential in late-eighteenth-century attempts to create a German intellectual tradition independent of French influences. The roles of Pierre-Louis Maupertuis, president of the Berlin Academy, and Voltaire, who held forth in the Prussian court of Frederick the Great, exemplify the extent of French intellectual dominance in Germany. Napoleon's defeat of Prussia, followed by the 1813 military overthrow of the French conquerors, further stimulated the desire to develop an independent German intellectual tradition that was part of a broader growth of German national consciousness.

This period, coinciding with the careers of some of the founders of modern German astronomy, predates the growth of German industrialization and capitalistic development that accompanied unification of the country in the 1860s. On the other hand, Germany's rapid economic and industrial development from about 1870 through World War I saw the birth of world-famous scientific, technological, and academic establishments. German astronomy in this period reflected these national achievements, and its success cannot be separated from the rise of the nation. Many of the developments in German astronomy can be understood as the result of technological advances or as refinements in astrometry. In turn, theoretical work in celestial mechanics deepened astronomers' understanding of the solar system.

Technological Development

Astronomy benefited from the new industrial technology. The popularity and status of astronomy made the manufacture and sale of telescopes and astronomical instruments profitable. From the beginning of the nineteenth century, the famous optical and instrument workshops of Hamburg and Munich produced instruments that made great improvements in astrometric precision. Joseph Fraunhofer, with the Reichenbach firm in Munich, equipped telescopes with filar micrometers and constructed a new kind of astrometric instrument, the heliometer. Fraunhofer also perfected large achromatic objective lenses up to about 9 inches in diameter and developed the German equatorial mount, so popular in the nineteenth century. After Fraunhofer's death, the firm continued to supply large telescopes to observatories worldwide and thus constituted a vital part of the international astronomical community. A handful of studies on Fraunhofer exist. The best is by Sang and provides detailed coverage of his life and work. The German tradition of astronomical instrumentation continued in the workshop of Ernst Abbe at the **Carl Zeiss** Werke of Jena, which by the beginning of the twentieth century was producing refracting telescopes with apertures in excess of 25 inches.

Improved instruments called for refined methods of observation and data reduction. **Friedrich Wilhelm Bessel** became director of the new Prussian imperial observatory in Königsberg in 1809 and established the German tradition of observational astrometry that would persist through the century. Bessel's *Fundamenta astronomiae* (1818) set a new standard for astrometric precision. Equipped with superior instruments, Bessel improved the accuracy of observation and the reduction of data through the analysis of instrumental and observational errors. Bessel's most important work in this area was the *Tabulae Regiomontanae* (1830), which made possible the ambitious star catalogues of the next generation. There is still no comprehensive account of Bessel's life and work.

Spectroscopy, which, with photometry and photography, was one of the fundamental technologies of astrophysics, owes much to German science. In 1817 Fraunhofer announced the discovery of dark lines (later named for him) in the solar spectrum, which he noticed while measuring indices of refraction in optical glass as a function of wavelength. However, scientific spectrum analysis began in 1859–1862, primarily as a result of the work of **Gustav Kirchhoff** and Robert Bunsen, at the University of Heidelberg, who formulated the empirical rules of spectrum analysis and identified the spectra of various elements.

The science of astronomical photometry was invented in Germany. Johann C.F. Zöllner, working first at Berlin and later Basel, developed a practical photometer and published his methods in 1861. Zöllner's later life, particularly his spiritualism and anti-Semitism, has been examined by Meinel. Astronomers worldwide purchased Zöllner's photometers. At Potsdam, Gustav Müller and Paul Kempf used a Zöllner photometer to measure stellar luminosities for their *Potsdamer Durchmusterung*. In the early twentieth century, photoelectric cells were used at Berlin and Tübingen for stellar photometry, providing far better measurements than were possible with conventional photometers.

The Solar System

Solar system studies were a major part of astronomy in the nineteenth century. Johann Franz Encke at Gotha analyzed observations of the 1761 and 1769 **transits of Venus** to determine the **solar parallax**. The 1874 and 1882 transits of Venus were observed by ten German expeditions scattered across the globe.

German work in **celestial mechanics** began with Wilhelm Olbers of Bremen and Carl Friedrich Gauss, director of the Göttingen Observatory. In 1797, Olbers published a method for determining the orbit of a comet that was a considerable improvement over the methods of Newton and Laplace and remained popular well into the nineteenth century. Much of Olbers's work is not well known, but some biographical and source materials have been assembled by Jaki. Gauss later provided a more general solution for the determination of an orbit using three observations, as well as new tools for data analysis, in the *Theoria motus corporum coelestium* (1809). Gauss also showed how to calculate gravitational perturbations on planetary orbits. For data reduction, astronomers began to adopt Gauss's least squares technique and the impartial use of all available observations, which has the effect of averaging out random errors. Such theories and techniques were essential to keeping track of new asteroids and comets and in the search for new planets. Much historical work has been done on Gauss, though it tends to focus on his mathematical achievements. Fortunately there is a comprehensive modern bibliography compiled by Merzback.

The Berlin Academy facilitated the search for asteroids by mapping the zodiacal region. Around 1891, Max Wolf at Heidelberg introduced a novel photographic method for detecting asteroids, and once again the number of asteroid discoveries surged. One of the most celebrated astronomical discoveries in history was accomplished by Johann Gottfried Galle at the Berlin Observatory in 1846. Galle, using predictions by the French astronomer Urbain J.J. Le Verrier and assisted by Heinrich d'Arrest, discovered the planet Neptune. Galle's search was greatly assisted by the Berlin Academy charts.

Planetary Science

Descriptive studies of solar system bodies benefited enormously from the growth of the German optical industry. Using a 4-inch Munich refractor, Wilhelm Beer and Johann Heinrich Mädler produced a lunar map in 1828 at their private observatory in Berlin. They also used the 9-inch refractor of the Berlin Observatory and determined the rotation period of Mars. Bessel at Gotha and Ernst Hartwig at Bamberg were among the first to measure planetary diameters, using Fraunhofer **heliometers**. Between 1877 and 1893, Müller and Kempf at Potsdam used a Zöllner photometer to measure the phase coefficients and albedos of Venus and Mercury and draw conclusions about their surfaces.

Stellar Statistics

The distribution of stars in the sky, in both two and three dimensions, received considerable attention by nineteenth-century German astronomers. Bessel's student **Friedrich Argelander** at Bonn produced the first modern celestial atlas, his *Uranometria nova* (1843). From 1852 to 1859, Argelander and assistants charted Northern Hemisphere stars to about the ninth magnitude. The result, the *Bonner Durchmusterung*, was used worldwide. Eduard Schönfeld, Argelander's successor at Bonn, extended the survey to –24 degrees. In 1871, the *Astronomische Gesellschaft* organized a major international astrometric project that included seventeen observatories.

Astrometry developed so rapidly that by the mid-nineteenth century astronomers were able to determine the proper motions and, in a few cases, the parallaxes of stars. In 1844 Bessel demonstrated that the proper motions of Sirius and Procyon are disturbed by then-unseen companions.

Astrometry also investigated the large-scale distribution of stars. Erwin Freundlich and Emanuel von der Pahlen at Potsdam discovered a pattern of radial velocities later explained by the rotation of the Milky Way Galaxy. Photography provided another method of collecting data on the distribution of stars, and, by 1869, Wolf at Heidelberg was one of several astronomers using relatively fast optical systems to photograph the Milky Way. Another approach involved the statistical investigation of large numbers of stars. **Hugo von Seeliger**, director of the Munich Observatory, derived the distribution function of stellar luminosities with the goal of finding the spatial distribution of stars in the Milky Way Galaxy. In 1910, building on von Seeliger's work, Karl Schwarzschild derived the theoretical relationship between the distribution of stars and the number of stars per unit volume in the Milky Way. But the existence of obscuring matter between the stars prevents this approach from yielding the true size and shape of our galaxy, which must be inferred by other methods.

Stellar Astronomy

New instruments also advanced the understanding of stars and star systems. Like Bessel and Mädler, **Friedrich G.W. Struve**, working at Dorpat (now Tartu in Estonia), used his Fraunhofer refractor with a filar micrometer to measure double stars. By 1850, orbits of about twenty binary stars had been determined.

Argelander in 1844 had called for systematic observation of variable stars. In 1919 Gustav Müller and Ernst Hartwig published a catalogue listing and classifying about one thousand variable stars. In 1889, Herrmann Carl Vogel and Julius Scheiner found evidence in the spectrum of Beta Persei that suggested the light varied because of periodic eclipses by an unseen companion. Beginning in 1899, Schwarzchild, Johannes Hartmann, and **Ejnar Hertzsprung**, a Dane working at Potsdam, developed techniques for very accurate photographic photometry of variable stars. Their methods led to the derivation of light curves for Cepheid variables, which are so important to the determination of galactic distances. With an accurate knowledge of stellar distances, it was possible to investigate the true luminosities of the stars.

The Twentieth Century

German scientists in the early twentieth century made theoretical contributions of the greatest importance. The formulation by Albert Einstein of the special and general theories of relativity and the development of quantum mechanics by Max Planck, Erwin Schrödinger, and Werner Heisenberg, among others, had enormous implications for cosmology, celestial mechanics, high-energy astrophysics, and other areas. In 1938, Carl Friedrich von Weizäcker, at Berlin, and **Hans Bethe**, working in the United States, theorized that the fusion of hydrogen nuclei into helium nuclei via the proton-proton reaction produced energy in the cores of main sequence stars.

War and social dislocation during the first half of the twentieth century cost German science dearly. Astronomy was affected by the international isolation imposed on German scientists after World War I, as well as by the westward flight of scientists before World War II. Bowen discusses astronomy under the Nazi regime.

After World War II, German astronomy regained its vigor and became a major partner in many international astronomical research organizations and projects. *Rosat* (the Röntgen Satellite), for example, is a major space astronomy project in collaboration with the United States. *Rosat*'s instruments are German-built and used to map the sky at X-ray and ultraviolet wavelengths. Germany is a major partner in the forthcoming Infrared Space Observatory. Germany also plays a role in European Space Association projects and in the construction and operation of the **European Southern Observatory**. **Radio astronomy** is strong in Germany. The 100-meter steerable radio telescope at Bonn has been operational since the early 1970s, and current plans call for major observational programs in millimeter and submillimeter wavelengths. Some of the best work in celestial mechanics, astrometry, and related areas has been carried out in Germany. The *Max Planck Gesellschaft* coordinates national funding of the various Max Planck Institutes, a significant number of which, such as the Institute for Radioastronomy and the Institute for Astrophysics, are devoted to astronomical research.

James M. Lattis

Bibliography

Baasner, R. *Das Lob der Sternkunst: Astronomie in der deutschen Aufklarung*. Göttingen: Vandenhoeck and Ruprecht, 1987.

Ben-David, J. *The Scientist's Role in Society*. Englewood Cliffs, N.J.: Prentice-Hall, 1971.

Bowen, R. *Universal Ice: Science and Ideology in the Nazi State*. London: Belhaven Press, 1993.

Chapman, A. "The Astronomical Revolution." In *Möbius and His Band: Mathematics and Astronomy in Nineteenth-Century Germany*, edited by J. Fauvel et al., 34–77. Oxford: Oxford University Press, 1993.

Drews, J., and H. Schwier, eds. *"Lilienthal oder die Astronomen": Historische Materialien zu einem Projekt Arno Schmidts*. Munich: edition text + kritik, 1984.

Forbes, E.G. *Tobias Mayer (1723–62): Pioneer of Enlightened Science in Germany*. Göttingen: Vandenhoeck and Ruprecht, 1980.

Gerdes, D. *Die Lilienthaler Sternwarte, 1781 bit 1818: Machinae Coelestes Lilienthalienses, Die Instrumente. Eine Zeitgeschichtliche Dokumentation*. Lilienthal: Heimatverein Lilienthal, 1991.

Hamel, J. *Friedrich Wilhelm Bessel*. Leipzig: BSB B.G. Teubner, 1984.

Hearnshaw, J.B. *The Analysis of Starlight: One Hundred and Fifty Years of Astronomical Spectroscopy*. Cambridge: Cambridge University Press, 1990.

Herrmann, D.B. "Das Astronomentreffen im Jahre 1798 auf dem Seeberg bei Gotha." *Archive for History of Exact Sciences* 6 (1969–1970): 326–344.

———. *History of Astronomy from Herschel to Hertzsprung*. Cambridge: Cambridge University Press, 1984.

Jackisch, G. *Johann Heinrich Lamberts "Cosmologische Briefe": Mit Beitragen zur Frügeschichte der Kosmologie*. Berlin: Akademie-Verlag, 1979.

Jaki, S.L. *Olbers Studies, with Three Unpublished Manuscripts by Olbers*. Tucson: Pachart, 1991.

Meinel, C. *Karl Friedrich Zöllner und die Wissenschaftskultur der Gründerzeit: Eine Fallstudie zur Genese Konservativer Zivilisationskritik*. Berlin: Sigma, 1991.

Merzback, U., comp. *Carl Friedrich Gauss: A Bibliography*. Wilmington, Del.: Scholarly Resources, 1984.

Paul, E.R. *The Milky Way Galaxy and Statistical Cosmology, 1890–1924*. Cambridge: Cambridge University Press, 1993.

Sang, H.-P. *Joseph von Fraunhofer: Forscher, Erfinder, Unternehmer*. Munich: Glas, 1987.

Schiebinger, L. "Maria Winkelmann at the Berlin Academy: A Turning Point for Women in Science." *Isis* 78 (1987): 174–200.

Zinner, E. *Geschichte der Sternkunde.* Berlin: Julius Springer, 1931.

Gill, David (1843–1914)

British astronomer and science administrator. Born in Scotland, David Gill trained as a clockmaker. He worked in his father's shop until 1872, when he accepted an invitation to plan and direct Lord Lindsay's private Dun Echt Observatory. After mastering the **heliometer**, he used it to determine the **solar parallax** with great accuracy from the diurnal shift of the position of minor planets and Mars. In 1879, Gill was named director of the Royal Observatory at the Cape of Good Hope. During his tenure, he transformed the dilapidated facility into an internationally respected research institution.

Gill is best known for his contributions to astronomical photography. A photograph he took of Comet 1882b showed background stars with sufficient clarity to suggest to him the value of photography to positional astronomy. He promoted this view, garnering support in the international astronomical community for two large-scale, collaborative photographic projects. In 1885, Gill began work on the *Cape Photographic Durchmusterung*, a catalogue of nearly a half-million stars in the southern sky, partially funded by the Royal Society and produced collaboratively with the Dutch astronomer **Jacobus C. Kapteyn**. That project's success encouraged Gill to solicit cooperation from observatories around the world to produce a photographic map of the entire sky, the *Carte du Ciel*. Although the methods used to produce this map were superseded during the more than seventy years it took to complete, it still stands as a monument to Gill's vision and the power of international scientific collaboration.

Barbara J. Becker

Bibliography

Brück, H.A. "Lord Crawford's Observatory at Dun Echt 1872–1892." *Vistas in Astronomy* 35 (1992): 81–138.

Evans, D.S. "Astronomical Institutions in the Southern Hemisphere: 1850–1950." In *Astrophysics and Twentieth-Century Astronomy to 1950: Part A*, edited by O. Gingerich. *The General History of Astronomy,* vol. 4, 153–165. Cambridge: Cambridge University Press, 1984.

Forbes, G. *David Gill, Man and Astronomer.* London: J. Murray, 1916.

Gill, D. *A History and Description of the Royal Observatory, Cape of Good Hope.* Edinburgh: Neill, 1913.

Lankford, J. "The Impact of Photography on Astronomy." In *Astrophysics and Twentieth-Century Astronomy to 1950: Part A*, edited by O. Gingerich. *The General History of Astronomy,* vol. 4, 16–39. Cambridge: Cambridge University Press, 1984.

Globes, Celestial

A Celestial globe is a sphere on which a map of the heavens is drawn, engraved, or pasted. Because it is a model of the firmament as seen from an external point, rather than from a geocentric point, the **constellation** figures were traditionally represented from the back side, as if they turned their faces toward the earth. In order for the globe to spin on its axis, the sphere was often held in a brass meridian ring, which was adjustable for the user's latitude within a wooden stand. The top of the stand served as the horizon circle, and a printed calendar and wind rose were pasted to it. Near the north pole of the meridian ring, there usually was an hour circle whose pointer turned as the globe revolved. Until the nineteenth century, celestial and terrestrial globes were always sold as a pair. In pocket globes, a seventeenth-century invention, the celestial hemispheres were projected on the concave interior of the spherical leather case that held the small terrestrial globe.

Celestial globes were used to represent the constellations without the distortions found on flat maps. They enabled graphical solutions to some basic problems of positional astronomy—for example, the relationship of the stars to the horizon, meridian, or ecliptic at a given time. As scientific instruments, they may have been less useful than maps, which were cheaper, more frequently updated, and could be drawn on a larger scale. As teaching tools, however, globes excelled. There is evidence that they were exhibited in public places and employed in schools as early as the third century B.C.E. In the early modern period, they were also used to educate navigators, and hundreds of manuals on the globes have been published since the sixteenth century. Globes, moreover, were valued initially by the wealthy because of their costliness and beauty. As costs came down, they served as icons of learning among merchants who wished to give evidence of their breeding and education.

The earliest extant celestial globe is that borne on the shoulders of the Farnese Atlas (a

Celestial Globe by Gerard Mercator, Louvain, 1551 (A-255). (Courtesy of the Adler Planetarium, Chicago, Illinois)

Roman statue currently preserved in the Museo Archeologico Nazionale in Naples), but more than five centuries earlier, Eudoxus of Cnidus possessed and described a globe. His instrument delineated the starry sky along with the principal celestial circles—the equator, tropics, arctic (ever-visible) circles, ecliptic, zodiac, and colures. Although his works have been lost, his globe made an impact. Aratus of Soli and Hipparchus were among those who commented on it, and the classical constellation figures have been only slightly modified since his time.

The exact nature of the Eudoxan globe is debated by scholars, who question, for instance, whether early globes were mounted in meridian and horizon rings, as was the case by Ptolemy's day. In the *Almagest*, Ptolemy offered advice on the making of a celestial globe. He recommended a dark background with yellow star points of a size commensurate with stellar magnitude. In contrast to the style of Eudoxus and his followers, Ptolemy dimly drew constellation figures so as not to take away from the stars.

Celestial globes were made very early in the Islamic world and entered Europe through Arabic channels in the Middle Ages. China had its own tradition of celestial globe production, dating back to about the fifth century C.E.

Nuremberg was the first center of globe production in Europe. It was there that Johann Schöner founded the first workshop to mass produce globes from printed gores in the 1520s. Another Nuremberg maker was Georg Hartmann. In 1537 in Louvain, Gemma Frisius issued a celestial globe whose gores were engraved by his pupil, Gerard Mercator. Mercator published his own celestial globe in 1551, and set standards for other makers to follow.

By the end of the sixteenth century, Amsterdam was the most important center for the production and international distribution of globes. Principal makers included Jodocus

Hondius, Willem Jansz Blaeu, and members of their families. Hondius and Blaeu made use of the southern constellations observed by Pieter Dircksz Keyser and Frederik de Houtman during recent Dutch voyages around the Cape of Good Hope. Blaeu had formerly studied with **Tycho Brahe** at Hven, and he incorporated Tycho's observations on his celestial globes.

Competition among makers encouraged the production of up-to-date globes in the first half of the seventeenth century, but no new globes were produced in Amsterdam during the second half. Globe production moved beyond the Netherlands. The most famous non-Dutch maker was Vincenzo Coronelli of Venice. He constructed an immense pair of globes (each measuring 3.9 meters in diameter) for Louis XIV in 1683, and collected his globe gores in an atlas, *Libro dei globi* (1697). Other notable makers included Joseph Moxon, John Senex, George Adams, and the Cary family in England; Nicolas Bion and Charles-François Delamarche in France; Johann Gabriel Doppelmayr and J.G. Klinger's Kunsthandlung in Germany. By the late eighteenth century, every country possessed its own globe-makers, many of whom seldom shipped beyond their national borders.

A large amount has been written on the history and cultural context of celestial and terrestrial globes, treating them as scientific instruments, teaching tools, cartographic documents, and pieces of furniture. In general, this information is packaged in inventories of museum collections; exhibition catalogues; essays on individual makers, their workshops, or cartographic productions; and a few general works. The first worldwide inventory of globes was that published by Stevenson in 1921, and it remains a touchstone in globe research. Stevenson considered it only a preliminary study, and since the early 1950s, the Internationale Coronelli-Gesellschaft für Globen- und Instrumentenkunde and others have been promoting the preparation of globe inventories by country. These inventories—which have been published in the society's journal, *Der Globusfreund*—briefly list each globe's maker or publisher, diameter, date, type (that is, terrestrial or celestial), and location. Other catalogues describe not only the sphere but also the mounting, and these have been published independently for Dutch collections, Bavarian collections, and the globes of Blaeu and Coronelli in Italy. American globes—both made in America and foreign globes held in U.S. collections—have not been so fully treated, but Warner has helped to make a start by alphabetically listing American makers along with brief biographical notes and references to their globes. The journal *Imago Mundi* contains many relevant discussions as well.

Among the numerous inventories, two deserve special mention for the study of celestial globes. One is Warner's catalogue of celestial cartographers, which provides detailed descriptions of a few important globe gores; the other is Savage-Smith's catalogue of Islamicate celestial globes, which uses that work as a springboard to examine differences in Western and Eastern traditions of globe-making. She shows, for example, that when Islamicate globes delineated the constellations, human figures faced outward with their backs turned toward a geocentric observer, in contrast to the figures on Greco-Roman and Byzantine globes. This raises a fascinating question pertinent to the way people in different cultures saw their relationship to nature: For whom were the constellations created, God or humanity?

Although Savage-Smith does not pose this question, a number of historians in recent years have begun to use celestial globes as vehicles to explore similar questions relevant to our understanding the social and cultural contexts of science. They have looked, for instance, at the way newly observed stars were formed into political constellations in order to flatter the cartographers' patrons, or how celestial globes were used allegorically in Elizabethan pageantry and portraiture to convey ideas about the English monarch's spiritual domain and imperial destiny. Others have focused their attention on the marketing strategies of globe-makers and the manifold ways globes were used by different target audiences, including men and women, schoolchildren and courtiers.

Sara Schechner Genuth

Bibliography

Dekker, E., and P. van der Krogt. *Globes from the Western World*. London: Zwemmer, 1993.

Fauser, A. *Die Welt in Händen: Kurze Kulturgeschichte des Globus*. Stuttgart: Schuler Verlagsgesellschaft, 1967.

Krogt, P. van der. *Old Globes in the Netherlands: A Catalogue of Terrestrial and Celestial Globes Made Prior to 1850 and Preserved in Dutch Collections*. Translated by W. ten Haken. Utrecht: HES, 1984.

Muris, O., and G. Saarmann. *Der Globus im Wandel der Zeiten: Eine Geschichte der Globen*. Berlin: Columbus Verlag, 1961.
Needham, J., with W. Ling. *Science and Civilisation in China*. Vol. 3, *Mathematics and the Sciences of the Heavens and the Earth*. Cambridge: Cambridge University Press, 1959.
Savage-Smith, E. *Islamicate Celestial Globes: Their History, Construction, and Use.* Washington, D.C.: Smithsonian Institution Press, 1985.
Stevenson, E.L. *Terrestrial and Celestial Globes.* 2 vols. New Haven: Yale University Press for the Hispanic Society of America, 1921; New York: Johnson reprint, 1971.
Wallis, H. "The Use of Terrestrial and Celestial Globes in England." *Actes du XIe Congrès International d'Histoire des Sciences* 4: 204–212. Wroclaw: Ossolineum Maison d'Édition de l'Académie Polonaise des Sciences, 1968.
———. "The Place of Globes in English Education, 1600–1800." *Der Globusfreund* 25–27 (1978): 103–110.
Warner, D.J. *The Sky Explored: Celestial Cartography, 1500–1800*. New York: Alan R. Liss, 1979; reprint, Amsterdam: Theatrum Orbis Terrarum, 1979.
———. "The Geography of Heaven and Earth." *Rittenhouse* 2 (1987–1988): 14–32, 52–64, 88–104, 109–137.
Zögner, L., ed. *Die Welt in Händen: Globus und Karte als Modell von Erde und Raum.* Berlin: Staatsbibliothek Preußicher Kulturbesitz, 1989.

Goodricke, John (1764–1786)

English astronomer. Deaf and mute from infancy, Goodricke became an astronomer with assistance from his neighbor, Edward Pigott. Goodricke discovered the variability of the star beta Persei (Algol) and developed its precise period. With Pigott's encouragement, Goodricke advanced theories that the variability was due either to spots or to periodic eclipses by another object. His second theory was later validated. Goodricke also discovered that delta Cephei was a variable star, and, with Pigott, he determined a light curve for beta Lyrae. Goodricke died at the age of twenty-two.

Thomas R. Williams

Bibliography

Hoskin, M. "Goodricke, Pigott and the Quest for Variable Stars." *Journal for the History of Astronomy* 10 (1979): 23–41.

Great Britain, Astronomy in

Sixteenth-century England inherited a rich tradition in both theoretical and practical astronomy that extended unbroken back to the twelfth century, while the Venerable Bede's *Computatus* (ca. 700 C.E.) was the first astronomy book written by an Englishman. But the century after 1500 brought new activity in the science, largely because of fresh intellectual priorities. Instead of the astronomer's being a person who watched the sky, primarily for calendrical purposes, the sixteenth century presented him with new problems about the composition of space and the earth's place in it. Although the court of King Henry VIII (reigned 1509–1548) brought foreign mathematicians like Nicholas Kratzer and Thomas Gemini to England, it was the impact of Copernicanism that opened up new possibilities. One of England's first Copernicans was Robert Recorde.

Protestant England was openminded about the ideas of **Nicholas Copernicus**, and while figures like John Dee embedded their astronomical ideas within a matrix of occult philosophy, some of Dee's disciples considered astronomical matters in less esoteric terms. When Leonard Digges's *Prognostication Everlastinge* (1555) was posthumously reissued by his son Thomas in 1576, it contained the first summary of the Copernican system written in English; **Thomas Harriot**, also of the Dee-Digges circle, was an early convert to the heliocentric theory. This late-sixteenth-century circle, moreover, seems to have experimented with lenses and mirrors, and scholarly opinion has been hotly divided as to whether Thomas Digges invented a form of reflecting telescope about 1560.

In spite of the ambiguity of the evidence surrounding the Tudor reflecting telescopes, it is certain that both Harriot and the Welshman William Lower were independently observing the craters on the moon by around 1609–1610. Their telescopes seem to have been of the well-documented Dutch spyglass type, however, and while they observed some of the phenomena reported by **Galileo Galilei**, they did not seize upon and use them for Copernican polemical purposes, as did Galileo.

During the seventeenth century, astronomy in England (as was also the case in Italy, France, Germany, and Holland) radically changed in academic status. It shifted from being a conservative part of the *quadrivium*, the medieval curricular division of the four sciences of proportion (alongside arithmetic, geometry, and music), to being the rapidly developing discipline that spearheaded the Scientific Revolution. Not only did the new and predominantly Copernican astronomical system challenge the very nature of ancient intellectual authority, it often did so using new handicraft-based technologies that provided a fresh class of evidence. Practical optics, mechanics, horology, and applied geometry produced the telescope, pendulum clock, micrometer, and precisely graduated instruments that revealed phenomena undetectable to the naked eye or unrefined senses. These instruments, some of which were invented and all of which were greatly improved in England, were fundamental in producing these major changes through which astronomy passed in the seventeenth century, for they provided new data about the heavens that the theoretician needed if astronomy was to become an inductive science.

Though professorships in astronomy and geometry were established in Gresham College, London, and Oxford University by the early seventeenth century, the Royal Observatory was founded at Greenwich in 1675, and the Royal Society actively encouraged astronomy after 1660, the overwhelming body of original research in the seventeenth century was conducted by private individuals holding no formal scientific positions. These men were not amateurs in the modern sense, however, for astronomy was much more than their hobby. As university-trained clergymen, lawyers, physicians, and gentlemen of leisure, they often possessed ample time and financial means to devote to science. Not all of them were wealthy, however, such as **Jeremiah Horrocks** in the 1630s, but if one possessed leisure, one could often improvise equipment that could still produce dramatic results if used in the right way.

The intellectual issue that dominated seventeenth-century astronomy was the dynamics of the solar system, and Jeremiah Horrocks made remarkable contributions that clearly defined and partially resolved many problems between 1635 and 1640. Working in rural Lancashire after leaving Cambridge without a degree, Horrocks displayed extraordinary talents as an observer, mathematician, and theoretician that effectively made him England's first astronomer of truly international standing. Collaborating with his local friends, **William Crabtree** and William Gascoigne, Horrocks demonstrated in 1637 that the moon follows a Keplerian, elliptical orbit around the earth. On November 24, 1639, he observed a transit of Venus across the sun's disk that he had predicted, and then went on to interpret his data in an aggressively pro-Copernican-Galilean manner. From it he drew conclusions about the size of the solar system, and the invisible force that held it together. Parts of Horrocks's work were first published by **Hevelius** in Danzig in 1662, while his achievements openly inspired Robert Hooke, John Wallis, and Isaac Newton, early members of the Royal Society. Horrocks's friend William Gascoigne, working in his Yorkshire manor house, also invented the telescopic reticular sight (eyepiece crosshairs), and the filar micrometer. Galilean ideas were also popularized by John Wilkins of Oxford, whose *Discovery of a New World in the Moone* (1638) was the first book in English to discuss the consequences of the earth's being a planetary body, while the second edition of his work (1640) contained one of the earliest discussions of possible space travel by means of mechanically powered vehicles.

Wilkins, as one of the formative influences on the early Royal Society, inevitably saw astronomy as taking a leading role in the society's program for the experimental investigation of nature. Seth Ward, John Wallis, and the young Christopher Wren were its early astronomical protégés, though the most influential of their number was Robert Hooke. As professor of astronomy at Gresham College, Hooke was active in all branches of astronomy. He strove to improve the quality of telescopes, popularized Gascoigne's filar micrometer as a way of measuring angles in the telescope field, and devised a zenith sector in 1669 with which he tried, unsuccessfully, to demonstrate the earth's motion in space by detecting a **stellar parallax**.

Optics and telescope improvement was a subject of great concern to the early Fellows of the Royal Society, and it was in this area of investigation that Isaac Newton first came to prominence, when he presented his prototype Newtonian reflector to the Royal Society in 1671. Though James Gregory had proposed a reflecting telescope in 1663, he had been unable to obtain a mirror of adequate quality to make the device work. But Newton, who was also a skilled craftsman in his own right, produced an instrument with a 1-inch diameter mirror of six inches focal length that gave an excellent image.

Newton's work on telescope design was in many ways an applied science offshoot from his investigations into the nature of light, made with a prism in the late 1660s, though not to be fully discussed until his *Opticks* in

1704. But Newton's most celebrated achievement lay in planetary dynamics. Working spasmodically on the problem from the mid 1660s and guided by Kepler's laws of planetary motion, Newton came to realize (after Kepler and Horrocks) that the force that caused objects to fall on earth was the same as that which produced the elliptical orbit of the moon and planets and that it was capable of precise mathematical expression. His laws of universal gravitation, presented to the Royal Society and published in *Principia Mathematica* (1687), was one of the great achievements of the human mind, and created a mathematical model for the explanation of all subsequent problems in dynamics. It also ensured the status of astronomy as the model or guide to the other sciences.

If planetary dynamics (followed closely by optics and the nature of light) was the principal intellectual concern of seventeenth-century astronomy, one must not forget that several more practical agendas were also present. The production of instruments of ever-increasing accuracy based upon the precise graduation of the circle was one of them, and saw the rise of a major instrument-making trade in London. Craftsmen like Thomas Tompion and his successor, George Graham, were fundamental in creating that crucial relationship between a scientific problem and a body of intelligent artisans who were capable of not only understanding the problem but also developing instruments with which to push back technical barriers and obtain better data. This problem-solving technology, which in the twentieth century lies at the heart of all the sciences, began in the astronomical community of late seventeenth-century London.

Nowhere was this concern for physical accuracy more clearly displayed than in the founding of the Royal Observatory, Greenwich, by King Charles II in 1675. The observatory was faced with the very practical problems of improving the determination of ships' longitudes at sea by the use of high-quality land-based tables of the moon and stars. **John Flamsteed**, as the first person to hold the office of Astonomer Royal, used the services of Abraham Sharp and other instrument-makers to develop a 7-foot equatorial sextant and a mural arc, both of which were divided to new levels of precision, while his micrometers (after Gascoigne and Hooke) and pendulum clocks made it possible for Greenwich to make the most precise angular measurements in the world by 1690. The Royal Observatory, moreover, was the only state-funded astronomical enterprise of seventeenth-century England, and though Flamsteed had to buy his own instruments, the observatory became one of the world's great standards of astronomical accuracy for the next three centuries, and was used after 1884 to define the Prime Meridian of the world and Greenwich Mean Time.

In many respects, eighteenth-century astronomy was concerned with working out and demonstrating Newtonian gravitation. **Edmond Halley**, who had encouraged Newton to write *Principia*, demonstrated the application of Newton's laws to comets in 1705. Halley's protégé James Bradley, in his discovery of the aberration (1728) of the list and nutation (1748), further demonstrated the observed cogency of gravitation theory. As Astronomer Royal (1720–1742), Halley reequipped the Royal Observatory with instruments by George Graham as a way of investigating the Newtonian lunar orbit, while in 1774 his successor, Nevil Maskelyne, weighed the Scottish mountain Schehallion by observing the mountain's attraction on a fine plumbline when compared with the position of a zenith star as seen in the field of a zenith sector. Upon finding that the earth was 4.5 times more dense than water (the actual figure is 5.5), astronomers were able to extract the respective masses of other solar system bodies.

London was the undisputed international center of precision instrument manufacture throughout the eighteenth century. Mathematical instrument makers like George Graham, John Bird, Jonathan Sisson, Jesse Ramsden, and Edward Troughton became famous across the world, as did the Gregorian reflecting telescope-maker James Short. In 1758, John Dollond senior succeeded in developing the achromatic lens for refracting telescopes, related to theoretical postulates contained in Newton's *Opticks*, thus transforming the history of the telescope. All of these craftsmen, moreover, enjoyed the complete respect of the scientific community, while Graham, Ramsden, and Troughton received its highest accolade, by being elected Fellows of the Royal Society. A century-long official concern with precision, moreover, led to two methods of finding the longitude at sea being made available by 1775, with John Harrison's chronometer and Tobias Mayer's lunar tables, which tables themselves had been compiled with the aid of a Bird quadrant at Mayer's Göttingen Observatory.

But in the last thirty years of the eighteenth century, a shift away from the intellectual and practical dominance of planetary dynamics took place in England, when **William Herschel** began to gauge the Milky Way and initiate the first systematic concern with observational deep-space astronomy. Using superb reflecting telescopes of his own design and manufacture, this Hanoverian musician who settled in England was regularly counting stars to create the first concept of a galaxy by 1785, though, unbeknown to Herschel, Thomas Wright (1711–1786) had spoken of the disklike nature of the Milky Way in 1755. Herschel's career was greatly enhanced in 1781, when he chanced upon a suspected comet that turned out to be a new planet, Uranus. This discovery won Herschel international fame and royal patronage.

In his brilliantly creative decade, 1782–1792, William Herschel laid the foundations of modern cosmology. In particular, his study of the relationship between stars and nebulae as physical systems that probably acted under gravitational influence led to space being regarded as dynamic and not static. But because Herschel possessed no research tools beyond a mirror and an eye, he inevitably ran up against barriers imposed by these limited investigative techniques. By the time of his death in 1822, he had come to ask many questions of his deep-space data that would constitute an agenda for **stellar statistics** and cosmology in the nineteenth and twentieth centuries. During the most important years of his career, William Herschel was assisted by his sister, Caroline Lucretia. Though this cooperation continued after William's marriage in 1788, Caroline came to establish an independent astronomical career of her own, as an observer, an authority on comets, and a mathematician who corrected many errors in Flamsteed's *Historia Coelestis Britannica* (1725), which was still one of the most comprehensive astrometric catalogues available. Caroline Herschel became one of the first women scientists to be formally honored when, in 1828, she received the Gold Medal of the Royal Astronomical Society, and in 1835 was elected an honorary member of the same society.

William Herschel's son, John Frederick William, took up his father's and aunt Caroline's work in 1816, first resurveying the Northern Hemisphere and then extending his father's sweeps to the nebula-rich southern skies between 1834 and 1838. John Herschel also made painstaking surveys of the Orion nebula and the Magellanic Clouds, looking for changes. Only after 1845, when William Parsons, Third Earl of Rosse (1811–1867), built a reflecting telescope with a 72-inch-diameter mirror at Birr Castle in Ireland, was it finally possible to see structure in certain nebulae, such as M51, and detect the spiral arms. Visual observers were never able to demonstrate conclusively changes in nebulae.

The intellectual issues that dominated nineteenth-century British astronomy were almost all of a kind that could be resolved only through improvements in instrumentation. High-precision astrometry to investigate the orbital elements of binary stars, as performed by John Herschel, James South, and Admiral William Henry Smyth, needed fine equatorial refractors similar to those being used by **Friedrich Georg Wilhelm Struve** and **Friedrich Wilhelm Bessel** in Germany. Similarly, the work of William Lassell into the surface details, rings, and satellites of the outer planets demanded the light grasp of large, equatorially mounted reflecting telescopes. Indeed, Lassell, a Liverpool brewer by profession, was the first person to successfully mount large reflecting telescopes (of 24- and 48-inch apertures) on equatorial mounts, and work with them in prime sky locations in Malta, away from the poor skies of England.

But the predominant issue in nineteenth-century astronomy was still the Herschelian one about the matter that occupied deep space. Lord Rosse's telescope, showing as it did the structure of certain nebulae, raised the question about the Laplacian model of the origin of star systems, and interpreters of astronomical data like John Herschel and John Pringle Nichol of Edinburgh discussed the possible nature of star and nebula formation and the existence of gas in deep space. Only when the spectroscope came of age as an astronomical tool in the 1860s, however, was it possible to establish the chemical and physical characteristics of stars and nebulae with a modicum of certainty. **William Huggins**, and after 1875 his wife, Margaret Lindsay Murray, working from their private observatory at Tulse Hill, South London, finally established the presence of gases in the spectra of stars and nebulae, and over the last thirty years of the century photographed and published the spectral characteristics of numerous stellar and nebulous objects.

Pure research in British astronomy in the Victorian age was performed almost entirely by grand amateurs: people of means and education, who had the time and resources to identify problems, commission specialist instruments, and use them effectively. Professional astronomy, by contrast, was more restricted in character, and largely confined to official observatories that performed astrometric, timekeeping, and navigation work for the Admiralty. Oxford, Cambridge, Durham, Edinburgh, and Dublin universities possessed observatories that were under the direction of astronomy professors, and while **George Biddell Airy** transformed the Royal Observatory at Greenwich after 1835, it was only to turn it into a more efficient institution. When John Couch Adams, after one of the most spectacular private investigations in planetary dynamics ever made, approached James Challis of the Cambridge University Observatory and Airy at Greenwich in 1845, to look for his computed Planet X, they were unable to do so due to the pressure of routine commitments. In consequence, Neptune was discovered in Berlin in 1846 on the quite separate computations of the Frenchman **Urbain Jean Joseph Le Verrier**.

Ireland possessed two well-equipped astrometric observatories by the early nineteenth century, both of which were near Dublin, at Armagh and Dunsink. Edinburgh's observatory was given the designation Royal in 1822 by King George IV, though it never had the official meridian functions of Greenwich. In the nineteenth century, both Ireland (which until 1922 was a part of Britain) and Scotland had their own Astronomers Royal, who generally held professorial appointments at Dublin and Edinburgh universities. These titles were largely honorary, however, and did not carry the official functions of the Astronomer Royal at Greenwich. Two of their most distinguished holders were **Charles Piazzi Smyth** in Edinburgh and Robert Stawell Ball in Ireland.

When the Royal Astronomical Society was founded in 1820, most serious astronomers in Britain were not paid for their work, though by 1890, when the British Astronomical Association was founded specifically for the membership of amateur astronomers, a distinct body of professional academic astronomers had come into being. These people, generally holding university posts, came to dominate astronomy in the twentieth century, as the escalating cost of instrumentation, and the necessity for a doctoral-level training as a prelude to research redefined the structure of British astronomy. But the British Astronomical Association received much of its early direction from a professional astronomer. This was Annie Russell Maunder, a mathematics graduate of Girton College, Cambridge, who was obliged to resign from her Royal Observatory post upon her marriage to the astronomer Edwin Walter Maunder. Over the next few decades, she, and sometimes her husband, traveled to many countries to photograph eclipses and conduct independent research into solar physics.

Spectroscopy, photography, relativistic physics, and cosmology formed the primary intellectual concerns in the twentieth century, though after 1945 the emerging science of radio astronomy gave a new lease on life to fundamental research in Britain, being unaffected by cloudy skies. Building on the breakthroughs made in radar and radio during World War II, astronomers at Cambridge and Manchester universities pioneered the new science, with Martin Ryle at Cambridge and Alfred Charles Bernard Lovell at Manchester. The 250-foot steerable radio dish at Jodrell Bank, Manchester (1957), long remained the largest in the world, and constant upgrading has kept it in the forefront. Apart from its early work as a satellite-tracking instrument, the Jodrell Bank telescope pioneered the development of interferometry, making it possible for radio astronomers to work closely with their visual colleagues to detect radio sources in complex regions such as nebulae and star fields.

Cosmology has also been spearheaded in Britain, especially since the 1940s, and in 1948 an alternative model to the Big Bang theory of the universe was proposed by Herman Bondi and others at a special Royal Astronomical Society meeting held in Edinburgh. This was the Steady State theory. Though no longer accepted today, the theory played a significant part in modern cosmological thought.

Astronomy, cosmology, and their related branches of physics are now researched in many British universities, most notably at Cambridge, Durham, Manchester, Edinburgh, London, Oxford, Sussex, and Cardiff. Very little professional optical astronomy has been performed in Britain since the 98-inch Isaac Newton reflector was taken from the Royal Greenwich Observatory to La Palma in the 1980s, as astronomers now use hardware in prime-sky locations around the world. Yet in spite of the increasingly international character of the science, the creativity of the British astronomical community is undiminished.

It nonetheless caused uproar when in 1986 the Conservative government reduced funding to the Royal Greenwich Observatory and sold Herstmonceux Castle, Sussex, to which the Royal Observatory had been moved during World War II. The much-reduced Royal Greenwich Observatory now operates on the same site as the Institute of Astronomy of Cambridge University. Active visual observation in Britain is almost entirely in the hands of a large and well-equipped body of dedicated amateurs. Patrick Moore has played a major role in stimulating amateur astronomy in Britain since the 1950s, and it is fitting that in a country where they took the research initiative for three centuries, amateur astronomers, in their monitoring of double stars, deep-sky, planetary, and other branches of the science, work closely with and are valued by the professional establishment.

No single scholarly study that sets out to examine the changing priorities of British astronomy over the last five hundred years has been produced, and historiographical interpretation has been focused instead upon the work of particular individuals, institutions, or localized research projects. Yet two studies which themselves are classics in the writing of astronomical history are those of Robert Grant and Agnes Mary Clerke.

One general trend, however, has been the move away from technical narrative accounts to historical studies that attempt to place a scientist's or an institution's work into a wider context of social, financial, and administrative processes. Yet the historiography of British astronomy has long contained polemical components, for when John Flamsteed, the first Astronomer Royal, wrote his account of the early years of the Royal Observatory, Greenwich, around 1715, he built into it attacks on the work, character, and motives of Newton and Halley that are invaluable to the modern historian who tries to comprehend the complex relations existing in the scientific community of the late seventeenth century.

Another marked trend, especially over the last century, has been a move away from reverential or eulogistic histories that often focused upon the greatness of particular individuals. Jeremiah Horrocks has been one of the most consistently eulogized individuals in British astronomy, for in the wake of Jeremy Shakerley's praises of 1649, no single century has passed without reverential publications appearing on Horrocks. Not only were Horrocks's very substantial contributions to planetary dynamics important, but also the facts that his career was brief, financially constrained, and that he died at twenty-two. The Victorians especially were fond of heroizing Horrocks as a martyr of science.

Isaac Newton, likewise, has been the subject of consistently reverential studies, in which it was often felt that a man of such genius must also be an exemplar of virtue and moral rectitude. David Brewster's classic biography of 1855 is redolent of this approach, though modern scholarship has been less value-laden and more critical, as in the case of the current standard biography by Richard S. Westfall. Modern studies of Newton, moreover, have concentrated more attention upon his extra-astronomical activities, such as his psychological makeup (as in the study of Frank Manuel) and his involvement in contemporary politics. Lesley Murdin has examined the careers of those astronomers who fell under Newton's shadow.

Two significant early biographical studies of astronomers are those of John Flamsteed and James Bradley, by respectively, Francis Baily (1835) and Stephen Peter Rigaud (1832). William Herschel has received a considerable amount of scholarly attention in recent years from Michael Hoskin, Angus Armitage, and other scholars, while Herschel's son, John Frederick William, after a long period of neglect, became the subject of a good popular biography by Gunther Buttmann and a Royal Society conference in his bicentenary year, 1992, and a volume of essays edited by Desmond King-Hele. There are still major gaps in the critical biography of British astronomers, though Allan Chapman is working on a biography of G.B. Airy.

In 1975, the tercentenary of the foundation of the Royal Observatory, Greenwich, stimulated much fundamental research into the history of that institution, and three major publications, by Derek Howse, A.J. Meadows, and Eric Forbes, were produced. Their work, and that of subsequent scholars, has gone a long way in reevaluating the interrelationship existing between official science and motives of the governments who finance it, and the relation of both to the world of grand amateur astronomers. The two histories of the Royal Astronomical Society by **Johann Louis Emil Dreyer** and Roger John Tayler et al., which cover between them the period 1820 to 1980, contain a wealth of detailed narrative, and some interpretation, of how high-level and increasingly professional astronomy worked within a major learned society. The autobiography of A.C.B. Lovell conveniently combines both a personal and an institutional history of a pioneer radio astronomer in his institutional and cultural context.

The studies of Hermann Brück and James Bennett have provided a sound scholarly context for understanding the development of observatories in Scotland and Ireland, respectively.

One very important branch of the historiography of British astronomy is also to be found in the history of scientific instruments and the trade that manufactured them. The relationship between technological innovation, discovery, business, and patronage in astronomy has been examined by Derek Howse, James Bennett, Anita McConnell, Allan Chapman, and others.

The historiography of five centuries of British astronomy has inevitably reflected changes in how historians have viewed the subject, from a primary concern with narrative, or genius, to an attempt to understand the science in conjunction with wider intellectual, technical, and social factors.

There are several large deposits of astronomical manuscripts in Britain. Cambridge University Library has perhaps the largest, and now contains the entire archive of the former Royal Greenwich Observatory, while the Royal Society and Royal Astronomical Society and Royal Observatory, Edinburgh, possess extensive holdings. There are also major holdings in Oxford University's Museum of the History of Science, while some archives are still preserved close to their original locations, as is the case with the Joseph Norman Lockyer archive, now lodged in Exeter University, and Lord Rosse's papers, which are still in private hands but easily accessible to scholars at Birr Castle, in Ireland. These archives tend to be used primarily, though, for the production of books and papers possessing very specific foci, and, considering the specialized character of modern research, it is unlikely that a single history of British astronomy covering several centuries in its scope will be produced in the near future.

Allan Chapman

Bibliography

Armitage, A. *William Herschel.* London: Thomas Nelson and Sons, 1962.

Bailly, F. *An Account of the Reverend John Flamsteed.* London, 1835.

Bennett, J.A. "On the Power of Penetrating into Space: The Telescopes of William Herschel." *Journal for the History of Astronomy* 7 (1976): 75–108.

———. *Church, State, and Astronomy in Ireland: 200 Years of the Armagh Observatory.* Belfast: Armagh Observatory with the Institute of Irish Studies, 1990.

Brück, H.A. *The Story of Astronomy in Edinburgh.* Edinburgh: Edinburgh University Press, 1983.

———. "Lord Crawford's Observatory at Dun Echt." *Vistas in Astronomy* 35 (1992): 81–138.

Brück, M.T. "Ellen and Agnes Clerke of Skibbereen, Scholars and Writers." *Seanchas Chairbre* 13 (1993): 22–43.

Chapman, A. "William Lassell (1799–1880): Practitioner, Patron and 'Grand Amateur' of Victorian Astronomy." *Vistas in Astronomy* 32 (1988): 341–370.

———. *Dividing the Circle: The Development of Critical Angular Measurement in Astronomy, 1500–1850.* New York: Ellis Horwood, Chichester, and Simon and Schuster, 1990.

———. "Jeremiah Horrocks, the Transit of Venus, and the 'New Astronomy' in Early Seventeenth-Century England." *Quarterly Journal of the Royal Astronomical Society* 31 (1990): 333–357.

Clerke, A.M. *A Popular History of Astronomy during the Nineteenth Century.* London: Adam and Black, 1885.

Dreyer, J.L.E. *History of the Royal Astronomical Society 1820–1920.* London: Royal Astronomical Society, 1923.

Flamsteed, J. *The 'Preface' to John Flamsteed's 'Historia Coelestis Britannica' of 1725.* Edited by A. Chapman, based on a translation by D. Johnson. *National Maritime Museum Monograph* 52. London, 1982.

Forbes, E. *Greenwich Observatory, I: Origins and Early History, 1675–1835.* London: Taylor and Francis, 1975.

Gingerich, O. *Astrophysics and Twentieth-Century Astronomy to 1950,* Part A. New York: Cambridge University Press, 1984.

Grant, R. *A History of Physical Astronomy.* London, 1852.

Hoskin, M.A. *William Herschel and the Construction of the Heavens.* London: Oldbourne, 1963.

Howse, D. *Greenwich Observatory, III: The Buildings and Instruments.* London: Taylor and Francis, 1975.

———. *Greenwich Time and the Discovery of the Longitude.* Oxford: Oxford University Press, 1980.

Hunter, M., and S. Schaffer. *Robert Hooke, New Studies.* Woodbridge: Boydell Press, 1989.

Kelly, H.L., ed. The *British Astronomical Association: The First Fifty Years.* London: British Astronomical Association, 1948.

King-Hele, D.G., ed. *John Herschel (1792–1871): A Bicentennial Celebration*. London: Royal Society, 1992.

Lovell, A.C.B. *Astronomer by Chance*. London: Macmillan, 1991.

McConnell, A. *Instrument Makers to the World: A History of Cook, Troughton and Simms*. York: William Sessions, 1992.

McLean, A. *Humanism and the Rise of Science in Tudor England*. London: Heinemann, 1972.

Meadows, A.J. *Greenwich Observatory, I: Recent History, 1836–1975*. London: Taylor and Francis, 1975.

Moore, P. *The Astronomy of Birr Castle*. Birr, Ireland: Tribune Press, 1971.

———. *Caroline Herschel: Reflected Glory*. Bath: William Herschel Society, 1988.

Murdin, L. *Under Newton's Shadow: Astronomical Practices in the Seventeeth Century*. Bristol and Boston: Adam Hilger, 1985.

Murray, C.A. 'The Distance of the Stars.' *The Observatory* 108 (1988): 199–217.

Ronan, C.A., et al. "Was There a Tudor Telescope?" *Bulletin of the Scientific Instruments Society* 37 (1993): 2–10.

Rigaud, S.P. *The Miscellaneous Works of the Reverend James Bradley*. Oxford: Oxford University Press, 1832.

Tayler, R.J. *History of the Royal Astronomical Society 1920–1980*. Oxford: Blackwells, for the Royal Astronomical Society, 1987.

Taylor, E.G.R. *The Mathematical Practitioners of Tudor and Stuart England*. Cambridge: Cambridge University Press, 1968.

———. *The Mathematical Practitioners of Hanoverian England*. Cambridge: Cambridge University Press, 1966.

Westfall, R.S. *Never at Rest. A Biography of Isaac Newton*. Cambridge: Cambridge University Press, 1980.

Wilkins, John. *Mathematical and Philosophical Works of John Wilkins*. London, 1802; reprint London: Frank Cass and Co., 1970.

Great Pyramid

There are about eighty pyramids known in Egypt, and the Great Pyramid at Giza is the largest of them. It is located about 7 miles southwest of central Cairo, on a desert plateau just west of the old course of the Nile. The pyramids were monumental tombs for the pharaohs of the Old Kingdom period (2650–2134 B.C.E.), and, because the ancient Egyptians associated the west and the setting of celestial objects with death, all of the pyramids were constructed on the west bank of the Nile.

Mortuary rituals were staged in temples constructed next to the pyramids. Many smaller tombs for high-ranking officials and aristocratic families accompany the pyramid complex at Giza and confirm that the entire area was an elite cemetery. The Great Pyramid was built by the Fourth Dynasty pharaoh Khufu. The pyramid of Khafre (or Rakhaef), who was one of Khufu's sons, and the pyramid of Menkaure, probably the son of Khafre, are just southwest of the Great Pyramid. The Great Sphinx, a massive outcrop sculpted in the shape of a crouching lion with a pharaoh's head, is just southeast of the Great Pyramid. As the vigilant guardian of the Giza necropolis, the Great Sphinx faces due east, the direction of sunrise and rebirth. In the New Kingdom period (1550–1070 B.C.E.), the Great Sphinx was associated with the rising sun and known as Horus-in-horizon.

The ancient name for the Great Pyramid has been translated as Horizon of Khufu, and the Egyptian word for horizon—*akhet*—links the Great Pyramid with the sun lodged on the skyline.

Egyptologist Mark Lehner has noted that the pyramids of Khufu and Khafre, when viewed from the vicinity of the Sphinx, or farther to the southeast, create the shape of the *akhet* and that the summer solstice sun sets between the two silhouetted peaks.

According to Egyptologist Zahi Hawass, Khufu restructured the Egyptian theocracy by declaring himself to be the living incarnation of Re, the sun god, and dismissing the priests of Heliopolis, the center of the cult of the sun. Hawass believes that the two boats that were buried on the south side of the Great Pyramid were intended to represent the boats on which the sun traveled—across the sky during the day and through the netherworld during the night.

Many pseudoscientific claims have been made for astronomical symbolism in the dimensions of the Great Pyramid and for astronomical function in its design. These are false, but the Great Pyramid does have some astronomical significance. It was planned and constructed with more care and refinement than any other pyramid, and its four sides are accurately aligned with the cardinal directions. The east side, which departs most from true cardinal alignment, is only 5½ arcminutes west of north. To the Old Kingdom Egyptians, the cardinal directions were the pillars

The north face of the Great Pyramid at Giza is cut open near the base to reveal the orihuban, the star closest to the north celestial pole at the time of the pyramid's construction. That circumpolar zone of the sky was one of the celestial spiritual destinies of the deceased pharaoh. (Courtesy of E.C. Krupp)

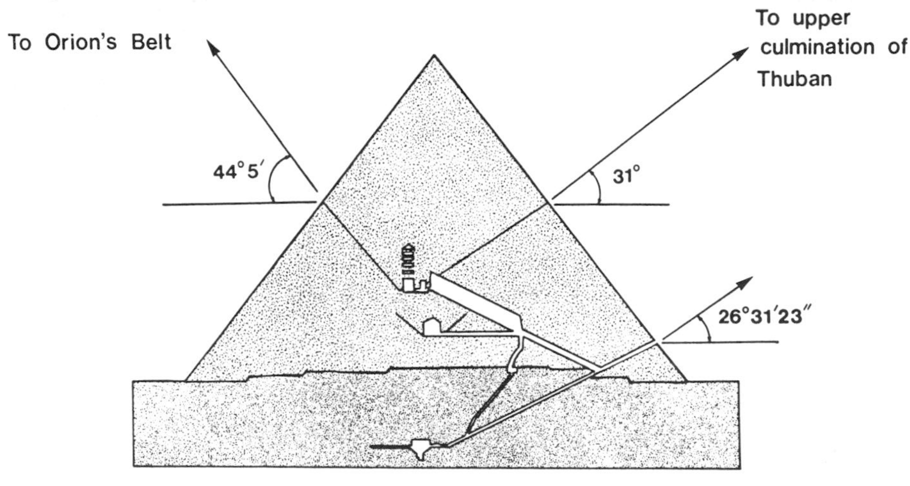

In section, the Great Pyramid of Giza reveals two shafts from the King's Chamber. The shaft on the south was angled in alignment with the transit of the Belt of Orion. The stars of Orion were regarded as the celestial incarnation of the god Osiris and were another destination on the dead pharaoh's itinerary to the sky. (Courtesy of the Griffith Observatory)

of the sky. They originate with the diurnal motion of the sky and order the landscape. By incorporating accurate cardinal orientation into the Great Pyramid, the Egyptians fortified its symbolic power with a principle of cosmic order.

The King's Chamber, deep within the Great Pyramid, is believed to have been the burial site of the dead pharaoh. It is reached, from the north side, via the Descending Corridor, the Ascending Corridor, and the Grand Gallery, which penetrate the interior at steep angles. It has been said that the Descending Corridor, which is inclined to the north at an angle of 26 degrees, 31 minutes, 23 seconds, was originally aligned with Thuban, the North Star at the time of construction of the Great Pyramid (about 2650 B.C.E.), but that is incorrect. There are, however, two other features within the Great Pyramid that probably were designed to have astronomical meaning. These are the two so-called air shafts that emerge at different angles from the north and south sides of the King's Chamber. Although the practical function of ventilation has been attributed to these narrow shafts, that makes little sense in terms of economy of construction and design. Egyptologist Alexander Badawy and astronomer Virginia Trimble have demonstrated that both shafts are well targeted on significant stars. The angle of the south shaft, 44 degrees, 5 minutes, corresponds to the transit of Orion's belt, and in fact aligns best with Alnilam, the belt's middle star in 2650 B.C.E. The upper culmination of Thuban, in Draco, matches the altitude angle, 31 degrees, of the north shaft. The funerary inscriptions, religious incantations, and magical spells carved upon the chamber walls of Fifth Dynasty (2465–2323 B.C.E.) pyramids and known as the *Pyramid Texts* identify the stars of Orion and the circumpolar stars as stellar destinations of the deceased pharaoh. Orion was the stellar embodiment of the god Osiris, who governed the resurrection of souls. Thuban was regarded as the leader of the circumpolar stars, which the Egyptians called imperishable and considered to be immortal.

Independent scholar John Charles Deaton argues that the play of light upon the smooth, white, triangular sides of the pyramid dramatized and activated the celestial ascent of the dead king. He notes that the names of several other pyramids indicate that the pyramid was equated with the luminous, airborne *ba*, or soul, of the deceased king.

Stellar connotations of the Great Pyramid imply that Khufu's tomb facilitated his spiritual transformation and the transfer of his soul to the realm of celestial power.

Edwin C. Krupp

Bibliography

Badawy, A. "The Stellar Destiny of Pharaoh and the So-Called Air-Shafts of Cheops' Pyramid." *Mitteilungen des Instituts für Orientforschung*, Band X (1964): 189–206.

Deaton, J.C. "The Old Kingdom Evidence for the Function of Pyramids." *Varia Aegyptiaca* 4 (1988): 193–200.

Hamblin, D.J. "A Unique Approach to Unraveling the Secrets of the Great Pyramids." *Smithsonian* 16, 1 (April, 1986): 78–93.

Hawass, Z. *The Funerary Establishments of Khufu, Khafra, and Menkaura* (Doctoral thesis, University Microfilms, Ann Arbor, Michigan). Philadelphia: University of Pennsylvania, 1987.

Krupp, E.C. *Echoes of the Ancient Skies*. New York: Harper and Row, 1983.

———, ed. *In Search of Ancient Astronomies.* Garden City, N.Y.: Doubleday, 1978.

———, ed. *Archaeoastronomy and the Roots of Science*. Boulder, Colo./Washington, D.C.: Westview Press/American Association for the Advancement of Science, 1984.

Lehner, M. "An Overview of the Complex at Giza." Lecture presented in program "Ancient Egypt: The Pyramid Age." Los Angeles: Los Angeles County Museum of Natural History, July 20, 1991.

Petrie, W.M.F. *The Pyramids and Temples of Gizeh (with an Update by Zahi Hawass)* [1883]. London: Histories and Mysteries of Man, 1990.

Trimble, V. "Astronomical Investigation concerning the So-Called Air-Shafts of Cheops' Pyramid." *Mitteilungen des Instituts für Orientforschung*, Band X (1964): 183–187.

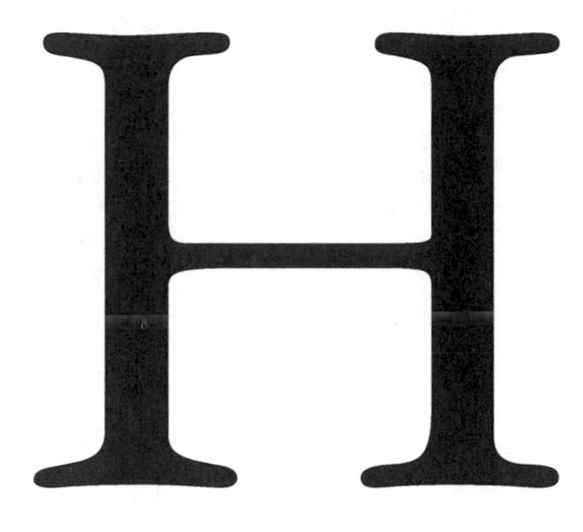

Hagihara, Yusuke (1897–1979)

Japanese celestial mechanician. Hagihara received his Ph.D. from the University of Tokyo in 1930, where he was already a member of the faculty. He remained there until his retirement in 1957. In 1946 he was appointed director of the Tokyo Astronomical Observatory, which had been destroyed during the war. He developed the observatory into a major center of astrophysical research. His own research was centered in celestial mechanics, especially perturbation theory and the stability of the solar system. His five-volume *Celestial Mechanics* is a survey of the field comparable to those that Laplace and Tisserand prepared for their eras.

LeRoy E. Doggett

Bibliography

Kozai, Y. "Yusuke Hagihara." *Quarterly Journal of the Royal Astronomical Society* 20 (1979): 325–328.

Hale, George Ellery (1868–1938)

As a Scientist

Almost all of Hale's original researches were in solar physics. Between 1890 and 1904, he invented the **spectroheliograph** for securing monochromatic images of the sun, investigated various techniques for detecting the corona without eclipse, and devised spectrographs suitable for making detailed comparative studies of solar and stellar spectra. Thereafter, Hale and his staff at the new Mount Wilson Solar Observatory built three solar telescopes with auxiliaries. Superbly equipped, they established the existence of strong magnetic fields in sunspots (1908) and the twenty-two-year cycle of solar magnetic activity (1924). They were unable, however, to build a compelling case for the claimed detection of the sun's general magnetic field. In his last years, Hale developed the **spectrohelioscope** for visual monitoring of chromospheric phenomena and helped create a cooperative global network devoted to that task.

Historians have generally approached Hale as a heroic figure in solar physics who, in the words of one colleague, "was the leader at all times . . . the driving force and inspiration" in Mount Wilson's early program of solar research (Adams, 623). Only one study—Hetherington—has paid more than cursory attention to Hale's interactions with his staff in the development of new observational claims about the sun or to the reception of these claims by the solar physics community. Investigation of these issues would provide interesting insights on Hale's and his community's scientific practices.

A gifted instrumentalist and organizer, Hale dramatically augmented solar observing capabilities and initiated research on solar magnetic phenomena. His relations with his colleagues and community need closer scrutiny.

Hale as a Statesman of Science

Together with Alexander Dallas Bache in the nineteenth century and Vannevar Bush in the mid-twentieth, Hale ranks as one of the great statesmen of American science. A builder of scientific and cultural institutions, Hale played a significant role in organizing American science to support World War I. The fruit of his wartime activities, the National Research Council, later became the operating arm of the National Academy of Sciences. Among his memorials are three major observatories, the premier journal in astrophysics, and the California Institute of Technology. Hale was perhaps the first leading American scientist to understand the importance of the new philanthropic foundations as patrons for pure research. Hale was also skilled in securing the financial support of individual philanthropists.

With financial support from his father, Hale established the Kenwood Physical Observatory (1891) soon after graduation from the Massachusetts Institute of Technology. By 1892 he was an associate professor at the new University of Chicago and would soon create the **Yerkes Observatory**, with its great 40-inch refractor, the largest operating instrument of its kind in the world. With support from the Carnegie Institution of Washington, Hale went on to establish the Mount Wilson Observatory in 1904. Soon it was equipped with the largest reflecting telescope in the world as well as a wide range of state-of-the-art instrumentation for research in solar physics and stellar spectroscopy. After retirement, Hale championed a 200-inch reflector and spent his later years securing funding and overseeing its construction.

Concerned with scientific and technical education on the West Coast, Hale, along with physicist Robert Millikan and chemist Arthur Noyes, transformed the Throop Polytechnic Institute in Pasadena into the California Institute of Technology. He was also active in the creation of the Huntington Library, where many of his papers are now deposited.

Hale played a principal role in building the infrastructure for the new science of astrophysics. It was Hale who effectively set the research agenda for observational astrophysics in the United States, an agenda not modified until the 1930s. With W.W. Payne he was co-editor of *Astronomy and Astrophysics* (1892–1895), with James E. Keeler founding co-editor of the *Astrophysical Journal* (1895), and the father of the International Union for Cooperation in Solar Research (1905). His deep commitment to cooperation in science eventuated in the International Research Council (later known as the International Council of Scientific Unions), as well as his participation in the revitalization of the National Academy of Sciences. Hale was one of the principal leaders in the construction of a permanent home for the academy in Washington, D.C.

George Ellery Hale was a man of enormous energy and enthusiasm, but often pushed beyond the physical and psychological limits of his constitution. Periods of great creativity were followed by long months of nervous exhaustion. Many of Hale's activities as a fundraiser and science organizer were carried out during times when he lacked the physical and emotional strength to continue scientific research. A deeper understanding of the rhythms and cycles of his life—that is, the ways he alternated scientific research with fundraising and institution-building—would be a valuable contribution. But even more important is the need for a full-scale biography of Hale that explores his scientific life and activities as a statesman of science, carefully located in the context of American culture and society, and in light of his own extraordinarily complex personality.

Karl Hufbauer
John Lankford

Bibliography

Adams, W.S. "Early Solar Research at Mount Wilson." *Vistas in Astronomy* 1 (1955): 619–623.

Goodstein, Judith R. *Millikan's School: A History of the California Institute of Technology.* New York: Norton, 1991.

Hetherington, N.S. "Adriaan van Maanen's Measurements of Solar Spectra for a General Magnetic Field." *Quarterly Journal of the Royal Astronomical Society* 16 (1975): 235–244.

Hufbauer, K. *Exploring the Sun: Solar Science since Galileo.* Baltimore: Johns Hopkins University Press, 1991.

Kevles, D.J. "George Ellery Hale, the First World War, and the Advancement of Science in America." *Isis* 59 (1968): 427–437.

Osterbrock, D.E. "Failure and Success: Two Early Experiments with Concave Gratings in Stellar Spectroscopy." *Journal for the History of Astronomy* 17 (1986): 119–129.

———. *Pauper & Prince: Ritchey, Hale & Big American Telescopes.* Tucson: University of Arizona Press, 1993.

Wright, H. *The Great Palomar Telescope.* London: Faber and Faber, 1953.

———. *Explorer of the Universe: A Biography of George Ellery Hale.* New York: Dutton, 1966.

Wright, H., J.N. Warnow, and C. Weiner,

eds. *The Legacy of George Ellery Hale: Evolution of Astronomy and Scientific Institutions in Pictures and Documents.* Cambridge: MIT Press, 1972.

Halley, Edmond (1656?–1743)

English mathematician and astronomer. Already a serious telescopic observer before entering Oxford in 1673, Edmond Halley pursued astronomy while a student there, communicating his observations to the Astronomer Royal, **John Flamsteed**. With Flamsteed's support, Halley—barely twenty years old—saw his first scientific paper, on determining a planet's orbital elements from observations, published in the Royal Society's *Philosophical Transactions*. He soon embarked on an ambitious expedition to map the southern sky and compiled his observations in *Catalogues Stellarum Australium* (1679), which extended existing star catalogues and won him both recognition from leading Continental astronomers and a place in the circle of such notable English mathematicians and scientists as Christopher Wren, Robert Hooke, and Isaac Newton.

By January 1684, Halley's interest in planetary orbits led him to investigate the nature of the force that determines their characteristic ellipticity. Equating Christian Huygens's expression for a centrally directed force with the harmonic ratio in Kepler's third law, Halley concluded that, whatever the physical cause of the force, its strength decreased in proportion to the square of the distance from the sun. Nearly five years earlier, Hooke had arrived at a similar conclusion and shared it with Newton. Although Newton considered the problem in some detail at that time, he revealed his thoughts only after an opportune visit from Halley in August 1684. Halley was so impressed with Newton's demonstration of the necessity of the inverse square force that he convinced Newton to make it public. Halley shepherded the resulting manuscript through the press, providing deft diplomacy during priority disputes, essential financial backing, expert editing, and favorable reviews when *Philosophiae Naturalis Principia Mathematica* finally appeared in print in 1687.

Recognizing the explanatory and predictive power of Newton's universal attractive force, Halley championed it as a basis for mathematical representation of observed planetary motion with far-reaching implications for both physical astronomy's emerging research agenda and cosmological theory. It informed his subsequent thinking about the behavior of all celestial bodies. Halley rejected the prevailing view that comets were random celestial phenomena in favor of including them in the family of bodies governed by the sun's gravitational attraction, and he successfully predicted the return of the comet that now bears his name. He also argued persuasively for an infinite universe on the grounds that a finite universe would possess a center toward which all matter would gravitate.

Halley pursued wide-ranging research interests throughout his long career: determining longitude at sea, measuring the solar parallax, studying variations in terrestrial magnetism, designing underwater diving apparatus, detecting the proper motion of stars, and speculating on the nature of nebulae. In 1720, he succeeded Flamsteed as Astronomer Royal. Finding the instruments and furnishings removed from the Greenwich Observatory by Flamsteed's executors, Halley obtained government support for their replacement. As Astronomer Royal, Halley concentrated on the problem of finding longitude at sea, resuming and refining his own interrupted program of lunar observations. He recorded the moon's position at numerous points in its orbit throughout one complete saros cycle, thus bolstering the confidence of his successors in the promise this method held for longitude determination.

Barbara J. Becker

Bibliography

Cotter, C.H. "Captain Edmond Halley, R.N., FRS." *Notes and Records of the Royal Society* 36 (1981): 61–77.

Freitag, R.S. *Halley's Comet: A Bibliography.* Washington, D.C.: Library of Congress, 1984.

Halley, E. *The Three Voyages of Edmond Halley in the Paramore 1698–1701.* 2 vols. Edited by N.J.W. Thrower. London: Hakluyt Society, 1981.

MacPike, E.F., ed. *Correspondence and Papers of Edmond Halley.* New York: Arno Press, 1975.

Ronan, C.A. *Edmond Halley: Genius in Eclipse.* Garden City, N.Y.: Doubleday, 1969.

Hansen, Peter Anderas (1795–1874)

German celestial mechanician. Trained in clock-making and self-educated in mathematics, Hansen became an assistant to the Danish astronomer Heinrich Christian Schumacher in 1820. In 1825 he became director of the private observatory of the Duke of Mecklenburg and retained that position until his death. Hansen's most important work was in planetary theory and lunar theory. His lunar theory set a standard for accuracy in the mid nineteenth century. In addition, Hansen worked on the theory of asteroid and comet orbits. His skill with instruments led to advances in the theory and use of heliometers and transit instruments.

LeRoy E. Doggett

Bibliography

Kopal, Z. "Peter Anderas Hansen." In *Dictionary of Scientific Biography,* edited by C.C. Gillispie, vol. 6, 103–104. New York: Scribner, 1972.

Harriot, Thomas (1560?–1621)

Elizabethan natural philosopher. An Oxford graduate with a lifelong interest in navigation and a natural gift for mathematics, Thomas Harriot provided technical expertise to Walter Raleigh's crew as they prepared to sail the Atlantic in 1584. Harriot made at least one voyage to the New World, serving as natural historian and conducting a linguistic and ethnographic study of the Algonquins.

Throughout his life, Harriot investigated a wide range of physical phenomena. He methodically recorded his findings and shared them with close associates. His failure to publish his notes, however, left the nature and content of his accomplishments open to dispute and misrepresentation until recently when a more thorough examination of his papers has been possible.

Although Harriot was among the first to examine celestial objects telescopically, he did not publish his efforts. From 1609–1613 he observed the lunar surface, Jupiter's moons, and conducted a longitudinal study of sunspots. The near synchrony of these observations with those of a similar nature made by **Galileo Galilei** has stimulated interest among modern historians concerning the degree to which Harriot was influenced by Galileo in both subject and method. Examination of Harriot's papers has revealed that he made use of Galileo's observations of Jupiter's moons recorded in *Sidereus Nuncius* to guide his own observations in 1610. But Harriot anticipated Galileo in viewing the moon's surface with a telescope in 1609. His study of sunspots, begun in 1611, was undertaken before information about similar efforts by others had been disseminated.

Barbara J. Becker

Bibliography

North, J. "Thomas Harriot and the First Telescopic Observations of Sunspots." In *Thomas Harriot: Renaissance Scientist,* edited by J.W. Shirley, 129–165. Oxford: Clarendon Press, 1974.

Rigaud, S.P. *Miscellaneous Works and Correspondence of James Bradley, Together with the Supplement.* Oxford: Oxford University Press, 1832–1833; reprint, New York: Johnson Reprint, 1972.

Shirley, J.W. *Thomas Harriot: A Biography.* Oxford: Clarendon Press, 1983.

Harvard College Observatory

From inauspicious beginnings in 1839, when its first director, William Cranch Bond, served without pay and used his own instruments to make observations from a special cupola mounted on the roof of the Dana House, the Harvard College Observatory (HCO) developed by century's end into a large, well-equipped, well-endowed institution that became a world leader in astrophysical research.

A permanent observatory was established in 1846, and a 15-inch telescope installed the following year. Made by the German firm of Merz and Mahler and paid for by funds raised by the citizens of Boston, the Great Refractor was the largest telescope in the United States.

Within months of its mounting, Bond used it in an attempt to obtain photographs of the sun. With the aid of John A. Whipple, a professional Boston photographer, by 1850 he succeeded in obtaining not only photographs of the sun, moon, and planets, but also the stars. The HCO was the first American observatory to apply photography to astronomy. Bond's pioneering work in this area was continued and expanded by his son George Phillips Bond, who served as director from 1860 to 1865.

When Joseph Winlock became director in 1866, he ordered a new meridian circle from Troughton and Simms in England. On its arrival in 1870, it was used by William A. Rogers in the international cooperative effort sponsored by the Astronomische Gesellschaft to revise Argelander's *Bonner Durchmusterung.* In addition to continuing the HCO's experiments in photography, Winlock began new researches in photometry, placing them under the direction of Charles S. Peirce.

At the time of **Edward C. Pickering**'s appointment as director in 1877, he was a professor of physics at the Massachusetts Institute of Technology. It was natural, therefore, for him to approach astronomy from the perspective of physics. From the beginning of his tenure, he shifted the observatory's research program to the new field of astrophysics.

Pickering held a Baconian concept of science. Eschewing speculation as far as possible, he instituted vast research projects, often of a routine nature, so that a sufficient basis in fact could be established for the solution of stellar problems by future astronomers.

His first major project was a quantitative determination of the visual magnitudes of the stars. When photographic methods largely supplanted visual ones, he turned to photographic photometry. An increasing part of his later work was devoted to establishing a standard system of stellar photographic magnitudes. He succeeded in this endeavor, and the Harvard system was adopted for universal use by the International Union for Cooperation in Solar Research in 1913.

Pickering's second major project was a photographic study of the spectra of the stars. The Henry Draper Fund supported his program of photographing, measuring, and classifying the spectra of the stars. Pickering worked hard for the universal acceptance of the Harvard system and the Draper classification system was adopted at the 1913 Solar Union meeting.

One of the most important achievements of his administration was the establishment in 1891 of an auxiliary observatory in the Southern Hemisphere in Arequipa, Peru. Made possible by the U.A. Boyden Fund, this station enabled Pickering to cover the entire sky in both his photometric and spectroscopic investigations.

Additionally, studies carried out there with the 24-inch Bruce Telescope led to many of the HCO's greatest achievements, such as the discovery by Henrietta S. Leavitt of Cepheid variables in the Small Magellanic Cloud (which led to the calibration of the period-luminosity law), Solon I. Bailey's discovery of short-period cluster-type variable stars in globular clusters, and William H. Pickering's discovery of Phoebe, the first known retrograde satellite. More than anything else, it was the results yielded by the Arequipa-Cambridge axis that catapulted the HCO into the forefront of astrophysical research.

Pickering was succeeded by **Harlow Shapley**, who served as director from 1921 to 1952. Throughout his tenure, Shapley was always proud of the existence of a southern station. In an attempt to find a better observing location, he moved the station from Arequipa to Bloemfontein, South Africa, in 1927. Almost simultaneously he secured funds from the Rockefeller Foundation for a 60-inch telescope for the new site. With it, he made extensive investigations of the Magellanic Clouds, establishing a virtual monopoly on their study.

In addition to Shapley's research on Cepheid and cluster-type variable stars, he encouraged **Annie Jump Cannon** and her associate Margaret W. Mayall to complete and extend the Draper catalogue of stellar spectra, and undertook an extensive survey of the distribution of galaxies in both hemispheres.

Aside from his own investigations, one of Shapley's greatest contributions was his training of graduate students. Prior to the mid-1920s, there was no graduate program in astronomy at Harvard. Under Shapley's direction, the program turned out distinguished students who became leaders in other graduate programs throughout the country.

Another major contribution included Shapley's efforts to promote international cooperation in astronomy. He brought many astronomers from all over the world to study and work at the HCO. During the late 1930s, he helped rescue European refugee scientists, bringing them and their families to the United States.

The HCO became the great institution it is today primarily through the efforts of Pickering and Shapley. By combining celestial photography, introduced by W.C. Bond, with spectroscopy, begun by Winlock, Pickering brought together two techniques that defined the observatory's research program. A southern station enabled the HCO to extend its investigations to the whole sky. Pickering further enhanced the status of the observatory by establishing a vast network of contacts with leading astronomers and observatories around the world. Shapley built on this foundation. He created such an extraordinarily stimulating environment at the HCO that it became a mecca for astronomers throughout the world. Under his directorship, the HCO long maintained its leading position in astronomy.

The Harvard University archives contain rich materials of use to the students of the history of science. The post-1920 period of HCO history is an especially inviting field of inquiry; topics range from the history of women in Harvard astronomy to the impact of World War II on the HCO.

Howard N. Plotkin

Bibliography

Bailey, S.I. *The History and Work of Harvard Observatory, 1839 to 1927*. New York: McGraw-Hill, 1931.

Elliott, C.A. "The History of Harvard Astronomy—A View from the Archives." *Journal for the History of Astronomy* 21 (1990): 3–8.

Gingerich, O. "Through Rugged Ways to the Galaxies." *Journal for the History of Astronomy* 21 (1990): 77–88.

———. "Two Astronomical Jewels from Peru, 1889–1927." In *Mundialización de la ciencia y cultura nacional. Actas del Congreso Internacional "Ciencia, descubrimiento y mundo colonial,"* edited by A. Lafuente, A. Elena, and M.L. Ortega, 707–713. Madrid: Doce Calles, 1993.

Jones, B.Z., and L.G. Boyd. *The Harvard College Observatory. The First Four Directorships, 1839–1919*. Cambridge: Harvard University Press, 1971.

Plotkin, H. "Harvard College Observatory." In *Astrophysics and Twentieth-Century Astronomy to 1950, Part A,* edited by O. Gingerich, 121–124. *The General History of Astronomy,* edited by M. Hoskin. New York: Cambridge University Press, 1984.

———. "Edward C. Pickering." *Journal for the History of Astronomy* 21 (1990): 47–58.

———. "Harvard College Observatory's Boyden Station in Peru: Origin and Formative years, 1879–1898." In *Mundialización de la ciencia y cultura nacional. Actas del Congreso Internacional "Ciencia, descubrimiento y mundo colonial,"* edited by A. Lafuente, A. Elena, and M.L. Ortega, 689–705. Madrid: Doce Calles, 1993.

Shapley, H. *Through Rugged Ways to the Stars*. New York: Scribner, 1969.

Stephens, C.E. "Astronomy as Public Utility: The Bond Years at the Harvard College Observatory." *Journal for the History of Astronomy* 21 (1990): 21–35.

Heliometer

A telescope that produces double images for precision determination of angular sizes or separations. In 1743, Servington Savery appears to have had the original idea of using either a bisected objective lens or two fixed equal lenses to produce a double solar image for positional measurement, though Olaus Römer has also been credited. In Savery's concept, an auxiliary filar micrometer was required to measure the distance between the limbs of the two solar images. The first telescope actually termed a heliometer, however, was that of Pierre Bouguer, built in 1748. It had two object glasses of equal size and focal length that could be rotated as a pair and moved relative to each other by a micrometer screw, the displacement of the lenses being proportional to the relative angular shift between the two images. This Bouguer object-glass micrometer also was used for measuring the sun's apparent diameter. In 1754 John Dollond improved Savery's bisection concept by separately mounting the two lens halves, allowing motion relative to each by a micrometer screw.

Double-image telescopes also could be used to measure the angular separation between two stars, by bringing their images into coincidence. A Fraunhofer 6.25-inch heliometer, constructed after the Dollond design, was used in 1838 by **Friedrich W. Bessel** for measurement of the parallax of 61 Cygni at Königsberg Observatory. Other notable heliometers include the 7.5-inch Repsold instrument at Oxford Observatory, in 1848 the largest in England and perhaps the finest precision instrument of its era. **David Gill** measured the parallax of Mars from Ascension Island in 1877 with a 4-inch Repsold heliometer. Gill also obtained an excellent 7-inch Repsold heliometer for the Royal Observatory at the Cape for stellar parallax work and for asteroid observations from which a highly accurate value for the solar parallax was determined. In the United States, the Yale Observatory secured a heliometer in the 1890s. Heliometer measurements, however, were painstaking, and by the end of the nineteenth century, they were largely replaced by photographic methods.

Charles J. Peterson

Bibliography

Bouguer, P. "De la Mesure des Diamètres des plus grandes Planètes: Description d'un nouvel Instrument qu'on peut nommer Héliomètre, propre à les déterminer; & Observations sur le Soleil." *Mémorie de L'Académie de Sciences, Paris* (1748): 11–34.

Dollond, J. "An Explanation of an Instrument for Measuring Small Angles." *Philosophical Transactions* 48 (1754): 551–564.

King, H.C. *The History of the Telescope*. London: Charles Griffin, 1955.

Savery, S. "A New Way of Measuring the Difference between the Apparent Diameter of the Sun at the Times of the Earth's Perihelion and Aphelion, with a Micrometer Placed in a Telescope Invented for that Purpose, tho' the Charge or Magnifying Power of the Telescope is so Great, that the Whole Sun's Diameter does not Appear Therein at One View." *Philosophical Transactions* 48 (1754): 167–178.

Herget, Paul (1908–1981)

American dynamical astronomer. Herget's education and career were centered at the University of Cincinnati, from which he received a Ph.D. in 1935. Herget explored the possibilities of automating the calculation of orbits, beginning with early punched card equipment. From 1942 to 1946, he worked in the Nautical Almanac Office, automating the production of almanacs. Returning to Cincinnati, he created the Minor Planet Center of the **International Astronomical Union** and served as its director until retirement in 1978. In the 1950s he prepared the orbital software for the *Atlas, Mercury,* and *Vanguard* projects. His privately published textbook, *The Computation of Orbits* (1948), presents methods adapted to the electronic resources of the era.

LeRoy E. Doggett

Bibliography

Osterbrock, D.E., and P.K. Seidelmann. "Paul Herget." *Biographical Memoirs of the National Academy of Sciences* 57 (1987): 59–86.

Herschel, Alexander Stewart (1836–1907)

English expert on meteors, born in the Cape Colony, South Africa, the fifth of **John F.W. Herschel**'s twelve children. After graduating in 1859 from Cambridge University (twentieth Wrangler) and further training at the Royal School of Mines in London, in 1866 he became professor of mechanical and experimental physics at the Andersonian University of Glasgow and then in 1871 professor of physics and experimental philosophy at the University of Durham College of Science at Newcastle. Retiring in 1886, this bachelor don resided at the Herschels' Observatory House in Slough, England.

Meteors were Alexander Herschel's chief research interest. Of his eighty-three publications, over half dealt with these objects. Usually observing them with only his naked eye, but also at times employing a meteor spectroscope that he developed during the 1860s in conjunction with the optician John Browning, he published numerous observations and encouraged others to observe as well. His particular contributions include determining the radiant points for various meteor showers and compiling evidence indicating the association of meteor showers with comets.

Michael J. Crowe

Bibliography

Hollis, H.P. "Alexander Herschel." In *Dictionary of National Biography, Second Supplement,* 257–258. London: Oxford University Press.

Millman, P. "The Herschel Dynasty—Part III: Alexander Stewart Herschel." *Journal of the Royal Astronomical Society of Canada* 74 (1980): 279–290.

Moore, P. *Alexander Herschel: The "Meteor Man."* Bath: William Herschel Society, 1993.

Herschel, Caroline Lucretia (1750–1848)

Hanoverian-born astronomer. In 1772, Caroline Herschel moved to the English city of Bath to be with her brother, an organist and music teacher. She sang as her brother's engagements demanded, kept house, and also assisted in his astronomical endeavors. **William Herschel**'s discovery of Uranus in 1781 brought him a government pension, and the Herschels abandoned their musical careers. Caroline Herschel assisted her brother in astronomical work, from grinding and polishing mirrors to recording observations and reducing data for publication. She also began observing on her own, discovering her first comet in 1786. The following year, she too was awarded a government pension. When William Herschel married in 1788, Caroline moved to her own lodgings but continued to assist him and to observe, discovering a total of eight comets and three nebulae. After her brother's death in 1822 she retired to Hanover, but she aided her nephew, the astronomer **John F.W. Herschel**, in his work. In 1828, Caroline Herschel received the Royal Astronomical Society's Gold Medal for reducing and arranging her brother's observations of star clusters and nebulae into a manuscript catalogue used by John Herschel. Seven years later, she was elected an honorary Fellow of the Society.

Peggy A. Kidwell

Bibliography

Herschel, M.C. *Memoir and Correspondence of Caroline Herschel.* London: John Murray, 1876.

Hoskin, M.A. "Caroline Lucretia Herschel." In *Dictionary of Scientific Biography,* edited by C.C. Gillispie, vol. 6, 322–323. New York: Scribner, 1972.

Ogilive, M.B. "Caroline Herschel's Contributions to Astronomy." *Annals of Science* 32 (1975): 149–161.

Herschel, John Frederick William (1792–1871)

English astronomer. The son of the astronomer William Herschel, he attended Cambridge University, graduating in 1813 as Senior Wrangler and First Smith's Prizeman. After starting preparations for a career in law, he soon turned to science, including mathematics, chemistry, and, from 1816 on, astronomy. In 1821, he began observing double stars with James South, and in 1825 took up the study of the nebulae, as the hundreds of nebulous objects visible in powerful telescopes were then called. By the end of 1830, he had published a book on the methodology of science and book-length studies on light, sound, and physical astronomy, helped found the Royal Astronomical Society, nearly won election to the presidency of the Royal Society, and married (1829) Margaret Brodie Stewart, their union producing twelve children.

Raised to knighthood in 1831, he published in 1833 his *Treatise on Astronomy,* which was expanded in 1849 to be his *Outlines of Astronomy,* which Agnes Clerke described as "possibly the most completely satisfactory general exposition of a science ever penned" (Clerke, 715). In 1833, he journeyed to the Cape Colony in South Africa, remaining there for five years, observing the southern heavens with his 18.7-inch-aperture, 20-foot-focal-length reflecting telescope. Upon returning, he was raised to the baronetcy and began preparing his Cape observations for publication. These appeared in 1847 as his *Results of Astronomical Observations made during the Years 1834, 5, 6, 7, 8 at the Cape of Good Hope.* Although he ceased active observation with large telescopes after his return from the Cape, he continued to publish and to play an active role in many aspects of British science. From 1850 to 1855, he served as Master of the British Mint. The high esteem in which Herschel was held by his contemporaries is attested to by the fact that he was buried next to Isaac Newton in Westminster Abbey.

John Herschel's most important contribution to astronomy consisted in his pioneering and detailed observations of the celestial objects visible in the Southern Hemisphere. What his famous father had done for the nebulae, clusters, and double stars visible from England, he accomplished for the southern skies. Moreover, as the only astronomer of his day (possibly ever) who had carefully observed the thousands of objects, northern and southern, visible in a large telescope and who in addition possessed superior expertise in mathematical and physical astronomy, he was elevated by his British contemporaries to serve as the supreme court in Britain on matters astronomical.

The significance of Herschel's contribution to stellar astronomy is indicated by such facts as that before sailing for the Cape, he had discovered 525 new nebulae and while at the Cape added 1,279 more as well as preparing a map of the **Magellanic Clouds** showing 1,163 objects. His Cape researches also yielded an important study of the distribution of the nebulae, showing how markedly they cluster toward the galactic poles. In the final decade of his life, he prepared a consolidated catalogue of 5,079 nebulae, most of which had been discovered by him and his father. He was scarcely less active in observing double stars. He went to the Cape having already discovered 3,347 new doubles, and he added 1,202 more during his five years there. In the final years of his life, he did extensive work on a catalogue of 10,300 double stars that was finished by others and published in 1874.

Regarding the structure of the Milky Way, Herschel in his *Treatise on Astronomy* (1833) advocated his father's disk theory of its structure, even though his observations of M51 were already suggesting to him the possibility of a ringlike or annular structure. He found this view reinforced by his Cape observations. Yet when in 1849 he discussed this question in his *Outlines of Astronomy,* he retreated to the stratum view of his father.

John Herschel's position regarding the nature of the nebulae also shifted during his career. In 1826, he supported his father's claim that a shining fluid is a major constituent of nebulae, but seven years later in his *Treatise on Astronomy* he maintained that most nebulae are composed of stars. By 1847, when he published his Cape observations, his views seem to have shifted to the point that he labeled his father's notion of a shining fluid as "purely hypothetical" and suggested that most nebulae would eventually be resolved into individual stars. Nonetheless, he also noted in his 1847 volume that the Magellanic Clouds contain nebulae in all stages of resolution, an observation that was widely discussed and led some of his contemporaries, such as William Whewell, to the conclusion that not all nebulae are resolvable. A final shift occurred in the 1860s as a result of **William Huggins**'s spectroscopic determination that some nebulae consist of glowing gas. In the preface to the 1869 edition of his *Outlines of Astronomy,* Herschel accepted Huggins's result as demonstrating the existence of true nebulosity.

John Herschel is also known for his contributions to areas of science outside astronomy. As president of the Analytical Society, he led a movement to introduce Continental methods of the calculus into British mathematics. He made numerous contributions to photographic science, the most important of which was his discovery, published in 1819, that sodium thiosulphate (now known to photographers as "hypo") dissolves silver salts. In physics, his most significant contribution was his completion in 1827 of a book-length study of light, which work was soon translated into French and German. The fact that Herschel's list of published books contains such titles as *Meteorology* and *Physical Geography* as well as a translation of Homer's *Iliad* shows the remarkable range of his interests, whereas the fact that he had over 350 publications suggests the magnitude of his creativity. In addition, he served as Secretary of the Royal Society, president (1845) of the British Association for the Advancement of Science, and for three two-year terms as President of the Royal Astronomical Society.

Over ten thousand items of John Herschel's correspondence are preserved at the Royal Society and are now available on microfilm from University Publications of America. The second largest collection of Herschel's correspondence (around twenty-five hundred items) is at the University of Texas. An annotated calendar of his entire correspondence is in preparation at the John Herschel Correspondence Project at the University of Notre Dame.

Michael J. Crowe

Bibliography

Buttmann, G. *The Shadow of the Telescope: A Biography of John Herschel.* Translated by B.E.J. Pagel. New York: Scribner, 1970.

Cannon, W.F. "John Herschel and the Idea of Science." *Journal of the History of Ideas* 22 (1961): 215–239.

Clerke, A.M. "Herschel. Sir John Frederick William." In *Dictionary of National Biography,* vol. 9, 714–719. London: Oxford University Press, 1921–1922.

Crowe, M.J., ed. "Introduction." In *The Letters and Papers of Sir John Herschel: A Guide to the Manuscripts and Microfilm* (in the series *Collections from the Royal Society*), v–xxxvii. Bethesda, Md.: University Publications of America, 1991.

Evans, D.S., T.J. Deeming, B.H. Evans, and S. Goldfarb, eds. *Herschel at the Cape: Diaries and Correspondence of Sir John Herschel, 1834–1838.* Austin: University of Texas Press, 1969.

Hoskin, M. "John Herschel's Cosmology." *Journal for the History of Astronomy* 18 (1987): 1–34.

Lubbock, C.A. *A Short Biography of Sir John F.W. Herschel, Bt.* Cambridge, U.K.: privately printed, ca. 1938.

Schweber, S.S. "John F.W. Herschel: A Prefatory Essay." In *Aspects of the Life and Thought of Sir John Frederick Herschel,* edited by S.S. Schweber, vol. 1, 1–158. New York: Arno, 1981.

Warner, B., and N. Warner. *Maclear and Herschel: Letters and Diaries at the Cape of Good Hope, 1834–1838.* Rotterdam: A.A. Balkema, 1984.

Herschel, William (1738–1822)

English astronomer and cosmologist. Born in Hanover, Germany, the son of Isaac Herschel, a musician in the Hanoverian Guard. At age fifteen, William joined the guard as an oboist, but left it in 1757 to pursue a career in England as a musician. In 1766, he made his first recorded astronomical observation and moved to Bath, England, where in 1772 his sister **Caroline Herschel** joined him. By 1776, he had constructed a number of telescopes, including a 12-inch reflecting telescope with a 20-foot-focal-length mirror. On March 13, 1781, while searching for double stars, he discovered an object that he at first believed to be a comet, but that he eventually recognized as a new planet, Uranus. This discovery not only made him internationally famous, but also won financial support from King George III, which enabled Herschel to become a full-time astronomer. To be near the king, he moved to Datchet and then to Slough, where in 1788 he married Mary (Baldwin) Pitt, a wealthy widow. In the same year, he completed the construction of his 48-inch reflector with a 40-foot-focal-length mirror, which remained the world's largest telescope until the 1840s. The year 1792 saw the birth of their only child, John, who also became a prominent astronomer. In 1816, William Herschel was knighted and in 1821 elected the first president of England's newly founded Royal Astronomical Society. He continued to pursue astronomical research almost to the time of his death.

William Herschel's most important contribution consisted in his pioneering studies in stellar astronomy. It was he who first supplied extensive evidence for the claim that our Milky Way is a more or less disk-shaped structure consisting of millions of stars, and that the dim nebulous patches visible in large telescopes are in many cases immensely large and extremely remote structures composed of millions of stars—in effect, other Milky Ways or island universes. Herschel's interest in nebulae developed gradually. By December of 1781, he had observed only four such objects. Late in that year, he received a list published by Charles Messier of sixty-eight nebulae, and not long after Messier's expanded list of 103 objects. By 1783, Herschel had begun searching for these objects, using his 18.7-inch, 20-foot-focal-length reflector, the finest telescope then in existence. In 1784 he reported resolving most of Messier's nebulae into individual stars, and that he had detected 466 new nebulae. The next year Herschel published a study in which he reported seeing hundreds of new nebulae, suggested that the Milky Way consists of a vast stratum of stars, and maintained that nebulae are of comparable structure. The significance of all this was not lost on Herschel's contemporaries. After visiting him in 1786, the novelist Fanny Burney exclaimed that Herschel "has discovered fifteen hundred universes! How many more he may find who can conjecture?" (Lubbock, 170).

Herschel's next major paper in stellar astronomy, a study of objects he designated globular clusters, appeared in 1789 and is noteworthy because Herschel raised a host of questions about the evolution of these objects.

In 1791 Herschel backed away from the grand synthesis that had earlier emerged from his papers of 1784, 1785, and 1789. He had come to the conclusion, especially after his observations of a planetary nebula, that not all nebulae are resolvable into individual stars. In fact, he reported his conviction that the nebulous portion of this planetary nebula consists of "a shining fluid of a nature totally unknown to us" (Herschel, vol. 1, 422). By 1811, he had backed off the island universe theory to the point that he seemed to believe that most nebulae, rather than being other Milky Ways, are stars in the process of formation.

Herschel's hesitancy about—if not rejection of—the island universe theory (a theory not confirmed until the 1920s) should not obscure the fact that he deserves credit as the pioneer, both observationally and theoretically, of stellar astronomy. Not only did he discover and catalogue over twenty-five hundred new nebulae and star clusters, he also located 848 new double stars. Further, in papers published in 1803 and 1804, he provided observational evidence that some doubles, rather than being line-of-sight objects, are gravitationally linked pairs, thereby extending for the first time the law of gravitation beyond the solar system. On a more theoretical level, he presented evidence in 1783 analyzing the proper motion of various stars and showing that our sun is itself in motion, moving in the direction of Lambda Hercules. Overall, Herschel raised most of the questions that later stellar astronomers sought to answer.

Herschel's discovery of Uranus, although his premier contribution to solar system astronomy, was far from being his only such achievement. He increased the population of the solar system by detecting in 1787 two Uranian moons, Titania and Oberon, correctly arguing in 1798 that they move in retrograde fashion. His cautious report of sightings of four other Uranian moons proved incorrect. Herschel's reputation as an observer of solar system objects was enhanced by the discovery in 1789 of the Saturnian satellites Enceladus and Mimas, by his determination of the period of rotation of Saturn and of Mars, and by observations of the Martian polar caps. Comets were of less concern; Herschel left these objects to his sister Caroline, who is remembered not only as Herschel's faithful assistant but also for her discovery of eight comets.

Herschel's observations of and reflections on the sun led him to the claim, developed between 1795 and 1801, that the sun consists of a cool, possibly habitable core surrounded by a glowing layer. Sunspots in this scheme were holes in the exterior layer through which the cooler core could at times be seen. Herschel, like many of his contemporaries, viewed the planets as habitable bodies more or less comparable to the earth. More than most of his contemporaries, Herschel was interested in learning the physical constitution of the planets.

The interests of nearly all Herschel's astronomical contemporaries were confined to the solar system, including comets, and in most cases restricted either to accurate determinations of position or mathematical calculations. In contrast, this musician turned astronomer transformed astronomy by showing how much could be learned by using large reflecting telescopes and by raising questions about stars and nebulae. The widely accepted description of Herschel's approach as being that of a celestial naturalist points to the originality of his thought and to the degree to which his approach separated him from his astronomical contemporaries. The fact that no one among his contemporaries could rival him in access to large telescopes has sometimes obscured the fact that few if any of his contemporaries possessed comparable originality of insight. There is perhaps no finer testimony to the importance of Herschel's research than the fact that, many decades after his death, astronomers repeatedly returned to his writings and observations to derive fresh insights from them.

Michael J. Crowe

Bibliography

Armitage, A. *William Herschel.* London: Thomas Nelson and Sons, 1962.

Bennett, J.A. "'On the Power of Penetrating into Space': The Telescopes of William Herschel." *Journal for the History of Astronomy* 7 (1976): 75–108.

———. "Catalogue of the Archives and Manuscripts of the Royal Astronomical Society." *Royal Astronomical Society Memoirs* 85 (1978): 1–90.

Crowe, M.J. *The Extraterrestrial Life Debate 1750–1900: The Idea of a Plurality of Worlds from Kant to Lowell.* Cambridge: Cambridge University Press, 1986.

Herschel, W. *The Scientific Papers of Sir William Herschel.* 2 vols. Edited by J.L.E. Dreyer. London: Royal Society and Royal Astronomical Society, 1912.

Holden, E.S., and C.S. Hastings. "A Synopsis of the Scientific Writings of Sir William Herschel." In *Annual Report of the Smithsonian Institution for 1880,* 509–622.Washington, D.C., 1881.

Hoskin, M.A. *William Herschel and the Construction of the Heavens.* London: Oldbourne, 1963.

———. "Sir William Herschel." In *Dictionary of Scientific Biography,* edited by C.C. Gillispie, vol. 6, 328–336. New York: Scribner, 1972.

Lubbock, C. *The Herschel Chronicle.* Cambridge: Cambridge University Press, 1933.

Schaffer, S. "Uranus and the Establishment of Herschel's Astronomy." *Journal for the History of Astronomy* 12 (1981): 11–26.

Hertzsprung, Ejnar (1873–1967)

Danish astrophysicist and observational astronomer. Educated as a chemical engineer and photochemist, Hertzsprung turned to the photographic study of stars, discovering the existence of the giant and main (or dwarf) sequences. He displayed this result in the first published color-magnitude diagrams (now called **Hertzsprung-Russell diagrams** in recognition of their independent development by Henry Norris Russell). Hertzsprung studied the membership of the Pleiades and other clusters, developed photographic techniques for studying double and variable stars, and calibrated Henrietta Leavitt's period-luminosity relationship for Cepheid variables, determining a distance to the Small Magellanic Cloud. Hertzsprung worked at Potsdam Observatory (1909–1919) before becoming adjunct director (1919–1935) and director (1935–1944) of Leiden Observatory.

Joann Eisberg

Bibliography

Strand, K.A. "Ejnar Hertzsprung, 1873–1967." *Publications of the Astronomical Society of the Pacific* 80 (1968): 50–56.

Hertzsprung-Russell Diagram

The Hertzsprung-Russell diagram, more commonly the HR Diagram, depicts the relationship between the absolute magnitudes of a definable set of stars and their spectra, or color-index. Ejnar Hertzsprung, an astronomer in Denmark, and **Henry Norris Russell** of Princeton independently found between the years 1905 and 1910 that the majority of stars in the sky followed a definite relationship between absolute magnitude and spectral class. But most dramatically, they found that there were a few red stars of great intrinsic brightness and of enormous dimension.

The HR Diagram is a plot of stellar luminosity against a measure of stellar temperature. Luminosity is expressed as absolute magnitude (the apparent magnitude of a star at a standard distance of ten parsecs). Surface temperature may be directly expressed in degrees Kelvin, as a photometric color index (usually the B-V color index, where B is the stellar magnitude measured in a blue region of the spectrum and V in the visual region), or indicated by the spectral class (OBAFGKM) where O is the hottest spectral type and M the

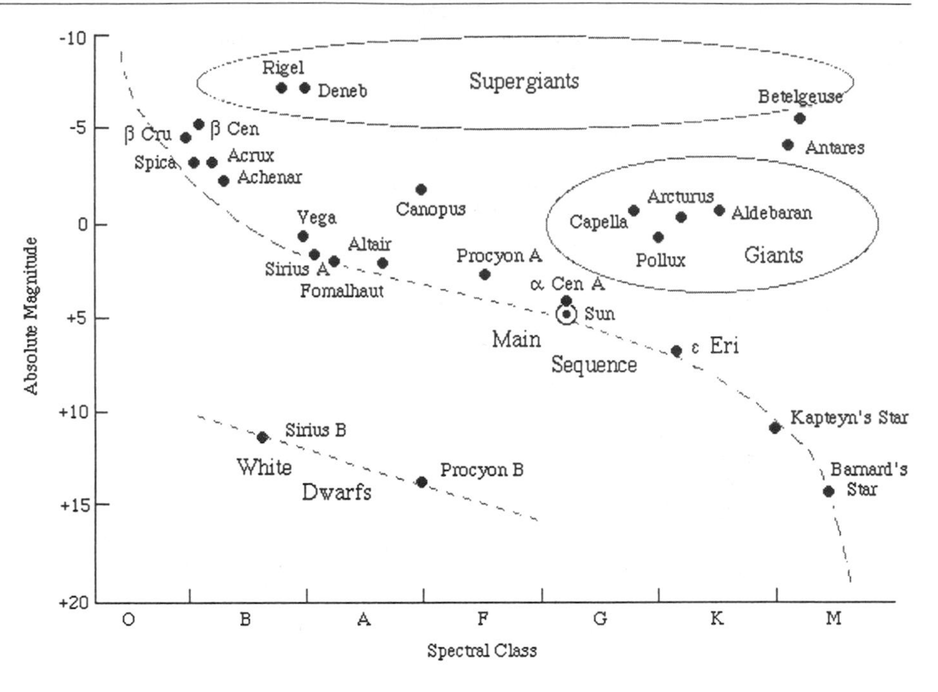

The four regions of stellar concentration are illustrated schematically in the HR Diagram, which plots absolute visual magnitude versus spectral class. Representative stars plotted in the diagram include the twenty brightest stars in the sky and a few fainter, nearby stars (such as Barnard's star and Kapteyn's star). (Diagram and explanation by C.J. Peterson)

coolest, with each class subdivided into ten subclasses.

Stars are not distributed uniformly at all luminosities and temperatures but concentrate in four regions on the HR Diagram:

1. A band termed the Main Sequence that runs diagonally across the diagram from high luminosity–hot surface temperatures to low luminosity–cool surface temperatures.
2. A sparsely populated region of very high luminosity at the top of the diagram. These stars are extremely large and called Supergiants.
3. A region of relatively cool stars with luminosities intermediate between the supergiants and the main sequence stars (these are termed Giants).
4. A region of relatively hot but very faint (and small) stars termed White Dwarfs.

Both Hertzsprung and Russell presented their findings graphically for different reasons—Hertzsprung to illustrate cluster membership, and Russell to depict a theory of stellar evolution. Even though the first publication of the diagram was by a Hertzsprung student in 1910, it gained prominence in 1913 as the Russell Diagram. In the 1930s, **Gerard Kuiper** campaigned for the name now in general use.

Russell did not continue to exploit the diagram that bears his name. Hertzsprung used it on a number of occasions to display improved data for open star clusters. Nonetheless, the diagram has become one of the most popular means of displaying data, both observational and theoretical, relevant to the study of the constitution and evolution of the stars.

David H. DeVorkin

Bibliography

DeVorkin, D.H. "Stellar Evolution and the Origins of the Hertzsprung-Russell Diagram in Early Astrophysics." In *Astrophysics and Twentieth-Century Astronomy to 1950,* edited by M.A. Hoskin and O. Gingerich, 90–108. Cambridge: Cambridge University Press, 1984.

Herrmann, D.B. "Ejnar Hertzsprung, Zur Strahlung der Sterne." *Ostwald's Klassiker* 255. Leipzig, 1976.

Jones, B.Z., and L.G. Boyd. *The Harvard College Observatory 1839–1919*. Cambridge: Harvard University Press, 1971.

Nielsen, A.V. "History of the Hertzsprung-Russell Diagram." *Centaurus* 9 (1963): 219–252.

Hevelius, Johannes (1611–1687)

Polish astronomer. Son of a prosperous brewer and property owner, Johannes Hevelius was born in Danzig (now Gdansk), Poland. His education prepared him for a business and civil service career, but he also studied mathematics, astronomy, and optics. Hevelius described his early astronomical work in *Selenographia* (1647), discussing existing telescope technology and describing his own instruments. This volume also included various observations of planets and detailed descriptions and maps of the lunar surface. Other publications included an extensive discussion of comets, *Cometographia* (1668), and a star catalogue that was published posthumously.

Hevelius discussed instrument-making in his two-volume *Machina Coelestis* (1673, 1679). He described various instruments of large size, including quadrants and sextants up to 6-foot radius. Convinced of the advantages of long focal-length telescopes, Hevelius described instruments ranging from 27 to nearly 140 feet in length. These larger telescopes could not be mounted in tubes, so Hevelius mounted the objective and the eyepiece on a spar suspended from a mast. The largest telescope of this design had a spar of 140 feet, a mast of 90 feet, and a lens of 8 inches diameter. Adjustments to such instruments proved exceptionally difficult and minimized the value of these telescopes.

In September of 1679, Hevelius's home and observatory burned, destroying most of his instruments, library, and equipment. Although the observatory was rebuilt by 1681, Hevelius could not replace his instruments with similar quality equipment. He continued to observe and publish, but his health began to deteriorate soon after the fire.

George E. Webb

Bibliography

Bell, L. *The Telescope*. New York: McGraw-Hill, 1922.

North, J.D. "Hevelius, Johannes." In *Dictionary of Scientific Biography,* edited by C.C. Gillispie, vol. 6, 360–364. New York: Scribner, 1972.

Hill, George William (1838–1914)

American celestial mechanician. Hill joined the Nautical Almanac Office in 1861 after receiving an A.B. from Rutgers College in 1859. He was associated with the office until his retirement in 1892. Hill's work on the lunar theory led to the study of periodic orbits in the three-body problem. His lunar theory was further developed by **E.W. Brown** to become a standard for the first half of the twentieth century. Working with **Simon Newcomb** at the Nautical Almanac Office, Hill helped develop a consistent set of theories for all the planets. He produced theories for Jupiter and Saturn that were used in the *American Ephemeris and Nautical Almanac* until 1960.

LeRoy E. Doggett

Bibliography

Brown, E.W. "George William Hill." *Biographical Memoir of the National Academy of Sciences* 8 (1916): 275–309.

Eisele, C. "George William Hill." In *Dictionary of Scientific Biography,* edited by C.C. Gillispie, vol. 6, 398–400. New York: Scribner, 1972.

Hipparchus of Rhodes (Second Century B.C.E.)

Hipparchus is generally considered to be one of the most influential astronomers of Antiquity, yet very little information available about him survives; his only extant work is a commentary on the astronomical poem of Aratus (third century B.C.E.). The *Almagest,* written by Ptolemy (second century C.E.), is the source of most of our knowledge about Hipparchus, whom Ptolemy considered to be his most important predecessor. In his own astronomical work, Ptolemy made extensive use of the work of Hipparchus, building on the foundation laid by him.

Hipparchus employed geometrical models, including the deferent-epicycle and eccentric previously used by Apollonius (fl. ca. 200 B.C.E.). Hipparchus was also interested in observation, using an instrument described by Ptolemy as a dioptra and producing the first known catalogue of stars. One of his contributions appears to have been the incorporation of numerical data based on observations into the geometrical models developed to account for the astronomical motions.

Hipparchus' discussion of the motion of the points of solstice and equinox slowly from east to west against the background of the fixed stars is perhaps his most famous achievement; he has been therefore credited with the discovery of the precession of the equinoxes. Neugebauer has suggested that Hipparchus, in fact, invented the theory of trepidation (Neugebauer, 298).

Perhaps most intriguing for historians of astronomy is Hipparchus' use of Babylonian astronomical material, including methods as well as observations. Many questions remain regarding the relationship between Babylonian and Greek astronomy; Hipparchus' work provides a clear link. Toomer has argued that Hipparchus was responsible for the direct transmission of both Babylonian observations and procedures.

Liba C. Taub

Bibliography

Jones, A. "The Adaptation of Babylonian Methods in Greek Numerical Astronomy." *Isis* (1991): 441–453.

Neugebauer, O. *A History of Ancient Mathematical Astronomy*. New York: Springer-Verlag, 1975.

Toomer, G.J. "Hipparchus." In *Dictionary of Scientific Biography,* edited by C.C. Gillispie, Supplement I: 207–224. New York: Scribner, 1978.

———. "Hipparchus and Babylonian Astronomy." In *A Scientific Humanist: Studies in Memory of Abraham Sachs,* edited by E. Leichty, M. de J. Ellis, and P. Gerardi, 353–365. Occasional Publications of the Samuel Noah Kramer Fund 9. Philadelphia: University Museum, 1988.

Hirayama, Kiyotsugu (1874–1943)

A Japanese astronomer who discovered families of the asteroids. Kiyotsugu Hirayama graduated from the Department of Astronomy of Tokyo Imperial University in 1897 and worked at Tokyo Observatory until his retirement. As an astronomer at Tokyo Observatory, he was sent to Sumatra in 1901 for the observation of solar eclipses and to Sakhalin in 1908 for determining the border between Japan and Russia. In 1916, he went to study astronomy under **Ernest W. Brown** at Yale University. Brown urged Hirayama to investigate the mean motion of asteroids, and Hirayama studied the subject for the rest of his life. The asteroids whose mean motion lay between 720 and 740 seconds a day, he discovered, appeared to cluster according to the inclination and eccentricity of their orbits. He called this group the Koronis family and successively found the Eos, Themis, and other asteroid families. He was also a serious student of ancient astronomical data in East Asia and studied calendrical systems in Japan and China.

Takehiko Hashimoto

Bibliography

Kiyotsugu, H. *The Asteroids* (in Japanese). Tokyo, 1935.

Horrocks, Jeremiah (1619?–1641)

English celestial mechanician and instrument maker. Among the first in England to adopt **Johannes Kepler**'s laws of planetary motion, Jeremiah Horrocks extended their explanatory power through rigorous observation. As early as 1635, he began to question the reliability of existing astronomical tables. Introduced to Kepler's new *Rudolphine Tables* by **William Crabtree** in 1637, Horrocks became persuaded of their superiority and embraced the physical theory on which they were based.

Horrocks believed that astronomers must observe celestial phenomena if they are to uncover the true structure of the heavens. Discrepancies in previous naked-eye observations convinced him that human eyesight is limited and subject to distortion. He advocated the use of telescopic instruments to improve human observing and recording capabilities.

Horrocks designed observational tests of contemporary astronomers' claims and constructed specialized precision instruments with which to carry them out. He thus refuted the notion that stars are extended objects, supported Kepler's theory of elliptical planetary orbits, and improved existing lunar theory. Horrocks is best known for his prediction and observation of the 1639 **transit of Venus**. With the data he collected, he determined Venus's orbital elements and made an improved measure of the **solar parallax** that challenged current estimates of scale in the solar system.

Locating Horrocks and his accomplishments more authentically within the context of his time has been a challenge for historians, particularly given the heroic place he has occupied in the lore of generations of astronomers.

Barbara J. Becker

Bibliography

Chapman, A. *Three North Country Astronomers*. Manchester: Neil Swinton, 1982.

———. "Jeremiah Horrocks, the Transit of Venus, and the 'New Astronomy' in Early Seventeenth-century England." *Quarterly Journal of the Royal Astronomical Society* 31 (1990): 333–357.

Horrocks, J. *The Transit of Venus across the Sun 1639*. Translated by A.B. Whatton. London: Macintosh, 1859.

———. *Opera Posthuma,* edited by J. Wallis. London: R. Scott, 1672–1673; reprint, M. Pitt, 1678.

Wilson, C. "Horrocks, Harmonies, and the Exactitude of Kepler's Third Law." In *Science and History: Studies in Honor of Edward Rosen,* edited by E. Hilfstein, P. Czartorysky, and F.D. Grande, 235–259. Wroclaw: Polish Academy of Sciences Press, 1978.

Hubble, Edwin Powell (1889–1953)

Generally regarded as the outstanding observational cosmologist of the twentieth century, Hubble was born in Marshfield, Missouri. He earned all of his degrees from the University of Chicago. In 1919, Hubble became staff member of the Mount Wilson Observatory where he had access to resources astronomers elsewhere could not match, especially the great 100-inch reflector.

In the early 1920s, Hubble determined distances to the Andromeda Nebula and other relatively large spiral nebulae. These findings ended the long-standing debate on the nature of the spirals, making clear that they are external to the Milky Way. In 1928, Hubble began to concentrate on the problem of whether or not galaxies (extragalactic nebulae, in his terminology) exhibited a red shift–distance relationship. Others had tried to find such a relationship, but astronomers judged the evidence as inconclusive. Hubble transformed this situation. With an initial paper in 1929 and a much more extensive one co-written with Milton Humason two years later, Hubble convinced his colleagues that there is indeed a red shift–distance relationship and that, to a first approximation, it is linear. Hubble's and Humason's researches were swiftly incorporated into models of the expanding universe, although Hubble took pains to point out that there might be another explanation for the red shifts besides radial velocities. Hubble developed an influential classification scheme for galaxies. His early researches are summarized in *The Realm of the Nebulae* (1936).

While a number of works detailing aspects of Hubble's life and scientific career (particularly his early scientific career) have been written, there is no good scholarly biography.

Robert W. Smith

Bibliography

Christianson, G.E. *Edwin P. Hubble: Mariner of the Nebulae.* New York: Farrar, Straus and Giroux, 1995.

Hetherington, N. "Philosophical Values and Observations in Edwin Hubble's Choice of a Model of the Universe." *Historical Studies in the Physical Sciences* 13 (1982): 41–67.

———. *The Edwin Hubble Papers: Previously Unpublished Manuscripts on the Extragalactic Nature of Spiral Nebulae: Edited, Annotated, and with an Historical Introduction.* Tucson: Pachart, 1990.

Hubble, E.P. *The Realm of the Nebulae.* New Haven: Yale University Press, 1936.

———. *The Observational Approach to Cosmology.* Oxford: Clarendon Press, 1937.

Osterbrock, D.E., R.E. Brashear, and J.A. Gwinn. "Self-Made Cosmologist: The Education of Edwin Hubble." In *Evolution of the Universe of Galaxies: Edwin Hubble Centennial Symposium,* edited by R. Kron, 1–8. San Francisco: Astronomical Society of the Pacific, 1990.

Smith, R.W. *The Expanding Universe: Astronomy's 'Great Debate' 1900–1931.* New York: Cambridge University Press, 1982.

———. "Edwin P. Hubble and the Transformation of Cosmology." *Physics Today* 43 (1990): 525–528.

Hubble Space Telescope

Initial discussions of an orbiting telescope, led by Lyman Spitzer and Leo Goldberg in the late 1940s, generally met with little enthusiasm. Ground-based astronomy remained more attractive to most astronomers, as shown by the national observatory campaign of the next decade. During the 1960s, however, NASA's Orbiting Astronomical Observatories program rekindled interest in the concept and led to suggestions for a federally funded Large Space Telescope with a 3-meter mirror. The telescope soon became linked with the proposed space shuttle as an important payload and as a target for later maintenance missions. As part of a continuous concern with costs, astronomers joined NASA officials to redraft plans for the instrument during the 1970s, ultimately decreasing the mirror size to 2.4 meters and minimizing scientific goals in favor of a program design that Congress would accept.

The instrument proved much more difficult to design than originally thought, leading to higher costs, further modifications, and a complete management shakeup in 1983. The choice of Lockheed to construct the Hubble Space Telescope (as it was renamed in 1983) proved of questionable value during the testing phase, which began in 1985. Lockheed had significant experience testing assembly-line military reconnaissance satellites, but the unique aspects of the space telescope required more time-consuming techniques. The *Challenger* disaster in January 1986 further delayed the project, but the many problems discovered during testing had already made unlikely the launch planned for later that year.

The successful launch of the telescope in April 1990 appeared to justify the $1.6 billion project cost (more than four times the original estimate), but the instrument soon proved seriously flawed. The main mirror had been ground to the wrong figure, making precise focusing impossible. Scientists quickly developed techniques to salvage the project

A photograph taken on April 25, 1990, by the crew of the Space Shuttle Discovery *shows the Hubble Space Telescope being deployed from the payload bay. (Courtesy of the National Aeronautics and Space Administration)*

through longer exposures and sophisticated computer enhancement programs, but these corrections could be achieved only at the expense of fewer observations. The NASA review panel report, issued in November, concluded that inadequate testing procedures had led to the misshapen mirror. The review panel also criticized NASA management for inadequate oversight and emphasized that cost-cutting and unreasonable time constraints underlay the various lapses.

Over the next three years, other problems emerged. Two of the six gyroscopes failed completely, while a third remained only marginally effective. Faulty electrical contacts in the High Resolution Spectrograph threatened the performance of that instrument, while instabilities in the solar cell panels threatened the entire telescope. Faced with numerous difficulties, NASA determined that the first maintenance visit by a shuttle crew, scheduled for 1993, offered an excellent opportunity to repair the ailing telescope. In mid-December, astronauts removed the High Speed Photometer and installed corrective optics to minimize the effects of the flawed mirror. The *Endeavor* crew also repaired other equipment and replaced the Wide Field/Planetary Camera with an improved instrument with its own corrective optics. At a total cost of more than $500 million, the repairs to the Hubble Space Telescope restored the instrument to its originally planned performance.

George E. Webb

Bibliography

Chaisson, E.J. "Early Results from the Hubble Space Telescope." *Scientific American* 266 (1992): 44–51.

O'Dell, C.R. "The Hubble Space Telescope Observatory." *Physics Today* 43 (1990): 32–38.

Schwarzschild, B. "Hubble Investigation Board Finds Out What Went Wrong." *Physics Today* 43 (1990): 19–21.

Smith, R.W. *The Space Telescope: A Study of NASA, Science, Technology, and Politics.* New York: Cambridge University Press, 1989.

Huggins, William (1824–1910)

English pioneer in astronomical spectroscopy. William Huggins worked in his family's London silk shop until the mid-1850s, when he turned full time to astronomy. In 1862, Huggins began analyzing starlight by attaching a spectroscope to his telescope, as did others like Giovanni Battista Donati, Lewis M. Rutherfurd, and **Angelo Secchi**. Huggins was the first to examine nebular spectra, measure stellar radial velocities, and identify hydrogen's ultraviolet spectrum. He worked in collaboration with his wife, née Margaret Lindsay Murray, following their marriage in 1875. She introduced photography into Huggins's toolkit, thus keeping him competitive with ambitious contemporaries like **J. Norman Lockyer** and **Henry Draper**. Huggins received international recognition for his contributions and served as president of the Royal Astronomical Society, the British Association for the Advancement of Science, and the Royal Society.

Historians have viewed Huggins's role in the rise of astrophysics in light of his own published accounts—in particular, a popular retrospective essay (Huggins 1897) and two self-edited volumes recounting his scientific contributions (Huggins and Huggins 1899, 1909). In these synthetic works, Huggins and his wife characterized the development of his research program as symbiotic with the growth of this new specialty. Becker's recent examination of his unpublished correspondence and notebooks, however, has revealed Huggins as a more eclectic and opportunistic observer who made his way from the periphery of a loosely structured community of serious British amateur astronomers to a place of prestige within an emerging elite core of international astrophysical experts.

Barbara J. Becker

Bibliography

Becker, B.J. "Eclecticism, Opportunism, and the Evolution of a New Research Agenda: William and Margaret Huggins and the Origins of Astrophysics." Ph.D. dissertation, Johns Hopkins University, 1993.

Huggins, W. *An Atlas of Representative Stellar Spectra.* London: Wesley, 1899.

———. "The New Astronomy: A Personal Retrospect." *Nineteenth Century* 41 (1897): 907–929.

Huggins, W., and M.L. Huggins. *The Scientific Papers of Sir William Huggins.* London: William Wesley and Son, 1909.

Maunder, E.W. *Sir William Huggins and Spectroscopic Astronomy.* London: T.C. and E.C. Jack, 1913.

Mills, C.E., and C.F. Brooke. *A Sketch of the Life of Sir William Huggins.* Richmond: Times Printing Works, 1936.

Ogilvie, M.B. "Marital Collaboration: An Approach to Science." In *Uneasy Careers and Intimate Lives: Women in Science 1789–1979,* edited by P. Abir-Am and D. Outram, 104–125. New Brunswick: Rutgers University Press, 1989.

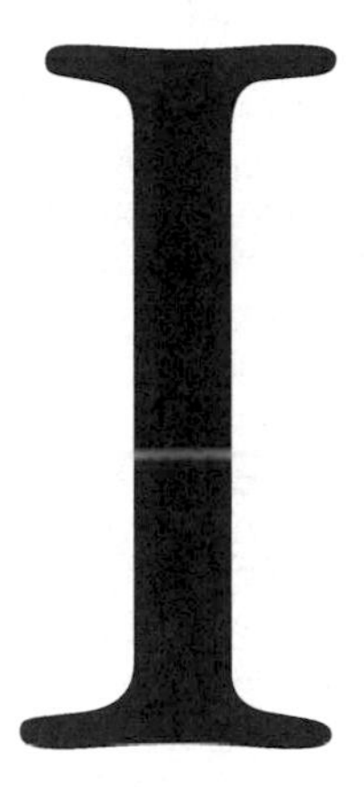

Infrared Astronomy

William Herschel reported in 1800 that the bulb of a thermometer registered a temperature even when placed in the invisible region of a solar spectrum beyond the red. Infrared eventually came to mean the spectral region between the far visible red, at a wavelength of about 7,000 angstroms, and the radio region around 1 mm, and convention settled on measuring wavelength in micrometers or microns. At the short end (the near infrared), conventional reflecting telescopes can be used, and photographic emulsions can be sensitized to respond. In the middle of the region, only electronic detectors work, and, in the far infrared, radio technology is more suitable. Herschel himself did little to exploit this newly opened region, but others in Europe and America during the nineteenth century used thermocouple devices to register infrared radiation from the moon and sun. With more sensitive radiometers, thermocouples enclosed in a vacuum, it became possible at the turn of the century to attempt measurements of the brighter stars and planets.

W.W. Coblentz of the U.S. Bureau of Standards took radiometric observations of stars at **Lick Observatory** in 1914, at the **Lowell Observatory** in 1921, then of Mars and other planets in collaboration with **Vesto Slipher** and Donald Menzel. During the same period Edison Pettit and Seth B. Nicholson conducted similar measurements from Mount Wilson using the 100-inch telescope.

Two problems plagued those interested in this region of the spectrum: suitably sensitive detectors and the variable opacity of the atmosphere in the infrared. The former produced various developments in photographic emulsions and electronics, spurred on by military needs and astronomical desires. The latter was solved by finding high, dry sites from which to make observations through the several atmospheric windows that allow narrow bands of infrared radiation to reach the surface of the earth, and by using new technological means (balloons, aircraft, rockets, and spacecraft) to rise above the absorbing atmosphere. Atmospheric molecules, notably water vapor and carbon dioxide, are the chief emitters and absorbers of infrared radiation.

Early photographic emulsions were most sensitive in the blue and violet, and completely ineffective in the red. During the 1930s, Eastman Kodak worked to develop special infrared sensitive emulsions for astronomers and for military customers as well. These emulsions were used in infrared spectroscopic studies of planetary atmosphere constituents. During the interwar years, electronic detectors also were developed and applied to radiometric measurements of the lunar surface, particularly its cooling rate during lunar eclipses, from which a few inferences were drawn concerning the probable mineralogical nature of lunar rocks and soil.

During World War II, tactical and strategic reconnaissance drove the development of more efficient electronic detectors, notably the Golay cell and the lead-sulfide cell of J. Cashman. The Cashman cell, sensitive to the 1–3 micron region, was exploited immediately after the war by several astronomers, including **Gerard P. Kuiper** and spectroscopist Gerhard Herzberg, who made observations of planets and satellites and laboratory comparison spectra Albert Whitford experimented at Chicago, and Harold Johnson, at the University of Arizona, used infrared measurements in an attempt to calibrate his emerging photometric system for reddening of starlight by interstellar dust. Improved radiometers were used at the focus of large telescopes at Mount Wilson and Mount Palomar. Some work was also done in brief flights of sounding rockets.

Infrared astronomy blossomed in the 1960s. Frank Low, at Texas Instruments Corporation, developed a series of germanium detectors cooled by liquid helium that opened up the 10-micron region. He moved to the University of Arizona, where Gerard Kuiper continued his long-standing interest in infrared observations with Harold Johnson and other collaborators. Other groups were active at several universities and laboratories around the world. Gerry Neugebauer and Robert Leighton at Caltech used an innovative telescope incorporating a metal-epoxy mirror to complete a survey of the entire sky through the 2-micron window. Again, military interest proved important: In order to track astronomically cool objects (missiles and spacecraft), the defense department needed accurate surveys of the infrared background of the whole sky.

Ground-based studies identified cool objects in the Orion Nebula and other regions where star formation was thought to take place, presumably gas and dust being warmed by the radiation of stars. As radio sources were observed in the infrared, their energy distributions became more recognizable and intelligible. Other objects held surprises when observed in the infrared. Some stars, for example Vega, showed an excess of infrared radiation compared with the extrapolation of energy distribution observed in the optical region. This excess suggested they were surrounded by cooler material, perhaps protoplanetary disks.

Infrared astronomers were most sensitive to the need for suitable sites. After promising sites were found in Arizona, Wyoming, Hawaii, and Tenerife island for near-infrared telescopes, the National Aeronautics and Space Administration (NASA) turned in the mid-1970s to locating a site for its 3-meter Infrared Telescope Facility (IRTF). A spirited and controversial site survey and competition ensued, resulting in the selection of Mauna Kea, Hawaii. Later in the decade the United Kingdom added a 3.8-meter infrared telescope nearby, joined by several other instruments from various international consortia. Because of its high altitude and low water vapor, Mauna Kea is a premier site for ground-based infrared astronomy. NASA also was an important sponsor of telescopes flown in various high-altitude aircraft above most of the absorbing atmospheric water vapor.

Topping the ground-based and balloon-borne work of the 1970s was the Infrared Astronomical Satellite (IRAS). The product of a collaboration between the United States, the United Kingdom, and the Netherlands, the IRAS satellite combined a solid-state detector sensitive to several important infrared channels with a telescope itself cooled to just above absolute zero by liquid helium. For nearly all of 1983, IRAS produced an all-sky survey entirely above the atmosphere, and numerous intensive studies of selected objects. A low-resolution spectrometer and a photometer also shared the focal plane. Among the many results produced by this mission were mapping the distribution of dust in the galactic and ecliptic planes, including two additional zodiacal bands of dust inclined to the ecliptic; a more diffuse infrared cirrus more broadly distributed; numerous asteroids; the structure of dust in comet tails; and unusual galaxies that radiate nearly all of their energy in the infrared (the Milky Way radiates about half).

Infrared astronomy does not enjoy a well-developed historiography, although certain themes and episodes have been treated in detail. Kidwell provides a thorough discussion of infared solar studies for the period up to 1860. Lovell discusses Herschel's experiments. Eddy gives an account of Thomas Edison's brief appearance in making infrared solar eclipse observations with an electrical detector. DeVorkin recounts the difficulties in disentangling terrestrial water vapor from near-infrared spectroscopic observations of Mars.

For broader treatments of infrared astronomy from ground-based instruments, balloons, rockets, and spacecraft, one is generally limited to a few memoirs, journalistic accounts, and scientific review articles. Tucker and Tucker devote three chapters to the Infrared Astronomical Satellite (IRAS) in their readable and informative but sparsely documented volume, providing some highlights of ground, balloon, rocket, and satellite-based developments and personalities. Allen, Field and Chaisson, Hanel et al., and various articles in *Annual Review of Astronomy and Astrophysics* provide scientific reviews ranging from popular to professional. Jennings gives a personal account of British developments. The growing literature on the history of radio astronomy, notably Sullivan, can be used to some advantage, since the far infrared shades into the radio region of the spectrum.

Joseph N. Tatarewicz

Bibliography

Allen, D.A. *Infrared: The New Astronomy.* New York: John Wiley and Sons, 1975.

Annual Review of Astronomy and Astrophysics. Palo Alto, Calif.: Annual Reviews, 1963–.

DeVorkin, D.H. "W.W. Campbell's Spectroscopic Study of the Martian Atmosphere." *Quarterly Journal of the Royal Astronomical Society* 18 (1977): 37–53.

Eddy, J.A. "Thomas A. Edison and Infra-Red Astronomy." *Journal for the History of Astronomy* 3 (1972): 165–87.

Field, G.B., and E. Chaisson. *The Invisible Universe: Probing the Frontiers of Astrophysics.* Boston: Birkhauser, 1985.

Hanel, R.A., B.J. Conrath, D.E. Jennings, and R.E. Samuelson. *Exploration of the Solar System by Infrared Remote Sensing.* New York: Cambridge University Press, 1992.

Henbest, N., ed. *Observing the Universe.* London: Basil Blackwell, 1984.

Jennings, R.E. "History of British Infrared Astronomy since the Second World War." *Quarterly Journal of the Royal Astronomical Society* 27 (1986): 454–461.

Kidwell, P.A. *Solar Radiation and Heat from Kepler to Helmholtz (1600–1860).* Ph.D. Dissertation. Cambridge: Harvard University, 1979.

Lovell, D.J. "Herschel's Dilemma in the Interpretation of Thermal Radiation." *Isis* 59 (1968): 46–60.

Schettino, E. "A New Instrument for Infrared Radiation Measurements: The Thermopile of Macedonia Melloni." *Annals of Science* 46 (1989): 511–17.

Sullivan, W.T., ed. *The Early Years of Radio Astronomy: Reflections 50 Years after Jansky's Discovery.* New York: Cambridge University Press, 1984.

Tucker, W., and K. Tucker. *The Cosmic Inquirers: Modern Telescopes and Their Makers.* Cambridge: Harvard University Press, 1986.

Willner, S.P. "The Cool Sky: Infrared Astronomy." In *Infinite Vistas: New Tools for Astronomy,* edited by J. Cornell and J. Carr, 152–180. New York: Scribner, 1985.

Ino, Tadataka (1745–1818)

A surveyor and maker of the first map of Japan. Originally a merchant, Ino entered the *samurai* class after demonstrating great courage. At the age of forty-nine, Ino retired and started to study astronomy under Yoshitoki Takahashi, the official astronomer in Edo. Russian encroachment prompted the government to survey Ezo, Japan's northernmost island. Takahashi seized this opportunity and ordered Tadataka Ino to perform a national survey with the aid of instruments designed by Shigetomi Hazama, based on Jesuit astronomical treatises. After a preliminary survey from Edo to Ezo, he received official approval to initiate the more comprehensive nationwide survey. He worked on this project for the next seventeen years, surveying coastlines with special care. He died while constructing the map based on the data he had gathered.

Takehiko Hashimoto

Bibliography

Otani, R. *Tadataka Ino.* In Japanese. Tokyo, 1917.

Instruments, Astronomical

The recovery of Ptolemaic astronomy in Renaissance Europe was not confined to the translation and discussion of original texts and the mastery of the planetary theory of the *Almagest.* The practice of the Ptolemaic program through practical observation and measurement was integral to the vision of a revitalized astronomy conceived by Georg Peurbach and Johannes Müller, called Regiomontanus, in Vienna in the later fifteenth century. In turn, this program developed from the ideas of mathematicians such as Alberti and Toscanelli, which takes the beginnings of this movement in European astronomy back to the Italian Renaissance.

The early designers, makers, and users of astronomical instruments in Renaissance Europe had two important resources: the account of instruments in the *Almagest* and later Islamic and other medieval patterns. The elements contributed by the *Almagest* were a form of quadrant for measuring altitude, an instrument known as **Ptolemy**'s rulers, comprising three pivoted rules for measuring zenith distance by subtended chords, several circles or rings set for measuring angles in a single coordinate, and the generalization of these rings into the complex and universal armillary sphere. In addition, Islamic practice added the torquetum and medieval astronomy the **cross-staff**, or radius astronomicus. There were also portable instruments, such as the **astrolabe** and horary quadrant, but although these were valuable teaching tools and although their ingenuity, usefulness, and desirability were factors in the spread of astronomical literacy, they were too small to contribute to astronomical measurement.

We must, however, be careful about accepting too readily assumptions of usefulness and purported applications to astronomical measurement. Both the **armillary sphere** and the torquetum present themselves as instruments adapted to measurement peculiarly suited to Ptolemaic planetary theory. The armillary sphere, for example, has an outer meridian ring and an adjustable polar axis to ensure that the system of rings mounted on it has an equatorial motion: It rotates in parallel with the apparent motion of the heavens. Within this a second axis is set at an angle to the first, equal to the obliquity of the ecliptic, and can therefore be rotated to point to the current position of the ecliptic pole. Two further rings carrying sights then permit direct measurement in ecliptic coordinates, the angles particularly required in Ptolemy's account of planetary motion. Such a mechanically complex instrument was scarcely suited to accurate positional work, but as a sculptural expression of the geometry the astronomers had projected onto the heavens, it was well adapted to teaching spherical astronomy.

The same points apply to the torquetum. This was a truly universal instrument, able to take measurements in all the coordinate systems operating in astronomy. In its simplest mode, a vertical circle on a horizontal base was adapted to measurement of altitudes and azimuths. However the hinged base could be propped at an angle appropriate to the local latitude, so as to swing the divided circles into the equatorial system. A second hinge, opened to receive a wedge equal to the obliquity of the ecliptic, could effect the final adjustment to ecliptic coordinates. The torquetum thus presents itself as a versatile instrument of measurement; in practice it must have been an invaluable demonstration of how the three coordinate systems were related to each other, which without such a demonstrational aid might well have been difficult to grasp.

The practical astronomers of the late fifteenth and sixteenth centuries made use of these precedents: Regiomontanus wrote on the armillary sphere and the torquetum and used Ptolemy's rulers and the cross-staff in the observatory he established in Nuremberg. This last instrument consisted of a graduated staff with a sliding cross-piece adjusted to extend between two target objects, so that its position on the staff indicated the angle the targets subtended at the eye of the observer. His disciple Bernard Walther, also in Nuremberg, had Ptolemy's rulers and a cross-staff as well as an armillary sphere with an ecliptic axis in the Ptolemaic style. While other sixteenth-century mathematicians contributed to this neo-Ptolemaic tradition in practical astronomy—Joannes Werner, Gemma Frisius, Wilhelm of Hesse with his observatory at Kassel—it was **Tycho Brahe** in Denmark who exploited it to the full and who was most successful in striking out in new directions.

Tycho's was a purpose-built observatory—Uraniborg—with an instrument workshop, a paper mill and a printing press, and accommodation for assistants as well as for instruments. He was equipped eventually with some two dozen instruments, a number of which were derived from the neo-Ptolemaic tradition. He had armillary spheres, for example, one a fully fledged Ptolemaic instrument with both equatorial and ecliptic axes. He had examples of Ptolemy's rulers, one based on an example he had acquired that had formerly belonged to Copernicus. He also had a modified version of the astronomer's cross-staff. Indeed each of his instruments, even these traditional designs, were modified to some extent, for he added features from his individual technical repertoire. Different forms of sights, for example, were added: Tycho was concerned that holes in traditional sights sufficiently large to admit enough light also admitted ambiguity in the line of sight: his design of cylindrical foresight and parallel double-slit nearsight was to overcome this. True alignment was achieved when the image in each slit, viewed tangentially to either side of the cylinder, was equally bright. Another vital ingredient in his technical repertoire was diagonal division, where subdivided diagonals were ruled between each scale division.

While Tycho added new features to existing patterns, more important for the future development of astronomical instruments were his new designs for quadrants and sextants. In the account he published of his observatory, the *Astronomiae instauratae mechanica* of 1598, he effectively ended the Ptolemaic tradition by explaining the care he had devoted to each design and then the inadequacies of its subsequent performance. The armillary sphere, for example, offered the convenience of direct measurement in celestial coordinates and the avoidance of much subsequent calculation, but for the most accurate fundamental measurement—for refounding the observational basis of mathematical astronomy, and this was Tycho's aim—the less an instrument moved the better. He thus found that his more accurate instruments were those operating in the most primitive of coordinate systems—altitude and azimuth, based on the local horizon—and the most accurate moved scarcely at all. It was a tension that would concern instrument-makers and users for centuries to come.

The altazimuth instruments were quadrants and sextants, some set in the meridian, others rotatable to any azimuth, but all with diagonal divisions and Tychonic sights. The most celebrated—by later historians as well as by Tycho himself—was the great mural quadrant of about 2 meters radius. This was mounted on a substantial wall built in the meridian, and the only moving parts were the nearsights (there were two, for different ranges of altitude). These sights ran on a divided brass arc let into the wall; the cylindrical foresight was fixed in an opening in a wall at right angles to the primary one. Since these sights indicated meridian altitudes, the measurements were easily converted from local to celestial coordinates—that is, declinations—by applying the local latitude. How was Tycho to deal with right ascensions? Contemporary illustrations show the great quadrant and beside it are two clocks and an assistant whose task is to call out the times of observation—the moment of transit across the meridian. If the clocks were regulated to the motion of the heavens (set to sidereal time), the time of transit would be the right ascension. With this arrangement Tycho adopted what would become the standard methodology of fundamental measurement in astronomy. However, the relatively new technology of the mechanical clock could not deliver the required accuracy or reliability, and Tycho had to depend on the azimuth measurements of movable instruments.

Tycho took measurements with open-sighted instruments to near perfection. For his mural quadrant he claimed accuracy in altitude to one sixth of a minute of arc, and modern studies certainly concede him fractions of a minute. Consistent performance, however, had been won at a great cost, for it derived not just from instrument design: The scale and dedication of an operation where instruments could be built, refined, and rebuilt under direct supervision and where teams of assistants could man different instruments at once in a coordinated and extensive program of observation could not readily be duplicated. As Tycho himself observed when he lost royal patronage and was obliged to move his observatory from Denmark: "It is very seldom that among the statesmen who wish to govern a state there are any so strongly attracted by these sciences that they consider it their duty to favor and support them, but are much more often repulsed by them and consider them futile, owing to their ignorance" (Raeder, 63).

The use of the telescope to examine the skies was scarcely relevant to the traditional practice of astronomy, since it did not involve measurement. Only with the introduction of the eyepiece micrometer and the application of telescopic sights to divided instruments did the telescope become an instrument of astronomy as traditionally understood. Christopher Wren, who was involved with just these applications, saw them in precisely this way: "We make the Tube an Astronomical Instrument, to observe to seconds" (Bennett 1987, 65). Before it had a measuring function, the "tube"—that is, the telescope—had not in contemporary terms been an astronomical instrument at all.

The optical arrangement that made this development possible was the one explained in Kepler's *Dioptrice* of 1611, where a positive eye-lens magnifies the real image formed by a positive objective. The earliest recorded introduction of a reference point, grid, or scale into the focal plane of the objective, which would therefore appear in focus with the image of a distant object, was by the English observer William Gascoigne in about 1640—more accurately, by a spider who obligingly spun a web precisely in the focal plane to surprise and inspire Gascoigne. Gascoigne went on to develop both an eyepiece micrometer, where two knife-edges were moved in opposite directions by a double screw attached to a pointer, and a telescopic sight—a telescope with a reference point—to replace the index rule (alidade) and open sights on a traditional measuring instrument. The new technology was becoming generally adopted in different parts of Europe, apparently through independent invention, by the later 1650s and the 1660s, in the work of astronomers such as Huygens in the Netherlands, Auzout, Petit, and Picard in France, and Wren, Hooke, and Flamsteed in England.

Despite this general European move to telescopic sights, the foremost and best equipped practical astronomer had set his face against them. **Johannes Hevelius** had built an observatory in Danzig after the manner of Tycho, adding and developing instrument after instrument until he had a range of equipment with which to pursue the same goal as Tycho, refounding the observational base of astronomy. He even published a full and detailed account of his instruments, after the manner of Tycho's *Mechanica,* but much larger. The most obvious difference between his observatory and Tycho's was that he had telescopes—prominent among his instruments on account of their great length and the apparatus required to hoist them into position. He even fitted eyepiece micrometers to his telescopes, but he firmly opposed replacing open-sighted alidades with telescopic sights, preferring to stick with Tycho's cylinder and double slit arrangement.

Through Hevelius's published account, the *Machina Coelestis* of 1673, his methods and techniques were being disseminated among astronomers at just the time when some were convinced that instrument design should be moving in quite a different direction. The task of countering this influence was taken up by the English astronomers, most vigorously by Hooke—not a trivial undertaking, for Hevelius was Europe's most experienced and respected observer. But Hooke was not one to be daunted by a reputation, and a bitter and protracted argument ensued. Hooke's position rested on his experimental demonstration of the resolving power of the human eye—the ability to distinguish an angular separation of less than a minute of arc was, he said, very rare, and half a minute impossible. Consequently, unless resolution were improved artificially by the use of telescopes, further subdivision and the building of large instruments to achieve greater accuracy wasted time, resources, and effort. Hevelius raised some objections to the manner of mounting telescopic sights, but basically he appealed to his record and considered he had no case to answer until the new instruments had achieved as much. He had, after all, devoted most of his life and estate to a program that the new instruments threatened to undermine.

In fact, the observatory of Hevelius was the last to be equipped on this scale with open-sighted instruments. It was also the last great private observatory of this type. Other private initiatives would have enormous influence in astronomy and some would even contribute to fundamental positional work, but in general astrometric research would pass to state-supported institutions. Hooke's designs were realized at the **Royal Observatory, Greenwich**, and the ideas of Auzout, Petit, and Picard influenced the establishment of the **Paris Observatory**.

The controversy with Hevelius had allowed Hooke to discuss some of his visionary schemes for new astronomical instruments, schemes presented, he explained, "that I may excite the World to enquire a little farther into the improvement of Sciences. . . . Let us see what the improvement of Instruments can produce" (Bennett 1987, 72). He sought to discredit Hevelius for looking backward to the age of Tycho and, in seeking to point out a different future, he added significant elements to the design repertoire. He proposed a quadrant rotatable on an equatorial axis moved by a driving clock controlled by a conical pendulum. Equatorial motion was a feature of the armillary sphere and the torquetum, but had not been tried with a large observatory instrument, and this first suggestion was integrated with a governor designed to deliver a smooth tracking motion. The use of mirrors would allow one observer to manage both telescopic sights, the movable one being adjusted by clamp and tangent screw, the screw position, read by a micrometer head, giving the final subdivision. He also incorporated the newly invented bubble-tube for leveling.

Hooke's equatorial quadrant was never built in the form he proposed, but elements did appear at the Royal Observatory, where there was an equatorial sextant with two telescopic sights and screw adjustment. Hooke also proposed divided instruments whose frames were mounted on meridian walls—Tycho's mural quadrant did not have a frame—and this became standard not only at Greenwich but in all observatories, along with the adoption of telescopic sights.

The observatories of Paris and Greenwich, both founded in the 1670s, came at just the right time to take advantage of the new telescopic sights, and both were equipped at an early stage with appropriate mural quadrants—the first example at Greenwich being designed by Robert Hooke. One of the astronomers at Paris, Ole Römer, introduced another instrument with a telescopic sight, the transit instrument, which would be fundamental to the work of observatories. Here the telescope was supported in the meridian by a horizontal axis mounted in bearings, which in Römer's instrument were attached to the wall on either side of a window but came more usually to be carried on the tops of stone piers. Here was a specialized instrument to apply Tycho's method for measuring right ascensions by timing meridian transits. An instrument of this sort was preferable to the mural quadrant for defining the meridian because its alignment was much more easily checked (for example, it could be reversed on its bearings) and adjusted.

Although such developments in instrument design were important, the new type of institutional setting was just as significant to the practice of astronomical measurement. National observatories could outlive the enthusiasm and dedication of individual founders, patrons, or observers. They could act as repositories of technical knowledge and practice, and provide points of reference for future designers and instrument makers, while the succession of astronomers in charge fostered a competitive dynamic that encouraged periodic reequipping and innovation. In time, orders from such observatories would be important in building the reputation and business of specialist instrument-makers.

A standard range of observatory instruments was established through the designs evolved by George Graham in supplying the Greenwich Observatory in the early eighteenth century. Instruments based on these models were then built for observatories across Europe by disciples and admirers of Graham, such as Jonathan Sisson and John Bird.

First came Graham's mural quadrant, built for **Edmond Halley** and mounted in 1725. The 8-foot-radius brass arc was carried by an iron framework, reinforced for maximum rigidity. There were two scales, divided respectively to 90 degrees and 96 parts, the latter being based on the radius stuck off the circumference as a chord subtending 64 parts (instead of 60 degrees) and so able to be subdivided to unity by successive bisection. The position of the telescopic sight was adjusted by a clamp and tangent screw and its position read by a vernier. Already in 1738 this instrument was given a whole chapter of Robert Smith's influential textbook *A Compleat System of Opticks,* and its fame was reinforced through the copy made for Greenwich by John Bird in 1750, which was subsequently commended and its description published by the British Board of Longitude.

Other influential designs by Graham were for the transit instrument and the zenith and equatorial sectors. The transit instrument, dedicated to the measurement of right ascension, was basically a telescope with reference hairs in the eyepiece, mounted so as to be conveniently and accurately adjusted to the observer's meridian. Timing the passages of bodies across the center of the field of view, using an astronomical clock, then yielded measures of right ascension. In Graham's general design the telescope was carried at the center of a horizontal axis comprising two opposed cones, whose apexes became cylindrical bearings resting in adjustable mounts carried by two stone piers. George Graham was also largely responsible for developing the seconds pendulum clock into a sufficiently precise instrument for taking the transit times, for he designed the two characteristic components of the astronomical clock—the deadbeat escapement and the temperature compensation pendulum. In the latter case the bob of his pendulum was a jar of mercury, which expanded upwards to compensate for the lengthening of the steel rod.

This division of labor between the two principal positional measurements—declination taken by the **mural quadrant**, right ascension by the transit instrument—established a pattern that lasted a century or more and allowed each specialized instrument to develop according to the priorities of its particular function. For special projects, however, more individual instruments might be devised, and the most celebrated of these among Graham's designs was the zenith sector, comprising a long telescopic sight hanging from a horizontal axis at the object end and moving across a meridian arc of 6 degrees or so on either side of the zenith. The aim was to capture a detectable stellar parallax and, although this specific project failed, the British Astronomer Royal James Bradley's discovery of stellar aberration with Graham's instrument—the first empirical proof that the earth was in motion—ensured the zenith sector a place in the equipment of many observatories. The less common equatorial sector, also first made by Graham for Bradley at Greenwich, was a sector mounted on a polar axis for measuring any small angles in right ascension and declination.

This range of designs by Graham, available from the celebrated succession of English makers in the eighteenth century—Sisson, Bird, Ramsden, Dollond, and Troughton—became the standard pattern of equipment in a growing number of newly founded official observatories. National, provincial, and metropolitan administrations, learned societies, universities, and church bodies were included in the vogue for establishing observatories as demonstrations of scientific patronage in its most prestigious, advanced, and unworldly aspect, in buildings that were also material evocations of permanence and security. It was the English makers who had a repertoire of instrument designs, tried at Greenwich, that could supply all that was required to join the ubiquitous commitment to fundamental astronomy, and throughout eighteenth-century Europe observatory instruments were predominantly London made.

In the second half of the century there was experimentation with equatorially mounted instruments for measurement. The tension between the convenience of off-meridian direct readings of right ascension and declination and the absolute need for stability in accurate measurement had been pointed out by Tycho, and astronomers since his time had settled for what would become known as "grinding the meridian" for fundamental work in positional astronomy. The makers, however, were attracted by the challenge of a design where equatorial motion would not compromise accuracy, and they had an economic interest in persuading astronomers that complex and novel instruments of this type could at last be admitted to the armory of a professional observatory. By the later eighteenth century, there was an accepted place for the measuring equatorial where a single universal instrument was required to cope with all measurement and needed to be portable, such as for expeditions and temporary observatories. Ramsden, Dollond, and Troughton produced designs to fill this need.

One of the most curious, though evidently fairly popular, measuring equatorials of this period was the relatively small portable observatory. This instrument had a polar axis adjustable for latitude, a full right ascension circle, and it carried above this a semicircle for declination and the telescopic sight. Of a very modest size—overall height of perhaps 50 cm or less—these instruments would have been of little use for measurement and yet at a technical level that can be their only purported purpose. One clue to the puzzle is that they are described and made by George Adams, who was catering principally for the fashionable interest in natural philosophy in the eighteenth century. There was a clear distinction in astronomy between interested amateurs who were concerned with qualitative observing and so required relatively large-aperture telescopes, such as Gregorian reflectors, and the professional practitioners whose observatories were equipped for taking measurements. The portable observatory, as well as having a didactic role, could allow the amateur a pretended association with the professional program.

Ambitious makers made serious attempts to go further and execute equatorials on a scale appropriate to an established observatory. By the end of the eighteenth century, the two leading makers in the dominant center of precision instrument-making—London—were Jesse Ramsden and Edward Troughton, and around 1790 both made large equatorials for precision work. Ramsden set a 4-foot declination circle in an enclosing cage of six pillars parallel to the 8-foot polar axis of what became known as an English mounting, at the base of which was the right ascension circle. His instrument was for the wealthy amateur Sir George Shuckburgh. Troughton's instrument was for the newly founded ecclesiastical observatory at Armagh. He used the same English mounting for the polar axis, but with the main structural pillars diverging from the upper and lower bearings and meeting at the center (as distinct from Ramsden's parallel structure); the right ascension circle was in the central equatorial plane.

Neither of these ambitious instruments was a practical success, but both contained an idea that was to dominate observatory instrument design into the new century. The full circle was preferable to the quadrant or sextant for a number of reasons—from mechanical balance and stability to accuracy of division and reading and reduction of errors—and features such as reading by micrometer microscopes at several points on the scales were already part of the early designs by Ramsden and Troughton. Ramsden in particular adapted his equatorial design to the more regular observatory arrangement of the altazimuth, when he built the celebrated Palermo circle for Piazzi and the 8-foot altitude circle (unfinished at his death in 1800) for the Observatory of Trinity College, Dublin.

The fundamental element of the divided circle was adapted to a variety of measuring instruments, with smaller arcs relegated to navigation or surveying, and even here the reflecting or repeating circle offered an alternative to the octant or sextant. For the smaller range of astronomical instruments, for expeditionary or temporary use, the altazimuth circle became much more common than the equatorial, while for permanent instruments in observatories hoping to contribute to the fundamental research in positional astronomy, a competition was to develop between the mural circle and the transit circle.

The adoption of the mural circle in observatories in Britain and her overseas colonies is to a large degree explained by the extraordinary reputation and esteem granted to their designer, Edward Troughton. It was an arrangement that preserved the traditional separation of right ascension and declination measurements in distinct instruments.

When Greenwich decided to replace the pair of mural quadrants of the Graham design (one made by Graham himself, the other by Bird), this was seen as a necessity in catching up with the adoption of circles by foreign observatories, mainly supplied by British makers. Troughton's answer, delivered in 1812, to the challenge of following the most successful design in fundamental astronomy was to maintain the stability of the wall but, naturally, since this was the principal desideratum, to substitute the quadrant for a circle. In the resultant mural circle, the 6-foot-diameter circle moved with the telescope on a horizontal axis and was read by six micrometer microscopes mounted on a massive, 4-foot-thick meridian wall. The axis was carried by bearings inside the wall, with much of the weight being taken off by a counterpoise.

Troughton had planned that both coordinates could be taken with this instrument—declination to tenths of a second by reading the micrometer microscopes, right ascension by timing transits in the telescope. However, the adjustments required to maintain the alignment of the telescope in the meridian could not be made with any facility and, just as had happened formerly with the mural quadrant, a transit instrument had to be added for right ascension. Thus the separation of the two measurements was maintained and, such was Troughton's reputation, that this model was followed in the British observatories.

To others, however, its disadvantages were obvious. It was possible to combine both functions in a single instrument—the transit circle—where a vertical circle was added to the horizontal axis of a transit instrument, to be read by micrometer microscopes carried by the piers. Free access to the ends of the axis, convenient adjustment, and the ability to reverse the whole instrument on its bearings were required of any instrument for transit measurements, and the declination measures were not compromised in the dual design. A single instrument was economical in the use of manpower and eliminated the risk of combining two coordinates of different objects.

The English dominance of the precision instrument trade was beginning to falter with the rise of alternative centers in Paris and Munich. With the English wedded to a problematic instrument regime, the opportunity to offer transit circles to observatories seeking to reequip was taken by German makers such as Reichenbach, Liebherr, Ertel, and later Repsold of Hamburg. German optical work had benefited enormously through the work of Fraunhofer and later opticians such as Merz and Steinheil, and in a succession of partnerships with the mechanics, their instruments came to be as characteristic of nineteenth century observatory equipment as those of the English makers were for the eighteenth. The problems with the mural circle are not the entire explanation of the rise of the German makers, but they did give the ambitious newcomers an important opening. The French also began to challenge the traditional dominance of British makers, first through the work of Lenoir and Fortin, both of whom had benefited by the upheavals of the French Revolution, not least from the changes to the old restrictive practices and privileges of artisan guilds. The names of Secretan, Gambey, and Gautier are found on innovative and substantial precision instruments of the nineteenth century.

By mid-century the British were realizing that they would be obliged to change to the Continental pattern of observatory equipment, and one of the most celebrated examples of the transit circle was the instrument designed by the Astronomer Royal **George Biddell Airy** and installed at the Greenwich Observatory in 1850—the instrument that would define the prime meridian adopted by an international conference in 1884. The building of this instrument, however, illustrates how the status of the British instrument-makers had changed since the heroic age of Ramsden and Troughton. The design was due to Airy, who commissioned mechanics and contractors he considered appropriate to fabricate various parts. It was a division of labor more appropriate to an industrial age, and Airy's attitude toward mechanics was also more typical of his society. They now worked, it seemed, to designs handed down by astronomers who concerned themselves with optical and mechanical questions.

Another Continental instrument led to the eventual admission of the equatorial telescope into the sanctuary of precision measurement. The admission ticket was the celebrated achievement of a long-standing goal in astronomy, the measurement of a **stellar parallax**. John Dollond had announced an original design for a micrometer in 1753, where a long focus lens was divided into two parts along its diameter and the parts mounted so that their lateral displacement could be adjusted and measured. If such a lens were applied to the incident end of a reflecting telescope, apparent separations of members of double star pairs, for example, could be taken by bringing the images of the different stars into coincidence and noting the displacement of the lens components.

A skilled optician such as Fraunhofer was able to apply this idea to a full-sized refractor on an equatorial mount, and it was with one of his heliometers that Bessell measured the parallax of the star 61 Cygni in 1838. Perhaps it was this achievement that finally brought the equatorial into the world of professional astronomy, for it became a popular and versatile instrument in the second half of the century. It was thus available to fully exploit the new tools of photography and spectroscopy, which extended the agenda of professional astronomy far beyond the narrow rigor of astrometric measurement.

James A. Bennett

Bibliography

Bennett, J.A. *The Divided Circle: A History of Instruments for Astronomy, Navigation and Surveying*. London: Phaidon-Christie's, 1987.

———. "The English Quadrant in Europe: Instruments and the Growth of Consensus in Practical Astronomy." *Journal for the History of Astronomy* 23 (1992): 1–14.

Chapman, A. *Dividing the Circle: the Development of Critical Angular Measurement in Astronomy 1500–1850*. Chichester: Ellis Horwood, 1990.

Daumas, M. *Scientific Instruments of the Seventeenth and Eighteenth Centuries and their Makers*. London: Barsford, 1972.

Howse, D. *Greenwich Observatory*. Vol. 3: *The Buildings and Instruments*. London: Taylor & Francis, 1975.

King, H.C. *The History of the Telescope*. New York: Dover, 1979.

Raeder, H., et al., eds. *Tycho Brahe's Description of his Instruments and Scientific Work*. Kobenhavn, 1946.

Turner, A. *Scientific Instruments: Europe 1400–1800*. London: Philip Wilson, 1987.

Interferometer

Albert A. Michelson developed the first high-precision optical interferometer in 1881, following James Clerk Maxwell's suggestion that a sensitive measuring tool could be based upon the interference patterns of light waves. The Michelson interferometer is sensitive to path length differences traversed by the two

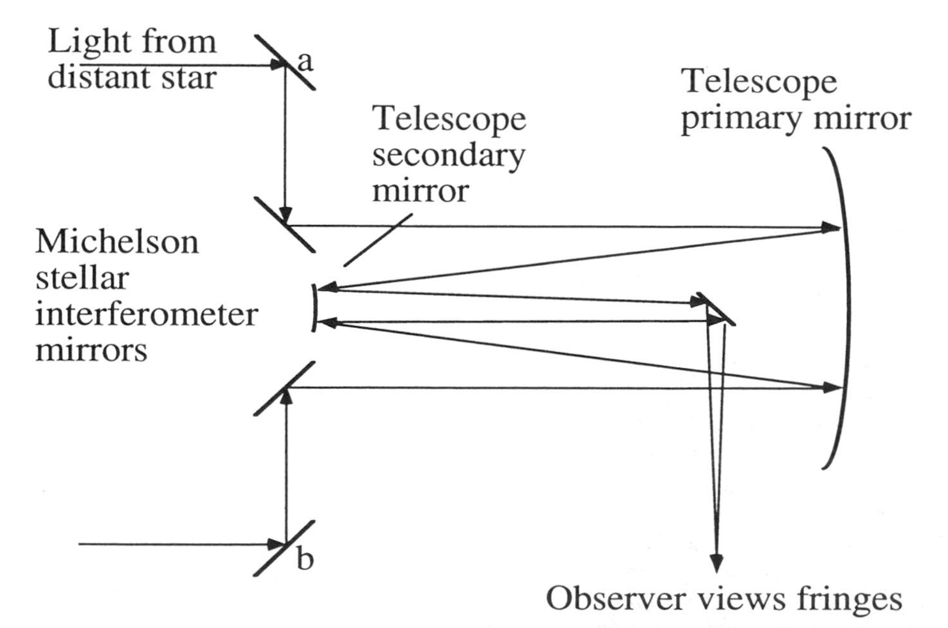

Stellar interferometer, showing paths for light from a distant star. The interferometer consists of four mirrors mounted over the entrance aperture of a large telescope. If mirrors a and b, which act as entrance slits for the starlight, are sufficiently close to each other, the diffraction image of the star will be crossed by interference fringes. If the separation between the mirrors is increased, the fringes become less distinct and finally disappear when the fringe pattern from one half of the star is completely canceled by the fringe pattern from the other half. For a star of diameter d located at a distance r, this will occur for monochromatic light (wavelength λ) at mirror separation given by the relation $d/r = 1.22\lambda/s$. *(Figure by C.J. Peterson)*

parts of a light beam that has been split and allowed to travel perpendicularly to one another before recombination to produce interference fringes.

With this interferometer, Michelson and J. René Benoît were the first to attempt to standardize the length of the meter against a selected wavelength (Cadmium 6438Å) in 1892. In 1887 Michelson, with Edward W. Morley, also attempted to exploit the device to investigate the motion of the earth relative to the hypothetical luminiferous aether. The failure of the Michelson-Morley experiment and subsequent work by Morley and Dayton C. Miller to show evidence for a motion (aether drift) was explained nearly two decades later by the special theory of relativity, which Albert Einstein developed, probably without knowledge of earlier interferometric results. The Michelson-Morley experiment since has come to be interpreted rather naively and anachronistically as the seminal evidence against the existence of an aether.

In 1868 Armand-Hippolyte-Louis Fizeau proposed interferometry be used for measurement of the diameters of celestial objects, such as the moons of Jupiter (accomplished in 1891) and stars. A stellar interferometer designed by Michelson was added as an auxiliary instrument for the 100-inch Hooker telescope in 1920, allowing Frances G. Pease and John A. Anderson to obtain the first diameter (0.047 seconds of arc for Betelgeuse) of a star other than the sun. Although a few other measurements were successfully attained, technical problems prevented widespread application of interferometry until the development of the radio interferometry by Robert Hanbury Brown in the 1950s and speckle interferometry by Antoine Labeyrie in the 1970s. Modern optical interferometers form the basis of fourier transform spectroscopy and have been proposed to measure distortions in the geometry of space due to the passage of gravitational waves (for example, the Laser Interferometer Gravitational Wave Observatory).

Charles J. Peterson

Bibliography

DeVorkin, D.H. "Michelson and the Problem of Stellar Diameters." *Journal for the History of Astronomy* 6 (1975): 1–18.

Livingston, D.M. *The Master of Light: A Biography of Albert A. Michelson*. Chicago: University of Chicago Press, 1973.

McAlister, H.A. "High Angular Resolution Measurements of Stellar Properties." *Annual Review of Astronomy and Astrophysics* 23 (1985): 59–87.

Swenson, L.D. "The Michelson-Morley-Miller Experiments before and after 1905." *Journal for the History of Astronomy* 1 (1970): 56–78.

———. *The Ethereal Aether: A History of the Michelson-Morley-Miller Aether-Drift Experiments, 1880–1930*. Austin: University of Texas Press, 1972.

International Astronomical Union (IAU)

As astronomical research became more specialized, late-nineteenth-century astronomers sought to create organizations for effective international cooperation. On the initiative of **George Ellery Hale**, the International Union for Cooperation in Solar Research was founded at the International Congress of Science held in conjunction with the 1904 St. Louis World Exposition. Originally designed to encourage international cooperation on the study of the sun, its efforts were expanded in 1910 to include promotion of all astrophysical studies.

All forms of international collaboration were disrupted by World War I. At its end, an International Research Council was created to promote international cooperation among the various sciences through the development of several International Unions. The International Astronomical Union absorbed the Union for Solar Research, the *Carte du Ciel* project, the Bureau Internationale de l'Heure, and other existing groups, to which were added various other commissions to make a total of thirty divisions. In spite of its mission to promote astronomy in all its endeavors through encouragement of international collaboration, initial membership was limited to scientists from the allied or neutral nations. German astronomers were not welcomed by the International Astronomical Union. Only in 1926 was this restriction removed and membership opened to all world scientists.

From an initial group of seven countries, the International Astronomical Union has grown (1992) to a membership of seventy-three hundred individuals representing fifty-six countries in which national organizations (for example, the National Research Council in the United States) adhere to its principles and make annual contributions to its financial support. Under the auspices of the International Astronomical Union, numerous international projects have been successfully conducted. In recent years special efforts have been addressed to the needs of astronomers in less developed nations.

The International Astronomical Union is the sole authority for astronomical nomenclature and the assignation of names to features on celestial objects. Its commissions deal with contemporary astronomical topics ranging from celestial mechanics to cosmology, from the history of astronomy to its teaching, as well as newer concerns dealing with the protection of observatory sites from light pollution and the search for extraterrestrial life. The International Astronomical Union holds a triennial general assembly, and most commissions produce a triennial review of scientific accomplishments in their area. The organization also has sponsored over 350 specialized scientific symposia and colloquia, the proceedings of which have been published under its authority.

A scholarly history of the institution has yet to be written.

Charles J. Peterson

Bibliography

Adams, W.S. "The History of the International Astronomical Union." *Publications of the Astronomical Society of the Pacific* 61 (1949): 5–12.

Blaauw, A. *History of the International Astronomical Union: The Birth and first Half-Century.* Dordrecht: Kluwer Academic Publishers, 1994.

Stratton, F.J.M. "International Co-operation in Astronomy." *Monthly Notices of the Royal Astronomical Society* 94 (1934): 361–372.

Italy, Astronomy in (from the Seventeenth Century)

Astronomy in Italy during the sixteenth and early seventeenth centuries is widely viewed by historians of science as a central part of the Scientific Revolution and the emergence of early modern science. Of course, the modern nation of Italy did not come to be until the late nineteenth century. Thus the term *Italian astronomy* is at best a vague one, but one that nevertheless may conjure up appropriate linguistic and geographical associations. Italians such as **Galileo Galilei**, Giovanni Magini, and Giambattista Riccioli were protagonists in the cosmological debates of that era and in the early development of telescopic astronomy. Societies such as the *Accademia dei Lincei* and *Accademia del Cimento* encouraged and sponsored astronomical pursuits. Giovanni Alfonso Borelli, who proposed a theory of celestial dynamics consistent with Keplerian orbits and applied it to the moons of Jupiter, was a member of the *Cimento*. At the *Accademia*'s request, he mediated the dispute between Christiaan Huygens and the Jesuit Honoré Fabri, a corresponding member, over the nature of Saturn's rings. Borelli decided for Huygens.

But Italian scientific societies, unlike their British and French counterparts, had dwindled to inactivity by the middle of the seventeenth century. Italy's northern neighbors pursued astronomy more vigorously in the eighteenth century, tending to organize and centralize their efforts. Thus studies of astronomers and astronomy in Italy from the mid-sixteenth to mid-seventeenth century (essentially the lifetime of Galileo) are plentiful, but generally speaking the literature is much sparser concerning the late seventeenth and eighteenth centuries. The studies that exist tend to focus on specific astronomical subjects and particular astronomers. This historiography suggests that the work of isolated individuals (as compared with private or public institutions) was relatively more important and longer lived in Italy than in Britain, France, or even Germany. This view is consistent with the chronic political instability of the peninsula, the late date at which it became a nation-state, and the late advent of significant industrialization. For these reasons, astronomy in Italy developed at a different rate and along different paths from the more northerly countries of Europe. Yet from Palermo to Milan, the lands that today constitute Italy have produced talented astronomers in every era.

Bologna was a center of early modern astronomy. Gian Domenico (later **Jean-Dominique) Cassini**, one of the preeminent astronomers of the second half of the seventeenth century, began his career in 1648 at a private observatory in Bologna, where he also studied under the Jesuit astronomers Riccioli and Francesco Maria Grimaldi, both of whom were skilled instrument-makers and observers. Cassini's work in Bologna, including measurements of the length of the year, theories of solar eclipses and atmospheric refraction, and accurate tables for the motions of the Jovian satellites, brought international recognition that led to his appointment, in 1669, as the first director of the new **Paris Observatory**. Cassini also contributed to the development of telescope technology in collaboration with the Roman lens-maker Giuseppe Campani, who is known for his own observations of Jupiter's moons and Saturn's rings. Cassini eventually introduced Campani's telescopes to Paris. Astronomical research in Bologna did not cease when Cassini left for France. Cassini's successor, Geminiano Montanari, for example, an accomplished instrument-maker, pioneered the systematic observation of variable stars and noted the cycle of Algol in 1667.

The University of Bologna observatory, planned from the late 1600s, was built between 1712 and 1725 in a tower (like the early observatories of Paris and Berlin) belonging to the university. Eustachio Manfredi and his assistants used a **mural circle** there to measure the phenomenon of aberration of starlight, a description of which he published, though without a theoretical explanation, in the same year (1729) in which James Bradley described and correctly explained the effect. The Bologna observatory was known through the eighteenth and early nineteenth centuries for its regularly published ephemerides. Political disturbances in the 1840s prevented Ignazio Calandrelli from putting new instruments into operation, but Lorenzo Respighi began some of the earliest astrophysical inquiries, primarily solar and stellar spectra, in the ancient observatory. Bologna's astronomers did not acquire a high-altitude observatory outside the city until 1936, when a Zeiss 60-cm reflector was installed at a site in Villa Aldina in the Apennines.

The decades that followed the establishment of the Bologna observatory in 1725 saw others established in Pisa (1730), Turin (1759), Milan (1760), Padua (1761), Florence (1774), Palermo (1786), and Naples (1788). This growth generally coincides with the decline of Spanish influence in much of Italy after about 1700 and the establishment of new political alignments toward the north, which may have favored the spread of reforming and secularizing aspects of the Enlightenment. The histories of Italian observatories have not been extensively studied.

Milan's Brera Observatory is an exception and much source material for it has been inventoried and published. The observatory began in a corner of the *Palazzo di Brera* in the 1760s, where the Jesuits of the *Collegio di Brera* had already been observing for many years. Indeed, the Jesuit observatories of that era in Brera, Bologna, and Rome were some of the best equipped of centers for experimental and observational work. The Dalmatian Jesuit Rudjer Bošković was a major influence in setting up the observatory, which included an assortment of meridian instruments and a small equatorial refractor. The observatory grew steadily under the tenure of Barnaba Oriani, who guided it through the tumultuous events of the Napoleonic wars, the transformation into a public institution, and the years of Austrian domination. In 1926 the observatory's operations were divided between the old site at Brera, which continued traditional positional astronomy, and a new site at Merate, which became the astrophysical branch.

The observatory created in Palermo by the Bourbon monarchy's viceroy of Sicily gained prominence under its first director, **Giuseppe Piazzi**. Piazzi, a member of the Theatine order, equipped the observatory with a 5-foot Ramsden mural quadrant and began an ambitious program typical of the age of positional astronomy—namely, the compilation of an exhaustive positional catalogue of all visible stars. Between 1792 and 1802 he carefully measured the positions of 6,748 stars, later increased to 7,646, within an accuracy of a few arcseconds. For some time Piazzi's observations were accepted as the most accurate available measurements, to be superseded only when Bradley's work was refined by **Friedrich Wilhelm Bessel** in 1818. Astrometry led to his most significant contribution, the first known minor planet, or asteroid, which he named Ceres. Piazzi's discovery, on January 1, 1801, that there were hitherto unknown planets that could be found by meticulous observation among the stars stimulated much of the positional and computational work of early nineteenth-century astronomy. Pietro Tacchini would later make Palermo an early site for astrophysics with his investigations of the solar spectrum before he moved to Rome in 1879.

Piazzi helped replace the original tower observatory in Naples with the new observatory at Capodimonte, begun in 1812 and completed in 1820. The development of astronomy, particularly larger telescopes, drove many observatories to follow the example of Capodimonte by moving away from urban areas and abandoning the tower configuration. At Capodimonte, as at the early-nineteenth-century observatories of **Pulkovo** and **Berlin**, the main building has a low profile above which rise the cupolas housing instruments mounted on sturdy piers. Positional astronomy at Capodimonte followed basic European patterns as exemplified by **Ercole Dembowski**, who specialized in detailed astrometric work such as determining the orbits of double stars.

Observatories have come and gone in Rome for centuries, and in the curial city they often had ecclesiastical sponsorship. Astronomy was a traditional specialty among the Jesuits of the *Collegio Romano* even in the late sixteenth century. The German Jesuit Christoph Clavius and his students, observing presumably from terraces and rooftops, were among the first to confirm independently Galileo's telescopic discoveries of 1609–1610. But the *Collegio Romano* seems not to have acquired a permanent observatory before 1787, when the Jesuit Giuseppe Calandrelli erected a slender tower on the roof of the *Collegio Romano* building and began a program of positional measurements. His successors distinguished themselves in observations of planets and comets. Papal observatories have existed at least since the Vatican's Tower of the Winds, designed by Ignazio Danti to house a meridian instrument, was built to make observations for the Gregorian calendar reform of 1582. The *Campidoglio* observatory in Rome, located on the eastern tower of the Senatorial *Palazzo,* was founded by Leo XII and completed in 1827. Ignazio Calandrelli, nephew of Giuseppe and former director of the Bologna observatory, became director of the *Campidoglio* observatory and there studied motions of **minor planets** and stellar **proper motions**. The *Campidoglio* observatory was eventually acquired by the Italian state, which transferred its equipment and operations to Monte Mario, immediately outside of Rome, beginning in 1925. The Vatican State retained the instruments of the *Collegio Romano* observatory, and in 1888 Leo XIII founded the Vatican Observatory, which quickly joined the international project to compile a comprehensive photographic star atlas (the *Carte du Ciel*). Pius XI approved the observatory's move from the Vatican gardens, amid the lights of Rome, to the site at Castel Gandolfo and provided modernized instrumentation that began operation in 1935.

The years after about 1830 saw a period of economic growth and industrial development in the Italian peninsula, except, as usual, in the south. Strong sentiments for Italian nationalism and relative prosperity had their effects on the growth of science, and the first congress of Italian scientists met in 1839. By the end of the *Risorgimento,* in 1870, the industrial base was still very small and would not grow rapidly until after 1900. Nevertheless, in the face of slow growth and political upheavals, Italian astronomy entered the age of astrophysics. The foremost example is the work of the Jesuit **Angelo Secchi**, who continued and greatly enhanced the long tradition of astronomical work at the *Collegio Romano*. Around 1850, Secchi brought his experiences in England and the United States back to Italy, where he obtained a modern 9-inch Merz refractor for the *Collegio Romano*. Secchi moved the operations of the observatory from its unsteady perch on the roof of the old building and installed the new instrument on solid piers atop the church of *Sant'Ignazio*. There he proceeded to apply thermography, photography, and especially spectroscopy to astronomical problems. He studied the chemical and physical characteristics of planets (first using the word *canale* for linear Martian features), comets, and the sun. He used an objective prism to compile a large catalogue of stellar spectra and developed a very influential classification of stellar spectral types.

Secchi and his work have been seen not only as signifying the excellence of Jesuit scientific traditions, but also as epitomizing a dedication to experimental work that is characteristic of Italian scientific culture in the first half of the nineteenth century. In this view, Secchi's system of classifying stellar spectra based on the accumulation of thousands of spectra is a product of a rigorously inductive procedure that yielded not only insights into nature, but also a conceptual widening of traditional astronomy into the modern discipline of **astrophysics**. Secchi was also a key figure in the new flowering of Italian scientific societies. In 1871, Secchi, Tacchini, Annibale Riccò, and Giuseppe Lorenzoni founded the *Società degli Spettroscopisti Italiani,* the publications of which constitute, in effect, the earliest journal of astrophysics. Respighi, at Bologna and later at Rome's *Campidoglio* observatory, and Giovan Battista Donati at Florence, also pioneered astrophysical spectroscopy in Italy.

While astrophysics advanced in Rome and elsewhere, Milan hosted a new era of planetary observations with the work of **Giovanni Schiaparelli**, who became director of the Brera Observatory in 1862. Schiaparelli updated the observatory's equipment, adding an 8-inch Merz refractor after 1874 and eventually acquiring a 50-cm Merz refractor on a Repsold mounting, thus making a major astrophysical instrument available to the Brera astronomers. Schiaparelli is best known for his planetary observations, but he also discovered the minor planet Hesperia, worked on comets and meteors (proving, in 1866, that the orbit of the Perseid meteor swarm is identical with the orbit of Comet Swift-Tuttle), made double star observations, and was an accomplished historian of ancient astronomy. His values for the rotation of Mercury and Venus were widely accepted. Schiaparelli charted the surface of Mars. His maps, done at Martian oppositions between 1877 and 1890, were internationally famous and stimulated great controversy over the reality and significance of the features on the planet and their apparent changes—particularly the *canali*.

In the late nineteenth and early twentieth centuries, Italian astronomers, like those in other nations, strove to acquire telescopes of ever larger apertures located at remote, high altitude sites. The Turin Observatory, for example, established a branch at the relatively high-altitude site of Pino Torinese in 1912. In 1942 the Padua observatory began operations at a site in the mountainous plain of Asiago with a 1.2-meter reflector, the largest in Europe at that time. In the wake of decades of war during the first half of the twentieth century, astronomy in Italy has followed the paths of professionalization and internationalization that have characterized astronomy in other nations. Major Italian universities, for example, now offer advanced degree programs in astronomy, and Italian astronomers maintain professional organizations for their various specialties. The *Istituto di Radioastronomia*, for example, operates the Italian Northern Cross radio telescope (a transit instrument near Bologna), the nearby 32-meter radio telescope at Medicina, and its twin in Noto, Sicily. These two instruments are primarily used for very long baseline interferometry. And the *Centro per l'Astronomia Infrarossa*, at the Arcetri Observatory, operates the Italian 1.5-meter infrared telescope at Gornergrat, in the Swiss Alps. Italian astronomers, and the Italian nation, participate at all levels in a wide variety of international endeavors, including collaboration in international space projects such as Giotto, Hipparchos, and the Hubble Space Telescope. Through the **European Space Agency**, Italy is a partner in the new space experiment named Solar Heliospheric Observatory. Italy is also a partner in the European Southern Observatory. Indeed, ground-based research remains a real Italian research strength, which can be seen by such projects as the Galileo Telescope (a new-technology 3.5-meter instrument at Santa Cruz de la Palma in the Canary Islands) and the Large Binocular Telescope. The last is a highly advanced telescope project in which Italy is a major partner. It will have twin telescopes with 8.0-meter thin mirrors atop Mount Graham in Arizona. The mirror technology for this project was tested and proven in the Vatican Advanced Technology Telescope, also at Mount Graham. Through such projects and powerful instruments, Italian astronomers continue to work in all areas of astronomy and astrophysics, with particular strengths in the structure and evolution of galaxies and galaxy clusters, stellar physics, and stellar evolution. Another traditional Italian strength is solar astronomy including radio, optical, and X-ray observations as well as high-resolution solar spectroscopy.

James M. Lattis

Bibliography

Abetti, G. *The History of Astronomy*. New York: Schuman, 1952.

Baldini, U. "L'attività scientifica nel primo Settecento." In *Scienza e technica nella cultura e nella società dal Rinascimento a oggi*, edited by G. Micheli, 469–526. Storia d'Italia. Annali 3. Turin: Einaudi, 1980.

———. "La scuola galileiana." In Micheli, 383–448.

Bozzolato, G., P. Del Negro, and C. Ghetti. *La specola dell'Università di Padova*. Brugine: Edizione 1+1, 1986.

Clerke, A.M. *A Popular History of Astronomy during the Nineteenth Century*. London: Adam and Charles Black, 1902.

Godoli, G. *Sfere armoniche: Storia dell' astronomia*. Turin: UTET Libreria, 1993.

Grant, R. *History of Physical Astronomy*. London, 1852; reprint, New York: Johnson Reprint, 1966.

Hearnshaw, J.B. *The Analysis of Starlight: One Hundred and Fifty Years of Astronomical Spectroscopy*. Cambridge: Cambridge University Press, 1990.

Herrmann, D.B. *History of Astronomy from Herschel to Hertzsprung*. Cambridge: Cambridge University Press, 1984.

Kranjc, A., ed. *Da Brera a Marte: Storia dell' Osservatorio Astronomico di Milano*. Milan: Nuovo banco ambrosiano, 1983.

Maffeo, S. *In the Service of Nine Popes: 100 Years of the Vatican Observatory*. Translated by G.V. Coyne. Vatican: Vatican Observatory and Pontifical Academy of Sciences, 1991.

Mandrino, A., G. Tagliaferri, and P. Tucci, eds. *Catalogo della corrispondenza degli astronomi di Brera, 1726–1799. Vol. 1*. Milan: Università degli Studi di Milano, 1986.

———. *Inventario di Archivo dell'Osservatorio Astronomica di Brera, 1726–1917.* Milan: Università degli Studi di Milano, Istituto di Fisica Generale Applicata, Sezione di Storia della Fisica, 1987.

Micheli, G., ed. *Scienza e technica nella cultura e nella società dal Rinascimento a oggi.* Storia d'Italia. Annali 3. Turin: Einaudi, 1980.

Miotto, E., G. Tagliaferri, and P. Tucci, eds. *La strumentazione nella storia dell' Osservatorio Astronomico di Brera.* Milan: Università degli Studi di Milano, 1989.

Osservatori astrofisici-astronomici e vulcanologici italiani. Ministero della Pubblica Istruzione, Direzione Generale dell'Istruzione Superiore. Rome, 1956.

Pannekoek, A. *History of Astronomy.* New York: Barnes and Noble, 1961.

Piazzi, G. *Sulle vicende dell'astronomia in Sicilia.* Giorgia Foderà Serio, ed. Palermo: Sellerio editore, 1990.

Redondi, P. "Cultura e scienza dall'illuminismo al positivismo." In *Scienza e technica nella cultura e nella società dal Rinascimento a oggi,* edited by G. Micheli, 685–809. Storia d'Italia. Annali 3. Turin: Einaudi, 1980.

Tagliaferri, G. "L'Osservatorio milanese di Brera tra la fine del XVIII e l'inizio del XIX secolo." *Giornale di Fisica* 32 (1991): 151–165.

Janssen, Pierre Jules César (1824–1907)

French solar physicist. Janssen was educated at home and at the University of Paris. He worked as a bank clerk and teacher before turning full time to science. Janssen joined the *Ecole Spéciale d'Architecture* in 1865, and in 1876 he was founding director of the national astrophysical observatory at Meudon. Janssen received many honors, including membership in scientific societies throughout Europe, the Royal Society's Rumford Medal (1877), and a special gold medal from the French Academy (1868).

In 1862 Janssen began studying the effects of the earth's atmosphere on the solar spectrum. In 1868, he and English astronomer **J. Norman Lockyer** independently discovered a means of observing solar prominences outside of eclipse, inaugurating a new era of research on the solar atmosphere. Janssen built Meudon into one of the best equipped facilities in Europe. There, he conducted the work that would lead to his opus magnus, a photographic solar atlas published in 1903. Janssen also conducted research outside the observatory. His first scientific work was with a magnetic survey in Peru in 1857. His work on atmospheric absorption took him to the Alps in the 1860s, and he organized and directed four expeditions to Mont Blanc between 1888 and 1897. He also directed five expeditions to observe total solar eclipses in Algeria, India, and the Pacific, and observed the 1874 transit of Venus in Japan. No biography of Janssen exists in English.

Alex S.-K. Pang

Bibliography

Lévy, J.R. "Janssen, Pierre Jules César." In *Dictionary of Scientific Biography,* edited by C.C. Gillispie, vol. 7, 73–78. New York: Scribner, 1976.

Knobel, E. "Janssen, Pierre Jules César." *Monthly Notices of the Royal Astronomical Society* 68 (1908): 245–249.

Pluvinel, A. de la B. "Janssen, Jules César." *Astrophysical Journal* 28 (1908): 88–99.

Japan, Astronomy in

Astronomy as a science was introduced into Japan from China in the seventh century. Astronomy in East Asia was intimately connected with astrology and calendar-making. In Japan, such astronomical practice started when Koreans brought with them the Chinese calendrical system into Japan. Along with the Chinese calendar, Japan also introduced a governmental office responsible for various astronomical and astrological practice. Since ancient times, China had an astronomical observatory for the purpose of making and keeping calendars, and, from the second century, developed a large and elaborate governmental organization, the Office of the Grand Astrologer, where astronomical, astrological, and chronometric tasks were performed and their techniques were taught to students. Its Japanese version, the Yin-yang Board (*On'you-no-tsukasa*), had the following structure. Under the director, it consisted of four departments, assigned to perform Yin-yang art (divination), astrology, calendar-making, and timekeeping. Each department also trained students. Compared with the Chinese system, whose primary function was to make and keep a calendar, the Japanese office placed more emphasis on the task of divination. Its staff was originally selected from exceptional students of aristocratic origins, but, later in the tenth century, it changed to a hereditary system. The *Kamo* family was assigned to this task. Later, the astrological and calendrical tasks were performed by two different families. In the Edo period, from the seventeenth century, the *Tsuchimikado* family dominated this astronomical office.

Of various tasks of the astronomical office, the most politically important and technically demanding was the reform of the calendar. Especially in China, where every new ruler demanded the change of the prevalent calendar, new calendars were developed very often, even several times within a century. Their calendars were solar and lunar calendar, and each new calendar aimed at more precise values of the periods of a year and a month.

Japan imported Chinese calendars and its astronomical office performed functions following the original Chinese office until the ninth century, when it ceased its regular cultural exchange with China. With the decline of aristocratic ruling with which astrological and calendrical rituals were closely connected, Japan ceased the regular task of calendrical reform and continued to use the one adopted in 862 for more than eight hundred years, during which Chinese rulers, in contrast, made calendrical reforms twenty-five times.

In the late seventeenth century, the official calendar produced a two-day difference at the solstice. Several intellectuals attempted to introduce a new Chinese calendar and reform the Japanese one. Although the importation of Chinese books expounding Western ideas was officially forbidden at the time, Chinese astronomical treatises were freely introduced. Through such books, the mathematician Takakazu Seki studied the *Shou-shih* calendrical treatise made by Kuo Shouching in 1280. The astronomer Harumi Shibukawa studied the theory of the *Shou-shih* calendrical system indirectly from a Korean astronomer. Based on this calendrical system, Harumi devised his original system. Unlike other Japanese calendar-makers, he made astronomical observations, which were, however, crude when compared with Chinese official observations. He took into account the difference of longitude between China and Japan, utilizing a world map he had obtained from a foreigner. Like the *Shou-shih* calendar, Shibukawa's also considered the gradual decrease in the length of a year; he employed the method of its calculation called *shocho-hou*. Since he was also a professional *go* player, Shibukawa was able to exercise his influence upon politicians and bureaucrats inside the government, leading to the adoption of his *Jokyo* calendar in 1684 despite the opposition from astronomers in Kyoto. Because of this achievement, Shibukawa was assigned as newly created *Tenmongata,* official astronomer to the shogun, whose task was to develop new calendars.

The *Tenmongata* was a hereditary profession, and all belonged to the Shibukawa and a few other officially designated families. But, because of the technical nature of the work, eight out of twelve inherited officials were adopted from outside these families. Decades later, Masayoshi Nishikawa of *Tenmongata* attempted to introduce Western astronomy in making a new calendrical system. The Tsuchimikado family criticized Nishikawa's attempt by pointing out his weakness in technical matters. When Tsuchimikado instead of Nishikawa took the initiative in reforming a new *Horyaku* calendar in 1754, he disregarded Western astronomy and basically continued the traditional calendrical system.

Japan was introduced to Western learning through Portuguese missionaries and Dutch merchants. With the advent of Jesuit missionaries in Japan in the late sixteenth century, some political and military leaders became interested in Western learning. In 1605, a Japanese Christian cosmologist wrote a tract on Western astronomical science and explained the spherical nature of the earth. Although Razan Hayashi, a leading Confucian philosopher of that age, refuted the idea of the earth as a sphere, most intellectuals accepted it. Jesuits in China, under the leadership of Father Matteo Ricci, were allowed to introduce Western science, but those in Japan were not, especially after the official ban of Christianity by the Tokugawa government in 1613. The missionary Christovao Ferreira, who was captured and forced to convert in 1633, wrote a cosmological treatise based on a Western astronomical book. The treatise was published in 1656 together with the critical commentary by a Confucian philosopher and physician, Gensho Mukai, as *Kenkon Bensetsu* (Western cosmography with critical commentaries). After the government selected the Netherlands and China as their exclusive trade partners, there emerged a group of hereditary functionaries to translate Dutch for official purposes. Since the government forbade importing Chinese books conveying information from Jesuits, these translators were key persons in introducing Western learning into Japan. Of them, Ryoei Motoki and **Tadao Shizuki** were most famous in introducing Western astronomy. Motoki translated Dutch treatises on astronomy and geography, and introduced the heliocentric system. Shizuki, who had learned astronomy from Motoki, tackled the study of Newtonian physics and astronomy and published around 1800 *Rekisho shinsho,* a translation of the Dutch version of an astronomical and physical treatise by Newton's disciple John Keill. In translating the work, Shizuki interpreted some basic concepts of Newtonian mechanics in terms of Confucianism.

From the mid-eighteenth century, Japanese astronomers made rapid progress in theory and practice. Key to this development was **Goryu Asada**. Asada studied astronomy by himself, observed independently of any academic institutions, and yet produced disciples who would become official astronomers of the Tokugawa government. Born the fourth son of a feudal family, he had no officially assigned job and studied astronomy and medicine by himself. As an amateur astronomer, he devised his own calendar, which predicted the solar eclipse in 1763 better than the official calendar. In 1767, Asada was ordered to become an official doctor of the clan. But he was by then a devoted astronomer and decided to leave not only his profession but also the clan to become an independent scholar, because the resignation from an assigned post was not permissible.

After he moved to Osaka, Asada concentrated on astronomical research, constructing instruments, making observations, and devising a new calendrical system. He attracted many excellent disciples, most notably the brilliant theoretician Yoshitoki Takahashi and the instrument-maker Shigetomi Hazama. A wealthy merchant, Hazama, was Asada's disciple and patron. He built a workshop in his residence and employed craftsmen. He designed and made quadrants and theodolites, and engaged in observational work. Although pendulum clocks were unavailable, pendulums were used in counting time during astronomical observation. He also constructed barometers and thermometers and made meteorological observations with these instruments.

Hazama also possessed a rare Chinese book edited by a Jesuit astronomer that explained Kepler's three laws. Deeply impressed by the precise agreement between theory and observation, Asada and his students committed themselves to research in Western astronomy and developed new calendars. Learning of the reputation of the Asada group, the Tokugawa government requested that Asada develop an official calendar. Instead of doing so himself, Asada told Takahashi to develop a new calendrical system. Takahashi went to Edo and Kyoto to cooperate with official astronomers and calendar-makers and proposed a new *Kansei* calendar in 1797. Takahashi later studied Joseph-Jerôme L. de Lalande's *Traite de astronomie,* a widely circulated astronomical textbook in late-eighteenth-century-Europe, and left voluminous reading notes.

With the increase of precision in astronomical observations, Takahashi felt the need to determine the longitudes of major cities in Japan. Russian encroachment led the government to survey *Ezo,* Japan's northernmost island. Takahashi seized the initiative and asked Tadataka Ino to carry out a national survey with the aid of Hazama's instruments. Ino had started to study astronomy under Takahashi at the age of fifty, and was strongly interested in this project. After Takahashi's untimely death in 1804, his eldest son, Kageyasu Takahashi, managed Ino's survey work, which resulted in the production of the first map of Japan in 1821. Kageyasu was involved with the Seabolt scandal in 1829 after the discovery that he had given a copy of the map to Philipp Franz van Seabolt, a Dutchman who had taught science to young Japanese intellectuals. After Kageyasu's imprisonment, his younger brother, Kagesuke Shibukawa, took over his office. At the Bureau of Astronomy, official astronomers started more exact and detailed observational work. Within the bureau, an office was set up to translate Western books and documents. The office played a role in the founding of the University of Tokyo. At the end of the Tokugawa period, Dutch naval engineers taught astronomy and surveying at the Nagasaki Naval School.

After the Meiji Restoration in 1868, the post of official astronomer to the shogun was abolished. The new government needed the Western calendar for diplomatic reasons. To carry out this task, the *Tsuchimikado* family and Tokugawa astronomers temporarily cooperated at a new Office of Astronomy, which was abolished after they created a new solar calendar. Calendar reform was resisted, especially by farmers. Another urgent task for the new government was to establish standard time. It constructed the Tokyo Observatory under the Department of the Navy. The observatory was transferred to Tokyo Imperial University in 1888. The department of astronomy invited foreign astronomers including Thomas C. Mendenhall from Ohio State University and Henry M. Paul from the Naval Observatory, who taught courses in positional astronomy.

Japan was strategically positioned to cooperate with European and American astronomers. In 1898, the International Geodetic Association (IGA) requested that Japan build a station for the precise measurement of latitude. Predicted by Leohard Euler in the eighteenth century and independently observed by Friedrich Küstner and Seth Carlo Chandler in the 1880s, the variation of the latitude became an important research topic for late-nineteenth-century astronomers. For its observation, the IGA decided to set up six stations in the Northern Hemisphere along the thirty-ninth parallel. Aikitsu Tanakadate, physics professor at Tokyo, and Hisashi Kimura, a young specialist in latitude observation, selected Mizusawa, located about 250 miles north of Tokyo. The station opened in 1899 and Kimura became its director. German astronomer Carl T. Albrecht developed a formula to express the variation of latitude. In 1901 Kimura proposed another term, called the Z term, for Albrecht's formula. Kimura was appointed the first president of the Variation of Latitude Commission of the **International Astronomical Union**.

Another notable achievement of Japanese positional astronomy was **Kiyotsugu Hirayama**'s discovery of the families of asteroids. A graduate of Tokyo Imperial University in 1897, Hirayama went to study at Yale University, where he worked with celestial mechanician **Ernest W. Brown**. Hirayama found groups of asteroids by identifying those with similar mean motion. These families of asteroids, he argued, derived from the explosion of large asteroids.

Some Japanese astronomers were well aware of the new development in astronomical discipline. Naozo Ichinohe, a 1903 graduate from the Tokyo Imperial University, went to study at the **Yerkes Observatory** of the University of Chicago. On his return, he became a scientific entrepreneur, organizing the Japanese Astronomical Society and campaigning for the construction of a new observatory with a large telescope. During his stay at Yerkes, Ichinohe had considered learning the art of telescope-making so that he could construct a major telescope in Japan. Inspired by Hale's construction of the Mount Wilson Observatory, Ichinohe proposed the bold idea of building such an observatory near the top of the Niitakayama in Taiwan. The plan, however, was unrealistic. Because of a disagreement with the director of the Tokyo Observatory, Ichinohe resigned and became the editor of a new scientific journal. He died in 1922.

Astronomers at Tokyo concentrated on positional astronomy. At Kyoto astronomers developed a different research agenda under the leadership of Shinzo Shinjo. A physics graduate from Tokyo University, Shinjo went to study geophysics at Gottingen, where he was influenced by Karl Schwarzschild and became interested in astronomy. He purchased several astronomical instruments in Germany and set them up in the observatory of Kyoto Imperial University. They launched a program of astrophysics in 1909 and opened a new observatory in the next year. Later some astronomers cooperated with theoretical physicists at this university. Shinjo also initiated an important research school in the history of Chinese science, and the department has provided many respected graduates. Shinjo later became a director at the Shanghai Research Institute.

The strong tradition of elementary particle physics helped to produce first-rate specialists in astrophysics in postwar Japan. Of them, the key figure is Chushiro Hayashi, who was encouraged by Hideki Yukawa to apply quantum mechanics to astronomy. Hayashi proposed a theory concerning the boundary of the forbidden region in the **Hertzsprung-Russell diagram** and introduced the concepts later known as the Hayashi phase and the Hayashi line. He also proposed a theory on the origin and evolution of the solar system based on his calculation that the disk in the solar nebula would become unstable and disintegrate. As a teacher, he produced a host of brilliant students who lead theoretical studies of astrophysics and cosmology in Japan.

Another key figure in the postwar development of Japanese astronomy was Minoru Oda, who entered **X-ray astronomy** around 1965 and, with his new collimators, was able to determine positions and distributions of X-ray sources. Since then he has led in this field as a teacher, researcher, and organizer. At his initiative, several artificial satellites were launched specifically to observe at X-ray wavelengths. The satellite *Hakucho* launched in 1979, for instance, brought in important data on periodic changes in the intensity and spectrum of radiations from X-ray stars.

Takehiko Hashimoto

Bibliography

Shigeru, N. *A History of Japanese Astronomy*. Cambridge: Harvard University Press, 1969.

Watanabe, T. *Shigetomi Hazama and His Family in the History of Astronomy* (In Japanese). Tokyo, 1943.

Jeans, James Hopwood (1877–1946)

English astronomer and physicist. Educated at Cambridge University, Jeans taught there (1904–1905; 1910–1912) and at Princeton University (1905–1909). After 1912, he worked from his Surrey home. Jeans studied the partition of energy in gases and in radiation, amending Lord Rayleigh's formula for black body radiation. He applied the dynamics of rotating, gravitating, fluid masses to theories of the origin of celestial systems. Debate with Jeans spurred **Arthur Stanley Eddington**'s work on the structure and evolution of stars. Jeans was physical secretary of the Royal Society (1919–1929) and revitalized its *Proceedings* as a research journal. He wrote textbooks and extremely successful popular works. Jeans was knighted in 1929.

Joann Eisberg

Bibliography

Milne, E.A. *Sir James: A Biography*. Cambridge: Cambridge University Press, 1952.

Jet Propulsion Laboratory, Astronomy at

The Jet Propulsion Laboratory (JPL), in Pasadena, California, is a **National Aeronautics and Space Administration** (NASA) field center operated by the California Institute of Technology (Caltech). JPL contributes to astronomical knowledge in three ways: the design, construction, and operation of unmanned solar-system exploration spacecraft; optical and radio astronomy investigations by staff astronomers at its own Table Mountain Observatory and other facilities; radio astronomy and planetary radar investigations using antennas of the Deep Space Network (DSN), the JPL-managed system by which NASA communicates with deep-space probes.

JPL began as an off-campus facility used by several Caltech graduate students in the late 1930s to conduct early rocket propulsion experiments. As an Army Ordnance facility in the 1940s and 1950s, it developed a jet-assisted takeoff engine for airplanes during World War II and the Corporal and Sergeant surface-to-surface missiles during the early Cold War years. Working with Wernher von Braun's rocket team at the army's Redstone Arsenal in Huntsville, Alabama, JPL engineers developed the upper stages and payload for the first United States satellite, *Explorer 1,* launched on January 31, 1958.

JPL's future, however, was shaped by a proposal, made within a few weeks after the Soviet Union's launching (October 4, 1957) of *Sputnik 1,* to launch a series of probes toward the moon. The Department of Defense subsequently approved the proposal, and one of the probes, *Pioneer 4,* launched on March 3, 1959, became the first United States spacecraft to escape the earth's gravity. To support the probes, JPL engineers hastily erected a 26-meter antenna in 1958 at Goldstone Dry Lake in the Mojave Desert of California. It subsequently became the cornerstone of the Deep Space Network.

After the Department of Defense agreed to transfer JPL to NASA in late 1958, it became the space agency's chief facility for designing, constructing, and operating unmanned solar-system exploration spacecraft. JPL also provides support to flight-project science investigators for developing their instruments and analyzing data obtained during a spacecraft's mission.

Under the leadership of directors William C. Pickering (1954–1976), Bruce Murray (1976–1982), Lew Allen (1982–1990), and Edward Stone (1990–present), JPL-built spacecraft have visited every planet in the solar system except Pluto and have studied many other objects as well. In the 1960s, three *Ranger* spacecraft took thousands of close-up pictures of the moon before impacting on the lunar surface, and five *Surveyor* spacecraft achieved soft landings on the moon and analyzed the lunar soil. During the same period, early *Mariner* spacecraft flew by Venus and Mars. They were followed by *Mariner 9,* the first spacecraft to orbit (1971) around another planet (Mars); *Mariner 10,* which flew (1973–1974) by Venus once and Mercury three times in the first gravity-assist mission; and two *Viking* orbiters inserted (1976) into orbit around Mars.

Taking advantage of a rare planetary alignment, *Voyagers 1* and *2* flew by Jupiter (1979) and Saturn (1980 and 1981), and the latter spacecraft also encountered Uranus (1986) and Neptune (1989). In addition to studying the atmospheres and magnetic fields surrounding each planet, spacecraft examined the satellites and ring systems of these outer planets; among their most important discoveries were active volcanoes on the Jovian satellite Io, numerous small satellites, and the complexity of Saturn's ring system. JPL's *Magellan* spacecraft, orbiting around cloud-shrouded Venus in the early 1990s, examined the planet's surface by radar. *Galileo,* an orbiter-probe spacecraft currently en route to Jupiter, made the first-ever close flybys of asteroids (Gaspra and Ida). A photograph and other data obtained during the latter encounter (August 28, 1993) provided the first clear evidence of a double asteroid.

Perceiving a need for in-house astronomy expertise to support the flight projects, JPL's leaders began hiring astronomers aggressively in the early 1960s. JPL astronomers were generally unsuccessful in obtaining observing time at existing large telescopes (particularly at the nearby Mount Wilson and Palomar Mountain observatories) and NASA Headquarters and Congress restricted them from obtaining a large telescope of their own. Headquarters officials did, however, allow them in 1961 to acquire a used Nishaimura 16-inch reflector, which they set up at Table Mountain in California. Subsequent additions to the observatory included a 10-foot radio antenna for research at millimeter wavelengths, an 18-foot Cassegrain radio antenna, and a 24-inch Cassegrain reflector with a Coudé room and Coudé spectrograph. Staff investigations using the telescopes at Table Mountain are generally in support of current and future JPL missions.

The JPL-managed Deep Space Network (DSN) is comprised of paraboloid antennas grouped at Goldstone; Tidbinbilla (near Canberra), Australia; and Robledo de Chavela (near Madrid), Spain. These stations are approximately 120 degrees apart in longitude in order to provide continuous coverage of space missions as the earth rotates. The primary mission of the antennas (currently 34 meters and 70 meters in diameter) is to support the space probes of JPL and other institutions (such as other NASA centers and the European, Japanese, and Russian space agencies). The support includes the transmission of commands, the reception of engineering and scientific data, and the determination of the distance and direction of the probes from earth. On a noninterference basis, however, various investigators have conducted radio astronomy and planetary radar investigations with the DSN antennas. The radio astronomy work has included collaborative very long baseline interferometry (VLBI) experiments conducted with institutions around the world.

The DSN first became involved in planetary radar because of the navigational needs of NASA's space-probe program. By measuring the time interval between the emission of a signal by a ground-based transmitter and reception of an echo reflected off a target planet, JPL engineers could obtain an extremely accurate measurement of the distance between the planet and the earth. Such a measurement would (by means of Kepler's third law of planetary motion) enable a more accurate measurement of the astronomical unit and in turn permit (by means of Newtonian gravitational theory) more accurately computed ephemerides of the future motions of the planets and other solar system objects. More accurate ephemerides would in turn enable JPL engineers to navigate a spacecraft closer to a target planet, satellite, asteroid, or comet.

In anticipation of two *Mariner* missions to Venus in 1962, DSN engineers attempted (with two antennas at Goldstone) a Venus radar experiment around the time of the inferior conjunction in 1961. Teams at the Massachusetts Institute of Technology and Jodrell Bank had made earlier claims of radar contact with Venus in 1958 and 1959. Planetary radar astronomers now generally agree, however, that the DSN team made the first definite radar contact with the planet on March 10, 1961.

JPL staff subsequently made radar contacts with the terrestrial planets (Mercury, Venus, and Mars), the major satellites of Jupiter and Saturn, the Saturnian ring system, and numerous comets and asteroids. These contacts provided much new information (such as rotation speeds and topographical features) about these objects. Various other facilities in the United States, the United Kingdom, and the Soviet Union were the sites of planetary radar investigations in the 1960s and early 1970s. Currently, however, planetary radar astronomers conduct their investigations only at Goldstone and the National Radio and Ionospheric Center in Arecibo, Puerto Rico.

Craig B. Waff

Bibliography

Burrows, W.E. *Exploring Space: Voyages in the Solar System and Beyond.* New York: Random House, 1990.

Ezell, E.C., and L.N. Ezell. *On Mars: Exploration of the Red Planet 1958–1978* (NASA SP-4212). Washington, D.C.: U.S. Government Printing Office, 1984.

Hall, R.C. *Lunar Impact: A History of Project Ranger* (NASA SP-4210). Washington,

D.C.: U.S. Government Printing Office, 1977.
Koppes, C.R. *JPL and the American Space Program: A History of the Jet Propulsion Laboratory*. New Haven and London: Yale University Press, 1982.
Morrison, D. *Voyages to Saturn* (NASA SP-451). Washington, D.C.: U.S. Government Printing Office, 1982.
Morrison, D., and J. Samz. *Voyage to Jupiter* (NASA SP-439). Washington, D.C.: U.S. Government Printing Office, 1980.
Murray, B. *Journey into Space: The First Thirty Years of Space Exploration*. New York and London: Norton, 1989.
Waff, C.B. "The Struggle for the Outer Planets." *Astronomy* 17 (1989): 44–52.
———. "Designing the United States' Initial 'Deep Space Networks.'" *IEEE Antennas and Propagation Magazine* 35 (1993): 49–57.
———. "The Road to the Deep Space Network." *IEEE Spectrum* 30 (1993): 50–57.

Jupiter

Galileo first saw the disk of Jupiter with his telescope on January 7, 1610. While the planet itself was featureless, it happened to be set against three stars that changed position from night to night. He quickly realized that these objects, together with a fourth, were revolving around Jupiter, and he was able to estimate their periods. This discovery provided support for the Copernican hypothesis; it demonstrated celestial motion about a center other than the sun, which was incompatible with the Aristotelian model.

Jupiter and its satellites attracted immediate attention from other observers and theoreticians. **Giovanni Domenico Cassini** at Bologna and later Paris, Christiaan Huygens, and Ole Römer refined the theory using timings of the satellites' eclipses. Römer became convinced that a 10-minute difference between tables based on opposition measurements and observations near conjunction was due to the finite velocity of light, and the additional distance, equal to earth's orbit, the light traversed.

In 1659, Huygens discerned two equatorial bands on Jupiter. In 1663, Cassini derived a 9-hour 56-minute rotation rate from features in the bands, and noted that spots near the equator had rotation periods about five minutes shorter than those close to the poles. Cassini and Robert Hooke noticed a conspicuous and long-lived spot in the southern portion, dubbed the Eye of Jupiter, possibly the first recorded observation of the Great Red Spot. In 1878 this most famous feature became conspicuous and has been under constant scrutiny since.

The tiny satellite Almathea, the first new satellite of Jupiter to be noticed since Galileo, was discovered in 1892 by **E.E. Barnard**; it was the last satellite to be discovered with the naked eye. Jovian satellites discovered later were all much smaller and farther from the planet than the Galileans.

At the beginning of the twentieth century, **Vesto Slipher** at **Lowell Observatory** found unidentified absorption bands in near infrared spectra of Jupiter, Saturn, Uranus, and Neptune, increasing in intensity with distance from the sun. Their source remained a mystery until **Rupert Wildt** at Göttingen tied them to laboratory lines of methane and ammonia in 1931–32, and Theodore Dunham was able to make a laboratory confirmation. In 1935 **Henry Norris Russell** showed that at the temperatures of these planets—and in the absence of oxygen—nitrogen, carbon, and hydrogen would combine into methane and ammonia as their most stable molecules, leaving a large amount of molecular hydrogen as a major constituent of the outer Jovian planets.

In 1938 Wildt proposed models of the outer planets in which each had a small earthlike core, surrounded by a layer of frozen condensed water and gases, in turn surrounded by highly compressed gases. These models were accepted by many astronomers despite problems concerning relative abundances of hydrogen and helium and the densities of the various layers.

Jupiter was found to be unusually active in the longer wavelengths. In the late 1950s, radio emission was detected from Jupiter, and **I.S. Shklovsky** identified it as synchrotron radiation from electrons trapped in the planet's magnetic field. This was the first discovery of a planetary magnetosphere from earth-based observations.

In 1969 Frank Low made infrared radiometric measurements from a Learjet, above the absorbing water vapor of the earth's atmosphere, showing that Jupiter radiated more than twice as much energy as it was receiving from the sun, suggesting the planet had an internal heat source.

Visual observers had from time to time detected features on the tiny disks of the Galilean satellites and followed the periodic photometric changes of the bodies. These observations supported a bound rotation rate, similar to that of the earth's moon, for all four. In the early 1970s, infrared spectroscopy of the Galilean satellites revealed the signature of water ice. When combined with estimates of satellite densities, these results suggested that the innermost, Io and Europa, were largely rocky bodies and the outermost, Callisto and Ganymede, about half rocky material and half ice. At about the same time, sodium was detected around the orbital path of Io, and theorists attempted to understand how this metal might be removed from a planetary body and inserted into the surrounding region.

In December of 1973 and 1974, the spacecraft *Pioneers 10* and *11* passed through the Jovian system. The spacecraft returned detailed color views of the bands, zones, and red spot, highlighting the structure of the boundaries between these dynamic features. The flyby was so swift, however, that the motions of the features could not be followed. While *Pioneer* did obtain images of the Galilean satellites, they showed little detail. Pioneer observations led to a more precise figure for the radiation budget of the planet, and showed the heat to be evenly distributed over the planet, equator-to-pole, and thus that the atmosphere was fairly efficient at transmitting energy. *Pioneer* also made the first determination of the ratio of hydrogen to helium, finding it to be about that of the sun, in general agreement with Rupert Wildt's models of the 1950s. *Pioneer 11* continued on a course that would take it to Saturn.

In March and July of 1979, *Voyagers 1* and *2* encountered Jupiter. About a month before encounter, the images exceeded the resolution of the *Pioneers,* in part due to the superior imaging system on the *Voyagers.* The wealth of detail and color in the carefully planned time-lapse images of the swirling atmosphere exceeded expectations and provided much information for the atmospheric physicists to digest. *Voyager* images also surprised scientists by disclosing a faint, narrow ring, about 128,000 km from Jupiter's center.

The geologists were not sure whether the icy surfaces of the Galilean satellites were durable enough to preserve impact craters for very long. They were ecstatic over the well-

Jupiter photographed at a distance of about 20 million miles (32.7 million kilometers) by Voyager 1 *on February 1, 1979. The resolution is such that objects as small as 375 miles (600 km) in diameter can be seen in this image. Note the Great Red Spot, which looks something like an eye, and the large number of smaller light and dark spots and clouds as well as bands. (Courtesy of the National Aeronautics and Space Administration)*

preserved record of bombardment on Ganymede and Callisto, having kept their form for many millions of years due to the rigidity of ice at only 120 degrees Kelvin. Europa showed a quite different surface, with a network of linear features over a smooth surface with few craters, suggesting internal activity. Io showed no craters at all, but a remarkable mottled surface in numerous hues of yellow-orange. A few days after encounter, enlargements of an image taken for navigation purposes showed that a volcano had been caught in near perfect profile, actively spewing sulphur compounds. Seven more active volcanoes were later identified, some with plumes rising 250 km above the surface. Six of these were still erupting, continually remaking the tiny satellite's surface, when *Voyager 2* arrived four months later.

The most comprehensive, albeit dated and not interpretive, work on ground-based observations of Jupiter remains that of Peek. Mark Washburn provides an excellent journalistic account of the *Voyager* encounters with Jupiter, mainly oriented toward imaging science and the first discoveries. Richard O. Fimmel et al. and Dave Morrison supplement their summary texts with brief historical overviews of the *Pioneer* and the *Voyager* missions, and valuable summaries of Jupiter studies in the present century. Tom Gehrels' volume provides a comprehensive and detailed scientific accounting of the state of knowledge of Jupiter just following the *Pioneer* encounters, but before those of *Voyager*. Relevant chapters of Beatty's successive editions provide snapshots of the state of consensus on Jupiter at critical times while new knowledge was being assimilated. Waff supplies a thorough popular discussion of the detailed and complex planning that went into the *Voyager* missions.

Interpretive historical treatments are few and concentrate on specific areas and problems. Débarbat and Wilson provide an authoritative treatment of studies of the Galilean satellites. Hockey (1991) examines a major observational activity of the nineteenth century, observations of the changing aspect of the Jovian belts, zones, and the Great Red Spot, as does Lankford, but with a different purpose. For more comprehensive discussions of astronomical work on Jupiter, one must consult the general histories of astronomy and the review literature.

Joseph N. Tatarewicz

Bibliography

Beatty, J.K., and A. Chaikin, eds. *The New Solar System*. New York: Cambridge University Press, 1981; 2nd ed., 1982; 3rd ed., 1990.

Débarbat, S., and C. Wilson. "The Galilean Satellites of Jupiter from Galileo to Cassini, Römer and Bradley." In *Planetary Astronomy from the Renaissance to the Rise of Astrophysics: Part A: Tycho Brahe to Newton*, edited by R. Taton and C. Wilson. In *The General History of Astronomy*, vol. 2A., edited by M. Hoskin, 144–158. New York: Cambridge University Press, 1989.

Fimmel, R.O., J. Van Allen, and E. Burgess. *Pioneer: First to Jupiter, Saturn, and Beyond*. Washington, D.C.: NASA SP-446, 1980.

Gehrels, T., and M.S. Matthews, eds. *Jupiter: Studies of the Interior, Atmosphere, Magnetosphere, and Satellites*. Space Science Series. Tucson: University of Arizona Press, 1976.

Hockey, T.A. "Nineteenth Century Investigations of Periodicities in the Jovian Atmosphere." *Vistas in Astronomy* 34 (1991), 409–415.

———. "Seeing Red: Observations of Colour in Jupiter's Equatorial Zone on the Eve of the Modern Discovery of the Great Red Spot." *Journal for the History of Astronomy* 23 (1992), 93–105.

Lankford, J. "Amateur versus Professional: The Transatlantic Debate over the Measurement of Jovian Longitude." *Journal of the British Astronomical Association* 89 (1979): 574–582.

Morrison, D., and J. Samz. *Voyage to Jupiter*. NASA SP-439. Washington, D.C.: Government Printing Office, 1980.

Morrison, D., ed. *Satellites of Jupiter*. Space Science Series. Tucson: University of Arizona Press, 1982.

Peek, B.M. *The Planet Jupiter: The Observer's Handbook* ([1958]). Revised by Patrick Moore. Boston: Faber and Faber, 1981.

Waff, C.B. "The Struggle for the Outer Planets." *Astronomy* 17 (1989): 44–52.

Washburn, M. *Distant Encounters: The Exploration of Jupiter and Saturn*. New York: Harcourt, Brace, Jovanovich, 1983.

Zeitner, M.E. "A History of the Theory of Io's Effect on Jupiter's Decametric Radiation." *Astronomy Quarterly* 6 (1989): 27–44.

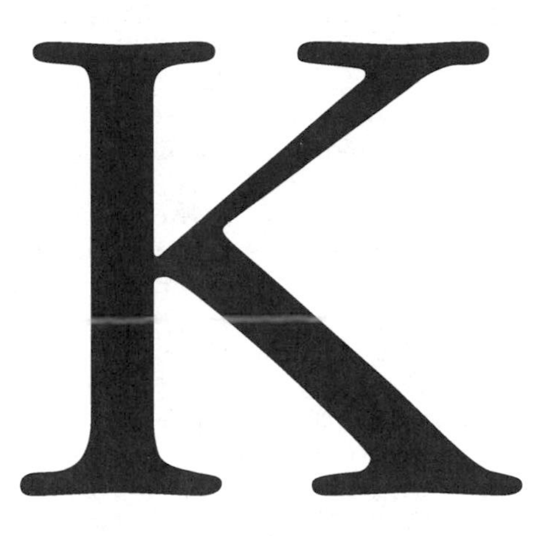

Kapteyn, Jacobus Cornelius (1851–1922)

Dutch astronomer. Born in Barneveld, Holland, J.C. Kapteyn attended his father's boarding school, matriculating to the University of Utrecht in 1869 where he took a doctorate in physics (1875). After three years at the Leiden observatory, he was elected to the chair of astronomy and theoretical mechanics at the University of Groningen (1878), where he remained until 1921. About 1890 he founded the world-renowned Astronomical Laboratory of Groningen, and in 1908 he became a research associate of the Mount Wilson Observatory, which he visited annually until the outbreak of World War I.

Throughout a long and distinguished career, Kapteyn was dominated by one scientific problem: What is the structure of the sidereal universe? Using mathematical and statistical techniques, his prerelativistic approach focused exclusively on understanding the distributions of the stars in space. His contributions to **stellar statistics** include the determination of the distribution, brightness, and motion of the stars. At the time it was thought that these principal relationships—the density, the luminosity, and the velocity laws—would provide a satisfactory explanation of the sidereal universe. Until 1902, Kapteyn focused on stellar velocity phenomena for his solution to the sidereal problem. As a result, he inadvertently discovered the phenomenon variously called star streaming, which suggested that the Milky Way Galaxy was composed of two intermingling but distinctly preferential star streams moving through one another. Afterwards he focused on the spatial distributions and stellar brightnesses of stars in order to understand the architecture of the sidereal universe. The culmination of nearly forty years of research resulted in a transparent, ellipsoidal stellar model, dubbed the Kapteyn Universe, in which star density at low galactic latitudes diminishes in all directions with increasing distance from his sun-centered system. Overall, the dimensions of this 1920 model were 8,000 light years toward the galactic poles and 60,000 light years in the galactic plane. His last major paper (1922) combined this model with his earlier discovery of star-streaming.

Kapteyn, along with **Hugo von Seeliger**, mounted the most important attempt to solve this problem using the mathematical and statistical tools available at the turn of the century. Kapteyn constantly sought to exploit international connections, and in 1904 he proposed the Plan of Selected Areas, in which he enlisted observatories worldwide in the collection of astronomical data needed to understand the cosmology of the heavens. Some twenty observatories participated in this mammoth project, achieving important results within a decade.

Kapteyn's Nachlass was destroyed during the bombing of Rotterdam in May 1940. As a result, the largest collection of Kapteyn's correspondence is preserved in the George Ellery Hale Microfilm Collection (Huntington Library), with additional important materials in the Karl Schwarzschild Microfilm Collection (American Philosophical Society), the Astronomical Laboratory at Groningen, the University of Groningen, and the **Yerkes Observatory** (Williams Bay, Wisconsin).

Finally, important technical and personal details not otherwise available are contained in the biography by Kapteyn's daughter Henrietta Hertzsprung-Kapteyn.

E. Robert Paul

Bibliography

Blaauw, A. "Kapteyn, Jacobus Cornelius." In *Dictionary of Scientific Biography*, edited by C.C. Gillispie, vol. 7, 235–240. New York: Scribner, 1973.

Hertzsprung-Kapteyn, H. *J.C. Kapteyn, zijn leven en werken*. Groningen, 1928. Translated and annotated by E.R. Paul. *The Life and Works of J.C. Kapteyn*. Dordrecht: Kluwer Academic Publishers, 1993.

Kepler, Johannes (1571–1630)

German astronomer and mathematician. Born in Weil der Stadt, Germany, Kepler attended Tübingen University from 1591 to 1594, pursuing a doctorate in theology, but before finishing he was diverted to a teaching position in mathematics in Graz. In 1600 he entered the employment of **Tycho Brahe** in Prague; when Tycho died in 1601, Kepler secured both Tycho's observations and his appointment as Imperial Mathematician. Kepler's patron, Rudolph II, died in 1612, and Kepler moved to Linz as provincial mathematician. He spent his last two years in Sagan and died of a fever in Regensburg on November 15, 1630. In addition to the works discussed below, Kepler published significant research on optics in 1604 and 1611, the widely read *Epitome of Copernican Astronomy* (1618–1621), the influential *Rudolphine Tables* (1627), and a pioneering work of science fiction, the *Dream* (posthumously, 1634).

Kepler is best known for his three laws of planetary motion, which he did in fact discover. However, Kepler's real importance in the history of astronomy lies in the novel approaches and beliefs that made the discovery of the laws possible.

Kepler was committed, first of all, to a full heliocentric astronomy, much more so than **Copernicus**, or indeed any of Kepler's contemporaries. In Copernican astronomy the earth still held a special position; it had a different type of orbit from the other planets, and the center of the earth's orbit, rather than the sun, was the basic reference point for all planetary motion. Kepler rejected this lingering terrestrial privilege; he required that the earth's orbit be similar to that of the other planets, and that step allowed him to discover that all planetary orbits are best referred to the true sun.

Kepler also held a deep belief that the solar system exhibited a harmonic structure that God had ordained at the Creation. This belief in cosmic harmony led to his proposal in the *Cosmographical Mysteries* (1596) that the six planetary orbits were determined by a successive nesting of the five perfect or Platonic solids, thus explaining both the number and

Ex l. 1. Apollonii Conicorum pag. XXI. *demonſtrat* COMMANDINVS *in commentario ſuper* V. *Sphæroideon* ARCHIMEDIS.

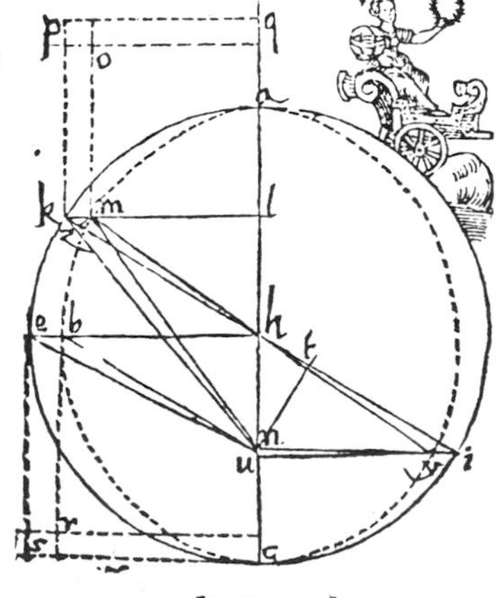

Sit enim circulus AEC. *in eo ellipſis* ABC *tangens circulum in* AC. *& ducatur diameter per* A. C. *puncta contactuum, & per* H *centrum. Deinde ex punctis circumferentiæ* K. E. *deſcendant perpendiculares* KL, EH, *ſecta in* M. B. *a circumferentia ellipſeos. Erit ut* BH *ad* HE, *ſic* ML *ad* LK. *& ſic omnes aliæ perpendiculares.*

II.

Area ellipſis ſic inſcriptæ circulo, ad aream circuli, habet proportionem eandem, quam dictæ lineæ

Vt enim BH *ad* HE, *ſic area ellipſeos* ABC *ad aream circuli* AEC. *Eſt quinta Sphæroideon* ARCHIMEDIS.

The first appearance of the ellipse in Kepler's Astronomia nova *(Prague, 1609). (Courtesy of the History of Science Collection, Linda Hall Library, Kansas City, Missouri)*

the spacing of the planets. While the scheme was not fully explanatory in its details, it was extremely pleasing to Kepler in that it made God a geometer, or rather, it made geometry divine. The continued search for harmonies culminated in Kepler's discovery, announced in the *Harmonies of the World* (1619), that the variation of each planet's velocity is a Pythagorean harmonic ratio and the discovery that planetary periods vary in regular ways with their distance from the sun. We honor this last discovery as Kepler's third or period law, but to Kepler, it was just another harmony.

The third profound innovation of Kepler was his belief that planetary orbits should be derived from a consideration of physical causes, rather than from hypothetical models. He refused to allow any kind of motion, such as epicycles, that could not be given a causal explanation. Early in his research on the orbit of Mars, Kepler proposed that a planet's varying speed as it drew near and away from the sun could be explained by a force emanating from the sun, which drove the planets around as the sun rotated. This in turn led to the discovery of the true elliptical nature of planetary orbits, which was announced, along with the area law, in the *New Astronomy* (1609).

The principal result of recent Kepler scholarship has been to show that Kepler's work was much more unified and coherent than previously allowed; he was not half mystic/half empiricist, or a sleepwalker, or a youthful dreamer who blossomed into a dedicated data-cruncher. His belief in physical causes and in an archetypal cosmic harmony were consistent with each other and were the driving force behind his career. Without them, his astronomical discoveries would have been impossible.

William B. Ashworth Jr.

Bibliography

Barker, P., and B.R. Goldstein. "Distance and Velocity in Kepler's Astronomy." *Annals of Science* 51 (1994): 59–73.

Beer, A., and P. Beer, eds. *Kepler: Four Hundred Years. Proceedings of Conferences held in Honour of Johannes Kepler. Vistas in Astronomy* 18 (1975).

Caspar, M. *Kepler*. Translated and edited by C.D. Hellman. London: Abelard-Schuman, 1959.

Donahue, W. "Introduction." In *Johannes Kepler, The New Astronomy,* 1–19. Cambridge: Cambridge University Press, 1993.

Field, J.V. *Kepler's Geometrical Cosmology*. Chicago: University of Chicago Press, 1988.

Gingerich, O. "Kepler, Johannes." In *Dictionary of Scientific Biography,* edited by C.C. Gillispie, vol. 7, 289–312. New York: Scribner, 1978.

———. "Johannes Kepler." In *Planetary Astronomy from the Renaissance to the Rise of Astrophysics, Part A: Tycho Brahe to Newton,* edited by R. Taton and C. Wilson. *General History of Astronomy,* vol. 2A, 54–78. Cambridge: Cambridge University Press, 1989.

———. *The Eye of Heaven: Ptolemy, Copernicus, Kepler*. New York: American Institute of Physics, 1993.

Jardine, N. *The Birth of History and Philosophy of Science: Kepler's 'A Defence of Tycho against Ursus' with Essays on Its Provenance and Significance.* Cambridge: Cambridge University Press, 1984.

Krafft, F. "The New Celestial Physics of Johannes Kepler." In *Physics, Cosmology, and Astronomy, 1300–1700: Tension and Accommodation,* edited by Sabetai Unguru, pp. 185–227. Dordrecht: Kluwer, 1991.

Stephenson, B. *The Music of the Heavens: Kepler's Harmonic Astronomy*. Princeton: Princeton University Press, 1994.

Kirchhoff, Gustav Robert (1824–1887)

German physicist and astronomer. Kirchhoff held professorships at Breslau, Heidelberg, and Berlin, but his years in Heidelberg (1854–1875), where he collaborated with Robert Bunsen, were his most productive in astronomy. In 1859 he concluded that the D lines seen in absorption in the solar spectrum were due to sodium atoms in the outer layers of the sun, and were the same lines as seen in emission in a laboratory flame. This discovery, which several other investigators had earlier proposed, opened the way for spectral analysis of the sun. In 1860 Kirchhoff and Bunsen catalogued the emission lines of different elements in the laboratory. Kirchhoff then made a detailed drawing of the positions of solar absorption lines, which he compared with those seen in the laboratory sources (1861, 1863). Six elements were definitely found to be present in the sun, while a further four were tentatively identified. At about the same time as his work on solar spectroscopy, Kirchhoff deduced his law of emission and absorption for bodies in thermodynamic equilibrium, which showed that the best absorbers are also the best emitters of radiation at a given wavelength, and he introduced the term black body for a perfect absorber at all wavelengths. Kirchhoff made several other contributions to physics, including his study of electrical currents in networks (1845–1849).

J.B. Hearnshaw

Bibliography

Hearnshaw, J.B. *The Analysis of Starlight*. Cambridge: Cambridge University Press, 1986.

Rosenfeld, L. "Gustav Robert Kirchhoff." In *Dictionary of Scientific Biography*, edited by C.C. Gillispie, vol. 7, 379–383. New York: Scribner, 1973.

Kitt Peak National Observatory

By the early 1950s, the status of American astronomy appeared to have declined in many ways. Most observatories, especially those associated with leading universities, were located in areas with inferior seeing conditions that severely limited the contributions those facilities could make. Educational and employment considerations were also topics of concern. Astronomers who completed one of the few graduate programs could often find employment only at small colleges that stressed teaching and offered no opportunities for research. Among the most intriguing proposals to solve astronomy's difficulties was the concept of a cooperative observatory that would be open to all astronomers. Discussions of this concept convinced the National Science Foundation to establish an advisory panel in January 1954. Chaired by distinguished astronomer Robert R. McMath, the panel was charged to develop a specific plan for a National Astronomical Observatory.

The location of the national observatory soon emerged as a prime consideration. Seeking a site with clear, steady air and appropriate weather patterns, the McMath Committee early limited its considerations to the American Southwest. Photographs of the region taken by missiles launched from White Sands, New Mexico, led to the identification of some 150 potential sites, which were examined more closely by site survey personnel. By the summer of 1956, five of these sites remained under consideration, one of which was the summit of Kitt Peak, 50 miles southwest of Tucson. The inclusion of this site was only made possible through the intercession of anthropologists and astronomers at the University of Arizona. The mountain lay within the Tohono O'odham (then known as the Papago) Reservation and represented a religiously significant spot for the tribe. Initially unwilling to open the site for development, the Tribal Council eventually reversed their decision after visiting the Steward Observatory in December 1955.

By the end of 1957, the southern-Arizona site had emerged as one of the three final locations and was undergoing extensive tests with various instruments, including a specially mounted 16-inch reflector. Program officials announced Kitt Peak as the site of the national observatory the following March. Details of the lease with the Tohono O'odham provided the tribe with specific payments and required astronomers to limit their activity to a 2,400-acre site on the mountain and to respect the religious traditions of the original inhabitants.

The development of Kitt Peak began immediately under a $3.1 million contract with the recently established **Association of Universities for Research in Astronomy** (AURA). Preparation of the mountain included the improvement of the road to the summit and significant construction to prepare the site for telescopes and various buildings. In Tucson, offices and laboratories were established, first in rented quarters but later in a separate building across the street from Steward Observatory. Erection of the telescopes planned for the national observatory began quickly as well. One of the 16-inch site survey reflectors was mounted in a simple dome in March 1959 and remained in active use until September 1962. Two other 16-inch instruments joined the growing collection in April 1962 and November 1963. The first major telescope for Kitt Peak, however, was a 36-inch reflector completed in March 1960. Although this instrument provided astronomers with valuable research opportunities, a national observatory required a much larger instrument. Late in 1958, Corning Glass Works had received the contract for a pyrex mirror blank of 84 inches diameter. Of ribbed construction with a honeycombed back to reduce weight, the Corning disk arrived in Tucson in October 1959, after which the mirror underwent 15 months of grinding and polishing. By the end of 1961, the telescope had been completed and installed in its dome on Kitt Peak as the world's fifth largest telescope.

In addition to its recommendations concerning the national observatory, the McMath Committee also urged the commitment of $3,500,000 for a large solar telescope. Although site requirements for solar and stellar telescopes proved significantly different, the National Science Foundation had insufficient funds to build both a national observatory and a solar telescope unless the two facilities were located on the same site. When Kitt Peak was announced as the site of the national observatory, therefore, officials included the solar telescope on the list of instruments to be located on the mountain. Designed around an 80-inch heliostat mirror, the solar telescope included a tower more than 100 feet high attached to a diagonal 500-foot shaft that extended 300 feet into the mountain. Construction of the mammoth instrument began in March 1960 and took slightly more than two years to complete.

Because of the superiority of the Kitt Peak site, the possibility of a very large telescope attracted much interest. AURA officials determined that a 158-inch telescope would represent a suitable major telescope for the national observatory. By 1963, the AURA board had decided to order a fused quartz mirror blank, awarding a contract the following year to General Electric Company. Completed in the fall of 1967, the huge mirror blank required three years to be figured. The housing on Kitt Peak reached completion at approximately the same time (late 1970), standing 187 feet tall and 108 feet in diameter. The telescope mounting, similar to that of the Hale Telescope on Mt. Palomar, took somewhat longer to complete because of the complexities of the 700,000-pound device. Dedicated in June 1973, the $10 million facility was, at the time, the second largest optical telescope in existence.

The erection of the 158-inch telescope completed the major instruments on Kitt Peak. For the next two decades, the observatory fulfilled its function as the nation's major supplier of telescope time and access to sophisticated equipment. Toward this end, technical advances became increasingly important. In 1983, for example, a remote observing link via satellite was established between the Royal Greenwich Observatory and the Kitt Peak 84-inch reflector. Unfortunately, the 1980s and early 1990s at Kitt Peak were also characterized by the dramatic decrease in financial support for American astronomy. As budgetary constraints continued to plague the facility, Kitt Peak National Observatory found itself struggling to maintain its position as the nation's center for optical astronomy.

George E. Webb

Bibliography

Edmondson, F.K. "AURA and KPNO: The Evolution of an Idea, 1952–1958." *Journal for the History of Astronomy* 22 (1991): 68–86.

Goldberg, L. "The Founding of Kitt Peak." *Sky & Telescope* 65 (1983): 228–232.

Kloeppel, J.E. *Realm of the Long Eyes: A Brief History of Kitt Peak National Observatory.* San Diego: Univelt, 1983.

Meinel, A.B. "The National Observatory at Kitt Peak." *Sky & Telescope* 17 (1958): 493–499.

Kuiper, Gerard Peter (1905–1973)

Stellar and solar system astronomer. After earning his doctorate at Leiden (1933), Kuiper held positions at Lick (1933–1935) and Harvard (1935–1937). He was then appointed to the Yerkes-McDonald observatories, administered by Chicago, and in 1960 became the director of what was ultimately named the Lunar and Planetary Laboratory (LPL) of the University of Arizona. This final move brought Kuiper greatly increased access to federal patronage, particularly from the **National Aeronautics and Space Administration**. Initially recognized for his contributions to stellar astrophysics, Kuiper turned to solar system astronomy after 1945, where he had enormous influence. He discovered the atmosphere of Titan, surveyed the properties of asteroids, and focused on lunar and planetary studies. Kuiper's edited compilations, beginning in 1948, stimulated much original research. The LPL, which he founded, became a world-class center for ground-based and spacecraft studies of solar system phenomena.

Ronald E. Doel

Bibliography

Cruikshank, D.P. "Gerard Peter Kuiper, 1905–1973." *Biographical Memoirs of the National Academy of Sciences* 62 (1992): 259–295.

Kukarkin, Boris Vasil'evich (1909–1977)

Soviet astronomer. Self-educated, Kukarkin began his career as an amateur astronomer in Nizhnii Novgorod before being invited to join the staff of the Tashkent Observatory (1931). In 1932 he moved to the Shternberg Astronomical Institute, which he later directed (1952–1956) and where he served as chairman of the divisions of variable stars and galactic studies. Kukarkin served as chairman of the **International Astronomical Union (IAU)**

Commission on Variable Stars (1952–1958) and as IAU vice president (1955–1961).

Kukarkin made the Soviet Union a leader in the study of variable stars. In 1928 he founded the bulletin *Peremennye zvezdy (Variable Stars),* and he coordinated the compilation and maintenance of the *Obshchii katalog peremennykh zvezd (General Catalogue of Variable Stars),* first published in 1948. Kukarkin also actively pursued studies of galactic structure, globular clusters, and interstellar absorption.

Robert A. McCutcheon

Bibliography

Kolchinskii, I.G., A.A. Korsun', and M.G. Rodriges. "Kukarkin, Boris Vasil'evich." In *Astronomy, biograficheskii spravochnik (Astronomers, a Biographical Handbook),* 172–173. Kiev: Naukova dumka, 1986.

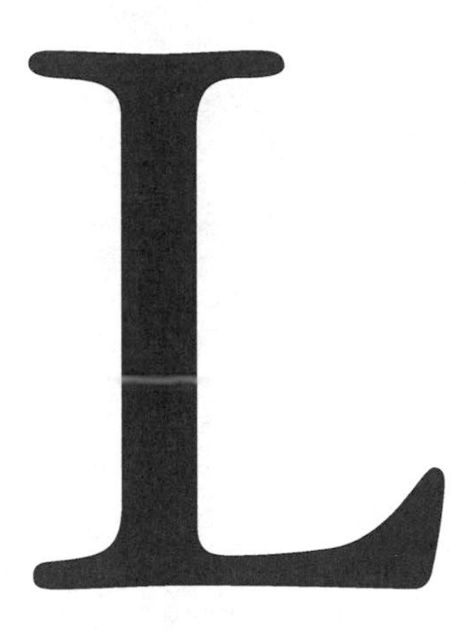

Lacaille, Nicolas-Louis de (1713–1762)

French astronomer and geodist. Born near Rheims, Lacaille was educated at the Collège de Lisieux and the Collège de Navarre in Paris; at the latter he developed a keen interest in mathematical astronomy. Between 1738 and 1741 he mapped (with Giovanni-Domenico Maraldi) the seacoast from Nantes to Bayonne and verified (with **César-Francois Cassini de Thury**) the great meridian of France. For the latter work, which supported Isaac Newton's view of the earth with an equatorial bulge rather than the Cartesian conception of it as a prolate spheroid, Lacaille was appointed (1739) professor of mathematics at the Collège Mazarin (where he primarily observed) and elected (1741) a member of the French Academy of Sciences.

His professorial duties led Lacaille to publish elementary textbooks in mathematics, mechanics, geometrical and physical astronomy, and optics that went through many editions and translations into foreign languages. He also computed three decennial volumes of astronomical almanacs, *Éphémérides de mouvements célestes*, that covered the years 1745 to 1775.

An industrious observer of celestial phenomena, Lacaille was principally concerned with the improvement of solar theory and the accurate determination of star places. His crowning achievement was an expedition to the Cape of Good Hope (1750–1754), during which he mapped nearly ten thousand stars; measured lunar, solar, and planetary parallaxes; named fourteen new constellations; and catalogued forty-two nebulae.

Craig B. Waff

Bibliography

Armitage, A. "The Astronomical Work of Nicolas-Louis de Lacaille." *Annals of Science* 12 (1956): 163–191.

Evans, D.S. "LaCaille: 10,000 Stars in Two Years." *Discovery* (1951): 315–319.

———. "Nicolas de La Caille and the Southern Sky." *Sky & Telescope* 60 (1980): 4–7.

Gingerich, O. "Lacaille, Nicolas-Louis de." In *Dictionary of Scientific Biography*, edited by C.C. Gillispie, vol. 7, 542–545. New York: Scribner, 1973.

Lacaille, N.-L. de. *Journal historique du voyage fait au Cap de Bonne-Espérance* (with a biography by the abbé Claude Carlier appended). Paris, 1776.

Taton, R. "Inventaire des publications et des manuscrits de Nicolas-Louis Lacaille (1713–1762)." In *Science and History: Studies in Honor of Edward Rosen (Studia Copernicana, vol. 16)*, 317–333. Wroclaw: Ossolineum, 1978.

Wilson, C. "Perturbations and Solar Tables from Lacaille to Delambre: The Rapprochement of Observation and Theory." *Archives for History of Exact Sciences* 22 (1980): 53–304.

Lagrange, Joseph Louis (1736–1813)

Italian/German/French mathematician. Born and educated in Turin, Lagrange spent his most scientifically productive period at the Berlin Academy (1766–1787) before settling in Paris, where he was treated as an eminent intellectual. He made important contributions to mathematics, especially developing the methods of analysis pioneered by Euler.

He applied these methods to planetary theory, satellite theory, and the three-body problem, for which he derived the equilibrium solutions that bear his name. His work on planetary theory dealt with the derivation and interpretation of periodic and secular terms. Much of this was done in enthusiastic competition with his younger colleague **Pierre-Simon Laplace**.

LeRoy E. Doggett

Bibliography

Itard, J. "Joseph Louis Lagrange." In *Dictionary of Scientific Biography*, edited by C.C. Gillispie, vol. 7, 559–573. New York: Scribner, 1973.

Wilson, C. "The Work of Lagrange in Celestial Mechanics." *Planetary Astronomy from the Renaissance to the Rise of Astrophysics*, Part B, edited by R. Taton and C. Wilson. In *The General History of Astronomy*, vol. 2A, edited by M. Hoskin. Cambridge: Cambridge University Press, in press.

Lalande, Joseph-Jérôme Lefrançais de (1732–1807)

French astronomer. After attending the lectures of the astronomers **Joseph-Nicolas Delisle** and Pierre Charles Le Monnier at the Collège Royale in Paris, Lalande traveled to Berlin to make simultaneous measurements with **Nicolas-Louis de Lacaille** (then at the Cape of Good Hope) for the determination of the lunar parallax. This work led to his election (1753) to the French Academy of Sciences. A professor of astronomy (1760–1806) at the Collège Royale, Lalande produced a standard textbook, *Traité d'astronomie* (1764), that contained much practical information on instruments and methods of calculation. He greatly expanded the astronomical almanac *Connaissance des temps* during the first of two terms (1760–1776, 1794–1807) as editor.

Craig B. Waff

Bibliography

Chapin, S.L. "Lalande and the Length of the Year: Or, How to Win a Prize and Double Publish." *Annals of Science* 45 (1986): 163–190.

Hankins, T.L. "Lalande, Joseph-Jérôme Lefrançais de." In *Dictionary of Scientific Biography*, edited by C.C. Gillispie, vol. 7, 579–582. New York: Scribner, 1973.

Jacquel, R. "L'astronome bressan et parisien Joseph Jérome de Lalande (1732–1807) et l'astronome balois et berlinois Jean III Bernoulli (1744–1807): Leur correspondence inédite (et presque inconnue) dans les Archives de la Bibliothèque Universitaire de Bale." In *Lyon, cité des savants*, 87–101. Paris: Comité des Travaux Historiques et Scientifiques, 1988.

Lalande, J.J. "Journal d'un voyage en Angleterre, 1763." Introduction by Hélène Monod-Cassidy. *Studies on Voltaire and the Eighteenth Century* 184 (1980).

Louyat, H. "Une astronome français: Jérome Lalande (1732– 1807)." *Mémoires de l'Académie des Sciences, Inscriptions, et Belles-Lettres de Toulouse* 145 (1983): 21–28.

Monod-Cassidy, H. "Une astronome philosophe, Jérôme de Lalande." *Studies on Voltaire and the Eighteenth Century* 56 (1967): 907–930.

Laplace, Pierre-Simon, Marquis de (1749–1827)

French mathematician and physicist. Born in Normandy, Laplace studied (1766–1768) in the Faculty of Arts at the University of Caen. There, under the encouragement of Christophe Gadbled and Pierre Le Canu, he developed an extraordinary talent in mathematics. Armed with a letter of recommendation to the mathematician Jean d'Alembert, Laplace traveled to Paris, where d'Alembert secured him a position of professor of mathematics at the École Militaire. After receiving at least thirteen papers on mathematical topics from Laplace, the French Academy of Sciences elected him to membership in 1773. Laplace remained a member until the Academy's suppression (1793) by the National Convention.

Two years later he became a member of the scientific class of the newly organized Academy. There he was not only elected to the honorific positions of vice president and president during its first two years, but also served on numerous influential committees concerning bylaws, weights and measures, finances, and the specification of topics for prize contests in mathematics and physics. Laplace was also influential in the development of the École Polytechnique, the Bureau of Longitude, the development of the metric system, and matters concerning navigation and astronomy in France.

After Napoleon seized power in 1799, Laplace served for six months as minister of the interior. Napoleon also appointed him chancellor of the senate (1803), a position that he retained during the subsequent Consulate and Empire periods; he awarded him the Legion of Honor in 1805, and ennobled him with title of count in 1806.

Laplace made important contributions to celestial mechanics. Comparison of observations made of Jupiter and Saturn in ancient and modern times indicated that the mean motion of the former was continually increasing and that of the latter was continually decreasing. The changes in the mean motions of these planets therefore appeared to be secular (changing continually in the same direction) rather than periodic (alternately increasing and decreasing). Such secular changes, if true, were both disturbing and challenging. If they continued indefinitely, they implied that the radius of the orbit of Jupiter would continually decrease (and thus Jupiter would either collide with one or more of the inner planets or fall into the sun) and that of Saturn would continually increase (thus Saturn would eventually leave the solar system). The challenge came from the fact that these apparent secular changes in the mean motions of the two planets had, despite the best efforts of mathematicians such as **Leonhard Euler** and **Joseph Lagrange**, defied explanation by Newton's inverse-square law of gravitation.

In a 1773 memoir, Laplace demonstrated that mutual attractions of the two planets and the sun could not produce any secular accelerations of the mean motions of the planets. He conjectured that the observed accelerations might be due instead to the actions of the large number of comets passing near Jupiter and Saturn. A dozen years later, however, Laplace discovered a gravitational explanation for the supposed secular accelerations of the planets. Observing that the mean motions of Jupiter and Saturn were nearly commensurable (in the ratio of nearly 5 to 2), he suspected that in the differential equations of these motions the terms having for arguments five times the mean longitude of Saturn minus two times the mean longitude of Jupiter could become sizable upon integration, even though they had as coefficients cubes and products of three dimensions of the eccentricities and inclinations of the orbits. Laplace demonstrated that there were indeed large equations of this type in the theories of the motions of the planets (+48 minutes 44 seconds for Saturn, –20 minutes 49 seconds for Jupiter) whose periods were approximately 929 years, and these equations and others could account for the observed motions of the planets.

Laplace presented his conclusions and demonstrations on this subject in a series of five memoirs on planetary and satellite motions presented to the academy between November 1785 and April 1788. Within this series he also demonstrated that the mean motions of the inner three satellites of Jupiter, which are commensurate (that of the first is about twice that of the second, and that of the second is about twice that of the third) became and will remain stable by virtue of their gravitational attractions; and that the observed secular acceleration of the earth's moon was due to the action of the sun combined with variations in the eccentricity of the earth's orbit, caused by the actions of the planets. The resulting inequality of motion, Laplace demonstrated, was in fact not secular but periodic over an interval of millions of years.

Laplace's overall work in celestial mechanics, summarized in his five-volume *Mécanique céleste* (1799, 1799, 1802, 1805, 1823–1825), introduced several new techniques, among them the calculation of perturbations proportional to the powers and products of the second and higher dimensions of the orbital eccentricities and inclinations, and the use of equations of condition in the corrections of orbital elements and in the evaluation of coefficients of perturbational terms. Euler, Tobias Mayer, and Roger Boscovich had used this method earlier, but Laplace was responsible for bringing it into general use. According to Curtis Wilson (Wilson 1985, 23), these techniques permitted "a marked reduction in the gap between tables and observations" and stimulated "a new period of advance, both theoretical and observational."

Laplace's *Exposition du Système du Monde* (1796), considered by Charles C. Gillispie as "one of the most successful popularizations of science ever composed" (Gillispie, 342) summarized for the lay person what was known about astronomy and cosmology at the end of the eighteenth century. At the end of the book Laplace speculated on the origin of the solar system, which has since become known as the nebular hypothesis.

Outside of astronomy, Laplace, between 1777 and 1783, investigated (with Antoine Laurent Lavoisier) evaporation and vaporization; dilation of glass and metals when heated; and specific heat. In mathematical physics, he demonstrated that a homogeneous shell of gravitating matter, bounded by similar and similarly situated concentric ellipsoids, exerts no attraction at any point inside it, and that all ellipsoids with the same foci for their principal sections attract a given external point with a force proportional to their masses (known today as Laplace's theorem). He also demonstrated that the velocity of sound in air given by a formula proposed by Newton had to be multiplied by the square root of the ratio of the specific heat of air under constant pressure and at constant volume.

The most extensive biography of Laplace and bibliography of works by and about him is that by Gillispie and collaborators in the *Dictionary of Scientific Biography*. Curtis Wilson has made several detailed studies of his work on celestial mechanics.

Craig B. Waff

Bibliography

Andoyer, H. *L'oeuvre scientifique de Laplace.* Paris: Payot, 1922.

Gillispie, C.C., R. Fox, and I. Grattan-Guinness. "Laplace, Pierre-Simon, Marquis de." In *Dictionary of Scientific Biography*, edited by C.C. Gillispie, vol. 15, 273–403. New York: Scribner, 1979.

Hahn, R. *Laplace as a Newtonian Scientist.* Los Angeles: Williams Andrew Clark Memorial Library, UCLA, 1967.

———. "Laplace and the Vanishing Role of God in the Physical Universe." In *The Analytical Spirit: Essays in the History of Science in Honor of Henry Guerlac*, edited by H. Woolf, 85–95. Ithaca, N.Y.: Cornell University Press, 1981.

———. *Calendar of the Correspondence of Pierre Simon Laplace.* Berkeley Papers in History of Science, vol. 8. Berkeley: Office for History of Science and Technology, University of California, 1982.

Jaki, S. "The Five Forms of Laplace's Cosmogony." *American Journal of Physics* 44 (1976): 4–11.

Levin, B.J. "Laplace, Bessel, and the Icy Model of Cometary Nuclei." *Astronomical Quarterly* 4 (1982): 167–70.

Whittaker, E. "Laplace." *Mathematical Gazette* 33 (1949): 1–12.

Wilson, C. "Perturbations and Solar Tables from Lacaille to Delambre: The Rapprochement of Observation and Theory." *Archives for History of Exact Sciences* 22 (1980): 53–304.

———. "The Great Inequality of Jupiter and Saturn: From Kepler to Laplace." *Archives for History of Exact Sciences* 33 (1985): 15–290.

Latin America, Astronomy in

After the success of the independence movements of the early nineteenth century, the initial development of astronomy in Latin America took place mostly under North American influence.

Eighteenth century European astronomers wanted to establish the shape of the earth and spent much of their energy measuring arcs of the meridian. A French expedition led by Pierre Bouguer measured the length of a 1-degree arc of latitude near the equator in what is now Ecuador as part of a study of the ellipsoidal form of the earth. However, Bouguer's results were challenged in 1752 by the findings of **N.-L. de Lacaille** working in South Africa. Bouguer also measured the effects of refraction on apparent positions of stars.

Astronomers from North America mounted a major expedition to Chile in 1847 under the leadership of James Melville Gilliss of the U.S. Naval Observatory. The party observed Mars in order to determine the **solar parallax** and also reobserved stars in the catalogue compiled by Lacaille in South Africa a century before. This was the first comprehensive survey of the southern sky. Gilliss made thirty-three thousand observations of stars within 24 degrees of the south celestial pole. The Mars project, however, was not a success because North American observers failed to make simultaneous observations with which those of Gilliss were to have been compared. The expedition produced three large volumes on the geography and fauna of Chile as well as astronomical results.

The 1882 **transit of Venus** was visible from many locations in Latin America and numerous expeditions were mounted. North Americans were stationed at Santa Cruz, Patagonia, and Santiago, Chile, where they used new photographic instruments. Belgian astronomers observed from Santiago, using a **heliometer**, and Louis Cruls established a station in Brazil. However, all the results were disappointing.

The indigenous development of astronomy in Latin America proceeded slowly. Argentine President Domingo Faustino Sarmiento met the astronomer Benjamin Apthorp Gould while serving as ambassador to the U.S. Sarmiento wanted to improve Argentina's image and international reputation by founding a national observatory at Cordoba, and he invited Gould to become its first director. Even before the official dedication (1871), Gould and four assistants compiled *Uranometria Argentina*, a catalogue of positions and magnitudes of all stars brighter than seventh magnitude within 10 degrees of the south celestial pole. The Franco-Prussian War delayed the arrival of astrometric instruments, but, once fully equipped, Cordoba became a productive institution. The *Cordoba Durchmusterung,* a catalogue with charts, includes the positions of stars brighter than tenth magnitude from –22 degrees to the pole. Gould retired in 1885 and was succeeded by John Macon Thome, and in 1909 by Lick Observatory astronomer Charles Dillon Perrine, the last American director. A second observatory was founded in 1882 at La Plata and directed by François Beuf.

While Cordoba remained the premier observatory in Latin America, other countries founded suit. For example, the Chilean National Observatory (1852) was established at Santiago, using meridian equipment left behind by the Gilliss expedition. Directors included Guillermo Modesta (1852–1865), José Ignacio Vergera (1865–1889), Alberto Obrecht (1889–1908; 1913–1923), and Frederick Ristenpart (1909–1913), who moved the observatory to Gran Avenida. In Ecuador a small observatory was set up at Quito under the direction of Father Menten.

In Brazil, Portuguese observations made from Rio de Janeiro in 1780 give currency to its claim of being the oldest Southern Hemisphere observatory. However, only in 1827 was an observatory founded in Brazil. It served as a school for training military officers in navigation and geodesy. The institution acquired new instruments after mid-century, and Emperor Pedro II, an amateur astronomer, invited Emmanuel Liais to become director in 1874. Liais ended the observatory's connection with the military. He was succeeded by a Belgian, Louis Cruls, in 1886. The flag of the Brazilian Republic (1889) represents the sky, with a bright star for each state.

The *Carte du Ciel*, a photographic catalogue and chart of the entire sky, was conceived by the International Astrographic Congress meeting in Paris in 1887. Four delegates attended from Latin America, including Luis Cruls from Rio de Janeiro and François Beuf, a captain in the French navy, who directed the La Plata Observatory in Argentina. The Congress assigned La Plata the zone from –24 degrees to –31 degrees, which was later completed by Cordoba, publishing the results between 1925 and 1932. The Observatory at Santiago, Chile, was assigned the zone from –17 degrees to –23 degrees, but the work was finished by the Hyderabad in India. The Observatory at Rio de Janeiro undertook the zone from –32 degrees to –40 degrees, but again the challenge proved too much and the zone was completed by the Observatory at Perth, in Western Australia. It must be remembered that the *Carte*, which required each participating observatory to make about twenty-two thousand plates for the catalogue and chart, was the most expensive and ambitious program of astronomical research ever conceived. Expenses connected with each zone of the *Carte* amounted to about fifteen million 1990 dollars. Observatories that did not have stable, long-term financial support could not succeed in the project.

In many ways, the southern heavens are more interesting than the sky visible from most North American observatories. The Milky Way and the Magellanic Clouds are of special importance to students of stellar and galactic astronomy and are best observed from south of the equator. Toward the end of the nineteenth century, North American observatories began establishing stations in Latin America. Harvard led the way with a station at Arequipa (8,055 feet above sea level) in Peru (1889). The Arequipa station was directed by a series of distinguished Harvard astronomers including Solon Irving Bailey and William Henry Pickering. The station permitted the extension of Harvard programs in stellar spectroscopy and photometry to the southern sky. The Arequipa station was equipped with the 24-inch Bruce photographic refractor, a state-of-the-art instrument that demonstrated the power of wide-field astronomical photography. Programs at the Harvard Station led to the discovery of a large number of variable stars. That, in turn, resulted in the discovery of the period-luminosity law for Cepheid variables by Henrietta Swann Leavitt (1913) that played an important role in establishing galactic distances. In 1927 the station moved to a site near Bloemfontein, South Africa.

Harvard was not the only North American observatory to establish a station in Latin America. From 1903 to 1929, the **Lick Observatory** of the University of California maintained a station in Chile as part of the Lick program of measuring the radial velocities of bright stars. The Lick Station, located near Santiago, used a 37-inch Cassegrain reflector and spectrograph for radical velocity work. The spectra of nebulae were also investigated. In 1929 the equipment was sold to the Catholic University of Chile.

The Harvard and Lick stations were devoted to astrophysical investigations. In the early twentieth century, the Dudley Observatory sent an expedition to western Argentina to determine the positions of stars not visible from Albany. The catalogue produced as a result of the Dudley expedition raised astrometric research on southern stars to new levels of precision. Other astrometric projects include the Yale-Columbia and Naval Observatory stations in Argentina.

In the twentieth century, the development of indigenous astronomical research in Latin America continued. The Rio de Janeiro Observatory, long inactive, was moved to a new site with modern instruments and São Paulo, originally a meteorological station, began work in astronomy in 1912. São Paulo expanded after World War II. Its primary research fields are astrometry and celestial mechanics. Radio astronomy has recently been added. At Cordoba, Perrine was dismissed before his program to move the institution into astrophysical research was completed. Only in 1942 was Perrine's dream of a large reflector (1.54 meters) located at a high-altitude site (Bosque Alegre), realized. Felix Aguilar succeeded Perrine. He promoted spectroscopy. Ernesto Gaviola became director in 1940, and fifteen years later the Observatory became a part of the University of Cordoba.

After World War II, Argentina developed a core of astrophysicists, including Jorge Sahade, Carlos U. Cesco, Carlos and Mercedes Jaschek, J. Landi Dessy, and J.L. Sérsie. This group was especially interested in spectral classification, photoelectric photometry, multiple star systems, and galaxies with emphasis on the **Magellanic Clouds**. In 1961 a new observatory was dedicated to the memory of Felix Aguilar in San Juan Province.

La Plata fell on hard times after Beuf. For a while the director of the University of Michigan astronomy program, William J. Hussey, shuttled between Ann Arbor and La Plata, but the arrangement did not prove satisfactory. Aguilar sought to establish closer ties to North American observatories and introduce astrophysical research. In 1928, the mirror of the 80-cm reflector was broken. The instrument was later replaced by a 90-cm reflector. Other research centers include solar physics at the Observatory of Cosmic Physics, Buenos Aires (1950); the National Institute of Radio Astronomy (1963); and the Argentine Institute of Space Physics, Buenos Aires (1971), whose director, Jorge Sahade, was president of the **International Astronomical Union** (1985–1988).

Since the Gilliss expedition in the 1840s, Chile has been regarded as an ideal spot for observational astronomy. The national observatory was established at Santiago, but not until the directorship of German-born Frederick Ristenpart (1909–1913) did the institution prosper. He moved the observatory to Gran Avenida, increased the staff, and initiated major programs in **astrometry**. After Ristenpart, the National Observatory languished until the directorship of Federico Rutllant (1950–1963), who moved the institution to Cerro Calan (altitude 860 meters), added a 60-cm Grubb refractor, and undertook a vigorous observing program in astrometry and **photometry**. The Chilean National Observatory has been active in international cooperation, but its work has been interrupted by political and economic upheavals.

In 1962 Soviet astronomers began working with scientists at the Chilean National Observatory on a program of absolute determinations of declinations to improve the positions of southern stars in the international fundamental catalogue. Soviet astronomers also worked in Chile on photometry and proposed a Russian astrophysical observatory, but after the overthrow of the Allende government the Russians withdrew, leaving their instruments to the University of Chile.

Chile became the site for the **Cerro Tololo Interamerican Observatory** (2,200 meters). Instrumentation includes a 4-meter telescope (1976), two 41-cm reflectors, the $^{61}/_{91}$-cm Curtis Schmidt telescope on loan from the University of Michigan, a 91-cm Cassegrain, and a 1.52-meter Ritchey-Chrétien reflector. The institution emphasizes cooperation between astronomers in the hemisphere.

A consortium of five nations (West Germany, Belgium, France, Netherlands, and Sweden) created the **European Southern Observatory** (ESO) in 1965. The consortium selected a site at La Silla about 150 km north of La Serena. Telescopes include a 1-meter Schmidt, a 1.5-meter Cassegrain/coudé reflector, a 1-meter photometric telescope. a 50-cm photometric telescope, a $^{25}/_{40}$-cm double astrograph, the 3.6-meter Cassegrain/coudé reflector, and a New Technology 3.5-meter telescope.

At Las Campanas, in northern Chile, the **Carnegie Institution of Washington** and the **California Institute of Technology** established a southern station in 1969. At an elevation of 2,300 meters, observing conditions are exceptional. Instruments include the 2.5-meter du Pont telescope, the 1-meter Swope telescope, and the Magellan Telescope (6.5 meters). The administrative history of Las Campanas has been complex, at one time involving cooperation with the California Institute of Technology. After the closing of the Mount Wilson Observatory (1989), Las Campanas became the principal observatory supported by the Carnegie Institution of Washington.

Dark skies and favorable observing sites in North America are more and more difficult to locate. In the next century, observational astronomy and astrophysics carried out at sites in Latin America will become more and more important.

David S. Evans

Bibliography

Evans, D.S. *Under Capricorn: A History of Southern Hemisphere Astronomy*. Bristol and Philadelphia: Adam Hilger, 1987.

Hodge, J.E. "Charles Dillon Perrine and the Transformation of the Argentine National Observatory." *Journal for the History of Astronomy* 8 (1977): 12–25.

Le Verrier, Urbain Jean Joseph (1811–1877)

French astronomer. Le Verrier studied at the *École Polytechnique*, which he entered in 1831 and where he was named lecturer in astronomy and geodesy in 1837. He became a member of the French Academy of Sciences in 1846. His research, like that of the English mathematical astronomer John Couch Adams, focused on a hypothetical planet that would provide an explanation for the anomalies in the orbit of Uranus. On September 23, 1846, Johann-Gottfried Galle and Henri Louis d'Arrest of the Berlin Observatory discovered the new planet (Neptune) within 52 minutes of the position indicated by Le Verrier. Le Verrier directed the **Paris Observatory** from 1854 to 1870 and again from 1873 to 1877. In 1853 he was instrumental in removing the observatory from the administrative control of the Bureau des Longitudes, an arrangement that dated from 1795. Le Verrier established the first general, coherent theory of the solar system. However, his theory could not account for certain discrepancies, including the secular advance of the perihelion of Mercury. Albert Einstein explained this discrepancy in the general theory of relativity. Le Verrier created the first meteorological service covering all of Europe. His papers are in the archives of the Paris Observatory.

Suzanne Débarbat

Bibliography

Hind, J.R. "Urbain Jean Joseph Le Verrier." *Monthly Notices of the Royal Astronomical Society* 38 (1878): 155–166.

Levert, P., F. Lammotte, and M. Lantier. *Le Verrier 1811–1877*. Coutances: OCEP, 1977.

Lick Observatory

Lick Observatory was completed and went into operation in 1888 with the largest refracting telescope in the world, the 36-inch objective by **Alvan Clark** and Sons and the mounting by Warner and Swasey. The observatory was built with funds provided by James Lick, the generous miser whose fortune was based in real estate in San Francisco at the time of the 1849 gold rush. Joseph Henry and Louis Agassiz played a part in awakening Lick's interest in perpetuating his name by founding a great observatory, but George Davidson, the head of the Pacific Coast branch of the U.S. Coast and Geodetic Survey, was the key, the persistent enthusiast who finally persuaded the old man to sign the deed of trust.

The observatory was built by the Lick Trust and only turned over to the University of California on completion. Richard S. Floyd, a wealthy ex-Confederate naval officer, planned the observatory and presided over its construction. **Simon Newcomb**, at the Nautical Almanac Office, was his chief astronomical adviser, and recommended his younger colleague, Edward S. Holden, for the directorship long before the observatory was completed. Thus when it began operations on June 1, 1888, Holden, **Sherburne W. Burnham**, **James E. Keeler**, **Edward E. Barnard**, and John M. Schaeberle made up its scientific staff. Holden, a West Point graduate, was an excellent planner, writer, cataloguer and librarian, but a mediocre research astronomer and a disaster in human relations. Keeler, Burnham, and Barnard all did important work, in spectroscopy, double stars, and wide-field astronomical photography, but within a few years all three were gone, Burnham and Barnard after bitter clashes with the director. Holden himself was forced out in 1897 by a staff revolt supported by the University of California regents he had antagonized and by other important figures in the West Coast educational world, including Davidson and Stanford president David Starr Jordan.

Keeler returned from the Allegheny Observatory as the second Lick director in 1898. He pioneered in nebular photography with the 36-inch Crossley reflector (a gift from

England that had precipitated the revolt against Holden) and recognized for the first time the great number of spiral nebulae in the sky. He realized that they are similar objects at different distances, from the nearby Andromeda nebula to the smallest, barely resolvable spirals. Keeler reported them as an important constituent of the universe, but to him and other astronomers of his time the universe meant the Milky Way Galaxy, and he thought of the spirals as stars or solar systems in formation. In 1900 Keeler's untimely death ended a brilliant but all too short career.

He was succeeded as director by **William Wallace Campbell**, who first came to Lick as Keeler's summer volunteer assistant in 1890 and had replaced him in 1891. Campbell built Lick into the leading radial-velocity measuring factory in the world. One of his first moves was to raise the money to establish a Southern Hemisphere station at Santiago, Chile, from Darius O. Mills, a wealthy financier who had been a member of James Lick's first board of trust. It had a 36-inch reflecting telescope designed to measure the radial velocities of stars and nebulae all over the sky. Campbell's long directorship formed Lick Observatory in his own image: careful, conservative, accurate, data-intensive, with very little theoretical guidance and no speculation. In Campbell's time Lick graduate students Edward A. Fath and Roscoe F. Sanford, and especially staff member Heber D. Curtis, made important advances in understanding spiral nebulae as island universes, galaxies like the Milky Way, composed of stars.

Campbell was also a dedicated leader of solar expeditions, heading eight in all, from Jeur, India, in 1898 to Wallal, Australia, in 1922. Although Campbell himself did little with the data, Donald H. Menzel, the astrophysicist hired to analyze and interpret them, developed the modern theory of the chromosphere. After 1912 Campbell made the effort to test Albert Einstein's special theory of relativity (1905), and then the general theory of relativity (1916), his chief eclipse program. The Lick expedition to Brovary, Russia, in 1914 was clouded out, and the one to Goldendale, Washington, in 1918 had to use second-rate cameras, as the best had been marooned in Russia by the outbreak of World War I. But at Wallal, Campbell and Robert J. Trumpler succeeded brilliantly, confirming the general theory prediction to very high accuracy, as the famous British expedition in 1919 had not, in fact, done.

After Campbell the next three Lick directors were his former assistants, Robert G. Aitken, William H. Wright, and Joseph H. Moore, and after them came his former student C. Donald Shane. Aitken, a double star observer, was the associate director who lived and worked at Mount Hamilton and actually ran the observatory, while Campbell was president of the university in Berkeley, still actively in control of overall policy at Lick. Aitken succeeded Campbell as director in 1930. Wright (director, 1935–1942) and Moore (1942–1945) worked chiefly on astronomical spectroscopy, the latter as longtime straw boss of the radial-velocity program under Campbell's general supervision. Shane, who had done his Ph.D. thesis on the spectroscopy of carbon stars, had been a Berkeley faculty member until he was offered the Lick directorship to start in 1942, but he did not accept it. During World War II he worked on the Manhattan (atomic bomb) Project at Berkeley and Los Alamos.

Before 1919 Wright had conceived of measuring stellar **proper motions** with respect to a reference system fixed in the universe and defined by the distant galaxies, which Curtis by then had shown were what the spiral nebulae actually are. Aitken, in one of his last acts as director, obtained the money to build the necessary wide-field Ross camera (invented by Frank E. Ross, a very early Lick Ph.D.) from the Carnegie Corporation. Wright pushed it through to completion and tested the concepts. Shane and Carl Wirtanen began the program after World War II, and Stanislavs Vasilevskis developed the automatic measuring techniques that made it work.

The Lick astronomers had long wanted a telescope larger than 36 inches in aperture, but during Campbell's later years he was too busy as president to try to raise the money to build one. He probably would have been able to do it in the 1920s, but by the time Aitken took over the directorship the Great Depression had struck, and neither he nor Wright succeeded in their many efforts. However, after Paul W. Merrill declined the offered Lick directorship (to succeed Wright in 1942), President Robert G. Sproul realized that a big telescope was a real necessity. He put it in the postwar building budget, and work on the 120-inch reflector began under Shane. Albert E. Whitford, who took over in 1958, the first director since Holden from outside the Lick staff, completed the Shane reflector.

Lick Observatory was America's first permanent mountaintop observatory. It is significant as one of the world's leading research observatories, a conservative institution that has survived and made real contributions for over a century. It may be considered America's first Big Science center, built around a large, expensive telescope, intended for use by a staff of research scientists working more or less independently on a variety of problems.

The Mary Lea Shane Archives of the Lick Observatory, located in the University Library, University of California, Santa Cruz, contains 375 linear feet of holdings, including the surviving papers of all the directors, many other astronomers, and the Lick Trust. Other significant sources for its early history are the George Davidson Papers and the Richard S. Floyd Papers in the Bancroft Library, University of California, Berkeley, and the Simon Newcomb Papers in the Library of Congress.

Donald E. Osterbrock

Bibliography

Crelinsten, J. "William Wallace Campbell and the Einstein Problem: An Observational Astronomer Confronts the Theory of Relativity." *Historical Studies in the Physical Sciences* 14 (1984): 1–91.

Lick, R. *The Generous Miser: The Story of James Lick of California.* Menlo Park: Ward Ritchie Press, 1967.

Osterbrock, D.E. "Lick Observatory Solar Eclipse Expeditions." *Astronomy Quarterly* 3 (1980): 67–79.

———. *James E. Keeler, Pioneer American Astrophysicist: And the Early Development of American Astrophysics.* Cambridge: Cambridge University Press, 1984.

———. "The Rise and Fall of Edward S. Holden." *Journal for the History of Astronomy* 15 (1984): 81–127, 151–176.

Osterbrock, D.E., J.R. Gustafson, and W.J.S. Unruh. *Eye on the Sky: Lick Observatory's First Century.* Berkeley: University of California Press, 1988.

Wright, H. *James Lick's Monument: The Saga of Captain Richard Floyd and the Building of Lick Observatory.* Cambridge: Cambridge University Press, 1987.

Wright, W.H. "William Wallace Campbell 1862–1938." *Biographical Memoirs of the National Academy of Sciences* 25 (1949): 35–74.

Lindblad, Bertil (1895–1965)

Swedish astrophysicist and dynamicist. Lindblad studied at Uppsala University, taught there, worked at Lick and Mount Wilson Observatories, and, after 1927, directed the Stockholm Observatory. Lindblad improved spectroscopic methods for determining stellar luminosity by identifying criteria visible in low dispersion spectra. He explained star streaming as a consequence of the structure of the galactic system, which, he argued, consists of subsystems of different degrees of flatness, rotating at different speeds around a single, distant center. Lindblad also studied the dynamics and stability of spiral structure in galaxies, considering the role of density waves and the distribution of dark matter.

Joann Eisberg

Bibliography

Oort, J.H. "Bertil Lindblad." *Quarterly Journal of the Royal Astronomical Society* 7 (1966): 329–336.

Literature and Astronomy

From Prehistory to the Late Medieval Era

Literature and astronomy have been conjoined since time immemorial. Ethnographers suggest that people of ancient oral cultures throughout the world, like their contemporary counterparts, created myths and narratives to transmit knowledge of the celestial bodies and beliefs about their origins. Artifacts of **archaeoastronomy** are encoded with early sophisticated observational astronomy. Solar, lunar, and stellar phenomena were recorded by the structure and positioning of lodges, kiva, earthworks, burial mounds, pyramids, temples, and city grids. Astronomical information was also marked upon the ground with stones, stakes, chalk, or pigment. Many examples of early forms of writing—paintings on cave walls, buckskin, and sand; bone and antler markings; decorative art; designs on woven fabric and headdresses; petroglyphs and pictograms—have astronomical content. The astronomy in ancient literatures greatly contributes to our understanding of cultures' religious myths and rituals, cosmological speculations, agriculture, animal husbandry, timekeeping, and social and political organizations. As these cultures framed perceptions of the cosmos, the linkage of literature and astronomy was driven by forces simultaneously connecting religion and astronomy: necessity, curiosity, wonder, fear. Successful farming, hunting, and survival itself were dependent on determining the interrelation of seasonal patterns with solar and lunar cycles, and the preservation of this vital information.

As conditions permitted, poets, priests, and astronomers—when their functions were not embodied by a single figure—pondered questions concerning the nature of human existence and the cosmos. They recorded celestial observations and speculations in various preliterate and literary forms. Oral astronomical narratives (often poems or songs) were practical mnemonic devices integral to the enactment and perpetuation of religious rituals and social functions. These narratives fulfilled aesthetic goals as they communicated cosmogonic myths and agriculturally useful information. In syllabic and alphabetical literatures, poetry was the genre chosen to inscribe astronomy, astrology, meteorology, and cosmology for many centuries. So rich was the scientific content in some of these works (Hesiod, Parmenides, Empedocles, Aratus, Lucretius, Manilius, and others) that critics questioned whether the genre should even be classified as poetry. Images and references from astronomy, broadly defined, are also present in Greek drama (Aristophanes, Aeschylus), Homeric epic, and various forms of Latin verse and prose (Vergil, Ovid, Varro). Plutarch treated popular astronomical lore in *De Facie in Orbe Lunae*. The earliest extant works of science fiction, Lucian's *True History* and *Icaromenippus*, exerted a strong influence, as did Cicero's cosmic dream *Somnium Scipionis*. The visionary cosmologies of Hildegard of Bingen and other early church figures are fascinating variations of this genre.

Dante's *Divine Comedy* is no doubt the best known of all medieval philosophical-cosmological verse. *Image du monde* is an important descriptive astronomical poem, probably written by the French poet Gossouin in the mid-thirteenth century. Translated as *The Mirror of the World* by William Caxton, this work (drawing upon the same sources as Sacrobosco) is perhaps the most comprehensive account of medieval astronomy available in English until the mid-sixteenth century (Johnson, 70). Geoffrey Chaucer's eminent place in the astrological-meteorological poetic tradition has been in part explained by J.D. North's expert analysis of the poet's command of technical astronomy.

In the half century preceding publication of Copernicus's *De Revolutionibus*, the concerns and conventions of star-crossed lovers and starry nights predominate in lyric poetry. Meanwhile, astronomical-philosophical and astrological-meteorological poems became increasingly encyclopedic. Such works include Vincent de Beauvais's *Speculum naturale*, *De proprietatibus rerum* of Bartholomaeus Anglicus, *Zodiacus vitae* of Marcellus Palingenius, and "shepherd's calendars" in various vernaculars. The quality of versification and levels of cosmological and philosophical complexity in these poems vary widely, as do their authors' technical understanding and characterizations of the Aristotelio-Ptolemaic system.

After Copernicus: Introduction

Human intellectual development may have allowed for a roughly simultaneous sophistication of natural philosophy and literary arts. But however natural the combination and whatever cultural reasons writers had for employing specialized literary forms to relate astronomical ideas and information, doing so was challenging. Writers sought and achieved some level of understanding of astronomy, astrology, or cosmology, past and contemporary. They crafted their account according to the unique formal requirements of their chosen genre: rhyme schemes, rhythms, conventions, tropes, rhetorical traditions, dramatic unities, characterization, and so on. They expressed both intellectual and emotional responses to the cosmic dilemmas posed by the phenomena in the sky and our mortal condition here below. Although inspired by these challenges, such works often exhibit the tension of rendering the truths of natural philosophy both technically and aesthetically whole. At its best, the artistic interplay of literature and astronomy further elevates the already ennobled investigations of natural philosophy and science by literally embodying and re-creating the essence of the quest.

The sophistication of the astronomical content of literature can vary proportionally or inversely to the aesthetic achievement of the works themselves. Successful poetic adaptation of an astronomical concept or discovery to metaphor is not guaranteed by technical expertise nor necessarily thwarted by inaccuracy or anachronism. Bad astronomy does not negate the aesthetic value of a poem or play otherwise well written and conceived. The poetic effect of John Keats's *On First Looking into Chapman's Homer* is not particularly intensified by his correct allusion to the new planet, Uranus, nor reduced by his erroneous reference to Cortez as the discoverer of the Pacific. Only rarely has good astronomy saved poor verse from obscurity. For this reason, the examples readily available are those considered canonically sound. Coincidentally, these works treat issues commonly considered central to the development of astronomy since the Scientific Revolution (thus most mentioned here are in Latin, English, French, Italian, and German).

Myriad works with significant astronomical content, and from non-Western literatures, previously unacclaimed, are continually coming under deserved scholarly scrutiny. Such works may be discovered by consulting the Modern Language Association's *Bibliography* and the list of relevant works at the end of this entry.

The surprising range of astronomical phenomena and theoretical issues employed in literary works, in all historical periods, impresses readers not previously alerted to it. Allusions to the earth as a planet include discussions of the four elements, the sublunary realm, technical aspects of Aristotelian physics, and comparisons of geocentric and Tychonic systems. Magnetism, meteorology, electricity, auroras, and the earth's rotation appear in literary imagery. Myriad references, poetic and prosaic, draw upon solar and lunar cycles, eclipses, sunspots, the inequality of the seasons, corona, *anima motrix*, solar retinopathy, heliocentrism, lunar topography, the tides, and two- and three-body systems. Literature documents the development of concepts concerning planetary phenomena from the music of the spheres, crystalline spheres, intelligences, Ptolemaic and Copernican models, through Galilean telescopic discoveries (satellites of Jupiter, rings of Saturn, phases of Venus), to circular and elliptical orbits, Keplerian laws, Newtonian gravitation, retrograde motion, the plurality of worlds, and extraterrestrials. Literary references to stellar observations and theories range from the astrological to the astrophysical, including the fixed stars, trepidation, constellations, cosmic influences, the Milky Way, the infinity of stars, their distances and proper motion, novae, variable stars, the nebular hypothesis, and pulsars. The muse of astronomy, Urania, has inspired plentiful allusions to comets, space, the void, plenum, extension, the infinity of the universe, entropy, and the role of the supernatural in the establishment and maintenance of natural law.

In all periods, writers enlist their astronomical knowledge to discuss such themes as the world in decay, the argument from design, sympathetic nature, the cruelty of nature, and the anthropomorphic fallacy. Astronomical figures illustrate philosophical relations of faith and reason, the role of imagination in poetic and scientific creativity, problems of the reason-sense dichotomy, and the place of emotion in natural investigation. References to astronomical ideas and discoveries, allusions to the lives and works of historical astronomers as well as the creation of fictional ones, bring important social issues to public notice. Such examples fuel the ancients' and moderns' debate concerning the utility of astronomical science, the educational value of the mathematical arts, the mathematization of nature, public attitudes toward astronomers as scientists, and astronomy's role in cosmology, especially in relation to evolution and geology.

Major Genres and Representative Primary Works

In the first post-Copernican century, the major genres discussed above—philosophical, cosmological, and astrological-meteorological verse, drama, epic, lyric, popularizations, cosmic voyages—were variously modified. Some early modern writers continued to draw upon ancient and medieval astronomy. Others adapted significant astronomical developments and observational discoveries concurrently with astronomers themselves. In England, the first vernacular treatments of Copernicanism—popular texts and astrological almanacs—were printed within a dozen years of *De Revolutionibus*. Like astronomical-philosophical poems, these prose works were intended to delight and instruct (for example, Robert Recorde, Thomas Digges). Soon after, popular considerations of heliocentrism appeared in encyclopedic cosmological poetry. Of long influence was Guillaume de Saluste Du Bartas's *La Sepmaine, ou Création du monde,* which countered the nonsensical physics of the Copernican system with Christianized Aristotelian arguments primarily drawn from medieval encyclopedists (Johnson, 186–189).

In the classical and medieval periods, great poets composed great astronomical-philosophical poems. Curiously, then, William Shakespeare's use of astronomy, astrology, and cosmology was conventional and tangential to the central themes of his drama. Christopher Marlowe, however, gave the astronomical quest serious evaluation. Dr Faustus's cosmic voyage, taken to gain insight into the ways of Heaven, ends in Hell—a dramatic condemnation of the dangers of overreaching in all human sciences. In fashionable satiric comedies, Ben Jonson alluded to Galileo's telescopic discoveries in the same breath as daily headlines and horoscopes (*News from the New World Discovered in the Moon*, *The Staple of News*). Modeled upon classical and medieval originals, Edmund Spenser's *Shepheardes Calender*, *The Fairie Queene*, and *Epithalamion* incorporated contemporary astronomical and astrological concepts into conventional tropes and compliments appropriate to Christian values and court verse.

John Donne's mastery and use of astronomy is unparalleled. With equal virtuosity he adapted (sometimes ad absurdum) complex astronomical analogies to rakish purposes of seduction or the serious pledging of wedded love and loyalty (*A Lecture upon a Shadow*, *The Sunne Rising*, *Valediction: Forbidding Mourning*). From his first-hand knowledge of the astronomy of Copernicus, Clavius, Galileo, and Kepler, he constructed unique syntheses of natural philosophy and faith (*Good Friday 1613*, *The Anniversaries*). He ingeniously satirized the philosophical and political excesses of the Jesuits by modifying the genre of the cosmic voyage (*Ignatius His Conclave*). This mixed genre blended fanciful and scientifically speculative fictions of space travel with social, political, and religious allegory and themes (Kepler's *Somnium*, Savinien Cyrano de Bergerac's *L'autre monde* and *Les états et empires de la Lune et du soleil*, and Francis Godwin's *Man in the Moone*). John Wilkins's thoughtful popularization of the major features of Galilean lunar topography and Keplerian selenography in *Discovery of a World in the Moon* (1638) may have struck his audience as comparatively mundane.

Abraham Cowley so effectively adopted the plain style advocated by Thomas Sprat to his *Ode to the Royal Society* that even an allusion to novae falls flat. The high-flown goals and modest achievements of the Royal Society are lampooned in Samuel Butler's burlesque satire *Hudibras* and the delightful *Elephant in the Moon*. Butler recognized the human limitations inherent in natural philosophy, including the unreliability of sensory perceptions (even when aided by instruments) and the mixed motivations of investigators of nature—personal fame and imperial-minded greed. In the satiric comedy *The Virtuoso*, Thomas Shadwell ridiculed actual experiments and astronomical work undertaken by Royal Society members.

The tradition of popular astronomical-philosophical works is represented by divergent forms in the late seventeenth century. Jean de La Fontaine's homely *Fables* gave accessible accounts of contemporary astronomical concepts while emphasizing the fraud of judicial astrology. Of a "romanticical [sic] . . . philosophical . . . fantastical" type, as designated by the author herself, is Margaret Cavendish's contribution to the genre of lunar voyages, *The Description of a New World.* This work was almost as universally scorned as her atomistic cosmological poetry. Precise poetical descriptions of the Copernican universe and seventeenth-century natural philosophy are featured in Henry More's Neoplatonic cosmological poems *Psychathanasia* and *Insomnium Philosophicum*. On a grander scale still resides John Milton's *Paradise Lost*, the principal example in English of a Christian metaphysical and cosmological poem in classical epic form. Synthesizing what he learned from astronomical and cosmological poetry (*Du Bartas*) and encyclopedias, Milton adapts the classical device of a cosmic voyage to Satan's journey through primal chaos (Book Two) and the astrological-meteorological perspectives of Aratus and Manilius to his dialogue on astronomy in Books Seven and Eight. Milton's personal contact with **Galileo** informs the discussion of two chief world systems and the conclusion that faith and revelation are ultimately more reliable than human knowledge of nature. In his earthly prose writings, Milton enlists astronomy, solar lore, and Galileo in his call for educational and political reforms (*On Education*, *Aeropagitica*).

After the publication of the *Principia* (1687), Isaac Newton, his achievements in astronomy, physics, optics, and the Royal Society, Newtonianism's social and theological implications, and mechanical philosophy in general, all find a place in astronomical literature. Aphra Behn's farcical *Emperor of the Moon* (1687) draws upon Godwin, Wilkins, Jonson, and Butler to satirize mechanical philosophy, hermeticism, enthusiasm, and the lunatic antics of a learned doctor obsessed with observing the moon. Her translation of Bernard le Bovier de Fontenelle's *Conversations on the Plurality of Worlds* provided a popular critique of contemporary astronomy. Jonathan Swift relentlessly parodied the learned controversies of real-life astrologers and astronomers (John Flamsteed, Edmond Halley, and Newton) in a series of pamphlets known as the *Bickerstaff Papers* and the poem *The Progress of Beauty*. In *Gulliver's Travels* (a conflation of the cosmic voyage and travelogue), he ridiculed the peculiarities of theoretical astronomy by characterizing its practitioners as the absent-minded Laputans. In Book Four, Swift suggested that human attempts to understand the celestial phenomena should be limited to what is necessary for timekeeping and agriculture. In one of the earliest modern novels, *Tristram Shandy*, Laurence Sterne cleverly incorporated aspects of Newtonian physics (flying off on a tangent) and mechanical philosophy (matter in motion) into the very structure of his rowdy, rambling tale, taking every opportunity to contrast lofty discoveries with commoners' views of them.

Alexander Pope's famous two-line epitaph for Newton is emblematic of the literary praises of the natural philosopher in the early eighteenth century. Probably taking inspiration from the themes introduced by Halley's *Ode* (prominently prefacing the *Principia*), writers repeatedly described Newton, his genius, and his work in terms of the divine. Writers of memorial verses, physico-theological, and nature poems exalted his insights into the mysteries of the natural world, the conquering of the comet, and discovery of universal law, in terms previously reserved for the powers of Christ (James Thomson's *To the Memory of Sir Isaac Newton* and *The Seasons*, Richard Blackmore's *Creation*, works by John Ray, William Derham and others). Essayists, Boyle lecturers, and other popularizers (for ladies as well as gentlemen) exercised no greater restraint (for example, Voltaire, William Whiston, James Ferguson, Richard Steele).

Only a few years later, however, in Pope's *Essay on Man*, the greatest mind of the age served to illustrate the limitations of human intellect. In *The Dunciad*, the final destruction of all intellectual light (once symbolized by Newton) is brought about by a disordering *vis inertiae* and the universal gravity of mental dullness. Samuel Johnson admired Newton's intellect and was well versed in his conceptualizations of the plenum, matter, and vacuity, but he reminded his readers that eternal benevolence and wisdom are behind extraordinary God-given talents. Astronomy could be a practical science as long as it worked toward the salvation of the experimenter or observer (*Rasselas*).

As the age of revolutions dawned, William Blake whirled with the vortices of the nebular hypothesis to effect a revolution of his own. Transforming astronomical-philosophical verse with the physics of his visionary poetry (*Vala*, *Jerusalem*, *Book of Urizen*, *Milton*), Blake countered the action of Newtonian reason with the energizing reaction of imagination. Blake's shorter verse, and the works of other Romantics, rarely drew upon astronomy. William Wordsworth depicted a disappointing first-hand experience with a public telescope in *Star-Gazers*, although he was among the first to predict that science would increasingly inspire literary imagery (for example, Samuel Taylor Coleridge's discussion of cosmology and Newton in *Religious Musings*, P.B. Shelley's treatment of the earth-moon system in *Prometheus Unbound*, and Keats's allusion to the Newtonian rainbow in *Lamia*). In the United States, Ralph Waldo Emerson contemplated atomistic cosmology in prose and verse. While Mark Twain experimented with fictional time travel in *A Connecticut Yankee in King Arthur's Court*, Walt Whitman preferred to encounter the heavens without the interference of astronomical apparatus (*When I Heard the Learn'd Astronomer*), as did Emily Dickinson (*Arcturus*).

Throughout the Victorian period, popular astronomical information was available in a variety of forms: essays (William Whewell), texts (**Richard Proctor, John Herschel**), illustrated journals, astronomical histories and encyclopedias (Agnes Clerke), children's books and women's magazines (**Maria Mitchell**), public lectures, observatories and exhibitions. These, added to the notice given international astronomical expeditions, the controversial ideas of Robert Chambers, Herbert Spencer, Charles Darwin, and others, the formation of interdisciplinary philosophical societies, and the personality of William Herschel and family, fostered intellectual interest in astronomy for some of the most important British writers of the age. Novels began to rival poetry as important forms of popularization.

Alfred Lord Tennyson, a student of Whewell and amateur astronomer, developed a sound knowledge of cosmology and evolutionary theory, synthesizing them as manifestations of a single process in *In Memoriam*. Thomas Hardy used astronomical imagery as scene-setting, timekeeping, and foreshadowing devices in most of his major novels. His poems *The Comet at Yel'ham* and *At a Lunar Eclipse* attest to his firsthand knowledge of contemporary astronomical events. In the melodramatic romance *Two on a Tower*, the most astronomical novel of the age, Hardy traced the career of an astronomer, while employing a comet, lunar eclipse, the Milky Way, and variable stars as plot devices and insightful analogues to the central characters. Norman Lockyer's ideas about Stonehenge inspired the concluding scenes of *Tess of the D'Urbervilles*. With similar sophistication, Hale White used the crafting of an orrery as a symbolic act embodying the union of romantic and scientific imaginations in his novelette *Miriam's Schooling*.

In the lyric mode, the union of sound and sense, of poetry and cosmology, in Algernon Swinburne's *Hertha* and *Anactoria* is utterly unique. In the latter, Sappho seeks to fuse her grief, her identity, her aesthetic vision into the eternity of an elemental cosmos. George

Meredith's *Meditation under Stars* is an optimistic exploration of ethical and aesthetic responses to the possibility that humanity shares its origin with the inorganic stars. In *A Dead Astronomer*, Francis Thompson describes the spiritual forces that draw a soul toward salvation in terms of planetary dynamics.

In science fiction novels, Jules Verne's *From Earth to the Moon* and H.G. Wells's *First Men in the Moon* are important adaptations of the scientific romance or cosmic voyage. Wells joins social commentary and the satiric elements introduced by Lucian and Swift with the technical detail and political allegory utilized by Kepler (*In the Days of the Comet*). At the end of the century, utopian visions of space travel are countered by a darker literary treatment of the laws of physics (for example, entropy in Joseph Conrad's *Heart of Darkness*).

Although volumes of poems do not top the twentieth century's best-seller lists (as Tennyson's often did), poets still draw upon recent developments and ideas in astronomy, astrophysics, and physics. The genre of astronomical-philosophical poetry is well represented by Mary Barnard's free verse *Time and the White Tigress*. In long poems, T.S. Eliot (*The Wasteland*), William Carlos Williams (*St. Francis Einstein of the Daffodils*, *Paterson*), W.H. Auden (*New Year Letter*), and Alfred Noyes (*The Torch-Bearers*) address concepts of contemporary or historical astronomy, entropy, relativity, post-Einsteinian time and space, and quantum mechanics. In shorter verse forms, John Updike writes playfully about the invasive properties of solar neutrinos (*Cosmic Gall*) as Robert Frost maintains a humanist stance toward scientific progress (*The Star-Splitter*, *Canis Major*). Other directly astronomical or astrophysical poems include Archibald MacLeish's *Einstein*, A.E. Housman's *Revolutions* and *Astronomy*, Julian Huxley's *Cosmic Death*, Siv Cedering's *Letter from Caroline Herschel,* and Robinson Jeffers's *Star-Swirls*.

Dramatists' traditional concern with contemporary science can be found in plays addressing historical and contemporary interactions of astronomy, religion, and politics (Bertolt Brecht's *Life of Galileo*) as well as the social consequences and human costs of astrophysics (Friedrich Dürrenmatt's *The Physicists*). The subject matter and structure of Samuel Beckett's plays and fiction deal with relativity, chaos, and uncertainty. Increasingly, dramatic presentations of astronomical subjects occur in the media of radio, television, film, or video rather than on stage (as in radio dramas: Wells's *War of the Worlds*; Douglas Adams's *Hitchhiker's Guide to the Galaxy*). On television, Rod Serling's *Twilight Zone* and the less cerebral *Lost in Space* enacted the themes and plots of time and space travel previously treated in lunar plays, cosmic voyages, or early science fiction novels. Gene Roddenberry's *Star Trek* (perhaps our closest approximation to a modern epic) has evolved into a new generation of spinoffs, serial novels, feature-length movies, starship models, and toys.

Although the popularization of astronomy is occurring through more avenues than were available previously, some astronomers and cosmologists still like to bring us word from above themselves. Carl Sagan is notable and notorious for his "billion" public "interfaces"—on the television series *Cosmos*, on talk shows, articles in *Parade* magazine, and his novel *Contact*. Stephen W. Hawking tried to present a popular account of his cosmology in *A Brief History of Time*, although Errol Morris's film version may have more successfully aided the public in visualizing the gist of the matter. Mainstream educational programming and science documentary series (*The Astronomers*, *Nova*, *Renaissance*) have reached millions of classrooms, homes, and VCRs with well-researched and well-produced presentations of the history of astronomy and its current events. Television pictures direct from the Apollo moon-landings, Voyager flybys, space shuttles, and the personal testimony of astronauts themselves are unsurpassed in their ability to bring home the awful actuality of our place in the solar system.

Not surprisingly in the post-atomic and post-Apollo age, astronomical subject matter in various media has become increasingly futuristic. Science fiction books, comics, film (*2001: A Space Odyssey*, *The Man who Fell to Earth*, *E.T.*), music (from Gustav Holst to David Bowie), video games, computer programs, virtual reality simulations, and hypertexts all explore the final frontier of space travel emphasizing human encounters with extraterrestrials. These media have virtually eclipsed, in popularity and influence, the more traditional literary treatments of astronomy.

Twentieth-century authors persisting in the use of print formats, however, continue to meet the challenges of increasingly sophisticated astronomy and astrophysics. Early in the century, authors developed experimental literary forms modeling Einsteinian concepts of space and time, relations of subject and observer, uncertainty, and indeterminacy (for example James Joyce's *Ulysses*, *Finnegans Wake*; Virginia Woolf's *To the Lighthouse*, *The Waves*; Lawrence Durrell's *Alexandria Quartet*; Vladimir Nabokov's *Bend Sinister*, *Ada*). Award-winning and best-selling authors tried their hand at moon voyage fiction almost immediately after the first lunar landing (Norman Mailer, Saul Bellow, Updike). Jorge Luis Borges, Italo Calvino, and Thomas Pynchon are innovators in structural and narrative uses of entropy, non-Euclidean geometry, relativity theory, quantum mechanics, and information theory. Isaac Asimov and Arthur C. Clarke contributed countless sci fi novels of technical mastery and successful popularizations. On the verge of the twenty-first century, Robert Coover (*The Universal Baseball Association*), Ursula Le Guin (*The Dispossessed*) and Alan Lightman (*Einstein's Dreams*) continue to explore for us the nature of the post-Einsteinian universe and its implications for human individuals and societies.

Interpretations and Conclusion

Given the fantastic abundance of primary materials, the relative dearth of secondary literature bewilders. A handful of book-length surveys and multiauthor studies are available, as are several single-author works. A goodly sum of interdisciplinary articles treating specific authors and works have been written by historians of science and literary critics, but the number of these has steadily declined since the 1960s. Most historiographic attention to literature and astronomy has focused on identifying the astronomical content of the literature and locating its sources. The old biographical or old historical criticism asked: What astronomy did the authors know? How did they know it? How current was their knowledge compared with that of contemporary astronomers? What are the scientific, social, intellectual, and literary contexts for the use of astronomy? Marjorie Nicolson's premier work on the sources and interpretation of astronomical imagery is still eminently worth consulting. In fact, she may have done her work too well. Daunted perhaps by her achievement, only a few scholars of literature and astronomy are among those currently working in literature and science studies.

Nicolson's preeminence has had other interesting consequences. Drawing upon her interpretations (inadequately mindful of other intellectual and religious influences she describes), historians of science (and others) have supported the hypothesis that Copernican astronomy engendered a revolutionary crisis in the surrounding culture. Literary scholars joined in determining the degree and kind of scientific crisis detectable in astronomical literature—not asking *whether* "new philosophy calls all in doubt," but *how*. Scholars relying upon the two world systems propaganda of Milton and Galileo oversimplified the cosmological choices available (Ptolemy versus Copernicus) to nonscientific writers. Thus, much astronomy has been misidentified, scientific perspectives have been skewed, and interpretations of literary responses to astronomical developments obscured. The doubt of Donne, for example, has been read as ambivalence over, or hesitancy to choose between, geo- and heliocentric models when, almost certainly, he had moved beyond such debates to embrace a sophisticated Keplerian cosmos.

As authors failed the litmus test of revolutionary awareness, such critiques may have reinforced the appearance of a lack of understanding between scientific and literary communities. In our own century's two cultures debate, the biochemist Michael Yudkin responded to C.P. Snow by arguing that one culture, primarily scientific, might be the inevitable result of such an ever-widening gap. He doubted that the sympathetic awareness of writers could ever be enhanced by a technical knowledge of modern astrophysics (Yudkin, 60). Of course, as we have seen, it already had. Personal and local ignorance of the other culture is not strong evidence of a universal or traditional disciplinary incompatibility. The majority of intellectuals in any age may never have been able to claim mastery of both literature and astronomy, or even an interest in both. Yet it should be heartening to find that some at least always could. As outlined above, poets, novelists, dramatists, essayists, natural philosophers, astronomers, and physicists, throughout history, have combined literary and astronomical approaches to understanding, and communicating knowledge about, the phenomena of the cosmos and our human relation to it.

Emergent approaches to the study of literature and science question the nature of the audience for scientific literature, the hermeneutics of scientific metaphor, and authors' use of scientific language per se, examining primary scientific texts as literature. Although nothing inherent in the texts of astronomical literature precludes them from consideration, few have commanded attention from scholars employing linguistic and rhetorical modes of critique. This trend may be partly attributable to the fact that the field of history of astronomy has been mined so well for so long. The discipline itself has been traditionally conservative in valuing internalist studies of technical astronomy over contextual analyses. Fresh appreciation for the importance of studying the confluence of literature and astronomy, in history, is gaining strength among interdisciplinary scholars. New awareness of the value of literary analyses of astronomical discourse is likewise burgeoning.

Because literature and astronomy are so inextricably interconnected, studying them in tandem can illuminate interactions of scientific and nonscientific communities, the popularization of science, aesthetics and science, humanism and science, and the history of science itself. New perspectives from diverse disciplines will continue to enrich our understanding of the technical achievement of astronomy and astrophysics while offering intriguing insights into the nature of the human sensibility that has undertaken the quest

To follow knowledge like a sinking star,
Beyond the utmost bound of human thought
(*Tennyson,* Ulysses)

Pamela Gossin

Bibliography

Beer, G. "Science and Literature." In *Companion to the History of Modern Science*, edited by R.C. Olby et al., 783–798. London: Routledge, 1990.

Cornell, J. *The First Stargazers: An Introduction to the Origins of Astronomy*. New York: Scribner, 1981.

Curry, W.C. *Milton's Ontology, Cosmology and Physics*. Lexington: University of Kentucky Press, 1957.

Eade, J.C. *The Forgotten Sky: A Guide to Astrology in English Literature*. Oxford: Clarendon Press, 1984.

Friedman, A.J., and C.C. Donley. *Einstein as Myth and Muse*. Cambridge: Cambridge University Press, 1985.

Gossin, P. *Poetic Resolutions of Scientific Revolutions: Astronomy and the Literary Imaginations of Donne, Swift and Hardy*. Ph.D. dissertation. University of Wisconsin-Madison, 1989.

Johnson, F.R. *Astronomical Thought in Renaissance England: A Study of the English Scientific Writings from 1500 to 1645*. Baltimore: Johns Hopkins Press, 1937.

Meadows, A.J. *The High Firmament: A Survey of Astronomy in English Literature*. Leicester: Leicester University Press, 1969.

Nicolson, M. *Science and Imagination*. Ithaca, N.Y.: Great Seal Books, 1962.

North, J.D. *Chaucer's Universe*. Oxford: Clarendon Press, 1988.

Schatzberg, W., et al., eds. *The Relations of Literature and Science: An Annotated Bibliography of Scholarship, 1880–1980*. New York: Modern Language Association, 1987.

Yudkin, M. "Sir Charles Snow's Rede Lecture." In *Two Cultures? The Significance of C.P. Snow*, edited by F.R. Leavis, 51–64. New York: Pantheon, 1963.

Lockyer, Joseph Norman (1836–1920)

British solar physicist and man of letters. Educated at provincial grammar schools, J. Norman Lockyer worked in the War Office from 1857 to 1871, when he became secretary of the Devonshire Commission on Scientific Instruction. From 1873 to 1913 he directed the Solar Physics Observatory at South Kensington, London. He was also the founder and editor of *Nature*. Lockyer was elected to the Royal Astronomical Society, Royal Society (which awarded him the Rumford Medal), and other societies.

Lockyer became active in astronomy in 1862. He achieved international fame in 1868 when he and **Pierre Janssen** independently discovered a means of observing solar prominences, which had previously been visible only during solar eclipses. His subsequent scientific research was conducted in the observatory, laboratory, and the field. He led his first solar eclipse expedition in 1870 and participated in another dozen expeditions as an observer or organizer. In 1873 he began building the Solar Physics Observatory at South Kensington. Lockyer was a forceful and unorthodox thinker. In 1868 his solar observations led him to announce the discovery of a previously unknown element that he dubbed helium. The element was isolated in the laboratory in 1895. Other theories on the relationship between sunspots and climate change, the constitution of the sun, spectrum analysis, and the meteoric origins of celestial objects were widely publicized but won few converts. Lockyer also plunged into archaeoastronomy in the 1890s, writing about British, Greek, and Egyptian monuments and ruins.

Lockyer was at least as important as a science popularizer and propagandist. He wrote numerous books and articles on science for both specialized and general audiences, and was much in demand as a lecturer. In 1869 he founded the journal *Nature*, which he edited until 1919. Under his direction *Nature* became one of the foremost scientific journals in the English-speaking world. Finally, he joined with T.H. Huxley and other leading Victorian scientists who argued for the importance of science in British life and lobbied for increased government support of research and education.

Alex S.-K. Pang

Bibliography

Barton, R. "The X Club: Science, Religion, and Social Change in Victorian England." Ph.D. dissertation, History and Sociology of Science. University of Pennsylvania, 1986.

Hufbauer, K. *Exploring the Sun: Solar Science since Galileo*. Baltimore: Johns Hopkins University Press, 1991.

Lockyer, T.M., and W.L. Lockyer, eds. *Life and Work of Sir Norman Lockyer*. London: Macmillan, 1928.

McGucken, W. *Nineteenth-century Spectroscopy: Development of the Understanding of Spectra 1802–1897*. Baltimore: Johns Hopkins University Press, 1969.

Meadows, A.J. *Science and Controversy: A Biography of Sir Norman Lockyer*. Cambridge: MIT Press, 1972.

Pang, A.S.-K. "Spheres of Interest: Imperialism, Culture, and Practice in British Solar Eclipse Expeditions, 1860–1914." Ph.D. thesis, University of Pennsylvania, 1991.

Turner, F.M. "Public Science in Britain, 1880–1914." *Isis* 71 (1980): 589–608.

Williams, M.E.W. "Astronomy in London: 1860–1900." *Quarterly Journal of the Royal Astronomical Society* 28 (1987): 10–26.

Lowell Observatory

Founded by Percival Lowell in Flagstaff, Arizona, in 1894, the Lowell Observatory has been an important private research institution ever since, particularly noted for the study of solar system objects. The origins of the institution stem from Harvard astronomer William H. Pickering's interest in observing the 1894 opposition of Mars from a temporary observatory in Arizona territory. Harvard, however, was short of money. Although not an astronomer by profession, Percival Lowell, wealthy and well connected in Boston scientific circles, was already fascinated by the red planet. At first he agreed to fund part of the expedition. Lowell, however, was anxious to ensure his observatory not be seen simply as a Harvard station. He therefore decided to fund the entire expedition, announced himself as the first director, and christened the temporary institution the Lowell Observatory. However, the apparatus was loaned from Harvard, and W.H. Pickering and A.E. Douglass, the first astronomers, were both on leave from Harvard.

Flagstaff in northern Arizona was selected as the site. Lowell, although choosing to keep an observatory here after the 1894 opposition, nevertheless continued to search for a superior site and conducted tests in the Saharan desert, for example. But in time Flagstaff became the observatory's permanent home.

During Lowell's lifetime, the staff numbered no more than about ten people, including computers in Boston, and often the number was smaller. Lowell also made it clear that the first priority of the staff was to pursue those tasks he set and not to question his judgments. The observatory under Lowell functioned as a benign dictatorship, but a dictatorship nevertheless, as Douglass found to his cost when he was fired in 1901 for criticisms of Lowell's claims of canals on Mars.

Lowell's association with a one-time assistant, Wilbur Cogshall of Indiana University's Kirkwood Observatory, led to three Indiana graduates becoming assistants in the 1900s: **V.M. Slipher**, C.O. Lampland, and E.C. Slipher (V.M.'s younger brother). Between them they would achieve nearly 150 years' service to the Observatory. The most accomplished was V.M. Slipher, who made several fundamental discoveries in astronomical spectroscopy. Most significantly, starting in 1912, he secured results on the red shifts of spiral nebulae that were later to be interpreted as key evidence of an expanding universe and so among the most important observational results of twentieth-century astronomy.

But Lowell's energetic and polemical engagement in the public debate on Martian canals and the existence of life on Mars, and the consequent suspicion with which some professionals viewed Lowell, left a legacy for the observatory that reached far beyond his death in 1916. For years the Lowell staff avoided taking public positions on interpretive issues in astronomy for fear of criticism. Instead, they labored to secure observational results that they judged to be beyond reproach. The interpretation of these results, and the disputes that might arise, were left to others. The observatory emphasized long-term observing programs, not conceptual innovations.

For decades after Lowell's death, the senior staff also continued lines of research that Lowell had initiated or directly encouraged. The result was that in a period when U.S. observatories were generally devoting little attention to the astrophysical study of solar system objects, Lowell astronomers bucked this trend. One important solar system investigation was the search for Lowell's Planet X. These researches were crowned triumphantly in 1930 with the discovery of Pluto.

Despite this and a few other innovative researches, after Lowell's death the observatory entered a long period of relative decline. One major problem was the long, grinding, and financially devastating battle with Lowell's widow over his estate in which the settlement provided much less money to the observatory than Percival Lowell had planned. In fact, from 1916, when V.M. Slipher became acting director (he was officially appointed director in 1926), until the early 1950s the observatory was generally strapped for cash, and, in resources, people, and equipment, was left behind by larger and more prosperous institutions. That the institution survived at all was an achievement and owed much to its sole trustee from 1927 to 1967, Roger Lowell Putnam, who at times aided the observatory with his own money.

The observatory was saved from extinction by federal patronage for science after World War II. One of the projects at Lowell made possible by this largesse focused on the atmospheres of the planets, and brought together astronomers and meteorologists with the help of federal and military contracts, a mix that was typical of the support for U.S. astronomy in the 1940s and 1950s. With the arrival in 1958 of John Hall as director (a post he was to hold for nineteen years), the institution secured not only a leading astronomer, but also a scientist whose skill in attracting government patronage was to be key to the observatory's future. Following the establishment of the **National Aeronautics and Space Administration** in 1958, funds became available for **solar system astronomy,** and the new space agency would play a key role in the rapid growth of planetary science. The changed relationship between the federal government and the observatory was symbolized by the Lowell Planetary Research Center, opened in 1963.

While some important books and papers have been written on aspects of the history of Lowell, there is no scholarly history of the observatory, and there are no scholarly biographies of its two leading figures, Percival Lowell and V.M. Slipher. Hoyt's two books, while excellent in many ways, are hobbled by the fact that they rest alone on published materials and sources available in the Lowell Archives.

Robert W. Smith

Bibliography

Doel, R.E. "Unpacking a Myth: Interdisciplinary Research and the Growth of Solar System Astronomy, 1920–1958." Unpublished Ph.D. dissertation, Princeton University, 1990.

Hoyt, W.G. *Lowell and Mars.* Tucson: University of Arizona Press, 1976.

———. *Planets X and Pluto.* Tucson: University of Arizona Press, 1980.

———. "Vesto Melvin Slipher." *Biographical Memoirs of the National Academy of Sciences* 52 (1980): 411–449.

Putnam, W.L., et al. *The Explorers of Mars Hill: A Centennial History of the Lowell Observatory.* Published for the Lowell Observatory. West Kennebunk, Maine: Phoenix Publishing, 1994.

Strauss, D. "Percival Lowell, W.H. Pickering and the Founding of the Lowell Observatory." *Annals of Science* 51 (1994): 37–58.

Webb, G.E. *Tree Rings and Telescopes: The Scientific Career of A.E. Douglass.* Tucson: The University of Arizona Press, 1983.

Magellanic Clouds

The nearest external galaxies to the Milky Way Galaxy, located in the southern constellations Dorado (Large Magellanic Cloud, LMC, distance ~50 kiloparsecs) and Tucana (Small Magellanic Cloud, SMC, distance ~60 kiloparsecs); also known respectively as Nubeculae Major and Minor. They were known to early navigators as the Cape Clouds but were later renamed after the Portuguese navigator Ferdinand Magellan. In 1867 Cleveland Abbe appears to have been the first to consider their astronomical nature, but detailed investigation did not begin until 1889 when the **Harvard College Observatory** southern station at Arequipa was established. The existence of the clouds was a primary scientific reason in the 1960s for the establishment of the major astronomical observatories in Chile and Australia.

As the nearest external galaxies, the LMC and SMC comprise an invaluable observational laboratory for study of stellar birth, evolution (for example, Super Nova 1987A), and stellar populations in a galactic environment rather different than that of the Milky Way (the LMC is deficient in heavy elements by a factor of 1.4, and the SMC by a factor of 4, compared with the sun). Cloud stars are also fundamental for calibration of stellar magnitudes. Of major importance, the period-luminosity relation of Cepheid variables was established in 1912 by Henrietta Leavitt from photographic surveys of the SMC at Arequipa. Study of the Cepheids and other stars continues today and still plays a major role in the establishment of the extragalactic distance scale.

Charles J. Peterson

Bibliography

Feast, M.W. "The Magellanic Clouds and the Extragalactic Distance Scale." In *The Extragalactic Distance Scale*, edited by S. van den Bergh and C.J. Pritchet, 9–22. San Francisco: Astronomical Society of the Pacific, 1988.

Mathewson, D. "The Clouds of Magellan." *Scientific American* 252 (1985): 106–114.

van den Bergh, S., and K. de Boer, eds. *Structure and Evolution of the Magellanic Clouds, I.A.U. Symposium No. 108.* Dordrecht: Reidel, 1984.

Westerlund, B.E. "The Magellanic Clouds: Their Evolution, Structure and Composition." *Astronomy and Astrophysics Review* 2 (1990): 29–78.

Mars

With its proximity to earth and distinctive atmosphere, Mars has occupied a special place in the history of astronomy. As early as the seventeenth century, the planet's prominence for observers made it the preferred source of evidence among positional astronomers. In 1605, **Johannes Kepler**, drawing on **Tycho Brahe**'s naked-eye observations of Mars's changing position, proposed that planetary orbits were elliptical in shape and that orbital velocity was a function of the planets' distance from the sun. Since Mars was the only planet whose surface markings could be seen through a telescope, it rapidly attracted attention from **Galileo** and his successors. As early as 1610, Galileo was able to determine that Mars was spheroidal.

Galileo's successors recorded their observations of Mars in drawings which, taken sequentially, provide a record of progress in identifying surface features of the planet. From these features, in turn, astronomers were able to refine their notions of the planet's postion, composition, and motion in space. Christiaan Huygens in 1659 discovered a V-shaped mark, now known as Syrtis Major. By following its movement, he found the rotational period of Mars. In 1666, **Giovanni Domenico Cassini** discovered icelike white deposits on the two poles of the planet. He also calculated correctly the distance between Mars and Earth. From observations made between 1777 and 1783, **William Herschel** established that the inclination of the Martian axis gave rise to seasons whose dates he noted along with corresponding color changes on the planet's surface. By the early 1830s Wilhelm Beer and J.H. von Madler had drawn the first modern map of the Martian surface that located and identified the various details.

A new era of Martian observation opened in 1877 with Asaph Hall's discovery of the moons of Mars and **Giovanni Schiaparelli**'s reports of a network of forty channels that crisscrossed the planet. The latter report had the most dramatic impact on the study of Mars. For centuries, astronomers had been interested in the possible existence of extraterrestrial life, for which they imagined various possible locations. Once the moon had been ruled out for lack of atmosphere, Mars, as the most earthlike of the planets in the solar system, was regarded as the most likely location of intelligent life. Schiaparelli's discovery of the canals helped to buttress this proposition, especially among astronomers who believed that the canals had been produced by artificial rather than natural forces. The canals, along with other Martian conditions such as temperature and atmosphere that might yield evidence of the planet's suitability as the abode for intelligent life, became the focus of much astronomical research.

The research agenda for Mars changed little over the next century. Even after Percival Lowell's canal observations were rejected by most professional astronomers, research on Mars continued to focus on the question of habitability. Spectroscopic evidence was sought regarding the atmosphere and new measurements were taken of the planet's tem-

Mars based on about one hundred images taken in red and violet light by the Viking Orbiter *in 1980. Note the impact craters. Some of the bright white areas in this photograph are covered with frozen carbon dioxide. (Courtesy of the National Aeronautics and Space Administration)*

perature. With the development of powerful rockets after 1945, a closer Martian encounter became a real possibility. Indeed, the *Mariner* and *Viking* missions conducted from 1965 to 1976 were driven in large part by a desire to settle the question of Mars's habitability.

The space era brought to a close a century of debate about intelligent life on Mars while opening up new questions. The *Viking* mission established conclusively that no intelligent life exists on Mars, and that, given the paucity of water and oxygen, the prospect of any life, even at the microorganismic level, is dim. At the same time, findings raised other questions regarding the origins and character of the planet. While astronomers had once regarded Mars as having an earthlike environment, the *Mariner 4* probe, showing an abundance of craters, convinced them momentarily of its moonlike character. Later *Mariner* and *Viking* expeditions provided images of channels, mountains, and volcanoes that stunned scientists by establishing the distinctive character of the Martian surface and atmosphere.

Research on Mars responded more slowly to trends in the profession than stellar research. Amateur astronomers like Percival Lowell working at smaller observatories continued to play a significant role in planetary research long after larger observatories had come to dominate stellar astronomy. This role was possible in some measure because the larger observatories concentrated their attention on stellar research. Furthermore, planetary astronomers engaged in more modest data-gathering projects that could easily be performed at smaller observatories. However, the matter of equipment and methodology remained an area of dispute between Lowell and astronomers at larger observatories. He never succeeded in persuading his colleagues that telescopes with objectives that were diaphragmed down were superior to larger instruments in discerning surface detail on the planets.

In other respects, Lowell adopted modern practices for the study of Mars, including photography and spectroscopy. And he anticipated today's interdisciplinary approach to planetary study by proposing in 1905 the new science of planetology, which would ally astronomy to geology and zoology in order to understand planetary evolution. Lowell's concept, however, has been applied in a way that he could hardly have anticipated or approved of. Consistent with current notions of Big Science, the *Viking* and *Mariner* expeditions have relied upon teams of highly specialized scientists from different disciplines and the application of sophisticated and expensive technology, all underwritten by government patronage.

The most important debates on Mars have involved scientists, not historians, and have been related to the **extraterrestrial life** issue. Chief among these have been questions about the reality of the canals and the presence of atmosphere, water, and oxygen on the planet.

The materials in the **Lowell Observatory** Archives provide information about the first systematic Martian research project. Historians will also wish to consult the National Archives and Records Center for documents on pre-*Viking* probes and the *Viking* Project Office at Langley Research Center, Virginia, for records of the *Viking* mission.

Research on Mars and on the history of our understanding of Mars has been skewed for over a century by the obsession with the possible existence of intelligent life on the planet. Hence, studies of Mars have emphasized the search for evidence to support or refute claims of intelligent life. Too little attention has been paid to the composition of the Martian surface and the planet's evolution. Further, historians of science have given disproportianate attention to the most sensational pre-*Viking* chapter in the search for extraterrestrial life on Mars from 1894 to 1916, while the continuing research on Mars over the next fifty years has largely been neglected. Furthermore, with the passage of nearly two decades, the time is now ripe for historians to dig into the mountainous documentation dealing with the *Viking* and *Mariner* missions. The apparent success of these projects, however, creates a dilemma. Rarely has current research in quantity and quality improved understanding of a scientific problem so dramatically in so short a time. Historians will need to resist the temptation to judge too harshly the contributions of earlier students of Mars and to overemphasize the discontinuities between the space era and its antecedents.

David Strauss

Bibliography

Antoniadi, E.M. *La planete mars*. Paris: Librairie scientifique Hermann, 1930.

Carr, M. *The Surface of Mars*. New Haven: Yale University, 1981.

Ezell, E.C., and L. Newman. *On Mars: Exploration of the Red Planet, 1958–1978*. Washington, D.C.: NASA Scientific and Technical Information Branch, 1984.

Flammarion, C. *La planete mars et ses conditions d'habitabilite*. 2 vols. Paris: Gauthier-Villars, 1892, 1909.

Hall, A. *Observations and Orbits of the Satellites of Mars*. Washington, D.C.: Government Printing Office, 1878.

Herschel, W. "On the Remarkable Appearances at the Polar Regions of the Planet Mars." *Philosophical Transactions* 74 (1784).

Horowitz, N.O. *To Utopia and Back: The Search for Life in the Solar System*. New York: W.H. Freeman, 1986.

Mutch, T.A., et al. *The Geology of Mars*. Princeton: Princeton University, 1976.

Vaucouleurs, G. de. *Physics of the Planet Mars*. London: Faber and Faber, 1954.

Masevich, Alla Genrikhovna (1918–)

Soviet astronomer. Masevich graduated from the Moscow Pedagogical Institute and worked first in the Shternberg Astronomical Institute (1946–1952) before becoming assistant chairman of the Astronomical Council of the USSR Academy of Sciences (1952). Since 1972 she has been a professor of space geodesy at the Moscow Institute of Geodesy and Cartography.

Masevich's scientific activities relate primarily to space geodesy and stellar interiors. She has carried out numerous studies concerning questions of stellar evolution—for example, the mass-luminosity dependency as a function of stellar structure. She has been very active in international scientific organizations and has served in a number of commissions concerned with space geodesy, stellar evolution, and observations of artificial earth satellites.

Robert A. McCutcheon

Bibliography

Kolchinskii, I.G., A.A. Korsun', and M.G. Rodriges. "Masevich, Alla Genrikhovna." In *Astronomy, biograficheskii spravochnik (Astronomers, a Biographical Handbook)*, 209–210. Kiev: Naukova dumka, 1986.

Medieval Astronomy

If we looked only at the mainstream of geometrical astronomy during the thousand years from the fall of Rome to the Renaissance, we would see a simple historical pattern: preservation from the fifth to the ninth centuries, rediscovery through Arabic and Greek sources from the tenth to the early thirteenth centuries, and full assimilation of ancient astronomy from the thirteenth century onward. But this would tell only part of the story. A series of practical astronomies devoted to keeping time and the calendar complemented this learned tradition and were central to the preservation of astronomy through the stormy twilight after the collapse of Rome. By stimulating a quest for ancient learning between the tenth and thirteenth centuries, these practical astronomies provided the impetus for the full rebirth of astronomy in the Latin West.

Medieval astronomy, like other elements of medieval culture, was influenced by the traditional practices of the Celtic and Germanic peoples of Northwest Europe. Archaeological studies of British megalithic monuments have shown a concern with a calendar that divides the year into four, eight, or more equal parts by watching the rising and setting sun, divisions that survive in nineteenth-century folklore.

A number of early computistical texts continued to divide the seasons on days falling midway between the solstices and equinoxes. In a number of well-documented cases, pagan festivals on the solar mid-quarter days were transformed into Christian feasts. The relationship of the Christian feasts in the Julian calendar to the traditional feasts in the solar calendar indicates that some kind of solar observation, tied to the uniform, reproducible, fourfold division of the year, continued through the early Middle Ages.

This astronomy served social as well as ritual functions. The saints whose feasts were celebrated on the mid-quarter days (Abbess Brigit of Kildare, 1 Feb.; Bishop Justus of Lyon, 4 Aug.; and King Oswald of Northumbria, 5 Aug.) were not ascetics noted for their piety but powerful leaders of their communities. As such, their cults were sponsored by local elites and represented local rather than universal centers of temporal and spiritual power. Assemblies on their feasts continued the ancient pattern by which the solar mid-quarter days contributed to trade and political and social interactions that animated and strengthened those communities.

If saints' cults and observational solar astronomy were connected with local centers of power, Easter (the Sunday after the full moon after the vernal equinox) was a feast of the universal Church. Regulating the date of Easter was not based upon astronomical observation, which could vary from place to place, but upon mathematical cycles that ensured ritual uniformity throughout Christendom. The chief computistical solutions were successively an eighty-four-year Easter cycle, adopted at Rome in the fourth century, and a nineteen-year lunar cycle (which, when combined with the twenty-eight-year cycle of weeks and leap years, yielded a 532-year Easter cycle) that became dominant at Rome early in the sixth century.

None of these computistical techniques were concerned with a geometrical model of the heavens. *Computus* used simple arithmetical techniques to find the date of the Paschal Full Moon each year. Although these computations called for none of the subtleties of Greek astronomy, in time they gave astronomy a secure place in the monastic curriculum.

Central issues in the early disputes over the correct method of computing Easter were the astronomical symbolism of the growing light of spring and the full moon rather than astronomical precision. These issues need not concern us. What is important is that the controversy stimulated the study of the rudiments of ancient astronomy, beginning in Ireland where the debate was especially heated and the study of alien Roman learning was encouraged. Easter *computus* became the guiding rationale for an introductory course in astronomy.

Early in the eighth century a Northumbrian monk, Bede of Jarrow, composed a series of treatises to justify the 532-year cycle against its eighty-four-year rival. His magisterial *On the Reckoning of Times* enlarged the computistical tradition, adding Pliny's *Natural History* and Virgil's *Georgics* to Macrobius's *Saturnalia,* Isidore's encyclopedic works, and other sources known to the Irish. These materials are unnecessary for Easter computations, but they enriched the student's understanding of the astronomical concepts underlying the Easter question.

Bede's works, and later works derived from them, were primers in astronomy and the calendar, including rules for computing the date of Easter and the approximate positions of the sun and moon. Although computists mentioned the periods of the planets, analogous to the periods of the sun and moon, computing planetary positions required geometrical knowledge beyond the scope of *computus*. By the ninth century, as the reckoning of the date of Easter became a part of the drive for clerical education and liturgical uniformity sponsored by Charlemagne and his successors, an educated cleric was expected to know these rudiments of astronomy.

Besides calculation of lunar cycles, observation of the order of the heavens guided the orderly cycle of prayer in the monasteries. Each day before dawn monks rose to praise God, who has given his creation *a law that cannot be altered* (Psalm 148:6). The regular laws of nature, established by God, resonate with the regular cycle of prayer, specified in monastic rules.

Determining the time for these prayers, especially of prayers before daybreak, required knowledge of the changing length of day and night and of the changing appearances of the stars with the seasons. Scattered throughout a wide range of monastic texts from the fifth to the thirteenth century are requirements that those who keep time should know what stars to watch, allusions to specific monks and nuns who were accustomed to watch the stars at night, and a few specific guides for this very practical form of astronomy.

But monks relied solely on unaided observation of the course of the stars. Pacificus of Verona invented a simple instrument to determine the time of night by watching the rotation of Polaris around a faint fifth magnitude star that in his day marked the pole. Around the year 1000 Gerbert (or one of his students) described the astrolabe as too accurate for ordinary timekeeping but especially suited for regulating the times of prayer (*De utilitatibus astrolabii,* 5.4).

Academic astronomy, unlike these practical astronomies, reflected the ancient Greek ideal of astronomy as a mathematical discipline, but without Ptolemy's geometrical precision or the observational detail of the practical astronomies. Astronomy was studied as one of the liberal arts for its philosophical and ethical value. Contemplating the order of the universe and humanity's place within it taught one to live well. Since ancient education aimed to form the leaders of the community rather than expert astronomers, this astronomy saw that almost inevitable simplification that we see today in introductory science courses for nonmajors.

After the breakdown of Roman municipal education, works in this tradition by Chalcidius, Martianus Capella, Boethius, and Cassiodorus, as well as encyclopedic compilations by Pliny and Seneca, survived to provide the only hints of ancient astronomy. Such Christian writers as Isidore of Seville could transmit a few scraps of ancient astronomy to reinforce the concept of a universe governed by a divinely established order, but they could not go beyond their limited sources.

The content of this astronomy was rudimentary, an introduction to celestial coordinates, sometimes a mention of something as advanced as the inclined path of the zodiac or the nature of epicycles, but the discussion seldom reached the level of an elementary-school text. The techniques for calculating the position of the sun, moon, stars, and planets found in Ptolemy's *Almagest* and *Handy Tables* were lost, and would remain so until the twelfth century. Even **Ptolemy** himself had become a legendary figure, an Egyptian king who had studied astronomy, and something of a model for later rulers who wished to be seen as philosopher kings.

This ideal of a royal sage took on new life in the court of Charlemagne and his successors. Charlemagne observed the heavens and asked his friend and colleague Alcuin of York why his observations did not agree with calculations. But this interest went beyond idle curiosity; as part of his goal to ensure uniformity of ritual throughout the empire, Charlemagne decreed that clerics be taught computus. The Carolingian court sponsored the production of deluxe astronomical manuscripts and scholarly anthologies combining late Roman and computistical texts that further enriched the study of astronomy.

During the ninth century, schoolmasters such as John Scottus Eriugena and Remigius of Auxerre began to draw on their knowledge of computus to clarify, and sometimes even correct, the astronomy of the liberal arts. This theoretical astronomy, however, lacked the connection to exact astronomical observation and calculation shared by Greek and Arab astronomy.

Early in the tenth century diplomatic contacts between the empire and the Caliphate of Córdoba give the first hints of scholarly communication. There are more than hints for knowledge of the **astrolabe**. By the end of the century instructions for its use and manufacture, and the instruments themselves, were making their way from Muslim Spain to the Latin West.

The astrolabe revolutionized European astronomy by incorporating a quantitatively exact geometrical model of the heavens into an instrument for computing time by observing the altitude of a heavenly body. As a time reckoning instrument the astrolabe fit easily into the tradition of monastic timekeeping and soon found a place in the curriculum of monastic and cathedral schools. Early in the eleventh century the noted schoolmaster Fulbert of Chartres composed a brief mnemonic rhyme to help his students remember the Arabic names and places of eight astrolabe stars that would be useful for timekeeping.

In time, the astrolabe contributed to a more revolutionary change. About an hour before dawn on October 18, 1092, Prior Walcher of Malvern saw the moon begin to grow dark. Since he needed the precise time of a lunar eclipse for more exact lunar tables, he took his astrolabe and measured the height of the moon at its darkest and found it to be 15 degrees above the western horizon. From this one eclipse observation, Walcher computed a set of tables covering seventy-six years that gave the time of each new moon to the nearest quarter hour. Walcher's investigation drew on two medieval astronomical traditions, timekeeping and computus, but with a decidedly new precision. Heretofore lunar tables were adequate if they gave the date of the new moon. By increasing computistical precision a hundredfold, Walcher posed new astronomical problems. As Walcher compared the results of his tables with subsequent eclipses, he assembled a disturbing collection of disagreements.

Walcher had rediscovered anomalies in the lunar orbit, anomalies already incorporated in Arabic astronomy, as he soon learned from the physician Peter Alfonsi. Peter partly translated the astronomical tables (or *zīj*) of Muḥammad ibn Mūsā al-Khwārizmī in 1116. Al-Khwārizmī's *zīj,* and many subsequent astronomical tables, revolutionized astronomical computations in an unrevolutionary way. Computists were familiar with finding the approximate time and place of new moons using rudimentary arithmetical techniques. These tables provided simple arithmetical procedures to find true positions; their geometrical foundations remained hidden. Yet they set the stage for the recovery of astronomical theory.

This recovery did not occur in a vacuum; the conquest of the European outposts of Arabic culture in Spain and Sicily, the growing prosperity of medieval cities, and the emergence of medieval universities all contributed to the naturalization of Greek and Arab geometrical astronomy into the Latin world.

The first step was the translation of texts dealing with astronomical theory—as opposed to the mere calculating techniques presented in the *zījes*—from Greek and Arabic into Latin. Among these translations were al-Farghani's introductory text *On the Science of the Stars,* first translated in 1135; Ibn al-Muthanna's detailed commentary on al-

Khwārizmī's *zīj*,, translated about the same time; and Ptolemy's *Almagest,* translated twice, from Greek and from Arabic, in the 1160s.

The new translations led to a recognition that the computists had used inaccurate data and inadequate methods to compute the equinoxes and the motion of the moon. As early as 1175 an anonymous English computist was citing Greek and Arabic sources as evidence for the correct date of the vernal equinox.

This was followed in the thirteenth century by a torrent of original texts that applied the new theory to familiar practical problems and presented it in forms suited to the university curriculum. This *corpus astronomicum* came to encompass all the texts needed for an introduction to the new astronomy; some were selected from the new translations but most were new works. The subjects covered in the *corpus astronomicum* display striking parallels to the topics of early medieval astronomies.

The annual cycle of seasonal festivals continued in ecclesiastical calendars of increasing sophistication. Robert Grosseteste, Roger Bacon, and others continued the tradition of Easter computus, while criticizing it on the basis of new astronomical knowledge. Instructions for using the astrolabe and newer instruments, the old and new quadrants, continued the tradition of observational timekeeping. The greatest changes were in the astronomy of the liberal arts, where treatises *de Sphaera,* most notably that of John of Sacrobosco, and new texts on the theory of the planets provided increasingly detailed descriptions of the geometrical structure of the heavens. Near the end of the century Campanus of Novara's *Theorica planetarum* went beyond mere description to present a series of instruments or *equatoria* that modeled planetary deferents and epicycles. These *equatoria* could be used to compute the positions of the planets without extensive use of astronomical tables. Computational astronomy, itself, was last to enter the university curriculum with the appearance of the *Toledan Tables,* and later the **Alfonsine Tables**, in fourteenth-century manuscripts of the *corpus astronomicum.*

As the new astronomy settled into a routine place within the medieval curriculum, it appears to have undergone no further theoretical transformations. The chief change was the continuing diffusion of astronomical knowledge beyond the university milieu with the appearance of astronomical works in the vernacular, such as William of St. Cloud's *Kalendarium Regine* (ca. 1290) and Geoffrey Chaucer's *Tretis of the Astrolabe* and *Equatorie of the Planetis* (ca. 1390).

Yet the place of astronomy in the university curriculum, the influence of Aristotelian natural philosophy on the teaching of astronomy, and the internal development of the discipline expressed in the *corpus astronomicum* and commentaries still remain to be studied with the care that has been directed toward other elements of the medieval curriculum.

Stephen C. McCluskey

Bibliography

Benjamin, F.S., and G.J. Toomer. *Campanus of Novara and Medieval Planetary Theory:* Theorica planetarum. Madison: University of Wisconsin Press, 1971.

Borst, A. *Computus: Zeit und Zahl in der Geschichte Europas.* Berlin: Verlag Klaus Wagenbach, 1990.

Bubnov, N., ed. *Gerberti postea Silvestri II papae Opera Mathematica.* Hildesheim: Georg Olms Verlagsbuchhandlung, 1963.

Butzer, P.L., and D. Lohrmann, ed. *Science in Western and Eastern Civilization in Carolingian Times.* Basel, Boston, Berlin: Birkhäuser Verlag, 1993.

Coyne, G.V., et al. *Gregorian Reform of the Calendar.* Proceedings of the Vatican Conference to Commemorate Its 400th Anniversary. Vatican City: Specolo Vaticana, 1983.

Duhem, P. *Le Système du Monde: Histoire des doctrines cosmologiques de Platon à Copernic.* Vols. 3–4. Paris: Hermann, 1954.

Eastwood, B.S. "Origins and Contents of the Leiden Planetary Configuration (MS Voss Q.79, Fol. 93v), an Artistic Astronomical Schema of the Early Middle Ages." *Viator* 14 (1983): 1–40.

Gingerich, O., and J. Dobrzycki, ed. *Proceedings of the Joint Symposium of the IAU and the IUHPS, cosponsored by the IAHS. Astronomy of Copernicus and Its Background, Torun 1973.* Colloquia Copernicana III, Studia Copernicana XIII. Wroclaw, Warsaw, Cracow, Gdansk: Polish Academy of Sciences, 1975.

Haskins, C.H. *Studies in the History of Mediaeval Science.* New York: Frederick Ungar, 1960.

Jones, C.W. *Bedae Opera de Temporibus.* Cambridge: Mediaeval Academy of America, 1943.

McCluskey, S.C. "Gregory of Tours, Monastic Timekeeping, and Early Christian

Attitudes to Astronomy." *Isis* 81 (1990): 9–22.
Pedersen, O. *Early Physics and Astronomy: A Historical Introduction*. Cambridge: Cambridge University Press, 1993.
Walsh, M., and D.Ó. Cróinín, ed. *Cummian's Letter De Controversia Paschali and the De Ratione Conputandi.* Toronto: Pontifical Institute of Mediaeval Studies, 1988.

Mercury

Mercury, the most difficult planet to observe, received scant attention during the early telescopic era. Galileo tried to observe the phases, but they were beyond the power of his telescope. In 1639 an Italian Jesuit, Giovanni Zupus, claimed to have seen them, as did **Johannes Hevelius** in 1644. Late in the eighteenth century Johann Hieronymus Schröter published some drawings of faint albedo features from which he derived a rotation period of twenty-four hours. He inferred a rough surface from the blunt appearance of one of the horns. Observing the transit of 1799, Schröter suspected that he had seen evidence of an atmosphere, but this turned out to have been an effect of the extreme contrast between the bright solar disk and the tiny dot of a planet. During the 1707 transit **John Flamsteed** had seen the same phenomenon, and during the transit of 1631 Pierre Gassendi had been amazed at the smallness of the disk.

Schröter, a persistent worker, took to observing Mercury in the daytime. Daytime observations eliminated the tight constraints of the planet's low altitude and rapid setting in twilight, and also reduced the glare of the planet against a twilight sky. In his *Mercurian Fragments* (1800–1816) he suggested a twenty-four-hour rotation. By 1881 **Giovanni Schiaparelli**, observing that faint visible streaks kept the same position relative to the planet's night-day boundary, concluded that Mercury's rotation took place not in twenty-four hours but in eighty-eight days—the same as its orbital period. He still held out for clouds on the tiny planet, and thought that the existence of bodies of water could not be positively refuted. He produced a map of the planet, showing the streaks but without nomenclature. T.J.J. See claimed to have seen craters on the tiny planet.

Antoniadi, Lowell, Lyot, and others produced many detailed maps replete with conflicting features and names. Some of the albedo features on these maps, and on drawings made at Pic du Midi by Audouin Dollfus in the 1960s (Lyot's successor) were later thought to correlate with large features on spacecraft images.

In 1832 **Friedrich Wilhelm Bessel** had derived a reasonably good diameter of only 4,855 km, from which in 1835 Encke could determine a mass of 1/4,686,571 that of the sun. The fortuitous appearance of the comet named for Encke allowed this mass to be calculated from the planet's perturbing force on the comet. Without a satellite, there was no other means for estimating the planet's mass. Anomalies in the planet's orbit led several astronomers to believe they had found an additional planet or companion dubbed Vulcan. The anomalous advancement of the planet's perihelion was not understood until Einstein's general theory of relativity.

Bernard Lyot made polarimetric observations of Mercury in the 1920s and compared them to terrestrial samples. His observations of Mercury resembled those of the moon, reinforcing the results from photometric studies that showed the two bodies to be probably composed of similar volcanic materials.

Radiometric measurements at **Lowell Observatory** and at Mount Wilson at about the same time showed little deviation from a black body, about 610 degrees Celsius, and seemed to reinforce the theory of synchronous rotation. But in 1965 Mercury was brought within range of advancing radar technology. The Doppler shift of the reflected radar waves revealed a rotation period of 58.6 days, two thirds of the orbital period. This turned the same side of the planet toward earth during times of its easiest visibility, thus providing the appearance of synchronous rotation.

In the early 1970s a *Mariner* spacecraft was sent into solar orbit from which it was able to encounter both Venus and Mercury in several passes, the first use of gravity assist. Passing Venus on November 3, 1973, *Mariner 10* then encountered Mercury on March 29, 1974, September 21, 1974, and March 16, 1975.

Without a satellite, Mercury's mass and density had been difficult to estimate. From perturbations of *Mariner's* orbit and refined measures of the planet's diameter, Mercury was found to have a large iron core, surrounded by a thin shell of rock. Equally surprising, the planet had a weak magnetic field, even though it did not exhibit rapid rotation and lacked a liquid core.

Mariner arrived to photograph Mercury after more than a decade of intensive study of the moon calibrated by returned lunar

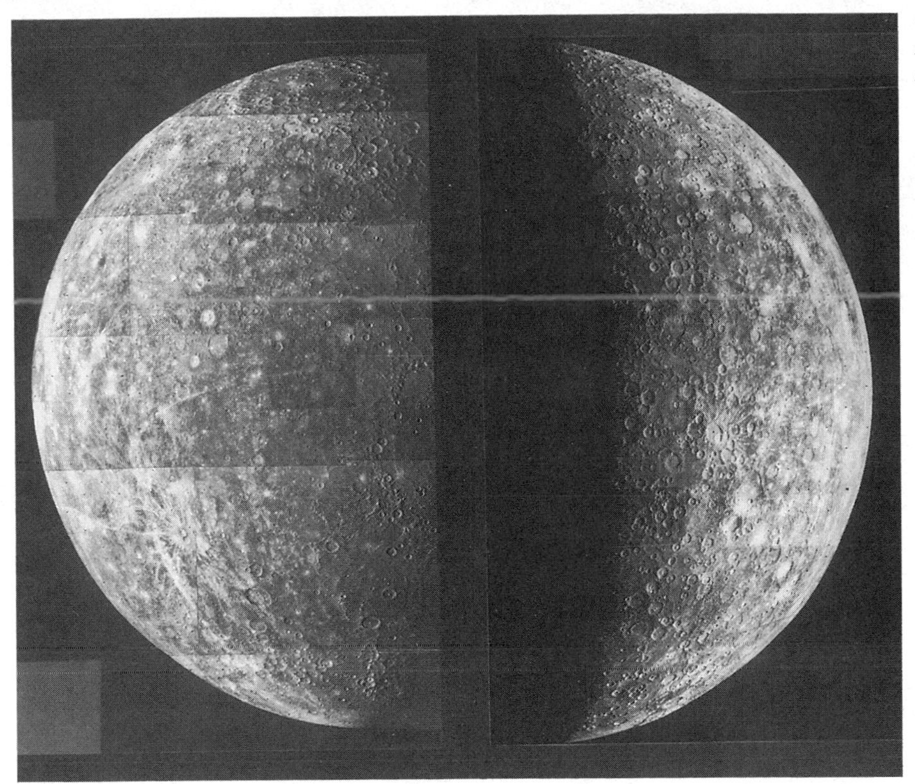

Mercury, the innermost planet, is shown here as photographed by Mariner 10 *in 1974. This photograph is based on a number of images. The surface of Mercury is heavily cratered and looks like earth's moon. (Courtesy of the National Aeronautics and Space Administration)*

samples. Hence planetary geologists were well prepared to analyze the similar surface. Cratering on Mercury confirmed and refined the bombardment history of the inner solar system. The cratering rate at Mercury seemed to have been about twice that at the Moon. Mercury showed the same basic features as the moon—cratered highlands, smooth plains where material melted in large impacts later solidified, and large circular basins surrounded by concentric rings. The most spectacular of these latter features was the Caloris Basin, which indicated an impact so massive that the shock waves converged on the opposite side of the planet and deformed the terrain there. The greater surface gravity of Mercury keeps impact ejecta from spreading as far as they do on the moon, and the smooth plains may represent an underlying older surface. Also different from the moon, extremely long scarps are visible on Mercury, probably the result of substantial shrinkage of the crust as it cooled.

Mariner's three encounters remain the only close inspection of the planet. Earth-based radar astronomy of Mercury has continued, however, and while it does not have the resolution of the *Mariner* observations it has helped characterize the planet more comprehensively. Radar observations also produced the somewhat surprising finding in 1991 that frozen water is to be found at the north pole.

Mercury itself has attracted only passing attention by historians, although issues of its orbit and the role of transit observations in defining the value of the astronomical unit have been treated extensively. Robert G. Strom provides the first book-length treatment of the planet since Antoniadi, and presents modern scientific results authoritatively but without references. Dunne and Burgess, as well as Murray and Burgess, provide a good summary of the *Mariner* mission as well as some interesting behind-the-scenes vignettes, as does Murray (1989). Roseveare, Verloren, and Campbell treat the anomalous motion of Mercury's perihelion, the search for intramercurial planets, and the problem's resolution.

Joseph N. Tatarewicz

Bibliography

Antoniadi. *The Planet Mercury {La Planete Mercure et la Rotation Des Satellites}.* Translated by Patrick Moore. Shaldon, England: K. Reid, 1974.

Campbell, W.W. "The Closing of a Famous Astronomical Problem." *Publications of the Astronomical Society of the Pacific* 21 (1909): 103–115.

Dunne, J.A., and E. Burgess. *The Voyage of Mariner 10: Mission to Venus and Mercury*. Washington, D.C.: NASA SP-424, 1978.

Lankford, J. "A Note on T.J.J. See's Observations of Craters on Mercury." *Journal for the History of Astronomy* 14 (1983): 129–132.

Lyttleton, R.A. "History of the Mass of Mercury." *Quarterly Journal of the Royal Astronomical Society* 21 (1980): 400–413.

Murray, B.C. *Journey into Space: The First Three Decades of Space Exploration*. New York: Norton, 1989.

Murray, B.C., and E. Burgess. *Flight to Mercury*. New York: Columbia University Press, 1977.

Roseveare, N.T. *Mercury's Perihelion from Le Verrier to Einstein*. Oxford: Oxford University Press, 1982.

Strom, R.G. *Mercury: The Elusive Planet*. Smithsonian Library of the Solar System. Washington, D.C.: Smithsonian Institution Press, 1987.

Van Helden, A. "The Importance of the Transit of Mercury in 1631." *Journal for the History of Astronomy* 7 (1976): 1–10.

Verloren Van Themaat, W.A. "Hindsight and the Definition of Research Success: Illustrated by the History of Planetary Discovery." *Zeitschrift Fur Allgemeine Wissenschaftstheorie* 15 (1984): 272– 277.

Meridian Instruments

Meridian instruments are specialized astronomical devices designed to observe the positions of celestial objects as they cross the local meridian of the observer. In the pretelescopic era they reached their height in **Tycho Brahe**'s mural quadrant, with positional accuracies of about a minute of arc; telescopic sights for quadrants were pioneered by Flamsteed, and eventually the telescope itself became the meridian instrument. Because these instruments were generally rigidly mounted and could move only in the north-south line (unlike equatorially mounted instruments), their stability gave them increased accuracy for the precise measurement of celestial positions. The family of meridian instruments includes not only the mural arcs (which were mounted on a wall), but also the transit instrument, so-called because it observes objects as they transit the meridian, and the transit (or meridian) circle, which includes a circle for the measurement of the declination coordinate. A variety of zenith instruments carried the meridian principle to its ultimate extreme, restricting pointing to the zenith for added stability at the cost of greatly reducing the number of observable objects. The transit instrument and transit circle, refined over the past three centuries at observatories around the world, have provided the fundamental stellar coordinate system and tracked the motion of solar system bodies against this reference frame.

The transit instrument was first used by Ole Römer in Copenhagen in 1689; by 1721 **Edmond Halley** had mounted one at Greenwich. The English came to excel in the manufacture of meridian instruments, and the first successful transit circle was made by Troughton in 1806. A Troughton mural circle was installed at Greenwich in 1812. They vied with each other to produce accurate declinations, but in the course of the nineteenth century the transit circle generally won out over the mural circle, giving positional accuracies of about 1 arcsecond. By the mid-nineteenth century every observatory of any size had its transit instrument or transit circle, which could be used not only for stellar positions but also for time determination. By this time the Germans began to overtake the English in meridian instruments, and when the **U.S. Naval Observatory** equipped its new building in 1842, it turned primarily to German makers. A major transit circle, such as that installed by Airy at Greenwich beginning in 1851, could make hundreds of thousands of individual observations in the course of its lifetime. The positions so determined could then be used as reference points for the photographic surveys of the sky, among its other uses.

The modern transit circle is used in conjunction with an atomic clock that can time the passage of a star to thousandths of a second, and with a circle with 7,200 divisions (0.05 degree), read with charge-coupled devices at six points around the circle to take into account any eccentricity. During the minute-and-a-half the object is in the field of view, the measurements in right ascension and declination may be made by an observer using a filar micrometer at the eyepiece, by a photoelectric detector, or by a charge-coupled device. A computerized data acquisition system gathers the data, which is then reduced to determine star positions, which may reach an internal accuracy of about 0.07 of an arcsecond with several observations. In addition to a computerized data acquisition system, the movement of the modern transit circle may also be computer-controlled.

The chief barrier to accuracy for modern meridian instruments has been the refraction correction necessary when observing through the earth's atmosphere. Despite heroic efforts at increased accuracy, fewer than a dozen transit circles are still in operation in the world. Barring unforeseen developments, the era of meridian instruments is probably passing, their function superseded by spacecraft techniques such as the *Hipparcos* satellite and ground-based radio and optical interferometry.

Steven J. Dick

Bibliography

Howse, D. *Greenwich Observatory: The Royal Observatory at Greenwich and Herstmonceux, 1675–1975, Vol. 3: The Buildings and Instruments*. London: Taylor and Francis, 1975.

Messier, Charles (1730–1817)

French astronomer. Messier was appointed (1755) as a clerk to the astronomer Joseph-Nicolas Delisle at the observatory in the Hotel de Cluny in Paris. He became a member of the French Academy of Sciences in 1770. Messier independently recovered Halley's comet on January 21, 1759, but was preceded by the German amateur astronomer Johann Georg Palitzsch. An assiduous comet observer, Messier discovered sixteen of these objects. A by-product of his comet searching was the cataloguing (1774–1784) of 103 nebulae and star clusters, known as Messier objects, including the Crab Nebula and the Andromeda Galaxy.

Craig B. Waff

Bibliography

Gingerich, O. "Messier, Charles." In *Dictionary of Scientific Biography*, edited by C.C. Gillispie, vol. 9, 329–331. New York: Scribner, 1974.

Jones, K.G. *Messier's Nebulae and Star Clusters*. London: Faber and Faber, 1968.

Mallas, J.H., and E. Kreimer. *The Messier Album*. Cambridge, Mass.: Sky Publishing Corp., 1978.

Messier, C. *The Messier Catalogue of Charles Messier*. Translated and edited by P.H. Niles. Clifton Park, N.Y.: Auriga, 1981.

Waff, C.B. "The First International Halley Watch: Guiding the Worldwide Search for Comet Halley, 1755–59." In *Standing on the Shoulders of Giants: A Longer View of Newton and Halley,* edited by N.J.W. Thrower, 373–411. Los Angeles and Oxford: University of California Press, 1990.

Meteoric Astronomy

That ordinary shooting stars, fireballs, and meteorites differed mainly in mass was not well understood until well into the twentieth century. Although the ancient Greeks believed that meteors and meteorites were of cosmic origin, by the Middle Ages and through the eighteenth century it was more generally thought that shooting stars were of purely atmospheric origin, analogous to lightning. **Johannes Kepler** proclaimed they should play no part in astronomy. Meteorites were considered ordinary rocks struck by lightning, and it was firmly believed that stones simply could not fall from heaven, witnesses notwithstanding. Nevertheless, some were venerated, for example, the Ensisham meteorite of 1492, which Emperor Maximilian considered as a sign from heaven that his enemies, the Turks, would be defeated. American Indians (ca. 900–1300) revered meteorites, as exemplified by the occurrence of meteorites in their burial mounds, particularly the Hopewell Mounds in Ohio.

In 1794 Ernst F.F. Chladni deduced a relationship between bright fireballs and meteorites that indicated their extraterrestrial origin. Yet it was not until after the fall of meteorites at l'Agile, France, in 1803, and at Weston, Connecticut, in 1807, that the scientific community finally conceded a cosmic origin for meteorites.

The first systematic attempts to determine the heights of meteors were carried out in 1798 by two Göttingen students, Heinrich Wilhelm Brandes and Johann Friedrich Benzenberg, demonstrating for the first time that the atmosphere of the earth extended well above 50 miles. Little progress followed until the advent of celestial photography. Between 1893 and 1910, William Lewis Elkin set up one battery of cameras at Yale, and another a few miles distant. For determining velocities, he also designed a rotating sector to occult the lenses six to ten times a second. Although the base line between the two stations was too short for the desired accuracy, Elkin's methods were imitated at Harvard, mainly under Fred. L. Whipple in the 1930s, but with adequate base lines and faster cameras and emulsions than had previously been available.

Alexander Humboldt, witnessing the spectacular Leonids in 1779, discovered their radiant point, noting that it signified that the meteors were traveling in parallel paths. Yet this discovery was overlooked in 1833 when Denison Olmsted at Yale and Alexander C.

Twining at West Point were given the credit for this discovery. As Leonids appeared several years in succession, Olmsted believed their period was a year or less. Later, Hubert A. Newton traced the shower back to 902 C.E. and found that any one of five interrelated periods could satisfy all the observations; and he was the first to predict its next return in 1866. However, it remained for John C. Adams to rule out all but the 33.25-year period.

In 1867, it became evident that the Leonids travel in the same orbit as Comet Temple. Comet Biela had been observed to split in 1846, and the Andromedid meteors, observed since 1772, were later found to travel in its orbit. The Lyrid meteors, associated with comet 1861I, were traced back to 687 B.C.E., over twenty-five hundred years. By 1879, H.A. Newton believed that not just meteors but also meteorites were once parts of comets.

More recently, it was believed that while shower meteors were derived from comets, meteorites and bright fireballs were related to asteroids. Orbits of several meteorites were found to have had aphelia close to the asteroid belt, including the spectacular fall at Sikhote-Alin on February 12, 1947. Then in 1983, a new Apollo-type asteroid, named Phaethon, was discovered moving in an elliptical orbit with aphelion near the asteroid belt. F.L. Whipple was quick to point out that the Geminid meteors travel in its path—the first apparent instance of an ordinary meteor shower associated with an asteroid. But then the question arose, Was Phaethon really an asteroid or an unusual comet? Other Apollo-type asteroids were found with associated meteor swarms. Theories had been advanced, in particular by Ernst J. Öpik in 1963, that Apollo-type asteroids may be extinct or moribund comets. Then, in 1985, infrared observations cast doubt on the extinct-comet model. Phaethon appeared to be a unique object showing properties of solid rock inconsistent with models of cometary nuclei.

Theoretically, perturbations of cometary orbits by the major planets could change some originally elliptical into hyperbolic orbits, leading to the ejection of some comets or meteors from the solar system. Alternatively, some interstellar material might have been captured by the solar system, entering at hyperbolic velocities. Indeed, Edmund Halley believed that meteors and comets originated in interstellar space. Extensive searches have been made for hyperbolic orbits, especially during a Harvard-Cornell program in Arizona in the early 1930s under the direction of Öpik and Samuel L. Boothroyd. Many meteor orbits have been suspected of being hyperbolic but none has ever been confirmed.

Mineralogical and chemical analyses of meteorites were carried out even before the famous fall at l'Agile in 1803, indicating minerals differing from the soil in which they fell; and their nickel-iron content was not characteristic of known terrestrial rocks. Determination of the chemical constitution of meteors, on the other hand, required spectrum analysis. Between 1897 and 1925 nine photographs of meteor spectra had been obtained serendipitously at several American and European observatories. As a graduate student at Harvard, Peter M. Millman analysed these and in 1931 initiated a program for obtaining objective prism spectra during the Leonid and Geminid showers, obtaining fourteen more spectra. He found that nearly all could be classified into either of two categories: those showing strong H and K lines of calcium, and those lacking these lines. Eight of the spectra corresponded to Leonids, proving these to be stony particles.

In 1929, radio engineers detected sporadic ionospheric radiations that were correlated with meteor displays. Ultimately, largely through the efforts of scientists in Canada and at Jodrell Bank Radio Observatory in England, daytime meteor showers were discovered, about a dozen by 1952. Much earlier, however, a daylight shower had been observed during the solar eclipse of August 7, 1869, possibly the same shower as one observed by radio from Jodrell Bank on August 4 and 8, 1947. Some dark bodies observed to transit the sun in 1090, 1203, 1547, and on May 12, 1706, and June 17, 1707, could concievably be associated with modern discoveries of daytime meteor showers.

As meteoritic research continues to advance our knowledge of meteors and meteorites, it also contributes to our understanding of the earth's atmosphere and of some geological features. Since World War II, measurements of the decelerations of ordinary meteors along their visible paths have resulted in determinations of the density of the upper atmosphere and have given indications of atmospheric oscillations related to solar and lunar cycles. The largest and oldest terrestrial scars, sometimes called fossil craters, that have been attributed to meteoritic impacts, were discovered through aerial surveys in the 1940s and 1950s. With diameters ranging from about 1 to 100 km, they are so large and so covered with subsequent deposits and overgrowth that their characteristic contours could not be recognized from the ground. Their meteoritic origin was inferred from the characteristics of the underlying fractured rocks, which differ from ancient volcanic formations. Drillings at these sites yielded information on the earth's crust to deeper layers than had previously been possible. Moreover, at craters in regions where carbonaceous rocks were present, commercially valuable diamonds were found, created by the impact of massive high speed meteorites—forces more powerful than could be matched in any laboratory.

Dorrit Hoffleit

Bibliography

Biot, E.C. *Catalogue General des Étoiles Filantes*. Paris: Imprimerie, 1846.

Hoffleit, D. "Yale Contributions to Meteoric Astronomy." *Vistas in Astronomy* 32 (1988): 117–143.

Hughes, D.W. "The History of Meteors and Meteor Showers." *Vistas in Astronomy* 26 (1982): 325–345.

Humboldt, A. von. *Kosmos*. Vols. 1–5b. Stuttgart: Gotta'scher Verlag, 1845–1862.

Kopff, A. "Kometen und Meteore." *Handbuch der Astrophysik* 4 (1929): 426–428, 477–485.

Krinov, E.L. *Principles of Meteoritics*. Translated from Russian by I. Vidziunas and edited by H. Brown. Oxford: Pergamon Press, 1960.

———. *Giant Meteorites*. Translated from Russian by J.S. Romankiewicz. Oxford: Pergamon Press, 1966.

Lovell, B. *Meteor Astronomy*. Oxford: Clarendon Press, 1954.

Millman, P.M. *Meteorite Research*. Dordrecht: Reidel,1969.

Olivier, C.P. *Meteors*. Baltimore: Williams and Wilkins, 1925.

Valentiner, W. "Kometen und Meteore." In *Handwörterbuch der Astronomie,* vol. 2, 49–228. Breslau: Eduard Trewendt, 1898.

Meudon Observatory

Part of the **Paris Observatory** since 1926, the Meudon Observatory is located on a site that was part of a royal domain of Louis XIV, including the Château Neuf and a public park built on a ridge located southwest of Paris at an altitude of 160 meters. **Jules Janssen**, who gained fame in 1868 for the discovery of helium (simultaneously with **J.N. Lockyer**), obtained authorization in 1876 to establish in the park at Meudon an astrophysical observatory, of which he was named director. Two wings of the Château Neuf burned in 1871. The remainder, slated for demolition, was saved in 1878 when Janssen proposed making it the location for a large refracting telescope, at the time the second largest in the world, after the 36-inch Lick telescope in the United States. The refractor had two objectives: one for photography (83 cm) and one for visual work (62 cm) with a focal length of 16 meters; it was located in a dome 18.5 meters in diameter. At the same time two other refractors (with 25- and 21-cm objectives) and a 1-meter reflecting telescope were installed.

After 1897 Janssen was assisted by Henri Deslandres, who became director in 1908 and embarked on a great expansion project. A spectroscopy laboratory was established and other instruments were set up on the hill overlooking Paris. While at the Paris Observatory, Deslandres invented the **spectroheliograph,** an instrument that permitted photographs to be taken of the outer layers of the solar atmosphere. He transferred the instrument to Meudon and installed a second in 1906. Deslandres constructed siderostats with mirrors of 0.75 and 0.50 cm and began a long series of solar observations. He also equipped the great refractor (still the largest in Europe and third largest in the world) for the measurement of **stellar radial velocities**. He also added an objective prism to the 1-meter telescope, with which observations were made of Halley's Comet in 1910 and of **Wolf-Rayet stars**. The activity of the observatory was reduced considerably during World War I with the mobilization of the Observatory astronomers. Acting on an idea suggested a few years earlier, Deslandres began (1922) construction on an equatorial table 2.3 meters in diameter, capable of supporting a ton and a half of instrumentation.

The Meudon Observatory lost its independence when Deslandres negotiated its merger with the Paris Observatory. Meudon became the *Section d'Astrophysique* of the Paris Observatory. From 1927 to 1932 Deslandres was the first director of this important complex. In 1920 a young astronomer named Bernard Lyot joined the solar research team at Meudon. He developed new instruments to be installed on the equatorial table. The coronograph (later duplicated at the Pic-du-Midi Observatory), which now bears his name, permits the observation of the solar corona in times other than eclipses.

With the appointment of André Danjon to the directorship in 1945, Meudon entered a new phase of development. Solar research was principally carried out by Lucien and Marguerite d'Azambuja and by Lyot. The expansion of the facility continued with the arrival of the **radio astronomy** group, and within a few years the personnel numbered several hundred. Meudon maintains a continuous survey of solar activity, as well as responsibility for compiling worldwide data on solar activity and predicting future activity. Meudon also organized the observation of artificial satellites with the launching of *Sputnik I*. In 1961 a **Schmidt Telescope** (60 cm, focal length 1 meter, corrector plate 40 cm) was placed on the equatorial table. Between 1963 and 1969, a 36-meter solar tower was built and equipped with a coelostat with 85-cm mirrors that send light to a laboratory at the base of the tower where a solar image of 41 cm is produced. Between 1967 and 1971 the 1-meter Cassegrain telescope was modernized. A 10-meter ultraviolet vacuum spectrograph, operational since 1972, permits a high-resolution study of ultraviolet laboratory sources to supplement satellite research. Space astronomy, research in theoretical and observational astrophysics and cosmology, relativity studies, radio astronomy in different wavelengths, and solar astronomy compose the work at Meudon.

Suzanne Débarbat

Bibliography

Biver, P. *Histoire du Château de Meudon {1923}*. Marseille: Lafitte Reprints, 1981.

Michard, R. *L'Observatoire de Paris*. Paris: Observatoire de Paris, 1975.

Michelson, Albert Abraham (1853–1931)

The first American recipient of a Nobel Prize in physics (1907). Michelson was born in Strelno, Prussia (now Poland), but his family soon immigrated to the United States, where Michelson was raised in mining camps in California and Nevada. Educated in San Francisco and at the U.S. Naval Academy, he joined the Annapolis science faculty in the mid-1870s and quickly focused his attention on improved techniques for optical measurements. Securing an appointment to the new Case School of Applied Science in Cleveland 1882, he continued his experiments and began a collaboration with Western Reserve University chemist Edward W. Morley. The two scientists developed a sensitive **interferometer** to determine whether wavelengths of light could provide a standard unit of length, but are today remembered for their 1887 experiment to test the relative motion of the earth against a stationary aether. Although the direct impact of the experiment's null result on the development of Einstein's special relativity theory remains ambiguous, the Ohio scientists' work attracted much attention.

Following four years at Clark University, Michelson moved to the new University of Chicago in 1893 as head of the physics department. He grew increasingly interested in astrophysical spectroscopy and improved existing techniques for the production of diffraction gratings. During the 1920s, Michelson frequently visited Mount Wilson Observatory and the California Institute of Technology, where he made measurements of the velocity of light and crafted a stellar interferometer for the 100-inch relector. Michelson retired from the University of Chicago in 1928 and moved to Pasadena.

George E. Webb

Bibliography

Holton, G. "Einstein, Michelson, and the 'Crucial' Experiment." *Isis* 60 (1969): 133–197.

Livingston, D.M. *The Master of Light*. New York: Scribner, 1973.

Swenson, L.S., Jr. *The Ethereal Aether: A History of the Michelson-Morley-Miller Aether-Drift Experiments, 1880–1930*. Austin: University of Texas Press, 1972.

Micrometer

A wide variety of devices employed for accurate measurement of small angles, achieved either by direct comparison of the field of telescopic view with adjustable or fixed fiducial markers or by creation of double images that can be moved relative to each other.

In 1612 **Galileo** made the first known micrometrical device, a cross-hatched disk attached to the side of his telescope. Viewed with the left eye, its image appeared superimposed on that seen through the telescope with the right eye. **William Herschel** used the same technique. Pinholes in his lamp micrometer produced two adjustable artificial stars viewed with the left eye for comparison with double stars viewed by the right eye through the telescope.

In 1639 William Gascoigne placed the first micrometer in the optical path of a tele-

A micrometer formerly used at the U.S. Naval Observatory in Washington, D.C. The eyepiece was fitted into the center hole. The dials on the right recorded distances and angles between celestial objects. Double star astronomy relied on the micrometer to measure the separation between stars and the position angle of the companion. The positions of comets and asteroids were measured from stars whose location was known. Solar system astronomers used the micrometer to locate the position of features on the moon and planets. (Courtesy of the National Museum of American History)

scope, at the position of the real image viewed by the eyepiece. His knife-edge micrometer consisted of two parallel metal bars, equidistant from the optical axis, that could be moved in opposite directions by an external screw. The edges of the bars were adjusted to bracket the object being measured. Thirty years later, Robert Hooke replaced the bars with fine hairs.

Christiaan Huygens preferred a metal wedge that could be moved until the object of interest was exactly covered. Adrien Auzout constructed the first moving-wire or filar micrometer, with two parallel silk threads, one fixed and the other movable, a design soon elaborated to six fixed threads and three movable ones. In 1662 the Marquis Carlo-Cesare Malvasia made a grid of many fine silver wires to divide the telescope field into squares of known size, while Philippe de la Hire etched lines on a glass reticule placed at this position. Thin thread or wire designs, mechanically perfected by Joseph Fraunhofer, have been the basis for the most widely used micrometers until the present era, when astrometrical techniques have been largely replaced by photographic and photometric means.

Alternatively, designs to produce double images that could be moved relative to each other include the divided object glass micrometer of Servington Savery in 1743 and the double object glass telescope (**heliometer**) of Pierre Bouguer. Double image designs have also employed one or two movable prisms or wedges placed into the optical path, bisection of the secondary mirror of a Cassegrain reflector, placement of two movable half-lenses in the focal plane, or use of birefringent crystal plates.

Charles J. Peterson

Bibliography

Drake S., and C.T. Kowal. "Galileo's Sighting of Neptune." *Scientific American* 243 (1980): 74–81.

Gill, D. "Micrometer." In *Encyclopaedia Britannica,* vol. 16, 242–256. New York: Henry G. Allen, 1899.

King, H.C. *The History of the Telescope*. London: Charles Griffin, 1955.

Mikhailov, Aleksandr Aleksandrovich (1888–1983)

Soviet astronomer. A graduate (1911) of Moscow University, Mikhailov served as a professor of astronomy at Moscow University (1918–1947) and a professor of geodesy at the Moscow Institute of Geodesy (1919–1947). Beginning in 1947 Mikhailov oversaw the reconstruction of **Pulkovo Observatory**, which had been destroyed during World War II. At Pulkovo he served both as director (1947–1964) and as chairman of the department of astronomical constants (1964–1977). Mikhailov also served as **International Astronomical Union** vice president (1946–1948).

Mikhailov's scientific work spanned practical and theoretical gravimetry, solar eclipse theory, stellar astronomy, astrometry, and the history of astronomy. He was an active solar eclipse observer, and he conducted numerous experiments to measure the Einstein effect during totality. He wrote textbooks on gravimetry and the theory of the earth's figure, and he served as the USSR's permanent representative on the Baltic Geodetic Commission. Mikhailov published historical works on Copernicus, Kepler, and F.G.W. Struve, among others.

Robert A. McCutcheon

Bibliography

"A.A. Mikhailov, 1888–1983." *Astronomicheskii zhurnal* 61 (1984): 412– 413.

Kolchinskii, I.G., A.A. Korsun', and M.G. Rodriges. "Mikhailov, Aleksandr Aleksandrovich." In *Astronomy, biograficheskii spravochnik (Astronomers, a Biographical Handbook),* 220–221. Kiev: Naukova dumka, 1986.

Milne, Edward Arthur (1896–1950)

English astrophysicist and cosmologist. Educated at Cambridge University, Milne taught there (1921–1925) and at the University of Manchester (1925–1928) and Oxford University (1928–1950). Anti-aircraft research during World War I broadened Milne's interests from pure mathematics to atmospheric theory. He studied radiative transfer and the ionization, opacity, and structure of stellar atmospheres. He collaborated with Ralph Howard Fowler to extend **Meghnad Saha**'s work relating spectral lines to stellar temperature. Milne challenged **Arthur Stanley Eddington**'s theory of stellar interiors, suggesting alternative models including nongaseous zones. He developed kinematic relativity, an alternative to general relativity, likening the expansion of the universe to a diffusion process.

Joann Eisberg

Bibliography

McCrea, W.H. "Edward Arthur Milne." *Monthly Notices of the Royal Astronomical Society* 111 (1951): 160–170.

Minkowski, Rudolph Leo Bernhard (1895–1976)

German-American astronomer. Minkowski graduated from Breslau (1921), became a professor at the Physikalisches Staatsinstitut, Hamburg (1922–1935), and joined the Mount Wilson Observatory in 1935. His early research at Mount Wilson centered on planetary nebulae and supernovae. With **Walter Baade**, Minkowski pioneered the optical identification of celestial radio sources. Minkowski continued to study these peculiar objects, which were usually either supernova remnants or what he and Baade believed to be colliding galaxies. In 1949, Minkowski was made supervisor of the National Geographic–Palomar Sky Survey. Minkowski retired from the Mount Wilson and Palomar Observatories in 1960 and joined the Radio Astronomy Laboratory at Berkeley.

Ronald S. Brashear

Bibliography

Osterbrock, D.E. "Rudolph Leo Bernhard Minkowski." *Biographical Memoirs of the National Academy of Sciences* 54 (1983): 271–298.

Mitchell, Maria (1818–1889)

American astronomer. Born and raised in a Quaker family on the island of Nantucket, Mitchell assisted her father, William, at the telescope from an early age, and, in 1847, discovered a comet. This brought her both minor celebrity and, in 1849, a medal from the king of Denmark, the first award for astronomical work granted by a foreign government to any American. She was soon elected to the American Academy of Arts and Sciences and to the American Association for the Advancement of Science, the first woman chosen by either organization. In the following years, Mitchell continued to work as librarian at the Atheneum on Nantucket. Charles H. Davies also hired her to perform calculations for the Nautical Almanac Office.

In the early 1860s, the wealthy brewer Matthew Vassar decided to endow a college in Poughkeepsie, New York, that would offer women a college education equivalent to that available to men. The equipment of Vassar College included a 12-inch telescope, one of the largest in the United States. Vassar hired Mitchell as the first director of the observatory and professor of astronomy. She and her widowed father moved to Poughkeepsie in 1865 and took up residence at the observatory.

As a professor at Vassar, Mitchell was most concerned with educating undergraduates, not with carrying out a research program of her own. Her students included both astronomers such as her successor, Mary Whitney, and the spectroscopist Antonia Maury, as well as women who became scientists in other disciplines, such as the chemist Ellen Swallow Richards. Mitchell also took a more general interest in women's education, serving as president of the Association for the Advancement of Women.

Peggy A. Kidwell

Bibliography

Belserene, E.P. "Maria Mitchell: Nineteenth Century Astronomer." *Astronomical Quarterly* 5 (1986): 133–150.

Kendall, P.M. *Maria Mitchell: Life, Letters, and Journals*. Boston: Lee and Shepard, 1896.

Kohlstedt, S.G. "Maria Mitchell and Women in Science." In *Uneasy Careers and Intimate Lives: Women in Science 1789–1979*, edited by P.G. Abir-Am and D. Outram, 129–146. New Brunswick: Rutgers University Press, 1987.

Wright, H. *Sweeper in the Sky: The Life of Maria Mitchell*. New York: Macmillan, 1950.

Moon (Earth's)

The first telescopic observations of **Galileo** and his contemporaries included detailed scrutiny of the moon. Its rugged and mountainous appearance had serious implications for the Copernican debate, since an Aristotelian celestial body would have to be smooth and unblemished. With the aid of the telescope, attention turned to mapping and naming the wealth of topographic detail that could be seen and speculating on its origins. The desire for a reliable means of determining longitude at sea and on land motivated numerous mathematical efforts to develop a theory of lunar motion, but this proved a most difficult enterprise and was not successful until well into the eighteenth century. Isaac Newton grappled with the problem of lunar theory, only to cede its solution to others. Subsequent giants of mathematics working in the Newtonian tradition of perturbation theory made small steps toward its solution until finally Tobias Mayer succeeded in producing usable lunar navigation tables. The theory of lunar motion eventually yielded not so much to analytic solution as to more accurate modeling and inclusion of empirical terms and corrections.

Initially the moon was thought to be habitable. Even after this became doubtful for most, many of the sober and careful students of the moon continued to write elaborate private or pseudonymous treatises that described the exotic but recognizable and congenial conditions. Friedrich Wilhelm Bessel's 1834 analysis of stars as they passed behind the limb of the moon, which found no measurable refraction, pushed the density of any atmosphere to imperceptible levels, and with it the likelihood of earthlike life. By the close of the nineteenth century most lingering hopes for life on the moon were gone. Still, some observers recorded a variety of changes on the lunar surface well into the twentieth century, and some even held out for some form of life. The possibility of microbial life was still plausible enough at the time of spacecraft voyages to require elaborate sterilization of spacecraft to avoid contamination, and quarantine of astronauts and samples to avoid back-contamination.

Early observers beginning with Galileo produced many drawings of the lunar disk, and had to come to terms with artistic and conventional standards for naming and depicting the various features, most of which took on very different appearances as the illumination changed during the lunar day. As mapping of the lunar surface became ever more popular and sophisticated, particularly in the nineteenth century, the issues of map scales and projections became more important. Since the seventeenth century thousands of lunar maps, charts, and atlases have been produced at various scales and in various styles. The profusion of nineteenth-century nomenclature schemes and other conventions such as coordinate systems prompted the **International Astronomical Union** to undertake to establish standards as one of its first tasks in the 1920s. These provided the basis for similar systems on the planets and their satellites.

The basis of detailed knowledge of lunar topography that flowed from depicting the lunar surface allowed informed speculation on the physical mechanisms that had produced those features. In 1873 **Richard Proctor** suggested that meteors formed the lunar craters by punching through the crust and generating waves of lava. Others looked for more internal mechanisms, similar to those that produce volcanoes on earth. The stage was set then for a debate over the primary forces that sculpted the moon's surface, a debate that would continue through the present century.

In the 1890s the chief geologist of the U.S. Geological Survey, Grove Karl Gilbert, became intrigued by two types of features—the craters of the moon and a large crater near Flagstaff, Arizona, known as Coon Butte. Based on fieldwork, he reluctantly concluded that the Flagstaff crater was the result of a subterranean volcanic steam explosion. Turning to the telescope, in the fall of 1892 he performed careful and perceptive observations that he subjected to the same rigorous criticism as his fieldwork at Coon Butte. But in this case they pointed toward meteoric impact as by far the most plausible mechanism for creating most of the features on the visible surface of the moon. Gilbert laid out a compelling case for impact, reserving volcanic mechanisms for a tentative, subsidiary role. It is all the more curious, Gilbert's several biographers and commentators note, that his conclusions failed to sway what then was the dominant view that lunar features were formed by volcanic means.

In 1925 the Carnegie Institution of Washington appointed a Committee on Study of the Surface Features of the Moon, including four astronomers, a mathematical physicist, a volcanologist, and two geophysicists. The committee worked part time until World War II disrupted its operation, but never reached the stage of synthesis. By then, consensus on the origin of the lunar surface features was tipping toward the impact hypothesis. However, the notion that the craters might in fact be extinct volcanic calderas remained very much alive until the lunar missions of the 1960s. After World War II, a great deal of additional empirical evidence on cratering dynamics helped move opinion toward the meteoric hypothesis, though volcanism would continue to be advanced through the Apollo program.

Wartime developments played an important role in stimulating two important figures in lunar science—Ralph B. Baldwin and Eugene M. Shoemaker—to develop theories of the origin of lunar craters. Baldwin, familiar with the physics of explosives and especially with the morphology of craters under varying conditions of impact, showed in the late 1940s how impacts of meteoric bodies on the moon could create all of the observed phenomena. Eugene Shoemaker, working in the U.S. Geological Survey, studied the morphology of volcanic craters as well as those produced by nuclear explosions. Fieldwork at the Flagstaff Crater led to the first thorough geological and, more important, stratigraphic study, establishing its origin as due to impact. He extended this stratigraphic analysis to the lunar crater Copernicus, and then to other lunar areas as well. His initiative and organizational acumen led to the establishment of a unique branch of the U.S. Geological Survey devoted to astrogeology. This organization became a major scientific focus for detailed earth-based study of the moon, and planning and executing spacecraft missions. After the studies of Baldwin and Shoemaker, impact was the generally accepted dominant mechanism for producing lunar craters and topography. Volcanism however continued to enjoy a strong following, some few remaining convinced it was the dominant mechanism.

During the 1950s, as spaceflight planning moved from vision to reality, the moon became a contested ground for competing theories of the origin of the solar system. Chemist Harold Urey and astronomer **Gerard P. Kuiper** each became interested in the moon and collaborated at Chicago during the early 1950s, but then parted ways. Urey was convinced the moon was a primordial object remaining from the formation of the solar system. Kuiper claimed it had undergone significant melting and internal differentiation. The hot moon–cold moon debate strongly influenced the scientific objectives of later spaceflight missions. These scientific questions, together with operational requirements of planning spacecraft missions, stimulated a resurgence during the 1950s and 1960s of direct telescopic lunar astronomy, sophisticated metric photography, and mapping for which existing observatories were conscripted and new instruments and observatories constructed.

The United States and the Soviet Union sent a string of automated spacecraft to the moon beginning in 1959. After President John F. Kennedy in 1961 set a piloted lunar landing as a major goal for the space program, the pace of automated reconnaissance quickened. A series of U.S. *Ranger* spacecraft relayed high-resolution television pictures of the lunar surface before being destroyed as they impacted. A series of soft-landing *Surveyor* spacecraft took in-situ pictures and performed mechanical and chemical analyses of the soil. *Lunar Orbiter* spacecraft mapped most of the surface at high resolution so that landing sites for Project Apollo could be selected, and piloted *Apollo 8* and *Apollo 10* missions provided a prelude to the landing missions by circumnavigating the moon.

The Soviets had in 1959 been first at flying close to the moon (*Luna 1*), hitting the moon (*Luna 2*), and returning the first image of the lunar farside (*Luna 3*). As the Apollo program and its automated precursors developed during the 1960s, the Soviets sent a variety of hard- and soft-landing craft that were only partially successful. Between 1969 and 1972 Apollos 11 through 17 landed at six geologically different sites, returning 382 kg of lunar material. Automated Soviet spacecraft returned smaller amounts and surveyed several other sites between 1970 and 1976. Spacecraft also carried out metric photography, remote sensing in several spectral ranges that allowed crude mineralogical surveys, and other scientific studies from lunar orbit. Automatic instruments emplaced by the astronauts continued to relay data for several years after Apollo, and reflectors on the equipment left behind continue to be used for laser ranging studies of the lunar orbit.

Samples, core tubes, and seismic, heat flow, and other data returned from the Apollo and Soviet missions led to a consensus on lunar evolution. An evolved and differentiated object rather than a primordial one, the moon was thought to be about as old as the earth (4.5 billion years). Most of the surface features were found to have been formed by meteoric impact that had varied in intensity over lunar history, including the large basins that contain the seas, or *maria*. The latter, however, were filled in at a later time by flowing volcanic lavas. The detailed sequence by which the major basins had been excavated three to four billion years ago, filled with lava, and in some cases had subsided was determined. The rugged highlands, or *terrae,* that occupy most of the lunar surface were found to be a jumble

Earth's moon, showing the Apollo landing sites. The large crater at the bottom of the photograph is Tycho. Note the rays that extend from the crater far across the lunar surface. They are thought to be material ejected by the impact that formed the crater. (Courtesy of the National Aeronautics and Space Administration)

of diverse material excavated and ejected by impacts at various times. In addition to establishing the sequence of lunar events, these analyses combined with statistical studies of cratering densities, distributions, and epochs of bombardment to allow comparative studies with the cratered surfaces of the other terrestrial planets and the satellites of the outer planets.

While the general course of lunar evolution was roughly agreed upon soon after Apollo, the origin of the moon and its history before it accreted, melted, and began to solidify was in no way so clear. The same few hypotheses that had been proposed and argued since the nineteenth century continued to be debated: portions of the earth's mantle spun off; coaccretion with the earth in the early solar nebula; and capture of the fully formed moon by the earth. Rather suddenly, at an important conference on the origin of the moon held at Kona, Hawaii, in 1984, a new theory emerged to become the leading explanation, with considerable assent. By this theory, a Mars-sized object struck the earth while it was still molten, but after its heavy core had begun to separate and sink toward the center. The proto-earth's and the impactor's cores eventually merged, and a mix of lighter mantle material thrown off from both bodies accreted to become the moon.

The moon enjoys a far more developed historiography than any other planetary satellite. Galileo's observations are discussed by Van Helden in his edition of *The Sidereal Messenger,* which includes a helpful bibliography. Important papers by Brush provide an exhaustive and thorough discussion of theories of the origin of the moon and many citations to the literature. Compton discusses the administrative and operational aspects of the Apollo missions, with summary discussions of their scientific implications. Wilhelms provides a thorough treatment of geological issues since 1946, and a more sketchy but reliable discussion for the fifty years before that. Crowe offers a comprehensive treatment of the moon as an abode for life. Doel discusses the Kuiper-Urey debate and the Carnegie committee. Whitaker is the authoritative source for lunar mapping. Taylor provides an account how the giant impactor hypothesis for lunar origin emerged and edged out its competitors. The scientific review literature is voluminous, particularly for the past three decades when spacecraft missions and concerted ground-based efforts provided a wealth of detailed information and a host of discoveries, fueling considerable theoretical work on all aspects. The review volume edited by Heiken, Vaniman, and French is an excellent and comprehensive guide to this period, with exhaustive bibliographies for the scientific literature. It is not generally reliable further into the past, however, and does not treat issues historically.

Joseph N. Tatarewicz

Bibliography

Brush, S.G. "Nickel for Your Thoughts: Urey and the Origin of the Moon." *Science* 217 (1982): 891–898.

———. "Early History of Selenogony." In *Origin of the Moon,* edited by W.K. Hartmann, 3–15. Houston: Lunar and Planetary Institute, 1986.

———. "A History of Modern Selenology: Theoretical Origins of the Moon from Capture to Crash 1955–1984." *Space Science Reviews* 47 (1988): 211–273.

Compton, W.D. *Where No Man has Gone before. A History of Apollo Lunar Exploration Missions.* SP-4212. Washington, D.C.: NASA, 1989.

Crowe, M.J. *The Extraterrestrial Life Debate, 1750–1900: The Idea of a Plurality of Worlds from Kant to Lowell.* Cambridge: Cambridge University Press, 1986.

Doel, R.E. *Unpacking a Myth: Interdisciplinary Research and the Growth of Solar System Astronomy, 1920–1958.* Ph.D. diss. Princeton: Princeton University, 1990.

Galileo, G. *The Sidereal Messenger.* Translated with an introduction by A. Van Helden, Chicago: University of Chicago Press, 1989.

Hall, R.C. *Lunar Impact: A History of Project Ranger.* SP-4210. Washington, D.C.: NASA, 1977.

Heiken, G.H., D.T. Vaniman, and B.M. French, eds. *The Lunar Sourcebook: A User's Guide to the Moon.* New York: Cambridge University Press, 1991.

Marvin, U.B. "Meteorites, the Moon and the History of Geology." *Journal of Geological Education* 34 (May 1986): 140–165.

Taylor, G.J. "The Scientific Legacy of Apollo." *Scientific American* 271 (July 1994): 40–47.

Whitaker, E.A. "Selenography in the Seventeenth Century." In *Planetary Astronomy from the Renaissance to the Rise of Astrophysics: Part A: Tycho Brahe to Newton,* edited by R. Taton and C. Wilson. *The General History of Astronomy,* Vol. 2A, edited by M. Hoskin, 119–143.

New York: Cambridge University Press, 1989.

Wilhelms, D.E. *To a Rocky Moon: A Geologist's History of Lunar Exploration.* Tucson: University of Arizona Press, 1993.

Moscow Observatory

The Moscow Observatory is the astronomical research and teaching department of the Lomonosov Moscow State University. Its official title is the Shternberg State Astronomical Institute. In 1955–1956 the headquarters of the observatory moved from its original location to the main campus of the university, where it has become one of the largest and most respected astronomical institutions in Russia. There are departments and laboratories in all the important research areas of modern astronomy (cosmology, astrophysics, stellar and extragalactic astronomy, radio astronomy, celestial mechanics, solar physics, planetology, astrometry, and geophysics). Graduate education is also a responsibility of the institute, carried out in conjunction with Moscow University. Given its urban location, the observatory has several branches in dark sky locations. The most important telescopes include 150-, 125- (two), 100-, and 70-cm reflectors and a 50-cm Maksutov with a 40-cm corrector plate. In addition, there are **astrographs** and **meridian instruments**. Moscow astronomers regularly are given observing time on the largest optical and radio telescopes of the country. The scientific personnel comprises over two hundred astronomers.

The Astronomical Observatory at Moscow University was founded in 1831 by Dmitry M. Perevoshchikov, who in 1848 became rector of the university. **F.W. Bessel**'s observatory at Königsberg was the prototype for the Moscow Observatory. At first the main purpose of the observatory was pedagogical. Among prominent graduates were two of Pulkovo's directors: academician Fiodor A. Bredikhin and academician Aristarch A. Belopolsky. The future Pulkovo director and vice president of the **International Astronomical Union** (1945–1948), academician **Alexander A. Mikhailov**, also trained at the Moscow Observatory and worked there afterwards. The well-known Estonian astronomer Ernst J. Opik was also a graduate.

In 1916 Pavel C. Shternberg was appointed director. He took an active part in the revolutionary underground and after the October Revolution became an important military leader. Science was important in the Soviet vision for a new society, and many new scientific institutions were established after the Revolution. In Moscow two new astronomical organizations appeared: the Institute for Astronomical-Geodetical Research (1922) and the State Astrophysical Institute (1923). In 1931 the three Moscow astronomical bodies were united into the Shternberg State Astronomical Institute. The astronomer Vsevolod V. Stratonov was one of the leaders of the political strike at Moscow University in 1922 that resulted in the deportation of many intellectuals. Luckily, not many Moscow astronomers became victims of Stalin's purges in the 1930s.

The work of the observatory in Moscow was suspended during World War II. Many of the students and faculty were involved in the war effort. Some are remembered as heroes, such as Evgenia M. Rudneva, who became a navigator in the Soviet Air Force. After her death in 1944, Rudneva was honored as a Hero of the Soviet Union. During the war some astronomers from Moscow worked at Alma-Ata (Kazakhstan) under the leadership of academician **Vasily G. Fesenkov** and laid the foundations for the new astrophysical institute.

In 1958 Shternberg Institute hosted the Tenth General Assembly of the International Astronomical Union. It was one of the first important international scientific meetings in the USSR during the Cold War. During those difficult years, one of the astronomy students, Kronid A. Lubarsky, played an important role in the struggle for human rights against the totalitarian regime. The Shternberg Institute took an active part in the International Geophysical Year and became involved in Soviet Space Science. The first photographs of the lunar farside were analyzed at the Shternberg and new names for lunar features were proposed. The astrophysicist **Iosif S. Shklovskii** was involved in creating the Institute for Space Research of the Academy of Sciences of the USSR (now the Russian Academy of Sciences) and was honored with the Lenin Prize, the most prestigious scientific award in the country. Fascinating glimpses of Shklovskii's life are contained in his remarkable book *Five Billion Vodka Bottles to the Moon* (English edition, 1991).

Other noteworthy astronomers of the Moscow Observatory include directors Vitold C. Tzerasky, noted for work in astronomical photography, and Sergei N. Blazhko, an expert in astrometry; solar system astronomer Sergei V. Orlov; celestial mechanician Nicolai D. Moiseev, vice president of the International

Astronomical Union (1955–1961); and variable star astronomer Boris V. Kukarkin.

At the Moscow Observatory there is a small group working in the history of astronomy. This group publishes important research including an annual volume, *Researches on History of Astronomy*. The founder of this annual was Piotr G. Kulikovsky of the Shternberg Institute.

Today in Moscow there are a number of important astronomical research centers: the Institute of Astronomy (formerly the Astronomical Council), the Institute for Space Research (astrophysics); the Lebedev Institute of Physics (radio astronomy), the Keldysh Institute for Applied Mathematics (celestial mechanics), the Institute for Geomagnetism and Propagation of Radio Waves (solar physics), the Shmidt Institute for Physics of the Earth (geophysics), and the Vernadsky Institute for Geochemistry and Analytical Chemistry (planetology and meteorics). In the 1990s, the Shternberg Institute is no longer the main astronomical center in Moscow, but one among many important research institutes advancing astronomical knowledge in Russia.

Alexander Gurshtein

Bibliography

A Century and a Half of Moscow University Observatory and the Shternberg State Astronomical Institute. Moscow University, 1981.

Blazhko, S.N. *The History of the Astronomical Observatory of Moscow University in Connection with Teaching in the University (1824–1920).* Uchenye zapisky MGU, LYIII, 1940.

Nicolaidis, E. *Le developpement de l'Astronomie en U.R.S.S. (1917–1935).* Observatoire de Paris, 1984.

Ponomarev, D.N. *Astronomical Observatories in the Soviet Union.* Moscow: Nauka, 1987.

Shklovsky, I. *Five Billion Vodka Bottles to the Moon: Tales of a Soviet Scientist.* Translated and edited by M.F. and H. Zirin with an introduction by M. Friedman. New York: Norton, 1991.

Moulton, Forest Ray (1872–1952)

American mathematician and celestial mechanician. Moulton received a Ph.D. from the University of Chicago (1899), and was a member of the astronomy faculty until retirement in 1926. With the geologist T.C. Chamberlin, Moulton developed a theory for the formation of planets from the solar nebula. Other research concerned periodic orbits in the three-body problem and, during World War I, artillery ballistics. Following retirement, Moulton was active in a variety of scientific enterprises, serving as secretary of the American Association for the Advancement of Science, 1936–1940. He wrote textbooks on celestial mechanics, descriptive astronomy, and ballistics. An *Introduction to Celestial Mechanics*, originally written in 1902, was the standard introductory text for more than half a century.

LeRoy E. Doggett

Bibliography

Carlson, A.J. "Forest Ray Moulton: 1872–1952." *Science* 117 (1953): 545–546.

Tropp, H.S. "Forest Ray Moulton." In *Dictionary of Scientific Biography*, edited by C.C. Gillispie, vol. 9, 552–553. New York: Scribner, 1974.

Multiple Mirror Telescopes

The completion of the 5-meter Hale Telescope in 1948 marked the practical limit of traditional reflecting telescopes. Weight, stability, and cost combined to restrict the size of reflectors to the 4-meter range for the next quarter century. Beginning in the early 1970s, however, serious discussion of a new technology began. Named the Multiple Mirror Telescope (MMT), the instrument entered the planning stage through the joint efforts of the University of Arizona and the Smithsonian Astrophysical Observatory. Recent improvements in laser and computer technology provided the means to guide the six 1.8-meter mirrors available to the university's Optical Sciences Center from a canceled military satellite project.

The multiple mirror design provided the equivalent of a single 4.5-meter instrument. Computer guidance of the mirrors allowed the use of an altazimuth mount, rather than the traditional equatorial, which permitted the construction of a rectangular dome to house offices and laboratory space. Construction of the MMT at the Smithsonian's Mount Hopkins site south of Tucson proved relatively rapid, with first light in 1978. A complication quickly arose, however, when astronomers discovered that the large number of moths on the mountain were interrupting the laser beams employed to coalign the mirrors. A mechanical self-collimation technique replaced the lasers by 1981, which also eliminated potential interference with infrared observations. The Multiple Mirror Telescope exceeded all expectations and dramatically confirmed the value of the new design. By the mid-1980s, however, other developments in telescope technology threatened to displace the MMT to a secondary position. Ironically, the most effective conversion of the Mount Hopkins facility appeared to be the replacement of the six existing mirrors with a single 6.5-meter honeycomb sandwich mirror.

The dramatic success of the MMT led to similar projects throughout the 1980s. As part of the National New Technology Telescope program, the National Optical Astronomy Observatories (Tucson) proposed a scaled-up MMT design based on four 7.5-meter mirrors, providing the equivalent of a 15-meter instrument. Another proposed facility emerged as the Columbus Project, planned for Mount Graham in southern Arizona. A binocular instrument of two 8.4-meter honeycomb sandwich mirrors, Columbus possesses the resolving power of an 11.8-meter instrument.

Another multiple mirror technology appeared in the form of segmented mirrors, a technique which revolutionized ground-based astronomy in the 1990s. The most advanced telescope based on this design is the 10-meter Keck Telescope on the summit of Mauna Kea, which achieved first light in November of 1990. Funded with a $70 million grant from the W.M. Keck Foundation to the University of California and California Institute of Technology, the instrument is composed of thirty-six 1.8-meter hexagonal mirrors. Each segment is supported individually, simplifying adjustment and control.

The Keck Telescope provided significant publicity for segmented mirror technology and encouraged various proposals. The University of Texas and Pennsylvania State University, for example, jointly designed the Spectroscopic Survey Telescope, which would employ eighty-five spherical segments to provide a 9-meter primary mirror. The German Large Telescope Project proposed a 12-meter primary mirror constructed of as few as four or as many as thirteen large segments. With continued technological developments, segmented mirror telescopes will remain one of the key elements in ground-based astronomy and represent an important evolutionary step from the original multiple mirror concept.

George E. Webb

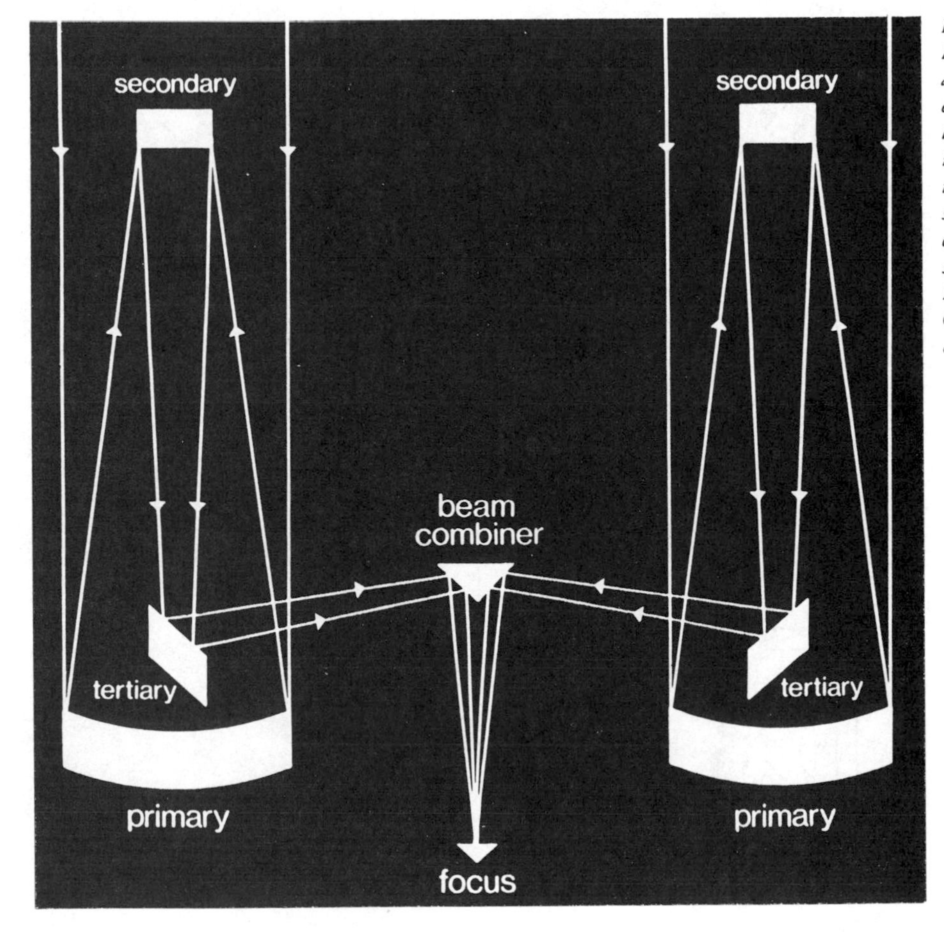

In the original Multiple Mirror Telescope design, an electronic control system employing computer and laser technology brought images from the six mirrors to a common focus. This schematic shows the optical configuration for two of the six mirrors. (Courtesy of the Multiple Mirror Telescope Observatory of the University of Arizona)

Bibliography

Carleton, N.P., and W.F. Hoffmann. "The Multiple-Mirror Telescope." *Physics Today* 31 (1978): 30–37.

Martin, B., et al. "The New Ground-Based Optical Telescopes." *Physics Today* 44 (1991): 22–30.

Waldrop, M.M. "The New Art of Telescope Making." *Science* 234 (1986): 1495–1497.

———. "Keck Telescope Mirror Is in Production." *Science* 243 (1989): 1010–1011.

Mural Quadrant

Attached to a north-south wall, the mural quadrant consisted of a 90-degree arc, 2 to 4 meters in radius, fitted with a device to sight and measure the meridian altitudes of stars. The plinth, a forerunner described by Ptolemy, had a peg to cast a shadow on its scale, while mural quadrants of medieval Islamic astronomers were equipped with alidades for use day or night. New levels of precision were achieved by **Tycho Brahe**, whose famous quadrant was divided by transversals to ten seconds of arc and ornamented with paintings depicting work at Uraniborg.

By the mid-eighteenth century, the mural quadrant was established as the principal instrument for meridian astronomy. Most observatories had one modeled after the quadrant designed by George Graham for **Edmond Halley** at Greenwich. Completed in 1725, with a radius of 2.4 meters, its frame was constructed with cross-bracing and mounted on a pier. It had a telescopic sight, a tangent screw for fine adjustment, and a vernier that gave readings to half a minute. The success of this instrument helped to position English makers, such as Jonathan and Jeremiah Sisson, John Bird, and Jesse Ramsden, as the primary suppliers of mural quadrants to both British and foreign observatories in the eighteenth century.

With the aid of a clock, astronomers used mural quadrants to fix star positions in two coordinates: Declinations were determined from observations of the stars' altitudes when

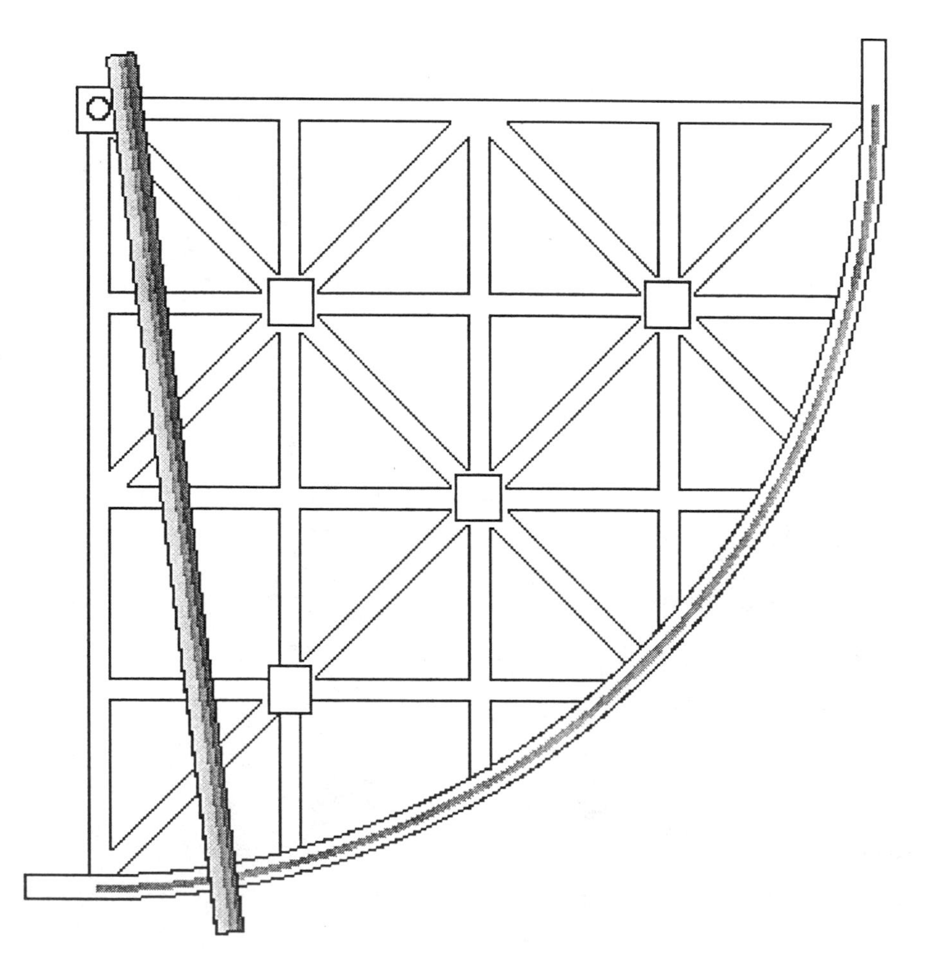

A schematic diagram of the 8-foot wall-mounted mural quadrant constructed in 1725 by George Graham for the Royal Greenwich Observatory. The vertical telescope (left) pivots about the axis of a 90 degree gradated arc (gray). Not shown is the vernier scale by which the angular position of the telescope is determined nor various rods used to move the telescope. (Drawing by Charles J. Peterson)

they crossed the meridian, and right ascensions were determined from the sidereal times of their transits.

In the late eighteenth century, specialized transit instruments took over the chore of determining right ascensions, and in the early nineteenth century, mural quadrants were replaced by mural circles as the chief meridian instruments of observatories in Britain and her colonies. European observatories, however, installed German-made transit circles, thereby avoiding the expense of maintaining two instruments. British observatories later followed suit.

Sara Schechner Genuth

Bibliography

Bennett, J.A. *The Divided Circle: A History of Instruments for Astronomy, Navigation, and Surveying*. Oxford: Phaidon-Christie's, 1987.

———. "The English Quadrant in Europe: Instruments and the Growth of Consensus in Practical Astronomy." *Journal for the History of Astronomy* 23 (1992): 1–14.

Dewhirst, D.W. "Meridian Astronomy in the Private and University Observatories of the United Kingdom: Rise and Fall." *Vistas in Astronomy* 28 (1985): 147–158.

Howse, D. *Greenwich Observatory*. Vol. 3, *The Buildings and Instruments*. London: Taylor and Francis, 1975.

———. *The Greenwich List of Observatories: A World List of Astronomical Observatories, Instruments, and Clocks, 1670–1850.* Chalfont St. Giles, England: Science History Publications, 1986.

Righini B., M. Luisa, and T.B. Settle. "Egnatio Danti's Great Astronomical Quadrant." *Annali dell'Istituto e Museo di Storia della Scienza di Firenze* 4 (1979): 3–13.

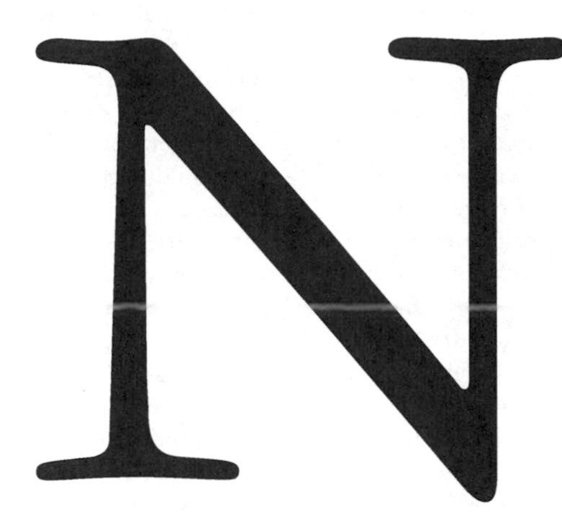

Nançay Radio Astronomy Station

At the beginning of the twentieth century, Henri Deslandes of the **Meudon Observatory** predicted the existence of electronic solar emissions, which were discovered by the American K. Jansky in 1932. After 1946 the discipline of **radio astronomy** developed rapidly. In France, M. Laffineur of the *Institut d'Astrophysique de Paris* and Y. Rocard of the *École Normale Supérieure* became involved in radio astronomy. Rocard was responsible in 1953 for the creation of a radio telescope station in the Sologne region that was to become an integral part of the **Paris Observatory** in 1956. A team led by J.-F. Denisse installed an array for solar observations, interferometers, and a large radio telescope inaugurated by Charles de Gaulle in 1965. Among the phenomena observed at the Nançay Station were emissions from the sun and from Jupiter, the radio spectrum of the solar corona, radio electric solar bursts, comets, interstellar molecules, galaxies, OH molecules, and pulsars. The data are analyzed in part at Nançay and in part at the Meudon Observatory.

Suzanne Débarbat

Bibliography

Bourgeois, G., E. Gérard, M. Pick, and J.-L. Steinberg. *Histoire du Centre de Radioastronomie de Nançay*. Paris: Observatoire de Paris, 1989.

National Aeronautics and Space Administration (NASA)

The National Aeronautics and Space Administration (NASA) was created in 1958 as the lead agency for U.S. civilian space exploration. NASA and its programs were the U.S. response to the perceived challenge of the first artificial satellite of the earth, the Soviet *Sputnik I*, orbited during the International Geophysical Year. With the National Advisory Committee on Aeronautics (NACA) as its base, the new agency acquired portions of other agencies and organizations already involved in rocketry and related scientific research. For the remainder of the Eisenhower administration (1958–1961), NASA emphasized developing reliable launch vehicles, a diverse program of scientific research using rockets and satellites, and a small effort aimed at putting human passengers into near-earth space. Responding to various pressures, President John Kennedy in May 1961 set the goal of landing a man on the moon (and returning him safely to earth) by the end of the decade. This program, Project Apollo, reoriented and expanded all facets of the agency. Carried to fruition by administrator James E. Webb and President Lyndon Johnson in the face of flagging enthusiasm and new national priorities later in the decade, Apollo culminated in a curtailed series of six successful lunar landings between 1969 and 1972.

NASA spent the decade after Apollo with its attention and steadily dwindling resources focused on developing the Space Shuttle, the only major new program for which it was able to gain approval. Remaining Apollo hardware was: (a) used to construct *Skylab*, a space station occupied by three successive three-man crews, 1973–1974; (b) transferred to the Apollo-Soyuz Test Project, a U.S.-Soviet docking in 1974; or (c) dispersed to various museums. *Skylab* carried the so-called Apollo

Telescope Mount, a suite of various specialized solar telescopes operated by the crew. The successor to the Orbiting Solar Observatory program (1962–1975), the *Skylab* solar telescopes were a welcome contribution to solar science.

During the Apollo era exploratory spacecraft were sent to fly by or orbit the **moon**, **Venus**, and **Mars**, and also to **Mercury**, **Jupiter**, **Saturn**, **Uranus**, and **Neptune** during the 1970s and 1980s. A suite of ever more sophisticated but relatively small scientific spacecraft were dispatched to study the physics of charged particles and magnetic fields near the earth. Because magnetospheric physics instruments were small and relatively inexpensive, they enjoyed many more flight opportunities than those of any other field, often hitchhiking on other spacecraft.

The benefits of astronomical observations from beyond the atmosphere were realized early in the century. Small instruments were lofted in balloons, on captured V-2 rockets immediately after the war, and then on small sounding rockets developed to replace the V-2. Early in the organization of NASA, proponents of continuing the incremental development of such instruments lost out to advocates of large, multipurpose satellites that would carry a suite of instruments. These observatory satellites (as opposed to the smaller explorer class) became the preferred basis for series of orbiting geophysical, solar, and astronomical observatories. Their complexity, however, pushed first flights of the *Orbiting Astronomical Observatory* (OAO) late into the 1960s. After one failure, *OAO-2* operated from 1968 to 1973 performing ultraviolet photometry and sky survey, and *OAO-3* from 1972 to 1980 performing ultraviolet spectroscopy. Two additional *OAO*s failed in orbit. Instrumentation for spectral ranges much beyond the optical proved more difficult to develop. Small satellites performed all-sky surveys in the X-ray region. Under budget pressure, the very large *High Energy Astronomical Observatories* (HEAO) was split in 1973 into three smaller spacecraft, which flew from 1977 to 1980. NASA cooperated with European agencies on the *International Ultraviolet Explorer* (IUE), a modest spacecraft placed into geosynchronous orbit in 1978 that proved surprisingly productive and long-lived. European cooperation was also essential in the cryogenically cooled *Infrared Astronomical Satellite* (IRAS), which performed an all-sky survey and detailed observations of selected objects during 1983.

Hoping for an expansive post-Apollo program based on already developed hardware, large follow-ons for the observatory class satellites were designed as attachments to Apollo hardware for earth-orbiting missions. The solar follow-on did fly on *Skylab*, but the proposed stellar modules for optical, ultraviolet, and high-energy astronomy never materialized. Instead, research on these instruments was incorporated into separate proposed satellites and the 3-meter-aperture Large Space Telescope, the first major free-flying scientific payload designed to be deployed from the Space Shuttle. Smaller astronomical telescopes for the ultraviolet and X-ray ranges were designed as so-called Shuttle sortie missions, intended to fly as attachments in the payload bay. The Hubble Space Telescope, downsized to 2.4-meter aperture, was finally deployed in 1990. The sortie telescopes, developed by several university groups, made a series of flights in the Shuttle's payload bay beginning in the mid-1980s as the Astro series.

NASA's ambitious plans for large facilities to follow the explorer and observatory class missions ran afoul of shuttle and budgetary problems in the mid-1980s. Having done space-based all-sky surveys at low resolution in all spectral ranges, NASA was faced with several communities of astronomers simultaneously poised to take the next step—Space Telescope–sized observatories now called facility-class. Plans were made and remade for the Advanced X-Ray Astrophysics Facility (AXAF) and the Space Infrared Telescope Facility (SIRTF). Even when these were belatedly packaged together with the Hubble Space Telescope and the Gamma Ray Observatory (GRO) as a suite of interdependent so-called "great observatories," those who held the pursestrings remained unwilling or unable to provide the funding. Plans for these X-ray and infrared astronomy facilities continued to be delayed or adjusted to the realities of budgets.

Another legacy of the Apollo era was the very institutional structure of NASA itself. Various portions of NASA retained the heritage and culture of their pre-NASA roots, on which was superimposed a very strong signature from their activity during the expansive Apollo years. NASA headquarters in Washington continued to try to exercise strong control in selecting and managing programs, relations with the executive branch and Congress, and budgets. The various field centers created, developed, and managed programs on a daily basis. The former NACA centers retained their aeronautics base and developed various expertise in space and science. Langley

(Virginia) worked on lunar orbiting satellites and the *Viking* Mars lander. Its Space Task Group in 1961 became the nucleus for a new Manned Spacecraft Center in Houston, Texas. Lewis (Ohio) specialized in propulsion. Ames (California) developed the *Pioneer* series of deep-space probes and also put astronomical telescopes on high-flying aircraft. Other field centers were acquired from existing organizations or created anew. The Jet Propulsion Laboratory of the California Institute of Technology early specialized in lunar and planetary exploration when it transferred from U.S. Army missile work to NASA. In addition to *Ranger, Surveyor, Mariner,* and *Voyager* spacecraft, during the 1970s it helped develop the IRAS. The Marshall Space Flight Center, formerly the Army Ballistic Missile Agency, was built around the rocketry expertise of Wernher von Braun and specialized in large boosters. Marshall developed expertise in astronomy while searching for scientific extensions for the Apollo hardware. This led to its work on the solar telescopes on *Skylab*, the *High Energy Astronomy Observatory,* and the Hubble Space Telescope. Rocket or experimental aircraft test ranges at Edwards Air Force Base (California), White Sands (New Mexico), Wallops Island (Virginia), and Cape Canaveral (Florida) were acquired from military agencies and were the sites from which rockets and aircraft lofted astronomical instruments. A new Goddard Space Flight Center was built in Greenbelt, Maryland. Initially staffed by personnel who had worked on the International Geophysical Year satellite and rocket programs, Goddard became the center for earth-orbiting scientific satellites (meteorology, geophysics, space physics, and astronomy) and for the worldwide tracking networks.

The best brief introduction to NASA is Bilstein, *Orders of Magnitude*. Newell, *Beyond the Atmosphere,* provides a comprehensive treatment of the science activities of the agency to the late 1970s, but includes a wealth of information about its institutional development and its other programs as well. Valuable compilations of data and capsule histories of major programs and offices are assembled in Ezell, *Historical Data Book* series, and the annual chronologies *Astronautics and Aeronautics*. *Research in NASA History* provides a comprehensive introduction to archives, the NASA History Series of publications, and a wealth of other information. It includes a complete listing of the many book-length histories of NASA centers and programs sponsored by the agency's history program. A valuable introductory guide to historical literature is Pisano and Lewis, *Air and Space History: An Annotated Bibliography*. Critical revisionist interpretations that also summarize earlier treatments can be found in McDougall, *The Heavens and the Earth,* and Bulkeley, *The Sputniks Crisis*. Smith, *The Space Telescope*, also discusses the previous NASA astronomy missions and programs. Tatarewicz, *Space Technology and Planetary Astronomy*, discusses the ground-based astronomy programs as well as the planetary exploration programs.

Joseph N. Tatarewicz

Bibliography

Bilstein, R.E. *Orders of Magnitude: A History of the NACA and NASA 1915–1990.* Washington, D.C.: NASA SP-4406, 1989.

Bulkeley, T. *The Sputnicks Crisis in the United States: An Examination of American Space Policy.* London: Macmillan, 1991.

Ezell, L.N., comp. *NASA Historical Data Book: Volume II: Programs and Projects, 1958–1968; Volume III: Programs and Projects, 1969–1978.* NASA SP-4012. Washington, D.C.: GPO, 1988.

Levine, A.S. *Managing NASA in the Apollo Era.* NASA SP-4102. Washington, D.C.: GPO, 1982.

McDougall, W.A. *The Heavens and the Earth: A Political History of the Space Age.* New York: Basic Books, 1985.

NASA History Division. *Research in NASA History: A Guide to the NASA History Program.* NASA HHR-55. Washington, D.C.: National Aeronautics and Space Administration, 1992.

NASA History Program. *Astronautics and Aeronautics: A Chronology of Science, Technology, and Policy* (Annual). NASA SP-4002 to SP-4025. Washington, D.C.: GPO, 1963–1979.

Naugle, J.E. *First among Equals: The Selection of NASA Space Science Experiments.* NASA SP-4215. Washington, D.C.: GPO, 1991.

Newell, H.E. *Beyond the Atmosphere: Early Years of Space Science.* Washington, D.C.: NASA SP-4211, 1980.

Pisano, D., and C.S. Lewis, eds. *Air and Space History: An Annotated Bibliography.* New York: Garland, 1988.

Roland, A. *Model Research: The National Advisory Committee for Aeronautics,* 1915–1958. Washington, D.C.: NASA SP-4103, 1985.

Rosholt, R.L. *An Administrative History of NASA, 1958–1963*. Washington, D.C.: NASA SP-4101, 1966.

Smith, R.W., with contributions by P.A. Hanle, R. Kargon, and J.N. Tatarewicz. *The Space Telescope: A Study of NASA, Science, Technology, and Politics*. Paperback edition with a new afterword. New York: Cambridge University Press, 1993.

Tatarewicz, J.N. *Space Technology and Planetary Astronomy*. Bloomington: Indiana University Press, 1990.

Van Nimmen, J., L.C. Bruno, and R.C. Rosholt, comps. *NASA Historical Data Book: Volume I: NASA Resources, 1958–1968*. NASA SP-4012. Washington, D.C.: GPO, 1988.

Nautical Almanac Offices

Nautical almanac offices are a government bureau that produces astronomical data needed by astronomers, navigators, surveyors, geodesists, oceanographers, and the general public. Because of the massive number of calculations, nautical almanac offices have been at the forefront in applying new computational methods and technologies. Indeed, it was in the nautical almanac offices that electronic computers were first applied to astronomical computations. Nautical almanac offices have employed a number of well-known scientists, in addition to countless unsung heros, the individuals who performed laborious calculations before the age of computing machines.

Since some of the terms and concepts used in this entry are highly technical, definitions are in order, especially for the terms *almanac, ephemeris* (plural, *ephemerides*), *table,* and *theory*. An ephemeris is a list of positions of a celestial body tabulated as a function of time. An almanac contains a collection of ephemerides. However, the word *ephemeris* has also been used in the sense of almanac to mean a collection of ephemerides (as in *The American Ephemeris and Nautical Almanac*). A theory for a planet or satellite is a set of trigonometric series from which one can compute an ephemeris. Since the sine and cosine functions of the series are very time consuming to evaluate, series were transformed into tables that required only simple arithmetic operations. A successful set of tables greatly reduced the work of computers, while maintaining the integrity of the original theory. Today, with electronic calculators performing the computations, tables are no longer needed.

The history of nautical almanac offices begins with the *Connaissance des Temps* (*CdT*), first produced for the year 1679 and annually thereafter. The first edition included a calendar, times of the rising and setting of the sun, moon and planets, circumstances of eclipses, and general information on astronomy. Originally produced by Joachim Dalencé for a private printer, it was taken over by the French Royal Academy of Sciences in 1702. The Academy published the *CdT* through contracts with specific astronomers until 1795, when it was assigned to the newly created *Bureau des Longitudes*. Although the *CdT* was not originally designed for navigators, it soon was applied to that purpose and subsidized by the French navy after 1785.

Navigation, particularly the problem of determining longitude, was a driving force in shaping the form and content of almanacs. Many methods have been suggested for determining longitude. **Galileo** proposed that the satellites of **Jupiter** could be used for this purpose. Galileo's method was based on the principle that if a celestial phenomenon could be observed simultaneously over a wide area of the earth, differences between local times of observation were principally due to difference in longitude between observers. Galileo proposed publishing an ephemeris giving the times, referred to a standard longitude, at which the satellites disappear and reappear from behind (or in front of) the disk of Jupiter. An observer would record the local time at which the phenomenon was observed. Comparison of the local time with the time in the ephemeris would give the observer's longitude.

The success of this method depended upon an accurate ephemeris of the phenomena. Despite considerable effort, Galileo was never able to achieve the required accuracy. Tables of the phenomena were first included in the *CdT* in 1690, and were successfully employed in determining longitudes on land. At sea, however, this method proved impractical, because of the difficulties of employing a telescope on a moving ship.

When Charles II founded the **Royal Observatory at Greenwich** in 1675, he was specifically interested in finding longitude at sea. Nearly a century later, the problem was still unsolved. In 1765 Nevil Maskelyne, the Astronomer Royal, proposed publication of an almanac that would give the angular distance of the moon from standard stars. Because the moon moves relatively quickly with respect to the stars, the time at which the moon is at a specified angular distance from a star can be considered a phenomenon to be observed simultaneously over a wide area of the earth.

Although the basic concept of lunar distances dated from the sixteenth century, it had not been applied earlier because there was no instrument for accurately measuring the distance between the **moon** and a star, and because the motion of the moon could not be predicted with sufficient accuracy. Further, the positions of reference stars were not known with enough precision. By the time of Maskelyne's proposal, however, the reflecting quadrant was available for shipboard measurements, the Royal Observatory had made significant advances in determining stellar positions, and Tobias Mayer's lunar tables, accurate to better than one minute of arc, were available.

Under the authority of the Board of Longitude, Maskelyne produced *The Nautical Almanac and Astronomical Ephemeris* (*NA&AE*) for 1767. In addition to the lunar tables, the almanac included celestial phenomena, positions of the sun and planets, and phenomena of the Galilean satellites. The lunar distance tables soon became a standard feature of scientific almanacs. They continued to be published until early in the twentieth century, well past the time when they were widely used.

The *CdT* was founded before Isaac Newton published the *Principia Mathematica* (1687), so its ephemerides were initially calculated from Johannes Kepler's *Rudolphine Tables*. By the time Maskelyne created the *NA&AE*, celestial mechanics, based on Newton's laws, had been developed by **Leonhard Euler**, **Alexis-Claude Clairaut**, and Jean d'Alembert. One of the first fruits of the new science was Mayer's lunar tables. For the planets, however, it was still necessary to use Keplerian models, with elements adjusted to more recent observations. Planetary tables that included perturbations due to other planets were not available until near the end of the eighteenth century.

Preparation of both the *CdT* and *NA&AE* was carried out by a staff of computers who performed calculations manually, under the direction of an astronomer. Maskelyne began with four computers and a comparer, who supervised the work. Computers worked at home and were paid on a piecework basis. Calculations had to be carried out independently and then checked; typesetting errors had to be corrected. Today, when scientific success is measured by exciting theoretical breakthroughs, the life of a computer may seem like endless drudgery. However, skill and enterprise were rewarded and the work was considered important and interesting. The number of computers grew as new solar system objects were discovered and more accurate theories were developed. As the preparation of almanacs became more complex, cooperation developed between the French and British almanac offices.

The *Connaissance des Temps*, unlike its sponsor, the Royal Academy of Sciences, survived the French Revolution. In 1795, the Convention passed a law establishing the *Bureau des Longitudes*, which was explicitly charged with producing the *CdT*. The Bureau was also charged with carrying on other work in astronomy, geodesy, navigation, and metrology. A group of distinguished scientists was elected as titular members of the Bureau and had an oversight role, while a permanent staff carried out day-to-day operations. This arrangement ensured that new developments in celestial mechanics and astronomy would quickly be introduced in the *CdT*. For the first half of the nineteenth century, tables derived from the theories of **Pierre-Simon Laplace** were used. In the middle decades, new theories and tables by **Urbain J.J. Le Verrier** were introduced and became the basis for the French, British, and American almanacs; with adjustments, they served in the *CdT* until 1984.

Following the death of Maskelyne, the *NA&AE* continued to be produced under the direction of successive Astronomers Royal, some of whom lacked Maskelyne's administrative skills and commitment. In 1818, responsibility for the almanac was transferred from the **Astronomer Royal** and, after a period of administrative confusion, the Nautical Almanac Office was created in 1832, under control of the Admiralty, becoming H.M. Nautical Almanac Office in 1904.

Until the middle of the nineteenth century, Americans relied on foreign almanacs—particularly from Great Britain—for astronomical and navigational data. In 1849, Congress established the Nautical Almanac Office (NAO) to prepare and publish an American almanac. From its home in Cambridge, Massachusetts, the NAO published *The American Ephemeris and Nautical Almanac* (*AE*) for 1855. The *AE* provided data needed by astronomers and surveyors, while *The American Nautical Almanac* was issued for mariners. These volumes served as a source of national pride, demonstrating the scientific prowess of the United States. However, despite the desire to create an almanac based on

American science, the underlying theories were European.

American theory would develop when **Simon Newcomb** became superintendent of the Nautical Almanac Office in 1877. Newcomb implemented a bold research program that would lead to new theories of the sun, moon, and all the planets. For the first time, orbital models were based on consistent theoretical methods and observational data. Fortunately he had assistance from the world-class mathematician G.W. Hill. Newcomb's efforts had an international impact. In 1896, his values for the **astronomical constants** (precession, nutation, the masses of the planets, and so on) were adopted by other nautical almanac offices. The Newcomb/Hill theories of the outer planets were used in the British and American almanacs until 1960, those for Mercury, Venus, Earth, and Mars until 1984.

Following Newcomb's retirement in 1897, the NAO reduced the scope of its research efforts. The new theories had to be implemented in the annual almanacs, and attention was devoted to improving the almanacs for marine navigation. By this time the office had become part of the **U.S. Naval Observatory**. Only in the 1940s did the NAO regain some of the reputation and international stature it had had in the days of Newcomb and Hill.

In the late 1920s, L.J. Comrie, pursuing ideas of Charles Babbage, introduced tabulating machines in H.M. Nautical Almanac Office, where they were used to evaluate lunar theory. Similar equipment would not appear at the NAO until Wallace Eckert became director in 1940, when mechanical computers were used to produce *The Air Almanac*. By producing camera-ready copy from a typewriter that was driven by punched cards, typesetting errors were virtually eliminated.

As mechanical computers developed, larger projects became possible. An important example is the numerical integration of the orbits of **Jupiter**, **Saturn**, **Uranus**, **Neptune** and **Pluto**, performed in the late 1940s. This cooperative effort of the Nautical Almanac Office, the International Business Machines Corporation, and Yale University produced ephemerides that were used in British and American almanacs until 1984. New forms of cooperation developed between the British and American almanac offices and eventually with scientists at the **Jet Propulsion Laboratory**. Beginning with the volumes for 1960, the nautical almanac offices in France, the United Kingdom, Germany, the United States, and the Soviet Union developed formal methods of cooperation. The British and American almanacs became identical in all but titles. During this period, the British Office, which had been an independent organization under the Ministry of Defence, became part of the Royal Greenwich Observatory. In 1965, the observatory itself was shifted from the Ministry of Defence to the newly formed Science Research Council, with long term impacts on both funding and scientific activities.

In the 1970s the French, British, and American offices began independently exploring means for presenting astronomical data in computerized formats. These efforts resulted in a series of publications giving efficient computational algorithms, and finally in software packages for microcomputers. In the meantime the Jet Propulsion Laboratory, responsible for guiding spacecraft on interplanetary missions, developed a complete new set of orbital calculations of the moon and planets. These were introduced in virtually all national almanacs in 1984.

By the 1980s some people regarded almanac offices as obsolete, providing paper products in an age of electronic information. Electronic methods of navigation were becoming much easier and, in many cases, more reliable than traditional celestial navigation. At the same time, however, the almanac offices faced ever increasing public demands for information, and remained important centers of expertise needed in many areas of science. With the aid of the French telephone system, for example, the *Bureau des Longitudes* produced a service that enables individuals to calculate astronomical phenomena with a home computer. At a time when dubious commercial software is widely used for astronomical calculations, the almanac offices are providing secure standards of accuracy.

There is no adequate historical study of the nautical almanacs or the institutions that produced them. Steven J. Dick and LeRoy E. Doggett have carried out oral history interviews with former members of the NAO; transcriptions of these are on file in the library of the U.S. Naval Observatory. The memoirs of Donald H. Sadler, who was director of H.M. Nautical Almanac, 1936–1971, have been edited by his successor, George A. Wilkins, but remain unpublished.

LeRoy E. Doggett

Bibliography

Bigourdan, G. "Le Bureau des Longitudes. Son histoire et ses travaux, de l'origine

(1795) à ce jour." *Annuaire du Bureau des Longitudes* A1–A117, 1928; C1–C92, 1929; A1–A110, 1930; A1–A145, 1931, A1–A117, 1932; A1–A91, 1933.
Davis, C.H. "On the Nautical Almanac." *Proceedings of the American Association for the Advancement of Science*. Fourth meeting, 1850. New York: G. Putnam, 1851.
Explanatory Supplement to the Astronomical Ephemeris and the American Ephemeris and Nautical Almanac. London: H.M. Stationery Office, 1961.
Forbes, E.G. "The Foundation and Early Development of the Nautical Almanac. *Navigation* 18 (1965): 391–401.
Howse, D. *Nevil Maskelyne, The Seaman's Astronomer*. Cambridge: Cambridge University Press, 1989.
Lévy, J. "La Creation de la Connaissance des Temps." *Vistas in Astronomy* 20 (1976): 75–77.
Newcomb, S. *Reminiscences of an Astronomer*. Boston: Houghton, Mifflin, 1903.
Sadler, D.H. "The Bicentenary of the Nautical Almanac." *Journal of the Royal Astronomical Society* 8 (1965): 161–171.
———. "Lunar Distances and the Nautical Almanac." *Vistas in Astronomy* 20 (1976): 113–121.
Wilkins, G.A. "The Expanding Role of H.M. Nautical Almanac Office, 1818–1975." *Vistas in Astronomy* 20 (1976): 239–243.
Woolard, E.W. "The Centennial of the American Nautical Almanac Office." *Sky & Telescope* 11 (1951): 27–29.

Navigation by Astronomical Methods

Until the middle of the twentieth century, it was necessary to use astronomical techniques for the navigation of ships on transoceanic voyages. The navigator is required to find his current position relative to the position of his destination and then to monitor the subsequent direction and distance of travel. Before the seventeenth century, observations of the stars at night and of the sun by day were used to establish direction and latitude, but it was not possible to determine longitude. Latitude was given by the altitude of the north celestial pole, and it was recognized that the position of the pole varied slowly with respect to the stars as a result of the precession of the earth's axis of rotation. Latitude was also given by the altitude of the sun at noon, but a correction for the declination of the sun, which varies throughout the year, was required.

As early as the second century B.C.E., Hipparchus recognized that the difference in the longitudes of two places is equal to the difference in the local times at those places. (Longitude is here expressed in time units at the rate of 1 hour for each 15 degrees of angle.) Local time could be measured at sea by observations of the sun, and so the solution of the problem of finding longitude depended on finding a way of simultaneously determining the local time at some distant reference place (usually a principal port). In 1514, Johann Werner of Nuremberg proposed the lunar-distance method, in which the apparent position of the moon with respect to the stars provides a measure of time that is not based on the rotation of the earth. In 1530, Gemma Frisius of Louvain suggested that a clock set to the local time of the port at which the voyage started should be carried on the ship. About 250 years elapsed before these two methods could be used to find longitude at sea with an accuracy of better than 100 km.

In addition to a nautical almanac containing the positions of the sun, moon, and stars, the navigator also needed charts that gave the latitudes and longitudes of the destination ports. The determination of these coordinates depended on the same principles, but the astronomical observations could be made with fixed instruments and could be repeated to improve the determination of the coordinates. At first, observations of the times of predicted eclipses of the satellites of Jupiter were used to determine the longitudes of the ports, but eventually observations of lunar distances were used. Later, astronomical observations were made regularly at the ports so that the clocks carried by the ships could be reset and so that their error rates could be determined; these clocks became known as chronometers.

Longitude from Lunar Distances

In the method of lunar distances for the determination of longitude, the navigator measured the angular distance between a star (or the sun) and the limb (edge) of the moon and compared this with the value predicted in the nautical almanac in order to derive the Greenwich time. A lunar distance increases by about 0.5 degree an hour and it had to be measured and predicted to an accuracy of 1 minute of arc (1') or better in order to obtain longitude to better than 0.5 degree. The navigator also needed to measure the altitudes of the moon and the star above the horizon in order to determine local time and other quantities that entered into the calculation of the longitude; such observations were best made in morning and evening twilight. The principal requisites for the successful use of the method were an instrument that could be used to measure the lunar distances and the altitudes, a catalogue of the positions of the bright stars in the zodiacal zone on either side of the ecliptic, theories of the apparent motions of the sun and moon with respect to the center of the earth, precomputed predictions of the lunar distances as well as of the positions of the sun, moon and stars, and a procedure for the calculation of the longitude from the observed distances and altitudes. In addition the navigator needed a watch that could be used to keep the time during each series of observations.

In 1675, King Charles II of England appointed John Flamsteed to be his Astronomical Observator and made funds available for the building of an observatory in the royal park at Greenwich in an endeavor to promote the development of the technique of lunar distances. Flamsteed concentrated on the observation of accurate positions of stars and of the moon for use in the preparation of a star catalogue and in the construction of the theory of the motion of the moon. Progress was slow, and in 1714 Queen Anne gave her assent to an act that offered rewards of up to £20,000 for practical methods of determining longitude at sea. Smaller rewards had been offered by other countries, but without success. Flamsteed's successors, **Edmond Halley** and James Bradley, continued to make the basic astronomical observations, while others gradually developed the practical techniques.

In about 1731 John Hadley in London and Thomas Godfrey in Philadelphia independently invented the reflecting quadrant for the accurate measurement of lunar distances. This was further developed in about 1757 by Captain John Campbell of the Royal Navy and the instrument-maker John Bird into the **sextant**, which with telescopic sights and a brass frame was capable of measuring angles accurately up to 120 degrees. By this time, spring-driven deck watches were capable of keeping good time over periods of up to six hours.

Many famous mathematicians worked on the development of the theory of the motion of the **moon**, but it was Tobias Mayer, a German astronomer, who in 1755 produced a set of tables that could be used to calculate the moon's position to the required accuracy; he used equations developed by **Leonhard Euler**, a Swiss mathematician. Bradley tested the tables against observations made at Greenwich, but the first trials at sea in 1757–1758 by Captain Campbell were inconclusive. In 1761, however, Nevil Maskelyne obtained successful results while on a voyage to and from St. Helena to observe the transit of **Venus**. His procedure for the calculation of the longitude from the lunar distance was based on a method devised by **Abbé Nicholas-Louis de Lacaille**, a French astronomer, who had also tested the technique several years earlier using inadequate lunar tables. In 1763, Maskelyne published an account of the technique in his *British Mariners' Guide* and put forward proposals for an appropriate nautical almanac.

Maskelyne became **Astronomer Royal** at the beginning of 1765 and the first edition of *The Nautical Almanac and Astronomical Ephemeris* was published in 1766 for the year 1767. In addition he published a set of *Tables Requisite to be used with the Ephemeris*, including a three-page illustration of the determination of the longitude from an observed lunar distance. The calculation was very laborious; account had to be taken of refraction in the atmosphere and of the difference between the place of the observation and the place, namely the center of the earth, for which the predicted lunar distances were computed. The calculations were made to a precision of 1 second of arc, although the use of 1 minute of arc would have been easier and more appropriate.

Predictions of lunar distances continued to be published in the *Nautical Almanac* until 1906, although the widespread use of chronometers made them largely obsolete before then. Maskelyne used Greenwich apparent time as the time-argument in the *Almanac*, and hence many charts were published using Greenwich to define the meridian of zero longitude. The argument was changed to Greenwich mean time after chronometers came into regular use. Other countries published their own almanacs in their own languages; some followed the British almanac, but others used a time argument appropriate to the principal port of the country concerned. Correspondingly, national charts used different zero meridians.

Chronometers and the Distribution of Time

John Harrison, an English clockmaker, was the first person to make a clock (1764) that satisfied the conditions of the 1724 Act. Copies of his chronometer were made by other clockmakers, and on James Cook's second voyage of exploration in the Pacific Ocean these proved satisfactory in a wide range of climatic conditions. The chronometers gave the required longitude whenever an observation, such as an altitude of the sun, could be made to determine local time; they were checked against the results from lunar-distance observations made under good conditions.

For commercial navigation, the ship's chronometers were checked and rated while the ship was in a principal port, where there would be an observatory for the determination of local mean time and a time-ball (as at Greenwich for the port of London from 1833) or a time-gun for making an accurate value of the time available to the ships in the port. (Greenwich time could be deduced directly, as the longitude of the port would be known.) In the second half of the nineteenth century, the laying of transoceanic cables for electric telegraphy led to the direct availability of Greenwich time and hence to the use on the East Coast of North America of standard times that differed from Greenwich time by an exact number of hours.

Since each major maritime country produced its own nautical almanacs and charts, using its capital or principal port as the reference point for the measurement of time and longitude, there was considerable confusion, sometimes with tragic consequences. Eventually an international conference held in Washington, D.C., in 1884 recommended that the meridian of the **Royal Observatory at Greenwich** be used as the prime meridian throughout the world for the measurement of longitude and for the establishment of a system of standard-time zones, in each of which the time kept for general use would differ from the mean time of the Greenwich zone by an integral number of hours. Henceforth, Greenwich time was regarded as the time to be determined from observations or carried by the chronometer for the determination of longitude.

New Techniques for Astronomical Navigation

Until the middle of the nineteenth century, the determination of position was based on independent determinations of latitude and longitude. Such determinations could not be made simultaneously, but it was possible to use estimates of the speed and direction of motion of the ship to connect the determinations and to make an estimate, or dead-reckoning (D.R), of the position at any subsequent time; such an estimate is known as a D.R. position. In 1837 Captain T.H. Sumner, an American, discovered that if he used three estimates of his D.R. latitude a single observation of the altitude of the sun could be used to give three D.R. positions that lay on a straight line; moreover this line was perpendicular to the direction of the sun. Such a Sumner line is strictly part of a circle centered on the sub-solar point and with radius equal to the observed zenith distance (90 degree altitude) of the sun. In 1874 Marcq St. Hilaire, a Frenchman, proposed a computational procedure that was based on a generalization of this principle, but which recognized that the position line is displaced from the D.R. position by an intercept that is equal to the difference between the observed and calculated values of the altitude. Two such position lines for objects that differ in azimuth meet in a point, but, because of the errors in the observed altitudes, it is normally found that three such position lines form a triangle or cocked hat within which the fix or estimated position lies. This soon became the most used method, but the latitude and longitude technique continued to be widely used.

The subsequent development of navigation by the use of observations of the altitudes of the sun, moon, planets, and stars may be seen as a series of gradual improvements in the instruments and, especially, in the techniques of calculation. The changes were primarily designed to simplify and so speed up the calculations, but others gave improvements in accuracy through the use, for example, of better formulae for the corrections for refraction, which are particularly large and liable to error at or near the horizon. The principal improvements came in two ways: first, through better design of the almanacs that contained the basic astronomical data and, second, through the publication of tables that gave altitude and azimuth directly in terms of the equatorial coordinates that were necessarily used in the almanacs. Such tables obviated the laborious calculations with logarithms that were otherwise required.

The necessity for the use of astronomical methods of navigation in aircraft, especially for military purposes during and after World War II, led to the greatest impetus for change, as speed of calculation was so much more important than on a slowly moving ship in the middle of the ocean. Almanacs that were specially designed for use in the air were introduced in the late 1930s. In them, all the data for each day were given at one opening and the coordinates were tabulated at an interval of 10 minutes, rather than of 1 hour or even of 1 day, as in the marine almanacs. Moreover, Greenwich hour angle was tabulated instead of right ascension, since this gave directly the longitude of the point at which the object was in the zenith. The unit of tabulation was increased from 0.1 minute to 1 minute and tabulations of altitude and azimuth were given for individual bright stars. The techniques that were introduced for use in the air led to corresponding changes in the practice of marine navigation.

International cooperation led to the use of standard data and techniques for astronomical navigation, and the same numerical data are published in almanacs with headings in different languages. These data are also made available in alternative forms for use in handheld calculators and in computers.

Alternative Methods of Position Finding

The principal disadvantage of the traditional astronomical method for marine navigation is its dependence on optical observations made with respect to the horizon, which may be indistinct or obscured by mist even when the sky is free of cloud. The bubble sextant was developed for use in the air; this defined an artificial horizon, but the technique proved to be incapable of giving good positions sufficiently quickly for commercial use. New methods of position finding that do not suffer from these disadvantages became available during the past half-century. First came radio-based systems such as the Loran system, which uses chains of radio stations that broadcast synchronized signals. In effect, the receiver measures the difference of its distances from a pair of stations in order to obtain a position line, which is an arc of a hyperbola; two such measurements give a fix at the intersection of the arcs, which are plotted on special charts. Inertial navigation systems, which are widely used on intercontinental flights, rely on the continuous monitoring and integration of the accelerations of the aircraft so as to provide an accurate D.R. position at all times.

The Transit Navigation system became operational in 1964; it was based on a set of five or six satellites in polar orbits. The receiver measured and analyzed the Doppler shifts of the signals transmitted by the satellites above the horizon at the time in order to obtain a fix that could be better than 0.5 km. This sytem has been largely superseded over the past few years by the Global Positioning System (GPS), which is based on a set of twenty-four satellites so that ideally at least four will be above the horizon at any place at any time. In this case the receiver measures its distances from the four satellites and derives the error of its clock and the three coordinates of its geocentric position, which is converted to latitude, longitude, and height with an accuracy of 100 meters or better.

Although the GPS system will soon become the principal technique for the determination of position at sea, in the air, and on land, it seems likely that the marine navigator will continue to wish to use each day astronomical data from *The Nautical Almanac* and he will wish to retain an independent capability of navigating his craft.

George Wilkins

Bibliography

Cotter, C.H. *A History of Nautical Astronomy*. London: Hollis and Carter, 1968.

Howse, H.D. *Greenwich Time and the Discovery of the Longitude*. Oxford: Oxford University Press, 1980.

———. "Navigation and Astronomy." *Journal of the British Astronomical Association* 92 (1982): 53–60; 92 (1983): 50–61.

Sadler, D.H. *Man Is Not Lost*. London: Her Majesty's Stationery Office, 1968.

Taylor, E.G.R. *The Haven-finding Art*. London: Hollis and Carter, 1971.

———. *The Mathematical Practitioners of Hanoverian England*. Cambridge: Cambridge University Press, 1979.

Nebular Hypothesis

Although Immanuel Kant had earlier suggested the formation of planets, stars, and galaxies from a chaos of atoms, **Pierre-Simon Laplace** developed a more detailed and convincing explanation of such phenomena. Initially announced in the popular work *System of the World* (1796), Laplace's nebular hypothesis argued that the planetary system formed from the primitive solar atmosphere, which extended beyond the orbit of the outermost planet. As this atmosphere cooled and condensed, it left a succession of rings in the plane of the solar equator that ultimately coalesced to form individual planets.

In the next five editions of *System of the World*, Laplace developed the details of his hypothesis, making significant use of the nebular investigations of **William Herschel**. The latter's suggestion of gravitational condensation of nebular matter led Laplace to posit that the early solar system resembled a slowly rotating hot nebula. As this body cooled and contracted, its rotational velocity increased to the point at which centrifugal force balanced gravitational attraction, eventually forming a series of concentric rings around the sun. These rings usually broke up into many small rotating bodies that formed planets and moons through a process of attraction and accretion. Laplace's nebular hypoth-

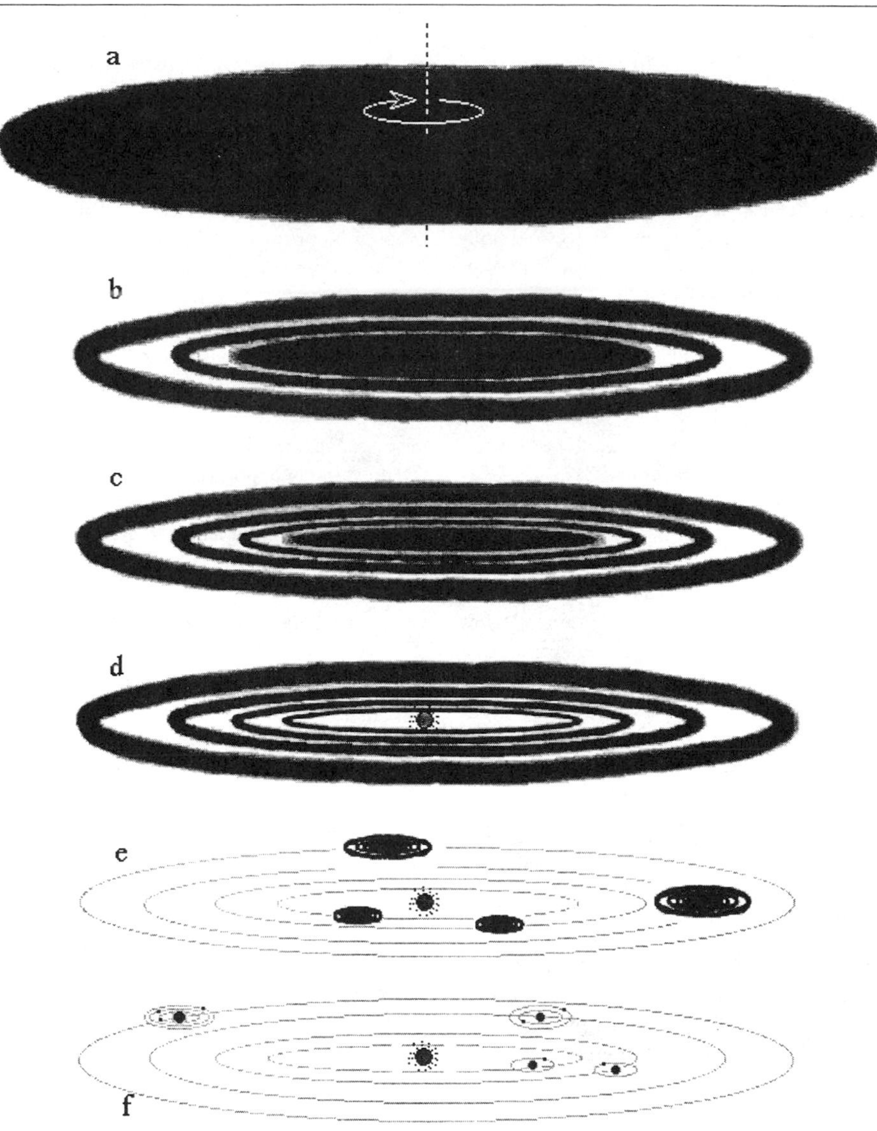

The Laplacian concept viewed the beginning of the solar system (f) as an initial hot, flattened, rotating mass (a) that proceeded to contract from self-gravitation. In successive stages of contraction (b and c), annular rings of material were left behind as gravity was balanced by the centrifugal force at the equator (left unexplained is why this process would produce a series of rings). The primary mass became the central sun (d), and each ring proceeded to contract to become a planet, a process that also left behind smaller rings (e) that became moons. (Figure by Charles J. Peterson)

esis had been largely accepted by the early decades of the nineteenth century.

By mid-century, however, challenges to Laplace's theory had emerged. Research conducted by Lord Rosse and others had resolved many nebulae into groups of individual stars, calling into question the earlier concept of nebulae as clouds of gas that would coalesce into stars and solar systems. Although later spectroscopic studies by **William Huggins** identified some nebulae as clouds of luminous gas, other questions remained. Critics stressed that condensation of a nebular cloud would result in a flat disk, rather than a series of large rings, and argued that a condensing nebula would not form planets with the observed rotational periods. By the early 1900s, the nebular hypothesis had largely been supplanted by the planetesimal hypothesis of Thomas C. Chamberlin and Forest Ray Moulton, but over the following decades the two hypotheses were combined to explain the formation of the solar system by processes of nebular condensation and planetesimal accretion.

George E. Webb

Bibliography

Brush, S.G. *Fruitful Encounters: The Origin of the Solar System and the Moon from Chamberlin to Apollo.* Vol. 3 of *A History of Modern Planetary Physics.* New York: Cambridge University Press, 1996.

Numbers, R.L. *Creation by Natural Law: Laplace's Nebular Hypothesis in American Thought.* Seattle: University of Washington Press, 1977.

Whitney, C.A. *The Discovery of Our Galaxy.* New York: Knopf, 1971.

Neptune

In October 1846, soon after the discovery of Neptune, William Lassell turned his 24-inch reflector toward the planet. His observations included a satellite (later named Triton) and a ring (later considered spurious and attributed to flexure in the telescope's mirror). A second satellite, Nereid, was discovered photographically by **Gerard P. Kuiper** in 1949. Triton's highly inclined (157-degree) and retrograde orbit was difficult to reconcile with the prevailing belief of a common origin for all the planets. It led to later speculations (after the discovery of **Pluto**) that the same catastrophic event had produced Pluto's extremely eccentric orbit and Triton's peculiar situation. *Voyager 2* revealed six more satellites in 1989.

Nineteenth-century **micrometer** measurements of the planet's diameter and estimates of its mass put it in the same class as the other outer planets, suggesting a large gaseous envelope around a small core. Spectroscopic and laboratory analyses in the 1930s implied the constituent gases were largely hydrogen and methane.

In 1977 James Elliot and his colleagues made the startling discovery of a ring system around **Uranus**, from stellar occultation observations made from the Kuiper Airborne Observatory. This led them to search for occultations of Neptune that might reveal a similar ring system. Occultation observations made of Neptune in 1968 had been negative, although observers had not been searching for rings at that time. When the *Pioneer 11* spacecraft observed a thin ring around Jupiter in 1981, hopes were raised for finding rings around Neptune. Stellar occultation measurements between 1977 and 1989 repeatedly produced suggestive but inconclusive results, the most likely hypothesis being that, if at all, Neptune was surrounded by partial ring arcs.

Observations of faint features on the difficult disk allowed estimates of rotation periods of around 17 to 18 hours, and an inclination of its polar axis of 29 degrees. In 1928 J.H. Moore and Donald Menzel derived a rotation period spectroscopically of 15.8 hours, but up until the *Voyager* spacecraft flyby of 1989 estimates continued to vary between 11 and 20 hours.

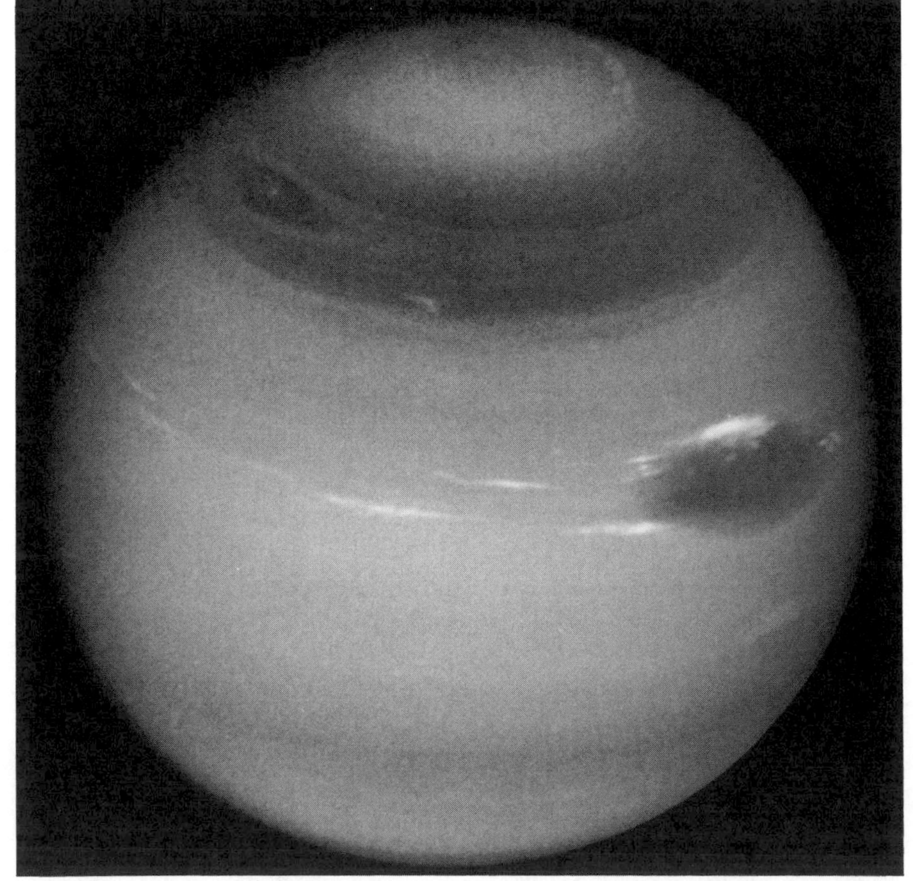

Neptune photographed in August 1989 by Voyager 2. *Note the belts and large dark spots as well as smaller bright spots, all of which are located at the top of Neptune's atmosphere. (Courtesy of the National Aeronautics and Space Administration)*

On August 25, 1989, *Voyager 2* made its closest approach to Neptune at about 5,000 kilometers above the cloud tops—the only spacecraft to visit the planet, and *Voyager's* last port of call. A Great Dark Spot, similar to the Great Red Spot on **Jupiter**, was observed at mid-southern latitudes, and several bright spots—cirrus clouds of methane ice—were observed at various latitudes, fixing the rotation periods of those atmospheric levels at around sixteen hours. The core was found by radio observations to rotate slightly more slowly, producing very high westerly shear winds in the clouds. The magnetic field's axis of rotation was found, like that of Uranus, to be offset from the planet's axis by about 60 degrees. The puzzling occultation results were clarified when *Voyager's* cameras revealed the narrow, dark, and wispy Uranian rings to include some more substantial clumps of material kept together by resonance interactions with newly discovered small satellites. Triton revealed a remarkably diverse mixture of young geological terrain, including active geysers at the subsolar point, presumably expelling nitrogen gas. Nereid was not seen very clearly due to the spacecraft's trajectory.

While there is an extensive historiography for the discovery of Neptune, only Lassell's putative observations of the Neptunian ring has attracted the attention of historians (and Baum, Hetherington, Hoyt, Smith). James Elliot, who led the team that discovered the rings of Uranus and who, along with others, searched for Neptunian rings, provides a clear and candid description of his and his colleagues' work. Popular accounts by Eric Burgess, Henry S.F. Cooper Jr., and Patrick Moore were all aimed at the *Voyager 2* encounter, and so provide only the most rudimentary historical details. Sheehan emphasizes the *Voyager 2* results as well.

Joseph N. Tatarewicz

Bibliography

Burgess, E. *Uranus and Neptune: The Distant Giants*. New York: Columbia University Press, 1988.

———. *Far Encounter: The Neptune System*. New York: Columbia University Press, 1991.

Cooper, H.S.F., Jr. "Annals of Space: The Planetary Community II—Neptune." *New Yorker* 66 (1990): 73–90.

Elliot, J., and R. Kerr. *Rings: Discoveries from Galileo to Voyager*. Cambridge: MIT Press, 1984.

Hetherington, N.S. "Neptune's Supposed Ring." *Journal of the British Astronomical Association* 90 (1979): 20–29.

Hoyt, W.G. "Reflections Concerning Neptune's 'Ring.'" *Sky & Telescope* 55 (1978): 284–285.

Moore, P. *The Planet Neptune*. New York: Halstead Press, 1988.

Sheehan, W. *Worlds in the Sky: Planetary Discovery from Earliest Times through Voyager and Magellan*. Tucson: University of Arizona Press, 1992.

Smith, R.W., and R. Baum. "William Lassell and the Ring of Neptune: A Case Study in Instrumental Failure." *Journal for the History of Astronomy* 1 (1984): 1–17.

"Special Issue on Voyager 2 Encounter with Neptune." *Science* 246 (December 15).

Neptune, Discovery of

The discovery of the planet Neptune at the Berlin Observatory in September 1846 was a direct result of calculations by the French mathematical astronomer **U.J.J. Le Verrier** and is one of the best known events in the history of astronomy. It sparked an extended priority battle that continues to rumble on and stir passions over credit for the predictions of the elements as well as the existence of the planet.

The bare outlines of the story (although little else) are generally agreed upon. By the early 1840s, the deviations of **Uranus** from its predicted orbital position constituted a worrying anomaly at the very heart of astronomy. One possibility was that the law of gravity acts in some unexpected manner at the enormous distance of Uranus. However, Newtonian theory appeared to the great majority, perhaps nearly all, of astronomers to be the impregnably true system of the world and beyond reproach. In consequence, the generally favored hypothesis was that a planet lay beyond Uranus and was perturbing it. One who thought so was the young Cambridge mathematician John Couch Adams. In 1843, after election to a college fellowship, he began a detailed investigation directed toward predicting the position, motion, and mass of the disturbing planet from the deviations in Uranus's motions. By September 1845, Adams was confident enough of his results to present to James Challis, Plumian Professor of Astronomy at Cambridge, the elements defining the orbit of the postulated planet as well as the position for it he had calculated. The Astronomer Royal, **George Biddell Airy**, became acquainted with Adams's results shortly after.

The problem of Uranus' motion had also been taken up, independently of Adams, by the brilliant French mathematical astronomer U.J.J. Le Verrier. In June 1846, Le Verrier published a paper predicting the disturber's position; a more detailed result followed a few weeks later. Frustrated by the lack of interest at the Paris Observatory, Le Verrier wrote to the Berlin Observatory and asked that a search be undertaken there. This search was crowned with success within a very short time when, on September 23, J.G. Galle and H. d'Arrest located the new planet very close to Le Verrier's predicted position. Despite Adams's having provided Challis and Airy with a good position a year earlier, Challis had begun a planet hunt only in July 1846 and, in the opinion of many of his countrymen, Adams had been scooped.

Following the planet's find there was a heated and sometimes bitter dispute over priority. French scientists were angry over English efforts to win credit for Adams despite the fact that he had not published the results of his researches prior to the discovery. The actual discovery was quickly accorded to Galle, but later in the century d'Arrest's role became accepted. The dispute therefore centered on the credit for the theoretical find. Recriminations even spilled over to the naming of the planet. Polemics were traded again when in 1847 the American astronomer Benjamin Peirce claimed that the visual discovery had been a "happy accident": The planet predicted by Adams and Le Verrier was not to be identified with Neptune. At stake in this argument was not only the extent to which Le Verrier and Adams deserved credit for the theoretical discovery of the planet, but also, by implication, the degree to which the discovery had been, as British and French scientists both contended—however much they might fight for credit among themselves—a demonstration of the power of theoretical science.

Most of the existing literature on the discovery is concerned with allocating blame to those who, in the authors' opinion, failed to search energetically enough for the postulated planet, particularly Challis and Airy. Neptune, in fact, has cast a very long shadow over both of their reputations. Airy and Challis have also found a few defenders. But attempts to vindicate or criticize Airy and Challis have worked to focus the existing literature quite narrowly on certain aspects of the discovery. A public account Airy presented in November 1846 of the circumstances of the discovery and in which he in part constructed history for his own purposes, has done much to structure the later historiography by posing the questions many writers have seized upon. But this is one part of a more general problem: These accounts have generally been hobbled by uncritical readings of the public writings of the participants published after the discovery in 1846. Some previously entrenched parts of the story have thus been overturned by more thorough and skeptical researches in the last few years. It had long been assumed, for example, that Challis was the only person in England to search for the new planet before its discovery in Berlin. However, J.R. Hind was also involved in the search (Smith, 407).

There have also been some attempts to interpret the discovery within broad social and political currents (Hubbell and Smith, Pannekoek, and Smith, as well as Grosser to some degree). For these authors, the lead-up to the find, as well as its aftermath, provide rich sites for exploring the nature of astronomy in Europe and the United States in the middle of the nineteenth century and its place in the wider culture.

Robert W. Smith

Bibliography

Chapman, A. "Private Research and Public Duty: George Biddell Airy and the Search for Neptune." *Journal for the History of Astronomy* 19 (1988): 121–139.

Grosser, M. *The Discovery of Neptune*. Cambridge: Harvard University Press, 1962.

Hubbell, J.G., and R.W. Smith. "Neptune in America." *Journal for the History of Astronomy* 23 (1992): 261–291.

Pannekoek, A. "The Discovery of Neptune." *Centaurus* 3 (1953): 126–137.

Rawlins, D."The Discovery of Neptune: Essential Revisions to the History." *Bulletin of the American Astronomical Society* 16 (1984): 734.

Smart, W.M. "John Couch Adams and the Discovery of Neptune." *Popular Astronomy* 55 (1947): 301–311.

Smith, R.W. "The Cambridge Network in Action: The Discovery of Neptune." *Isis* 80 (1989): 395–422.

Turner, H.H. *Astronomical Discovery*. London: Edward Arnold, 1904.

Netherlands, Astronomy in

Of particular importance to the reputation of Dutch astronomy is the historical role of the seventeenth-century scientist Christiaan Huygens and, in the twentieth century, **J.C. Kapteyn** and **Jan H. Oort**.

Christiaan Huygens, easily the greatest Dutch scientist in the seventeenth century and among Europe's greatest mathematicians, was preeminent in mechanics. His contributions to science were extensive and included high-caliber work in astronomy, time measurement, and optics. Huygens constructed a telescope and in 1655 discovered Titan, a satellite of Saturn. He also proposed that the arms of **Saturn** could best be explained as a ring circumscribing the planet. In addition, he determined the rotation of Mars, observed the Orion nebula, and built **micrometers** for the determination of the angular diameters of the planets. He was a defender of the Copernican system. His greatest contribution to science was the *Horologium oscillatorium* (1673), which advocated a mathematical approach to the study of nature. In the widely read, posthumously published *Cosmotheros* (1698), Huygens promoted the view of sentient life on other planets throughout the sidereal system. As an unaffiliated scholar, however, Huygens did not attract disciples, and therefore did not leave a direct scientific legacy.

An understanding of the development of astronomy in the Netherlands is, to a large degree, the history of astronomy at the four major universities, Leiden, Utrecht, Groningen, and Amsterdam.

Leiden

The founding of the Leiden Observatory, in 1633 by Jacob Golius, represents the first observatory connected with a university. Although the Vatican Observatory and **Tycho Brahe**'s observatory are older, they were private research institutions. Originally equipped with a great quadrant instrument with a radius of 7 feet and a circle divided by **transversalis** of 2 minutes, the Leiden Observatory was housed in a specially built octagonal, rotating turret above the main university building, from which observations of comets, eclipses, and the planets were made. By 1705 the observatory contained a **sextant**, additional quadrants, and various telescopes. The observatory, however, was a place of public demonstration and teaching, not a research institute. The first professor of astronomy was Willem Jacob s'Gravesande, appointed in 1717. He was succeeded by Petrus van Musschenbroek, who died in 1761.

The first important scientific research dates from the days of Johan Lulofs. Among numerous astronomical contributions, Lulofs observed Halley's comet and the transits of Mercury (1743 and 1753) and Venus (1761). Following Lulofs, there were several competent astronomers, including Johan Frederik van Beeck Calkoen, Cornelis Ekama, and Pieter Johannes Uylenbroek.

In 1837 Frederik Kaiser was appointed director of the Leiden Observatory and later full professor at the university. Kaiser had already distinguished himself with work on Halley's comet in 1835. In 1860 a new building was constructed and Kaiser acquired a 6-inch telescope by Merz-Fraunhofer, comparatively large for the day. Kaiser observed comets, minor planets, double stars, and planetary diameters. In 1869 Kaiser acquired a transit instrument. Hendrik Gerald van de Sande Bakhuyzen, Kaiser's favorite pupil and successor (1872), added a 13-inch photographic refractor in 1897.

Continuing Kaiser's policy, **astrometry** was the principal research interest under Bakhuyzen. Both Kaiser and Bakhuyzen filled important offices in the International Geodetic Association, while Bakhuyzen was active on the *Carte du Ciel* project. Following Bakhuyzen's retirement in 1908, his brother Ernst became director. He died in 1918. A major reorganization of the observatory took place under the guidance of the new director, Willem de Sitter. De Sitter managed the department of theoretical astronomy, and in 1919 the Danish astronomer **Ejnar Hertzsprung** was appointed to direct astrophysics. Antonie Pannekoek was originally offered the position but was rejected by the Ministry of Education because of his Marxist leanings. Following his retirement as director of the Groningen Observatory in 1918, J.C. Kapteyn, was appointed to direct the department of positional astronomy. De Sitter's main contributions were in **celestial mechanics** and relativity theory applied to cosmology; Hertzsprung is best known for studies that led to the development of the **Hertzsprung-Russell diagram**. Following de Sitter's death in 1934, Hertzsprung became director. In 1944, Jan Hendrik Oort, who joined the observatory staff in 1924 and became professor of astronomy at the university in 1935, was appointed director. Oort served until retirement in 1970. Oort is best known for the Lindblad-Oort model of galactic structure, and contributions to solar system and radio astronomy.

Utrecht

The second oldest university observatory was founded in 1642; Henricus Regius was instrumental in its organization. At the university, astronomy was undistinguished. Johannes de Bruijn, a professor of physics from 1652, devoted some time to the field, and later Jacobus Ode, professor of philosophy, taught astronomy. Petrus van Musschenbroek, remembered today for his invention of the Leiden Jar, held the chair of astronomy at the university from 1732 to 1740, when he became professor of astronomy at the University of Leiden. Johann Castillon followed as lecturer in mathematics and astronomy.

In 1805 Johan Frederik van Beeck Calkoen became director at Utrecht. He was succeeded by Gerald Moll, who also was professor of physics at the university. Moll was primarily interested in the observations of the transits of Mercury. R. van Rees succeeded Moll in 1838, and A.S. Rueb became lecturer in astronomy in 1843. C.H.D. Buys Ballot, who was one of the chief organizers of the science of meteorology, was professor of mathematics (1847) and physics (1867) at the university until 1888.

The first sustained astronomical research began with Martinus Hoek, who studied under Frederik Kaiser at Leiden and moved to Utrecht in 1856. He became professor of astronomy at the university. Hoek did original astronomical research and is chiefly known for discovering thirty-three comets belonging to six groups that occupy the same orbit, as well as for investigations of optical phenomena in moving bodies. In 1875 Jean Abraham Chretien Oudemans became professor of astronomy at Utrecht. He was followed in 1898 by Albertus A. Nijland.

Willem Henri Julius became professor of physics at the University of Utrecht in 1896 and, following the solar eclipse of 1901, he began to specialize in solar physics. He was known for observations of solar prominences and anomalous scattering, and during his tenure he set up a solar spectrograph, which at the time was the third one in the world.

The observatory was transformed into an astrophysical institute mainly for the study of solar and stellar spectra when Marcel Gilles Jozef Minnaert was appointed professor of physics at the university (1925) and later director of the Utrecht Observatory (1937). He was a pioneer in solar research, and in addition promoted the study of comets, nebulae, and lunar photometry.

Groningen

The first prominent astronomer at the University of Groningen was Nicolaas Mulerius, appointed in 1614. Interested in the motions of planets, he published astronomical tables and, although an opponent of heliocentrism, an annotated edition of Copernicus's *De Revolutionibus*. Nicolaas Engelhard, appointed at Groningen (1728), was able to refute the anti-Copernican views of the theologians. After Engelhard, interest in astronomy waned. The first significant revival occurred with the appointment of Jacob Baart de la Faille in 1789; he remained at Groningen until his death in 1823.

As a result of higher education reform in 1878, a chair of astronomy was established at the University of Groningen, to which **Jacobus Cornelius Kapteyn** was appointed. Kapteyn's extraordinary research career began in 1886 when he proposed to **David Gill**, Royal Astronomer at the Cape of Good Hope, that they cooperate in the production of the *Cape Photographic Durchmusterung* (1896–1899). Gill made the observations and Kapteyn measured the plates and carried out the reductions and analysis. In 1896 Kapteyn organized the Astronomical Laboratory at Groningen to assist astronomers with the reduction of astrometric data. He envisioned a twofold function for the Astronomical Laboratory. First, theoretical research and calculations needed for understanding the construction of the heavens: the mean-parallaxes, the luminosity law of the stars, and the number of stars in each magnitude class. Second, practical researches: the measurement of photographic plates in order to obtain data needed to understand the structure of the stellar system. The results appeared in numerous publications of the Astronomical Laboratory, starting in 1900.

Following Kapteyn's retirement in 1918, his student, colleague, and later assistant Pieter Johannes van Rhijn became professor of astronomy and director of the observatory. Van Rhijn continued Kapteyn's research in **stellar statistics**, including correlations between apparent magnitude, position, and proper motion. In 1923 he published a very important catalogue of the average stellar parallax according to spectral class. In 1925 van Rhijn completed his research on the luminosity function. With van Rhijn as president, stellar statistics was eventually incorporated into Commission 33, on the Structure and Dynamics of the Galactic System, of the **International Astronomical Union** (IAU). In 1953 the first symposium of the IAU—Coordination of Galactic Research—was held in Groningen. When van Rhijn retired in 1957, Adriaan Blaauw became director of the Kapteyn Astronomical Laboratory.

Amsterdam

In the eighteenth and nineteenth centuries, astronomy was occasionally taught at the University of Amsterdam, but not until the early twentieth century was astronomy organized as a program. The driving force behind these developments was Antonie Pannekoek, who studied astronomy at Leiden and began his career as a geodesist and observer at the Leiden Observatory. He soon grew disenchanted with astrometry, which he considered to have little scientific value, and became involved in Leftist political activities. When the ministry rejected Pannekoek's 1918 appointment as vice-director at the Leiden Observatory, the city of Amsterdam, which was not dependent on the state, appointed Pannekoek lecturer in mathematics and astronomy at the municipal university. In 1921 he established the modest but important astronomical institute, which embodied his interests in stellar atmospheres and spectral absorption. He is considered the founder of **astrophysics** in the Netherlands. After his retirement in 1942, Pannekoek published *A History of Astronomy* (1951, 1961), which has informed numerous practitioners and historians of astronomy.

It is widely believed among Dutch astronomers that in the twentieth century astronomy in the Netherlands was profoundly influenced by Kapteyn. Single-handedly, Kapteyn raised Dutch astronomy to an important place in the international astronomical community. There is a belief that virtually all twentieth-century Dutch astronomers are either pupils of Kapteyn or pupils of pupils of Kapteyn. Although Kapteyn had only eight doctoral students, all of them were successful. Van Rhijn and de Sitter became observatory directors, while Oort completed his Groningen Ph.D. under van Rhijn; so did Adriaan Blaauw. Oort became director at Leiden and Blaauw director at Groningen. An influential cohort of Dutch scientists received their astronomical training under Kapteyn's pupils. As a result, like Huygens in the seventeenth century, Kapteyn became, in spirit if not in fact, the guiding influence in modern Dutch astronomy.

E. Robert Paul

Bibliography

Blaauw, A., et al. *Sterrenkijken Bekeken.* Groningen, 1983.

Jager, C. de, H.G. van Bueren, and M. Kuperus. *Bolwerk van de sterren.* 1993.

Pannekoek, A. *A History of Astronomy.* New York: Interscience Publishers, 1961.

Sitter, W. de. *Short History of the Observatory of the University at Leiden, 1633–1933.* Haarlem, 1933.

Newcomb, Simon (1835–1909)

Canadian/American celestial mechanician. Born in Nova Scotia, Newcomb came to the United States as a youth. He was largely self-educated until he was employed by the Nautical Almanac Office as a computer in 1857. While there he studied at Harvard's Lawrence Scientific School, receiving a B.S. in 1858. In 1861 he joined the **U.S. Naval Observatory** as a transit circle observer. Soon he was directing the observing program and continuing his study of planetary and lunar theory.

From 1877 until his retirement in 1897, Newcomb was superintendent of the Nautical Almanac Office. He organized a program to develop a set of planetary theories based on a consistent set of observations and astronomical constants. **G.W. Hill** helped Newcomb achieve these goals. The resulting theories of the outer planets formed the basis for national almanacs until 1960; those of the inner planets were used until 1984.

In addition he wrote high-school textbooks and articles on science, economics, and politics for popular periodicals. He became one of the most famous and influential astronomers in America. He was the first president of the American Astronomical Society, 1899–1905.

LeRoy E. Doggett

Bibliography

Brown, E.W. "Simon Newcomb." *Bulletin of the American Mathematical Society* 16 (1910): 341–355.

Campbell, W.W. "Simon Newcomb." *Memoirs of the National Academy of Sciences* 17 (1916): 1–18.

Marsden, B.G. "Simon Newcomb." In *Dictionary of Scientific Biography*, edited by C.C. Gillispie, vol. 10, 33–36. New York: Scribner, 1974.

Moyer, A.E. *A Scientist's Voice in American Culture: Simon Newcomb and the Rhetoric of Scientific Method.* Berkeley: University of California Press, 1992.

Newcomb, S. *Reminiscences of an Astronomer.* Boston: Houghton Mifflin, 1903.

Norberg, A. *Simon Newcomb and Nineteenth-Century Positional Astronomy.* Unpublished Doctoral Dissertation, University of Wisconsin-Madison, 1974.

Newton, Hubert Anson (1830–1896)

Foremost American meteoricist of the nineteenth century. A Yale graduate (1850), Newton became the head of the Mathematics Department (1865–1896), and, in 1882, the first director of Yale's Winchester Observatory. He is noted for the discovery of relations between comets and meteors; for tracing the Leonid shower back to 902 C.E.; for the idea that families of comets were a consequence of capture by the major planets; and he was first to suggest meteoroid rotation from light variations along a fireball trail. He was a collector of meteorites, which he later turned over to Yale. Newton was the author of over fifty scientific publications.

Dorrit Hoffleit

Bibliography

Gibbs, J.W. "Hubert Anson Newton." *Biographical Memoirs of the National Academy of Sciences* 4 (1897): 101–124.

Newton, Isaac, Astronomy of

During his student days at Cambridge in the mid-1660s, Isaac Newton became acquainted with astronomy through reading Thomas Streete's *Astronomia Carolina* (1661) and Vincent Wing's *Harmonicon coeleste* (1651). Both works assumed elliptical orbits for the planets; neither mentioned **Johannes Kepler**'s area law; both employed modified equant devices to compute a planet's position in orbit. Streete, following **Jeremiah Horrocks**'s theory in the manuscript of his *Venus in sole visa* (completed in 1640 but not published until 1662), derived the relative solar distances of the planets from their periods by way of Kepler's third law; he was the first to do so in print.

In notes on the endpapers of Vincent Wing's *Astronomia Britannica* (1669), Newton showed himself doubtful of the ellipticity of the orbits; proposed a modified equant device of his own; and attributed the lunar anomalies to the compression of the circumterrestrial vortex by the circumsolar vortex. Some of the errors in Wing's tables, he opined, might be due to Wing's not following Kepler's third law for the planets' solar distances (Whiteside 1964).

In a letter to Newton of November 1679, Robert Hooke requested Newton's thoughts on the idea of compounding a planet's motion from "a direct motion by the tangent and an attractive motion towards the central body" (Turnbull, *Correspondence* vol. II, 297). This way of conceiving planetary motion was new to Newton, who up to then had assumed with Descartes that the planets, swept around the sun in a vortex, were subject to a centrifugal force generated by the orbital motion—Newton like Descartes called it a *conatus recedendo a centro*—that had to be neutralized. (In a manuscript of the late 1660s Newton had argued from Kepler's third law that this *conatus* must vary inversely as the square of the solar distance; see *Correspondence* I, 297.) But he soon deduced—without informing Hooke—that Hooke's central forces implied Kepler's area rule, and that an elliptical orbit with center of force at a focus implied an inverse-square law of force. Then he returned to his alchemical studies, which Hooke's letters had intruded upon.

A visit from **Edmond Halley**, probably in August 1684, triggered Newton's renewed assault on the problem of central forces; it expanded into the writing of the *Philosophiae Naturalis Principia Mathematica*, published in July 1687. The aether's resistance to the motion of pendulums, Newton inferred from experiments, probably in 1684 (Dobbs), was nonexistent; hence its role in planetary motion could be assumed to be nil. As Newton was to state in the preface to the *Principia*, "The whole burden of [natural] philosophy seems to consist in this—from the phenomena of motions to investigate the forces of nature, and then from these forces to demonstrate the other phenomena." The task he now set himself was to demonstrate from the phenomena the existence of a universal inverse-square force of gravity, and then to derive the further consequences of this force.

Newton's argument for the law of universal gravitation is complex and impressive, though not free of flaws. By *Principia* I.2 (Book I, Prop. 2), bodies moving uniformly in concentric circular orbits are subject to a central force, and by I.4 Kepler's third law holds of them if and only if the force is inverse-square. From the phenomena it then follows that the satellites of **Jupiter** and **Saturn** are subject to an inverse-square force toward their respective primaries (III.1). In the case of the primary planets circling the sun, I.4 is only approximately applicable since their orbits, though nearly circular, are variously eccentric; but here the inverse-square proportion is "with great accuracy, demonstrable from the quiescence of the aphelion points" (III.2). For by I.45, any departure from the inverse-square proportion causes the apsidal line of an elliptical orbit to progress or regress, and the ellipse with center of force at focus thus appears as the only possible fixed, eccentric orbit. That the planetary aphelia were stationary had been asserted by Streete in 1661 and Nicolas Mercator in 1676, while Kepler, Ismael Boulliau, and Wing had assigned motions to the apsides, albeit very slow ones.

In III.3 Newton argues that the force keeping the moon in its orbit is, very nearly, inverse-square, because the lunar apse advances only 3 degrees 3 minutes per revolution. According to I.45, Cor. 1, this much apsidal motion would be produced by a central force varying inversely as $r^{2.0165}$, r being the moon-earth distance; the small departure from the inverse-square proportion, Newton asserts, can be accounted for by the sun's perturbing force. The average radial component of this perturbing force, Newton added in the second edition, was to the earth's attractive force on the moon as 1 to $178^{29}/_{40}$, just enough, by I.45, Cor. 2, to cause the observed apsidal motion. Earlier, in an attempted derivation of the apsidal motion devised in the 1680s but not published, Newton correctly attributed the apsidal motion to both radial and transverse components of the perturbing force. In fact the true average radial component of the sun's perturbing force is only one-half as great as the ratio $1:178^{29}/_{40}$ implies. Mysteriously, in an illustrative calculation in I.45, Cor. 2, Newton uses the half-ratio 1:357.45.

III.4 introduces Newton's "Moon-test," a crucial step in the generalizing induction that leads to universal gravitation. The force retaining the moon in its orbit, already argued to be inverse-square, is now shown to be such that the moon, if brought down to the earth's surface, would fall with an acceleration almost exactly that found for a stone at the same distance from the earth's center. The calculation as Newton outlines it would lead to a fall of 15.009 Paris feet in the first second, but Newton obtains $15^1/_{12}$ Paris feet; having (without saying so) multiplied the initial result by the fraction $(178^{29}/_{40})/(177^{29}/_{40})$, as would be required to subtract out the average radial force on the moon due to the sun, assuming this radial force to be to the earth's force as 1 to $178\ ^{29}/_{40}$, hence double its true value. In the second edition, in further attempted refinements, Newton essayed to derive a value for surface gravity accurate to ninths of a Paris line (1 ligne = 2.256 mm). A recent commentator (Aoki) has described the effort as "something like building a castle in the air."

In III.5, generalizing from the case of the moon, Newton identifies the force on the circumjovial satellites toward Jupiter, that on the circumsaturnal satellites toward Saturn, and that on the circumsolar planets toward the sun, as gravity. **Venus**, **Mercury**, and **Mars**, being presumably bodies of the same sort, must be endowed with the same gravitational attraction (Cor. 1). Also by Cor. 1, "Since all attraction is mutual," Jupiter must gravitate toward its satellites, Saturn toward its satellites, the earth toward the moon, and the sun toward the circumsolar planets. This claim assumes the bodies to be acting on each other in the sense of Newton's law of action and reaction (Law III of motion)—which would not necessarily be so under an aethereal model of gravitational action.

By III.6, the weights of bodies toward any one planet at equal distances from its center are proportional to the quantities of matter the bodies contain. The primary confirmation is a terrestrial experiment (essentially the Eötvös experiment), in which Newton compares the periods of pendulums of the same lengths and with bobs of the same weight but of different materials; the outcome showed that, to within one part in a thousand, mass was proportional to weight. Most aethereal theories of gravity (including one that Newton had presented to the Royal Society in 1675; *Correspondence* I, 362ff) thereby became untenable.

III.7 invokes I.69 to show that the gravitational force is proportional to the mass of the attracting body as well as to that of the attracted body. This conclusion, like Cor. 1 of III.5, depends crucially on the assumption that the bodies are interacting in the sense of Newton's law of action and reaction.

In III.8 Newton uses I.75 and I.76 to establish that two spheres with mass distributed symmetrically about their centers attract with a force inversely proportional to the square of the distance between these centers. This result legitimates treating the planets as point-masses in reckoning their mutual attractions.

In the corollaries to III.8, Newton proceeds to compute the relative masses of the sun and the planets with known satellites, Jupiter, Saturn, and the earth; he finds them to be (in the third edition, here differing considerably from the earlier editions) as 1, $^1/_{1067}$, $^1/_{3021}$, $^1/_{169282}$, respectively; the last three numbers being in error by 1.8, 15.8, and 96.8 percent. The large error in the case of the earth's mass came from an excessive value for solar parallax. Newton's numbers for the masses of Jupiter and Saturn would figure in attempted calculations of perturbative effects until

Pierre-Simon Laplace revised them in the 1780s.

We have now entered the second phase of Newton's enterprise, the deduction of consequences from the principle of universal gravitation, taken as established. III.13 asserts the ellipticity of the planetary orbits—Kepler having, in Newton's view, "known ye Orb to be not circular but oval & guest it to be Elliptical" (letter to Halley of June 1686; *Correspondence* II, 436). But has Newton proved that the inverse-square law implies closed planetary orbits to be elliptical? In Props. 11, 12, and 13 of Bk. I he shows that conic-section orbits with center of force at a focus imply an inverse-square law; in Corollary 1 of Prop. 13 he asserts the converse. In the *Principia*'s second edition (1713) he gave a sketch for a proof of this converse, assuming that for given initial conditions of position and velocity, force-law, and strength of central force, one and only one orbit is possible.

Universal gravitation implies that the motions of the planets must be perturbed by their mutual attractions, and Newton recognized that the effects—oscillations in the eccentricity, aphelion, and mean motion—would be noticeable in the case of Saturn; but he did not succeed in finding how to compute these inequalities. Success here would depend on **Leonhard Euler**'s introduction (in 1748) of trigonometric series, and on Laplace's discovery (in 1785) that terms proportional to the squares and higher powers of the eccentricities were sizable.

As for the lunar inequalities, Newton showed (in I.66 and III.22) that universal gravitation implied those known in Antiquity as well as those discovered by **Tycho Brahe**. The second inequality, treated as menstrual from **Ptolemy** to Kepler, had been reformulated as a semiannual oscillation in the eccentricity and apse by Jeremiah Horrocks, and it is the inequality in this form that Newton accounted for qualitatively (I.66, Cors. 8 and 9). He obtained a good estimate of the annual regression of the moon's node (III.32), but none for the advance of the moon's apse: **Alexis-Claude Clairaut** in his *Théorie de la lune* (1752) would show that a good value depends on computing terms proportional to the square of the perturbing force. In seeking an accurate predictive theory of the moon (*Theory of the Moon's Motion*, 1702), Newton fitted up Horrocks's theory with new numerical parameters, incorporated annual oscillations in the motions of the apse and node, and added some small inequalities that may have been derived from observation alone; the errors in the resulting theory were found to go as high as 8 or 9 arcseconds, too large to permit determining the longitude at sea to within 1 degree.

Newton was the first to announce the true cause of the precession of the equinoxes, namely the attraction exercized by the moon and sun on the earth's equatorial bulge (I.66, Cor. 20). His attempt to derive this effect quantitatively (III.39), however, is deeply flawed, primarily for lack of a dynamics of rotational motion; the first essentially correct derivation is attributed to Jean le Rond d'Alembert in 1749.

Newton's attempts to account gravitationally for the shape of the earth (III.19), the libration of the moon (III.38), and the tides (III.24), although leaving much to be desired, provided the starting-points for the important later investigations of these problems—by Clairaut, **Joseph Louis Lagrange**, and Laplace, respectively.

Beginning in autumn 1684, Newton had been hoping that a major confirmation of his theory would be its application to cometary motions, generally assumed since Kepler to be rectilinear or but slightly inflected. After many fruitless efforts, in late 1686 or early 1687 he discovered a graphical method of fitting a parabolic orbit to observations, and applied this to the comet of 1680 (III.41). Halley determined the parabolic elements of twenty-four comets and predicted the return in 1758 or 1759 of the comet that would bear his name from its apparitions in 1531, 1607, and 1682; Clairaut in 1758–1759 was able to show that perturbations due to Jupiter and Saturn nearly accounted for the delay in the return. Halley and Newton were mistaken, however, in supposing the comet of 1680 to be periodic with a period of 575 years (*Principia* III.41, second edition).

Curtis Wilson

Bibliography

Aoki, S. "The Moon-Test in Newton's *Principia*: Accuracy of the Inverse-Square Law of Universal Gravitation." *Archive for History of Exact Sciences* 25 (1992): 147–190.

Cohen, I.B. *Isaac Newton's Theory of the Moon's Motions (1702)*. Folkestone: Dawson and Sons, 1975.

Dobbs, B.J.T. *The Janus Faces of Genius: The Role of Alchemy in Newton's Thought.* New York: Cambridge University Press, 1991.

Koyré, A., and I.B. Cohen. *Isaac Newton's*

Philosophiae Naturalis Principia Mathematica. 2 vols. Cambridge: Cambridge University Press, 1972.

Pourciau, B.H. "On Newton's Proof that Inverse-Square Orbits Must Be Conics." *Annals of Science* 48 (1991): 159–172.

Turnbull, H.W., ed. *The Correspondence of Isaac Newton*. 2 vols. Cambridge: Cambridge University Press, 1959, 1960.

Whiteside, D.T. "Newton's Early Thoughts on Planetary Motion: A Fresh Look." *British Journal for the History of Science* 2 (1964): 117–129.

———. "Before the *Principia*: The Maturing of Newton's Thoughts on Dynamical Astronomy, 1664–1684." *Journal for the History of Astronomy* 1 (1970): 5–19.

———, ed. *The Mathematical Papers of Isaac Newton* 6: 1684–1691. Cambridge: Cambridge University Press, 1974.

Wilson, C. "From Kepler's Laws, So-called, to Universal Gravitation: Empirical Factors." *Archive for History of Exact Sciences* 6 (1970): 89–170.

Novae and Supernovae

Novae and supernovae are stars or binary star systems that suddenly increase in magnitude, becoming million times brighter than the sun. They gradually fade over a period of weeks, months, or years. Novae and supernovae were once called new or temporary stars because people did not realize that these objects were faint stars before they exploded. Novae and supernovae provide astronomers with important information on stellar evolution.

Between 532 B.C.E. and 1604 C.E., Chinese astronomers recorded 581 novae. In most cases these discoveries were probably comets (Hoffleit, 77). In the West there was little interest in such phenomena, partly due to the influence of the Aristotelian theory of the permanence of the celestial sphere, and partly due to a lack of observational skills (Clark and Stephenson, 5). This was the situation until the appearance of two bright novae—one in 1572 and the other in 1604. These objects were studied extensively by **Tycho Brahe**, and Brahe's onetime assistant **Johannes Kepler**.

Early discoveries of novae occurred by chance rather than through systematic searching. From 1600 to 1875, only twenty-two novae were recorded. But with the development of astronomical photography in the late nineteenth century and the use of systematic searches, 197 novae were discovered over the next hundred years (Hoffleit, 78). This number continues to grow. The fourth edition of the *General Catalogue of Variable Stars* (Kholopov 1985) and the Central Bureau of Astronomical Telegrams list 221 confirmed novae discovered between 1670 and 1993.

Early Theories of Novae

One of the earliest explanations of novae came from Tycho Brahe, who believed that the cosmic vapors of the Milky Way coalesced to become a luminous new star. Other hypotheses stated that a nova was the result of an intrinsically bright star moving toward, then away from, the earth or that the brightening of a star was due to magma seeping out through cracks in its surface. In 1713, Isaac Newton proposed that novae are burnt-out stars that brightened when impacted by comets. Many later theories suggested collisions with meteor streams, comets, asteroids, planets, and other stars (Hoffleit, 88).

With the advent of spectroscopy in the second half of the nineteenth century, new theories were developed. **William Huggins** and William Miller interpreted the bright hydrogen lines in the spectrum of the nova T Coronae Borealis in 1866 as due to an explosion and the chemical combustion of hydrogen in the star (Friedjung and Duerbeck, 375). Also, William H. Pickering found evidence in the spectra of the bright nova GK Persei (1901) that collision theories were not valid physical explanations of novae.

The first evidence that novae are not new stars but existing faint stars came in 1918 with nova V603 Aquilae, the brightest nova of the century. This star appeared as a faint object on photographic plates made thirty years earlier. Its spectra also showed an expanding shell of nebulosity indicating that material was blown out at very high velocities.

The initial event that led to the distinction between novae and supernovae was the discovery of a new star in the Andromeda nebula in 1885. The brightness of this new star equaled the apparent brightness of the nebula, and its spectrum was very different from that of other novae (Clerke, 89). In the years following, about a dozen new stars were discovered in other galaxies. In the 1920s, when astronomers realized that nebulae were distant galaxies, it became apparent that new stars observed in galaxies had extreme intrinsic brightness, thousands of times brighter than ordinary novae. In 1934, **Walter Baade** and **Fritz Zwicky**, pioneers in supernovae research, introduced the term supernovae for new stars with extreme intrinsic brightness. Zwicky's extensive extragalactic surveys provided insight into the nature and importance of supernovae.

A breakthrough in understanding the nature of novae came in 1954 when observations by Merle F. Walker indicated that the old nova DQ Hercules (1934) was a close binary system. More observational evidence of the binarity of novae enabled Robert P. Kraft to conclude in 1962 that close binarity is necessary for the nova phenomenon. Further observations and theoretical research eventually provided a clearer understanding of the structure of close binary components and the cause of the explosions.

The Nature and Importance of Supernovae and Novae

A supernova marks the violent end to the evolution of a massive star during which the star blows out as much as ten solar masses of material at very high speeds and radiates as much light as the sun does in a hundred million years. Brightness changes and spectroscopic observations indicate that there are two types of supernovae.

A Type I supernova has a uniform light curve and spectrum, does not show any hydrogen lines in its spectrum, and is believed to occur among old, halo stars of spiral and elliptical galaxies. Type I supernovae occur in close binary systems in which one of the components is a massive white dwarf, an earth-sized, compact star that explodes when it receives too much material from a companion.

A Type II supernova has a heterogenous light curve and spectrum, and occurs only in the arms of spiral galaxies. It is the result of the gravitational collapse of a massive star when its ability to produce nuclear reactions comes to an end. The star's core collapses and creates enormous energy in the form of shock waves that carry away material surrounding the core and leave a rapidly rotating massive object.

The discovery of a supernova (1987A) in the Large Magellanic Cloud led to the detection of gamma rays having the specific decay energy of radioactive cobalt nuclei. This finding confirmed the theory that supernovae create heavy elements (Filippenko, 34). In addition, the detection of neutrinos from supernova 1987A supported the theory that enormous energies are created through the supernova explosion. The 1987A supernova also showed that if a galaxy has a lower abundance of heavier elements, as in the case of the Large Magellanic Cloud, the progenitor of the supernova need not be a red supergiant. A massive not rich in heavy elements can evolve rapidly and explode while it is a blue supergiant.

As astronomers studied supernovae, they learned that nuclear reactions in supernova explosions cause the synthesis of elements heavier than iron, such as gold, silver, and uranium. Many of these elements are created during the supernova explosion by the addition of neutrons to iron nuclei. The supernova explosion distributes these heavy elements in the interstellar medium, providing raw materials for the formation for new stars. Expanding nebulosities, extended sources for radio emission, cosmic rays, gravitational radiation, pulsars, and most galactic X-ray sources are all remnants of these spectacular explosions.

Based on data from the Central Bureau of Astronomical Telegrams and the Palomar Supernova Search master list, during the period between 1604 and 1994, 222 supernovae reached 15th magnitude or brighter at maximum.

Supernovae explosions resemble the explosions of novae, but the scale is much greater. In a typical nova explosion the energy released is less than ten one-thousandths of a supernova. While a supernova explosion is a one-time event marking the final destruction of a massive star, a nova explosion is only a temporary departure from a star's normal evolutionary path.

By the 1970s astronomers agreed that novae are close binary systems made up of a white dwarf orbiting around a solar type star where the solar type star transfers material to the white dwarf. This material (mostly hydrogen) falls onto the white dwarf and, under its strong gravitational field, is compressed and heated until a thermonuclear reaction is triggered that produces the explosive ejection of matter.

With space-based observatories, astronomers have observed novae across the spectrum, from gamma to radio wavelengths. Observations from ultraviolet and X-ray satellites help astronomers fix the distance of the nova and identify the characteristics of the explosion and the composition of ejected material. Observations from space also have shown that some novae are weak sources of energetic X-rays. The source of these X-rays has not yet been fully explained.

Observations in the longer wavelengths, such as the infrared, have helped in understanding the ejected material and the formation of dust particles in the ejected material. Images of Nova Cygni 1992 obtained with the **Hubble Space Telescope** reveal that the ejected material is not uniform, but clumpy.

More than any other astronomical phenomenon, novae and supernovae provide clues to help astronomers understand stellar evolution, especially the birth and death of stars, mass exchange in binary systems, stellar atmospheres, the ejection of mass, remnants such as pulsars and neutron stars, and the structure of the Milky Way and other galaxies.

Janet A. Mattei

Bibliography

Clark, D.H., and F.R. Stephenson. *The Historical Supernovae*. New York: Pergamon Press, 1977.

Clerke, A.M. *The Systems of Stars*. London: Adam and Charles Black, 1905.

Filippenko, A.V. "A Supernova with an Identity Crisis." *Sky & Telescope* (December 1993): 30.

Friedjung, M., and H. Duerbeck. "Models of Classical and Recurrent Novae." In *Cataclysmic Variables and Related Objects*, edited by M. Hack and C. la Dous, 371–412. Washington, D.C.: NASA Scientific and Technical Information Branch, 1993.

Hack, M., et al. "Classical Novae and Recurrent Novae—General Properties." In *Cataclysmic Variables and Related Objects*, edited by M. Hack and C. la Dous, 261–369. Washington, D.C.: NASA Scientific and Technical Information Branch, 1993.

———. "Typical Examples of Classical Novae." In *Cataclysmic Variables and Related Objects*, edited by M. Hack and C. la Dous, 413–510. Washington, D.C.: NASA Scientific and Technical Information Branch, 1993.

Hoffleit, D. "A History of Variable Star Astronomy to 1900 and Slightly beyond." *The Journal of the American Association of Variable Star Observers: 75th Anniversary Edition* 15 (1986): 77–106.

Kholopov, P.N., et al. *General Catalogue of Variable Stars*, 4th ed. Moscow: Nauka Publishing House, 1985.

Payne-Gaposchkin, C. *The Galactic Novae*. New York: Dover Publications, 1964.

Starrfield, S. and S. Shore. "Nova Cygni 1992: Nova of the Century." *Sky & Telescope* (February 1994): 20.

Trimble, V. "Supernovae: An Impressionistic View." *The Journal of the American Association of Variable Star Observers: 75th Anniversary Edition* 15 (1986): 181–188.

Numerov, Boris Vasil'evich (1891–1941)

Soviet astronomer. A graduate of Petersburg University, Numerov worked as an astronomer at **Pulkovo Observatory** (1913–1915) before founding the Computing Institute in 1919. He directed the Computing Institute, which in 1923 expanded to become the Leningrad Astronomical Institute, through 1936. Arrested in 1936 during the Great Purges, Numerov was executed in 1941.

Numerov was the most important Soviet specialist in applied **celestial mechanics** prior to World War II. Under his guidance the Astronomical Institute, since renamed the Institute of Theoretical Astronomy, became a leading center for celestial mechanics. He was also active in **astrometry** and proposed a method to use minor planet observations in determining the equator and equinox for star catalogues. In addition, Numerov helped identify Soviet ore and oil deposits using a pendulum gravimeter and other devices developed under his guidance.

Robert A. McCutcheon

Bibliography

Kulikovsky, P.G. "Numerov, Boris Vasil'evich." In *Dictionary of Scientific Biography*, edited by C.C. Gillispie, vol. 10, 158–160. New York: Scribner, 1981.

Numerova, A.B. *Boris Vasil'evich Numerov, 1891–1941*. Leningrad: Nauka, 1983.

Observatories

An astronomical observatory is a place where observations of celestial bodies are regularly made. The following discussion focuses on the changing form and function of observatories from the second half of the sixteenth century, with an emphasis on ground-based institutions. Today there are also space-based observatories.

A discussion of the changing form and function of observatories includes the development of telescopes, the buildings in which they are housed, their location, the scientific programs carried out at observatories, and some thoughts on what motivates various research programs.

The sixteenth-century astronomical observatory of **Tycho Brahe**, Uraniborg (Castle of the Heavens), was the first scientific research institution in postclassical Europe. It was built between 1576 and 1580 on the 2,000-acre island of Hven in the Danish sound between Copenhagen and Elsinore. The castle was a multistory wooden edifice 60 (Tychonian) feet on a side and 75 feet high, with a basement twelve feet deep. Tycho and his assistants observed with equatorial **armillaries, quadrants**, and parallactic instruments on balconies and in towers with folding pyramidal roofs (see Krisciunas, 1988, 49, for list of instruments). The southwest room contained a brass **mural quadrant** of 2.0 meters radius that had the remarkable resolution of 10 arcseconds. Thanks to generous royal patronage, Tycho's instruments were the most accurate ever constructed. Prior to Tycho, the best stellar and planetary positions had been accurate to 10 arcminutes, but Tycho was able to achieve positions to better than 1 arcminute. This was a full generation before Galileo's first use of a telescope for astronomical observations.

Having filled up Uraniborg, Tycho added an auxiliary site called Stjerneborg that housed five instruments of iron or brass, each situated in a half-sunken crypt (see Krisciunas, 1988, 53, for list of instruments). Two of these crypts were equipped with rotatable domes.

Tycho's goal was nothing less than a complete overhaul of **astrometry**—determining the positions of the naked eye stars with unprecedented accuracy and refining the ephemerides of the sun, moon, and planets without relying on the results of previous (mostly ancient Greek) astronomers. Tycho's *Astronomiae instauratae progymnasmata* (*Introductory Exercises Toward a Restored Astronomy*), published posthumously in 1602, contained his observations of the supernova of 1572, his innovative lunar and solar theories, and a catalogue of 777 stars. Because of his failure to detect **stellar parallaxes**, he concluded that the earth was stationary. Tycho believed that the planets orbited the sun, which in turn orbited the earth.

At the entrance to Stjerneborg, Tycho had engraved his motto: "Neither wealth nor power, but only knowledge, alone, endures" (Thoren, 184). In his pursuit of precise data Tycho relied on careful observational methods such as independent observations by two observers working with similar instruments. Using concepts to be developed later, he considered sources of systematic and random errors.

Part of Tycho's motivation lay in the ancient Hermetic tradition of wresting secrets from the world for near mystical purposes. In

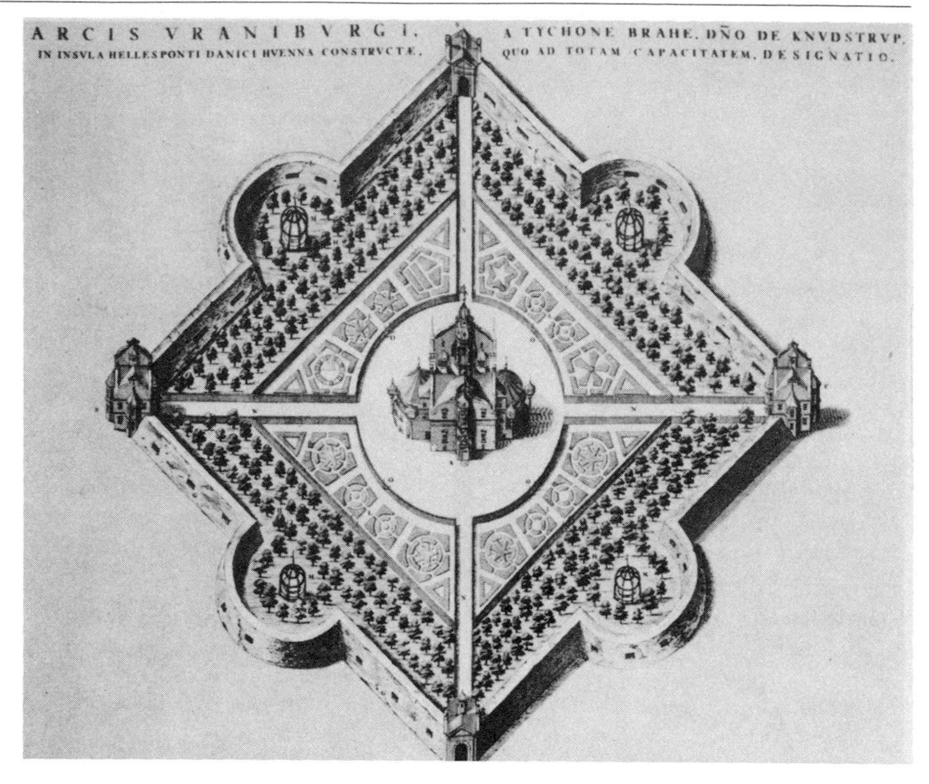

Tycho Brahe's observatory-castle, Uraniborg, was completed in 1580 on the island of Hven. Here we see the main building and its surrounding grounds, walls, and guard towers. Original from Tycho Brahe, Astronomiae instauratae mecanica, *Wandsbeck, 1598. (Courtesy of Kevin Krisciunas)*

his twenties and thirties Tycho pursued alchemical experiments, and the basement at Uraniborg contained such a laboratory. "There can be no doubt that he was influenced by the writings of Paracelsus" (Hannaway, 597). A principal hermetical concept was the belief that whatever ruled the heavens must also influence things on (or under) the earth. Tycho's description of his instruments and observatory (*Astronomiae instauratae mechanica*. Wandsbeck, 1598; Nuremberg, 1602) contains an engraving showing a godlike figure leaning on a globe with a pair of compasses in his hand. His gaze is directed skyward. It is labeled with the motto *suspiciendo despicio* ("In looking up, I look down"). A corresponding engraving shows the godlike figure holding some herbs and the snake of Aesculapius, the Greek god of medicine. There is also a view of underground furnaces and chemical apparatus. It is labeled with the motto *despiciendo suspicio* ("In looking down, I look up"). Tycho, who referred to chemistry as "terrestrial astronomy" (Hannaway, 597–598), had one foot planted in empirical science and the other in the Hermetic tradition.

In spite of Tycho's mystical leanings, he broke with the Hermetic tradition in one significant way: His work was not kept secret. While the castle on Hven rapidly fell into a state of disrepair after his departure in 1597, the observational material and the written descriptions Tycho left of his instruments and methods of work were of such significance that "the organization of every modern observatory derives from Uraniborg" (Sarton, 64).

By the time academies such as the Accademia dei Lincei (Rome, 1603), the Royal Society (London, 1662), and the Academie des Sciences (Paris, 1666) were founded, scientific research was undertaken for two reasons: pure intellectual curiosity, or reasons of state. The wealth of nations depended on commerce. Reliable means of navigating the seas were critical. The most important challenge to astronomers was determining longitude at sea, which depended on accurate lunar, planetary, and stellar positions and on the development of accurate timekeeping devices.

The **Royal Greenwich Observatory** was founded in 1675, primarily for the purpose of determining longitude. The first Astronomer Royal, **John Flamsteed**, and his assistants made many positional measures of the moon and planets, and by the time Flamsteed died they had produced a catalogue of 2,935 stars, accurate to about 10 arcseconds. The improvement over Tycho was entirely due to the use of telescopic sights.

Astronomers at the **Paris Observatory** (built ca. 1667–1682) were similarly motivated by the pursuit of accurate determinations of longitude. They also began various geodetic surveys. In addition to these practical matters, the French astronomers were avid observers of the planets and planetary satellites using extremely long focus telescopes.

Astrometry reached its zenith in the nineteenth century at the **Pulkovo Observatory** near St. Petersburg and at the **U.S. Naval Observatory** (completed in 1844). Like Tycho, Pulkovo astronomers endeavored to eliminate sources of systematic error in their observations. This involved new determinations of the fundamental constants of nutation, precession, and aberration, made with unrivaled accuracy. By the end of the nineteenth century, astronomers were able to produce ephemerides of the sun, moon, and planets and planetary satellites with an accuracy far beyond that required for practical navigation or timekeeping purposes.

The nineteenth century observatory contained one or more transit circles for astrometric research plus one or more visual refracting telescopes used to measure the positions of double stars, planetary satellites, comets, and asteroids. These observatories also housed extremely accurate clocks, keeping both solar and sidereal time. These precision instruments were often located in constant-temperature vaults that also protected the instruments from the effects of dust and humidity. Meteorological and geophysical instrumentation was also found in nineteenth-century observatories. Research in these areas was not, however, of primary concern to most astronomers. Most observatories provided space for offices and a library. A few also included living quarters for the director.

"Historians look at the forerunners of astrophysics and great discoverers, not at the men who spend their evenings in this very fundamental, very basic work [positional astronomy]" (Rothenberg, 32). Indeed, by the early nineteenth century astronomy was undergoing a major transition. Positional astronomy was the province of nationally funded observatories such as Greenwich, Pulkovo, and the U.S. Naval Observatory, while private observatories were making noteworthy advances in completely new fields of astronomical investigation.

In the late eighteenth and early nineteenth centuries, **William Herschel** and his son John carried out the first full-sky telescopic surveys of the heavens using telescopes as large as 20 inches in diameter. They discovered thousands of double stars and nebulae. William Herschel's most significant technical contribution was the development of large reflecting telescopes. The bigger the telescope mirror, the more light it collects. Faint (presumably very distant) objects become visible in larger telescopes. One of Herschel's goals (and herein lies his great theoretical contribution) was the search for evidence of evolution of the celestial bodies. William Herschel demonstrated that the fixed stars were not fixed at all. He showed, for example, that the components of a double star orbited the center of mass and that the sun and planets were moving toward a point in the constellation Hercules. Herschel also realized that he could investigate the evolution of nebulae

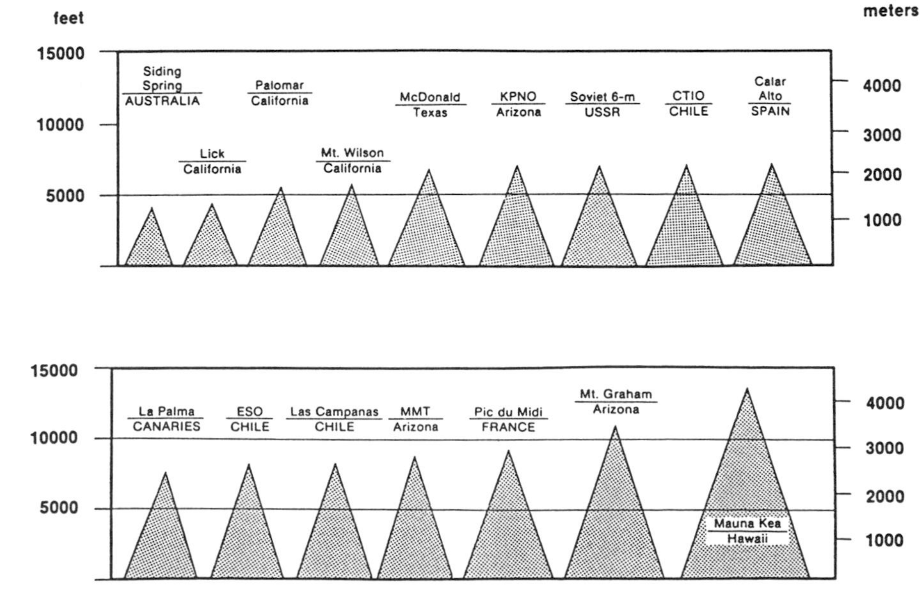

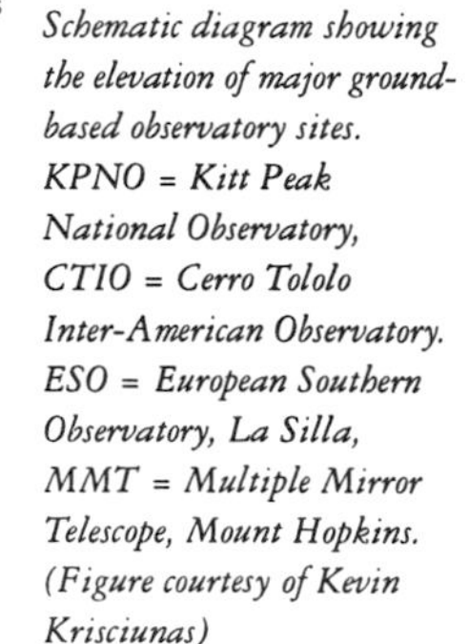
Schematic diagram showing the elevation of major ground-based observatory sites. KPNO = Kitt Peak National Observatory, CTIO = Cerro Tololo Inter-American Observatory. ESO = European Southern Observatory, La Silla, MMT = Multiple Mirror Telescope, Mount Hopkins. (Figure courtesy of Kevin Krisciunas)

by cataloguing their shapes and assuming that they represented different states of development, even though the evolution of an individual nebula was too slow to be noticed on human time scales.

In the nineteenth century, amateur astronomers built observatories and often equipped them with new forms of instrumentation. From these observatories frequently came important observational data. Astrophysics first developed in these institutions. National observatories like Greenwich, Paris, or the U.S. Naval Observatory were too busy with routine programs in astrometry to be concerned with a totally new research agenda.

"Before the nineteenth century only about three dozen important observatories existed. A century later there were more than 200, along with a large number of smaller stations, some of which only existed for a short time" (Herrmann, 179). Along with exponential growth in the number of observatories, which has continued almost unabated to the present day, came a consideration of where the telescopes would best be located.

Most observatories have been situated for convenient access, independent of site quality. Dunsink Observatory (established in 1785 near Dublin) was one of the first noteworthy exceptions. It was located far from sources of light and air pollution. In addition, it was the first observatory with a rotating hemispherical dome and a telescope mounting isolated from the rest of the building in order to reduce unwanted vibrations.

But this was only the beginning. In the *Opticks* (1704), Isaac Newton noted that to find "serene and quite air" one must go to a mountain top "to take away that confusion of rays which arises from tremors in the atmosphere." The first extensive astronomical observations from a mountain were carried out by the Scottish Astronomer Royal, Charles Piazzi Smyth, who in 1856 went to Tenerife in the Canary Islands and spent six months making astronomical and meteorological observations. The world's first permanent mountaintop observatory was established at Mount Hamilton, California (elevation 4,200 feet/1,280 meters), in 1888. Harvard astronomers opened a station in Arequipa, Peru (elevation 8,055 feet/2,455 meters), in 1889.

Following the research of Gustav Kirchhoff and Robert Bunsen, which put spectroscopy on a firm empirical foundation, it became possible to investigate the chemical composition and physical condition of stars and nebulae and their motions in the line of sight. With the development of dry photographic emulsions (1874) by the Englishman William Abney, the work of astronomers underwent a dramatic change. It became possible to build an astronomical data base of photographic plates. Long-exposure photographs replaced visual observations except in measuring the positions and separation of double stars and the study of planetary surfaces, where the observer waits for fleeting moments of good seeing.

After the success of the Crossley 36-inch reflector at Lick, and the 60-inch and 100-inch reflectors at Mount Wilson (elevation 5,700 feet/1,737 meters), reflectors supplanted the long-focus refractor as the instrument of choice for astronomers. At about the same time, **astrophysics** (the study of the physical state and evolution of celestial bodies) supplanted astrometry as the principal activity of astronomers.

Astrophysical observatories were generally equipped with one or more large reflecting telescopes. These were used for spectrographic investigations of the sun and stars as well as nebulae and star clusters. Astrophysical observatories also contained optical and machine shops that kept the instruments in order and permitted the construction of auxiliary instrumentation on site. Sometimes new telescopes were constructed in these shops as well.

In addition to astronomers, optical craftsmen, and machinists, the workforce at astrophysical observatories (especially in the United States) included a corps of assistants (generally women known as computers) who measured spectrograms and photometric plates and reduced the data. In the United States, astrophysical observatories were organized as knowledge factories. Data were acquired wholesale by photography and then reduced by semiskilled workers on an assembly line basis. These factory observatories were among the first twentieth-century Big Science institutions.

A comparison of conditions at the **Potsdam Astrophysical Observatory** (founded in 1876) and the **Yerkes Observatory** (opened in 1897) suggests interesting national differences. At Potsdam the inside of the dome housing the dual refractor (one objective was figured for visual observations and the other for photography) appears well appointed and decorated with curtains and valances as well as comfortable chairs, as if awaiting a state visit from the Kaiser or at least the rector of the University of Berlin. No auxiliary equipment is in sight; the polished hardwood floor is uncluttered. The dome is pierced by windows, an interesting architectural addition but one that implies the predominance of aesthetic over engineering considerations. At Yerkes bare brick walls, inexpensive chairs, and a small table suggest spartan simplicity. On the floor we see an observing ladder and two spectroscopes on their stands. This is a scientific institution American-style. Funds were spent on equipment and instruments, not on interior decorations.

Today the major national and international facilities are all situated on remote mountaintops, typically at elevations of about 7,500 feet (2,300 meters). The major exception is Mauna Kea in Hawaii (elevation 13,800 feet/4,205 meters). At such an altitude the water vapor content in the atmosphere is significantly diminished, allowing observations at infrared and submillimeter wavelengths that would be difficult or impossible at lower elevations. At most radio wavelengths the atmosphere is sufficiently transparent that radio telescopes may be situated at sea level.

Radio astronomy is a major branch of ground-based astronomical research. As with optical astronomy, radio astronomy facilities progressed from observatories that could be built by individual institutions such as universities to national facilities such as the National Radio Astronomy Observatory in Greenbank, West Virginia, or the Very Large Array in Socorro, New Mexico. Because radio telescopes can be linked over intercontinental baselines for very long baseline interferometry, radio astronomy research has involved international collaboration since the 1960s. The signals of radio telescopes situated thousands of miles apart can be combined to achieve a resolution of one milliarcsecond or better—the best of any branch of astronomy.

Astronomy is a technology-intensive science, expensive enough to justify careful archiving of data obtained with large and expensive instruments. When Pulkovo Observatory was the astronomical capital of the world and positional astronomy was at its peak of importance, observatory publications might contain every observation and the steps involved to reduce observations to their final values. As projects became larger, that became impractical.

Photography provided the means of obtaining and storing massive quantities of data. For example, in the Harvard College Observatory plate vault there are approximately 500,000 photographs taken since 1885, covering most of the sky. These plates are used for the study of variable stars. Also in the Harvard archives are all the objective prism spectrograms that went into the **Henry Draper Catalogue** (225,300 stars) and the Henry Draper Extension (47,000 stars). The plate vaults at Mount Wilson and Mount Palomar contain plates taken with the 60-inch and 100-inch telescopes at Mount Wilson, the Palomar 60-inch and 200-inch telescopes, and the Palomar Schmidt telescopes, as well as plates taken at Las Campanas, Chile.

Plates are no longer scanned by eye, but by a computerized measuring device. Because there is so much information on an individual plate (sometimes covering 6 by 6 degrees to a limit of 22nd magnitude), once an astronomer is done analyzing the numbers, shapes, sizes, and magnitudes of the objects under study, the scanned information is not stored. The most efficient way to store the data is on the original plate. It is much more economical to throw it away and scan the plate again later if necessary.

During the 1970s and 1980s, astronomical data acquisition became automated. In the past an astronomer had to sit in the dome looking through the guide telescope to make sure the large telescope remained centered on the object being photographed. The proper exposure involved a certain amount of guesswork. Today astronomers observe from a control room that is lighted and heated. Guiding is computer controlled. Optical and infrared instruments now use solid-state arrays, the output of which must be computer readable. Such arrays are often cryogenically cooled with liquid nitrogen to reduce electronic noise. These instruments are like a Thermos bottle but contain light-sensing elements, motors, mirrors, lenses, and gratings. By the mid-1990s an optical array might contain a chip with 8,192 by 8,192 picture elements (pixels) and be used to image a relatively large area of the sky. Infrared arrays are presently no bigger than 1,024 by 1,024 pixels in size.

Photographic plates obtained at an observatory officially belonged to the observatory, though the astronomer that took them might have kept them for a number of years. Once data were being stored at the telescope on magnetic media (tapes and floppy disks), it became difficult to keep track of. Today, many ground-based observatories have computer-readable data archives, but because of the ever more sensitive instruments (which render old observations somewhat unimportant) and the difficulty in reading old magnetic media, it can be argued that the most important data archive for most modern research happens to be the research journals. Thanks in part to standardized data reduction packages and the means by which data can be transferred in standard formats, astronomers may discuss the implications of the data in the literature without having to go into the details of the reduction procedures. State-of-the-art data archives also exist for astronomical satellites such as the *International Ultraviolet Explorer* and the Hubble Space Telescope.

Another way in which ground-based observatories are trying to emulate satellite operations involves remote observing. Satellites, of course, must operate this way, and it is very expensive. Communications networks have made it possible to take data comparatively inexpensively with a telescope situated on a mountaintop thousands of miles away, but this method of operation has not yet been fully implemented for any ground-based telescope. Presently, the closest thing to remote operation would be robotic telescopes, which are programmed to sense if it is raining or cloudy, and, if it is not, to open the dome and execute a prescribed series of observations. Some robotic telescopes have been operating since the early 1980s.

Mention should also be made of procedures required for astronomers to obtain access to a major astronomical research facility. An astronomer writes a proposal, justifying the science to be done and the number of nights on a given telescope needed to complete the project. Proposals are submitted to a telescope time committee. At most research observatories the time committee meets twice a year. For a major telescope the sum of all nights requested by applicants usually amounts to three times the number of nights in a year, so only about one-third are approved. Given that there are about four hundred large professional telescopes in the world and forty thousand scientists publishing some form of astronomical research, the competition for access to the best telescopes can be fierce. One serious drawback to this method of competing for telescope time is that long-term projects such as monitoring variable stars and quasars cannot be done at major professional facilities. As a result, there is still a role for the amateur to play in astronomy. It requires hundreds of dedicated amateurs to monitor thousands of variable stars. Amateurs often alert professionals to changes in variable stars so that professionals may train large telescopes on them. Amateurs are also active in discovering novae.

Finally, a major component of modern scientific research is the ever-shortening time scale for the dissemination of results. With reliable computer networks it is possible to write up exciting new observations in a matter of days, submit a paper to a journal to be refereed, and post a preliminary version of the paper on a computer bulletin board that automatically distributes the abstract to thousands of researchers, who may then retrieve the full paper and the associated graphics. In Tycho's day the time scale for judging the impact of one's work might have been decades. Nowadays it can be as short as one week.

Kevin Krisciunas

Bibliography

Dreyer, J.L.E. *Tycho Brahe: A Picture of Scientific Life and Work in the Sixteenth Century*. Edinburgh: Adam and Charles Black, 1890.

Hannaway, O. "Laboratory Design and the Aim of Science: Andreas Libavius versus Tycho Brahe." *Isis* 77 (1986): 584–610.

Herrmann, D.B. *The History of Astronomy from Herschel to Hertzsprung*. Cambridge: Cambridge University Press, 1984.

Howse, D. "The Greenwich List of Observatories: A World List of Astronomical Observatories, Instruments, and Clocks, 1670–1850." *Journal for the History of Astronomy* 17 (1986): i-iv, 1–100.

Krisciunas, K. *Astronomical Centers of the World*. Cambridge: Cambridge University Press, 1988.

———. "Pulkovo Observatory's Status in 19th Century Positional Astronomy." In IAU Symposium No. 141, *Inertial Coordinate System on the Sky*, edited by J.H. Lieske and V.K. Abalakin, 15–24. Dordrecht: Kluwer, 1990.

Lankford, J. "Amateurs and Astrophysics: A Neglected Aspect in the Development of a Scientific Specialty." *Social Studies of Science* 11 (1981): 275–303.

———. "The Impact of Astronomical Photography to 1920." In *Astrophysics and Twentieth-Century Astronomy to 1950,* edited by O. Gingerich, 4A, 16–39. Cambridge: Cambridge University Press, 1984.

———. "Women and Women's Work at Mt. Wilson Observatory before World War II." In *The Earth, the Heavens and the Carnegie Institution of Washington*, edited by G. Good, 125–127. *History of Geophysics* 5. Washington, D.C.: American Geophysical Union, 1994.

Lankford, J., and R.L. Slavings, "The Industrialization of American Astronomy, 1880–1940." *Physics Today* 49 (1996): 34–40.

Mueller, P. *Sternwarten in Bildern: Architektur und Geschichte der Sternwarten von den Anfangen vis. ca. 1950.* Berlin: Springer, 1992.

Rothenberg, M. "Observers and Theoreticians: Astronomy at the Naval Observatory, 1845–1861." In *Sky with Ocean Joined*, edited by S.J. Dick and L.E. Doggett, 29–43. Washington, D.C.: U.S. Naval Observatory, 1983.

Sarton, G. *Six Wings: Men of Science in the Renaissance.* Bloomington and London: Indiana University Press, 1957.

Thoren, V.E. *The Lord of Uraniborg.* Cambridge: Cambridge University Press, 1990.

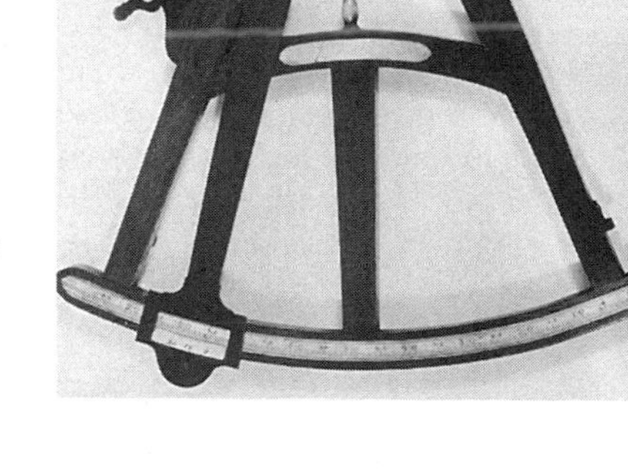

Octant. English, ca. 1770 (A-55). (Courtesy of the Adler Planetarium, Chicago, Illinois)

Octant

The octant—also known as Hadley's quadrant—was so named because its scale was calibrated for 90 degrees over an arc of 45 degrees. It was a reflecting instrument in which a mirror was used to bring the image of a target object (such as a star) into apparent coincidence with another (such as the horizon). The mirror was mounted at the pivot point of an index arm, whose lower portion slid over a degree scale. To measure a star's altitude, one viewed the horizon through a pin-hole sight and the clear portion of a half-silvered horizon glass. By adjusting the index arm, one "brought the star down to the horizon"—that is, caused the star's image to be reflected by the index mirror to the horizon glass. The angle between the mirror and glass was half of that between the star and the horizon. The angular separation was read off the octant's limb.

Because of its design, the octant was more accurate than the **cross-staff** and much easier to use on board a rocking ship. Reflecting instruments had first been discussed in the seventeenth century by Robert Hooke and **Isaac Newton**, and proposals for nautical quadrants were made independently by Thomas Godfrey of Philadelphia and John Hadley of London in the early eighteenth century. Hadley's design was widely adopted by the 1750s, and wooden octants were produced until the end of the nineteenth century.

At sea, the octant was used to measure altitudes and lunar distances of stars in order to find latitude and longitude respectively (although the sextant became the tool of choice for the lunar-distance method of longitude determination by the late eighteenth century). On land, it was used to measure the distances between fixed stars and comets by those who either desired portable apparatus or could not afford fixed instruments.

Sara Schechner Genuth

Bibliography

Bennett, J.A. *The Divided Circle: A History of Instruments for Astronomy, Navigation and Surveying.* Oxford: Phaidon-Christie's, 1987.

Cotter, C.H. *A History of the Navigator's Sextant.* Glasgow: Brown, Son and Ferguson, 1983.

May, W.E. "Early Reflecting Instruments." *Nautical Magazine* 145 (1945): 21–26.

Olbers's Paradox

Formulated as Olbers's Paradox in Hermann Bondi's *Cosmology* (1952), the riddle of the dark night sky has long been of interest. The concept of an infinite universe, presumably filled with an infinite number of stars, led to the intriguing question of why the night sky was not ablaze with light. In the mid-1570s, Thomas Digges examined the riddle within the context of Copernican heliocentrism. Abandoning the concept of an outer sphere of fixed stars, Digges concluded that stars were dispersed throughout infinite space. The sky was dark, he argued, because the most distant stars were too faint to be seen. Unlike Digges, **Johannes Kepler** recognized that the dark night sky clashed with the idea of an infinite universe filled with stars. Advocating a finite, bounded universe, Kepler argued that observers who viewed the night sky looked out between the stars to the dark wall that enclosed the universe.

The infinite and star-filled Newtonian universe defined the parameters of the debate for most of the eighteenth and early nineteenth centuries. **Edmond Halley** attempted to explain the darkness of the night sky by suggesting that the decrease in luminosity with distance (according to the inverse-square relationship) was greater than the decrease in separation between stars with distance. He also described the universe in terms of stellar shells surrounding the observer. An infinite number of such shells, however, would not result in infinite brightness because light from the outer shells was intercepted by stars closer to the observer. Beyond a certain background limit, distant stars remained invisible.

The Swiss astronomer Jean-Philippe Loys de Chéseaux further developed the concept of the background limit. In a brief appendix to his 1744 work on comets, he argued that although there existed an infinite number of star-filled shells, those beyond a radius of 3,000 trillion light years contributed no additional light because they were hidden by a continuous background of visible stars. Having eliminated the possibility of infinite brightness, Chéseaux explained the darkness of the night sky by positing that the interstellar medium absorbed starlight. Nearly eighty years later, Wilhelm Olbers introduced the line-of-sight argument. From the observer's eye, a line will eventually intersect the surface of a star, whether or not stars are distributed uniformly. Realizing that the brightness of starlight would be cumulative to the background limit, Olbers explained the dark night sky by the same absorption phenomenon as Chéseaux, although Olbers apparently developed this explanation independently.

The absorption explanation, however, contained a serious flaw that was pointed out by **John Herschel** in 1848. Radiant heat from stars would heat the absorbing medium, which would eventually emit radiant heat itself. Herschel explained the dark night sky by arguing that observers look out between stars to the blackness of infinite extragalactic space. He also suggested a hierarchical structure of the universe, in which stars cluster to form galaxies, galaxies cluster to form groups of galaxies, and on toward even larger combinations. Such a structure would eliminate a continuous background and leave the dark areas visible at night.

Another key insight concerning the dark night sky also emerged during the nineteenth century. In his *Eureka: A Prose Poem* (1848), Edgar Allan Poe speculated that certain areas of the night sky were dark because the light from stars in those regions had not yet reached earth. Qualitatively grasping that looking deep into space was also looking back into time, Poe envisioned a period before the birth of stars. It remained for William Thomson, Lord Kelvin, to provide the quantitative explanation for the dark night sky. In a paper published in 1901, Kelvin made the crucial distinction between the physical universe and the visible universe. Because the universe was much less than 3,000 trillion years old, the transit time of light from the background limit was far greater than the lifetime of stars or of the universe. The visible universe would be much smaller than that required to create a bright sky.

Kelvin's explanation assumed a static universe, a concept that was supplanted by the expanding universe model within a few years. Advocating a steady-state expanding universe, in which matter was continuously created throughout space, Hermann Bondi explained Olbers's Paradox by emphasizing that light from distant galaxies was red-shifted to invisibility. The night sky would remain dark because the universe was expanding. As astronomer Edward Harrison stressed in the 1980s, however, Bondi's explanation required a steady-state universe. In an expanding, Big Bang universe, another solution to the dark night sky riddle is more convincing. Because the universe has a finite age of some fifteen billion years, a very small proportion of the night sky is covered with stars. There is insufficient energy in the universe to provide a bright, starlit sky, even if all the matter in the universe were annihilated to form energy. The age of the universe is the principal factor that solves the riddle of the dark night sky.

George E. Webb

Bibliography

Bondi, H. *Cosmology.* Cambridge: Cambridge University Press, 1952.

Harrison, E. "Kelvin on an Old, Celebrated Hypothesis." *Nature* 322 (1986): 417–418.

———. *Darkness at Night: A Riddle of the Universe.* Cambridge: Harvard University Press, 1987.

Jaki, S.L. *The Paradox of Olbers' Paradox.* New York: Herder and Herder, 1969.

———. *Olbers Studies: With Three Unpublished Manuscripts by Olbers.* Tucson: Pachart, 1991.

Oort, Jan Hendrik (1900–1992)

Dutch astronomer. Born in Franeker, Oort earned his doctorate in 1926 in astronomy at the University of Groningen under **J.C. Kapteyn** and Pieter van Rhijn. He received an appointment at the Leiden Observatory in 1924, where he remained until his retirement in 1970. He was also a professor at the University of Leiden from 1935. From 1958 to 1961, he served as president of the **International Astronomical Union**. In 1962, he was instrumental in the establishment of the **European Southern Observatory**.

During his lifetime Jan Oort was considered by many as the greatest living astronomer of the twentieth century. Although his contributions were many, three areas stand out. First, after the Swedish astronomer **Bertil Lindblad** proposed a complicated mathematical model for galactic rotation (1925), Oort developed an elegant mathematical understanding of this phenomenon (1927). Known as differential galactic rotation, the Lindblad-Oort model of galactic structure supported the big-galaxy proposed by **Harlow Shapley**. In order to account for the increased mass of the larger galaxy, the model assumed the existence of large quantities of invisible matter. Known as missing mass, this undetected matter constitutes 90 percent of the mass content of the universe and as a result explains the gravitational clustering of stars into galaxies. For the next two decades Oort continued to make fundamental contributions to theories of galactic structure. Second, in 1947, Oort realized that no hyperbolic cometary orbits had ever been established. Oort subsequently proposed the existence of a huge cloud of cometary nuclei surrounding the sun at about a distance of one light year. The source of comets has come to be known as the Oort Cloud. Finally, from the 1940s, many of Oort's astronomical contributions have been in the field of **radio astronomy**. In 1951 Oort confirmed the 1944 prediction of his student Henk van de Hulst by discovering the 21-cm hydrogen line. In 1956, the world's largest radio telescope was built by Oort and his colleagues in Holland.

E. Robert Paul

Bibliography

van Woerden, H., W.N. Brouw, and H.C. van de Hulst, eds., *Oort and the Universe: A Sketch of Oort's Research and Person*. Dordrecht: D. Reidel, 1980.

Optical Astronomy from Space

Optical astronomy refers to observations in the spectral region to which the human eye is sensitive, and for which earth's atmosphere provides a clear window. Bounded by the infrared and the ultraviolet, the optical region of the spectrum ranges from wavelengths of about 900 to 300 nanometers.

From at least the time of Newton, it was apparent to astronomers that the turbulent air above the best earthbound observing site limited the usefulness of telescopes. Even without the added capability of detecting other spectral ranges, high-altitude or space-observing platforms held allure just for the removal of atmospheric defects. In addition to introducing unwanted spectral absorption and emission lines, airglow and sky background limited the magnitudes of objects that could be recorded even by the largest telescopes, and turbulence prevented clear images of extended objects and focusing of stellar images on the apertures of photometers and spectrographs.

Before World War II, those engaged in experimental rocketry speculated on the advantages of astronomy from space and the types of observatories that might be placed in orbit or on the moon. After the war, captured V-2 rockets and their successors developed for scientific research were used as platforms for observations of the sun and brighter planets and stars. Because of the instability of early rockets and the problem of retrieving data, observations were limited to photometry or spectroscopy. Balloons offered a more stable platform for instrumentation but operated within the atmosphere. Piloted balloons were flown during the 1950s and 1960s with astronomers operating and guiding the instruments, but they achieved limited success. Automated balloon instruments such as the Stratoscope series, flown during the 1960s and 1970s, did accomplish high-resolution imaging of the sun and planets, as well as of other astronomical objects.

Only a small number of astronomers became involved in space astronomy. Some historians have suggested that the West Coast astronomers, their observing needs amply provided for under favorable skies by the Mount Wilson, Lick, and Palomar telescopes, were less open to the promise of space astronomy than their East Coast counterparts, who had to contend with aging equipment and light pollution. Some have seen a generational divide, with the younger and presumably freer individuals willing to take the risks of space astronomy. Whatever the reasons, American and European astronomers seemed uneasy about space astronomy (Smith, 46–47).

With the availability of large launch vehicles based on intercontinental ballistic missiles, and a willingness to create a large space

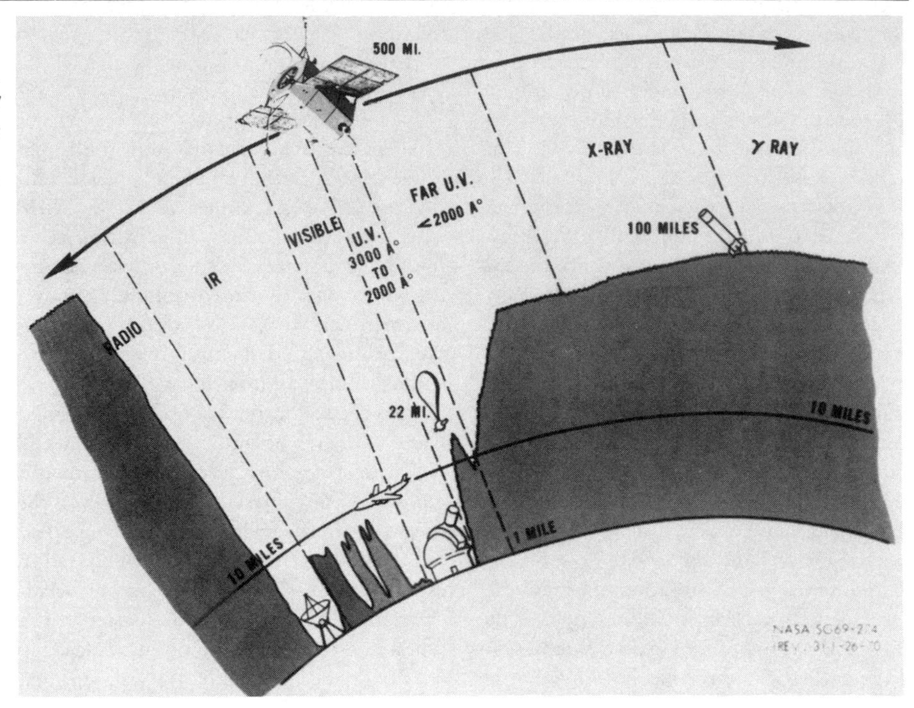

Earth's atmosphere acts as a filter. Only a small portion of the electromagnetic spectrum can penetrate to ground-based observatories. As the diagram suggests, the higher above earth's atmosphere one is able to locate an observing platform, the wider the spectral range that can be observed. (Courtesy of the National Aeronautics and Space Administration)

program in the aftermath of the Soviet satellite *Sputnik* in 1958, the way was open to optical astronomy from orbit. Lyman Spitzer, an astronomer at Princeton University, had written a report in 1946 for military patrons on the potential for astronomy from orbit. Since the report remained classified, it did not directly influence the development of space astronomy. Its author, however, became one of the more important leaders of the field.

The **National Aeronautics and Space Administration** (NASA) and its scientific advisors began to develop a space astronomy program almost immediately. Based on a common spacecraft outfitted for a succession of instruments, the *Orbiting Astronomical Observatory* (OAO) series was designed primarily for **ultraviolet astronomy**. In part, this was due to the rudimentary state of detector technology, which limited electronically transmittable data to measurements of point sources (that is, photometry or spectroscopy) or fairly low resolution images. Some consideration was given to physical retrieval of exposed film, either by astronauts or by remote control, but that was too problematic. Since the ultraviolet was an almost unexplored spectral range, it promised the most rapid rate of discovery. While space promised revelations in the ultraviolet, only incremental improvements could be expected in the optical, at least for the 1-meter class orbiting telescopes being planned for *OAO*.

However, a space-based optical telescope roughly comparable to the largest earth-based optical telescopes would be far more than an incremental advance. Beginning in the early 1970s, NASA undertook feasibility studies for a 3-meter general purpose observatory, the Large Space Telescope. Redesigned in response to budgetary pressures and delayed numerous times, the 2.4-meter **Hubble Space Telescope** (HST) was finally deployed from the space shuttle in 1990. The optical system was designed to span the spectral regions from near-infrared to far-ultraviolet, and the focal plane to accommodate a variety of instruments. With the large size of the primary mirror and its location above earth's atmosphere, the HST's diffraction-limited performance and large light grasp promised significant advances for optical astronomy. The telescope's first complement of instruments included two imaging cameras, two spectrographs, and a photometer.

Optical astronomy from space has been treated in a number of historical accounts. The best introduction to the historiography of the subject overall is Smith, which treats the Hubble Space Telescope in detail, but also within the broader context of space astronomy. DeVorkin (1992) discusses the use of V-2 and other rockets to loft instruments in part for ultraviolet spectroscopy, and DeVorkin deals with piloted and automated balloons as platforms for astronomy. Hevly discusses the Naval Research Laboratory's efforts during the 1940s and 1950s and is important for understanding the origins of the NASA program. Coyne is an early, limited effort covering the administrative history of NASA's efforts to establish an orbiting astronomical observatory program. Winter is the best source recounting the informed speculation of rocket pioneers on benefits for astronomy from space. Krige and Golay provide an important introduction to the regrettably sparse literature concerning European efforts.

There are numerous memoirs, journalistic accounts, and scientific review articles that deal with various aspects of astronomy from space. Spitzer is a valuable reprint with commentary of an otherwise difficult to obtain report, and one that is often cited in review literature as having been space astronomy's manifesto. Tucker and Tucker devote three chapters to the Hubble Space Telescope in their readable and informative but sparsely documented volume, providing highlights of relevant ground-, balloon-, rocket-, and satellite-based developments and personalities. Cornell and Carr, Henbest, and Field and Chaisson, as well as various articles in *Annual Review of Astronomy and Astrophysics* provide scientific reviews ranging from popular to professional.

Joseph N. Tatarewicz

Bibliography

Annual Review of Astronomy and Astrophysics. Palo Alto, Calif.: Annual Reviews, 1963– .

Cornell, J., and J. Carr, eds. *Infinite Vistas: New Tools for Astronomy.* New York: Scribner, 1985.

Coyne, E. *Astronomy in the Space Age.* Master's thesis. Case Institute of Technology (Cleveland), 1965.

DeVorkin, D.H. *Race to the Stratosphere: Manned Scientific Ballooning in America.* New York: Springer-Verlag, 1989.

———. *Science with a Vengeance: How the Military Created U.S. Space Sciences after World War II.* New York: Springer-Verlag, 1992.

Dupree, A.K. "The Ultraviolet Sky." In *Astronomy from Space: Sputnik to Space Telescope,* edited by J. Cornell and P. Gorenstein, 116–139. Cambridge: MIT Press, 1983.

Field, G.B., and E. Chaisson. *The Invisible Universe: Probing the Frontiers of Astrophysics.* Boston: Birkhauser, 1985.

Golay, M.. "1960: How Many European Astronomers Wanted a Space Telescope?" In *Science beyond the Atmosphere: The History of Space Science in Europe.* Proceedings of a Symposium Held in Palermo, Italy, November 5–7, 1992, edited by A. Russo. Noordwijk, The Netherlands: ESA HSR-Special, 1993.

Henbest, N., ed. *Observing the Universe.* London: Basil Blackwell, 1984.

Hevly, B.W. *Basic Research within a Military Context: The Naval Research Laboratory and the Foundations of Extreme Ultraviolet and X-Ray Astronomy, 1923–1960.* Ph.D. dissertation. Baltimore: Johns Hopkins University, 1987.

Kondo, Y., ed. *Exploring the Universe with the IUE Satellite.* Dordrecht: D. Reidel, 1987.

Kondo, Y., J.M. Mead, and R.D. Chapman, eds. *Advances in Ultraviolet Astronomy: Four Years of IUE Research.* Proceedings of a Symposium Held at NASA Goddard Space Flight Center, Greenbelt, Maryland, March 30–April 1, 1982. NASA Conference publication CP-2238. Washington, D.C.: GPO, 1982.

Krige, John. "The Rise and Fall of ESRO's First Major Scientific Project, the Large Astronomical Satellite (LAS) 1." *History and Technology* 9 (1992): 1–26.

Newell, H.E. *Beyond the Atmosphere: Early Years of Space Science.* Washington, D.C.: NASA SP-4211, 1980.

Smith, R.W., with contributions by P.A. Hanle, R. Kargon, and J.N. Tatarewicz. *The Space Telescope: A Study of NASA, Science, Technology, and Politics.* New York: Cambridge University Press, 1989.

Spitzer, L. "Astronomical Advantages of an Extra-terrestrial Observatory." Reprint with commentary of the RAND 1946 Memorandum. *Astronomy Quarterly* 7 (1990): 131–142.

Tucker, W., and K. Tucker. *The Cosmic Inquirers: Modern Telescopes and Their Makers.* Cambridge: Harvard University Press, 1986.

Winter, F.H. "Observatories in Space: 1920s Style." *Griffith Observer* (1982): 2–8.

Optical Glass-Making

Glasses for refracting optics are distinguished from all other glasses by their internal uniformity. Michael Faraday observed in 1829 that the essential condition that renders any glass

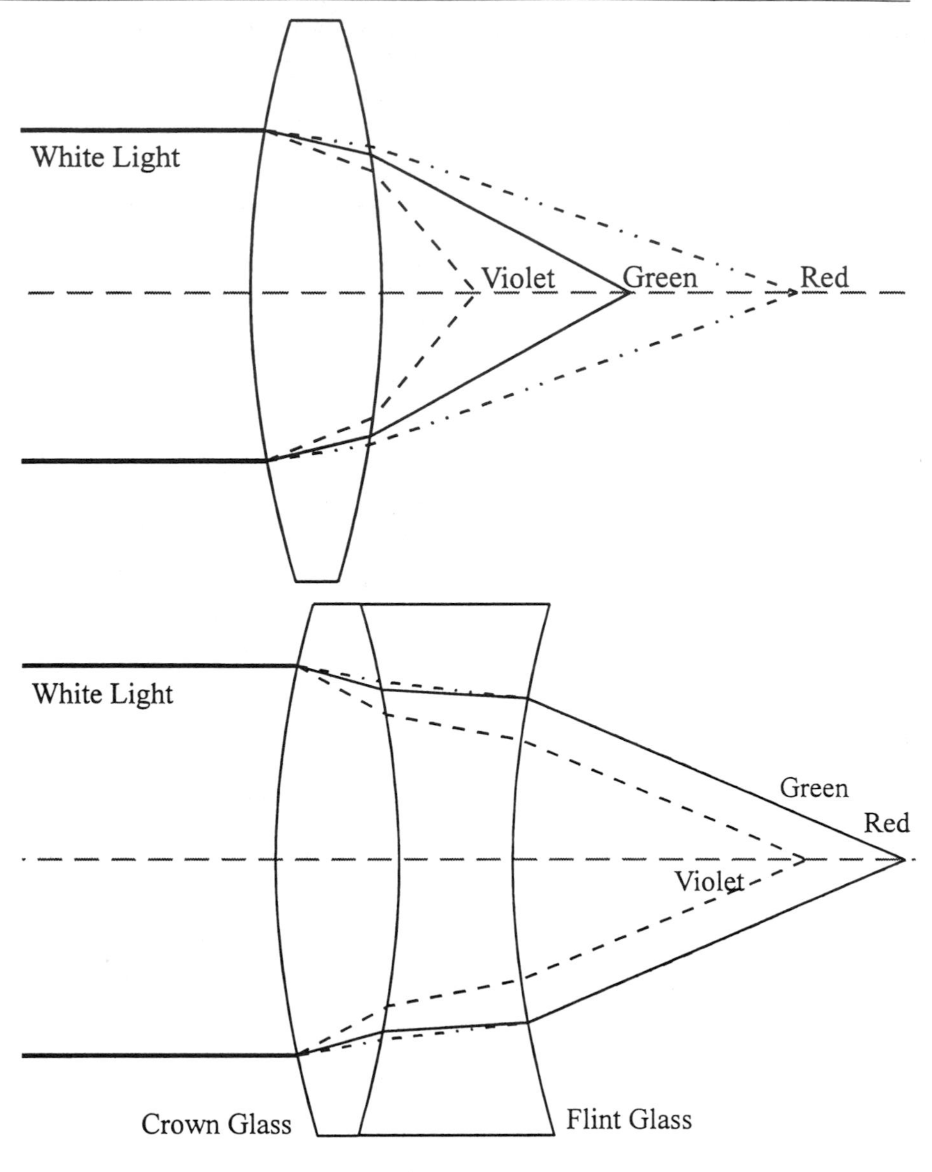

Chromatic aberration in a simple lens means that various colors of the spectrum (wavelengths of light) are not brought to focus at a single point. Under these conditions, point sources appear to be a blur of colors. (Figure by Frank E. Wooley)

An achromatic compound lens made of crown and flint glass, which have different indices of refraction, will focus red and green light at approximately the same point. However, the wavelengths represented by violet light will still be out of focus, and objects such as planets seen through this lens system will have a violet halo. (Figure by Frank E. Wooley)

useful as an optical agent is a perfectly homogeneous composition and structure. By that he meant that it should be free of striae (localized cordlike variations in the refractive index) and inclusions (both solid and gaseous). It also should be optically homogeneous (free of gradual changes in index of refraction across the piece). Since both striae and gradients of index of refraction arise from variations in chemical composition, optical glasses must be chemically homogeneous to an unusual degree.

Makers of refracting telescopes need glasses with special optical properties. Glasses that have different variations of index of refraction with wavelength (that is, different dispersions) are combined in multielement systems to eliminate chromatic and other aberrations of refracting optics. A modern manufacturer's catalogue of optical glasses may list more than two hundred different glasses, grouped by range of index and dispersion and labeled by their key chemical components. Optical glasses are broadly classified by their dispersion as crown glasses (lower dispersion) and flint glasses (higher dispersion), and by index of refraction as heavy (higher index) and light (lower index).

Before the eighteenth century, common window glass, an alkali-lime silicate glass called crown glass, was used for optical elements. Dispersion was considered a property of light, not of the optical material. In 1671 **Isaac Newton** first correctly explained the cause of chromatic aberration as the variation of index of refraction with wavelength. Because the index of refraction is greater at shorter wavelengths, a single spherical lens produces a series of images of different colors at varying distances from the lens; these are much exaggerated in the illustration.

The first of three major advances in optical glasses came in 1733 when Chester Moore Hall built on Newton's concept to invent an achromatic lens. He combined a converging crown lens with a diverging lens of flint glass, a potassium-lead silicate developed fifty years earlier for decorative tableware. This combination eliminated the strong color fringes on the image formed by a telescope but still left a much smaller colored edge, the secondary spectrum. The images for two wavelengths are made coincident, but all other images lie at different distances. Hall's achromatic lens was perfected and commercialized by John Dolland in 1758. The terms crown and flint persist in optical glass terminology today.

Another important development of the seventeenth and eighteenth centuries was the purification of raw materials to eliminate iron and other coloring elements. While this improved the transmission of light by lenses, it inadvertently led to reduction of the lime and alumina, components that were later found to be essential to resistance to attack by water. Glass during this period often exhibited crizzling, a surface cracking caused by hydration and subsequent dehydration. Only after methods of chemical analysis were developed in the late eighteenth century was this problem understood, but glasses of poor durability were produced well into the nineteenth century.

Early in the nineteenth century, Joseph von Fraunhofer, working with the glass-maker Utzschneider in Bavaria, began the search for elements other than lime and lead to add to the glass composition to eliminate the secondary spectrum. He found improved crown glasses, but the search was made difficult by the poor optical quality of the experimental melts. Michael Faraday was commissioned by the Royal Society in 1824 to improve the quality of optical glasses for telescopes. Practical techniques for mechanical stirring of optical glasses in platinum vessels had been developed by Pierre-Louis Guinand in Switzerland and by Fraunhofer two decades earlier, but Faraday's report in 1829 gave the first published instructions on mechanical stirring and fining in platinum vessels. William Harcourt and George G. Stokes, using a novel laboratory furnace to produce experimental melts through the mid-nineteenth century, showed the range of optical properties available if a larger selection of chemical elements were employed. But their glasses were inhomogeneous and their findings were not commercialized.

The second major advance in optical glasses came in the last quarter of the nineteenth century, when optical theory was sufficiently advanced to specify the optical properties of the glasses for the microscopes needed by biological and medical researchers. Theory and practice came together in Jena, Germany, in the remarkable collaboration, begun in 1881, of Otto Schott, a chemist/glass-maker, Ernst Abbe, a physicist, and **Carl Zeiss**, a manufacturer of optical instruments. They developed many improved glasses of the barium borosilicate family, and new glasses containing phosphorous and fluorine. By 1892 their Jenaer Glaswerke Schott und Genossen offered seventy-six optical glasses for sale.

The third major advance occurred after 1930, when lanthanum and other rare earth oxides were introduced in borate glasses by G.W. Morey. This made available a greatly expanded field of high-index, low-dispersion glasses for correction of optical aberrations.

Optical glasses are made much like any other glasses, but with greater attention to the elimination of striae and bubbles. The main steps are melting, forming, annealing, shaping, and finishing. Glasses used in larger volumes are melted continuously, while smaller volumes are produced in crucibles, normally made of platinum. Since the scale of production is small, continuous optical melters are quite different from those used for containers, sheet, or fibers. As with all glasses, the melting process involves (a) batch melting (conversion of powdered raw materials into a liquid and elimination of undissolved solids), (b) fining (elimination of bubbles), and (c) homogenizing, both chemically and thermally. For optical glasses, these three steps are carried out in separate chambers. Batch melting takes place in a shallow basin or tank constructed of refractory (heat-resistant ceramic) blocks. The tank is heated by combustion of natural gas above the glass or by passing electrical current through the glass. Fining and homogenization are carried out in a series of connected chambers made of platinum. Although platinum is very costly, its use is justified by the need to avoid contamination from the refractories. Striae are created in the molten glass by corrosion of the refractory container and by the loss of some components from the surface by volatilization. The glass is always stirred mechanically after melting and fining to obtain the required chemical homogeneity. It is possible to produce large lens blanks in which the index of refraction varies less than one part in a million.

Glass blanks are produced continuously by cutting the molten stream of viscous glass into gobs and pressing into metal molds. Large disks and long bars are cast from more fluid glasses. Large optical-quality castings have been made weighing several hundred kilograms. After forming, the glass is annealed by slow cooling from the temperature at which the material is plastic. Annealing removes the stress and therefore the birefringence that is caused by cooling different parts of the piece at different rates. The final optical elements are obtained by cutting and grinding to shape with abrasives, polishing, and then coating to reduce reflection losses.

The chemical composition of an optical glass is chosen to provide (a) the required optical properties, (b) resistance to devitrification (crystallization) during hot forming, and (c) sufficient chemical durability to avoid surface corrosion under the conditions of polishing and end use. Raw materials used to obtain the composition are carefully chosen to exclude coloring elements (such as, iron, chromium, and copper) that lower the transmission of light.

Glasses for the front-surface mirrors used in reflecting optics are not generally called optical glasses. Their optical properties are unimportant, since the glass is simply a substrate for the metallic reflecting coating. They should have low and uniform thermal expansion, to reduce distortion of the optical image due to temperature changes in the mirror. The first silver-on-glass mirrors, developed around 1860, used crown glass having a high coefficient of linear thermal expansion (CTE). In the early twentieth century low-alkali borosilicate glasses having a CTE three times lower were introduced, culminating in the 1933 casting by Corning of the 200-inch Pyrex™ mirror blank for the Hale Telescope. In the past thirty years, mirrors have been made of fused silica and silica-titania, and of glass-ceramics of the lithium-aluminosilicate family. These materials have CTE values ten to one hundred times lower than the borosilicate glasses.

Frank E. Wooley

Bibliography

Deeg, E.W. "Optical Glasses." In *Advances in Ceramics, Volume 18: Commercial Glasses*, edited by D.C. Boyd and J.F. MacDowell, 9–34. Columbus, Ohio: American Ceramic Society, 1986.

Douglas, R.W., and S. Frank. *A History of Glassmaking*. Henley-on-Thames, Oxfordshire: G.T. Foulis, 1972.

Izumitani, T. *Optical Glass*. Translated by Berkeley Scientific Translation Service. New York: American Institute of Physics, 1986. (Original work: *Kogaku Garasu*. Kyoritsu Shuppan, Tokyo, 1984.)

Engineers at the Corning Glass Company in New York study the newly cast 200-inch telescope disk in 1933. The disk was shipped by rail to the California Institute of Technology in Pasadena for grinding and polishing. This task was interrupted by World War II and only in 1948 did the great 200-inch Hale Telescope see first light. (Courtesy of Corning Incorporated, Department of Archives and Records Management, Corning, NY)

Oxford University, Astronomy at

Astronomy has been taught and practiced in Oxford University since at least the thirteenth century. The writings of the mathematicians active in Merton College, and several of their surviving astrolabes, indicate the intensity with which the science was cultivated in medieval Oxford. In the sixteenth century, Oxford provided academic domicile for Nicholas Kratzer, mathematician to King Henry VIII, as well as Robert Recorde, the English Copernican, and Leonard Digges, who wrote on optics. In 1619 Henry Savile, the mathematical Warden of Merton College, established the professorships of astronomy and geometry that still bear his name, and emphasized the importance of astronomy in a liberal education. John Bainbridge and Henry Gellibrand were distinguished holders of the Savilian Chairs, while Professor John Greaves traveled to Rhodes and Egypt to confirm the coordinates of some classical observing sites.

Between 1648 and 1659, that group which met under the aegis of Dr. John Wilkins at Wadham College and which after 1660 constituted the nucleus of the Royal Society actively cultivated astronomy and were especially interested in advancing Copernican ideas. This group, which included the young Christopher Wren (Savilian professor of astronomy 1660–1673) and Robert Hooke, not only made telescopic observations from Wadham College, but also discussed the possibility of life on other worlds, and space travel by means of flying chariots.

Edmond Halley, who was perhaps Oxford's most illustrious astronomer, won fame even as a student by spending the years 1676–1678 on the South Atlantic island of St. Helena to produce the first survey of the stars of the Southern Hemisphere made with telescopic instruments. Halley played a major role in encouraging Isaac Newton in Cambridge to complete his work on gravitation, and Halley even paid for the cost of publishing *Principia Mathematica* (1687) out of his own pocket. Halley's work extended across most of the branches of science that were known in his day, and his fundamental contributions included cometary orbits (1705), new and variable stars (1715–1716), proper motions (1718), and the nature of nebulae (1716, 1720). From 1705 to the end of his life, Halley held the Savilian Professorship of Geometry at Oxford, which he combined after 1720 with the office of **Astronomer Royal**.

The years 1650–1800 were a time of remarkable achievement for astronomy in Oxford, even beyond the work of Christopher Wren and Edmond Halley. Other Savilian professors of astronomy and geometry, such as David Gregory and John Keil, popularized Newtonianism in the university. Much of this teaching would have taken place in the Old Ashmolean Museum, which after 1683 provided Oxford University with its first specifically designed science building. Since the 1920s, this building has housed the priceless instrument collections of what became the Museum of the History of Science.

In 1721, Halley's protégé James Bradley became Savilian professor of astronomy, and continued to retain the chair upon succeeding Halley as Astronomer Royal in 1742. Bradley discovered the aberration of light (1728) and nutation (1748), made major advances in refining the techniques of precise observation, and demonstrated the physical action of Newton's laws.

Yet Oxford still lacked an established astronomical observatory, though Wadham College, Corpus Christi College, the tower in the Old Schools Quadrangle, and the residences of the two Savilian professors in New College Lane contained makeshift structures that housed portable instruments. In 1768, however, Bradley's successor as Savilian professor of astronomy, Thomas Hornsby, approached the Radcliffe trustees about the provision of such an institution. The resulting building, equipped with two quadrants, transit, zenith sector, and equatorial instrument in 1773 by John Bird and achromatic refractors by Peter Dollond, was considered in 1777 by the Danish visitor Thomas Bugge to be the best in Europe. Hornsby was a meticulous and regular observer, making a number of observations at the Radcliffe between 1773 and 1805, though unfortunately they remained unpublished until edited by Arthur Rambaut, Harold Knox-Shaw, and others in the 1930s.

In the early eighteenth century, three of Oxford's Savilian professors held the office of Astronomer Royal. They were Halley (1720–1742), Bradley (1742–1762), and Nathaniel Bliss (1762–1764).

By the early nineteenth century, the rapid advances in astronomical technology that had taken place since 1780 made the Radcliffe Observatory instruments obsolete for original research. Not until Stephen Peter Rigaud acquired a new mural circle by the instrument-maker Thomas Jones in 1836, and Manuel Johnson obtained the famous Repsold heliometer from Hamburg in 1848, was the observatory's instrumentation really brought up to date. The Repsold **heliometer** was used primarily for astrometry and stellar parallax work.

A peculiarity of Oxford astronomy at this period lay in the fact that the Radcliffe Observatory was never controlled directly by the university, but by a quite independent board of Radcliffe trustees. Since Hornsby's time, the trustees had appointed to the Radcliffe Observership the same man as the university quite separately appointed to the Savilian professorship of astronomy, to combine both offices. In 1839, however, this practice ended, with separate persons coming to hold the observership and professorship, and creating the awkward situation of the astronomy professor having no observatory of his own. But in 1875, Professor Charles Pritchard commenced work in the newly opened University Observatory, so that there were now two major observatories, under separate control, operating in the same academic community. This situation continued until 1935, when the Radcliffe trustees decided to close down the eighteenth-century observatory and move its greatly updated equipment to a prime-sky location in Pretoria, South Africa. After being used for a variety of purposes, the magnificent Radcliffe Observatory building became the central feature of the new Green College, Oxford, in 1979.

In addition to the equipment of formal, institutional astronomy in the Victorian period, two smaller observatories existed in Oxford. Botany professor Charles Giles Bridle Daubeny ran a teaching observatory in the university's botanical gardens, of which he was keeper, and the geologist and keeper of the Ashmolean Museum, John Phillips, maintained a substantial private observatory from which, in 1862, he completed the observations necessary to produce the first globe representing the surface of Mars. There was also Warren De La Rue, whose fine equatorial reflecting telescope came to the university observatory.

The Oxford observatories played active roles in the *Carte du Ciel* photographic survey under Herbert Hall Turner, though it was not until 1932, when Harry Hemley Plaskett became professor, that serious **astrophysics** really began in the university. Plaskett, a distinguished Canadian solar physicist who had worked under Harlow Shapley at Harvard, commenced an Oxford tradition in active solar physics that continued until 1988, when the university observatory was closed down. After 1960, however, astronomy at Oxford was conducted under a new Department of Astrophysics, although its researchers, who work primarily in the field of galaxy-formation, obtain their data from observatories around the world. Oxford never developed a **radio astronomy** observatory. On the other hand, Oxford laser scientists have developed and built the cameras used on the Isaac Newton 98-inch telescope on La Palma, and have pioneered adaptive and adoptive optics.

Yet another of the peculiarities of Oxford astronomy is that it has never been an undergraduate degree subject. In the past, it was taught as a cultural refinement to a predominantly arts university, while today it is part of the postgraduate department of Nuclear Physics.

Considering the duration over which astronomy has been practiced at Oxford, it has received surprisingly little historiographical attention. Some biographies of its practitioners in the university have been written that provide much detail, such as the works of Rigaud and Ada Pritchard, but critical historical interest is very recent. Robert Theodore Gunther included astronomy in his monumental *Early Science in Oxford*, but not until the chapters for the still incomplete *History of Oxford University* were commissioned in the 1980s was the university's astronomical legacy assessed—and even then, only as a part of general physics. Chapman's *Oxford Figures* deals at some length with Oxford astronomy between 1650 and 1850, though Sir William McCrea's obituary of H.H. Plaskett (1981) provides the best account of the establishment of astrophysics in Oxford.

Most of the relevant manuscript collections are held in the archives of the Museum of the History of Science, Oxford, with further collections in the Bodleian Library. The Royal Society and Royal Astronomical Society house many Oxford-related documents and citation of documents in their collections. One of the relatively few scholars actively engaged in research into the history of Oxford astronomy at the present time is Roger Hutchins of Magdalen College.

Allan Chapman

Bibliography

Chapman, A. "Edmond Halley and His Tradition." In *Oxford Figures: 800 Years of Mathematics*, edited by J. Fauvel, R. Flood, and R. Wilson. Oxford: Clarendon Press, 1994.

———. "John Wallis and the Savilian Professorships at Oxford." In *Oxford Figures: 800 Years of Mathematics*, edited by

J. Fauvel, R. Flood, and R. Wilson. Oxford: Clarendon Press, 1994.

———. "The Radcliffe Observatory." In *Oxford Figures: 800 Years of Mathematics*, edited by J. Fauvel, R. Flood, and R. Wilson. Oxford: Clarendon Press, 1994.

Feingold, M. *The Mathematicians' Apprenticeship: Science, Universities and Society in England, 1560–1640*. New York: Cambridge University Press, 1984.

Guest, I. *Doctor John Radcliffe and His Trust*. Oxford: Radcliffe Trust, 1991.

Gunther, R.T. *Early Science in Oxford*. Vols. II, XI. Oxford: R.T. Gunther, 1923, 1937.

Hutchins, R.D. "Magdalen's Astronomy Observatory." In *Magdalen College Record*. 44–51. Oxford: Oxford University Press, 1990.

———. "Professor John Phillips at Oxford, 1853–1874: Catalyst for the University Observatory." Oxford University Additional Honours School thesis, 1992. Deposited in the Museum of the History of Science, Oxford.

McCrea, W. "Harry Hemley Plaskett, F.R.S., 1893–1980." *Biographical Memoirs of the Royal Society* 27 (1981): 445–478.

Plaskett, H.H. *The Place of Observation in Astronomy*. Inaugural Lecture. Oxford: Oxford University Press, 1933.

Rigaud, S.P. *The Miscellaneous Works of Dr. James Bradley*. Oxford: Oxford University Press, 1832.

Ronan, C.A. *Edmond Halley, Genius in Eclipse*. London: MacDonald, 1970.

Simcock, A.V. *The Ashmolean Museum and Oxford Science 1683–1983*. Oxford: Museum of the History of Science, 1984.

Thackeray, A.D. *The Radcliffe Observatory 1772–1972*. Oxford: Radcliffe Trust, 1972.

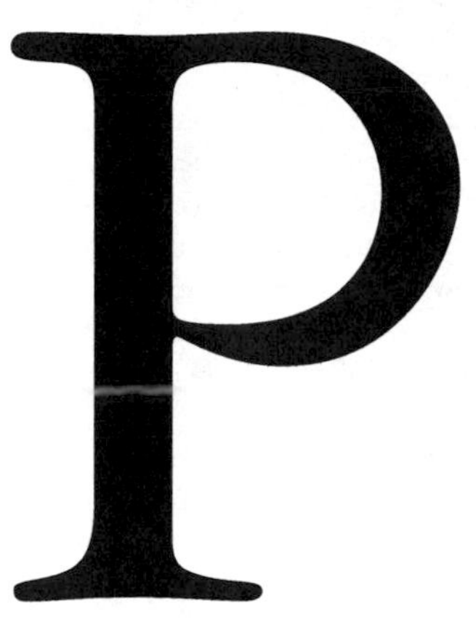

Palomar Observatory

American astronomical observatory. Palomar Observatory consists of several telescopes located 5,600 feet/1,700 meters above sea level on Palomar Mountain, 45 miles north-northeast of San Diego, California. The observatory is owned and operated by the California Institute of Technology (Caltech).

The origins of the Palomar Observatory can be traced to the mid-1920s, when **George Ellery Hale**, the retired director of the Mount Wilson Observatory, and the Mount Wilson astronomer Francis Gladheim Pease studied the possibility of constructing very large telescopes with mirrors 5 to 7.5 meters in diameter. Hale's efforts resulted in the Rockefeller Foundation's International Education Board decision in 1928 to fund the construction of a 200-inch/5-meter telescope. The Rockefeller Foundation did not want to award the telescope to the Carnegie Institution of Washington's Mount Wilson Observatory, however, but rather to Caltech, the nearby educational institution, even though the latter had no astronomy department. Caltech, in turn, raised the money to endow the operation and for maintenance of the telescope. Although Mount Wilson would not get the telescope, it was decided that their astronomers would be closely involved with the planning and the operation of the Caltech instrument.

Hale and Caltech quickly established the organizational elements to construct the telescope and its auxiliary instrumentation. After a failed attempt to produce a 200-inch mirror of fused quartz, a Pyrex glass mirror was cast at Corning Glass Works in 1934. That same year, after a site survey in Southern California and Arizona, Palomar Mountain was chosen as the location for the new observatory. Construction of the telescope building and dome began shortly thereafter, but work on grinding the mirror at Caltech progressed slowly and was effectively halted by World War II. The mirror was finally transported to Palomar Mountain in 1947 and the telescope was dedicated on June 3, 1948, as the Hale Telescope. The necessity of further testing prevented the telescope from entering service until November 1949, and regular spectroscopic observations could not begin until one year later. The Hale Telescope, as the largest telescope in the world, was used primarily on projects for which smaller telescopes would not suffice. The main focus of research with the Hale Telescope was on what astronomers termed the cosmological problem: the determination of the scale of the universe, the Hubble constant, and the limits of the deceleration parameter. Significant discoveries with the Hale Telescope have included the optical identification of distant radio sources and the discovery of quasars.

When the 200-inch telescope was nearing completion, Caltech and the Carnegie Institution of Washington finalized their plans for joint operation of the Mount Wilson Observatory and the Palomar Observatory. Both observatories were to function as one under a single director. In addition, a formal procedure was instituted whereby astronomers from outside institutions could apply and be granted time on the observatories' telescopes. The joint plan went into effect on April 1, 1948, and the two observatories became known as the Mount Wilson and Palomar

Observatories. The director was **Ira Sprague Bowen**, the head of Mount Wilson since 1946. While the plan for unified operation seemed a good one on paper, matters did not always proceed smoothly in its implementation. By the late 1960s, Caltech's astronomical operations had grown tremendously from its humble beginnings and it was necessary to revise the original agreement. A new operating agreement was effected in 1969 that included the addition of an associate director as well as a name change to the Hale Observatories.

While construction was just beginning on the 200-inch telescope, plans were underway to build other telescopes on Palomar Mountain. The potential of the recently developed Schmidt-type telescope led to Palomar's first instrument: an 18-inch/0.46-meter Schmidt in 1936. This telescope was soon used by Caltech astronomer **Fritz Zwicky** in his studies of supernovae in distant galaxies and his cataloguing of galaxies and clusters of galaxies. The success of the 18-inch led to the decision to construct a Schmidt telescope with a 48-inch/1.2-meter aperture, which went into operation on Palomar Mountain in January 1949. It was decided that the 48-inch would begin a large project of photographically mapping the entire sky visible from Palomar. The project involves approximately eighteen hundred exposures in blue and red light. The National Geographic Society agreed to fund the project which commenced in July 1949 as the National Geographic Society–Palomar Observatory Sky Survey. Despite some problems with the emulsions, the project was completed in 1956, with a southern extension of the Sky Survey added later. The complete atlas of 1,830 photographs was eventually distributed at cost to several hundred observatories around the world. The Sky Survey proved to be an effective research tool and an invaluable reference catalogue. When technical improvements allowed astronomers to install an achromatic corrector to the 48-inch Schmidt, a second Palomar Sky Survey was begun in 1985. In 1987, after a sizable gift from Samuel Oschin, the 48-inch was named the Oschin Telescope.

In the 1960s, increasing light pollution and electronic interference around Mount Wilson made conditions difficult for direct photography and photometry of faint sources with the telescopes. The observatories, therefore, with funding by the National Science Foundation and the Oscar G. Mayer family, constructed a 60-inch/1.5-meter telescope on Palomar Mountain, where sky conditions were darker. The telescope was completed in 1970.

The joint operation of the Hale Observatories by Carnegie and Caltech came to an end on July 1, 1980. Significant problems had arisen due to the different operating styles of the two parent institutions and with the dissimilar responsibilities of the Carnegie and Caltech staff. As a result of the breakup of the Hale Observatories, the Palomar Observatory became wholly operated by Caltech and Gerry Neugebauer was named director of Palomar Observatory.

A great deal has been written about the Hale Telescope and Palomar Observatory, but very little by historians. A number of works concentrate on the building of the Hale Telescope, but they do not touch upon the scientific use of the instrument. Those that do concentrate on the research performed with the Hale Telescope tend to be written by journalists or science writers for popular audiences. An institutional history of Palomar Observatory is needed, one that places it both in the context of Caltech and the development of its astronomy department, and the Carnegie Observatories, which operated it during its tenure as the site of the largest telescope in the world.

Ronald S. Brashear

Bibliography

Bowen, I.S. "The Palomar Observatory." *Scientific Monthly* 73 (1951): 141–149.

———. "Schmidt Cameras." In *Stars and Stellar Systems*, edited by G.P. Kuiper and B.M. Middlehurst, vol. 1, *Telescopes*, pp. 43–61. Chicago: University of Chicago Press, 1960.

———. "The 200-Inch Hale Telescope." In *Stars and Stellar Systems*, edited by G.P. Kuiper and B.M. Middlehurst, vol. 1, *Telescopes*, 1–15. Chicago: University of Chicago Press, 1960.

Hale, G.E. "The Possibilities of Large Telescopes." *Harper's* 156 (1928): 639–646.

———. "Building the 200-Inch Telescope." *Harper's* 159 (1929): 720–732.

Minkowski, R.L., and G.O. Abell. "The National Geographic Society–Palomar Observatory Sky Survey." In *Stars and Stellar Systems*, edited by G.P. Kuiper and B.M. Middlehurst, vol. 3, *Basic Astronomical Data*, 481–487. Chicago: University of Chicago Press, 1960.

Van Helden, A. "Building Large Telescopes." In *Astrophysics and Twentieth-Century Astronomy to 1950: Part A*, edited by O. Gingerich, 134–152. Cambridge: Cambridge University Press, 1984.

Wright, H. *Palomar, The World's Largest Telescope*. New York: Macmillan, 1952.

———. *Explorer of the Universe: A Biography of George Ellery Hale*. New York: E.P. Dutton, 1966.

Wright, H., J.N. Warnow, and C. Weiner, eds. *The Legacy of George Ellery Hale*. Cambridge: Massachusetts Institute of Technology Press, 1972.

Paris Observatory

Today the Paris Observatory is made up of three sections: the Observatory situated in Paris, the *Section d'astrophysique* located at the **Meudon Observatory**, and the **Nançay Radio Astronomy Station** in the Department of the Cher.

With the formation of learned societies and academies in Europe during the seventeenth century, the creation of a multidisciplinary scientific establishment in France was inevitable. The cornerstone of Louis XIV's Royal Observatory, situated just south of Paris, was laid on June 21, 1667, the summer solstice. The architect, Claude Perrault, designed the building so that its central axis coincides with the meridian of Paris. The first astronomers who worked and lived at this establishment, like Adrien Auzout and Jean Picard, were members of the French Academy of Sciences, established in 1666. Several foreigners, including Christiaan Huygens, **Jean-Dominique Cassini**, and Ole Römer, were invited to the observatory by Louis XIV's minister, Colbert. Most of the construction was completed by 1672, but work on the interior continued until 1683. The building, whose walls had a width of 2 to 2.5 meters, was constructed on the site of an old quarry, part of which, situated beyond the observatory, was, in the eighteenth century, the Catacombs of Paris. The depth of this basement, approximately 28 meters, is more or less that of the height of the building (27 meters). The building is three stories with a square tower on the north side and two stories on the south, flanked by octagonal towers to the west and the east. The original instrumentation of the observatory was of two principal types. First, there were very long focus aerial telescopes with objective lenses made by G. Campani and E. Divini. These instruments were used for the study of the planets and their moons. For positional astronomy there were mural sectors and quadrants equipped with the micrometer perfected by A. Auzout and J. Picard. These instruments were small and very stable. From its inception, the observatory was the site of constant discovery. For example, J.-D. Cassini discovered four of Saturn's moons and the division in its rings named after him; Römer demonstrated that light moves at a finite speed; and Picard created geodesic instruments. Astronomers at the observatory were engaged in one of the most fundamental tasks of that era, the precise determination of longitudes. The observatory was administered by the Academy of Sciences and had no official director. But in fact, four generations of the Cassini family reigned over the observatory, from 1671 to 1793.

During the eighteenth century the observatory was responsible principally for the development of geodesy and cartography. The observatory conducted several expeditions to measure the *Meridienne de France* based on the meridian defined in 1667. The survey of 1670–1671, which reduced the area of France by a fifth, was followed by a second (1701–1718), and finally the survey supervised by **Nicolas-Louis Lacaille** in 1739–1740. In 1795 Lacaille's measurements would serve as the basis of the provisional meter. During this period, **C.F. Cassini de Thury** completed his map of France (1756–1790), which was used to locate the new departments created by the Revolution. Starting in 1791, a survey along the French meridian was launched. Led by **Jean-Baptiste Delambre** and Pierre-François-André Méchain, the project led to the Law of September 10, 1799, defining the system of weights and measures founded on the meter, the ten-millionth of a quarter of the terrestrial meridian, a fraction of the so-called *Toise du Pérou,* which served as the basis of the measurements. The French Revolution gave rise to a major change in the observatory's administration: The office of general director, created in 1771, was abolished in 1795 when the newly created *Bureau des Longitudes* assumed administrative control. A more efficient administrative system was introduced with the appointment of Dominique F.J. Arago as director of observations in 1834. Arago was responsible for the construction of two new wings, an eastern wing for the transit instruments and a western wing that housed a large amphitheater for public lectures in astronomy inaugurated in 1813 by the *Bureau des Longitudes* and enormously popular among the general public. Arago ordered an equatorial refractor with a focal length of 9 meters over which a dome, today known as the *Coupôle*

Arago, was fitted on the eastern tower. The refractor was installed in 1855; its first objective, which rapidly deteriorated, was replaced with an objective made by the brothers Paul and Prosper Henry. The remarkable quality of this lens allows astronomers today to make photometric observations of Jupiter's moons and of asteroids.

Following the death of Arago, the government of Napoleon III requested Urbain J.J. Le Verrier to effect a complete reorganization of the observatory. The *Bureau des Longitudes* and the Paris Observatory were separated, and Le Verrier was named director of the latter. Le Verrier installed (1863) a large transit circle and began publication of the *Annales de l'Observatoire de Paris*. During Le Verrier's tenure, thirty-seven volumes of the *Annales* were published. They contained observations made at the observatory. Le Verrier's authoritarian rule was briefly interrupted when he was replaced by Charles-Eugène Delaunay, whose accidental death occasioned the return in 1873 of a somewhat wiser, more mellow Le Verrier. At Le Verrier's death, the new director, Admiral Ernest Mouchez, continued the programs envisioned by his predecessor. A modern meridian instrument was installed in 1878. Mouchez also began time determinations, produced astrometric catalogues, and encouraged the observation of double stars. He founded the *Bulletin Astronomique* and created the Museum of the Observatory. Mouchez was succeeded by **François Félix Tisserand**, author of the classic four-volume work, *Traité de Mécanique céleste* (1889–1896). The next director, Maurice Loewy, with the collaboration of Pierre Puiseux, was responsible for the creation (1896 to 1910) of a photographic atlas of the moon using a new equatorial instrument created by Loewy and nicknamed *coudé* because it was bent like an elbow. Loewy's successor, Benjamin Baillaud, was extremely active in international projects and became the first president of the **International Astronomical Union**. In 1910, Baillaud inaugurated the broadcast of time signals from the Eiffel Tower. The Bureau International de l'Heure, created by the International Astronomical Union, was established in France with Guillaume Bigourdan, an astronomer from the Paris Observatory, as director. The *Bureau* ceased operating in 1987. It was replaced by the *Section Temps Atomique International* of the *Bureau International des Poids et Mesures*, while research on the rotation of the earth was taken over by the International Earth Rotation Service, whose Central Bureau was also directed by the Paris Observatory.

In 1926 an important reorganization of the observatory took place. The new director, Henri Deslandres, since 1907 director of the Meudon Observatory, managed the merger of his establishment with the Paris Observatory. Deslandres's successor, Ernest Esclangon, named director in 1929, developed observatory clocks with dual dials, one for mean time and one for sidereal time, and invented the speaking clock in 1932, which was placed in public service on February 14, 1933.

In 1945, after the German occupation (during which work on time determinations and transmission continued), André Danjon directed the reconstruction of the Paris Observatory and the astrophysics section at Meudon. In Paris, the optics laboratory directed by André Couder was responsible for repairing French telescopes and restoring them as effective research instruments. Under Danjon's direction, the Nançay Radio Astronomy Station became an integral part of the Paris Observatory, a solar tower was constructed at the Meudon Observatory, French space research was born, and two new instruments were created: André Lallemand's electronic camera (1955), along with the photomultipliers that gave birth to the scanner; and the *astrolabe à micromètre impersonnel* (1952), known today as the Danjon astrolabe. The personnel of the Paris and Meudon observatories numbered fifty until the end of World War II; today some seven hundred are employed in various departments covering all branches of astronomical research, divided among Paris, Meudon, and Nançay. A central administration governs the whole, while there is one common general service, including a Computer Service. The archives of the Paris Observatory contain rich materials on its history and the activities of astronomers who worked there.

Suzanne Débarbat

Bibliography

Débarbat, S., S. Grillot, and J. Lévy. *Observatoire de Paris—Son histoire (1667–1963)*. Paris: Observatoire de Paris, 1984, 1990.

Pelletier, M. *La Carte de Cassini: l'extraordinaire aventure de la Carte de France.* Paris: Presses de l'Ecole Nationale des Ponts et Chaussées, 1990.

Wolf, C. *Histoire de l'Observatoire de Paris de sa création à 1793*. Paris: Gauthier-Villars, 1902.

Parsons, William, Third Earl of Rosse (1800–1867)

Anglo-Irish telescope maker. Heir to a distinguished Irish family, Parsons was educated at Birr Castle, the family seat in County Offaly. He received his university education at Trinity College, Dublin, and Magdalen College, Oxford, graduating with first-class honors in mathematics from the latter in 1822. Active in Irish affairs throughout his life, Parsons also contributed significantly to astronomy. Soon after graduation from Magdalen, Parsons began experiments on large aperture telescopes, concluding that such instruments would be more successful if they were reflectors. Developing an alloy of four parts copper to one part of tin as the best material for astronomical mirrors, Parsons designed a ventilated mold that would allow even cooling of the disk in an annealing oven. By 1840, he had successfully cast a 36-inch mirror using his new process. Parsons soon applied this new technology to the construction of the Leviathan of Parsonstown, completed in 1845 with a 72-inch mirror that weighed four tons.

For the next two decades, Parsons and his principal collaborator, the Reverend Thomas Romney Robinson, carried out various observations with the huge telescope. The most important of these studies examined the nebulae investigated a few years earlier by **John Herschel**. With his superior equipment, Parsons could resolve many of these nebulae into groups of individual stars, and he identified several spiral nebulae. His detailed drawing of M51 clearly showed the spiral pattern and helped to establish spirals as a new class of nebulae.

George E. Webb

Bibliography

Dewhirst, D.W., and M. Hoskin. "The Rosse Spirals." *Journal for the History of Astronomy* 22 (1991): 257–266.

Hoskin, M. "Rosse, Robinson, and the Resolution of the Nebulae." *Journal for the History of Astronomy* 21 (1990): 331–344.

North, J.D., and C.A. Ronan. "Parsons, William, Third Earl of Rosse." In *Dictionary of Scientific Biography*, edited by C.C. Gillispie, vol. 10, 328–329. New York: Scribner, 1974.

Payne-Gaposchkin, Cecilia (1900–1979)

American astronomer. Born and raised in England, Payne studied astronomy under **Arthur Eddington** and physics under Ernst Rutherford as a student at Newnham College of Cambridge University. In 1923, she came to the **Harvard College Observatory** as one of the first graduate students in astronomy. In her doctoral dissertation, *Stellar Atmospheres* (1925), Payne used quantum theory and Harvard photographs of stellar spectra to establish a temperature scale for stellar atmospheres. Her data also suggested that hydrogen and helium were far more abundant in stellar atmospheres than on earth, but, on the advice of **Henry Norris Russell**, she rejected this evidence as spurious. Payne remained at Harvard as a National Research Council fellow, a member of the observatory staff, and, from the 1950s, as a member of the Harvard University faculty. She wrote notable volumes on stars of high luminosity and on novae, and, particularly in collaboration with her husband, Sergei Gaposchkin, made extensive studies of variable stars.

Peggy A. Kidwell

Bibliography

Haramundanis, K., ed. *Cecilia Payne-Gaposchkin: An Autobiography and Other Recollections*. Cambridge: Cambridge University Press, 1984.

Kidwell, P. "Cecilia Payne-Gaposchkin: Astronomy in the Family." In *Uneasy Careers and Intimate Lives: Women in Science 1789–1979*, edited by P.G. Abir-Am and D. Outram, 216–238. New Brunswick: Rutgers University Press, 1987.

Phillips, Theodore Evelyn Reece (1868–1942)

English amateur astronomer, Phillips's major contribution was in planetary observation and analysis. From 1908 to 1940, he was the only observer to consistently make micrometrical belt and zone latitude measurements and transit timings of atmospheric features on Jupiter. As British Astronomical Association (BAA) Jupiter Section director, he improved the drift rate methods of A.S. Williams and W.F. Denning. The observations published under Phillips's care are the only satisfactory records of Jupiter from 1900 to 1933. Phillips also observed **Mars, Saturn, double stars,** and **variable stars**. His harmonic analysis of light curves first demonstrated that there are two distinct groups of long-period variables.

Thomas R. Williams

Bibliography

Peek, B.M. "Obituary—Theodore Evelyn Reece Phillips." *Journal of the British*

Astronomical Association 52 (1942): 203–208.

Photography, Astronomical

The 1838 success of Louis J.M. Daguerre in producing a recorded image was recognized by D.F.J. Arago for its astronomical potential even though Daguerre had failed to produce a clear image of the moon. By 1840, John W. Draper had begun his pioneering efforts to produce a daguerreotype of the moon. Nine years later William C. and George P. Bond at Harvard, in collaboration with commercial photographers, made more successful daguerreotypes, but it was Warren de la Rue who obtained the first really substantial lunar results with the newer wet collodion process introduced in 1851. In other experiments, Giovanni A. Majocchi attempted photography of the 1842 solar eclipse, but successful eclipse daguerreotypy at totality, recording the solar corona, was achieved only in 1851, by the professional photographer Berkowski at Königsberg Observatory. Draper recorded the solar spectrum in 1843, and in 1845 Jean-Bernard-Léon Foucault and Armand-Hippolyte-Louis Fizeau photographed two large sunspot groups. In 1850 G.P. Bond with John A. Whipple produced the first daguerreotypes of stars, though it was clearly recognized that the photographic process was still inferior to naked-eye observation.

De la Rue turned to wet collodion plates, which were ten times more sensitive than daguerreotypes, obtaining a long series of lunar photographs including stereoscopic pairs in 1859; he also designed in 1857 a photoheliograph for solar photography. From wet collodion photography he and **Angelo Secchi** conclusively showed in 1860 that the solar prominences seen at eclipse totality were of solar origin. G.P. Bond also experimented (1857–1860) with collodion plates to photograph stars, recognizing immediately their astrometric and photometric potential.

At the same time Lewis M. Rutherfurd embarked on research to improve photographic results, by 1864 producing the first American photographic refractor. He also experimented with photography of star clusters and spectroscopy, in 1875 obtaining the coronal spectrum during an eclipse. In the 1860s **Henry Draper** also undertook exhaustive experiments to develop a perfect photographic telescope with a more stable mount, a more reliable drive, and optical correction to the blue, not the visual. Draper worked on reflectors and instrumentation for stellar spectroscopy, obtaining in 1872 a spectrum of α Lyrae with the first photographic recognition of absorption lines. **William Huggins** also applied photography to stellar spectra in 1863, becoming highly successful in the following decade using dry photographic plates. In 1882 he detected emission lines in the spectrum of the Orion Nebula.

While scientific achievements in photographic astronomy occurred, there were setbacks in adoption of the technology. The 1874 international campaign on the transit of Venus involved a major application of photography, but accurate positional measurement proved impossible and use of the new technology was considered a failure by all parties. Generally, photography was rejected for the 1882 Venus transit work.

Nevertheless, the year 1880 saw the first promising results on extended objects, with Draper's Orion photography, followed shortly thereafter by Andrew A. Common's efforts, which revealed details not visible to the naked eye. Common also began design of large reflectors for photographic purposes. These first efforts were followed by the significant photographic accomplishments of Isaac Roberts on nebulae and star clusters after 1885.

At the same time, serious application of photography to stellar research was begun in 1885 by **David Gill**, in collaboration with **Jacobus C. Kapteyn**. His southern star catalogue, the *Cape Photographic Durchmusterung*, completed in 1900, reported positions and photographic magnitudes of 454,875 stars. The brothers Paul and Prosper Henry also turned to photography to complete their mapping of the sky within 5 degrees of the ecliptic when they ran into the Milky Way, leading **Paris Observatory** director E.B. Mouchez to suggest in 1885 an all-sky photographic star chart. The Astrographic Congress of 1887 established the *Carte du Ciel* project, involving more than twenty-two thousand sky fields of 2 degrees square. Undertaken prematurely, the project and its *Astrographic Catalogue* were completed only in 1964.

Nevertheless, by the close of the 1880s, photography had become an established part of astronomical research, primarily due to the advent of dry plates more than three orders of magnitude more sensitive than the original daguerreotypes. Long-exposure photography now surpassed the ability of the human eye. Photography was being applied to problems of classical **astrometry** as well as leading to new discoveries in astrophysics.

In the 1890s, short-focus photographic work with small telescopes became invaluable for mapping the sky and following variable stars. By the end of the first decade of the twentieth century, the photographic work of **James E. Keeler, George W. Ritchey**, and Max Wolf showed that large reflectors were also significant for astronomical study.

Equally important was the development of techniques of accurate quantitative analysis of photographic material. Charles Pritchard pioneered photographic astrometry by his 1873 study of lunar libration and then turned to parallax work, obtaining the first photographic parallax, of 61 Cygni, in 1887. **Frank Schlesinger** developed methods that became standard for long-focus refractor photographic determination of parallaxes. Photography also became the mainstay for stellar positions.

Photographic photometry was less tractable due to the difficulty of calibration of images on the photographic plates. **Harvard College Observatory** (1890) addressed this problem, by 1907 establishing a standard North Pole Sequence. At the same time, **Karl Schwarzschild**, who also developed the concept of photographic (blue)–visual (yellow) magnitudes as a color index, set up photographic standards about the equator. John A. Parkhurst pioneered in 1912 use of sensitometer images added to plates after exposure to the sky; Sydney Chapman and Philibert J. Melotte investigated in 1913 wire diffraction gratings to produce secondary images; and Frederick H. Seares worked on establishment of a uniform magnitude scale from 10th to 18th magnitude. In 1922, his values for the North Polar Sequence were adopted.

Photographic materials continued to improve, with C.E. Kenneth Mees of Eastman Kodak specifically addressing problems encountered by observational astronomers in the 1920s and 1930s. The ability to produce uniform large-scale photographic plates made possible the 1949–1957 National Geographic Society–Palomar Observatory Sky Survey, eighteen hundred photographs on red- and blue-sensitive emulsions in 6 degree by 6 degree fields, north of declination –30 degrees. Comparable southern sky surveys were accomplished in the 1970s and 1980s. The northern sky survey is being repeated (1987–1994) using finer grain emulsion plates that will achieve a fainter limit by about 5 times.

Establishment of basic photographic techniques and applications in research astronomy also included processes to increase the sensitivity of available emulsions through hypersensitization means. Other techniques—superposition of individual photographic plates and unsharp masking—were developed to bring out faint details present in photographic images.

As technological advance in emulsion sensitivity slowed, modern experimentation turned to intensification of the incident light or toward replacement of the photograph altogether. Development of phosphor output tubes began in the late 1940s, the most successful modern device being the so-called Carnegie image tube developed in the late 1960s. An alternative, the electronic camera or electronographic tube, developed in the 1950s by André Lallemand, Gerald E. Kron, and others, used fine-grain nuclear emulsions in place of the output phosphor. Other experimental work with television cameras (orthicon or vidicon tubes) has been applied to astronomy from the 1950s onward.

More successful have been solid state detectors with high quantum efficiencies (up to 80 percent). Linear silicon photodiode arrays (digicons, reticons) were introduced in the early 1970s to replace photographic plates in spectroscopy. The charge-coupled device (CCD), a two-dimensional array of silicon-based photosensitive detectors, is producing a modern revolution in imagery and data recording. CCDs not only have a high quantum efficiency, but also produce a digital output with a linear response and low noise. Because of their small size, CCDs still can not replace the photographic plate for many purposes.

Charles J. Peterson

Bibliography

Barnard, E.E. "The Development of Photography in Astronomy." *Popular Astronomy* 6 (1898): 425–455.

de Vaucouleurs, G. *Astronomical Photography: From the Daguerreotype to the Electron Camera*. New York: Macmillan, 1961.

Hoffleit, D. *Some Firsts in Astronomical Photography*. Cambridge: Harvard College Observatory, 1950.

Lankford, J. "The Impact of Photography on Astronomy." In *Astrophysics and Twentieth-century Astronomy to 1950*, edited by O. Gingerich. *The General History of Astronomy,* vol. 4A, 16–39. Cambridge: Cambridge University Press, 1984.

Malin, D., and P. Murdin. *Colours of the Stars*. Cambridge: Cambridge University Press, 1984.

Miller, W.C. "From the Dark Ages Onward." In *Modern Techniques in Astronomical Photography*, edited by R.M. West and J.-L. Heudier, 1–13. Garching bei München: European Southern Observatory, 1978.

Norman, D. "The Development of Astronomical Photography." *Osiris* 5 (1938): 560–594.

Photoheliograph

A small-aperture refracting telescope designed specifically for photographic observation of the sun.

The first attempt at solar photography, in 1845, was a daguerreotype by Armand-Hippolyte-Louis Fizeau and Jean-Bernard-Léon Foucault, who experienced great difficulty in attaining a sufficiently short exposure time. In 1857, at the urging of **John Herschel**, who argued the importance of a daily photographic record of sunspots, the Royal Society granted support to Warren de la Rue to undertake the design of a suitable instrument. The result was a 3.5-inch f/14 achromat, corrected for the violet (photographic) region of the spectrum. An enlarging lens placed behind the primary focus imaged a 4-inch solar disk onto a photographic plate. The telescope was installed briefly at Kew Observatory, then used in 1860 at Rivabellosa, Spain, to photograph the solar eclipse, revealing clearly that prominences were a solar phenomenon. Returned to Kew in 1861, the photoheliograph produced a daily record of the sun over a full solar cycle. After removal to **Royal Greenwich Observatory** in 1873, the daily photography of the sun recommenced. The telescope, the prototype for other photoheliographs, was placed in the South Kensington Science Museum in 1927.

Five additional photoheliographs were made by Thomas R. Dallmeyer in 1874 for use in observing the **transits of Venus**. Two of the Dallmeyer telescopes remained at Greenwich to continue the daily sunspot records, and others were sent to Mauritius, India, and the Royal Observatory at the Cape of Good Hope. Moved to Herstmonceux in 1949, a Dallmeyer instrument has continued in service to produce an essentially uninterrupted record of sunspot photographs for more than a century. More recent photoheliographs by Bernard Lyot and others in the 1940s and 1950s were designed for motion picture photography of sunspots and the solar photosphere.

Charles J. Peterson

Bibliography

Bray, R.J., and R.E. Loughhead. *Sunspots*. London: Chapman and Hall, 1964.

Howse, D. *Greenwich Observatory, Vol. 3: The Buildings and Instruments*. London: Taylor and Francis, 1975.

King, H.C. *The History of the Telescope*. London: Charles Griffin, 1955.

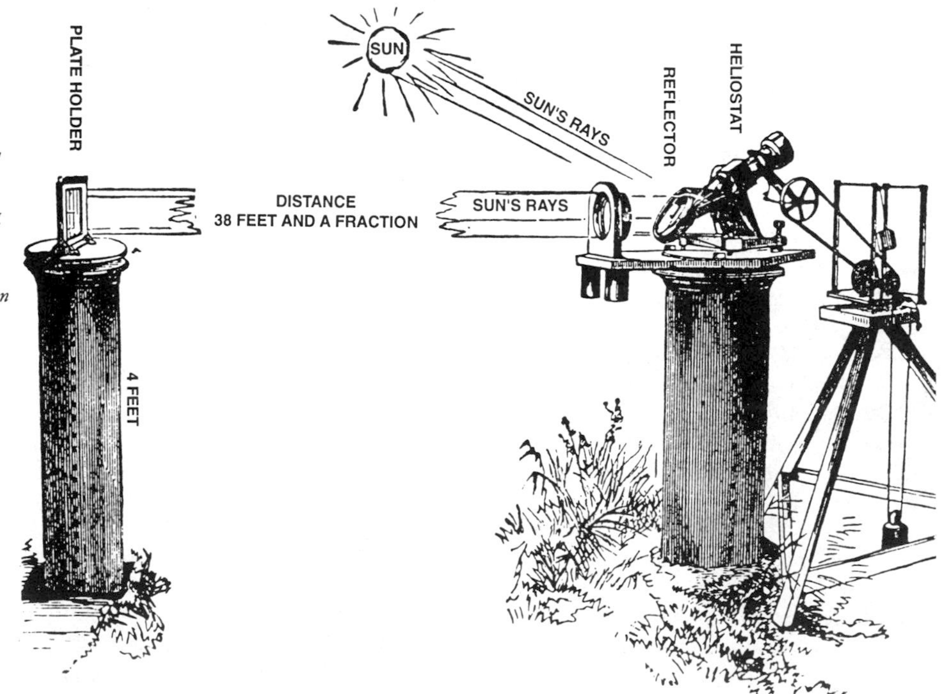

A schematic diagram of a photoheliograph. These instruments were used by French, American, and British observers to photograph solar eclipses as well as the 1874 and 1882 transits of Venus. The long focal length provided an extended image with high resolution. This illustration is from Simon Newcomb's Popular Astronomy, School Edition *(1882). (Courtesy of the United States Naval Observatory)*

Zöllner photometer of the Potsdam Astrophysical Observatory. Photograph taken from G. Müller, Photometrie der Gestirne *(Engelmann Verlag, Leipzig, 1897). (Courtesy photolabs of the Royal Observatory Edinburgh)*

Photometer

An astronomical photometer is an instrument for measuring the intensity of the light emitted by a celestial body. For point sources, such as stars, the photometer allows the brightness or apparent magnitude to be obtained. For extended objects a photometer normally records an image from which a surface brightness can be determined.

Stellar photometers can broadly be classified into visual, thermal, and photoelectric photometers, depending on the detector employed. Visual photometers use the eye and were popular for most of the nineteenth century. They in turn can be of the extinction or comparison type. The former render a star just invisible by inserting absorbing plates or a wedge in a telescope beam, the amount of absorption required indicating the magnitude. Such a device was first used by Anders Celsius in 1740 using glass plates, while wedge photometers were used by several observers from the 1830s and notably by Charles Pritchard in Oxford in the 1880s. Numerous physiological effects limit the accuracy attainable.

Comparison visual photometers rely on the diminution of the light from a comparison star, either real or artificial, to render it of equal brightness to the star observed. Carl von Steinheil's prism photometer of 1836 was the first successful instrument of this type. Later the Zöllner photometer (1861) was widely used, notably at Potsdam. Here polarizing Nicol prisms reduced the intensity of light from an artificial star from a lamp observed simultaneously with the real star. Pickering's meridian photometer at Harvard was also of the comparison type. Two stars, one normally the Pole Star, the other on the meridian, were compared, also using polarizing filters.

Thermal photometers include thermocouples and various types of bolometer and radiometer, and are sensitive over a wide wavelength range, especially in the infrared. **William Huggins** in 1866 attempted the detection of infrared stellar radiation using thermocouples, but with marginal results. Herman Pfund at Allegheny in 1913, William Coblentz at Lick (1914), and Edison Pettit and Seth Nicholson at Mount Wilson (1920s) used much improved vacuum thermocouples and did reliable photometry on

Early photoelectric photometer used by Paul Guthnick and Richard Prager on the 30-cm refractor at the Berlin-Babelsberg Observatory in 1914. Photo from P. Guthnick and R. Prager, "Veröffentlichungen der königl." Sternwarte zu Berlin-Babelsberg, 1 (1914).

bright stars to near infrared wavelengths. However, from 1961 Frank Low's germanium bolometer, which was cooled to 2 degrees Kelvin with liquid helium, revolutionized stellar infrared photometry at wavelengths to 20 micrometers (0.02 mm).

Photoelectric detectors for photometry can be classified into photovoltaic, photoconductive, and photoemissive devices. The last has been easily the most widely used, especially in the optical region, although photovoltaic (from 1893) and photoconductive (from 1907) photometers made earlier debuts. The first photoemissive cells, with potassium hydride photocathodes, by Julius Elster and Hans Geitel of Germany, were used for astronomy from 1912 by Paul Guthnick in Berlin and Hans Rosenberg at Tubingen. At the same time Joel Stebbins at Illinois (later Wisconsin) used Kunz photocells similar to those in Europe. Guthnick and Stebbins developed practical photometers in the 1920s using delicate electrometers to record the tiny photocurrents. Later developments were thermionic amplification (by Rosenberg in 1920 and Whitford at Wisconsin in 1932) and the use of cooled red-sensitive cells, with cesium oxide on silver photocathodes, by John Hall at Yale in 1931.

With the photomultiplier tube's development at RCA from 1937, the first really practical photometers became possible in the late 1940s. Gerald Kron at Lick was a notable pioneer in their use. The 1P21 had a blue-sensitive cesium-antimony photocathode and the photocurrents were amplified about a millionfold by secondary electron emission from the nine dynodes. The photomultiplier allowed pulse-counting to be introduced, by William Blitzstein (Pennsylvania) and Gilbert Yates (Cambridge) from 1949.

There has always been a close relationship between photometers and detector technology, and consequently some of the foremost pioneers in using new astronomical photometers were those with close links with physicists and electronic engineers.

J.B. Hearnshaw

Bibliography

Hearnshaw, J. *The Measurement of Starlight.* New York: Cambridge University Press, 1995.

Johnson, H.L. "Photoelectric Photometers and Amplifiers." In *Astronomical Techniques*, edited by W.A. Hiltner, *Stars and Stellar Systems*, vol. 2, 157–177. Chicago: University of Chicago Press, 1962.

Weaver, H.F. "The Development of Astronomical Photometry." *Popular Astronomy* 54 (1946): 211–230, 287–299, 339–351, 389–404, 451–464 and 504–526.

Whitford, A.E. "Photoelectric Techniques." In *Handbuch der Physik,* edited by S. Flugge, *Astrophysics V*, vol. 54, 240–288. Berlin, Gottingen, Heidelberg: Springer-Verlag, 1962.

Photometry, Astronomical

Astronomical photometry is the measurement of the brightness of celestial objects. The historical development of optical stellar photometry has always been closely linked to developments in instrumentation, especially detectors. Hence it is useful to classify astronomical photometry into a number of eras, based on the instruments used. They are discussed in the following sections in the order of their first introduction. However, many of these techniques extended over long periods of time in simultaneous developments. Indeed at present photographic photometry, photomultiplier photometry, and photometry with area detectors, especially Charge Couple Devices (CCDs), are all used for different astronomical applications.

Naked-Eye Visual Magnitude Estimates

Ptolemy's *Almagest* (ca. 137 C.E.) provides the earliest quantitative information on the brightness of the stars. The star catalogue of the *Almagest* listed 1,028 stars together with their positions and magnitudes. **Ptolemy** used a six-point scale, the brightest stars being assigned to magnitude one, the faintest visible to magnitude six. A few stars (156 in total) were given descriptions of a little more or a little less than the integral values.

Ptolemy's original catalogue has not survived, but there are numerous manuscript copies from the ninth to sixteenth centuries. Although these provide the earliest extant quantitative data on star brightness, it is possible that the magnitude scale of the *Almagest* was adopted from the work of **Hipparchus of Rhodes**, some three centuries earlier. Although this continues to be a topic of contentious debate, the arguments possibly favor Ptolemy as being the observer of many of the stars in his catalogue, in part because from Rhodes (about 5 degrees north of Ptolemy's Alexandria) the southernmost *Almagest* stars would be very close to the horizon and heavily dimmed by atmospheric extinction.

The *Almagest* magnitudes are precise to only about ±0.6 magnitude and were probably never intended as reliable quantitative measures. It is perhaps unfortunate that this arcane scale of measurement has survived to the present day, albeit in much modified form. It is a highly nonlinear scale of intensity and also an inverse scale, larger numbers pertaining to fainter stars.

The Persian astronomer Abu'l-Husayn al-Ṣūfī reestimated the magnitudes of the *Almagest* stars in the tenth century. This was the only significant work on stellar magnitudes between classical times and the sixteenth century. Only with the observations of the Danish astronomer **Tycho Brahe**, some fifteen centuries after Ptolemy, did substantial new data become available, but with little improvement in precision. At the end of the sixteenth century, Dutch sailors visited the Southern Hemisphere and recorded visual magnitudes in the uncharted southern constellations, which appeared on celestial globes and atlases from the early seventeenth century.

Visual Magnitude Estimates through the Telescope

The telescope revealed for the first time large numbers of faint stars, especially in the Milky Way. **Galileo** estimated that he could see stars down to about the twelfth magnitude, though in practice he did not record any stellar magnitudes.

The telescope was a mixed blessing for photometric astronomy in the seventeenth and eighteenth centuries. **John Flamsteed**, **Edmond Halley** (from St. Helena 1676–1678), and James Bradley all estimated stellar magnitudes through small sighting telescopes attached to their astrometric instruments. **J.-J.L de Lalande** in Paris and **N.-L. de Lacaille** at the Cape also engaged in this type of work. The problem was that the Ptolemaic magnitude scale was arbitrary, and hence not readily extrapolated to fainter stars without some agreed standards. Different observers therefore produced discordant results. A star's magnitude was an ill-defined parameter somehow corresponding to the visual sensation imparted to the eye. Until the time of **William Herschel**, many observers continued to regard magnitude as no more than an identification aid, and gave little thought to physiological effects in its estimation or to the extinction of starlight by the earth's atmosphere.

Herschel was the first astronomer to produce reliable magnitude estimates, both by naked eye and through the telescope. He adopted a method of sequences from 1781, in which stars in a certain area of sky were placed in order of their apparent brightness. An estimate was made of the magnitude difference of successive stars. Herschel's technique therefore relied on the direct comparison of neighboring stars, and his results were generally precise to about ±0.2 magnitude.

Herschel saw two applications for stellar magnitudes. He recognized the possibility of finding new variable stars, and also he considered that a star's brightness should depend primarily on its distance, which provided a means of estimating the distribution of stars in space. Herschel's star gauges attempted to delineate the size and shape of the Milky Way based on the numbers of stars to different magnitude limits.

Stellar magnitude estimation reached its zenith with the work of **Friedrich Argelander** and, later, of John Thome. Argelander at Bonn produced his *Uranometria Nova* in 1843, based on estimates of mainly bright stars. He also developed the method of sequences for studying variable stars (he listed eighteen known variables in 1844). But his main achievement was the *Bonner Durchmusterung*, a catalogue and atlas of nearly one third of a million northern stars to magnitude 9.5, based on an extrapolation of the *Almagest* scale in a 76-mm refracting telescope. This huge observational program was completed in 1859 by Argelander and two assistants. The Bonn magnitudes set the standard for all magnitude estimates brighter than tenth magnitude and provided a valuable statistical base for further studies of the sidereal universe. The precision was about a quarter of a magnitude for stars near the zenith.

The *Bonner Durchmusterung* was extended to −23 degrees by Eduard Schonfeld in Bonn, using a larger telescope but essentially the same techniques. Further south, Benjamin Gould estimated magnitudes to m = 7 in his *Uranometria Argentina* (1879), a work noted for its high precision of about ±0.15 magnitude. This was the forerunner of the much larger *Cordoba Durchmusterung* (1892–1900) of John Thome and Charles Perrine. This contained coordinates and magnitude estimates for over half a million stars to about magnitude 11 and north of −62 degrees declination.

The *Cordoba Durchmusterung* was the last major work of this kind. Although large numbers of southern stars were recorded for the first time, the work was undertaken at a time when photographic methods were becoming well established. In addition, simple magnitude estimates could not compete with the precision that visual photometers provided.

Visual Photometry

In the 1720s, Pierre Bouguer in France was the founder of quantitative photometry. He measured the decrease in the intensity of light rays in an absorbing medium and introduced visual comparison methods for estimating the illumination on a screen. He applied these techniques to astronomy by imaging both the sun and the moon onto a screen and compared the illuminations produced with that from a candle. An early application of Bouguer's techniques to astronomy was by Anders Celsius in Sweden in 1740. His method was to insert glass plates into a telescope beam so as just to render a star invisible. Each plate gave about half a magnitude of extinction; the number of plates used was therefore a measure of a star's brightness. William Wollaston in England in 1826–1827 also tried to apply the principles of photometry to measure the brightness ratio of Sirius to the sun, an extraordinarily difficult task, given the vastly greater brightness of the sun. His value of 2×10^{10} was within a factor or two of the modern value. Such a value implied a distance of over 10^5 astronomical units for the star, an early photometric indication of the great distances of the stars prior to the first trigonometric parallax determination.

Stellar visual photometry flourished in the nineteenth century. The Celsius technique is an example of extinction photometry. In principle the method is not as precise as comparison photometry, in which the brightness of two images (or illuminations) is brought to equality by changing the intensity of at least one of them. The comparison star can be a real star, or an artificial star provided by a lamp. Herschel experimented with comparison photometry in the early nineteenth century, using two identical telescopes, one of them being stopped down so as to render a brighter star apparently equal to that viewed in the unmodified aperture. Later **John Herschel** at the Cape used his "astrometer," a visual photometer that compared stars with a starlike image of the moon. However, the first really successful comparison photometer was Carl von Steinheil's prism photometer of 1836. The Steinheil instrument achieved high precision (less than 0.1 magnitude), but was limited to bright stars, a consequence of its using extrafocal images. It was used by Ludwig Seidel for a photometric catalogue of about two hundred stars in 1862.

The researches of Steinheil and Seidel spurred interest in stellar photometry in the second half of the nineteenth century. Three major photometric catalogues were produced, each using a photometer of different design. The first of these was Zöllner's comparison photometer (1861). It used polarizing Nicol prisms to reduce by a known amount the brightness of an artificial star produced by a lamp. Zöllner photometers were made commercially by the firm of Ausfeld in Gotha and were acquired by many observatories.

The Zöllner photometer was used by Gustav Müller and Paul Kempf for the famous *Potsdamer Durchmusterung*, published 1894–1907. This catalogue contained over fourteen thousand stars to magnitude 7.5 and was by far the most reliable photometric data available at that time, with random errors of about ±0.05 magnitude. Great care was taken to establish a network of standard comparison stars, to take the effects of stellar color into account, and to allow for the extinction in the earth's atmosphere.

The meridian photometer designed by **Edward Pickering** at Harvard was the most extensively used visual photometer, but only at **Harvard College Observatory** and at its southern Boyden Station in Peru. It made a direct comparison between a star and the Pole Star (or other bright star near either celestial pole). Its operation involved changing the intensity of both stars viewed simultaneously using polarizing filters, so as to achieve apparent equality of both images.

The first meridian photometer was in operation from 1877 and used for the *Harvard Photometry* of 1884, in which the visual magnitudes of over four thousand bright stars were catalogued. Later the *Revised Harvard Photometry* (1908) contained visual magnitudes for over nine thousand stars to magnitude 6.5 in both hemispheres. By 1910 Pickering had personally made about 1.4 million photometric observations with meridian photometers over three decades. The probable errors for bright star magnitudes in the *Harvard Photometry* were about ±0.10 magnitude, a precision inferior to that at Potsdam, a fact that Müller and Kempf ascribed to the undue haste of Pickering's observational work.

The third major catalogue of visual photometry in the late nineteenth century was the *Uranometria Nova Oxoniensis* (1885) of Charles Pritchard, who used a wedge extinction photometer on 3- or 4-inch telescopes in Oxford and Cairo. The neutral density wedge was displaced sideways in the beam to render a star just invisible, the wedge displacement thereby giving the stellar magnitude. The catalogue contained nearly three thousand stars.

Two features in common to these three catalogues of visual photometry were first, the practice of allowing for atmospheric extinction by reducing all the magnitudes to zenith values, and second, the use of the Pogson scale for the relation between intensity and magnitude. In 1856 Norman Pogson had proposed using the fifth root of 100, or about 2.512, for the intensity ratio corresponding to a one magnitude interval, which would, if adopted, closely follow Argelander's *Bonner-Durchmusterung* scale. By adopting the Pogson scale, relative intensity measurements could readily be converted into magnitudes. This uniformity of practice among photometrists of the late nineteenth century allowed their data to be intercompared. The adoption of the Pogson scale by the general consensus was therefore a unifying current in astronomy as practiced in America, Britain, and Germany in the late nineteenth century.

At this time the cataloging of stellar magnitudes was the main preoccupation of photometrists. The analysis of the magnitude data, to obtain the intrinsic properties of stars and their distribution within the galactic system, was not much considered until well into the twentieth century. The precision of visual photometry was poor by today's standards, and although the data themselves are now all obsolete, it would be a mistake to consider this era of photometry as wasted effort. The extension of photometric measurements to faint telescopic stars on the Pogson scale (in some cases to magnitude 13), the procedures for atmospheric extinction corrections, the cataloging of all stars to magnitude 7.5 and the discovery of several hundred new variable stars (393 were known by 1896) were the major achievements of this era.

Photographic Photometry

The earliest successful stellar photographs were taken at Harvard with the 15-inch telescope in the 1850s, using wet collodion plates. George Bond obtained a series of photographs of the double star Mizar, from which he attempted the first photographic stellar photometry. His method was to deduce a relationship between the apparent image diameter and the exposure time. If intensity and exposure time were inversely related for a given photographic impression (the so-called reciprocity law), then intensities and hence magnitudes could be obtained.

When astronomers returned to the problems of photographic photometry in the early 1880s, the much more practical dry gelatine plates were being used. Edward Pickering at Harvard experimented with a variety of techniques, including the estimation of photographic density in trailed stellar images, which could be calibrated by taking photographs using telescopes of different aperture. Using such techniques, Pickering published a catalogue of photographic magnitudes for over two thousand stars in 1890.

The optimism concerning photographic photometry toward the end of the nineteenth century spread rapidly among the astronomical community. In 1885 **David Gill** at the Cape embarked on a large program to photograph the southern skies using a 6-inch astrographic telescope. The aim was to record the positions and magnitudes of all the stars south of −18 degrees to at least magnitude 9.2. The plate measurements and reductions for nearly half a million stars were undertaken in collaboration with **Jacobus Kapteyn** at the University of Groningen in Holland. Thirteen years were required (twice the original estimate), but the resulting *Cape Photographic Durchmusterung* was one of the earliest and most fruitful international collaborations in astronomy.

Unfortunately, there were large systematic errors in the CPD magnitudes. Two fundamental problems had hardly been addressed, and in future years they were to become increasingly intractable. These were the failure of the reciprocity law and the fact that photographic plates recorded blue and ultraviolet light, and could therefore not readily be calibrated using visual magnitudes.

These problems had still only occasionally been alluded to when another very large international program, the *Carte du Ciel* and *Astrographic Catalogue*, was launched in Paris in 1887. One of the aims was to obtain magnitudes for about two million stars to magnitude 11. The work was divided among eighteen observatories using identical 33-cm astrographs. None of the participants were from North America and Pickering wisely took no part, although he offered advice at times.

The *Carte du Ciel* program quickly ran into the problem of how to transfer the scale of standard magnitudes that Pickering had set up around the north pole to other regions of the sky. The practice of double exposures of polar and other regions of the sky was fraught with photometric difficulties that were never satisfactorily resolved. In the end the program was terminated in 1962 after seventy-five years, with the work being performed in a very inhomogeneous and patchy manner. Some of the observatories did not even complete the necessary exposures, and none of them obtained satisfactory stellar magnitudes. It was one of the largest and most ambitious programs ever attempted in international science, and by most accounts an embarrassing failure.

In the early twentieth century many astronomers grappled with the problems of photographic photometry and some progress was made using extrafocal images. Some of the problems of the nonlinear response and saturation of the plates could be overcome by spreading the light uniformly over a small area whose density could be measured using a microdensitometer. **Karl Schwarzschild**'s *Gottinger Aktinometrie* (1910) contained magnitudes for some thirty-five hundred stars from smeared jiggle-camera images with random errors of about 5 percent, the best photographic photometry then available. John Parkhurst at **Yerkes Observatory** was another pioneer of extrafocal techniques. His *Yerkes Actinometry* (1912) was nearly as precise as Schwarzschild's work and introduced the photovisual (or yellow) magnitudes using orthochromatic plates with a yellow filter.

Meanwhile Pickering at Harvard was pursuing his own vigorous program of photographic photometry in both hemispheres. He had set up forty-eight standard regions over the sky with the aim of defining sequences of secondary standard stars in each region with magnitudes tied to the North Polar Sequence (NPS), and used for calibrating focal images on photographic plates. Henrietta Leavitt at Harvard did most of the work in establishing these standard magnitudes. By 1912 the NPS stars to magnitude 21 had been defined, supposedly on the Pogson scale, and by 1913 the Harvard International System of Photographic Magnitudes was adopted by the *Carte du Ciel*, even though no acceptable technique of transferring this scale to other regions of the sky had been found.

When Pickering died in 1919 and Miss Leavitt two years later, Frederick Seares at Mount Wilson became the champion of the International System and of the North Polar Sequence. He showed that substantial systematic errors pervaded the Harvard scale, and devoted almost his whole working life to resolving these problems. In 1922 Seares presented a new list of photographic and photovisual magnitudes for ninety-two NPS stars to the newly formed **International Astronomical Union**. These thenceforth defined the officially adopted International System.

Yet major problems still persisted; the faint stars were nearly all red, while many of the bright ones were white. This unfortunate distribution of color made the transfer to the International System difficult for observers using different instruments. Seares's work was mainly with the Mount Wilson 60-inch silvered reflector. Later this was aluminized, giving a greater ultraviolet response, while other observers used refractors with different color equations. Unfortunately, the spectral band of the unfiltered photographic magnitudes had never been defined, so the amount of ultraviolet light varied according to the telescope used, its altitude, and the air mass and color of the star being observed. The transfer of the NPS magnitudes to other regions of the sky, in particular to the Southern Hemisphere, was another awkward problem, in spite of huge efforts by many observers to overcome it.

Toward the end of his career, Seares was forced to admit that his life's work was still incomplete. In practice, the International System was finally abandoned as an official IAU system in 1955, by which time photoelectric photometry was giving results with both higher precision and accuracy.

The history of the NPS and the International System was the second major failure for photographic photometry after the *Carte du Ciel*. Nevertheless a huge amount of photographic photometry was accomplished in the first half of the twentieth century and many important results were forthcoming—notably those concerning new variable stars and the analysis of their light curves and those concerning **stellar statistics** and the structure of the Milky Way system. Ironically the most famous result of photographic photometry was obtained by **Harlow Shapley** in 1918, concerning the distances of the globular clusters from photographic observations of the variable stars they contained. He showed the distribution of these clusters define the center of the galaxy. His analysis used relatively crude determinations of photographic magnitude for which the errors in the International System scale were of little import, yet one of the most significant conclusions of astronomical research of that era came from this work.

After 1950 the photomultiplier considerably changed the way photographic photometry was undertaken. Photoelectric sequences were used to calibrate the stellar images on each plate, and these sequences were in turn tied to the standard stars of the UBV or other photoelectric systems. Moreover large **Schmidt telescopes** allowed wide-angle plates to faint limiting magnitudes to be recorded, and with the development of fully automatic plate measuring engines, notably in Edinburgh and Cambridge, large numbers of photographically determined magnitudes for faint stars have been obtained since about 1970.

Photoelectric Photometry with Simple Photocells

Photoelectric cells were developed by Julius Elster and Hans Geitel in Germany, and were first used in astronomy by Paul Guthnick in Berlin, by Hans Rosenberg at Tubingen, and by colleagues of Joel Stebbins at Illinois in the year 1912. The cathode was generally hydrogenated potassium, the cell was filled with a low-pressure inert gas, which amplified the photocurrent by collisional ionization, and photocurrents as small as 10–14 amps were detected with a delicate string electrometer. Guthnick with Richard Prager in Berlin and Stebbins at Illinois (then, from 1922, in Wisconsin, with Morse Huffer and Albert Whitford) were the undisputed masters of the new technique. From 1920 Kurt Bottlinger in Berlin used glass filters to obtain color indices, a technique that became a common practice elsewhere, though the passbands were not standardized. In the period 1912–1940 as many as thirty-seven observers at twenty-two observatories in Europe and North America attempted to emulate the success of these pioneers, but apart from Gerald Kron at Lick and John Hall at Yale and Sproul observatories in the 1930s, few of the others overcame the numerous technical difficulties to produce good astronomical data. The reasons were that few astronomers had practical experience in electronics, while those achieving success had the close support of physicists to supply and operate their cells: Guthnick from Elster and Geitel, Stebbins from Jakob Kunz at Illinois, and John Hall from Charles Prescott, who at Bell Labs produced the first red-sensitive cesium oxide on silver photocells, with which Hall made pioneering spectrophotometry and studied the law of interstellar reddening. In 1943 Stebbins and Whitford used red-sensitive cells of this type for six-color UVBGRI photometry to study further the reddening of B stars.

Photoelectric Photometry with the Photomultiplier

The introduction of the photomultiplier by Viktor Zworykin at RCA in the early 1940s greatly improved the ease of making photoelectric photometry from about 1945. This gave essentially noise-free amplification of about a million times and allowed relatively simple measurement techniques to be employed. By 1947 Kron at Lick was using the 931-A and soon afterwards the 1P21 tube, both with blue-sensitive cesium-antimony cathodes and nine stages of amplification. At first the 1P21 was used with blue and yellow

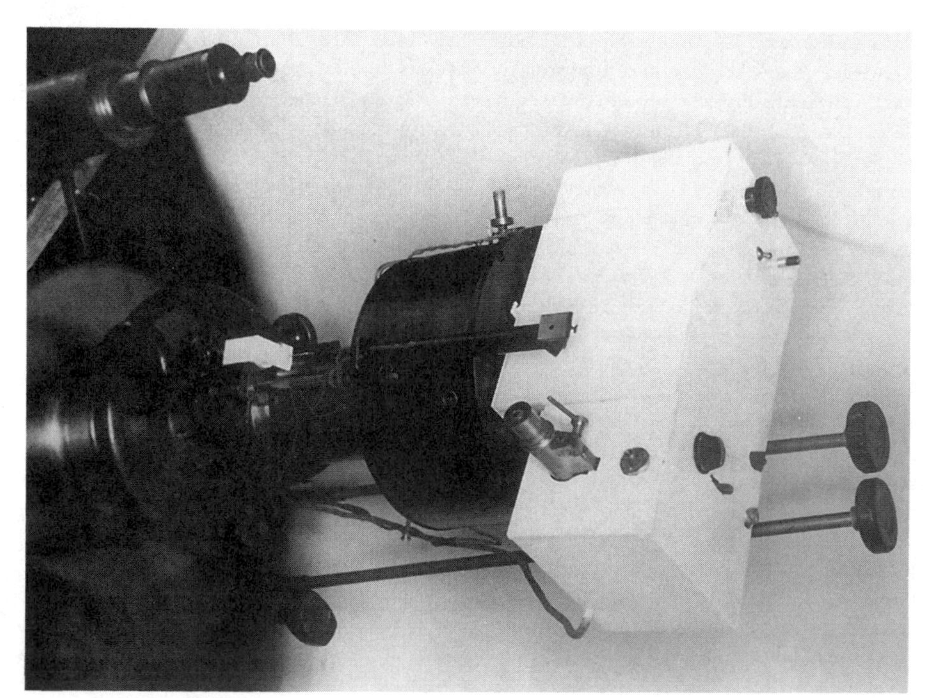

Photoelectric photometry with Cs-O-Ag red-sensitive photocell cooled in dry ice used by John S. Hall on the Amherst College Observatory 18-inch refractor in 1940. (Courtesy of the late John S. Hall)

filters designated P and V, designed roughly to match the International System of photographic photometry; from 1953 Harold Johnson and William Morgan devised the UBV three-color system, which became widely used at many observatories. Meanwhile **Bengt Stromgren** experimented with narrow-band systems, which led to his UVBY system's being widely used from 1960.

The relative ease with which photoelectric photometry could be undertaken with the photomultiplier allowed many observatories to undertake this type of work for the first time in the 1950s and 1960s. Many studies were made of stellar open clusters, mostly in the UBV system. The color-magnitude diagrams enabled the theory of stellar evolution to be tested, and also the composition, photometric distance, evolutionary age, and reddening of many clusters were obtained. Photometry thus became the tool for astrophysical analysis. Photometric indices to measure a range of parameters, such as temperature, luminosity, and metallicity for individual stars were also devised. Other applications of photometry were the study of pulsating stars, the analysis of eclipsing-binary light curves, and the measurement of the polarization of starlight by interstellar dust grains.

Electronic Area Detectors for Photometry

Image intensifier tubes made their first appearance in astronomy in the 1930s. In particular, Andre Lallemand's electronic camera (1936) recorded electron images on a nuclear-track emulsion inside the glass envelope of the tube. The glass was broken to recover the plate for development. This tube was first used after the war for spectroscopy, but also for photometry when Lallemand took the electronic camera to Lick in 1959. Various electrographic tubes followed, notably those designed by Kron and James McGee, but the small cathode size and the technical difficulty in their use prevented widespread photometric application.

Meanwhile image tubes with phosphors and conventional photographic recording were widely used detectors for astronomy from the 1960s, but with few advantages for photometry over direct photography, especially for sky-limited work. Likewise the development of electron-scanned television tubes such as the image orthicon and videcon in the 1950s led to these devices primarily being used for spectroscopic work at observatories.

The ideal imaging photometric detector combines the qualities of a large sensitive area, high quantum efficiency, wide spectral bandpass, a linear response over a large dynamic range, and low readout noise. Such qualities were first available with the charge-coupled device from the early 1970s, which has now become the preferred detector for area photometry in astronomy.

J.B. Hearnshaw

Bibliography

Hearnshaw, J.B. *The Measurement of Starlight.* Cambridge University Press, 1995.

Lundmark, K. "Luminosities, Colours, Diameters, Densities, Masses of the Stars." In *Handbuch der Astrophysik,* vol. 5 (part 1), 210–574. Berlin: Springer-Verlag, 1932.

Müller, G. *Photometrie der Gestirne.* Leipzig: Engelmann Verlag, 1897.

Sterken, C., and J. Manfroid. *Astronomical Photometry: A Guide.* Dordrecht: Kluwer, 1992.

Weaver, H.F. "The Development of Astronomical Photometry." *Popular Astronomy* 54 (1946): 211–230, 287–299, 339–351, 389– 404, 451–464, and 504–526.

Physics and Astronomy

Underlying all astronomical thinking today is the belief that cosmic processes obey the laws of physics. Accordingly, all interpretive work falls under the aegis of **astrophysics**. Among professional astronomers, only those determined to restrict themselves to purely descriptive observational work can escape the need for physical interpretation.

Otto Neugebauer, writing in *The Exact Sciences in Antiquity,* describes late Babylonian work that developed ways of calculating the times of appearance and disappearance of planets with respect to the horizon and provided a lunar theory, without developing any physical model to describe these phenomena. Instead, Babylonian scholars developed algorithms permitting them to compute times of lunar and planetary phenomena well into the future.

Babylonian and Greek astronomy was astrologically inspired. But Greek astronomy from the times of Thales developed models for stellar and planetary motions. With Empedocles we see the early recognition of the causes of night and day and a discussion of eclipses in terms of shadows cast by one solar system body on another. With **Aristarchus**, geometric methods were introduced for determining the size and distance of the moon and sun, and a consistent emphasis on physical explanations of the universe began to prevail.

Not that all of the Greek theories were correct. But then, even the turnover in ideas since the year 1900 has been astonishing, and there is no reason to believe that modern astrophysics has approached anything like an ultimate truth. Nevertheless, our current views share with Greek astronomy a faith in the rationality of the heavens, and that belief has maintained a measure of continuity for over two millennia.

Innovations in Theoretical Physics

The acceptance of physical explanations for cosmic processes is so widespread that complex theories, comprising layer upon layer of extrapolation, abound, even where observational evidence is entirely lacking or at best fragmentary. This reflects an astonishing measure of confidence in physical theory, particularly in view of the fact that modern physics in general has only been tested on scales as small as the laboratory or, in exceptional cases, as in the theory of gravitation, on a scale as large as the solar system or binary pulsars—a scale of order 10^{14} cm. This needs to be contrasted to the scale of the universe, roughly 10^{28} cm, where for all we know the laws of physics could take quite different forms.

A particular example of this layering of extrapolations is the theory of stellar structure and evolution and the closely allied theory of the origin of the heavy chemical elements. In 1939, **Hans Bethe** published a detailed theory that related the luminosity of the sun to the rate at which nuclear reactions were converting hydrogen into helium at the sun's center. Hydrostatic and thermodynamic arguments permitted Bethe to calculate the density and temperature at different radial distances from the center of the sun. Laboratory measurements on some nuclear reactions and theoretical calculations of others allowed him to compute the nuclear reaction rates for converting hydrogen into helium. He found the corresponding rates of energy generation to just match the outpouring of energy in the form of sunlight, thereby convincingly proving his case.

No part of Bethe's theory could be directly verified. Nevertheless astrophysicists began a detailed series of further extrapolations, calculating and quantitatively predicting the nuclear processes that would be set in motion after all the hydrogen at a star's center was depleted. By the late 1950s, the theory of energy and chemical-element generation in the cores of stars was widely accepted and summarized in a paper published by E. Margaret Burbidge, Geoffrey R. Burbidge, William A. Fowler, and Fred Hoyle. This theory explained, in some detail, the relative abundances of heavy elements found on earth, in meteorites, and in the spectra of celestial objects.

Meanwhile work on yet a third layer of extrapolation had begun. It focused on the evolution of a massive star after depletion of all nuclear energy sources. This theory predicted a free-fall collapse of the stellar core, whose density would shoot up by tens of orders of magnitude within a second, generating a huge abundance of neutrinos, which in turn could escape through the entire body of the star, depriving the star of a significant portion of its mass through energy transported away by neutrinos.

The supernova 1987A observed in the Large Magellanic Cloud generated just such a burst of neutrinos, dramatically vindicating for the first time the nearly half-century-long process of computation that had been initiated by Bethe's work. Until this outburst in 1987, direct examination of neutrinos generated in celestial sources and the sun had yielded ambiguous results, and the prime evidence supporting stellar evolution theory had come from relative abundances of the chemical elements found in the photospheres of various types of stars, in interstellar space, and in supernova remnants.

Innovative Instrumentation and Marginals

Theory is not the only place where physics has had a leading impact on astronomy. Most of the modern observational tools that have permitted a charting of the heavens and the discovery of new phenomena detectable primarily at gamma-ray, X-ray, ultraviolet, infrared, and radio wavelengths were introduced into astronomy by physicists. David O. Edge and Michael J. Mulkay discuss this prevalence of contributions from physicists with particular attention to the birth of radio astronomy. In their book *Astronomy Transformed*, they argue that marginals (practitioners who work at the margins of a discipline and occasionally contribute new techniques imported from another field) are best poised to effect the transfer of new instrumentation into astronomy. However, an additional factor could be the size of the physics community, which is so much larger than that of astronomy. The 1991 membership directory of the American Astronomical Society listed roughly fifty-five hundred members. In contrast, the American Physical Society listed about forty-five thousand members in the same year. The role of marginals in science remains under active study.

How Far will Astrophysics Reach?

How far can physics go in explaining the universe? The answer to that question is not at all clear. Until the mid-1940s, cosmology was primarily an exercise in geometry and general relativity. Then, in the late 1940s, Ralph A. Alpher, Robert Herman, and George A. Gamow began to search for the origin of the chemical elements in nuclear reactions that should have taken place if the universe had once been hot and far denser than it is today. Because a hot, explosive cosmic origin could also explain today's rapid expansion of the universe, this idea seemed attractive. By the late 1950s it had become clear that helium and some other light nuclei could be formed within the first few hundred seconds of a cosmic explosion, though the heavy elements would have to be formed in stars.

Given these successes, we can ask whether astrophysics and cosmology will ultimately also permit us to explain phenomena such as the observed prevalence of matter over antimatter, or the precise equality of charge and mass of electrons all over the universe. Will all of those observables ultimately be explained on the basis of known physical processes, or will astrophysics be forced to stop questioning at some point and simply postulate initial conditions that, for no good reason, just happened to prevail at the birth of the universe?

We do not know. Despite its many other strengths, astrophysics can not forecast its own future.

Martin Harwit

Bibliography

Alpher R.A., R. Herman, and G.A. Gamow. "Thermonuclear Reactions in the Expanding Universe." *Physical Review* 74 (1948): 1198–1199.

Bethe, H. "Energy Production in Stars." *Physical Review* 55 (1939): 434–456.

Burbidge, E.M., G.R. Burbidge, W.A. Fowler, and F. Hoyle. "Synthesis of the Elements in Stars." *Reviews of Modern Physics* 29 (1957): 547–650.

Edge, D.O., and M.J. Mulkay. *Astronomy Transformed—The Emergence of Radio Astronomy in Britain*. New York: John Wiley and Sons, 1976.

Harwit, M.O. *Cosmic Discovery—The Search, Scope and Heritage of Astronomy*. New York: Basic Books, 1981.

Heath, T. *Aristarchus of Samos—The Ancient Copernicus*. New York: Dover, 1981.

Hufbauer, K. *Exploring the Sun: Solar Science since Galileo*. Baltimore: Johns Hopkins University Press, 1991.

Neugebauer, O. *The Exact Sciences in Antiquity*. 2nd ed. New York: Dover, 1969.

Piazzi, Giuseppe (1746–1826)

Italian astronomer. Born in Valtellina, Italy (now Switzerland), Piazzi studied philosophy and mathematics in Milan and Rome. Beginning in 1769, he taught in various Italian cities before securing appointment to the chair of higher mathematics at the Academy of Palermo in 1780. Encouraged by the Bourbon viceroy of Sicily to establish an observatory, Piazzi traveled to England to obtain instruments for the facility, which opened in 1790.

Piazzi's research focused on **astrometry**. A catalogue of nearly seven thousand stars was published in 1803 and was expanded over the next decade to include an additional nine hundred entries. Near the end of his first research program, Piazzi made the discovery that would become his most famous contribution. During the first six weeks of 1801, he observed a new body that he concluded could only be a comet or a planet. Using Piazzi's published observations, Karl Friedrich Gauss calculated the required orbital elements, which allowed F.X. von Zach of the Gotha Observatory to locate the asteroid in late December. Piazzi named this minor planet Ceres in 1802.

Following the completion of his expanded star catalogue, Piazzi published a two-volume introductory astronomy text in 1817. In that same year, King Ferdinand I asked the astronomer to supervise the completion of the Naples observatory and appointed him director general of both the Palermo and Naples facilities. Dividing his time between the two cities, Piazzi discharged his responsibilities but seriously weakened his health. Following retirement in 1824, Piazzi moved to Naples, where he died.

George E. Webb

Bibliography

Abetti, G. "Piazzi, Giuseppe." In *Dictionary of Scientific Biography*, edited by C.C. Gillispie, vol. 10: 591–593. New York: Scribner, 1974.

Cunningham, C.J. "Giuseppe Piazzi and the 'Missing Planet.'" *Sky & Telescope* 84 (1992): 274–275.

Serio, G.F. "Giuseppe Piazzi and the Discovery of the Proper Motion of 61 Cygni." *Journal for the History of Astronomy* 21 (1990): 275–282.

Pickering, Edward Charles (1846–1919)

American astronomer and observatory director. Born in Boston, he graduated from the Lawrence Scientific School in 1865. After teaching there and at the Massachusetts Institute of Technology, Pickering was appointed director of the **Harvard College Observatory** (HCO) in 1877, a position he held until his death. From 1903 until his death he served as president of the American Astronomical Society.

Pickering approached astronomy from the perspective of physics. Under his directorship, the new field of **astrophysics** became the main research program at the HCO. With a Baconian concept of science, he instituted vast, often routine, projects that collected large and valuable amounts of data.

A skillful entrepreneur, he was highly successful in raising money. Deeply concerned with matters of efficiency and productivity, he ran the HCO like a factory. Although this led to splendid successes, it also raised difficult questions, such as how much credit he deserved for discoveries made by his assistants.

He devoted most of his time and effort in his later years to securing the universal acceptance of the Harvard systems of spectral classification and photographic magnitudes. Both systems were adopted by the International Union for Cooperation in Solar Research in 1913.

It is difficult—and in a fundamental way unnecessary—to separate Pickering's achievements from those of the HCO. His real significance lies in the institutional development of astronomy.

The Harvard University Archives house sixty-eight linear feet of his personal and official correspondence. To date, there is no full-length biography of Pickering.

Howard N. Plotkin

Bibliography

Bailey, S.I. *The History and Work of Harvard Observatory, 1839 to 1927*. New York: McGraw-Hill, 1931.

Jones, B.Z., and L.G. Boyd. *The Harvard College Observatory. The First Four Directorships, 1839–1919*. Cambridge: Harvard University Press, 1971.

Plotkin, H. "Edward C. Pickering, the Henry Draper Memorial, and the Beginnings of Astrophysics in America." *Annals of Science* 35 (1978): 365–377.

———. "Edward C. Pickering." *Journal for the History of Astronomy* 21 (1990): 47–58.

Planetariums

Planetariums represent the motions of the planets by systems of mechanical gears or by optical projection. Mechanical representations of celestial motion were diverse in form and use. The **armillary spheres** developed by Muslim scholars suggest the calculation of astronomical events, while the highly embellished marble globes of Greece presented a complete visualizable cosmology. The seventeenth-century Gottorp globe, a hollow copper sphere made for Duke Frederick III of Holstein-Gottorp, in which up to ten observers could view gilded stars and constellations, must be understood in the context of courtly spectacle. However, the planetarium's combination of faithful representation and impressive display made it ideal as a pedagogical instrument.

In 1682, Johannes van Ceulen built a model to the design of Christiaan Huygens in which the planets were globes carried by gear-wheels with the number of teeth in proportion to the planet's period. The mechanism was placed in an octagonal box, and the planets were carried on spindles with off-centered circular tracks to mimic the nonuniform motion of elliptical orbits. The Huygens planetarium emerged from the burgeoning commercial culture of the European capitals of the late seventeenth century: At one extreme they became recognized symbols of wealth, and at the other became necessary tools of the lecturer in natural philosophy. Such use was exemplified in the work of London instrument-makers. George Graham and the clock-maker Thomas Tompion made working models of the sun, moon, and earth between 1704 and 1709. Desaguliers recorded that four copies of this machine were made by a fellow London instrument-maker, John Rowley, of which one was sent to Charles Boyle, Fourth Earl of Orrery (hence the name *orrery* for this and similar devices). The Rowley orreries were highly valued both as works of art and as scientific curiosities, and other instrument-makers began constructing them. Thomas Wright at his London Orrery and Globe workshop designed and built the Grand Orrery, an instrument showing the movements of the earth, moon, and five planets.

Special mention should be made of the large orrery built between 1774 and 1781 by Eise Eisinga, a wool-comber of Franeker in West Friesland. Its huge, heavy, pendulum-driven mechanism was concealed in a double ceiling, so that the planetarium appeared over the head of the observer. The planets revolve at their natural periods (thus Saturn took twenty-nine and a half years to complete one revolution).

The large, impressive planetarium became part of the stage act of the renowned lecturer of astronomy. A poster from the 1780s announced that Adam Walker had displayed his Eidouranion, or transparent orrery, at the Royal Theatre in London. The Eidouranion was not without competitors: the Eidophusikon of Philip de Loutherbourg, the Aetheroedies of Mr. Didier, while the Dioastrodoxon could boast both minor planets and the Georgium Sidus, Uranus.

With the design of Walther Bauersfeld, of the **Carl Zeiss** optical works at Jena, the construction of planetariums shifted profoundly. The stars were produced by thirty-one optical projectors that studded a 20-inch ball, in the middle of which was a 200-watt light bulb. This was placed on an equatorial mount to show the sky at Munich's latitude. At 23½ degrees from the equatorial axis were a series of movable cylinders that held the projectors for the planets, the sun, and the moon. The light show could be viewed at a range of speeds. When installed at the Deutsches Museum in Munich in August 1923, the first Zeiss projection planetarium presented an artificial sky to fifty thousand visitors in six months. Walter Villiger modified this design in 1924 so that the device could be used at any latitude. The Zeiss universal planetarium was a dumbbell consisting of two star globes, one for each hemisphere, with the planetary, solar, and lunar projectors arranged along an interlinking bar. Ten such instruments were opened in German and Austrian cities between 1925 and 1928. Rome had a Zeiss universal planetarium in 1928, and Moscow the following year. The Adler Planetarium was installed in Chicago to great acclaim in May 1930, and it was swiftly followed by Philadelphia (1933), Los Angeles (1935), New York (1935), Pittsburgh (1939), and Chapel Hill (1940). The Carl Zeiss Werke of Jena divided after 1945, with planetarium production continuing in both East and West Germany. They were joined in an expanding market for optical projectors by Spitz Laboratories of Yorklyn, Delaware.

The Griffith Observatory Mark IV Zeiss Planetarium Projector was installed in 1964. (Courtesy of the Griffith Observatory)

The standard source for the history of the planetarium is King's study of orreries, planetariums, and astronomical clocks. His emphasis is very much on mechanical and geared models. King makes the etymological distinction between orreries as models of the earth accompanied by an orbiting moon ball, and the planetarium, in which the model is dominated by the demonstration of planetary motion. However, it must be stressed that the term *planetarium* has had diverse meanings for historical actors. With regard to the optical projection planetarium, the key questions of the contexts in which they were used, the relations between planetarium directors and astronomers, and in particular the reactions of the planetarium audience, have been largely undiscussed. Contemporary writers have described the planetarium as variously a cathedral, temple, and a combination of school, theater, and cinema. In the lectures that accompanied shows with the Zeiss instrument, such as at the Adler Planetarium under Philip Fox in the 1930s, the attention of the audience was often directed as much to the capabilities of the projector as to astronomical instruction. Planetarium lectures, from the Eidouranion to the optical projectors, have included subjects tailored to popular culture: the star of Bethlehem, the sky seen by Admiral Byrd in 1940 from the Antarctic, or by the poet Goethe in the summer of 1828. The reception of planetariums varied with different national cultures: from the large numbers and close association with the professional scientific community in Germany, to their late, commercial arrival in Britain. There is no detailed history of the growth of small planetariums after World War II, but nonhistorical sources for descriptions of individual instruments are *Sky & Telescope* and the journal of the International Planetarium Society, *The Planetarian*.

Jon Agar

Bibliography

Fox, P. *Adler Planetarium and Astronomical Museum*. Chicago: Lakeside Press, 1933.

King, H.C. *Geared to the Stars: The Evolution of Planetariums, Orreries, and Astronomical Clocks*. Bristol: Adam Hilger, 1978.

Letsch, H. *Das Zeiss-Planetarium: Captured Stars*. Translated by H. Spitzbardt. Jena: VEB Gustav Fisher Verlag, 1959.

Villiger, W. *The Zeiss Planetarium*, translated by R.G. Aitken. Jena: Zeiss, 1927.

Planetary Satellites

The first telescopic observations of **Galileo** and his contemporaries focused on the startling phenomenon of the four inner satellites of **Jupiter**. In addition to demonstrating celestial motion about a center other than the sun and the implications for the Aristotelian-Copernican debate, these observations were also used to produce tables of the satellites' motions. The desire for a reliable means of determining longitude motivated efforts to develop theories of motion based on positions and eclipse timings, as well as practical procedures and tools that might be used by navigators and surveyors.

The prestige associated with discovering a new satellite and the leverage provided by the discoverer's prerogative of naming the new objects provided powerful motivation. Galileo, for example, named the four Jovian satellites the Medician Stars, after his patron. However, the names from mythology assigned by his contemporary Simon Marius became generally accepted. As telescopes increased in size and power, and observing techniques became more sophisticated, satellite discovery remained a favorite activity, as did precise determinations of the satellite motions.

Huygens directed his new telescope toward **Saturn** in March 1655, a favorable time for discovering satellites since the rings were oriented edge-on and their distracting glare was at a minimum. He discovered a satellite later named Titan. During Cassini's first few years at the Paris Observatory he discovered two additional satellites (1671–1672), and yet another two in 1684.

Isaac Newton drew on observations of Jupiter's four Galilean satellites, showing in his *Principia* that they obeyed Kepler's laws, and by the second edition in 1713 he was able to add five Saturnian satellites as well. Showing that gravitation operated on satellites as well as planets was a crucial element in demonstrating its universal character.

The development of large reflecting telescopes in the late eighteenth century and the widespread adoption of reflectors in the nineteenth led to fresh discoveries. **William Herschel** found two Uranian satellites. In 1851, six years after discovering the planet itself, William Lassel added two more. Lassel used his large instruments to discover Neptune's Triton in 1846, which was in a most unusual retrograde orbit. This was an anomaly, for the nebular hypothesis of the origin of the solar system predicted that all satellites orbited planets in the same direction.

The largest moons of the solar system photographed by various NASA spacecraft. Earth's moon, with a diameter of 3,476 km (2,160 miles), is shown in the center. Io (3,632 km), Europa (3,126 km), Ganymede (5,276 km), and Callisto (4,820 km) are satellites of Jupiter while Titan (5,150 km) is a satellite of Saturn. (Photograph courtesy of the National Aeronautics and Space Administration)

Lassel also shared discovery of Saturn's Hyperion in 1848 with the Bonds at Harvard.

Refracting telescopes, of course, remained useful. During the favorable opposition of 1877, Asaph Hall, observing with U.S. Naval Observatory's 26-inch telescope in Washington, discovered two satellites of **Mars**. With the orbits of these satellites, the mass of Mars could be determined much more accurately than from its perturbations on Jupiter's orbit. The satellites also produced a puzzle in celestial mechanics. Both satellites are very small and close to the planet. Phobos, the innermost, has a period of only 7 hours and 39 minutes, making it the only satellite that revolves in less time than its host planet rotates, another anomaly for the nebular hypothesis. Surveys were made from ground-based telescopes and later spacecraft, but no additional satellites were found.

The introduction of photography into astronomy permitted long-exposure photographs, bringing fainter companions into range. The tiny moon Almathea, the first new satellite of Jupiter to be discovered since Galileo, was located in 1892 by **E.E. Barnard** and was destined to be the last satellite discovered visually.

By 1960, some thirty satellites were known to be orbiting Mars, Jupiter, Saturn, **Uranus**, and **Neptune**; **Mercury**, **Venus**, and **Pluto** so far were without known companions. During the next thirty years, the number doubled. Many of these discoveries were made by spacecraft, but some were made from ground-based instruments in support of spacecraft mission planning, operations, and analysis. A companion to Pluto, named Charon, was discovered using a ground-based telescope employing electronic detectors in 1978. Elaborate and sometimes controversial schemes of identifying, certifying, and naming these objects were worked out under the auspices of the **International Astronomical Union**.

Beyond facilitating discovery, the spacecraft missions also revealed these bodies as more than just points of light with mathematically characterized orbits, masses, and densities. Well before spacecraft visits, the tiny disks of the Galilean satellites of Jupiter had been mapped visually by various indefatigable observers. Infrared reflectance spectroscopy and other techniques revealed an atmosphere on Saturn's Titan, ices on the Galilean satellites, and other characteristics. But this was a prelude to the enormous increase in knowledge provided by spacecraft that flew by or orbited Mars, Jupiter, Saturn, Uranus, and Neptune. The detailed images alone provided geologists with a wealth of information on the processes that shaped the planetary companions—cratering from without, as well as melting and tectonic activity from within. Even exotic active volcanic eruptions were observed on Jupiter's Io and Neptune's Triton. The *Voyager* mission provided much information on the thick methane atmosphere that enshrouds Titan, and on the plasma interactions of the Jovian satellites with Jupiter's magnetic field.

The amazing extent and complexity of the Saturnian ring system, and the discovery of rings surrounding Jupiter, Uranus, and Neptune, brought new attention to the kind of celestial mechanics and resonance theory first applied to the **asteroids** by the American Daniel Kirkwood in the nineteenth century. Satellites large and tiny were found to play a role in shepherding thin rings and keeping them from dispersing, as well as in clearing paths through the ring particles by ejecting material in resonance with various satellite orbits. A unique discovery of the *Voyager* mission was the existence of co-orbital satellites, two or more companions sharing the same orbit, sometimes at one or another of the stable Lagrangian points. With greater awareness of the close association and interaction of rings and satellites, planetary rings were increasingly treated mathematically as vast swarms of small satellites, providing new challenges to **celestial mechanics**.

The historiography of planetary satellites (exclusive of the **earth's moon**) is mixed. Most thorough historical studies consist of journal articles on narrowly circumscribed aspects, and most often treat the circumstances of discovery and confirmation of planetary satellites. For Mars, the articles by Gingerich are authoritative. For the Galilean satellites of Jupiter, the best place to begin is the survey by Débarbat and Wilson, and Westfall for the issue of patronage. For Saturn and the rest of the outer planets see the articles listed in the bibliographies for those entries in this encyclopedia. Often, the best available historical source is the *Dictionary of Scientific Biography* entry for the discoverer of the satellite.

The scientific review literature is voluminous, particularly for the past two decades when spacecraft missions and new ground-based instruments provided a wealth of detailed information and a host of satellite discoveries, fueling considerable theoretical work on all aspects of planetary satellites. The review volumes edited by Atreya, Burns, and Morrison are excellent guides, with comprehensive bibliographies for the scientific literature of the past two decades. However, they are not generally reliable farther into the past and they do not treat issues historically.

Joseph N. Tatarewicz

Bibliography

Atreya, S.K., J.B. Pollack, and M.S. Matthews, eds. *Origin and Evolution of Planetary and Satellite Atmospheres*. Space Science Series. Tucson: University of Arizona Press, 1989.

Blunck, J. *Mars and Its Satellites: A Detailed Commentary on the Nomenclature*. Smithtown, N.Y.: Exposition Press, 1982.

Burns, J.A., and M.S. Matthews, eds. *Satellites*. Space Science Series. Tucson: University of Arizona Press, 1986.

Cruikshank, D.P. "Barnard's Satellite of Jupiter." *Sky & Telescope* 64 (1982): 220–224.

Débarbat, S., and C. Wilson. "The Galilean Satellites of Jupiter from Galileo to Cassini, Römer and Bradley." In *Planetary Astronomy from the Renaissance to the Rise of Astrophysics: Part A: Tycho Brahe to Newton*, edited by R. Taton and C. Wilson. In *The General History of Astronomy,* vol. 2A, edited M. Hoskin, 144–158. New York: Cambridge University Press, 1989.

Gillispie, C.C., ed. *Dictionary of Scientific Biography*. 15 vols. New York: Scribner, 1970.

Gingerich, O. "The Satellites of Mars: Prediction and Discovery." *Journal for the History of Astronomy* 1 (1970): 109–115.

———. "The Discovery of the Satellites of Mars." *Vistas in Astronomy* 22 (1978): 127–132.

Greenberg, R., and A. Brahic, eds. *Planetary Rings*. Space Science Series. Tucson: University of Arizona Press, 1984.

Holmes, F.L., ed. *Dictionary of Scientific Biography: Supplement II*. 2 vols. New York: Scribner, 1990.

Lévy, J. "L'intérêt Pratique Des Satellites de Jupiter." In *Roemer et la Vitesse de la Lumière*. Paris: J. Vrin, 1978.
Morrison, D., ed. *Satellites of Jupiter*. Space Science Series. Tucson: University of Arizona Press, 1982.
Mozel, P. "In Search of Sprites: The Discovery of Ariel and Umbriel." *Journal of the Royal Astronomical Society of Canada* 80 (1986): 344–350.
Roche, J.J. "Harriot, Galileo and Jupiter's Satellites." *Archives Internationale D'Histoire Des Sciences* 32 (1982): 9–51.
Westfall, R.S. "Science and Patronage: Galileo and the Telescope." *Isis* 76 (1985): 11–30.

Plaskett, John Stanley (1865–1941)

Canadian astrophysicist. Born near Woodstock, Ontario, Plaskett worked as a machinist, then took a B.A. at Toronto in 1899. He organized the Dominion Observatory astrophysics group (1905–1917), specializing in spectroscopic binaries, solar rotation, and spectrograph design. Plaskett was responsible for the **Dominion Astrophysical Observatory**. There, his primary study was radial velocities of O and B stars. In 1928, he and J.A. Pearce corroborated Oort's and Shapley's ideas on galactic rotation, while providing a value for the solar galactic rotation. In 1930, they also confirmed Eddington's and Struve's predictions of calcium II rotation. Plaskett later acted as consultant for the McDonald Observatory.

Richard A. Jarrell

Bibliography

Jarrell, R.A. *The Cold Light of Dawn: A History of Canadian Astronomy*. Toronto: University of Toronto Press, 1988.

Plato, Astronomy of (427–348/347 B.C.E.)

The Athenian philosopher Plato is well known for his doctrine of the Forms, which is a theory that what really exists can be understood only through thought and cannot be comprehended by the senses. Because of his views regarding the Forms, Plato has sometimes been accused of having discouraged the study of the natural world. Yet Plato has also been seen as having strongly encouraged the study of astronomy, and his dialogue the *Timaeus* provided an important cosmological model during Antiquity and the Middle Ages. Furthermore, Plato argued that the study of astronomy provided an ethical function, enabling humans to imitate the cosmic order. While in the *Republic* the study of astronomy was required for future philosopher-guardians, in the *Laws* all citizens must acquire a basic familiarity with the heavens.

A detailed cosmology is presented in the *Timaeus*, but as with all Platonic dialogues, it is not clear whether the views of the main speaker, Timaeus, represent those of Plato himself. Nevertheless, the work is of great historical interest, having been the subject of debate and commentary during Antiquity.

In the *Timaeus*, the speaker after whom the dialogue is named sets out a detailed account of creation and of cosmology. According to what Timaeus himself describes as a likely story, the universe was fashioned by a divine Craftsman (*Demiurgos*, the Demiurge), to be perfectly spherical and turning uniformly in place. The universe as a whole was endowed with a soul. Taking the stuff of this world-soul, the Demiurge constructed something rather like an armillary sphere, with the outer ring (known as the Same) corresponding to the equator, revolving to the right (that is, east to west) and representing the motion of the fixed stars, while the inner ring corresponded to the zodiac (the Different) moving toward the left (that is, west to east) along the diagonal. The motion of the Different was further divided into seven concentric and nested rings; these represent the motions of the seven planets (the wandering stars, namely the moon, sun, Venus, Mercury, Mars, Jupiter, and Saturn). The order and the motions of the planets are further described by Timaeus, but scholars have debated the precise meaning of the text without reaching a consensus. Nevertheless, it is generally agreed that the apparent daily motions of the heavens and the slow drifting of the planets against the background of the fixed stars are explained by this model. Further, the planets are living beings with souls and move in circles in an orderly way, the visible motions of the planets having been designed as a measure of time. Astronomy is thereby useful and beneficial to humans.

In several of his works, Plato suggested an ethical philosophy based on the divinity of the heavens; such a philosophy gave a high value to astronomical knowledge. In the *Timaeus*, the heavenly bodies are gods who, together with the traditional mythological gods, created the other living beings; significantly, every human soul was given a portion of the world-soul. Humans have many ways in which they can gain comprehension of the universe by means of astronomy; these are discussed in various Platonic works. For example, in the *Timaeus*, before acquiring its body each human soul rode a star through the universe and was shown the laws of destiny; this prenatal knowledge was available to humans by means of recollection. Further, that the astronomical bodies were visible is significant and was intentionally planned, to enable humans to see gods who visibly demonstrate order and regularity. This visual access offers humans the opportunity to imitate the order and regularity of the universe. In addition to these methods of learning about the eternal cosmic order, Plato described more sophisticated means available only to philosophers. The nature of this type of astronomy has been much discussed by scholars, who have disagreed about the importance of the phenomena within Plato's astronomy.

Plato was credited by Simplicius (sixth century C.E.), quoting Sosigenes (second century C.E.), with having posed the classical problem of astronomy: to account for the astronomical phenomena using uniform, orderly motions—that is, to use geometrical models to explain the appearances. Whether or not the story is true, the association of Plato with astronomy was a strong one, and questions regarding the status of the phenomena in Plato have continued to interest philosophers and historians of science. In the *Republic*, Plato outlined the type of education necessary for philosopher-kings, which included training in arithmetic, geometry, stereometry, astronomy, and harmonics. Scholars have debated exactly what kind of astronomy Plato had in mind, agreeing, generally, that it was a very special sort. In a crucial passage in the *Republic,* 530 B.C.E., Socrates claimed that "it is by means of problems . . . that we shall proceed in astronomy, in the same way as we do in geometry, and we shall let the things in the heavens alone if, by doing real astronomy, we are to turn from disuse to use that part of our soul whose nature it is to be wise" (translated by Vlastos in 1980, 3).

There has been an extensive literature on this topic, the product, for the most part, of scholars particularly interested in Plato's philosophy. A variety of interpretations have been suggested. On the one hand, there are those who claim that Plato advocated an *a priori* astronomy, leaving the things in the heaven alone. Others stress the importance of the suggestions to "proceed by means of problems" and "save the phenomena." Those scholars who occupy a middle ground argue that if Plato had really meant to "dismiss the things in the heaven," that would have resulted in the abandonment of astronomy itself. This middle ground has much to commend it, not least of all because of the apparent impact of Plato's advocacy of the study of astronomy. One measure of this impact may be the significant contributions of several of his students, including Eudoxus (ca. 400 B.C.E.-ca. 347 B.C.E.) and Aristotle (384–322 B.C.E.) to astronomical theory.

Liba C. Taub

Bibliography

Alexander, P.D.M. "Astronomy and Kinematics in Plato's Project of Rationalist Explanation." *Studies in the History and Philosophy of Science* 12 (1981): 1–32.

Allan, D.J. "Plato." In *Dictionary of Scientific Biography*, edited by C.C. Gillispie, vol. 11, 22–31. New York: Scribner, 1975.

Anton, J.P., ed. *Science and the Sciences in Plato*. New York: Eidos, 1980.

Bulmer-Thomas, I. "Plato's Astronomy." *Classical Quarterly* 34 (1984): 107–112.

Cornford, F.M. *Plato's Cosmology: The "Timaeus" of Plato Translated with a Running Commentary*. London: Routledge and Kegan Paul, 1937.

Dicks, D.R. *Early Greek Astronomy to Aristotle*. Ithaca: Cornell University Press, 1970.

Duhem, P. *To Save the Phenomena: An Essay on the Idea of a Physical Theory from Plato to Galileo*. Translated by E. Doland and C. Maschler. Chicago: University of Chicago Press, 1969.

Lloyd, G.E.R. "Saving the Appearances." In *Methods and Problems in Greek Science: Selected Papers*, 248–277. Cambridge: Cambridge University Press, 1991. (Reprinted, with a new introduction, from *Classical Quarterly* 28 (1978): 202–222.)

Mourelatos, A.P.D. "Plato's Science—His View and Ours of His." In *Science and Philosophy in Classical Greece*, edited by A.C. Bowen, 31–42. New York: Garland, 1991.

Taylor, A.E. *A Commentary on Plato's Timaeus*. Oxford: Clarendon Press, 1928.

Vlastos, G. *Plato's Universe*. Seattle: University of Washington Press, 1975.

———. "The Role of Observation in Plato's Conception of Astronomy." In *Science and the Sciences in Plato*, edited by J.P. Anton, 1–31. New York: Eidos, 1980.

Pluto

After some of the enthusiasm over the discovery of **Neptune** had died down, there remained questions among celestial mechanicians whether Neptune was the object—or perhaps the only object—pointed to by the residuals in Uranus's orbit. Buoyed by optimism over using Uranus's orbit as a guide to finding Neptune, several astronomers wondered whether the method might lead to other planetary discoveries. This came to naught in the search for Vulcan, a putative intra-Mercurial planet postulated as the cause of the anomalous advancement of Mercury's perihelion. However, it did lead eventually to the discovery of Pluto, the only planet discovered in this century.

Percival Lowell, whose primary interest was the study of **Mars**, gave serious thought to searching for a trans-Neptunian planet. From first considerations in 1902, Lowell moved to an active search between 1905 and 1909. This first search included photography of a portion of the ecliptic and mathematical analysis of the orbits and residuals of Uranus and Neptune. The second search, 1910–1915, involved far more sophisticated mathematics and more careful searches guided by the analysis. Lowell worked feverishly and secretly on the project, employing a host of assistants in Flagstaff and Boston to assist in the photography and the analysis. Ironically, Pluto does appear on plates taken in 1915, but it was unnoticed. Lowell broke the secrecy in an address to the American Academy of Arts and Sciences wherein he summarized his analytical methods. The address was received without enthusiasm, and appeared nearly a year later as a **Lowell Observatory Publication**. Apparently, Lowell lost interest in the project, for he did not pursue the search with his characteristic vigor. The photographic work continued, but Lowell spent little if any time on the project, limiting himself to hopeful queries to the staff whether they had found anything.

What William Graves Hoyt calls the third search for Planet X did not begin until the mid 1920s. The Lowell Observatory staff built new equipment, and hired a young self-taught amateur astronomer from Kansas as an assistant. Clyde W. Tombaugh arrived in Flagstaff just ahead of the new 13-inch photographic telescope. Tombaugh began exposing plates in April 1929, and by summer he was devising ways to make the tedious process of examining the plates for candidate objects more systematic and efficient.

Tombaugh's persistence and cleverness paid off in remarkably short order. In February 1930, analyzing plates in Gemini taken the previous month, he detected an object beyond the orbit of Neptune. The Lowell staff reacted cautiously, and then moved ahead with the announcement, timing it to occur on the 75th anniversary of Percival Lowell's birth, which happened to be the 149th anniversary of Herschel's discovery of Uranus. The public acclaim was enormous, and secured for Tombaugh and the Lowell Observatory a permanent place in history.

Beneath the public acclaim, however, there lurked some controversy and lingering doubts. Harvard's William H. Pickering, Lowell's sometime friendly rival in the planet search, had himself made many predictions. One of these was actually slightly closer to Pluto's discovery position than Lowell's prediction. Pickering raised objections and alternated between gracious acceptance and occasional indignation. More serious, however, was the realization that Pluto's diminutive size was probably insufficient to account for the residuals in Neptune's orbit. Without a mass for Pluto, nobody could be sure. But its extremely faint magnitude required that it be extremely dark, if it were to have substantial mass.

Two serious issues were at stake here. First, was there another perturbing body, yet to be found, that had acted in concert with Pluto? Second, was the discovery of Pluto merely an accident, unrelated to the predictions? Both of these questions would continue to be debated over the next fifty years. Had Pluto been discovered between the orbits of Mars and **Jupiter** it would easily have been called an asteroid. Since it was beyond Neptune, and that region failed to disclose any other similar objects over the years, Pluto enjoyed the status of planet—but just barely and not without controversy.

New observational technology combined with Pluto's nearing perihelion (its closest opposition since 1742 occurred in May 1990) combined to allow an important discovery. In 1978 James W. Christy identified a satellite of Pluto, named Charon, locked in a roughly seven-day orbit around the planet, the same period as Pluto's rotation. Pluto and Charon entered a series of mutual eclipses 1985–1990, allowing even more precise determinations of their orbital elements and the thin methane atmospheres that arise when the frost covering the bodies is heated around perihelion. Since Charon is nearly half the mass of

Pluto, it makes more sense to consider them a system of double planets, if indeed objects that small merit the name at all. The mass determination finally seemed to settle the question of whether Pluto was Lowell's Planet X—its mass was far too small to have caused all of the inequalities in the orbit of Neptune. Planet X remains an elusive and controversial quarry.

The most comprehensive and reliable treatment of the search for and discovery of Pluto remains that of William Graves Hoyt. Clyde Tombaugh has recounted his story in several places, most extensively in his book with Patrick Moore. David Levy's appreciative biography is based on more recent extensive interviews and research in Tombaugh's and other manuscripts. The continuing search for Planet X, and modern dynamical, telescopic, and spectroscopic studies of Pluto and Charon must be followed in the astronomical literature, although good popular summaries can be found in the works of Burgess on Uranus and Neptune and in Sheehan. Hoyt does provide some coverage of these latter topics as well, but the discovery of Charon came just as his book was being finished.

Joseph N. Tatarewicz

Bibliography

Burgess, E. *Uranus and Neptune: The Distant Giants*. New York: Columbia University Press, 1988.

———. *Far Encounter: The Neptune System.* New York: Columbia University Press, 1991.

Crosswell, K. "The Pursuit of Pluto." *American Heritage of Invention & Technology* 5 (Winter 1989): 50–57.

Grosser, M. "The Search for a Planet Beyond Neptune." *Isis* 55 (1964): 163–183.

Hoyt, W.G. "W.H. Pickering's Planetary Predictions and the Discovery of Pluto." *Isis* 67 (1976): 551–64.

———. *Planets X and Pluto*. Tucson: University of Arizona Press, 1980.

Kemp, K.W. "Pluto and the Patterns of Planetary Discovery." *Astronomy Quarterly* 7 (1990): 19–33.

Levy, D.H. *Clyde Tombaugh: Discoverer of Planet Pluto*. Tucson: University of Arizona Press, 1991.

Sheehan, W. *Worlds in the Sky: Planetary Discovery from Earliest Times through Voyager and Magellan*. Tucson: University of Arizona Press, 1992.

Tombaugh, C.W., and P. Moore. *Out of the Darkness, the Planet Pluto*. Harrisburg, Pa.: Stackpole Books, 1981.

Verloren Van Themaat, W.A. "Hindsight and the Definition of Research Success: Illustrated by the History of Planetary Discovery." *Zeitschrift Fur Allgemeine Wissenschaftstheorie* 15 (1984): 272–277.

Whyte, A.J. *The Planet Pluto*. New York: Pergamon Press, 1980.

Poincaré, Jules Henri (1854–1912)

French mathematician and celestial mechanician. Poincaré completed his doctorate in mathematics at the University of Paris in 1879 and became a mathematics instructor at the University of Caen. In 1881 he became a professor at the University of Paris, where he taught until his death. The breadth and importance of his contributions to pure mathematics, **celestial mechanics** and mathematical physics are comparable to those of Euler and Gauss. Poincaré's mathematical work included the theories of functions and numbers, geometry, algebra, topology, differential equations, and the foundations of mathematics.

Celestial mechanics was a lifelong interest of Poincaré's. He proved that the trigonometric series used in planetary theory were not, despite the hopes of astronomers, convergent. Instead, they were useful because of asymptotic convergence. He applied his work in the qualitative theory of differential equations to the three-body problem, where he established methods for studying the behavior of periodic orbits. Poincaré considered the behavior of orbits subjected to small changes in initial conditions. His revolutionary work in these areas is presented in his three-volume *Les méthodes de la mécanique céleste*, which has inspired theoretical work in celestial mechanics to the present day.

LeRoy E. Doggett

Bibliography

Darboux, G. "Éloge historique d'Henri Poincaré." *Mémoires de l'Académie des sciences* 52 (1914): lxxxi–cxlviii.

Dieudonné, J. "Jules Henri Poincaré." In *Dictionary of Scientific Biography*, edited by C.C. Gillispie, vol. 11, 51–61. New York: Scribner, 1975.

Goroff, D.L. "Editor's Introduction" to the English translation of Poincaré's *New Methods in Celestial Mechanics*, 1–193. New York: American Institute of Physics, 1992.

Potsdam Astrophysical Observatory

The Potsdam Astrophysical Observatory (*Astrophysikalishen Observatorium Potsdam*) was founded in 1874 by Kaiser Wilhelm I as a royal Prussian scientific institute. It was the first observatory dedicated specifically to **astrophysics**, the new branch of astronomy emphasizing physical and chemical inquiry using the techniques of **photometry**, **spectroscopy**, and photography (in contrast to classical astronomy, which employed positional measurements of stars and planets and descriptive observations of celestial objects). The early spectroscopist Herrmann Carl Vogel became the first official director of the Potsdam Astrophysical Observatory (PAO) in 1882, which position he held for the rest of his life.

The PAO was one of the earliest centers devoted to astrophysics. Because North American scientists dominated early astrophysics, PAO is particularly notable as one of the very few European sites for astrophysical research in the late nineteenth century. The immediate impetus for the founding of the observatory seems to have come from Wilhelm Foerster, who urged German Kaiser Wilhelm I to create an institute for the study of the sun, knowledge of which, Foerster argued, was crucial and of great practical importance to us on earth. Viewed in a broader context, the PAO came into existence during the period of greatest growth of industry and science in Germany, growth that was accompanied by the founding of many research establishments and considerable national pride in their achievements.

The work of the observatory began, in a sense, before construction was even finished in 1879. Vogel, still working in Berlin in the period 1874–1877 but already holding an appointment as observer at PAO, spent his time planning research at the new observatory. Though his work on the solar spectrum began in Berlin, it became the subject of one of the first of the Potsdam observatory publications. Vogel's teacher, Johann C. F. Zöllner, famous as the inventor of quantitative astronomical photometry, exercised his influence on the early research program of the PAO and was perhaps the inspiration for one of its most significant contributions—the *Potsdamer Durchmusterung* (Herrmann, 1975). Zöllner's early involvement in the establishment and work of the PAO underscores the astrophysical mission of the institution from its inception, as do the unsuccessful attempts to interest **Gustav Robert Kirchhoff**, the co-founder of spectroscopy, in taking the job as the observatory's first director.

The PAO was planned in combination with sibling institutions for meteorological and geodetic studies all sharing the same tract of land on the *Telegraphenberg* south of the town of Potsdam. Construction was finished in 1879 at a cost (not including scientific instruments) of approximately 862,000 marks. The ground plan is similar to that of the university observatory at Babelsberg, Berlin, but at Potsdam the side domes are separated from the main dome by long corridors. The greater distance from the main dome was intended to lessen instability of air over the smaller domes and thus improve the seeing—an important consideration for astrophysical applications often requiring observations at low light levels. The original building is a striking Italianate design with a square water tower reminiscent of a Tuscan campanile. This style is in strong contrast to the later Einstein Tower solar telescope, which is a streamlined modernistic edifice.

The original main dome housed a refractor with a 30-cm Schröder objective and Repsold mounting. A larger dome was erected in 1896 for an astrographic double refractor. The double refractor had Steinheil objectives of 50 and 80 cm and a Repsold mounting. The double refractor ceased operations in 1967. The Einstein Tower, housing a solar observatory, was completed in 1924. The vertical tower telescope has a Zeiss 60-cm objective and a coelostat for directing sunlight into the stationary telescope. A horizontal spectrograph is below ground. The tower's name refers to tests there, by Erwin F. Freundlich, of Einstein's general theory of relativity.

The most famous product of PAO research was the *Potsdamer Durchmusterung* catalogue of stellar luminosities, which became a fundamental work for astrophysicists. Vogel assigned PAO observers, primarily Gustav Müller and Paul Kempf, to measure the luminosities of all stars in the *Bonner Durchmusterung* down to magnitude 7.5 using a special Zöllner photometer. The accuracy of the PD was much higher than that of E.C. Pickering's comparable Harvard catalogue (though the Harvard survey included the Southern Hemisphere). The PD was begun in 1886 and completed in 1907. Photometry at PAO also included planetary work, such as Müller and Kempf's measurements of the phase coefficients and albedos of Venus and Mercury (which allowed conclusions about the nature of the planetary surfaces), and completion of luminosity surveys down to 12th magnitude of the regions assigned as part of J.C. Kapteyn's Plan of Selected Areas. Vogel's spectroscopic work with Julius Scheiner at Potsdam in 1889–1890 produced proof of the existence of eclipsing binary stars, such as *Algol*. Vogel and Müller also published an early catalogue of stellar spectral types. Scheiner and J. Wilsing applied Potsdam's early expertise in spectrophotometry to produce some of the earliest estimates of the surface temperatures of stars. Wilsing also applied spectrophotometry to nonstellar objects, demonstrating for example that reflection from the moon's surface makes sunlight more yellow. Potsdam spectroscopists Freundlich and Emanuel von der Pahlen discovered the pattern of radial velocities in Milky Way stars that Jan Oort later showed to be consistent with general orbital motion about the center of the galaxy.

A fundamental source on the history of PAO is Hassenstein's article, which contains extensive lists of PAO researchers and their publications through 1939. Dieter Herrmann's investigations of the early development of astrophysics focus on the important place that the PAO held in the late nineteenth century and use its research and publishing activities as a principal comparison against the development of astrophysics in the United States (Herrmann, 1973). His work on the early history of the PAO (Herrmann, 1975) sheds light on the formative influences of the institution and offers observations on the interactions between academic, scientific, and political interests in the development of German astrophysics.

James M. Lattis

Bibliography

Hassenstein, W. "Das Astrophysikalischen Observatorium Potsdam." *Mitteilungen des Astrophysikalischen Observatoriums Potsdam* 1 (1941): 1–56.

Herrmann, D.B. "Zur Frühentwicklung der Astrophysik in Deutschland und in den USA: Ein quantitativer Vergleich." *NTM-Schriftenreihe für Geschichte der Naturwissenschaften, Technik und Medizin* 10 (1973): 38–44.

———. "Zur Vorgeschichte des Astrophysikalischen Observatorium Potsdam (1865 bis 1874)." *Astronomische Nachrichten* 296 (1975): 245–259.

———. "Wilhelm Foerster und die Gründung des Astrophysikalishen Observatoriums Potsdam." In *Sternzeiten*, edited by G. Jackisch, band 2, 29–34. Veröffentlichungen des Forschungbereichs Geo- und Kosmoswissenschaften, heft 7. Berlin: Akademie-Verlag, 1977.

Müller, P. *Sternwarten in Bildern: Architektur und Geschichte der Sternwarten von den Anfängen bis ca. 1950*. Berlin: Springer-Verlag, 1992.

Spieker, P. *Die Königlichen Observatorien für Astrophysik, Meteorologie und Geodäsie auf dem Telegraphenberg bei Potsdam*. Berlin, 1895.

Princeton University, Astronomy at

Instruction in astronomy at Princeton (before 1896 called the College of New Jersey) began in the late eighteenth century. Walter Minto, author of a treatise on the discovery of Uranus, taught astronomy as an aspect of natural philosophy in 1787, while a Princeton graduate, Andrew Hunter Jr., became professor of mathematics and astronomy in 1804. Already by 1771, Princeton was home to a large, precision-built orrery, used to demonstrate planetary motions, constructed by the Philadelphia instrument-maker **David Rittenhouse**. Its first research facility, however, was not built for another century. In 1872, Stephen Alexander, appointed professor in astronomy in 1840, oversaw construction of the Halstead Observatory, funds for which he had secured while developing distinct courses in astronomy. Completion of this building helped persuade Charles A. Young, noted for his solar research at Dartmouth College, to become Alexander's successor.

Young's directorship (1877–1905) marked the start of the modern era of astronomy at Princeton. Under Young, Princeton acquired an observatory office and residence in 1878, and a 23-inch refracting telescope—then one of the largest instruments of its kind—in 1882. Complementing it was the John C. Green Student Observatory, constructed in 1877 and equipped with a 9.5-inch refracting telescope, a meridian circle, spectroscope, and other instruments. Young, with one assistant, also continued an eclectic program of solar studies and wrote several authoritative textbooks that greatly influenced the teaching of astronomy in the United States.

After a brief period (1905–1908) in which the department was led by the celestial mechanician Edgar Odell Lovett, later president of Rice University, Princeton astronomy was directed by Young's former student **Henry Norris Russell**. Russell's term as chair of Princeton's Department of Astronomy (1912 to 1947) established the observatory as a leading center of astronomy, even though staff was limited to two professors in the decade beginning in 1910 and three the following decade. One of the most eminent American astronomers of the early twentieth century, Russell made fundamental contributions to studies of stellar evolution and astrophysical interpretations of solar and stellar spectra; he independently developed the **Hertzsprung-Russell diagram** relating stellar luminosities to temperatures, and, with his Harvard colleague F.A. Saunders, he explained an anomaly in the intensities of lines of excited atoms later known as Russell-Saunders coupling. Widely interested in all fields of astronomy, Russell also made important contributions to cosmogony and served as advisor to several American observatories.

A forceful advocate of interdisciplinary research, Russell worked closely with Princeton physicists, particularly Allen Shenstone. Although Russell did not seek outside funds to promote the rapid growth of Princeton astronomy, he joined colleagues in other fields in successful efforts to secure foundation grants for Princeton science in the 1920s, which helped sustain research there during the Great Depression. An influential textbook author as well, Russell made Princeton a small but important center for graduate training in astronomy, producing such students as Harlow Shapley (Ph.D., 1913) and Donald H. Menzel (Ph.D., 1924), both subsequently directors of the Harvard College Observatory.

In 1934, Princeton constructed the FitzRandolph Observatory (also known as the New Observatory) to house the Halstead Observatory's venerable 23-inch at a site on the edge of campus, still close to city lights. Devoted solely to R.S. Dugan's photometric studies of eclipsing variables, the FitzRandolph Observatory was neither large enough nor suitably located to compete with the major observatories established in the American southwest early in the twentieth century. During the 1930s, Princeton's 23-inch refractor was employed for astrometric research, including Raymond S. Dugan's studies of eclipsing binaries. But by the early 1950s, following Russell's lead, most Princeton astrophysicists used the large reflecting telescopes at Mount Wilson or Mount Palomar for observational work.

After World War II, and particularly during the 1950s, Princeton astronomy became largely devoted to theoretical astrophysics and space-based research. In 1947, when Russell retired as director, he was replaced by Lyman Spitzer Jr., a former student. Spitzer's research focused on the nature of interstellar clouds and the formation of stars; his colleague Martin Schwarzschild, also appointed in 1947, studied physical processes in stellar interiors and contributed to theoretical understanding of the Hertzsprung-Russell diagram. During Spitzer's directorship, the department developed further ties with physics, and pursued innovative research strategies.

In 1951, with funds from the Atomic Energy Commission, Spitzer co-launched Project Matterhorn, designed to create fusion reactions by gas contained within a strong magnetic field. While the Stellerator device that Spitzer initially constructed did not succeed, the effort led to further research on solar nuclear reactions and plasma physics, and in 1961 Project Matterhorn formally became the nucleus of Princeton's Plasma Physics Laboratory, directed by Spitzer. Spitzer also pursued studies of space-based telescopes (having first proposed the concept in 1946), while Schwarzschild, employing a 12-inch telescope attached to a balloon, made pioneering studies of solar granulation in mid-1957. With expanded departmental resources, Princeton increasingly supported visiting astronomers from the United States and abroad. The department also benefited from the nearby Institute for Advanced Studies, where in 1957 **Bengt Strömgren** became the first astronomer to hold an appointment.

Astronomy at Princeton shared in the rapid growth of the discipline in America after 1960. The 23-inch telescope was briefly mothballed in the early 1960s. It was replaced by a 36-inch reflector. Faculty members substituted Astrophysical Sciences for Astronomy as the name of their department in 1963 and in 1966 moved into Peyton Hall. Primarily a graduate program since the early twentieth century, the department swelled from six faculty members at the assistant professor level or above in 1961–1962 to ten (1964–1965) and soon eighteen (1969–1970). As patronage for astronomy and the market for astronomers mushroomed in the 1950s, Princeton became a major center for graduate training and benefited from grants from numerous federal agencies. In the early 1970s, Spitzer and his colleagues used the earth-orbiting satellite *Copernicus*, equipped with a 32-inch telescope, to study the ultraviolet composition of interstellar gas and extended stellar atmospheres. By the mid-1980s, departmental associates enjoyed access to the Tokamak Fusion Test Reactor, the world's largest fusion research apparatus. Increasingly oriented toward theoretical astronomy, graduate training and faculty research expanded to include atomic and molecular physics, far ultraviolet astronomy, and (by the 1980s) galactic research.

Historians have recognized the significance of the Princeton Orrery as an example of late-eighteenth-century precision instrument-making, and its role as a pedagogical tool. Recent work on the history of solar research has helped place Young's work within the context of solar astronomy and astrophysics in the late nineteenth century. David H. DeVorkin has focused particularly on Russell's research and his contributions to stellar astrophysics; his work underscores Russell's centrality to early-twentieth-century astronomy and to many of astronomy's component fields. Other studies have suggested that Princeton, like other East Coast observatories, shifted increasingly toward big science projects and nontraditional instrumentation after World War II as a result of disciplinary competition, wartime research experiences, and patronage opportunities. Studies of the history of the space telescope project have illuminated the role that Spitzer played in developing this instrument and in steering Princeton colleagues toward large-scale programs, while other investigations analyze Spitzer's contributions to Project Matterhorn and to plasma research. Research on patronage for U.S. universities has also served to underscore the historically small size of the department until the early 1960s and the degree of interdisciplinary cooperation among Princeton's science departments in the early twentieth century.

Nonetheless, much of Princeton's involvement in astronomy remains unexplored. Little has been written about the teaching of astronomy at Princeton in any period. While new work has addressed solar eclipse expeditions in the Victorian era, Young's influence on this style of research has not been reconnoitered. The extent of Russell's impact on theoretical astrophysics in the United States makes him a prime candidate for a scientific biography. Particularly lacking are studies of Princeton astronomy after 1945. Sharply increased funding from defense and military patrons, the influence of Princeton research on plasma phenomena and stellar nuclear reactions, and the development of satellite-based research all await investigation. No less warranted are investigations of Princeton's contributions to balloon- and satellite-instrument design and engineering, as well as the role Princeton researchers played in debates over steady-state and big-bang cosmologies, the nature and distribution of interstellar matter, and galactic structure. No historical studies yet address how the burgeoning growth of astronomy after 1960 affected Princeton as a center of graduate education, or its relation with other science departments.

Young's correspondence is available at the Dartmouth College archives in Hanover, New Hampshire, and at Princeton. The Princeton University library houses the extensive papers of Russell and Spitzer, as well as departmental records and collections for other astronomy faculty, including R.S. Dugan and J.Q. Stewart.

Ronald E. Doel

Bibliography

Bedini, S. *Thinkers and Tinkers: Early Men of Science*. New York: Scribner, 1975.

Bromberg, J. *Fusion: Science, Politics, and the Invention of a New Energy Source*. Cambridge: MIT Press, 1982.

DeVorkin, D. "A Fox Raiding the Hedgehogs: How Henry Norris Russell Got to Mount Wilson." *History of Geophysics* 5 (1993): 103–112.

DeVorkin, D., and R. Kenat. "Quantum Physics and the Stars (II): Henry Norris Russell and the Abundances of the Elements in the Atmospheres of the Sun and Stars." *Journal for the History of Astronomy* xiv (1983): 180–222.

Doel, R.E. *Science on the Periphery: Solar System Astronomy in America, 1920–1960.* New York: Cambridge University Press, 1996.

Field, G. "Princeton and Astronomy." *Princeton Alumni Weekly* 62, no. 13 (1962): 8–22.

Hufbauer, K. *Exploring the Sun: Solar Science since Galileo*. Baltimore: Johns Hopkins University Press, 1991.

Pang, A. S.-K. "The Social Event of the Season: Solar Eclipse Expeditions and Victorian Culture." *Isis* 84 (1993): 252–277.

Smith, R.W., et al. *The Space Telescope: A Study of NASA, Science, Technology, and Politics*. New York: Cambridge University Press, 1989.

Proctor, Richard Anthony (1837–1888)

English astronomer and science writer. In 1860, Proctor graduated from Cambridge University as twenty-third Wrangler. The failure in 1866 of the New Zealand Banking Company, in which he was a major investor, forced him to earn his living as a writer and lecturer, especially on astronomical subjects, at which he achieved remarkable success. After the death of his first wife, he married a widow from St. Joseph, Missouri, taking up residence there and later in Orange Lake, Florida. He died in New York City, probably from yellow fever.

In the English-reading world from 1870 to 1890, Richard Proctor was the most widely read writer on astronomical subjects. The more than seventy books and hundreds of essays, including eighty-three papers in the *Royal Astronomical Society Monthly Notices*, suggest his importance. Proctor's opposition to the claim that other universes exist beyond our Milky Way played a key role in the eclipse of that theory during the final decades of the nineteenth century. Moreover, his championing of an evolving solar system largely bereft of living forms was no less influential. Rarely has astronomy had a more eloquent, effective, and sober advocate and expositor.

Michael J. Crowe

Bibliography

Clerke, E.M. "Richard Anthony Proctor." In *Dictionary of National Biography,* vol. 16, 419–421. London: Oxford University Press, 1921–1922.

Crowe, M.J. *The Extraterrestrial Life Debate 1750–1900: The Idea of a Plurality of Worlds from Kant to Lowell.* Cambridge: Cambridge University Press, 1986.

North, J.D. "Richard A. Proctor." In *Dictionary of Scientific Biography,* edited by C.C. Gillispie, vol. 11, 162–163. New York: Scribner, 1975.

Proctor, R.A. "Autobiographical Notes." *New Science Review* 1 (1895): 393–397.

Proper Motion

Proper motion is the motion of the stars as viewed from earth due to their own movement in space and the motion of the solar system. The proper motion of the stars is extremely small; the largest (for Barnard's star) is only about 10 seconds of arc per year. In contrast to the planets, the Greeks believed the stars were fixed, and not until 1718 did **Edmond Halley** show that the bright stars Aldebaran, Sirius, and Arcturus had changed their positions since Antiquity. Although the motions are small, they are cumulative over time, and this property allowed Halley to discover proper motion; this was later disproved, and similar cases remain unconfirmed.

After Halley's discovery the measurement of proper motions became one of the prime goals of **astrometry**. Proper motions are important because their study can be used to determine a variety of effects, including invisible stellar companions due to gravitational perturbations, the motion of the sun through space, and the structure of our galaxy. In 1783 **William Herschel** deduced the solar motion from such an analysis of proper motions. Thanks to new photographic techniques, by the turn of the twentieth century enough proper motions had been measured to allow **J.C. Kapteyn** to detect the phenomenon of star streaming. In the 1920s **Jan Oort** and **Bertil Lindblad** used proper motions to determine galactic rotation. **Friedrich Wilhelm Bessel** was the first to detect perturbations in the proper motions of stars; he thereby deduced the existence of stellar companions to Procyon and Sirius, later confirmed visually. In 1962 Peter van de Kamp first claimed a planetary companion to Barnard's star, based on extremely small perturbations in its proper motion over a quarter of a century. This has since been disproved, and similar cases remain unconfirmed.

Hundreds of thousands of proper motions may be found in modern star catalogues.

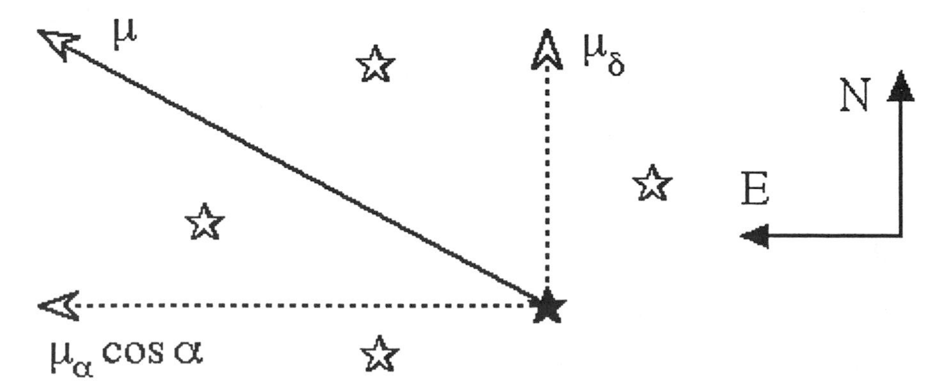

Stellar proper motion. Relative to very distant "fixed" stars (open symbols) a nearby or high-velocity star (filled symbol) will show an annual change in position, or proper motion μ*, measured in seconds of arc per year. In terms of the rate of change of the declination and right ascension of the star, the components of proper motion are* $\mu\delta$ *and* $\mu\alpha \cos \delta$*, respectively. (Drawing by Charles J. Peterson)*

The *Smithsonian Astrophysical Observatory Star Catalogue* (1966) contains positions and proper motions for 258,997 stars. The Astrographic Catalog Reference Stars, completed at the U.S. Naval Observatory in 1991, gives positions and proper motions for 325,416 stars. In 1989 the Germans produced a catalogue of 181,731 proper motions to replace the northern portion of the SAO catalogue, and by 1991 they had also replaced the southern part. The Lick Observatory Northern Proper Motion program, and its southern counterpart, the Yale Southern Proper Motion program, are mammoth surveys of stellar proper motions measured with respect to an extragalactic reference frame.

Steven J. Dick

Bibliography

Eichhorn, H. *Astronomy of Star Positions: A Critical Investigation of Star Catalogues, the Methods of Their Construction, and Their Purpose.* New York: Ungar, 1974.

Ptolemy of Alexandria (second century C.E.)

Claudius Ptolemy occupies a special place in the history of astronomy, and many of his works have survived in their entirety; his great work of mathematical astronomy, generally referred to as the *Almagest*, is among the most important works in the whole of the history of science. His writings represent the culmination of the Greek astronomical achievement; his influence in astronomy can be traced throughout the Middle Ages up to the work of **Nicolas Copernicus** in the early modern period. In addition to his astronomical work, he produced important writings in several other areas, including music, optics, and geography.

Very little is known about the life of Ptolemy; from his own reports in the *Almagest* we know that he made observations at Alexandria, Egypt, between the years 127 and 141 C.E.; there is no compelling reason to believe that he lived elsewhere. Yet Ptolemy must be understood as culturally Greek; he wrote in Greek and worked within the traditions of Greek mathematics and philosophy.

Ptolemy's writings provide valuable information about his predecessors. In the *Almagest* Ptolemy acknowledged his debts, particularly to Apollonius and **Hipparchus**; Ptolemy is the source of most of our information regarding their contributions to astronomy. The *Phases of the Fixed Stars* contains historical information regarding the *parapegmata* tradition, in which the risings and settings of certain bright stars are correlated with weather phenomena, of which that work forms a part. His astronomical works include the *Mathematical Syntaxis* (or *Almagest*); the *Handy Tables*; the *Planetary Hypotheses*; the *Tetrabiblos*; the *Phases of the Fixed Stars; On the Analemma*; and the *Planisphere*. Further, Book III of the *Harmonics* is concerned with the relation of astronomy to music.

The *Almagest* is Ptolemy's most important and influential astronomical work. The work, which contains thirteen books, begins with a philosophical preface explaining why astronomy is the highest intellectual pursuit. Ptolemy then briefly outlined the cosmological assumptions upon which his mathematical astronomy rested. These assumptions are that the heavens move spherically; that the earth, taken as a whole, is sensibly spherical; that the earth is in the middle of the heavens, with regard to the senses; that the earth has the ratio of a point relative to the size of the heavens; that the earth makes no motion involving change of place; that there are two different primary motions in the heavens.

While in many ways it has been regarded as a summary of Hellenistic astronomy, the bulk of the *Almagest* is devoted to the presentation of geometrical models to describe the planetary motions, including those of the sun and moon. Books VII and VIII contain a star catalogue, based on an earlier version by Hipparchus, listing the longitude, latitude, and magnitude of 1,022 fixed stars.

In the *Almagest*, the model for the motion of each planet is treated individually; although there are similarities in the models of the planets, there is no unified treatment of the planets collectively. Several geometrical models, developed by Ptolemy's predecessors, notably Apollonius (third century B.C.E.) and Hipparchus (second century B.C.E.) are used to describe the motions; of these the most important are the deferent-epicycle and the eccentric.

Ptolemy credited Apollonius with the introduction of several important mathematical devices; each planet was described as moving in an epicycle (from the Greek for "on" and "circle"), the center of which moved on a deferent (from Latin, "to carry"). The use of the deferent-epicycle allows the distance of the planet to vary from the center of the circle. The eccentric (from Greek, "out of center," opposed to concentric—that is, having the same center) circle allows the earth (as the center of the universe) to be shifted from the center of the deferent, and results in the apparent speeding up and slowing down of the planets. Ptolemy used the deferent-epicycle and the eccentric, and he introduced another center of motion, the point of a circle from which motion would appear to be uniform, thereby allowing the center of the epicycle to move along the deferent at varying speeds. This point was called the equant during the Middle Ages; from the equant, equal angles are swept out in equal times. In the view of some, this constituted a redefinition of the principle of uniform circular motion, which was the basis of Greek astronomy. Nevertheless, Ptolemy's astronomy was widely accepted for a number of reasons; it was consistent with the accepted cosmological postulates, mathematically rigorous, and in agreement with the data.

Ptolemy collected together the various planetary tables that are found throughout the *Almagest* in a later work, known as the *Handy Tables*; this, as does his interest in instruments, indicates that he was committed to producing tools that would be useful for the practicing astronomer. That Ptolemy was interested in the design and use of astronomical instruments is clear from his detailed descriptions of several instruments used to make astronomical observations in the *Almagest*; these instruments were also described in later commentaries by Pappus (fourth century C.E.), Theon of Alexandria (fourth century C.E.), and Proclus (fifth century C.E.). In some cases the instruments were known to Hipparchus and may have been in use even earlier; in other cases it appears that Ptolemy was the inventor. Each instrument was built for a specific purpose; for example the equinoctial, or equatorial armillary, was used (by Hipparchus, according to Ptolemy) to determine the dates of the equinoxes. The meridian quadrant, or plinth, was used to find the altitude of the sun at midday; these measurements were used to determine the observer's latitude as well as the obliquity of the ecliptic.

Ptolemy described a new instrument, which he called an *astrolabon*, designed to help with the problem of accounting for the positions of the moon relative to the sun; observed positions taken with the *astrolabon* could then be compared with calculated positions. He described in detail the design of an observational armillary sphere consisting of seven nested rings, of which the innermost was fitted with a pair of sights. This instrument could be used to determine the longitude and latitude (with respect to the ecliptic) of a star; this type of instrument may have been used by both Hipparchus and Ptolemy for making the observations included in their star catalogues. The name of this instrument, *astrolabon*, has led to some confusion with the planispheric astrolabe, which was apparently called a horoscopic instrument by Ptolemy. Other instruments described in the *Almagest* include the parallactic ruler designed to measure zenith distances and an instrument invented by Hipparchus, the dioptra, used to obtain a value for the apparent angular diameter of the moon.

Two separate smaller works are each devoted to topics that are relevant to a particular instrument. In the *Analemma*, Ptolemy explained the determination of angles necessary for the construction of sundials. In the *Planisphere*, Ptolemy, who was relying on the work of his predecessor Hipparchus, described the construction and use of a stereographic projection to map a spherical surface onto a flat plane; while this is the projection that was customarily used in the planispheric astrolabe, it is unknown whether Ptolemy knew of this instrument.

Ptolemy's interest in instruments is noteworthy in several regards. First of all, it indicates his commitment to making observations. Additionally, as he explained in the *Planetary Hypotheses*, he was concerned with making his planetary models useful to instrument makers and to those interested in building equatoria. Devices such as these would be handy for quick computations and could be useful for teaching and demonstration, but Ptolemy's care in this regard suggests that he was also interested in physical representations of his models of planetary motion. Further, his remarks suggest that ownership and use of scientific instruments was not restricted to the most accomplished astronomers. The extent to which these instruments were actually used by Ptolemy as part of a program of observation is unknown; nevertheless the written descriptions of these instruments served as instructive models for readers of the *Almagest* in the medieval and early modern period.

Further evidence for the importance of observations is indicated in the *Planetary Hypotheses*, a work that in many ways may be regarded as a companion piece to the *Almagest* and that incorporated the findings of new observations, which in some cases required that changes be made in the planetary models previously presented in the *Almagest*. The work was divided into two parts; Book One summarizes the planetary models in mathematical terms and discusses the order and distance of the planets. Book Two is concerned with the physics of the celestial realm, including the material substance of which the heavens and the heavenly bodies consist, as well as the cause of motion of the celestial objects. In many ways this book may be read as an attack on Aristotle's celestial physics, as described in his *Metaphysics*. While Ptolemy has often been regarded as an Aristotelian in terms of his cosmology, careful reading of his astronomical writings indicate that this was not the case.

Several of Ptolemy's writings indicate that he thought that there were important correlations between celestial and terrestrial phenomena. His *Phases of the Fixed Stars* fits into the Greek tradition of providing lists of stellar risings and settings correlated to weather phenomena; here any physical explanation of such correlations is entirely absent. In his *Harmonics*, Ptolemy pointed to analogous structures and relationships occurring between music, the heavens, and also the human soul, claiming that the same formal, mathematical relationships are present in each. He argued that harmonic ratios play an important role in the celestial realm; as an example, he pointed to the analogies between the twelve divisions of the zodiac and the twelve-tone musical scale. However, it was in the *Tetrabiblos*, a work that deals primarily with astronomical prognostication, that Ptolemy offered his most extensive treatment of the relationship and influence between the celestial and the terrestrial regions. Here he explained that the astronomy presented in the *Almagest* enables the prediction of configurations of the sun, moon, and stars, while the *Tetrabiblos* discusses the nature of those configurations and the ensuing changes.

These various astronomical works must all be consulted to piece together Ptolemy's cosmological views, since he does not present them in a unified fashion. Briefly, for Ptolemy, the earth is approximately spherical, very small in comparison to the size of the universe, and in the middle of the universe, kept there by pressure. The earth does not experience any local motion. The heavens and the heavenly bodies move spherically; there are two primary motions, namely the daily motion from east to west and the motion of the planets from west to east along the ecliptic. The order of the planets is as follows: earth, moon, Mercury, Venus, sun, Mars, Jupiter, and Saturn. Each heavenly body moves itself independently of other bodies, but the motions of the celestial bodies are affected by nearby terrestrial elements, just as terrestrial occurrences are affected by celestial motions. There is no space between the celestial spheres. The motions of the celestial bodies are based on formal, mathematical relations that also underlie the human soul and music, relationships that give mathematicians special access to knowledge about those subjects.

In order to gain a fuller understanding of Ptolemy's astronomy the philosophical ideas that underlie his astronomical writings must be considered; within his astronomical works he presented his natural philosophical, epistemological, and ethical views. For example, in the philosophically oriented preface to the *Almagest* Ptolemy made it clear that he considered mathematics, and astronomy in particular, to be the highest form of philosophy. Further, Ptolemy's conception of the celestial bodies as divine beings shaped his ideas about natural philosophy, epistemology, and ethics, and the practice of astronomy; these ideas in turn play a significant role in his study of the heavens.

Plato emphasized the important role that astronomy can play in ethical philosophy, suggesting that it is ethically necessary for all humans to be acquainted with the celestial bodies and their motions. While many of the students of Plato (427–348/347 B.C.E.) had been interested in astronomy, including Eudoxus of Cnidus (ca. 400-ca. 347 B.C.E.) and Aristotle (384–322 B.C.E.), they did not seem to be particularly concerned about the ethical benefits to be derived from the study of astronomy. However, in the second century C.E., several influential writers, including Ptolemy, picked up the thread of Plato's thought and wove it into their work.

In the *Almagest*, Ptolemy placed an especially high ethical value on knowledge of the heavens. By studying astronomy, he believed that he was engaging in the highest form of philosophy, particularly by teaching and making progress in astronomical theories. This statement concerning the value of the study of astronomy occurs at the very beginning of a widely used book; given the unique place of the *Almagest* in the history of astronomy education, Ptolemy's claim about the special status of the study of astronomy must be taken seriously.

Questions regarding Ptolemy's attitude toward the phenomena have been debated, primarily on two fronts. On the one hand, there is the question as to whether or not Ptolemy's models were meant to be strictly mathematical, or whether he was also interested in the physical world. The discussion of the physical hypotheses that underlie the *Almagest* and Book Two of the *Planetary Hypotheses* indicate that he wanted his models to be viable physically. Ptolemy's detailed descriptions of observing instruments and his concern with being able to provide useful information for builders of planetariums give further evidence of his interest in the phenomena.

There has been something of a historical tradition of criticism regarding Ptolemy's handling of observational data. Most recently, he has been accused by Robert R. Newton of having been a mediocre astronomer with a rather cavalier attitude toward observations. Others, in turn, have rallied to defend Ptolemy against the various crimes attributed to him by Newton. Britton completed a detailed study of the solar and lunar observations reported in the *Almagest*, and of the related models, with a view to evaluating Ptolemy's skills in practical astronomy and the role of observations in the development of his astronomical theory. He concluded that the relatively high accuracy of Ptolemy's parameters can be explained by assuming that they represent the average of many determinations from a much larger number of observations than are reported by Ptolemy. In his view, that Ptolemy did not describe the procedure he used for arriving at his parameters does not suggest that Ptolemy was attempting to mislead his readers. Rather, the overall character of the *Almagest* is didactic; Ptolemy did not intend to present an account of how he arrived at his theories. Furthermore, Ptolemy tended to try to present his demonstrations in a logically rigorous manner, in keeping with the standards of Greek mathematics; being unable to present his methodology in this way, he may have chosen not to discuss it in detail. The relationship between observation and scientific theory is one that is continually debated by historians and philosophers of science and is certainly not restricted to the field of ancient Greek astronomy. Ptolemy's procedures may have been more sophisticated and more similar to those of modern astronomers than has been previously realized (Britton, xiv).

Scholarship on Ptolemy has tended to focus on his mathematical achievement. He was the most influential mathematical astronomer of Antiquity, the Middle Ages, and well into the early modern period. Yet although Ptolemy's historical importance has long been recognized, there remains much work to be done in order to fully appreciate his achievement. For example, no single study has attempted to understand fully the relationships between Ptolemy's different works. Further, Ptolemy's work should be considered within the broader context of Alexandrian philosophical and intellectual life.

Liba C. Taub

Bibliography

Britton, J.P. *Models and Precision: The Quality of Ptolemy's Observations and Parameters*. New York: Garland, 1992.

Evans, J. "On the Function and Probable Origin of Ptolemy's Equant." *American Journal of Physics* 52 (1984): 1080–1090.

———. "Ptolemaic Planetary Theory;" "Ptolemy;" "Ptolemy's Cosmology." In *Encyclopedia of Cosmology: Historical, Philosophical, and Scientific Foundations of Modern Cosmology*, edited by Noriss Hetherington, 513–544. New York: Garland, 1993.

Neugebauer, O. *A History of Ancient Mathematical Astronomy*. 3 vols. Berlin: Springer-Verlag, 1975.

Newton, R.R. *The Crime of Claudius Ptolemy.* Baltimore: Johns Hopkins University Press, 1977.

Pederson, O. *A Survey of the Almagest*. Odense: Odense University Press, 1974.

Price, D.J. "Precision Instruments: to 1500." In *A History of Technology*, edited by C. Singer, E.J. Holmyard, A.R. Hall, and T.I. Williams, vol. 3, 582–619. Oxford: Clarendon Press, 1957.

Swerdlow, N.M. "Ptolemy on Trial." *American Scholar* 48 (1979): 523–531.

Taub, L.C. *Ptolemy's Universe: The Natural Philosophical and Ethical Foundations of Ptolemy's Astronomy*. Chicago: Open Court, 1993.

Toomer, G.J. "Ptolemy." In *Dictionary of Scientific Biography*, edited by C.C. Gillispie, vol. 11, 186–206. New York: Scribner, 1975.

Publications, Astronomical

The earliest scientific journals covered all areas of science, much as *Science* and *Nature* do today. The earliest strictly astronomical publications included learned correspondence and ephemerides. Among the earliest ephemeris still being published is the French *Connaissance des Temps,* first published in 1679. The *Philosophical Transactions* of the Royal Society of London and other general science publications regularly contained astronomical papers. The first astronomical journal is generally considered to be Baron Franz Xaver von Zach's *Monatliche Correspondenz*. As the title implies, this was a periodical based upon extensive correspondence with a late-eighteenth-century astronomer and his colleagues, along with book reviews, translations, and progress reports on the status of astronomy all over Europe. It was published from 1800 through 1813 in Germany. It was followed by another periodical of Zach's, published in French, from 1818 to 1826. Through his *Correspondenz*, Zach became known as the most prominent promoter of astronomy of his era (Hermann, 101).

Astronomische Nachrichten is among the oldest of the astronomical periodicals still being published. It began publication in 1821. After that, regular publication of other journals and observatory publications began. One of the earliest U.S. publications, *Astronomical Journal*, closely followed the format of *Astronomische Nachrichten*. Journals were typically published on a regular basis (monthly, quarterly, semiannually), but observatory publications came out when funds were available for publication and sufficient data were collected. Political upheaval also played a part; as European conflicts caused borders to change, titles were suspended. There could be a gap of five or ten years or more between numbers in the series.

Despite some problems with publication schedules, the volume of material increased phenomenally. The *Astrophysical Journal*, for example, published approximately 850 pages in its first year on a 5- by 8-inch page. In 1993, pages numbered over 19,000 on 8- by 10-inch pages. As the number of "Communications," "Publications," "Memoirs," and commercial journals grew, the need to index them became evident. *Astronomischer Jahresbericht* (1899–1968) was the first major index of the subject; it was continued by *Astronomy and Astrophysics Abstracts*. Compiled at the Astronomische Rechen-Institut, Heidelberg, it still provides the most complete index to astronomical/astrophysical sources, in four large volumes per year. Indexed by author and subject, it is available electronically via the data base PHYS, which is online retrievable via STN International, c/o Fachinformationszentrum Karlsruhe, P.O. Box 2465, 76344 Karlsruhe, Germany.

Publication of an observatory's annals or reports was a method of exchanging information among colleagues all over the world and of building the observatory library. Many observatories developed a formal exchange program in which they agreed to send their publication series to one another. Some observatories began a publication series with original material, but began issuing a numbered reprint series with the same title. Other observatories issued a reprint series with a separate title. Reprints were often published in journals which most observatories received, but sometimes were originally part of a university's general science series or an even more obscure title—and thus might not be part of an observatory library. If more than one author was involved, from more than one institution, it was likely that the same paper might appear in an observatory collection in several forms. There is at least one astronomy paper that was issued in five reprint series and two report forms (Kemp, viii).

Observatory publications became the vehicle for large cooperative survey catalogues published in the late nineteenth century into the twentieth. Large catalogues such as the *Bonner Durchmusterung*, Henry Draper Catalog, *Cordoba Durchmusterung*, *Astronomische Gesellschaft Katalog*, and the Astrographic Catalogue (*Carte du Ciel*) were published as part of observatory publication series. The Astrographic Catalogue was compiled at nineteen different observatories.

Large, formal exchange programs are now virtually nonexistent because of the costs involved; very few observatories continue to publish an original (that is, not reprint) series. More common now are annual reports and newsletters, although a few observatories may publish a special catalogue of observations and number it as a volume of a publication series.

The practice of sending reprints as a series had more or less been discontinued as printing and postal costs increased and journals became more readily available and affordable. As reprint series were discontinued, the practice of sending preprints began. Some preprints are issued in numbered series and sent out to large numbers of institutions on mailing lists; others are sent to individuals who the author of the preprint believes would like to see a copy of the material in advance of publication. This practice too may become outmoded as more and more electronic publishing becomes routine and authors mount their preprints on a server and make it available through Mosaic™ or Gopher™ and the World Wide Web.

Judy L. Bausch

Bibliography

Armitage, A. "Baron von Zach and His Astronomical Correspondence." *Popular Astronomy* 57 (1949): 326–333.

DeVorkin, D.H. *The History of Modern Astronomy and Astrophysics: A Selected, Annotated Bibliography*. New York: Garland, 1982.

Hermann, D.B. "B.A. Gould and His *Astronomical Journal*." *Journal for the History of Astronomy* 2 (1971): 98–108.

Kemp, D.A. *Astronomy and Astrophysics, A Bibliographical Guide*. London: Archon Books, 1970.

Seal, R.A. *A Guide to the Literature of Astronomy*. Littleton, Colo.: Libraries Unlimited, 1977.

Seal, R.A., and S.S. Martin. *A Bibliography of Astronomy, 1970– 1979*. Littleton, Colo.: Libraries Unlimited, 1982.

Union List of Astronomy Serials. Compiled by J.A. Lola (Bausch). Special Libraries Association, Physics-Astronomy-Mathematics Division, 1983; 2nd ed. available electronically via anonymous ftp. Contact jab@yerkes.uchicago.edu (Internet) for information.

Pulkovo Observatory

The Pulkovo Observatory, officially the Main (Pulkovo) Astronomical Observatory of the Russian Academy of Sciences, is known to every astronomer in the world as the symbol of Russian astronomy. The nineteenth-century American astronomer B.A. Gould characterized Pulkovo as the astronomical capital of the world.

After World War II, astronomy in the Soviet Union expanded rapidly, but Pulkovo continued to occupy an important position in Soviet astronomy. Traditionally Pulkovo was concerned with **astrometry**, but its astronomers also work in many other fields. The observatory has some involvement with graduate education.

Major instruments at Pulkovo include a 65-cm astrometric refractor, a 120-meter radio telescope constructed by Semen E. Khaikin and Naum L. Kaidanovsky that became the prototype for the RATAN-600 of the Special Astrophysical Observatory on the Caucasus, a horizontal solar telescope, and various astrometric instruments. The observatory has several branches, including a mountain station for solar research near Kislovodsk (in the Caucasus), the station for measuring the variation of latitude at Blagoveshchensk (on the river Amur), large telescopes at Pamirs, and some temporary stations. Pulkovo staff carry out astrometric investigations in Chile with a new transit instrument and a 70-cm Maksutov wide-field astrograph. Pulkovo astronomers have observed the southern skies from other locations in Latin America as well. Pulkovo personnel helped to develop the 6-meter reflector at the Special Astrophysical Observatory in the North Caucasus Mountains. Pulkovo astronomers pioneered in observing the sun from balloons and took part in space research.

The Pulkovo Observatory was founded in 1839 under the leadership of **Friedrich Georg Wilhelm Struve**, a German-born astronomer educated at Dorpat University (now Tartu University in the Baltic republic of Estonia). Struve modeled Pulkovo on Bessell's observatory at Königsberg. After the Napoleonic wars, it was obvious that the vast Czarist empire needed a national observatory similar to Greenwich or Paris to provide the state with astronomical and geodetic information and expertise. Pulkovo was established by Czar Nicolaus the First and located on the Pulkovo Hills not far from St. Petersburg, the imperial capital.

For fifty years the observatory was directed by F.G.W. Struve and his son **Otto W.** The observatory played a leading role in training personnel for geodesy and cartography. F.G.W. Struve was a leader in the project to measure the arc of the meridian from the Danube to the Arctic Ocean. The great 30-inch refractor was installed in 1885. Following the Struves, the most prominent directors were academicians Fiodor A. Bredikhin, who was recognized as an expert on comets, and the astrophysicist Aristarkh A. Belopol'sky. Pulkovo became the center for astrometry in Russia, but lost ground with the rise of astrophysics in the late nineteenth century. In spite of the 1917 Revolution, the level of research at the observatory continued to be impressive and Pulkovo astronomers continued to cooperate with colleagues abroad. In 1926 the Grubb 40-inch reflector was installed at the Crimean Pulkovo branch, located at Simeis and in 1927 a new **astrograph** by Zeiss. In 1940 a large horizontal solar telescope went into operation. It was built by a Leningrad optical factory to a design by Pulkovo astronomer Nicolai G. Ponomarev.

The decline of the Pulkovo Observatory began in the 1930s during Stalin's purges. Stalin hated revolutionary Leningrad and its intellectuals. Pulkovo director **Boris P. Gerasimovich** and many other leading scientists were executed or died in prison. The history of this tragedy is discussed by Robert A. McCutcheon. During World War II, Leningrad was besieged by the German army and the observatory was in the line of fire; its buildings were leveled. The largest telescopes perished; only some optics could be saved. Part of the famous library and archive of astronomical photographs were also destroyed. Many astronomers survived the Stalin purges only to die from starvation inside the besieged city or to be killed in battle.

The priority given to science by the Soviet government after World War II is reflected in the decision to rebuild Pulkovo. The observatory was reconstructed in its original nineteenth-century form with one exception; modern hemispherical domes replaced the original octagonal turrets. The restoration was the symbolic gesture of government concern for soviet science. From a scientific point of view, Pulkovo should have been moved from Leningrad to a dark-sky site from which observations could have been made.

The principal role in the renovation of Pulkovo belonged to Aleksandr A. Mikhailov, director from 1947 to 1964, vice president of the International Astronomical Union (1946–1948). The restored observatory opened in May 1954, with astronomers from around the world in attendance. For soviet astronomers it was a dress rehearsal for the General Assembly of the **International Astronomical Union** in 1958. At that time the Pulkovo staff numbered about one hundred. The importance of the event was emphasized with a special commemorative postal stamp issued by the Soviet government. A second commemorative stamp was issued in 1989 in connection with the 150–year anniversary of Pulkovo.

Following the fall of the Soviet Union, the financial situation at the Pulkovo Observatory as well as many other scientific institutions is very uncertain.

Alexander Gurshtein

Bibliography

Abalkin, V.K., ed. *One Century and a Half of Pulkovo Observatory*. In Russian. Leningrad, 1989.

Batten, A.H. *Resolute and Undertaking Characters: The Lives of Wilhelm and Otto Struve*. Astrophysics and Space Science Library, 139. Dordrecht, 1988.

Dadaev, A.N. *Pulkovo Observatory: an Essay on its History and Scientific Activity*. In Russian. Leningrad, 1972. English translation by Kevin Krisciunas, Pulkovo Observatory, NASA Technical Memorandum TM-75083. Springfield, Mass.: National Technical Information Service, 1978, 239.

———. "The Second Birth of Pulkovo." In Russian. In *Researches on History of Astronomy*, edited by A. Gurshtein, vol. 21, 17–49. Moscow: Nauka, 1989.

———. "The Events of One Hundred Years Old (The Retirement of Otto Struve and the Directorship of Fiodor Bredikhin)." In Russian. In *Researches on History of Astronomy*, edited by A. Gurshtein, 24. Moscow: Nauka, 1993.

Gnevyshev, M.N. "Accomplishments and Alarms of Pulkovo." In Russian. In *Researches on History of Astronomy,* edited by A. Gurshtein, vol. 21, 342–368. Moscow: Nauka, 1989.

Krisciunas, K. "A Short History of Pulkovo Observatory." *Vistas in Astronomy* 22 (1978): 27–37.

———. "The End of Pulkovo Observatory's Reign as the Astronomical Capital of the World." *Quarterly Journal of the Royal Astronomical Society* 25 (1984): 301–305.

———. *Astronomical Centers of the World.* Cambridge: Cambridge University Press, 1988.

McCutcheon, R.A. "Stalin's Purge of Soviet Astronomers." *Sky & Telescope* 78, no. 4 (October 1989): 352–357.

———. "The 1936–1937 Purge of Soviet Astronomers." *Slavic Review* 50, no. 1 (1991): 100–117.

Mikhailov, A.A. "Pulkovo Observatory." In *Astrophysics and Twentieth-Century Astronomy to 1950 (The General History of Astronomy) Part A*, edited by O. Gingerich, vol. 4, 119–122. Cambridge: Cambridge University Press, 1984.

Nicolaidis, E. *Le developpement de l'astronomie en U.R.S.S. 1917–1935*. Observatoire de Paris, 1984.

———. "Astronomy and Politics in Russia in the Early Stalinist Period." *Journal for the History of Astronomy* 21 (1990): 345–351.

Struve, F.G.W. *Description de l'Observatoire Astronomique Central de Poulkova*. St.-Petersbourg, 1845.

Pythagoras of Samos, Astronomy of

Pythagoras (sixth century B.C.E.) himself remains a sage-like figure shrouded in mystery; he is known only through later authors. Surviving fragments of the writings of Philolaus (fifth century B.C.E.) probably represent the earliest written account of Pythagorean ideas; no complete work exists. Knowledge of Pythagorean astronomy is derived from other sources, including Plato (427–348/347 B.C.E.) and Aristotle (384–322 B.C.E.).

Important ideas associated with Pythagorean astronomy include the existence of a central fire about which revolve a "counter-earth," which is invisible, the inhabited earth, the moon, the sun, the five planets visible to the naked eye (Venus, Mercury, Mars, Saturn, and Jupiter), and the so-called fixed stars. This view of the universe was in sharp contrast with the more widely held idea that the earth was in the center. The Pythagorean doctrine of the "harmony of the spheres" is well attested, although not present in the writings of Philolaus. That cosmic music exists is an idea that fits well with the general interest of the Pythagoreans in musical theory, but it is unlikely that they produced any detailed account.

The division of the study of mathematics into the four fields of arithmetic, music, geometry, and astronomy is sometimes associated with the Pythagoreans and was very influential in the history of education; further, the close association between geometry and astronomy was an essential characteristic of ancient Greek astronomy.

While some scholars, including Burkert, have questioned the extent to which Pythagorean astronomy was scientific, the influence of ideas that have been labeled "Pythagorean" has been considerable. Ancient commentators believed that the Pythagoreans were the source of Plato's ideas on astronomy; the belief that astronomy owes a great debt to Pythagoras was long-lived.

Liba C. Taub

Bibliography

Burkert, W. *Lore and Science of Ancient Pythagoreanism.* Translated by Edwin L. Minar. Cambridge: Harvard University Press, 1972.

Fritz, K. von. "Pythagoras of Samos." In *Dictionary of Scientific Biography*, edited by C.C. Gillispie, vol. 11, 219–225. New York: Scribner, 1975.

Huffman, C. *Philolaus of Croton: Pythagorean and Presocratic.* Cambridge: Cambridge University Press, 1993.

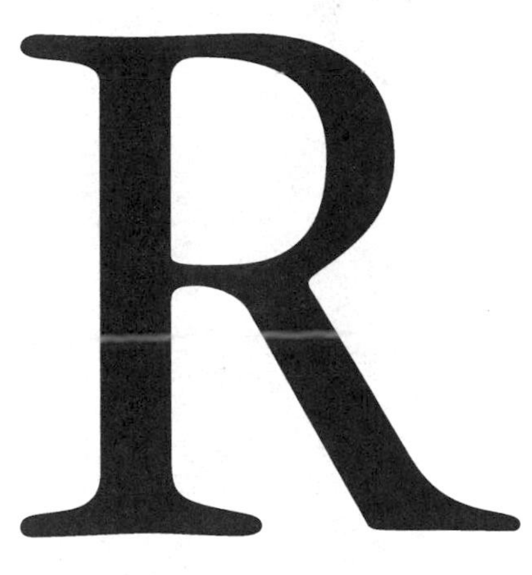

Radial Velocity (Stellar)

The radial velocity of a star is the component of its velocity relative to the observer along the line of sight. The determination of stellar radial velocities can be made from a spectrum by measurement of the small wavelength shifts of the spectral lines from their rest positions. In 1842 Christian Doppler predicted that a frequency (or wavelength) change should occur as a result of the radial motion of either light source or observer, but he incorrectly believed this would induce a color change in the stars. Later Armand Fizeau and Ernst Mach correctly predicted that a spectral line shift should in principle be observable. From 1868 **William Huggins** in London and **Angelo Secchi** in Rome attempted to detect Doppler line shifts by the visual observation of stellar spectra, but it was not until Hermann Carl Vogel and Julius Scheiner in Potsdam photographed stellar spectra in 1888–1892 that reliable Doppler shifts, for some fifty stars, were first observed. The first spectroscopic binary stars were discovered in 1889 as a result of this program.

These techniques were then applied by many observers, most notably by **William Wallace Campbell** at the **Lick Observatory**, who with his colleagues undertook a program to measure the radial velocities of the stars visible from both hemispheres to magnitude 5.51. An observatory in Santiago, Chile, was established in 1903 for this work on the southern stars, and a catalogue was published in 1928 by Campbell and Joseph Moore with results for 2,771 stars. Other large programs on fainter stars were undertaken by **Walter Adams** and Alfred Joy at Mount Wilson, by John Plaskett at Victoria, British Columbia, and by Edwin Frost at the Yerkes Observatory. The discovery of the high-velocity stars of the galactic halo and of galactic rotation were the results of these programs.

At Victoria, Joseph Pearce from the 1930s, later with Robert Petrie, developed the concepts of standard rest wavelengths and of standard stars to help overcome systematic errors in radial-velocity work.

Several radial-velocity catalogues have been compiled. Moore's catalogue of 1931 contained data for 6,739 stars, a fifth of them with apparently variable velocity due to pulsation or orbital motion in a binary. Ralph Wilson's compendium of 1953 contained data for over 20,000 stars from twenty-four observatories. Practically all these results were from photographic spectrograms with slit spectrographs. Slitless objective-prism radial velocities, first attempted by Edward Pickering in 1887, never gave very precise results. At the Cambridge Observatories, Roger Griffin has pioneered since 1967 the photoelectric determination of radial velocity using the real-time cross-correlation with a mask, while Bruce Campbell at Victoria was one of those using digital cross-correlations of two spectra recorded with a diode array to obtain relative velocities of high precision. For many years accuracy of about ±1 km/s from photographic spectra of late-type stars was regarded as good. With the most recent techniques, this value has been reduced to between 10 and 100 m/s at several observatories.

J.B. Hernshaw

Bibliography

Campbell, W.W. *Stellar Motions, With Special Reference to Motions Determined by*

Means of the Spectrograph. New Haven: Yale University Press, 1913.

Hearnshaw, J.B. *The Analysis of Starlight*. Cambridge: Cambridge University Press, 1986.

———. "Doppler and Vogel—Two Notable Anniversaries in Stellar Astronomy." *Vistas in Astronomy* 35 (1992): 157–177.

Radio Astronomy

Radio astronomy is the study of the extraterrestrial universe through the reception of naturally emitted radio waves. The first detection of such radiation was in 1932, but the technique came to fruition only at the end of World War II, when a corpus of physicists and engineers who had developed military radar during the war turned to peacetime pursuits. Within five years, discoveries by these investigators revealed a universe at radio wavelengths that was in many respects wholly unsuspected, since all previous astronomy had been confined to the narrow range of wavelengths detectable by the human eye and the photographic plate. Within ten years, the terms *radio astronomy* and *radio astronomer* were firmly established, and, indeed, for the first time a more specific term, *optical astronomy,* was needed for what had previously been all of astronomy. By 1960 radio astronomy was an established part of astronomy in many countries, with England and Australia the clear leaders, and since that time it has continued to play a major part in the development of astronomy. Most of the major discoveries in radio astronomy have been crucially aided by steady advances in technology that have increased the ability to detect faint signals and to make fine-scale maps by many powers of ten.

Shortly after Heinrich Hertz established the existence of electric (radio) waves in the laboratory in 1886–1888, several unsuccessful attempts were made in Europe to detect these waves from the sun. It was not until 1942, however, that James Stanley Hey, a radar physicist, deduced that puzzling signals being received on British radar sets, taken at first to be intentional jamming by the Germans, were in fact emanating from the sun. By the end of the war, several others had made preliminary studies of the unexpectedly high levels of solar radio emission in the forms of both quiescent (steady) emission and bursts. The major findings of the postwar decade were that the solar corona emitted at a temperature of two million degrees Kelvin, and that powerful radio bursts of many kinds often accompanied sunspots, flares, and prominences. These bursts, as well as the quiescent radiation, made possible much more detailed and complete models of the outer solar atmosphere.

Solar observations dominated early radio astronomy, but the most exciting discoveries were made in the nonsolar realm. In fact, the first detection of extraterrestrial radio waves had not been from the sun, but rather from the Milky Way. In 1932 Karl Jansky, a radio physicist at the Bell Telephone Laboratories in New Jersey, accidentally discovered faint cosmic noise coming from all parts of the Milky Way. Its source remained unexplained until the 1950s, when it was shown that cosmic ray electrons, spiraling around weak interstellar magnetic fields, would emit synchrotron radiation. In 1945 Hey's group in England discovered that one portion of this radiation, in the constellation of Cygnus, was behaving as if it were a discrete source, rather than a general background emission. This was called Cygnus A. Many other examples of radio stars were subsequently found. Their nature was hotly debated: some concluded that they were a new form of dark star, relatively close to the sun, while others argued that they were distant galaxies. By the mid-1950s the latter view held sway largely because of work by John Bolton of the Radiophysics Laboratory in Sydney and Graham Smith of the Cavendish Laboratory at Cambridge University on the radio side and **Walter Baade** and Rudolph Minkowski, who with the Mount Palomar 200-inch telescope demonstrated an association between many peculiar galaxies and the radio sources.

Once scientists understood that radio sources could be detected at distances far exceeding those of the faintest optical galaxies, radio astronomers used them as a cosmological probe and became embroiled in the debate between defenders of the Big Bang universe and those of the Steady State universe. Martin Ryle at Cambridge argued that the distribution of the sources indicated that the early (distant) universe contained many more sources than does today's universe, in direct contradiction to the central Steady State idea. But Bernard Mills in Sydney had his own extensive surveys of sources, which disagreed with Ryle's and provided Fred Hoyle, one of the creators of the Steady State model, with powerful ammunition. The debate went on for a decade and eventually was resolved for most parties only by another startling, accidental radio discovery, the cosmic microwave background. Arno Penzias and Robert Wilson, working at Bell Labs, discovered in 1965 that the entire sky emitted as if it were at a uniform temperature of 3 degrees Kelvin. This radiation could be nicely explained as a relic of the Big Bang, but had no home in Steady State theory. Penzias and Wilson received the Nobel Prize in Physics for this discovery, as did Ryle for his work on radio galaxies, cosmology, and the development of radio interferometers. In the 1960s studies of quasars, distant luminous objects that had been discovered in 1963 through radio and optical observations, also presented persuasive evidence for an evolving Big Bang universe. In the early 1990s researchers took radio astronomy outside the atmosphere and used the COBE (cosmic background explorer) satellite to establish the existence of weak mottling in the cosmic microwave background, predicted as a consequence of galaxies forming shortly after the Big Bang.

In 1967 the Cambridge group, led by Antony Hewish and his student Jocelyn Bell, discovered radio sources that emit pulses with unprecedented accuracies. These pulsars were soon explained as rapidly spinning neutron stars, the collapsed remnant cores of the supernova explosions of massive stars. For this Hewish shared the Nobel Prize with Ryle, and the field of pulsar astronomy, now extended to many other wavelength regions, has become one of the most fundamental in astronomy. For example, long-term precision monitoring of one particular pulsar, rapidly orbiting a companion star, has allowed Joseph Taylor to infer the existence of gravitational waves, one of the necessary consequences of Einstein's general relativity.

Radio astronomy has also revealed a host of spectral lines that provide probes of the motions and physical properties of colder regions of interstellar space. The most important line is that at 21 cm wavelength from hydrogen, discovered in the United States in 1951 by Harold Ewen and Edward Purcell but predicted and later successfully exploited by Dutch astronomers Hendrik van de Hulst and Jan Oort. In 1968 radio lines from molecules of ammonia and water vapor were discovered by a group led by Charles Townes, and within a few years an entire organic interstellar chemistry became evident. By the early 1990s almost one hundred different molecules had been studied.

Besides the intellectual history summarized above, radio astronomy presents an excellent case study for historical questions dealing with the development of new research areas, patronage, national styles, institutions, and the relation between science and technology. For instance, we can now see that radio astronomy was the first of many steps in opening new electromagnetic windows on the universe. During the 1960s, when scientific satellites were placed in orbit, astronomy for the first time gained access to those portions of the spectrum cut off by the earth's atmosphere. The subdisciplines of infrared, ultraviolet, X-ray, and gamma-ray astronomy were born, and they, like radio astronomy before them, provided new opportunities for workers to do astronomy despite their lack of formal training in the subject. The pioneering study in the social history of radio astronomy is by Edge and Mulkay (1976), who focused on radio sources and the cosmological debate of 1955–1965 and on how the leadership styles of the two major groups in England led to sharply different research strategies. Sullivan (1993) has analyzed the reasons for the lag in U.S. radio astronomy in the postwar decade, especially compared with England and Australia (Sullivan 1988, Robertson 1993), and finds it a result of the abundant funding available to American researchers, the dominance of U.S. optical astronomy, and the directions of military research. He has also studied the nature of the gradual integration of the former wartime radar workers into the astronomical community. An extensive oral history collection is available at the American Institute of Physics, Center for the History of Physics, in College Park, Maryland.

Woodruff T. Sullivan III

Bibliography

Edge, D.O., and M.J. Mulkay. *Astronomy Transformed: The Emergence of Radio Astronomy in Britain.* New York: John Wiley and Sons, 1976.

Hey, J.S. *The Evolution of Radio Astronomy.* London: Elek Science, 1973.

Kellermann, K., and B. Sheets, ed. *Serendipitous Discoveries in Radio Astronomy.* Green Bank, W.Va.: National Radio Astronomy Observatory, 1983.

Robertson, P. *Beyond Southern Skies: Radio Astronomy and the Parkes Telescope.* Cambridge: Cambridge University Press, 1993.

Sullivan, W.T. III. *Classics in Radio Astronomy.* Dordrecht: Reidel, 1982.

———. "Early Radio Astronomy." In *Astrophysics and Twentieth-century Astronomy to 1950*, edited by O. Gingerich, 190–198. Cambridge: Cambridge University Press, 1984.

———. "Early Years of Australian Radio Astronomy." In *Australian Science in the Making*, edited by R.W. Home, 308–344. Cambridge: Cambridge University Press, 1988.

———. "The Entry of Radio Astronomy into Cosmology: Radio Stars and Martin Ryle's 2C Survey." In *Modern Cosmology in Retrospect*, edited by R. Bertotti et al., 309–330. Cambridge: Cambridge University Press, 1990.

———. "The Federal Patron and Postwar Radio Astronomy: A Case where Big Bucks and the Latest Technology Failed in the USA." In *Science and the Federal Patron,* edited by N. Reingold and D. Van Keuren. Washington, D.C.: Smithsonian Institution, 1993.

———, ed. *The Early Years of Radio Astronomy: Reflections Fifty Years after Jansky.* Cambridge: Cambridge University Press, 1984.

Radio Telescopes

A radio telescope is a structure that intercepts radio waves of extraterrestrial origin and, together with associated receiving electronics, permits the measurement of various properties of the incident radio waves such as their intensity, wavelength or frequency, direction of arrival, polarization, and the like. The forms of radio telescopes range from simple antennas, not unlike those for commercial radio and television reception, to specialized antennas in the shapes of tepees or helices or trumpet horns, to the more familiar dishes or parabolic reflectors. The history of radio astronomy has seen a continual interaction between the scientific problems under investigation and the technology of antennas and receivers. Often it has been the technologically possible that has driven scientific observations, rather than a scientific problem that has led to the development of new techniques.

The first antenna designed for extraterrestrial radio waves was a 31-foot dish built by Grote Reber in 1937, shortly after Karl Jansky's accidental discovery of radio emission from the Milky Way. Such reflectors were analogous to optical telescopes except that they observed wavelengths a million times larger and could discern detail only on the order of 10–100 arcminutes. They also turned out to be most suitable for detecting microwaves, those with wavelengths of less than 1 meter. Most astronomical radio sources, however, turned out to be most intense at the longer wavelengths. This, combined with the relative insensitivity and instability of microwave receivers during the pre-1960 period, meant that the greatest advances were possible at longer wavelengths, where other types of radio telescopes were more flexible and less expensive. The simplest were arrays of antennas either closely spaced as a single unit, or widely separated and connected by cable as an interferometer. Martin Ryle's group at Cambridge University steadily developed the interferometer technique, analogous to Michelson's interferometer at optical wavelengths, to the point that the very rotation of the earth was employed to effect changes in the orientations and lengths of the interferometer elements relative to the radio source. This technique of earth rotation aperture synthesis was also developed during the 1950s and 1960s primarily for solar work by W.N. Christiansen of the Radiophysics Laboratory in Sydney. Also at the same laboratory, Joseph Pawsey and John Bolton intensively developed the sea-cliff interferometer, an arrangement whereby a single antenna on a seaside cliff observing a source just above the horizon could in effect act as an interferometer. But by the mid-1950s the greater flexibility and accuracy of Ryle's technique had won out. Aperture synthesis interferometers are today central to much of radio astronomy. The largest and most sensitive arrays have been at Westerbork, Holland (in operation since the late 1960s), near Socorro, New Mexico (late 1970s, the Very Large Array of twenty-seven dishes movable on railroad tracks over several tens of kilometers), and in New South Wales (late 1980s, the Australia Telescope).

During the 1950s at the Jodrell Bank Observatory of Manchester University, Robert Hanbury Brown and colleagues pioneered the effort to increase the separation of antennas making up an interferometer in order to gain finer angular resolution of radio sources. The first step was to discard cable connections and instead use radio links (much as telephone calls are routed today), and by the 1960s even that became unnecessary when timing and tape recording techniques allowed dispensing with any real-time link and then combining the recorded signals later in a computer. This technique of very long baseline interferometry (VLBI) allowed one to conduct simultaneous observations at sites on separate continents and to discern detail in some cases even smaller than a milliarcsecond. In the early 1990s VLBI and aperture synthesis techniques have merged most fully and powerfully with the building of the Very Long

The Owens Valley 40-meter radio telescope. (Courtesy E.C. Krupp, Griffith Observatory)

Baseline Array (VLBA) of ten dishes scattered over the United States.

As interferometry has developed, the single dish has not languished as a tool of the radio astronomer. Bernard Lovell, director at Jodrell Bank, built a 250-foot dish in the mid-1950s that long reigned supreme in many respects. The other dominant antenna in terms of sheer collecting area arrived in the 1960s in central Puerto Rico near Arecibo: a 1000-foot, partially steerable spherical reflector nestled into a valley. With the continual march to shorter wavelengths over the years, it became important that the surface of a dish not just be large, but also accurate enough to focus these wavelengths. From 1970 onward a 36-foot dish on Kitt Peak in Arizona pioneered work at millimeter wavelengths, in particular the detection of dozens of new species of interstellar molecules. Today the largest dish usable at millimeter wavelengths is 45 meters in diameter, at Nobeyama, Japan.

Woodruff T. Sullivan III

Bibliography

Christiansen, W.N., and J.A. Högbom. *Radiotelescopes*. Cambridge: Cambridge University Press, 1969, 1985.

Kraus, J. *Radio Astronomy*. New York: McGraw-Hill, 1966, 1986.

Lovell, A.C.B. *The Story of Jodrell Bank*. London: Oxford University Press, 1968.

———. *Out of the Zenith: Jodrell Bank 1957–1970*. London: Harper and Row, 1973.

———. *The Jodrell Bank Telescopes*. London: Oxford University Press, 1985.

Moran, J.M., G.W. Swenson Jr., and A.R. Thompson. *Interferometry and Synthesis in Radio Astronomy*. New York: John Wiley and Sons, 1986.

Pawsey, J.L., and R.N. Bracewell. *Radio Astronomy*. London: Oxford University Press, 1955.

Sullivan, W.T. III. "Some Highlights of Interferometry in Early Radio Astronomy." In *Radio Interferometry: Theory, Techniques and Applications*, edited by T.J. Cornwell and R.A. Perley, 132–149. San Francisco: Astronomical Society of the Pacific, 1991.

Relativity and Astronomy

Astronomy has long been intimately connected with the subject of gravitation and relativity. Observation of planetary motions led to Johannes Kepler's laws, which were then explained by Isaac Newton's theory of gravitation. Astronomy provided further tests of Newtonian gravity: **Edmond Halley** determined that the comets that had appeared in 1531, 1607, and 1682 were one and the same, following a single Newtonian orbit; **Leonhard Euler** and **Joseph Lagrange** showed that the observed changes in the period of Jupiter and Saturn were periodic rather than secular, and **Alexis Clairault** demonstrated in 1749 that Newtonian gravity correctly accounted for the motion of the lunar perigee. But in the nineteenth century, observations of the motion of Mercury revealed a discrepancy with Newtonian gravity that resulted in a triumph for Albert Einstein's general relativity.

In the latter part of the twentieth century, astronomy played a dual role in the development of general relativity. Discoveries of exotic astronomical objects such as quasars, pulsars, binary X-ray sources containing black holes, and gravitational lenses, pointed to an important role for general relativity in astrophysics, and helped fuel a renaissance in the subject. And new high-precision astronomical techniques, such as very long baseline radio interferometry, radar ranging, and precise timing of radio pulsars, provided tests of general relativity at unheard of precision.

When Einstein completed the general theory of relativity in November 1915, he had in hand three testable predictions: an explanation of the perihelion advance of **Mercury**, the deflection of starlight, and the gravitational red shift of light. The first was an immediate success.

In 1859, U.J.J. Le Verrier in France had announced that, after the perturbing influences of the other planets on the orbit of Mercury were taken into account, there remained a discrepancy of about 43 arcseconds per century between the observed advance of the perihelion, 575 arcseconds per century, and the theoretical advance. This discrepancy remained unexplained until the twentieth century. Einstein found that the general relativistic contribution to Mercury's perihelion advance neatly accounted for the difference. He reported that he had "palpitations of the heart" on making this discovery (Pais, 253). The accurate general relativistic prediction for the effect is 42.98 arcseconds. Since 1966, the ability to bounce radar signals off Mercury has resulted in determinations of its orbit to the level of one kilometer, leading to an observed value in agreement with the prediction to one part in one thousand.

The second great success of general relativity was also provided by astronomy. The theory predicts that the path of a light ray near a gravitating body should be deflected. For the sun, the maximum deflection is 1.75 arcseconds for a grazing ray. In May 1919, this deflection was measured by British astronomers led by **Arthur Stanley Eddington**, who journeyed to the path of totality in order to photograph stars near the sun. The results agreed with general relativity with stated uncertainties between 10 and 20 percent, although hindsight suggests that much larger errors are warranted, given the inadequately understood systematic effects. Since 1968, radio interferometry has provided accurate measurements of the deflection of light from quasars and radio galaxies, reaching 1 percent by 1975. Recently, measurements of sources distributed over the entire celestial sphere using very long baseline radio interferometry have confirmed general relativity to one part in one thousand.

The deflection of light has a cosmological counterpart in gravitational lenses, first discovered in 1979. These are galaxies or clusters of galaxies whose gravitational field deflects the light from a more distant galaxy or quasar, producing multiple images, arcs, and rings. By using the general relativistic predictions for the deflection, it is now possible to study the mass distribution in the lensing object from the distribution, brightness, and shapes of the images. This may yield important information about the distributon of dark matter in the universe.

Closely related to the deflection of light is the Shapiro time delay, a retardation of a light signal in the curved space region around a body such as the sun, named after **Irwin I. Shapiro**, who discovered it as a prediction of general relativity in 1964. He and others then measured the effect using radar ranging to planets and interplanetary spacecraft between 1966 and 1976. The retardation causes a delay in a round-trip signal from earth to **Mars** of about 200 microseconds for a ray that grazes the sun. Radar ranging to the 1976 *Viking* Mars landers and orbiters verified the prediction to one part in one thousand.

The third famous prediction made by Einstein was initially an astronomical failure. This was the gravitational red shift, a change in the wavelength of light emitted by an atom in a gravitational field. Early attempts to measure this effect in spectral lines of white dwarfs or the sun failed because of complicating physical effects. The first true test of this effect came from the Harvard laboratory of Robert V. Pound, who measured the change in frequency of gamma rays emitted by iron nuclei as they ascended or descended a tower. The most accurate test, at 0.02 percent, was carried out in 1976, using a hydrogen maser atomic clock launched on a *Scout* rocket over the Atlantic Ocean. Only recently have astronomers measured the red shift of solar spectral lines with any accuracy, reaching 2 percent.

Radio astronomy provided a dramatically new test of general relativity by confirming its predictions for gravitational radiation. This resulted from the serendipitous discovery in 1974 of the pulsar PSR 1913+16, found to be in a binary system with another neutron star with an orbital period of about 8 hours. The pulsar's intrinsic 59 millisecond pulse period turned out to be extremely stable, allowing precise measurements of its orbit through the variations in pulse arrival times caused by the varying propagation path. This accuracy permitted measurement of a number of general relativistic effects in the system, such as the analogue of the perihelion shift, which in this case is 4.22663 degrees per year, with an accuracy of four parts per million. According to general relativity, a binary system should emit gravitational radiation. This radiation carries energy from the system, causing it to spiral inward, resulting in a decrease of the orbital period at a predicted rate of 75.8 microseconds per year. The measured rate, first reported in 1979, agrees with the prediction to an accuracy that now stands at 0.5 percent.

Gravitational radiation may provide a new form of astronomy in the twenty-first century. Large-scale detectors using laser interferometers are currently being constructed by the United States and other countries that will be sensitive enough to observe sources of gravitational waves, such as supernovae and inspiraling neutron-star and black-hole binary systems, to great distances. This will open a new window onto cataclysmic events in the universe.

Clifford M. Will

Bibliography

Pais, A. *'Subtle is the Lord . . .': The Science and the Life of Albert Einstein.* New York: Oxford University Press, 1980.

Roseveare, N.T. *Mercury's Perihelion from Le Verrier to Einstein.* Oxford: Clarendon Press, 1982.

Will, C.M. "Experimental Gravitation from Newton's *Principia* to Einstein's General Relativity." In *300 Years of Gravitation*, edited by S.W. Hawking and W. Israel. Cambridge: Cambridge University Press, 1987.

———. *Theory and Experiment in Gravitational Physics.* 2nd ed. Cambridge: Cambridge University Press, 1992

———. *Was Einstein Right? Putting General Relativity to the Test.* 2nd ed. New York: Basic Books, 1993.

Reward System in Modern Astronomy

Science is a very competitive activity. Scientists aggressively compete in the race to create new knowledge and to gain recognition. The reward system in science provides recognition for outstanding achievement. Hagstrom (168) suggests that scientists exchange new information about the natural world for recognition and that the prospect of honors and awards is an important factor in motivating scientific research. Honors and awards represent scarce commodities; otherwise, they would have no value. The reward system of science is arranged hierarchically. In each discipline there is a reward system, likewise in each national scientific community. At the level of the international scientific community there is also a reward system. The following discussion focuses primarily on the American experience.

In American astronomy the reward system is structured as follows: Local honors come from a scientist's home institution and are of limited value. The American Astronomical Society offers prizes, medals, and lectureships. These are much more prestigious than local awards. The National Academy of Sciences (founded in 1863) is the premier honorary body of the American scientific community. Its Astronomy Section includes most of the distinguished researchers in the field. Election to the academy is a signal honor. Two lesser academies (the American Academy of Arts and Sciences and the American Philosophical Society) also provide honors for scientists, but membership in these organizations does not carry the prestige of the National Academy.

At the level of the international astronomical community, American astronomers look to election as a foreign associate of the Royal Astronomical Society of London, the Royal Society of London, or the French Academy of Sciences as marks of major recognition. These European academies also bestow prizes and medals that are highly coveted. The Bruce Medal of the Astronomical Society of the Pacific in the United States is also numbered among major international honors. Astronomers from around the world compete for the award. The Nobel Prize in Physics has recently been awarded for research in astrophysics. The Nobel marks the capstone award of the international scientific community.

Lankford has shown that before World War II there was a significant correlation between the accumulation of honors and power in the American astronomical community. Astronomers who had a number of national and international awards to their credit and were members or foreign associates of major academies were also directors of leading observatories, controlled the important publications of the community, presided over its most important institutions, and had power over the distribution of other resources.

The allocation of honors and awards in the American astronomical community does not reflect decisions made exclusively on the basis of merit. Lankford has found that both patronage and merit determine the allocation of honors and awards, with patronage more important early in the career and merit of greater significance later in the career.

The study of the reward system of modern science has been the province of sociology of science. R.K. Merton pioneered in the field and his students J. and S. Cole and H. Zuckerman have made important contributions. Social historians of modern science have recently provided fresh insights into the topic. For example, Lankford's work examines the reward system in relation to the larger problem of the scientific career. A great deal remains to be done in this field. Especially needed are comparative studies between different scientific communities in the same national context or between scientific communities in different national contexts. The comparative social history of modern science is an inviting research frontier, and the reward system provides a challenging starting point. Major European and American academies publish biographical memoirs of deceased members. These memoirs provide a convenient and valuable resource for social historians interested in the reward system of modern science.

John Lankford

Bibliography

Cole, J.R. and S. Cole. *Social Stratification in Science.* Chicago: University of Chicago Press, 1973.

Hagstrom, W.O. *The Scientific Community.* New York: Basic Books, 1965.

Lankford, J. *American Astronomy: Community, Careers and Power, 1859–1940.* Chicago: University of Chicago Press, forthcoming.

Storer, N.W., ed. *Robert K. Merton: The Sociology of Science, Theoretical and Empirical Investigations.* Chicago: University of Chicago Press, 1973.

Zuckerman, H. *The Scientific Elite: Nobel Laureates in the United States.* New York: Free Press, 1977.

Ritchey, George Willis (1864–1945)

American telescope-maker, astronomical photographer, and prophet of large reflecting telescopes. Ritchey was born in the tiny hamlet of Tuppers Plains, Ohio. He attended the University of Cincinnati for two years, and taught himself to make mirrors from the writings of **Henry Draper** and A.A. Common. A manual training teacher in Chicago, he met **George Ellery Hale** in 1890 and began working at his Kenwood Observatory.

Ritchey worked for Hale at Chicago, then at **Yerkes Observatory**, then at Mount Wilson, as optician, superintendent of construction, and superintendent of the instrument shop. He completed the 24-inch reflector at Yerkes, and built the 60-inch reflector at Mount Wilson. With them, and with the 40-inch Yerkes refractor, he took outstanding photographs of nebulae, galaxies, globular clusters, and the moon. In 1910 Ritchey and his volunteer assistant, Henri Chrétien, invented the Ritchey-Chrétien concept that has been the basis for almost all large reflecting telescopes built after the 200-inch. Ritchey completed the mirror for the 100-inch, but the rest of the telescope was taken out of his hands, and Hale fired him in 1919 after it was finished.

Ritchey went to France in 1924, to build a large telescope, which was never funded, but he did make the world's first Ritchey-Chrétien reflector there, and later, for the Naval Observatory, a 40-inch research telescope of this type. Ritchey conceived many ideas for large telescopes, such as control of the seeing, rapidly interchanging secondary mirrors and instruments, cellular mirrors, and super apertures, that were far ahead of the technology of his own time, but that have become standard practice for the most successful telescopes of the 1990s.

Donald E. Osterbrock

Bibliography

Hall, J.S. "The Ritchey-Chrétien Reflecting Telescope: Half a Century from Conception to Acceptance." *Astronomy Quarterly* 5 (1987): 227–251.

Osterbrock, D.E. *The Pauper and the Prince: George Willis Ritchey, George Ellery Hale, and Big American Telescopes.* Tucson: University of Arizona Press, 1994.

Ritchey, G.W. "The Two-Foot Reflecting Telescope of the Yerkes Observatory." *Astrophysical Journal* 14 (1901): 217–233.

———. "The 60-inch Reflector of the Mount Wilson Solar Observatory." *Astrophysical Journal* 29 (1909): 198–210.

———. *L'Evolution de l'Astrophotographie et les Grands Télescopes de l'Avenir.* Paris: Sociéte Astronomique de France, 1929.

Rittenhouse, David (1732–1790)

American instrument-maker and astronomer. Born on a farm near Germantown, Pennsylvania, the third of ten children of Matthias and Elizabeth (Williams) Rittenhouse. At age nineteen, Rittenhouse opened a shop in Norriton, Pennsylvania, in which he made and repaired clocks and various mathematical instruments. He made a telescope in 1756. In 1767–1771 he designed and built two elaborate vertical orreries—one purchased for the College of New Jersey (now Princeton University); the second, for the University of Pennsylvania.

Rittenhouse built an observatory, a transit telescope, an equal-altitude instrument, and a clock, to observe the **transit of Venus** of 1769. In Philadelphia, where he moved in 1770, he made astronomical observations, lectured on astronomy, and provided astronomical data for almanacs. He invented the collimating telescope (1785), introduced spider lines in the eyepiece of instruments (1786), and made a plane transmission grating and studied diffraction spectra (1786).

In 1763 Rittenhouse participated in the Mason-Dixon survey of the boundary between Pennsylvania and Maryland. In subsequent years he surveyed several other colonial and state boundaries, as well as canals and rivers, often with instruments of his own construction. He served in various technical and administrative capacities during the Revolution, and was appointed first director of the U.S. Mint in 1792. He followed Benjamin Franklin as president of the American Philosophical Society in 1791, and was elected a foreign member of the Royal Society of London in 1795.

Deborah Jean Warner

Bibliography

Hindle, B. *David Rittenhouse.* Princeton: Princeton University Press, 1964.

Rowland, Henry Augustus (1848–1901)

American physicist. Rowland received a civil engineering degree from Rensselaer Polytechnic Institute in 1870. Never a particularly effective classroom teacher, Rowland welcomed the opportunity to join the faculty of the research-oriented Johns Hopkins University. After a year of study in Europe, he assumed his duties as professor of physics in 1876, establishing a well-equipped laboratory and conducting experiments on magnetism, electromagnetism, and the determination of various physical constants.

Rowland's research focus and mechanical abilities led to his most significant and best-known work, the development of concave gratings that revolutionized spectroscopy in the 1880s. Existing gratings were of poor quality because uniform line spacings were impossible to obtain. To correct this problem, Rowland designed an exceptionally accurate screw to move the carriage that scribed lines on the grating. Once perfected, the new ruling engine could rule as many as forty-three thousand lines per inch and could produce a grating more than twice the size of existing gratings. Rowland also developed a method to produce spherically concave gratings that were self-focusing, thus eliminating the need for lenses which absorbed infrared and ultraviolet radiation. Equally valuable, the optical properties of concave gratings allowed the reflected light to focus directly on a photographic plate, thus simplifying the observation of spectra.

Rowland used his grating to map the solar spectrum lines, publishing the results in *Preliminary Table of Solar Spectrum Wave-lengths* in 1898. This volume remained the standard reference for the next thirty years.

George E. Webb

Bibliography

Henry, R.C., D.H. DeVorkin, and P. Beer, eds. "Henry Rowland and Astronomical Spectroscopy." *Vistas in Astronomy* 29 (1986): 119–236.

Kevles, D.J. "Rowland, Henry Augustus." In *Dictionary of Scientific Biography*, edited by C.C. Gillispie, vol. 11, 577–579. New York: Scribner, 1975.

Moore, A.D. "Henry A. Rowland." *Scientific American* 246 (1982): 150–161.

Royal Greenwich Observatory

The Royal Observatory at Greenwich, in greater London, was chartered by Charles II in 1675 for the purpose of finding reliable ways to determine longitude, especially for ships at sea. The task required precise measurements of time and the positions of the stars, moon, and planets; tasks that remained central during most of the history of the observatory. Until the late nineteenth century, the successive directors completely controlled research programs.

John Flamsteed was the first Astronomer Royal and director of the observatory. During his long tenure, Flamsteed and assistants made thousands of observations of stars, planets, comets, sunspots, and Jovian satellites. An unauthorized version of observations at Greenwich appeared in 1712, but the authorized edition of Flamsteed's observations was not published until 1725, six years after his death. His great catalogue gave the positions of some twenty-nine hundred stars.

Flamsteed improved on the accuracy of previous observers by using a telescopic sight.

Edmond Halley succeeded Flamsteed in 1720. Using historical observations, Halley concluded that four comets observed over two hundred years were really the same comet. His insight was later vindicated by the return of the comet, which is named for him. Halley used observations from antiquity, along with new observations, when he demonstrated that stars display **proper motions**. Halley discovered the secular acceleration of the **moon**, and argued that transits of **Venus** were the best means for determining the distance of the sun. He also provided support and encouragement for Isaac Newton. In 1721, Halley set up the first English transit instrument at Greenwich, a telescope that rotates in a fixed plane about a horizontal east-west axis, so that the line of sight through the telescope always lies in the meridian. The transit instrument defined, in effect, the Greenwich meridian.

In 1742, James Bradley succeeded Halley. Prior to the appointment, Bradley had discovered that the apparent position of a star described a small ellipse, with a period of one year. This apparent motion, or stellar aberration, was due to the finite speed of light. Bradley's determination of that speed was comparable to the velocity derived in another way by the Danish astronomer Ole Römer. Over a longer period, Bradley found a small motion of the axis of rotation of the earth, in addition to the known precession of earth's axis. This second effect is now known as nutation. Both of Bradley's discoveries relied on extreme accuracy of observation.

Four years before his appointment as **Astronomer Royal** in 1765, Nevil Maskelyne traveled to the island of St. Helena to observe a transit of Venus. During the sea voyage, he used lunar observations to derive longitude and publicized the method upon his return. After appointment, Maskelyne recommended the regular publication of a nautical ephemeris to assist seamen in the determination of longitude. The British *Nautical Almanac* first appeared in 1766, and specified the position of the moon at three-hour intervals for the entire year. The *Almanac* continued to appear annually. Thus under Maskelyne, the fifth Astronomer Royal (Nathaniel Bliss had preceded him), the Royal Observatory fulfilled the mission assigned to it ninety years before by Charles II.

With its original purpose accomplished, the observatory changed after Maskelyne, but the Greenwich longitude became entrenched in the global reckoning of location and time. Use of the British *Nautical Almanac* spread to mariners of many nations, and Greenwich began to appear on the charts they used. The trend continued into the nineteenth century. The U.S. government decided to use Greenwich as a nautical reference point in 1850; in 1853 the admiral of the Russian fleet began to draw on the *Almanac* (Howse, 131). An International Geographical Congress in Antwerp in 1871 chose to adopt the Greenwich meridian for oceanic maps. In 1884, the United States government called an International Meridian Conference, which voted to recommend the Greenwich transit instrument as marking the prime meridian, zero degrees longitude, of the world.

The only other Astronomer Royal to serve as long as Maskelyne (forty-six years) was **George Biddell Airy**, appointed in 1835. Under Airy, the Royal Observatory rapidly became modernized, and the role of the Astronomer Royal became that of a factory manager. Positional astronomy was routinized and mechanized, and observations were reduced and made available more quickly. Airy, knowledgeable in engineering, stressed efficiency and productivity. With few scientists in the civil service, Airy acted as a general scientific advisor to the government. Employment at the observatory increased during the nineteenth century, but conditions of employment changed. Turnover among observing assistants had been high under Maskelyne, and Pond had regarded the assistants as "mere drudges" (Forbes, 156), but Airy introduced "a severe disciplinary regime" that sought to minimize the differences of individuals in taking observations (Schaffer, 120). He developed a mechanical "artificial star" that could be used to determine reaction time of each observer, and introduced self-registering machines to make observations more exact. Prior to the transit of Venus in 1874, Airy had carefully trained observers, and furnished identical equipment for each of five observing stations. The development of photography during his term conformed with his objective of eliminating the human factor.

Under Airy's successor, William Christie, supervision became more relaxed, staff size increased, and more attention was given to **astrophysics**. Christie pursued visual research in stellar radial velocities but stopped when the **Astrophysical Observatory at Potsdam** introduced superior photographic methods. The Royal Observatory largely preserved a traditional emphasis on astrometry and celestial mechanics that kept it away from some of the important fields of twentieth-century astronomy.

The Nautical Almanac Office, which was separate from the Royal Observatory for a century, was rejoined to it in 1936. The office is responsible for the national time service. The importance of the Astronomer Royal to British astronomy has declined in the twentieth century. Air pollution caused deteriorating seeing conditions at Greenwich, and during World War II the site sustained extensive bomb damage.

The Royal Observatory, Greenwich, moved in 1948 to Herstmonceux Castle in rural Sussex, where sky conditions were better. The name was then changed to the Royal Greenwich Observatory at Herstmonceux. The prime meridian of course remained at the old Greenwich site. Observations at Herstmonceux became secondary to the support of observations at other sites. In 1965, authority over the Royal Greenwich Observatory passed from the Board of Admiralty to the Science and Engineering Research Council (SERC). In 1972, the positions of Astronomer Royal and director of the observatory were separated. The SERC announced a controversial decision in 1986 to move the observatory again. It chose to locate the Royal Greenwich Observatory at the Institute of Astronomy at Cambridge University; the move was completed in 1990.

Historians generally agree that the directorship of Airy marked a turning point for the observatory. Prior to his appointment, the Astronomer Royal took a greater proprietary interest and maintained a more personal involvement in the control of observation and publication. Airy's rationalization and automation of work made the observatory resemble the industrial factories of the day. Of course, insistence on the highest degree of accuracy was not new to the nineteenth century. New in Airy's time was the quantification of individual variation, which entailed "a loss of the observer's authority within the discipline of astronomy" (Schaffer, 125–126). Afterward the history becomes one of systems as well as individuals.

A large literature on the Royal Greenwich Observatory exists, including works occasioned by the tercentenary in 1975. The practical problem of finding longitude, up to the nineteenth century, has received much attention. Recent scholarship has analyzed Airy's managerial innovations. The high accuracy of observation across the long history of the observatory might serve broadly as a theme that can connect disparate eras and unite the study of practical work at the observatory with the study of fundamental insights achieved along the way.

Archival material on the Royal Greenwich Observatory is very extensive; the Airy papers alone run to some seven hundred volumes (Krisciunas, 74). The archives probably tell of many developments that have not yet made their way into the historical record.

George Sweetnam

Bibliography

Forbes, E.G., D. Howse, and A.J. Meadows. *Greenwich Observatory*. 3 vols. London: Taylor and Francis, 1975.

Howse, D. *Greenwich Time and the Discovery of the Longitude*. Oxford: Oxford University Press, 1980.

Krisciunas, K. *Astronomical Centers of the World*. Cambridge: Cambridge University Press, 1988.

Maunder, E.W. *The Royal Observatory Greenwich*. London: Religious Tract Society, 1900.

Schaffer, S. "Astronomers Mark Time: Discipline and the Personal Equation." *Science in Context* 2 (1988): 115–145.

Smith, R.W. "A National Observatory Transformed: Greenwich in the 19th Century." *Journal for the History of Astronomy* 45 (1990): 5–20.

Russell, Henry Norris (1877–1957)

American astronomer. The first of three sons of a Presbyterian minister, Russell was sent to the Princeton Preparatory School in 1890 and entered the College of New Jersey (later Princeton University) in 1893. Russell took his bachelor's degree in 1897, and a Ph.D. in astronomy under C.A. Young and H.B. Fine in 1900. After postgraduate study at Cambridge University, he returned to Princeton in 1905 as an instructor, becoming full professor, chairman of the department, and director of the observatory by 1913. Russell's career was spent in Princeton, where he concentrated on research and teaching. Although he shunned committee work and professional organizations, he eventually held high positions in his discipline and was active in the American Philosophical Society and the American Association for the Advancement of Science. His chief activity external to Princeton was as associate editor for astronomy for *Scientific American* from 1900 until 1943.

Russell concentrated in stellar astronomy and **astrophysics**, although at different times of his life he maintained active research in all areas of planetary, solar, and stellar astronomy. After the appearance of Meghnad Saha's theory of ionization equilibrium and Miguel Catalán's theory of multiplet structure in the early 1920s, Russell's major field of interest was observational and theoretical spectroscopy. His main contribution, through essays and by example, was his constant urging of the importance of the role of physical theory in the analysis of astronomical observations, and the importance of theoretical prediction in directing effective astronomical observing programs. He campaigned for this research strategy at major American observatories where he found the data necessary to pursue his many research interests.

Russell's name has been linked to many astronomical techniques and concepts. He independently discovered the relationships between the characteristics of the stars embodied in the **Hertzsprung-Russell Diagram**, and was one of the first to appreciate that the physical characteristics of stars were determined by two parameters, mass and chemical composition, expressed in the Vogt-Russell theorem. With physicist F.A. Saunders, Russell developed a model for two-electron interactions, known as Russell-Saunders coupling. At the end of the 1920s Russell established the modern picture of the solar composition—known as the Russell mixture—confirming the efforts of earlier workers that hydrogen dominated in the solar atmosphere.

Russell's voluminous correspondence and working papers are housed in the Firestone Library Manuscripts Division of Princeton University. There is a microfilm edition.

David H. DeVorkin

Bibliography

Cogan, B.C. "Russell, Henry Norris." In *Dictionary of Scientific Biography*, edited by C.C. Gillispie, vol. 12, 17–24. New York: Scribner, 1971.

DeVorkin, D.H. "Henry Norris Russell." *Scientific American* 260 (1989): 126–133.

———. "A Fox Raiding the Hedgehogs: How Henry Norris Russell Got to Mount Wilson." In *The Earth, the Heavens, and the Carnegie Institution of Washington: Historical Perspectives after Ninety Years,* edited by G. Good, 103–111. Washington, D.C.: American Geophysical Union, 1994.

Philip, A.G.D., and D.H. DeVorkin, eds. *In Memory of Henry Norris Russell.* Proceedings of IAU Symposium #80. Dudley Observatory Report #13, 1977.

Shapley, H. "Henry Norris Russell." *Biographical Memoirs. National Academy of Sciences* 32 (1958): 354–378.

Russian Astronomy (to the Revolution)

Before the 1917 Bolshevik Revolution, Russian astronomy had developed rich traditions and a record of scientific productivity. Astronomy had an eminent position in the Russian scientific community and was well respected abroad. But the roots of Russian astronomy did not go back to the ancient world as is the case in the Orient, the Near East, or Western Europe. While there are some scholarly discussions of the history of Russian astronomy during the Middle Ages, the development of modern astronomy can be traced to the reforms of Czar Peter the Great. These reforms stimulated Russian economic and cultural development, including the creation of the Academy of Sciences in the Czar's new capital of St. Petersburg. The czar was interested in astronomy and visited the Paris and Greenwich observatories.

It was the czar's advisor, Jacob Bruce, a Scottish nobleman born in Moscow, who played a key role in early Russian astronomy. Bruce established a Naval Observatory in Moscow (1699) and secured the services of European experts to teach there. Later Bruce transferred the observatory to St. Petersburg (1703). He was editor of the first Russian astronomical almanac and the first Russian star chart (1707). He also wrote a preface to the Russian translation of *Cosmotheoros* by Christiaan Huygens. Bruce was also interested in the development of telescopes.

Soon after the St. Petersburg Academy was established, a famous French astronomer, **Joseph-Nicolas Delisle**, was elected to the academy and from 1726 to 1747 worked in Russia. Delisle can be credited with founding Russian astronomy. He attracted a circle of outstanding pupils and together they made important contributions to astronomy, geodesy, and cartography. Delisle's observatory was placed in a special tower on the main academic building at St. Petersburg.

Michailo V. Lomonosov made numerous contributions to eighteenth-century science, including the discovery of the atmosphere of Venus during the 1761 transit. The physicist, astronomer, and diplomat Franz Aepinus organized expeditions to observe the **transit of**

Venus in 1769. This marked Russia's entry into the international scientific community. It was, however, the great Swiss mathematician Leonhard Euler who placed Russian astronomy on solid foundations and gained for it full international recognition during his years as a member of the Academy at St. Petersburg.

After the consolidation of the Russian Empire by Catherine the Second, Russian higher education expanded. In addition to the old universities at Dorpat (now the city of Tartu in Estonia), Vilno (now the city of Vilnius in Lithuania), and Moscow, three new institutions were established: Kazan (1804), Kharkov (1804; now in Ukraine), and St. Petersburg (1819). These developments provided a powerful impetus to Russian science.

After the partition of Poland, the city of Vilno became a part of the Russian empire and soon the Vilno Academy became a university with an astronomical observatory. The director was Abbot Martin Poczobut, a fellow of the Royal Society of London (1771) and corresponding member of the French Academy of Sciences (1780). He was succeeded by the Polish astronomer Jan Snjadetsky, who was also rector of the university. Vilno University was closed in 1832, and its observatory became a branch of the St. Petersburg Academy of Sciences.

The university in the Estonian city of Tartu, at various times known as Dorpat (before 1893) or Yur'ev, played an important role in Russian astronomy. The university was founded by the Swedish king in 1632 and reestablished as Dorpat University in 1802. The university had close connections with several German states and the language of instruction was German. Ernst Knorre was the first director of the Dorpat Observatory. He was succeeded in 1818 by **Friedrich Georg Wilhelm Struve**, a Dorpat graduate. Struve directed the Dorpat Observatory until 1839 and determined the first **stellar parallax**. He equipped the observatory with a Fraunhofer refractor, at the time perhaps the best telescope in the world. After Struve, Johann Madler became director. Such well-known astronomers as A.N. Sawitch and G. Sabler were among Struve's pupils at Dorpat.

The astronomy department at the university of Kazan opened in 1810 under the direction of K.L. von Littrow. In 1816 von Littrow became director of the Vienna Observatory, but his students continued the astronomical research in Kazan. The great Russian mathematician Nicolai Ivanovich Lobachevsky, creator of non-Euclidian geometry, worked at Kazan, as did astronomer-explorer Ivan M. Simonov. Dmitry M. Perewostchikoff, the founder of **Moscow Observatory**, graduated from Kazan. One of the best known astronomers from Kazan was Marian A. Kowalski, who analyzed the proper motions of stars in Bradley's catalogue.

A department of astronomy was formed at Moscow University in 1804, but it did not prosper until 1832 under the direction of D.M. Perewostchikoff. The most prominent leaders of Moscow astronomy were Fiodor A. Bredikhin, an expert on comets, and Vitold K. Tserasky, who modernized the observatory at the end of the nineteenth century.

The first professor of astronomy in Kharkov was I.S.G. Huth, but he left Kharkov for Dorpat after a few years and astronomy languished until 1883. Graduates of Kharkov include such distinguished scientists as the Russian-American astronomer **Otto Struve**, who directed the **Yerkes Observatory**, and **Boris P. Gerasimovich**, who directed Pulkovo.

In 1819 St. Petersburg Pedagogical College was transformed into the university and Vikenty K. Wisniewski became professor of astronomy. Together with academician F.T. Schubert, he established an observatory at Nicolaev on the Black Sea.

After the Napoleonic Wars, the government decided that it was time to develop a national observatory similar to those at Paris or Greenwich in order to provide a time service and technical aid for navigation, and to support research in geodesy and cartography. In 1839, with the backing of Czar Nicolas the First, F.G.W. Struve was called from Dorpat to found the **Pulkovo Observatory**, outside St. Petersburg. In 1873, the military established an observatory at Tashkent (now Uzbekistan). Its primary responsibility was to provide technical assistance for the exploration of Central Asia. This observatory played a significant role in the development of practical astronomy and the theory of the figure of the earth. In 1899 the International Latitude Service was established with one of its six stations at Tchardjui, near Tashkent. This reminds us that Russian astronomers took part in almost all nineteenth-century international projects, including the Transits of Venus and the *Carte du Ciel*.

The Pulkovo Observatory sent an expedition to observe the 1887 solar eclipse from a station at the small town of Yur'evetz near Nijny Novgorod on the river Volga. The eclipse stimulated the development of **amateur astronomy** in Russia and led to new publications. As a result of a gift from a wealthy amateur, the Simeis Observatory was established in the Crimea. Amateur observatories developed in many Russian cities.

By the end of the nineteenth century, Russian astronomy had fallen behind other nations. As was the case with many other European observatories, Pulkovo was not able to keep up with the development of **astrophysics**. By the time of the October Revolution, there was no significant tradition of astrophysics, but Russian astronomy was well respected in the fields of **celestial mechanics** and astrometry.

Alexander Gurshtein

Bibliography

Boss, V. *Sir Isaac Newton and Russia*, Vol. 1. Cambridge: Harvard University Press, 1972.

Centennial Anniversary of Astronomical Institute. In Russian. Uzbek Academy of Sciences. Tashkent: Fan, 1974.

Chenakal, Valentin L. *Essays on History of Russian Astronomy*. In Russian. Moscow: Academy Publishing House, 1951.

Erpylev, Nicolai P. "Development of Stellar Astronomy in Russia During 19th Century." In Russian. In *Researches on History of Astronomy*. 4 (1958): 13–252. Moscow: Gostechizdat.

Kazan University. *The Essays on History 1804–1979*. In Russian. Kazan, 1979.

Kolchinsky, I.G., A.A. Korsun, and M.G. Rodriges. *Astronomers (Reference Book of Biographies)*. In Russian. 2nd rev. Kiev: Naukova Dumka, 1986.

Lavrova, N.B. *Bibliography of Russian Astronomical Literature 1800–1900*. In Russian. Moscow: Moscow University, 1968.

Levitsky, G. *Astronomers of Yur'ev University from 1802 up to 1894*. In Russian. Yur'ev: Mattisen, 1899.

Nevskya, N.I. *Astronomical School of Petersburg during 18th Century*. In Russian. Leningrad: Nauka, 1984.

Progress of Natural Sciences in Russia (from 18th up to beginning of 20th Century). Edited by S.R. Mikulinsky and A.P. Yushkevich. Moscow: Nauka, 1977.

Rainov, T.I. *Science in Russia, 11th–17th Centuries*. In Russian. Moscow-Leningrad, 1940.

Seleshnikov, S.I. *Astronomy and Cosmonautics*. In Russian. Kiev, 1974.

Svyatsky, D.O. "The Essays on History of Astronomy in Ancient Russia. Parts 1–3." In *Researches on History of Astronomy*, vol. 7 (1961), 71–130; vol. 8 (1962), 9–82; vol. 9 (1966), 11–126. Moscow: Nauka.

Vorontsov-Vel'yaminov, B.A. *Essays on History of Astronomy in Russia*. In Russian. Moscow: Gostechizdat, 1956.

Saha, Meghnad (1893–1956)

Indian physicist, educator, and social reformer. Saha was the fifth of eight children. His father was a shopkeeper in East Bengal. Saha's early education was funded by local patrons and by government scholarship, which he lost after protesting the partition of Bengal. He received a B.Sc. in 1913 from Calcutta Presidency College with honors in mathematics, and an M.Sc. in applied mathematics in 1915 while supporting himself and a brother by tutoring students. In 1916 Saha obtained a lectureship in the Department of Mathematics, which allowed him to continue his studies to the award of a D.Sc. in 1918 from Calcutta for work in electromagnetic theory and radiation pressure.

Saha, lionized in Calcutta for his promotion of science as well as his political activism (Sen, 56; Anderson, 65), is best known in the West as a physicist who developed the concept of thermal ionization equilibrium and applied it to astrophysical problems, providing a theoretical basis for the Harvard spectral sequence and a means to calibrate that sequence in terms of temperature. His first application was to interpret the character of the solar spectrum, finding that temperature was its primary determinent, followed by pressure. Saha's theory was quickly exploited in the West to demonstrate the explanatory powers of quantum mechanics for astrophysics (DeVorkin and Kenat).

Saha was elected fellow of the Royal Society in 1927 and traveled to the West on several occasions, but he spent his professional life in India, first in Calcutta, then in Allahabad, returning to Calcutta in 1938. He was an outspoken critic of Indian science policy, forming the progressive Science and Culture group in 1934, becoming a member of the National Planning Committee of the Indian National Congress in 1938, and being elected to the Indian Parliament in 1951 as an independent. He remained politically active until his death. Saha's personal and professional papers have been deposited at the Nehru Memorial Museum and Library, Teen Murti House, New Delhi.

David H. DeVorkin

Bibliography

Anderson, R.S. *Building Scientific Institutions in India: Saha and Bhabha*. McGill University: Centre for Developing-Area Studies, Occasional Paper Series No. 11, 1975.

DeVorkin, D.H. "Saha's Influence in the West: A Preliminary Account." In *Meghnad Saha Birth Centenary Commemoration Volume*, edited by S.B. Karmohapatro, 154–202. Calcutta: Saha Institute of Nuclear Physics, 1993.

DeVorkin, D.H., and R. Kenat. "Quantum Physics and the Stars (I); (II)." *Journal for the History of Astronomy* 14 (1983): 102–132; 180–222.

Kothari, D.S. "Meghnad Saha." *Biographical Memoirs of the Fellows of the Royal Society* 5 (1959): 217–236.

Sen, S.N., ed. *Professor Meghnad Saha, His Life, Work, and Philosophy*. Calcutta, 1954.

Saturn

In July 1610 **Galileo** thought he observed two satellites of Saturn, but unlike those of **Jupiter**, these kept the same relative position on either side of the planet's disk, just barely discernible. They disappeared in 1612, reappeared in 1613, and then took on the appearance of handles. This puzzling phenomenon was later explained by Christiaan Huygens and publicly announced in his *Systema Saturnia* (1659). Combining his own observations with those of observers for over forty years and arguing from Cartesian principles, he proposed that Saturn was surrounded by a thin ring. This conclusion was by no means immediately accepted.

When Huygens directed his new telescope toward Saturn in March 1655, he noticed a satellite later named Titan. The rings were then oriented edge-on, a favorable situation for discovering satellites. During **Gian Domenico Cassini**'s early years at the **Paris Observatory**, he found two additional satellites. In 1675 he discerned a dark line in the ring now known as Cassini's division, although its existence as a true gap was the subject of considerable controversy. In 1684 Cassini added another two satellites to his list of discoveries. Sporadic observations of the very faint belts on the globe of the planet, similar to those much more prominent features of Jupiter, continued. So did some **micrometer** measurements of the rings, and discussions over whether they were solid. Until the large reflecting telescopes of **William Herschel** in the late eighteenth century, little more could be seen.

In 1793–1794, William Herschel derived a rotation period of 10 hours and 16 minutes, differing only by minutes from the modern accepted value, and he later found the rotation rate at other latitudes to differ only slightly from the equatorial period. In general, Saturn's cloud surface appeared to be similar to Jupiter's, only far less energetic.

Early observers doubted whether a solid ring could maintain its stability; Cassini thought it had to be a swarm of small satellites. In 1785 Pierre-Simon Laplace showed on Newtonian gravitational grounds that a single, solid ring would inevitably shear itself to pieces, and he instead proposed a nested succession of thin rings. In the nineteenth century, Cassini's Division was joined by a variety of disputed gaps or whispy structures in the rings. In 1855 James Clerck Maxwell, who would later become known for his researches into electromagnetism, showed that anything other than a swarm of particles orbiting according to Newtonian mechanics would be unstable. Observational proof was not forthcoming until 1895, when **James E. Keeler** identified different Doppler shifts for the light from the inner and outer edges of the rings, indicating they were moving at different speeds.

Toward the end of the nineteenth century the density of Saturn was determined to be less than that of water. Spectroscopists noted strong absorption bands at the far red end of the spectrum of Saturn and the other jovian planets, and **Rupert Wildt** at Göttingen University identified them with laboratory lines of methane and ammonia in 1931–1932. In 1938 Wildt proposed models of the outer planets in which each had a small earthlike core surrounded by a layer of frozen condensed water and gases, in turn surrounded by highly compressed gases. These models were accepted by many astronomers despite problems concerning relative abundances of hydrogen and helium and the densities of the various layers.

In 1943–1944 **Gerard Kuiper**, observing from McDonald Observatory in Texas, identified methane absorption bands in the infrared spectrum of Titan, making it the only satellite known to have an atmosphere. Larger telescopes and the periodic orientation of the rings edge-on continued to provide opportunities for discovering additional satellites and to revise, ever downward, estimates of the thickness of the rings. By the 1960s, five main ring systems were recognized although visual observers differed over the reality of a wealth of fine structure.

In 1970 near-infrared spectra of the rings suggested they were composed almost entirely of water ice, and radio and radar observations three years later seemed to confirm this. In 1972 infrared observations of Titan suggested that it, like Jupiter and Saturn, was warmer than would be expected for a body in equilibrium with incoming solar radiation. This caused a flurry of excitement and model-building, some astronomers arguing that, like **Venus**, Titan was undergoing a greenhouse effect. Infrared spectra of the other satellites identified water ice, and newly derived densities suggested they might be composed mainly of ice.

After its 1974 encounter with Jupiter, *Pioneer 11* had been targeted toward Saturn. Arriving September 1, 1979, its imaging system at first showed the globe of the planet to be disappointingly bland. The images of the rings just barely showed a new, narrow ring, called the F-ring. Infrared measurements showed a temperature of –180 degrees C, sub-

Saturn photographed by the Hubble Space Telescope in 1990. The resolution is such that Saturn would appear like this to the naked eye if its distance were only twice that of the moon. In this photograph, the north pole of the planet is tilted toward the earth by about 24 degrees and the ring system is open and its major components visible. (Courtesy of the National Aeronautics and Space Administration)

stantially higher than expected, and showing that Saturn was radiating more than twice as much heat as it received from the sun. *Pioneer 11* found Saturn's magnetic field to be far weaker than Jupiter's, but curiously closely aligned with its rotational axis. Refined measurements showed Saturn was composed mostly of extremely compressed hydrogen, with a small rocky core of about ten times the mass of earth, similar to the models proposed by Rupert Wildt in the 1950s. Polarization measurements of sunlight through the Cassini division showed that it was not empty at all, but filled with fine material. Flight controllers were relieved they had decided not to fly the spacecraft through Cassini's division.

In the year between *Pioneer 11* and *Voyager 1* Saturn encounters, ground-based observation of Saturn was frenzied, with the additional impetus of the earth's ring plane crossing. Searching for additional satellites, astronomers at several observatories identified a new phenomenon—two pairs of co-orbital satellites. Twelve satellites were recognized before 1980.

As *Voyager 1* approached Saturn in the summer of 1980, the planet finally began to show features similar to those observed at Jupiter—belts, zones, and rotating spots. In early November a startling new phenomenon was seen in the B-ring—dark spokes that rotated around the ring, but in a seemingly non-Keplerian fashion. Several new very small satellites were seen, apparently shepherding the narrow F-ring and keeping it from dispersing. Observations of Titan could not penetrate the dense layer of banded clouds. On November 12, 1980, *Voyager 1* dove through the plane of the rings, passed under Saturn, and then northward. One after another, the icy satellites displayed the cratered terrain familiar from the Jupiter encounter, although there was evidence that internal activity may have shaped the surface of some. Scientists were prepared for more structure in the rings than just the five major systems, and had analyzed numerous resonances among the many Saturnian satellites. They were not prepared, however, for more than a thousand rings, including eccentric rings and a tripartite heliacal braiding of the F-ring. In August of 1981 *Voyager 2* flew through the Saturn system, on a course that complemented that of *Voyager 1* and also allowed it to continue on a course to **Uranus**.

The most comprehensive, albeit dated and not interpretive, work on Saturn remains that of A.F.O'D. Alexander. Henry S.F. Cooper Jr. and Mark Washburn provide excellent journalist accounts of the *Voyager* encounters with Saturn, mainly oriented toward imaging science and the first discoveries. Richard O. Fimmel, et al. and Dave Morrison supplement their summary texts with brief historical overviews of the *Pioneer* and the *Voyager* missions, and valuable summaries of Saturn studies in the present century. Tom Gehrels's edited volume provides a comprehensive and detailed scientific accounting of the state of knowledge of Saturn just after the *Voyager* encounters. Relevant chapters of Beatty's successive editions provide snapshots of the state of consensus on Saturn at critical times while new knowledge was being assimilated. Waff supplies a thorough popular discussion of the detailed and complex planning that went into the *Voyager* missions.

Interpretive historical treatments are few and concentrate on specific areas and problems. The works of Van Helden remain the standard for the early telescopic era, and his "Saturn through the Telescope: A Brief Historical Survey" is a selective but historically more reliable place to begin. Brush et al. provide excellent commentary on James Clerck Maxwell's work on the stability of Saturn's rings.

Joseph N. Tatarewicz

Bibliography

Alexander, A.F.O'D. *The Planet Saturn: A History of Observation, Theory, and Discovery*. London: Faber and Faber, 1962.

Beatty, J.K., and A. Chaikin, eds. *The New Solar System*. 1st ed. New York: Cambridge University Press, 1981; 2nd ed., 1982; 3rd ed., 1990.

Cooper, H.S.F., Jr. *Imaging Saturn: The Voyager Flights to Saturn*. New York: Holt, Rinehart, Wilson, 1985.

Fimmel, R.O., J. Van Allen, and E. Burgess. *Pioneer: First to Jupiter, Saturn, and Beyond*. Washington, D.C.: NASA SP-446, 1980.

Gehrels, T., and M.S. Matthews, eds. *Saturn*. Space Science Series. Tucson, Ariz.: University of Arizona Press, 1984.

Maxwell, J.C. *Maxwell on Saturn's Rings*. Edited by S.G. Brush, C.W.F. Everitt, and E. Garber. Cambridge: MIT Press, 1983.

Morrison, D. *Voyages to Saturn*. NASA SP-451. Washington, D.C.: GPO, 1982.

Osterbrock, D.E., and D.P. Cruikshank. "Keeler's Gap in Saturn's A Ring." *Sky & Telescope* 64 (1982): 123–126.

Shapley, D. "Pre-Huygenian Observations of Saturn's Ring." *Isis* 40 (1949): 12–17.

Van Helden, A. "The Accademia del Cimento and Saturn's Ring." *Physics* 15 (1973): 237–259.

———. "'Annulo Cingitur': The Solution of the Problem of Saturn." *Journal for the History of Astronomy* 5 (1974): 155–174.

———. "Saturn and His Anses." *Journal for the History of Astronomy* 5 (1974): 105–121.

———. "A Note about Christiaan Huygens's *De Saturni Luna Observatio Nova*." *Janus* 62 (1975): 13–15.

———. "Saturn through the Telescope: A Brief Historical Survey." In *Saturn*, edited by T. Gehrels and M. Shapley Matthews, 23–43. Space Science Series. Tucson, Ariz.: University of Arizona Press, 1984.

Waff, C.B. "The Struggle for the Outer Planets." *Astronomy* 17 (1989): 44–52.

Washburn, M. *Distant Encounters: The Exploration of Jupiter and Saturn*. New York: Harcourt, Brace, Jovanovich, 1983.

Scheiner, Julius (1858–1913)

German astrophysicist. His doctorate (1882) at Bonn Observatory was on the variable star Algol. In 1887 Scheiner obtained a position at Potsdam under Hermann Carl Vogel, and together they measured the first reliable radial velocities of stars using photography. Scheiner's expertise in photographic spectroscopy enabled him to catalogue the line spectra of some fifty stars. Also his $7^1/_2$-hour exposure of the Andromeda nebula (1899) was the first to show absorption lines similar to those of the sun, a vital clue to its extragalactic nature.

Later Scheiner worked with Johannes Wilsing to obtain the first stellar color temperatures from visual spectrophotometry (1905–1909), by fitting Planck functions to the flux gradients for 109 stars. He also made useful contributions to stellar photography and the photographic photometry of stars.

Scheiner's books were highly influential, notably *Die Spectralanalyse der Gestirne* (1890) and *Die Photographie der Gestirne* (1897).

J.B. Hearnshaw

Bibliography

Frost, E.B. "Julius Scheiner." *Astrophysical Journal* 41 (1915): 1–9.

McGucken, W. "Julius Scheiner." In *Dictionary of Scientific Biography*, edited by C.C. Gillispie, vol. 12, 152–153. New York: Scribner, 1975.

Scheiner, J. *Die Spectralanalyse der Gestirne*. Leipzig: Engelmann, 1890.

———. *Die Photographie der Gestirne*. Leipzig: Engelmann, 1897.

Schiaparelli, Giovanni Virginio (1835–1910)

Italian astronomer. Schiaparelli studied civil engineering at the University of Turin. After graduation in 1854, he turned to astronomy, training under J.F. Encke at the Berlin Observatory and **Otto Struve** at Pulkova. In 1860 he was appointed astronomer at the Brera Observatory in Milan, and became director in 1862.

Schiaparelli's most important investigation was into the relationship between comets and meteors. In 1866, he showed that the debris responsible for the Leonid meteor shower followed the orbit of Comet Tempel-

Tuttle. He later showed a similar association between the Perseids and the Great Comet of 1862 (Swift-Tuttle). In 1877, he produced a more accurate map of **Mars** than previously available; it was based on micrometric measures of the positions of key features and introduced a new nomenclature that is the basis of that now in use. He also recorded the *canali* (canals), highly regular linear features on Mars that in the view of some (though not Schiaparelli himself) were engineering works constructed by inhabitants of the planet. Their discovery started a violent controversy; however, these features are now known to have been illusory and due to the eye's tendency to connect small, irregular features into continuous lines. In 1889 Schiaparelli announced that the rotation of Mercury was eighty-eight earth days, the same as its period of revolution—a result that was accepted until 1965, when radio astronomers found the correct period, 58.65 days. In addition to his observational prowess, he was a highly respected historian of astronomy and wrote classic treatises on the planetary theory of Eudoxus and on early versions of the heliocentric theory.

William Sheehan

Bibliography

Crowe, M. *The Extraterrestrial Life Debate, 1750–1900: The Idea of a Plurality of Worlds from Kant to Lowell.* Cambridge: Cambridge University Press, 1986.

Schlesinger, Frank (1871–1943)

American astronomer specializing in the photographic astronomy of star positions. Schlesinger graduated in 1890 from the City College of New York and took a Ph.D. from Columbia University in astronomy in 1898. A pioneer in photographic methods for the determination of **stellar parallax**, he undertook this work first with the 40-inch refractor at Yerkes Observatory (1903–1904) and continued it as director of Allegheny Observatory (1905–1920) and Yale University Observatory (1920–1941). In 1925 he established the first Southern Hemisphere parallax program, undertaken from a station he established in South Africa. While at Allegheny, Schlesinger also participated in spectroscopic binary work, and during his Yale years he led the wide-angle photographic astrometry effort to reobserve the Astronomische Gesellschaft catalogue between declinations +30 degrees and –30 degrees. He published the first edition of the famous *Catalogue of Bright Stars* in 1930.

Steven J. Dick

Bibliography

Brouwer, D. "Biographical Memoir of Frank Schlesinger." In *Biographical Memoirs of the National Academy of Sciences* 24 (1945): 105–141.

Schmidt Telescopes

Astronomers early realized the potential of photography for making permanent records of the sky. However, conventional telescopes suffered serious limitations as cameras, requiring long exposures and yielding small usable fields. The need for a wide-field telescopic camera for astronomical survey work was acute.

A concave spherical mirror offers a starting point for a wide-field telescopic camera, but it forms images blurred by spherical aberration. If, however, a corrector plate could be figured to minimize these aberrations, the result would be a very powerful photographic instrument.

These seemingly simple concepts were finally brought together for the first time by a brilliant but eccentric Estonian optician, Bernhard Voldemar Schmidt. Schmidt lost his right forearm in an explosion in a laboratory when he was fifteen years old, but his interest in science was undiminished. After studying engineering at Gothenburg, Sweden, Schmidt migrated to Mittweida, near Jena, Germany. He studied at the Mittweida Technical Institute for four years and associated with optical workers employed by the Carl Zeiss Institute. He remained there as a highly respected but independent optical worker for over twenty-five years.

In 1926, Schmidt became an associate of the Hamburg Observatory at Bergedorf. By

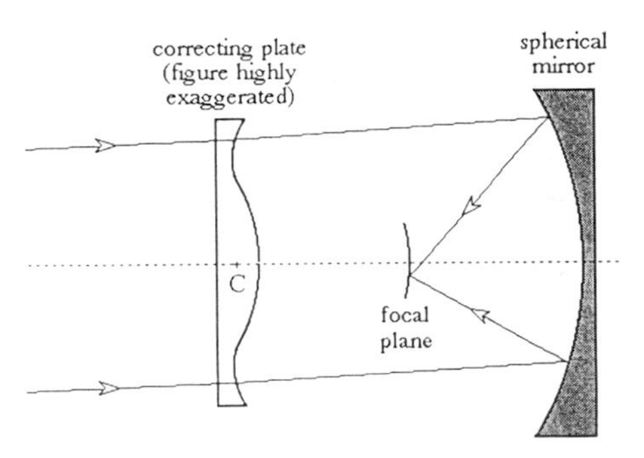

The basic Schmidt optical design consists of a spherically curved mirror and a correcting plate located at the position of the center of curvature (C) of the primary mirror. This combination produces a curved focal plane. Note that the diameter of the correcting plate may be less than that of the main mirror to minimize vignetting effects. (Figure by Charles J. Peterson)

The 48-inch Schmidt telescope on Palomar Mountain. Astronomer W.A. Baum is at the guide telescope. This photograph was taken in 1956. (Courtesy of the Huntington Library and the Carnegie Observatories)

1929, he had worked out most of the details for the Schmidt telescope, but had not yet invented a technique for polishing the thin corrector lens. Schmidt solved this problem by using a vacuum to distort a thin glass plate on a mandrel and then polishing the distorted glass flat to produce the aspheric corrector. Photographs were taken with the first Schmidt telescope (14-inch) in early 1930.

In 1931, Walter Baade, who had been a colleague of Schmidt's at Bergedorf, showed photographs made with Schmidt's first telescope to **Edwin P. Hubble** and other astronomers at the Mount Wilson Observatory. Their response was immediate and enthusiastic. The Mount Wilson/Palomar optical shops experimented with Schmidt systems of progressively larger apertures during the 1930s. Fields of up to 15 degrees were found to be possible in Schmidt telescopes, compared with only $^1/_2$ degree fields with conventional telescopes. The photographic plate had to be curved to match the curvature of the focal surface, but that proved acceptable in practice.

The 48-inch Schmidt telescope was placed in service on Palomar Mountain in 1948. A survey of the northern two-thirds of the sky on both red- and blue-sensitive photographic plates was completed with the 48-inch Schmidt in 1956.

Eleven large (corrector plates >25-inches) and numerous smaller Schmidt telescopes have been installed around the world. The Schmidt telescope at the Karl Schwarzchild Observatory in Tautenburg, Germany (1960), with a 53-inch corrector plate, is the world's largest. Schmidt corrector plates with a small wedge between surfaces serve as objective prisms and are used for spectrascopic surveys. Schmidt telescopes are employed for studies of **variable stars**, extended nebulae, **galaxies**, galaxy clusters, for identifying optical counterparts of radio objects, and for discovering small, fast-moving objects in the solar system.

Thomas R. Williams

Bibliography

Hendrix, D.O., and W.H. Christie. "Some Applications of the Schmidt Principle in Optical Design." In *Amateur Telescope Making, Book III*, edited by A.G. Ingalls. New York: Scientific American, 1959.

Hodges, P.C. "Bernard Schmidt and His Reflector Camera: An Astronomical Contribution to Radiology. Paper I." *The American Journal of Roentgenology and Radium Therapy* 59 (1948): 122–131.

King, H.C. *The History of the Telescope*. New York: Dover Publications, 1955.

Pasachoff, J.M. "Schmidt Camera." In *Optics Source Book*, edited by S.P. Parker. New York: McGraw-Hill Book Co., 1988.

Wachmann, A.A. "From the Life of Bernhard Schmidt." *Sky & Telescope* 15 (1955): 4–9.

Schröter, Johann Hieronymus (1745–1816)

German astronomer. Born at Erfurt, he studied theology at the University of Gera and jurisprudence at the University of Göttingen, and in 1777 he became secretary of the Royal Chamber (of George III) in Hanover. There he became acquainted with William Herschel's brothers, who encouraged his interest in astronomy. The turning point in his career occurred in March 1781, when **William Herschel** discovered the planet Uranus. Thereafter Schröter, in a spirit of emulation, resolved to devote himself chiefly to astronomy; he relinquished his post in Hanover for that of chief magistrate of Lilienthal, a sleepy village near Bremen, where his light official duties allowed him time to pursue his astronomical goals. He went on to establish at Lilienthal the largest observatory on the continent. From 1796 to 1804 he was assisted by Karl Ludwig Harding and from 1804 to 1810 by **Friedrich Wilhelm Bessel**. He was also closely associated with the Bremen physician and astronomer Heinrich Wilhelm Matthäus Olbers. In April 1813, the Lilienthal observatory was destroyed by French troops retreating before the Cossacks after Napoleon's Russian debacle; Schröter never recovered from the shock, and he died three years later.

Schröter opened a new era with his detailed studies of individual formations on the surface of the **moon** under varying angles of illumination. He also made systematic observations of the planets, which initiated the comparative study of planetology, as the field was later designated by Percival Lowell, who, of course, did not acknowledge he had been anticipated. Some of Schröter's conclusions were farfetched. He believed, on insufficient grounds, that he had found evidence of changes on the lunar surface; he gave incorrect rotation periods for **Mercury** and **Venus**, published measures of improbably high mountains on Venus, was possessed of the strange delusion that the fixed surface features on Mars were clouds, and believed that **Saturn**'s ring was a solid body, studded with mountains and possessing an atmosphere. Nevertheless, though he was a clumsy draftsman and made mistakes, his work laid the foundation of descriptive astronomy in Germany, and many of his results were unsurpassed in their field for decades.

William Sheehan

Bibliography

Gerdes, D. *Die Lilienthal Sternwarte 1781 bis 1818*. Lilienthal: Heimatverein Lilienthal, 1991.

Schwarzschild, Karl (1873–1916)

German astronomer. Born in Frankfurt, Karl Schwarzschild received his Ph.D. from the University of Munich in 1896. He taught at Munich, and then became an assistant at an observatory in Vienna, In 1901, Schwarzschild joined the faculty of the University of Göttingen. The following year, he became full professor and director of the observatory. Schwarzschild moved to Potsdam in 1909 as director of the Astrophysical Observatory. He was accompanied in the move by **Ejnar Hertzsprung**. When World War I broke out, Schwarzschild entered military service. He manned a weather station in Belgium and calculated the trajectories of artillery shells in France and on the Russian front. While in the military, Schwarzschild contracted a fatal skin disease. He was awarded a posthumous Iron Cross.

At the turn of the century, estimates of stellar magnitude were still often made by eye. Schwarzschild developed new methods of photographic photometry. He found that doubling the exposure time did not necessarily produce a photographic image equal in intensity to a star twice as bright. Rather, the exposure time followed a more complicated formula, which became known as Schwarzschild's law. Schwarzschild also used a technique of recording stellar images slightly out of focus, for more even exposure. At Göttingen, Schwarzschild published the photographic magnitudes of thirty-five hundred stars, to magnitude 7.5. Photographic and visual magnitudes differed, but Schwarzschild suggested that the difference, or color index, could specify the spectral type of a star.

Schwarzschild proposed that transfer of energy in the sun depended mainly on radiation, rather than convection, as previously thought. He developed a theory of radiative equilibrium, in which the weight of material above any layer of a star must be offset by pressure within that layer. He also created a model in which the photosphere of a star emitted a continuous black-body spectrum, while absorption lines arose in a reversing layer above, which scattered light at discrete wavelengths. **Arthur S. Eddington**'s model of stellar structure later prevailed over Schwarzschild's.

Fifteen years before the publication of Einstein's general theory of relativity (1915), Schwarzschild became one of the first astronomers to take seriously the possibility of curved or non-Euclidean space and calculate minimum possible sizes for the universe. After Einstein's publication, Schwarzschild wrote two papers on the theory. The first dealt with the case of a single point object in space. In the second, Schwarzschild examined the properties of an object that would allow no light to escape from it. Today such an object is called a black hole, and the Schwarzschild radius is the size, for a given mass, below which the object becomes a black hole.

Schwarzschild also studied comet tails, the flash spectrum of the sun during an eclipse, and stellar radial velocities. He advised the **Carl Zeiss Werke in Jena** on the development of optical instruments and made an unsuccessful attempt to measure gravitational red shift in the sun. In addition to his technical work, Schwarzschild gave popular lectures on astronomy.

A 79-inch reflecting telescope near Jena, erected in 1960, is named for him. A son, Martin, born in 1912, is also an eminent astronomer. He immigrated to the United States in 1937. Karl Schwarzschild awaits his biographer.

Most of Schwarzschild's papers from the University of Göttingen were microfilmed and are available in the United States at the Niels Bohr Library of the American Institute of Physics, College Park, Maryland; the Library of the American Philosophical Society at Philadelphia; and the University of California at Berkeley.

George Sweetnam

Bibliography

Dieke, S.H. "Schwarzschild, Karl." In *Dictionary of Scientific Biography*, edited by C.C. Gillispie, vol. 12, 247–253. New York: Scribner, 1975.

Scientific Revolution, Astronomy in

The Scientific Revolution is the term commonly applied to the period between **Johannes Kepler** (b. 1571) and Isaac Newton (d. 1727), and is more or less coterminous with the seventeenth century. This period saw the mathematization of science, the establishment of a new scientific method, the development of the mechanical philosophy, a new emphasis on experiment, the organization of the scientific enterprise, and the general acceptance of a heliocentric cosmology. Major figures who were not astronomers include Francis Bacon, William Harvey, Gottfried Leibniz, Robert Boyle, Marin Mersenne, John Ray, and Pierre Gassendi. **Copernicus** is sometimes included as the inaugurator of the Scientific Revolution, but he is more properly a figure of late Renaissance science and is treated separately in this encyclopedia.

Astronomy played a major role in the Scientific Revolution. When the seventeenth century opened, Copernicanism was almost sixty years old, but was advocated by only a handful of astronomers. Aristotelian cosmology remained dominant and Ptolemaic astronomy the norm. Even Copernican astronomers used the techniques and devices of classical astronomy, with only a change in reference frame. Within fifty years, however, heliocentrism became widely accepted. As the authority of Aristotle and **Ptolemy** was called into question, so too in other areas of learning did ancient authority falter under the probings of skeptical investigators.

A key part in inaugurating the Scientific Revolution was played by Johannes Kepler. Kepler grew up at a time when some aspects of Aristotelian cosmology (such as the immutability of the heavens) were already being challenged. Observations of the nova of 1572 suggested to **Tycho Brahe** and others that change could take place in the celestial regions, and the motion of the comet of 1577 indicated that even the celestial spheres themselves were of doubtful existence. However, from the perspective of predictive astronomy, there was little reason to choose Copernicus over Ptolemy. Both used the same devices of epicycles, eccentrics, and deferents. Ptolemy used an additional device called an equant, which Copernicus discarded, since it seemed to violate the classical axiom of uniform circular motion; some astronomers preferred Copernicus for that reason alone. Otherwise, Copernican astronomy was no better at accounting for the movement of the planets than Ptolemaic. The Copernican system did have one real advantage: It established for the first time the order and spacing of the planets, which in geocentric astronomy was quite arbitrary. In addition, heliocentrism explained retrograde motion and the close association of Mercury and Venus with the sun. But these were not necessarily seen as advantages at a time when cosmology was largely the province of natural philosophers and astronomy was strictly a science of mathematical prediction of planetary positions.

Kepler dramatically changed the nature of Copernican astronomy. He demonstrated that the actual path of a planet through space is an ellipse and that the traditional predictive devices of epicycles and eccentrics are unnecessary, indeed irrelevant. Kepler simply discarded uniform circular motion, the principle that Copernicus and most of his followers thought fundamental to astronomical practice. The virtue of the ellipse was that it was not a device at all, but a real orbit, and predictions based on Keplerian orbits were many times more accurate than those based on circular orbits, whether Ptolemaic, Copernican, or Tychonic.

Kepler also made the universe truly heliocentric. In Copernican astronomy the sun was indeed the body around which every major planet moved, but it was almost a bystander. The true center of the universe was the center of the earth's orbit. For Copernicus, the earth was still a very special body, even though now in motion. It also had an orbit that differed from that of other planets. Kepler showed that all planets, including the earth, moved in elliptical paths and that the body at the focus of each orbit was the sun. Thus all planetary planes passed through the sun and every trace of terrestrial privilege was eradicated.

Kepler was also the first astronomer to consider the problem of celestial dynamics: What are the forces that keep the planets in motion? In traditional astronomy the planets were on spheres, which either moved on their own with uniform motion, or were directed to do so by planetary intelligences. When Tycho and others dissolved the celestial spheres, the planets were set adrift, and it was Kepler who first attempted to rein them in. Kepler proposed that a force emanated from the sun, a force that diminished with distance, and that as the sun rotated, this force swept through the cosmos and moved the planets before it. He thought the force was magnetic in nature and interacted with each planet's inherent magnetism to produce the elliptical path. Kepler's version of the solar force proved to be ultimately unworkable, but the idea would prove attractive to later investigators.

Perhaps Kepler's greatest contribution to the scientific revolution was his demonstration that the planets obey simple mathematical laws. Very few mathematical laws of nature were known at the time and practically all were classical, such as the law of the lever or balance and the laws of floating bodies. When Kepler showed that a planet sweeps out equal areas in equal times (his second, or area, law), or that the period of a planet varies with its mean distance from the sun (the third, or period, law) or (erroneously) that a planet's velocity is inversely proportional to its distance, he was demonstrating that nature is regular and that simple mathematical relationships can describe and predict those regularities. Other scientists would seek the same kind of relationships, and it is no exaggeration to see Huygens's law of centrifugal force or Newton's law of universal gravitation as a natural outgrowth of Kepler's quest for cosmic harmonies.

The second major astronomical event of the Scientific Revolution was the introduction of the telescope. The telescope was invented by an unknown Dutch lens-maker around 1608, but when Galileo made his telescope and turned it on the moon in 1609, it became an astronomical instrument and a brand new kind of instrument at that. Astronomical instruments were traditionally used for measuring, and they measured only one quantity: divisions of a circle. All of Tycho's twenty-odd instruments did the same thing in different ways—they measured angles. So the telescope was not properly an instrument at all, since it did not measure anything. It was a magic glass. Thus it is not surprising that only **Galileo**, and **Thomas Harriot** in England, thought of bringing such a toy to the aid of astronomy. Indeed, the surprise is that anyone thought of it at all. By doing so, Galileo began the

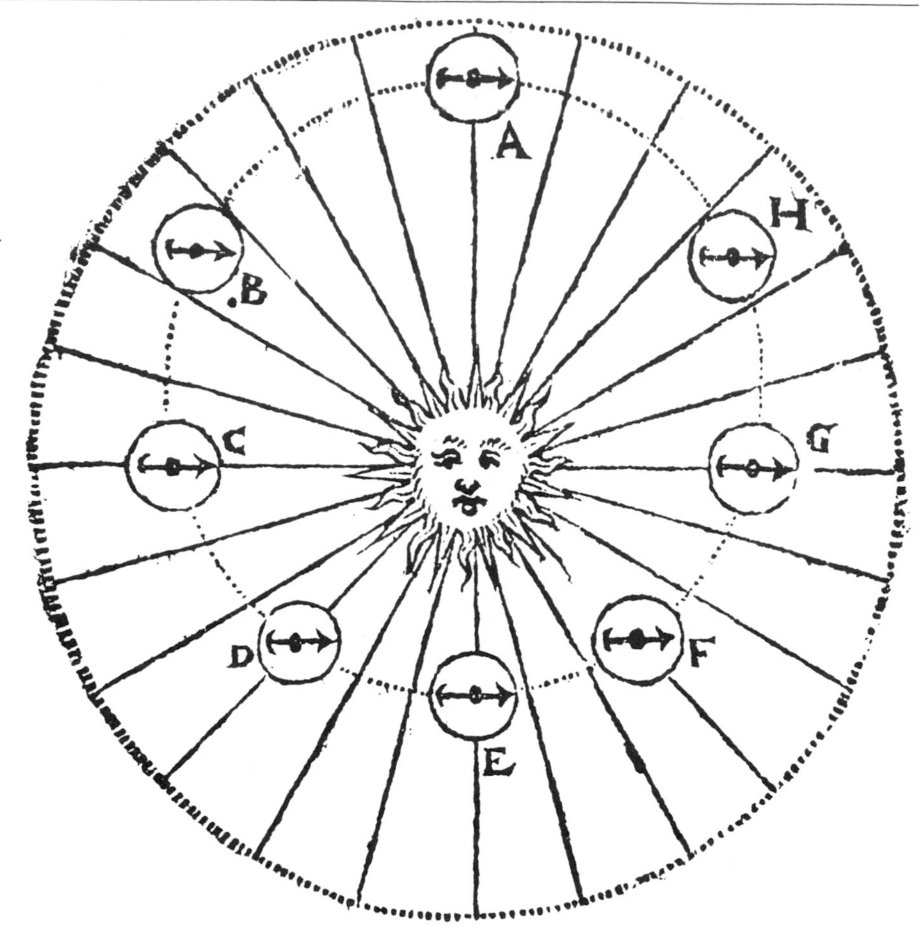

Kepler's diagram illustrating his conception of a magnetic force emanating from the sun that interacts with the earth's magnetism to produce an eccentric orbit, from his Epitome *(Linz, 1618-1622). (Courtesy of the History of Science Collection, Linda Hall Library, Kansas City, Missouri)*

transformation of the nature of the contemporary debate over cosmologies. Galileo's telescopes revealed an unexpected universe. The moon appeared as an irregular, earthlike body, contrary to the Aristotelian doctrine of celestial perfection. Four satellites circled Jupiter. The sun had spots, further evidence of heavenly imperfection, and it rotated on its axis. Venus was observed to have phases like the moon, which could only mean that it orbited the sun. All these novelties were observed within a year, and the implications were immediate and far-reaching. In the short run the telescope and its revelations turned Galileo into an ardent Copernican and an equally ardent anti-Aristotelian, who would soon convert others.

In a larger sense, the telescope was emblematic of a new kind of astronomy that would permeate the entire century. It was a new tool, unknown to the ancients, and it revealed a universe that was unknowable without it. Much of the effort of later astronomers would go into improving the telescope, enlarging the sphere of new discoveries, and, ironically, inventing crosshairs and micrometers that would allow the telescope itself to be turned into a measuring instrument.

The third major development of the Scientific Revolution that involved astronomy was a momentous confrontation with Church authority. Astronomers in the medieval period and the Renaissance had rarely run afoul of religious authority, and even the work of Copernicus was not seen as threatening by the sixteenth-century Church, since astronomy dealt with mathematical hypotheses, not the true nature of things. But around 1613, when Galileo began publicly arguing that Scripture, if properly interpreted, was perfectly compatible with heliocentric cosmology, he set in motion a series of events that would ultimately result in his own trial and condemnation, and cause the Church to declare heliocentrism heretical. The details will not be recapitulated here, but the effects should be noted. In Italy, theoretical astronomy came to a halt. Astronomers limited themselves to building telescopes, observing, and measuring. Speculation and theorizing were dangerous, and it is no coincidence that all the major advances in cosmology and astronomical theory would be made elsewhere. In other Catholic countries, such as France, some alarm was apparently felt, but the strictures did not prevent Descartes, Mersenne, Boulliau, and others from advocating heliocentrism. In the Netherlands and England, both Protestant countries, the astronomical revolution went forward without interruption.

There was a fourth major development in astronomy that contributed significantly to the Scientific Revolution: the reintroduction of an astronomy deduced from first principles. Since the first principles were those of René Descartes, and not Aristotle or Ptolemy, the implications were quite novel. Descartes had deduced that the only essential property of matter was extension and that matter could act on other matter only by contact. This meant that the universe must be filled with matter. Since a planet could move only if something pushed on it, the solar system must be a vortex of matter in motion, with the planets carried along in the flow.

The vortex theory of planetary motion, as it came to be called, addressed the same problem that had faced Kepler—namely, what moves the planets, but it produced quite a different result. Kepler gave us a tidy system of mathematically described orbits; Descartes offered instead a flotilla of inert bodies mechanically pushed along by a sea of invisible matter. Descartes's cosmology was totally incapable of explaining or even utilizing the mathematical regularities discovered by Kepler. But it did have the virtue of dispensing with mysterious forces, and as a model it was easily understood. Consequently, the vortex theory attracted a wide following and remained popular well into the eighteenth century.

Descartes also played a major role in what has been called the seventeenth-century transformation from a closed world to an infinite universe. Even as innovative a mind as Kepler had retained the concept of a finite stellar sphere. Descartes was really the first important thinker (excepting such predecessors as Giordano Bruno) to envision each star as a sun, and to picture a universe filled with a plurality of suns and perhaps a plurality of worlds revolving around those suns. The concept was not testable in the seventeenth century, since **stellar parallax** could not be measured, but even those who later rejected Cartesian cosmology (such as Newton) came to accept his proposal of stars uniformly distributed through an indefinite and perhaps infinite space.

There were many other developments in the seventeenth century that loom large in the history of astronomy, but that did not really contribute to the fundamental change in outlook that characterizes the Scientific Revolution. Most of these are examples of what Thomas Kuhn has called normal science and would include such notable events as the discovery of the rings of Saturn and its moon Titan by Huygens (1656); the discovery of Jupiter's Great Red Spot by Cassini (1664); the invention of the filar micrometer by Auzout and Picard in 1666; the invention by Isaac Newton and John Gregory of the reflecting telescope; and the founding of the **Paris Observatory** in 1667 and the **Royal Observatory** at Greenwich in 1675. However, one of these apparently normal enterprises seems to transcend the others and its significance merits discussion: the measurement of the parallax of Mars by **Gian Domenico Cassini** and Jean Richer in 1672.

It seems astonishing that with telescopic discoveries and insights provided by Kepler's laws, in 1670 no one had the slightest idea of the size of the solar system. Or, more precisely, their ideas were wildly inaccurate. The key to determining the size of the solar system was an accurate measurement of the earth-sun distance, which involved determination of the **solar parallax**. This proved an intractable problem, and the most common estimate (around 2 arcminutes) was more than twenty times greater than the value accepted today. Consequently, the solar system in 1672 was considered to be twenty times smaller than it actually is. Cassini hit on a new approach to the problem. At opposition in 1672 Mars would be about $2^1/_2$ times closer than the sun and would have a parallax that much greater. Cassini believed he could successfully measure the Martian parallax. He sent Richer to the island of Cayenne, off South America, and from these widely separated stations (Cassini was observing from Paris) they made a series of simultaneous measurements of Mars against the background of the stars. When the observational data were compared, a Martian parallax of 25 arcseconds was detected. This translated into an earth-sun distance of 87 million miles, not too far from the current value. We now know that this figure was extremely underdetermined and that the data would have supported just about any result, so Cassini had other reasons for preferring a large earth-sun distance. Nevertheless, astronomers by Newton's time had a new picture of the solar system to reckon with, one dominated by a truly gigantic sun, with two much smaller but still giant outer planets, and with four truly tiny terrestrial planets not much bigger than the moons of Jupiter. It was another significant step in the gradual diminution in the stature of our earthly abode, a process that began with Copernicus and would culminate in Shapley's 1918 demonstration of the sun's peripheral position in the Milky Way Galaxy.

The culminating event of the Scientific Revolution was Isaac Newton's proposal of a universal force of gravitation in 1687, and it provided fitting closure to the innovations begun by Kepler. Instead of a tangentially acting force that radiates out from the sun, Newton proposed a central force of attraction that, together with a planet's own inertial motion, yielded a perfect Keplerian elliptical orbit. The power of the Newtonian hypothesis was that it could explain and predict not only Kepler's laws of planetary motion, but also Galileo's laws of falling bodies, Huygens's

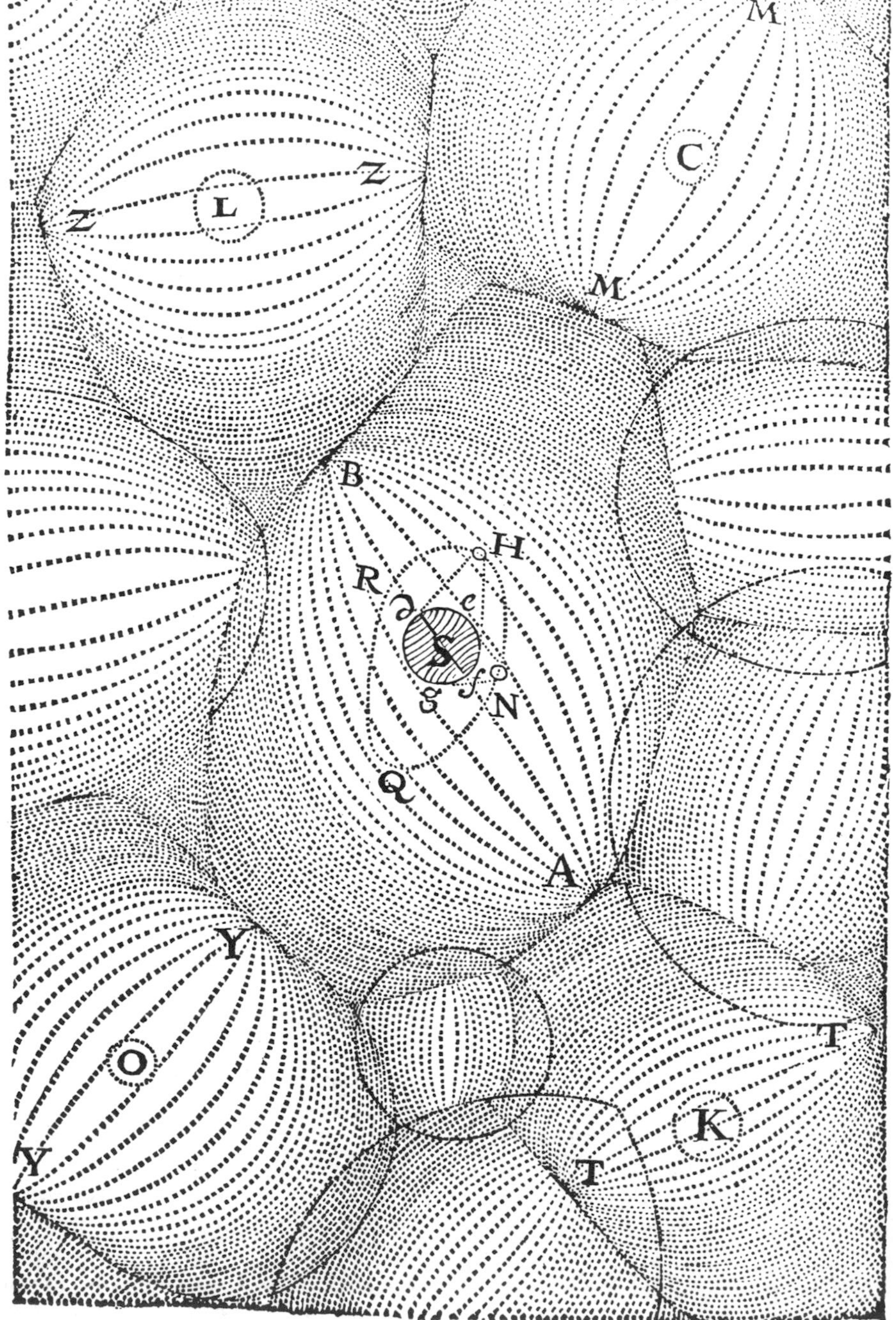

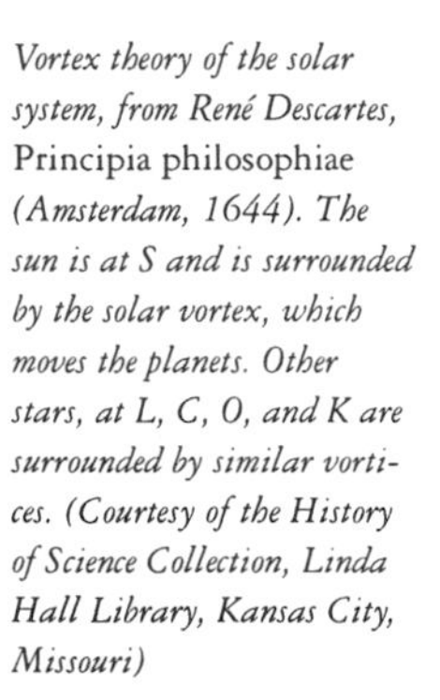
Vortex theory of the solar system, from René Descartes, Principia philosophiae *(Amsterdam, 1644). The sun is at S and is surrounded by the solar vortex, which moves the planets. Other stars, at L, C, O, and K are surrounded by similar vortices. (Courtesy of the History of Science Collection, Linda Hall Library, Kansas City, Missouri)*

law of the pendulum, and sundry other phenomena, such as the tides, and even the shape of the earth. The hypothesis was contested, since the notion of a force that acts at a distance seemed to be a throwback to the magical sympathies of the Renaissance, and many, such as Christiaan Huygens, preferred the mechanical certainty of the Cartesian explanation. However, no one was able to achieve Newton's results with any kind of mechanically generated force, and ultimately Newton prevailed. Terrestrial physics, celestial physics, astronomy, and cosmology were now united and explained by one set of laws.

William B. Ashworth Jr.

Bibliography

Aiton, E.J. *The Vortex Theory of Planetary Motions*. New York: American Elsevier, 1972.

———. "The Cartesian Vortex Theory." In *Planetary Astronomy from the Renaissance to the Rise of Astrophysics, Part A: Tycho Brahe to Newton,* edited by R. Taton and C. Wilson. *The General History of Astronomy*, vol. 2A, 207–221. Cambridge: Cambridge University Press, 1989.

Dick, S.J. *Plurality of Worlds: The Origins of the Extraterrestrial Life Debate from Democritus to Kant*. Cambridge: Cambridge University Press, 1982.

Koyré, A. *From the Closed World to the Infinite Universe*. Baltimore: Johns Hopkins University Press, 1957.

———. *The Astronomical Revolution: Copernicus—Kepler— Borelli*. Translated by R.E.W. Maddison. Ithaca, N.Y.: Cornell University Press, 1973.

Kuhn, T.S. *The Structure of Scientific Revolutions*. 2nd ed. Chicago: University of Chicago Press, 1970.

———. "Mathematical vs. Experimental Traditions in the Development of Physical Science." *Journal of Interdisciplinary History* 7 (1976): 1–32.

Lindberg, D.C., and R.S. Westman, eds. *Reappraisals of the Scientific Revolution*. Cambridge: Cambridge University Press, 1990.

Schuster, J.A. "The Scientific Revolution." In *The Companion to the History of Modern Science,* edited by R.C. Olby et al., 217–242. London: Routledge, 1990.

Van Helden, A. *Measuring the Universe: Cosmic Dimensions from Aristarchus to Halley*. Chicago: University of Chicago Press, 1985.

———. "Galileo, Telescopic Astronomy, and the Copernican System." In *Planetary Astronomy from the Renaissance to the Rise of Astrophysics, Part A: Tycho Brahe to Newton*, edited by R. Taton and C. Wilson. *The General History of Astronomy*, vol. 2A, 81–105. Cambridge: Cambridge University Press, 1989.

———. "The Telescope and Cosmic Dimensions." In *Planetary Astronomy from the Renaissance to the Rise of Astrophysics, Part A: Tycho Brahe to Newton*, edited by R. Taton and C. Wilson, vol. 2A, 106–118. *The General History of Astronomy*. Cambridge: Cambridge University Press, 1989.

Wilson, C.A. "From Kepler's Laws, So-Called, to Universal Gravitation: Empirical Factors." *Archive for History of Exact Sciences* 6 (1970): 89–170.

———. "Predictive Astronomy in the Century after Kepler." In *Planetary Astronomy from the Renaissance to the Rise of Astrophysics, Part A: Tycho Brahe to Newton*, edited by R. Taton and C. Wilson. *The General History of Astronomy*, vol. 2A, 161–206. Cambridge: Cambridge University Press, 1989.

Secchi, (Pietro) Angelo (1818–1878)

Italian astronomer and Jesuit priest. After a brief time at Georgetown University in Washington, D.C., Secchi returned to Italy to become the director of the new Collegio Romano Observatory in Rome (1849). Here he installed a 24-cm Merz equatorial refractor, with which he studied the sun, planetary surfaces, comets, and the moon. His solar observations of prominences, sunspots, and the chromosphere were especially notable, and his book *le Soleil* (Paris, 1876) became a classic.

In December 1862, Secchi turned his attention to the visual observation of stellar spectra. His main interest was spectral classification. He classified about four thousand stars into five main classes according to their spectral lines. Those of class IV were the carbon stars, of which Secchi was the discoverer (1868). In the late 1860s Secchi attempted to measure stellar radial velocities using visual spectroscopy, but he was largely unsuccessful. However his observation in 1870 of a velocity difference between the east and west solar limbs due to solar rotation was among the first confirmations of the Doppler effect for light. Secchi was a prolific writer; he wrote a second book, *le Stelle* (Milan, 1877), and over five hundred papers.

J.B. Hearnshaw

Bibliography

Abetti, G. "Angelo Secchi." In *Dictionary of Scientific Biography*, edited by C.C. Gillispie, vol. 12, 266–270. New York: Scribner, 1975.

Hearnshaw, J.B. *The Analysis of Starlight*. Cambridge: Cambridge University Press, 1986.

Seeing, Astronomical

The concept of seeing—the effect of atmospheric conditions on the sharpness and steadiness of telescopic images—was first recognized by Christiaan Huygens at the end of the seventeenth century. Huygens pointed out that quality of telescopic optics was not always to blame for poor images: Even on seemingly serene nights the atmosphere caused the stars to twinkle and the limbs of the **moon** and planets to appear tremulous, while on many nights the images boiled so badly as to make observing useless. As Isaac Newton remarked in the *Optics* (1704), even if **telescopes** were made optically perfect, they would continue to be troubled with that "confusion of the Rays which arises from the Tremors of the Atmosphere," and he suggested that the only remedy would be to place the instruments at the tops of mountains.

By the mid-nineteenth century, improvements in telescope optics had reached the point where atmospheric conditions began to be the limiting factor in critical observations, and astronomers began to take Newton's suggestion seriously. In 1856, **Charles Piazzi Smyth** set up a temporary observing station on Tenerife, a volcanic peak in the Canary Islands (elevation 3,716 meters). The first permanent mountaintop observatory, the Lick, was established on Mount Hamilton in California in 1888, and other high-altitude observing stations were founded at Arequipa, Peru (1892), Mont Blanc (1893), and Flagstaff, Arizona (1894).

The larger the telescope, the more it tends to be vulnerable to poor seeing conditions. Therefore, small telescope users in the late Victorian period argued that they had the advantage over large telescopes in mediocre conditions when it came to imaging the moon and planets. Sociologically sensitive historians have seen in this an indication of a larger turf struggle by amateurs faced with an increasingly sophisticated and specialized professionalism in astronomy. Certainly there were rhetorical aspects to these discussions, nowhere better illustrated than in the case of Percival Lowell's attempts to use arguments from seeing to buttress his embattled Martian observations. Other scholars have begun to examine how astronomical seeing is related to the problem of seeing more broadly—the question of how seeing, which tends to become perfectly steady only for brief flashes, interacts with the perceptual system's ability to interpret what is seen.

William Sheehan

Bibliography

Hoyt, W.G. *Lowell and Mars*. Tucson: University of Arizona Press, 1976.

Lankford, J. "Amateurs versus Professionals: The Controversy over Telescope Size in Late Victorian Science." *Isis* 72 (1981): 11–28.

Sheehan, W. *Planets and Perception*. Tucson: University of Arizona Press, 1988.

Seeliger, Hugo Ritter von (1849–1924)

German astronomer. After graduating with a doctorate from Leipzig (1872) and subsequently holding positions at Leipzig and at the observatories at Bonn and Gotha, Seeliger became professor of astronomy and director of the Munich Observatory (1882–1924) and president of the Astronomische Gesellschaft (1896–1921). One of the principal founders of modern statistical astronomy, he formulated statistico-mathematical models of the galaxy using his now famous fundamental equation of stellar statistics. Along with **J.C. Kapteyn**, Seeliger established the mathematical study of the distribution of the stars in the Milky Way Galaxy. This allowed him to discuss the mass-density of the galaxy in order to explain (in prerelativistic terms) the gravitational and optical paradoxes and the anomalous motion of the perihelion of Mercury.

E. Robert Paul

Bibliography

Kienle, H. "Seeliger Nekrolog." *Vierteljahrsschrift der Astronomische Gesellschaft*, 60 (1925): 2–23.

Selenography

The mapping and charting of the moon. The first telescopic observations of the moon were made by **Thomas Harriot** in July 1609. Galileo's more accurate observations, which have been dated by Whitaker, commenced on November 30, 1609. **Galileo** made beautiful sepia ink-wash drawings, established that the dark areas were lower elevations than the light areas, described the dominant features of the lunar surface, the craters, and made early estimates of the heights of lunar mountains by observing their peaks catching the sunlight while their bases were still in the shadowed area beyond the terminator. In addition, Galileo discovered the moon's libration in latitude. Recent historians such as Cohen have stressed the importance of Galileo's Copernicanism in guiding him to the correct interpretation of the features he viewed indistinctly through his small telescopes (Cohen, 188–193).

Early maps were produced by **Hevelius** and Giambattista Riccioli. The latter introduced the system of nomenclature that is the basis of that still used today, in which the names of scientists are given to the craters. These early maps were drawn entirely freehand. After the initial excitement following Galileo's discoveries died out, there was a loss of interest that Ashbrook has referred to as the "long night of selenography" (Ashbrook, 237). In part this was due to the imperfect optics and the inconvenience of using the long aerial telescopes. Christiaan Huygens made a few important observations; in 1686, he became the first to depict lunar features such as Straight Wall, Schröter's Valley, and Hyginus Rille. Moreover, a contemporary, Gian D. Cassini, was responsible for a new map, which was more artistic than accurate. By and large, however, lunar studies languished.

A new era was begun in the eighteenth century by Tobias Mayer, a cartographer who became interested in mapping the moon in order to improve terrestrial longitude determinations. A very old method had been to make timings of the beginning of a lunar eclipse as viewed from two widely separated places; the difference between the two local times gave the longitude difference. Hevelius had suggested that the accuracy of this method could be improved if instead of timing the beginning of the eclipse, observers noted the exact moment at which individual lunar craters entered the earth's shadow. However, he had never attempted to put the method into practice, and Mayer realized that it would not prove useful unless observers were furnished with a better map. In 1748, Mayer carefully measured the positions of two dozen points on the lunar surface, from which he worked out the selenographic coordinates as the basis for a map, on a scale of 18 cm to the diameter of the moon. Unfortunately, it did not appear during his lifetime; it was published only in 1775.

William Herschel, the greatest observer of his age, made observations of the moon but confided them only to the pages of his private observing books, and they remained unknown until long after his death. They give fascinating insights into his methods, but have yet to be systematically studied. However, in 1787 he did publish reports of what he took to be three volcanoes erupting on the night side of the moon; this was one of his rare blunders—as we now know, he was seeing only the bright rayed craters Aristrarchus, Kepler, and Copernicus shining dimly by light reflected from the earth. These reports stimulated the lunar investigations of **Johann Hieronymus Schröter**, chief magistrate of Lilienthal, a small village near Bremen, and who in 1782 established the largest observatory on the continent. Two of his telescopes had mirrors fashioned by Herschel. At first Schröter planned to draw a new lunar map, but he changed his mind. Since his main interest was in showing that the moon was an active world, the site of ongoing atmospheric, vegetative, and especially geologic changes (he believed that the moon was the scene of volcanic eruptions), he devoted himself to sketching a large number of individual surface features as they appeared under varying conditions of illumination. With the help of his friend Heinrich W.M. Olbers, he also worked out a new method for determining the heights of lunar mountains from the shadows they cast across the surface, and his measures were a marked improvement over those made by his predecessors. Schröter's research was published as his *Selenotopographische Fragmente* (vol. 1, 1791; vol. 2, 1802). He was a keen observer, though a clumsy draftsman, and his worth has been greatly underappreciated.

The same may be said of Franz von Paula Gruithuisen, a Munich physician who shared some of Schröter's romantic ideas about the moon. With a keen eye and small refractors of 6 and 9 cm aperture, he discovered many delicate rills (including the intricate Triesnecker system, south of Mare Vaporum), and was an early advocate of the impact theory of crater origin. But his adherence to the view that the moon was a living world led him, in July 1822, to report the discovery of nothing less than a lunar city, near the dark area now known as Sinus Aestuum. As later observers found, it consists only of a curious though completely natural-looking arrangement of low walls, and henceforth many astronomers of the day regarded Gruithuisen as a crank. Modern historians familiar with the notion that perception is an active process, conditioned by expectations, may approach his work with more sympathy. In any case, the body of his work—he was extraordinarily prolific—has never been systematically studied, in part because so much of it is buried in obscure journals that were in many cases founded by himself, simply because the standard journals of the day refused to publish him.

Opposed to what might be called the romantic school of selenography of Schröter and Gruithuisen, there arose a classical school, founded by Wilhelm Gotthelf Lohrmann. Like Mayer a professional cartographer—he was responsible for carrying out a geodetic survey of the Kingdom of Saxony—Lohrmann started a geodetic survey of the moon, which was to serve as the basis of a large map. He started work in the winter of 1821–1822 but abandoned the project after publishing the first four of a projected twenty-five sections of his map in 1824; nevertheless, his overall plan was taken up by Wilhelm Beer and Johann Heinrich Mädler. Beer, a wealthy banker, established a small observatory on the roof of his villa in Berlin and equipped it with a first-rate instrument, a 9.5-cm refractor by Fraunhofer. Their moon-mapping project began in April 1830, with almost all of the actual work being done by Mädler. The result was a map on a scale of 97.5 cm to the diameter of the moon, the same as that which Lohrmann had hoped to complete, and it was published in four sections between 1834 and 1836, followed in 1837 by their great book, *Der Mond.*

Beer and Mädler were hostile to Schröter, and dismissed the Lilienthal astronomer's claims of lunar changes as unfounded. The moon, they pronounced, was a dead world; it was airless and moistureless, and presumably changeless. It was, then, in their famous phrase, "No copy of the Earth." In fact, they left the impression that there was little left to achieve in lunar studies, and the next thirty years saw the virtual abandonment of the moon as an object of serious scientific study.

The Mädlerian paralysis finally ended in 1866, when Julius Schmidt, director of the Athens Observatory, published his report of changes in the small crater Linné, in Mare Serenitatis. Though it is now certain that Linné cannot have undergone any real change—the much-maligned Schröter had depicted the crater in essentially its modern form in 1788, and the feature has now been shown to be an ordinary, fresh-impact crater—Schmidt's report had a seismic effect and gave rise to renewed interest in the moon. Schmidt himself produced a new topographic map on a scale of 183 cm to the moon's diameter that was published in 1876. Other observers of the moon—most of whom looked at it in terms of the dominant volcanic theory of crater formation—sought evidence of obscurations and eruptions, concluding on the basis of uncertain evidence that new features had appeared, since they had not been recorded by Schröter and other early observers. At the same time the fascination with producing ever larger and better maps—what E.E. Both has called the "Holy Grail" of selenography—revived (Both, 19).

At the end of the nineteenth century, the impact of photography began to be felt. Early atlases were produced by Maurice Loewy and Pierre Puiseux at the Paris Observatory, and by Harvard's William H. Pickering. At last the project envisioned by Schröter, of recording the lunar features under different conditions of illumination, became a reality. Earth-based mapping efforts continued into the early Space Age, reaching their culmination in the U.S. Air Force mapping project led by **G.P. Kuiper** of the University of Arizona. The moon's far side was photographed for the first time by the Russian *Lunik 3* spacecraft in 1959, and most of the moon was mapped at high resolution by the five American *Lunar Orbiter* spacecraft in 1966–1967. Only a small region around the lunar south pole, which was not well covered by the *Orbiters*, has had to be filled in on the basis of earth-based observations of limb features under conditions of favorable libration. Now the moon has been completely mapped, and the triumph of the impact theory of crater formation over the volcanic theory has all but laid to rest the expectation of changes of the sort sought by earlier observers. Once more the situation is as it was in the years after 1837: The moon is viewed as a dead world, static and unchanging, and there seems to be no compelling need for further maps.

As yet there is no full-length study of selenography. Many of the source materials are in German and have thus far been little studied by scholars in the English-speaking world. Schröter's observatory in Lilienthal is currently being reconstructed. Meanwhile he is much in need of a sympathetic reevaluation—his reputation still suffers largely from the harsh criticisms of Beer and Mädler. Mädler has been the subject of a recent study. An investigation into the methods and instruments that led to a gradual improvement of the measures of positions, diameters and elevations of the moon's features would also be valuable, but has yet to be attempted.

William Sheehan

Bibliography

Ashbrook, J. *The Astronomical Scrapbook: Skywatchers, Pioneers, and Seekers in Astronomy.* Cambridge, Mass.: Sky Publishing, 1984.

Both, E.E. *A History of Lunar Studies*. Buffalo, N.Y.: Buffalo Museum of Science, 1961.

Cohen, I.B. *The Birth of a New Physics*. New York: W.W. Norton, 1988.

Eelsalu, H., and D.B. Hermann. *Johann Heinrich Mädler (1794–1874)*. Berlin: Akademie Verlag, 1985.

Forbes, E.G. *Tobias Mayer (1723–62): Pioneer of Enlightened Science in Germany*. Göttingen: Vandenhoeck & Ruprecht, 1980.

Kopal, Z., and R.W. Carder. *Mapping of the Moon, Past and Present*. Dordrecht: Reidel, 1974.

Whitaker, E.A. "Selenography in the Seventeenth Century." In *Planetary Astronomy from the Renaissance to the Rise of Astrophysics, Part A: Tycho Brahe to Newton*, edited by R. Taton and C. Wilson, 119–143. *The General History of Astronomy*. Cambridge: Cambridge University Press, 1989.

Wilhelms, D.E. *To a Rocky Moon*. Tucson: University of Arizona Press, 1993.

SETI (Search for Extraterrestrial Intelligence) Project

SETI, an acronym for Search for Extraterrestrial Intelligence, is the generic term applied to those scientific programs attempting to detect by means of **radio telescopes** signals of intelligent origin from outer space. Although the tradition of inhabited worlds dates to the ancient Greeks, and though Percival Lowell's idea of intelligence on **Mars** (spurring attempts to intercept Martian radio signals) pervaded popular culture in the early twentieth century, the modern era of SETI dates only from 1959. In that year the physicists Giuseppe Cocconi and Philip Morrison proposed a strategy for interstellar communication, as the enterprise was first called. The early search programs often went under the acronym CETI (Communication with Extraterrestrial Intelligence), but in a conscious attempt to downplay the communication aspects and emphasize a more passive search, the NASA workshops in 1975–1976 chaired by Morrison adopted the name of SETI for their proposed research program. Although specific observing programs (including NASA's) now go by their own distinctive names, SETI still encompasses the overall enterprise. Dozens of SETI programs of varying power have thus far detected no intelligent signals, but the program is intrinsically filled with immense strategic difficulties, including where and how to search.

It is a measure of the compelling nature of the question of extraterrestrial intelligence that the radio search began almost immediately when the technology became available to detect at interstellar distances signals comparable in power to artificial signals produced by radar on earth. Frank Drake undertook the first such search in Project Ozma at the National Radio Astronomy Observatory (NRAO) in Green Bank, West Virginia. Months before Cocconi and Morrison had proposed the radio region of the spectrum as optimal for interstellar communication and suggested more specifically the 21-cm emission line of hydrogen as an obvious wavelength to monitor (the first landmark event in modern SETI history), Drake had independently begun building equipment for just such a project. Encouraged by NRAO's first director, Otto Struve (who had for years believed in the abundance of planetary systems based on his studies of stellar rotation), Drake also chose the 21-cm hydrogen line because hydrogen was the most abundant element in the universe. The 21-cm line was therefore perhaps a frequency that might draw universal attention; furthermore, it was the only astrophysical emission line known to terrestrials at the time. Drake's ensuing two-hundred-hour examination of radio signals from two solar-type stars in the spring of 1960 failed to detect any intelligence but was the second landmark in the annals of SETI.

Another SETI landmark occurred when the National Academy of Sciences sponsored the first conference on interstellar communication, hosted at NRAO by Struve and Drake in 1961. This small gathering brought together scientists from a broad range of disciplines to discuss the probabilities of extraterrestrial intelligence, and resulted in the famous Drake Equation, first used as the agenda for the meeting. In the ensuing three decades the Drake Equation has become a paradigm for discussing the number of communicative civilizations in the galaxy. Although subsequently elaborated in a number of ways, the equation was originally written as $N = R^{*} f_p n_e f_l f_i f_c L$, where R^{*} is the rate of star formation, f_p the fraction of stars forming planets, n_e the number of planets per star with environments suitable for life, f_l the fraction of suitable planets on which life develops, f_i the fraction of life-bearing planets on which intelligence appears, f_c the fraction of intelligent cultures that are communicative, and L the lifetime of the civilization. The components of this equation may be divided in astronomical, biological, and social factors, but values for most of the parameters are extremely uncertain. Even the existence of planetary systems outside our own is uncertain, to mention nothing of the origin and evolution of life in extraterrestrial environments. (The negative findings of the Mars *Viking* mission seem not to have had much effect on SETI proponents). Thus values of N over the last three decades, proposed by a multitude of individuals and conferences, have ranged from a hundred million or more communicative civilizations in our galaxy to only one—our own. Perhaps never in the history of science has an equation been devised yielding values differing by eight orders of magnitude. In a measure of the uncertainty at the core of what some have called a branch of the new discipline of exobiology or bioastronomy, each scientist seems to bring his own prejudices and assumptions to the problem. Although these discussions have been extremely interesting, astronomers have increasingly emphasized that the only way to find a solution is to observe.

The problems of which radio frequencies to search and in what way have remained challenging, but the chances of a solution have been greatly enhanced by advances in computer power and chip technology. These advances have been gradually taken advantage of in search programs around the world during the 1970s and 1980s, including the long-running project at Ohio State University, Project META at Harvard and Argentina, and Project SERENDIP sponsored by the University of California, Berkeley. No search has been more powerful than the SETI program developed by NASA and inaugurated on October 12, 1992—the Quincentennial of Columbus's landing in the New World. Individuals within NASA had first expressed interest in SETI in 1969, and the first concrete results of their efforts was the publication in 1971 of a feasibility study, directed by Bernard M. Oliver and John Billingham, known as Project Cyclops. Its projected ten-billion-dollar cost was much too ambitious for government funding, but the Morrison workshops of 1975–1976 laid out a more reasonable strategy, and after further study, minimal funding and much political wrangling, a sustained research and development (R&D) effort began in 1983. The heart of NASA's detector system was the Multi-Channel Spectrum Analyzer (MCSA), a device that could search millions of radio channels simultaneously for an intelligent signal. The MCSA, developed at NASA's Ames Research Center, and a similar detector developed at the Jet Propulsion Laboratory, are the heart of NASA's ten-year dual strategy incorporating a targeted search of nearby solar-type stars at high sensitivity and an all-sky survey at lower sensitivity. The effect of technology advance on SETI is evident in the fact that NASA's program (now known as High Resolution Microwave Survey, or HRMS) exceeded in its first several minutes the scope of all previous SETI observations. After less than a year of observing, Congress terminated funding for the project in 1993.

SETI has undergone many crises of rationale and funding, none more so than in the mid-1970s, when skeptics proposed that the Fermi paradox should be taken more seriously. In 1950 Enrico Fermi had innocently asked, "Where is everybody?" implying that if extraterrestrials were so abundant, they should have undertaken interstellar travel and reached the earth, given time scales of billions of years available in the history of our galaxy during which intelligence might have evolved. SETI advocates replied in a variety of ways, insisting that radio signals were much more economical and efficient than interstellar travel, and reaffirming that the empirical tradition of science was the only way to a solution of the question of extraterrestrial intelligence. No small part of their task has been to build a consensus in many national and international organizations that SETI is a program worth pursuing.

During its brief modern history, SETI has been viewed in many ways. It has been seen as frontier science by most of its practitioners, as a pseudoscience by skeptics, as exploration, as a test of the biophysical cosmology, and as mythology in the broad positive sense of a deeply ingrained thought system. From whatever viewpoint one chooses, SETI, together with its broader background in the plurality of worlds debate and the discipline of exobiology, is a rich subject for study by historians, philosophers, and sociologists of science interested in how science functions at its limits on a subject of wide popular interest and high scientific stakes—one essential to resolving the age-old question of humanity's place in the universe. Although few historical studies have been carried out on the twentieth century, aside from reminiscences by some of the scientists involved, NASA's SETI History Project now underway promises to remedy this in part.

Steven J. Dick

Bibliography

Crowe, M.J. *The Extraterrestrial Life Debate, 1750–1900: The Idea of a Plurality of Worlds from Kant to Lowell.* Cambridge: Cambridge University Press, 1986.

Dick, S.J. *Plurality of Worlds: The Origins of the Extraterrestrial Life Debate from Democritus to Kant.* Cambridge: Cambridge University Press, 1982.

———. "The Concept of Extraterrestrial Life—An Emerging Cosmology?" *Planetary Report* 9 (1989): 13–17.

———. "From the Physical World to the Biological Universe: Historical Developments Underlying SETI." In *Bioastronomy: The Search for Extraterrestrial Life—The Exploration Broadens,* edited by J. Heidmann and M.J. Klein, 356–363. Berlin, 1991.

———. "The Search for Extraterrestrial Intelligence and the NASA High Resolution Microwave Survey (HRMS): Historical Perspectives." *Space Science Reviews* 64 (1993): 93–139.

———. *The Biological Universe: The Twentieth Century Extraterrestrial Life Debate and the Limits of Science.* New York: Cambridge University Press, 1996.

Drake, F., and D. Sobel. *Is Anyone Out There? The Scientific Search for Extraterrestrial Intelligence.* New York: Delacorte Press, 1992.

Guthke, K.S. *The Last Frontier: Imagining Other Worlds from the Copernican Revolution to Modern Science Fiction.* Ithaca, N.Y.: Cornell University Press, 1990.

Morrison, P. "Twenty-Five Years of the Search for Extraterrestrial Communications." In *The Search for Extraterrestrial Life: Recent Developments*, edited by M. Papagiannis, 13–19. Dordrecht: D. Reidel, 1985.

Papagiannis, M. "A Historical Introduction to the Search for Extraterrestrial Intelligence." In *The Search for Extraterrestrial Life: Recent Developments*, edited by M. Papagiannis, 5–12. Dordrecht: D. Reidel, 1985.

Swift, D.W. *SETI Pioneers.* Tucson: University of Arizona Press, 1990.

Sextant

In modern usage, a small, handheld navigational instrument used to measure the altitude of a celestial object. Longitude can be determined if the time of measurement is known.

The term *sextant* refers to a calibrated arc of one-sixth a circle, but any similar instrument regardless of arc length is generally called a sextant: modern instruments may be as long as 90 degrees. To bring together into the same field of view the horizon and an object in the sky, two mirrors are used. Viewing is done through a small movable telescope (the first sextants used a pinhole sight) aligned toward a half-silvered horizon mirror, which

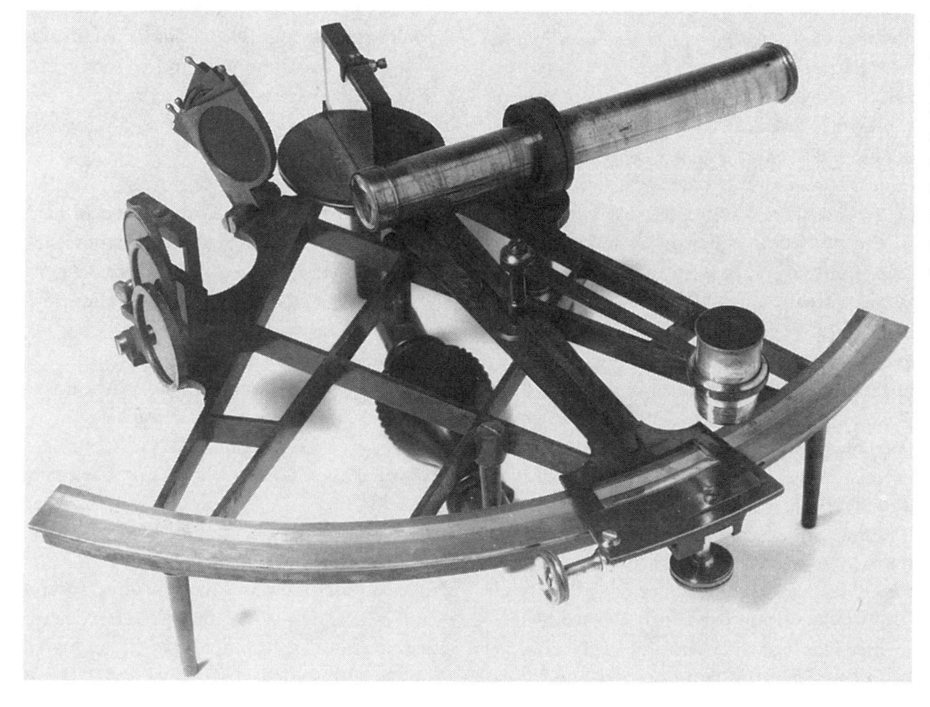

The sextant was an important tool for marine navigation. This late-nineteenth-century example shows the telescope, filters, graduated scale, and magnifying lens used to read the scale. (Courtesy of the National Museum of American History)

catches on its silvered side an image of the Sun (or other object) reflected from the first or index mirror. The ocean horizon is seen through its clear half. The position on the graduated arc of the movable index arm yields the angle between the sun and horizon. The index mirror is mounted at the pivot of the index arm and is fixed with respect to it. The mirrors are parallel when the angle between horizon and an object is 0 degrees. As the use of a mirror halves the angle to be measured, the arc of a true sextant is calibrated from 0 to 120 degrees.

This scheme was described in 1699 by Isaac Newton (1642–1727) who modified a 1644 single-reflection concept of Robert Hooke (1635–1703), but his design was not published until after 1730. By then, John Hadley (1682–1744) in England and Thomas Godfrey in America independently had developed instruments based on the same idea.

Hadley's sea-octant was first employed for navigation by Captain John Campbell, who proposed in 1757 its enlargement to a 60-degree length. Campbell's form of the instrument, variously termed a nautical, marine, or reflecting sextant, became the standard form by 1770. The greater arc length allowed more accurate measurement of the position of the moon relative to a given star; when compared to ephemeris tables this allowed determination of Greenwich time in an era before the existence of reliable chronometers. Measurement of the solar altitude gave local time. The difference between the two times is the observer's longitude.

Earlier instruments, either employing a calibrated arc of one-sixth a full circle or sometimes one-sixth a half circle, have also been called sextants. Two radial arms, one fixed and the other movable about the axis of the arc, were aligned toward two objects in the sky, their angle of separation being read from the arc. In the tenth century, Abu'l Wefa, working at the Baghdad Observatory erected by the Caliph Al-Ma'mûn, apparently employed a stone sextant of 56 foot radius. **Tycho Brahe** built sextants with a 30- or 60-degree sector, including a small portable instrument that could be used in his travels. It was **Edmond Halley** who added a telescope to a sextant. **John Flamsteed** at Greenwich Observatory equipped a 7-foot sextant with two telescopes that necessitated two observers to sight along the arms. Such instruments were used into the mid-eighteenth century; for example, by **Nicholas-Louis de Lacaille**, who carried one to the Cape of Good Hope in 1751 to survey bright southern stars. These instruments passed out of use when more accurate telescopic techniques were developed for determination of angular position.

Charles J. Peterson

Bibliography

Campbell, W.W. *The Elements of Practical Astronomy,* 89–121. New York: Macmillan, 1913.

Shain, Grigorii Abramovich (1892–1956)

Soviet astrophysicist. Having studied at Iur'ev (Dorpat) University, Shain joined the staff of **Pulkovo Observatory** in 1921. In 1925 he moved to Pulkovo's Simeis station, where he supervised the installation of a 1-meter reflector—the largest telescope in the Soviet Union at that time. Shain was elected a member of the USSR Academy of Sciences in 1939, and after World War II (1944–1952) he directed the new **Crimean Astrophysical Observatory**.

Shain's main contributions to astronomy were in stellar spectroscopy and the physics of gaseous nebulae. Together with O. Struve, in 1929 Shain proposed a method to determine the rotational velocity of stars of early spectral class. In 1940 Shain studied the content of C13 in stellar atmospheres, from which he determined that the ratio of C13 to C12 on the earth and sun is much smaller than in most stars. During the Stalinist repressions Shain exerted great efforts to aid the families of imprisoned astronomers and to secure the release of these astronomers.

Robert A. McCutcheon

Bibliography

Kolchinskii, I.G., A.A. Korsun', and M.G. Rodriges. "Shain, Grigorii Abramovich." In *Astronomy, biograficheskii spravochnik* (Astronomers, a Biographical Handbook) 2nd ed., 368–369. Kiev: Naukova dumka, 1986.

Kulikovsky, P.G. "Shayn, Grigory Abramovich." In *Dictionary of Scientific Biography*, edited by C.C. Gillispie, vol. 12, 367–369. New York: Scribner, 1981.

Shapley, Harlow (1885–1972)

American astronomer. Shapley, after several years as a small town newspaper reporter (Chanute, Kansas; Joplin, Missouri) graduated from the University of Missouri in 1910 and earned his Ph.D. at Princeton in 1914. Then he was appointed astronomer at Mount Wilson (1914–1920) and director of **Harvard College Observatory** (1921–1952). His research included the determination of orbits of eclipsing binaries (1913); proof that Cepheids are not eclipsing binaries, as previously believed, but single pulsating stars (1914); and extensive investigations of stellar clusters, including proof that the solar system is far removed from the center of the Milky Way (1918). At Harvard he discovered clusters of galaxies in Fornax and Virgo, and a remote cloud of galaxies in Hydra-Centaurus, the Shapley Supercluster. His hobby was research on ants, deriving for them a temperature-speed relation.

Shapley established the graduate program in astronomy at Harvard. The first Ph.D. was awarded to Cecilia Payne in 1925. During his thirty years as director, fifty Ph.D. degrees were awarded. Of the recipients, twelve became directors of observatories. Shapley was also involved in the founding of the National Science Foundation and the United Nations Economic, Scientific, and Cultural Organization.

A pacificist at heart, Shapley felt that bringing scientists of all nations and religions together in cooperative research should ultimately lead to better international relations. For example, he succeeded in getting astronomers from North Ireland and the Republic of Ireland to collaborate with Harvard in research with a new telescope at the Harvard southern station in Bloemfontein, South Africa. He named the telescope ADH for Armagh-Dunsink-Harvard. He enabled Jewish refugee astronomers from Germany and Italy to find employment in America, and after World War II to bring foreign visitors, especially Russian, to Harvard. Unfortunately his purely humanitarian and scholastic motives were misinterpreted by political extremists, Senator Joseph McCarthy and Congressman John Rankin, who unjustly attacked Shapley as un-American.

Dorrit Hoffleit

Bibliography

Bok, B.J. "Harlow Shapley." *Biographical Memoirs of the National Academy of Sciences* 49 (1978): 241–291.

Mather, K.F. "Harlow Shapley, Man of the World." *American Scholar* 40 (1971): 475–481.

Shapley, H. *Through Rugged Ways to the Stars.* New York: Scribner, 1969.

Shizuki, Tadao (1760–1806)

An astronomer and physicist in the middle Edo period. Tadao Shizuki, whose original family name was Nakano, became an assistant translator at the age of sixteen. He was adopted into the Shizuki family, whose hereditary function was to translate Dutch for the government. The next year, however, he retired from the post because of poor health and began the private study of Western science. He studied astronomy with Ryoei Motoki, a member of another translator family, who taught Western geography and astronomy, especially the idea of the heliocentric system.

Shizuki is best known for his introduction of Newtonian cosmology and mechanics into Japan. The key text he relied upon was the Dutch translation of John Keill's Newtonian textbooks, *Introductio ad veram physicam* (Introduction to true physics) (London, 1701) and *Introductio ad veram astronomiam* (Introduction to true astronomy) (London, 1718). The outcome of this decade-long investigation was his translation of and commentary on Keill's *Rekisho shinsho* (A new treatise of calendrical phenomena) (3 vols., 1798–1802). In translating this work, Shizuki attempted to interpret some Newtonian concepts and theories in terms of Chinese concepts such as *chi*. Shizuki wrote numerous treatises on mathematics, mechanics, astronomy, surveying, and Dutch grammar. He is also known for his translation of a chapter from Engelbert Kaempfer's *Beschrijving van Japan* (The history of Japan), which supported Japan's policy of remaining closed to foreigners.

Takehiko Hashimoto

Bibliography

Nakayama, S. *A History of Japanese Astronomy*. Cambridge: Harvard University Press, 1969.

Shklovskii, Iosif Samuilovich (1916–1985)

Soviet astrophysicist. A graduate of Moscow State University (1938), Shklovskii joined the staff of the Shternberg Astronomical Institute (1941), where he later (1944) became head of the radio astronomy department. In 1967 he founded the department of astrophysics in the USSR Academy of Sciences' Space Research Institute.

Shklovskii is regarded as one of the most important post–World War II Soviet astrophysicists. Shklovskii's principal works were in theoretical astrophysics. In the 1940s he elaborated a general theory of the solar corona and a theory of the sun's radiation at radio wavelengths. Beginning in the late 1940s, Shklovskii studied the origins of galactic radio waves. He predicted the observability of the 21-cm hydrogen line as well as the OH and CH lines. Shklovskii developed an original method for determining the distances to planetary nebulae.

Shklovskii published numerous works on the philosophy of science and on man's place in the universe. Shklovskii's book *Intelligent Life in the Universe* has been translated into English and many other languages.

Robert A. McCutcheon

Bibliography

Kardashev, N.S., and L.S. Marochnik. "The Shklovskii Phenomenon." *Astronomy Quarterly* 7 (1990): 219–242.

Kolchinskii, I.G., A.A. Korsun', and M.G. Rodriges. "Shklovskii, Iosif Samuilovich." In *Astronomy, biograficheskii spravochnik* (Astronomers, a biographical handbook). Kiev: Naukova dumka, 1986.

Slipher, Vesto Melvin (1875–1969)

American astronomer. Born in Indiana and a graduate of Indiana University, Slipher moved to Flagstaff, Arizona, in 1901 to become Percival Lowell's chief assistant, and succeeded him as director of **Lowell Observatory** in 1916. He was a pioneering spectroscopist who obtained spectra of the planets, carried out radial velocity measurements of spectroscopic binaries that led to his independent discovery of the sharp, stationary absorption lines of Ca II, which he correctly interpreted as resulting from interstellar gas, and he was the first to recognize that the Pleiades nebulosity was a reflection nebula. In 1912, he obtained a long-exposure spectrogram of the Andromeda Nebula—a remarkable technical feat at the time. He later added those of other spiral nebulae, establishing that most of them appeared to be receding from the earth at rapid velocities, in some cases as great as 1,000 km/second, thus providing the first evidence of what became known as the expanding universe.

William Sheehan

Bibliography

Hoyt, W.G. "Vesto Melvin Slipher (1875–1969)." *Biographical Memoirs of the National Academy of Sciences* 52 (1980): 410–449.

Smyth, Charles Piazzi (1819–1900)

British astronomer. Born in Naples, Italy, Smyth's father was Admiral William Henry Smyth, hydrographer in the Royal Navy. In 1825 William set up a private observatory at Bedford, England, and through him Smyth became acquainted with many of the leading astronomers of his day. Smyth never received more than a grammar school education. Through his father's influence, Smyth became assistant to Thomas Maclear at the Cape of Good Hope (1835–1845). He later served as Astronomer Royal for Scotland (1845–1888).

A brilliant designer of spectroscopes and an early advocate of high-altitude observatories, in 1856 Smyth took one of his instruments to Tenerife, a volcanic peak in the Canary Islands (altitude 3,716 meters). Though he fell short of his goal of observing the solar corona from Tenerife, he made important studies of the near infrared spectrum, and was the first to distinguish telluric (spectrum lines produced by the earth's atmosphere) from solar lines. Among his other achievements, he correctly explained the Zodiacal Light as the reflection of sunlight from meteoric material surrounding the sun.

Regrettably, after a visit to the **Great Pyramid of Gaza** in 1863, Smyth became obsessed with the eccentric theories of John Taylor, a London bookseller and publisher, who argued that ancient wisdom was concealed in mathematical form in the structure of the pyramid. He followed up on a suggestion of **John Herschel**, with whom he had first become acquainted at the Cape, that the length of the earth's axis could be made equal to 500 million inches if that unit were increased by one thousandth part, and in his book *Our Inheritance in the Great Pyramid* (1864) worked out his theory that the pyramid had been constructed using Herschel's geometrical inch. His monomaniacal obsession with the Great Pyramid lasted for the rest of his life, and has unfortunately overshadowed his genuine achievements.

William Sheehan

Bibliography

Warner, B. *Charles Piazzi Smyth, Astronomer Artist: His Cape Years, 1835–1845.* Accord, Mass.: A.A. Balkena, 1983.

Brück, H.A., and M.T. Brück. *Charles Piazzi Smyth: The Peripatetic Astronomer.* Bristol and Philadelphia: Adam Hilger, 1988.

Solar Constant

In 1838, Claude Pouillet defined the solar constant as the amount of solar radiation impinging vertically on a unit area of the earth's outer atmosphere in a unit of time and estimated this quantity's value by correcting ground-level measurements of the incident heat for atmospheric absorption. His value figured prominently in the calculations of the solar radiative output used in the initial inquiries into the sun's energy source. From the 1880s until the 1950s, Samuel Pierpont Langley and his successor as director of the Smithsonian Astrophysical Observatory, Charles Greeley Abbot, steadfastly sought to improve the value of the solar constant and to establish its variability with solar activity. These matters remained more or less unsettled, however, until observations from above the atmosphere became possible. In 1980, Richard C. Willson's radiometer on the *Solar Maximum Mission* (*SMM*) provided the first unambiguous evidence of what is now called solar irradiance variability. During the ensuing decade, concurrent measurements from *SMM* and *Nimbus* 7 demonstrated that solar irradiance varies directly with solar activity.

Recent historical studies have done much to illuminate the main stages of research on the solar constant. However, only DeVorkin has dealt at any length with the full range of strategies used by observers to establish confidence in their empirical claims. Much could be learned about trust-engendering processes in modern astronomy by studies that paid more attention to these strategies as well as to the criteria used by the observers' audiences when deciding whether or not to rely upon specific solar irradiance measurements for theorizing about the sun's temperature, energy generation, and solar-terrestrial relations.

Karl Hufbauer

Bibliography

DeVorkin, D.H. "Defending a Dream: Charles Greeley Abbot's Years at the Smithsonian." *Journal for the History of Astronomy* 21 (1990): 121–135.

Hoyt, D.V. "The Smithsonian Astrophysical Observatory Solar Constant Program." *Reviews of Geophysics and Space Physics* 17 (1979): 427–458.

Hufbauer, K. *Exploring the Sun: Solar Science since Galileo*. Baltimore: Johns Hopkins University Press, 1991.

Kidwell, P.A. "Prelude to Solar Energy: Pouillet, Herschel, Forbes and the Solar Constant." *Annals of Science* 38 (1981): 457–476.

Willson, R.C., and H.S. Hudson. "The Sun's Luminosity over a Complete Solar Cycle." *Nature* 351 (1991): 42–44.

Solar Parallax

Solar parallax, the shift in the sun's position as seen from widely separated parts of the earth (or from the same part after the earth's rotation has carried it to a widely separated position), is a measure of the distance to the sun. This quantity, one of the fundamental astronomical constants, cannot be observed directly because of atmospheric effects on the solar limb. But by observing the positional shift in a nearby planet such as Mars or Venus, the relative proportions of planetary distances being known from Kepler's third law, the solar parallax and the scale of the solar system may be inferred.

Because solar parallax held the key to the scale of the solar system, it was a long-sought quantity. In 1672 Richer at Cayenne and Cassini in Paris observed Mars and determined a solar parallax of 9.5 seconds of arc, corresponding to 87 million miles. Venus approaches closer to the earth and therefore has a larger parallax than Mars, but since it is so close to the sun, its parallax can be observed only when Venus passes in front of the sun, the so-called transits of Venus. This phenom-

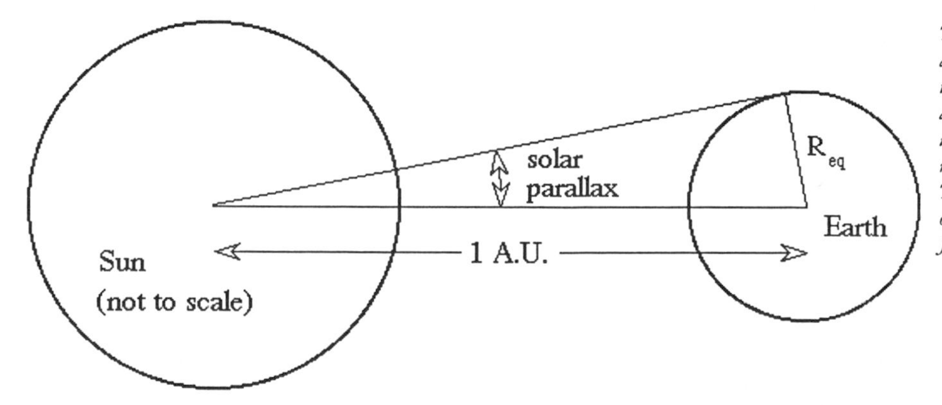

The solar parallax is the angle subtended by the equatorial radius of the earth at a distance of 1 astronomical unit, that is the mean annual distance to the sun. This angle is 8.8 seconds of arc. (Figure by Charles J. Peterson)

enon occurs only every 105 and 121 years, and then in pairs, so their occurrence was the occasion for great expeditions beginning in 1761 and 1769. These results gave a solar parallax of 8.5776 arcseconds (95.5 million miles), but problems with the data did not give cause for confidence in this result. The improvement in instrumentation and the application of photography to astronomy caused astronomers to redouble their efforts in 1874 and 1882. The results even from those observations gave values between 8.76 and 8.85 arcseconds, still leaving an uncertainty of about 1.5 million miles.

In 1897 the minor planet Eros was discovered; because it occasionally approaches the earth closer than Mars and Venus it was used in 1900 and 1930 to give a value of 149,670,000 km, with an uncertainty of 25,000 km. Modern radar measurements give the distance to the sun as 149,597,892 km with an uncertainty of only a few kilometers; the associated solar parallax is 8.794148 seconds of arc.

Steven J. Dick

Bibliography

Woolf, H. *The Transits of Venus: A Study of Eighteenth Century Science.* Princeton: Princeton University Press, 1959.

Solar Physics

Tracing its origins back to the discovery of sunspots, solar physics takes the sun's constitution and behavior as its purview. This astronomical field has passed through four epochs since the early seventeenth century and is now well into its fifth. Throughout these centuries, tools for investigating the sun have become ever more diverse and discriminating; the phenomena under scrutiny, ever more numerous and precisely characterized; and the models for relating the phenomena to one another, ever more inclusive and robust. It is small wonder that successive generations of scientists interested in the sun have been confident that their knowledge of our star surpassed that of preceding generations.

The founding epoch of modern solar science (ca. 1610–1810) began when a handful of investigators directed the first telescopes at the sun. Making the most of his observations, **Galileo Galilei** argued that sunspots revealed that the sun is not only rotating but also, contrary to Aristotelian doctrine, mutable. Galileo's stance on this as well as a host of related issues helped set the stage for René Descartes's advocacy three decades later of an infinite universe in which the sun is a star and all stars are suns. Some four decades later, **Gian Domenico Cassini**, **John Flamsteed**, and Isaac Newton inaugurated a tradition of mensuration and calculation that by the 1780s yielded values for the sun's distance, size, and mass within 10 percent of today's values. All the while, curiosity as to the nature of sunspots—which Galileo had likened to clouds and Descartes to dross—continued unabated. The most prominent astronomer to take up this issue in the late eighteenth century was **William Herschel**. Embracing Alexander Wilson's hypothesis, he maintained that sunspots were holes in the sun's incandescent atmosphere that give glimpses of its solid surface. He even went so far as to contend that the sun and other stars must, in accord with the principle of plenitude, all be inhabited.

The first narrative account of solar science's development between Galileo and Herschel appeared in Hufbauer (1991), who stitched it together by drawing upon earlier biographical and thematic work (see his bibliographical essay and references). A useful recent study is Legrand et al.'s review of seventeenth-century sunspot and auroral observations, which refines the argument built during the last two decades for the occurrence of a sustained minimum in solar activity between 1670 and 1710. More scholarly attention should be given in future studies to the ways in which new facts and ideas about the sun figured in the emergence of modern science during the seventeenth and eighteenth centuries. What role, for instance, did Galileo's arguments from sunspots about the nature of the sun have in the debates over and the ultimate triumph of Copernicanism? How did successive observers interested in the sun's rotation rate use their views on scientific progress to interpret the discrepancies between their predecessors' and their own results? And how effectively, to judge from textbooks and encyclopedias, were the broader scientific intelligentsia in Britain, France, and Germany kept abreast of the growth of knowledge about the sun?

Solar science's second epoch (ca. 1810–1910) commenced with the establishment of observing programs and interpretive frameworks of such puissance that they gave rise in the 1860s to the specialty of solar physics. The new observing programs were devoted to mapping the dark-line spectrum of sunlight, to studying the sun's chromosphere and corona during eclipse, and to monitoring sunspot numbers and distribution. In 1817, Joseph Fraunhofer reported that the solar spectrum contains many fixed lines, publishing a map of nearly five hundred of them. Some fifteen years later, David Brewster mapped about two thousand Fraunhofer lines in an unconvincing attempt to prove that they arise from absorption by nitrous oxide. Soon thereafter, James Forbes (who was skeptical about Brewster's work) and Francis Baily observed the 1836 annular eclipse, not with the traditional goal of determining its precise timing, but rather to study the spectral and lucent phenomena near the sun's limbs. Their reports, particularly Baily's vivid description of the annulus, inspired numerous astronomers to station themselves along the path of totality during the 1842 total eclipse. Clear views of prominences and the corona along with animated debates concerning their nature induced more and more observers to focus on these phenomena during the 1851 and 1860 total eclipses. In the meantime, Heinrich Schwabe reported in 1843 and again in 1851 that the number of sunspots follows a slow cyclical pattern. Shortly after the second report, Edward Sabine found that the sunspot cycle correlated with a cycle in terrestrial magnetic activity, and Rudolf Wolf adduced historical evidence that the sunspot cycle's average duration is eleven years. These results prompted others to join Schwabe in monitoring sunspots by visual means (notably Wolf and Richard Carrington) and with the aid of photography (Warren de la Rue and his colleagues at Kew Observatory). Before the decade was out, Carrington deduced from his observations that the latitudinal distribution of spots decreases in the course of the sunspot cycle and that the sun rotates faster at the equator than toward the poles.

Meanwhile, other scientists—mostly physicists—were theorizing about thermodynamic and spectroscopic phenomena in ways that would revolutionize ideas about the sun's constitution. In the early 1840s, J. Robert Mayer and John James Waterston independently recognized that chemical and electrical processes are quite insufficient to sustain the sun's output of heat for any sizable length of time, an output that Claude Pouillet had recently estimated could melt terrestrial ice at the rate of 31 meters/year. Both suggested that solar radiation must originate in the conversion of gravitational energy into heat. A decade later, Hermann Helmholtz and William Thompson popularized this idea as they expounded the new principle that energy is conserved. They argued first that simple gravitational contraction powers the sun, and second, that meteoric infall does so. Some five years later yet (1859), Robert Bunsen and Gustav Kirchhoff made a good case that each element has a distinctive spectral signature and started decoding the sun's Fraunhofer lines. Perhaps inspired by the nebular cosmogony that implied that all solar system bodies are composed of the same elements, Kirchhoff looked for evidence of the common terrestrial element iron in the solar spectrum. He soon found that the bright lines in iron's flame spectrum coincided with several of the lines on Fraunhofer's original map.

During the 1860s, scientists on both sides of the Atlantic seized the opportunities inherent in the new observing programs and theoretical tools to create a specialty oriented community focused on solar physics. Unlike most earlier contributors to solar science, many of these pioneers—notably, de la Rue, Balfour Stewart, and **J. Norman Lockyer** in England, **P. Jules Janssen** in France, **Angelo Secchi** and Pietro Tacchini in Italy, Wolf in Switzerland, Gustav Spörer in Germany, Anders-Jonas Ångström in Sweden, and Charles Young in the United States—dedicated all, or at least a large fraction, of their research to the goal of expanding scientific knowledge of the sun. They monitored the sunspot cycle, made atlases of the solar absorption spectrum and identified numerous lines, improved the characterization of the sun's differential rotation, registered the profiles of the sun's atmospheric layers during eclipses, and devised spectroscopic methods for monitoring prominences outside eclipse. Expecting that all this research should be transformative, these men were open to arguments against solid- and liquid-body models of the sun. By 1870, following the lead of Secchi, Thompson, and especially Hervé Faye, most solar physicists pictured the sun as a rotating gaseous sphere in which gravitational contraction generates heat that is convected turbulently to the photosphere and chromosphere and then radiated through the lucid corona into space.

The ensuing two decades were a period of consolidation. In addition to improving instrumentation and becoming comfortable with photography, pioneering solar physicists, their recruits, and other scientists interested in the sun managed to establish solar observing programs at several astrophysical as well as ordinary observatories. But their results seemed anticlimactic when compared with those from the 1850s and 1860s. Disappointed, some recruits—such as Hermann Vogel, **Edward Pickering**, and **James Keeler**—turned their attention from the sun to the stars.

George E. Hale rang out solar physics' second epoch by revitalizing the field during the quarter century before World War I. He won a name for himself in the early 1890s with his invention of the **spectroheliograph** for securing monochromatic images of the sun. Capitalizing on this feat, Hale went on to become the University of Chicago's first professor of astrophysics (1892), to establish the *Astrophysical Journal* (1895), to found **Yerkes Observatory** (1897) and then Mount Wilson Solar Observatory (1904), to organize the International Union for Cooperation in Solar Research (1904), and to show that sunspots are seats of intense magnetic fields (1908). His successes as an organizer and fundraiser were due in no small part to his eloquence in using the solar-stellar analogy to argue that solar and stellar research were mutually reinforcing activities. Notwithstanding his rhetorical, and practical, support for stellar research, Hale was optimistic that solar physics, with its focus on the nearest star, would set the pace in laying bare the secrets of all the stars.

Solar science's second epoch has received considerable attention from historians. Clerke included several sections about solar research in her magisterial history of nineteenth-century astronomy, deftly interweaving thumbnail sketches of key figures into a lively narrative of the main observational and interpretive advances. Seventy years later, Meadows seems to have relied heavily on Clerke's history in assembling and introducing many seminal texts of early solar physics. Hufbauer (1991) definitely did so in his treatment of the era even though he ended up paying much greater attention than either Clerke or Meadows to the social and institutional dimensions of the solar-physics community's emergence and early history. The rich biographical and thematic literature cited by Hufbauer has recently been augmented in important ways by three historians. Pang (1991, 1993) has explored how British scientists both depended upon and gave expression to their nation's imperialistic culture as they organized for, conducted themselves on, and reported about eclipse expeditions during the half century before World War I. Becker has described William Huggins's solar researches—especially his promising but ultimately unsuccessful attempts to photograph the corona outside of eclipse—in her discerning analysis of his astrophysical research agenda. Lastly, Hentschel (1993) has examined how Henry Rowland's improvement of spectroscopic gratings enabled him and an assistant to discover in the early 1890s that many Fraunhofer lines have slight red shifts when compared with the corresponding laboratory lines.

There remain, of course, many questions regarding nineteenth-century solar science that deserve closer scholarly attention than they have yet received. How rapidly and for what reasons, for instance, did support among astronomers and natural philosophers for Herschel's solid-body model of the sun wane between 1840 and 1870? When and how did those eclipse observers who regarded the corona as a solar feature prevail over those who attributed this phenomenon to the earth's or moon's atmosphere? How did the solar-physics community's membership, structure, and relations with the disciplines of physics and astronomy evolve during the community's first half-century? And how did these changes influence the ways in which the community argued over interpretations of solar phenomena and its leaders presented solar physics's claims to the larger world?

Solar physics' third epoch (ca. 1910–1940) opened with advances in physics and astronomy that soon dissipated any expectations that the specialty would set the pace in deciphering the stars. In physics, Ernest Rutherford and Niels Bohr laid what became the basis for solving basic stellar, including solar, problems by establishing that atoms are nuclei surrounded by electrons in quantized orbits. And in astronomy, **Arthur Stanley Eddington** and **Henry Norris Russell** adumbrated the role that theorizing would henceforth play in solar and stellar research by analyzing the equilibrium of giant stars.

This is not to say that solar physics ceased to exist during the interwar years. Quite the contrary. Monitoring of solar phenomena became ever more thorough and inclusive after World War I as a result both of increasing patronage for solar observing programs and of increasing coordination from the International Astronomical Union's solar commissions and the International Research Council's Solar-Terrestrial Commission. Moreover, Hale and his colleagues at Mount Wilson Observatory demonstrated the existence of a twenty-two-year magnetic cycle in solar activity and helped establish an association between solar flares and sudden ionospheric disturbances causing fadeouts in short-wave radio transmission. Finally, instrumentalists not only improved the standard tool kit for observing the sun but also augmented it—most notably with Hale's spectroheliscope, Bernard Lyot's coronagraph, and Robert McMath's spectroheliokinematograph. But, solid as these and similar achievements were, they contributed much less to the basic changes in the picture of the sun that occurred during this epoch than did the researches of those using the new physics to theorize about the sun and other stars. Four lines of inquiry yielded results of particular significance.

Inaugurated by Eddington in 1916–1917, the first line of theorizing focused at the outset on the structure of giants—that is, stars that Russell and independently **Ejnar Hertzsprung** had found to be exceptionally large and hence diffuse. Eddington, supposing that the giants are essentially huge gas balls, maintained that these stars are in equilibrium because gravity is counterbalanced by the pressure of the outflowing radiation. Following up on Eddington's theory, Russell soon examined the restorative processes that would maintain the equilibrium of such a star. For all its attractiveness, however, the theory of the radiative equilibrium was at first limited in its applicability to the rarified, and rare, giants. In 1924, Eddington stunned the astronomical world by using available data regarding stellar luminosities and masses to argue that the sun and other ordinary stars, despite having a central density well above that of water, are also in radiative equilibrium. He supported this counterintuitive conclusion by pointing out that the temperatures in stellar interiors are so high that the matter there would consist not of atoms, but rather of their constituent electrons and nuclei. Thus, drawing on **stellar statistics** and atomic theory, Eddington made what was rapidly judged by most astronomers to be a convincing case that the sun behaves in accord with the simplest gas laws.

The second line of inquiry was initially devoted to ascertaining elemental abundances in the atmospheres of the sun and stars by analyzing their spectra with the aid of atomic theory. In the early 1920s, **Meghnad Saha**, and following him, E. Arthur Milne and Ralph Fowler, prepared the way for such work with theoretical studies of the influence of temperature, pressure, and relative abundances on line intensities. Not long after, Cecilia Payne used their results to interpret stellar spectrograms in **Harvard College Observatory** collection. Her research strongly indicated that hydrogen is much more abundant than all the other elements in stellar atmospheres. However, deferring to Russell's then-persuasive arguments for the late-nineteenth-century idea that the sun and stars are composed of a terrestrial mix of elements, she ended up rejecting this prescient conclusion as spurious. Over the next few years, as it happened, Russell's ongoing efforts to ascertain elemental abundances from solar spectra led him to Payne's conclusion. His arguments in 1929 for hydrogen's preponderance in the sun's atmosphere quickly won assent for this recently heretical idea. Three years later, Eddington and **Bengt Strömgren**, impelled by Milne's questioning of Eddington's theory of stars, went on independently to argue that hydrogen must be quite abundant not only in stellar atmospheres but also in stellar interiors. By the mid-1930s, therefore, the theorists had built a strong case that hydrogen is far and away the most common element in the sun.

The third line of theorizing was directed at identifying the source of stellar energy, a problem that had been posed anew between 1917 and 1920 when Eddington and **Harlow Shapley** established that stars have ages greatly in excess of gravitational contraction's paltry time scale of tens of millions of years. Eddington suggested in 1920 that the source would almost certainly turn out to be either electron-proton annihilation or element building, subatomic processes that would afford stellar lifetimes in the trillions or billions of years respectively. Through the 1920s, he and most other theorists favored the annihilation hypothesis. Attention shifted during the early 1930s to the element-building hypothesis. One reason for this shift was that quantum mechanics and then accelerator experiments indicated that protons could penetrate into nuclei at the temperatures thought to prevail in stellar interiors. Another was that studies of the universe's expansion and the dynamics of star clusters pointed to a cosmic time scale of billions of years. Several theorists—most of them, physicists—attempted to identify the energy-generating thermonuclear reactions. Finally in 1938, **Hans Bethe** came up with a robust scenario. He maintained that ordinary stars are powered by two reaction chains that cook protons up into helium nuclei—cooler stars by a chain beginning with proton-proton fusion, hotter stars by a cycle starting with proton-carbon fusion. Accepting the theoretical astrophysicists' values for the sun's central temperature, density, and composition, Bethe built a powerful case that the helium-building CNO cycle is the main source of solar energy. Immediately hailed as a breakthrough, his solution to the stellar-energy problem became the new starting point for most research on the internal constitution and evolution of the sun and stars.

The fourth line of theoretical inquiry concentrated on deciphering the corona's unique emission spectrum. This spectrum, which numbered about twenty bright lines by 1930 and, thanks to Lyot's researches with the coronagraph, twenty-four by 1938, had been attributed for decades to an unknown element dubbed "coronium." Although theoretically minded spectroscopists no longer accepted this view in the 1930s, they were not convinced that any of the many attempts at linking lines to familiar elements had yielded anything other than a coincidental match. Such skepticism was the prevailing response in 1939 to Walter Grotrian's attribution of two lines to rare transitions of highly ionized iron atoms. The only one to follow up was Bengt Edlén, whose experimental results had served as one basis for Grotrian's proposal. By extrapolating from his published and unpublished data, the Swedish spectroscopist managed to attribute another thirteen lines to highly ionized iron, nickel, and calcium. Once announced in 1941, Edlén's solution to the coronal-line problem was swiftly acclaimed. At the same time as he resolved this enigma, however, he created a more profound one—to explain why the corona's temperature exceeds the photosphere's by two orders of magnitude.

Hufbauer (1991) drew upon his own prior researches as well as a goodly number of historical studies in fashioning the first overview of solar science's development during its third epoch. In later studies (1993a, 1994), he has examined the origins, character, and reception of Lyot's and Edlén's respective breakthroughs on the problems of observing the corona outside eclipse and of identifying the coronal lines. Meanwhile, in the course of analyzing the astronomical response to general relativity, Hentschel (1992) has written a superb monograph on the Einstein-Turm that reveals the inner workings of Germany's leading center for solar research between the world wars and two articles (1992b, 1993) on gravitational red shift that skillfully delineate the practice of precision solar spectroscopy between 1917 and 1925. In addition, DeVorkin (1993) has presented a sensitive account of Saha's early researches and their crucial role in stimulating work on elemental abundances in solar-stellar atmospheres.

Despite fairly intense scholarly labors on this epoch for the last decade and a half, many issues still await full historical treatment. How, for instance, did eclipse experts, who were primarily interested in the sun, pursue their research agendas while simultaneously responding to the widespread interest in using eclipses to test general relativity? How did Albrecht Unsöld and other theorists incorporate quantum mechanics into solar spectroscopy and with what consequences for the practices of data acquisition and theories about the sun's atmosphere? How did theoretical astrophysicists and physicists depend upon and compete with one another in seeking to identify the energy-generating processes in the sun and stars? And why, how, and with what success did solar physicists join into the investigation of solar-terrestrial relations?

Opening with World War II, solar physics' fourth epoch (ca. 1940–1960) was mainly characterized by the growth of solar observing capabilities. During the war, solar physicists in Germany, the United States, England, Australia, and the Soviet Union worked with radio scientists and the military to establish or reorient solar monitoring programs in hopes that the resulting data would facilitate wartime communications. These programs left a legacy consisting not only of new monitoring stations (especially in Germany) but also of a postwar readiness by military and civil authorities to fund solar research, especially in the United States, Australia, and the Soviet Union. Indeed, this readiness gave rise to three major solar observatories—the High Altitude Observatory in Boulder, Colorado; the Sacramento Peak Observatory at Sunspot, New Mexico; and the Astrophysical Observatory in the Crimea.

As solar physicists were acquiring new telescopes and improving their instrumentation, outsiders were extending the range of phenomena that could be observed. During World War II, three radio scientists—James Hey, George Southworth, and Grote Reber—independently detected radio emissions from the sun. Once hostilities were over, several groups followed up these discoveries. Joseph Pawsey and his colleagues at the Radiophysics Laboratory near Sydney were the most successful. In 1946, they strengthened Hey's case that sunspots emit radio waves and, with the aid of ionospheric physicist David Martyn, interpreted the continuous component of solar radio emission as confirmation that the corona is every bit as hot as indicated by Edlén's line identifications. During the next decade or so, the Australians continued to lead the way in observing the radio sun by constructing, most notably, the first radiospectrograph (1949) and the first radioheliograph (1957).

Meanwhile, scientists using rocket-borne instruments were securing the first observations of the ultraviolet and X-ray sun. During World War II, Erich Regener coordinated efforts in Germany to instrument a V-2 rocket for scientific observations from above most of the earth's atmosphere. Although Regener's group did not get a launch before the war's end, scientists in the United States were soon invited by the military to equip captured V-2s with scientific payloads. In 1946, Richard Tousey's group at the Naval Research Laboratory obtained the first solar ultraviolet spectrum with the aid of a spectrograph aboard the twelfth V-2 launched at White Sands Proving Ground. Three years later, a group led by Tousey's colleague Herbert Friedman acquired the first electronic record of solar ultraviolet and X-rays by means of telemetry from a photon counter aboard the forty-ninth V-2. During the 1950s, these and a few other groups in the United States and Soviet Union steadily increased the versatility of rockets as platforms for studying radiation from the sun and, in doing so, helped set the stage for the use of satellites as solar observing platforms.

A third important extension of the observational range was achieved in the early 1950s by Horace Babcock, a stellar physicist at Mount Wilson Observatory. At the behest of his father (who had participated in Hale's studies of solar magnetism), Babcock took on the challenge of devising a means of observing weaker fields than those found in sunspots. He drew on knowledge of electronics gained during World War II to devise the first solar magnetograph. This enabled Babcock and his father to map field patterns on the solar disk and hence to inaugurate research on the links between detailed features of the sun's magnetic field and numerous solar phenomena besides sunspots.

The International Geophysical Year (IGY), which took place during 1957–1958, gave those who had been developing solar observational capabilities since World War II ample opportunity to prove themselves. The organizers of this huge cooperative study of the earth's constitution and behavior regarded the collection of extensive solar data as crucial for advancing knowledge of solar-terrestrial relations. Accordingly, IGY participants observed the sun from around, and above, the globe with optical telescopes, coronagraphs, magnetographs, radio telescopes, and rocket-borne ultraviolet and X-ray instruments. Among their many results, the most striking was Friedman's demonstration that X-ray bursts from solar flares cause the sudden ionospheric disturbances that are responsible for short-wave fadeouts. However, another IGY result lacking any immediate connection to solar physics—the *Sputnik*-triggered space race—would soon be recognized as IGY's largest contribution to solar observing.

Compared with the expansion of the solar armamentarium during and after World War II, concurrent advances in solar theory were, for all their importance, unspectacular. Throughout the epoch, theoretically minded solar physicists and theoretical astrophysicists interested in solar spectra labored steadily, and with numerous successes, at deciphering the details of the sun's absorption and emission spectra. This theorizing about the solar atmosphere was complemented by separate researches on both the interior of and material effluxes from the sun. In the late 1940s, theoretical astrophysicists interested in stellar structure concluded from systematic endeavors to model the sun that its internal temperature is around 15 million degrees and consequently that its main power source is the helium-building reaction chain beginning with proton-proton fusion instead of the CNO cycle. And during the 1950s, Ludwig Biermann and especially Eugene Parker argued that the hot corona expands outward as a solar wind that causes disturbances in the geomagnetic field, auroras toward the terrestrial poles, and a persistent antisolar orientation of cometary ion tails.

Hufbauer (1991) utilized many sources and historical studies, especially some ongoing projects about early solar research with radio antennae and rocket-borne instruments, in surveying the growth of solar observational capabilities from World War II through the IGY. He also described the work of Biermann and especially Parker on the solar wind. Wolfschmidt has since scrutinized Karl-Otto Kiepenheuer's success in creating a wartime solar-monitoring network for Germany and its partial survival into the postwar era. More important, DeVorkin (1992) has published a superb monograph about the American conduct of upper-atmosphere and solar research with V-2 rockets. Opportunities still abound in this epoch for historical work on large questions. How, for example, did entrepreneurial solar physicists like Leo Goldberg, Walter O. Roberts, John W. Evans, and Andrei Borisovich Severny harness Cold War patronage and with what consequences for their research programs? How, as radio and rocket scientists obtained solar spectra of higher quality during the 1950s, did theoretically minded solar physicists weave these data into their evolving picture of the photosphere and its relations to the chromosphere and corona? And how did the ambitious IGY solar-monitoring programs influence the structure and goals of the solar-physics community?

Because solar physics' present epoch (since ca. 1960) is not only very rich but also incomplete, any attempt to sustain the narrative style used for the preceding four epochs would be folly. It suffices for the present purposes to note that patronage for solar research grew substantially between the early 1960s and mid-1970s and, despite many setbacks thereafter, remains well above its earlier levels; that ever more sophisticated instruments for observing solar radiations and particles have been mounted at ground-based facilities, placed on rockets and spacecraft, and even located in deep caverns; that the observers using these instruments have significantly augmented empirical knowledge of the sun; that theorists working with the new observational results have elaborated increasingly robust solar models; and that, accompanying all these changes, solar physics has evolved from a specialty into a subdiscipline with its own journal (*Solar Physics*, 1967–) and distinct sections in national disciplinary associations.

With the aid of a few specialized historical and sociological studies, Hufbauer (1991) sought to explain and characterize the growth of solar observational capabilities and the evolution of the solar-physics community's institutions since *Sputnik*. He also recounted the labors of space scientists and those theorists having access to their data to establish the solar wind's existence and explore its structure and the multipronged campaign by instrumentalists and solar physicists to demonstrate and then explain the variability of the sun's radiant output. In a subsequent study (1993b), he examined the role of European space scientists in securing approval of a joint out-of-ecliptic mission to observe the sun from high heliographic latitudes.

Even more so than for the fourth epoch, opportunities abound in the present epoch for historical work on large questions. For instance, how effectively have the planners and decision-makers at the National Aeronautics and Space Administration—the largest patron of solar research since the early 1960s—gone about allocating resources for solar instruments, missions, data collection and analysis, and theorizing? How have reductions in funding for solar research since the mid-1970s affected the solar-physics community's recruitment and retention, structure, and aspirations? How have solar theorists interacted with observers in modeling the solar dynamo since Horace Babcock's pioneering theory of the early 1960s? (Or in developing helioseismology since Franz-Ludwig Deubner's confirmation in 1975 of the proposal that the 5-minute solar oscillations are acoustic waves? Or in modeling solar structure since the second-generation neutrino detectors came on line in the early 1990s?) And how, as the ability to observe phenomena like activity cycles, coronae, and winds elsewhere in the galaxy has improved, have solar and stellar physicists cooperated and competed in unriddling the stars?

Karl Hufbauer

Bibliography

Becker, B.J. "Eclecticism, Opportunism, and the Evolution of a New Research Agenda: William and Margaret Huggins and the Origins of Astrophysics." Ph.D. dissertation, Johns Hopkins University, 1993.

Clerke, A.M. *A Popular History of Astronomy during the Nineteenth Century*. 4th ed. London: Black, 1902.

DeVorkin, D. *Science with a Vengeance: How the Military Created the U.S. Space Sciences after World War II*. New York: Springer, 1992.

———. "Saha's Influence in the West: A Preliminary Account." In *Meghnad Saha Birth Centenary Commemoration Volume*, edited by S.B. Karmohapatro, 154–202. Calcutta: Saha Institute of Nuclear Physics, 1993.

Hentschel, K. *Der Einstein-Turm: Erwin F. Freundlich und die Relativitätstheorie—Ansätze zu einer 'dichten Beschreibung' von institutionellen, biographischen und theoriengeschichtlichen Aspekten*. Heidelberg: Spektrum Akademischer Verlag, 1992a.

———. "Grebe/Bachems photometrische Analyse der Linienprofile und die Gravitations-Rotverschiebung: 1919 bis 1922." *Annals of Science* 49 (1992b): 21–46.

———. "The Conversion of St. John: A Case Study on the Interplay of Theory

and Experiment." *Science in Context* 6 (1993): 137–194.
———. "The Discovery of the Redshift of Solar Fraunhofer Lines by Rowland and Jewell in Baltimore around 1890." *Historical Studies in the Physical and Biological Sciences* 23 (1993): 219–277.
Hufbauer, K. *Exploring the Sun: Solar Science since Galileo*. Baltimore: Johns Hopkins University Press, 1991.
———. "Breakthrough on the Periphery: Bengt Edlén and the Identification of the Coronal Lines, 1939–1945." In *Center on the Periphery: Historical Aspects of 20th-Century Swedish Physics*, edited by S. Lindqvist, 199–237. Canton, Mass.: Science History Publications, 1993a.
———. "European Space Scientists and the Genesis of the Ulysses Mission, 1965–1979." In *Science beyond the Atmosphere: The History of Space Research in Europe: Proceedings of a Symposium Held in Palermo, 5–7 November 1992,* edited by A. Russo, 171–191. Florence: European Space Agency, 1993b.
———. "Artificial Eclipses: Bernard Lyot and the Coronagraph, 1929–1939." *Historical Studies in the Physical and Biological Sciences* 24 (1994): 337–394.
Legrand, J.-P., M. le Goff, C. Mazaudier, and W. Schröder. "L'activité solaire et l'activité aurorale au XVIIe siècle." *Académie des Sciences: Comptes rendus: La Vie des Sciences* 8 (1991): 181–219.
Meadows, A.J. *Early Solar Physics*. Oxford: Pergamon, 1970.
Pang, A.S.-K. "Spheres of Interest: Imperialism, Culture, and Practice in British Solar Eclipse Expeditions, 1860–1914." Ph.D. dissertation, University of Pennsylvania, 1991.
———. "The Social Event of the Season: Solar Eclipse Expeditions and Victorian Culture." *Isis* 84 (1993): 252–277.
Wolfschmidt, G. "Kiepenheuers Gründung von Sonnenobservatorien im Dritten Reich: Kontinuität der Entwicklung zur internationalen Kooperation." *Deutsches Museum: Wissenschaftliches Jahrbuch* (1992/1993), 283–318.

Solar System Astronomy

Until the mid-twentieth century, solar system research was an integral component of astronomy. After the launch of *Sputnik* in 1957, the Soviet Union, the United States, and other nations dramatically increased funding for planetary exploration, creating greatly expanded training programs, dedicated publications, new instruments (including direct investigation by spacecraft), and interdisciplinary research institutes. Thereafter, solar system astronomy became increasingly separate from its parent discipline. In time, solar system astronomy emerged as an interdisciplinary undertaking linked to developments in geochemistry, geophysics, meteorology, and geology as well as to **astrophysics**. The history of solar system research in the twentieth century thus encompasses two distinct historical periods; its history is also intertwined with that of other scientific communities bordering on astronomy.

By the end of the nineteenth century, solar system astronomy consisted of two distinct branches: **celestial mechanics** and physical studies of the moon, planets, satellites, and smaller bodies gravitationally bound to the sun. Because of the great importance many nations placed on the production of nautical almanacs for navigation and for surveying, celestial mechanics remained a central program at national observatories. Many astronomers concentrated on making improvements to planetary theories developed by **J.L. Lagrange**, **P.-S. Laplace** and their French contemporaries in the late eighteenth century. Determining the precise dimensions of the solar system was critical to this endeavor, and the **transits of Venus** in 1874 and 1882 provided important opportunities to measure the **solar parallax**. Other astronomers—including the growing number of researchers associated with private observatories and academic institutions—focused on computing orbits for comets and asteroids using new analytical methods. **Giovanni Schiaparelli** at Milan's Brera Observatory investigated connections between comets and meteor showers during the 1860s. American astronomers **Hubert A. Newton** of Yale and Daniel Kirkwood of Indiana University were also active in this field.

Astronomers also attempted to assess the physical characteristics of the moon and planets. Making sketches of Mars and the major planets were commonplace activities at many observatories in the United States and Europe. Efforts to map the lunar surface continued through the late nineteenth century, including the work of James Nasmyth, James Carpenter, W.H. Pickering, and J.F.J. Schmidt. These activities were aided by the construction of large refracting telescopes. Astronomers with access to large refractors carried out inventories of the solar system. In 1877,

Asaph Hall used the U.S. Naval Observatory 26-inch refractor to discover the two satellites of Mars, while **E.E. Barnard** found Jupiter V (Almathea) with the 36-inch refractor at Lick in 1892. The application of photography to astronomy in the late nineteenth century led to a dramatic rise in the number of known asteroids, particularly through the research of the German astronomer Max Wolf. Another stimulant to planetary astronomy was speculation about the possibility of life on other planets, an old tradition reinvigorated by observations of Mars with large refracting telescopes. In the 1890s, Percival Lowell used his private fortune to build the first major American observatory dedicated to the study of solar system objects. He also championed the idea that **Mars** was crossed by canals constructed by intelligent beings, an idea that quickly entered American popular culture and created intense controversy among astronomers, particularly in the United States and Great Britain.

In the early twentieth century, studies of planetary gravitational theory remained a primary interest of astronomers at national observatories such as Greenwich and Pulkovo, although leadership in this field increasingly passed to individuals at university research centers. Henri Poincaré's influential investigations of the equilibrium of rotating liquids and his mathematical research on the tides of the oceans strongly influenced the astronomical-geophysical investigations of George Darwin and later Harold Jeffreys, both at Cambridge University. In America, **Ernest W. Brown** at Yale continued the work of **G.W. Hill**, concentrating on the theory of the moon's orbit. New research schools of celestial mechanics emerged at a number of universities, including that of Willem de Sitter at Leiden. The extremely rapid rate of discovery of asteroids through photographic surveys inspired researchers to focus on this subject. By the 1930s, August Kopff made asteroid orbital studies a major undertaking at the Berlin Recheninstitut, while the Soviet astronomer **B.V. Numerov** made the Leningrad Astronomical Institute a center for this work. While World War II disrupted research programs, military interest in applying high-speed computing devices to ballistics led to new theoretical and applied studies of planetary orbits. In less than a decade, the prospect of launching artificial satellites and spacecraft caused the rapid expansion of celestial mechanics, principally in the United States and the Soviet Union.

Astrophysical studies of solar system phenomena also increased during the twentieth century. Although astronomers found it easier to apply photographic, spectroscopic, and photometric techniques to stellar and galactic phenomena than to solar system bodies (in part because of technical factors such as the difficulty of photographing extended images), some researchers brought these tools to bear on variety of solar system problems. Bernard

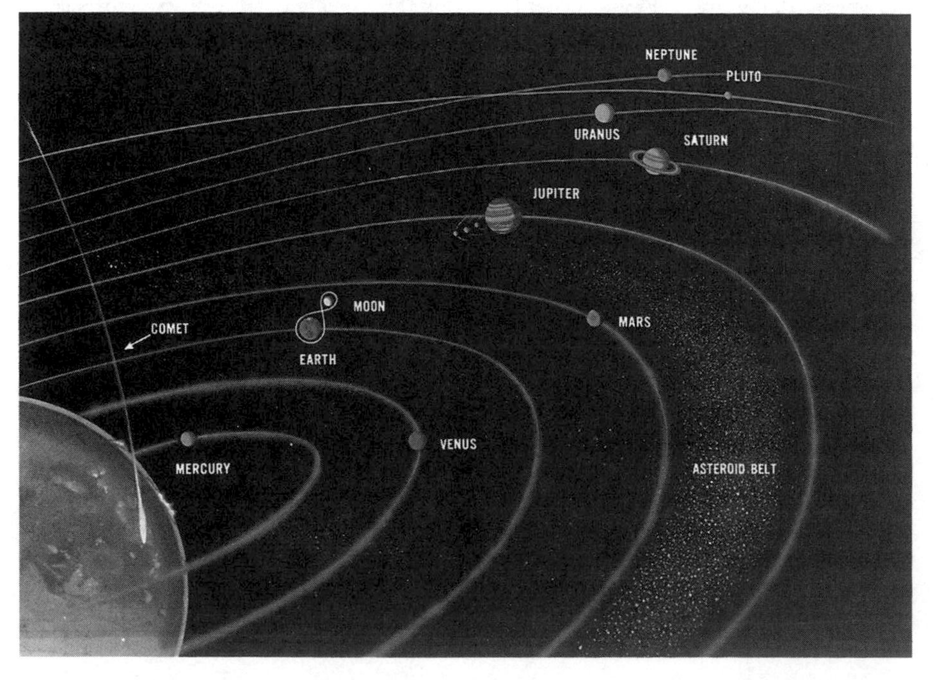

The solar system. The first four planets are solid objects composed of rock. Mercury is the innermost planet, followed by Venus and earth. Comets often pass between Mercury and the sun and a few crash into the sun, drawn by its gravity. Beyond earth lies Mars and the asteroid belt. Then come the giant planets, composed primarily of gas. Jupiter is the largest, followed by Saturn, Uranus, Neptune, and Pluto. Note that the orbit of Pluto is so eccentric that at times it moves inside the orbit of Neptune. (Courtesy of the National Aeronautics and Space Administration)

Lyot investigated the polarization of planetary atmospheres and the lunar surface from the Pic du Midi Observatory, while astronomers at the Mount Wilson, Lick, and Lowell observatories in the United States investigated the composition of planetary atmospheres.

Many astronomers were interested in understanding the origin and boundaries of the solar system as well as its relation to interstellar material. The early twentieth century saw important investigations in the origin and physical structure of meteors, comets, and asteroids. Sometimes these programs were inaugurated by smaller observatories such as Cincinnati and Iowa. Major programs developed at leading astronomical centers including Harvard and Berlin-Babelsberg. In the Soviet Union, research programs involving planetary atmospheres, polarization studies, and meteor investigations were led by S.V. Orlov, V.V. Sharonov, and Nicolas P. Barabashov. Cosmogony remained an especially attractive topic to many astronomers and astrophysicists. **Henry Norris Russell**, Carl F. von Weizsäcker, **Gerard P. Kuiper**, and **Viktor Ambartsumian** all contributed to this field, as did researchers at the Schmidt Institute of Geophysics in Moscow.

Because of its interdisciplinary nature, solar system research was particularly concerned with professional boundaries separating astronomy from neighboring disciplines. These boundaries varied from nation to nation. Patronage was also an important influence on the growth of the field. Government support, especially after World War II, made it possible to develop interdisciplinary research projects, such as Carlyle S. Beals's efforts at the Dominion Observatory (Ottawa) to search for ancient meteorite craters on the Canadian Shield. Military patronage proved critical to the growth of this field. Interest in using meteors to probe the upper atmosphere led to military support for Fred L. Whipple's extensive meteor program at Harvard and Bernard Lovell's radar meteor work at Manchester University's Jodrell Bank. Organizations such as the British Astronomical Association and the U.S. Association of Lunar and Planetary Observers supported visual studies of the moon and planets. The **International Astronomical Union** (IAU) maintained commissions devoted to planets and satellites, celestial mechanics, comets, meteors, and the zodiacal light. These commissions coordinated research programs.

Controversies over theories in solar system astronomy often showed evidence of national styles in science. U.S. astronomers reached different conclusions concerning the origin of comets than their counterparts in Great Britain because of differing emphasis on mathematical models. Interdisciplinary work in solar system astronomy was not always easy to maintain. The efforts of Gerard Kuiper and the physical chemist Harold C. Urey to build a field of planetary astrochemistry ended in bitter controversy over methodology and professional standards.

After the launch of *Sputnik* in October 1957, solar system astronomy expanded rapidly and became a distinct field of research. Soviet and American spacecraft began reaching the moon and nearby planets in the late 1950s and early 1960s. The U.S. government established the **National Aeronautics and Space Administration** (NASA) to promote space and solar system exploration in 1958 and the European Space Research Organization, predecessor to the European Space Agency, was founded in 1964. Astronomers were recruited by these agencies. Numerous journals were created, including *Planetary and Space Science, Astronomiia Solntse, Luna, Planety* (Solar system astronomy), and *Icarus*. International symposia on solar system topics multiplied rapidly. New research institutions devoted to solar system astronomy were also founded, including the Lunar and Planetary Laboratory of the University of Arizona, while the **Pulkovo Observatory** and the Sternberg State Astronomical Institute in Moscow developed research programs in the field. Despite increasing conflicts with astrophysicists over access to telescopes, disputes over graduate training, and attempts by professional geophysics organizations to appropriate solar system research, many American solar system astronomers remained affiliated with astronomy. In 1968, U.S. astronomers created the Division of Planetary Sciences as a division of the American Astronomical Society. The field continued to fragment into overlapping subspecialties as research programs matured.

Until recently, virtually all historical accounts of solar system astronomy have emphasized its intellectual aspects. In the last few years, more attention has been paid to the institutional and social context in which research was conducted, including the influence of patronage on research programs and instrumentation, and the relation of solar system astronomy to its parent discipline. New work on nineteenth-century astronomy has emphasized the ways in which priority disputes, national rivalries, and observing strategies influenced research programs; while other studies have focused on the production of knowledge at the major government observatories. Robert W. Smith, for example, has demonstrated the influence of the Cambridge network in the discovery of **Neptune**. Smith and others have examined the deployment of skilled workers and routinized patterns of observations and reduction at the Greenwich Observatory, suggesting a factory structure of organization. Since solar system research remained a principal task of national observatories during this period, these accounts are relevant to the history of the subject as a whole. Other works analyze traditions of mathematical astronomy within various national and institutional contexts.

The historiography of the field in modern times is less well defined. A number of works have treated the founding of the **Lowell Observatory** and the Mars canal controversy that Lowell precipitated; most conclude that the controversy cost Lowell Observatory professional support from American astronomers and dampened professional enthusiasm for visual studies of the planets. Other works have addressed specific research problems that bordered on solar system astronomy, including efforts to investigate possible impact features on the earth and the moon and research into cosmogony. Aside from these detailed studies, few historians have addressed the twentieth-century history of this field. Until recently, most writers have termed this a period when solar system astronomy was abandoned by astronomers in favor of stellar and galactic research, and defined the post-*Sputnik* era as a virtual rebirth of the field. New studies have challenged this view by examining the continuing development of research programs in planetary atmospheres, meteors, and celestial mechanics from the early twentieth century. With few exceptions, most accounts of planetary exploration in the NASA era have been written by participants and journalists. While many contain useful information, most devote relatively little attention to institutional issues and focus on individual missions rather than underlying research problems or conflicts over instrumentation. A few historians have examined U.S. institutions central to solar system astronomy after 1960, including the **Jet Propulsion Laboratory** and NASA itself, and a valuable account of lunar exploration in the NASA era has recently appeared. These studies, Tatarewicz (133) writes, indicate that the "pace and direction" of solar system research after 1960 "depended on considerations far beyond the scientific desiderata developed by the research community itself." Among these considerations were strategic military planning and political judgments about the international prestige value of space exploration during the Cold War. Historical studies of Soviet cosmogony during the 1930s and 1940s, by contrast, have focused on the political and ideological battles that clouded this research.

Very few aspects of solar system astronomy have received extended historical treatment. Research is needed on celestial mechanics in the nineteenth and twentieth centuries, particularly on the relationships that emerged between mathematical astronomers and university departments of mathematics. Little is known about the emergence of interdisciplinary solar system research in Europe or the Soviet Union. Also absent are comparative studies aimed at revealing how existing disciplinary boundaries in different national contexts shaped research in this field. Additional work is required to assess the ways in which solar system research influenced work in other fields of astronomy, as well as in neighboring disciplines such as geochemistry and geophysics. Another important area of investigation still virtually untouched is the relationship between amateur and professional research in the twentieth century, particularly for nations (including France and the USSR) where amateur activity was often a prelude to professional training. Equally neglected, given their importance to mid-twentieth-century science and politics, are the lunar and planetary missions that began in the late 1950s and early 1960s. While several studies place them within the context of Big Science, additional work is needed on the design and planning of planetary missions, the construction of new instruments, and the theoretical agendas that mission planners addressed. Conspicuously absent are studies of solar system research in the Soviet Union and China during the twentieth century, except for Soviet work on cosmogony. Within these national contexts, attention should be given to political and ideological factors no less than intellectual and institutional issues. A synthetic overview of the field's growth and external relations in the mid- and late twentieth century is also needed.

Manuscript collections of individual astronomers who undertook research in solar system astronomy during the nineteenth century, including **E.E. Barnard** (Vanderbilt University Library) and William H. Pickering

(Harvard Archives) are particularly helpful for understanding solar system astronomy in the late nineteenth and early twentieth centuries. Archival holdings are also available for twentieth-century astronomers including G.P. Kuiper (University of Arizona Library), F.L. Whipple (Harvard University Archives), B. Lyot (Archives of the Observatoire de Paris), and N.P. Barabashov (State Archives of Kharkov District, Ukraine). Institutional and organizational records include the Lowell Observatory (Flagstaff, Arizona), the National Aeronautics and Space Administration (NASA History Office, Washington, D.C.), the archives of the Jet Propulsion Laboratory (Pasadena, California), and the Department of Space History, National Air and Space Museum, Smithsonian Institution, Washington, D.C. Oral history interviews with solar system astronomers are available at the Department of Space History at National Air and Space Museum as well as at the Center for History of Physics of the American Institute of Physics, College Park, Maryland.

Ronald E. Doel

Bibliography

Brush, S.G. "Planetary Science: From Underground to Underdog." *Scientia* 113 (1978): 771–787.

———. "From Bump to Clump: Theories of the Origin of the Solar System 1900–1960." Edited by P. Hanle and V.D. Chamberlain. In *Space Science Comes of Age: Perspectives in the History of the Space Sciences.* Washington, D.C.: Smithsonian Institution, 1981.

———. "A History of Modern Selenography: Theoretical Origins of the Moon, from Capture to Crash, 1955–1984." *Space Science Reviews* 47 (1988): 211–273.

Burrows, W.E. *Exploring Space: Voyages in the Solar System and Beyond.* New York: Random House, 1990.

Crowe, M. *The Extraterrestrial Life Debate: The Idea of a Plurality of Worlds from Kant to Lowell.* New York: Cambridge University Press, 1986.

DeVorkin, D. "W.W. Campbell's Spectroscopic Study of the Martian Atmosphere." *Quarterly Journal of the Royal Astronomical Society* 18 (1977): 37–53.

Doel, R.E. "Evaluating Soviet Lunar Astronomy in Cold War America." *Osiris* 2nd series 7 (1992): 238–264.

———. *Science on the Periphery: Solar System Astronomy in America, 1920–1960.* New York: Cambridge University Press, 1996.

Herrmann, D.B. *The History of Astronomy from Herschel to Hertzsprung.* Rev. ed. Translated by K. Krisciunas. New York: Cambridge University Press, 1984.

Hoyt, W.G. *Lowell and Mars.* Tucson: University of Arizona Press, 1976.

———. *Coon Mountain Controversies: Meteor Crater and the Development of Impact Theory.* Tucson: University of Arizona Press, 1987.

Koppes, C.R. *JPL and the American Space Program: A History of the Jet Propulsion Laboratory.* New Haven: Yale University Press, 1982.

Levin, A.E. "The Otto Schmidt School and the Development of Planetary Cosmogony in the USSR." In *The Origin of the Solar System: Soviet Research, 1925–1991,* edited by A. Levin and S. Brush, New York: American Institute of Physics, forthcoming.

Logsdon, J.M. "Missing Halley's Comet: The Politics of Big Science." *Isis* 80, no. 302 (1989): 254–280.

Mikhailov, A.A., et al. *Astronomiya v SSSR za Sorok Let 1917–1957.* (Forty years of astronomy in the USSR, 1917–1957.) Translated by J. Willis et al. St. Louis, Mo.: Aeronautical Chart and Information Center, Linguistic Section, 1960.

Murray, B.C. *Journey into Space: The First Thirty Years of Space Exploration.* New York: Norton, 1989.

Smith, R.W. 1989. "The Cambridge Network in Action: The Discovery of Neptune." *Isis* 80, no. 303 (1989): 395–422.

———. "A National Observatory Transformed: Greenwich in the Nineteenth Century." *Journal for the History of Astronomy* 22, no. 67, part 1 (February 1991): 5–20.

Tatarewicz, J.N. *Space Technology and Planetary Astronomy.* Bloomington: Indiana University Press, 1990.

Taton, R., and C. Wilson, eds. *Planetary Astronomy from the Renaissance to the Rise of Astrophysics. The General History of Astronomy, vol. 2B.* New York: Cambridge University Press, forthcoming.

Taylor, R.J., ed. *The History of the Royal Astronomical Society. Vol. 2: 1920–1980.* Oxford: Blackwell Scientific Publishers, 1987.

Vucinich, A. *Empire of Knowledge: The Academy of Sciences of the USSR.* Berkeley: University of California Press, 1984.

Whitaker, E. *The University of Arizona's Lunar and Planetary Laboratory: Its Founding and Early Years*. Tucson: University of Arizona, 1985.

Wilhelms, D.E. *To a Rocky Moon: A Geologist's History of Lunar Exploration*. Tucson: University of Arizona Press, 1993.

Solar Tower Telescope

This is the name for a solar telescope designed to have a very long focal length (usually hundreds of feet), with the optics arranged vertically on top of a tower. The long focal length is simply to provide a large solar image; the vertical deployment of the optical path was conceived to improve the stability of an image over that obtained with a horizontal path.

The first tower telescope was erected at the Mount Wilson Solar Observatory in 1907 by **George Ellery Hale**. It was a 65-foot steel tower that held a coelostat and second mirror, and a 12-inch objective with a 60-foot focal length. The coelostat and second mirror support were provided by the Brashear Optical Shops and were probably designed by Frank Wadsworth. Hale noted that the tower telescope accomplished the purposes for which it was designed, namely to provide a better defined image than his horizontal Snow telescope and to keep the figure of the mirror stable in spite of the heat of the sun.

In his analysis of the proposed telescope, Hale notes that he was led to the vertical path concept by his own observations on Mount Wilson, by comments of astronomer Edwin Frost, and a published paper by H.C. Plummer on coelostats used with long-focal-length telescopes.

Hale's success ultimately led to the construction of tower telescopes of varying heights and design at every observatory whose research involved solar physics. Famous telescope-makers such as **Zeiss**, Grubb-Parsons, and Warner and Swasey were active in the design and construction of many systems. Modern designs include vacuum telescopes (the light passes from the objective to the photographic plate in a tube from which the air has been evacuated) with objectives up to 60 inches in diameter.

Louis F. Drummeter Jr.

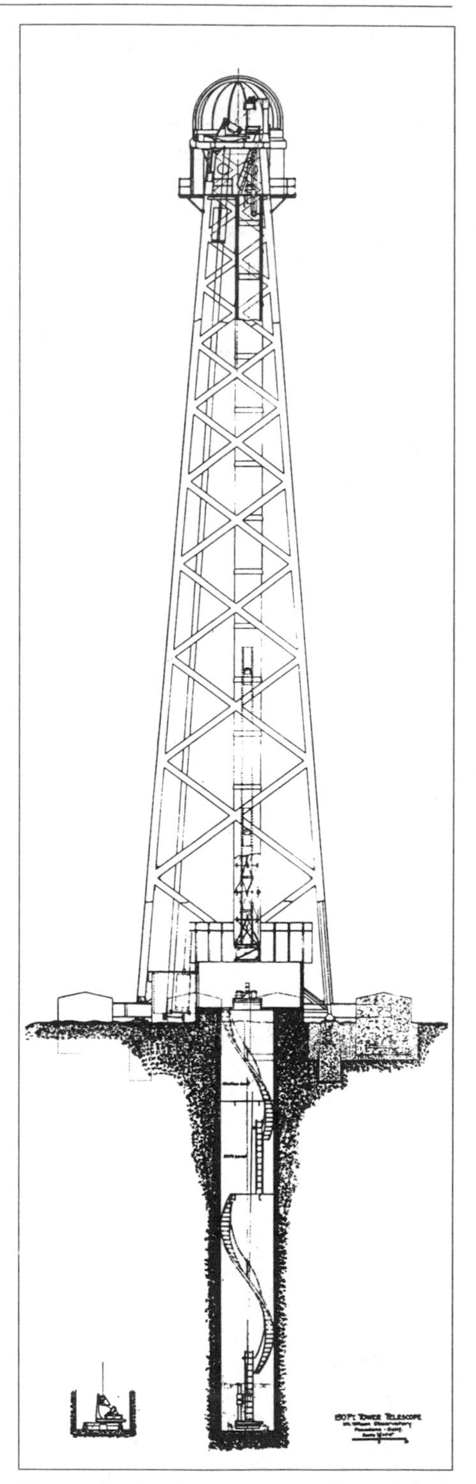

The 150-foot solar telescope on Mount Wilson. Sunlight falls on a 19-inch coelostat mirror that sends the beam to a 15-inch flat mirror. This mirror reflects the sunlight vertically to a 12-inch objective lens with a focal length of 150 feet. The lens forms an image of the sun in the observing room at the base of the tower. The area below ground houses a spectrograph that makes it possible to observe the solar spectrum at very high resolution. (Courtesy of the Huntington Library and Carnegie Observatories)

Bibliography

Abetti, G. "Solar Physics." In *Das Sonnensystem, Handbüch der Astrophysik*, edited by G. Eberhard, A. Kohlschütter, and H. Ludendorff, vol. 4, 57–230. Berlin: Springer, 1929.

Hale, G.E. "A Vertical Coelostat Telescope." *Astrophysical Journal* 25 (1907): 68–74.
King, H.C. *The History of the Telescope*, 338–342, 381–382, 388. High Wycombe: Charles Griffen, 1955; reprint, Dover, New York (1979).

Somerville, Mary Fairfax Greig (1780–1872)

Scottish scientific expositor. Somerville was largely self-taught in mathematics and astronomy. Encouraged by her second husband, the physician William Somerville, she carried out an extensive correspondence with contemporary British mathematicians and astronomers. This, combined with her own diligence, led to *Mechanism of the Heavens* (1831), an annotated English translation of the first four books of Pierre-Simon Laplace's *Mécanique céleste*. The book established her reputation for clearly representing scientific ideas. In *On the Connexion of the Physical Sciences* (1834), she offered a lucid account of contemporary physics and astronomy. Somerville also published two papers on possible physical effects of sunlight. She was elected an honorary member of the Royal Astronomical Society, and awarded a government pension in recognition of her contributions to science.

Peggy A. Kidwell

Bibliography

Patterson, E.C. *Mary Somerville and the Cultivation of Science 1815–1840*. Boston/The Hague/Dordrecht/Lanchester: Martinus Nijhoff, 1983.
Somerville, Mary. *Personal Recollections from Early Life to Old Age of Mary Somerville with Selections from her Correspondence.* Edited by Martha Somerville. London: John Murray, 1874.

South African Astronomical Observatory

Founded in 1820 for the improvement of astronomy and navigation by the British Government as the Royal Observatory at the Cape of Good Hope, it was located near Cape Town, capital of Cape Colony. The observatory site was chosen by the first astronomer, the Rev. Fearon Fallows, a Cambridge graduate. The stone building comprised two double-story residences connected by an east-west structure where the mural circle and transit circle were housed. After Fallows died, Thomas Henderson took over in April 1832 but remained only a short time before becoming **Astronomer Royal** for Scotland in 1834. Only after his return to Europe did he find time to analyze observations of alpha Centauri that provided the first measured stellar parallax. German astronomers, however, published before Henderson.

Thomas Maclear, a medical doctor and active member of the group that founded the Royal Astronomical Society (London) arrived in January 1834. Sir **John Herschel** came to the Cape at about the same time and spent four years observing the southern skies from a location near the observatory. Maclear and Herschel worked closely together. In 1835 **Charles Piazzi Smyth**, son of the distinguished double star observer Admiral W.H. Smyth, became Maclear's assistant. Steeped in astronomy from birth (he was named for the great Sicilian astronomer Giuseppe Piazzi), Smyth was a dedicated observer, mechanically ingenious, and a pioneer in several areas of astronomical research. Smyth became Astronomer Royal for Scotland in 1846. Maclear's instructions included repetition of the measurement of the arc of the meridian made by the French astronomer **Nicolas-Louis de Lacaille** in 1752. That result, used to measure the polar flattening of the earth, was not in agreement with other observations carried out in Europe and Latin America. After much difficulty, the error in Lacaille's work was traced to gravitational deflection caused by mountains. The survey was extended beyond Lacaille's original arc to northern Namaqualand. During Maclear's tenure, new instruments were added, the staff increased, and a time ball erected for the benefit of shipping. Maclear retired in 1870. He and his wife are buried at the observatory. Edward James Stone, from the **Royal Observatory at Greenwich**, replaced Maclear, but was mainly concerned with publishing his predecessor's work.

In 1879 **David Gill** was appointed Astronomer Royal at the Cape. Born in Aberdeen and educated at the university under James Clerk Maxwell, Gill was especially adapt in the development and manipulation of new forms of astronomical instrumentation and in 1870 became director of the observatory of Lord Lindsay at Dun Echt. Gill developed new observing programs to determine the **solar parallax** using the **heliometer**. His success in this work led to the Cape appointment. Gill modernized the observatory and, aided by a young American, W.L. Elkin, began a series of heliometer observations in order to refine the value of the solar parallax. He also used this information to improve the value for the lunar mass as well as the mass of the earth. In addition, Elkin and Gill measured nine stellar parallaxes. With the aid of a local photographer, Gill obtained images of the great comet of 1882. These plates also revealed many stars. This led to the first use of photography for astrometric purposes, the *Cape Photographic Durchmusterung*. The plates were made at the Cape using a specially designed telescope and measured at Groningen, Holland, by **Jacobus C. Kapteyn**. Gill helped organize the International Astrographic Congress, which met in Paris in 1887. Out of the 1887 meeting came the *Carte du Ciel*, an international project designed to map the whole sky using photography. Gill undertook the zone between –40 to –52 degrees.

In 1883 Gill promoted geodetic surveys carried by the army along the border of German South West Africa (now Namibia) and into tropical East Africa. Gill designed a new transit circle of vastly improved performance and acquired a twin refractor with a 24-inch photographic objective and 18-inch visual objective (the Victoria Telescope). At retirement in 1907, Gill left the Cape the premier southern observatory with a tripled staff, expanded facilities, and modern instrumentation.

Gill was succeeded by his chief assistant, Sydney Samuel Hough, whose interest lay in the study of **stellar statistics**. He was succeeded in turn by Harold Spencer Jones, a Cambridge graduate and former chief assistant at Greenwich. During his years at the Cape, Spencer Jones produced an enormous output of astrometric and astrographic data as well as some spectroscopy. He also began a large project for the precise determination of the solar parallax using the minor planet Eros. He became Astronomer Royal in 1933. In spite of problems connected with World War II, John Jackson continued Spencer Jones's programs.

Richard Hugh Stoy became chief assistant in 1935, and was appointed H.M. Astronomer at the Cape in 1950. Important work in photometry developed at the Cape after the appointment of Durban amateur A.W.J. Cousins in 1946. Stoy and Cousins developed the standard photometric system of the southern sky and reconciled it with work in the north. After the war, programs at the Cape continued to change. In 1951, Cape astronomers were given substantial observing time on the 74-inch reflector at Radcliffe Observatory, Pretoria, and David S. Evans moved from Pretoria to become chief assistant. Evans undertook research in stellar spectroscopy, especially of nearby stars. The Cape Observatory was active in the International Geophysical Year, monitoring solar flares and tracking satellites.

There were many changes in the postwar years. The nominal merger of the Cape Observatory with the Royal Greenwich Observatory (by then relocated to Herstmonceux) submerged the Cape's identity, but did lead to useful staff exchanges. Supervision passed from the Admiralty to the British Science and Engineering Research Council. In 1965 Evans led a search for a new remote dark-sky site. He also urged a merger of the three major South African astronomical research institutions (the Cape, Radcliffe, and Republic observatories). Subsequent political developments led to a number of staff resignations, and it appeared that the Cape would be closed down. However, an agreement with the South African Council for Scientific Research led to the creation of the South African Astronomical Observatory (1972), and after some difficulty establishing new administrative patterns, the staff was increased, instruments modernized, and the new institution has since turned out important research in all fields of astrophysics from gamma rays to the infrared.

David S. Evans

Bibliography

Evans, D.S. *Under Capricorn: A History of Southern Hemisphere Astronomy*. Bristol and Philadelphia: Adam Hilger, 1987.

Gill, D. *History and Description of the Cape Observatory*. London: Admiralty, 1913.

Warner, B. *Astronomers at the Royal Observatory Cape of Good Hope*. Cape Town and Rotterdam: Balkema, 1979.

Soviet Astronomy

Like most Russians, Russian astronomers greeted the popular revolution that toppled the czarist government in March 1917 with enthusiasm. Like most of the academic and professional communities, however, they were much less accepting of the Bolshevik coup d'etat that followed eight months later. The Russian Civil War of 1918–1920 and the Entente naval blockade that accompanied it completely cut off Russian astronomers from their international colleagues. Supplies of photographic plates and even astronomical ephemerides, all of which came from the West, dried up, and Russian astronomers were able to continue their observing programs only with the greatest of difficulties. The Civil War disrupted normal commerce, and astronomers were forced to plant vegetable gardens in order to avoid starvation. Electrical power was spotty, and the severely inflated money supply made it difficult to purchase even such basic supplies as candles. Moreover, the principal Russian observatory at Pulkovo served as a battleground on two occasions.

Despite the severe strains of war, famine, and social disruption, Russian astronomy survived the Civil War to continue its work in the new Soviet state. The difficulties of the period even forced improvisations that would later blossom into scientific schools and institutions. Most notably, in 1919 **Boris Vasil'evich Numerov** founded the Computing Institute to calculate astronomical ephemerides, filling the void left by the disappearance of ephemerides from abroad. In the following years this modest undertaking expanded and gained in stature as it became the Leningrad Astronomical Institute and later the Institute of Theoretical Astronomy. Today it is recognized as one of the world's leading centers for theoretical astronomy and **celestial mechanics**.

The New Economic Policy (NEP) pursued by the Soviet government in the 1920s provided a respite for Soviet astronomers. International ties were restored, and a number of Soviet astronomers were able to travel to the West for conferences and to accept temporary appointments at Western observatories. Astronomers from throughout the Soviet Union gathered on four occasions for astronomical conventions, and the *Astronomicheskii zhurnal* (Astronomical journal) made its appearance. Amateur astronomy enjoyed great popularity during the 1920s, and such future leaders of Soviet astronomy as **Viktor Amazaspovich Ambartsumian** and Boris Vasil'evich Kukarkin began their careers in the amateur organizations during the 1920s. In 1928 Kukarkin published the first issue of *Peremennye zvezdy* (Variable stars), which helped to turn the Soviet Union into a recognized leader in the field of variable stars.

The 1920s were problematical for astrophysics, however. The severe lack of funds for even basic maintenance of existing observatories obviated the possibility of building new Soviet observatories that could equal the standard of American and European institutions such as Mount Wilson. Thus the State Astrophysical Institute, founded in 1921 and later renamed the Shternberg Astronomical Institute, remained an organization without any significant observational potential. Nevertheless, **Vasilii Grigor'evich Fesenkov**, **Boris Petrovich Gerasimovich**, and a handful of other Soviet astrophysicists began to acquire world-class reputations during this period.

If the 1920s allowed Soviet astronomers a measure of autonomy, the 1930s were to bring severe repression. Joseph Stalin replaced NEP with a policy of rapid industrialization and collectivization of agriculture. This was accompanied by a period of cultural revolution from 1928 through 1931 in academic and professional circles during which any scientist with a pre-1917 education was considered politically unreliable and during which all scientific disciplines were required to demonstrate their relevance to the industrialization program. The Russian Association of Astronomers was forced to disband in 1930 and was replaced by the government-controlled All-Union Astronomical-Geodesical Society. The directors of a number of observatories were removed and replaced by non-astronomers who were appointed by the government.

The political climate moderated somewhat from 1932 through 1935, but the onset of the Great Purges in 1936 brought disaster to Soviet astronomy. Over two dozen astronomers were arrested between March 1936 and July 1937—almost all of them perishing in prison, labor camps, or in front of firing squads. This represented between 10 and 20 percent of all professional astronomers in the Soviet Union at that time. Given that the list of those arrested included the most outstanding Soviet astronomers, the consequences for astronomical science in the Soviet Union were devastating. Many research programs were abandoned, and many of the most important observatories and committees lost their directors and chairmen. The situation deteriorated still further during World War II, when several observatories, including Pulkovo, were destroyed and many astronomers became casualties of war. Other astronomers were evacuated to research centers in Siberia and the Central Asian republics of the Soviet Union.

The end of World War II brought great hopes for moderation of Soviet domestic and foreign policies. Indeed, the period from 1945 through 1947 gave Soviet astronomers some reasons for optimism after eight years of repression and war. The Academy of Sciences announced that **Pulkovo Observatory** would be rebuilt, and one of the most respected Soviet astronomers, the astrometrist **Aleksandr Aleksandrovich Mikhailov**, was named to direct the rebuilt observatory. Construction of the **Crimean Astrophysical Observatory** (CAO), the first Soviet observatory with true astrophysical capabilities, began in 1944, and it was soon followed by other new observatories such as the Biurakan Observatory in Armenia and the Main Astronomical Observatory of the Ukrainian Academy of Sciences.

The period from 1945 to 1947 brought renewed contacts between Soviet and Western astronomers. CAO director **Grigorii Abramovich Shain** was allowed to lead a delegation of Soviet astronomers on an eight-month trip to the United States to purchase new astronomical instruments, and in 1947 A.A. Mikhailov led an expedition to observe a total solar eclipse in Brazil.

All causes for optimism had vanished by 1948, however. With the Cold War deepening, a new wave of repressions and xenophobia swept through the Soviet Union. This period was characterized by ideological rigidity in all fields. The science of genetics was outlawed, and at a 1948 conference Soviet astronomers loudly denounced Western cosmologists for their ideological errors. Soviet scientists, including astronomers, could publish their works only if they acknowledged the superiority of dialectical materialist methodology and included obligatory testimonials to Stalin. They also had to claim Russian precedence for nearly all discoveries. The inclusion of such claims and political statements in scientific works combined with the nearly complete isolation of Soviet astronomers caused great consternation in the international astronomical community.

A definite and long-lasting improvement in the political climate in the Soviet Union came only with the death of Joseph Stalin in 1953. This event and the thaw in political and cultural life ushered in by Nikita Khrushchev reopened the doors to international cooperation. The **International Astronomical Union** (IAU) held its 1958 general assembly in Moscow, and V.A. Ambartsumian served as IAU president from 1958 through 1961. Exchanges and cooperative research programs, cut off since the 1930s, were resumed.

In the 1950s and 1960s Soviet astronomy expanded into new fields. **Iosif Samuilovich Shklovskii** led Soviet advances in radio **astronomy** and the search for extraterrestrial civilizations. Alla Genrikhovna Masevich, a specialist in stellar structure and evolution, pioneered the field of space geodesy.

Following the launch of *Sputnik-1* in 1957, the Soviet Union began an impressive series of missions for space astronomy and interplanetary exploration. These have ranged from the initial *Luna-3* mission of 1959 to photograph the far side of the moon through the *Vega* missions to Venus and Comet Halley in the 1980s. The USSR Academy of Sciences founded the Space Research Institute in 1965 specifically to coordinate Soviet research in the space sciences.

Leonid Brezhnev put an end to the liberalizing policies of Khrushchev, and so once again contacts between Western and Soviet astronomers became problematical as Soviet scientists found it difficult to obtain permission to travel abroad. During this period the Soviet Union built the largest optical and radio telescopes in the world: the 6-meter altazimuth reflector and the 600-meter RATAN-600 radio telescope at the Special Astrophysical Observatory in the Caucasus Mountains.

The policy of openness and economic restructuring under Mikhail Gorbachev and the final break-up of the Soviet Union into its constituent republics has brought astronomers of the former Soviet Union to a new crossroads. Political restrictions and repressions have been removed completely, but they have been replaced by economic restrictions that may force a dramatic reorganization of astronomical institutions. The future of astronomy in the former Soviet Union will depend on the progress that astronomers and politicians make in facing and solving the problems associated with making the transition from a command to a market economy.

Robert A. McCutcheon

Bibliography

Dadaev, A.N. *Pulkovskaia Observatoriia: Ocherk istorii i nauchnoi deiatel'nosti* (Pulkovo Observatory: An outline of its history and scientific activity). Leningrad: Nauka, 1972.

Graham, L.R. *Science and Philosophy in the Soviet Union*. New York: Alfred A. Knopf, 1972.

Istoriko-astronomicheskie issledovaniia (Historical-astronomical investigations) 1–21 (1955–1989).

Kolchinskii, I.G., A.A. Korsun', and M.G. Rodriges. *Astronomy, biograficheskii spravochnik* (Astronomers, a biographical handbook). 2nd ed. Kiev: Naukova dumka, 1986.

Lutskii, V.K. *Istoriia astronomicheskikh obshchestvennykh organizatsii v SSSR* (History of voluntary astronomical organizations in the USSR). Moscow: Nauka, 1982.

McCutcheon, R. "The 1936–1937 Purge of Soviet Astronomers." *Slavic Review* 50, no. 1 (1991): 100–117.

Mikhailov, A.A., ed. *Astronomiia v SSSR za sorok let, 1917–1957* (Astronomy in the USSR for forty years, 1917–1957). Moscow: Physical-Mathematical Literature, 1960.

Nicolaidis, E. *Le Developpement de L'Astronomie en U.R.S.S., 1917–1935.* Paris: Observatoire de Paris, 1984.

———. "Astronomy and Politics in Russia in the Early Stalinist Period (1928–1932)." *Journal for the History of Astronomy* 21 (1990): 345–351.

Shklovsky, I. *Five Billion Vodka Bottles to the Moon: Tales of a Soviet Scientist.* Translated by M.F. Zirin and H. Zirin. New York: Norton, 1991.

Vorontsov-Veliaminov, B.A. *Ocherki istorii astronomii v SSSR* (Outline of the history of astronomy in the USSR). Moscow: Physical-Mathematical Literature, 1960.

Vucinich, A. *Empire of Knowledge, The Academy of Sciences of the USSR (1917–1970).* Berkeley: University of California Press, 1984.

Spectroheliograph

The spectroheliograph, generally credited to **George Ellery Hale**, is used to obtain a monochromatic photographic image of the sun in a chosen wavelength. Hale's device was a two-slit spectrograph with a photographic plate. The two slits, movable perpendicular to their length, were the entrance and exit slits of a spectroscope. The sun was imaged on the first (entrance) slit, and the second (exit) slit isolated a narrow spectral band. The sun's image was scanned by moving the entrance slit, and since this caused the spectrum to move, the exit slit was moved at a compensating rate so that the observed wavelength remained unchanged. The image passing through the exit slit was, in spatial detail, the same as that accepted by the entrance slit, hence a monochromatic spatial image of the sun was scanned onto a photographic plate behind the exit slit. This is not the only scanning possibility. For example, the slits can be stationary, and the image and the plate moved. This became the configuration most frequently used. The wavelength chosen is usually a strong solar line: the H or K lines of calcium, or one of the lines of hydrogen.

This device opened up a new era in solar research. It permitted observers to probe the characteristics of various levels of the sun, and temperature, excitation levels, and magnetic fields were revealed with the aid of the invention. Hale used the device regularly from 1891, but noted that he had invented the spectroheliograph in 1889. He was unaware that the idea had been around since about 1870, and that it had even been tried unsuccessfully by several workers. He was also unaware that Henri Deslandres, at the **Meudon Observatory** in France, had also developed a similar device. Both men claimed credit for the invention, and the priority debate was acrimonious. Historians suggest that Hale was the first to get the device to work successfully.

In 1926 Hale developed the spectrohelioscope, a fairly natural extension of the original idea. He wanted some way of watching the transient behavior on the sun, and replaced the slow moving slits with fast oscillating slits, and the photographic plate with the eye. The persistence of vision permitted the observer to see a spatially integrated monochromatic image of the sun and to observe fairly fast variations. Later versions of the device used rotating prisms as scanners, but the subsequent development of reliable, narrow-band optical filters by Bernard F. Lyot and others made the spectrohelioscope obsolete.

Louis F. Drummeter Jr.

Bibliography

Hale, G.E. "Solar Photography at the Kenwood Astro-Physical Observatory." *Astronomy and Astro-physics* 11 (1892): 407–417.

———. "The Spectroheliograph." *Astronomy and Astro-physics* 12 (1893): 241–247.

———. "The Spectrohelioscope and Its Work; Part I." *Astrophysical Journal* 70 (1929): 265–311.

Struve, O., and V. Zebergs. *Astronomy of the 20th Century.* New York: Macmillan, 1962.

Spectroscopes and Spectrographs

A spectroscope disperses white light composed of different wavelengths into a spectrum, which is normally viewed through an eyepiece. One of the simplest arrangements of astronomical spectroscope was the objective prism instrument used by Fraunhofer for solar and stellar spectroscopy in 1814–1815, with which he observed the absorption lines in solar and stellar spectra. A prism was mounted in front of the objective lens of a small telescope in this instrument.

In the mid-nineteenth century, prism spectroscopes employing a slit and collimator were developed for laboratory studies and manufactured by instrument-makers such as Steinheil and Merz in Germany, by Simms, Browning, and the Hilger brothers in England, and by Hoffmann in Paris. Such instruments with one or several flint glass prisms gave improved spectral resolving power (a purer spectrum) and could be mounted at the focus of a refracting telescope. Robert Bunsen and **Gustav Kirchhoff** used a slit spectroscope in 1859 for laboratory and solar spectroscopy, while Lewis Rutherfurd, **William Huggins**, and **Angelo Secchi** all used prism spectroscopes for stellar spectroscopy from 1862 or 1863. For stellar work a cylindrical lens was often employed so as to broaden the star's image on the slit and hence give a widened spectral image.

In 1872, the American **Henry Draper** built an astronomical spectrograph (his term) with which he photographed the first stellar spectrum. These pioneering experiments were taken up by Huggins in London using a quartz optics spectrograph on a reflecting telescope, so as to record ultraviolet stellar spectra for the first time (1876). Similar spectrographs became common at other observatories in the 1880s and 1890s, notably at **Potsdam**, **Lick**, **Yerkes**, **Pulkovo**, Bonn, Cambridge, and Ottawa, though generally mounted on the equatorial refractors then in vogue. Considerable problems were experienced in their use, especially differential flexure and thermal effects, which blurred the photographic image, thereby limiting their use to short exposures.

The objective prism spectrograph was another simple, slitless arrangement of the astronomical spectrograph that proved especially valuable for low-resolution classification spectrography. Edward Pickering at Harvard from 1885 was its most famous promoter, and the **Draper Catalogue of Stellar Spectra** (1918–1924) became the crowning achievement of some three decades of spectral classification work at Harvard.

Diffraction gratings were also used in spectroscopes and spectrographs in the nineteenth century, but their inefficiency initially made the spectral images too weak for all but solar work. Both Anders Ångström (1868) and later **Henry Rowland** exploited for solar spectroscopy their property of a uniform dispersion that they provided. Gratings ruled by Rutherfurd or Rowland were used in astronomical spectroscopes by, for example, Secchi in Rome and **James Keeler** at Lick, but with limited success for stellar sources.

The development of the blazed grating by John Anderson, Rowland's successor at the Johns Hopkins University, revolutionized astronomical spectrography. This grating has a specially shaped groove profile able to concentrate most of the light into a single diffraction order and hence greatly to improve the luminous efficiency. **John Plaskett** in Canada in 1912 and Paul Merrill at Mount Wilson a decade later were the early pioneers. The blazed grating proved valuable for photography in the red and near infrared, where prisms provided inadequate dispersion. Often the

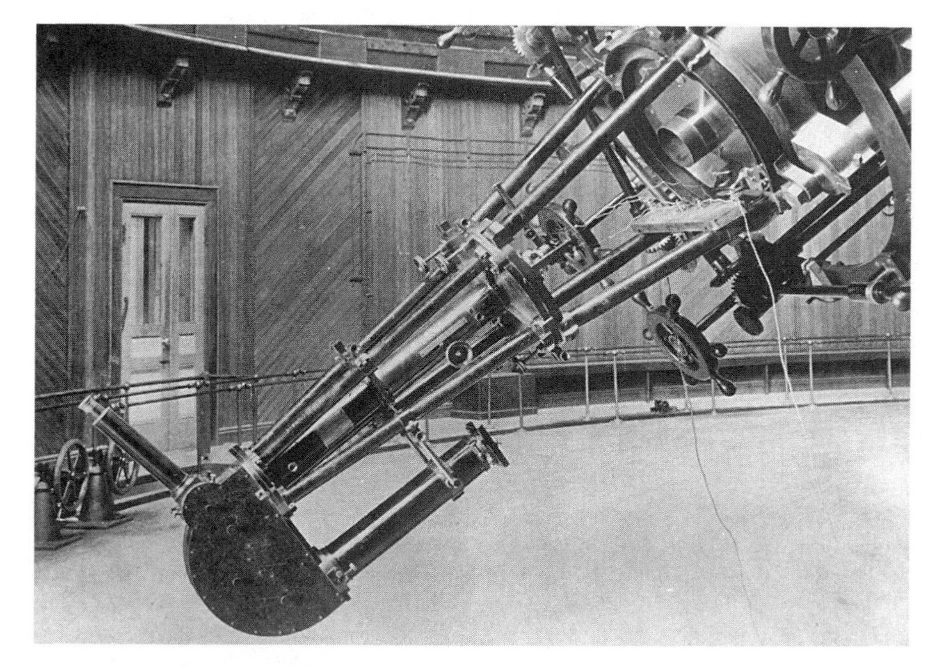

The original Mills spectrograph on the Lick Observatory 36-inch refractor in 1896. From W.W. Campbell and J.H. Moore, Publications of the Lick Observatory *16 (1928).*

blue and red regions could be recorded in one exposure with blazed grating spectrographs.

Although the coudé spectrograph, with its stationary telescope focus, was first devised by Maurice Loewy in Paris in 1883, this concept was really exploited by George Ellery Hale at Mount Wilson on the 60-inch reflector in 1911 and then copied and further refined by **Walter Adams** for the 100-inch coudé in 1925. Initially these were both prism instruments, but Theodore Dunham and Adams in the 1930s made further improvements, installing a large blazed grating in 1931 and Schmidt cameras in 1934 to give a versatile high dispersion stellar spectrograph able to reach relatively faint stars. Flexure problems were completely eliminated in such instruments, while their thermal stability was far superior to cassegrain spectrographs.

After World War II, coudé spectrographs became increasingly popular and were constructed for large telescopes at McDonald, Mount Palomar, Radcliffe, Haute Provence, and Mount Stromlo observatories in the 1950s and 1960s. On the other hand, efficient cassegrain grating instruments were used for lower dispersion observations of fainter stars and nebulae, sometimes in conjunction with image tubes or television cameras to record the spectrum.

J.B. Hearnshaw

Bibliography

Dunham, T. "Methods in Stellar Spectroscopy." In *Vistas in Astronomy* 2 (1956): 1223–1283.

Hearnshaw, J.B. *The Analysis of Starlight.* Cambridge: Cambridge University Press, 1986.

King, H. *The History of the Telescope.* London: Charles Griffin, 1955.

Spectroscopy, Astronomical

Astronomical spectroscopy entails the dispersion of starlight by a prism or grating and the visual inspection or recording of the resultant spectral image. The intensity distribution with wavelength of the continuous spectrum and the strengths, wavelengths, and profiles of the absorption or, occasionally, emission lines in stellar spectra give information on the temperatures, pressures, composition and other physical conditions prevailing in stellar atmospheres (or sometimes in circumstellar or interstellar space), and also on the radial (line-of-sight) and rotational velocities of stars.

This entry discusses the historical development of stellar spectroscopy, but with occasional reference to solar or nebular spectroscopy. The subject is closely linked to developments in laboratory physics, in theoretical physics (especially atomic and quantum physics), and to developments in optical instrumentation and detectors.

In the nineteenth century, stellar spectroscopy developed along three parallel but largely separate paths, namely spectral classification, stellar radial velocities, and spectral analysis. These three branches had relatively few cross-fertilizing interactions until about 1920, and really only merged into one subject of stellar astrophysics in the 1950s. The reasons for these three separate paths and their eventual convergence will be outlined.

Early Stellar Spectral Classification (1814–1922)

The earliest visual observations of stellar spectra were made by Joseph Fraunhofer in 1814–1815. He used an objective prism spectroscope to record numerous absorption lines in the solar spectrum and to describe the spectra of a few bright stars and planets. Later, in 1823, he commented on the clear differences between the spectra of Sirius, Betelgeuse, and Venus, which represents the earliest attempt at stellar spectral classification.

Fraunhofer's work was cut short by his premature death in 1826. His observations were not repeated until the early 1860s, when Giovanni Donati, Lewis Rutherfurd, **William Huggins**, **Angelo Secchi**, **George Biddell Airy**, and probably Carl von Steinheil all independently made observations of stellar spectra. The manufacture of reliable prism spectroscopes in the mid-nineteenth century was one major cause of this rebirth, as well as an understanding for the origin of the spectral lines in the solar spectrum from the work of **Gustav Kirchhoff**, who showed them to arise from the absorption by different elements in the sun's outer layers.

Of these new stellar spectroscopists, Lewis Rutherfurd in New York, like Fraunhofer, placed stars into three broad divisions, based on the appearance of their absorption line spectra. But Angelo Secchi, with his 25-cm Merz refractor at the Collegio Romano Observatory in Rome, soon surpassed Rutherfurd in devising a more comprehensive classification scheme and in observing a larger number of stars (over four thousand). In 1866 he adopted three classes based on Sirius, the sun, and Betelgeuse as type stars, with Orion stars like Rigel being a subtype of Class I. By 1868 he had identified a new, rare, fourth type of star (such as 19 Piscium), which he correctly identified as carbon stars, and in 1877 he assigned emission-line stars (including gamma Casiopeiae) to a fifth class. Secchi's work was highly influential, and his classification was widely used until 1922.

In Germany, Hermann Carl Vogel devised his own independent classification scheme in 1873, initially with seven spectral classes, but he revised this in 1895 following the discovery of helium to include as many as ten classes or subclasses (type Ib showed lines of the new element). Vogel's revised scheme was based on photographic spectra.

Meanwhile, **Edward Pickering** at Harvard launched a large program of stellar spectral classification using objective prism plates in 1885 under the name of the Henry Draper Memorial. The *Draper Memorial Catalogue* (1890) placed over ten thousand stars in a continuous sequence of thirteen spectral types. Later this was developed by **Annie Cannon** and Pickering into the ***Draper Catalogue of Stellar Spectra*** (1918–1924) with nearly a quarter of a million stars. It arranged stars into ten principal spectral types (O, B, A, F, G, K, M, R, N, and S) and nearly fifty subtypes. The Harvard sequence was later recognized as essentially a temperature sequence from hot to cool, except that types R, N, and S represented abundance peculiarities among cool stars. Also sometimes used at Harvard were types P for planetary nebulae and Q (or Pec.) for peculiar emission-line stars, such as novae.

These were not the only spectral classification schemes devised. For example, Antonia Maury at Harvard had an innovative two-dimensional scheme that took line width as well as strength into account, but her work was not favored by Pickering. Joseph Norman Lockyer also classified stars in his own scheme, believing they represented an evolutionary sequence, an idea later supported by **Henry Norris Russell**. However, when the newly founded **International Astronomical Union** (IAU) first met in 1922, the HD Catalogue classification of Pickering and Cannon was officially adopted, thereby making rival schemes obsolete. By this time **Walter Adams** at Mount Wilson with Arnold Kohlschutter had made major progress by taking luminosity effects in classification into account, following the discovery by **Ejnar Hertzsprung** in 1905 that stars classified by Antonia Maury as narrow-lined (or c-type) were in fact high-luminosity or distant stars, since described as supergiants. This discovery of a luminosity effect in stellar spectroscopy, together with other effects based on line-strength ratios, allowed the Mount Wilson observers to classify stars into dwarfs (d), giants (g), or supergiants (c) from 1914, using mainly slit spectrograms from the 60-inch telescope.

By 1922 there were clear indications that the spectral-type sequence was in reality a temperature sequence, based on measurements of stellar energy distributions, stellar colors, and the new Saha theory of ionization, even though the actual temperature scale was poorly determined. That it might also be an evolutionary sequence was advocated by Russell, along the lines proposed earlier by Lockyer. In practice, stellar structure and evolution theory was not nearly advanced enough to give definitive answers to such speculations at this time.

Stellar Radial Velocities (1842–1922)

Christian Doppler's original suggestion of 1842 concerning the colors of stars in motion along the line of sight was corrected by Armand Fizeau (1848) and Ernst Mach (1860) so as to become an effect observable through wavelength shifts of spectral lines. It was not until 1888 that Vogel at Potsdam was able to obtain reliable measurements of stellar Doppler shifts by photography. By the 1890s or early 1900s, several observatories were engaged in measuring Doppler shifts of stars from prismatic slit spectrograms at blue wavelengths. The most active observatory was Lick, where **William Wallace Campbell** undertook a large program from 1903 to measure the Doppler shifts of all stars to magnitude 5.51 in both hemispheres, using the large Lick refractor and a reflector in Santiago, Chile. At Mount Wilson, Walter Adams was also engaged in a large program on fainter stars with large proper motions, using the 60-inch, and, later (with Alfred Joy) the 100-inch telescopes; data for over one thousand stars had been obtained by 1923, while, at Victoria, British Columbia, **John Plaskett** had obtained radial-velocity data for some six hundred proper motion stars on the 72-inch telescope by 1921. Edwin Frost at Yerkes was another noteworthy observer, specializing in the velocities of B-type stars using the 40-inch refractor.

The data on stellar radial velocities had an impact in three areas. First, it was used to explore stellar space motions, by combining the radial-velocity results with those from parallaxes and proper motions. The Mount Wilson observers (Adams, Joy, and Gustav Stromberg) were able to investigate the velocity distribution of stars in the solar neighborhood and to explore the asymmetric distribu-

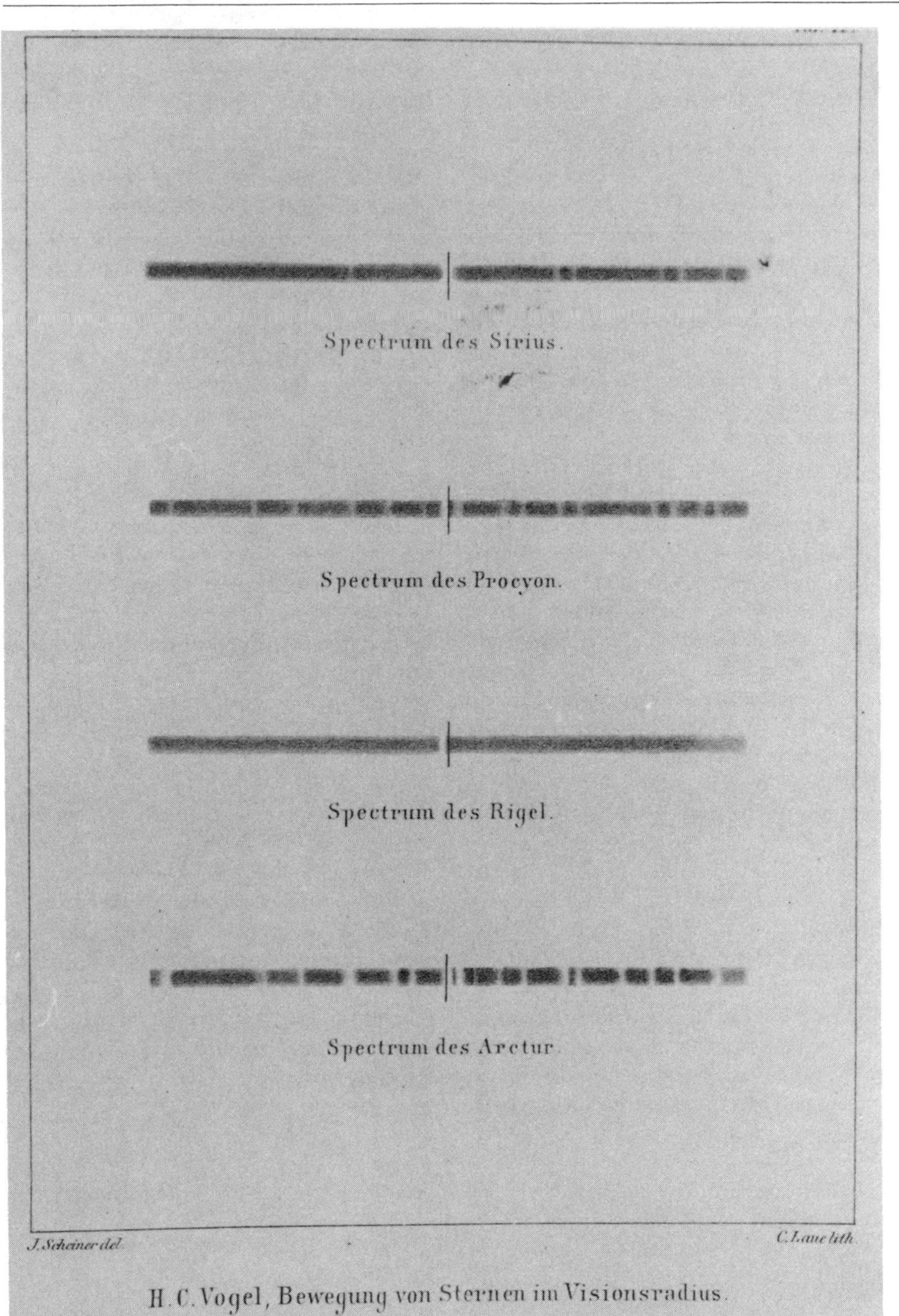

Photographic spectra obtained by H.C. Vogel at the Potsdam Astrophysical Observatory in 1888. These photographs were the first to reliably demonstrate stellar motion in the line of sight. The H-beta line was compared with the spectra produced by a discharge lamp. From H.C. Vogel, "Sitzungsberichte der Königl." *Preussischen Akademie der Wissenschaften zu Berlin (1888).*

tion of velocities due to the high-velocity stars in the galactic halo. The discovery of galactic rotation was the result of this program. Campbell at Lick, on the other hand, investigated the sun's motion relative to the local standard of rest (defined by the mean velocity of nearby stars), and found our peculiar velocity to be nearly 20 km/s.

The other applications of radial-velocity data were the study of orbital motion in binary stars (Vogel and Pickering were the independent discoverers in 1888) and the study of pulsating stars. At first all variable-velocity stars were considered to be binaries, but **Harlow Shapley** and **Walter Baade** showed that the Cepheid variables must be pulsating single stars by analyzing both the radial-velocity and photometric data.

Stellar Spectral Analysis (1814–1922)

Here spectral analysis refers to the interpretation of spectra to determine the composition of and physical conditions prevailing in the source of radiation. The coincidence in wavelength of the solar D lines in absorption with the bright yellow lines seen in many flame spectra had been noted by Fraunhofer in 1814. But several decades of painstaking laboratory analysis by several workers were required before Gustav Kirchhoff was able to announce in 1859 that the sun contains sodium atoms, which are also the cause of the bright yellow lines seen in the laboratory. A key experiment in reaching this conclusion had been performed by Leon Foucault in 1849, when he passed sunlight through a carbon arc containing sodium vapor and found that the D lines were now more strongly in absorption, yet the arc by itself gave these lines in emission. In 1860 Kirchhoff and Robert Bunsen proposed that a detailed analysis of the solar spectrum could now be undertaken. Kirchhoff the following year was able to find wavelength coincidences for at least six elements by comparing solar and laboratory spectra.

When stellar spectroscopy was launched in the 1860s, William Huggins in London was the preeminent pioneer of spectral analysis. His results, at first with the collaboration of William Miller, a chemistry professor, were entirely qualitative, and showed that the same elements present on the earth and in the sun were also distributed throughout the sidereal universe.

Stellar spectra presented a bewildering complexity of spectral lines. By 1897 **Henry Rowland** had catalogued many thousands in the solar spectrum, while at the same time **Julius Scheiner** at Potsdam gave wavelength and element identifications for the spectra of forty-seven bright stars covering a wide range in spectral type. Many important identifications followed, including the carbon bands by Secchi in his Class IV stars, TiO bands by Alfred Fowler (1904) in M stars, and the CH molecule for the solar G-band by Henry Newall (1916). But the most famous identification was Lockyer's discovery in 1868 of helium in the sun's chromospheric spectrum. This was an element at that time unknown on earth and not studied in the laboratory until 1895 by William Ramsay, when it was immediately also found in B stars. However the ionized helium lines in O stars, which Pickering, from his observation of the zeta Puppis spectrum, believed to be due to hydrogen, took some years more to identify, in part because of the difficulty in reproducing them in the laboratory. The problem was solved in 1912 when Fowler reproduced the zeta Puppis lines, which appeared to be between the well-known hydrogen lines of the Balmer series, using a mixture of hydrogen and helium gas in his laboratory. This observation allowed Niels Bohr to identify them with helium, at about the same time that his quantum theory of atomic structure was being devised. The story of helium in solar and stellar spectra thus involved an excellent example of interaction between astronomers, laboratory physicists, and a theoretical physicist.

By the time of the first IAU General Assembly in Rome in 1922, the origin of the green emission lines in gaseous nebulae presented a major problem. The problem became all the more acute as the laboratory spectra of the common light elements in the periodic table became increasingly well catalogued. It was not solved until Ira Bowen in 1928 showed that the lines once ascribed to a new element, nebulium, were in fact due to ionized oxygen, excited under conditions of very low density.

At this time little quantitative analysis of stellar spectra had been undertaken. One exception was the attempt by Johannes Wilsing and Julius Scheiner at Potsdam to measure color temperatures in 1909. They compared the flux gradients (that is, dependence of a star's brightness on color or wavelength) with the theoretical predictions of a Planckian black body, using the data from visual spectrophotometry. A few years later, Hans Rosenberg in Tubingen undertook photographic spectrophotometry for the same purpose. Although substantial systematic errors were made, due to the departure of the energy distribution of stellar radiation from that of black bodies, the first indication that the spectral-type sequence was in fact a temperature sequence came from this important work.

The Birth of Quantitative Astrophysics (1920–1945)

The birth of quantitative astrophysics really began only in the 1920s, spurred by the quantum and atomic theories of Max Planck (1901) and Niels Bohr (1913), and by the work of **Meghnad Saha** (1921) on ionization equilibrium and of Edward A. Milne (1922) on local thermodynamic equilibrium, which governed the structure of stellar atmospheres as well as the degrees of ionization and excitation that prevailed therein.

The stars provided a natural extension of the conditions that could be produced in the laboratory for testing and applying the theories of the new quantum and atomic physics. Saha himself had applied his theory to the Harvard sequence of spectral types in 1921 and, by considering the temperatures at which different lines should show marginal appearances, he demonstrated that this was indeed a temperature sequence. This result was later described by Russell as one of the most important applications of the new physics to the interpretation of stellar spectra. On the other hand, Ralph Fowler and Milne in 1923 criticized Saha for the apparent lack of excitation effects in his analysis and for the unrealistically high pressures he assumed to prevail in stellar atmospheres. Indeed, the details of Saha's temperature calculations are not fully described in his paper. In spite of the remarkable success of his conclusions, some criticism of his methods appears to be justified.

The way was now open for a much more detailed analysis of the lines in stellar spectra of different type, with a view to a quantitative analysis of stellar composition. Cecilia Payne at Harvard for her doctoral thesis under Shapley tackled just this problem by applying Saha's theory of ionization to the great wealth of objective prism spectra obtained at Harvard for classification purposes. The most important outcomes of this work were first, to show the general uniformity of composition from spectral types O to M. This was truly a temperature sequence, or, more strictly, a sequence in which the degrees of ionization and excitation were changing for stars of one type to the next. But composition was essentially the same for all types. Secondly, she demonstrated the great preponderance of the lightest elements, hydrogen and helium, in stars, a tentative result that Cecilia Payne herself may at first have doubted. The implications of the overwhelmingly high abundance of these two elements and the trace amounts of all others were very considerable for theories of stellar structure and evolution, as well as for stellar energy generation and for cosmology. **Otto Struve** described Payne's Harvard dissertation as "the most brilliant ever written."

If Payne had initially had some doubts about the correctness of her conclusions, the detailed spectroscopic analysis of the sun by Russell in 1929, in which the abundances of fifty-six elements were derived after a calibration of the Rowland scale of solar line strengths, fully confirmed the very high abundance of hydrogen. For the heavier elements relatively high abundances of carbon, nitrogen, oxygen and iron were also demonstrated for the first time.

Further advances in quantitative analysis had to await a more complete understanding of the theory of line broadening, of the source of the continuous opacity in stellar atmospheres and the theoretical modeling of stellar atmospheric structure. During the 1930s the new physics and astronomy were developing a fruitful relationship. Thus Marcel Minnaert and his colleagues in the Netherlands (1930) constructed the first curves of growth for spectral lines, which related line strength to element abundance for a given star, while Louis Berman in California in 1935 applied the curve of growth to study the peculiar carbon star R Coronae Borealis, one of the rare hydrogen-deficient stars with a markedly nonsolar composition. The first nongrey stellar atmospheres were also computed at this time, in 1931 by William McCrea for hot stars with neutral atomic hydrogen opacity, and for the sun by **Bengt Strömgren** (1944), based on the discovery by **Rupert Wildt** in 1939 that the negative hydrogen (H-) ion was the principal opacity source for cooler stars.

During the 1940s detailed abundance analyses were undertaken for the first time using these new techniques. Probably the best known and most thorough was that of Albrecht Unsöld in Kiel for the B star tau Scorpii, which he showed to have a nearly solar composition, consistent with the results derived by Payne using far more rudimentary methods. Jesse Greenstein, Kenneth Wright, and Lawrence Aller also made substantial contributions to quantitative spectral analysis during these years for several B and F stars. The essential groundwork for these quantitative studies was the interaction between astrophysics and theoretical physics. Between 1906 and 1939 the contributions of **Karl Schwarzschild**, Meghnad Saha, Edward Milne, **Arthur Stanley Eddington**, William McCrea, Rupert Wildt, and Albrecht Unsöld were all very influential in our understanding of physical processes in stellar atmospheres, including the formation and broadening of spectral lines in stellar spectra and the structure of stellar atmospheres.

Instrumental improvements also greatly helped the development of stellar spectral analysis, in particular the construction of large coudé grating spectrographs at Mount Wilson in the 1930s and elsewhere after World War II, and the development of recording microdensitometers for turning a photographic spectrum into a strip-chart record. Notable early examples were used by Minnaert in Utrecht

(1930s) and by Robley Williams and Albert Hiltner in Michigan (1940s).

Finally, laboratory physicists also played an essential role, not only in providing tables of line wavelengths for identifications in stellar spectra, but also by measuring the oscillator strengths of different transitions of astrophysical interest. The work of Arthur and Robert King at Mount Wilson Observatory from 1935 was one notable example.

Astrophysics from 1945

After 1945 astrophysics became a more unified and a more quantitative subject, and the links with theoretical physics, laboratory physics, and instrumentation technology became closer. The 1950s and 1960s were decades in which reliable quantitative analyses of stellar spectra using the curve of growth method were undertaken for the first time. The principal groups involved were Unsöld and his co-workers in Kiel, Greenstein at the California Institute of Technology, Wright at Victoria, British Columbia, and Aller at Michigan.

An excellent example of the interaction between spectral classification, radial-velocity determination, and quantitative analysis is provided by the discovery of a class of weak-lined stars by Nancy Roman in 1950. She found that high-velocity stars (velocity in excess of 70 km/second) are nearly always in this group. The most extreme members were labeled subdwarfs or halo population stars, designations that came from the renewed interest in stellar evolution in the **Hertzsprung- Russell diagram** (following **Hans Bethe**'s discovery in 1939 of the nuclear fusion processes in main-sequence stars) and from the work of **Walter Baade** (1944) on stellar populations. By 1951, Aller's group in Michigan had analyzed the spectra of two of the high-velocity subdwarfs and found them to be between ten and one hundred times deficient in calcium and iron (relative to the sun). The low abundances found for these and other halo stars led to the theory of galactic evolution by Olin Eggen, Donald Lynden-Bell, and Allan Sandage (1962), in which the galaxy underwent a rapid collapse to a disk after the formation of the metal-deficient halo stars. In addition the data on stellar element abundances was an essential clue for the origin of the elements by nuclear reactions in stars, as first proposed in detail by Geoffrey and Margaret Burbidge, William Fowler, and Fred Hoyle (1957).

Other examples came from the wealth of peculiar stars that classifiers were discovering and that did not fit into the categories of the Morgan-Keenan MK system of two-dimensional spectral classification (1943, revised 1953). Thus the peculiar A-type stars, the metallic-line A stars, the hydrogen-deficient carbon stars, and barium stars were all types with spectral peculiarities that could be ascribed to abnormal (that is, nonsolar) abundances of certain elements in the stars' atmospheres.

The 1960s was also the era when electronic computers made a significant impact on astrophysics, and in particular they allowed physically more complex stellar models to be calculated. In turn, the theoretical line strengths predicted by these atmospheres could be compared with those observed in high-dispersion coudé spectra, thus enabling the physical parameters for stars (temperature, pressure, gravity, luminosity, rotation rate, magnetic field strength, and chemical composition) to be obtained. This was therefore the era of quantitative spectral analysis, which unified stellar astrophysics into a single subject, instead of the three parallel and largely separate courses that it had followed in earlier times.

Finally we remember that detector technology and laboratory astrophysics played an increasing role in observational stellar spectroscopy from the 1950s. Image intensifier tubes and television tubes were used for recording stellar spectra of fainter stars, while digital microdensitometers were built to convert photographic images directly into digital files for computer analysis. In the laboratory the measurement of line strengths, line wavelengths, atomic energy levels, and oscillator strengths was an essential adjunct to astronomical spectroscopy. Many physicists contributed to this work, but the twenty-five-year program of William Meggers at the National Bureau of Standards to catalogue the line strengths and wavelengths of thirty-nine-thousand lines for seventy elements was the most notable. In addition, Charlotte Moore's Multiplet Table of Astrophysical Interest (1933, 1945) was an invaluable compendium of element wavelengths and transitions.

J.B. Hearnshaw

Bibliography

Hearnshaw, J.B. *The Analysis of Starlight*. Cambridge University Press, 1986.

———. "The Analysis of Starlight: Some Comments on the Development of Stellar Spectroscopy, 1815–1965." *Vistas in Astronomy* 30 (1988): 319–375.

Star Names

Most peoples and civilizations have developed a nomenclature for conspicuous celestial objects, stars, and larger configurations such as asterisms and constellations. Star names today are the result of a historical process of growth and development over three millennia. Modern stellar nomenclature is a conglomerate of Babylonian, Greek, Roman, Arabic, and medieval Latin elements.

The constellations we know today were devised by the ancient Greeks. The Greeks, in turn, were influenced by the Babylonians. They received from the Babylonians the figures of many constellations for which they partly retained the names, in Greek, and partly introduced or substituted names of their own tradition. Babylonian constellations and star names, including the twelve signs of the zodiac, were fully developed, after more than a thousand years of growth, around 1000 B.C.E. The Greek astronomer Ptolemy, around 150 C.E., summed up the Greek picture of the sky in a catalogue of 1,025 stars arranged in forty-eight constellations published in his *Almagest*. Of the eighty-eight constellations acknowledged by the **International Astronomical Union** since 1928, fifty-one are based on Ptolemy. The others were added in modern times.

The line of transmission runs from the Greeks to the Arabs. During the ninth century in Baghdad, Islamic scholars translated a number of Greek scientific texts, among them Ptolemy's *Almagest*. Ptolemy was translated from Arabic into Latin in twelfth-century Spain. Arabicized Greek stellar nomenclature plus genuine Islamic discussions of astronomy spread through Europe, often in distorted spellings. From the sixteenth century, European scholars tried to analyze and explain the Arabic or Greek-Arabic star names. However, because they lacked the original sources and had only a limited knowledge of Arabic, they introduced many incorrect or purely speculative forms of star names. From that time on, astronomers plundered philological studies and picked up names that they assigned, more or less correctly. Where historical tradition did not supply any star names, they invented new ones.

The following examples illustrate the historical growth of modern stellar nomenclature and demonstrate some of the linguistic difficulties connected with the explanation of these names.

Regulus (α Leonis)

This star was called by the Sumerians and the Babylonians the King star. The name lived on in Greek astronomy as *basiliskos*, the King. The medieval Latin translation of the *Almagest* from Arabic rendered the word as *rex*, the King. In the Renaissance, a Latin diminutive form was introduced, *regulus*, imitating Ptolemy's Greek form, which was also in the diminutive. It was not Copernicus who introduced this form in the *De revolutionibus* of 1543, as is frequently maintained. *Regulus* can be documented as early as 1522 in Johannes Werner, *Libellus . . . super vigintiduobus elementis conicis,* and in 1524 in Peter Apian, *Cosmographicus liber*.

Altair (α Aquilae)

The Babylonians called this star the Eagle. The name was used by the Greeks (Ptolemy: *aëtos*) and the Arabs in their indigenous star lore, which predated contact with Greek astronomy. The star was called *al-nasr al-ṭā'ir*, the Flying Eagle—in contrast to the Falling Eagle, Vega, α Lyrae. In a late-tenth-century Latin treatise on the astrolabe, the Arabic name was borrowed as altair, and in this spelling it lives on to the present.

Betelgeuse (α Orionis)

The star was called in indigenous Arabic star lore *yad al-jawzā',* the Hand of *al-jawzā'. Al-jawzā'* is a feminine name of unknown meaning given by the Arabs to a zodiacal constellation corresponding to the sign of Gemini but located in the stars of Orion. In a Latin star table of 1246, the Arabic name was wrongly spelled *bedalgeuze* (misreading the first Arabic letter *y* as *b*). Renaissance scholars explained the unintelligible name by unfounded speculation, mistaking the initial *bed* as *bet*, for an assumed Arabic word *bāṭ*, "armpit," which does not exist in this spelling. From that time, the name has continued to be used in the revised, incorrect spelling as Betelgeuze (and Beteigeuze in German, with an old misprint, i for l).

Fomalhaut (α Piscis Austrini)

Ptolemy described the star as marking the mouth of the Southern Fish. From this description the name was derived as the Mouth of the Southern Fish. Its Arabic form was borrowed by medieval Latin translators in various spellings. Today the spelling found in Johannes Bayer's *Uranometria* (1603) is used.

Alwaid (β Draconis)

Like many others, this name was introduced by **Giuseppe Piazzi**, in the second edition (1814) of his star catalogue. He collected these names from Thomas Hyde's edition of **Ulugh Beg**'s star catalogue, published at Oxford in

1665. In Piazzi's catalogue there are many spelling errors and mistaken identifications. The name Alwaid, for example, corresponds to an old Arabic asterism name, *al-'awa'idh*, the Mother Camels (in Hyde's transliteration *AlAwâïd),* the name the Arabs gave to the stars Ny, Beta, Xi, and Gamma Draconis. Piazzi arbitrarily assigned the name, with corrupted spelling, to β Draconis alone.

Apart from many names of Arabic origin, a number of Latin names exist that derive from medieval translations of Arabic, such as Ancha (θ Aquarii) or Graffias (β Scorpii).

Well-known classical Greek and Roman star names were revived in the Renaissance and continue in use today; for example Arcturus (α Bootis), or Spica (α Virginis). Modern astronomers have borrowed forms of Babylonian star names (such as Girtab, θ Scorpii, or Nunki, σ Sagittarii), the last one an outdated interpretation. Modern scholarship takes Nunki to be α Carinae or some stars in that area. Astronomers have even used Chinese names such as Cih or Tsih for γ Cassiopeiae or Koo She for δ Velorum.

When necessary, modern astronomers have not hesitated to invent new names for stars that were unnamed in traditional sources, such as Atria for alpha Trianguli Australis or Gacrux for gamma Crucis.

Finally, a group of roughly a dozen star names that appear for the first time in Antonín Bečvář 's *Atlas Coeli* (1950) should be mentioned. So far it has been impossible to identify the language or the civilization from which these names were borrowed. To this group belong Achird (η Cassiopeiae), Arich (γ Virginis), and Hassaleh (ι Aurigae).

Research in the history and linguistic origins of star names started in 1553 with a book by the French orientalist Guillaume Postel, *Signorum coelestium vera configuratio aut asterismus*. Since then, the subject has attracted considerable interest. The most important contemporary studies are Kunitzsch (1959) and Kunitzsch and Smart (1986). The work of R.H. Allen (1899, 1963) is rich in mythological and literary material, but is unreliable for Arabic and other oriental matters.

Paul Kunitzsch

Bibliography

Allen, R.H. *Star Names, Their Lore and Meaning*. New York: Dover, 1963.

Kunitzsch, P. *Arabische Sternnamen in Europa*. Wiesbaden: Harrassowitz, 1959.

———. *The Arabs and the Stars*. Northampton: Variorum Reprints, 1986.

———. "Rätselhafte Sternnamen." In *Der Himmel hat viele Gesichter: Winfried Petri zum 80. Geburtstag,* edited by W. Kokott. München: Institut für Geschichte der Naturwissenschaften, 1994.

Kunitzsch, P. and T. Smart. *Short Guide to Modern Star Names and Their Derivations*. Wiesbaden: Harrassowitz, 1986.

Stellar Energy Problem

How the sun and stars generate their prodigious energy outputs is arguably the most fundamental question of stellar physics. Even in its earliest guise, the question's bearing on the issue of stellar perdurance was clear. As solutions to the stellar-energy problem have become increasingly robust during the last century and a half, energy generation has been linked as well to the stellar properties of mass, chemical composition, internal structure, and evolutionary pathway.

Inquiries about the processes that keep the stars shining have occurred in four main stages. First, from Isaac Newton's day to the mid-nineteenth century, natural philosophers occasionally pondered whether some mechanism had replenished the sun's outpouring of light during the millennia since Creation. Then in the 1840s and 1850s, several of the founders of thermodynamics—Julius Robert Mayer, John James Waterston, Hermann Helmholtz, and William Thomson (later Lord Kelvin)—used the principle of energy conservation to reformulate the problem in terms of energy sources and expenditures. Thomson, the most persistent physicist writing on the problem, soon came to believe that gravitational contraction was the only process capable of powering the sun and other stars and hence that the geologists and evolutionists must adapt their ideas to its relatively short time scale of tens of millions of years. During the problem's third stage, which opened with the discovery of radium's heating effect in 1903, most astronomers and physicists searching for energy sources directed their attention to subatomic processes that, if operative, would make much longer stellar lifetimes possible. Their search culminated in the late 1930s with **Hans Bethe**'s convincing identification of helium-building thermonuclear reactions that could sustain the main-sequence stars for billions of years. Finally, during the current stage, which was initiated by Bethe's breakthrough, a maturing stellar-evolution research community has conducted ever more sophisticated theoretical, experimental, and observational investigations of energy generation in stars of different initial mass and chemical composition all along their distinct evolutionary pathways.

This summary suffices to indicate that the history of the stellar energy problem offers ample opportunity for illuminating a number of general issues in the history of science. For instance, because of the problem's theoretical character, its history nicely exemplifies how theorists' relations with observers and experimentalists have changed over time. Similarly, on account of the problem's position in the borderlands between astronomy and physics since the mid-nineteenth century, its history is an excellent site for studying how the motives for and organization of interdisciplinary research have changed during the last century and a half. Again, on account of the problem's longevity, its history can be used for analyzing how the scientists serving as a problem's self-appointed custodians go about reformulating their precise statement of the problem and their expectations for its solution in response to relevant developments in their own and related fields. However, before these general issues can be fully illuminated, there is a need—as the ensuing discussion of the historical literature on each of the stellar energy problem's four stages suggests—for many further specialized studies of the problem's history.

Two historians have delved into the problem's first stage. Schaffer did so in the course of sketching out the background of **William Herschel**'s researches on the sun's constitution. Throughout the eighteenth century, partisans of Newton's corpuscular theory of light had discussed whether, and if so, how, the sun and other stars were replenished to compensate for mass loss due to the emission of light particles. Schaffer, situating Herschel within this tradition, traced the investigative path that led him to regard the sun as a chemical laboratory refueled by luminous matter from passing comets. Taking an entirely different approach, Kidwell examined the gradual convergence of ideas, instruments, and techniques that led during the 1820s and 1830s to the first measurements of the sun's heat impinging on the earth. She found that, though English natural philosophers began discussing the sun's maintenance in the late seventeenth century, this speculative tradition played no discernible role in motivating the initial determinations of the solar constant. Instead, this work was variously inspired by Claude Pouillet's interest in the physics of heat transfer and **John Herschel**'s and David Forbes's interest in the sun's influence on terrestrial climate. Taken together, Schaffer's and Kidwell's studies raise the issue whether scientific curiosity about the sun's replenishment survived the triumph of the wave theory of light in the early decades of the nineteenth century.

Several scholars have investigated the history of the stellar-energy problem during the six decades following the establishment of the principle of energy conservation in the 1840s. Burchfield began the discussion with his account of the struggles over the age of the earth. In making the case for an age between ten and a hundred million years, Thomson frequently argued that this time scale was in accord with the sun's age as calculated on the assumption that its energy source was gravitational contraction. Burchfield described Thomson's path to and development of this argument, his success in using this and other arguments to persuade many contemporary scientists to reduce estimates of the earth's age, and his dismissive treatment of the theories of those like the geologist James Croll and the engineer William Siemens who sought alternatives to his restricted view of the sun's lifetime.

Since Burchfield, historians have greatly enriched—but not transformed—this basic narrative line. Kidwell (1979) and James detailed the connections between the founding of thermodynamics in the 1840s and 1850s and the earliest formulations of the problem in energetic terms. Smith and Wise devoted two chapters of their insightful biography of Thomson to delineating his researches on the dissipation of the sun's energies. Among other things, they substantiated Burchfield's hunch that Thomson's anti-Darwinian sentiments played a strong role in motivating his decision around 1861 to shift from his own meteoritic theory of energy generation to Helmholtz's contraction theory. More generally, Smith and Wise established that Thomson's profound commitment to the second law of thermodynamics underlay his recurrent advocacy of the inevitability of the sun's death. In studies of early theorizing about stellar evolution and structure, DeVorkin (1978, 1984) and Schwarz showed that the contraction theory of energy generation served from the 1860s as a background framework for most such research. Likewise, Powell found that the engineer J. Homer Lane's adherence to the contraction doctrine played a definite, yet modest, role in his development in 1869–1870 of the first mathematical theory of the sun's structure. Finally, in addressing the cultural impact of rhetoric about the sun's death, Beer provocatively suggested that this prediction engendered widespread anxieties which, in turn, gave rise to the Victorians' fascination not only with speculative works about solar mythology but also with Charles Darwin's prosaic treatise on earthworms—creatures that, despite being continually hidden from the sun's rays, had great fructifying powers.

Notwithstanding the many valuable studies dealing with the stellar energy problem's second stage, at least two historical questions warrant more detailed attention than they have yet received. How and to what depth did the physicists' contraction theory of energy generation enter into the astronomers' worldview during the last four decades of the nineteenth century? What intellectual resources did Croll, Siemens, and others draw upon in devising rival theories, and why did most astronomers, despite some doubts about the contraction theory because of its paltry time scale, refuse to take these alternatives seriously?

The transition from the second to third stage in the stellar energy problem's history that occurred during the first two decades of the twentieth century has received scrutiny from four historians. In concluding his history of the age-of-the-earth controversy, Burchfield discussed how the evidence for subatomic energies that emerged from investigations of radioactivity in 1903 undermined the credibility of Kelvin's contention that the sun's energy source was gravitational contraction. Deepening Burchfield's account of Kelvin's final stance in their biography, Smith and Wise demonstrated that the aged physicist's cocksure confidence in the contraction theory never wavered. Hufbauer (1981) opened a new line of inquiry by focusing on the astronomers' response to the discovery of subatomic energies. He found that they were quick to accept the possibility that the stars were powered by subatomic processes. But since they were unable to discern how this possibility might be relevant to ongoing astronomical research, they did not rush to take up the stellar energy problem. Indeed, it was only around 1919–1920, after **Arthur Stanley Eddington** and **Harlow Shapley** had made strong cases for stellar ages greatly in excess of the Helmholtz-Kelvin time scale, that Eddington and **Henry Norris Russell** began using the former's new theory of stellar structure together with recent results from atomic physics to search for likely energy-generating processes.

Only two historians have paid more than incidental attention to the important researches on the stellar energy problem during the next two decades. Kenat did so in the course of analyzing Eddington's theory of stellar structure. In 1924, this pioneering theoretical astrophysicist succeeded, despite his avowed ignorance of the energy-generating process, in building a robust case that main-sequence stars, like giant stars, behaved in accord with the perfect-gas laws. Kenat showed that it was in consequence of this success that Eddington relegated the stellar energy problem to a subordinate position in his *Internal Constitution of the Stars* (1926) by insisting that the problem's importance lay primarily in its relevance to the evolutionary pathways taken by stars. Hufbauer (1991), who also discussed Eddington's breakthrough of 1924, put this achievement into the context of the general development of stellar theory during the interwar years. Eddington continued to play the lead role in the field into the early 1930s, arguing, for instance, that **Edwin Hubble**'s discovery of the expansion of the universe pointed to a stellar time scale of billions of years. In doing so, he was implicitly taking a stance against the theory that electron-proton annihilation, with its time scale of trillions of years, was the source of stellar energy. Instead, he was siding with the physicists Robert d'Escourt Atkinson and Friedrich Houtermans, who had recently used quantum-tunneling theory to bolster the idea that helium-building nuclear reactions powered the stars. Thereafter, in Hufbauer's view, younger theoretical astrophysicists—notably **Bengt Strömgren** and Thomas G. Cowling—assumed the leadership in specifying the conditions under which energy was liberated deep in stellar interiors. Meanwhile, a string of young theoretical physicists—notably George Gamow, Carl Friedrich von Weizsäcker, and Lev Landau—attempted to identify the energy-generating nuclear reactions. Finally in 1938, Bethe used his unsurpassed knowledge of nuclear physics to marshal a compelling case that cooler main-sequence stars drew their energy from a helium-building reaction chain that began with proton-proton reactions, and that hotter main-sequence stars drew their energy from a helium-building reaction cycle that began with proton-carbon reactions.

The available historical literature on the stellar energy problem's third stage makes it clear that additional studies of at least four questions are needed. How did theoretical astrophysicists go about drawing on the latest developments in atomic physics and observational astronomy to keep the formulation of the stellar energy problem up to date between 1920 and 1938? Why, despite their interest in the problem, did they end up leaving the actual problem-solving work to theoretical physicists? How did the physicists learn about the problem and what motivated them to venture outside their own domain to propose solutions? When confronted with putative solutions, how did the theoretical astrophysicists decide whether to reject them out of hand, treat them as proposals warranting further development, or, in the case of Bethe's solution, acclaim it as a breakthrough?

While any number of scientists have written narratives and quasi-historical reviews about stellar-evolution theory since Bethe's breakthrough, Pinch is the lone nonparticipant to examine any part of this stage's history. He used an extended case study of the first direct observational test of Bethe's theory as a vehicle for advancing constructivism within the sociology of science. In Pinch's generally credible portrayal, nuclear astrophysicists—especially John Bahcall—played a crucial role in generating funding for and interest in the nuclear chemist Ray Davis's efforts to detect neutrinos released by one of the thermonuclear reactions that were thought to be powering the sun. In 1968, within a year of the completion of his subterranean detector, Davis began reporting neutrino fluxes that were well below Bahcall's predictions. Within another three or so years, nuclear astrophysicists and others were debating whether the persistent discrepancy should be attributed to a faulty understanding of stellar energy generation or neutrinos. Although the debate was still unresolved when Pinch published, it may well—thanks to data from new neutrino detectors—achieve closure during the 1990s.

Insightful though it is, Pinch's study deals with only a few developments in the post-1938 stage of the stellar energy problem's history. How, for instance, did theoretical astrophysicists, theoretical physicists, and observational astrophysicists cooperate during the next decade in moving beyond Bethe's breakthrough to explore energy generation by gravitational contraction and a wider range of nucleosynthetic reactions in the late stages of stellar evolution? Why and how did William A. Fowler take on the challenge of developing the new specialty of experimental nuclear astrophysics? How during the 1950s did these lines of research come together in the development of a reasonably comprehensive theory of stellar nucleosynthesis? How since the late 1950s has the stellar-evolution community gone about acquiring access to and using ever more powerful computing capabilities and the results from ever more varied and sensitive stellar-emission detectors to refine its understanding of energy generation in the stars? Why and how, despite the solar-neutrino problem, have most members of the stellar-evolution community continued to express confidence in the underlying soundness of their basic theoretical framework? And why, how, and with what consequences have producers of astronomy series for television and writers of science-fiction novels and scripts done so much since the mid-1970s to popularize the prevailing scientific view of energy generation and nucleosynthesis in the stars?

In order to answer most of the questions posed in this entry, scholars will have to go beyond the standard scientific literature. Whatever their period, they will need to consult correspondences, referee reports, and institutional records for evidence about and insights into the motives, assumptions, practices, and standards of the scientists who have worked on the stellar energy problem. Those interested in the half century between roughly 1925 and 1975 will also want to see the many interviews of modern astrophysicists conducted under the auspices of the American Institute of Physics for such information.

The preceding account of the stellar energy problem's history since the late seventeenth century gives rise to curiosity about the prospects that the present stage will end in the near future. This outcome seems quite likely, for there is an excellent chance, given the numerous empirical constraints satisfied by contemporary stellar-evolution theory, that the mystery of the missing solar neutrinos will be resolved in a way that preserves the essential features of that theory. Should things work out that way, it seems reasonable to anticipate that the ensuing stage of the stellar energy problem's history will be extremely technical and, compared with the excitement of the second through fourth stages, rather boring.

Karl Hufbauer

Bibliography

Beer, G. "'The Death of the Sun': Victorian Solar Physics and Solar Myth." In *The Sun Is God: Painting, Literature and Mythology in the Nineteenth Century*, edited by B. Bullen, 159–180. Oxford: Clarendon Press, 1990.

Burchfield, J.D. *Lord Kelvin and the Age of the Earth*. New York: Science History, 1975.

DeVorkin, D.H. "An Astronomical Symbiosis: Stellar Evolution and Spectral Classification (1860–1910)." Ph.D. dissertation, University of Leicester, 1978.

———. "Stellar Evolution and the Origin of the Hertzsprung-Russell Diagram." In *Astrophysics and Twentieth-century Astronomy to 1950*, edited by O. Gingerich. *The General History of Astronomy, vol. 4A,* edited by M.A. Hoskin, 90–108. Cambridge: Cambridge University Press, 1984.

Hufbauer, K. "Astronomers Take up the Stellar-Energy Problem, 1917–1920." *Historical Studies in the Physical Sciences* 11 (1981): 277– 303.

———. *Exploring the Sun: Solar Science since Galileo*. Baltimore: Johns Hopkins University Press, 1991.

James, F.A.J.L. "Thermodynamics and Sources of Solar Heat, 1846–1862." *British Journal for the History of Science* 15 (1982): 155–181.

Kenat, R.C., Jr. "Physical Interpretation: Eddington, Idealization and the Origin of Stellar Structure Theory." Ph.D. dissertation, University of Maryland at College Park, 1987.

Kidwell, P.A. "Solar Radiation and Heat from Kepler to Helmholtz (1600–1860)." Ph.D. dissertation, Yale University, 1979.

———. "Prelude to Solar Energy: Pouillet, Herschel, Forbes and the Solar Constant." *Annals of Science* 38 (1981): 457–476.

Pinch, T.J. *Confronting Nature: The Sociology of Solar-Neutrino Detection. Dordrecht: Reidel, 1986.*

Powell, C.S. "J. Homer Lane and the Internal Structure of the Sun." *Journal for the History of Astronomy* 19 (1988): 183–199.

Schaffer, S. "The 'Great Laboratories of the Universe': William Herschel on Matter Theory and Planetary Life." *Journal for the History of Astronomy* 11 (1980): 81–111.

Schwarz, O. "Zur historischen Entwicklung der Theorie des innern Aufbaus der Sterne von 1861 bis 1926." *Veröffenlichung der Archenhold-Sternwarte Berlin-Treptow* 22 (1992): 1–169.

Smith, C., and M.N. Wise. *Energy and Empire: A Biographical Study of Lord Kelvin*. Cambridge: Cambridge University Press, 1989.

Stellar Parallax

Stellar parallax is the apparent annual motion of the stars due to earth's motion in its orbit. Unlike proper motion, it is only an apparent motion; since it is inversely proportional to the distance of the star, stellar parallax is the basis for the entire cosmic distance scale. When combined with astrophysical data, it is an essential datum for the determination of stellar evolution.

Because stellar parallax is a direct implication of the Copernican theory, it was a long-sought measurement in proof of that theory. Although many claimed to have measured stellar parallax, the measurements made by **Friedrich Bessel, F.G.W. Struve**, and Thomas Henderson between 1838 and 1840 were the first to withstand the test of time. Their measurements, made with a variety of instruments, showed parallaxes of a few tenths of an arcsecond. The largest parallax now known is 0.76 arcseconds for Alpha Centauri, making it the nearest star. Parallaxes were subsequently determined largely by long-focus refractors, although Adriaan van Maanen used the large reflectors at Mount Wilson. The introduction of photographic techniques increased the accuracy and number of parallaxes. Parallaxes determined by these methods are called trigonometric parallaxes; spectroscopic, dynamical, and statistical parallaxes may be determined by other means.

In 1952 Yale University published the *General Catalogue of Trigonometric Stellar Parallaxes* with 5,822 parallaxes; 600 more were added in the 1963 *Supplement*. These are being superseded by a new *General Catalogue*, also produced at Yale. Modern ground-based parallaxes are measured at the rate of about one hundred per year, largely with the 61-inch astrometric reflector of the U.S. Naval Observatory. Photographic parallaxes determined with this instrument can produce milliarcsecond accuracies, and with a charge-coupled device (CCD) submilliarcsecond accuracies are achieved. About 10,000 stellar parallaxes are now known, but *Hipparcos* (High Precision Parallax Collecting Satellite) in the 1990s will

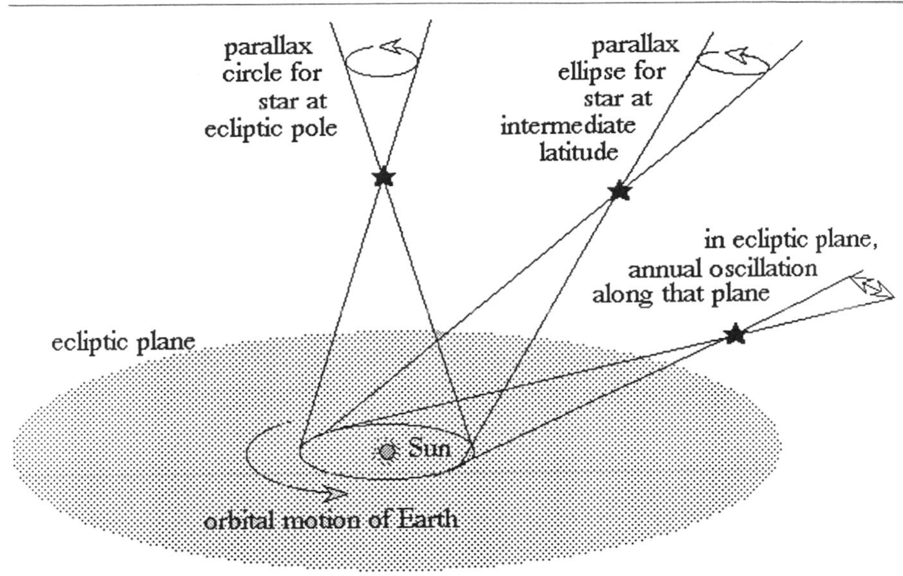

Due to the annual orbital motion of the earth about the sun, nearby stars are observed to change their directional position by a small amount. For a star situated near the pole of the ecliptic plane, the parallax effect produces an annual motion in a small circle, the angular diameter of which represents the angle subtended by 2 astronomical units at the distance to the star. For a star in the ecliptic plane the parallax effect is a small oscillation in position parallel to the ecliptic plane. At intermediate latitudes, nearby stars appear to describe a small ellipse over the course of a year. (Figure by Charles J. Peterson)

observe parallaxes for more than 100,000 stars with an accuracy at the milliarcsecond level.

Steven J. Dick

Bibliography

Fernie, J.D. "The Historical Search for Stellar Parallax." *Journal of the Royal Astronomical Society of Canada* 69 (1975): 153–161; 222–239.

Stellar Statistics

Stellar statistics refers to that field of astronomy that employs statistics and probability to examine two major problems. What are the real motions of stars in the aggregate? How are stars distributed collectively? Theoretically, these developments were expressed in the velocity law, which relates the motions of stars to their brightness, and in the luminosity law and density law, which describe the distribution of stellar brightness from the faintest stars to the brightest, and the distribution of stars in space. By about 1900 stellar statistics had become a major research enterprise that cut across the entire astronomical landscape.

The application of statistics to astronomy began during the eighteenth century with the discovery of stellar **proper motions** and continued with James Bradley's discovery of the aberration of starlight. But it was **William Herschel** who developed stellar statistics as a method for understanding the architecture of the universe. Herschel referred to this project as the study of the Construction of the Heavens. In the nineteenth century it became known as the sidereal problem. The central, empirical concern dealt with the kind of data that could be used to measure stellar distances accurately. Herschel suggested that distance is proportional to stellar brightness on the principle that brightness means nearness. He built his cosmology on this idea even though he was aware of the contradiction implied by the existence of binary and multiple star systems with members of different luminosities.

During the last half of the nineteenth century, the view that stars move randomly through space was widely accepted. By the 1870s astronomers were also arguing that distance was inversely proportional to proper motion on the principle that proper motion means nearness. For each known trigonometric parallax, there were hundreds of measured proper motions. Thus more stellar distances could be determined if proper motion data, rather than trigonometric parallax or stellar brightness, were used. Using Carl Friedreich Gauss's least-squares techniques, **Friedrich Argelander** and **George Biddell Airy** identified random fluctuations in stellar motions, concluding that random irregularities were due, not to observational errors, but to the motions of stars relative to one another. By 1875, most astronomers accepted the assumptions that stellar distances were inversely proportional to proper motions and that stellar motions were random.

Although dynamic models were proposed that relied on Newtonian arguments, the sheer immensity of the sidereal problem prevented these ideas from providing a satisfying conceptual basis for understanding the arrangement of stars in space. Prior to the 1890s, astronomers had not succeeded in relating a distance measure based on a few thousand proper motions to the demands of survey catalogues containing the positions of hundreds of thousands of stars.

During the 1890s the Dutch astronomer **Jacobus C. Kapteyn** obtained a statistical relationship correlating trigonometric parallaxes with proper motions and magnitudes. Generalizing his results over large numbers of stars, he derived a statistical function that expressed mean distances to the stars. These investigations were based on the assumption that stellar motions were the key to understanding the distribution of the stars using the velocity law. Conclusive observational evidence for Kapteyn's velocity law was entirely lacking. The hypothesis of random motions was not valid.

Kapteyn's failure to harmonize observation with theory reaffirmed the anomalous nature of stellar motions, and led him to discover in 1902 that there were two star streams. Finding that the stars tend to move in two distinct and diametrically opposite directions, Kapteyn suggested that this phenomenon resulted from two once distinct but now intermingled populations of stars moving relative to one another. Prior to the recognition of differential galactic rotation by **Bertil Lindblad** and **Jan Oort** during the later 1920s, **Arthur S. Eddington** (1906) and **Karl Schwarzschild** (1907) developed complementary theories explaining star streaming using mathematical and statistical ideas.

Concurrent with these motion studies were investigations dealing with the spatial distribution of the stars. This line of investigation also began in the late eighteenth century with Herschel's research into the Construction of the Heavens. The basic method behind investigations of the distribution of stars was to locate the position of large numbers of stars in three-dimensional space. Consequently, astrometric and photometric catalogues became critical because they contained the positions and brightnesses of many stars. Initially adopting the brightness-nearness principle, astronomers were able to construct architectures of the sidereal system.

Following Herschel's attempts, the first sustained attacks on the problem were produced by **F.G.W. Struve** of the **Pulkovo Observatory** and **John Herschel** working at the Cape of Good Hope. They used the most reliable data available, and their analyses demonstrated the possibilities inherent in stellar statistics based on stellar counts.

The most pressing need was for the production of catalogues containing large numbers of stars. The first modern astrometric catalogue was Argelander's *Bonner Durchmusterung* (1859) for the northern sky, containing 324,000 stars. This was subsequently followed by Eduard Schönfeld's survey (1886) of the southern sky (down to -23 degrees declination) containing 133,000 stars. Others, principally Edward Pickering and Georg Auwers, also produced useful catalogues of the naked-eye stars and refinements of the *Bonner* catalogues.

The first sustained analysis of the *Bonner Durchmusterung* was by Karl L. von Littrow. He partitioned space into concentric spheres and placed stars using the brightness-nearness principle. Others, principally Benjamin A. Gould, **Richard A. Proctor**, **Edward C. Pickering**, and **Giovanni Schiaparelli**, applied mathematical models to the data and argued on theoretical grounds that the numbers of stars contained in successive spherical shells should increase by a factor of four. Christened by Eddington as the fundamental theorem, research in stellar distribution was based on the unproven assumption that stars are nearly uniformly bright.

The German **Hugo von Seeliger** and Kapteyn spent several decades devising statistical methods for determining the distribution of stars in space. Using star counts and data on luminosities, Seeliger employed a probability function to represent the Gaussian distribution of luminosities and developed a series of increasingly refined solutions to the sidereal problem using a technique later christened the fundamental equation of stellar statistics. In 1910 Karl Schwarzschild refined Seeliger's solutions using Fourier analysis.

Although Seeliger was the first to provide a complete solution (1898) to the sidereal problem, his analysis was mathematically abstract and it was not based on all the available observational data. Kapteyn had also been working on the sidereal problem, but he had a greater command of empirical data, particularly proper motions and parallaxes. By 1901 Kapteyn had developed a technique for obtaining the luminosity law that correlated the magnitudes of stars with their motions and hence their mean distances. Recognizing the essential importance of relating star counts, the density distribution, and the luminosity law, Seeliger and Kapteyn elevated stellar statistics to a powerful technique in stellar studies. During the early 1920s, Seeliger and Kapteyn fashioned their final solutions to the sidereal problem, using the luminosity and density laws. These relationships were based on statistical and mathematical ideas.

E. Robert Paul

Bibliography

Paul, E.R. *The Milky Way Galaxy and Statistical Cosmology, 1890–1924*. New York: Cambridge University Press, 1993.

Stonehenge

Stonehenge is a prehistoric monument in southern England and is the archaeological site most closely identified with the idea of astronomical alignment. It was built, used, and modified over more than one thousand years by Neolithic and Bronze Age farmers and herders. Construction on its earliest phase was begun around 2800 B.C.E., and at that stage Stonehenge comprised a circular earthen bank, an outlying upright stone known as the Heel Stone, a ring of fifty-six small pits known as the Aubrey Holes, possibly the rectangular arrangement of four Station stones and mounds, and several other features. In 1979, a pit that could have once held another large upright was discovered just to the northwest of the Heel Stone, and this appears to belong to the earliest period of Stonehenge. At about 2150 B.C.E., a double horseshoe of bluestone uprights was installed in the center, and the Avenue was extended to the northeast. There is some uncertainty about the Stations, which actually may have been added in this era. Between 2000 and 1550 B.C.E., a variety of architectural changes occurred. The most significant of these was the removal of the bluestone horseshoes and their replacement with the massive linteled circle of sarsen sandstone and the accompanying horseshoe of five trilithons. This arrangement of monumental archways opened to the northeast.

Astronomical significance was first attributed to Stonehenge in 1721 when the English antiquary William Stukeley, in the company of another investigator, Roger Gale, observed that the Avenue continued toward the direction of summer solstice sunrise. Writing about the monument in 1740, Stukeley recognized that the stones themselves were not oriented exactly to summer solstice sunrise, but in 1771 Dr. John Smith claimed that

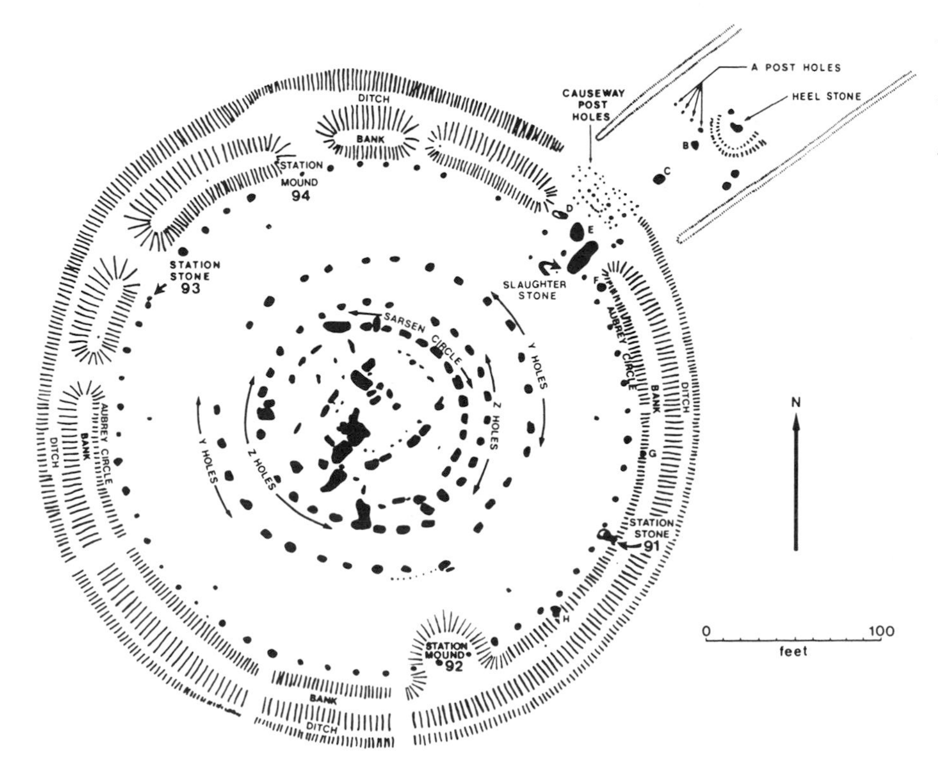

All of the principal features of more than a thousand years of construction and use of Stonehenge appear in this plan. The main axis is the line of bilateral symmetry that continues from the center to the northeast. This line also coincides with summer solstice sunrise. (Courtesy of the Griffith Observatory)

The view northeast along the primary axis of Stonehenge includes the Heel Stone, an outlier that appears offset in the archway of the circle of large uprights. For years, astronomical significance has been given to this line of sight, for, from the center, the summer solstice sun appears to rise over the Heel Stone. When Stonehenge was first built, however, the sun rose to the left—perhaps between the Heel Stone and another stone that is now gone. The socket for that other stone was discovered beneath the surface through salvage excavation in 1979. (Courtesy of E.C. Krupp)

the summer solstice sun rose directly over the Heel Stone.

In 1901, **J. Norman Lockyer** became interested in the possibility of astronomical significance in Stonehenge after he surveyed Egyptian temple alignments. Believing that the principal axis of Stonehenge was intended to coincide with summer solstice sunrise, Lockyer attempted to define that axis with precision and establish its orientation. With this information he intended to estimate astronomically the date of Stonehenge's construction. Lockyer concluded that Stonehenge III was erected between 1900 and 1500 B.C.E., but he was criticized for arbitrarily adjusting his measurements to fit a preconceived notion. These differences in assumed azimuth were actually very small—less than two arcminutes. There are, however, too many uncertainties to permit Stonehenge to be dated with precision through astronomy. Despite that limitation, Lockyer's assumption of solstitial orientation provided a date that is roughly consistent with what is known archaeologically.

After Lockyer, Stonehenge astronomy was ignored until 1965, when Gerald S. Hawkins published an analysis of possible astronomical alignments and the statistical likelihood of their having been intended. Hawkins concluded that a variety of astronomical sightlines—solstice sunrises and sunsets and the maximum and minimum monthly extremes of moonrise and moonset—were part of the plan of Stonehenge from the beginning and were carried over into the later stages as well. Hawkins also interpreted the circle of Aubrey Holes as a lunar eclipse predictor. Hawkins turned Stonehenge into a prehistoric observatory and computer.

The Hawkins interpretation of Stonehenge generated great interest and controversy. In time, specialists in archaeoastronomy became particularly skeptical of his eclipse predictor. Although disputes over other details of his pattern of solar and lunar alignments continued, Hawkins had a great deal to do with the revival in the 1970s of the study of ancient and prehistoric astronomy.

The most convincing astronomical alignment at Stonehenge is the axis of the Avenue, which points accurately toward the sun's first gleam on summer solstice at about 2150 B.C.E., when the Avenue was constructed. The discovery of a stone hole near the Heel Stone opens the possibility that the rising summer solstice sun was framed in the Avenue by a pair of stones viewed from the center. If so, the rising summer solstice sun may be interpreted as a dynamic component of seasonal ritual conducted in the most architecturally ambitious sacred precinct of prehistoric Britain.

Edwin C. Krupp

Bibliography

Atkinson, R.J.C. *Stonehenge*. Harmondsworth, U.K.: Penguin Books, 1979.

———. "Aspects of the Archaeoastronomy of Stonehenge." In *Archaeoastronomy in the Old World*, edited by D.C. Heggie, 107–116. Cambridge: Cambridge University Press, 1982.

Hawkins, G.S. *Beyond Stonehenge*. New York: Harper and Row, 1973.
Hawkins, G.S. and J.B. White. *Stonehenge Decoded*. Garden City, N.Y.: Doubleday, 1965.
Krupp, E.C. *Echoes of the Ancient Skies*. New York: Harper and Row, 1983.
———, ed. *In Search of Ancient Astronomies*. Garden City, N.Y.: Doubleday, 1978.
Lockyer, J.N. *Stonehenge and Other British Stone Monuments Astronomically Considered*. 2nd ed. London: Macmillan, 1909.
Thom, A. and A.S. Thom. *Megalithic Sites in Britain and Britanny*. Oxford: Oxford University Press, 1978.

Strömgren, Bengt (1908–1987)

Danish astrophysicist, son of Svante Elis Strömgren, celestial mechanician and director of Copenhagen Observatory. Educated at Copenhagen University, Bengt Strömgren divided his career between those institutions, the University of Chicago, Yerkes and McDonald observatories, and the Institute for Advanced Study, Princeton. He was director of Copenhagen, Yerkes, and McDonald observatories, and a founder and president of the **European Southern Observatory**. Strömgren identified hydrogen as the major constituent of stellar interiors. He analyzed the ionization of interstellar hydrogen in sharply defined regions (H II regions) surrounding O and B stars. He modeled the solar atmosphere, studied stellar classification, constitution, and evolution, and developed techniques in photoelectric photometry.

Joann Eisberg

Bibliography

Strömgren, B. "Scientists I Have Known and Some Astronomical Problems I Have Met." *Annual Reviews of Astronomy and Astrophysics* 21 (1983): 1–11.

Struve, Friedrich Georg Wilhelm (Vasily Yakovlevich) (1793–1864)

Russian astronomer, geodesist, and science administrator. Born in Altona, Germany, he immigrated to Dorpat in Russia (now Tartu, Estonia), where, in 1813, he earned a doctorate in astronomy and joined the staff of the Dorpat Observatory, becoming its director in 1819. Struve was also a professor of astronomy at Dorpat University.

In 1839 he was appointed director of the newly established **Pulkovo Observatory** near St. Petersburg. Pulkovo was built under his supervision. He was succeeded in 1862 by his son Otto Wilhelm.

Struve worked in **astrometry**. He equipped both Dorpat and Pulkovo with the best instruments available. Transit circle observations under his direction provided the basis for a series of important star catalogues. He also was active in double star work, and his catalogue of double stars set new standards for research in the field. Otto Wilhelm collaborated with his father in these investigations. In 1837, Struve announced a value for the parallax of Vega (Alpha Lyrae). Struve was one of the first to successfully measure the parallax of a star. He also made important contributions to **stellar statistics**. Struve cooperated with the Russian government in various projects in geodesy. Of these, the most important was a project to measure an arc of the meridian over 25 degrees in length. This difficult task was completed in 1855. Many young scientists studied with Struve, and a number became observatory directors or leaders in geodesy.

Struve as elected a foreign associate of the Royal Society of London and of the Royal Astronomical Society, as well as being honored by many other academies and scientific societies around the world.

His name was attached to the minor planet 768 Struveana, discovered in 1913 by the Russian astronomer Grigory Neujmin, and a lunar crater is named after him.

Vitaly A. Bronshten

Bibliography

Batten, A.H. "The Struves of Pulkovo—A Family of Astronomers." *Journal of the Royal Astronomical Society of Canada* 71, no. 5, (1977): 345–372.
———. *Resolute and Undertaking Characters: The Lives of Wilhelm and Otto Struve*. Dordrecht: Reidel, 1988.
Berry, A. *A Short History of Astronomy*. New York: Dover Press, 1961.
Clerke, A.M. *A Popular History of Astronomy during the Nineteenth Century*. 4th ed. London: Adam and Charles Black, 1902.
Dadaev, A.N. *Pulkovo Observatory* [Leningrad, 1972.] Translated by K. Krisciunas. NASA TM-75803. Springfield, Va.: National Technical Information Service.
Frost, E.B. "The Family of Astronomers." *Popular Astronomy* 29, no. 9 (1921) 536–541.
Mikhailov, A.A. "Pulkovo Observatory." In *Astrophysics and Twentieth-Century Astronomy to 1950: Part A*, edited by

O. Gingerich, 119–122, 132. Cambridge University Press, 1984.
Novokshanova (Sokolovskaja), Z.K. *Vassily Yakovlevich Struve.* In Russian. Moscow: Nauka Press, 1964.
Struve, O. *Wilhelm Struve. Zur Erinnerung an der Vater den Geschwistern Dargebracht.* Karlsruhe, 1895.
Vassily Yakovlevich Struve. In Russian. Edited by A.A. Mikhailov. Moscow: Nauka Press, 1964.

Struve, Georg Otto Hermann (1886–1933)

German astronomer. Born at Tsarskoe Selo (near St. Petersburg), he was the son of astronomer **Karl Hermann Struve**. After study at Heidelberg and Berlin, he earned his doctorate in 1910 for a thesis in celestial mechanics. Following positions at Bonn, Berlin, and Bergedorf, he became an astronomer at the Naval Observatory in Wilhelmshaven. In 1919 Georg Otto Hermann Struve moved to the Berlin-Babelsberg Observatory, where he was promoted to astronomer in 1929. Struve continued his father's work on **planetary satellites** and the ring system of Saturn. He was also active in the Eros campaign of 1930–1931, when observations of the minor planet were used to determine the value of the solar parallax.

Struve traveled widely using astronomical facilities in Africa and the United States. During a visit to the **Yerkes Observatory**, he undertook, with his cousin Otto W. Struve (son of Gustav Wilhelm Ludwig) a reanalysis of observations of the complex multiple star system zeta Cancri made by their grandfather, Otto Wilhelm.

Vitaly A. Bronshten

Bibliography

Batten, A.H. "The Struves of Pulkovo—A Family of Astronomers." *Journal of the Royal Astronomical Society of Canada* 71, no. 5 (1977) 345–372.
———. *Resolute and Undertaking Characters: The Lives of Wilhelm and Otto Struve.* Dordrecht: Reidel, 1988.

Struve, Gustav Wilhelm Ludwig (Ludwig Ottovich) (1858–1920)

Russian astronomer and science administrator. Born in Pulkovo, son of Otto W. Struve, Gustav Wilhelm Ludwig graduated from Dorpat University (now Tartu in Estonia). After a period at **Pulkovo Observatory**, he studied at Bonn, Milan, and Leipzig, and from 1886 to 1894 was an astronomer at Dorpat. In 1894 he became professor of astronomy and geodesy at Kharkov University (now in Ukraine) and director of the observatory. Dismissed by the Bolsheviks, Struve died within the year.

Gustav Wilhelm Ludwig Struve was a student of **astrometry**. At Dorpat he took part in observing a zone for the international star catalogue sponsored by the Astronomische Gesellschaft. He also continued the family tradition of double star astronomy. He used occultatons of stars by the moon in order to refine the value of the lunar radius. In 1887 he developed a theory of the rotation of the Milky Way Galaxy. At Kharkov, Struve worked on a catalogue of circumpolar stars.

In keeping with Struve family traditions, Gustav Wilhelm Ludwig was a hardworking and able astronomer who excelled both as an observer and administrator.

Vitaly A. Bronshten

Bibliography

Batten, A.H. "The Struves of Pulkovo—A Family of Astronomers." *Journal of the Royal Astronomical Society of Canada* 71, no. 5 (1977) 345–372.
Frost, E.B. "The Family of Astronomers." *Popular Astronomy* 29, no. 9, (1921): 536–541.
Kolchinskii, I.G., A.A. Korsun' and M.G. Rodriges. *Astronomers.* In Russian. 2nd ed. Kiev, 1986.
Vorontsov-Velyaminov, B.A. *Essays on the History of Astronomy in Russia.* In Russian. Moscow, 1956.

Struve, Karl Hermann (Hermann Ottovich) (1854–1920)

Russo-German astronomer and science administrator. He was born in Pulkovo, Russia, son of astronomer Otto W. Struve. In 1877 Karl Hermann graduated from Dorpat University and went on to study at Strasbourg, Paris, Berlin, and Graz under such luminaries as Hermann Helmholz, Gustav Robert Kirchhoff, and Ludwig Boltzmann. Struve worked at the **Pulkovo Observatory** until 1895, when he was called to Königsberg as professor and director of the observatory. In 1904 Struve became head of the Berlin-Babelsberg Observatory and in 1913 director of the Neubabelsberg Observatory, where he remained until his death.

The main scientific contributions of Karl Hermann Struve were in observational astronomy and celestial mechanics. He continued the tradition of double star astronomy begun by his grandfather, Friedrich Georg

Wilhelm, and carried on by his father. Karl Hermann carried out a remarkable series of micrometric observations of the satellites of Mars, Saturn, and Neptune and developed mathematical models of their orbits. In 1888 he discovered the libration effect in the orbit of Hyperion, the seventh satellite of Saturn, and attributed this phenomenon to the gravitational influence of Saturn's sixth satellite, Titan. In 1892 he discovered the libration effect for two other satellites of Saturn, Mimas and Enceladus. His observations of the Martian satellite Phobos led to later investigations of the secular acceleration of its orbit. Struve also carried out extensive observational and theoretical investigations of Saturn's rings.

For these researches Struve was awarded the Damoiseau Prize by the Paris Academy of Sciences (1897) and the Gold Medal of the Royal Astronomical Society (1903).

Vitaly A. Bronshten

Bibliography

Clerke, A.M. *A Popular History of Astronomy during the Nineteenth Century*. 4th ed. London: Adam and Charles Black, 1902.

Frost, E.B. "The Family of Astronomers." *Popular Astronomy* 29, no. 9 (1921): 538–541.

Kolchinskii, I.G., A.A. Korsun' and M.G. Rodriges. *Astronomers*. In Russian. 2nd ed. Kiev, 1986.

Struve, Otto (1897–1963)

Otto Struve ranks with **Edwin Hubble**, **Harlow Shapley**, and **Henry Norris Russell** as one of the most influential American astronomers of the mid-twentieth century. Struve was born in Kharkov, Ukraine. He and his cousin Georg represent the fourth generation of astronomers in the Struve family, all of whom carried out work at the highest level, much of which dealt with double stars, ranging from the discovery and measurement of visual pairs to the spectroscopic study of interacting binaries.

The Struve family tradition also involved administrative responsibilities. After Struve earned his Ph.D. in 1923 at the University of Chicago with a study of short-period spectroscopic binaries, he moved up through the ranks at the **Yerkes Observatory**, becoming director in 1932. He held that post until 1947. In 1932 Struve also became founding director of McDonald Observatory, which was a joint endeavor of the universities of Texas and Chicago. At the end of his career (1959–1961) he became the first director of the National Radio Astronomy Observatory.

Struve published more than nine hundred papers and books, ranking him near the top among prolific astronomers. His most important work dealt with spectroscopic studies of stars. With G.A. Shain and C.T. Elvey, he studied spectral line widths as a function of spectral type and found that the implied rotational rates of the stars decreased monotonically from type O through type F. This suggested to Struve that a significant process in the evolution of a star was mass loss due to rotation, and that the most rapidly rotating stars might be on the verge of rotational instability, able to throw off rings of material or even to split into two stars.

In addition to stellar rotation, Struve also studied the Stark effect in stellar spectra, the broadening of spectrum lines due to the presence of electric fields in stellar atmospheres. He also studied turbulence in stellar atmospheres and published many papers on expanding shells around such stars as P Cygni. Much of this work required a larger telescope than those at Yerkes, and throughout the 1940s Struve availed himself of the greater light-gathering power of the 82-inch telescope at McDonald Observatory, which was then the second largest telescope in the world.

One of Struve's greatest accomplishments was rebuilding the astronomy department at the University of Chicago. He hired **S. Chandrasekhar**, **G. Kuiper**, **B. Strömgren**, G. Herzberg, W.W. Morgan, and J. Greenstein, and after World War II brought in visiting astronomers from Europe such as P. Swings, **J. Oort**, M. Minnaert, H.C. van de Hulst, and A. Unsöld. Yerkes Observatory and the University of Chicago became among the most significant astronomical research centers in the United States.

From 1932 to 1947 Struve served as editor of the *Astrophysical Journal*. He was also one of the instigators of modern cooperative research, having been significantly involved in the establishment of **Kitt Peak National Observatory** and the National Radio Astronomy Observatory. He was awarded many honors, the two highest being the Gold Medal of the Royal Astronomical Society (1944) and the presidency of the **International Astronomical Union** (1952–1955).

Kevin Krisciunas

Bibliography

Cowling, T.G. "Otto Struve 1897–1963." *Biographical Memoirs of Fellows of the Royal Society* 10 (1964): 283–304.

Evans, D.S., and J.D. Mulholland. *Big and Bright: A History of the McDonald Observatory*. Austin: University of Texas Press, 1986.

Herbig, G.H., ed. *Spectroscopic Astrophysics: An Assessment of the Contributions of Otto Struve*. Berkeley: University of California Press, 1970.

Krisciunas, K. "Otto Struve." *Biographical Memoirs of the National Academy of Sciences* 61 (1992): 350–387.

Struve, Otto Wilhelm (Otton Vasilievich) (1819–1905)

Russian astronomer, geodesist, and science administrator. Son of astronomer **Friedrich Georg Wilhelm Struve**, he was born in Dorpat, Russia (now Tartu, Estonia). In 1837 he was appointed assistant at the Dorpat Observatory and two years later received a doctorate from Dorpat University and moved to **Pulkovo Observatory**, where his father was director. Otto Wilhelm succeeded his father in 1862, retiring in 1889. He was honored with membership in the St. Petersburg Academy of Sciences and the French Academy of Sciences. For a decade Struve was president of the Astronomische Gesellschaft.

Otto Wilhelm Struve collaborated with his father in double star work, discovering more than five hundred pairs. He determined **stellar parallaxes** and observed Saturn's rings. Struve also tried to obtain observational evidence of star formation in nebulae. His value for the constant of precession was accepted for many years.

Like his father, Struve devoted much of his energy to geodesy and was involved in training military officers in this work. During his directorship, the great 30-inch Alvan Clark refractor (1883), at that time the largest telescope in the world, was installed at Pulkovo. Struve also helped organize new observatories in Kiev (now in the Ukraine), Tashkent (now in Uzbekistan), and Tiflis (now Tbilisi, Georgia). The development of astrophysics in the second half of the nineteenth century led Struve to open an astrophysical laboratory at the Pulkovo Observatory and institute astrophysical observations.

He was an astronomer of international reputation and a worthy successor to his distinguished father.

Vitaly A. Bronshten

Bibliography

Clerke, A.M. *A Popular History of Astronomy during the Nineteenth Century*. London: Adam and Charles Black, 1902.

Dadaev, A.N. *Pulkovo Observatory* [Leningrad, 1972]. Translated by K. Krisciunas. NASA TM-75803. Springfield, Va.: National Technical Information Service.

Frost, E.B. "The Family of Astronomers." *Popular Astronomy* 29, no. 9 (1921): 536–541.

Mikhailov, A.A. "Pulkovo Observatory." In *Astrophysics and Twentieth-Century Astronomy to 1950: Part A*, edited by O. Gingerich. *The General History of Astronomy,* edited by M. Hoskin, 119–122, 132. Cambridge: Cambridge University Press, 1984.

Vorontsov-Velyaminov, B.A. *Essays on the History of Astronomy in Russia*. In Russian. Moscow, 1956.

Yerpylev, N.P. "Development of the Stellar Astronomy in Russia in the Nineteenth Century." In Russian. In *Studies on the History of Astronomy*, vol. 4, 13–249. Moscow, 1958.

Sundials

A sundial determines the local time by means of a shadow cast by a gnomon onto a surface marked in hours. Although sundials date back to Antiquity, these time-finders were especially popular in the sixteenth through eighteenth centuries when mechanical clocks were becoming more and more common. The reason for this was that clocks required sundials to check if they were keeping correct time. The situation changed in the 1830s, when railroads began to use the telegraph to transmit a common time signal to all stations along their routes. This effectively established time zones and made the sundial—which indicated local rather than standard time—obsolete.

There are three basic classes of sundial. The design of instruments in each class depends on the apparent motion of the sun, which daily appears to rise in the east, climb into sky until it crosses the meridian, and set in the west. One class uses the variation in the sun's altitude; the second uses its variation in east-west position, given in terms of hour-angle or azimuth; and the third uses a combination of the two. In the early modern period, common altitude dials included pillar, ring, rectilinear, and skaphe dials. Directional dials, which measured the sun's hour-angle, included horizontal, vertical, polyhedral, and equatorial dials, such as those frequently found in gardens, fixed to the walls of buildings, or carried in pockets. Magnetic-azimuth dials also measured the sun's east-west varia-

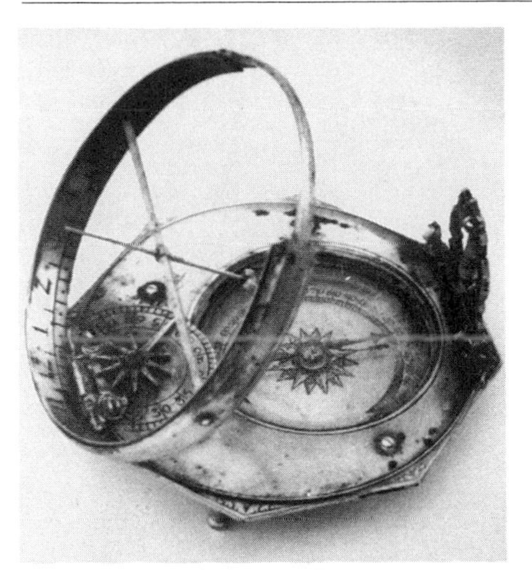

Augsburg-type pocket sundial by Johann Mathias Willebrand, Augsburg, ca. 1700 (A-158). (Courtesy of the Adler Planetarium, Chicago, Illinois)

tion. The universal ring dial is a good example of an instrument combining altitude and directional properties. Although some of these dials were fixed for a particular latitude, many were adjustable for different latitudes and so were popular with travelers. The major centers for the manufacture of sundials included Nuremberg, Augsburg, London, Paris, and Dieppe. Each region had its own distinctive style.

Thousands of sundials are preserved in museum and private collections worldwide. Copious publications on gnomonics testify further to the popularity of sundials. Written by scholars and instrument-makers, these tracts served as technical manuals on the design, construction, and use of different types.

For many years, sundials have fascinated curators, collectors, and hobbyists; and numerous publications have emanated from and been directed to these audiences. Although all these texts describe the history, theory, construction, and use of sundials, their emphasis varies in accordance with the target audience. Museum catalogues, for instance, focus on the hardware of historical instruments, whereas do-it-yourself manuals guide hobbyists in making their own dials. Despite the different levels of stress placed on the historical narrative, most works have tended to focus on the makers of dials rather than on the roles sundials have played in the social and cultural domain. In recent years, however, a few scholars have begun to study sundials in an interdisciplinary way, looking at them as scientific instruments, decorative objects, and artifacts of consumer culture. They have begun to study the economic and social conditions that gave rise to their production in specific regions at specific times, how the instruments were marketed and distributed, and how members of different social classes favored different styles.

Sara Schechner Genuth

Bibliography

Bobinger, M. *Alt-Augsburger Kompassmacher.* Augsburg: Rösler, 1966.

Bryden, D.J. *Sundials and Related Instruments.* Whipple Museum of the History of Science, Catalogue 6. Cambridge: Whipple Museum of the History of Science, 1988.

Chandler, B., and C. Vincent. "A Sure Reckoning: Sundials of the 17th and 18th Centuries." Metropolitan Museum of Art Bulletin 26 (1967): 154–169.

———. "Three Nürnberg Compassmacher: Hans Troschel the Elder, Hans Troschel the Younger, and David Beringer." *Metropolitan Museum Journal* 2 (1969): 211–216.

Gouk, P. *The Ivory Sundials of Nuremberg, 1500–1700.* Cambridge: Whipple Museum of the History of Science, 1988.

Higgins, K. "The Classification of Sundials." *Annals of Science* 9 (1953): 342–358.

Lloyd, S.A. *Ivory Diptych Sundials, 1570–1750.* Introductions by P. Gouk and A.J. Turner. Catalogue of the Collection of Historical Scientific Instruments, Harvard University. Cambridge: Collection of Historical Scientific Instruments, Harvard University, 1992.

Mayall, R.N., and M.W. Mayall. *Sundials: Their Construction and Use.* 3rd ed.Cambridge, Mass.: Sky Publishing, 1994.

Rohr, R.R.J. *Sundials: History, Theory, and Practice.* Translated by Gabriel Godin. Toronto: University of Toronto Press, 1970.

Waugh, A.E. *Sundials: Their Theory and Construction.* New York: Dover, 1973.

Zinner, E. *Deutsche und niederländische astronomische Instrumente des 11.-18. Jahrhunderts.* Munich: Beck, 1956.

Tables and Ephemerides, Astronomical

An annual calendar giving solar, lunar, and possibly planetary positions, plus other information (for example, ecclesiastical or meteorological) is commonly called an almanac. A tabulation of such positions for an entire year is usually designated as an ephemeris, although the distinction is often blurred, as in *The American Ephemeris and Nautical Almanac.* In previous centuries multiyear compendia of positions were often published, generally referred to by the plural word *ephemerides.* The planetary positions in these earlier ephemerides were not computed directly from the underlying mathematical theory but through the intermediary of tables, of which Kepler's Rudolphine Tables *(Tabulae Rudolphinae)* is perhaps the most famous example.

The first practical theory for predicting planetary positions arose in Babylon around 450 B.C.E. In its earliest form, this **Babylonian astronomy** was concerned with predicting times and places of certain specific phenomena such as first and last appearances, oppositions, and the beginning and ending of retrogression. In later centuries, owing to the rise of horoscopic astronomy, a demand arose for planetary positions on arbitrary days not associated with the specific phenomena, and Babylonian astronomers developed various tables to assist in the interpolation of planetary positions for any specified dates.

Comprehensive and unified tables for finding positions of the sun, moon, and the five naked-eye planets on any chosen date apparently originated with Ptolemy, who, in his *Almagest,* not only produced the underlying geometrical models and parameters for such predictions but also showed how to construct the necessary tables to simplify these procedures. Essentially, the process began with mean motion tables, which could be used in conjunction with a base position, or *radix,* to find approximately how far a planet had moved from that starting point. After determining the mean position, the astronomer would next apply a series of corrections, called by Ptolemy *prosthaphaereses* (literally, additio-subtractions), or, in the Middle Ages, equations. These corrections took into account the fact that the sun and planets do not move with uniform velocity around the sky, and, in the case of the planets, the fact of retrograde motion.

Ptolemy arranged his tables in a highly ingenious fashion, so that corrections depending on two variables—that is, those that might normally require a double-entry table—were split apart into multiplicative components each depending on a single variable. This form of table persisted into the seventeenth century. Ptolemy himself abstracted his tables from the *Almagest,* and, with several improvements of parameters and procedures, prepared the so-called Handy Tables (ca. 150 C.E.), which in turn became the basis of astronomical tables in the Islamic period.

Collections of tables in Arabic or Persian are called *zīj*es. In 1956, E.S. Kennedy published a list of over one hundred Islamic *zīj*es written from the eighth through fifteenth centuries of the common era. Besides mean motion and equation tables, the *zīj*es might typically include calendrical or chronological tables, trigonometric or spherical astronomy tables, geographical lists with latitudes and longitudes, and positions of the fixed stars. Among the more famous of these is the ninth-century *zīj* of the Baghdad astronomer al-Khwārizmī (which adopts some trigonometric methods commonly used by medieval Hindus) and the Hakimite *Zīj* of the tenth-century Cairo astronomer Ibn Yunus, which survives only in fragments. In contrast, the Ilkhani *Zīj* by Nasir ad-Dīn at-Tūsī and his collaborators at the Maragha Observatory in northwestern Iran, ca. 1270, is found in numerous copies, and parts of it were printed by the Oxford scholar John Greaves in 1652. Although only a single example of al-Battānī's *zīj* survives, its publication (1537) in Latin translation by Plato of Tivoli made it influential in the development of European astronomy (and won for Battānī a place on the moon under his Latinized name of Albategnius). A monumental edition of his work by C.A. Nallino, in three volumes (Milan, 1899–1907), provided the foundation for the modern study of Islamic astronomy.

In Moorish Spain, a set of astronomical tables today known as the Toledan Tables were assembled in the eleventh century, based primarily on the work of al-Zarqāllu, al-Battānī, and al-Khwārizmī. The radices, or starting positions, for the planets were given for the date of the Hijra. While the other parameters differed somewhat from those of Ptolemy's Handy Tables, they were very much in the same Ptolemaic form. The Toledan Tables were used, for example, as the basis of an *Almanach perpetuum* commencing with March of 1300 written by the Jewish-Provençal astronomer Prophatius Judaeus (ca. 1236–ca. 1307). Around the same time, these tables were rewritten in Christianized form by giving the radices for the Incarnation (A.D. 1) and also by setting the times for the longitudes of other European cities. Thus we find, for example, the Toulousean Tables or the Marseillan Tables.

Sometime after 1320, the **Alfonsine Tables** rapidly superseded the *Toledans.* Concerning the origins of the *Alfonsines,* there is a surprising amount of controversy. Alfonso X, king of Castile from 1273 to 1284, encouraged his astronomers and translators to prepare a major corpus of astronomical texts in Castellan Spanish. Included in the extant materials is a set of instructions, or canons, for planetary tables, but the tables themselves have not been found. What survives as the Alfonsine Tables seems in crucial ways different from the Castellan canons, and there is strong evidence that the form in which the tables were widely disseminated in Europe originated in Paris in the 1320s. What particularly distinguishes the Alfonsine Tables is an advanced precessional theory (which includes a periodically varying term called trepidation), and an ingenious sliding sexagesimal scheme that allows the mean motion tables to be used with an arbitrary set of radices. Hence it is possible to compute for dates in the Muslim calendar as readily as with the Christian Julian calendar. One can imagine that such a flexibility would have been even more desirable in Spain than in France, but the specific surviving alternative canons that match the existing tables are certainly well documented as arising in Paris.

With the advent of printing, the fifteenth-century German astronomer Johannes Regiomontanus decided to exploit the new technology for the advance of his science. He computed a monumental ephemeris for 1474 to 1506, and printed it in his own shop in Nuremberg. His work was essentially based on the Alfonsine Tables. (Those tables had first propagated in manuscript form, but in 1483 the first of a number of printed editions appeared.) The Regiomontanus *Ephemerides* were reprinted several times, and as their expiration date drew near, they were extended by Jacob Pflaum and Johannes Stoeffler of Tübingen through 1531. In turn, several astronomers tried their hand at extending the run in 1532, but Stoeffler himself had prepared the major calculation, going to 1551.

Regiomontanus devised a format for ephemerides that became standard for several centuries—namely, to tabulate the daily positions for a month on the left side of the opening, and to display the astrological aspects of the planets with the moon and with each other on the right-hand side. The accuracy of the Alfonsine Tables was sufficiently poor that discrepancies with the observations could be readily noticed, especially in the times of conjunctions shown in the astrological tabulation. Thus, for example, Copernicus recorded in a manuscript note in one of his books that "Mars exceeds the numbers by more than two degrees, and Saturn is exceeded by a degree and a half." Modern calculations show that this situation prevailed at the time of the great conjunction of Jupiter and Saturn in 1503–1504.

Nicholas Copernicus, in his *De revolutionibus* (1543), gave planetary tables by which positions could be calculated, but he did not live long enough to issue handy tables based on his astronomy. This fell to Erasmus Reinhold, the astronomer at the University of Wittenberg, who published the Copernican-based *Prutenicae tabulae* in 1551. These Prutenic Tables were cast in essentially the same form as the Alfonsine Tables, so astronomers could use them without making any commitment to the heliocentric cosmology of Copernicus's book, and the predictive procedures depended in no way on heliocentrism. Nor did the accuracy of the new tables—for they were essentially based on the Ptolemaic observations, with only minor adjustments that the much longer temporal baseline allowed. Copernicus never mentioned in print the observational discrepancies he had found in 1504, and for practical purposes his tables were not conspicuously better. **Tycho Brahe** was one of the few astronomers who made systematic comparisons with different predictive methods. He had been propelled into astronomy in part because the Copernican ephemerides predicted the great conjunction of Jupiter and Saturn in 1563 by an error of nearly two days. At the same time, the Alfonsine ephemerides showed an error of about a month, but this disparity between the two was unusual, as generally the errors were comparable, and, as **Johannes Kepler** was later to complain, the Copernican predictions for Mars went off by nearly 5 degrees in 1625.

In the second half of the sixteenth century, several ephemeris-makers, including Johannes Stadius and G.A. Magini, published their own tables, which scarcely differed in effect from the *Prutenics,* although Magini later published a supplement to his tables that was the first to adopt some of Kepler's innovations. The first radical departure came with Kepler's *Tabulae Rudolphinae* of 1627. While all previous tables had incorporated the effect of the solar (or terrestrial) motion into the procedure for each planet independently, Kepler arranged the Rudolphine calculation to find separately the heliocentric position of the earth and of the planet in question, and then to combine these trigonometrically to establish the geocentric coordinates. For Kepler, the calculation of the planetary latitude was an integral part of the procedure, including a projection to the ecliptic plane. Furthermore, because the transcendental Kepler's equation was involved in correction of the mean motions, Kepler provided a novel (and necessarily unfamiliar) technique of logarithmic interpolation to facilitate this part of the procedure. With this attention to detail, the Rudolphine Tables provided positions thirty times more accurate than previous procedures allowed. A decisive moment came with the prediction of a transit of Mercury on November 7, 1631. J.B. Riccioli remarked in 1665 that Ptolemy, Copernicus, and Longomontanus (Tycho Brahe's apprentice) each erred by about 5 degrees in predicting the event, whereas Kepler missed by less than 10 minutes of arc.

Kepler computed the first ephemerides using the new tables, for 1617–1628, and then with his protégé Jacob Bartsch for 1629–1636. Subsequently, Lorenz Eichstadt continued the series from 1636 through 1665, and after him Johannes Hecker carried on through 1680. When Hecker's ephemerides ran out, the French *Connaissance des Temps* began its series of annual volumes, which has continued to this day, essentially providing an unbroken sequence from the time of Kepler. An independent ephemeris tradition in England, involving the astrologers Vincent Wing, John Gadbury, and John Wing, provided a connected series of ephemerides from 1652 until 1708. In Italy, an even longer sequence, with the names Andrea Argoli and Francisco Montebruni heading the list, continued into the nineteenth century. In Bologna, a sequence of ephemerides by Flamino Mezzavacca beginning in 1675 held an unchallenged supremacy, but after his death Eustachio Manfredi began an alternative series, which created some animosity with Antonio Ghisilieri, who considered himself Mezzavacca's heir. Ghisilieri in 1731 published nearly a hundred pages of errors in Manfredi's ephemerides, although modern computations show that Manfredi's positions were generally better. Meanwhile, the French either used the Italian ephemerides for control on their own work, or else copied them outright.

During this time, the underlying tables were continually improved. In particular, the tables of Philippe de La Hire (Paris 1687, 1702) and of **Jacques Cassini** (Paris, 1740) provided the basis for the French calculations. In England, **Edmond Halley**'s posthumously published *Tabulae astronomicae* (London, 1749) came on the scene too late to have much practical effect on the computation of ephemerides, but his book is notable for its remark on the perturbing interactions of Jupiter and Saturn. Although Isaac Newton's *Principia* (London, 1687) had pointed the way to theoretical improvement of planetary positions through the concept of mutual perturbations, it was not until the latter part of the eighteenth century that practical calculations benefited from these insights. During that century, more specialized tables appeared, such as those for the sun and moon by Johann Tobias Mayer, which shared the prize from the

English Parliament for finding longitude at sea. Nevertheless, Mayer's tables were essentially empirical and based on observations rather than theory for the new terms included in the calculations.

In 1767, the annual English *Nautical Almanac* began its sequence under the instigation of the Astronomer Royal, Nevil Maskelyne, and in 1776 Johann Elert Bode's *Berliner astronomisches Jahrbuch* inaugurated its series. The *American Ephemeris and Nautical Almanac* began for the year 1855, and from 1981 has been combined with the British *Nautical Almanac* under the title *The Astronomical Almanac.*

In the nineteenth century, the annual national almanacs virtually replaced ephemerides containing positions for many years. Planetary tables developed by **Simon Newcomb** at the Nautical Almanac Office began to serve as the basis for American and English calculations, while the French used those devised by **U.J.J. Le Verrier** at the **Paris Observatory**. The lunar tables of the German astronomer **Peter Andreas Hansen**, published at the expense of the British government in 1857, caused Astronomer Royal **George Biddell Airy** to remark, "Probably in no recorded instance has practical science ever advanced so far in a single stride." His tables were superseded only in 1919, by those of **Ernest W. Brown** at Yale University.

The development of electronic computers opened a new era in calculating ephemerides. In 1951 **Wallace Eckert**, **Dirk Brouwer**, and **Gerald Clemence** published ephemerides of the five outer planets that were computed from step-by-step numerical integrations. Further, computers made it possible to calculate almanacs directly from the trigonometric series of gradational theories, without the intermediary of tables.

In this century several rather sophisticated sets of tables were generated especially for chronological use, including those by P.V. Neugebauer (Leipzig, 1914; Berlin, 1929) and Karl Schoch (Berlin, 1927). The Schoch tables plus the advent of electronic computers made possible a long ephemeris for chronological purposes, William D. Stahlman's and Owen Gingerich's *Solar and Planetary Longitudes for Years –2500 to +2000* (Madison, 1963).

The last great set of printed ephemerides is Bryant Tuckerman's *Planetary, Lunar and Solar Positions,* which gives geocentric longitudes and latitudes accurate to about 0.01 degree for 601 B.C.E. to 1649 C.E. These are based on the trigonometric formulae of U.J.J. Le Verrier for the inner planets (1855–1861) and on those of A. Gaillot for Jupiter (1913) and Saturn (1904). Today, these formulae are used in various personal computer programs that can quickly calculate positions for any historical date, which makes the printed form of the ephemerides essentially obsolete. At the same time, vastly refined step-by-step integrations of planetary positions have made possible the far more precise Jet Propulsion Laboratory (JPL) Ephemerides, which are available in various computer-accessible forms from the JPL in Pasadena, California.

Owen Gingerich

Bibliography

Gingerich, O. "Early Copernican Ephemerides." In *The Eye of Heaven: Ptolemy, Copernicus, Kepler,* edited by O. Gingerich, 205–220. New York: American Institute of Physics, 1993.

Gingerich, O., and B.L. Welther. "The Accuracy of Historical Ephemerides." In *Planetary, Lunar, and Solar Positions, New and Full Moons, A.D. 1650–1805, Memoirs of the American Philosophical Society* 59S (1983).

Kennedy, E.S. "A Survey of Islamic Astronomical Tables." *Transactions of the American Philosophical Society* 46, part 2 (1956).

Kepler J., *Gesammelte Werke,* Band X, *Tabulae Rudolphinae.* Munich: C.H. Beck'sche Verlag, 1969.

Magini, G.A. *Supplementum Ephemeridum ac Tabularum Secundorum Mobilum.* Venice: Heirs of Damian Zenarius, 1614.

Neugebauer, P.V. *Astronomische Chronologie.* Berlin and Leipzig: 1929.

Poulle, E. *Les Tables Alphonsines.* Paris: Centre National de la Recherche Scientifique, 1984.

———. "The Alfonsine Tables and Alfonso X of Castile." *Journal for the History of Astronomy* 19 (1988): 97–113.

Schoch, K. *Planeten-Tafeln für Jedermann.* Berlin-Pankow: Linser-Verlag, 1927.

Seidelmann, P.K., ed. *Explanatory Supplement to the Astronomical Almanac.* Mill Valley, Calif.: University Science Books, 1992.

Toomer, G. "A Survey of the Toledan Tables." *Osiris* 15 (1968): 5–174.

Tuckerman, B. *Planetary, Lunar, and Solar Positions, 601 B.C. to A.D. 1, Memoirs of the American Philosophical Society* 56 (1962).

———. *Planetary, Lunar, and Solar Positions, A.D. 2 to A.D. 1649, Memoirs of the American Philosophical Society* 59 (1964).

Telescope, Invention of (to ca. 1630)

The origins of the telescope are still shrouded in mystery. Although the early history of the instrument has now been well established, its prehistory is sketchy and speculative due to the paucity of sources.

The prehistory of the telescope begins with the use of eyeglasses late in the thirteenth century. Thanks to the work of Edward Rosen, we know that convex pieces of glass (called lenses after *lens,* the Latin word for lentil), either in a frame or attached to the bill of a cap, came into use as reading glasses for scholars suffering from presbyopia. These are the same as the off-the-shelf reading glasses that can be bought in drug stores today. Concave eyeglasses came somewhat later: The earliest sources for these date from the middle of the fifteenth century, and they were used to correct the weak vision of the young. Although convex and concave mirrors were treated fully in medieval optical treatises, little is known about their manufacture and use. But such mirrors were clearly becoming common, as the work of Flemish painters testifies. Having established that lenses and mirrors of all necessary varieties were available in Europe by about 1500, it must be said that very little is known as yet about their qualities, especially in the case of mirrors.

In the speculative magical and mathematical literature of the sixteenth century, a number of allusions to devices for seeing faraway things can be found. Some of these are clearly miraculous, such as the instrument by which King Ptolemy could see his enemies at 600 miles. Others, such as the perspective glass mentioned by **Thomas Harriot** in *A Briefe and True Report of the New Found Land of Virginia* (1588) are surely single lenses or mirrors. There are, however, several references that are not so easy to dismiss.

Among the mathematical practitioners in Elizabethan England, Leonard Digges seems to have experimented with combinations of mirrors and lenses, and his son, Thomas, testified to his father's "continual painfull practices" in this area (Van Helden, 30). Thomas Digges's description of the effects his father had achieved were fanciful and have therefore usually been discounted. But an acquaintance of his, William Bourne, wrote about optical devices on several occasions. In his *Inventions and Devices* (1578), the 110th device is one for seeing "any small thing a great distance of from you" (Van Helden, 30). Bourne states here that one should receive the beam of light in a very large burning glass 14 or 16 inches in diameter—a size that surely could not be made at that time—and then focused on a concave mirror. Although Bourne's argument is rather fanciful (harking back to the miraculous effects speculated on by Roger Bacon, three centuries earlier), it contains a description of a device that will actually work as a telescope. This has recently been shown beyond a shadow of a doubt by Colin Ronan, who has actually built a telescope to Bourne's specifications. We can speculate about the quality of the lenses and mirrors available to Digges (whom Bourne mentions elsewhere) and Bourne, and point out that this instrument, even with modern components, is difficult to use and does not produce very good images, but the essential point is that Bourne's instrument entails the telescopic effect.

One difficulty remains. Inasmuch as the description of the device appeared in a published work, why is there no evidence of its being used by anyone after Digges and Bourne? Perhaps the image was too poor to be of any practical use; the field of view was certainly minuscule.

The other tantalizing reference is found in the second edition of Giovanni Battista Della Porta's *Magia naturalis* of 1589. Porta, a polymath with great interest in magical and playful devices, turned his attention to the powers of lenses and mirrors in Book X, where we find the following statement: "With a Concave [glass] you shall see many small things afar off, very clearly; with a Convex, things [nearer to be greater,]" but more obscurely: "if you know how to fit them both together, you shall see things both afar off, and things neer hand, both greater and clearly" (Van Helden, 35). **Johannes Kepler** and others later ascribed the invention of the telescope to Porta on the basis of this statement. When Porta himself saw a spyglass in 1609, he stated that it was a hoax and based on his writings, although he referred to another book that does not, in fact, contain anything like a description of such an instrument.

In the passage in *Magia naturalis,* Porta was referring to the correction of defective vision: Immediately after the sentence cited above, he writes: "I have much helped some of my friends, who saw things afar off, weakly; and what was neer, confusedly, that they might see al things clearly." When it came to extending normal vision, however, Porta gave a confused description of a magical device that led nowhere.

It is clear that by 1600 the interest in extending normal vision was piqued. Perhaps also the quality and strengths of lenses had reached the point at which a combination of lenses that gave noticeable and useful magnification became possible. From the above, one would expect that the telescope would first have made its official appearance in Italy or England; in fact, it happened in the northern part of the low countries, a region that earlier had been an intellectual backwater. With the founding of the Dutch Republic, in 1579, and the fall of Antwerp to the Spanish in 1585, trade, industry, and intellectual life in the north entered a period of great flowering. It is interesting to note that Italian glass-makers moved to Middelburg at this time and that Thomas Digges may have been with the English expeditionary forces in the province of Zeeland.

It was in Middelburg, the capital of Zeeland, that the telescope began its public career. On or about September 25, 1608 (Gregorian), a person left Middelburg for The Hague with a letter from the provincial government to its delegation to the States-General. The letter described the bearer as one "who claims to have a certain device by means of which all things at a very great distance can be seen as if they were nearby, by looking through glasses which he claims to be a new invention," and asked the delegates to be helpful in his efforts to gain advantage from the device. A week later, the States-General discussed the patent application of Hans Lipperhey, a spectacle-maker of Middelburg on "a certain instrument for seeing far" (Van Helden, 36).

Although the States-General were very interested in this device because of its obvious military and naval applications, Lipperhey did not receive a patent on the telescope. Within weeks two other claimants came forward, Jacob Metius of Alkmaar and another spectacle-maker from Middelburg, identified by Cornelis de Waard as Sacharias Janssen. In the face of these competing claims, the States-General decided that the instrument was too easy to copy to be protected by a patent. Metius was voted a small sum for his efforts, and Lipperhey received a large sum for making several binocular instruments with lenses made of rock crystal for the use of the nation.

At the time, the Dutch government was negotiating for an armistice in its long-standing war with the Spanish Crown. The Hague was therefore filled with foreign observers. News of Lipperhey's patent application spread rapidly through diplomatic pouches, and before the end of the year it had reached France, England, Italy, and Germany. Since the invention was easy to duplicate, spyglasses quickly became available abroad. In April 1609 they were for sale in Paris. In May a traveler offered one to the Count of Fuentes in Milan, and in August of that year Porta in Naples saw one and described it in a letter. Simon Marius in Ansbach probably obtained his first spyglass as early as October 1608, and although it is not known when Thomas Harriot in England made his first instrument, we know that by the beginning of August 1609 he had turned a six-powered spyglass to the heavens.

Over the years scholars have championed all three of the claimants for the invention. In the seventeenth century René Descartes and Christiaan Huygens gave priority to Metius, while Pierre Borel made an elaborate case for Janssen. In the nineteenth century archival research in The Hague uncovered the claim of Lipperhey, for whom we now have the oldest indisputable evidence. At the beginning of the twentieth century, Cornelis de Waard uncovered numerous sources in the archives of Middelburg. From these has emerged a fuller picture of the mysterious Janssen (who turns out to have been a shady character) and a confirmation of Lipperhey's priority. In his later studies of the journal of Isaac Beeckman, de Waard found the statement by Janssen's son, Johannes Zachariassen, that his father had made the first telescope in 1604 after the example of one in the possession of an Italian and bearing the date "190," presumably 1590 (Van Helden, 6–9).

Zachariassen's statement is plausible enough; de Waard's archival searches certainly documented the presence of Italians in the glass works of Middelburg around 1590. We can speculate that Janssen presented a spyglass to Prince Maurice some time between 1604 and 1608 and that Maurice managed to keep it a state secret until Lipperhey, a colleague of Janssen's in Middelburg, came forward with his own version of the instrument and made it public. In the absence of further evidence, it remains a likely story. What is perhaps more important is that Zachariassen's statement calls into question the nature of this particular historical question. Although it would be nice to know the identity of the inventor of the instrument, how can we be sure that there was an inventor, and what does it mean to have invented the telescope?

It appears from Porta's statement in *Magia naturalis* that he had combined convex and concave lenses of various strengths. Perhaps some of these combinations, using a stronger concave and a weaker convex lens, magnified one and a half or two times. If Porta was looking for a device such as King Ptolemy had with which he could discover his enemies at 600 miles, would he think much of such a mundane combination of lenses? Another Italian, Raffaello Gualterotti, wrote to Galileo in 1610 that he had made such a device in 1598, but that he had considered it a "feeble thing" and ignored it (Van Helden, 45–46).

This argument means that the telescope was there before anyone realized it and that at some point when, say, strong enough concave lenses became available, someone—surely a spectacle-maker—realized that the combination of the strongest concave and weakest convex lenses in his inventory gave a useful magnifying effect, say two and half or three diameters. Presumably this realization came to someone in Middelburg in or shortly before 1608, and then others, such as Jacob Metius, realized that they had been using the same device but at a lower magnification, probably for other purposes. No wonder that when Porta finally saw a spyglass, almost a year later, he called it a hoax.

Little information exists concerning these spyglasses. The earliest surviving description and depiction is one made by Porta in August 1609. Porta wrote to Federico Cesi: "It is a small tube of silvered tine, one palm long and three inches in diameter, which has a convex glass in the end. There is another tube of the same [material], four inches long, which enters into the first one, and in the end it has a concave [glass], which is soldered like the first. . . . And it goes in and out like a trombone, so that it adjusts to the visions of the observers, which are all different" (Van Helden, 44).

The Neapolitan and Roman palms were about 25 cm in length, so the combined length of the two tubes was about 33 cm. Let us assume that this instrument had the same magnification—three—as the first spyglass constructed by Galileo a month or two earlier. Since the length of a simple telescope is equal to the sum of the focal lengths of the two lenses (in this case the focal length of the ocular is negative), the focal length of the objective was about 50 cm and that of the ocular about (–) 17 cm.

What Porta's description does not mention but the sketch shows is that the aperture of this instrument was very small, perhaps a centimeter at most. We may surmise that the lens curvature was so poor that a large aperture made the device useless. It did not increase light-gathering power; it merely magnified.

Such were the first spyglasses that spread through Europe between October 1608 and the summer of 1609. To point them to the heavens was an obvious thing to do, and even at such low magnifications (and poor quality) they showed that there were many more fixed stars than were visible with the naked eye. Serious exploration of the heavens required higher magnifications and larger apertures. In August 1609 Harriot turned a six-powered instrument to the moon; later that same month Galileo presented an eight-powered device to the Venetian Senate. By the end of the year, Galileo was examining the heavens with a twenty-powered instrument and began his discoveries that ushered in the age of telescopic astronomy. The instrument received the name *telescope* at a banquet in Rome in April 1611.

It is interesting to note that the small field of view of the Galilean telescope quickly became the limiting factor to higher magnifications. At a power of twenty, the field is about fifteen arcminutes. Although slow improvements in lens quality allowed a gradual increase in apertures (Galileo's ranged from $1\frac{1}{2}$ to $2\frac{1}{2}$ cm), the potential of this instrument for celestial discovery was reached within three or four years of Lipperhey's patent application.

Albert Van Helden

Bibliography

De Waard, C. *De Uitvinding der Verrekijkers.* The Hague, 1906.

Drake, S. *The Unsung Journalist and the Origin of the Telescope.* Los Angeles: Zeitlin and Ver Brugge, 1976.

Ilardi, V. "Eyeglasses and Concave Lenses in Fifteenth-Century Florence and Milan: New Documents." *Renaissance Quarterly* 29 (1976): 341–360.

Rosen, E. "The Invention of Eye-Glasses." *Journal for the History of Medicine and Allied Sciences* 11 (1956): 13–46, 183–218.

Van Helden, A. "The Invention of the Telescope." *Transactions of the American Philosophical Society* 67, no. 4 (1977): 5–67.

Telescopes, from Galileo to Fraunhofer

The earliest telescopes emerged from opticians' experiments. Spectacles made from convex lenses to correct far-sightedness were available as early as the thirteenth century; similar spectacles made from concave lenses to correct near-sightedness followed in the 1500s. By 1600, suitable lenses were available in optical shops to allow the construction of telescopic devices of two or three power. Dutch spectacle-maker Hans Lipperhey attempted to obtain a patent for such an instrument in 1608, but Dutch officials denied his application because other similar devices were available. Descriptions of these instruments spread quickly throughout Europe, providing optical craftsmen with sufficient information to copy the Dutch spyglass.

Among the earliest experimenters was **Galileo Galilei**, who heard of the Dutch instrument during the summer of 1609. Galileo soon crafted a three-power instrument, followed by a nine-power telescope that he showed to the Venetian Senate. The Galilean telescope, constructed of a concave lens eyepiece and a convex lens objective, was relatively easy to make, provided an erect image, and was characterized by a sharp field. Various problems with materials and production methods, however, impeded the development of the telescope. The lack of clear and homogeneous glass and the absence of commercial abrasives led to lenses of marginal quality, as indicated by the estimate that no more than 10 percent of Galileo's own instruments proved satisfactory. Nonetheless, Galileo continued to improve the telescope, constructing instruments of as much as thirty power. The largest of these devices was 49 inches long with an aperture of 1¾ inches.

An important advance in telescope design emerged from the theoretical treatment of lens systems in **Johannes Kepler**'s *Dioptrice* (1611). Kepler concluded that a telescopic device could be constructed from two convex lenses. The disadvantage to this astronomical telescope was its inverted image, but the advantages of a larger field of view and greater

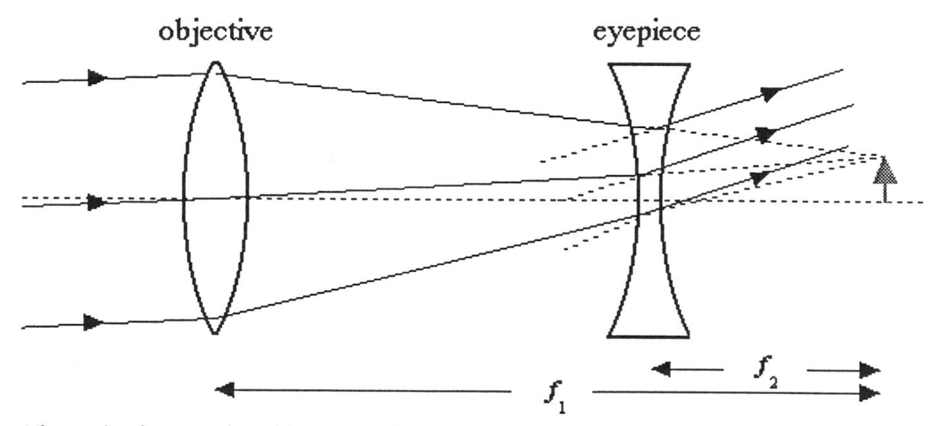

The optical configuration of a Galilean telescope. By use of a convex objective lens and a concave eyepiece, a Galilean telescope produced an erect image. The path of three representative rays of light are shown. For an object (the arrow) at infinity, an intermediate image is formed at the common focal point of the two lenses. The magnification of the telescope is given by the ratio of focal lengths: f_1 / f_2. (Figure by Charles J. Peterson)

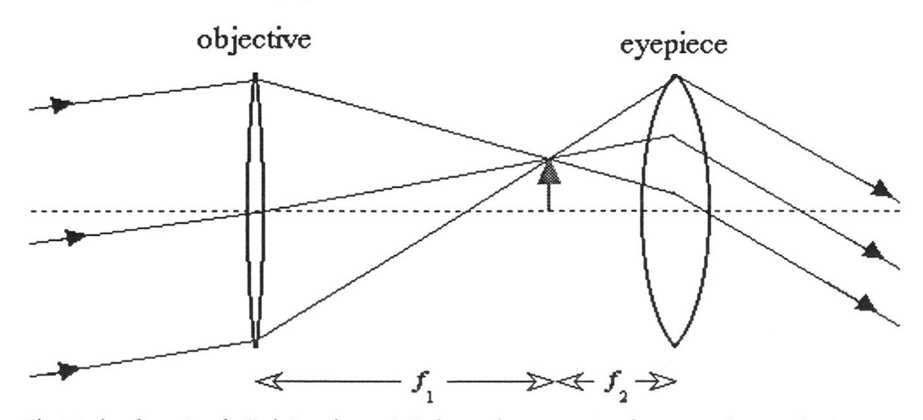

The optical configuration of a Keplerian telescope. A Keplerian telescope consisting of two concave lenses produced an inverted image, as illustrated by the paths of three light rays coming from an object at infinity. The position of the intermediate image formed by the objective is shown by an arrow. The telescope magnification is given by the ratio of focal lengths: f_1 / f_2. (Figure by Charles J. Peterson)

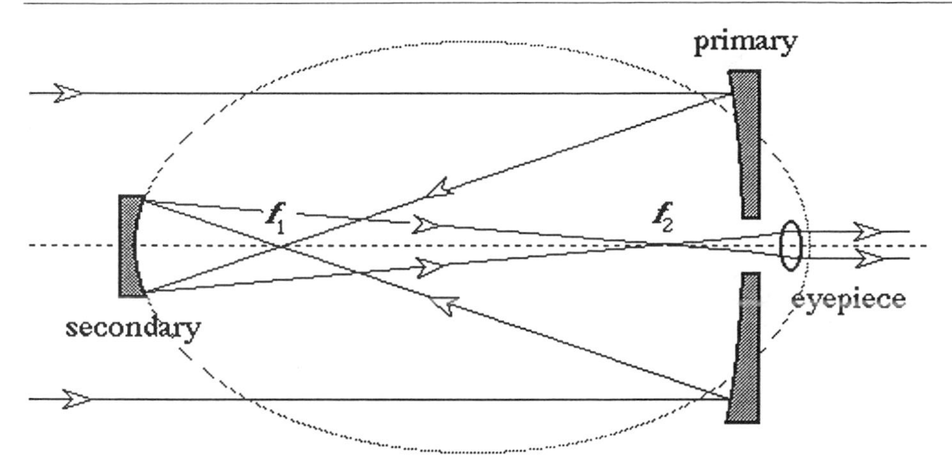

A Gregorian reflector combines a parabolic primary mirror (with a hole in the center) and an ellipsoidal secondary mirror. The focal point f_1 is common to both mirrors. F_2 is the focus of the secondary mirror. Light from a star forms an image at F_2 and is observed with an eyepiece. (Figure by Charles J. Peterson)

magnification could not be ignored. Unfortunately, the higher magnification was accompanied by greater spherical and chromatic aberration (geometric distortion and false color), particularly evident when using the instrument for celestial observations. Improved lens-grinding techniques in the mid-seventeenth century provided better spherical lenses of decreased curvature (and increased focal length), which led to longer telescopes of good quality. The greater focal length gave a larger image and minimized the apparent effects of spherical and chromatic aberration.

Among the most noteworthy early work on very-long-focus telescopes was that of Johannes Hevelius. As described in his *Machinae Coelestis* (1673), Hevelius constructed telescopes with focal lengths of as much as 150 feet and lenses up to 8 inches in diameter. Existing mounting techniques proved inadequate, leading Hevelius to design an open structure for his instruments. A long plank carried the objective and eyepiece and was suspended from a high mast. The telescope was adjusted by a complex system of ropes and pulleys, which required several assistants. The largest of these telescopes, however, proved virtually worthless. The open frame flexed significantly and produced severe vibrations in the slightest breeze.

Contemporaries of Hevelius included the brothers Christiaan and Constantine Huygens. Constructing telescopes with focal lengths up to 210 feet, the Huygens brothers developed the aerial telescope by mounting the objective in an iron tube at the top of a high pole. The objective could be raised and lowered on the mast and was connected to the eyepiece by a long string. When the string was taut, the eyepiece and objective were in approximate alignment. Although somewhat steadier than other designs, the Huygens mounting remained cumbersome and proved to be a short-lived experiment.

The second half of the seventeenth century also witnessed the initial efforts to design and construct reflecting telescopes. Scottish mathematician James Gregory described the Gregorian reflector in his *Optica Promota* (1663), proposing a parabolic primary mirror (with an eyepiece in its center) and an elliptical secondary mirror. Gregory announced that this arrangement would give an erect image, no spherical aberration, and minimal chromatic aberration. Although theoretically sound, the Gregorian telescope could not be constructed at the time because of opticians' inability to produce aspherical surfaces. Attempts to construct such an instrument with a spherical primary mirror proved disappointing.

The most significant impetus to the development of reflectors came from the early work in optics of Isaac Newton. From superficial research in the 1660s, Newton concluded that refracting telescopes would always have chromatic aberration because dispersion was directly proportional to refraction in all media. Newton quickly turned his attention to the construction of reflecting telescopes, presenting to the Royal Society in 1672 an instrument with a spherical mirror slightly less than 1½ inches in diameter. Providing a magnification of no more than forty, the small device held a mirror made of a bright metal alloy of six parts copper and two parts tin, to which Newton added one part arsenic to improve polishing characteristics. A small flat secondary mirror inclined at a 45-degree angle to the instrument's axis reflected the beam from the primary mirror to an eyepiece mounted in the side of the tube. Although Newton remained convinced of the superiority of reflectors to refractors, the small size of his instruments obscured design flaws. Larger Newtonian reflectors would have displayed significant spherical aberration and would probably have been no more effective than contemporary large refractors.

The key early improvements to reflecting telescopes were the work of John Hadley in the 1720s. Assisted by his brothers, Hadley constructed an impressive Newtonian reflector of 6-inch aperture and 62-inch focus. Although cast as a spherical mirror, the primary was carefully polished to give a good approximation of a parabolic shape. Equally important was a significant advance in mounting technique. Large instruments required a technique to set the telescope on the observed object and to follow it as it moved across the night sky. Hadley developed the altazimuth mount to achieve this goal, with the altitude axis parallel to the horizon and the azimuth axis perpendicular to it. The simplicity of this mounting was compromised by the need to move the telescope along both axes simultaneously to keep an object in view, but the ease with which this could be done in Hadley's instrument represented an important advantage.

As a result of Hadley's work, reflectors became increasingly common in the eighteenth century. Among the most successful telescope-makers was James Short of London, who began building superior Gregorian instruments in the early 1740s. Polishing mirrors with a combination of strokes to create a parabolic curve, Short produced instruments up to 18-inch aperture and 12-foot focus. Although most of Short's telescopes were equipped with altazimuth mounts, he also experimented with an equatorial mounting. By 1749, he had developed a mounting in which one axis was parallel to the earth's axis of rotation. Because movement along this axis canceled the diurnal rotation, the other axis (perpendicular to the first) represented the only one that needed to be moved to track an object. Once perfected in the late eighteenth century, the equatorial mounting greatly simplified astronomical observations.

Early reflector technology peaked in the final quarter of the eighteenth century through the work of **William Herschel**. By the late 1770s, the musician-turned-astronomer had built several reflectors of up to 9-inch aperture and 10-foot focus. The most successful of Herschel's early telescopes was a 7-foot Newtonian (6¼-inch aperture) completed in late 1778. With this instrument, Herschel compiled the first catalogue of double stars and, in 1781, discovered the planet Uranus.

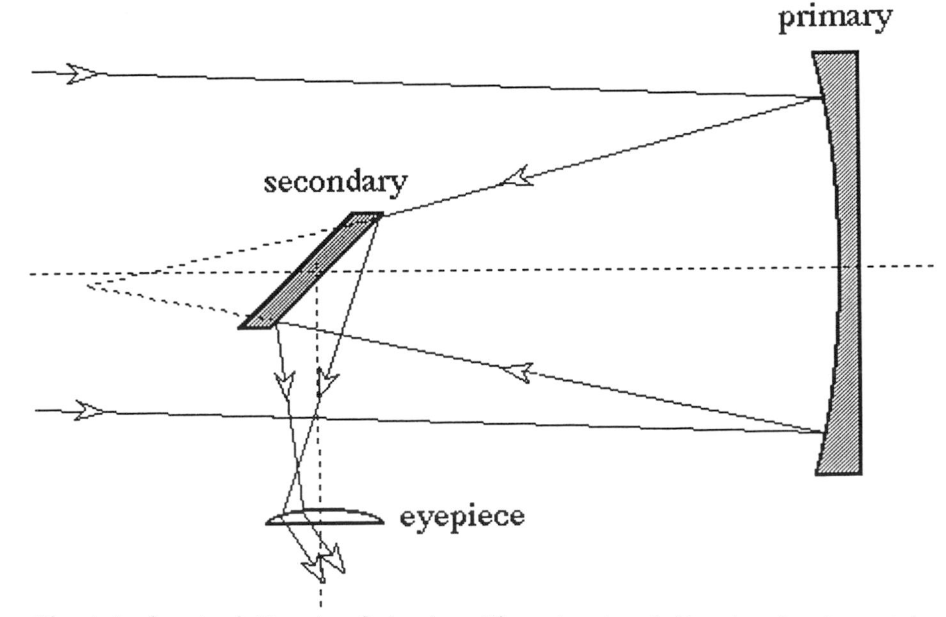

The optical configuration of a Newtonian reflecting telescope. The secondary mirror of a Newtonian reflector is an optical flat that reflects light to an eyepiece at right angles to the optical axis of the parabolic primary mirror. (Figure by Charles J. Peterson)

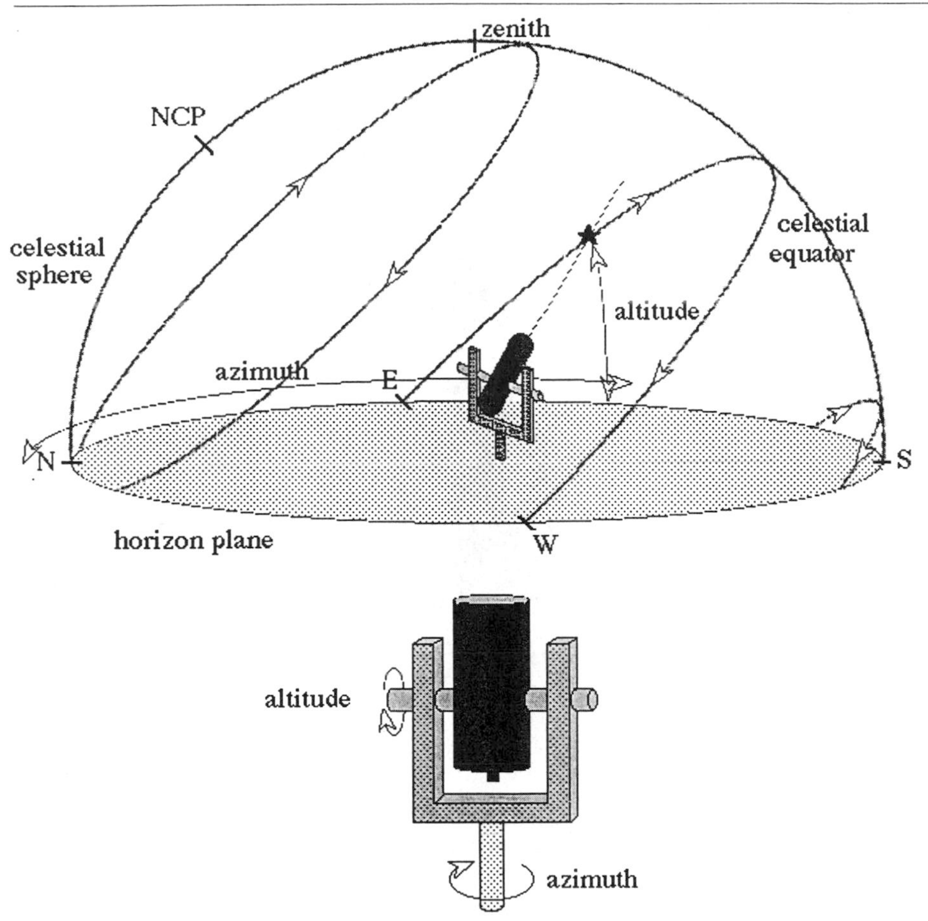

Schematic diagram of the operation of an altazimuth telescope mounting. An altazimuth mount (pictured at the bottom of the diagram) utilizes two axes, one vertical and one horizontal, to point the telescope to any position in the sky. The horizontal axis allows rotation to any elevation or altitude above the horizon. The vertical axis allows the telescope to sweep in a cone about the zenith as indicated in the upper portion of the diagram. To track a star across the sky (the motion of the star is caused by the earth's rotation), both angles must be continually changed. In addition, the orientation of the field viewed through the eyepiece of the telescope on an altazimuth mount will rotate as the instrument follows an object across the sky. (Figure by Charles J. Peterson)

He completed a 12-inch instrument in 1782 and spent much of the next six years perfecting a 20-foot Newtonian reflector with an 18.8-inch mirror and altazimuth mount. Perhaps the best of all Herschel's instruments, this reflector was later changed to a front-view focus by tilting the primary mirror to redirect its focus to the front edge of the tube.

Despite the superiority of the large 20-foot reflector, Herschel also attempted to develop a much larger instrument. In 1785, he began to design a 40-foot-long telescope with a 4-foot-diameter mirror. For the rest of the decade, Herschel battled with difficulties casting the speculum, perfecting the front-view focus, constructing the tube, and erecting the wooden structure to hold the instrument. He began observations in the fall of 1789, quickly discovering the sixth and seventh satellites of Saturn (Enceladus and Mimas). Although the greater light-gathering power of this huge instrument was an advantage, Herschel's reflector saw only intermittent service. Imperfect polishing and flexing of the mirror resulted in poor images, while the English weather was rarely good enough to make full use of the large aperture. The most serious weakness, however, was the rapid tarnishing of the speculum metal, which required frequent repolishing and, thus, refiguring. Tarnishing had become a major concern by the end of the eighteenth century, causing reflectors to decline in popularity during the following decades.

Fortunately for astronomers, the refracting telescope had been resurrected through the development of new techniques and knowledge. By 1730, students of optical phe-

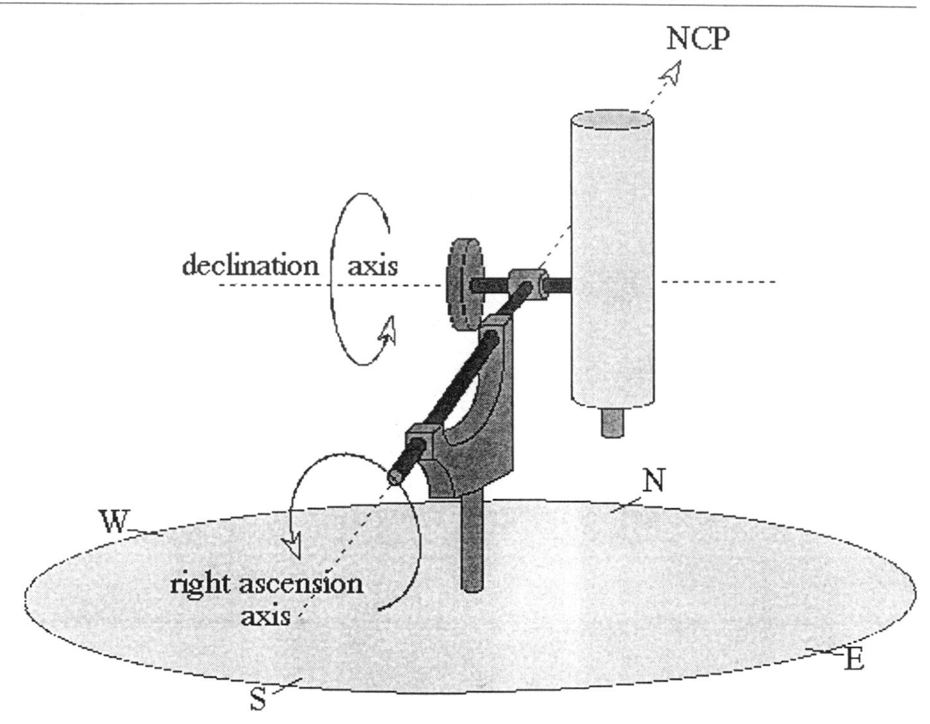

An equatorially mounted telescope is shown here as viewed from the east. One of the two axes about which the telescope may be rotated is parallel to the axis of the earth. Rotation about this axis allows a star to be tracked as it moves across the sky. This is generally accomplished with a mechanical drive that makes one rotation every 23 hours and 56 minutes, the length of the sidereal day. The second axis is perpendicular to the first and allows the telescope to be moved north or south across the sky, according to the declination of the object being observed. (Figure by Charles J. Peterson)

nomena had concluded (incorrectly) that the human eye was achromatic because it was constructed of media with different indices of refraction. Opticians attempted to apply this concept to the construction of achromatic objectives. In 1733, British barrister Chester Moore Hall combined a concave lens of flint glass with a convex lens of crown glass in a telescope with a 2½-inch objective. A few similar instruments were constructed during the 1730s, but the poor quality of available flint glass limited the influence of this new technique.

The 1750s, however, witnessed the introduction of workable achromatic lenses through the efforts of English optician John Dolland. Learning of Hall's earlier work, Dolland ultimately combined a concave flint and convex crown lens of the correct focal lengths to eliminate chromatic aberration. Dolland received a patent for this design, but by the time of his death in 1761 other opticians were making similar objectives. Dolland's son Peter successfully challenged these patent infringements during the 1760s, while developing a triple objective to further correct for the poor quality of flint glass.

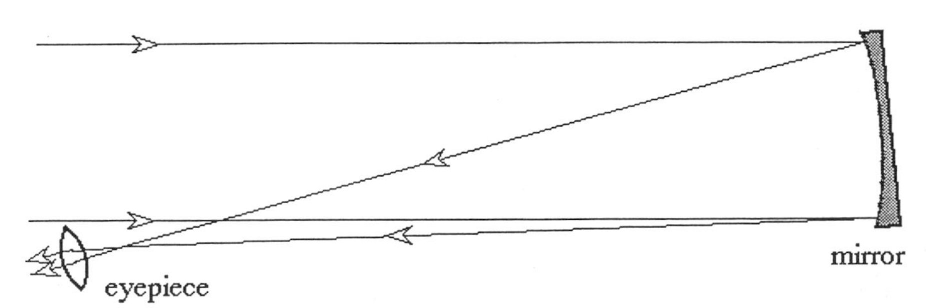

To avoid loss of light because of a second reflection, Herschel tilted the primary mirror with respect to the direction of view. The image at the primary focus was viewed with an eyepiece. This configuration also provided a more comfortable position for the observer. (Figure by Charles J. Peterson)

Despite the knowledge of achromatic lenses, refracting telescopes remained severely limited by glass-making technology. The development of high-quality optical glass was the work of Swiss artisan Pierre Louis Guinand, who began experimenting with flint glass manufacture in 1783. By the end of the decade Guinand had isolated lead as an important constituent of flint glass and as the cause of defects. During melting, lead separated from the glass and appeared on the surface of the melt, forming bubbles and globules. The lead then oxidized and sank, forming trails of small threads. By the late 1790s, Guinand was able to produce high-quality blanks of as much as 6 inches in diameter by allowing the mix to cool rapidly and split into irregular pieces, the best of which were cut and polished on one side. The key development came in 1805, however, when Guinand replaced the long wooden rods used to stir the glass with porous fireclay rods. Where the wooden rods had caused the lead oxide to mix unequally and form streaks, the fireclay stirrers brought the bubbles to the surface and kept the glass thoroughly mixed to produce nearly flawless flint glass.

The new technique attracted the attention of a German optical firm that convinced Guinand to move to Munich. This association proved difficult for Guinand, who returned to Switzerland in 1814 and began constructing and selling complete refracting telescopes. During his stay in Munich, however, Guinand agreed to train a company-nominated assistant in his methods. This apprentice optician was Joseph Fraunhofer, who had joined the Munich firm in 1806 and quickly established himself as a gifted craftsman. Working with Guinand from 1809 to 1813, he took the cru-

William Herschel's 40-foot (focus) reflector. Mounted as an altazimuth, this giant instrument required the labor of several workmen to move. The observer on the platform viewed objects through an eyepiece located at the side of the tube, as the instrument was configured as a Herschelian reflector. Often Caroline Herschel, the astronomer's sister, sat at a table nearby and recorded his observations. (Courtesy of the National Museum of American History)

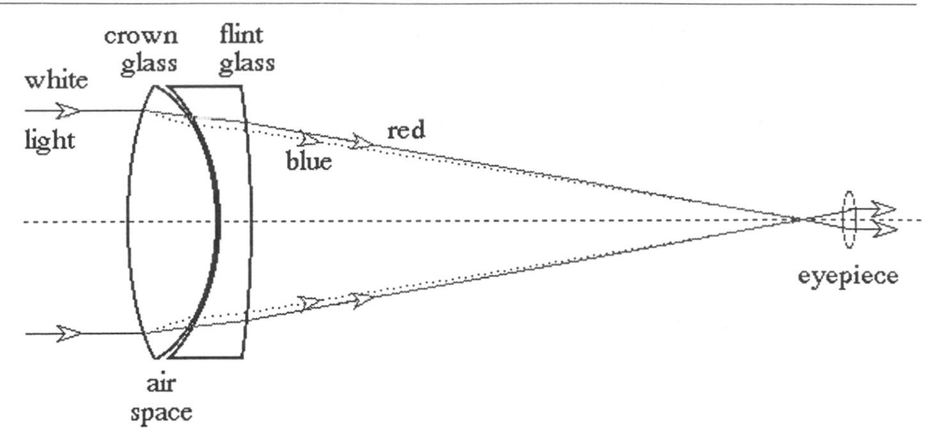

To minimize chromatic aberration in a refractor, Fraunhofer replaced the single objective lens with a doublet consisting of a convex lens made of crown glass (index of refraction $n \approx 1.5$) followed by a concave lens of flint glass ($n \approx 1.6$), the two separated by an airspace that is thinnest at the center. The second surface of the crown glass lens is strongly curved, with a radius of curvature one-third that of the first surface. The exit surface of the flint glass is weakly curved. (Figure by Charles J. Peterson)

Fraunhofer's masterpiece, the 9½-inch refractor constructed for the Dorpat Observatory in 1824. In the hands of F.G. Wilhelm Struve, the Dorpat refractor made important contributions to astrometry. Note the equatorial mounting including weights to power the driving mechanism (on the far side of the wooden stand) and a complex system of counterweights (two on long rods with the weights at the eye end of the telescope and a third projecting along the right ascension axis) to balance the telescope as it tracked an object across the sky. (Courtesy of Owen Gingerich and Sky & Telescope*)*

cial step forward in telescope design by more accurately calculating the required lens curvatures, based on more careful measurements of glass characteristics. The figure to the left shows the optical characteristics of a Fraunhofer objective lens. In addition to his theoretical work, Fraunhofer also improved furnaces and annealing ovens to remove remaining defects in the glass.

Fraunhofer's new techniques and knowledge led to the construction of superior instruments, including the famous 9½-inch achromatic refractor for the Dorpat Observatory in Russia. Installed at the observatory in 1824 by noted astronomer F.G. Wilhelm Struve, the 14-foot-focal-length instrument represented the largest refracting telescope of the time and provided immediate and superior results. Struve used this instrument in his northern sky survey of some 120,000 stars and also employed the Dorpat refractor in his micrometric measurements of nearly three thousand double stars, approximately twenty-three hundred of which were unknown previously. Equally significant was the modern equatorial mounting of the Dorpat refractor. Counterpoises enabled the telescope tube to be easily moved into position, after which the polar axis slowly rotated at the rate of one revolution every sidereal day. Fraunhofer's most significant modification to the equatorial mount was his use of a falling weight controlled by a clock mechanism to drive the polar axis, a technique that soon became standard.

Combining superior achromatic optics with functional equatorial mountings, Fraunhofer's telescopes established refractors as the leading astronomical instruments of the early 1800s. His work also led to the emergence of the German optical industry. For the next forty years, refracting telescopes with German optics represented the standard against which all other astronomical instruments were judged.

George E. Webb

Bibliography

Bedini, S.A. "The Aerial Telescope." *Technology and Culture* 8 (1967): 395–401.

Bell, L. *The Telescope*. New York: McGraw-Hill, 1922.

King, H.C. *The History of the Telescope*. London: Charles Griffin, 1955.

Van Helden, A. "The Telescope in the Seventeenth Century." *Isis* 65 (1974): 38–58.

———. "The Invention of the Telescope." *Transactions of the American Philosophical Society* 67 (1977): 5–67.

Telescopes since 1820

By 1820, the telescope emerged from an embryonic state in which it was valued chiefly for the novelty of the discoveries it made possible, and became a precision instrument, valued as a scientific tool. The refracting telescopes produced at the Fraunhofer Institute in Munich empitomized this transition. Fraunhofer's telescopes were equipped with both high-quality optics and stable, clock-driven equatorial mountings. However, using his larger reflecting telescopes, though they were crude by comparison, **William Herschel** had already demonstrated the importance of large apertures for observing faint objects.

The refracting telescope was the instrument of choice for most professional and amateur astronomers in 1820. That choice was dictated by ease of use and maintenance, as well as by the limited objectives set for telescopic astronomy. For a few amateur astronomers, however, Herschel's discoveries with large reflecting telescopes opened a new window on the heavens. Many of the nebulae, double stars, and other objects in his catalogues could not be observed in the smaller refracting telescopes used by professional astronomers. Thus, after 1820, both types of telescopes continued to evolve, but in different hands and for different purposes.

The Golden Age of the Refracting Telescope

In 1820, the main task of the astronomer was rather narrowly defined. As Bennett aptly notes, "Much of the astronomers' time was devoted to fundamental measurements of positions—mostly of stars—using instruments designed to measure angles as precisely as possible in one or the other coordinate" (Bennett, 1990, 6). It was less important to see faint objects than it was to increase the accuracy with which the positions of the brighter objects were known. Accordingly, the quality and stability of the telescope mounting, the precision with which its circles were engraved and read, and the accuracy of micrometers and clocks received more attention than the objective lens of the telescope.

The size of objective lenses was limited by the availability of suitable glass. Merz and Mahler, the successors to Fraunhofer in Munich, enjoyed a competitive advantage because of their glass manufacturing capability. English telescope-makers, lacking a domestic supply, were forced to rely on expensive imported glass that was available only in small sizes, mainly from Guinand in France. It is not surprising, then, that Dolland, Tulley, and the Troughton and Simms firms specialized in the manufacture of mural telescopes, transit circles, and portable telescopes of relatively small apertures. The situation in England began to change in 1837 when the Chance Brothers of Birmingham purchased the Guinand technology, and employed the former Guinand owner when he took refuge in England during the 1848 Revolution.

As glass and optical technology improved, larger objectives gradually became available. In 1839, Merz and Mahler completed a 15-inch refractor for the **Pulkovo Observatory**. They provided a similar telescope to the **Harvard College Observatory** in 1847. Discoveries made with these telescopes contributed to the popularity of astronomy, and led many individuals and institutions to acquire large telescopes.

The drive for larger apertures accelerated in 1859, when F.A.P. Barnard, an astronomer turned university president, persuaded **Alvan Clark** to undertake the construction of an 18.5-inch refractor, the largest in the world. This telescope was for the observatory of the University of Mississippi, constructed on the plans of the Pulkovo Observatory. After the American Civil War broke out, Barnard was unable to pay for the telescope. However, the completed lens was already famous. While testing the 18.5-inch lens, Clark's son, **Alvan Graham Clark**, discovered a faint companion to the bright star Sirius. The Chicago Astronomical Society outbid Harvard College Observatory, so the 18.5-inch Clark was installed at the Dearborn Observatory in 1866.

The Clarks were also involved in the next increase in aperture. The U.S. Navy convinced Congress that the instrumentation at the Naval Observatory (USNO) was inadequate, and received authorization for a large, new telescope. The largest glass blanks available to the Clarks (from Chance Brothers) were approximately 26 inches in diameter. Finished in 1873, the USNO refractor was, at first, plagued by reflected images. This problem was later corrected. An identical 26-inch Clark telescope was installed at the University of Virginia in 1884. In the decades that followed, other large refractors were built. The Clarks provided the Lowell 24-inch, Pulkovo 30-inch, and the Lick 36-inch refractors. Several other manufacturers of large refractors were active, including P. Gautier and the Henry Brothers of Paris, who supplied the 29-inch Bischoffsheim refractor at Nice and the 32.7-inch refractor at Meudon. Howard Grubb of Dublin supplied the Vienna 27-inch, and the Greenwich 28-inch refractors.

The largest refracting telescope in the world, the Yerkes 40-inch telescope, was the crowning achievement of Alvan Clark and Sons. Alvan Graham Clark who, by 1897, was the only family member active in the firm, worked at the limits of existing technology to achieve the appropriate balance of adequate edge thickness to avoid sagging of the lens, while minimizing light losses due to the central thickness of the glass. Optical performance of the telescope met the high standards of the Clarks.

The Yerkes telescope and observatory were the first major projects undertaken by **George Ellery Hale**, then an associate professor at the University of Chicago. Hale conceived of the telescope as the primary instrument for the first American observatory designed expressly for astrophysical research. From a historical perspective, however, the Yerkes 40-inch refractor is more appropriately seen as the culmination of the giant astronomical refractor. Although there were more than a dozen large (20- to 30-inch) refractors built after the completion of the Yerkes telescope, these tended to be specialized astrometric instruments.

Large Reflecting Telescopes Emerge

William Parsons, Third Earl of Rosse, dedicated his considerable talents and resources to the task of continuing William Herschel's research on nebulae. On his estate, Birr Castle, near Parsonstown, Ireland, Lord Rosse cast many speculum metal mirrors, experimenting with alloy compositions and molding techniques. His 36-inch telescope, completed in 1839, was judged a success when it gave satisfactory star disks and resolved moderately close (1.5 arcsecond) double stars. **John Herschel** considered the Rosse 36-inch telescope the most powerful then built. This mirror was later remounted in an equatorial fork mounting and used for many years.

Lord Rosse then set out to cast a 72-inch mirror. His efforts to cast the larger mirror began in April 1842, but a finished mirror was not available until 1845. The telescope mounting was completed in 1844 and consisted of a tube slung between two masonry piers. The arrangement allowed observing within half a degree on either side of the meridian. Observers at Birr Castle concentrated on objects that were previously identified as nebulae. Many were resolved into masses of faint stars, but a few remained unresolved,

The 18.5-inch Clark refractor (1866) of the Chicago Astronomical Society. During the testing process, A.G. Clark discovered the companion of Sirius *predicted by Bessel. The telescope was later transferred to Northwestern University. (Courtesy of the National Museum of American History)*

whirlpool-like spirals. However, difficulties in using the 72-inch were substantial. In addition, severe limitations were imposed by poor seeing conditions. The 72-inch was therefore put to very limited use.

The results at Parsonstown encouraged other astronomers to experiment with reflecting telescopes. The obvious starting points were lighter mirrors and mountings that would allow extended periods of observation. An English amateur, William Lassell, was the first to mount a large reflecting telescope on an equatorial mounting. With his 24-inch equatorially mounted Newtonian reflector, he observed first in England, and then in 1852 from Malta. In 1861, Lassell returned to Malta to assemble a 48-inch equatorial Newtonian. With these telescopes, Lassell made a number of important discoveries and confirmed the value of a larger-aperture instrument on an equatorial mounting and the importance of seeing conditions. The polar axis for Lassell's 48-inch was a cone-shaped casting that presaged mountings of the twentieth century. The telescope and declination bearings were carried on a fork mounted on the wide end of the cone. From the available drawings, the mounting appears to have made it impossible to access the north polar region of the sky.

A New York physician and amateur astronomer, **Henry Draper**, was working, without much success, on metal mirrors when Sir John Herschel advised him that Steinheil, in Munich, and Foucault, in Paris, were both having good results with silver on glass mirrors. Draper taught himself to make parabolic glass mirrors by producing about one hundred mirrors of various sizes over a three-year period. His largest mirror was a 28-inch Cassegrain finished in 1872. Though his was a trial-and-error process, Draper learned about directional effects and stress in glass, thermal effects in testing and polishing, and other aspects of mirror-making. Draper's remarkable photographs and a comprehensive monograph published by the Smithsonian Institution encouraged other astronomers to consider reflecting telescopes with silvered-glass mirrors.

The next step was taken by English amateur astronomer Andrew Ainslie Common, who mounted a 36-inch silvered glass reflector on an equatorial mount. After several years of debugging and careful adjustments, Common produced extraordinary photographs of the Orion nebula, containing detail that had never been observed or photographed. Common sold the telescope to Edward Crossley, who later donated it to **Lick Observatory**. **James E. Keeler** patiently worked with the Crossley reflector and, in 1898, favored by outstanding seeing conditions at Mount Hamilton, undertook a photographic survey of nebulae.

At the Yerkes Observatory, Hale's colleague, **George Willis Ritchey**, built a 24-inch Newtonian reflector. The quality of the photographs Ritchey made with this telescope exceeded even those taken by Keeler with the Crossley. Photographs taken with the Ritchey and Crossley reflectors proved conclusively that a silver-on-glass reflecting telescope, on a well designed equatorial mounting and in the hands of a skilled observer, would yield scientifically useful astronomical photographs.

Hale wasted no time in acting on this conclusion. He persuaded the Carnegie Institution of Washington to fund a 60-inch reflecting telescope at a new observatory on Mount Wilson. The project was approved in 1904 and Ritchey's silvered-glass mirror, in an equatorial fork mounting, saw first light in 1908. After a year of fine tuning, primarily to control mir-

The 24-inch reflecting telescope built by G.W. Ritchey for the Yerkes Observatory of the University of Chicago (1900). Astronomical photographs made with the instrument were of such high quality that they stimulated the Yerkes director, G.E. Hale, to move forward with a project to construct a 60-inch reflecting telescope and locate it on a mountaintop to escape poor seeing conditions at lower elevations. (Courtesy of the National Museum of American History)

The 100-inch Hooker reflector on Mount Wilson (1917). In this 1949 photograph, the control panel is in the foreground. (Courtesy of the Huntington Library and Carnegie Observatories)

ror temperature, it was clear that the telescope would meet or exceed expectations for its performance as an astrophysical research tool.

Even before the performance of the 60-inch reflector was proven, Hale again sought funding for a larger instrument. He persuaded a wealthy Los Angeles merchant, J.D. Hooker, to finance a 100-inch mirror. The Carnegie Institution of Washington provided the remaining funds. The first glass blank from the St. Gobain Glass works in France was clearly imperfect. But after waiting two years for a better disk, Hale agreed to start work on the original blank. The grinding, polishing, and silvering of the main mirror and secondary optics were again under the direction of Ritchey. The mounting, an English cross-axis yoke, limited access to the polar region but provided exceptional stability. When the telescope was completed in 1917, comparison of spectrographic results with those of the 60-inch clearly demonstrated the benefits of the nearly threefold increase in light grasp.

Mount Palomar and the Hale Telescope

With two powerful instruments and an outstanding staff, Mount Wilson rapidly became a major astrophysical research center. Never satisfied, Hale started dreaming about a telescope with an aperture of at least 200 inches. In 1928, the Rockefeller Foundation agreed to fund the project as a joint venture with the California Institute of Technology as owner and the Mount Wilson Observatory as operator. Once again, Hale demonstrated his genius in selecting associates as he assembled the project team, including astronomers John Anderson and Francis Pease from Mount Wilson, many Caltech scientists and engineers, amateur astronomer Russell W. Porter, and a battleship builder, Captain C.S. McDowell of the United States Navy, as construction manager. As the project executive officer, Anderson personally took charge of the site selection process. By 1935, site development was underway on Palomar Mountain.

The thermal characteristics of the glass in the 60- and 100-inch mirrors were a dis-

The 200-inch Hale telescope (1948) on Palomar Mountain. The photograph was taken in 1956. (Courtesy of the Huntington Library and Carnegie Observatories)

tinct limitation in both polishing the mirrors and the nightly use of the telescopes. Borosilicate glass, which has a low coefficient of thermal expansion, was finally made available in large disks suitable for telescopic mirrors. As Van Helden noted, solving the glass problem was critical to the success of all future large telescopes. By 1940, Pyrex glass was in use in the 72-inch Dominion telescope in British Columbia and the 82-inch McDonald telescope in Texas, as well as in the 200-inch disk that was being figured for the Mount Palomar telescope. In addition to the choice of Pyrex glass, the 200-inch mirror broke new ground in other ways. The mirror blank was ribbed to reduce its weight. Complex counterweight assemblies were installed in cells in the back of the mirror to counteract stresses in the mirror as it changed position. Finally, John Strong's process of aluminizing mirrors for greater ultraviolet reflectivity and longer service, developed with the 200-inch mirror in mind, was proven at Mount Wilson and the Dominion and McDonald observatories before the 200-inch mirror was finished.

Pease, Porter, and E.P. Burrell of Warner and Swasey were the key figures in the selection of the unique mounting for the 200-inch telescope. The horseshoe shaped north bearing and the hemispherical south bearing for the polar axis were supported on oil-pad bearings. Mark Surrerier saw that it was impossible to make the tube completely rigid. So instead, he designed a truss structure that allowed both the mirror cell and the prime focus to flex an equal amount in the same direction. There were many other technical innovations in the mounting, which was constructed by Westinghouse in Philadelphia and transported to California via the Panama Canal.

World War II delayed completion of the project, but in 1948 the mirror was installed. For the next three decades, the Hale telescope was the largest and most productive telescope in the world. No telescope pushed the frontiers of astronomical knowledge further or faster.

A New Generation of Telescopes

In 1954, leading American astronomers recommended the establishment of a national optical observatory. The **National Science Foundation** supported this project, which ultimately led to the construction of three nearly identical 155-inch (4-meter) telescopes at the **Kitt Peak National Observatory** in 1973, the **Cerro Tololo International Observatory** (1974), and the Anglo-Australian Telescope (1975) at Siding Spring, Australia.

Many of the design innovations embodied in the Hale telescope were incorporated in the 4-meter telescopes, including the ribbed, low-expansion glass mirrors, oil-pad bearings, and Surrerier truss tubes. Many other advances in technology were built into these telescopes—for example, use of the wider field Ritchey-Crétien optics and helical, counteracting gears to replace worm gears in critical drive trains.

From 1954 to 1980, thirty or more telescopes with apertures greater than 1 meter were completed. This was the greatest burst of large telescope construction ever undertaken. These new telescopes blended design concepts from the Palomar project with other innovations as new technology emerged or new observing opportunities were identified.

Major innovations were attempted in the 236-inch *Bolshoi Telescop Azimutal'ny* at Mount Pastukhov in the Caucasus Mountains in Russia. This 1975 installation was the first large telescope to move from the equatorial to the alt-azimuth mounting. Computer technology to drive the telescope simultaneously on two axes near the zenith proved inadequate for this task, so a few degrees of the sky directly overhead are inaccessible. In addition, the enclosure of the telescope in a large dome resulted in thermal management problems. Climate and wind conditions at this site place some additional constraints on the use of this instrument, but with a new mirror and improved ventilation, the telescope performs very well given these limitations.

The 4-meter Mayall telescope at the Kitt Peak National Observatory. The telescope and mounting weigh 375 tons but are so well balanced that a one-half horsepower motor moves the instrument as it follows celestial objects across the sky. (Courtesy of the National Optical Astronomy Observatories)

In the Western Hemisphere, innovations in telescope design accelerated after about 1976; two principle changes account for this. First, the widespread availability of high-speed computers impacted nearly every aspect of telescope construction including optical design, mirror blank design, manufacture and polishing, mounting design and operation, instrument design and operation, as well as data acquisition and analysis. Second, development of sophisticated new detectors (for example the Charge Coupled Device, or CCD) with high quantum efficiencies enlarged the potential utility of all telescopes.

The Apache Point, New Mexico, 138-inch (3.5-meter) telescope and supporting facilities, which were placed in service in 1994, embody most of these new technologies. The primary mirror for the Apache Point telescope features a very short focal length (f1.75) and was spun-cast at the University of Arizona. The borosilicate glass is relatively thin and, together with its altazimuth mounting, weighs only one-third as much as similar telescopes using conventional mirrors in equatorial mountings. This saving in weight translates directly to reduced cost and increased effectiveness.

Up to eleven axillary instruments can be accessed at any time with the light beam of the Apache Point telescope. The time required to change instruments, which are mounted on nine access ports directly on the mirror mounting and at two Nasmyth foci, is less than five minutes. The Apache Point Observatory telescope represents a new level of achievement in telescope and observatory design. Many of these innovations will be included in multimirror instruments in the next generation of telescopes.

Conclusion

While professional astronomers focused on precise positional measurements using small refracting telescopes, amateur astronomers pioneered the use of large, equatorially mounted reflecting telescopes. The discoveries made using these instruments demonstrated the value of large apertures for both visual observation and for photography. With growing awareness of the need for more light to feed cameras, **spectrographs**, and other astrophysical instruments, astronomers began a drive for more aperture. In the span of only 170 years the largest telescope in the world grew from the 18-inch Herschel reflector to the 236-inch *Bolshoi* reflector, an increase of more than 170 times in light grasp, with a substantial increase in the spectral range available for examination. Changes in every aspect of telescope design and construction were required to make this transition.

A revolution in optics was necessary to support the growth in telescope size. The refracting telescope reached its upper limits before the turn of the century. The reflecting telescope proved more adaptable, and has formed the basis for optical telescope design since that time. With the adoption of Ritchey-Chrétien optics, telescopes of wider fields and shorter tube lengths became possible, simplifying telescope mounting design. An interesting question that has not been explored in the literature on the history of telescopes is the eyepiece. As every telescope user knows, even the best objective lens or mirror is compromised by a poor-quality eyepiece. Did the evolution of eyepiece design keep pace with or limit the effectiveness of telescopes as they grew in size during this period?

In the long process of development, mountings improved, first to accommodate precision measuring instruments, and then to accommodate heavy astrophysical instruments. Driving mechanisms and photographic equipment were improved to make possible continuous observation over many hours, extending in some cases for several nights. The mounting could no longer be supplied as an accessory by the telescope manufacturer, and instead became a precision machine, constructed by mechanical contractors.

There are interesting historical questions that should be examined. For example, new technology emerged during the last forty years for construction of lightweight aerospace vehicles. Was the acceptance of this technology impeded by earlier technology embodied in the Hale telescope? Major mechanical contractors, those who built bridges, boilers, and battleships, have been involved in the construction of most large telescopes, but did the availability of their expertise enhance or impede the technological evolution of lighter, lower-cost telescopes?

Computers and advanced detectors revolutionized telescope design, construction, and operation. These advances were retrofitted to older telescopes, greatly enlarging their capabilities. These advances also made possible the next generation of telescopes, those with multiple primary mirrors and adaptive optics. These instruments will define observational astronomy in the coming century.

Thomas R. Williams

Bibliography

Bennett, J.A. "The Giant Reflector, 1780–1870." In *Human Implications of Scientific Advance,* edited by E.G. Forbes, 553–558. Edinburgh: Edinburgh University Press, 1978.

———. *Church, State and Astronomy in Ireland—200 Years of Armagh Observatory.* Belfast. Armagh Observatory in Association with the Institute of Irish Studies and the Queen's University of Belfast, 1990.

Chapman, A. "William Lassell (1799–1880): Practitioner, Patron and 'Grand Amateur' of Victorian Astronomy." *Vistas in Astronomy* 32 (1988): 341–370.

Draper, H. "On the Construction of a Silvered Glass Telescope, Fifteen and a Half Inches in Aperture, and Its Use in Celestial Photography." In *Smithsonian Contributions to Knowledge,* vol. 14, 1–55. Washington, D.C.: Smithsonian Institution, 1865.

Hoskin, M. "Apparatus and Ideas in the mid-19th Century." *Vistas in Astronomy* 9 (1967): 79–85.

King, H.C. *The History of the Telescope.* New York: Dover, 1955.

Learner, R. *Astronomy through the Telescope.* New York: Van Nostrand Reinhold, 1981.

Osterbrock, D.E. *Pauper & Prince—Ritchey, Hale & Big American Telescopes,* Tucson: University of Arizona Press, 1993.

Ritchie, G.W. "On the Modern Reflecting Telescope and the Making and Testing of Optical Mirrors." In *Smithsonian Contributions to Knowledge,* vol. 34, 2. Washington, D.C.: Smithsonian Institution, 1904.

Shane, C.D. "Astronomical Telescopes since 1890." In *The Legacy of George Ellery Hale,* edited by Helen Wright et al., 209–219. Cambridge: MIT Press, 1972.

Van Helden, A. "Telescope Building, 1850–1900" and "Telescope Building, 1900–1950." In *Astrophysics and Twentieth-Century Astronomy to 1950: Part A,* edited by O. Gingerich. *The General History of Astronomy,* edited by M. Hoskin, vol. 4, 40–58, 134–152. Cambridge: Cambridge University Press, 1984.

Warner, D.J. *Alvan Clark & Sons: Artists in Optics.* Washington, D.C.: Smithsonian Institution Press, 1968.

Tidal Theory

Theory of the origin of the planetary system as a result of gravitational interaction of the sun with another star. The Chamberlin-Moulton planetesimal hypothesis is a tidal theory, but the term applies primarily to its modification by **James H. Jeans** and Harold Jeffreys, though two-body interactions had been proposed as early as 1745 by the Comte de Buffon. Jeans envisioned that by itself the gravitational forces of the close approach of another star would draw a single massive cigar-shaped filament of liquid material out of the tidal bulge raised upon the sun. While the base of this filament fell back into the sun (thus ensuring a rotation in the same direction as the planetary orbital motion) and the outer part may have escaped, much of the filament fragmented directly into planetary-sized bodies, the largest forming in the middle of the filament. Their original elliptical orbits would have been circularized by interaction with the remaining gaseous material (the resisting medium). Subsequent tidal disrup-

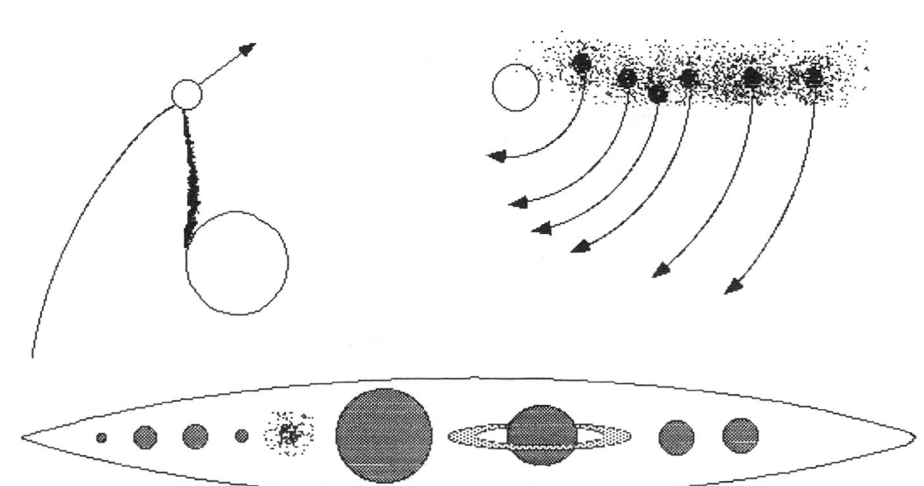

According to tidal theory, a passing star draws a single, cigar-shaped filament of matter out of the sun (top left); it quickly condenses into the planets (top right). The bottom drawing emphasizes the relationship between the shape of the assumed filament and the size distribution of planets. (Figure by Charles J. Peterson)

tion of the primary bodies at perihelion while they still had highly eccentric orbits must have produced most of the satellites, whose properties mimic the properties of the solar system as a whole. While considered a competitor to the Chamberlin-Moulton idea, the tidal theory actually differs only in details.

Major dynamical objections were voiced against the tidal theory—its inability to account for the regularity of planetary spacing (Titius-Bode Law) and the actual angular momentum distribution of the solar system, the questionable assumption of fragmentation of a filament into planetary-sized bodies, and the role of comets. Jeffreys later proposed, in 1929, that the encounter was actually a grazing collision between the two objects, but within a decade he admitted that no satisfactory theory existed. In lieu of more plausible alternatives, the tidal theories remained popular up through the 1940s, but since they have been supplanted by models in which the origin of the planets is a natural consequence stemming from the formation of the sun.

Charles J. Peterson

Bibliography

Jaki, S.L. *Planets and Planetarians: A History of Theories of the Origin of Planetary Systems.* New York: John Wiley and Sons, 1977.

Jeans, J.H. *Problems of Cosmogony and Stellar Dynamics.* Cambridge: Cambridge University Press, 1919.

Russell, H.N. *The Solar System and Its Origin.* New York Macmillan, 1935.

Time and Timekeeping Instruments

Time finding, time measuring and timekeeping provide three categories into which instruments of time may be divided. Devices such as **sundials**, **astrolabes**, nocturnals, **sextants**, and transit instruments, designed to find time by determining the position of a location on the earth in relation to the heavens, fall into the first category. Instruments intended to measure specific intervals of time, including certain types of waterclocks, sandglasses, fire clocks, mechanical timers, and some atomic clocks, belong to the second category. The third timekeeping category relates to instruments designed to make time accessible on demand: These include water-clocks, mechanical, electric, and quartz clocks and watches, as well as atomic clocks.

Dividing the Day

One of the earliest records of a time-measuring instrument relates to an outflow water clock being used for dividing the periods of daylight and darkness. The reference appears in a fragmentary inscription on an Egyptian official's tomb, dating from about 1580 B.C.E. The inscription claims that the deceased, Amenemhet, made the first water clock of this type in honor of the deceased King Amenhotep I. The earliest archaeological fragments of such a device, found at the temple of Amon in Karnak in Upper Egypt, date from the reign of Amenhotep III (1415–1380 B.C.E.). The Egyptians evolved a system of dividing each period of daylight and darkness into twelve equal parts: In summer, there were twelve long hours during the day and twelve short hours at night, and in the winter, the opposite. Only at the spring and autumn equinoxes were the hours of daylight and darkness equal. These hours of variable length were known as temporal, unequal, or sometimes planetary hours.

Temporal hours were adopted by the Greeks and Romans and continued to be used in Europe until the advent of the mechanical clock at the end of the thirteenth century. The mechanical clock was more suited to keeping equal hours than to being constantly adjusted for temporal hours. The different equal hour systems that evolved varied according to when the hours of the day began and how the hours were counted: The astronomical, whole clock, Babylonian, and Italian hour systems all divided the day into twenty-four hours, but astronomical hours were counted from noon, whole clock hours from midnight, Babylonian hours from sunrise, and Italian hours from sunset. Nuremberg hours also divided the day into twenty-four hours, but daylight hours were counted from dawn and nighttime hours from dusk; the number of hours of daylight and darkness therefore were adjusted throughout the year. Small clock or French hours, which divided the day into two groups of twelve hours beginning at midnight, became the system generally adopted for civil purposes in Europe by the middle of the seventeenth century.

The mechanical clock was made possible by the invention of the escapement, a device through which the timekeeper rations energy, counts the beats, and transmits impulse: The escapement releases the energy of the power source at regular intervals to maintain the motion of the oscillator governing the speed at which the mechanism operates. The origins of the mechanical clock are obscure. Early references are confused by the fact that the word *horologium* was a generic term applied to all instruments of time, including the sundials and water clocks that were the principal instruments used for finding and keeping time before the mechanical clock. The mechanical clock had several advantages over all these devices: Unlike the sundial, it would work at night as well as during the day; unlike the water clock, it could operate in both warm and in freezing temperatures; its time and rate could be easily adjusted; in the tradition of astronomical geared devices, it was naturally suited to show any number of indications; and, most important, it could be made to ring a large bell automatically, so that an entire community would be made aware of the time. The description of the *horologium* installed at Dunstable Priory in Bedfordshire, England, in 1283 is the earliest of several references that reveal mechanical clocks were being used by the end of the thirteenth century. Similar documents in France and Italy from the same period reveal that knowledge of these new devices also existed on the Continent. By the second quarter of the fourteenth century, mechanical clocks were well known throughout Europe: When Richard of Wallingford described his highly complicated astronomical clock in 1327, he referred only briefly to the timekeeping part of the mechanism, implying that such knowledge was commonplace.

Dividing the Hour

The division of the hour into minutes was made in the fifteenth century. Although no timekeepers made before 1550 with this feature are known to survive, a manuscript written about 1475 by a German monk named Paulus Almanus illustrates a clock with a dial indicating minutes. In the text, Almanus actually described this dial as being associated with the time of sunrise, an error that would suggest that the division of the hour into minutes was unusual at that time. The famous Nuremberg astronomer Bernhard Walther would have been pleased to have had such a clock when he attempted to measure the difference in time between the rising of Mercury and sunrise on January 16, 1484: To time the event with a clock that indicated only hours, he noted the revolutions of the hour wheel and expressed a fraction of its rotation by counting the number of gear teeth. During this period, the division of hours into minutes would have had no application in civil or domestic life; it became necessary only when the clock was used as a scientific instrument. Because these smaller units of time were first introduced for use in astronomy, it is not surprising that they were based on the sexagesimal system, which had long been established in astronomy for the division of a degree. Divisions of a degree were called *minuta,* the primary sixty divisions being the *minuta prima,* the secondary sixty divisions the *minuta secunda*. These were abbreviated to *minuta* and *secunda,* from which the words *minutes* and *seconds* are derived. During the course of the next hundred years, clocks incorporating minutes and seconds were made, but surviving examples are rare. The Danish astronomer **Tycho Brahe** used clocks with these indications to determine star positions, but he found his angular measuring instruments more reliable. Such precise divisions of time are seldom seen on clocks made before the application of the pendulum in 1657 or on portable timekeepers made before the invention of the spiral balance spring in 1675.

From Minutes to Seconds

The mechanical clock did not become a reliable instrument for measuring and keeping time until the pendulum was used to control its operation. Because its intrinsic frequency is controlled by the force of gravity, the pendulum proved to be significantly more accurate than the devices used to regulate earlier timekeepers. The pendulum is known to have been used as a time-measuring device before it was applied as a regulator for clocks. Leonardo da Vinci, Benvenuto Volpaia, and others made drawings of pendulums, but there is no evidence that their schemes were ever put into practice. **Galileo** devised a mechanism to maintain the motion of a pendulum, but this instrument had no provision for telling the time. The first person to apply the pendulum to a mechanical clock and thereby introduce a substantial improvement in the accuracy of timekeepers was the celebrated Dutch mathematician Christiaan Huygens. Pendulum clocks, which were first produced in Holland in 1657, were soon being manufactured in France and England. During the next fifteen years, the accuracy of the pendulum clock was further improved by the introduction of the long pendulum and the invention of the anchor escapement.

In 1675, the accuracy of portable timekeepers was transformed by the introduction of the spiral balance spring. By applying a spiral spring to the balance, the balance's motion could be controlled in a similar way to which gravity controls the motion of a pendulum. Huygens's priority in this invention was challenged by the English experimental philosopher Robert Hooke, in the same way that his invention of the pendulum clock had been challenged by Galileo's supporters.

Finding the Time

Sundials were commonly used to set clocks and watches. Improvements in the accuracy of timekeepers, however, revealed variations between sun time and clock time. The difference between these times, known as the equation of time, is caused by the tilt of the earth's axis relative to its path and the earth's elliptical orbit around the sun. Apparent solar time (the time shown by a sundial) and mean solar time (the time shown by a clock) agree only four times a year (on or about April 15, June 13, September 2, and December 25) and can differ by as much as sixteen minutes. Although this discrepancy had been observed since the time of Ptolemy, it was of no consequence for timekeeping until precision clocks were developed. To regulate a clock correctly by a sundial, the equation of time must be taken into account. Tables showing the equation of time for each day of the year were produced for this purpose. To avoid this problem completely, a few clock-makers designed clocks that kept solar time instead of mean time.

Sidereal Time

Owing to the variations of solar time, pendulum clocks used in observatories were regulated by the observation of the transit of a star from one night to the next. This system of time measurement, which measured the rotation of the earth on its axis relative to the stars, is known as sidereal time (from the Latin *siderius,* relating to the stars). In the course of one year, the earth, because of its orbit around the sun, will rotate one more time with respect to the sun than it will with respect to the stars. In other words, in 365.2422 days, the time it takes the earth to travel from vernal equinox to vernal equinox, sidereal time will differ from solar time by twenty-four hours. A sidereal day is, therefore, 3 minutes 56.4 seconds shorter than a mean solar day. Clocks that were designed specifically for keeping sidereal or mean solar time were called regulators, because they provided the standard time by which other clocks were regulated. A regulator incorporates several special features to maintain the high standards of timekeeping required: a pendulum that automatically compensates for variations in temperature, a special escapement to provide a regular impulse to the pendulum, maintaining power to keep the clock running while it is being wound, and a dial especially designed to indicate clearly minutes and seconds. Regulators were made generally without striking mechanisms.

Time and Longitude

Improvements in the accuracy of timekeepers revealed new opportunities for science. One of these concerned the problem of determining longitude. Longitude and time are related because the earth rotates on its axis once in a period of twenty-four hours, so there is a change of fifteen degrees of longitude every hour. Longitude may be expressed in hours, minutes, and seconds of time, and time may be expressed in degrees, minutes, and seconds of longitude. Thereby, the difference in longitude between two places can be determined by knowing the difference in their local times.

The idea of using a timekeeper to provide a reference for the longitude of a ship at sea was first proposed in 1530 by the Flemish astronomer Gemma Frisius in *De principiis astronomiae et cosmographiae*. In theory, the method was simple: A clock showing the time at the place of known longitude would be taken on board the ship. When the local time of the ship was found by astronomical observation and compared with the time shown on the clock, the time difference, and hence the longitude difference, could be quickly determined. In practice, however, this straightforward method required accurate timekeeping under the most adverse conditions.

With the growth of maritime traffic during the seventeenth century, the number of ill-fated voyages caused by ignorance of the longitude increased, at great cost to trade, colonization, and exploration. Major seafaring countries offered substantial rewards for a solution to the problem. Notwithstanding the doubt that such a device could be produced, an English horological autodidact named John Harrison pursued the task of developing an accurate and reliable marine timekeeper and succeeded. His fourth marine timekeeper, completed in 1759, satisfied the conditions for the £20,000 prize offered by the British government in 1714. By 1790, the marine chronometer, as this specialized form of timekeeper came to be known, had been developed into a sophisticated machine, although its basic design remained unchanged. The regulator and the marine chronometer, which established new standards of accuracy, had a major influence on astronomy, navigation, surveying, and many other branches of science.

Standardizing Time

Before the advent of the railroad, each community lived by its own local time, determined by the position of the sun at noon. The variation in the local time of one community to that of another was of no consequence. When the railroad substantially reduced the time that it took to travel from one region to another, there arose a need for uniform time by which the operation of trains could be regulated. Mass production of clocks and watches increased the growing consciousness and importance of time in the rapidly expanding industrialized society. The development of the electric telegraph enabled time to be distributed over great distances from observatories that served as the source from which each region's time was determined. The first public time service, introduced in December 1851, was based on clock beats telegraphed from the **Harvard College Observatory** in Cambridge, Massachusetts. The **Royal Observatory at Greenwich** introduced its public time service in August 1852. Time zones in the United States were established in 1883. In October 1884, at the International Meridian Conference in Washington, D.C., the world was divided into twenty-four time zones and the Prime Meridian was established on the main transit instrument at the Royal Observatory at Greenwich. Greenwich Mean Time thereby became the standard time reference, that was gradually adopted throughout the civilized world.

Time and Frequency

The properties of quartz crystal as a frequency standard were investigated in 1928 by Warren Morrison of the Bell Telephone Laboratories. By 1939, the first quartz crystal clock had been installed at the Greenwich Observatory, and nine years later, the first complete atomic clock system, using an absorption line of ammonia to stabilize a quartz crystal oscillator, had been developed at the National Bureau of Standards in Washington, D.C. During the next few years, with the improvements in stability and reliability achieved with the introduction of the cesium beam atomic clock, it was confirmed that the earth's rotation was not constant. Therefore in 1967, the atomic second (defined as the duration of 9,192,631,770 periods of the radiation corresponding to the transition between the two hyperfine levels of the ground state of the cesium-133 atom) was adopted internationally as the fundamental unit of time measurement. By 1972, the average rates of several atomic clocks in different parts of the world had determined that the earth was slowing down by approximately one second per year. The world's time signals (referred to as Coordinated Universal Time) are coordinated at present by the *Bureau International de Poids et Mesures* in Paris. These signals are based on atomic time, determined from both cesium beam atomic clocks and hydrogen masers, and are adjusted as required by a leap second, usually on June 30 or December 31, to keep them within nine-tenths of a second of astronomical time (UT2—Universal Time 2). UT2, coordinated by the International Earth's Rotation Service in Paris, is the time determined by observation of the heavens with corrections made for polar motion and other irregularities in the earth's rotation. Atomic time (TAI—*Temps Atomique International*) is based on the weighted average of approximately 180 atomic clocks in 30 countries.

Will Andrewes

Bibliography

Andrewes, W. "Time for the Astronomer, 1484–1488." In *Vistas in Astronomy,* vol. 28, 69–86. Oxford: Pergamon Press, 1985.

———. "Time and Clocks." In *Astronomy and Astrophysics Encyclopedia*. New York: Van Nostrand Reinhold, 1992.

Brusa, G. "Early Mechanical Horology in Italy." In *Antiquarian Horology,* vol. 5, 485–513. Ticehurst, East Sussex: Antiquarian Horological Society, 1990.

Howse, D. *Greenwich Time and the Discovery of Longitude*. Oxford: Oxford University Press, 1980.

Jespersen, J., and J. Fitz-Randolph. *From Sundials to Atomic Clocks—Understanding Time and Frequency*. Washington, D.C.: National Bureau of Standards Monograph 155, 1978.

Landes, D.S. *Revolution in Time*. Cambridge: Harvard University Press, 1983.

Tisserand, François Félix (1845–1896)

French celestial mechanician. Tisserand joined the **Paris Observatory** in 1866 after graduation from the École Normale Supérieure. Following completion of his doctorate (1868), he served as director of the Toulouse Observatory (1873–1878), as a member of the Paris Faculty of Sciences, and as director of the Paris Observatory (1892–1896), where he pursued development of the *Catalogue photographique de* *la carte du ciel* (Astrographic catalogue). Tisserand's extensive publications are concerned with the lunar theory, three-body problem, and planetary theory. His four-volume *Traité de mécanique céleste* (1889–1896) surveyed nineteenth-century work in **celestial mechanics** in the same way that Laplace's *Mécanique céleste* surveyed eighteenth-century research.

LeRoy E. Doggett

Bibliography

Bassot, L., H. Poincaré, and M. Loewy. "Discours prononcés à l'inauguration de la statue de F. Tisserand à Nuits-St. Georges." *Annuaire de Bureau des longitudes* 1900, E1–E19.

Lévy, J.R. "François Félix Tisserand." In *Dictionary of Scientific Biography*, edited by C.C. Gillispie, vol. 3, 422–424. New York: Scribner, 1976.

Ultraviolet Astronomy

Ultraviolet astronomy refers to observations in the spectral region between the far-visible violet, at a wavelength of about 3,000 angstroms, and the X-ray region, around 100 angstroms. Objects with temperatures between 10,000 and 1,000,000 degrees Kelvin radiate most of their energy in the ultraviolet region of the spectrum. These include stars slightly hotter than the sun as well as more exotic stellar objects. In addition, the interstellar and interplanetary medium, atmospheric gases of stars, comets and planets produce emission and absorption features in the ultraviolet. Atoms and molecules of the most abundant elements and compounds in the universe produce characteristic spectral signatures in the ultraviolet, making this a key spectral region for a variety of purposes.

It was apparent to astronomers early in the century that the ultraviolet would be an important observational regime, and that the atmosphere of the earth (chiefly the ozone layer) prevented such radiation from reaching the ground. Initially it was called the vacuum ultraviolet, because laboratory spectroscopy had to be carried out in evacuated apparatus. Early experiments by Theodore Lyman of Harvard and others attempted to probe the cutoff altitude by taking instruments to high mountains or in balloons. Only after World War II, when rockets became available for lofting instruments, was it possible to observe celestial objects in this region.

In October 1946, Richard Tousey and his colleagues from the Naval Research Laboratory (NRL) used a captured V-2 rocket to loft a spectrograph, obtaining the first ultraviolet spectrum of the sun. A succession of flights using new scientific rockets obtained more detailed spectra from higher altitudes. More sophisticated instruments, capable of being pointed at the sun and at other objects, evolved. These helped investigators understand the dynamics, composition, and temperature of various layers of the sun, and the composition and dynamics of the upper atmosphere of the earth as well. The ultraviolet, in addition, provided key data in understanding how solar energy initiated magnetic and electrical activity in the earth's upper atmosphere.

In 1957 the NRL group obtained the first ultraviolet observation of a star. Rocket ultraviolet astronomy continued to be pursued vigorously, and also provided the basis on which later spacecraft instruments were designed and tested. Even before satellite ultraviolet astronomy, rocket data had led to a variety of discoveries and new theoretical interpretations concerning the evolution of hot stars, the composition of the interstellar medium, and characteristics of the atmospheres of planets and comets.

A series of four *Orbiting Astronomical Observatories (OAOs)* for ultraviolet photometry and spectroscopy were incorporated into the space research program of the **National Aeronautics and Space Administration** (NASA) almost immediately after its formation. Technologically challenging, the *OAO* series did not achieve successful observations until the late 1960s. Two *OAO* spacecraft actually achieved orbit and returned data—*OAO-2* beginning in 1968 and *OAO-3* in 1972. *OAO-2* surveyed the entire sky using a University of Wisconsin ultraviolet photometer and a Smithsonian

Astrophysical Observatory suite of survey telescopes. *OAO-3,* called Copernicus, carried a 32-inch Princeton University high-resolution spectrometer, making six years of observations between 1972 and 1978. The companion *Orbiting Solar Observatory* series included ultraviolet observations of the sun.

Handheld ultraviolet photography of stars was part of the *Gemini* piloted missions of the 1960s. During the *Apollo 16* mission a Naval Research Laboratory ultraviolet telescope was set up on the moon for observations of stars and of the earth's aurorae and airglow. Some of the multiple telescopes on the *Skylab* space station were devoted to ultraviolet observations of the sun, and the chance appearance of Comet Kohoutek in 1974 resulted in the first intensive study of a comet in the ultraviolet, particularly mapping of its surprisingly large hydrogen envelope.

In Europe, British investigators carried out rocket flights during the 1960s, making observations from the Southern Hemisphere as well. The European Space Research Organization's 1972 satellite *TD-1* carried out an all-sky survey and spectroscopy in the ultraviolet. The Astronomical Netherlands Satellite in 1974 did broad-band ultraviolet photometry.

In 1978 the *International Ultraviolet Explorer (IUE)* began a mission devoted entirely to ultraviolet spectroscopy that continues as of this writing, making it the longest-lived astronomical space observatory. Carrying a 45-cm telescope feeding both high- and low-resolution spectrometers, IUE obtained spectra of many thousands of objects and has been used by a substantial fraction of the world's astronomers.

Beginning in the early 1970s, NASA began feasibility studies for a 3-meter general purpose observatory, the Large Space Telescope. Redesigned in response to budgetary pressures and delayed numerous times, the 2.4-meter **Hubble Space Telescope** (HST) was finally deployed from the *Space Shuttle* in 1990. The optical system was designed from the start to span the spectral regions from near-infrared to far-ultraviolet. With the large size of the primary mirror and its location above the atmosphere of the earth, the HST's diffraction-limited performance and large light grasp promised significant advances for optical astronomy. These features were especially important for its performance in the ultraviolet, and the telescope's first complement of instruments, including two imaging cameras, two spectrographs, and a photometer, were designed for the best ultraviolet performance possible.

Ultraviolet astronomy has most often been treated in conjunction with **optical astronomy** from space, since instruments were usually also sensitive to the latter spectral range as well. Coyne gives an early account covering the administrative history of NASA's efforts to establish an orbiting astronomical observatory. DeVorkin treats the use of V-2 and other rockets to loft instruments in part for ultraviolet spectroscopy. Hevly discusses the Naval Research Laboratory's efforts during the 1940s and 1950s, important for understanding the origins of the NASA program. Smith treats ultraviolet astronomy as part of a broader program in space astronomy, and insofar as it was directly relevant to the development of the Hubble Space Telescope.

There are numerous memoirs, journalistic accounts, and scientific review articles that deal at least in part with ultraviolet astronomy. Tucker and Tucker devote three chapters to the Hubble Space Telescope in their readable and informative but sparsely documented volume, providing highlights of ground, balloon, rocket, and satellite-based developments and personalities. Cornell, Dupree, Henbest, Field and Chaisson, Kondo (1982), Kondo et al. (1987), and various articles in *Annual Review of Astronomy and Astrophysics* provide scientific reviews ranging from popular to professional.

Joseph N. Tatarewicz

Bibliography

Annual Review of Astronomy and Astrophysics. Palo Alto, Calif.: Annual Reviews, 1963–.

Cornell, J., and J. Carr, eds. *Infinite Vistas: New Tools for Astronomy.* New York: Scribner, 1985.

Coyne, E. *Astronomy in the Space Age.* Master's thesis. Cleveland: Case Institute of Technology, 1965.

DeVorkin, D.H. *Science with a Vengeance: How the Military Created US Space Sciences after World War II.* New York: Springer-Verlag, 1992.

Dupree, A.K. "The Ultraviolet Sky." In *Astronomy from Space: Sputnik to Space Telescope,* edited by J. Cornell and P. Gorenstein, 116–140. Cambridge: MIT Press, 1983.

Field, G.B., and E. Chaisson. *The Invisible Universe: Probing the Frontiers of Astrophysics.* Boston: Birkhauser, 1985.

Henbest, N., ed. *Observing the Universe*. London: Basil Blackwell, 1984.
Hevly, B.W. *Basic Research within a Military Context: The Naval Research Laboratory and the Foundations of Extreme Ultraviolet and X-ray Astronomy, 1923–1960*. Ph.D. dissertation. Baltimore: Johns Hopkins University, 1987.
Kondo, Y., ed. *Exploring the Universe with the IUE Satellite*. Dordrecht: D. Reidel, 1987.
Kondo, Y., J.M. Mead, and R.D. Chapman, eds. *Advances in Ultraviolet Astronomy: Four Years of IUE Research*. Proceedings of a Symposium Held at NASA Goddard Space Flight Center, Greenbelt, Maryland, March 30–April 1, 1982. NASA Conference Publication CP-2238. Washington, D.C.: Government Printing Office, 1982.
Smith, R.W., with contributions by P.A. Hanle, R. Kargon, and J.N. Tatarewicz. *The Space Telescope: A Study of NASA, Science, Technology, and Politics*. New York: Cambridge University Press, 1993.
Tucker, W., and K. Tucker. *The Cosmic Inquirers: Modern Telescopes and Their Makers*. Cambridge: Harvard University Press, 1986.

Ulugh Beg (1394–1449)

Patron of Islamic astronomy. A grandson of Tamerlane, he is best known by his title, Ulugh Beg (great prince). Raised at court, Ulugh Beg became ruler of the province of Maverannakhr (currently southeastern Uzbekistan) in 1409. Although a noted public figure, he remained primarily interested in science, establishing an educational institution in Samarkand in 1420 that stressed astronomy as its most important subject. Four years later, Ulugh Beg erected a three-story observatory whose main instrument was a **sextant** of 40 meters' radius. Placed in a 2-meter-wide trench along the line of the meridian, this device was designed chiefly for solar observations, but was also used for lunar and planetary investigations. Numerous measurements with this and additional equipment led to accurate determinations of the inclination of the ecliptic, the point of the vernal equinox, and other astronomical constants.

The Samarkand investigations resulted in the volume known as the *Zīj* of Ulugh Beg. Although it included extensive trigonometric tables, this work was primarily an astronomical encyclopedia. From data gathered at the Samarkand observatory, the *Zīj* recorded tables of calendar calculations and planetary positions, and included an extensive star catalogue. Although some stellar positions were determined by the Samarkand astronomers, others were taken from an existing Arabic catalogue based on **Ptolemy**'s investigations. Ulugh Beg was assassinated by order of his son. He was buried as a martyr in the mausoleum of Tamerlane.

George E. Webb

Bibliography

Kari-Niazov, T.N. "Ulugh Beg." In *Dictionary of Scientific Biography*, edited by C.C. Gillispie, vol. 13, 535–537. New York: Scribner, 1976.
Piini, E.W. "Ulugh Beg's Forgotten Observatory." *Sky & Telescope* 71 (1986): 542–544.
Shevchenko, M. "An Analysis of Errors in the Star Catalogues of Ptolemy and Ulugh Beg." *Journal for the History of Astronomy* 21 (1990): 187–201.

United States Naval Observatory

The U.S. Naval Observatory, located in Washington, D.C., was the first national observatory of the United States, comparable to the Greenwich, Paris, and Pulkovo observatories that preceded it. Founded in 1830 as a Depot of Charts and Instruments for the navy, new facilities provided in 1844 made it a naval observatory; it was very quickly proclaimed a national observatory. It also performed the functions of a hydrographic office until 1866, and in 1893 it acquired the Nautical Almanac Office. With the possible exception of the quasi-governmental Smithsonian Astrophysical Observatory (1891), the Naval Observatory remained the only national observatory in the United States until the founding of **Kitt Peak National Observatory** in 1957. While quite young by international standards, the Naval Observatory is one of the oldest government scientific institutions in the United States.

Like the national observatories of many other nations, the U.S. Naval Observatory was founded for practical purposes. Lt. Louis M. Goldsborough instituted the Depot of Charts and Instruments in 1830 for purely navigational reasons: The chronometer was coming into widespread use in the U.S. Navy, and navigational instruments and charts needed a centralized location for calibration, repair, and distribution. In particular the delicate chronometers used for determining longitude needed to be rated so that their rates of running fast or slow—rates peculiar to each instrument—could be applied to the longitude calculation. Here was the link to astronomy, for the most accurate clock known for comparison was the earth's rotation, as determined by the sun or a star passing over the meridian. Goldsborough and his successors used increasingly specialized instruments for this purpose over the years—first the **sextant** and circle, then the transit instrument and transit circle. In the process they not only determined time for use by scientists and the public, they also began to prepare star catalogues for other purposes. Thus from its earliest days, time and **astrometry** (positional astronomy) were the two prime functions of the Naval Observatory, joined by **celestial mechanics** in 1893.

The history of the Naval Observatory may be divided into five eras, each reflecting technical, social, and political events in the United States. The Founding Era (1830–1865) was dominated by the conversion of the Depot to a national observatory and was marked by tensions associated with both the hydrographic and astronomical duties that fell to the office. For twelve years, Goldsborough, Charles Wilkes, and James Melville Gilliss carried out the routine duties of the Depot, until Gilliss broadened the observing program and then agitated for a new observatory. The historian A. Hunter Dupree has correctly characterized the creation of the Naval Observatory as surreptitious, in the sense that Congress—for political reasons centering around animosity toward President John Quincy Adams and the founding of the Smithsonian—appropriated funds for a Depot of Charts and Instruments with only a small observatory attached. With the approval of the secretary of the navy, however, Gilliss purchased instruments and constructed a building far beyond the immediate needs of the navy, and Matthew Fontaine Maury seized for the institution the title of national observatory. The early schizophrenia of the institution is borne out by dual title pages in its first volume of observations in 1846. Maury gathered about him an able staff, however, the observatory was troubled by constant tensions between military and civilians. During these years Maury labored mightily to carry out the twin tasks of astronomy and hydrography, and in the end placed his resources mainly in hydrography: the famous wind and current charts emerged from this period, while astronomical observations remained unpublished. Upon Maury's defection to the Southern cause, Gilliss took over and despite Civil War difficulties restored the astronomical side of the observatory. By his death in 1865, Gillis had laid the foundations for the future path of the observatory.

The decades after the Civil War (1865–1893) may truly be described as a golden era at the observatory. In 1873 the 26-inch refractor went into operation, the largest telescope in the world. With it Asaph Hall discovered the two moons of Mars in 1877. In 1874 and 1882 **transits of Venus** occurred, and the Naval Observatory sent far-flung expeditions to observe this phenomenon, which was crucial to determining the **solar parallax** and thereby the scale of the solar system. During this period **Simon Newcomb** built a reputation as the premier astronomer in America, first at the Naval Observatory and after 1877 as superintendent of the Nautical Almanac Office. This was also the golden age of solar eclipse expeditions, of which the Naval Observatory sponsored many. Finally, during these years Naval Observatory time began to spread nationwide, thanks to the telegraph and the services of Western Union. Altogether, this was a period when an observatory that specialized in positional astronomy could still be the premier observatory in the United States, a situation that was soon to change through advancements in astrophysics.

The years between 1893 and the Depression of the 1930s were an era of opportunity at the Naval Observatory, as it moved to new quarters in Georgetown Heights, a few miles outside of Washington. The great refractor was remounted by Warner and Swasey; a new 6-inch transit circle was constructed, destined to become the workhorse instrument for positional astronomy; radio time signals superseded telegraphic signals, and Newcomb's successors struggled after his departure to maintain research at the Nautical Almanac Office. However, all of this work was placed in shadow by developments in astronomy. The Naval Observatory, faced with decisions about expanding its work to photographic, photometric, and spectroscopic techniques, embraced none of them, and thus in the eyes of many astronomers the institution was left behind. It still pursued those fields in which it had always excelled, but these were no longer the leading edge of astronomy.

The Naval Observatory experienced an era of modernization between 1927 and 1957. In 1935 **G.W. Ritchey** completed at the observatory a 40-inch reflecting telescope of unique design, known as a Ritchey-Chrétien reflector. Although both the observatory and the outside world were slow to realize its potential, this design eventually came into widespread use (including much later for the Space Telescope mirror). By the late 1940s, however, the telescope was being used at the Naval Observatory for pioneering work on interstellar polarization. In the area of time, quartz crystal clocks began to replace pendulum clocks, showing for the first time the irregularity in the earth's rotation. Beginning in 1934 the observatory began to determine time with a Photographic Zenith Tube. Facilities were expanded to include a station near Miami, Florida, in 1949, and in 1955 the 40-inch telescope was moved to a dark-sky site near Flagstaff, Arizona.

The era since 1957 has been dominated by the Space and Computer Age, with computers having a more decisive effect on the Naval Observatory. Although the Space Age undoubtedly had an indirect effect on the observatory in providing money for new projects such as the 61-inch astrometric reflector operated since 1963 near Flagstaff, the observatory has not become directly involved in satellite or spacecraft work. Computers, on the other hand, have altered every aspect of life at the observatory, especially in the areas of data acquisition and analysis. While research was undertaken in limited areas of astrophysics, the unique work of the Naval Observatory is still done in astrometry and timekeeping. The determination of stellar positions is now vigorously pursued in both the Northern and Southern hemispheres, the latter at a station on the South Island of New Zealand. Where once pendulum clocks kept the nation's time, now atomic clocks of the cesium beam, hydrogen maser, and mercury ion variety lead the way.

Although the chronometer and instruments functions left the Naval Observatory in 1950, navigation is still a primary driver of research at the institution, in the form of time service, celestial reference frames, and celestial mechanics. The synergism between pure and practical research at a mission-oriented naval institution still persists today, no less than when Maury made his choices between astronomy and hydrography in the mid-nineteenth century.

Steven J. Dick

Bibliography

Dick, S.J. "John Quincy Adams, the Smithsonian Bequest, and the Origins of the U.S. Naval Observatory." *Journal for the History of Astronomy* 22 (1991): 31–44.

———. "National Observatories: An Overview." *Journal for the History of Astronomy* 22 (1991): 1–4.

———. "Centralizing Navigational Technology in America: The U.S. Navy's Depot of Charts and Instruments, 1830–1842." *Technology and Culture* 33 (1992): 467–509.

Dick, S.J., and L.E. Doggett, eds. *Sky with Ocean Joined: Proceedings of the Sesquicentennial Symposia of the U.S. Naval Observatory, December 5 and 8, 1980.* U.S. Naval Observatory, 1983.

Dupree, A.H. *Science in the Federal Government: A History of Policies and Activities to 1940.* Cambridge: Harvard University Press, 1957.

Nourse, J.E. *Memoir of the Founding and Progress of the United States Naval Observatory*. Washington, D.C., 1873.

Plotkin, H. "Astronomers versus the Navy: The Revolt of American Astronomers over the Management of the United States Naval Observatory." *Proceedings of the American Philosophical Society* 122 (1978): 385–399.

Weber, G.A. *The Naval Observatory: Its History, Activities and Organization*. Baltimore: Johns Hopkins University Press, 1926.

United States of America, Astronomy in

European astronomy (this entry ignores astronomical practices of Native Americans and focuses on Euroamericans) was brought to British North America by the first wave of settlers to New England and quickly took root. The second book to be published in British North America was an almanac (1639); thereafter almanacs were published regularly in Massachusetts, and appeared in other colonies, including Pennsylvania and New York, before the end of the century. Readers could keep abreast of developments in European astronomy—in particular the displacement of the geocentric view by the Copernican heliocentric model of the solar system, and the subsequent refinement of **Copernicus**'s theory by **Kepler**—through these almanacs, which often relied on British publications for their information. The first astronomical telescope to appear in the colonies, a refractor with a focal length of 10 feet, was purchased by John Winthrop Jr., fellow of the Royal Society and governor of Connecticut. He was using it as early as 1660. In 1672, he donated a refracting telescope with a focal length of 3.5 feet to Harvard College. Neither Winthrop nor any subsequent observers in seventeenth-century British North America observed regularly, but some astronomically significant observations were made and transmitted to Britain. The most famous were of the comet of 1680 by Thomas Brattle. Brattle sent his observations to the Astronomer Royal, **John Flamsteed**, who in turn gave them to Isaac Newton. The observations were acknowledged in the *Principia*.

Colonial astronomy grew slowly during the eighteenth century, peaking with the observations of the transit of Venus of 1769. Thanks to an unprecedented outpouring of resources by colonial governments, institutions, and individuals, twenty-two sets of observations were obtained. These observations were made available to European astronomers through publication in the *Philosophical Transactions* or the first volume of the *Transactions of the American Philosophical Society* (1771).

This level of activity could not be sustained after the outbreak of the Revolutionary War in 1775. A people engaged in war and subsequent nation-building were unable to provide its astronomical community sufficient resources to be competitive with Europe. For the next two generations American astronomers were, for all intents and purposes, peripheral to the international astronomical community, with astronomical practice in the United States frozen roughly at the level it had attained when the nation declared independence. The astronomical textbooks used in American colleges were usually adaptations or reprints of British texts, and they reflected the state of British astronomy around 1750. Periodically, there were efforts to build an astronomical observatory, but none of these ever got beyond the design phase. Existing observatories gave no hint of the great changes wrought in refracting telescopes by the Germans or in reflecting telescopes by **William Herschel**. Individuals interested in astronomy could earn a living as surveyors, through the publication of almanacs, by making instruments, or teaching, but not through research. As a result, although there was some astronomical activity during the years from 1776 through 1830, it was sporadic and of little scientific value.

It took an infusion of money and what might be termed an intellectual revolution to transform this group of surveyors and almanac publishers into the independent astronomical community of international reputation that existed by 1875. Astronomy became one of the most generously supported sciences in nineteenth-century America. The money came from a variety of public and private sources. For example, the great refractor of **Harvard College Observatory** was paid for by the local gentry and business community in response to appeals to local pride. The view that the study of astronomy, within the context of natural theology, was a means of acquiring knowledge of the attributes of God, also played a role. The same sort of appeals (local pride and religious significance) to a much broader audience led to the raising of funds to build the Cincinnati Observatory. The establishment of the Naval Observatory was an acknowledgement by the federal government that astronomy was a utilitarian pursuit that should be supported by the taxpayer.

The concurrent intellectual revolution involved the recognition that there had been a massive transformation of astronomy in Europe during the two generations since the outbreak of the Revolutionary War. Nathaniel Bowditch issued what was perhaps the first call urging the revitalizing of astronomy in the United States and pointing to European advances in two articles in the *North American Review* (1820, 1822). Others soon took up the cause. From Europe, Americans obtained ideas, techniques, and instruments, as well as models for the organization of an observatory and training programs for astronomers. From about 1820, the first to be imported were French analytical mathematical techniques. During the 1840s and 1850s, Americans adopted the German method of astronomy, characterized by mathematical rigor and exemplified in the work of Carl F. Gauss, Friedrich W. Bessel, and Johann F. Encke. Coinciding with this latter development was a switch from English to German instrument-makers, from whom Americans bought telescopes and other apparatus. Finally, in the 1860s, Americans recognized the significance of European advances in spectroscopy, setting the stage for American participation in the development of **astrophysics**.

Americans used two techniques to transfer European astronomy to the Western Hemisphere. The first was through the printed page: reprints, translations, and adaptations of textbooks and articles. This transfer was facilitated by the lack of international copyright agreements. Two of the most significant publications were Bowditch's translation, annotation, and exposition of Laplace's *Méchanique Celeste* (1829–1839), which introduced Americans to the latest methods of analysis in **celestial mechanics**, and **John Herschel**'s *Treatise on Astronomy* (first American edition, 1834), which alerted Americans to European developments in astronomy since the last quarter of the eighteenth century.

The second means of obtaining knowledge of European astronomy was through personal interaction. This took place in two ways. Thanks to the increasing availability of funds and improvements in transportation, the number of American astronomers touring Europe swelled during the nineteenth century. They visited observatories and instrument-makers. Some attended university lectures or formally studied with European astronomers. Alternatively, the interaction took place in the United States. Especially after 1848, European astronomers were employed in American observatories and universities. Among the most notable were F. Brünnow at the University of Michigan and C.H.F. Peters at Hamilton College. These Europeans helped educate the next generation of American astronomers.

By 1875, the combination of money and knowledge had produced an American astronomical community able to offer educational, research, and employment opportunities. In the subsequent quarter-century, this community would diverge from European models as it became part of the emerging system of research universities, whose scale and mission were vastly different from its overseas counterparts.

Efforts to establish an American astronomical periodical were short-lived—for example, O.M. Mitchel's *Sidereal Messenger* (1846–1848) and B.A. Gould's *Astronomical Journal* (1848–1861)—and the attempt to form an astronomical society in 1859 was abortive. Notwithstanding, the growth of American astronomy was phenomenal. In 1835, there was only one observatory in the United States. Fifteen years later, only the German states collectively surpassed the United States in the number of observatories. By 1875, the United States had pulled ahead of Germany. Contributions to the *Astronomische Nachrichten,* the leading continental research journal in astronomy, are another indicator of the growth and significance of the American astronomical community. Prior to 1840, Americans wrote less than 1 percent of the papers in that journal. By 1875, Americans were annually contributing 15 percent of the papers, and the number was growing.

Five themes are helpful in exploring the history of American astronomy from the last quarter of the nineteenth century. Instruments, the institutions in which they are located, patronage, the research interests of American astronomers, and American astronomy as the first of the big sciences, all provide useful ways of explaining its growth.

Astronomy is a data-driven science and the quest for more and better observations entails ever larger, generally more expensive instrumentation. The growth of instrumentation, measured in both aperture and number of telescopes, led to the restructuring of research observatories as factories for the production of scientific knowledge. Other institutional changes came as a result of astronomy's increasingly close association with American higher education. By the 1890s, astronomy was playing an important role in the new American research universities. The creation of a national professional organization for astronomers (1899), the revival of the *Astronomical Journal* (1886), and the founding of the *Astrophysical Journal* (1895) further added to the institutional infrastructure of American astronomy.

New instrumentation and new institutions rested, in turn, on patronage. The federal government supported **astrometry** and **celestial mechanics** at the Nautical Almanac Office and the Naval Observatory. Otherwise, astronomers had to look to philanthropists and from the early years of the twentieth century, philanthropic foundations, for support. The demographic growth of the American astronomical community is interesting. The table on the following page reports data on the demography of the American astronomical community. By the 1880s, America probably had more astronomers than any other nation in the western world. While the numbers vary as a consequence of economic and political conditions, the trend from the 1880s through the 1930s was upward. The 1959 personnel data suggest that American astronomy recovered slowly from the effects of war, but the increasing number of observatories points to continued growth.

In 1886, the cognitive concerns of American astronomers were divided between the majority who worked in celestial mechanics and astrometry and a minority who gave their attention to astrophysics. By 1900 the balance was rapidly shifting, and in the twentieth century astrophysics came to dominate the profession.

Through the third quarter of the nineteenth century, observatory directors had to settle for one large new instrument during their professional lifetimes. By the 1890s, however,

Growth of the American Astronomical Community, 1886–1959

	1886	1907	1931	1959
Observatories				
Total Number	40	102	90	99
National	2	2	2	6
College and University	29	71	64	80
Private Research	8	13	11	6
Joint Research	—	—	—	6
Public	—	—	—	1
Amateur	1	16	13	—
Personnel				
Total Number	128	294	378	315
Astronomers	89	153	170	240
Professors	29	53	104	75
Computers	10	88	104	—

Source: Adapted from Lankford and Edge, "Astronomy, 1850–1950, A Social-Historical Overview."

These data are drawn from a series of reports published by the Royal Belgian Observatory at Uccle. All but the first survey were based on self-reporting questionnaires. Private research observatories include institutions such as the Mount Wilson or Dudley observatories. Computers refer to assistants who performed various measurements and made computations under the supervision of astronomers. The data on personnel probably underrepresent the actual size of the community.

astrophysics, with its rapidly expanding research agenda, demanded constant innovation in the design and construction of instruments. Researchers in solar physics, stellar spectroscopy, and stellar photometry all required new instruments and axillary equipment.

The most striking development was the shift from refractors to reflectors. The process was initiated by amateurs such as **Henry Draper** in the 1870s, and by the 1890s professional astronomers became interested in the reflector. In relatively quick succession the 36-inch reflector at the **Lick Observatory** and then the 60-inch and 100-inch reflectors at Mount Wilson marked the transition from the age of the great refractor to the epoch of large reflectors.

Key to the process of developing new instrumentation was the introduction of photography into astronomy. By the 1890s, dry plates were readily available and photography was rapidly replacing the visual observer in most areas of astronomical research. By 1920, fundamental transit circle astrometry and double star research were among the few research fields that did not rely on photography. Photography was especially important in stellar photometry and for solar and stellar spectroscopy. Photography produced a record that could be examined at leisure with auxiliary equipment, resulting in measurements of great precision. In the early twentieth century, photography was applied to astrometry, especially the study of **stellar parallaxes** and the determination of stellar positions. During the second decade of the twentieth century, photography was also applied to the study of nebulae and star clusters.

Photography not only meant a significant increase in accuracy, it also led to an increase of many orders of magnitude in the rate of data acquisition. In large part, spiraling rates of data acquisition drove the growth of the unskilled and semiskilled labor force employed by large American research observatories.

From the 1870s to the 1950s, telescope-building in America falls into three distinct periods. The era from the 1870s through World War I might be called the golden age of great American telescopes. Beginning with the Lick 36-inch refractor (1888), through the Mount Wilson 100-inch reflector (1917), American telescopes grew in number and aperture. The interwar period saw a dramatic downturn in the rate of telescope construction that can be explained, in part, by economic conditions. After World War II, the 200-inch Hale reflector came on line (1948), and until the advent of optical telescopes in space, it served as the prototype for American ground-based instrumentation. Toward the end of the century, **multiple mirror telescopes** and dramatic innovations in electronic auxiliary instrumentation made their appearance.

The golden age of telescope construction rested on two generations of skilled American optical craftsmen, including the Clarks of Cambridgeport, Massachusetts, and the Brashear works of Pittsburgh, as well as such skilled engineers as Warner and Swasey of Cleveland. Glass-makers such as Corning were responsible for important technical contributions. In addition, craftsmen associated with observatories such as **George W. Ritchey** at the Yerkes and later Mount Wilson observatories, and optical theorists such as Charles Hastings of Yale, were important in the process of innovation.

Patronage for the construction of new instruments and institutions, as well as for specific research projects, came from a variety of sources. In contrast to Europe, the national government supported only astrometry and celestial mechanics. Astrophysical investigations had to rely on private donors and, after 1900, philanthropic foundations. Workers in both astrophysics and the older fields of celestial mechanics and astrometry were aided by small grants from the National Academy of Sciences, the American Philosophical Society, and the American Academy of Arts and Sciences. After the Carnegie Institution of Washington opened its doors in 1902, astronomy accounted for the largest single category of support, a pattern that continued through the 1940s. World War II marked a watershed in patronage for science in America. After the war the federal government became the most important patron of astronomy and astrophysics.

Through the third quarter of the nineteenth century, celestial mechanics and astrometry were the dominant research concerns of American astronomers. Developing theories for the orbits of solar system objects, testing those models against observation, and the publication of ephemerides were the primary concerns of celestial mechanicians. They also made contributions to pure and applied mathematics and devoted considerable attention to the problem of the long-term stability of the solar system. Workers in astrometry compiled ever more accurate catalogues of stellar positions. These provided data to measure the proper motions of the stars and to help construct models of the sidereal universe. American astrometry also pioneered in the use of photography in determining stellar positions and parallax.

Unlike celestial mechanicians who relied primarily on pen and paper and observations made by others, researchers in astrometry used state-of-the-art instrumentation to collect data. Both fields were mathematically demanding. The computation of an orbit for a comet or asteroid was an exacting process. The development of a new mathematical theory of a planet or the moon involved the help of assistants who did the routine calculating. Astrometry began with an understanding of the errors of the instrument, and the observer and went on to include corrections that had to be applied to the observations before they could be taken to represent the places of the stars or solar system objects. Both fields involved long-term projects, often stretching over a professional career. In neither celestial mechanics nor astrometry could an individual expect to make many dramatic discoveries.

Simon Newcomb, who became director of the Nautical Almanac Office in 1877, and his collaborator, **G.W. Hill**, earned international recognition for their work in celestial mechanics. They were followed in the next generation by **E.W. Brown** of Yale and **F.R. Moulton** of the University of Chicago. By the 1920s, however, celestial mechanics in America appeared to have reached a dead end. Events after 1950 would revitalize the field.

American astrometry came of age under the direction of Lewis Boss at the Dudley Observatory. Working with a large staff funded by the Carnegie Institution of Washington, the Dudley Observatory became one of the leading centers for astrometry in the world. Its work culminated in the *General Catalogue of 33,342 Stars* (1937). In the second generation, **Frank Schlesinger**, long-time director of the Yale Observatory, was the recognized leader of American astrometry. However, like celestial mechanics, interest in astrometry declined, only to revive as a consequence of the space age.

At first, astrophysics in America was the province of amateurs. L.M. Rutherfurd and Henry Draper were pioneers in the 1860s and 1870s, applying photography to solar and stellar spectroscopy and developing new forms of instrumentation that would become standard in astrophysical observatories by the end of the century. Professionals had such heavy career investments in existing problems and instrumentation that the process of change in American astronomy was sluggish. Astrophysics grew slowly through the 1890s, but by 1920 had come to dominate the American astronomical community.

Astrophysics developed in several stages. **E.C. Pickering**, a physicist who became director of the **Harvard College Observatory** in 1877, instituted large-scale research programs in photometry and then spectroscopy. At first observations were made visually, but soon Pickering introduced photography and data begin to accumulate at an astonishing rate. In the 1880s, Pickering organized the Harvard Observatory along the lines of a knowledge factory. Astronomers planned projects, supervised their execution, and interpreted the results. Semiskilled workers (generally male) spent long nights at the telescope exposing plates. An unskilled labor force composed of women analyzed the plates and reduced the data.

Soon the role of observatory director became similar to that of a chief executive officer in a major industrial corporation, and research observatories became factories organized for the mass production of scientific knowledge, similar in organization to the United States Steel Corporation or other industrial giants.

Solar physics under C.A. Young at Dartmouth and then Princeton and, in the second generation, led by **G.E. Hale**, founder of the Yerkes and Mount Wilson observatories, quickly gained a foothold in America. Young was a pioneer in solar spectroscopy and Hale argued that the sun was the nearest star and that astronomers could learn much by carefully investigating its physical and chemical characteristics. Hale carried out important work in solar physics at Yerkes. He equipped Mount Wilson with special instruments designed for solar research and a large reflecting telescope (with a 60-inch mirror) to study stellar spectra.

It was Hale who defined the research agenda for American astrophysics from the 1890s through the 1920s. Influenced by European developments in experimental spectroscopy, he sought to apply the techniques and methods of physics to the sun and stars. Hale encouraged two generations of solar and stellar spectroscopists and made several important contributions to instrumentation and observational astrophysics, including the invention of the **spectroheliograph** and the discovery of solar magnetism.

At the Mount Wilson Observatory, Hale's large telescopes were soon used to study nebulae and galaxies. In time, this research, pioneered by **Harlow Shapley** and **Edwin Hubble**, produced data that redefined the size of the universe, the nature of the Milky Way Galaxy, and the expansion of the universe. These investigations would lead to dramatic new conceptions in cosmology.

From the beginning in mid-nineteenth-century Europe, astronomers working in stellar spectroscopy often believed that stars could be arranged in a sequence according to temperature. Before World War I, the Princeton astronomer **H.N. Russell**, working independently of **E. Hertzprung** in Europe, developed a model relating absolute magnitude to spectral type and positing the existence of both giant and dwarf stars. These ideas remain an important part of the foundation on which theories of stellar evolution rest.

From the 1920s, a few American astronomers became interested in the physical processes that produce radiation in the sun and stars. Before World War II the physics on which these investigations rested came from Europe. In the late 1930s, **Hans Bethe** of Cornell proposed a mechanism to explain the production of stellar energy based on nuclear reactions in the interiors of stars. Physical processes in nebulae were under investigation at the same time, most notably by Donald Menzel and his team at Harvard.

Theoretical and observational astrophysics developed rapidly after World War II. Innovation in instrumentation, ranging from electronic computers to large telescopes, highly efficient auxiliary photon detectors, and close collaboration between physicists and astronomers resulted in greatly increased understanding of the physical processes operating in stars and nebulae. Indeed, by the 1960s, many practicing astronomers had earned a Ph.D. in physics before entering the field.

The coming of the space age rejuvenated celestial mechanics under the new label of dynamical astronomy. The success of space missions rested on the careful calculation of orbits for probes and later manned vehicles. This, in turn, stimulated renewed interest in theories of solar system objects, especially new methods of calculating models using Einstein's general theory of relativity, and the application of high speed electronic computers to the process. Astrometry experienced a modest resurgence as space telescopes demanded new catalogues of faint stars in order to carry out their scientific missions.

Indeed, in many ways the old distinctions between astrophysics, celestial mechanics, and astrometry faded after 1950, as new research agendas emerged. For example, investigations of the kinematics of nebulae and galaxies and their distribution in space require the tools of both astrophysics and dynamical astronomy.

Astronomy played an important role in the Cold War and benefited from federal patronage. Both the military and agencies such as the **National Science Foundation** (NSF) provided funds for the expansion of American astronomy. Especially important was a system of national optical and radio observatories funded by the NSF. Solar physics was often supported by the military, which saw its potential for understanding long-term weather patterns as well as short-term effects on electronic communications.

Beginning in the 1970s, space-based telescopes and new ground-based telescopes observing in various portions of the electromagnetic spectrum (such as X-ray, gamma-ray or infrared) provided exciting new information that greatly enhanced the knowledge of the physics of stars and galaxies. Of special importance were observations that confirmed the Big Bang origin of the universe and revealed its large-scale structure. Physics and astronomy merged in the study of the Big Bang and the very early universe.

Lankford and Edge have argued that astronomy was the first of the big sciences in America. By World War I, the scale and organization of astronomical research institutions, and the cost of astronomical research at observatories such as Mount Wilson, Lick, Dudley, and Yerkes, were greater than those for any of the other sciences in America. The only competitors were the laboratories of industrial chemists and the Berkeley cyclotron project. American astronomy built on these foundations and enjoyed a period of remarkable growth in the postwar era. However, as is the case for all the physical sciences, the end of the Cold War means a new and uncertain future for American astronomy.

Marc Rothenberg
John Lankford

Bibliography

DeVorkin, D.H. "Stellar Evolution and the Origin of the Hertzsprung-Russell Diagram." In *Astrophysics and Twentieth-Century Astronomy to 1950*, edited by O. Gingerich, vol. 4A, 90–108. Cambridge: Cambridge University Press, 1984.

Dick, S.J. "How the United States Naval Observatory Began, 1830–1865." In *Sesquicentennial Symposia of the United States Naval Observatory,* edited by S.J. Dick and L.E. Doggett, 167–181. Washington, D.C.: USNO, 1983.

Jones, B.Z., and L.G. Boyd. *The Harvard College Observatory: The First Four Directorships, 1839–1919*. Cambridge: Harvard University Press, 1971.

Lankford, J. "Amateurs and Astrophysics: A Neglected Aspect in the Development of a Scientific Specialty." *Social Studies of Science* 11 (1981): 275–303.

———. "The Impact of Astronomical Photography to 1920." In *Astrophysics and Twentieth-Century Astronomy to 1950,* edited by O. Gingerich, vol. 4A, 16–39. Cambridge: Cambridge University Press, 1984.

———. *American Astronomy: Community, Careers and Power, 1859–1940.* University of Chicago Press, forthcoming.

Lankford, J. and D. Edge, "Astronomy 1850–1950: A Social-Historical Overview." In *Astrophysics and Twentieth-Century Astronomy to 1950,* edited by O. Gingerich, vol. 4B, Cambridge: Cambridge University, forthcoming.

Lankford, J. and R.S. Slavings. "The Industrialization of American Astronomy, 1880–1940." *Physics Today* 49 (1996): 34–40.

Loomis, E. *The Recent Progress of Astronomy, Especially in the United States* [1856]. New York: Arno, 1980.

Musto, D.F. "A Survey of the American Observatory Movement, 1800–1850." *Vistas in Astronomy* 9 (1968): 87–92.

Rothenberg, M. "The Educational and Intellectual Background of American Astronomers, 1825–1875." Ph.D. dissertation, Bryn Mawr College, 1974.

———. "History of Astronomy." In *Historical Writings on American Science: Perspectives and Prospects,* edited by S.G. Kohlstedt and M.W. Rossiter, 117–131. Baltimore: Johns Hopkins University Press, 1986.

Struve, O., and V. Zebergs. *Astronomy of the Twentieth Century*. New York: Macmillian, 1962.

Warner, D.J. "Astronomy in Antebellum America." In *The Sciences in the American Context: New Perspectives,* edited by N. Reingold, 55–75. Washington, D.C.: Smithsonian Institution Press, 1979.

Wright, H. *Explorer of the Universe: A Biography of George Ellery Hale*. New York: E.P. Dutton, 1966.

Yeomans, D.K. "The Origin of North American Astronomy—Seventeenth Century." *Isis* 68 (1977): 414–425.

University of Arizona, Astronomy at

Since the 1950s, the University of Arizona in Tucson has played a leading role in the development of American astronomy. The institution's recent achievements represent the culmination of nearly a century of endeavors. The University of Arizona's astronomy program began with the arrival of A.E. Douglass in 1906. A former assistant at the **Harvard** and **Lowell observatories,** Douglass recognized the superior seeing conditions of southern Arizona and early on launched a campaign to obtain a suitable telescope. Within three years, he borrowed an 8-inch refractor from Harvard, but was unable to secure funds for a larger telescope. In 1916, however, local resident Lavinia Steward provided $60,000 for an astronomical facility to honor her late husband. Committing most of the bequest to the telescope itself, Douglass decided on a 36-inch reflector. American involvement in World War I delayed work on the Steward telescope, as did difficulties casting the mirror blank. Despite Douglass's incessant pleas, the telescope remained unfinished until the summer of 1922.

Because Douglass wanted as large a telescope as possible, he agreed to locate the instrument on campus and to accept an observatory building that had space for little more than the telescope itself. The university had few resources to augment the Steward budget, leaving Douglass and his successor, Edwin F. Carpenter, to administer a skeleton facility. Despite the lack of support, the Steward astronomers contributed to the discipline. In 1923, Douglass led an eclipse expedition to Puerto Libertad, Sonora, returning one of the best photographic records of that eclipse. Five years later, the Steward Observatory joined Yerkes, Mount Wilson, Lick, and Lowell observatories in a systematic survey of bright nebulae coordinated by **Edwin Hubble**. Such contributions, as well as superior viewing conditions, attracted the attention of astronomers without access to large telescopes. The Tucson installation regularly hosted visitors who pursued a variety of research projects.

In the mid-1950s, the fortunes of astronomy at the University of Arizona began to improve, as southern Arizona emerged as one of the leading sites for the proposed national observatory. When Kitt Peak was chosen as the site for this facility in 1958, the Steward Observatory found itself a close neighbor to an institution expected to grow into the optical astronomy center of the nation. The most important impact of the Kitt Peak selection on the University of Arizona, however, may well have been a new view of the existing astronomy facility on campus. Finally convinced that the observatory represented an important part of the university community, officials approved proposals to expand the campus building, hire new staff, and secure a site on Kitt Peak for a Steward Observatory station.

The fall of 1960 witnessed another important development for the university, when noted planetary astronomer **Gerard P. Kuiper** and his staff arrived as the nucleus of the Lunar and Planetary Laboratory. Formerly a director of the **Yerkes Observatory**, Kuiper had focused on lunar studies throughout the 1950s. Anxious to establish a separate planetary institute to expand his research, the Dutch-born astronomer realized the potential value of relocating to Tucson to take advantage of the growing astronomical resources of the area. University of Arizona officials welcomed the prospect of a distinguished faculty member and arranged for Kuiper to assume a joint appointment with the Institute of Atmospheric Physics and the Steward Observatory.

Kuiper's reputation as a planetary astronomer and lunar expert led to his appointment to several National Aeronautics and Space Administration (NASA) committees during the 1960s. He and the Lunar and Planetary Laboratory (LPL) were instrumental in both the *Ranger* and *Surveyor* programs, as well as many other NASA efforts. The accompanying expansion of the LPL staff (119 by fall of 1967) convinced NASA to provide additional funding for a separate Space Sciences building on campus. The five-story structure was completed by the fall of 1966 through a NASA grant of more than one million dollars. The LPL also expanded during the 1960s, installing various optical and infrared telescopes at several sites in the Catalina Mountains north of Tucson.

As Kuiper's laboratory achieved fame, another element of the university's astronomy program began to emerge. During the 1963–1964 academic year, astronomy department chairman Aden B. Meinel began coordinating plans for an interdisciplinary Optical Sciences Center on campus. Under Meinel's direction, the Optical Sciences Center quickly gained prominence, preparing mirrors for reconnaissance satellites and performing much of the optical work for the various observatories in southern Arizona. Beginning in 1970, the center's primary concern was the design and development of the **Multiple Mirror Telescope** (MMT), using mirrors from a cancelled satellite project.

The growth of astronomy at the University of Arizona also included the Steward Observatory and the Department of Astronomy. External funding from NASA, the National Science Foundation (NSF), and other agencies provided the means to expand the observatory and department. During the 1965–1966 academic year, for example, the observatory received a grant of $1,400,000 from the NSF, most of which was earmarked for a 90-inch reflector to be installed at the Steward station on Kitt Peak. Under the directorship of the eminent astronomer Bart J. Bok, the observatory and department grew dramatically during the late 1960s. The discovery of the first optical pulsar by astronomers using the 36-inch reflector was a major achievement of the Steward Observatory. The department's educational program proved similarly successful. During the 1970–1971 academic year, the American Council on Education rated the University of Arizona fifth in "overall effectiveness" of its graduate program in astronomy.

The 1970s and 1980s also witnessed developments at the University of Arizona that fundamentally changed an important aspect of astronomy: telescope design. Among the leaders in the design and construction of the new technology telescopes, the university's various astronomy facilities played crucial roles in the creation of a new generation of astronomical instruments. The first example of the new technology was the MMT, jointly developed by the Steward Observatory, the Optical Sciences Center, and the Smithsonian Astrophysical Observatory. Located on the latter's Mount Hopkins site south of Tucson, the MMT employed six 1.8-meter mirrors that were focused to provide the equivalent resolution of a single 4.5-meter telescope. Using sophisticated laser and computer guidance technology, the MMT proved a remarkably successful instrument. Beginning in 1980, another innovation in telescope design emerged from the University of Arizona, under the leadership of J. Roger Angel. In an attempt to create lightweight, relatively inexpensive mirrors, Angel produced short focal-length mirror blanks of a lightweight honeycomb design that were cast in a spinning furnace. This technique provided mirrors that required less grinding than those cast by traditional methods, saving time and expense. The short focal length also allowed the use of smaller, less expensive support structures. By the end of the decade, Angel's technique had been well established and was one of the leading technologies for new telescopes. Among the mirrors planned by Angel's laboratory were a 6.5-meter replacement for the MMT, an 8-meter mirror for the Carnegie Institution's Las Campanas Observatory in Chile, and four 7.5-meter mirrors for the National New Technology Telescope.

As the University of Arizona's reputation continued to grow, southern Arizona emerged once again as a leading site for a new observatory. In contrast to the situation in the 1950s, however, the university would be the guiding force behind this new facility. Arizona astronomers had long been intrigued with the potential of Mount Graham (some 70 miles northeast of Tucson) for astronomy. By the early 1980s, university astronomers began planning for an international observatory on the site, to include a collection of telescopes supported by various institutions. The centerpiece of the proposed facility emerged a few years later in the form of a binocular telescope constructed of two 8-meter mirrors supplied by Angel's laboratory in Tucson. Estimated to cost some $60 million, this telescope was to be jointly funded by the University of Arizona, Ohio State University, and the Arcetri Astrophysical Observatory in Florence, Italy. Although Ohio State withdrew from the project in 1991, the Mount Graham site remained an important goal for the American astronomical community as well as the University of Arizona.

In addition to ground-based astronomy, the University of Arizona continued to participate in many of the most dramatic accomplishments of space astronomy. Astronomers of the Lunar and Planetary Laboratory participated in virtually all NASA probes in the 1970s and 1980s, frequently serving as team leaders. The most dramatic example of the university's role was the *Voyager 2* mission to the outer planets, which included more than a dozen university scientists in various important positions. Actively involved in space and ground-based astronomy, as well as in the development of new astronomical technology, the University of Arizona moved toward the next century with a secure reputation and the potential for continued significant contributions.

George E. Webb

Bibliography

Martin, B., et al. "The New Ground-Based Optical Telescopes." *Physics Today* 44 (1991): 22–30.

Stiles, L. "Uranus Flyby: 'Everything Went Right.'" *Arizona Alumnus* 63 (1986): 32–34.

Waldrop, M.M. "The New Art of Telescope Making." *Science* 234 (1986): 1495–1497.

Webb, G.E. *Tree Rings and Telescopes: The Scientific Career of A.E. Douglass*. Tucson: University of Arizona Press, 1983.

Whitaker, E.A. *The University of Arizona's Lunar and Planetary Laboratory: Its Founding and Early Years*. Tucson: University of Arizona, 1986.

University of California, Astronomy at

In the early days of the University of California (it began operation in 1863), an engineering professor taught astronomy. The first astronomer on its faculty was Armin O. Leuschner, who came to the campus as an instructor in mathematics in 1890. He was Lick Observatory's first graduate student. He was working on a thesis under its director, Edwin S. Holden, when he began his instructorship. At Berkeley, Leuschner began teaching astronomy, and in 1894 he became assistant professor of astronomy and geodesy. He had abandoned his thesis, and he and Holden were constantly at swords' points.

During this period Leuschner had two graduate students, although there was no formal graduate program. They were William H. Wright and Frederick H. Seares. Neither received a Ph.D., but they went on to long and successful careers at Lick and Mount Wilson observatories, respectively. In 1896–1897 Leuschner went on leave to the University of Berlin for one year in celestial mechanics and returned with his Ph.D.

Holden's successor, **James E. Keeler**, was a former Lick staff member whom Leuschner knew well. He had worked with Keeler at Lick and at Allegheny Observatory. Furthermore, Keeler was convinced of the value of having young, active graduate students at the observatory. He transferred the funds in the budget to create three **Lick Observatory** fellowships (each at $600 per year when the program began in 1898 and for many years thereafter). Keeler and Leuschner worked out a program under which the Lick fellows would spend the summer and the fall semester (the good observing season) at Mount Hamilton, and the winter-spring semester at Berkeley taking graduate courses. The first fellows, Frank E. Ross, R. Tracy Crawford, and Harold K. Palmer, were all Berkeley graduates. Ross ended by getting his Ph.D. in mathematics, but he became an outstanding research astronomer. Crawford, the first Berkeley astronomy Ph.D. (1901), was immediately hired by Leuschner as the second faculty member in the department.

Keeler died unexpectedly in 1900, but his successor as director, **William Wallace** Campbell, continued the Lick fellowships on the same basis. Gradually Leuschner built up the Berkeley Astronomical Department, adding Sturla Einarsson to the faculty in 1913, William F. Meyer in 1920, and C. Donald Shane in 1924. All earned Ph.D.s from the Berkeley department. Leuschner hired them for their teaching abilities, and they normally taught from six to twelve class hours per week, depending on rank.

Lick Observatory had the status of a separate department of the university. Its faculty members had no teaching duties but could serve as thesis advisers and on thesis committees. Occasionally a Lick astronomer would spend a semester teaching on campus, in an exchange with a Berkeley professor who would do research at Mount Hamilton.

In 1913, at the fiftieth anniversary commencement of the University of California, six Ph.D.s were awarded in astronomy, the largest number given in any year until after World War II. There were only three Ph.D.s and one Sc.D. awarded in all the other departments that year. Many outstanding astronomers came from the University of California. For years it was the largest and best graduate astronomy department in the United States. In a study of graduate schools published in 1925, a panel ranked Berkeley best in the nation in astronomy, with Chicago a distant second. By then there were so many astronomy graduate students at Berkeley that only a few got the fellowships that enabled them to spend a full year or more on the mountain. Leuschner and Campbell (and after him, **Robert G. Aitken**) cooperated very closely in deciding who would get the Lick fellowships, other research fellowships, and the teaching fellowships that were the last line of support.

Under Leuschner's leadership the department was strongly oriented toward **celestial mechanics** and orbit theory. Only Shane taught **astrophysics**, with help from Donald H. Menzel during two semester-long exchanges from Lick observatory, in 1928 and 1931. Campbell wanted to get more physics into the standard curriculum, but Leuschner insisted that the theoretical astronomy that he loved was necessary.

Leuschner retired in 1936, and Crawford, his successor, in 1941. Shane succeeded Crawford as chairman, but in 1942 went on leave to work on the atomic bomb project, first at the Radiation Laboratory in Berkeley, then at Los Alamos. Einarsson became the next chairman, and made it his mission to rebuild the department after the war ended. Shane did not return, but became director of Lick Observatory. In 1947 Einarsson succeeded in bringing Louis G. Henyey from Yerkes Observatory, an astrophysicist, to a permanent faculty position in the department. Three years later **Otto Struve** came as chairman, bringing John G. Phillips from Yerkes with him. They, with Harold F. Weaver, led the Berkeley Astronomical Department into its current place as a modern, astrophysics-oriented research and graduate-training center.

The main collection of papers of the Berkeley Astronomical Department is at the University of California Archives, Berkeley, in the Department of Astronomy, College of Letters and Science Papers. There are also significant collections in the Armin O. Leuschner Papers and the Otto Struve Papers, Bancroft Library, University of California, Berkeley, and in the Mary Lea Shane Archives of the Lick Observatory, University of California, Santa Cruz.

Donald E. Osterbrock

Bibliography

Herget, P. "Armin Otto Leuschner." *Biographical Memoirs of the National Academy of Sciences* 49 (1978): 129–147.

Hughes, R.M. *A Study of the Graduate Schools of America*. Oxford, Ohio: Miami University, 1925.

Leuschner, A.O. "History of the Students' Observatory." *Publications of the Astronomical Society of the Pacific* 16 (1904): 68–77.

Makemson, M.W. "Russell Tracy Crawford." *Publications of the Astronomical Society of the Pacific* 71 (1959): 503–505.

Osterbrock, D.E. *James E. Keeler, Pioneer American Astrophysicist: And the Early Development of American Astrophysics*. Cambridge: Cambridge University Press, 1984.

———. "Armin O. Leuschner and the Berkeley Astronomical Department." *Astronomy Quarterly* 7 (1990): 95–115.

Osterbrock, D.E., J.R. Gustafson, and W.J.S. Unruh. *Eye on the Sky: Lick Observatory's First Century*. Berkeley: University of California Press, 1988.

Phillips, J. "Sturla Einarsson." *Mercury* 4 (1975): 7, 23.

University of Chicago, Astronomy at

Astronomy at the University of Chicago began with Kenwood Physical Observatory in the yard next to William Ellery Hale's family mansion at 4545 Drexel Boulevard, two miles from the Hyde Park site at which the campus was to be built. The senior Hale had the observatory, with a 12-inch refractor optimized for solar spectroscopy and spectroheliography, built for his son George Ellery Hale the year after he graduated from the Massachusetts Institute of Technology. The telescope optics and the **spectroheliograph** (first used by Hale for his 1890 senior thesis at MIT) were made by **John A. Brashear**, and the sturdy telescope mounting was made by Warner and Swasey, all to young George's specifications; the Chicago architectural firm of Burnham and Root designed the dome. The whole Kenwood Physical Observatory belonged to William E. Hale; he had built it so that his son could do research at his home. It was dedicated in June 1891, just as William Rainey Harper was agreeing to become the founding president of the University of Chicago.

By 1892 Harper had worked out an agreement with the elder Hale by which his son became an associate professor of astrophysics (at no salary for the first three years), the university got the use of Kenwood Observatory for students under his supervision, and Hale promised to give the observatory, the telescope, and all the instruments to the university if George wanted to keep the job, and if Harper succeeded in raising $250,000 or more for a larger telescope within three years. He did so in just a few months, but until **Yerkes Observatory** was completed in 1897, Kenwood was where Hale, his assistant Ferdinand Ellerman, **George Willis Ritchey**, and Edward E. Barnard worked and observed under University of Chicago auspices. The 12-inch refractor and its dome, spectrograph, and spectroheliograph were moved to Yerkes that year.

Thomas Jefferson Jackson See began the tradition of mathematical astronomy on the University of Chicago campus. It was the old astronomy of orbit theory and planetary motion, much more familiar to classical scholars like Harper than astrophysics. A Missourian with a Berlin Ph.D., See began as an assistant professor in 1892. In a pattern he was to repeat later in his career, See made a brilliant first impression but soon clashed with Hale, then with Harper. See claimed great importance for his research work, but any expert who examined it in detail found it derivative, and its author arrogant if not dishonest. Harper declined to promote See, who drifted off to **Lowell Observatory** on leave, then resigned his Chicago position when he got a job at Lowell but soon lost that too.

Forest Ray Moulton was a much more successful University of Chicago mathematical astronomer. In 1897, while he was still a graduate student there, geologist Thomas C. Chamberlin asked for his help with calculations dealing with the evolution of the earth's atmosphere, under the nebular hypothesis of the origin of the solar system. After receiving his Ph.D. in 1899, Moulton remained on the Chicago faculty, and became a full-fledged, if junior, collaborator with Chamberlin. They developed their planetesimal hypothesis of the origin of the planets, as a result of the gravitational interaction between the sun and another star in a disruptive close approach. Chamberlin provided most of the central ideas and the geological reasoning, while Moulton worked out the orbital dynamics. Moulton was promoted rapidly, ultimately to full professor in 1912. He continued working on celestial mechanics with various Ph.D. students, especially in applications to this picture of the formation of the solar nebulae. Moulton was a good teacher, and among his students was **Edwin Hubble**, whom he recommended strongly for the Rhodes scholarship that took the young man to Oxford after his graduation in 1910. After Hubble's return from England Moulton recommended him strongly for a graduate scholarship at Yerkes Observatory. Moulton resigned from the Chicago faculty in 1926 to enter the business world as a director and adviser to the president of a Chicago utilities holding company, and after 1937 was the longtime permanent secretary of the American Association for the Advancement of Science.

Other mathematical astronomers on the University of Chicago campus faculty were Kurt Laves and William D. MacMillan; like Moulton they were closely connected with the Mathematics Department, but unlike him they did little significant research in astronomy. When MacMillan retired in 1935, **Otto Struve**, the chairman of the Astronomy Department, whose headquarters and most of its faculty and graduate students were at Yerkes Observatory, determined to capture the vacant position for astrophysics. In 1936 he hired **Bengt Strömgren**, from Copenhagen Observatory, specifically for this post. However, Strömgren proved so valuable for research that after his first half year on the campus, Struve had him move to Williams Bay to be with the rest of the faculty members there. Struve had considered stationing **S. Chandrasekhar**, whom he also hired in 1936, on campus, but Dean Henry G. Gale's intransigent prejudice against anyone with a dark skin made this impossible. Philip C. Keenan then briefly filled the astronomy teaching post on campus, as later did Thornton L. Page and various other astrophysicists on short-term, temporary bases. Almost all the astronomy graduate courses continued to be taught at Yerkes Observatory.

However, in the late 1940s, with Gale long departed from the scene and overt racism on the decline in academic circles, Chandrasekhar began regular weekly trips to the campus. He found his contacts with members of the physics department valuable, and he moved permanently to Chicago in 1964. Other members of the faculty were also commuting, and in the 1970s the center of gravity shifted decisively to the campus. Since then nearly all the graduate courses have been taught in Chicago, and most of the faculty members, including several observers who use national ground-based, airborne, and space observatories, have their offices there.

The main but fragmentary sources for the history of astronomy on the University of Chicago campus are its various presidents' papers in the Special Collections Department of its Regenstein Library. The Yerkes Observatory Archives, in Williams Bay, Wisconsin, also contains many letters dealing with departmental affairs. Several of George Ellery Hale's letterbooks from Kenwood Observatory are in the Mount Wilson Observatory Collection in the Huntington Library, San Marino, California.

Donald E. Osterbrock

Bibliography

Gasteyer, C.E. "Forest Ray Moulton." *Biographical Memoirs of the National Academy of Sciences* 41 (1970): 341–355.

Goodspeed, T.W. *A History of the University of Chicago: The First Quarter-Century*. Chicago: University of Chicago Press, 1916.

Osterbrock, D.E. *Pauper and Prince: Ritchey, Hale, and Big American Telescopes*. Tucson: University of Arizona Press, 1993.

Peterson, C.J. "A Very Brief Biography and Popular Account of the Unparalleled T.J.J. See." *Griffith Observer* 54, no. 7 (1990): 2–16.

Storrs, R.S. *Harper's University: The Beginnings*. Chicago: University of Chicago Press, 1966.

Wali, K.C. *Chandra: A Biography of S. Chandrasekhar*. Chicago: University of Chicago Press, 1991.

Wright, H. *Explorer of the Universe: A Biography of George Ellery Hale*. New York: E.P. Dutton, 1966.

Uranus

William Herschel, an accomplished musician whose general interest in science grew into a devotion to astronomy in the 1770s, discovered the planet Uranus in March 1781. Self-taught, meticulous, and patient, he made several Newtonian telescopes, reaching diameters of 19 inches and focal lengths of 20 feet. The quality of his mirrors allowed him to use extremely high powers of magnification—so high, in fact, that they were at first met with disbelief among the English astronomical establishment.

While working on a star survey in the constellation Gemini in March of 1781, he noticed a very bright object that he took for a comet. Herschel relayed the information to Nevil Maskeleyne, the **Astronomer Royal**, who spread the word. After a few months of observation, the orbit could be calculated—it was in a roughly circular solar orbit well beyond Saturn, nearly nineteen times the distance of the earth to the sun—the first new planet to be discovered in historic time. Although the English scientific establishment still was somewhat skeptical of Herschel, they nonetheless lobbied to find a position for him. King George III awarded Herschel a not-so-royal annual pension of £200, but it was enough that he could use his musical profession and telescope-making as supplements and devote the majority of his time to astronomy. Herschel reciprocated by calling the planet Georgium Sidus, but the name Uranus (after Urania, the muse of astronomy), used elsewhere in Europe, stuck.

Uranus had been recorded a number of times before its discovery but mistaken for an ordinary star. Prediscovery observations revealed discrepancies in calculated orbits for the planet, which led eventually to the discovery of Neptune.

While observing his new planet in 1787, Herschel detected two new satellites, Oberon and Titania, as well as a ring. The ring, although seemingly confirmed by others at the time, turned out to be spurious. In 1851 William Lassel detected the satellites Ariel and Umbriel. (All of the satellites were given their current names later by Sir **John Herschel**, William's son). In 1948 **Gerard P. Kuiper** discovered Miranda photographically. The spacecraft *Voyager 2* added ten more satellites in 1986.

Herschel had measured a very high oblateness for the planet, but later observers disputed his results. The discrepancies were not resolved until realizing, in 1829, the planet's peculiar inclination of 98 degrees to the plane of its orbit. This added another to the growing number of anomalies in the Laplacian **nebular hypothesis**. If the solar system had formed together out of a rotating nebula, then the planets and their satellites should all rotate and revolve in the same directions, and their axes of rotation should be inclined little if at all. Now, Uranus joined the peculiar orbital period of **Mars** innermost satellite and several other satellites in highly inclined or even retrograde orbits as anomalies to be explained.

Visual observations of the planet were difficult, although some observers attempted to derive rotation rates by tracking the faint and elusive features they thought they saw on the planet's disk. **Vesto Slipher** at **Lowell Observatory** in 1911 derived spectroscopically a rotation period of 10.7 hours, correlating with the very high measured oblateness. In 1930 J.H. Moore and Donald Menzel derived a rotation period spectroscopically of 10.8 hours, but up until the *Voyager* spacecraft flyby of 1986 estimates continued to vary between 11 and 24 hours. Photographic attempts did not reveal any structure on the disk, even from balloon-borne telescopes, and electronic imaging attempted in the late 1970s revealed only limb darkening.

Nineteenth-century micrometer measurements of the planet's diameter and estimates of its mass put it in the same class as the other outer planets, suggesting a large gaseous envelope around a small core. Uranus' and **Neptune**'s relatively higher densities, however, suggested a middle layer of water. Spectroscopic and laboratory analyses in the 1930s implied the constituent gases at the surface were largely hydrogen and methane.

On March 10, 1977, James Elliot and his colleagues made the startling discovery of a ring system around Uranus from stellar occultation observations made from the Kuiper Airborne Observatory. Their primary quarry on the flight had been photometry of Uranus' atmosphere, to attempt to refine measures of its oblateness, size, and its atmospheric composition and structure. At first they mistook the five photometric dips for belts of small satellites (no narrow rings then being known in the solar system). With corroborating observations from other observing teams, it became accepted that Uranus was surrounded by a system of very narrow rings. Ground-based observations of another occultation a year later revealed a total of nine rings, and *Voyager 2* revealed another, also using stellar occultation.

On January 24, 1986, *Voyager 2* passed through the Uranian system. It found a magnetic field, as in the case of Neptune, inclined 60 degrees to the pole. This confirmed suggestive observations by earth-orbiting satellites in 1973 and 1982–1983. The core rotated with a period of seventeen hours, slightly slower than the atmospheric features, resulting in easterly wind shears. The zonal

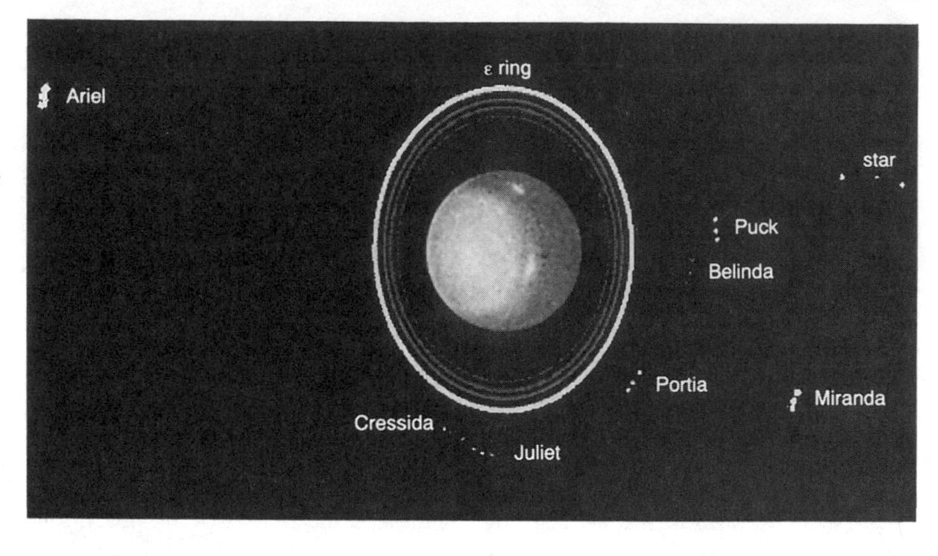

The rings and five of the inner moons (multiple images) of the planet Uranus photographed by the Hubble Space Telescope on August 14, 1994. Also visible are bright clouds in the southern hemisphere of the planet. (Courtesy of the National Aeronautics and Space Administration)

structure of Uranus' atmosphere revealed by the *Voyager* images suggested that an outer planet's rotation—and not solar energy—drives zonal flow. Uranus' rotational pole was pointed toward the sun during the encounter, yet it showed the same zonal structure as **Jupiter** and **Saturn**, whose poles were nearly perpendicular to the ecliptic. Observations and analysis confirmed and refined the general model of Uranus' interior: a rocky core surrounded by water and ice, surrounded by an atmosphere rich in hydrogen, helium, and methane. As at Saturn and Neptune, *Voyager* radio, occultation photometry, and imaging revealed new complexity in the ring system and confirmed that small, newly discovered satellites were indeed shepherding at least some of the rings. Resonances with the larger satellites also played a role in keeping the ring structure stable.

Uranus' satellites were seen in detail for the first time. The relatively dark surfaces of the satellites (as compared with the icy satellites of Saturn and Jupiter) were attributed to their spending a large portion of their time in the radiation environment of the planet, where trapped ions acted on the methane ice to darken it. Miranda showed the greatest variety of terrain, a bewildering assemblage of old and young features visibly displaced from earlier locations. Geologists suspected the moon had formed, been cratered, broken apart by a catastrophic impact, and gravitationally reassembled. There was even evidence that it had been tectonically active. The other large satellites displayed equally interesting varieties of terrain. The surfaces of Titania and Ariel seemed relatively younger than those of Oberon and Umbriel, and all seemed to have been reworked by impacting short-period comets.

While there is an extensive historiography for the discovery of Uranus, only A.F.O'D. Alexander discusses in detail the various observations and interpretations after discovery, and that from the standpoint of an active visual observer. Most of the historical treatment of Uranus is focused on the scientific career of William Herschel and his interactions with his contemporaries. James Elliot, who led the team that discovered the rings of Uranus, provides a clear and candid description of his and his colleagues' work. Popular accounts by Eric Burgess and William Sheehan focus on the *Voyager 2* encounter, and so provide only the most rudimentary historical details. Jay T. Bergstrahl et al. summarize the scientific knowledge gained from the *Voyager 2* encounter and provide by way of review papers some discussion of previous work.

Joseph N. Tatarewicz

Bibliography

Alexander, A.F.O'D. *The Planet Uranus: A History of Observation, Theory, and Discovery*. London: Faber and Faber, 1965.

Austin, R.H. "Uranus Observed." *British Journal for the History of Science* 3 (1967): 275–284.

Bennett, J.A. "The Discovery of Uranus." *Sky & Telescope* 61 (1981): 188–191.

Bennett, J.A. "Herschel's Scientific Apprenticeship and the Discovery of Uranus." In *Uranus and the Outer Planets,* edited by G. Hunt, 35–54. Proceedings of the IAU/RAS Colloquium No. 60. New York: Cambridge University Press, 1982.

Bergstrahl, J.T., E.D. Miner, and M.S. Matthews, eds. *Uranus*. Space Science Series. Tucson: University of Arizona Press, 1991.

Burgess, E. *Uranus and Neptune: The Distant Giants*. New York: Columbia University Press, 1988.

Elliot, J., and R. Kerr. *Rings: Discoveries from Galileo to Voyager*. Cambridge: MIT Press, 1984.

Hoskin, M.A. "Herschel and the Construction of the Heavens." In *Uranus and the Outer Planets,* edited by G. Hunt, 55–66. Proceedings of the IAU/RAS Colloquium No. 60. New York: Cambridge University Press, 1982.

Hunt, G., ed. *Uranus and the Outer Planets*. Proceedings of the IAU/RAS Colloquium No. 60. New York: Cambridge University Press, 1982.

Mozel, P. "In Search of Sprites: The Discovery of Ariel and Umbriel." *Journal of the Royal Astronomical Society of Canada* 80 (1986): 344–350.

O'Meara, S.J. "A Visual History of Uranus." *Sky & Telescope* 70 (1985): 411–414.

Porter, R. "William Herschel, Bath, and the Philosophical Society." In *Uranus and the Outer Planets,* edited by G. Hunt, 23–34. Proceedings of the IAU/RAS Colloquium No. 60. New York: Cambridge University Press, 1982.

Schaffer, S. "Uranus and the Establishment of Herschel's Astronomy." *Journal for the History of Astronomy* 12, no. 1 (1981): 11–26.

Sheehan, W. *Worlds in the Sky: Planetary Discovery from Earliest Times through Voyager and Magellan*. Tucson: University of Arizona Press, 1992.

Smith, R.W. "The Impact on Astronomy of the Discovery of Uranus." In *Uranus and the Outer Planets,* edited by G. Hunt, 81–90. Proceedings of the IAU/RAS Colloquium No. 60. New York: Cambridge University Press, 1982.

"Special Issue on Voyager 2 Encounter with Uranus." *Science* 233 (July 4, 1986).

Variable Star Astronomy

Oriental astronomers recorded the earliest observations of stellar variability. At least seventy-five of their guest stars dating from 532 B.C.E. to 1604 C.E. are now classified as **novae** or **supernovae**. One of their new stars in Cassiopeia marked the beginning of variable star observation in Europe. Observed by **Tycho Brahe**, Thomas Digges, and others in 1572, this star was placed among the fixed stars by Tycho's observations. A similar conclusion was reached in 1604 for Kepler's star in Ophiuchus.

Discovery, Observation, and Cataloguing of Variable Stars

Observations of the new stars of 1572 and 1604 helped break the Aristotelian grip on Western astronomy. Once philosophers understood that the stars were not always of constant brightness, discoveries of variable stars slowly began to accumulate. The first of these was observed in 1596 by David Fabricius; its regular variability was confirmed by Holwarda and Fullenius in 1638. In 1603, Bayer included the star in his atlas as omicron Ceti. It was later named Mira (The Magnificent). There were other discoveries by Blaeu, Kirch, Maraldi, Montanari, and Koch, but by 1715, **Edmond Halley** could describe only six variable stars as convincingly documented (Hoskin, 23).

Two English colleagues, John Goodricke and Edward Pigott, were the leading variable star astronomers in the late eighteenth century. Under Pigott's tutelage, Goodricke discovered the variability of delta Cephei and beta Lyrae, and determined a very accurate period for the eclipsing binary beta Persei (Algol). Pigott himself discovered eta Aquilae, R Coronae Borealis, and R Scuti. In this same period, **William Herschel** discovered the variability of 44i Boötis and alpha Herculis. However, in 1786 Pigott could reliably add only two novae and four other stars to Halley's catalogue. Pigott appended a list of thirty-nine suspected variable stars, making his catalogue a valuable resource for astronomers.

In spite of Pigott's legacy, by 1844 only eighteen variable stars were reliably documented. **John F.W. Herschel**, **Friedrich W.A. Argelander**, and **Edward C. Pickering** urged astronomers, including amateurs, to take up the study of variable stars. The first two organizations formalized for variable star study were the British Astronomical Association Variable Star Section in 1890, and the American Association of Variable Star Observers in 1911. Systematic observations by members of these and similar organizations in France, Japan, and other countries contributed substantially to variable star astronomy.

After the invention in the 1870s of dry emulsion photographic plates, a number of observatories instituted photographic surveys for variable stars and other objects. At about the same time, spectrographic discovery techniques emerged, and the discovery of variable stars accelerated. Pigott's list of suspected variable stars also grew. Seth Carlo Chandler's 1893 catalogue of variable stars included one hundred suspected variable stars. This grew to 14,810 stars in the 1982 *Catalogue of Suspected Variable Stars*. Chandler's first catalogue (1888) contained epochs and elements for the prediction of maxima for clearly periodic variable stars.

Variable Stars Catalogued 1715–1980

Year	*Compiler*	*Variable Stars*
1715	Halley	6
1786	Pigott	12
1850	Argelander	24
1854	Pogson	53
1865	Chambers	113
1888	Gore	243
1903	Pickering	701
1915	Müller and Hartwig	1,687
1930	Prager	4,581
1947	Kukarkin	14,708
1980	Kholopov	28,435

The history of visual and photographic photometric and spectroscopic techniques applied to the discovery and study of variable stars is outlined briefly by Hoffleit and Percy. However, the history of the application of photoelectric photometry to variable stars is not well developed.

Classification and Theory Evolution for Variable Stars

Early theories about the origin of stellar variability included the nonuniform distribution of surface brightness on a rotating body (Riccioli in 1651; Boulliau in 1667), the precession of an ellipsoidal body (Maupertuis in 1732), periodic appearance of large spots similar to sunspots (Secchi in 1869), collisions of swarms of meteors in orbit around the star (Lockyer in 1887), and numerous theories related to double star evolution. These early attempts at theory development confronted major uncertainties as to the nature of a star as well as the lack of reliable, systematic observations and classifications of variable stars with which to distinguish theoretical opportunities.

Pickering's First Classification of Variable Stars

Class I	New or temporary stars
Class II	Variables of Long Period
IIa	Ordinary Long Period Variables
IIb	U Gem/SS Cyg Type Variables
Class III	Variables of Small Range or Irregular Variation according to laws as yet unknown
Class IV	Variables of Short Period
IVa	Ordinary Short Period Variables
IVb	Beta Lyrae Short Period Variables
Class V	Variables of the Algol Type

As discoveries and observations accumulated, astronomers characterized each star as to the amplitude, period, and character of its brightness variation over time. In 1881, Pickering proposed classification of variable stars in five groups, a system that was only slightly modified in the next few decades (see Furness). At the time of Pickering's first classification effort, it was still unclear whether the variations in brightness that formed the basis for his system were caused by external factors or were intrinsic to the nature of the star.

The first break in resolving this dilemma came in 1889, when Hermann Carl Vogel confirmed Goodricke's brilliant speculation (in 1783) that Algol's variability was caused by an eclipse of the bright star by a dark object. Vogel discovered that Algol was a spectroscopic binary in which conjunctions of the two stars coincide with light minima. This discovery confirmed that geometric considerations provided at least one explanation for stellar variability. As the full details were worked out by **Henry Norris Russell**, **Harlow Shapley**, and others, Pickering's Algol Type classification emerged as five distinct classes of extrinsically variable stars.

Theories to account for intrinsic stellar variability emerged as part of more general models of stellar evolution. As early as 1879, August Ritter suggested that variability of some stars was intrinsic and due to adiabatic radial pulsation. However, theory development in this direction was delayed until the classification of Cepheid variables, could be resolved.

In 1913, H.C. Plummer suggested that spectral line shifts observed in Cepheids could actually reflect the radial pulsations of one star rather than the orbital motions of two stars. Although **Ejnar Hertzsprung** and Russell independently characterized Cepheids as giants, Shapley was the first to point out, in 1914, that the diameters of these stars substantially exceeded the computed orbits of the hypothetical binary systems. Shapley supported the pulsation theory with a demonstration that the periods of pulsation observed were those expected for the mean density of these giant stars.

In a brief period of intense activity that included a famous debate with **James Jeans** on the whole theory of stellar evolution, **Arthur Stanley Eddington** developed a successful theory of stellar pulsation based on radiative equilibrium. However, the exact cause of the instability and pulsations remained elusive. It was not until after mid-century that work by S.A. Zhevakin (in 1953), and by John P. Cox and Charles A. Whitney (in 1958) clearly identified a second stage of helium ionization as the source of instability leading to Cepheid pulsation. Other investigations extended this theory to Mira long-period variables and several other classes of pulsating intrinsic variable stars. A second, less regular form of intrinsic pulsation was identified in 1945 when Alfred H. Joy called attention to the nebular or T Tauri stars. By 1947, **Viktor Ambartsumian** correctly identified the T Tauri stars as new stars condensing out of the surrounding clouds of gas and dust.

In the early 1950s, Merle F. Walker and Joy discovered that the recurrent nova DQ Herculis and the dwarf nova SS Cygni were both close binary star systems with unusually short periods. In 1962, Robert P. Kraft confirmed that five additional dwarf novae and seven additional recurrent novae and nova remnants are also short period binary systems. Kraft concluded that membership in a binary system was a necessary condition for a star to become a nova. The eruptions in brightness observed in novae, cataclysmic, and symbiotic stars were eventually shown to be a consequence of the close proximity of an evolved, cool red giant star and a white dwarf or degenerate partner in these binary systems. There remain a number of classes of eruptive variable stars for which no satisfactory theoretical model exists—for example, R Coronae Borealis stars, which suddenly and rapidly fade from their normal levels of brightness on irregular intervals.

Importance of Variable Stars

Three major developments in the history of astronomy illustrate the importance of variable stars. In 1912, Henrietta Swan Leavitt at Harvard observed that as the brightness of Cepheid variables in the Small Magellanic Cloud increases, the periods of their light variations also increase in a regular manner. Since the Magellanic Cepheids are all at effectively the same distance from earth, this implies a direct relationship between the period and absolute magnitude or luminosity of Cepheid variables. Once calibrated, the period-luminosity relationship became a vital tool for determining the distances of globular clusters, thus defining the scale of the Milky Way Galaxy. Cepheid variable stars were also used as standard candles to determine the distances of nearby galaxies. The Cepheid period-luminosity relationship is a vital link in the determination of the scale of the universe.

In the 1940s, **Walter Baade** realized that the Cepheid variables occurred in two distinct classes, which differed significantly in metallicity, and therefore in age. The older Population II Cepheids were characteristically low in metals and found in the galactic bulge of spiral galaxies, in elliptical galaxies, and in globular clusters. The younger, comparatively metal-rich Population I Cepheids were concentrated in the spiral arms of the galaxy. This distinction provided a significant new tool for interpreting the structure of stellar systems. In a crucial step in this process, the lowest-mass, shortest-period variables, the RR Lyrae stars, were recalibrated as the standard candles for the globular clusters associated with the Milky Way Galaxy.

Finally, there are at least ten discrete locations in which various classes of variable stars are concentrated on the **Hertzsprung-Russell diagram**. A successful theory of stellar evolution must explain these concentrations to remain credible. Such explanations must be able, for example, to distinguish between the red and blue sides of the rather narrow strip identified as the Cepheid instability zone, a severe test by any measure. Thus, variable stars provide a critically selective diagnostic tool with which to evaluate alternative theories of stellar evolution.

Variable star astronomy offers interesting challenges from a historian's perspective. The historiography of theoretical developments in variable star astronomy needs greater development. Also, orbiting observatories working at wavelengths from the infrared to the X-ray portions of the spectrum are providing new challenges to theoreticians. These observational contributions as well as those of ground-based observers deserve early historiographic attention.

Thomas R. Williams

Bibliography

Clark, D.H., and F.R. Stephenson. *The Historical Supernovae*. Oxford: Pergamon, 1977.

Furness, C.E. *An Introduction to the Study of Variable Stars*. Boston: Houghton Mifflin, 1915.

Hoffleit, D. "A History of Variable Star Astronomy to 1900 and Slightly Beyond." *Journal of the American Association of Variable Star Observers* 15 (1986): 77–106.

Hogg, H.S. "Variable Stars." In *Astrophysics and Twentieth-Century Astronomy to 1950: Part A,* edited by O. Gingerich. *The General History of Astronomy,* edited by M. Hoskin, 73–89. Cambridge: Cambridge University Press, 1984.

Ho, P.Y. "Ancient and Medieval Observations of Comets and Novae in Chinese Sources." In *Vistas in Astronomy* 5 (1962): 127–226.

Hoskin, M. "Goodricke, Pigott and the Quest for Variable Stars." *Journal for the History of Astronomy* 10 (1979): 23–41.

Joy, A.H. "Some Early Variable Star Observers." *Astronomical Society of the Pacific, Leaflet* 99. April, 1937.

Kopal, Z. *An Introduction to the Study of Eclipsing Variables.* Harvard Observatory Monograph No. 6. Cambridge: Harvard University Press, 1946.

Lang, K.R., and O. Gingerich, eds. *A Source Book in Astronomy and Astrophysics, 1900–1975.* Cambridge: Harvard University Press, 1979.

Ledoux, P., and T. Walraven. "Variable Stars." In *Handbuch der Physik*, edited by S. Flüge, vol. 51, *Astrophysik II: Sternaufbau,* 353–605. Berlin: Springer-Verlag, 1958.

Merrill, P.W. *The Nature of Variable Stars.* New York: Macmillan, 1938.

Percy, J.R. "Variable Stars: A Historical Perspective." In *Variable Star Research: An International Perspective,* edited by J.R. Percy, J.A. Mattei, and C. Sterken, 11–20. Cambridge: Cambridge University Press, 1992.

Variation of Latitude

The earth is not an ideal ellipsoid, but has a somewhat irregular shape due to mass inhomogeneities in its interior. **Leonhard Euler** showed in 1765 that an angular displacement of the maximum moment of inertia from a rotational axis will produce a small oscillation of a body with respect to its spin axis that can be considered instantaneously fixed in space. On the earth, therefore, the positions of the poles on the surface move (polar motion) and latitude and longitude are affected.

Variation of latitude was detected astrometrically (but unintentionally) by Karl Friedrich Küstner in 1888 at the **Berlin Observatory**. More thorough investigation in 1892 by Seth C. Chandler found two oscillations, an intrinsic 1.2-year period (Chandler component) attributable to the shape of the earth, and a forced 1.0-year period (annual component) due to seasonal changes between the Southern and Northern Hemisphere air masses, polar ice caps, and ground water. Their respective amplitudes, approximately 30 feet and 26 feet, correspond to a maximal latitude variation of less than 0.5 second. Each motion is counterclockwise as viewed from above the North Pole. There also exists a small secular drift of the polar positions, of the order of 0.0036 second per year, possibly the result of delayed response to late Pleistocene melting of the polar ice caps. With the relatively recent introduction of Very Long Baseline Interferometry using **radio telescopes** and Satellite Laser Ranging methods with positional accuracies of better than 0.001 second, irregular oscillations, apparently due to meteorological and various geophysical influences, have been detected with periods of a few days to a few years. Other decade-long variations due to torques between the core and mantle of the planet also may be present.

Charles J. Peterson

Bibliography

Lambeck, K. "The Earth's Variable Rotation: Some Geophysical Causes." In *The Earth's Rotation and Reference Frames for Geodesy and Geodynamics, I.A.U. Symposium #128*, edited by A.K. Babcock and G.A. Wilkins, 1–20. Dordrecht: Kluwer, 1988.

Mueller, I.I., and B. Kolaczek, eds. *Developments in Astrometry and Their Impact on Astrophysics and Geodynamics, I.A.U. Symposium #156*. Dordrecht: Kluwer, 1993.

Munk, W.H., and G.J.F. MacDonald. *The Rotation of the Earth*. Cambridge: Cambridge University Press, 1960.

Venus

In the fall and winter of 1610, **Galileo** claims to have completed a series of observations that showed Venus to go through an entire cycle of phases, just like those of the moon. This was a decisive blow to the Ptolemaic system, in which Venus would never show the entire cycle of phases. Soon after Galileo's observations became known, the Ptolemaic system fell into disuse for most astronomers, although it would take some time for Copernicanism to take hold in other quarters. There has been some debate whether Galileo actually made these observations precisely when he says he did, or whether he asserted the observations based on what he was certain he would find and then made them later (Westfall).

In spite of Venus' brilliance and prominence in the morning and evening skies, telescopically it is a difficult object, showing only the most subtle of markings. F. Fontana in 1645 produced a map showing seas and continents. **J.D. Cassini** in 1667 derived a rotation period of 23 hours 41 minutes, but several years later he was unable to recover the bright patches he had used as a reference. In 1728 Francesco Bianchini at Rome published a map of Venus based on two years of observations. He estimated the Venusian day to be about twenty-four days, and had the rotational axis almost in the orbital plane. As on Mercury, **J.H. Schröter** inferred a mountainous surface in 1792 because one of Venus' horns appeared blunted. **William Herschel** rejected the mountains but agreed with Schröter that the visible surface was a layer of clouds. Schröter seems to have been the first to see the horns of Venus merge near inferior conjunction, when the solar light shines through the atmosphere of the planet and forms a ring effect. In 1789–1792, Schröter affirmed a rotation period of 23 hours 21 minutes. He also reported the so-called ashen light, a controversial observation of a glow from the unlit hemisphere of Venus frequently reported by subsequent observers.

Venus was quickly given other earthly characteristics. Features on drawings and later maps were named as mountains, lakes, and seas; some claimed to be able to see bright reflections off mountain peaks or even glimpses of the surface. The clouds were unproblematically interpreted as composed of water and presumably produced earthly weather conditions. However, by the late nineteenth century the consensus was that the clouds were impenetrable, and Percival Lowell embroiled himself in controversy in 1896 by claiming to have seen the surface of the planet.

The Russian Mikhail Lomonosov detected an atmosphere from observations during the 1761 transit across the sun, when he could see the planet in its rare back-lighted perspective. **David Rittenhouse** confirmed this at the 1769 transit, but Herschel's own observations of this effect were published well before those of Lomonosov, giving him priority. Venus was observed intensively during its transits across the sun in the eighteenth and nineteenth centuries. However, physical observations were opportunistic and secondary to timing the transits so that the value of the astronomical unit could be refined.

Giovanni Schiaparelli broke with tradition in 1890, claiming a synchronous rotation rate of 225 days from observations of the subtle markings. Ultraviolet photographs obtained by F. Ross at Mount Wilson in 1928 showed distinct patterns but they could not be identified from day to day and it was impossible to deduce a rotation rate. Bernard Lyot and Audouin Dollfus made extensive visual observations and photographs in various wavelengths in the 1940s and 1950s but could conclude only that certain permanent markings seemed to indicate a synchronous rotation rate, overlaid by more irregular and rapidly moving clouds visible in the ultraviolet.

Photometric observations in the nineteenth century and later polarization measurements established that the thick cloud layer was optically impenetrable. Lyot and Dollfus concluded from their polarization measurements that the clouds were made of water vapor. Percival Lowell, in reaction to the disbelief with which his visual observations of Venus had been met, set **Vesto M. Slipher** to work determining the rotation rate spectroscopically. Slipher's results in 1902 were inconclusive, but were a blow to the earthly rotation rate. In the 1920s several spectroscopists detected lines in the Venus spectrum that could not be identified. In 1932 **Walter S. Adams** and Theodore Dunham at Mount Wilson succeeded in identifying them with carbon dioxide at high pressure. They were unable to detect either water vapor or oxygen, and so the possible concentrations of these substances in Venus' clouds were pushed downward.

Radio observations in the 1950s gave rise to two interpretations—an extremely hot surface or a relatively benign surface temperature with the observed radiation due to ionospheric nonthermal emission. Debate was intense, and many models of the Venus atmosphere and surface were advanced to try to explain the observations, including the greenhouse effect, where the carbon dioxide in the atmosphere traps incoming solar radiation. Infrared radiometers carried on the U.S. *Mariner 2* spacecraft in December 1962 seemed to confirm the high surface temperature interpretation. There was still considerable room for debate, however, and the debate took a few more years to reach consensus.

Beginning in 1956 Venus was the target of radar attempts to refine the value of the astronomical unit. In 1961 Soviet and American investigators produced varying estimates of the planet's rotation rate, converging by 1964 on a retrograde rotation of 243 days.

Venus, photographed by the Pioneer-Venus *spacecraft in 1983, is shrouded in clouds. (Courtesy of the National Aeronautics and Space Administration)*

Near-ultraviolet photographs of the cloud features had by then settled on only a four-day rotation rate, suggesting intense winds at the surface. By this time, although some still held out for more hospitable conditions at the surface, Venus was no longer considered a possible abode for life. By the early 1970s, as Venus was receiving increasingly frequent visits from Soviet and American spacecraft, ever more powerful radar beams were scanning the planet from earth and producing the first maps of the surface.

Venus was the easiest planet to reach by spacecraft, and so it received early attention from Soviet and American programs. However, after the 1962 encounter by *Mariner 2*, the United States concentrated on Mars for the rest of the decade. Perhaps because of the impenetrable clouds and the inhospitable conditions, the United States seemed to neglect Venus. It sent only one other *Mariner* to Venus in 1967 (and that was an afterthought) and one in 1974 (and in that case, *Mariner 10* was en route to Mercury and using Venus for a gravity assist). The Soviets, however, made Venus the object of a concerted campaign with spacecraft sent at every favorable launch opportunity, ten attempts between 1961 and 1975.

After several failed attempts, the Soviets finally succeeded with *Venera 4* in 1967, which returned data during a 94-minute descent toward the surface of Venus. It measured temperatures from 40 to 280 degrees C, and pressures from 0.7 to 20 atmospheres—in situ confirmation of the high temperatures near the surface. Some oxygen and water vapor were detected, but the atmosphere was found to be 90 percent carbon dioxide. Shortly thereafter, *Mariner 5* probed the atmosphere with its radio transmitter and the extrapolated estimates gave a surface temperature of 527 degrees C and 100 atmospheres pressure. In 1969–1970, *Veneras 6–9* provided similar data. Finally, in July of 1972 *Venera 8* reached the surface of Venus and survived for 50 minutes, confirming in situ the high temperatures and pressures. In 1973 *Mariner 10* flew by Venus, the first spacecraft to carry cameras to that planet. The ultraviolet images of cloud rotation confirmed features seen in earthbound photographs and the four-day cloud rotation.

Between 1975 and 1978, Venus became host to a much more sophisticated suite of Soviet and American spacecraft—combinations of orbiters with radar mapping instruments and suites of atmospheric probes and landers. In 1978, *Pioneer* mapped the planet from orbit and sent a battery of four probes into the atmosphere and to the surface. In 1982 *Venera 13* produced the first color pictures from the surface, and also sampled and analyzed the soil. During the 1980s a suite of Soviet orbiters and flyby probes visited the planet, followed by the U.S. *Magellan* spacecraft, which began high-resolution radar mapping from orbit in 1990.

The historiography of Venus is extremely uneven. Galileo's observations and the impact on Copernicanism have received considerable attention, as have the transits of Venus in the eighteenth and nineteenth centuries. Visual observations into the twentieth century have received spotty attention, as have spectroscopic observations and their theoretical interpretation. Mostly, however, one is limited to the extensive scientific review literature and a variety of popular accounts.

Joseph N. Tatarewicz

Bibliography

American Philosophical Society. *The Planet Venus: Past, Present, and Future. Papers Read at the Autumn General Meeting, November 14, 1968, in the Symposium Commemorating the Society's Participation in Observations of a Transit of Venus, June 3, 1769*. Proceedings, vol. 113, no. 5. Philadelphia: American Philosophical Society, 1969.

Ariew, R. "The Phases of Venus before 1610." *Studies in History and Philosophy of Science* 18 (March 1987): 81–92.

Barsukov, V.L. *Venus Geology, Geochemistry, and Geophysics*. Edited by A.T. Basilevsky, V.P. Volkov, and V.N. Zharkov. Space Science Series. Tucson: University of Arizona Press, 1992.

Burgess, E. *Venus: An Errant Twin*. New York: Columbia University Press, 1985.

Chapman, A. "Jeremiah Horrocks, the Transit of Venus, and the 'New Astronomy' in Early 17th-Century England." *Quarterly Journal of the Royal Astronomical Society* 31 (1990): 333–357.
Cooper, H.S.F., Jr. *The Evening Star: Venus Observed.* New York: Farrar, Straus and Giroux, 1993.
Drake, S. "Galileo, Kepler, and the Phases of Venus." *Journal for the History of Astronomy* 15, no. 3 (1984): 198–208.
Dunne, J.A., and E. Burgess. *The Voyage of Mariner 10: Mission to Venus and Mercury.* Washington, D.C.: NASA SP-424, 1978.
Hunt, G.E., and P. Moore. *The Planet Venus.* London: Faber and Faber, 1982.
Hunten, D.M., ed. *Venus.* Space Science Series. Tucson: University of Arizona Press, 1983.
Keating, G.M., ed. *The Venus Atmosphere.* Proceedings of Workshop IX of the COSPAR Twenty-Seventh Plenary Meeting Held in Espoo, Finland, July 18–29, 1988. Advances in Space Research. New York: Pergamon, 1989.
Lankford, J. "Photography and the 19th-Century Transits of Venus" *Technology and Culture* 28 (July 1987): 648–657.
Luhmann, J.G., M. Tatrallyay, and R.O. Pepin, eds. *Venus and Mars: Atmospheres, Ionospheres, and Solar Wind Interactions.* Washington, D.C.: American Geophysical Union, 1992.
Meadows, A.J. "The Discovery of an Atmosphere on Venus." *Annals of Science* 22 (1966): 117–127.
National Research Council. Space Science Board. Ad Hoc Panel on Planetary Atmospheres. *The Atmospheres of Mars and Venus, a Report Prepared by William W. Kellog and Carl Sagan.* Washington, D.C.: National Academy of Sciences—National Research Council, 1961.
Robertson, D.F. "Venus—A Prime Soviet Objective." *Spaceflight* 34 (May, June 1992): 158–161, 202–205.
Westfall, R.S. "Science and Patronage: Galileo and the Telescope." *Isis* 76: 11–30.
Woolf, H. *The Transits of Venus: A Study of Eighteenth-Century Science.* Princeton: Princeton University Press, 1959.

Venus, Transits of

As the Copernican system replaced the system of **Aristotle** and **Ptolemy** in the seventeenth century, Kepler's third law gave the distances of all planets from the sun in terms of the earth-sun distance. If in cosmology it was nice to know the exact length of this astronomical unit, in technical astronomy it was essential, for it fixed the solar parallax, the angle subtended by the earth's radius as seen from the center of the sun. In the seventeenth-century efforts to improve solar theory, several considerations, including attempts to measure the parallax of Mars, brought about a rough consensus of 8 to 12 seconds for the **solar parallax.** As **Edmond Halley** argued, however, the actual measurements of parallaxes (those of Mercury, Mars, and Venus) were all inadequate. As early as 1678 he argued that only transits of Venus provided an opportunity to measure a parallax (other than the moon's) accurately. In 1691 he published a paper in the *Philosophical Transactions* in which he calculated past and future Venus transits, and although he was not entirely accurate, he correctly predicted the transits of 1761 and 1769. He returned to the subject once more, in 1716, when he published "A Singular Method by which the Parallax of the Sun or its Distance from the Earth can be Determined Securely, by Means of Observing Venus in the Sun" in the *Philosophical Transactions.* Here he argued that Venus' parallax relative to the sun could be determined accurately to one part in five hundred by comparing transit observations made at widely separated places. These observations could be made with simple instruments. Halley's paper was the clarion call, and as the transit of 1761 approached, European astronomers made preparations to observe the event close to home and in faraway places.

The major expeditions were planned and executed under the auspices of the French Académie Royale des Sciences and the English Royal Society. It should not be thought that the impetus for these expeditions was limited to national pride: In the spirit of the Enlightenment, scientists saw them as opportunities for international cooperation and convinced their respective governments to act accordingly. Thus, although England and France were at war (the Seven Year's War, or, in U.S. history, the French and Indian War), their governments instructed their respective navies not to molest enemy ships engaged in these expeditions—orders that were, however, not always obeyed.

Since 1724, when he visited Halley in London, **Joseph-Nicolas Delisle** had been convinced that Venus transits provided the only opportunities for measuring solar parallax. After Halley's death in 1742, Delisle became the main advocate for these observations, and in preparation he refined the method by means of observations of Mercury transits and revised Halley's Venus tables. The transit of 1761 would not everywhere be visible from beginning to end; the best locations would be India and the East Indies. Delisle advocated observations in Tobolsk, Batavia, Yakoutsk, Kamchatka, the Cape of Good Hope, St. Helena, Peking, Macao, Archangel, Torneo, and St. Petersburg—and, of course, in Europe.

The French Academy organized the following expeditions: Alexandre-Guy Pingré was sent to the island of Rodrigue in the Indian Ocean, Guillaume-Joseph-Hyacinthe-Jean-Baptiste le Gentil de la Galaisière obtained independent funding for an expedition to Pondicherry on the east coast of India, **César-François Cassini de Thury** was sent to Vienna, and Jean-Baptiste Chappe d'Auteroche was sent to Tobolsk in cooperation with the St. Petersburg Academy. By the time le Gentil arrived at his destination, Pondicherry had fallen to the British, and his ship retreated toward Mauritius: le Gentil observed the transit from the deck of the ship.

Across the Channel, the Royal Society sent Charles Mason and Jeremiah Dixon to Benkulen, but their ship was attacked in the Channel. The delay made it impossible for the two to reach their goal, and they therefore stopped at the Cape of Good Hope to make the observation there. Another British expedition under Neville Maskelyne went to St. Helena. In the British colonies in North America, John Winthrop of Harvard College organized an expedition to St. John's, Newfoundland.

To these expeditions must be added the organized observations made in European nations and those made by European residents in various locations around the world. Altogether more than 120 observations of the transit were made in places ranging from Peking to Newfoundland. In many of these places only parts of the transit were visible. Single ingress or egress observations nevertheless proved useful.

Halley's predicted accuracy of one part in five hundred turned out to be very optimistic. The precision of the observations varied greatly, and there was the systematic problem

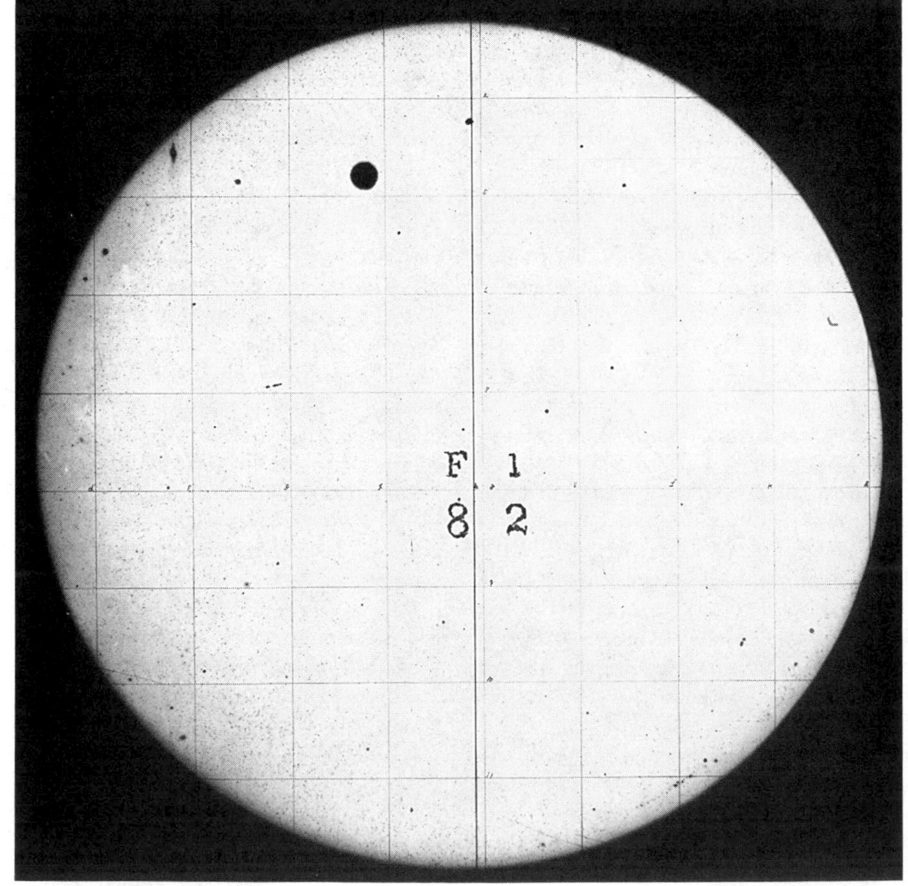

A photograph of one of the nineteenth-century transits of Venus (probably 1874, but the location is unknown) taken by one of the expeditions sent out by the U.S. Transit of Venus Commission. The dark lines were used as reference points from which to measure the position of Venus. This image was made using a wet plate and the small dots are defects in the emulsion, not sunspots. (Courtesy of the United States Naval Observatory)

of the black drop effect, which prevented an exact timing of first and last internal contacts. The quality of the data therefore varied greatly, and in the absence of statistical methods of data analysis astronomers picked and chose their data, often with the object of making the solar parallax larger or smaller to fit their preconceived notions. Further, since there was no international agreement on the sharing and joint publication of data, it took considerable time before all the data were published. As a result, the value of solar parallax calculated from the various subsets of the data pool ranged from 8.28 seconds to 10.60 seconds, and there was no particular consensus.

With the lessons learned from the 1761 transit, astronomers set out to improve their observations of the 1769 transit. Le Gentil (who had stayed in the area) went to Pondicherry; Pingré observed in Saint Domingue, Chappe went as part of a joint French and Spanish expedition to Baja California; Charles Green with James Cook's expedition observed in Tahiti; the British Crown also sent expeditions to northern Norway and County Donegal in Ireland. In North America the transit was observed at no fewer than nineteen locations. Maximillian Hell, S.J., was invited by the Danish-Norwegian Crown to observe on the island of Vardö, off the eastern coast of Norway. The St. Petersburg Academy organized a number of expeditions covering locations from Russia to the Far East. As in the 1761 transit, the Swedes were again very active in organizing observations in their country. The transit was observed at seventy-seven stations spread over most of the globe.

The solar parallax derived from these observations ranged from 8.43 to 8.8 seconds. The most influential value was that arrived at by Lalande, 8.6 seconds, which was adopted by many as the consensus value. It was confirmed by Laplace who, in his *Exposition du Système du Monde* of 1796 derived it from the parallactic inequality of the moon. In the nineteenth century astronomers returned to the published observations of the 1761 and 1769 transit on several occasions, using new methods of data reduction. Between 1822 and 1835 Johann Franz Encke successfully narrowed down the error margin, using Carl Friedrich Gauss' method of least square. His final result was 8.57116 seconds ±0.0371. In the middle of the century a larger value became desirable in order to fit with solar parallax values derived by other means, such as the parallactic equation, the earth's perturbations of the orbits of Mars and Venus, and the aberration of light. From the observations of the eighteenth-century Venus transits they now derived values close to 8.9 seconds. In preparation for the 1874 and 1882 transits, Karl Rudolph Powalky reexamined the eighteenth-century data one more time, and after rejecting many observations teased a value of 8.83 seconds out of the remaining ones.

The nineteenth-century transits were observed at locations all over the world, and from them values ranging from 8.76 to 8.88 seconds derived. Although the results were again disappointing and astronomers concluded that transit observations were inadequate for determining the solar parallax to the desired accuracy, it was now clear that by these observations the value could be determined to the nearest 0.1 second at any rate.

In the late nineteenth century, astronomers returned to measuring the parallax of Mars, and in the twentieth century planetoids have been used. Measurements of Eros at its close opposition of 1930–1931 yielded a solar parallax of 8.790 seconds ±0.001. In 1976 the **International Astronomical Union** adopted 8.794148 as its value of the mean horizontal solar parallax. Since 1984 this constant has been used for all the national ephemerides.

Albert Van Helden

Bibliography

Lankford, J. "Photography and the Nineteenth Century Transits of Venus." *Technology & Culture* 28 (1987): 648–657.

Nunis, D.B., Jr., ed. *The 1769 Transit of Venus. The Baja California Observations of Jean-Baptiste Chappe d'Auteroche, Vicente de Doz, and Joaquín Velázquez Cárdenas de León.* Translated by J.D. Maynard, J. Geiger, and I.W. Engstrand. Los Angeles: Natural History Museum of Los Angeles County, 1982.

Woolf, H. *A Study of Eighteenth-Century Science.* Princeton: Princeton University Press, 1959; reprint, New York: Arno Press, 1981.

W

Wildt, Rupert (1905–1976)

German-American astrophysicist. Born in Munich, Rupert Wildt received a Ph.D. in physical chemistry at Berlin in 1927. He worked as an astronomical observer in Bonn and also Göttingen, before coming to Mount Wilson Observatory (1935–1936) as a Rockefeller fellow. Wildt was at the Institute for Advanced Study (1936–1937), Princeton University (1937–1942), and the University of Virginia (1942–1946). He joined the faculty of Yale University in 1947, and remained there until retirement.

Wildt interpreted bands appearing in the spectrum of **Jupiter** as evidence for the presence of ammonia and methane. Theodore Dunham confirmed Wildt's conclusion. Wildt also studied the atmosphere of **Venus** and reasoned that the surface might be much hotter (as high as 408 degrees Kelvin) than the outer atmosphere, due to the greenhouse effect caused by carbon dioxide, which is abundant on Venus. Observation eventually confirmed Wildt's idea.

Wildt also investigated the role of negative hydrogen ions in the origin of the continuous solar spectrum. Hans Bethe showed in 1929 that the negative hydrogen ion was potentially stable, although there was little hope of studying it in the laboratory. Wildt studied the equilibrium theoretically, and reached the startling conclusion that, in the upper levels of the sun, where free electrons are common, the negative hydrogen ion must be more abundant than the neutral hydrogen atom in the ground state of the Balmer series. These hydrogen ions could contribute to continuous absorption, or opacity, in the sun. The opacity was not well understood prior to Wildt's research (1939).

Wildt's papers are in the Manuscripts and Archives Division of the Yale University Library, New Haven, Connecticut.

George Sweetnam

Bibliography

"Obituary of Rupert Wildt," *Sky & Telescope* 51:156 (1976).

Wolf-Rayet Stars

Wolf-Rayet stars (WR) have spectra showing broad emission features of nitrogen or carbon—stars that have consumed the hydrogen in their cores and are burning helium or carbon. The first three were discovered in 1867 by Charles Joseph Etienne Wolf and Georges Antoine Pons Rayet in France. Today nearly four hundred are known. From the widths of the spectral lines, Carlyle S. Beals in Canada and Donald Menzel at Harvard in 1929 independently inferred that matter was streaming outward from the stars. In 1933 Cecilia Payne at Harvard made an extensive investigation of sixty-five, including eleven nuclei of planetary nebulae. Different lines in the same spectrum indicated temperatures that suggested a compact core with a stratified envelope.

Among those brighter than 10th magnitude about half are spectroscopic binaries with orbits indicating masses from five to fifty solar. However, the planetaries are less than one solar mass. On the **Hertzsprung-Russell diagram** the massive WR stars fall slightly to the right of the main sequence, the planetaries far to the left. Payne in 1979 stated that from their location on the HR diagram it was difficult to judge whether the massive WR were approaching or leaving the main sequence. In either case they would be young, whereas the planetaries are very old. Thus there may actually be two separate classes of WR stars. Various current theories are controversial. Numerous recent papers speculate that WR stars are progenitors of **supernovae**.

Dorrit Hoffleit

Bibliography

Lamers, H.I.G.L.M., A. Maeder, W. Schmutz, and J.P. Cassinelli. "Wolf-Rayet Stars as Starting Points or as Endpoints of the Evolution of Massive Stars." *Astrophysical Journal* 368 (1991): 538–544.

Lortet, M.C., and A. Pitault, eds. *Wolf-Rayet Stars: Progenitors of Supernovae?* Proceedings of a Workshop Held at Observatoire de Paris-Meudon: France, 1983.

Underhill, A.B. "About the Stage of Evolution of Wolf-Rayet Stars." *Astrophysical Journal* 383 (1991): 729–738.

Women in Astronomy

From at least the time of Hypatia, women have assisted their male relatives in astronomical work. Fathers, husbands, and brothers have taught women how to make and use astronomical instruments, to perform computations, and to report results to the scholarly community. Particularly from the nineteenth century, expanding educational opportunities for women, exploding demands for routine data reduction associated with techniques such as astronomical photography, and a more general acceptance of women workers and professors in much of the world have led to more extensive contributions to astronomy by women. Examining women's work in astronomy not only sheds light on women's history, but also draws attention to the contributions of women who worked as translators, teachers, and computers (that is to say, people doing computations, but later a generic term for female assistants in astronomical observatories), and whose activities have been an essential part of astronomy. The experiences of women who have tried to join scientific societies also reveals the inner workings of these elite institutions.

From Antiquity through the Eighteenth Century

The best known female astronomer of antiquity was Hypatia (ca. 370–415 C.E.), daughter of the mathematician Theon of Alexandria. She is thought to have assisted her father in preparation of a treatise on Ptolemy's *Almagest* and to have written commentaries (now lost) on works by **Ptolemy**, Diophantes, and Apollonius. Hypatia was not the first woman remembered for her knowledge of astronomy—Aglaonice (or Agnice) of Thessaly reputedly predicted eclipses centuries earlier. Other women were commended for their general learning, which included some knowledge of astronomy. Examples include the Greek Cynic philosopher Hipparchia (fourth century B.C.E.); Catherine of Alexandria (fourth century); the Greek Eudocia (396–460), wife of the emperor Theodosius II; and the Greek Asclepigenia (fifth century B.C.E.), daughter of Plutarch. Similarly, in the twelfth century, the wide learning of the nun Hildegard of Bingen reportedly included a knowledge of astronomy.

In the twelfth and thirteenth centuries, the center of learning in Western Europe shifted from monasteries and nunneries to universities. Women were largely barred from these institutions. Occasional noblewomen, such as the French countess Thiéphaine Raguenel du Guesclin; Renée of France, the duchess of Ferrara, and the Italian Catherine de Medici learned something of astronomy.

The sixteenth and seventeenth centuries saw fundamental changes in science, with the overthrow of Aristotelian physics, the acceptance of a heliocentric model of the universe, the introduction of new instruments such as the telescope, and the birth of scientific societies, outside the universities, that served as new centers of inquiry. Women were on the periphery of the new natural philosophy. At least one, the English noblewoman Margaret Cavendish, published at some length on the new physics. Another, the Frenchwoman Jeanne Dumée, wrote a dialogue on Copernican views concerning the motion of the earth that survived in manuscript. The Silesian Maria Cunitz, wife of the physician and amateur astronomer Elias Löven or Lewen, published a revision of Kepler's *Rudolphine Tables*. Other women were faithful assistants to their astronomer husbands. The Pole Catherine Hevelius worked over a quarter century with her spouse, **Johannes Hevelius**. The German Maria Clara Eimmart Müller, daughter of the astronomer Georg Christoph Eimmart and wife of Johann H. Müller, is remembered for her scientific drawings, especially of the lunar surface.

Most of the new scientific societies, like the universities, excluded women from even minor participation. Maria Winkelmann Kirch did work without pay in the observatory of the Berlin Academy of Sciences, assisting her husband, Gottfried Kirch, with observations and computations. In 1702 Maria Kirch discovered a comet, although the discovery was published under her husband's name. After Gottfried died in 1710, Maria applied for the position of assistant calendar-maker to the Berlin Academy. Although Gottfried Leibniz favored the idea, other members of the academy rejected it as unseemly. Kirch found other astronomical positions, and even discovered the periodic variable star Chi Cygni in 1716. She also trained both her daughters in astronomy. Indeed Christine Kirch computed the calendar for the Berlin Academy from at least 1720 until her death.

Throughout the Middle Ages and Renaissance, Latin served as the common language of scholars. Increasing use of modern languages brought with it a demand for translations, some of which were provided by women. In 1579, the Frenchwoman Marie de Coste-Blanche published a French translation of a Spanish treatise on the relative sizes of the sun, moon, and planets. In 1722, Eleonora Barbapiccola published an Italian translation of René Descartes's *Principia philosophiæ*. Undoubtedly the best known of these translators was the French noblewoman Gabrielle-Émilie Châtelet, an intimate of Voltaire who published the definitive French translation of Newton's *Principia*. Mme. Châtelet also published several original treatises on subjects in physics.

From the eighteenth century, women also began to fulfill a demand for elementary instruction in astronomy. At mid-century, Sophie Granchamp offered a public course on the subject in Paris. Louise Dupierry, who computed tables of refraction and of the length of day and night, began to teach an astronomy course for women in Paris in 1789. In England, Margaret Bryan published astronomy textbooks in the late eighteenth and early nineteenth centuries. Similarly, M.N. Calemard, a Frenchwoman who probably taught in England, published a textbook on astronomy for girls in London in 1801.

The Nineteenth Century

These traditions of translation and instruction continued and expanded in the nineteenth century. In England, **Mary Somerville** not only prepared an English translation with commentary of the first four books of Pierre-Simon Laplace's *Mécanique céleste* but wrote a text used by both men and women entitled *On the Connexion of the Physical Sciences* (1834). Other Englishwomen did likewise. Elizabeth Sabine, wife of the geophysicist Edward Sabine, published an English translation of Alexander von Humboldt's *Cosmos* (1846–1847). Winifred Lockyer, the first wife of the astronomer J. Norman Lockyer, translated French works of Camille Flammarion and of A.V. Giullemin. Later in the century, Agnes Mary Clerke wrote a series of influential books and articles describing recent developments in astrophysics. Clerke worked closely with contemporary scientists, and her books are still consulted by historians.

Winifred Lockyer not only translated astronomical books but also continued the ancient tradition of acting as an unpaid assistant to her astronomer relative. Other examples of women who played this role include Marie-Jeanne Lefrançais de Lalande, wife of Michel-Jean-Jêrome Lefrançais de Lalande of the Paris Observatory, Marie Rümker, the English-born wife of an astronomer at the Hamburg Observatory, and most especially **Caroline Herschel**, who assisted her brother **William Herschel** in observing and telescope-making. Caroline Herschel also searched for comets on her own account, and eventually received a government stipend for her contributions to astronomy. Later in the century, Margaret Murray Huggins, the Irish-born wife of **William Huggins**, also brought her talents to bear on astronomical problems. In the United States, **Maria Mitchell** of Nantucket learned astronomy from her father, William, and won acclaim as the discoverer of a comet.

Women not raised in astronomical households sometimes took bold steps to acquire the education they needed. The Russian Sofia Kovalevskaia entered into an arranged marriage so that she could go abroad to study. Kovalevskaia wrote her dissertation on the rings of Saturn, although most of her research focused on purely mathematical topics. California native Dorothea Klumpke also left home to study astronomy, obtaining a doctorate in mathematical sciences from the Sorbonne. Like Kovalevskaia, she wrote on the rings of Saturn. Klumpke then worked at the **Paris Observatory**, directing a group of women measuring and reducing data for the *Carte du Ciel*. In 1901, she married an English amateur astronomer, Isaac Roberts, and went to work at his observatory. Other American women studied at newly established women's colleges like Vassar, where Maria Mitchell taught and directed the observatory from 1865 until her retirement in 1888. In England, several women's colleges also were established, particularly in conjunction with the universities of Cambridge and Oxford. Annie Scott Dill Russell graduated from Girton College, Cambridge, in 1889, and soon was hired by the Royal Observatory, Greenwich. There she met and, in time, wed the astronomer Edward W. Maunder. Annie Maunder resigned from her job but continued to do research with her husband. Britain's Royal Astronomical Society had declined to admit Russell as a member before her marriage. In part for this reason, both Maunders joined enthusiastically in the activities of the new British Astronomical Association, and Annie Maunder edited its *Journal* for several years.

Relatively few women were hired to do routine data reduction at observatories in Great Britain. However, in France, South Africa, Australia, and the United States, computing and the measurement of photographic plates often was deemed woman's work. At first, most women hired as computers had no college training. However, such women's college graduates as **Annie J. Cannon**, **Antonia Maury**, and Henrietta Leavitt did distinguished work at the **Harvard College Observatory**, and scores of other American women found astronomical work elsewhere.

Women's education also expanded in Russia, with courses for women opened in four cities in the 1860s and 1870s. All but the St. Petersburg course closed down in 1886. In 1900, a new course began in Moscow, with additional programs for women in other cities by 1905–1906. Restrictions resumed in 1908, but did not have the effect of the 1886 cutbacks. Russian observatory directors sought to draw on this pool of skilled workers. In the mid-1890s, J.O. Backlund, the newly appointed director of the **Pulkovo Observatory**, asked permission to hire women with a college education as permanent staff members. His request was refused, and women were hired at Pulkovo only temporarily on a piecework basis. Soon after the Revolution of 1917, this policy was reversed, and women joined the permanent staff of the observatory. By the 1930s, at least ten Russian observatories had female staff, in positions ranging from computers and graduate students to senior scientists. These women shared the hazards as well as the privileges of Soviet life. Several suffered privations of war and famine, and at least three of them apparently lost their posts and were imprisoned in the 1936–1937 purge.

The scientific societies founded in the seventeenth and eighteenth centuries had no women members. In the nineteenth century, societies specifically devoted to the study of astronomy such as Britain's Royal Astronomical Society (established 1820), the German *Astronomische Gesellschaft* (1863), the *Société Astronomique de France* (1887), and the American Astronomical Society (1899) were founded. The venerable Caroline Herschel and Mary Somerville were elected honorary members of the Royal Astronomical Society in 1835, although no women were elected as regular members of the institution until 1916. Indeed, the British Astronomical Association was founded in 1890 in part to give voice to women. The *Société Astronomique de France* admitted women members at least from the turn of the century, and had a special prize for women. Similarly, the American Astronomical Society had women members from its inception. Women served as officers in some of these organizations. Hence it is not surprising that when the **International Astronomical Union** was established in 1920, women were on several of its commissions.

In the first quarter of the twentieth century, both male and female astronomers increasingly obtained advanced degrees. Women quickly discovered, however, that a distinguished dissertation from a major university in no way guaranteed a prestigious job. Cecilia Payne, for example, obtained her Radcliffe College Ph.D. in 1925 with a remarkable dissertation on the temperature and composition of stellar atmospheres. Although there were several vacancies for astrophysicists at the time, neither her native Britain nor Canada, or the United States offered a permanent post in which she could pursue her research. Instead, she stayed on at the **Harvard College Observatory**, first as a National Research Council fellow, then as a staff member, and finally, from the mid-1950s, as a member of the Harvard University faculty. Other women doctorates had similar experiences. Moreover, women astronomers increasingly married, often to other astronomers or physical scientists. Particularly with the introduction of antinepotism policies in the 1930s, women found it difficult to find paying positions in the same location as their husbands.

For women, then, advanced education and skillful research did not necessarily bring tangible rewards. Women did not serve as directors of observatories, except those privately owned or at women's colleges. Indeed, as recently as 1965, such a major American observatory as Mount Wilson officially barred women from observing with its telescopes. Similarly, women were not elected to prestigious scientific societies. The first woman astronomer elected to the Royal Society of London was E. Margaret Burbidge in 1964. In 1978, Burbidge became the first woman astronomer elected to the National Academy of Sciences in the United States. The Parisian Academy of Sciences and the Academy of Sciences in the U.S.S.R. proved equally hesitant when it came to admitting women into the ranks of their astronomers.

Research of women such as Beatrice Tinsley, Vera Rubin, Margaret Geller, Margaret Burbidge, Virginia Trimble, and Jocelyn Bell Burnell, to list only a few names, has had a major influence on contemporary astronomy. Women also have gained considerable influence as administrators at institutions such as the Greenwich Observatory, the Harvard College Observatory, and the National Optical Astronomy Observatories. At the same time, however, the portion of the American astronomical community that was female decreased substantially from 1940, so that by 1973 the percentage of the American Astronomical Society members who were women was lower than at any time in the history of the society. Although this trend has reversed somewhat, women, at least in the United States, still report significant discrimination in their attempts to pursue astronomical careers.

Peggy A. Kidwell

Bibliography

Cowley, A., R. Humphreys, B. Lynds, and V. Rubin. "Women in Astronomy: Report to the Council of the AAS from the Working Group on the Status of Women in Astronomy—1973." *American Astronomical Society Bulletin* 6 (1974): 412–422.

Flam, F. "Still a 'Chilly Climate' for Women?" *Science* 252 (1991): 1604–1606.

Hill, E. *My Daughter Beatrice: A Personal Memoir of Dr. Beatrice Tinsley, Astronomer*. New York: American Physical Society, 1986.

Hoffleit, D. "The Evolution of the Henry Draper Memorial." *Vistas in Astronomy* 34 (1991): 107–162.

———. *Women in the History of Variable Star Astronomy*. Cambridge, Mass.: American Association of Variable Star Observers, 1993.

Kidwell, P.A. "Women Astronomers in Britain 1780–1930." *Isis* 75 (1984): 534–546.

Koblitz, A.H. *A Convergence of Lives: Sofia Kovalevskaia, Scientist, Writer, Revolutionary*. Boston: Birkhäuser, 1983.

Lankford, J. "Women and Women's Work at Mount Wilson Observatory before World War II." In *The Earth, the Heavens, and the Carnegie Institution of Washington*, edited by G. Good, vol. 5, 125–128. Washington, D.C.: American Geophysical Union, 1994.

Lankford, J. and R.L. Slavings. "Gender and Science: Women in American Astronomy, 1859–1940." *Physics Today* 43 (1990): 58–65.

McCutcheon, R.A. "The Purge of Soviet Astronomy: 1936–37 with a Discussion of Its Background and Aftermath." M.A. dissertation, Georgetown University, 1985.

Mack, P.E. "Straying from Their Orbits: Women in Astronomy in America." In *Women of Science*, edited by G. Kass-Simon and P. Farnes, 72–116. Bloomington: Indiana University Press, 1990.

Morrison-Low, A.D. "Women in the Nineteenth-Century Scientific Instrument Trade." In *Science and Sensibility: Gender and Scientific Enquiry, 1780–1945*, edited by M. Benjamin, 89–117. Oxford: Basil Blackwell, 1991.

Nicolaidis, E. "Le Developpement de l'astronomie en U.R.S.S. 1918–1933." Ph.D. dissertation, École des Hautes Études en Sciences Sociales, 1982.

Rossiter, M. *Women Scientists in America: Struggles and Strategies to 1940*. Baltimore: Johns Hopkins University Press, 1982.

Schiebinger, L. *The Mind Has No Sex? Women in the Origins of Modern Science*. Cambridge: Harvard University Press, 1989.

Stites, R. *The Women's Liberation Movement in Russia: Feminism, Nihilism, and Bolshevism, 1860–1930*. Princeton: Princeton University Press, 1978.

Warner, D.J. "Women Astronomers." *Natural History* 88 (1979): 12–26.

X

X-ray Astronomy

X-ray astronomy is a branch of astronomy, pursued largely after World War II, concerned with detecting X-rays from space, determining their source, and studying their spectral and temporal characteristics. X-ray photons have wavelengths in the range of 1 to 100 angstroms, far shorter than photons of visible light, which have wavelengths from 4000 to 7000 angstroms. The ozone layer of the earth's atmosphere, which is between 20 and 40 kilometers in altitude, prevents radiation at wavelengths of less than approximately 3000 angstroms from penetrating. Therefore, X-rays from astronomical sources cannot reach the earth's surface. As a result, X-ray astronomy is exclusively a space-based science, which makes it highly dependent on space-borne technologies and government support to fund its development. Prominent X-ray sources include the sun, whose emission originates mainly in the corona, **supernova** remnants in the Milky Way Galaxy, and several extragalactic sources. In general, X-ray astronomy has contributed to the view that violent and high-temperature phenomena, such as black holes accreting matter from binary companions, exist in space to a degree previously unimagined.

The history of X-ray astronomy can be traced to 1924 when the Naval Research Laboratory (NRL) was established in Washington, D.C. One of the NRL's primary missions was to study radio waves. When Edward O. Hulbert and others observed the propagation of radio waves, they discovered that solar flares affected the radiation. The scientists hypothesized that the sun could influence the ionosphere only if it "produced an invisible flux of high-energy radiation" (Tucker and Giacconi, 19). To detect that radiation directly, they realized the need to send detectors above the radiation-absorbing atmosphere.

X-ray astronomy flourished after World War II as new technologies (and government support to pay for them) permitted scientists to observe X-rays from above the atmosphere. The most important technology consisted of rocket hardware, which became available after the war when the U.S. Army offered captured German V-2 rockets to scientists. In 1946, Hulbert and co-workers first attempted to send instruments above the atmosphere, but the rocket's crash destroyed the equipment. An NRL team headed by Herbert Friedman had more luck in 1949 when it launched a V-2 rocket carrying detectors sensitive to ultraviolet and X-radiation. The X-ray counters registered a strong signal coming from the sun. Measurements of X-ray and ultraviolet emissions supported the hypothesis that temperatures of up to 1,000,000 degrees Kelvin existed in astronomical objects. Throughout the next decade, Friedman's group continued studying solar X-ray emissions with instruments carried on short-lived sounding rockets. By routinely monitoring X-ray emissions throughout the eleven-year cycle of solar activity, the group became the first to detect strong X-radiation released from solar flares.

While searching for other X-ray emitters as well as for solar X-rays reflected off the moon in 1962, Riccardo Giacconi detected the first nonsolar X-ray source using a Geiger counter carried on a small rocket. Found in the constellation of Scorpio and named Sco X-1, the source emitted more X-radiation than any sunlike star. Freidman's group corroborated the discovery a year later, and also found a second source in the Crab Nebula, a remnant of a supernova explosion. The X-ray emissions from the nebula predated discoveries of other X-ray sources found in supernova remnants.

The unusual brightness of cosmic X-ray sources caused the field's popularity to soar, and scientists developed new experimental and theoretical approaches to understand the enigmatic emitters. New technologies, such as long-lived satellites and specialized X-ray detectors, proved critical to the science's rapid growth. The first X-ray astronomy satellite, named *Uhuru,* the Swahili word for "freedom," was launched by Giacconi's group in Kenya on the country's independence day, December 12, 1970. The satellite's detectors revealed flickering X-ray emissions from Cygnus X-1, a source that had previously been detected with sounding rockets. The emissions differed from those of the Crab Nebula, which pulsated at regular intervals. Following comprehensive experiments and theoretical work, astronomers determined that Cygnus X-1 consisted of a binary system made up of a blue star orbiting an unseen companion having a mass twenty times that of our sun. Because the invisible star is so massive, astronomers suggested that it is a black hole that slowly strips away its companion star's outer atmosphere. As the material is pulled into the black hole, it rotates, thereby creating a disklike structure called an accretion disk. The spiraling material becomes superheated and emits X-rays.

Following *Uhuru* and other X-ray satellites launched by England and the Netherlands, the High Energy Astronomical Observatories (HEAO) next carried sensitive X-ray detectors into space. The American HEAO-2, referred to as the Einstein Observatory after reaching orbit in late 1978, employed a grazing-incidence telescope that reaped an unprecedented body of data. In 1983, the European Space Agency launched *Exosat*, while Japan sent up its *Ginga* satellite in 1987.

The most prolific X-ray satellite to date, *Rosat,* achieved orbit in 1990. The satellite's name comes from the German word *Röntgensatellit*, which honors the German discoverer of X-rays, Wilhelm Röentgen. Because the satellite resulted from a collaboration between the United States, Germany, and Great Britain, astronomers from all three countries had access to its data. *Rosat*'s unprecedented ability to locate X-ray sources within areas a thousand times smaller than the area of the full moon has led to many startling discoveries. First, *Rosat* detected the weak X-radiation emitted from ordinary stars. *Rosat* also has found that the faster a star rotates, the more X-radiation it produces. Astronomers have therefore theorized that X-radiation can reveal information about the age of stars and the nature of their atmospheres. Furthermore, these observations may indicate the level of activity in the sun's atmosphere soon after its birth, giving astronomers new insights into the formation of the planets.

Rosat has also provided information for use by scientists trying to locate the missing mass that may have originated in the Big Bang and that may determine whether the universe will continue expanding forever. The cold, dense gas that permeates the space between stars is patchy with superheated bubbles that may have been created by supernova explosions. *Rosat* has detected some of these superheated patches as they emit X-radiation. By mapping the distribution of hot gas, astronomers will acquire a more comprehensive view of the interstellar medium and a possible answer to the riddle of the missing mass.

Rosat also revealed that the sky is not uniformly bright in X-radiation, as was previously supposed. Quasars may be one type of phenomenon that can explain the apparently non-uniform X-ray glow, since they account for about 45 percent of the background emission. Some scientists, such as Joachim Treumper and Geunther Hasinger of the Max Planck Institute for Extraterrestrial Physics, argue that the remaining background radiation comes from more distant clusters of quasars and starburst galaxies—powerful X-ray emitters "in which stars are forming at an extraordinary rate, triggered perhaps by a close encounter with a galactic neighbor" (Powell, 26). If this hypothesis is verified and the quasars are not uniformly distributed across space, then cosmologists will have to reevaluate the Big Bang theory.

The success of *Rosat* underscores the fact that X-ray astronomy is no longer a science dominated by American practitioners. As the field advanced from inexpensive sounding rocket experiments to elaborate satellite-based probes, funding for X-ray astronomy's technologies became more involved in interest group politics. Because of Congressional funding cutbacks, for example, launch of the

Advanced X-Ray Astrophysics Facility (*AXAF*) has been delayed until at least the year 2000. Even though information garnered from existing and past satellites will keep X-ray astronomers busy for many years, this example suggests again how much advances in X-ray astronomy depend on technological innovation and the government support to pay for it.

Richard F. Hirsh
Voula Saridakis

Bibliography

Cowen, R. "ROSAT Revelations: Satellite Provides a New View of the X-ray and Ultraviolet Universe." *Science News* 139 (1991): 408–410.

Dyer, A. "ROSAT's Penetrating X-ray Visions." *Astronomy* 19 (1991): 42–49.

Friedman, H. "Discovering the Invisible Universe." *Mercury* 20 (1991): 2–22.

Henbest, N. "The Universe through X-ray Eyes." *New Scientist* 132 (1991): 42–46.

Hirsh, R.F. *Glimpsing an Invisible Universe: The Emergence of X-ray Astronomy*. Cambridge: Cambridge University Press, 1983.

"Japan Developing Advanced Spacecraft for Deep Space X-ray, Radio Astronomy." *Aviation Week & Space Technology* 133 (1990): 80–81.

Margon, B. "Exploring the High-Energy Universe." *Sky & Telescope* 82 (1991): 607–612.

Marshall, E. "X-ray Astronomy: The Unkindest Cut." *Science* 254 (1991): 508–510.

Patchett, B.E. "X-ray Astronomy." *Contemporary Physics* 30 (1989): 77–88.

Powell, C.S. "X-ray Riddle: Cosmic Background Is Still Unexplained." *Scientific American* 264 (1991): 26.

Tucker, W., and R. Giacconi. *The X-ray Universe*. Cambridge: Harvard University Press, 1985.

Yale University, Astronomy at

Almost from the inception of the college in 1701, at least one basic course in astronomy was taught at Yale. Yale was primarily a liberal arts college in which the sciences played a secondary role. In 1847 a Scientific Department was added, later called the Sheffield School in honor of its chief benefactor, who in 1866 provided a 9-inch Alvan Clark telescope. In 1861, the first Ph.D. degree for a thesis in astronomy (on meteors) was awarded to Arthur W. Wright. Through 1971, Yale awarded seventy-eight Ph.D. degrees in astronomy.

Research was slower than teaching in getting started. Through most of the nineteenth century, research was devoted primarily to meteors, meteorites, and comets. The reasons for this were twofold. The occurrence of spectacular fireballs and meteor showers, especially the fall of meteorites at Weston, Connecticut, in 1807, inspired investigations. A lack of proper scientific equipment deterred stellar research. Early on, important research on meteors could be carried out simply on the basis of naked-eye observations. It had been generally believed that meteors were purely atmospheric effects analogous to lightning, and that meteorites were ordinary terrestrial rocks struck by lightning. Yale scientists contributed significantly to the rectification of these beliefs. Geologist Benjamin Silliman proved that the Weston meteorites differed in composition from terrestrial rocks, and that they had originated in outer space. Astronomer **Hubert A. Newton** was influential in establishing the cosmic origin of meteors and their association with comets. Between 1894 and 1910, William Lewis Elkin carried out pioneering photographic work for the determination of heights and velocities of meteors—programs perfected a generation later at Harvard.

In 1830, Yale acquired a 5-inch Dollond telescope, at the time the largest refractor in America. A return of Halley's comet was expected in 1835, and with that telescope Professor Denison Olmsted and Elias Loomis enjoyed the distinction of being the first in America to recover the comet before it reached naked eye visibility.

The Yale University Observatory, founded in 1880 by Oliver Winchester, acquired the only heliometer in America, an instrument designed for astrometric work. With this, Elkin determined more stellar parallaxes (163) than had been determined elsewhere. When Frank Schlesinger came to Yale in 1920, his chief interest was in photographic astrometry. He established the Southern Station at Johannesburg, South Africa, and, with a specially designed 26-inch photographic refractor, determined stellar parallaxes in great number. Moreover, he initiated the *Yale Zone Catalogues,* which ultimately provided the proper motions of some 227,000 stars. Schlesinger also published a *General Catalogue of Steller Parallaxes* and the *Catalogue of Bright Stars,* catalogues that are continually being updated.

Celestial mechanics at Yale was begun by **Ernest W. Brown** with his meticulous investigations of the motions of the moon, published in 1919. Brown's disciple and later director of the observatory, **Dirk Brouwer,** developed celestial mechanics to the extent that Yale became a world leader in the field at a time when advanced training in celestial mechanics was essential to space flight endeavors. Brouwer established a Summer Institute in Dynamical Astronomy, sponsored by the **National Science Foundation** and the **National Aeronautics and Space Administration**. Between 1959 and 1966, six hundred college teachers and government and industry scientists received training in celestial mechanics.

Pioneering work in infrared photometry was carried out in the 1930s and early 1940s, first by graduate student John S. Hall (Ph.D. 1933), then by Arthur Bennett. From 1946 to 1953 Joseph Ashbrook observed variable stars, and Harlan Smith made photoelectric observations of short-period variables between 1953 and 1963.

From 1956 through 1965, a small group headed by Harlan Smith started a promising program on planetary **radio astronomy**. This project, including the radio equipment, was transferred to the University of Texas when the key investigators obtained more favorable appointments there.

Astrophysics played a lesser role than celestial mechanics or astrometry during the Schlesinger and Brouwer directorships, **Rupert Wildt**'s outstanding achievements, particularly in planetary astrophysics, notwithstanding. Wildt was an inspiring thesis advisor to half a dozen exceptionally talented students. With the appointment of Pierre Demarque as department head in 1968, astrophysics became the predominant field for research, since the need for celestial mechanics was no longer pressing.

After World War II, Yale could no longer support enough observers to operate its Southern Station full time. An arrangement was reached with Columbia University for joint operation of the station; this lasted until 1970. By 1952, seeing conditions at Johannesburg had deteriorated and the station was moved to the Commonwealth Observatory in Australia. By 1962 that site also proved unsatisfactory. The 26-inch telescope, which had provided over sixty-six thousand parallax plates since 1925, was donated to the Commonwealth Observatory. The Southern Observatory was then transferred to El Leoncito, Argentina, where a modern 20-inch double astrograph was erected to extend to the South Pole the proper motion survey relative to faint galaxies that was being carried out at **Lick Observatory** for zones north of −30 degrees. The southern extension is being carried out with the collaboration of Argentinian astronomers.

In the Northern Hemisphere, an observing station was acquired in 1955 at Bethany, some ten miles from New Haven. The largest telescope there is a 20-inch reflector, used largely for training purposes. A versatile 40-inch reflector, intended by Brouwer for Bethany, was eventually removed to the more favorable **Association of Universities for Research in Astronomy** (AURA) site at **Cerro Tololo**, Chile.

Clearly, with successive observatory directors, the primary fields for research changed. Nevertheless, whatever predominated in any era, in that field Yale achieved outstanding leadership, successively in meteoritics, astrometry, celestial mechanics, and finally, astrophysics.

Dorrit Hoffleit

Bibliography

Elkin, W.L. *Transactions of Yale University Observatory*. Vol. 1, v–vii. New Haven, Conn.: The Observatory, 1904.

Hoffleit, D. "Yale Contributions to Meteoric Astronomy." In *Vistas in Astronomy,* vol. 32, 117–143. Oxford: Pergamon Press, 1988.

———. *Astronomy at Yale, 1701–1968. Memoirs of the Connecticut Academy of Arts and Sciences*. New Haven, Conn.: Academy of Arts and Sciences, 1992.

McKeehan, L. *Yale Science, the First Hundred Years, 1701–1801.* New York: Henry Schuman, 1947.

Musto, D. "Yale Astronomy in the Nineteenth Century." *Ventures* 8 (1968): 7–17.

Yerkes Observatory

The Yerkes Observatory of the University of Chicago went into operation in 1897, built around the largest refracting telescope in the world, the 40-inch refractor. The unscrupulous tycoon Charles T. Yerkes provided the funds to build it. William Rainey Harper, the president of the University of Chicago, then in its second year of existence, and **George Ellery Hale**, his associate professor of astronomy, persuaded Yerkes to put up the funds in October 1892. An essential part of their sales talk was that the 40-inch would "lick the Lick"—that is, would be bigger than the Lick Observatory 36-inch, at the time the largest refractor in existence. All the astronomers recommended building the observatory outside of low, smoky Chicago, and Harper ultimately decided on a site at Williams Bay, Wisconsin.

Alvan G. Clark figured and polished the 40-inch lens, and the Warner and Swasey company made the telescope mounting. Hale, only twenty-nine years old at the time of the dedication in 1897, was devoted to astrophysics and specialized in solar research. He planned the observatory building with spectroscopic laboratories, photographic darkrooms, and smaller, auxiliary telescopes for specialized physical measurements. His announced aim was to compare the spectra of the sun and stars, to understand their physical nature and evolution.

The first staff members at Yerkes Observatory included **Sherburne W. Burnham**, the great double star observer, **Edward E. Barnard**, the wide-field astronomical photographer and keen-eyed planetary observer, and Edwin B. Frost, the astronomical spectroscopist who had studied at Dartmouth, Princeton, and Potsdam. Burnham and Barnard were essentially self-taught astronomers of the old school. **George Willis Ritchey** was the optician, skilled astronomical photographer, and eventually head of the shop and superintendent of instrument construction.

Hale, a demon of organizational energy, played an extremely important role in founding the *Astrophysical Journal,* setting up scientific meetings and congresses, and raising money to hire additional staff members at Yerkes Observatory, but had little time to do research of his own. Ritchey completed the 24-inch reflector, the first professional-quality reflecting telescope in America, and began using it for nebular photography in 1901. He and Hale were convinced that large reflectors, not refractors, would be the great telescopes of the future. Hale's wealthy father purchased a 60-inch glass disk and Ritchey was rough grinding it, as the first step for making it into a primary mirror, by the time of the dedication in 1897.

The 40-inch refractor was not well suited to the high-dispersion spectroscopy that Hale wanted to do, and he abandoned it to set up a University of Chicago remote observing station on Mount Wilson in 1903. At the end of 1904 he succeeded in getting a large grant from the Carnegie Institution of Washington, which enabled him to break away from the University of Chicago and found the Mount Wilson Solar Observatory. As the nucleus of its staff, he took his first team from Yerkes with him: Ritchey, observing assistant Ferdinand Ellerman, and former graduate student **Walter S. Adams**.

Frost then succeeded Hale as director of Yerkes Observatory. Frost had already started a radial-velocity program with the 40-inch, with Adams as his collaborator, and continued it with other staff members. This program resulted in fundamental data on the motions of stars. However, the same type of program was underway at Lick Observatory, where the clear skies, excellent seeing, and systematic, engineering approach of the director, **W.W. Campbell**, enabled it to outproduce the Yerkes program significantly. Nevertheless, Frost continued it until he retired in 1932. He was a notably uncreative research worker, who tried to keep the observatory much as it had been when Hale had left. Thus when Burnham retired, Frost replaced him with double star observer George van Biesbroeck, and when Barnard died, he hired wide-field photography expert Frank E. Ross in his place. Both were good research astronomers, but under Frost's direction few new ideas came to the observatory. He had poor eyesight and became completely blind in 1921. From then on he depended upon readers to keep him in contact with the world of science. He was extremely courageous and a wonderful human being, but he could not keep Yerkes Observatory in the forefront of astronomy. It deteriorated badly as a research institution during his directorship. Nevertheless it produced several almost completely self-taught Ph.D.s, two of whom were to have outstanding research careers, **Edwin Hubble** and **Otto Struve**, and two more who received much of their training from Struve, William W. Morgan and Philip C. Keenan.

Struve had arrived in the United States in 1931, and, in two years as a graduate student had proved himself an extremely energetic worker. Frost put him on the staff as an instructor and promoted him rapidly, so that by 1930 Struve was an associate professor. He served as acting director during Frost's serious illness in 1931, and became director on the latter's retirement the following year. Struve had started on Frost's radial velocity program, but made himself into an astrophysicist, using the available rich store of radial-velocity spectrograms to draw important new conclusions on interstellar matter.

Struve knew that, to survive, Yerkes Observatory needed a larger telescope at a better site. He brought about an agreement under which he supervised the building of the new McDonald Observatory with its 82-inch reflector for the University of Texas. Under the agreement the Yerkes staff operated McDonald Observatory for the first twenty-five years of its existence. This was a new concept, the first observatory shared between two universities, and thus the distant forerunner of later national observatories. Even before the 82-inch was completed in 1939, Struve and other Yerkes astronomers were doing research with small telescopes and a nebular spectrograph at the dark-sky site in the mountains of west Texas.

Struve faced opposition or at least suspicion in his early years as director, because of his youth and his foreign birth and upbringing. However, he gained and kept the support of President Robert M. Hutchins and Dean Henry G. Gale by his complete concentration on astronomical research, and his successes in it. He gradually consolidated his power, and in 1935–1936 added **Gerard P. Kuiper, Bengt Strömgren**, and **S. Chandrasekhar**, all foreign-born astronomers, to the faculty. They, with Morgan, whom Frost had kept on the staff after he received his Ph.D., were the nucleus of Struve's outstanding research team of the later 1930s and the 1940s (except for Strömgren, who returned to Denmark in 1938). Chandrasekhar and Strömgren represented the solution to Struve's conviction that American astronomy was seriously deficient in theorists. The whole group, with several younger faculty members who came later and numerous visiting astronomers from abroad, produced important research results at a fantastic rate, particularly after the 82-inch McDonald reflector went into operation in 1939.

However, nearly all the young astronomers were called to technical and scientific development work during World War II. After the war ended Yerkes Observatory was still one of the most important astronomical research centers in the world, but Struve had tired of administration. The formerly young astronomers were now important figures in their own right, who wished to make their own decisions rather than meekly accept Struve's orders. He resigned in 1950 and moved to the Berkeley campus of the University of California.

Strömgren came back from Copenhagen to succeed to the directorship, but then left for the Institute for Advanced Study in Princeton in 1957. Kuiper became the next director, but went to the University of Arizona in 1960 to found the Lunar and Planetary Laboratory. By then several other universities had large telescopes in dark-sky sites, and within a few years Kitt Peak opened up the possibilities for observational work from many other universities. The University of Texas had built up its own astronomy department, and took control of McDonald Observatory, under the terms of the original agreement. Yerkes Observatory was no longer one of the preeminent astronomical research institutions in the world.

After Kuiper left, subsequent directors of Yerkes Observatory were Morgan (1960–1963), W. Albert Hiltner (1963–1966), C. Robert O'Dell (1966–1972), Lewis M. Hobbs (1974–1982), D.A. Harper (1982–1989), and Richard G. Kron (1989–). The 40-inch, still the largest refractor in the world, had become a small telescope in comparison with numerous larger reflectors at better sites. But Yerkes Observatory is now the administrative center for the Center for Astrophysical Research in Antarctica, a consortium project that came into existence in 1991. The space for laboratories and shops, the attractive living conditions, the library, and above all the scientific research tradition have kept it going productively for nearly a century.

Yerkes Observatory was and remains the site of the largest refracting telescope in the world. It is especially important for its contributions to astronomy and astrophysics, and for blazing a trail by operating a distant observatory cooperatively with another university. Its history is also a striking illustration of the importance of individual human beings in setting the tone, policies, and productivity of a scientific institution.

The Yerkes Observatory Archives, located at the observatory in Williams Bay, Wisconsin, consists of approximately three hundred boxes of correspondence of the directors from Hale through Strömgren. In addition there are several letterbooks from Hale's early Yerkes Observatory days, and a few boxes of Barnard's papers. The other significant sources for its history are the various collections of University of Chicago presidents' papers, in the Special Collections Department, Regenstein Library, on the campus in Chicago.

Donald E. Osterbrock

Bibliography

Adams, W.S. "Some Reminiscences of the Yerkes Observatory." *Science* 106 (1947): 196–200.

Evans, D.S., and J.D. Mulholland. *Big and Bright: A History of McDonald Observatory*. Austin: University of Texas Press, 1986.

Frost, E.B. *An Astronomer's Life*. Boston: Houghton Mifflin, 1933.

Krisciunas, K. "Otto Struve." *Biographical Memoirs of the National Academy of Sciences* 61 (1992): 351–387.

Osterbrock, D.E. *James E. Keeler, Pioneer American Astrophysicist: And the Early Development of American Astrophysics*. Cambridge: Cambridge University Press, 1984.

———. *Pauper and Prince: Ritchey, Hale, and Big American Telescopes*. Tucson: University of Arizona Press, 1993.

Storrs, R.S. *Harper's University: The Beginnings*. Chicago: University of Chicago Press, 1966.

Struve, O. "The Story of an Observatory: The Fiftieth Anniversary of the Yerkes Observatory." *Popular Astronomy* 55 (1947): 227–244.

Wali, K.C. *Chandra: A Biography of S. Chandrasekhar*. Chicago: University of Chicago Press, 1991.

Wright, H. *Explorer of the University: A Biography of George Ellery Hale*. New York: E.P. Dutton, 1966.

Zeiss, Carl (1816–1888)

German instrument-maker. Born in Weimar, Carl Zeiss was apprenticed to a mechanician in Jena in 1834. Zeiss also attended academic lectures during his apprenticeship. From 1838 to 1845, he trained in optical and machine shops in Stuttgart, Darmstadt, Vienna, and Berlin. In 1846 he founded the optical works at Jena. In 1860, Zeiss was appointed mechanician to the University of Jena.

Initially, the optical works produced microscopes. In 1866, Zeiss retained physicist Ernst Abbe, at the University of Jena, to collaborate in transforming instrument production and development into a systematic process. Zeiss also consulted with glass chemist Otto Schott, who developed new optical glasses at his own firm in Jena. With the help of Abbe and Schott, the Zeiss works produced an apochromatic lens, which brought light of all colors to a focus at the same point, to eliminate chromatic aberration. By the 1880s, the Zeiss optical company had an international reputation. In recognition of Abbe's role, Zeiss made him a partner in the firm in 1876. Abbe, who was director of the observatory at the University of Jena, persuaded Zeiss to produce astronomical instruments. The Zeiss works led the German optical industry into a highly profitable era.

An extensive literature on the Zeiss works exists in German.

George Sweetnam

Bibliography

Schomerus, F. *Geschichte des Jenaer Zeisswerkes, 1846–1946*. Stuttgart: Piscator Verlag, 1952.

Zenith Telescope

The original zenith telescope was a geodetic instrument consisting of a transit telescope equipped with a sensitive leveling system, plus a micrometer eyepiece. It was used, in the field, for the precise determination of latitude via the use of the Talcott method, which used the difference of the zenith distances of a star north of the zenith, and one south of the zenith.

The telescope also came into use at fixed locations, where it was used for the determination of the variation of latitude, and for the determination of astronomical aberration—the shift in star positions caused by the finite velocity of light.

It is a particular example of the general class of vertical telescopes, which have existed in various forms. Robert Hooke used a vertical telescope in 1669 in an attempted parallax measurement, and observations with a vertical telescope led Bradley to discover astronomical aberration in 1729.

In an attempt to obviate problems associated with precision leveling, various attempts were made to utilize liquid surfaces. **David Gill** lists a variety of floating instruments, beginning in 1825, but notes that micrometer measurement was precluded in the instruments because it disturbed the floating system. At the turn of the century, Bryan Cookson developed a photographic zenith telescope that floated on mercury, and used it for measurements of the variation of latitude.

In 1911, Frank E. Ross constructed the first photographic zenith tube, an interesting variant of the zenith telescope. It used liquid mercury as an optical reflecting surface

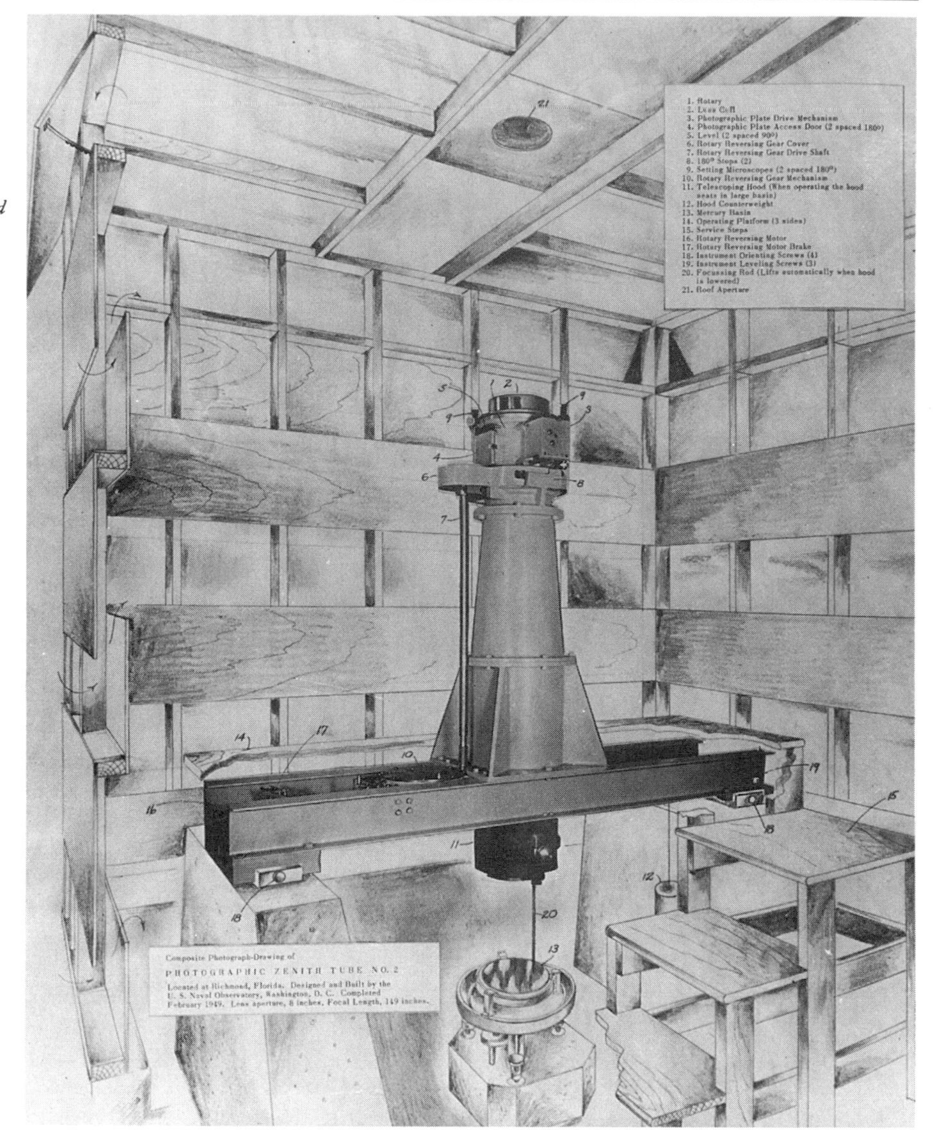

The photographic zenith tube at the U.S. Naval Observatory. This class of instrument, dating back to the seventeenth century, took positional astronomy to a very high level of precision, but at a cost. Since it pointed only to the zenith, it was very stable, but limited to observing those objects passing directly overhead. (Courtesy of the U.S. Naval Observatory)

to establish a zenith line of sight. Ross used his zenith tube to measure variation of latitude, but the arrangement lent itself readily to the precise determination of time, and was used for that purpose at a number of observatories, most notably at the U.S. Naval Observatory, until very recently.

Louis F. Drummeter Jr.

Bibliography

Fehrenbach, C. "Twentieth Century Instrumentation." In *Astrophysics and Twentieth Century Astronomy to 1950: Part A,* edited by O. Gingerich, vol. 4, 184, *The General History of Astronomy*, edited by M. Hoskin. Cambridge: Cambridge University Press, 1984.

Gill, D. "Telescope." In *Encyclopedia Britannica.* 11th ed., edited by Hugh Chisholm, 571–573. Cambridge: Cambridge University Press, 1911.

King, H.C. *The History of the Telescope.* High Wycombe: Charles Griffen, 1955.

Zwicky, Fritz (1898–1974)

Swiss-American physicist and astronomer. Born in Bulgaria to Swiss parents, Zwicky remained a Swiss citizen all his life. He received a Ph.D. in physics from the Federal Institute TMof Technology in Zurich in 1922. In 1925, Zwicky came to the California Institute of Technology as a physics fellow of the International Education Board, and remained at Caltech until his death in 1974. When Caltech received a large grant in 1928 for the construction of the Mount Palomar Observatory, Zwicky was drawn into astronomy. In 1928, Zwicky received an additional appointment as astronomer at Mount Wilson and Palomar observatories. Through much of his career he was regarded as a maverick.

The work most appreciated in Zwicky's own lifetime was his theory, with **Walter Baade**, of supernovae and neutron stars. Baade and Zwicky predicted in 1934 that **supernovae** would produce cosmic rays and would leave behind a new kind of object, a neutron star. Zwicky launched a search for galactic supernovae, so that more spectra, until then extremely rare, might be obtained. Supernovae could also be used as distance indicators for the galaxies. The prediction of neutron stars was confirmed by radio astronomers in the 1960s.

Zwicky was among the first astronomers to formulate the dark matter problem. He decided in the 1930s that the two established methods of deriving galaxy masses, through the mass/luminosity ratio and the speed of rotation, were inadequate. Instead, he studied galaxy clusters. From the velocities of component galaxies and the assumption that clusters are bound by gravity, Zwicky derived a mass/luminosity ratio for the galaxies in the Coma cluster of 500:1, compared with an accepted figure of 3:1 for the Milky Way. Zwicky also suggested the gravitational lensing effect as another means by which to obtain galaxy masses.

In one of Zwicky's first papers in astronomy, in 1929, he suggested that the large red shifts observed in some galactic spectra did not, as **Edwin Hubble** stated, reflect velocities of recession. Rather, Zwicky asserted, the red shift occurred as light from distant galaxies transferred energy and momentum to gravitating matter that it passed. Zwicky's maverick standing resulted in part from this claim.

Zwicky systematically photographed large numbers of galaxies and published catalogues of them. He advocated what he dubbed morphological astronomy, a systematic approach to discovering new objects and new physical laws. Zwicky carried out many of his observations with an 18-inch Schmidt telescope at Mount Palomar Observatory.

George Sweetnam

Bibliography

Hufbauer, K. "Zwicky, Fritz." In *Dictionary of Scientific Biography* 18 (Supplement II): 1011–1013. New York: Scribner, 1990.

Müller, R. *Fritz Zwicky: Leben and Werk des grossen Schweizer Astrophysikers, Raketenforschers und Morphologen (1898–1974)*. Glarus: Verlag Baeschlin, 1986.

Wilson, A. "Fritz Zwicky." *Quarterly Journal of the Royal Astronomical Society* 16 (1975): 106–108.

Index

Page references for main entries are in **boldface**; page numbers for illustrative and tabular materials are in italic.